BIOMEDICAL ENGINEERING FUNDAMENTALS

BIOMEDICAL ENGINEERING FUNDAMENTALS

Myer Kutz Editor

Third Edition

McGraw Hill

McGraw Hill Education (India) Private Limited

Information contained in this work has been obtained by McGraw-Hill Education from sources believed to be reliable. However, neither McGraw-Hill Education nor its authors guarantee the accuracy or completeness of any information published herein, and neither McGraw-Hill Education nor its authors shall be responsible for any errors, omissions, or damages arising out of use of this information. This work is published with the understanding that McGraw-Hill Education and its authors are supplying information but are not attempting to render engineering or other professional services. If such services are required, the assistance of an appropriate professional should be sought

Mc Graw Hill

Biomedical Engineering Fundamentals, Third Edition

McGraw Hill Education (India) Reprint 2021

RZDZYYRBJLRBY

Reprinted in India by arrangement with McGraw Hill Global Education Holdings, LLC, New York

Sales territories: India, Pakistan, Nepal, Bangladesh, Sri Lanka and Bhutan

Library of Congress Control Number: 2020952464

ISBN-13: 978-93-5460-188-0
ISBN-10: 93-5460-188-X

01 02 03 04 05 SAN 25 24 23 22 21

Published by McGraw Hill Education (India) Private Limited, Anjana Complex No: 5/90 A, Butt Road, St. Thomas Mount, Chennai – 600016, Tamil Nadu, India, and Printed and bound in India at Sanat Printers, EPIP, HSIDC, Kundli, Sonipat, Haryana

Visit us at: www.mheducation.co.in; Phone (Toll free in India): **1800 103 5875**
Write to us at: info.india@mheducation.com

CIN: U80302TN2010PTC111532

For Arlene, forever

ABOUT THE EDITOR

MYER KUTZ is founder and president of Myer Kutz Associates, Inc., a publishing and information services consulting firm.

CONTENTS

CONTRIBUTORS

Crystal Anderson-Cunanan *Boston Scientific Corporation, Marlborough, Massachusetts* (Chap. 18)

Ronald E. Barr *University of Texas, Austin, Texas* (Chap. 9)

Christopher Batich *University of Florida, Gainesville, Florida* (Chap. 15)

Ravi V. Bellamkonda *Georgia Institute of Technology/Emory University, Atlanta, Georgia* (Chap. 21)

Anthony J. Brammer *University of Connecticut Health, Farmington, Connecticut* (Chap. 13)

Thomas S. Buchanan *University of Delaware, Newark, Delaware* (Chaps. 8, 14)

Hsiang-Han Chen *University of Minnesota, Minneapolis, Minnesota* (Chap. 3)

Vladimir Cherkassky *University of Minnesota, Minneapolis, Minnesota* (Chap. 3)

Shmuel Einav *Tel Aviv University, Tel Aviv, Israel* (Chap. 5)

David Elad *Tel Aviv University, Tel Aviv, Israel* (Chaps. 5, 7)

Michele J. Grimm *Michigan State University, East Lansing, Michigan* (Chap. 20)

Paul Grimshaw *University of Adelaide, Adelaide, Australia* (Chap. 11)

James B. Grotberg *University of Michigan, Ann Arbor, Michigan* (Chap. 6)

Pinchas Halpern *Tel Aviv Medical Center, Tel Aviv, Israel, and Sackler School of Medicine, Tel Aviv University, Tel Aviv, Israel* (Chap. 7)

Michael N. Helmus *Medical Devices, Drug Delivery, and Nanotechnology, Worcester, Massachusetts* (Chap. 18)

William Hersh *Oregon Health & Science University, Portland, Oregon* (Chap. 2)

Arif Iftekhar *University of Minnesota, Minneapolis, Minnesota* (Chap. 16)

Dentcho Ivanov *Microelectronics Fabrication Center, New Jersey Institute of Technology, Newark, New Jersey* (Chap. 25)

Teena James *Department of Biomedical Engineering and Microelectronics Research Center, New Jersey Institute of Technology, Newark, New Jersey* (Chap. 25)

Chris Jones *Independent Researcher, Adelaide, Australia* (Chap. 11)

Tony M. Keaveny *University of California, San Francisco, California, and University of California, Berkeley, California* (Chap. 10)

David H. Kohn *University of Michigan, Ann Arbor, Michigan* (Chap. 17)

Patrick Leamy *LifeLink Foundation, Tampa, Florida* (Chap. 15)

Hyunjung Lee *Georgia Institute of Technology, Atlanta, Georgia* (Chap. 21)

Merilyn Lock *University of South Australia, Adelaide, Australia* (Chap. 11)

Eric J. Madsen *University of Michigan, Ann Arbor, Michigan* (Chap. 17)

Kurt T. Manal *University of Delaware, Newark, Delaware* (Chap. 8)

Manu Sebastian Mannoor *Department of Biomedical Engineering and Microelectronics Research Center, New Jersey Institute of Technology, Newark, New Jersey* (Chap. 25)

Nancy J. Meilander *National Institute of Standards and Technology, Gaithersburg, Maryland* (Chap. 21)

Elise F. Morgan *University of California, Berkeley, California* (Chap. 10)

Jit Muthuswamy *Arizona State University, Tempe, Arizona* (Chaps. 23, 26)

Roger J. Narayan *University of North Carolina and North Carolina State University, Raleigh, North Carolina* (Chap. 24)

Michael D. Nowak *University of Hartford, West Hartford, Connecticut* (Chap. 12)

Govind Pandey *King George Medical University, Lucknow, India* (Chap. 24)

Prem C. Pandey *Banaras Hindu University, Varanasi, India* (Chap. 24)

Marcus G. Pandy *University of Melbourne, Melbourne, Australia* (Chap. 9)

Donald R. Peterson *Northern Illinois University, DeKalb, Illinois* (Chap. 13)

Bonnie Pierson *University of North Carolina and North Carolina State University, Raleigh, North Carolina* (Chap. 24)

Shrirang V. Ranade *Genentech Inc., a member of the Roche Group, South San Francisco, California* (Chap. 18)

Anat Ratnovsky *Afeka College of Engineering, Tel Aviv, Israel* (Chap. 7)

Narender P. Reddy *University of Akron, Akron, Ohio* (Chap. 1)

Qi Shao *University of Delaware, Newark, Delaware* (Chap. 14)

Bruce C. Towe *Arizona State University, Tempe, Arizona* (Chap. 22)

Bradley Jay Willenberg *University of Central Florida, Orlando, Florida* (Chap. 15)

Oscar C. Yeh *University of California, Berkeley, California* (Chap. 10)

Roya Zandparsa *Tufts University School of Dental Medicine, Boston, Massachusetts* (Chap. 19)

Liang Zhu *University of Maryland, Baltimore County, Baltimore, Maryland* (Chap. 4)

PREFACE

The purpose of this handbook is to provide engineers, physicians, and other medical professionals with fundamental information that will help them use engineering sensibilities and methodologies to invent, design, properly operate, and evaluate medical instruments, devices, and machines. This third edition is an expanded and updated version of Vol. 1, *Fundamentals*, of the *Biomedical Engineering and Design Handbook,* Second Edition, published in the summer of 2009, and follows the same outline. Again, there are four major parts: Biomedical Systems Analysis, which now has three chapters instead of one; Biomechanics of the Human Body, with 11 chapters in both editions; Biomaterials, with seven chapters in both editions; and Bioelectronics, with five chapters in both editions.

Of the 26 chapters in the third edition—two chapters more than in the second edition—four chapters are entirely new and nine have been updated. Two second edition chapters have been dropped: Biodynamics: A Lagrangian Approach and Biomedical Signal Processing. I should point out that the first volume of the second edition constituted a substantial revision of the corresponding parts of the first edition. So the overall revision from first to third editions has been extensive, in keeping with the growth of knowledge in the biomedical engineering discipline.

The four new chapters in this edition cover the following important topics, which add value for readers: Biomedical Informatics (Chap. 2, contributed by William Hersh), which deals with the efficient storage, acquisition, and use of information in healthcare; Machine Learning for Biomedical Engineering (Chap. 3, contributed by Vladimir Cherkassky and Hsiang-Han Chen), which involves methodological issues and assumptions important for applying machine learning to biomedical data so that limitations of predictive data-analytic models can be understood properly, available data can be modeled mathematically, and the right questions can be asked of the data; Biomechanics of the Foot and Knee (Chap. 11, contributed by Paul Grimshaw, Chris Jones, and Merilyn Lock), fundamental knowledge which underlies, for example, treatment of injury to the anterior cruciate ligament; and Neural Interfaces (Chap. 26, contributed by Jit Muthuswamy), which can be implanted so that electrical activity from single neurons in the brain and peripheral nervous system can be recorded.

As noted above, nine chapters from the second edition have been updated for this edition. Comments regarding those updates are presented in the following paragraphs.

Liang Zhu, contributor of Chap. 4, Heat Transfer Applications in Biological Systems, writes: "There are quite a lot of updates due to my teaching of bioheat transfer and my research in the past 10 years. In addition to the major updates, including some figures, many new references after 2007 were added to the manuscript." Among the sections updated are those dealing with the Pennes bioheat equation, bioheat transfer modeling, temperature, thermal properties and blood flow measurements, hyperthermia, and thermal damage assessment.

Marcus G. Pandy, co-contributor with Ronald E. Barr, of Chap. 9, Biomechanics of the Musculoskelatal System, writes: "I have removed the text that appeared in the very last section of the previous version and replaced this with a description of running biomechanics, which I believe the reader will find interesting plus it follows nicely from the description of walking biomechanics appearing immediately above. I also have included two new figures."

In Chap. 12, Finite-Element Analysis, contributor Michael D. Nowak has added text on coronary artery disease, vascular assist devices, and aortic valve replacement, plus two complex figures.

Donald R. Peterson, co-contributor with Anthony J. Brammer, of Chap. 13, Vibration, Mechanical Shock, and Impact, writes: "The chapter has significant updates as some of the second edition version is obsolete now." Among the sections with major updates are Biodynamic Models in the section on Models and Human Surrogates; Occurrence of Health Effects and Injury in the section on Countermeasures; Protection against Hand-Transmitted Vibration in the section on Countermeasures.

In Chap. 15, Polymeric Biomaterials, the contributors, led by Christopher Batich, added an extensive new section on biocompatibility and tissue engineering by Bradley Jay Willenberg, as well as a major new section on sterilization by Patrick Leamy. Part of the section on tissue scaffolds has been rewritten.

David H. Kohn, co-contributor of Chap. 17, Bioceramics, writes: "The main changes to the chapter included an expansion of the inorganic/organic hybrid section, especially discussion of peptide conjugation to calcium phosphates and nanotechnology."

Michael N. Helmus, co-contributor of Chap. 18, Cardiovascular Biomaterials, wrote to me with a lengthy list of changes, including updates to tables that were in the second edition; addition of new tables, together with discussion; a new section, Special Risks Associated with the Use of Materials of Animal Origin; plus five new discussions on other topics.

Michele J. Grimm, contributor of Chap. 20, Orthopedic Biomaterials, writes: "Sections on mechanobiology were added to the discussions of bone, cartilage, and ligament/tendon. References were updated where key new information was available (e.g., tantalum, zirconia, calcium sulfate injectables, wear particles, metal-on-metal hip implants, and others). A section on biodegradable metal was added."

Chapter 24, Biosensors (lead contributor, Roger J. Narayan), was updated with several changes to the text and the addition of two figures.

Although the majority of this handbook's contributors work in the United States, there is a noteworthy international component. Contributors of two chapters, Biomechanics of the Musculoskelatal System, which was updated, and Biomechanics of the Foot and Knee, which is new, are located in Australia. Two chapters, carried over unchanged from the second edition, were written by contributors located in Israel. A co-contributor of the chapter on Vibration, Mechanical Shock, and Impact is based part-time in Canada, and contributors of updates to the chapter on Biosensors are located in India. Most contributors work in academia, with a smattering of them in industry and government. I am immensely grateful to all of the contributors—those who contributed new and updated chapters, as well as those whose chapters from the second edition have been carried over unchanged into this one. I know how difficult it is to find the time to do any kind of writing, particularly a scholarly chapter on a technical subject, in these days when professionals in academia and industry are so hard-pressed. Thank you all.

Thanks also to my wonderful wife, Arlene, whose love is the thing I cherish most in all the world.

Myer Kutz
Delmar, New York

P · A · R · T · 1

BIOMEDICAL SYSTEMS ANALYSIS

CHAPTER 1
MODELING OF BIOMEDICAL SYSTEMS

Narender P. Reddy
University of Akron, Akron, Ohio

Models are conceptual constructions which allow formulation and testing of hypotheses. A mathematical model attempts to duplicate the quantitative behavior of the system. Mathematical models are used in today's scientific and technological world due to the ease with which they can be used to analyze real systems. The most prominent value of a model is its ability to predict as yet unknown properties of the system. The major advantage of a mathematical or computer model is that the model parameters can be easily altered and the system performance can be simulated. Mathematical models allow the study of subsystems in isolation from the parent system. Model studies are often inexpensive and less time consuming than corresponding experimental studies. A model can also be used as a powerful educational tool since it permits idealization of processes. Models of physiological systems often aid in the specification of design criteria for the design of procedures aimed at alleviating pathological conditions. Mathematical models are useful in the design of medical devices. Mathematical model simulations are first conducted in the evaluation of the medical devices before conducting expensive animal testing and clinical trials. Models are often useful in the prescription of patient protocols for the use of medical devices. Pharmacokinetic models have been extensively used in the design of drugs and drug therapies.

There are two types of modeling approaches: the black box approach and the building block approach. In the black box approach, a mathematical model is formulated based on the input-output characteristic of the system without consideration of the internal functioning of the system. Neural network models and autoregressive models are some examples of the black box approach. In the building block approach, models are derived by applying the fundamental laws (governing physical laws) and constitutive relations to the subsystems. These laws together with physical constraints are used to integrate the models of subsystems into an overall mathematical model of the system. The building block approach is used when the processes of the system are understood. However, if the system processes are unknown or too complex, then the black box approach is used. With the building block approach, models can be derived at the microscopic or at the macroscopic levels. Microscopic models are spatially distributed and macroscopic models are spatially lumped and are rather global. The microscopic modeling often leads to partial differential equations, whereas the macroscopic or global modeling leads to a set of ordinary differential equations. For example, the microscopic approach can be used to derive the velocity profile for blood flow in an artery; the global or macroscopic approach is needed to study the overall behavior of the circulatory system including the flow through arteries, capillaries, and the heart. Models can also be classified into continuous time models and models lumped in time domain. While the continuous time modeling leads to a set of differential equations, the models lumped in time are based on the analysis of discrete events in time and may lead to difference equations or sometimes into difference-differential equations. Random walk models and queuing theory models are some examples of discrete time models. Nerve firing in the central nervous system can be modeled using such discrete time event theories. Models can be classified into deterministic and stochastic models. For example, in deterministic modeling, we could describe the rate of change of volume of an arterial compartment to be equal to rate of flow in minus the rate of flow out of the compartment. However, in the stochastic approach, we look at the probability of increase in the volume of the compartment in an interval to be dependent on the probability of transition of a volume of fluid from the previous compartment and the probability of transition of a volume of fluid from the compartment to the next compartment. While the deterministic approach gives the means or average values, the stochastic approach yields means, variances, and covariances. The stochastic approach may be useful in describing the cellular dynamics, cell proliferations, etc. However, in this chapter, we will consider only the deterministic modeling at the macroscopic level.

The real world is complex, nonlinear, nonhomogeneous, often discontinuous, anisotropic, multilayered, multidimensional, etc. The system of interest is isolated from the rest of the world using a boundary. The system is then conceptually reduced to that of a mathematical model using a set of simplifying assumptions. Therefore, the model results have significant limitations and are valid only in the regimes where the assumptions are valid.

1.1 COMPARTMENTAL MODELS

Compartment models are lumped models. The concept of a compartmental model assumes that the system can be divided into a number of homogeneous well-mixed components called compartments. Various characteristics of the system are determined by the movement of material from one compartment to the other. Compartment models have been used to describe blood flow distribution to various organs, population dynamics, cellular dynamics, distribution of chemical species (hormones and metabolites) in various organs, temperature distribution, etc.

Physiological systems (e.g., cardiovascular system) are regulated by humoral mediators and can be artificially controlled using drugs. For instance, the blood pressure depends on vascular resistance. The vascular resistance in turn can be controlled by vasodilators. The principle of mass balance can be used to construct simple compartment models of drug distribution. Figure 1.1 shows a general multicompartmental (24-compartment) model of drug distribution in the human body. The rate of increase of mass of a drug in a compartment is equal to the rate of mass flowing into the compartment minus the rate of mass leaving the compartment, minus the rate of consumption of the drug due to chemical reaction in the compartment. In the model shown in Fig. 1.1, the lungs are represented by three compartments: Compartment 3 represents the blood vessels (capillaries, etc.) of the lung, the interstitial fluids of the lung are represented by compartment 4, and the intracellular components of the lung are represented by compartment 5. Each other organ (e.g., kidneys) is represented by two compartments consisting of the blood vessels (intravascular) and the tissue (extravascular consisting of interstitial and intracellular components together). Let us consider the model equations for a few compartments.

For compartment 3 (lung capillaries),

$$V_3 dC_3/dt = Q_2C_2 - Q_3C_3 - K_{3\text{-}4}A_{3\text{-}4}(C_3 - C_4) \tag{1.1}$$

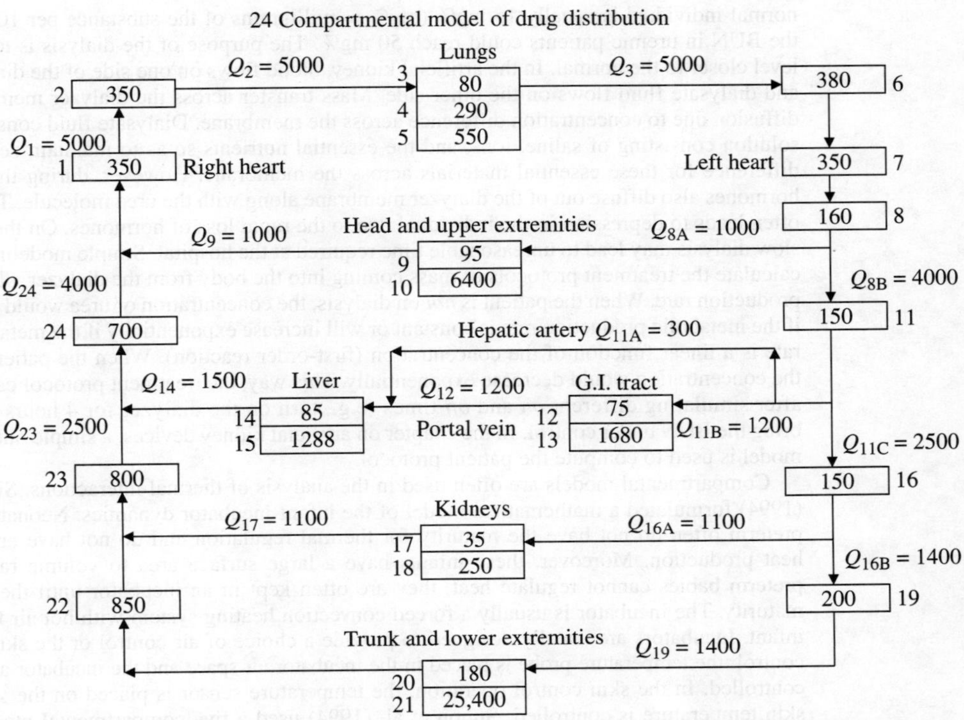

FIGURE 1.1 A generalized multicompartment (24) model of the human body to analyze drug distribution in the body. The numbers in the compartments represent volumes in milliliters. The numbers on the lines are flow rates in mL/min.

Q_2C_2 is the rate of mass flowing into compartment 3 from compartment 2, and Q_3C_3 is the rate of mass flowing out of compartment 3 into compartment 6. In addition, there is the interface mass transfer (diffusion) from capillaries into the interstitial spaces. This is represented by the last term. $K_{3\text{-}4}$ is the diffusional permeability of lung capillary. The diffusional permeability depends on capillary pore size, the number of pores per unit area, the diffusion coefficient for the drug molecule, the ratio of the diameter of the drug molecule, and the pore diameter. This permeability is different from the hydraulic permeability. $A_{3\text{-}4}$ is the lung capillary (interface) surface area. Mass is equal to volume times concentration. The change in volume occurs over a longer duration when compared to the changes in concentration. Consequently, volumes are assumed to be constant.

For the interstitial compartment,

$$V_4 dC_4/dt = K_{3\text{-}4} A_{3\text{-}4} (C_3 - C_4) - K_{4\text{-}5} A_{4\text{-}5} (C_4 - C_5) \tag{1.2}$$

For the intracellular compartment,

$$V_5 dC_5/dt = K_{4\text{-}5} A_{4\text{-}5} (C_4 - C_5) - M_R \tag{1.3}$$

where M_R is the rate of metabolic consumption of the drug. This could be a constant at high concentrations and a function of concentration at low concentrations. Recently, Kim et al. (2007) have developed a whole body glucose homeostasis during exercise and studied the effect of hormonal control.

Simple one compartmental models can be used for the prescription of treatment protocols for dialysis using an artificial kidney device. While the blood urea nitrogen (BUN) concentration in the normal individual is usually 15 mg% (mg% = milligrams of the substance per 100 mL of blood), the BUN in uremic patients could reach 50 mg%. The purpose of the dialysis is to bring the BUN level closer to the normal. In the artificial kidney, blood flows on one side of the dialyzer membrane and dialysate fluid flows on the other side. Mass transfer across the dialyzer membrane occurs by diffusion due to concentration difference across the membrane. Dialysate fluid consists of a makeup solution consisting of saline, ions, and the essential nutrients so as to maintain zero concentration difference for these essential materials across the membrane. However, during the dialysis, some hormones also diffuse out of the dialyzer membrane along with the urea molecule. Too rapid dialysis often leads to depression in the individual due to the rapid loss of hormones. On the other hand, too slow dialysis may lead to unreasonable time required at the hospital. Simple modeling can be used to calculate the treatment protocols of mass coming into the body from the dialyzer, plus the metabolic production rate. When the patient is *not* on dialysis, the concentration of urea would increase linearly if the metabolic production rate is constant or will increase exponentially if the metabolic production rate is a linear function of the concentration (first-order reaction). When the patient is *on* dialysis, the concentration would decrease exponentially. This way, the treatment protocol can be prescribed after simulating different *on* and *off* times (e.g., turn on the dialyzer for 4 hours every 3 days) to bring the BUN under control. In the chapter on artificial kidney devices, a simple one compartmental model is used to compute the patient protocol.

Compartmental models are often used in the analysis of thermal interactions. Simon and Reddy (1994) formulated a mathematical model of the infant-incubator dynamics. Neonates who are born preterm often do not have the maturity for thermal regulation and do not have enough metabolic heat production. Moreover, these infants have a large surface area to volume ratio. Since these preterm babies cannot regulate heat, they are often kept in an incubator until they reach thermal maturity. The incubator is usually a forced convection heating system with hot air flowing over the infant. Incubators are usually designed to provide a choice of air control or the skin control. In air control, the temperature probe is placed in the incubator air space and the incubator air temperature is controlled. In the skin control operation, the temperature sensor is placed on the skin and infant's skin temperature is controlled. Simon et al. (1994) used a five-compartmental model (Fig. 1.2) to compare the adequacy of air control and skin control on the core temperature of the infant. They considered the infant's core, infant's skin, incubator air, mattress, and the incubator wall to be four separate well-mixed compartments.

The rate of change of energy in each compartment is equal to the net heat transfer via conduction, convection, radiation, evaporation, and the sensible heat loss. There is a convective heat loss from the infant's core to the skin via the blood flow to the skin. There is also conductive heat transfer from the core to the skin. The infant is breathing incubator air, drawing in dry cold air at the incubator air temperature and exhaling humidified hot air at body temperature. There is heat transfer associated with heating the air from incubator air temperature to the infant's body (core) temperature. In addition, there is a convective heat transfer from the incubator air to the skin. This heat transfer is forced convection when the hot air is blowing into the incubator space and free convection when the heater manifolds are closed. Moreover, there is an evaporative heat loss from the skin to the incubator air. This is enhanced in premature infants as their skin may not be mature. Also, there is a conductive heat transfer from the back surface of the skin to the mattress. Also, exposed skin may radiate to the incubator wall. The incubator air is receiving hot air (convective heat transfer) from the hot air blower when the blower is in the *on* position. There is convective heat transfer from the incubator air to the incubator wall and to the mattress. In addition, there is metabolic heat production in the core. The energy balance for each compartment can be expressed as

$$mCp(dT/dt) = \Sigma Q_{\text{in}} - \Sigma Q_{\text{out}} + G \tag{1.4}$$

where m is the mass of the compartment, T is the temperature, t is the time, Q is the heat transfer rate, and G is the metabolic heat production rate. G is nonzero for the core and zero for all other compartments. G is low in low-birth-weight and significantly premature babies. Simon et al. (1994) investigated infant-incubator dynamics in normal, low birth weight, and different degrees of prematurity under skin and air control. Recently, Reddy et al. (2008) used the lumped compartmental

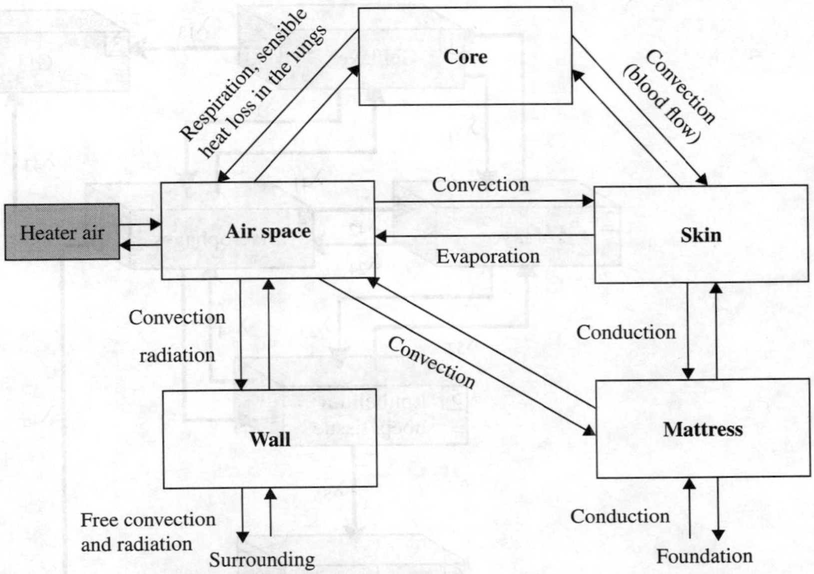

FIGURE 1.2 A lumped parameter model of the infant-incubator dynamics used by Simon et al. (1994) to simulate the effect of various control modes in a convectively heated infant incubator. Infant's core and skin are modeled as two separate compartments. The incubator air space, the incubator wall, and the mattress are treated as three compartments. Heat interactions occur between the core (infant's lungs) and the incubator air space through breathing. Skin-core heat interactions are predominantly due to blood flow to the skin. Heat transfer between the infant's skin and the incubator air is due to conduction and convection. Heat transfer from the skin to the mattress is via conduction, and heat transfer to the wall is via radiation from skin and convection from the air.

model of Simon et al. (1994) to evaluate the efficacy of air control, skin, control, and fuzzy logic control which incorporates both skin and air temperatures.

Compartmental models have been used to model particle dynamics. The growing number of cases of lung diseases, related to the accumulation of inhaled nonsoluble particles, has become a major problem in the urban population. Sturm (2007) has developed a simple multicompartment model for the clearance of nonsoluble particles from the tracheobronchial system (Fig. 1.3). While most of the particles are rapidly transported toward the pharynx by the beating celia, the particles caught in between celia in the highly viscous gel layer (compartment 1) may enter the low viscous sol layer (compartment 2) via diffusion. From the sol layer, they could enter the epithelium (compartment 5) and eventually enter the regional lymph node (compartment 6) or enter the blood circulation. Alternatively, they could be captured by the macrophages (compartment 4) in any of these layers and could reach the regional lymph node or the blood circulation (compartment 6) or the gastrointestinal tract (GIT; compartment 3). Macrophages could release phagocytosed particles into any of these layers. In addition, the particles could defuse among all three layers (gel, sol, and epithelium) in both directions. Sturum (2007) has derived model equations based on the diffusion of particles and other modes of transport.

1.2 ELECTRICAL ANALOG MODELS OF CIRCULATION

Electric analog models are a class of lumped models and are often used to simulate flow through the network of blood vessels. These models are useful in assessing the overall performance of a system or a subsystem. Integration of the fluid momentum equation (longitudinal direction, in cylindrical

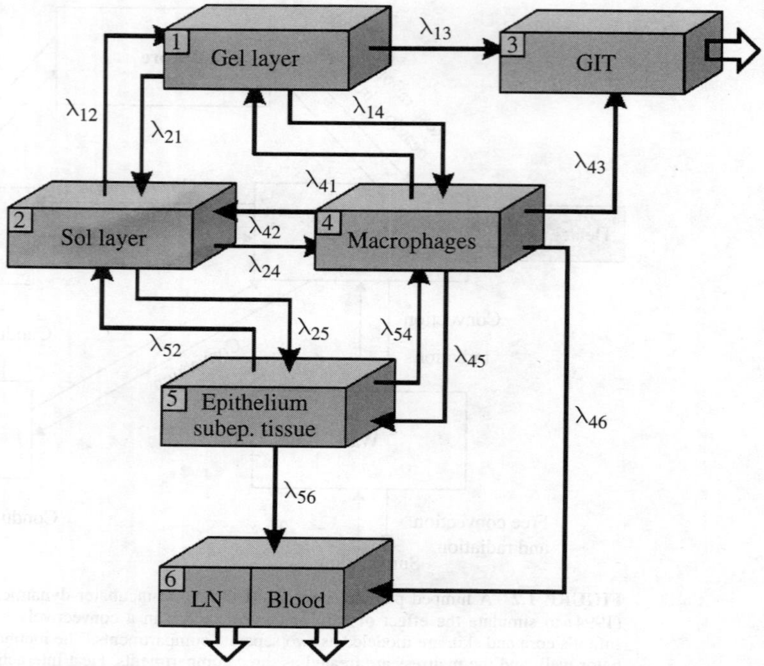

FIGURE 1.3 A multicompartmental model for the clearance of inhaled insoluble particles from the lung. [*Reproduced with permission from Sturm (2007).*]

coordinates) across the cross section results in the following expression (Reddy, 1986; Reddy and Kesavan, 1989):

$$\rho dQ/dt = \pi a^2 \, \Delta P/\ell 2a\tau_w \tag{1.5}$$

where ρ is the fluid density, Q is the flow rate, a is the wall radius, P is the pressure, ℓ is the length, and τ_w is the fluid shear stress at the wall. If we assume that the wall shear stress can be expressed using quasisteady analysis, then the wall shear stress can be estimated by $\tau_w = 4\mu Q/a^3$. Upon substituting for the wall stress and rearranging, the results are

$$[\rho\ell/(\pi a^2)]dQ/dt = \Delta P - [8\mu\ell/(\pi a^4)]Q \tag{1.6}$$

The above equation can be rewritten as

$$LdQ/dt = \Delta P - RQ \tag{1.7}$$

where $L = \rho\ell/(\pi a^2)$ and $R = 8\mu\ell/(\pi a^4)$.

It can be easily observed that flow rate Q is analogous to electrical current i, and ΔP is analogous to the electrical potential drop (voltage) ΔE. In the above equation, L is the inductance (inertance) and R is the resistance to flow. Therefore, Eq. (1.5) can be rewritten as

$$Ldi/dt = \Delta E - Ri \tag{1.8}$$

Fluid continuity equation, when integrated across the cross section, can be expressed as

$$dV/dt = \Delta Q = Q_{\text{in}} - Q_{\text{out}} \tag{1.9}$$

where V is the volume. However, volume is a function of pressure. Momentum balance for the vessel wall can be expressed as

$$P = P_{ext} + (h/a_0)\sigma \tag{1.10}$$

where P_{ext} is the external pressure on the outside of the vessel wall, h is the wall thickness, and σ is the hoop stress in the wall. The hoop stress is a function of wall radius a and modulus of elasticity E of the wall, and can be expressed as

$$\sigma = (E/2)[(a/a_0)^2 - 1] \tag{1.11}$$

where a_0 is the unstretched radius. Since the length of the segment does not change, the above equation can be expressed as

$$\sigma = (E/2)[(V/V_0) - 1] \tag{1.12}$$

where V is the volume of the vessel segment and V_0 is the unstretched volume. Equations (1.10), (1.11), and (1.12) can be combined as

$$dV/dt = CdP/dt \tag{1.13}$$

where

$$C = (2V_0\, a_0/hE) \tag{1.14}$$

C is often referred to as the compliance or capacitance.

Substituting Eq. (1.13) in Eq. (1.9) results in

$$CdP/dt = Q_{in} - Q_{out} \tag{1.15}$$

Equation (1.15) can be expressed in terms of an electrical equivalent as follows:

$$\overline{E} = (1/C)\int idt \tag{1.16}$$

Equations (1.7) and (1.16) can be used to simulate either a segment of a blood vessel or the entire blood vessel itself. In small blood vessels, the inductance L is very low when compared to the resistance term R, and therefore, the inductance term can be neglected in small arteries, arterioles, and capillaries. Since there is no oscillation of pressure in the capillaries, the inductance term can be neglected in vessels downstream of the capillary including venules, veins, vena cava, etc. (Chu and Reddy, 1992).

An electrical analog model of the circulation in the leg is illustrated in Fig. 1.4. Let us consider the flow from the femoral artery into the small leg arteries. There is no inductance in small leg arteries, and there is only the resistance. Since the small arteries are distensible, they have capacitance (compliance). The muscular pressure (P_{MP}) acts as the external pressure on the majority of small leg arteries. Consequently, P_{MP} is used as the reference pressure across the capacitor. The arterioles do not have inductance, but have a variable resistance which is controlled by neurogenic and metabolic factors. In this model, the precapillary sphincters and the capillaries are lumped together. Since the capillaries are rather rigid, they do not have any capacitance (compliance), but the combined resistance of the sphincters and capillaries is variable subject to metabolic control. For instance, precapillary sphincters dilate in the presence of lactic acid and other end products of metabolism. Venules have resistance and a variable capacitance. This capacitance is subject to neurogenic control since the diameter of the venule is under neurogenic control. From the venules, the flow goes into leg small veins which have a resistance and a variable capacitance subject to neurogenic control. In addition, the venules have valves which only permit unidirectional flow. These valves can be modeled as diodes. Again, the reference pressure for the capacitor is the muscle pressure P_{MP}. It is well known that the blood flow in the legs is aided by the muscle pump which is essentially the external pressure oscillations on the blood vessel wall due to periodic skeletal muscle contractions during walking, etc. The muscle pump is absent in bedridden patients. Extremity pumps are used on such patients to enhance blood flow to the legs. These extremity pumps provide a periodic a graded sequential external compression of the leg. The electrical analog model shown in Fig. 1.4 can be easily modified to simulate the effect of these extremity pumps.

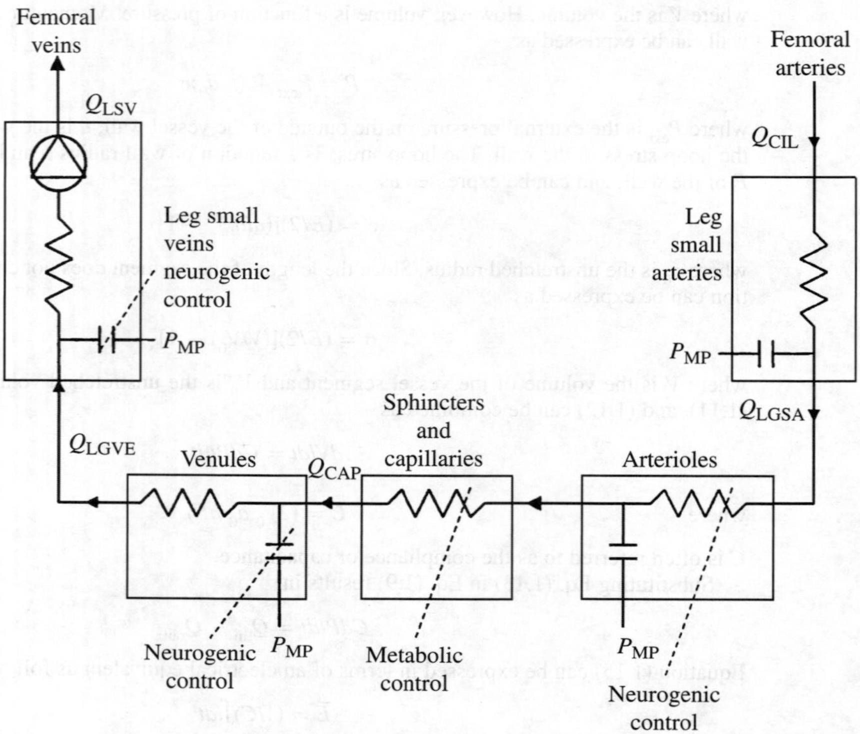

FIGURE 1.4 Electrical analog model of the circulation of the leg P_{MP} is the muscle pump which exerts a periodic external pressure on the blood vessels, Q is the flow rate, Q_{LGSA} is the flow through the leg small arteries, Q_{CAP} is the flow rate through the capillary, and Q_{LGVE} is the flow through the leg small veins. The elasticity is simulated with capacitance. The nonlinear capacitance of the leg small veins and the nonlinear resistance of arterioles and venules are under neurogenic control. The resistance of precapillary sphincters and capillaries is subject to metabolic control. The valves in the veins are simulated using diodes which permit only the unidirectional flow.

An electric analog model of pulmonary circulation is shown in Fig. 1.5. The flow is considered from node to node where the pressure is defined. The model equations for flow from compartment 1 (right ventricle) to the pulmonary arteries can be expressed by

$$L(dQ_1/dt) = P_1 - P_2 - R_1Q_1 \tag{1.17}$$

The pressure in compartment 2 can be expressed as

$$P_2 - P_{ith} = (1/C_1)\int(Q_1 - Q_2)dt \tag{1.18}$$

where P_{ith} is the intrathoracic pressure, which is pressure acting on the outside of the pulmonary vessels. Similarly,

$$P_2 - P_3 = R_2Q_2 \tag{1.19}$$

$$P_3 - P_{ith} = (1/C_2)\int(Q_2 - Q_3)dt \tag{1.20}$$

$$P_3 - P_5 = R_3Q_3 \tag{1.21}$$

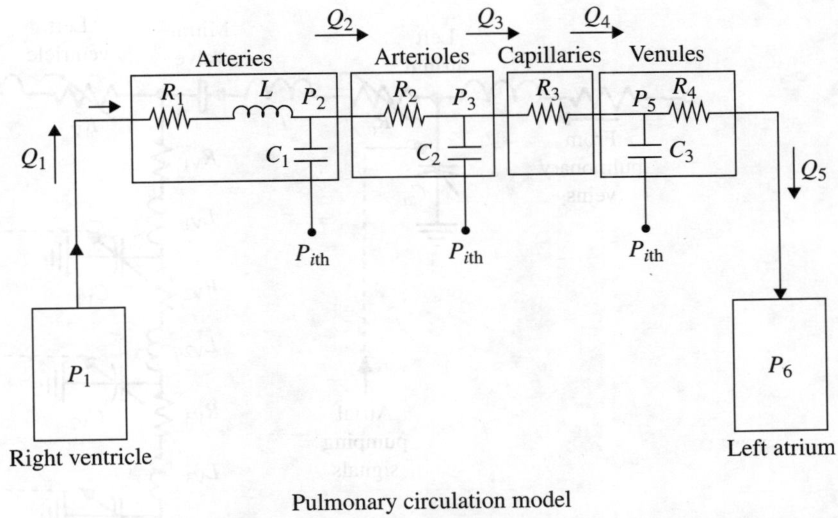

FIGURE 1.5 A model of pulmonary circulation. P_{ith} is the intrathoracic pressure which is the external pressure on the pulmonary blood vessels.

$$P_5 - P_{\text{ith}} = (1/C_3)\int(Q_4 - Q_5)dt \tag{1.22}$$

$$Q_3 = Q_4 \tag{1.23}$$

$$P_5 - P_6 = R_4 Q_5 \tag{1.24}$$

The capacitance is due to distensibility of the vessel. The capillaries are stiffer and less distensible, and therefore have minimal capacitance.

Electrical analog models have been used in the study of cardiovascular, pulmonary, intestinal, and urinary system dynamics. Recently, Barnea and Gillon (2001) have used an electrical analog model to simulate flow through the urethra. Their model consisted of a simple L, R, C circuit with a variable capacitor. The time varying capacitor simulated the time-dependent relaxation of the urethra. They used two types of resistance: a constant resistance to simulate Poiseouille-type viscous pressure drop and a flow-dependent resistance to simulate Bernoulli-type pressure loss. With real-time pressure-flow data sets, Barnea and Gillon (2001) have used the model to estimate urethral resistance and changes in urethral compliance during voiding, and have suggested that the urethral elastance (inverse of compliance) estimated by the model provides a new diagnostic tool. Ventricular and atrial pumping can be modeled using similar techniques. The actual pump (pressure source) can be modeled as a variable capacitor. Figure 1.6 shows a model of the left heart with a multisegment representation of the ventricle (Rideout, 1991). Kerckhoffs et al. (2007) have coupled an electrical analog model of systemic circulation with a finite element model of cardiac ventricular mechanics.

1.3 MECHANICAL MODELS

Mechanical models consisting of combinations of springs and dashpots are very popular in numerous disciplines. Spring dashpot models have been used to model the mechanical behavior of viscoelastic materials and can be used to represent the one dimensional behavior of tissue and other biological materials. In a linear spring, the force is proportional to the change in length or the strain.

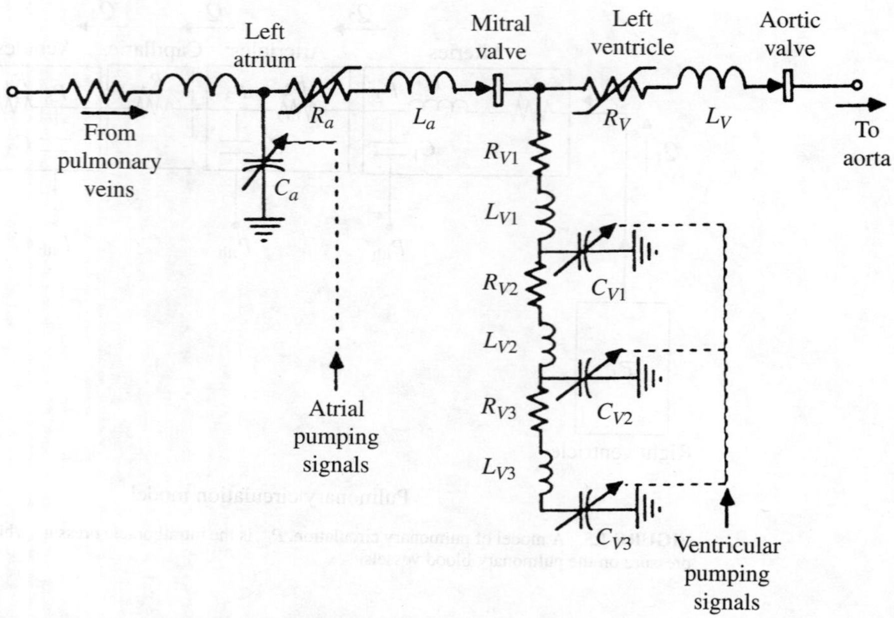

FIGURE 1.6 Electrical analog model to simulate atrial and ventricular pumping. Variable capacitances simulate the muscle contractions, and the filling and emptying through the ventricle can be simulated by a series of inductance and resistance elements. [*Adapted from Rideout (1991).*]

On the other hand, the force in a dashpot is proportional to the rate of change in strain. Consider a mass supported by a spring and a dashpot in parallel. Let a force F be acting on the mass. Force in a dashpot is $b(dX/dt)$ since the force in a fluid depends on strain rate. Here, b is a constant. The force in the spring is given by kX, where k is the spring constant.

Application of Newton's law results in

$$m(d^2X/dt^2) + b(dX/dt) + kX = F \tag{1.25}$$

where X is the elongation or change in length with respect to the steady-state value, b is the constant of the dashpot, and k is the spring constant.

It should be pointed out that the above mechanical equation is similar to the following electrical equation:

$$L(di/dt) + Ri + (1/C)\int i dt = E \tag{1.26}$$

where L is the inductance, R is the resistance, i is the current, and E is the voltage. This equation can be expressed in terms of the charge q instead of the current as

$$L(d^2q/dt^2) + R(dq/dt) + (1/C)q = E \tag{1.27}$$

Equations (1.25), (1.26), and (1.27) are similar. Therefore, mass is analogous to the inductance, the dashpot is analogous to the resistor, and the spring is analogous to the capacitor. The spring and the capacitor are storage units, whereas the dashpot and the resistor are the dissipaters of energy. The charge is analogous to the deformation or elongation, the current is similar to the velocity, and force is analogous to the voltage. Therefore, any electrical system can be modeled using mechanical analogs and any mechanical system can be modeled using electrical analogs.

Lumped mechanical models have been used to analyze the impact dynamics. Generally, muscle is represented by a combination of a spring and a dashpot, whereas a ligament is modeled using a spring.

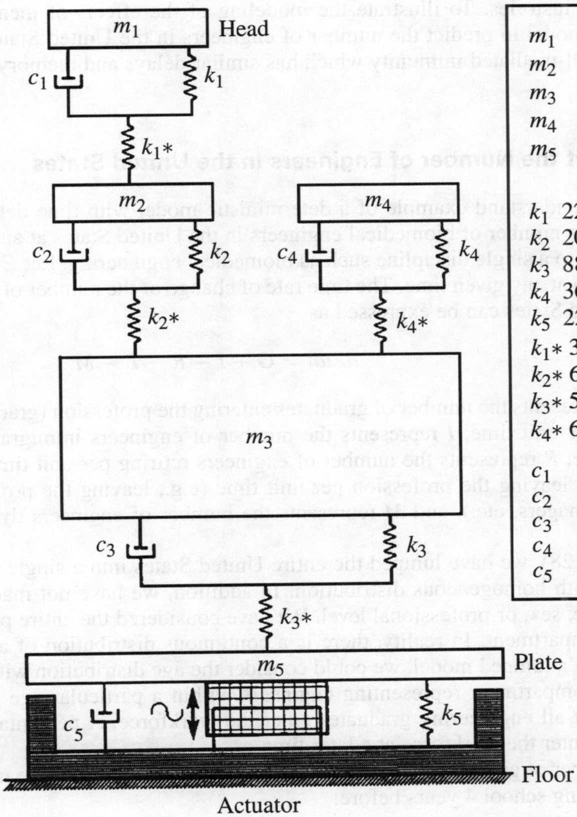

Parameter	Value
m_1	8.25 kg
m_2	8.05 kg
m_3	44.85 kg
m_4	13.86 kg
m_5	5 kg
k_1	22×10^8 N·m^{-1}
k_2	20.13×10^4 N·m^{-1}
k_3	88.56×10^3 N·m^{-1}
k_4	36.47×10^3 N·m^{-1}
k_5	22.2×10^4 N·m^{-1}
k_1*	36×10^7 N·m^{-1}
k_2*	65×10^9 N·m^{-1}
k_3*	52.34×10^4 N·m^{-1}
k_4*	69.30×10^3 N·m^{-1}
c_1	748.1 N·s·m^{-1}
c_2	578.0 N·s·m^{-1}
c_3	2964.0 N·s·m^{-1}
c_4	901.8 N·s·m^{-1}
c_5	84 N·s·m^{-1}

FIGURE 1.7 A lumped mechanical analog model for the analysis of vibration in relaxed standing human. [*Reproduced with permission from Fritton et al. (1997).*]

Human body vibrations can be analyzed using similar lumped models. Fritton et al. (1997) developed a lumped parameter model (Fig. 1.7) to analyze head vibration and vibration transmissibility in a standing individual. The model results are in good agreement with the experimental results. Such models are useful in the design of automobile seat cushion, motorcycle helmet design, etc.

1.4 MODELS WITH MEMORY AND MODELS WITH TIME DELAY

Time delay and memory processes occur in several biomedical disciplines. An example of such an application occurs in modeling of the immune system (Reddy and Krouskop, 1978). In cellular immune response, lymphocytes are sensitized to a foreign material and have memory. The immune response is significantly enhanced if the similar material is reintroduced after certain lag time. Another example could be the application to stress-induced bone remodeling. Modeling of the nervous system would involve time delays and memory. Similar hereditary functions are used to describe the material responses of viscoelastic materials. The effect of environmental pollutants can be modeled using such hereditary functions. Stress-induced bone remodeling involves time lags between the actual application of stress and actual new bone formation, and also involves stress/strain histories. To illustrate the modeling of the effects of memory and time delay, let us consider a model to predict the number of engineers in the United States. Then we will consider a model of cell-mediated immunity which has similar delays and memory functions.

1.4.1 A Model to Predict the Number of Engineers in the United States

An easy-to-understand example of a deterministic model with time delay and memory is a model to predict the number of biomedical engineers in the United States at any given time. Let us restrict our analysis to a single discipline such as biomedical engineering. Let E be the number of engineers (biomedical) at any given time. The time rate of change of the number of engineers at any given time in the United States can be expressed as

$$dE/dt = G + I - R - L - M \tag{1.28}$$

where G represents the number of graduates entering the profession (graduating from an engineering program) per unit time, I represents the number of engineers immigrating into the United States per unit time, R represents the number of engineers retiring per unit time, L represents the number of engineers leaving the profession per unit time (e.g., leaving the profession to become doctors, lawyers, managers, etc.), and M represents the number of engineers dying (before retirement) per unit time.

In Eq. (1.28), we have lumped the entire United States into a single region (a well-stirred compartment) with homogeneous distribution. In addition, we have not made any discrimination with regard to age, sex, or professional level. We have considered the entire pool as a well-stirred homogeneous compartment. In reality, there is a continuous distribution of ages. Even with this global analysis with a lumped model, we could consider the age distribution with a series of compartments with each compartment representing engineers within a particular age group. Moreover, we have assumed that all engineering graduates enter the workforce. A percentage of them go to graduate school and enter the workforce at a later time.

The number of graduates entering the profession is a function of the number of students entering the engineering school 4 years before:

$$G(t) = k_1 S(t - 4) \tag{1.29}$$

where $S(t)$ is the number of students entering the engineering school per unit time. The number of students entering the engineering school depends on the demand for the engineering profession over a period of years, that is, on the demand history.

The number of engineers immigrating into the United States per unit time depends on two factors: demand history in the United States for engineers and the number of visas that can be issued per unit time. Assuming that immigration visa policy is also dependent on demand history, we can assume that I is dependent on demand history. Here we have assumed that immigrants from all foreign countries are lumped into a single compartment. In reality, each country should be placed in a separate compartment and intercompartmental diffusion should be studied.

The number of engineers retiring per unit time is proportional to the number of engineers in the profession at the time:

$$R(t) = k_2 E(t) \tag{1.30}$$

The number of engineers leaving the profession depends on various factors: the demand for the engineering profession at that time and demand for various other professions at that time as well as on several personal factors. For the purpose of this analysis, let us assume that the number of engineers leaving the profession in a time interval is proportional to the number of individuals in the profession at that time:

$$L(t) = k_3 E(t) \tag{1.31}$$

The number of engineers dying (before retirement) per unit time is proportional to the number of engineers at that time:

$$M(t) = k_4 E(t) \tag{1.32}$$

The demand for engineers at any given time is proportional to the number of jobs available at that time ($J(t)$) and is inversely proportional to the number of engineers available at that time:

$$D(t) = kJ(t)/E(t) \tag{1.33}$$

The number of jobs available depends on various factors such as government spending for R&D projects, economic growth, sales of medical products, number of hospitals, etc. Let us assume in this case (biomedical engineering) that the number of jobs is directly proportional to the sales of medical products (p), directly proportional to government spending for health care R&D (e), and directly proportional to the number of new medical product company startups (i):

$$J(t) = (k_6 e + k_7 c + k_8 i + k_9 + kp) \tag{1.34}$$

Although we assumed that the number of jobs at the present time is dependent on $e(t)$, $c(t)$, $h(t)$, $i(t)$, and $p(t)$, in reality the number of jobs at present may depend on previous values of these parameters, or on the history of these parameters.

Let us now analyze the demand history. This history depends on the memory function. Let us assume that the effect of demand existing at a time decays exponentially (exponentially decaying memory). The net effect of demands from time = 0 to t can be expressed as

$$H_1(t) = {}_{\tau=0}I^{\tau=t}\{D(\tau)\exp[-k_{10}(t-\tau)]\}d\tau \tag{1.35}$$

The number of students entering the engineering school per unit time is

$$S(t) = k_{11} H_1(t) \tag{1.36}$$

Immigration rate can similarly be expressed as

$$I(t) = k_{12} H_2(t) \tag{1.37}$$

where

$$H_2(t) = {}_{\tau=0}I^{\tau=t}\{D(\tau)\exp[-k_{13}(t-\tau)]\}d\tau \tag{1.38}$$

H_1 and H_2 are called hereditary functions. Instead of an exponential decay of memory, we could have a sinusoidal or some other functional form of memory decay, depending on the physical situation.

$$dE/dt = k_1 k_{10} H_1(t-4) + k_{11} H_2(t) - (k_2 + k_3 + k_4)E(t) \tag{1.39}$$

In this analysis, making various assumptions, we have formulated a lumped parameter deterministic model to predict the number of engineers (biomedical) present in the United States at any given time. If we want to know the geographical distribution, we can take two approaches. We can divide the entire United States into a number of compartments (e.g., northeast, east, west, etc.) and study the intercompartmental diffusion. Alternatively, we can make E a continuous variable in space and time $I(x, y, t)$ and account for spatial diffusion.

1.4.2 Modeling the Cell-Mediated Immunity in Homograft Rejection

In cell-mediated immunity, lymphocytes in the tissue become sensitized to the target (graft) cells and travel to the regional lymph nodes where they initiate an immunological response by increasing the production of immunocompetent lymphocytes. The newly produced lymphocytes are then transported into the blood stream via the thoracic duct. Lymphocytes recirculate from the blood stream through the tissue and return to the blood stream via the lymphatic system. When foreign cells are introduced into the tissue, blood lymphocytes migrate into the tissue at an increased rate and bring about the destruction of the target cells. Lymphocytes have memory and they exhibit an increased secondary response, e.g., if after the rejection of the first graft, a second graft is introduced into the host, the second graft is rejected much faster. A similar situation occurs in delayed hypersensitivity, which is another cell-mediated reaction. In this analysis, let us assume that blood and tissue are well-stirred compartments and that the newly produced lymphocytes are introduced into the blood compartment (Reddy and Krouskop, 1978).

For sensitization to occur, a lymphocyte has to come in contact with a target cell. The number of lymphocytes becoming sensitized at any given time ($L_s(t)$) is a function of the number of lymphocytes in the tissue ($L_T(t)$) and the number of target (foreign) cells ($g(t)$)

$$L_s(t) = C_1 L_T(t) g(t) \tag{1.40}$$

Certain lymphocytes, upon encountering target cells, are transformed into memory cells. The memory cell formation depends upon the number of lymphocytes in the tissue and the number of target cells. The number of memory cells formed at any time (t) may thus be expressed as

$$L_{ms}(t) = C_1 L_T(t) g(t) \tag{1.41}$$

Sensitized lymphocytes stimulate the production of immunocompetent lymphocytes and the effect of each sensitized cell lasts for a given period of time. For the purpose of the present analysis, it is assumed that the effect of each sensitized lymphocyte decays exponentially over a period of time. The production rate of blood lymphocytes at any time (t) due to the primary response $(dL_B/dt)_{prim}$ would then be equal to the sum of the residual effect of all the lymphocytes sensitized between time 0 and time $t - \Phi_1$, where Φ_1 is the time lag between sensitization and production of the lymphocytes.

The number of lymphocytes produced due to primary response between time t and time $(t - \Phi_1)$ would be

$$L_B(t) - L_B(t - \Delta t) = C_3\{\underbrace{L_S(t - \Phi_1)\Delta t}_{\text{Due to lymphocytes sensitized at } t - \Phi_1} + \underbrace{L_S(t - \Phi_1 - \Delta t)\Delta t}_{\text{Due to lymphocytes sensitized at } t - \Phi_1 - \Delta t} + \underbrace{L_S(t - \Phi_1 - 2\Delta t)e^{-K1\Delta t}\Delta t}_{\text{Due to lymphocytes sensitized at } t - 2\Phi_{1-} - \Delta t}$$

$$+ \underbrace{L_S(t - \Phi_1 - r\Delta t)e^{-K1\, r\Delta t}\Delta t}_{\text{Due to lymphocytes sensitized at } t - \Phi_{1-} = r\Delta t} + \cdots\} \tag{1.42}$$

$$= C_3 3 L_S(t - \Phi_1 - r\Delta t)e^{-K1\, r\Delta t}\Delta t \tag{1.43}$$

Dividing by Δt and taking the limits as $\Delta t\ \Pi\ 0$, the left-hand side becomes a derivative and the right-hand side can be represented as an integral in terms of the hereditary function

$$(dL_B(t)/dt)_{primary} = C_3 \int_0^{t - \Phi_1} L_S(\tau) e^{-K1(t - \Phi_1 - \tau)} d\tau \tag{1.44}$$

Substituting for L_S in terms of L_T,

$$(dL_B(t)/dt)_{primary} = k_2 \int_0^{t - \Phi_1} L_T(\tau) e^{-K1(t - \Phi_1 - \tau)} d\tau \tag{1.45}$$

For the secondary response to appear, a memory cell must encounter a target cell, and therefore the secondary response depends upon the number of memory cells and the number of target cells. Similar to (Eq. 1.45), Reddy and Krouskop (1978) expressed the secondary response in terms of a hereditary function

$$(dL_B(t)/dt)_{secondary} = k_3 \int_0^{t - \Phi_2} L_T(\tau) g(\tau) e^{-K4(t - \Phi_2 - \tau)} g(t - \Phi_3) d\tau \tag{1.46}$$

In developing the above equation, it is assumed that the effect of a memory cell also decays exponentially over a period of time. Thus the production rate of blood lymphocytes at time (t) due to secondary response $(dL_B/dt)_{second}$ is due to the sum of the residual effects of all the memory cells formed between 0 and time $t - \phi_2$, where ϕ_2 is the time lag between memory cell formation and the appearance of the secondary response.

The net rate in change of blood lymphocytes may then be described as

$$dL_B/dt = \underbrace{k_2 \int_0^{t-\Phi_1} L_T(\tau)e^{-K1(t-\Phi_1-\tau)}d\tau}_{\text{Due to primary response}} + \underbrace{k_3 \int_0^{t-\Phi_2} L_T(\tau)g(\tau)e^{-K4(t-\Phi_2-\tau)}g(t-\Phi_3)d\tau}_{\text{Due to secondary response}}$$

$$+ \underbrace{K_5L_T}_{\text{Recirculation}} - \underbrace{K_6L_B - K_7L_B}_{\text{Death in the blood}} - \underbrace{K_8L_Bg}_{\text{Migration into tissue due to target cell presence}} \tag{1.47}$$

The rates of change of tissue lymphocytes and the number of target cells can be described using similar mass balance

$$dL_T/dt = \underbrace{K_8L_B\,g}_{\text{Increased migration}} \underbrace{- K_5L_T + K_6L_B}_{\text{Recirculation}} \underbrace{- K_9L_Tg}_{\text{Loss due to target cell destruction}} \tag{1.48}$$

$$dg/dt = (dg/dt)_{input} - k_{10}L_Tg \tag{1.49}$$

These equations were simulated by Reddy and Krouskop. Figure 1.8 shows the production rate of lymphocytes and the number of target cells when the target cells were introduced on day 0 and again on day 4. Figure 1.9 shows the production rate of lymphocytes and the number of target cells present in the tissue when the target cells were introduced continuously.

1.5 ARTIFICIAL NEURAL NETWORK MODELS

Neural network models represent the black box type of model. These models are used where the precise functioning of the system is not understood but the sample input-output data are known. Neural networks represent a new generation of information processing systems that are artificially (virtually) constructed to make use of the organizational structure of the neuronal information processing in the brain. A neural network consists of several interconnecting neurons also called as nodes. These nodes are organized into an input layer, one or more hidden layers, and an output layer. The number of input layer nodes in the input layer depends on the number of input variables. The number of nodes in the output layer is determined by the number of output parameters. Each input parameter is represented by a node in the input layer, and the each output parameter is represented by a node in the output layer. The number of nodes in the hidden layer could be variable. Each node in a feed-forward neural network is connected to every node in the next level of nodes. That means each input node is connected to all the nodes in the hidden layer neurons. Let us, for simplicity, consider only one hidden layer. Now, each node in the hidden layer is connected to all the nodes in the output layer. Figure 1.10 shows a network with four output nodes and five input nodes with four hidden layer nodes. The connection strengths are determined by the weights.

Let us assume that $W_{i,j}$ represents the weight of the connection from the jth node in the hidden layer to the ith node in the output layer, and let us assume that $w_{j,k}$ represents the weight of connection from the kth input node to the jth node in the hidden layer. Let X_k represents the value of kth input node.

The sum of weighted inputs to the jth node in the hidden layer is

$$I_j = \Sigma w_{j,k} X_k \tag{1.50}$$

In other words, $I_1 = w_{1,1}X_1 + w_{1,2}X_2 + w_{1,3}X_3 + w_{1,4}X_4$, where X_1, X_2, X_3, and X_4 are the values of the four input parameters.

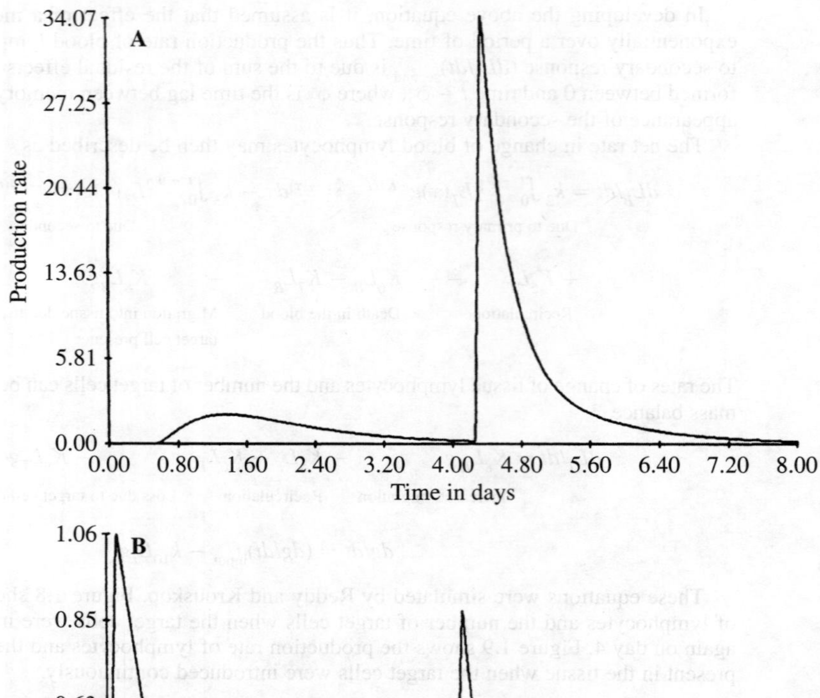

FIGURE 1.8 The simulation results of the production rate of lymphocytes (A), and the number of target cells or foreign cells (B) plotted as a function of time in days. In the simulation, the target cells were introduced on day 0 and again on day 4. [*Reddy and Krouskop (1978).*] Note the increased secondary response.

The output of a hidden layer neuron is a function of its input

$$H_j = f(I_j) \tag{1.51}$$

This function f is called the activation function. An example of this function is the sigmoid function

$$H_j = k[2/(1 + \exp(-aI_j + B) - 1] \tag{1.52}$$

where k, a, and B are constants. B is called the bias. B can be a zero. In general, any monotone, nondecreasing differentiable signal function can be used as the activation function.

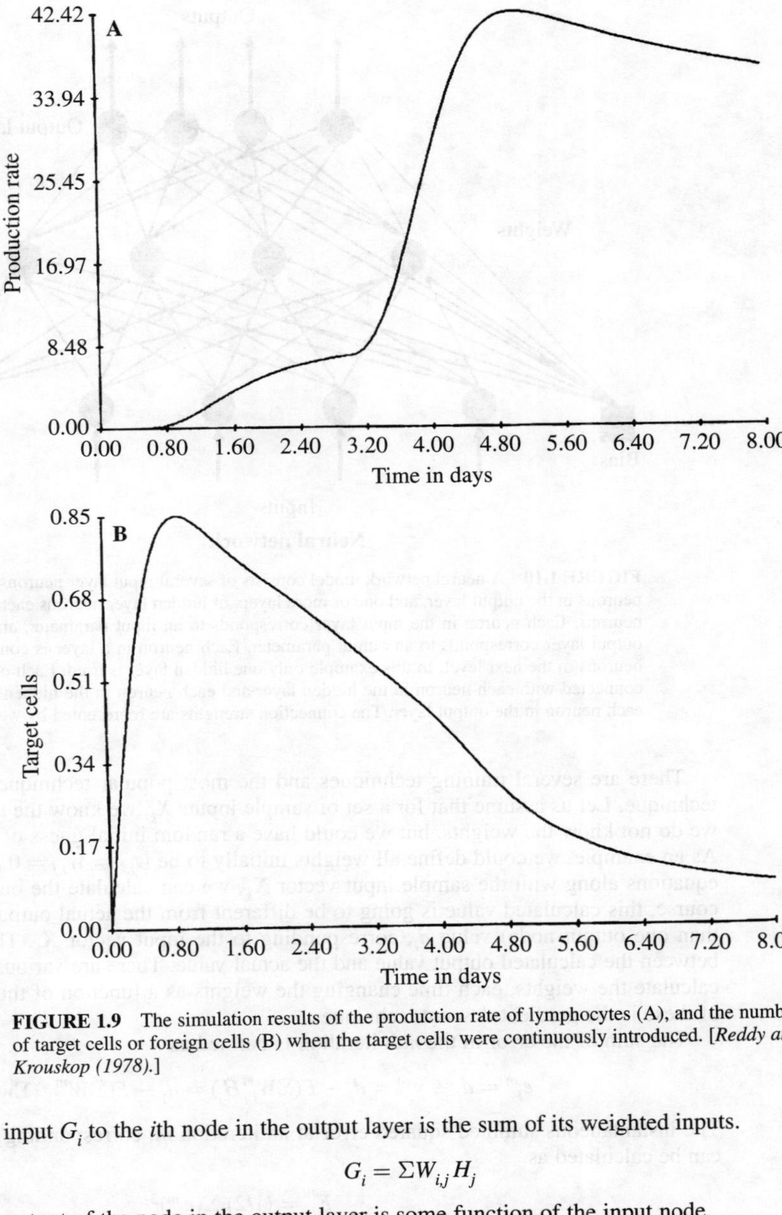

FIGURE 1.9 The simulation results of the production rate of lymphocytes (A), and the number of target cells or foreign cells (B) when the target cells were continuously introduced. [*Reddy and Krouskop (1978).*]

The input G_i to the ith node in the output layer is the sum of its weighted inputs.

$$G_i = \Sigma W_{i,j} H_j \tag{1.53}$$

The output of the node in the output layer is some function of the input node.

$$Y_i = F(G_i) \tag{1.54}$$

The activation function F of the output neurons can be any monotone, nondecreasing differentiable function. Sigmoid or logistic functions are usually used.

If the weights $w_{j,k}$, and $W_{i,j}$ are all known, then given the input X_k, the output Y_i of the system can be calculated. The weights are determined through a training algorithm using the sample input-output data.

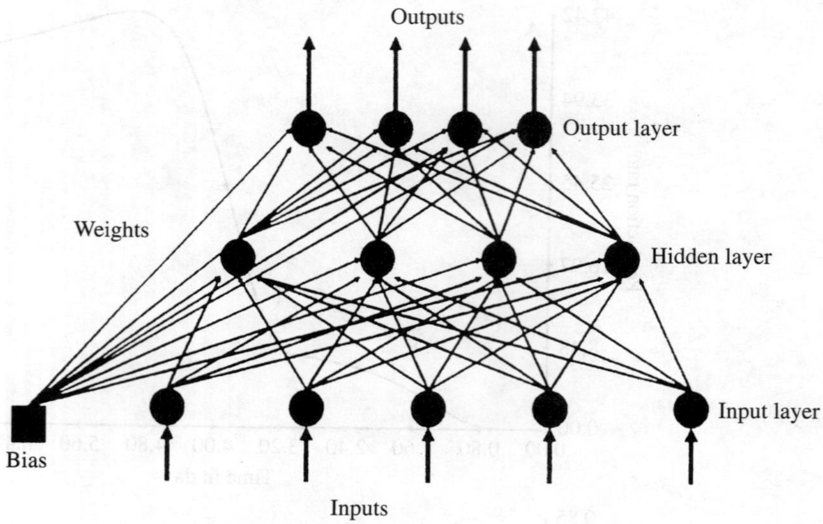

Neural network

FIGURE 1.10 A neural network model consists of several input layer neurons (nodes), one or more neurons in the output layer, and one or more layers of hidden layer neurons each consisting of several neurons. Each neuron in the input layer corresponds to an input parameter, and each neuron in the output layer corresponds to an output parameter. Each neuron in a layer is connected to each of the neurons in the next level. In this example only one hidden layer is used. Each of the input neurons is connected with each neuron in the hidden layer and each neuron in the hidden layer is connected to each neuron in the output layer. The connection strengths are represented by weights.

There are several training techniques and the most popular technique is the back propagation technique. Let us assume that for a set of sample inputs X_k, we know the actual outputs d_i. Initially, we do not know the weights, but we could have a random initial guess of the weights $w_{j,k}$ and $W_{i,j}$. As an example, we could define all weights initially to be $w_{j,k} = W_{i,j} = 0.2$ or 0.5. Using the above equations along with the sample input vector $\mathbf{X}_k$, we can calculate the output of the system Y_i. Of course, this calculated value is going to be different from the actual output (vector if there is more than one output node) value d_i, corresponding to the input vector $\mathbf{X}_k$. The error is the difference between the calculated output value and the actual value. There are various algorithms to iteratively calculate the weights, each time changing the weights as a function of the error. The most popular of these is the gradient descent technique.

The sum of the error in the mth iteration is defined as

$$e_i^m = d_i - y_i^m = d_i - F(\Sigma W_{i,j}^m H_j) = d_i - F(\Sigma W_{i,j}^m f(\Sigma w_{j,k}^m X_k) \tag{1.55}$$

The instantaneous summed squared error at an iteration m, corresponding to the sample data set n, can be calculated as

$$E_n^m = (1/2)\ \Sigma(e_i^m)^2 \tag{1.56}$$

The total error E at each iteration, for all the sample data pairs (input-output), can be calculated as the sum of the errors E_n for the individual sample data.

Adjusting the weights for each iteration for connections between the hidden layer neurons and the output layer neurons $W_{i,j}$ can be calculated as

$$W_{i,j}^{m+1} = W_{i,j}^m - \eta(\delta\ E^m/\delta W_{i,j}) \tag{1.57}$$

where η is the learning rate.

The error gradient can be expressed as

$$(\delta E^m/\delta W_{i,j}) = (\delta E^m/\delta F)(dF/dW_{i,j}) \tag{1.58}$$

For a sigmoid function (F), it turns out that the differential is a simple function of the sigmoid as follows:

$$dF = b(1 - F)F \tag{1.59}$$

where b is a constant. Thus,

$$(dF/dW_{i,j}) = b(1 - F(W_{i,j}))F(W_{i,j}) \tag{1.60}$$

For adjusting the weights for connections between the input and the hidden layer neurons, the error is back propagated by calculating the partial derivative of the error E with respect to the weights $w_{j,k}$ similarly (Haykin, 1999).

The whole process of calculating the weights using the sample data sets is called the training process. There is a neural network package in the MATLAB which can be easily used in the training process. There are several algorithms in the package, including the back propagation, modified back propagation, etc. which the user can choose in the MATLAB software. Once the weights are calculated using MATLAB or any other software, it becomes a matter of obtaining the output vector for a given input vector using matrix multiplications. The most important aspect of a neural network is that it should be tested with data not used in the training process.

Neural networks have been used for classification and control. For instance, Reddy et al. (1995) used neural networks to classify the degree of the disease in dysphagic patients using noninvasive measurements (of throat acceleration, swallow suction, pressure, etc.) obtained from dysphagic patients during swallowing. These measurements were the inputs to the network and the outputs were normal, mild, moderate, and severe. Neural network performance depends on the sample data, initial weights, etc. Reddy et al. (1995) trained several networks with various initial conditions and activation functions. Based on some initial testing with known data, they recruited the best five networks into a committee. A majority opinion of the committee was used as the final decision. For classification problems, Reddy and Buch (2003) and Das et al. (2001) obtained better results with committee of neural networks (Fig. 1.11) when compared to a single network, and the majority opinion of the committee was in agreement with clinical or actual classification.

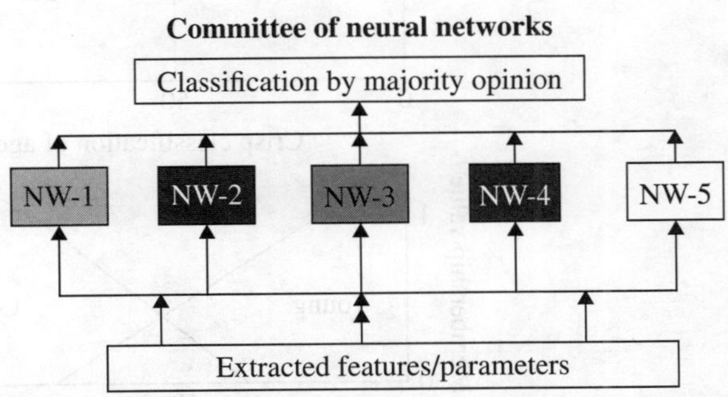

FIGURE 1.11 The committee of neural networks. Each of the input parameters is simultaneously fed to several networks working in parallel. Each network is different from the others in terms of initial training weights or the activation function (transfer function at the nodes). A majority opinion of the member networks provides the final decision of the committee. This committee of networks simulates the parliamentary process, and emulates a group of physicians making the decision. [*Reddy and Buch (2000).*]

1.6 FUZZY LOGIC

Most real world systems include some element of uncertainty and cannot be accurately modeled using crisp logic. Moreover, some of these systems require modeling of parameters like human experience, intuition, etc., which involve various degrees of conceptual uncertainties and vagueness. Several of these applications require fuzzy definition of boundaries and fuzzy classes, whose membership values are in the form of degree of membership, rather than in the form of true or false. In crisp logic, a parameter can belong to only one class. However, in fuzzy logic, a parameter could belong to more than one class at the same time. Let us assume that we want to classify the age of a person into two classes: young and old. In crisp logic, the individual belongs to either old or young, as the crisp logic requires a clear boundary between the two classes. In fuzzy logic, the individual can belong to both classes at the same time. Figure 1.12 provides a general comparison of a crisp and a fuzzy variable and its membership to subsets. The variable x is divided into two subsets "young" and "old." For example, if $x = 40$, the crisp classification would be "young." On the other hand, the fuzzy classification would be (0.7, 0.3), indicating that the individual belongs to both classes (70 percent young and 30 percent old). The individual's membership to the subset "young" would be 0.7, and his membership to subset "old" would be 0.3. The function which defines the boundaries of the domains (or subsets) is called "membership function" and the values 0.7 and 0.3 are called the membership values.

Overall scheme of the fuzzy logic system is shown in Fig. 1.13. In the fuzzy logic, each measured parameter is fuzzified by calculating the membership values to various subsets using predefined membership functions. The membership values for the parameters are then sent to a predefined rule base to provide a fuzzy output. The fuzzy output is then defuzzified using a defuzzification scheme. Usually, the centroid defuzzification is used to come up with a crisp output. The first step in designing a fuzzy logic system is to first define the number of subsets, and the membership functions which define the subset domains. The membership functions can be linear, triangular, trapezoidal, or sigmoidal, or can be of irregular geometry. Fuzzy logic can be used for classification (Suryanarayanan et al., 1995; Steimann and Adlassnig, 1998; Sproule et al., 2002; Sakaguchi et al., 2004; Mangiameli et al., 2004) and control problems (Suryanarayan and Reddy, 1997; Kutava et al., 2006). Examples of both of these are presented below.

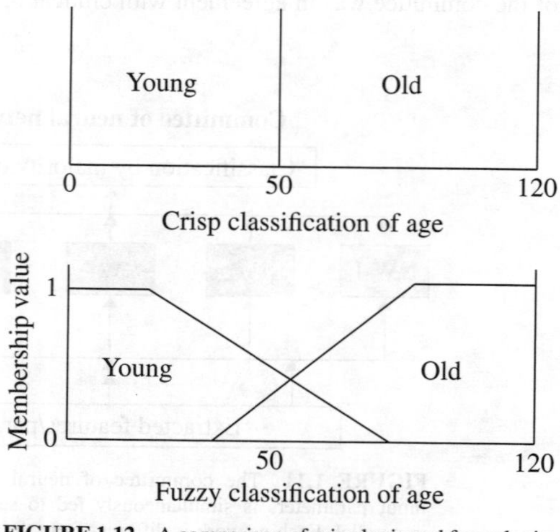

FIGURE 1.12 A comparison of crisp logic and fuzzy logic. In crisp logic a variable (age of an individual in this example) belongs to a single subdomain. In fuzzy logic, a variable can belong to a number of subdomains with varying degree of membership value. The domain boundaries are defined by membership functions.

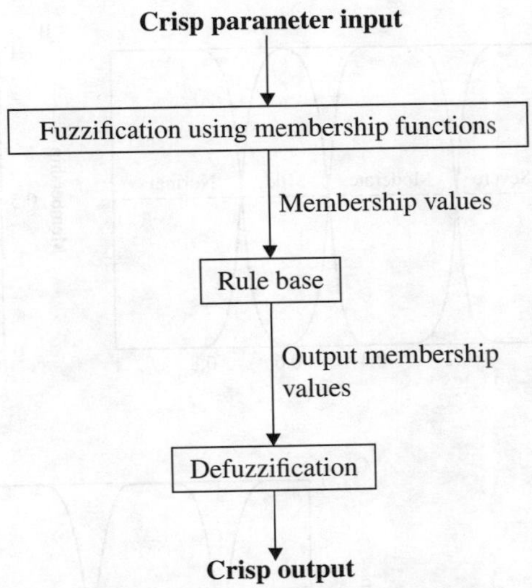

FIGURE 1.13 The overall scheme of fuzzy logic. The measured crisp parameters are first fuzzified with the aid of membership functions to obtain the membership value to various subdomains. The membership values are then subjected to a predefined rule base. The output of the rule base is in the form of output membership values to various subdomains. This fuzzy output is then defuzzified to obtain a crisp output.

1.6.1 Fuzzy Classification of Risk for Aspiration in Dysphagic Patients

Suryanarayanan et al. (1995) developed a fuzzy logic diagnosis system to classify the dysphagic patient into "normal, mild, moderate, and severe dysphagia" based on several parameters measured from the dysphagic subject. Dysphagia denotes dysfunction of the swallowing mechanism and presents a major problem in the rehabilitation of stroke and head injury patients. Dysfunction of the pharyngeal phase of swallow can lead to aspiration, chocking, and even death. Consequently, the assessment of risk for aspiration is important from a clinical point of view. Reddy et al. (1990, 1991, 1994) have identified and developed instrumentation and techniques to noninvasively quantify various biomechanical parameters that characterize the dysphagic patient and clinically evaluated the technique by correlating with the videofluorography examination (Reddy et al., 2000). For the assessment of the pharyngeal phase, they have placed an ultraminiature accelerometer at the throat at the level of thyroid cartilage and asked the patient to elicit a swallow (Reddy et al., 1991, 1994). Swallowing in normal subjects gave rise to a characteristic acceleration pattern which was distorted or absent in dysphagic individuals. In addition to the acceleration measurements, they measured swallow suction pressure (with a catheter placed toward the posterior aspect of the tongue), and the number of attempts to swallow before eliciting a swallow response, etc. Suryanarayanan et al. (1995) fuzzified these measurements by defining membership functions for each of these parameters (magnitude of acceleration, swallow pressure, and number of attempts to swallow) which defined the four subdomains (severe risk, moderate risk, mild risk for aspiration, and normal) for each of these parameters (Fig. 1.14). Membership functions were constructed using the function

$$\mu = 1/(\exp(\alpha x + \beta)) \tag{1.61}$$

where μ is the membership value, x is the measured parameter, and α and β are constants. The slope of the sigmoid function can be changed by changing the value of α.

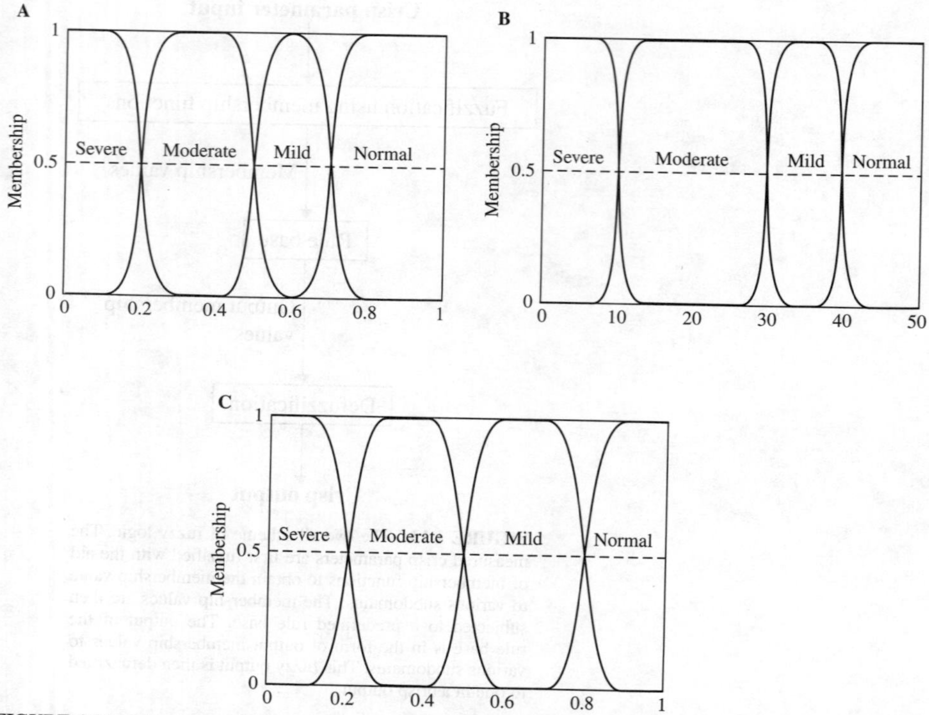

FIGURE 1.14 The membership functions are used to compute the membership values corresponding to the measured parameters: (A) membership functions for the acceleration magnitude (peak-to-peak value); (B) membership functions for the peak swallow pressure; and (C) the measured number of attempts to swallow. The variable number of attempts to swallow n, was transformed by a linear transfer function given by defining a new variable $f = (8 - n)/7$ and membership functions defined on the new variable f. *[Reproduced with permission from Suryanarayanan et al. (1995).]*

The membership values are represented as $\mu_{i,j}$, where i represents the parameter and j represents the subset. Corresponding to each parameter a, we have a vector of membership values given by

$$\mu_a(X) = [\mu_{a,1}(x), \mu_{a,2}(x), \mu_{a,3}(x), \mu_{a,4}(x)] \tag{1.62}$$

where a is the parameter, $\mu_{a,j}$ is the membership to the jth subset corresponding to parameter a. For instance, $\mu_{a,1}$ refers to membership value related to severe distortion in the acceleration magnitude, $\mu_{a,2}$ refers to moderate distortion in acceleration magnitude, $\mu_{a,3}$ refers to mild distortion in acceleration magnitude, and $\mu_{a,4}$ refers to normal acceleration magnitude. Similarly, the elements in $\mu_{b,1}$, $\mu_{b,2}$, $\mu_{b,3}$, and $\mu_{b,4}$ refer to severe distortion in the swallow pressure magnitude, moderate distortion in swallow pressure magnitude, mild distortion in swallow pressure magnitude, and normal swallow pressure.

For each patient, the measured parameter values are fuzzified to obtain the four membership values for each of the three parameters. These values are then fed to a rule base R. The function R is defined as a relation between the parameters defined. A typical relation between input and output parameters is the IF-THEN rule. The output is given by the rule set R acting upon the membership values computed for the measured parameters and is represented as

$$\Phi = R \cdot [(\mu_a(x), \mu_b(y), \mu_c(z)] \tag{1.63}$$

where subscript a refers to the parameter "acceleration magnitude" and x is the corresponding value, subscript b refers to the parameter "swallow pressure magnitude" and y is the corresponding value of this parameter, and subscript c refers to the parameter "number of attempts to swallow" and z is the corresponding value of this parameter. The rule base can be in the form of a lookup table or in the form of a minimum or maximum operation. Since the dysphagia classification involves estimating the severity of the disease, Suryanarayanan et al. (1995) used the maximum rule.

Using the maximum rule, the output membership value corresponding to the severe risk (Φ_1) can be calculated as

$$\Phi_1 = [\mu_{a,1}(x) V \mu_{b,1}(y) V \mu_{c,1}(z)] \tag{1.64}$$

The output membership value corresponding to the moderate risk can be expressed as

$$\Phi_2 = [(\mu_{a,2}(x) V \mu_{b,2}(y) V \mu_{c,2}(z)] \tag{1.65}$$

The output membership value corresponding to the mild risk can be expressed as

$$\Phi_3 = [(\mu_{a,3}(x) V \mu_{b,3}(y) V \mu_{c,3}(z)] \tag{1.66}$$

The output membership value corresponding to the normal risk can be expressed as

$$\Phi_4 = [(\mu_{a,4}(x) V \mu_{b,4}(y) V \mu_{c,4}(z)] \tag{1.67}$$

where V indicates the maximum operator.

The output can be defuzzified using centroid defuzzification scheme to obtain a crisp value C.

$$C = \left[\frac{\sum_{j=1}^{j=4} j\Phi_j}{\sum_{j=1}^{j=4} \Phi_j} \right] \tag{1.68}$$

This crisp output gives a continuous value. In the present case, C has a value between 1 and 4 where 1 represents severe risk for dysphagia, 2 represents moderate risk for dysphagia, 3 represents mild risk for dysphagia, and 1 represents normal. Figure 1.15 compares the classification made by the fuzzy logic diagnosis system and the classification made by the clinician. There was complete agreement between the fuzzy logic system and the clinician classification. In four cases, the fuzzy logic system overestimated the risk by half a category. It should be noted that the clinician classification itself is subjective based on qualitative observations.

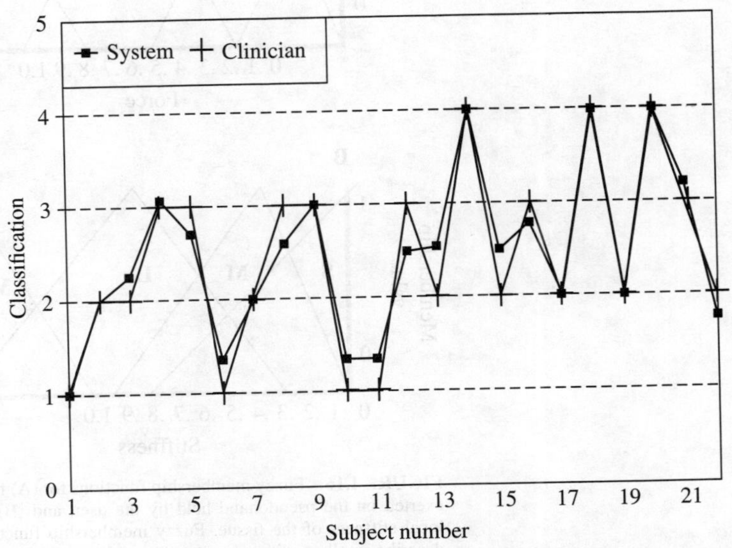

FIGURE 1.15 A comparison of the classification made by the fuzzy logic system and the clinician. [*Reproduced with permission from Suryanarayanan et al. (1995).*]

1.6.2 Fuzzy Mechanics

Virtual reality (VR) is gaining importance in every discipline, including medicine and surgery. VR is a computer-generated pseudo space that looks, feels, hears, and smells real, and fully immerses the subject. Potential applications of VR include medical education and training, patient education, VR-enhanced rehabilitation exercises, VR-induced biofeedback therapy and teletherapy, VR-aided emergency medicine, VR surgical simulations, etc. Surgical simulations in VR environment can aid the surgeon in planning and determining the optimal surgical procedure for a given patient, and also can aid in medical education. Song and Reddy (1995) have demonstrated the proof of concept for tissue cutting in VR environment. They have developed a technique for cutting in VR using interactive moving node finite element models controlled by user-exerted forces on instrumented pseudocutting tool held by the user. In Song and Reddy's system, the user (surgeon) holds the instrumented wand (instrumented pseudotool) and manipulates the tool. The forces exerted by the wand (on a table) together with the orientation and location of the wand are measured and fed to a finite element model of the tissue and the deformations are calculated to update the model geometry. Cutting takes place if the force exerted is larger than the critical force (computed from local tissue properties) at the node. Otherwise, tissue simply deforms depending on the applied force. However, finite element models require significant amount of computational time and may not be suitable for cutting large amount of tissue. Recently, Kutuva et al. (2006) developed a fuzzy logic system for cutting simulation in VR environment. They fuzzified the force applied by the operator and the local stiffness of the tissue. The membership functions for the force and stiffness are shown in Fig. 1.16. They have developed

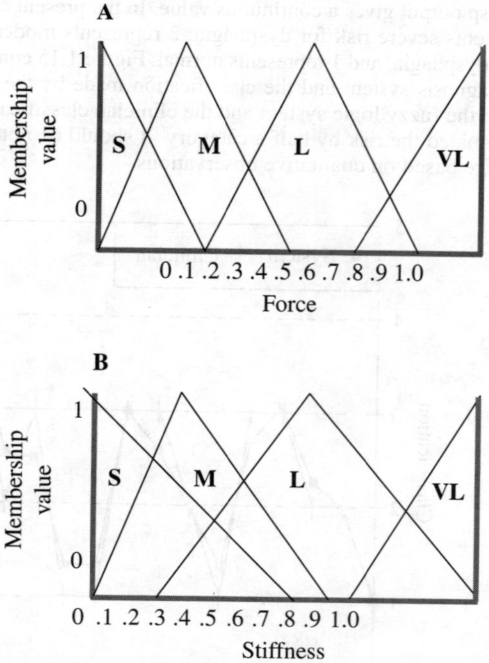

FIGURE 1.16 Fuzzy membership functions for (A) force exerted on the pseudohand held by the user, and (B) the local stiffness of the tissue. Fuzzy membership functions describe small, medium, large, and very large subdomains. [*Reproduced with permission from Kutava et al. (2006).*]

TABLE 1.1 Fuzzy-rules lookup table

Stiffness \ Force	Small	Medium	Large	Very large
Small	No cut	Small	Medium	Large
Medium	No cut	No cut	Small	Medium
Large	No cut	No cut	No cut	Small
Very large	No cut	No cut	No cut	No cut

The force subdomains are in the horizontal column and the stiffness domains are described in the vertical column. The corresponding output subdomain is given in the cells.

a lookup table (IF-THEN rules) to compute the cutting depth. Table 1.1 shows the lookup table. For instance, if the normalized force is 0.4, the membership values are (0, 0.5, 0.3, 0). The membership value for small is zero, for medium is 0.5, for large is 0.3, and zero for very large. If the normalized stiffness at the cutting location is 0.32, the membership values for stiffness are (0.4, 0.8, 0.4, 0). The stiffness membership value is 0.4 for small, 0.8 for medium, 0.4 for large, and 0 for very large. The contribution to the output domain small cut is calculated from the lookup table by adding all the possibilities for small cut. Small cut is possible if the force is medium (0.5) and the stiffness is small (0.4) which results in 0.4 times 0.5 which is 0.2; additional possibility is if force is large (0.3) and stiffness is medium (0.8) which results in $0.3 \times 0.8 = 0.24$ for small cut. Another possibility is if force is very large (0) and stiffness is large (0.4) which results in 0. Now, the membership value for the output subdomain small cut is calculated by adding all these possibilities: $0.2 + 0.24 + 0 = 0.44$. Similar calculation for medium cut results in $0.3 \times 0.4 = 0.12$. The membership value for no cut results in $0.5\,(0.8 + 0.4) + 0.3 \times 0.4 = 72$. The output membership values for this example are (0.72, 0.44, 0.12, 0). The fuzzy output of the cutting depth is then defuzzified using the centoid defuzzification scheme to calculate a crisp value for the cutting depth. In the above example, the crisp value is calculated as

$$C = \frac{0.75 \times 1 + 0.44 \times 2 + 0.12 \times 3 + 0 \times 4}{0.72 + 0.44 + 0.12 + 0} \tag{1.69}$$

At each epoch, the force exerted by the user on the pseudocutting tool is measured, fuzzified, and the cutting depth is calculated. The virtual cutting tool is then advanced to the depth computed by the fuzzy logic system. The node(s) along the cutting path are released, and the display is updated with cut view. Then, the user's input force exerted on the pseudocutting tool is measured, defuzzified, and the cutting is performed by advancing the tool to the new location by the amount of cutting depth. The procedure is repeated as long as the pseudocutting tool is in the cutting space. The procedure is continued until the pseudocutting tool is withdrawn out of the virtual tissue space. Figure 1.17 provides a demonstration of fuzzy-logic-based tissue cutting in VR environment using two-dimensional models.

1.7 MODEL VALIDATION

This chapter discussed the art of modeling with few examples. Regardless of the type of model developed, a mathematical model should be validated with experimental results. Validation becomes very important in the black box type of models such as the neural network models. Moreover, the model results are valid only to certain regimes where the model assumptions are valid. Sometimes, any model can be fit to a particular data by adjusting the parameter values. Moreover, the techniques of parameter estimation were not presented in this chapter. In addition, the presentation was limited to lumped parameter analysis or macroscopic modeling.

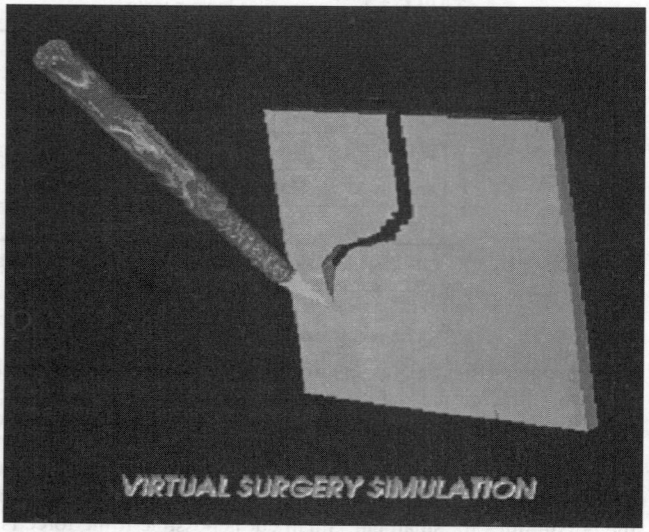

FIGURE 1.17 A demonstration of the fuzzy logic cutting. [*Reproduced with permission from Kutava et al. (2006).*]

REFERENCES

Barnea, O., and Gillon, G., (2001), Model-based estimation of male urethral resistance and elasticity using pressure-flow data. *Comput. Biol. Med.* **31**:27–40.

Chu, T. M., and Reddy, N. P. (1992), A lumped parameter mathematical model of the splanchnic circulation. *J. Biomech. Eng.* **114**:222–226.

Das, A., Reddy, N. P., and Narayanan, J. (2001), Hybrid fuzzy logic committee neural networks for recognition of acceleration signals due to swallowing. *Comput. Methods Programs Biomed.* **64**:87–99.

Fritton, J. C., Rubin, C. T., Quin, Y., and McLeod, K. J. (1997), Whole body vibration in the skeleton: development of a resonance-based testing device. *Ann. Biomed. Eng.* **25**:831–839.

Haykin, S. (1999), *Neural Networks: A Comprehensive Foundation,* 2nd ed., Prentice Hall, Upper Saddle River, N.J.

Kerckhoffs, R. C., Neal, M. L., Gu, Q., Bassingthwaighte, J. B., Omens, J. H., and McCulloch, A. D. (2007), Coupling of a 3D finite element model of cardiac ventricular mechanics to lumped system models of the systemic and pulmonic circulation. *Ann. Biomed. Eng.* **35**:1–18.

Kim, J., Saidel, G. M., and Cabrera, M. E. (2007), Multiscale computational model of fuel homeostasis during exercise: effect of hormonal control. *Ann. Biomed. Eng.* **35**:69–90.

Kutuva, S., Reddy, N. P., Xiao, Y., Gao, X., Hariharan, S. I., and Kulkarni, S. (2006), A novel and fast virtual surgical system using fuzzy logic. *Proceedings of IADIS Multi Conference on Computer Graphics and Visualization 2006* (Nian-Shing Chen and Pedro Isaias, eds.) IADIS Press, pp. 277–281.

Mangiameli, P., West, D., and Rampal, R. (2004), Model selection for medical decision support systems. *Decis. Support Syst.* **3**:247–259.

Reddy, N. P. (1986), Lymph circulation: physiology, pharmacology and biomechanics. *CRC Crit. Rev. Biomed. Eng.* **14**:45–91.

Reddy, N. P., and Krouskop, T. A. (1978), Modeling of the cell mediated immunity in homograft rejection. *Int. J. Biomed. Comp.* **9**:327–340.

Reddy, N. P., and Kesavan, S. K. (1989), Low Reynolds number liquid propulsion in contracting tubular segments connected through valves. *Math. Comput. Modeling.* **12**:839–844.

Reddy, N. P., Costerella, B. R., Grotz, R. C., and Canilang, E. P. (1990), Biomechanical measurements to characterize the oral phase of dysphagia. *IEEE Trans. Biomed. Eng.* **37**:392–397.

Reddy, N. P., Canilang, E. P., Casterline, J., Rane, M. B., Joshi, A. M., Thomas, R., Candadai, R. (1991), Noninvasive acceleration measurements to characterize the pharyngeal phase of swallowing. *J. Biomed. Eng.* **13**:379–383.

Reddy, N. P., Thomas, R., Canilang, E. P., and Casterline, J. (1994), Toward classification of dysphagic patients using biomechanical measurements. *J. Rehabil. Res. Dev.* **31**:335–344.

Reddy, N. P., Prabhu, D., Palreddy, S., Gupta, V., Suryanarayanan, S., and Canilang, E. P. (1995), Redundant neural networks for medical diagnosis: diagnosis of dysphagia, In *Intelligent Engineering Systems through Artificial Neural Networks: Vol. 5 Fuzzy Logic and Evolutionary Programming* (C. Dagli, A. Akay, C. Philips, B. Fernadez, J. Ghosh, eds.) ASME Press, N.Y., pp. 699–704.

Reddy, N. P., Katakam, A., Gupta, V., Unnikrishnan, R., Narayanan, J., and Canilang, E. P. (2000), Measurements of acceleration during videofluorographic evaluation of dysphagic patients. *Med. Eng. Phys.* **22**:405–412.

Reddy, N. P., and Buch, O. (2003), Speaker verification using committee neural networks. *Comput. Methods Programs Biomed.* **72:**109–115.

Reddy, N. P., Mathur, G., and Hariharan, H. I. (2008), Toward fuzzy logic control of infant incubators. (in press)

Rideout, V. C. (1991), *Mathematical and Computer Modeling of Physiological Systems.* Prentice Hall, Englewood Cliffs, N.J.

Sakaguchi, S., Takifuji, K., Arita, S., and Yamaeu, H. (2004), Development of an early diagnostic system using fuzzy theory for postoperative infections in patients with gastric cancer. *Diagn. Surg.* **21**:210–214.

Simon, B. N., Reddy, N. P., and Kantak, A. (1994), A theoretical model of infant incubator dynamics. *J. Biomech. Eng.* **116**:263–269.

Song, G. J., and Reddy, N. P. (1995), Tissue cutting in virtual environments, In *Interactive Technology and the New Paradigm for Healthcare* (R. M. Satava, K. Morgan, H. B. Seiburg, R. Mattheus, and J. P. Cristensen, eds.), IOP Press and Ohmsha, Amstardam, pp. 359–364.

Sproule, B. A., Naranjo, C. A., and Tuksen, I. B. (2002), Fuzzy pharmacology: theory and applications. *Trends in Pharmacol. Sci.* **23:**412–417.

Steimann, F., and Adlassnig K. P. (1998), Fuzzy medical diagnosis. In *Handbook of Fuzzy Computation.* IOP Press, Oxford, pp. 1–14.

Sturm, R. (2007), A computer model for the clearance of insoluble particles from the tracheobronchial tree of the human lung. *Comput. Biol. Med.* **37**:680–690.

Suryanarayanan, S., Reddy, N. P., and Canilang, E. P. (1995), A fuzzy logic diagnosis system for classification of pharyngeal dysphagia. *Int. J. Biomed. Comput.* **38:**207–215.

Suryanarayanan, S., and Reddy, N. P. (1997), EMG based interface for position tracking and control in VR environments and teleoperation. *PRESENCE: teleoperators and virtual environ.* **6:**282–291.

CHAPTER 2
BIOMEDICAL INFORMATICS

William Hersh
Oregon Health & Science University, Portland, Oregon

2.1 INTRODUCTION

The modern healthcare system, and professionals and patients within it, spends a substantial portion of its time collecting, analyzing, and using data and information, not only during patient care but also for research, quality measurement and improvement, and public health. The discipline devoted to the efficient storage, acquisition, and use of information in healthcare is called *biomedical and health informatics* (BMHI, or often biomedical informatics for short) [1]. The term *informatics* itself usually refers to the confluence of people, information, and technology [2] (see Fig. 2.1). While information technology (IT) infrastructure (i.e., the networks, devices, and software) is essential for effective application of informatics, the larger goal is the benefit that information provides, in the case of BMHI, to healthcare and optimal health of individuals and populations.

2.2 AREAS WITHIN BIOMEDICAL AND HEALTH INFORMATICS

Although informatics is a relatively new discipline compared to others in medicine, it has accumulated a history over a half-century that has evolved with advances in IT [3]. The term *informatics* has been attributed to Dreyfus from 1962 [4]. The word was used initially mostly throughout Europe—starting in France as the term *informatique* and then later around the rest of Europe—all through the 1960s. In Europe, the focus of the term has been on computing issues related to information use, which is somewhat different from how we use informatics now, especially in the context of BMHI. The term *medical informatics* is purported to first have been used in 1974 [5]. There are two books that have been published by the late Dr. Morris Collen—an initial volume in 1995 [6] and then an updated volume that he finished shortly before his death in 2015 [3]. At present, the term *informatics*

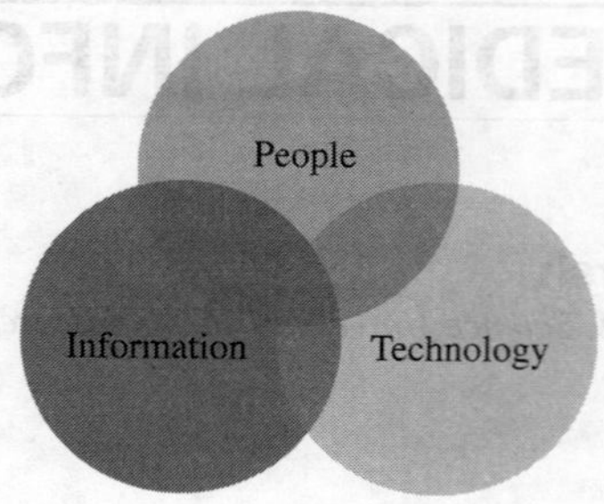

FIGURE 2.1 Venn diagram of essential components of informatics. (*Adapted from Ref. 2.*)

is most substantially used in the biomedical arena, although there are fields such as legal informatics, chemoinformatics, social informatics, and so forth.

As shown in Fig. 2.1, modern usage of informatics focuses on it as the confluence of people, information, and technology. One adage about the field is that it is more about information than technology. Friedman has defined the "fundamental theorem" of informatics, which states that informatics is more about using technology to help people perform their work better than about building systems to mimic or replace human expertise [7]. He has also described what informatics is (information sciences applied in a biomedical application domain with the aim of helping people) and is not (any use of IT in healthcare) [8].

The various areas within BMHI are depicted in Fig. 2.2. Sometimes narrower words appear in front of the term *informatics*. Other areas of BMHI include:

- *Bioinformatics*—the application of informatics in cellular and molecular biology, often with a focus on genomics [9].
- *Imaging informatics*—informatics with a focus on imaging, including the use of systems to store and retrieve images across all types of informatics [10].
- *Clinical informatics*—informatics applied in healthcare settings [11].
- The application of informatics focused on specific healthcare disciplines, such as nursing (*nursing informatics*) [12], dentistry (*dental informatics*), pathology (*pathology informatics*), etc. [13].
- *Consumer health informatics*—the field devoted to informatics from a consumer view, often with a focus on mobile health [14].

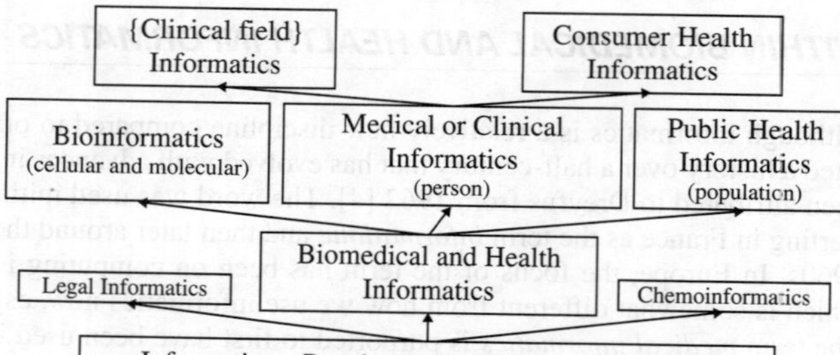

FIGURE 2.2 Biomedical and health informatics and areas within it. (*Adapted from Ref. 2.*)

- *Clinical research informatics*—the use of informatics to facilitate clinical research, with increasing emphasis on *translational research* that aims to accelerate research findings into clinical practice [15].
- *Public health informatics*—the application of informatics in areas of public health, including surveillance, reporting, and health promotion [16].

We can also view the continuum of bioinformatics, clinical informatics, and public health informatics as a spectrum of informatics applied to cellular and molecular processes to people to populations, although there is considerable overlap, as exemplified through the use of genomics technologies to investigate public health outbreaks. Some use the term *health informatics* to describe the field, which Shortliffe and Cimino denote as the combination of clinical informatics and public health informatics [17].

2.3 MAJOR APPLICATIONS OF BIOMEDICAL AND HEALTH INFORMATICS

There are many applications of BMHI that vary based on the focus of the subarea of the field. One application that has relevance to most areas of BMHI is the *electronic health record* (EHR), which serves several key functions to improve care delivery, not only in documenting data and information of care delivery but also in providing access to other participants in the system, most importantly the patient. But there are many other important applications as well.

2.3.1 Electronic Health Record

One of the most central applications of clinical informatics is the EHR. In the past, the term *electronic medical record* (EMR) was more commonly used, but EHR implies a broader and more longitudinal collection of information about the patient. There is also increasing use of the term *personal health record* (PHR). This usually refers to the patient-controlled aspect of the health record and may or may not be *tethered* to one or more EHRs from healthcare delivery organizations. Growing numbers of health systems have adopted the Open Notes approach that provides patients access to clinical notes along with a substantial amount of other data [18–20].

The EHR is not meant to be a mere replacement for the paper-based record, rather it should ideally serve as a tool to transform and improve healthcare delivery. One major component of the EHR is *clinical decision support* (CDS), which allows detection of errors and adverse events and can facilitate improved care delivery and quality [21]. The most critical time for intervention is when the physician is entering patient orders, so the optimal time to make CDS readily available is within the functioning of *computerized physician/provider order entry* (CPOE). Related to CPOE is *electronic prescribing* (e-prescribing), which focuses more narrowly on the electronic ordering of medications. The major categories of CDS include:

- *Information display*—showing general or patient-specific information in context of the current clinical situation.
- *Reminder systems*—reminding clinicians to perform actions, such as preventive measures, when they are due.
- *Alerts or notifications*—alerting to critical clinical situations, e.g., interacting drugs or abnormal lab values, that may negatively impact patient safety and health outcomes.
- *Clinical practice guidelines*—guiding treatment to promote consistent care based on best evidence.

An exemplar EHR has been the *Veterans Health Information Systems and Technology Architecture* (VistA) system, which is used in 1800 locations across the world including all U.S. Department of Veterans Affairs medical centers as well as several national health systems. Figure 2.3 shows the

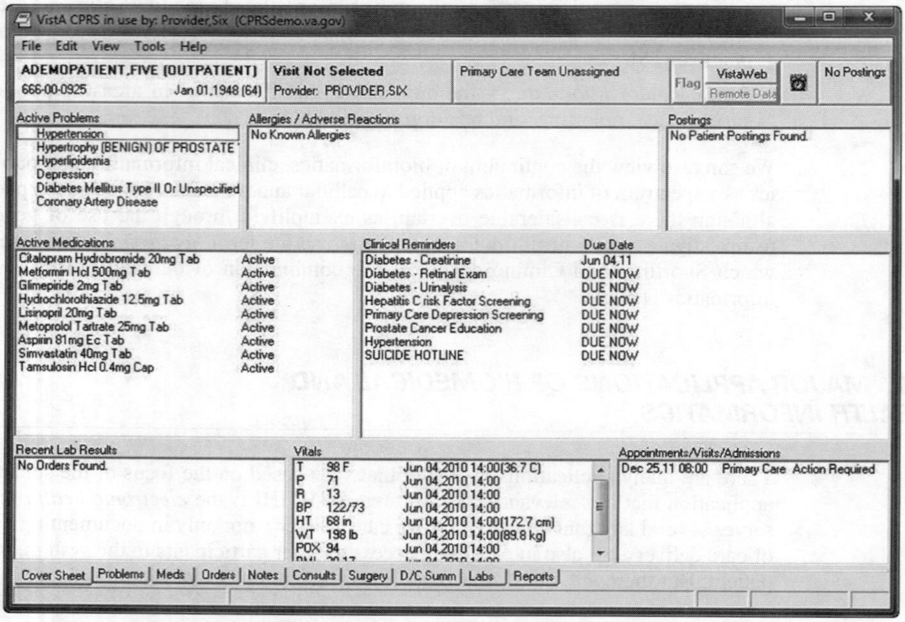

FIGURE 2.3 Cover page of the Veterans Health Information Systems and Technology Architecture (VistA).

cover page of the VistA EHR, which provides an overview of the patient, including their active problems and medications as well as recent results. This page also shows an example of CDS, listing relevant clinical reminders. The tabs at the bottom of the screen allow the user to drill down into more details on specific aspects of the patient's care, such as medications and laboratory results. Many of these screens feature additional CDS, such as indicating drug–drug interactions. Current Department of Veterans Affairs plans include replacing VistA with a commercial EHR over the next decade to better align with the commercial EHR system being adopted by the Department of Defense so that the care of military personnel can be seamlessly integrated as they transition to veteran status.

As the use of EHRs has grown, it has become apparent that information does not seamlessly flow among healthcare providers, and across different healthcare organizations. This has led to growing advocacy for *health information exchange* (HIE), which is the exchange of health information for patient care across traditional business boundaries in healthcare [22]. Even many healthcare organizations that have exemplary HIT systems have difficulty providing their patient information to other entities where the patient may receive care. An increasingly mobile population demands "data following the patient" as patients move in, out, and across healthcare systems.

One of the impediments to HIE has been suboptimal *interoperability* of EHR systems, with systems unable to seamlessly exchange data. Optimal interoperability requires adoption and adherence to *standards* to define data structures and formats. Although many standards exist for exchange of information and consistent use of terminology, they have not been consistently applied for a variety of reasons [23]. The major categories of standards include:

- *Identifiers*—of patients, clinicians, health plans, insurance companies, etc.
- *Transactions*—eligibility, enrollment, payments, etc.
- *Message exchange*—transmission of data, images, documents, etc.
- *Terminology*—standard descriptions of diagnoses, tests, treatments, etc.

The longest-standing and most widely used messaging standard in healthcare is Health Level 7 (HL7) Version 2. However, there are no formal standard terminology requirements for names of diagnoses, tests, and treatments in HL7 Version 2 as well as a number of other technological limitations, which limits its accomplishing of interoperability. These limitations have led to a new messaging standard, the *Fast Healthcare Interoperability Resources* (FHIR) [24]. A key element of FHIR is Resources, which provide structured and standardized modeling of all data components of healthcare, from patients to observations to medications [25, 26]. A complementary standard is *Substitutable Medical Apps, Reusable Technology* (SMART), which provides a standardized platform for building EHR and PHR "apps" (which can be Web-based or run on mobile devices). These two have been married to form *SMART on FHIR*, which aims to provide new forms of interaction based on standardized data on top of the EHR [27].

The presence of standardized interoperable data and systems not only leads to improved direct care of patients but also enables *reuse* (also called *secondary use*) of clinical data, where data from clinical settings is used for other applications, such as quality measurement and improvement, clinical and translational research, and public health [28].

2.3.2 Beyond the EHR

BMHI is not limited to EHRs. Another vital component for optimal patient care is access to information and knowledge. The field devoted to indexing and retrieval of knowledge-based information is called *information retrieval* (IR) or *search* [29]. IR systems are ubiquitous in modern life, and a large majority of people search for health-related information using Google or other general search engines [30]. In addition, virtually all healthcare professionals search the scientific literature, including electronic journals, books, and other websites, in their professional practice [31].

Searching is a requisite skill in the practice of *evidence-based medicine* (EBM), a process that includes the proper phrasing of clinical questions, seeking the best evidence to answer such questions, critically appraising what was retrieved, and applying such evidence to patient care. One recent textbook of EBM notes, "Searching for current best evidence in the medical literature has become a central skill in clinical practice. On average, clinicians have 5 to 8 questions about individual patients per daily shift … Some now even consider that 'the use of search engines is as essential as the stethoscope'" [32]. The importance of search goes beyond EBM, as clinicians must have skills in finding high-quality information for use by professionals and patients alike.

Additional important applications of clinical informatics are telemedicine and telehealth [33]. *Telemedicine* is the delivery of healthcare when the participants are separated by time and/or distance, while *telehealth* has a larger aspect of all telecommunications applications devoted to health. As with informatics, the "tele-" terms sometimes reflect medical specialties in which they are applied, e.g., teleradiology and telepathology. A variety of practice models embracing telehealth have now emerged, including e-ICU and telestroke services which are commonly employed to deliver expertise to a broader population. The uptake of telemedicine and telehealth increased substantially at the start of the COVID-19 pandemic.

There are also a number of related terms used that refer to informatics in specific contexts. The term *eHealth* usually refers to health-related applications that use information and communications technology [34]. The term *mHealth* refers to informatics applied to mobile devices such as smartphones [35]. The definition of *digital health* varies, but has been defined to include genomics [36].

Other applications of BMHI focus on bioinformatics. This work began with the sequencing of the human genome but has now spread to other "omes and omics." Not only have next-generation sequencing technologies led to rapidly lowering costs [37], but other biomolecular technologies have produced many applications relevant not only to genomics but also to other omes and omics [38]. These include:

- *Gene expression and transcriptomics* to measure expression of DNA and RNA.
- *Proteomics* to elucidate structure and function of proteins.
- *Microbiome*—microorganisms in other living organisms.
- *Mapping phenotype to genotype*—closing the circle of genomics to clinical data.

A rich source of data and tools, especially but not limited to bioinformatics, comes from the National Center for Biotechnology Information (NCBI) of the U.S. National Library of Medicine (NLM) [39]. A larger catalog of data and systems is published annually in the database issue of the journal, *Nucleic Acids Research* [40].

Another example of the various subareas of BMHI converging is in *precision medicine,* where diagnosis and therapy are driven by identifying genetic, environmental, and lifestyle factors related to disease [41]. Pharmacogenomics is a subset of precision medicine that studies how genetics affect a person's response to particular drugs [42]. The U.S. government has recently committed a substantial investment in research around precision medicine in the AllOfUs initiative [43].

2.4 HISTORY OF BIOMEDICAL AND HEALTH INFORMATICS

The scientific origin of the field of informatics is often attributed to the paper by Ledley and Lusted (1959) [44], which is one of the most widely cited papers in the field. This paper aimed to model and understand physician reasoning through:

- *Symbolic logic*—representing concepts such as patient findings, tests, and diagnoses.
- *Probability*—likelihood of outcomes (e.g., diagnosis) based on concepts (symbols).
- *Value theory*—complexity of values going into medical decision making.

This paper led to early attempts at computer-based decision making in medicine and led to the first era of *artificial intelligence* (AI). The focus of this era was on hand-crafted knowledge bases with algorithms to provide "artificial" intelligence. One early application of applying AI included a mathematical model for diagnosing congenital heart disease, predicting diagnosis with the highest conditional probability given a set of symptoms [45]. Another approach was to use "problem-knowledge couplers" that aimed to connect patient findings and diagnoses [46].

This was followed by the emergence of "expert systems," which were computer programs that aimed to mimic human expertise. One line of work focused on rule-based expert systems, including the PhD dissertation of Shortliffe [47] and subsequent work [48]. Another early AI approach applied scoring algorithms. INTERNIST-1 [49] and DxPlain [50] used disease profiles and scoring aiming to cover all of general internal medicine. These early systems, based on computer technology of the time that included time-share networks and command-line user interfaces, were slow and time-consuming to use. They also did not provide much value in everyday clinical practice, leading one early researcher to write a paper on the "Demise of the Greek Oracle" approach to AI and advocating that systems instead aim to provide supportive rather than independent role [51]. This coincided with the general decline of interest in the first era of AI and led to the more focused type of CDS that emerged in the 1990s [21].

The 1960s also saw the first work that led to early EHR systems. Most of these systems were primitive by today's standards but set BMHI on the path to learning about implanting EHRs in clinical settings. Some well-known early systems included:

- *COmputer STored Ambulatory Record (COSTAR)*—from Massachusetts General Hospital [52], based on the MUMPS programming language, which is still used in many modern EHR systems [53].
- *Health Evaluation through Logical Processing (HELP)*—from LDS Hospital in Utah [54].
- *The Medical Record (TMR)*—from Duke University [55].
- *Regenstrief Medical Record System (RMRS)*—from Indiana University [56], which led to development of Gopher [57].
- El Camino Hospital in California [58].
- *Veterans Health Information Systems and Technology Architecture (VistA) and Computerized Patient Record System (CPRS)*—from the U.S. Veteran's Health Administration [59].

A critical early leader in BMHI was the NLM [60]. One of the first and still one of the most important applications was the ability to search bibliographic databases. This started with the paper volumes of *Index Medicus* that were used before the widespread availability of systems such as command-line ELHILL [61], PC-based Grateful Med [62], and Web-based PubMed that is now used ubiquitously. The NLM has also developed other information resources for clinicians, researchers, and consumers. It has also been a leader in terminology development and standardization [63] as well as a funder of research and training. The NLM was led for over 30 years by Donald Lindberg, MD, who recently passed the torch to Patricia Brennan, PhD, RN [64].

Another important historical event for BMHI was the *Human Genome Project* to sequence human genome. The project started in 1988 and in 2001, NIH-based project published "first draft" [65] simultaneously with private effort from Craig Venter of Celera Genomics [66]. The project was declared to be "completed" in 2003 [67]. The sequencing of more humans and other organisms has increased understanding of genomic variation and complexity and led to continued advances in bioinformatics.

Also important to BMHI was the thought leadership of a series of reports published by the Institute of Medicine (IOM; now National Academy of Medicine):

- *The Computer-Based Patient Record*—paper records illegible, inefficient, and error-prone; computer-based record vital to modern healthcare [68].
- *For the Record: Protecting Electronic Health Information*—benefits of electronic health information compromised by inadequate protection; informed HIPAA legislation [69].
- *Networking Health*—value of computer networks and the Internet for health [70].
- *To Err is Human*—medical errors are common and a systems problem [71].
- *Crossing the Quality Chasm*—set of aims and rules for high-quality twenty-first century healthcare [72].

Another important concept to emerge from the IOM was that of the *learning health system*—must measure provision and outcomes of care to know what works [73]. Components of learning health system included transparency of data and information; rewarding of outcomes and value, not volume; and errors promptly identified and corrected [74]. The IOM also noted that although health IT systems may improve healthcare, they may also introduce error and cause harm if not designed and applied properly [75].

The importance of clinical informatics in healthcare delivery began to emerge in the latter part of the twentieth century. A series of seminal reports from the National Academy of Medicine (NAM), known at the time as the Institute of Medicine (IOM), documented significant problems in healthcare delivery and led to proposed solutions based on best information technology (IT) and evidence supporting its use. The first NAM report documented the harms resulting from incomplete and illegible paper-based medical records [68]. Probably the most high profile of these reports focused on errors in hospitals estimated to result in up to 96,000 deaths per year [71]. Another NAM report described deficiencies in the quality of healthcare as a "chasm" between known, evidence-based best practices and their actual use in the healthcare system. Constraints on exploiting the revolution in information technology were named as one of the underlying reasons for inadequate quality of care, and increasing the use of information technology was cited as a means of improving quality of care [72].

A number of studies supported the conclusions of these reports. In 1995, Bates et al. documented error rates of 6.5 adverse drug events (ADEs) per 100 hospitalized patients [76]. Quality problems were quantified more clearly in 2003 by McGlynn et al., who assessed the records of 6259 patients in 12 metropolitan areas and found that only 54.9 percent of care delivered was consistent with evidence-based known best practices [77]. Paper-based medical information was associated with clinical decisions being made with incomplete information, as Smith et al. showed that information was missing and impacted up to 44 percent of patients in primary care settings [78].

Additionally, there was emerging evidence for the value of health IT. In 1993, Tierney et al. documented that CPOE in hospitals was associated with a 12.7 percent decrease in total charges and 0.9 days shorter length of stay [79]. Shortly afterwards, Bates and colleagues showed that CPOE reduced serious medication errors by 55 percent, with adverse drug events reduced by 17 percent [80]. Other studies showed CPOE led to a reduction in redundant laboratory tests [81] and increased prescribing of equally efficacious but less costly medications [82]. Much of this work culminated in a systematic review of 257 studies of health IT documenting its association with increased adherence to guideline-based care, enhanced surveillance and monitoring, and decreased medical errors [83].

Modeling studies were also being published demonstrating return on investment for EHRs as well as HIE, the exchange of information across the boundaries of healthcare organizations [84]. Johnston and colleagues assessed the potential benefit of CPOE in ambulatory settings and noted savings of up to $28,000 per practice per year, although most of the savings went to laboratories and insurance companies, and not the physician practices making the investment [85]. Another modeling study by Hillestad et al. applied results of known research in an attempt to scale to entire U.S. healthcare system, finding that HIE could potentially result in savings of $81 billion per year to the system and a reduction of 200,000 ADEs per year [86].

Another important happening for BMHI was the *American Recovery and Reinvestment Act* (ARRA), the economic stimulus package passed by Congress in early 2019. Within ARRA was the *Health Information Technology for Economic and Clinical Health* (HITECH) Act, which allocated around $30 billion for incentives for EHR adoption in the United States. This led to the so-called "meaningful use" program that required adherence to criteria to qualify for incentive payments. While the program overall substantially increased EHR adoption in the United States up to 96 percent in hospitals and 85 percent among office-based physicians [87], there were also criticisms of inadequate attention paid to usability and interoperability of systems [88].

Even though not limited to the work of physicians, clinical informatics has been recognized as a medical subspecialty [11] and has been defined by the Accreditation Council for Graduate Medical Education (ACGME) as the field that "transforms healthcare by analyzing, designing, implementing, and evaluating information and communication systems to improve patient care, enhance access to care, advance individual and population health outcomes, and strengthen the clinician-patient relationship" [89]. Since 2013, physicians who have worked in the field or completed a fellowship in informatics and have a primary board certification in their specialty have been eligible to become additionally board certified in clinical informatics. That subspecialty certification is available to physician specialists who are certified by any of the 24 member boards of the American Board of Medical Specialties, which endorses the broad clinical relevance of expertise in clinical informatics [11]. Since the first certification exam was offered in 2013, over 2000 physicians have become board-certified.

2.5 DATA SCIENCE AND ANALYTICS

One of the promises of the growing critical mass of clinical data accumulating in the EHR is secondary use (or reuse) of the data for other purposes, such as quality improvement, operations management, and clinical research [28]. There has also been substantial growth in other kinds of health-related data, most notably through efforts to sequence genomes and other biological structures and functions. This has led to the application of the related areas of data science and data analytics to biomedicine and health.

Data science is "the science of learning from data; it studies the methods involved in the analysis and processing of data and proposes technology to improve methods in an evidence-based manner" [90]. *Data analytics* may be viewed as the practical application of data science, i.e., "the extensive use of data, statistical and quantitative analysis, explanatory and predictive models, and fact-based management to drive decisions and actions" [91].

Hospitals and other healthcare organizations are generating an exploding amount of data. Clinical data takes a variety of forms, from structured (e.g., images and lab results) to unstructured (e.g., textual notes including clinical narratives, reports, and other types of documents). Additionally, healthcare organizations capture and generate data as a byproduct of the care delivery process. This can include billing, quality, management, and other financial data which is increasingly important in the optimization of healthcare delivery. Kaiser-Permanente estimated in 2013 that its data store for its 9+ million members exceeded 30 petabytes of data [92].

These two areas have been enabled by both the massive increase in the collection and availability of data, along with the development of new techniques to make predictions and recommend actions from that data. Another facilitator of this advance has been the capabilities of *machine learning,* the subarea of computer science defined as the ability of computer programs to learn without being explicitly programmed [93] or the use of computers to optimize a performance criterion using example data or past experience [94]. Many of the recent successes in machine learning come from the use of neural networks that, when used in deep layers, called *deep learning,* have led to impressive results [95].

As noted above, one of the reasons for the growth and success of data analytics and deep learning has been the development of *Big Data,* which refers to the large and ever-increasing quantities of data that adhere to the following attributes [96]:

- *Volume*—ever-increasing amounts.
- *Velocity*—quickly generated.
- *Variety*—many different types.
- *Variability*—variation in amounts, generation, and types.

Bates et al. have elucidated a number of use cases where big data methods might lead to improved patient outcomes [97]:

- *High-cost patients*—looking for ways to intervene early.
- *Readmissions*—preventing.
- *Triage*—providing appropriate level of care.
- *Decompensation*—alerting when patient's condition worsens.
- *Adverse events*—raising awareness.
- *Treatment optimization*—especially for diseases affecting multiple organ systems.

Adams and Klein authored a primer on data analytics in healthcare that defines different levels of the application of analytics and describes their attributes [98]. They note three levels of analytics, each with increasing functionality and value:

1. *Descriptive*—standard types of reporting that describe current situations and problems, e.g., reports of patients with certain diagnoses or outlier test results.
2. *Predictive*—simulation and modeling techniques that identify trends and portend outcomes of actions taken, e.g., lists of patients who may be at risk for poor outcomes or repeated admissions to the hospital.
3. *Prescriptive*—optimizing clinical, financial, and other outcomes, e.g., recommendations for patients to maintain health or to prevent poor outcomes.

Much work is focusing now on *predictive analytics,* especially in clinical settings attempting to optimize health and financial outcomes, including in clinical practice [99].

Deep learning algorithms have been developed for many tasks, especially those in physician specialties that use imaging. A sampling of these studies includes:

- *Radiology*—diagnosis comparable to radiologists for pneumonia [100], tuberculosis [101], and intracranial hemorrhage [102].
- *Dermatology*—detecting skin cancer from images [103–105].
- *Ophthalmology*—detecting diabetic retinopathy from fundal images [106, 107], diagnosing plus disease [108], and predicting cardiovascular risk factors from retinal fundus photographs [109].
- *Pathology*—classifying various forms of cancer from histopathology images [110, 111] and detecting lymph node metastases [112].

- *Cardiology*—cardiac arrhythmia detection [113] and interpreting electrocardiograms [114] comparable to cardiologists.
- *Gastroenterology*—assessing endocytoscopic images for diagnose-and-leave strategy for diminutive, nonneoplastic, rectosigmoid polyps [115].

Success has not been limited to images, however, and deep learning algorithms have also been able to process data in EHRs to predict:

- Several dozen diseases [116].
- Length of stay, mortality, readmission, and diagnosis at two large medical centers [117].
- Prognosis in palliative care [118].
- Thirty-day readmission in heart failure [119].
- Patient mortality from coronary artery disease more accurately than traditional cardiovascular risk models [120].
- Early risk of chronic kidney disease in patients with diabetes [121].
- Many pediatric diagnoses at a major referral center [122].
- Clinical outcomes in rheumatoid arthritis [123].

The world's growing base of scientific literature is another source of data, and can be linked with EHR and other patient data to improve outcomes of care. One approach to this problem that has generated attention is the IBM Watson project, which was made famous by winning at the TV game show Jeopardy! [124]. One of the areas where IBM and its partners have been applying Watson is in the healthcare arena [125].

A more peripheral but related term is *business intelligence,* which in healthcare refers to the "processes and technologies used to obtain timely, valuable insights into business and clinical data" [98]. A major motivator for data-driven decision making in healthcare is the move from volume-driven (e.g., fee for service) to value-driven (where health systems and providers share risk) reimbursement [126].

A concern for more intensive use of data is that data generated in the routine care of patients may be limited for analytical purposes [127]. For example, such data may be inaccurate or incomplete. It may be transformed in ways that undermine its meaning (e.g., coding for billing priorities). For example, services or diagnoses that are highly reimbursed may be coded more reliably than other entities. It may exhibit the well-known statistical phenomenon of *censoring*, i.e., the first instance of disease in record may not be when it was first manifested (left censoring) or the data source may not cover a sufficient time interval to reflect the full course of disease (right censoring). Data may incompletely adhere to well-known standards, which makes combining it from different sources more difficult.

2.6 BENEFITS AND CHALLENGES OF INFORMATICS

With the massive adoption of EHRs in the United States driven by the HITECH Act, focused research on current systems and their impact on medical practice demonstrates a dichotomy between specific benefits and general dissatisfaction. Following an original systematic review in 2006 [83], three subsequent reviews using a similar methodology published in 2009 [128], 2011 [129], and 2014 [130] have shown persistent benefits.

At the same time, a growing number of problems have been identified related to the EHRs in clinical practice. One of these is excess focus on the computer over the patient [131, 132]. Another is the demise of traditional communications during care, such as radiology rounds [133]. There are also problems with documentation losing the patient's story through use of documentation templates that replace the narrative with elements such as checkboxes [134]. While this structuring of data assists with the use of data for other purposes, it loses the nuance of the patient's and clinician's narrative.

Finally, there is the problem of inappropriate use of "copy and paste," which may propagate errors and lead to uncertainty as to which provider rendered specific observations and recommendations (attribution) [135].

Another challenge is the increased time EHRs require of physicians and other clinicians, which takes time away from direct care of patients. Several recent time-motion studies have found that physicians spend up to half their workday interacting with the computer [136–138]. This has been shown to be one of the major causes of the growing epidemic of physician burnout [139]. It is important to note that studies of physician time over several decades, even in the pre-EHR era, have shown that physicians spend up to half of their time in "indirect care" not in the presence of patients, performing tasks such as documentation; in communication with patients, other physicians, and other clinical staff; and in transit [140, 141]. One reason for excess time requirements for the EHR in the United States is the increased billing and regulatory burden, as evidenced by the fact that physician notes in U.S. EHRs are longer, sometimes several-fold, than notes of physicians in other countries where EHRs are used [142]. There is no question that U.S. physicians spend too much time entering data into the EHR, but it must also be determined what is the optimal time devoted to documentation to enter data that informs the system to enable improved care.

Although EHRs have been touted to improve patient safety, there are also growing concerns that some aspects of their use may introduce new safety problems [75]. Two recent high-profile mishaps included CDS leading to massive overdosing of a common antibiotic [143] and poor communication between clinicians resulting in accidental discharge of a patient infected by the Ebola virus [144]. There are also growing concerns over the security of health information [145]. The year 2015 saw several massive security breaches, leading to exposure of records of over 100 million Americans [146–148]. The black market value of a medical record has been estimated to be 10 times that of a credit card number due to its containing larger quantities and more sensitive information [149].

It is clear that we must continue to improve EHRs and leverage their benefits to improve healthcare delivery. Two high-profile reports from several professional organizations have issued white papers specifying improvements in the EHR [150] and patient documentation [151]. The American Medical Association has laid out a set of principles for improved usability and interoperability [152]:

- Enhance physicians' ability to provide high-quality patient care.
- Support team-based care.
- Promote care coordination.
- Offer product modularity and configurability.
- Reduce cognitive workload.
- Promote data liquidity.
- Facilitate digital and mobile patient engagement.
- Expedite user input into product design and postimplementation feedback.

A recent report from the Pew Charitable Trusts, the American Medical Association, and MedStar Health focused on methods for improving EHR safety [153]. The report noted seven usability or safety issues where efforts should be focused:

1. *Data entry:* EHR data entry is difficult or not possible given the clinicians' work process, preventing the clinician from appropriately entering desired information.
2. *Alerting:* EHR alerts or other feedbacks from the system are inadequate because they are absent, incorrect, or ambiguous.
3. *Interoperability:* Interoperability is inadequate within components of the same EHR or from the EHR to other systems, hindering the communication of information.
4. *Visual display:* EHR display of information is confusing, cluttered, or inaccurate, resulting in clinicians having difficulty interpreting information.
5. *Availability of information:* EHR availability of clinically relevant information is hindered because information is entered or stored in the wrong location or is otherwise inaccessible.

6. *System automation and defaults:* EHR automates or defaults to information that is unexpected, unpredictable, or not transparent to the clinician.
7. *Workflow support:* EHR workflow is not supported due to a mismatch between the EHR and intent of the end user.

2.7 THE PEOPLE OF INFORMATICS

We noted at the beginning of the chapter that informatics was defined as the intersection of information, technology, and people. While we have focused so far mostly on the information and technology aspects, let us now focus on the people's aspects of BMHI. There are a number of types of people who make use of and lead BMHI. Informatics professionals lead the way in healthcare and other industries, academia, and government. Equally important are healthcare and other professionals who apply informatics tools in their work and consumers and patients who use informatics to maintain health, prevent disease, and treat disease.

While informatics started as a research endeavor, typically in academic medical centers, the field has grown to accompany a diverse array of professionals who bring expertise in computing and information technology applied to biomedicine and health [154, 155]. The professional and, for some, academic work of BMHI spans all of the areas shown in Fig. 2.4. The growing numbers of physicians who assume roles in healthcare settings such as *Chief Medical Informatics Officer* (CMIO) have led to the designation of the new medical subspecialty of clinical informatics [11]. A recent practice analysis of physicians [156] and other [157] informatics professionals shows five "domains" of expertise required for their work:

1. Fundamental Knowledge and Skills.
2. Improving Care Delivery and Outcomes.
3. Enterprise Information Systems.
4. Data Governance and Data Analytics.
5. Leadership and Professionalism.

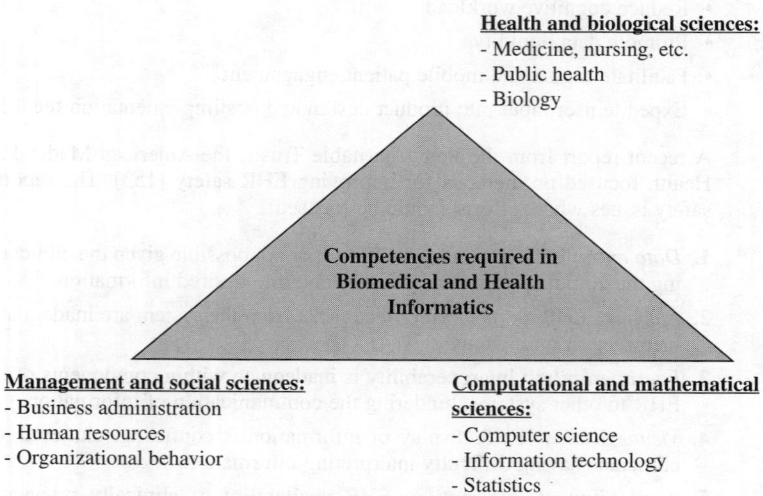

FIGURE 2.4 Competencies required in biomedical and health informatics.

Healthcare professionals also make use of informatics in their work. Not only must they be facile in using the EHR and accessing knowledge, but they also must be competent with the growing number of BMHI applications from clinical decision support to telemedicine [158]. As patients also want to interact with the healthcare system in manners similar to the ways they interact with airlines, banks, and retailers, i.e., through digital means, they too must have basic skills and knowledge of informatics [159].

REFERENCES

1. Hoyt, R. and W. Hersh, eds., *Health Informatics: Practical Guide,* 7th ed., 2018, Lulu.com, Pensacola, FL.
2. Hersh, W., A stimulus to define informatics and health information technology, *BMC Medical Informatics & Decision Making*, 2009, **9**:24.
3. Collen, M. and M. Ball, eds., *The History of Medical Informatics in the United States*, 2015, Springer, New York.
4. Fourman, M., Informatics, in *International Encyclopedia of Information and Library Science,* 2nd ed., J. Feather and P. Sturges, eds. 2002, Routledge, London, pp. 237–244.
5. Collen, M., The origins of informatics. *Journal of the American Medical Informatics Association*, 1994, **1**: 91–107.
6. Collen, M., *A History of Medical Informatics in the United States 1950–1990*, 1995, American Medical Informatics Association, Bethesda, MD.
7. Friedman, C., A "fundamental theorem" of biomedical informatics. *Journal of the American Medical Informatics Association,* 2009, **16**:169–170.
8. Friedman, C., What informatics is and isn't. *Journal of the American Medical Informatics Association,* 2012, **20**: 224–226.
9. Lesk, A., *Introduction to Bioinformatics,* 4th ed., 2014, Oxford University Press, Oxford, England.
10. Bui, A. and R. Taira, eds., *Medical Imaging Informatics*, 2010, Springer, New York.
11. Detmer, D. and E. Shortliffe, Clinical informatics: prospects for a new medical subspecialty, *Journal of the American Medical Association,* 2014, **311**:2067–2068.
12. Ball, M., et al., eds., *Nursing Informatics: Where Technology and Caring Meet,* 4th ed., 2011, Springer, New York.
13. Pantanowitz, L., J. Tuthill, and U. Balis, eds., *Pathology Informatics: Theory and Practice*, 2011, American Society for Clinical Pathology, Chicago, IL.
14. Wetter, T., *Consumer Health Informatics—New Services, Roles, and Responsibilities*, 2016, Springer, New York.
15. Richesson, R. and J. Andrews, eds., *Clinical Research Informatics,* 2nd ed., 2019, Springer, New York.
16. Magnuson, J. and P. Fu, eds., *Public Health Informatics and Information Systems*, 2014, Springer, New York.
17. Shortliffe, E. and J. Cimino, eds., *Biomedical Informatics: Computer Applications in Health Care and Biomedicine,* 4th ed., 2014, Springer, London.
18. Delbanco, T., et al., Open Notes: doctors and patients signing on, *Annals of Internal Medicine*, 2010, **153**:121–125.
19. Meltsner, M., A patient's view of OpenNotes, *Annals of Internal Medicine,* 2012, **157**:523–524.
20. Nazi, K., et al., VA OpenNotes: exploring the experiences of early patient adopters with access to clinical notes, *Journal of the American Medical Informatics Association,* 2014, **22**:380–389.
21. Greenes, R., *Clinical Decision Support: The Road to Broad Adoption,* 2nd ed., 2014, Elsevier, Amsterdam, Netherlands.
22. Dixon, B., *Health Information Exchange: Navigating and Managing a Network of Health Information Systems*, 2016, Elsevier, Amsterdam, Netherlands.
23. *Connecting Health and Care for the Nation: A Shared Nationwide Interoperability Roadmap version 1.0 (Roadmap)*, 2015, Department of Health and Human Services, Washington, DC.

24. Braunstein, M., *Health Informatics on FHIR: How HL7's New API Is Transforming Healthcare*, 2018, Springer, New York.
25. Comstock, J., Apple to launch Health Records app with HL7's FHIR specifications at 12 hospitals, *Healthcare IT News*, 2018.
26. Hay, D., *FHIR for Clinicians: How to Blaze through Health IT Projects*, 2016, Orion.
27. Mandel, J., et al., SMART on FHIR: a standards-based, interoperable apps platform for electronic health records, *Journal of the American Medical Informatics Association,* 2016, **23**:899–908.
28. Safran, C., et al., Toward a national framework for the secondary use of health data: an American Medical Informatics Association white paper, *Journal of the American Medical Informatics Association*, 2007, **14**:1–9.
29. Hersh, W., *Information Retrieval: A Biomedical and Health Perspective,* 4th ed., 2020, Springer, New York.
30. Fox, S. and M. Duggan, *Health Online 2013*. 2013, Pew Internet & American Life Project, Washington, DC.
31. *From Screen to Script: The Doctor's Digital Path to Treatment*, 2012, Manhattan Research; Google, New York.
32. Guyatt, G., et al., eds., *Users' Guides to the Medical Literature: A Manual for Evidence-Based Clinical Practice,* 3rd ed., 2014, McGraw-Hill, New York.
33. vanDyk, L., A review of telehealth service implementation frameworks. *International Journal of Environmental Research and Public Health,* 2014, **11**:1279–1298.
34. Oh, H., et al., What Is eHealth (3): a systematic review of published definitions, *Journal of Medical Internet Research,* 2005, **7**(1):e1.
35. Cerrato, P. and J. Halamka, *The Transformative Power of Mobile Medicine: Leveraging Innovation, Seizing Opportunities and Overcoming Obstacles of mHealth*, 2019, Academic Press, San Diego, CA.
36. Sonnier, P., *The Fourth Wave: Digital Health*, 2017, Amazon.com, Seattle, WA.
37. Goodwin, S., J. McPherson, and W. McCombie, Coming of age: ten years of next generation sequencing technologies, *Nature Reviews Genetics,* 2016, **117**:333–351.
38. Lesk, A., *Introduction to Genomics,* 3rd ed., 2017, Oxford University Press, Oxford, England.
39. Sayers, E., et al., Database resources of the National Center for Biotechnology Information. *Nucleic Acids Research,* 2019, **47**:D23–D28.
40. Rigden, D. and X. Fernández, The 2019 Nucleic Acids Research database issue and the online molecular biology database collection, *Nucleic Acids Research*, 2019, **47**:D1–D7.
41. *Toward Precision Medicine: Building a Knowledge Network for Biomedical Research and a New Taxonomy of Disease*, 2011, National Academies Press, Washington, DC.
42. Beitelshees, A. and D. Veenstra, Evolving research and stakeholder perspectives on pharmacogenomics, *Journal of the American Medical Association*, 2011, **306**:1252–1253.
43. Collins, F. and H. Varmus, A new initiative on precision medicine, *England Journal of Medicine*, 2015, **372**:793–795.
44. Ledley, R. and L. Lusted, Reasoning foundations of medical diagnosis, *Science*, 1959, **130**:9–21.
45. Warner, H., et al., A mathematical approach to medical diagnosis. Application to congenital heart disease. *Journal of the American Medical Association*, 1961, **177**:177–183.
46. Weed, L., *Medical Records, Medical Education, and Patient Care*, 1969, Year Book, Chicago, IL.
47. Shortliffe, E., et al., Computer-based consultations in clinical therapeutics: explanation and rule acquisition capabilities of the MYCIN system, *Computers and Biomedical Research,* 1975, **8**:303–320.
48. Clancey, W. and E. Shortliffe, *Readings in Medical Artificial Intelligence: The First Decade*, 1984, Addison-Wesley, Reading, MA.
49. Miller, R. A., H. E. Pople, and J. D. Myers, INTERNIST-1: an experimental computer-based diagnostic consultant for general internal medicine, *New England Journal of Medicine*, 1982, **307**:468–476.
50. Barnett, G. O., J. J. Cimino, J. A. Hupp, E. P. Hoffer, DXplain: an evolving diagnostic decision-support system. *Journal of the American Medical Association*, 1987, **258**:67–74.
51. Miller, R. and F. Masarie, The demise of the "Greek Oracle" model for medical diagnostic systems, *Methods of Information in Medicine,* 1990, **29**:1–2.

52. Barnett, G., et al., COSTAR: a computer-based medical information system for ambulatory care, *Proceedings of the IEEE,* 1979, **67**:1226–1237.

53. Greenes, R., et al., Design and implementation of a clinical data management system, *Computers and Biomedical Research,* 1969, **2**:469–485.

54. Kuperman, G., R. Garnder, and T. Pryor, *HELP: A Dynamic Hospital Information System*, 1991, Springer-Verlag, New York.

55. Stead, W. and W. Hammond, Computer-based medical records: the centerpiece of TMR, *MD Computing,* 1988, **5**(5):48–62.

56. McDonald, C., et al., The Regenstrief medical records, *MD Computing,* 1988, **5**(5):34–47.

57. Duke, J., et al., Regenstrief Institute's Medical Gopher: a next-generation homegrown electronic medical record system, *International Journal of Medical Informatics,* 2014, **83**:170–179.

58. Carter, K., Patient care computer system vital to El Camino, *Modern Healthcare*, 1987, 84–86.

59. Brown, S., et al., VistA-U.S. Department of Veterans Affairs national-scale HIS, *International Journal of Medical Informatics*, 2003, **69**:135–156.

60. Miles, W., *A History of the National Library of Medicine: The Nation's Treasury of Medical Knowledge*, 1982, U.S. Department of Health and Human Services, Bethesda, MD.

61. Lindberg, D. and H. Schoolman, The National Library of Medicine and medical informatics, *Western Journal of Medicine*, 1986, **145**:786–790.

62. Lindberg, D., The NLM and Grateful Med: promise, public health, and policy, *Public Health Reports*, 1996, **111**:552–555.

63. Humphreys, B., et al., The Unified Medical Language System: an informatics research collaboration, *Journal of the American Medical Informatics Association,* 1998, **5**:1–11.

64. Brennan, P., Crafting the third century of the National Library of Medicine, *Journal of the American Medical Informatics Association*, 2016, **23**:858.

65. Collins, F. and V. McKusick, Implications of the Human Genome Project for medical science, *Journal of the American Medical Association*, 2001, **285**:540–544.

66. Venter, J., et al., The sequence of the human genome, *Science,* 2001, **291**:1304–1351.

67. Collins, F., M. Morgan, and A. Patrinos, The Human Genome Project: lessons from large-scale biology, *Science*, 2003, **300**:286–290.

68. Dick, R., E. Steen, and D. Detmer, eds., *The Computer-Based Patient Record: An Essential Technology for Health Care,* Revised Edition, 1997, National Academies Press, Washington, DC.

69. *For the Record: Protecting Electronic Health Information*, 1997, National Academies Press, Washington, DC.

70. *Networking Health: Prescriptions for the Internet*, 2000, National Academies Press, Washington, DC.

71. Kohn, L., J. Corrigan, and M. Donaldson, eds. *To Err Is Human: Building a Safer Health System*, 2000, National Academies Press, Washington, DC.

72. *Crossing the Quality Chasm: A New Health System for the 21st Century*, 2001, National Academies Press, Washington, DC.

73. Eden, J., et al., eds., *Knowing What Works in Health Care: A Roadmap for the Nation*, 2008, National Academies Press, Washington, DC.

74. Smith, M., et al., *Best Care at Lower Cost: The Path to Continuously Learning Health Care in America*, 2012, National Academies Press, Washington, DC.

75. *Health IT and Patient Safety: Building Safer Systems for Better Care*, 2012, National Academies Press, Washington, DC.

76. Bates, D., et al., Incidence of adverse drug events and potential adverse drug events. Implications for prevention. ADE Prevention Study Group, *Journal of the American Medical Association,* 1995, **274**:29–34.

77. McGlynn, E., et al., The quality of health care delivered to adults in the United States. *New England Journal of Medicine*, 2003, **348**:2635–2645.

78. Smith, P., et al., Missing clinical information during primary care visits, *Journal of the American Medical Association*, 2005, **293**:565–571.

79. Tierney, W., et al., Physician inpatient order writing on microcomputer workstations: effects on resource utilization, *Journal of the American Medical Association*, 1993, **269**:379–383.

80. Bates, D., et al., Effect of computerized physician order entry and a team intervention on prevention of serious medication errors, *Journal of the American Medical Association*, 1998, **280**:1311–1316.

81. Bates, D., et al., A randomized trial of a computer-based intervention to reduce utilization of redundant laboratory tests, *American Journal of Medicine*, 1999, **106**:144–150.

82. Teich, J., et al., Effects of computerized physician order entry on prescribing practices, *Archives of Internal Medicine*, 2000, **160**:2741–2747.

83. Chaudhry, B., et al., Systematic review: impact of health information technology on quality, efficiency, and costs of medical care, *Annals of Internal Medicine*, 2006, **144**:742–752.

84. Williams, C., et al., From the Office of the National Coordinator: the strategy for advancing the exchange of health information, *Health Affairs*, 2012, **31**:527–536.

85. Johnston, D., et al., *The Value of Computerized Provider Order Entry in Ambulatory Settings*, 2003, Center for Information Technology Leadership, Boston, MA.

86. Hillestad, R., et al., Can electronic medical record systems transform health care? *Health Affairs*, 2005, **24**:1103–1117.

87. Washington, V., et al., The HITECH era and the path forward, *New England Journal of Medicine*, 2017, **377**:904–906.

88. Halamka, J. and M. Tripathi, The HITECH era in retrospect, *New England Journal of Medicine*, 2017, **377**:907–909.

89. *ACGME Program Requirements for Graduate Medical Education in Clinical Informatics*, 2014, Accreditation Council for Graduate Medical Education, Chicago, IL.

90. Donoho, D., 50 years of Data Science, *Journal of Computational and Graphical Statistics*, 2017, **26**:745–766.

91. Davenport, T., *Analytics 3.0: The Era of Impact*, 2013, International Institute for Analytics, Portland, OR.

92. Gardner, E., The HIT approach to big data, in *Health Data Management*, March 2013, p. 4.

93. McCarthy, J. and E. Feigenbaum, In memoriam Arthur Samuel: Pioneer in machine learning, *AI Magazine*, 1990, p. 10–11.

94. Alpaydin, E., *Machine Learning: The New AI*. 2016, MIT Press, Cambridge, MA.

95. Esteva, A., et al., A guide to deep learning in healthcare, *Nature Medicine*, 2019, **25**:24–29.

96. Chang W. and N. Grady, *NIST Big Data Interoperability Framework: Volume 1, Definitions*, 2019, National Institute for Standards and Technology, Gaithersurg, MD.

97. Bates, D., et al., Big data in health care: using analytics to identify and manage high-risk and high-cost patients, *Health Affairs*, 2014, **33**:1123–1131.

98. Adams, J. and J. Klein, *Business Intelligence and Analytics in Health Care: A Primer*, 2011, The Advisory Board Company, Washington, DC.

99. Sniderman, A., R. D'Agostino, and M. Pencina, The role of physicians in the era of predictive analytics, *Journal of the American Medical Association*, 2015, **314**:25–26.

100. Rajpurkar, P., et al., CheXNet: radiologist-level pneumonia detection on chest x-rays with deep learning. arXiv.org, 2017: arXiv:1711.05225.

101. Lakhani, P. and B. Sundaram, Deep learning at chest radiography: automated classification of pulmonary tuberculosis by using convolutional neural networks, *Radiology*, 2017, **284**:574–582.

102. Arbabshirani, M., et al., Advanced machine learning in action: identification of intracranial hemorrhage on computed tomography scans of the head with clinical workflow integration. *Digital Medicine*, 2018, **1**:9.

103. Esteva, A., et al., Dermatologist-level classification of skin cancer with deep neural networks, *Nature*, 2017, **542**:115–118.

104. Haenssle, H., et al., Man against machine: diagnostic performance of a deep learning convolutional neural network for dermoscopic melanoma recognition in comparison to 58 dermatologists, *Annals of Oncology*, 2018, **29**:1836–1842.

105. Han, S., et al., Classification of the clinical images for benign and malignant cutaneous tumors using a deep learning algorithm, *Journal of Investigative Dermatology*, 2018, **138**:1529–1538.

106. Gulshan, V., et al., Development and validation of a deep learning algorithm for detection of diabetic retinopathy in retinal fundus photographs, *Journal of the American Medical Association*, 2016, **316**:2402–2410.

107. Ting, D., et al., Development and validation of a deep learning system for diabetic retinopathy and related eye diseases using retinal images from multiethnic populations with diabetes, *Journal of the American Medical Association*, 2017, **318**:2211–2223.

108. Brown, J., et al., Automated diagnosis of plus disease in retinopathy of prematurity using deep convolutional neural networks, *JAMA Ophthalmology*, 2018, **136**:803–810.

109. Poplin, R., et al., Prediction of cardiovascular risk factors from retinal fundus photographs using deep learning, *Nature Biomedical Engineering*, 2018, **2**:158–164.

110. Bejnordi, B., et al., Context-aware stacked convolutional neural networks for classification of breast carcinomas in whole-slide histopathology images, *Journal of Medical Imaging*, 2017, **4**(4):044504.

111. Liu, Y., et al., Detecting cancer metastases on gigapixel pathology images, arXiv.org, 2017:arXiv:1703.02442.

112. Bejnordi, B., et al., Diagnostic assessment of deep learning algorithms for detection of lymph node metastases in women with breast cancer, *Journal of the American Medical Association*, 2017, **318**:2199–2210.

113. Rajpurkar, P., et al., Cardiologist-level arrhythmia detection with convolutional neural networks, arXiv.org, 2017:arXiv:1707.01836.

114. Smith, S., et al., A deep neural network learning algorithm outperforms a conventional algorithm for emergency department electrocardiogram interpretation, *Journal of Electrocardiology*, 2018, **52**:88–95.

115. Mori, Y., et al., Real-time use of artificial intelligence in identification of diminutive polyps during colonoscopy: a prospective study, *Annals of Internal Medicine*, 2018, **169**:357–366.

116. Miotto, R., et al., Deep Patient: an unsupervised representation to predict the future of patients from the electronic health records, *Scientific Reports*, 2016, **2016**:26094.

117. Rajkomar, A., et al., Scalable and accurate deep learning for electronic health records, *Digital Medicine*, 2018, **1**:18.

118. Avati, A., et al., Improving palliative care with deep learning, *BMC Medical Informatics & Decision Making*, 2018, **18**:122.

119. Golas, S., et al., A machine learning model to predict the risk of 30-day readmissions in patients with heart failure: a retrospective analysis of electronic medical records data, *BMC Medical Informatics & Decision Making*, 2018, **18**:44.

120. Steele, A., et al., Machine learning models in electronic health records can outperform conventional survival models for predicting patient mortality in coronary artery disease, *PLoS ONE*, 2018, **13**(8):e0202344.

121. Ravizza, S., et al., Predicting the early risk of chronic kidney disease in patients with diabetes using real-world data, *Nature Medicine*, 2019, **25**:57–59.

122. Liang, H., et al., Evaluation and accurate diagnoses of pediatric diseases using artificial intelligence, *Nature Medicine*, 2019, **25**:433–438.

123. Norgeot, B., et al., Assessment of a deep learning model based on electronic health record data to forecast clinical outcomes in patients with rheumatoid arthritis, *JAMA Network Open*, 2018, **2**(3):e190606.

124. Ferrucci, D., et al., Building Watson: an overview of the DeepQA Project, *AI Magazine*, 2010, **31**(3):59–79.

125. Ferrucci, D., et al., Watson: beyond Jeopardy! *Artificial Intelligence*, 2012, **199–200**:93–105.

126. Burwell, S., Setting value-based payment goals: HHS efforts to improve U.S. health care, *New England Journal of Medicine*, 2015, **372**:897–899.

127. Hersh, W., et al., Caveats for the use of operational electronic health record data in comparative effectiveness research, *Medical Care*, 2013, **51**(Suppl 3):S30–S37.

128. Goldzweig, C., et al., Costs and benefits of health information technology: new trends from the literature, *Health Affairs*, 2009, **28**:w282–w293.

129. Buntin, M., et al., The benefits of health information technology: a review of the recent literature shows predominantly positive results, *Health Affairs*, 2011, **30**:464–471.

130. Jones, S., et al., Health information technology: an updated systematic review with a focus on meaningful use, *Annals of Internal Medicine*, 2014, **160**:48–54.

131. Toll, E., The cost of technology, *Journal of the American Medical Association*, 2012, **307**:2497–2498.

132. Patel, J., Writing the wrong., *Journal of the American Medical Association*, 2015, **314**:671–672.

133. Jersild, S., The cause of—and solution to—radiology's problems, *Diagnostic Imaging*, 2012, November 27.

134. Lewis, S., Brave new EMR, *Annals of Internal Medicine*, 2011, **154**:368–369.

135. O'Reilly, K., EHRs: "Sloppy and paste" endures despite patient safety risk, *American Medical News*, 2013, February 6.

136. Sinsky, C., et al., Allocation of physician time in ambulatory practice: a time and motion study in 4 specialties, *Annals of Internal Medicine*, 2016, **165**:753–760.

137. Tai-Seale, M., et al., Electronic health record logs indicate that physicians split time evenly between seeing patients and desktop medicine, *Health Affairs*, 2017, **36**:655–662.

138. Arndt, B., et al., Tethered to the EHR: primary care physician workload assessment using EHR event log data and time-motion observations, *Annals of Family Medicine*, 2017, **15**:419–426.

139. Shanafelt, T., et al., Relationship between clerical burden and characteristics of the electronic environment with physician burnout and professional satisfaction. *Mayo Clinic Proceedings*, 2016, **91**:836–848.

140. Mamlin, J. and D. Baker, Combined time-motion and work sampling study in a general medicine clinic, *Medical Care*, 1973, **11**:449–456.

141. Tipping, M., et al., Systematic review of time studies evaluating physicians in the hospital setting, *Journal of Hospital Medicine*, 2010, **5**:353–359.

142. Downing, N., D. Bates, and C. Longhurst, Physician burnout in the electronic health record era: are we ignoring the real cause? *Annals of Internal Medicine*, 2018, **169**:50–51.

143. Wachter, R., *The Digital Doctor: Hope, Hype, and Harm at the Dawn of Medicine's Computer Age*, 2015, McGraw-Hill, New York.

144. Cortese, D., et al., *The Expert Panel Report to Texas Health Resources Leadership on the 2014 Ebola Events*, 2015, Texas Health Resources, Arlington, TX.

145. Perakslis, E., Cybersecurity in health care, *New England Journal of Medicine*, 2014, **371**:395–397.

146. Rubenfire, A., Hackers breach Anthem; 80M exposed, *Modern Healthcare*, 2015, February 4.

147. Rubenfire, A., Cyberattack on New York Blues plan Excellus affects 10 million, *Modern Healthcare*, 2015, September 9.

148. Vinton, K., Premera Blue Cross breach may have exposed 11 million customers' medical and financial data, *Forbes*, 2015, March 17.

149. Humer, C. and J. Finkle, Your medical record is worth more to hackers than your credit card, *Reuters*, 2014, September 24.

150. Payne, T., et al., Report of the AMIA EHR-2020 Task Force on the status and future direction of EHRs, *Journal of the American Medical Informatics Association*, 2015, **22**:1102–1110.

151. Kuhn, T., et al., Clinical documentation in the 21st century: executive summary of a policy position paper from the American College of Physicians, *Annals of Internal Medicine*, 2015, **162**:301–303.

152. *Improving Care: Priorities to Improve Electronic Health Record Usability*, 2014, American Medical Association, Chicago, IL.

153. *Ways to Improve Electronic Health Record Safety*, 2018, Pew Charitable Trust, Washington, DC.

154. Hersh, W., The health information technology workforce: estimations of demands and a framework for requirements, *Applied Clinical Informatics*, 2010, **1**:197–212.

155. Hersh, W., K. Boone, and A. Totten, Characteristics of the healthcare information technology workforce in the HITECH era: underestimated in size, still growing, and adapting to advanced uses, *JAMIA Open*, 2018, **1**:188–194.

156. Silverman, H., et al., Domains, tasks, and knowledge for clinical informatics subspecialty practice: results of a practice analysis, *Journal of the American Medical Informatics Association*, 2019, 26(7):586–593.

157. Gadd, C., E. Steen, and C. Caro, Domains, tasks, and knowledge for health informatics practice: results of a practice analysis, *Journal of the American Medical Informatics Association*, 2019, 26(7):845–852.

158. Hersh, W., et al., Beyond information retrieval and EHR use: competencies in clinical informatics for medical education, *Advances in Medical Education and Practice*, 2014, **5**:205–212.

159. Dameff, C., B. Clay, and C. Longhurst, Personal health records - more promising in the smartphone era? *Journal of the American Medical Association*, 2019, **321**:339–340.

CHAPTER 3

MACHINE LEARNING FOR BIOMEDICAL ENGINEERING

Vladimir Cherkassky and Hsiang-Han Chen
University of Minnesota, Minneapolis, Minnesota

3.1 INTRODUCTION

There is a growing interest in application of machine learning (ML) to biomedical data. This chapter describes methodological issues and assumptions important for such applications. In particular, understanding statistical assumptions underlying ML methods is important for understanding limitations of predictive data-analytic models. Understanding of biomedical application domain is necessary for "asking the right question" about biomedical data, i.e., proper mathematical formalization for modeling available data. Methodological issues and limitations of data-analytic modeling are illustrated using several real-life application studies.

3.2 PREDICTIVE LEARNING VERSUS STATISTICAL METHODOLOGY

In classical statistics, linear regression and logistic regression models are used as a tool for understanding the importance of input variables in explaining the output. This approach is reasonable when the sample size is "large," relative to the number of inputs, and the "true" parametric form of unknown distribution is known (or assumed to be known). For example, such approach can be used to describe a few hundred samples using a probabilistic model depending on two or three predefined input variables. In many cases, explanatory variables are not specified, but have to be selected from a large set of possible inputs. In this case, a statistician tries to consider several possible models, searching for the "best" parsimonious model involving a small subset of the variables. Then a statistician estimates model parameters using available data. The resulting "simple" model has *both explanatory and predictive value*. That is, the model is interpretable because it is simple, and it can be used for prediction because its analytic form is designed by the experts and assumed to be true.

The problem with this approach is an assumption that a statistician can specify an analytic model for data generated by unknown mechanism designed by Nature. This disconnect (between modeling assumptions and unknown data distributions) becomes increasingly problematic for modeling high-dimensional data and multivariate data (with many input variables). In particular, it is not possible (for a statistician) to provide realistic parametric models for high-dimensional data, and yet such data sets become quite common in modern biomedical applications, ranging from genomics to brain imaging (Choy, Samir & Brink, 2018; Huang, Cai & Pacheco, 2018; Lemm, Blankertz, Dickhaus & Müller, 2011; Min, Lee & Yoon, 2017; Zou et al., 2019).

Many modern data-analytic applications, such as data-driven discovery of biomarkers, do not follow the classical statistical framework. That is, analytic form of the model is not known, and the input (explanatory) variables are not specified a priori. In such applications, data modeling techniques are commonly used to pursue two different goals:

1. *Exploratory data analysis* having the purpose of suggesting relationships, i.e., selecting a few genetic inputs "associated" with the disease.
2. *Confirmatory data analysis*, when relationships/hypotheses suggested in (1) are tested for statistical significance.

The challenge for both tasks is due to the high dimensionality of the data relative to sample size, so that the number of possible input variables may be larger than the number of samples. In such a setting, it is not feasible to estimate data distributions. For such sparse data settings, it may be still possible to estimate *predictive* models with such data, as advocated by ML approaches.

The *predictive modeling* paradigm is based on statistical learning theory (Cherkassky & Mulier, 2007; Vapnik, 1995) that provides mathematical conditions for estimating good predictive models from finite samples, i.e., for estimating accurate predictive models from limited data. Another important consideration is that classical statistical methodology is biased toward the *controlled experiment* setting, whereas many biomedical applications use *observational* data (e.g., genetic data). Typically, controlled experiments are designed based on solid scientific understanding of a physical or biological system, and estimated models have just a few "strong, informative" input variables. In contrast, data analytic models based on observational data usually have very large number of variables that may have only weak informative value. However, some "smart combinations" of these variables may result in good predictive models, as shown in many ML studies (Cruz & Wishart, 2006; Kourou, Exarchos, Exarchos, Karamouzis & Fotiadis, 2015).

In summary, reliable predictive modeling of modern biomedical data does not conform to the usual statistical assumptions (small number of variables, large sample size, simple parametric model, and controlled experiment setting). Modeling of complex biomedical data is similar to typical ML applications such as image recognition. For example, many ML algorithms can classify handwritten digits with very high prediction accuracy (~98%), using all pixels of an image as input variables for making classification decision. For a 16 × 16 grayscale image, there are 256 pixels used as input variables. The classification decision boundary in a 256-dimensional input space is estimated from training data, i.e., labeled examples of handwritten digits. Such ML approaches make no assumptions about the parametric form of unknown distributions and can achieve high prediction accuracy (generalization) with sparse high-dimensional data. However, it may be difficult or impossible to define the decision boundary in terms of a simple model, i.e., a function of a small subset of inputs (say, 5 pixels). Prediction performance of ML methods is similar to human recognition capability. Humans can recognize faces in a complex image very well, but they cannot "explain" their decision in terms of simple rules using a few "informative" variables (a small subset of pixels). Likewise, predictive modeling approaches can provide accurate prediction, but may lack interpretation capability of statistical methods.

Predictive modeling is often used for identification of reliable biomarkers from heterogeneous high-dimensional data. Here "heterogeneous" patient's data includes *genetic, clinical, and demographic* inputs for estimating complex predictive model. All these input variables that *may* contain informative value for prediction, e.g., predicting disease outcome. This is consistent with current understanding in the medical research community, that

1. Biomarker evaluation and validation must be done in the context of clinical application and in a population of interest.
2. Biomarker performance is affected by disease-specific factors (i.e., clinical variables) and nondisease-specific factors (i.e., demographic variables).

Machine learning models can only estimate *certain properties* of complex biological or clinical phenomena (Cherkassky & Mulier, 2007). Meaningful interpretation of such predictive models remains a challenge.

This chapter describes development of ML models for several biomedical applications. Our presentation will focus on methodological issues, rather than on technical aspects of ML algorithms. Such methodological issues include various modeling assumptions (common for all ML methods) as they relate to practical goals of different biomedical applications.

In particular, data-analytic modeling usually reflects various human modeling biases. These biases may lead to misinterpretation of estimated models and false conclusions. The problem is especially evident in medical research and life sciences. For example, according to statistics compiled in 2011 by Thomson Reuters for *The Wall Street Journal*, during the previous 10-year period the number of medical papers that has been retracted climbed more than 15-fold, even though the number of published papers increased just 44 percent. While some of these retractions are caused by fraud and academic plagiarism, a large number is due to cognitive biases hidden in the data-analytic modeling process. For example, many application studies assume that data-analytic models are objective because they are derived from observed data. The methodological framework of predictive learning can safeguard against such cognitive biases (Cherkassky, 2013). It is easy to come up with a model *explaining* available data, but much more difficult to construct a model that has (objective) predictive value. This observation implies that many biomedical application studies should yield negative results, i.e., that many data-analytic models are likely to have little predictive capability. However, such negative findings are rarely reported.

Many biomedical application studies start with an "intelligent speculation" which is confirmed or disproved by empirical data. As the amount of data grows (due to digital technology), the speculation less intelligent and more vague in a hope is that statistical learning algorithms can utilize large volumes of data to compensate for the lack of scientific knowledge. Such an approach, however, works only under well-defined methodological constraints. Application studies discussed in Secs. 3.4 and 3.5 illustrate the importance of understanding methodological issues in data-analytic modeling.

3.3 SUPPORT VECTOR MACHINES FOR MODELING HIGH-DIMENSIONAL DATA

This section describes popular ML technique called support vector machine (SVM), because application studies presented in Secs. 3.4 and 3.5 use SVM classifiers for data-analytic modeling.

SVM classifiers (Vapnik, 1995) have been successfully used in many real-life applications ranging from medical diagnosis to functional MRI imaging, genomics, drug discovery, and financial engineering. Camps-Valls, José Luis, and Martínez-Ramón (2007) provide review of SVM applications in biomedical engineering. SVM approach is based on solid theoretical foundations provided by statistical learning theory, and practical success of SVMs is due to their robustness for estimating predictive models from high-dimensional data, like biomarkers. The main distinction between conventional statistical methods and SVMs is the way they control model complexity. Many statistical methods control complexity by selecting a small number of informative inputs, whereas SVMs use a new concept, called *margin*, for complexity control. The margin (for a classification problem) can be viewed as the "width" of decision boundary separating positive and negative training samples.

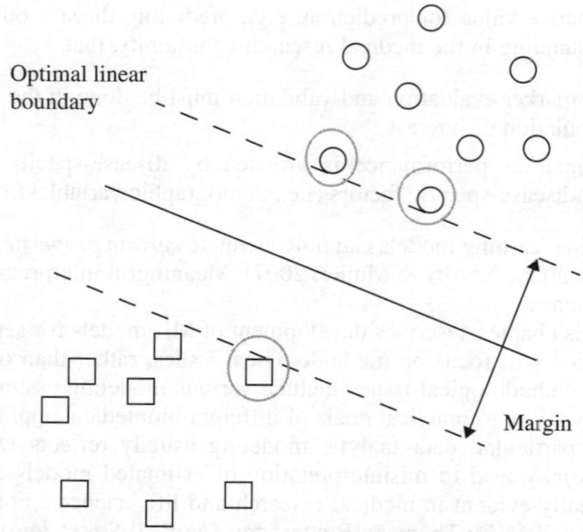

FIGURE 3.1 Linear decision boundary with maximum margin. Data samples lying on the margin borders are called support vectors (enclosed by circles).

The optimal decision boundary separating data samples from two classes would have *maximum separation margin,* defined as the distance between the decision boundary and the closest points from each class. For example, Fig. 3.1 shows optimal linear decision boundary separating data points from two classes.

Intuitively, it is clear that large separation margin provides more confidence in classification decisions. Moreover, Fig. 3.1 also suggests two important observations:

1. The decision boundary *depends only* on a few data points called support vectors (SVs) (circled in Fig. 3.1). SVs are data points that are most difficult to classify, because they are closest to decision boundary. In fact, removing all other data points (except SVs) from the data set would yield *the same* decision boundary. This illustrates an important concept: SVM classifiers do not attempt to estimate class distributions yet do separate the input space into regions corresponding to distinct classes.
2. SVM model complexity is controlled by margin size, rather than the dimensionality of the input space. So a large-margin decision boundary can ensure good prediction accuracy (generalization) even for high-dimensional data sets, such as using complex biomarkers.

Because complex biomedical data is heterogeneous and output class distributions may be overlapping in many characteristics, SVM tries to find an optimal trade-off between the large margin size (better discrimination between different classes) and the number of errors, or data samples falling on the "wrong side" of margin borders. SVM technology can be also extended to model nonlinear decision boundaries through a so-called "kernel trick." Figure 3.2 shows a nonlinear SVM decision boundary for Haberman's Survival Data Set available from UCI Data Repository. This data set contains survival data from studies of patients with breast cancer. The two input variables are patient's age at the time of transplant and the number of tumor-involved axillary nodes. The binary output represents a patient survival or death within 5 years after surgery. In the figure, patients' data samples (where both input variables are independently normalized to [0,1] range) and the nonlinear SVM decision boundary are estimated using RBF kernel. Data samples from the two classes are heavily overlapped, and many samples lie inside the margin borders. This suggests poor prediction accuracy, in comparison with well-separated data set in Fig. 3.1. In fact, the test error of this SVM model for Haberman's Survival Data Set, estimated via resampling, is about 22 percent.

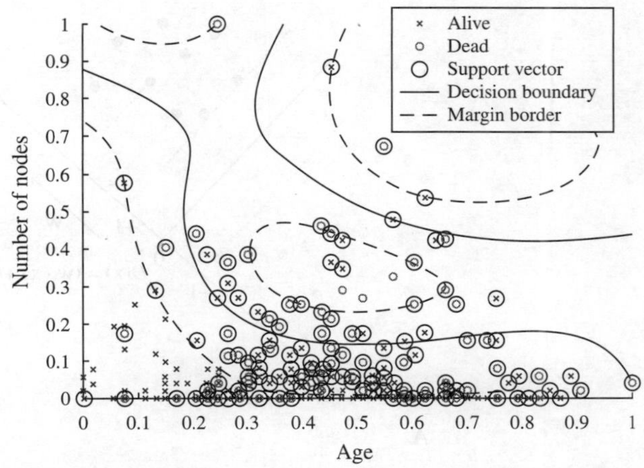

FIGURE 3.2 Nonlinear SVM decision boundary for breast cancer survival data. Nonlinear decision boundary is shown in solid line and margin borders in dashed lines. Support vectors (SVs) correspond to data samples on the wrong side of margin border (circled samples).

Although SVM models may not offer significant advantages over classical statistical techniques for low-dimensional data sets, they typically yield superior prediction accuracy for high-dimensional data. The next example illustrates application of SVM to 30-dimensional data. The Wisconsin Diagnostic Breast Cancer data set includes results of a medical test for 599 female patients suspected of having breast cancer. Each patient record has 30 input variables representing measurements from a fine-needle aspirate of a breast mass. These measurements describe characteristics of the cell nuclei present in the breast, such as radius, area, and symmetry. The output is a binary diagnosis of whether the cells are benign or malignant. There are total of 599 data points, of which 375 are classified as benign and 212 as malignant. In this case, because the data is high-dimensional and sparse, it can be effectively modeled by linear SVM decision boundary $D(\mathbf{x}) = \mathbf{w} \cdot \mathbf{x} + b$ where $\mathbf{x}$ is a 30-dimensional input vector, $\mathbf{w}$ is a vector of model parameters (estimated from training data), and $\mathbf{w} \cdot \mathbf{x}$ denotes the dot product. The test error of linear SVM classifier, estimated via resampling, is about 2.6 percent, far superior to what could be estimated by applying classical statistical methods to this high-dimensional data set.

The main difference between SVM and classical statistical methods is in their approaches to controlling model complexity. It is well known that good reproducibility (i.e., prediction accuracy) of data-analytic models depends on choosing appropriate model complexity, aka *model selection* (Hastie, Tibshirani & Friedman, 2001). In this respect, statistical and SVM methods adopt different strategies for implementing complexity control:

- Classical methods control model complexity by selecting a *small subset* of strong (informative) input variables, usually based on prior knowledge provided by experts. Thus, for high-dimensional data sets where the number of inputs (say SNPs) is very large, only a small subset of input variables is included in a statistical model.
- SVM classifiers control model complexity via two parameters: margin size and the chosen kernel, where the kernel function effectively specifies the flexibility of nonlinear model (Cherkassky & Mulier, 2007; Hastie et al., 2001). Note that both SVM complexity parameters (margin size and kernel) do not relate to the number of input variables. This makes the SVM approach particularly attractive for high-dimensional data, where all inputs can be used for modeling.

Most ML methods (including SVM) represent black box models that are not intelligible. Indeed, it is not possible to visualize 30-dimensional SVM hyperplane $D(\mathbf{x}) = \mathbf{w} \cdot \mathbf{x} + b$ estimated for the

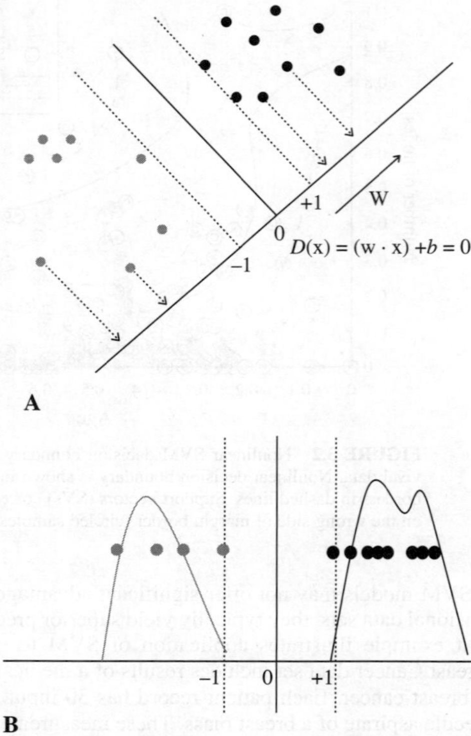

FIGURE 3.3 Interpretable representation of multivariate classification (SVM) models using univariate histograms of projections: (A) projecting available data onto univariate direction provided by the normal vector **w** of the SVM classifier; (B) univariate histogram of projections. *Note:* Data samples from the two classes are indicated by dark and light-shaded circles.

Wisconsin Breast Cancer data. Hence, medical practitioners are hesitant to make diagnostic decisions based on such black box models. So there is a clear need for techniques aimed at improved understanding of SVM models. One simple but effective approach for better interpretability of high-dimensional SVM models is to display the distances between data samples and SVM decision boundary. Then the distribution of (univariate) distances can be conveniently represented as a histogram. Such a histogram is easily interpretable, even though it corresponds to distances in a high-dimensional input space. These distances represent projections of data samples onto vector **w** orthogonal to linear SVM decision boundary, as shown in Fig. 3.3A. Training samples from each class are projected *separately* onto vector **w** and histograms are used to show the distribution of the two classes in the projected one-dimensional space. The resulting histogram is called the "histogram of projections" (HOP). An example of such HOP is shown in Fig. 3.3B, where one can clearly see the distribution of distances, relative to decision boundary (marked as "0") and to the margin borders for positive and negative class (marked as $+1/-1$).

The degree of separability between the two classes can be visualized by projecting the input samples onto the normal vector **w**. Training samples from each class are projected *separately* onto vector **w** and histograms are used to show the distribution of the two classes in the projected one-dimensional space.

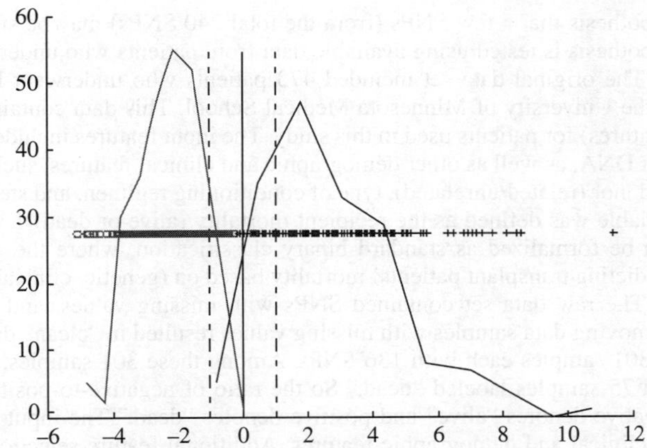

FIGURE 3.4 Histograms of projections for the Wisconsin Breast Cancer data, where "0" corresponds to SVM decision boundary, and margin borders are shown by dashed vertical lines.

While Fig. 3.3 shows the HOP for linear SVM where data samples (for the two classes) are well-separable, the same visual representation can be used for nonseparable data and nonlinear SVM models. For example, Fig. 3.4 shows HOP for 30-dimensional Wisconsin Breast Cancer data. This histogram illustrates nonseparable data set where class distributions are overlapping, and some samples fall on the "wrong side" of margin borders. This HOP shows the degree of separability between the two classes (in 30-dimensional space), which may be helpful for making diagnostic decisions for this data set. Likewise, the HOP representation can be helpful for diagnostic decisions with other (complex) biomarker data sets.

3.4 CASE STUDY: PREDICTIVE MODELING OF TRANSPLANT-RELATED MORTALITY

As noted in Sec. 3.2, data-analytic modeling may be affected by various human modeling biases that often lead to false conclusions. Such biases typically violate methodological assumptions underlying data-analytic modeling. This section describes a case study to illustrate this problem.

Let us consider the problem known as predictive data modeling of transplant-related mortality (TRM). TRM occurs due to complications of allogeneic hematopoietic cell transplantation (HCT). HCT is performed for patients with life-threatening diseases of the blood, bone marrow, or certain cancers. This is a risky procedure with many possible complications, and about one-third of all patients die within one year after HCT (Arora et al., 2007; Balduini et al., 2001; Cavet et al., 1999; Cooley et al., 2009; Couriel et al., 2004; Ferrara & Deeg, 1991). There are several clinical and demographic factors known to impact the outcome of HCT, such as recipient and donor age, type of donor (related/unrelated), type of conditioning (prior to transplant), and stem cell source (peripheral blood, marrow, and umbilical cord blood). The purpose of this study was to identify additional genetic biomarkers for predicting TRM (Cai, 2010).

Most patients undergoing allogeneic HCT receive pretransplant conditioning involving chemotherapy along with ionizing radiation. Tissue damage caused by these agents is determined by the balance of prooxidant and antioxidant enzymes present in recipient cells. The DNA damage caused by these agents is repaired by DNA repair pathways. Medical experts specified 240 genetic inputs, or SNPs, that can potentially affect the damaging effect of this procedure. This leads to clinical hypothesis that a few SNPs (from the total 240 SNPs) may be strongly associated with TRM. This hypothesis is tested using available data from patients who underwent HCT procedure.

The original data set included 473 patients who underwent HCT in the pilot study performed at the University of Minnesota Medical School. This data contained donor-recipient characteristics (features) for patients used in this study. The input features included genetic information about recipient DNA, as well as other demographic and clinical features, such as recipient/donor age, race, type of donor (related/unrelated), type of conditioning regimen, and stem cell source. The binary response variable was defined as the recipient mortality (alive or dead) 1 year after transplant. This problem can be formalized as standard binary classification, where the goal is to estimate a classifier for predicting transplant patients' mortality based on (genetic, clinical, and demographic) input features.

The raw data set contained SNPs with missing values, and patient data with missing values. Removing data samples with missing values resulted in "clean" data (used for actual data modeling) of 301 samples each with 136 SNPs. Among these 301 samples, 226 samples were labeled "alive" and 75 samples labeled "dead." So the ratio of negative-to-positive samples was about 3:1, where negative denotes "alive" and positive denotes "dead." The input variables included 136 SNPs plus 11 clinical and demographic features. Additional feature selection was performed to select smaller number of most informative input features. This feature selection process is usually performed prior to model estimation (classifier training). In this study, feature selection resulted in the following set of seven features: recipient's age at transplant, and six genetic inputs (SNPs).

An important part of this problem formalization is the specification of misclassification costs, i.e., relative importance of false-positive (FP) and false-negative (FN) errors. For this application, FN error occurs when a transplant patient is incorrectly predicted "alive" one year posttransplant. Likewise, FP error occurs when a transplant patient is incorrectly predicted as "dead." These costs reflect the consequences of misclassification errors, and they are provided by medical experts. For this application, the cost ratio of FN-to-FP errors was specified as $C_{fn}/C_{fp} = 3{:}1$. In medical applications, it is quite common to assign larger cost (importance) to false-negative errors, in situations where the positive class denotes a severe binary outcome (in this case, death). So the quality of a binary classifier is estimated by its weighted test error:

$$\text{weighted\_test\_error} = C_{fp}P_{fp} + C_{fn}P_{fn} \tag{3.1}$$

Here P_{fp} and P_{fn} denote the fraction (or probability) of false-positive and false-negative test errors. Standard linear SVM classifier was used to estimate a decision rule used for prediction. The decision rule has the form:

$$\hat{y} = \text{sign}(\mathbf{w} \cdot \mathbf{x} + b) \tag{3.2}$$

where $\mathbf{x}$ is the vector of selected input features, and SVM decision function $f(\mathbf{x}) = \mathbf{w} \cdot \mathbf{x} + b$ is estimated from the training data. Here the input vector $\mathbf{x}$ encodes patient's input features, and output y is a binary class label with values $+1$ or -1 encoding transplant-related mortality ("dead" or "alive").

Estimation of test error is difficult because future (test) data is not known during model estimation. In medical research, test data is often obtained from a separate pilot study used to validate the model developed in the original study. During the first stage of this project, such additional data (from a separate study) was not available. So the test error is estimated using resampling. Specifically, tenfold cross-validation was used to estimate test error. That is, all available data (301 samples) is partitioned into 10 subsets, so that 90 percent is used for training and 10 percent is used for measuring the test error. The test error averaged over 10 different partitions is reported as the final test error. In addition, another level of resampling (via fivefold cross-validation) was used for SVM model selection.

For the University of Minnesota data set (301 samples), the final SVM model had 29 percent test error rate. Note that performance indices represent weighted error (3.1). The 29 percent test error rate indicates certain prediction capability of estimated model. For comparison, a simple rule that always makes "negative" prediction (majority class) will have weighted test error 50 percent corresponding to zero predictive capability.

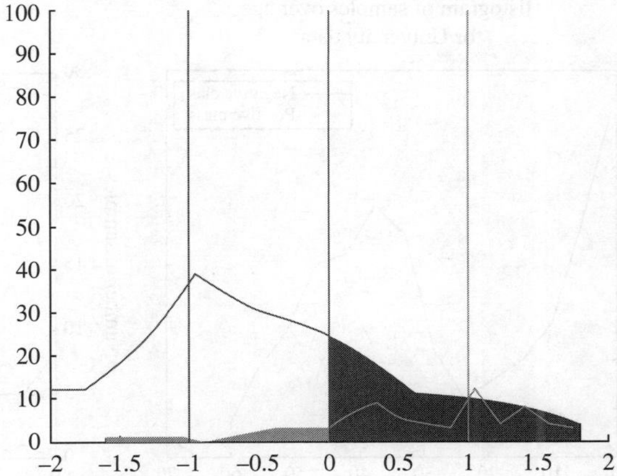

FIGURE 3.5 Univariate histograms of projections for SVM model. Histograms of projections for negative class (~"alive" patients) and positive class (~"dead" patients). These two histograms are heavily overlapping, so that light-shaded area represents false-negative (FN) errors, and dark-shaded area represents false-positive (FP) errors.

For better understanding of this SVM model, consider the histogram of projections shown in Fig. 3.5. This histogram shows projections of all data samples onto the SVM decision boundary. It clearly displays the unbalanced nature of the data (there are three times more "alive" than "dead" patients), and also reflects uneven misclassification costs. In particular, this SVM model makes accurate negative predictions ("alive") but very inaccurate positive predictions. This observation can be helpful if the model is used in clinical practice. The asymmetric nature of the SVM model is a direct result of unequal misclassification costs. Using different misclassification costs will result in a different model, estimated from the same data. Thus we emphasize:

- The importance of choosing misclassification costs appropriate for particular biomedical application.
- The fact that specification of these costs is not a part of the data-analytic method used to estimate predictive model. That is, these costs are fixed and should not be tuned by a learning algorithm.

Analysis of this SVM model has not confirmed the original modeling hypothesis about the existence of a strong genetic biomarker for predicting TRM. In fact, the *recipient age* was consistently identified as the most influential input in SVM model. Further, SVM classifiers using just a few genetic inputs consistently yielded poor prediction accuracy.

The second phase of this study involved data-analytic modeling of another data set of blood-and-marrow transplant patients from a pilot study performed at the Mayo Clinic. The Mayo Clinic study followed the same protocol as the University of Minnesota study, and presumably had patients with similar statistical characteristics (according to medical experts). So the reasonable approach was to use the Mayo Clinic data as an independent test set for validating the SVM model estimated from the University of Minnesota data set. However, using this approach produced very poor results, i.e., about ~46 percent weighted test error (for the Mayo Clinic data set). Likewise, using the Mayo data set for estimating an SVM model, and then testing it on the University of Minnesota data, also yielded poor prediction accuracy. These results suggested that the two data sets had different statistical characteristics. Indeed, additional analysis revealed that the patients' age distribution in these two data sets was quite different, as shown in Fig. 3.6. In particular, for the University of Minnesota study, an average age of patients from "alive" class was ~40 years, whereas for the Mayo Clinic data the average age was 50 years (for "alive" class). The input variable "age" was very informative for the University of Minnesota data. In contrast, the Mayo Clinic data had fewer younger

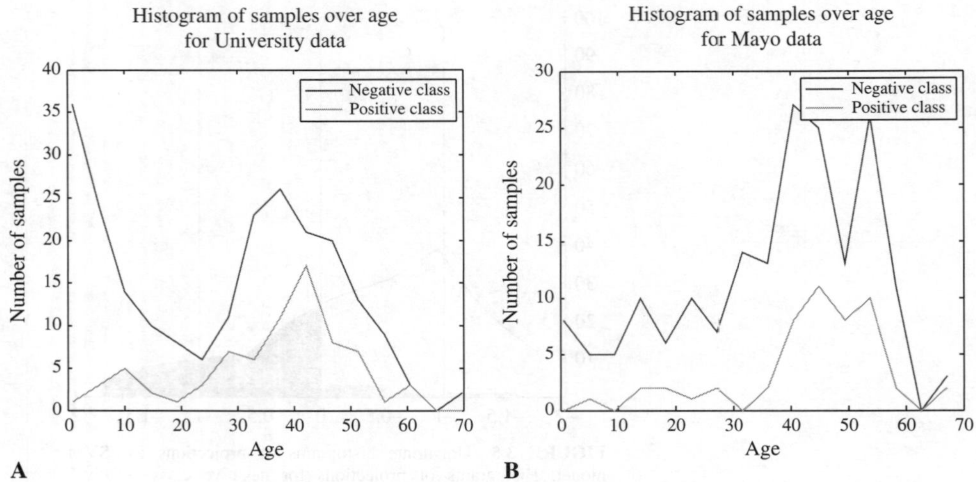

FIGURE 3.6 Patient age distribution: (A) University of Minnesota data, (B) Mayo Clinic data.

patients, and the age distribution of the two classes was very similar. Hence, for this data set the age input had much less informative value for prediction. In summary, results of these study show that when the assumption about similarity of statistical distributions for past (training) and future (test) data is violated, then accurate prediction via data-analytic modeling is not possible.

This study underscores rather trivial (but very important) point that data-analytic modeling makes sense only under (several) statistical assumptions, such as close statistical similarity (between training and test data distributions) and independent identically distributed (IID) sampling. Such assumptions must be critically evaluated in the context of particular biomedical application that generates available data.

3.5 CASE STUDY: PREDICTION OF EPILEPTIC SEIZURES FROM iEEG SIGNAL

3.5.1 Background

Epilepsy is one of the most common neurological disorders. About 50 million people worldwide have epilepsy (WHO, 2019). Currently available anticonvulsant medications are ineffective in 25 to 30 percent of patients (Dalic & Cook, 2016; Kwan & Brodie, 2000). For these patients, seizure prediction may be an alternative solution for managing their condition and improving quality of life.

Prediction of epileptic seizures has attracted significant attention over the past two decades. There is general consensus among clinical experts that abnormal brain activity preceding seizures can be captured from electroencephalogram (EEG) signal (Lange, Lieb, Engel & Crandall, 1983; Litt & Echauz, 2002; Litt et al., 2001; Petrosian, 1995). Based on this assumption, seizure prediction can be viewed as a binary classification problem for classifying EEG segments as *preictal* (preceding seizure) or *interictal* (far away from seizure). Here a *segment* refers to EEG signal of fixed duration (say, 1 hour) that contains useful information (for prediction). The decision rule for discriminating between interictal and preictal segments is estimated from past (known) observations, and then used for predicting future EEG segments. Often, ML methods are used to estimate an effective decision rule.

This chapter describes several challenging issues for application of ML for seizure prediction. The problem is difficult because the biological mechanisms and causes of epilepsy are often unknown. Therefore, decision rule (for prediction of preictal segments) cannot be derived from biological models, and this motivates application of data-analytic methods for prediction. However, application of ML methods is also challenging problem because seizure is rare and preictal data is very sparse.

There are two main assumptions underlying all data-analytic methods for seizure prediction from EEG signal:

1. *Physiological assumption:* Electrical activity of the brain changes before epileptic seizures. These abnormal changes in EEG are very brief (a few seconds long), and they may occur a few hours before seizure..
2. *Mathematical assumption:* Statistical characteristics of EEG signal do not change with time. In other words, we assume similarity between (past, known) training data and (future, unknown) test data.

The physiological assumption has been well studied and confirmed in several studies (LeVan Quyen, Martinerie, Navarro, Baulac & Varela, 2001; LeVan Quyen et al., 2001; Navarro et al., 2002). In addition, these studies suggest that the brain activity (as measured by EEG) is very individualized and patient-specific. As a result, all data-analytic predictive models should be *patient-specific*.

The mathematical assumption (stationarity of EEG signal) is implicitly assumed in all data-analytic modeling approaches. However, it may not hold, especially for long-term EEG recordings, when training and test periods are a few months away. To account for nonstationarity of EEG signal, predictive model is re-estimated every few weeks (using most recent EEG data). This is known as "retraining" in ML.

Design of seizure prediction system requires specification of the following important time parameters (Chen & Cherkassky, 2020; Chen, Shiao & Cherkassky, 2019):

- *Prediction period*, i.e., the length of time interval that may contain predictive signals (about impending seizure).
- *Prediction horizon*, i.e., the length of time interval when predicted seizure may occur.

These time parameters are shown in Fig. 3.7. A seizure prediction system generates prediction or warning (Yes/No) *at the end* of each prediction period (PP), and this prediction holds for the duration of prediction horizon (PH). Typical values are PP = 1 hour, and PH = 1–4 hours. Another important time parameter is the duration of short window (W) where abnormal changes in EEG may occur, with typical values in the range W = 10–30 seconds. All these time parameters reflect physiological assumptions about epileptic seizures. Specifically, the value of W reflects the *short duration* of

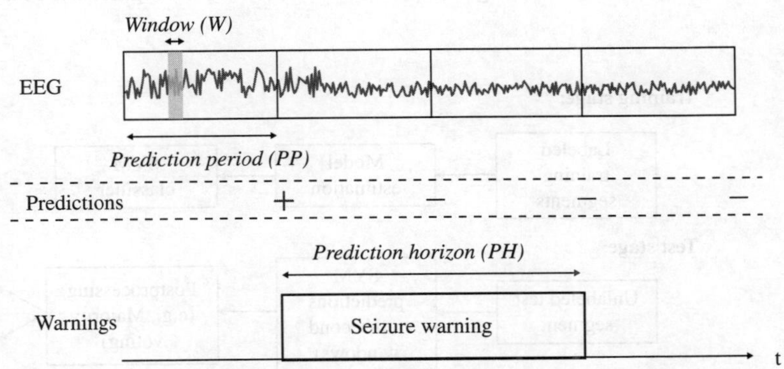

FIGURE 3.7 Three time parameters for seizure prediction system: prediction period (PP), and prediction horizon (PH), and window size (W). Positive (+) or negative (−) predictions are derived from EEG signal within time segment of length PP.

abnormal changes in EEG, and the time interval where these changes may occur corresponds to PP (prediction period). These three time parameters (*W*, PP, and PH) effectively define three time scales important for design and evaluation of seizure prediction systems. These parameters reflect a priori knowledge and they are independent of classification method (used for seizure prediction). Prediction performance of seizure prediction system *depends on both* (a) the values of these time parameters and (b) classification method. Consequently, performance comparisons (of different seizure prediction systems) can be done only if these systems adopt the same values of *W*, PP, and PH. However, many existing studies specify different values of time parameters, even when proposed prediction systems are evaluated on the same data set. For example:

1. Freiburg dataset (https://epilepsy.uni-freiburg.de/freiburg-seizure-prediction-%20project/eeg-database):
   - PH = 5 minutes is used in Netoff, Park, and Parhi (2009).
   - PH = 30 minutes is used in Park, Luo, Parhi, and Netoff (2011).
2. American Epilepsy Society Seizure Prediction Challenge data (Brinkmann et al., 2016):
   - *W* = 60 seconds is used in Assi, Nguyen, Rihana, and Sawan (2017) and Howbert et al. (2014).
   - *W* = 30 seconds is used in Nejedly et al. (2019).
   - *W* = 20 seconds is used in Shiao et al. (2016).

3.5.2 Description of Seizure Prediction System

We now describe the structure of a typical seizure prediction system that performs classification of EEG segments as positive or negative (corresponding to *Yes* or *No* prediction). Such a system, shown in Fig. 3.7, makes binary prediction for consecutive time segments of EEG signal. Typically, nonoverlapping time segments are used. Assuming that each segment is 1 hour long, the system will generate predictions every hour. Based on analysis of past EEG data (with observed known seizures), past (training) segments are labeled as negative or positive. These labeled segments represent training data set used to estimate a binary classifier. Then this classifier is used to predict future segments as positive or negative. Such operation corresponds to training and test (prediction) stages, as shown in Fig. 3.8 (Shiao et al., 2016), where an SVM classifier is used, for the sake of discussion. Notably, each time segment (say, 1 hour long) consists of many small windows (say, 20 seconds long). So a classifier is trained using many EEG windows (with known class labels). Then during operation (test stage), SVM predictions are made for every 20-second window; however, all these predictions need to be combined, in order to make final prediction for the whole segment. The task of combining many window predictions is known as *postprocessing* (see Fig. 3.8). Note that in the system shown in Fig. 3.8, predictions for 1-hour test segments are made by a classifier trained on

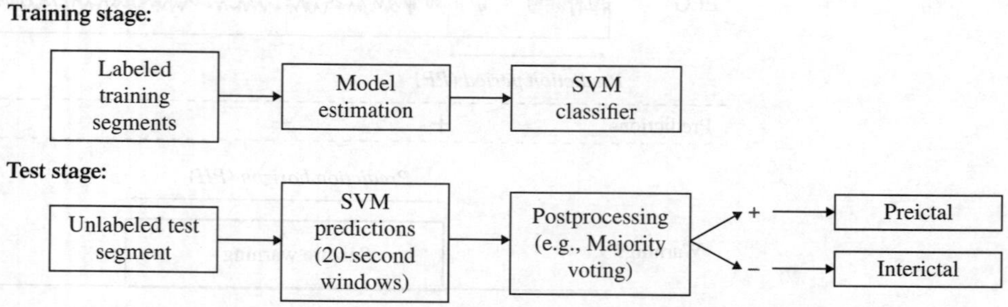

FIGURE 3.8 Seizure prediction system. During training, a classifier is estimated using labeled 20-second windows. During test stage, predictions made for 20-second windows are combined to make final prediction for 1-hour segments.

20-second windows. This is direct consequence of different time scales used for seizure prediction (shown in Fig. 3.7).

Next, we describe a set of features for representing 20-second window of EEG signal. This set of features is used as input to SVM classifier in Fig. 3.8. As shown in Fig. 3.9, EEG data is collected from 16 electrodes (implanted in the brain) also known as channels. For each channel, a 20-second signal is represented by six numbers corresponding to signal energy in six Berger frequency bands. These Berger frequency bands are 0.1–4, 4–8, 8–12, 12–30, 30–80, and 80–180 Hz. Therefore, each 20-second window (for all 16 channels) is represented by $6 \times 16 = 96$-dimensional feature vector, and seizure prediction system in Fig. 3.8 uses 96-dimensional feature vectors for training SVM classifier. During test stage, SVM classifier makes predictions for each 20-second window, and then 180 predictions are combined to make the final prediction for 1-hour segment.

3.5.3 Characteristics of Seizure Data

The difficulty of accurate seizure prediction is reflected in statistical properties of real-life seizure data. Specifically, seizure data is:

- Very sparse, due to rare occurrence of seizures and patient-specific modeling.
- Very unbalanced, meaning that there are many more interictal (negative) than preictal (positive) EEG segments. This complicates training a classifier.
- High-dimensional, i.e., each 20-second window is represented as 96-dimensional feature vector.
- Very noisy, so that positive and negative class distributions are highly overlapping.

The lack of EEG seizure data for humans is due to the fact that such data is typically obtained only for short time periods, e.g., for 24 to 48 hours, corresponding to duration of patient's hospitalization. On the other hand, only long-term recordings of seizure data can be used for training a classifier for seizure prediction system (shown in Fig. 3.8). Therefore, most seizure prediction studies utilize *long-term EEG recordings* from dogs with naturally occurring seizures (Assi et al., 2017; Brinkmann et al., 2015; Howbert et al., 2014; Nejedly et al., 2019; Shiao et al., 2016). Canine seizure data can be used to evaluate seizure prediction for humans, due to (known) similarity of biological mechanisms for epilepsy in humans and dogs.

In this chapter, we specifically consider modeling using long-term EEG recordings, i.e., several months or more. For such long-term data, occurrence of seizures is highly nonuniform. That is, seizures are clustered (in time), for most patients (and canines). For example, a cluster of seizures may occur once every 1 to 2 months, and each cluster may have three to five seizures separated by just a few hours. The first seizure (in a cluster) is called a *lead seizure*. Prediction of lead seizures

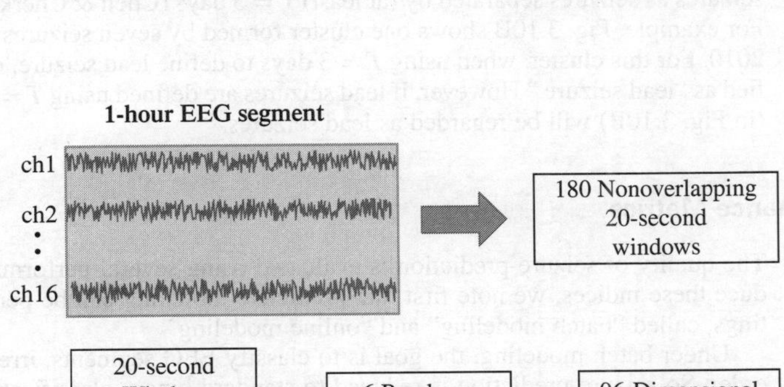

FIGURE 3.9 Feature encoding for 20-second windows.

is most important for patients and for clinicians. Lead seizures become more important in the field of seizure prediction in recent years. Therefore, practical seizure prediction system should use only lead seizures (for both training and testing), and prediction performance indices should be reported only for lead seizures. This brings up the question of how to select lead seizures from all (observed) seizures. Selection of lead seizures is controlled by (user-defined) parameter T. That is, a lead seizure is defined as seizure preceded by seizure-free duration of length T (or longer). Of course, the issue is how to define T, because sufficiently small values of T would qualify all seizures as lead ones, and sufficiently large T-values would yield no lead seizures. From clinical perspective, the pattern of seizure clustering is known to be patient-specific, so it may be difficult to provide the same definition of lead seizures for all patients (Epilepsy Foundation, 2008).

Many seizure prediction studies use different T-values (for defining lead seizures), even when using the same data set. For instance, for American Epilepsy Society Seizure Prediction Challenge data set:

- $T = 4$ hours was used in Brinkmann et al. (2015); Howbert et al. (2014); Nejedly et al. (2019); Shiao et al. (2016); Varatharajah, Iyer, Berry, Worrell, and Brinkmann (2017).
- $T = 80$ minutes was used in Assi et al. (2017), even though it was not explicitly stated in their paper.

Likewise, for Melbourne-University AES-MathWorks-NIH Seizure Prediction Challenge data set:

- $T = 8$ hours was used in Cook et al. (2013).
- $T = 4$ hours was used in Kuhlmann et al. (2018).

These studies do not provide explanation for their selection; however, all studies used rather short T values. It appears that such short T values are used in order to achieve better prediction performance since shorter T yields larger number of lead seizures, which is beneficial for modeling. We argue that typical value of $T = 4$ hours is too short, because it takes longer than 4 hours for the brain to transition to "normal" interictal state following a seizure.

It may be possible to specify appropriate T values by identifying natural clusters in (long-term) seizure recordings. This approach is illustrated in Fig. 3.10, using seizure data Dog L2 provided by Mayo Systems Electrophysiology Lab (see http://msel.mayo.edu)—which was also used in American Epilepsy Society Seizure Prediction Challenge. This data set has 45 annotated seizures during recording period (July 2009 to November 2010). Figure 3.10A shows all 45 seizures (indicated as crosses). These seizures form eight clusters clearly visible in Fig. 3.10A. The time duration of each cluster (e.g., time from the first to last seizure in a cluster) varies in the range of ~1 to 3 days, and successive clusters are separated by ~26 to 41 days (except for the large gap, from January 2010 to May 2010, due to missing recording). Based on this analysis, it is reasonable to define lead seizures as seizures separated by (at least) $T = 3$ days (Chen & Cherkassky, 2020; Chen et al., 2019). For example, Fig. 3.10B shows one cluster formed by seven seizures during time period June 3 to 5, 2010. For this cluster, when using $T = 3$ days to define lead seizure, only the first one will be identified as "lead seizure." However, if lead seizures are defined using $T = 4$ hours, then all seven seizures (in Fig. 3.10B) will be regarded as lead seizures.

3.5.4 Performance Metrics

The quality of seizure prediction is evaluated using several performance indices. In order to introduce these indices, we note first that predictive modeling can be performed under two distinct settings, called "batch modeling" and "online modeling."

Under batch modeling, the goal is to classify EEG segments, irrespective of their chronological order. So seizure prediction is reduced to standard binary classification (of EEG segments). Under this formalization, prediction accuracy (of a binary classifier) is evaluated using two indices: sensitivity and specificity. Assuming that classification refers to prediction of lead seizures, sensitivity is simply the fraction of lead seizures that are correctly predicted (during test stage). Specificity index is usually defined as the false-positive rate (FPR), or the fraction of false-positive predictions relative

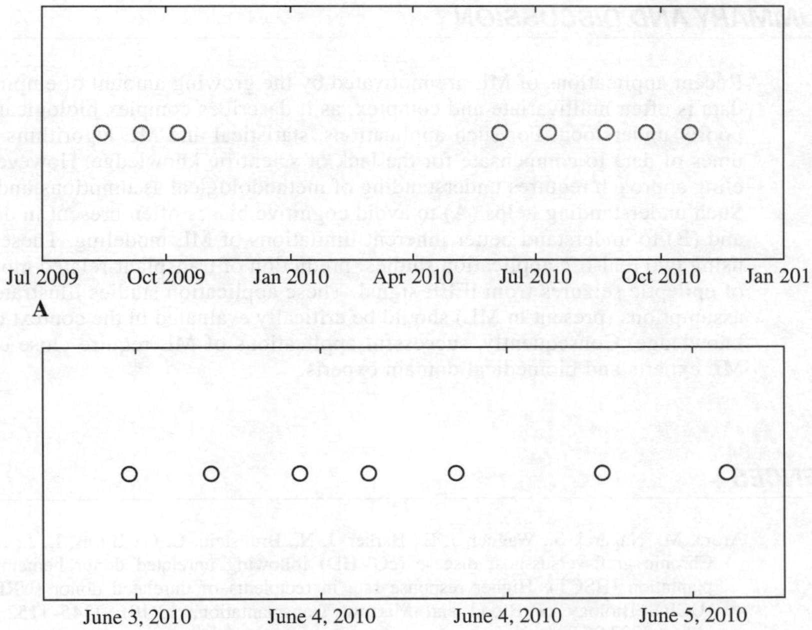

FIGURE 3.10 Clustering of seizures for canine data (dog L2): (A) all 45 seizures (represented by 45 circles) during the whole period (July 2009 to November 2010), indicating strong clustering in time; (B) distribution of seven seizures (represented by 7 circles) within one cluster, during time period June 3 to 5, 2010.

to the number of all test segments. Note that batch modeling provides optimistic estimates of prediction performance, because it may use future EEG data to predict past seizures.

Under online modeling setup, the classifier (in Fig. 3.8) is always trained using past data and makes prediction for future events. Clearly, online modeling provides more realistic set up; however, the modeling becomes more challenging (compared to batch modeling), because the amount of training data is reduced significantly. Moreover, dealing with nonstationarity of EEG becomes more challenging, because future data is not used for training. Nonstationarity of EEG is usually addressed by periodically retraining a classifier (in Fig. 3.8) using most recent data. To further reduce the effect of nonstationarity, new development of learning methods is required. Evaluating prediction accuracy (for online modeling) requires more sophisticated performance indices. Referring to Fig. 3.7, performance indices for online prediction should take into account the duration of the prediction horizon (PH), in addition to the usual specificity and sensitivity (used for batch modeling). This additional index, called time-in-warning (TIW), is defined as the fraction of test period when "warnings" are generated. A good prediction system should keep TIW as small as possible because spending much time in warning affects patients' quality of life. Further, for online modeling FPR is defined as the number of false warnings per day (or per hour).

Finally, we emphasize that performance metrics (for online prediction) are affected by system design parameters (i.e., PP and PH) (Chen & Cherkassky, 2020). Referring to Fig. 3.7, the system with longer prediction horizon is likely to have higher sensitivity and TIW. Hence, these system design parameters should be carefully specified *prior to* design of prediction system (shown in Fig. 3.8). However, many studies on seizure prediction focus on start-of-the-art classification algorithms while using ad hoc specification of system design parameters in their systems.

3.6 SUMMARY AND DISCUSSION

Recent applications of ML are motivated by the growing amount of empirical data. Biomedical data is often multivariate and complex, as it describes complex biological mechanisms that are poorly understood. For such applications, statistical and ML algorithms can utilize large volumes of data to compensate for the lack of scientific knowledge. However, data-analytic modeling approach requires understanding of methodological assumptions underlying ML methods. Such understanding helps (A) to avoid cognitive biases often present in data-analytic modeling and (B) to understand better inherent limitations of ML modeling. These issues are illustrated using two real-life application studies: prediction of transplant-related mortality, and prediction of epileptic seizures from iEEE signal. These application studies illustrate that methodological assumptions (present in ML) should be critically evaluated in the context of application domain knowledge. Consequently, successful applications of ML require close collaboration between ML experts and biomedical domain experts.

REFERENCES

Arora, M., Nagaraj, S., Wagner, J. E., Barker, J. N., Brunstein, C. G., Burns, L. J., …Weisdorf, D. J. (2007). Chronic graft-versus-host disease (cGVHD) following unrelated donor hematopoietic Stem cell transplantation (HSCT): Higher response rate in recipients of unrelated donor (URD) umbilical cord blood (UCB). Biology of Blood and Marrow Transplantation, 13(10), 1145–1152. https://doi.org/10.1016/j.bbmt.2007.06.004

Assi, E. B., Nguyen, D. K., Rihana, S., & Sawan, M. (2017). A functional-genetic scheme for seizure forecasting in canine epilepsy. IEEE Transactions on Biomedical Engineering, 65(6), 1339–1348. https://doi.org/10.1109/TBME.2017.2752081

Balduini, C. L., Frassoni, F., Noris, P., Klersy, C., Iannone, A. M., Giorgiani, G., …Locatelli, F. (2001). Donor–recipient incompatibility at CD31-codon 563 is a major risk factor for acute graft-versus-host disease after allogeneic bone marrow transplantation from a human leucocyte antigen-matched donor. British Journal of Haematology, 114(4), 951–953.

Brinkmann, B. H., Patterson, E. E., Vite, C., Vasoli, V. M., Crepeau, D., Stead, M., …Worrell, G. A. (2015). Forecasting seizures using intracranial EEG measures and SVM in naturally occurring canine epilepsy. PLoS ONE, 10(8), 1–12. https://doi.org/10.1371/journal.pone.0133900

Brinkmann, B. H., Wagenaar, J., Abbot, D., Adkins, P., Bosshard, S. C., Chen, M., …Worrell, G. A. (2016). Crowdsourcing reproducible seizure forecasting in human and canine epilepsy. Brain, 139(6), 1713–1722. https://doi.org/10.1093/brain/aww045

Cai, F. (2010). Predictive modeling of transplant-related mortality. Journal of Medical Devices, 4(2), 027527.

Camps-Valls, G., José Luis, R.-Á., & Martínez-Ramón, M. (2007). Kernel methods in bioengineering, signal and image processing. Idea Group.

Cavet, J., Middleton, P. G., Segall, M., Noreen, H., Davies, S. M., Dickinson, A. M., …Dickinson, A. M. (1999). Recipient tumor necrosis factor and interleukin-10 gene polymorphisms associated with early mortality and acute graft-versus-host disease severity in HLA-matched sibling bone marrow transplants. Blood, 94(11), 3941–3946.

Chen, H.H., Shiao, H. T., & Cherkassky, V. (2019). Online Prediction of Lead Seizures Using Long-term iEEG Recordings [Manuscript submitted for publication].

Chen, H. H., & Cherkassky, V. (2020). Performance metrics for online seizure prediction. Neural Networks, 128, 22–32. https://doi.org/10.1016/j.neunet.2020.04.022

Cherkassky, V. (2013). Predictive learning. VCtextbook.com.

Cherkassky, V., & Mulier, F. (2007). Learning from data: concepts, theory and methods (2nd ed.). Hoboken, NJ: John Wiley & Sons. https://doi.org/10.1097/EDE.0b013e3181e13328

Choy, G., Samir, A. E., & Brink, J. A. (2018). Current applications and future impact of machine learning in radiology. Radiology, 288(2), 318–328.

Cook, M. J., O'Brien, T. J., Berkovic, S. F., Murphy, M., Morokoff, A., Fabinyi, G., …Himes, D. (2013). Prediction of seizure likelihood with a long-term, implanted seizure advisory system in patients with drug-resistant epilepsy: A first-in-man study. The Lancet Neurology, 12(6), 563–571. https://doi.org/10.1016/S1474-4422(13)70075-9

Cooley, S., Trachtenberg, E., Bergemann, T. L., Saeteurn, K., Klein, J., Le, C. T., …Weisdorf, D. J. (2009). Donors with group B KIR haplotypes improve relapse-free survival after unrelated hematopoietic cell transplantation for acute myelogenous leukemia. Blood, 113(3), 726–732. https://doi.org/10.1182/blood-2008-07-171926.

Couriel, D. R., Saliba, R. M., Giralt, S., Khouri, I., Andersson, B., Lima, M.De, …Champlin, R. (2004). Acute and chronic graft-versus-host disease after ablative and nonmyeloablative conditioning for allogeneic hematopoietic transplantation. Biology of Blood and Marrow Transplantation, 10(3), 178–185. https://doi.org/10.1016/j.bbmt.2003.10.006

Cruz, J. A., & Wishart, D. S. (2006). Applications of machine learning in cancer prediction and prognosis. Cancer Informatics, 2, 59–77. https://doi.org/10.1177/117693510600200030

Dalic, L., & Cook, M. J. (2016). Managing drug-resistant epilepsy: Challenges and solutions. Neuropsychiatric Disease and Treatment, 12, 2605–2616. https://doi.org/10.2147/NDT.S84852

Epilepsy Foundation. (2008). Seizure clusters. Retrieved January 6, 2020, from https://www.epilepsy.com/learn/professionals/refractory-seizures/potentially-remediable-causes/seizure-clusters

Ferrara, J. L., & Deeg, H. J. (1991). Graft-versus-host disease. New England Journal of Medicine, 324(10), 667–674.

Hastie, T., Tibshirani, R., & Friedman, J. (2001). The elements of statistical learning. Springer series in statistics. New York: Springer. https://doi.org/10.1198/jasa.2004.s339

Howbert, J. J., Patterson, E. E., Stead, S. M., Brinkmann, B., Vasoli, V., Crepeau, D., …Worrell, G. A. (2014). Forecasting seizures in dogs with naturally occurring epilepsy. PLoS ONE, 9(1)–PLoS One 9, e81920. https://doi.org/10.1371/journal.pone.0081920

Huang, S., Cai, N., & Pacheco, P. P. (2018). Applications of support vector machine (SVM) learning in cancer genomics. Cancer Genomics and Proteomics, 15, 41–51. https://doi.org/10.21873/cgp.20063

Kourou, K., Exarchos, T. P., Exarchos, K. P., Karamouzis, M. V., & Fotiadis, D. I. (2015). Machine learning applications in cancer prognosis and prediction. CSBJ, 13, 8–17. https://doi.org/10.1016/j.csbj.2014.11.005

Kuhlmann, L., Karoly, P., Freestone, D. R., Brinkmann, B. H., Temko, A., Barachant, A., …Cook, M. J. (2018). Epilepsyecosystem.org: Crowd-sourcing reproducible seizure prediction with long-term human intracranial EEG. Brain, 141(9), 2619–2630. https://doi.org/10.1093/brain/awy210

Kwan, P., & Brodie, M. J. (2000). Early identification of refractory epilepsy. The New England Journal of Medicine, 342(5), 314–319.

Lange, H., Lieb, J., Engel, J. J., & Crandall, P. (1983). Temporo-spatial patterns of pre-ictal spike activity in human temporal lobe epilepsy. Electroencephalography and Clinical Neurophysiology, 56(6), 543–555.

Lemm, S., Blankertz, B., Dickhaus, T., & Müller, K. (2011). NeuroImage Introduction to machine learning for brain imaging. NeuroImage, 56(2), 387–399. https://doi.org/10.1016/j.neuroimage.2010.11.004

LeVan Quyen, M., Martinerie, J., Navarro, V., Baulac, M., & Varela, F. J. (2001). Characterizing neurodynamic changes before seizures. Journal of Clinical Neurophysiology, 18(3), 191–208. https://doi.org/10.1097/00004691-200105000-00001

LeVan Quyen, M., Martinerie, J., Navarro, V., Boon, P., D'Havé, M., Adam, C., …Baulac, M. (2001). Anticipation of epileptic seizures from standard EEG recordings. Lancet, 357(9251), 183–188. https://doi.org/10.1016/S0140-6736(00)03591-1

Litt, B., & Echauz, J. (2002). Prediction of epileptic seizures. Lancet Neurology, 1(1), 22–30. https://doi.org/10.1016/S1474-4422(02)00003-0

Litt, B., Esteller, R., Echauz, J., D'Alessandro, M., Shor, R., Henry, T., …Vachtsevanos, G. (2001). Epileptic seizures may begin hours in advance of clinical onset: A report of five patients. Neuron, 30(1), 51–64. https://doi.org/10.1016/S0896-6273(01)00262-8

Min, S., Lee, B., & Yoon, S. (2017). Deep learning in bioinformatics. Briefings in bioinformatics, 18(5), 851–869. https://doi.org/10.1093/bib/bbw068

Navarro, V., Martinerie, J., LeVan Quyen, M., Clemenceau, S., Adam, C., Baulac, M., & Varela, F. (2002). Seizure anticipation in human neocortical partial epilepsy. Brain, 125(3), 640–655. https://doi.org/10.1093/brain/awf048

Nejedly, P., Kremen, V., Sladky, V., Nasseri, M., Guragain, H., Klimes, P., …Worrell, G. A. (2019). Deep-learning for seizure forecasting in canines with epilepsy. Journal of Neural Engineering, 16(3), 036031. https://doi.org/10.1088/1741-2552/ab172d

Netoff, T., Park, Y., & Parhi, K. (2009). Seizure prediction using cost-sensitive support vector machine. In 2009 Annual International Conference of the IEEE Engineering in Medicine and Biology Society (pp. 3322–3325). IEEE. https://doi.org/10.1109/IEMBS.2009.5333711

Park, Y., Luo, L., Parhi, K. K., & Netoff, T. (2011). Seizure prediction with spectral power of EEG using cost-sensitive support vector machines. Epilepsia, 52(10), 1761–1770. https://doi.org/10.1111/j.1528-1167.2011.03138.x

Petrosian, A. (1995). Kolmogorov complexity of finite sequences and recognition of different preictal EEG patterns. In Proceedings Eighth IEEE Symposium on Computer-Based Medical Systems (pp. 212–217). IEEE. https://doi.org/10.1109/CBMS.1995.465426

Shiao, H. T., Cherkassky, V., Lee, J., Veber, B., Patterson, E. E., Brinkmann, B. H., & Worrell, G. A. (2016). SVM-based system for prediction of epileptic seizures from iEEG signal. IEEE Transactions on Biomedical Engineering, 64(5), 1011–1022. https://doi.org/10.1109/TBME.2016.2586475

Vapnik, V. (1995). The nature of statistical learning theory. New York: Springer-Verlag.

Varatharajah, Y., Iyer, R. K., Berry, B. M., Worrell, G. A., & Brinkmann, B. H. (2017). Seizure forecasting and the preictal state in canine epilepsy. International Journal of Neural Systems, 27(01), 1650046. https://doi.org/10.1142/S0129065716500465

WHO. (2019). Epilepsy. Retrieved January 6, 2020, from https://www.who.int/news-room/fact-sheets/detail/epilepsy

Zou, J., Huss, M., Abid, A., Mohammadi, P., Torkamani, A., & Telenti, A. (2019). A primer on deep learning in genomics. Nature Genetics, 51(1), 12–18. https://doi.org/10.1038/s41588-018-0295-5

P · A · R · T · 2

BIOMECHANICS OF THE HUMAN BODY

CHAPTER 4
HEAT TRANSFER APPLICATIONS IN BIOLOGICAL SYSTEMS

Liang Zhu
University of Maryland, Baltimore County, Baltimore, Maryland

4.1 INTRODUCTION

Over the past 100 years, the understanding of thermal and mechanical properties of human tissues and physics that governs biological processes has been greatly advanced by the utilization of fundamental engineering principles in the analysis of many heat and mass transport applications in biology and medicine. During the past two decades, there has been an increasingly intense interest in bioheat transfer phenomena, with particular emphasis on therapeutic and diagnostic applications. Relying on advanced computational techniques, the development of complex mathematical models has greatly enhanced our ability to analyze various types of bioheat transfer process. The collaborations among physiologists, clinicians, and engineers in the bioheat transfer field have resulted in improvements in prevention, treatment, preservation, and protection techniques for biological systems, including use of heat or cold treatments to destroy tumors or to improve patients' outcome after brain injury, and protection of humans from extreme environmental conditions.

Section 4.2 starts with fundamental aspects of thermal interaction between blood and its surrounding tissue. Discussions on how thermal effect of blood is modeled in biological systems then follow in Sec. 4.3. Section 4.4 shows different approaches for theoretically modeling the blood flow in the tissue. In particular the assumptions and validity of several widely used continuum bioheat transfer equations are evaluated. Different techniques to measure temperature, thermophysical properties, and blood flow in biological systems are described in Sec. 4.5. Section 4.6 focuses on one of the medical applications of heat transfer, hyperthermia treatment for tumors, with emphases on traditional and current heating techniques and advanced modeling approaches.

4.2 FUNDAMENTAL ASPECTS OF BIOHEAT TRANSFER

One of the remarkable features of the human thermoregulatory system is that we can maintain a core temperature near 37°C over a wide range of environmental conditions and during thermal stress. The value of blood flow to the body varies over a wide range depending upon the need for its three primary functions:

1. *Mass transfer in support of body metabolisms:* Blood transports oxygen to the rest of the body and transports carbon dioxide and other waste from the cells.
2. *Regulation of systemic blood pressure:* The vascular system is a primary effector in the regulation of systemic blood pressure through its ability to alter the distribution of blood flow and regulate the cardiac output and thereby buffer systemic pressure fluctuations.
3. *Heat transfer for systemic thermoregulation.*

As for the last primary function, blood is known to have a dual influence on the thermal energy balance. First, it can be a heat source or sink, depending on the local tissue temperature. During winter time, blood is transported from the heart to warm the rest of the body. On the other hand, during hyperthermia treatment for certain diseases where tissue temperature is elevated to as high as 45°C by external devices, relatively cold blood forms cold tracks that can decrease the treatment efficacy. The second influence of blood flow is that it can enhance heat dissipation from the inside of the body to the environment to maintain a normal body temperature. Theoretical studies have shown that if the heat produced in the central areas of the body at rest condition could escape only by tissue conduction, the body temperature would not reach a steady state until it was about 80°C. A lethal temperature would be reached in only 3 hours. During exercise, our body temperature would have typically risen 12°C in 1 hour if no heat were lost by blood flow. Maintaining a core temperature of 37°C during thermal stress or exercise in the body is achieved by increasing the cardiac output by central and local thermoregulation, redistributing heat via the blood flow from the muscle tissue to the skin, and speeding the heat loss to the environment by evaporation of sweat.

Thermal interaction between blood and tissue can be studied either experimentally or theoretically. However, for the following reasons it is difficult to evaluate heat transfer in a biological system:

- *The complexity of the vasculature:* It is not practical to develop a comprehensive model that includes the effect of all thermally significant vessels in a tissue. Therefore, the most unusual and difficult basic problem of estimating heat transfer in living biologic systems is modeling the effect of blood circulation.
- *Temperature response of the vasculature to external and internal effects:* It is also a complex task. In a living system, the blood flow rate and the vessel size may change as a response to local temperature, local pH value, and the concentration of local O_2 and CO_2 levels.
- *The small thermal length scale involved in the microvasculature:* Thermally significant blood vessels are generally in a thermal scale of less than 300 μm. It has been difficult to build temperature-measuring devices with sufficient resolution to measure temperature fluctuation.

For the above reasons, even if the heat transfer function of the vascular system has been appreciated since the mid-nineteenth century, only in the past four decades, has there been a revolution in our understanding on how temperature is controlled at the local level, i.e., how local microvascular blood flow controls the local temperature field and how the local tissue temperature regulates local blood flow.

Until 1980, it was believed that, like gaseous transport, heat transfer took place in the capillaries because of their large exchange surface area. Several theoretical and experimental studies (Chato, 1980; Chen and Holmes, 1980; Lemons et al., 1987; Weinbaum et al., 1984) have been performed to illustrate how individual vessels participate in local heat transfer and thus to understand where the actual heat transfer between blood and tissue occurs. Since heat transfer requires temperature difference, it is essential to identify blood vessels where their temperatures are higher or lower than the temperature of their surrounding tissue. In these analyses, the concept of thermal equilibration length was introduced. Thermal equilibration length of an individual blood vessel was defined as a distance over which the temperature difference between blood and tissue drops a certain percentage. For example, the axial variation of the tissue and blood temperature difference can be expressed as $\Delta T = \Delta T_0 e^{-\frac{x}{x_{cr}}}$, where ΔT_0 is the temperature difference at the vessel entrance, and x_{cr} and $4.6x_{cr}$ are the thermal equilibration length over which ΔT decreases to 37 percent and 1 percent, respectively, of its value at the entrance. A blood vessel whose thermal equilibration length is comparable to its physical length L is considered thermally significant, and thus, its thermal effect on tissue temperature field should be included in theoretical modeling. If the thermal equilibration length is much longer than the physical length, the blood temperature changes very little along its length. However, when the thermal equilibration length is much shorter than L, the blood temperature along the vessel should be very close to the local tissue temperature, and thus, the thermal effect of those blood vessels can often be neglected in theoretical modeling.

Chato (1980) first theoretically investigated the heat transfer from individual blood vessels in three configurations: a single vessel, two vessels in countercurrent flow, and a single vessel near the skin surface. It was shown that the Graetz number, proportional to the blood flow velocity and radius, is the controlling parameter determining the thermal equilibration between the blood and tissue. For blood vessels with very low Graetz number, blood quickly reaches the tissue temperature. It was also demonstrated that heat transfer between the countercurrent artery and vein is affected by the vessel center-to-center spacing and mass flow rate between them.

In an anatomic study performed on rabbit limbs, Weinbaum et al. (1984) identified three vascular layers (deep, intermediate, and cutaneous) in the outer 1-cm tissue layer. Subsequently, three fundamental vascular structures were derived from the anatomic observation: (1) an isolated vessel embedded in a tissue cylinder, as shown by the intermediate tissue layer; (2) a large artery and its countercurrent vein oriented obliquely to the skin surface, as shown in the deep tissue layer; and (3) a vessel or vessel pair running parallel to the skin surface in the cutaneous plexus. These three vascular structures served as the basic heat transfer units in the thermal equilibration analysis in Weinbaum et al. (1984).

As shown in Weinbaum et al. (1984), 99 percent thermal equilibration length of a single blood vessel embedded in a tissue cylinder was derived as

$$x_{cr} = 1.15 * a * \mathrm{Pr} * \mathrm{Re}_D [0.75 + K * \ln(R/a)] \tag{4.1}$$

where a and R are the blood vessel and tissue cylinder radius, respectively, Pr and Re_D are the blood flow Prandtl number and Reynolds number, respectively, and K is the ratio of blood thermal conductivity to tissue thermal conductivity. It is evident that x_{cr} is proportional to the blood vessel size and its blood flow velocity. Substituting the measured vascular geometry and the corresponding blood flow rate number for different blood vessel generations (sizes) from a 13-kg dog (Whitmore, 1968), one could calculate the thermal equilibration length as listed in Table 4.1.

Several conclusions were drawn from the comparison between x_{cr} and L. In contrast to previous assumptions that heat transfer occurs in the capillary bed, for blood vessels smaller than 50 μm in diameter, blood temperature quickly reaches the tissue temperature; thus, all blood-tissue heat transfer must have already occurred before entering into these vessels. For blood vessels larger than 300 μm in diameter, there is little change in blood temperature in the axial direction because of their much longer thermal equilibration length compared with the vessel length. The medium-sized vessels between 50 and 300 μm in diameter are considered thermally significant because of their comparable thermal equilibration length and physical length. Those blood vessels are primary contributors to tissue heat transfer. Note that the conclusions are similar to that drawn by Chato (1980).

It was observed that virtually all the thermally significant vessels (>50 μm in diameter) in the skeletal muscle were closely juxtaposed artery-vein pairs (Weinbaum et al., 1984). The countercurrent heat exchange mechanism, if dominant, was suggested as an energy conservation means since it provides a direct heat transfer path between the vessels. Therefore, it leads to a small thermal resistance between the warm artery and its countercurrent vein. Thermal equilibration in the artery

TABLE 4.1 Thermal equilibration length in a single vessel embedded in a tissue cylinder

Vessel radius a, μm	Vessel physical length L, cm	R/a	x_{cr}, cm
300	1.0	30	9.5
100	0.5	20	0.207
50	0.2	10	0.014
20	0.1	7	0.0006

(50~300 μm in diameter) in a countercurrent pair was estimated based on a simple heat conduction analysis in the cross-sectional plane. It was noted that the thermal equilibration length in the countercurrent artery was at least three times shorter than that in a single vessel of the same size embedded in a tissue cylinder (Weinbaum et al., 1984). A short thermal equilibration length indicates a smaller thermal resistance due to the short cut of heat transfer pathway between the countercurrent artery and vein. Significantly short thermal equilibration length in comparison with that of a single vessel suggests that the primary blood tissue heat exchange mechanism for vessels larger than 50 μm in the deep layer is the incomplete countercurrent heat exchange. Therefore, for modeling heat transfer in these tissue regions, reasonable assumptions related to the countercurrent heat exchange mechanism can be made to simplify the mathematical formulation.

Theoretical analyses of the thermal equilibration in a large vessel in the cutaneous layer (Chato, 1980; Weinbaum et al., 1984) demonstrated that its thermal equilibration length was much longer than its physical length during normal and hyperemic conditions despite the close distance from the skin surface. It was suggested that the large vessels in the cutaneous layer can be far from thermal equilibration and are therefore capable of delivering warm blood from the deep tissue to the skin layer. This superficial warm blood shunting is very important in increasing the normal temperature gradient at the skin surface and therefore plays an important role in losing heat during heavy exercise. On the contrary, during surface cooling there is rapid cutaneous vasoconstriction in the skin. The minimally perfused skin, along with the underlying subcutaneous fat, provides a layer of insulation, and the temperature gradient from the skin surface into the muscle becomes almost linear (Bazett, 1941) yielding the lowest possible heat transfer from the body.

4.3 BIOHEAT TRANSFER MODELING

The effects of blood flow on heat transfer in living tissue have been examined for more than a century, dating back to the experimental studies of Bernard in 1876. Since then, mathematical modeling of the complex thermal interaction between the vasculature and tissue has been a topic of interest for numerous physiologists, physicians, and engineers. A major difficulty to theoretically predict temperature distribution in tissue is the assessment of the thermal effect of blood circulation, which is the dominant mode of heat removal or release and is an important cause of tissue temperature inhomogeneity.

Because of the complexity of the vascular geometry, there are two theoretical approaches describing the effect of blood flow in a biological system. Each approach represents two length scales over which temperature variations may occur.

1. *Continuum models,* in which the effect of blood flow in the region of interest is averaged over a control volume. Thus, in the considered tissue region, there is no blood vessel present; however, its effect is treated by either adding an additional term in the conduction equation for the tissue or changing some of the thermal/physical parameters in the conduction equation. The continuum

models are simple to use since the detailed vascular geometry of the considered tissue region need not be known as long as one or two representative parameters related to the blood flow are available. The shortcoming of the continuum model is that since the blood vessels disappear, no point-by-point variation in the blood temperature is available. Another shortcoming is associated with the assumptions introduced when the continuum model was derived. For different tissue regions and physiological conditions, these assumptions may not be valid.

2. *Vascular models,* in which blood vessels are represented as tubes buried in tissue. Because of the complicated vascular geometry one may only consider several blood vessels and neglect the others. Previous studies (Crezee and Lagendijk, 1990; Dorr and Hynynen, 1992; Roemer, 1990; Wang and Zhu, 2007; Wang et al., 2008) have demonstrated that blood flow in large, thermally unequilibrated vessels is the main cause for temperature nonhomogeneity during hyperthermia treatment. Large blood vessels may significantly cool tissue volumes around them, making it very difficult to cover the whole tumor volume with therapeutic thermal exposure. In applications where point-to-point temperature nonuniformities are important, vascular model has been proved to be necessary to predict accurately the tissue temperature field (Wang and Zhu, 2007; Zhu et al., 1996a). In recent years, with the breakthrough of advanced computational techniques and resources, vascular models (Raaymakers et al., 2000) for simulating vascular networks have grown rapidly and already demonstrated its great potential in accurate and point-to-point blood and tissue temperature mapping.

4.3.1 Continuum Models

In continuum models, blood vessels are not modeled individually. Instead, the traditional heat conduction equation for the tissue region is modified by either adding an additional term or altering some of the key parameters. The modification is relatively simple and is closely related to the local vasculature and blood perfusion. Even if the continuum models cannot describe the point-by-point temperature variations in the vicinity of larger blood vessels, they are easy to use and allow the manipulation of one or several free parameters. Thus, they have much wider applications than the vascular models. In the following sections, some of the widely used continuum models are introduced and their validity is evaluated on the basis of the fundamental heat transfer aspects.

Pennes Bioheat Equation. It is known that one of the primary functions of blood flow in a biological system is their ability to heat or cool the tissue, depending on the relative local tissue temperature. The existence of a temperature difference between the blood and tissue is taken as evidence of its function to remove or release heat. On the basis of this speculation, Pennes (1948) proposed his famous heat transfer model, which is called Pennes bioheat equation. Pennes suggested that the effect of blood flow in the tissue be modeled as a heat source or sink term added to the traditional heat conduction equation. The Pennes bioheat equation is given by

$$\rho_t c_t \frac{\partial T_t}{\partial t} = k_t \nabla^2 T_t + q'''_{\text{blood}} + q'''_m \tag{4.2}$$

where q'''_m is the volumetric metabolic heat generation rate in the tissue, and the second term on the right side of the equation (q'''_{blood}) takes into account the contribution of blood flow to the local tissue temperature distribution. The strength of the perfusion source term can be derived as follows.

Figure 4.1 shows a schematic diagram of a small tissue volume perfused by a single artery and vein pair. The tissue region is perfused via a capillary network bifurcating from the transverse arterioles, and the blood is drained by the transverse venules. The blood flow rate in the supply artery decreases while that in the supply vein increases. Mass conservation requires that the amount of the blood flow rate change in the supply artery or vein is the same, i.e.,

$$Q_{\text{in},a} - Q_{\text{out},a} = Q_{\text{out},v} - Q_{\text{in},v} = \Delta Q_{\text{O}_2-\text{CO}_2} \tag{4.3}$$

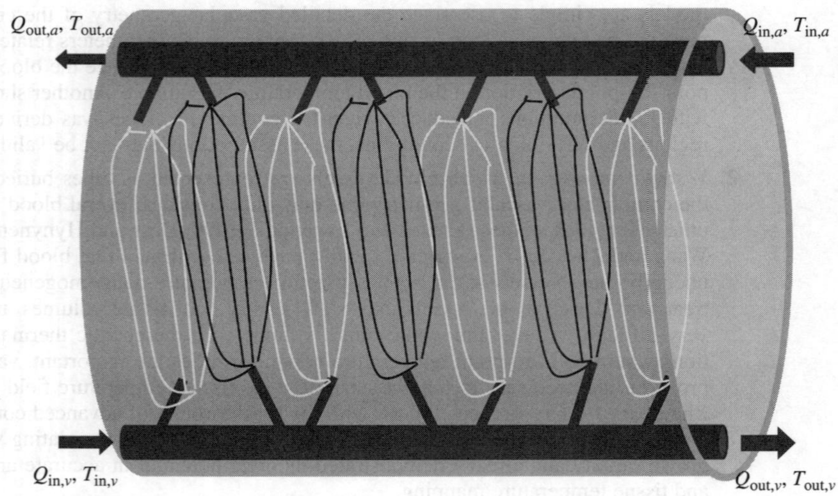

FIGURE 4.1 Schematic diagram of a tissue volume perfused by a single artery and vein pair.

If one assumes that both the artery and vein keep a constant temperature when they pass through this tissue region, the total heat released is equal to the total amount of blood perfusing this tissue volume per unit time, $\Delta Q_{O_2-CO_2}$, multiplied by its density ρ_b, specific heat c_b, and the temperature difference between the artery and vein, and is given by

$$\rho_b c_b \Delta Q_{O_2-CO_2}(T_a - T_v) \quad \text{(W)} \tag{4.4}$$

The volumetric heat generation rate q'''_{blood}, defined as the heat generation rate per unit tissue volume V, is then derived as

$$q'''_{\text{blood}} = \frac{\rho_b c_b \Delta Q_{O_2-CO_2}(T_a - T_v)}{V} = \frac{\Delta Q_{O_2-CO_2}}{V}\rho_b c_b (T_a - T_v) = \omega \rho_b c_b (T_a - T_v) \quad \left(\frac{\text{W}}{\text{mL}} \ or \ \frac{\text{W}}{\text{m}^3}\right) \tag{4.5}$$

where ω is defined as the amount of blood perfused per unit volume tissue per second and it is given by the following equation:

$$\omega = \Delta Q_{O_2-CO_2}/V \quad \left(\frac{1}{\text{s}}\right) \tag{4.6}$$

Notice the slight difference of the unit in Eq. (4.6) for the blood perfusion rate from the one in medical literature, where the blood perfusion rate usually carries a unit of mL/g tissue*s. When the density of tissue is known, one should be able to convert it from the value given in medical literature to the one defined in Eq. (4.6).

Both T_a and T_v in Eq. (4.5) are unknown. Applying the analogy with gaseous exchange in living tissue, Pennes believed that heat transfer occurred in the capillaries because of their large area for heat exchange. As shown in Fig. 4.2, Pennes stated that the local arterial temperature T_a could be assumed as a constant and equal to the artery blood temperature from the heart, T_{b0}. As for the local venous blood, it seems reasonable to assume that it equilibrates with the tissue in the capillary, and when the blood enters the venules from the capillary, it has a similar temperature as the local tissue temperature. Figure 4.2 also illustrates that when the countercurrent heat exchange between the paired large artery and vein is neglected, the temperature of the venous blood in systemic circulation

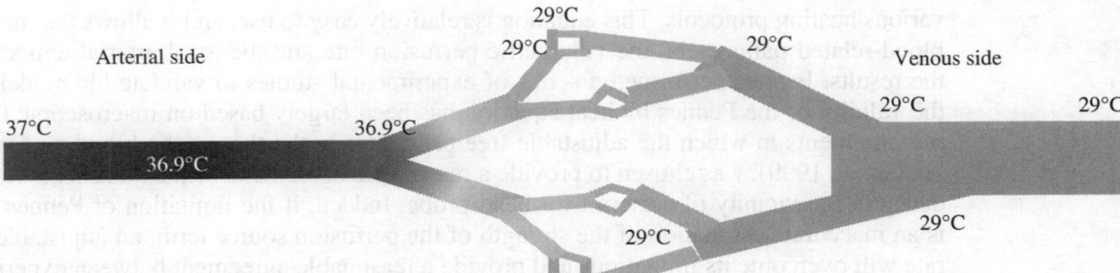

FIGURE 4.2 Schematic diagram of temperature variations in the vasculature and its surrounding tissue assumed by Dr. Pennes.

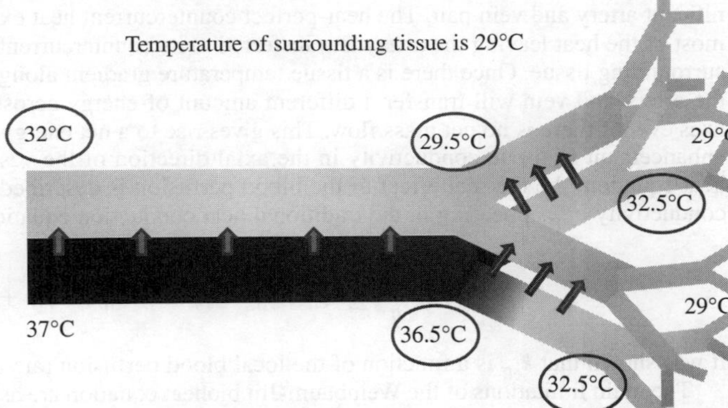

FIGURE 4.3 Schematic diagram of realistic temperature variations in the vasculature and its surrounding tissue considering heat exchange between blood and tissue, as well as between countercurrent artery and vein.

T_v would remain the same as its surrounding tissue temperature T_t. Then, the Pennes bioheat equation becomes

$$\rho_t c_t \frac{\partial T_t}{\partial t} = k_t \nabla^2 T_t + \omega \rho_b c_b (T_{b0} - T_t) + q'''_m \tag{4.7}$$

This is a partial differential equation for the tissue temperature field, when T_{b0} is often prescribed as 37°C. As long as an appropriate initial condition and boundary conditions are prescribed, the transient or steady-state temperature field in the tissue can be determined.

The limitations of the Pennes equation come from the basic assumptions introduced in this model. First, it is assumed that the temperature of the arterial blood does not change when it travels from the heart to the capillary bed. As shown in Fig. 4.3, small temperature variations occur only in blood vessels with a diameter larger than 300 μm. Another assumption is that the venous blood temperature is approximated by the local tissue temperature. This is valid only for blood vessels with a diameter smaller than 50 μm. Thus, without considering the thermal exchange between the countercurrent artery and vein in different vessel generations, the Pennes perfusion source term obviously overestimates the effect of blood perfusion. To accurately model the effect of blood perfusion, the temperature variation along the artery and the heat recaptured by the countercurrent vein must be taken into consideration.

Despite the limitations of the Pennes bioheat equation, reasonable agreement between theory and experiment has been obtained for the measured temperature profiles in perfused tissue subject to various heating protocols. This equation is relatively easy to use, and it allows the manipulation of two blood-related parameters, the volumetric perfusion rate and the local arterial temperature, to modify the results. Pennes performed a series of experimental studies to validate his model. Over the years, the validity of the Pennes bioheat equation has been largely based on macroscopic thermal clearance measurements in which the adjustable free parameter in the theory, the blood perfusion rate (Xu and Anderson, 1999), was chosen to provide a reasonable agreement with experiments for the temperature decay in the vicinity of a thermistor bead probe. Indeed, if the limitation of Pennes bioheat equation is an inaccurate estimation of the strength of the perfusion source term, an adjustable blood perfusion rate will overcome its limitations and provide a reasonable agreement between experiment and theory.

Weinbaum-Jiji Bioheat Equation. Since 1980, researchers (Chato, 1980; Chen and Holmes, 1980; Weinbaum et al., 1984) have begun to question the validity of the Pennes bioheat equation. Later, Weinbaum and Jiji (1985) developed a new equation for microvascular blood tissue heat transfer, based on an anatomic analysis (Weinbaum et al., 1984) to illustrate that the predominant mode of heat transfer in the tissue was the countercurrent heat exchange between a thermally significant artery and vein pair. The near-perfect countercurrent heat exchange mechanism implies that most of the heat leaving the artery is transferred to its countercurrent vein rather than released to the surrounding tissue. Once there is a tissue temperature gradient along the countercurrent vessel axes, the artery and vein will transfer a different amount of energy across a plane perpendicular to their axes even if there is no net mass flow. This gives rise to a net energy transfer that is equivalent to an enhancement in tissue conductivity in the axial direction of the vessels. In the Weinbaum-Jiji bioheat equation, the thermal effect of the blood perfusion is described by an enhancement in thermal conductivity k_{eff}, appearing in the traditional heat conduction equation,

$$\rho_t c_t \frac{\partial T_t}{\partial t} = k_{\text{eff}} \nabla^2 T_t + q_m''' \qquad k_{\text{eff}} = k_t [1 + f(\omega)] \tag{4.8}$$

It was shown that k_{eff} is a function of the local blood perfusion rate and local vascular geometry.

The main limitations of the Weinbaum-Jiji bioheat equation are associated with the importance of the countercurrent heat exchange. It was derived to describe heat transfer in peripheral tissue only, where its fundamental assumptions are most applicable. In tissue area containing big blood vessels (>200 μm in diameter), the assumption that most of the heat leaving the artery is recaptured by its countercurrent vein could be violated; thus, it is not an accurate model to predict the temperature field. In addition, this theory was primarily developed for closely paired microvessels in muscle tissue, which may not always be the main vascular structure in other tissues, such as the renal cortex. Furthermore, unlike the Pennes bioheat equation, which requires only the value of local blood perfusion rate, the estimation of the enhancement in thermal conductivity requires that detailed anatomical studies be performed to estimate the vessel number density, size, and artery-vein spacing for each vessel generation, as well as the blood perfusion rate (Zhu et al., 1995). These anatomic data are normally not available for most blood vessels in the thermally significant range.

A New Modified Bioheat Equation. The Pennes and Weinbaum-Jiji models represent two extreme situations of blood-vessel thermal interaction. In the original Pennes model, the arterial blood releases all of its heat to the surrounding tissue in the capillaries and there is no venous rewarming. Pennes did not realize that thermal equilibration was achieved in vessels at least an order of magnitude larger than the capillaries. In contrast, in the Weinbaum-Jiji model the partial countercurrent rewarming is assumed to be the main mechanism for blood-tissue heat transfer. The derivation of the Weinbaum-Jiji equation is based on the assumption that heat transfer between the artery and the vein does not depart significantly from a perfect countercurrent heat exchanger. In other words, most of the heat lost by the artery is recaptured by its countercurrent vein rather than lost to the surrounding tissue. Subsequent theoretical and experimental studies have shown that this is a valid assumption only for vessels less than 200 μm diameter (Charny et al., 1990; Zhu et al., 1996a).

Several theoretical studies have suggested that one way to overcome the shortcomings of both models was to introduce a "correction coefficient" in the Pennes perfusion term (Baish, 1994; Brinck and Werner, 1994; Chato, 1980; Weinbaum et al., 1997; Zhu et al., 2002). In 1997, Weinbaum and coworkers (Weinbaum et al., 1997) modified the Pennes source term on the basis of the thermal analysis of a basic heat transfer unit of muscle tissue, a 1-mm-diameter tissue cylinder containing blood vessels smaller than 200 μm in diameter, as shown in Fig. 4.4. The countercurrent heat exchange between the *s* artery and vein defined in the anatomical studies of Myrhage and Eriksson (1984) led to the estimation of the heat loss recaptured by the *s* vein. The strength of the source term was then rederived taking into account the rewarming of the countercurrent venous blood in the *s* tissue cylinder. The thermal equilibration analysis on the countercurrent *s* artery and vein in the tissue cylinder led to the following bioheat transfer equation:

$$\rho_t c_t \frac{\partial T_t}{\partial t} = k_t \nabla^2 T_t + \varepsilon \omega \rho_b c_b (T_{a0} - T_t) + q_m''' \tag{4.9}$$

Note that the only modification to the Pennes model is a correction coefficient ε in the Pennes perfusion source term. This correction coefficient can be viewed as a weighting function to correct the overestimation of the original Pennes perfusion term. An easy-to-use closed-form analytic expression was derived for this coefficient that depends on the vessel spacing and radius. From the anatomic studies of the vascular arrangements of various skeletal muscles, the correction coefficient was found to vary from 0.6 to 0.8 under normal physiological conditions, indicating that there is a 20 to 40 percent rewarming of the countercurrent vein. Similarly, one early work (Baish, 1994) was based on a generated vascular network following diffusion of angiogenic factors in tissue and it has shown that the Pennes perfusion source term overestimates the strength of heat released to or absorbed by the local blood perfusion by approximately 20 percent, implying a correction coefficient of 0.8. Note that it is close to neither unity (the Pennes model) nor zero (the Weinbaum-Jiji model). Thus, both the Pennes and Weinbaum-Jiji bioheat equations are not valid for most muscle tissue. The accuracy of

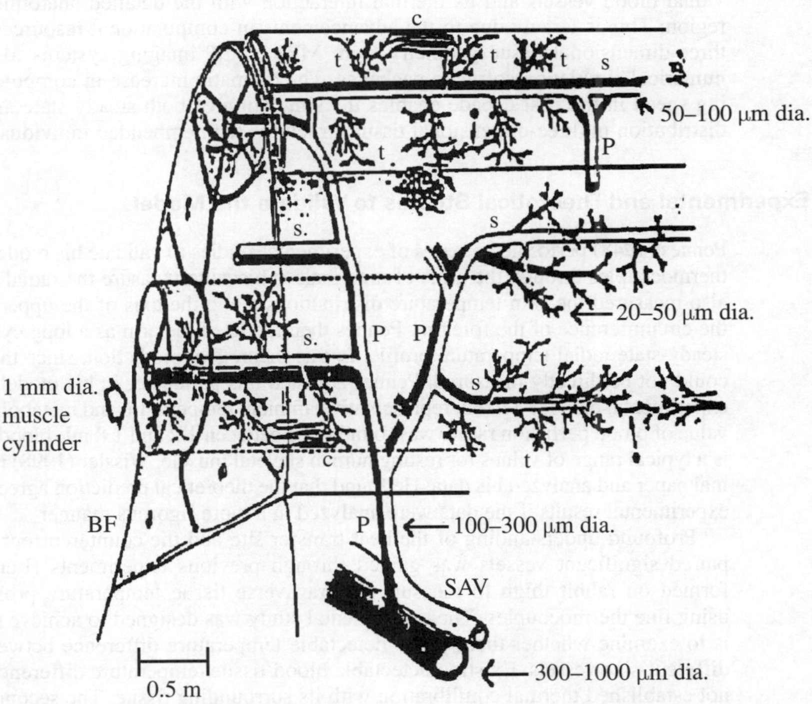

FIGURE 4.4 Macro- and microvascular arrangement in skeletal muscle. The blood supply for the muscle tissue cylinder comes from a branching countercurrent network of supply vessels. The primary (*P*) vessels originating from the *SAV* vessels run obliquely across the muscle tissue cylinders and then branch into the long secondary (*s*) vessels. [*From Myrhage and Erriksson (1984) with permission.*]

the calculated correction coefficients in the previous studies still depends on the precise description of the local vasculature arrangements and whether a repeatable tissue unit can be identified in the targeted tissue region. Unfortunately, in tissue region such as tumors, the blood flow patterns are often irregular and unpredictable, making the derivation of the correction coefficient a difficult task. Furthermore, as shown in Zhu et al. (2002), the arterial temperature T_{a0} may not be approximated as a constant either, unless the local blood perfusion is very high. In most physiological conditions, it is a function of the tissue depth, blood vessel bifurcation pattern, and the local blood perfusion rate.

Current Status of Bioheat Transfer Modeling. There were only a few attempts to develop alternative bioheat transfer models in the past 10 years based on volume averaging temperatures of porous media (Nakayama and Kuwahara, 2008; Shrivastava and Vaughan, 2009). One thing that is not clear from those models is the calculation of the "to-be-determined" parameters appearing in those equations. The determination of those parameters still requires development of a vasculature-tissue unit for establishing their relationship to the specific vasculature and blood perfusion rate.

Although developments of new bioheat transfer models have attracted a lot of attention in the 1980s and 1990s, most of the developed bioheat models have not yet been applied regularly by bioengineering researchers due to the uncertainty of estimating the parameters such as the enhancement in tissue thermal conductivity and the correction coefficient. The Pennes bioheat equation, utilizing only local perfusion rate and arterial blood temperature, is relatively easy to use without detailed anatomic knowledge of their detailed vasculature. In the past 10 years, very limited efforts have been focused on developing a better bioheat transfer models, with a few exceptions (Nakayama and Kuwahara, 2008; Shrivastava and Vaughan, 2009). Currently, the thermal effects of small blood vessels are still normally modeled by the Pennes perfusion source term, with special treatments to the large vessels. The emphases of bioheat transfer modeling have been shifted to model large individual blood vessels and its thermal interaction with the detailed anatomic geometry in the tissue region. This is largely due to the advancements in computational resources which allow import of three-dimensional tissue geometry from MRI or CT imaging systems to commercially available numerical simulation software packages. The dramatic increase in computer memory and calculating speed in the past decade enables the simulation of both steady state and transient temperature distribution in three-dimensional tissue structures with embedded individual large blood vessels.

4.3.2 Experimental and Theoretical Studies to Validate the Models

Pennes (1948) performed a series of experimental studies to validate his model. He inserted and pulled thermocouples through the arms of nine male subjects to measure the radial temperature profiles. He also measured the skin temperature distributions along the axis of the upper limb, as well as around the circumference of the forearm. Pennes then modeled the arm as a long cylinder and calculated the steady-state radial temperature profile. In this theoretical prediction, since the blood perfusion rate ω could not be directly measured, Pennes adjusted this parameter in his model to fit the solution to his experimental data for a fixed, representative ambient temperature and metabolic heating rate. The fitted value of blood perfusion rate ω was found to be between 1.2 and 1.8 mL blood/min/100 g tissue, which is a typical range of values for resting human skeletal muscle. Wissler (1998) reevaluated Pennes' original paper and analyzed his data. He found that the theoretical prediction agrees very well with Pennes' experimental results if the data were analyzed in a more rigorous manner.

Profound understanding of the heat transfer site and the countercurrent heat exchange between paired significant vessels was gained through previous experiments (Lemons et al., 1987) performed on rabbit thigh to measure the transverse tissue temperature profiles in the rabbit thigh using fine thermocouples. The experimental study was designed to achieve two objectives. The first is to examine whether there exists detectable temperature difference between tissue and blood for different-size vessels. Existing detectable blood-tissue temperature difference implies that blood has not established thermal equilibration with its surrounding tissue. The second is to examine the temperature difference between the countercurrent artery and vein. If the countercurrent heat exchange is dominant in blood tissue heat transfer, the vein must recapture most of the heat leaving the artery; thus, the venous blood would have a temperature significantly higher than the surrounding tissue temperature. Using thermocouples to mapping temperature profiles in tissue, Lemons et al. (1987) performed in vivo experiments and considered local temperature bumps along the temperature profile as indications of existence of a warmer artery or vein nearby.

Experimental measurements by Lemons et al. (1987) recorded small temperature bumps of up to 0.5°C along the tissue path in the deep tissue region. The irregularities in the tissue temperature profiles were closely associated with the existence of blood vessels in the vicinity of the thermocouple wire. It was shown that temperature fluctuation was observed in all the blood vessels larger than 500 μm, in 67 percent of the vessels between 300 and 500 μm, and in 9 percent of the vessels between 100 and 300 μm. No temperature bump was observed in blood vessels less than 100 μm in diameter. This finding indicates that the assumption in the Pennes model that arterial blood reaches the capillary without significant prior thermal equilibration is inaccurate for this vascular architecture, and thus most of the significant blood-tissue heat transfer occurs in the larger vessels upstream. It was also observed that the temperature field near a large countercurrent artery and vein pair showed two temperature bumps rather than one temperature bump. This implies that the venous blood in the vein receives heat from its warm countercurrent artery nearby; thus, the temperature of the venous blood is raised close to the arterial blood temperature, rather than close to the local tissue temperature, as illustrated in the schematic diagram in Fig. 4.3.

Similar experiments were performed by He et al. (2002, 2003) to measure directly the temperature decays along the femoral arteries and veins and their subsequent branches in rats, using thermocouples attached to the surfaces of countercurrent artery and vein pairs of difference vessel generations. The experimental results have demonstrated that the venous blood in mid-size blood veins recaptured up to 41 percent of the total heat released from their countercurrent arteries under normal conditions. As expected, the contribution of countercurrent rewarming is reduced significantly to less than 15 percent for hyperemic conditions.

In a series of experiments with an isolated perfused bovine kidney, Crezee and Lagendijk (1990) inserted a small plastic tube into the tissue of a preserved bovine kidney and measured the resulting temperature fields in a plane perpendicular to the tube while heated water was circulated through it, with the kidney cortex perfused at different perfusion rates. They also used thermocouples to map the temperature distribution in the tissue of isolated bovine tongues perfused at various perfusion rates (Crezee et al., 1991). By examining the effect of increased perfusion on the amplitude and width of the thermal profile, they demonstrated that the temperature measurements agreed better with a perfusion-enhanced k_{eff} as opposed to the perfusion source term in the Pennes equation.

Charny et al. (1990) developed a detailed one-dimensional (1D) three-equation model. Since this model was based on energy conservation and no other assumptions were introduced to simplify the analysis of the blood flow effect, it was viewed as a relatively more accurate model than both the Pennes and Weinbaum-Jiji equation. The validity of the assumptions inherent in the formulation of the Weinbaum-Jiji equation was tested numerically under different physiological conditions. In addition, the temperature profile predicted by the Pennes model was compared with that by the three-equation model and the difference between them was evaluated. The numerical simulation of the axial temperature distribution in the limb showed that the Weinbaum-Jiji bioheat equation provided very good agreement with the three-equation model for downstream vascular generations that are located in the outer layer in the limb muscle, while the Pennes model yielded better description of heat transfer in the upstream vessel generations. Considering that vessels bifurcate from approximately 1000 μm in the first generation to 150 μm in the last generation, one finds that the Pennes source term, which was originally intended to represent an isotropic heat source in the capillaries, is shown to describe instead the heat transfer from the largest countercurrent vessels, more than 500 μm in diameter. The authors concluded that this was largely attributed to the capillary bleed-off from the large vessels in these tissue regions. The capillary bleed-off appeared to result in a heat source type of behavior that matches the Pennes perfusion term. The Weinbaum-Jiji model, on the other hand, significantly overestimated the countercurrent heat exchange in the tissue region containing larger blood vessels. The validity of the Weinbaum-Jiji equation requires that the ratio of the thermal equilibration length L_e of the blood vessel to its physical length L be less than 0.2. This criterion was found to be satisfied for blood vessels less than 300 μm in diameter under normothermic conditions.

4.3.3 Heat Transfer Models of the Whole Body

As outlined above, due to the complexity of the vasculature, continuum models appear more favorable in simulating the temperature field of the human body. In the Pennes bioheat equation, blood temperature is considered to be the same as the body core temperature or the arterial temperature at the heart; in the Weinbaum-Jiji bioheat equation, on the other hand, the effect of the blood temperature serves as the boundary condition of the simulated tissue domain. In either continuum model (Pennes or Weinbaum-Jiji), blood temperature is an input to the governing equation of the tissue temperature. However, in situations in which the blood temperature is actively lowered or elevated, both continuum models seem inadequate to account for the tissue-blood thermal interactions and to accurately predict the expected body temperature changes.

The human body has limited ability to maintain a normal, or euthermic, body temperature. The vasculature facilitates the redistribution and transfer of heat throughout the body preserving a steady core temperature for all vital organs and making the human body relatively insensitive to environmental temperature changes. In extreme situation such as heavy exercise or harsh thermal environment, the body temperature can shift to a high or low level from the normal range. Active control of body temperature is increasingly employed therapeutically in several clinical scenarios, most commonly to protect the brain from the consequences of either primary (i.e., head trauma, stroke) or secondary injury (i.e., after cardiac arrest with brain hypoperfusion). Mild to moderate hypothermia, during which brain temperature is reduced to 30 to 35°C, has been studied, among others, as an adjunct treatment for protection from cerebral ischemia during cardiac bypass injury (Nussmeier, 2002), carotid endarterectomy (Jamieson et al., 2003), and resection of aneurysms (Wagner and Zuccarello, 2005) and it is also commonly employed in massive stroke and traumatic brain injury patients (Marion et al., 1996, 1997). Even mild reductions in brain temperature as small as 1°C and importantly, the avoidance of any hyperthermia, can substantially reduce ischemic cell damage (Clark et al., 1996; Wass et al., 1995) and improve outcome (Reith et al., 1996). It seems that either the Pennes or Weinbaum-Jiji bioheat equation alone is unable to predict how the body/blood temperature changes during those situations.

Understanding the blood temperature variation requires a theoretical model to evaluate the overall blood-tissue thermal interaction in the whole body. The theoretical models developed by Wissler and other investigators (Fu, 1995; Salloum, 2005; Smith 1991; Wissler, 1985) similarly introduced the whole body as a combination of multiple compartments. The majority of the previously published studies introduced a pair of countercurrent artery and vein with their respective branching (flow system) in each compartment and then modeled the temperature variations along this flow system to derive the heat transfer between the blood vessels and tissue within each flow segment. The accuracy of those approaches of applying a countercurrent vessel pair and their subsequent branches has not been verified by experimental data. Such an approach is also computationally intensive although the models are capable of delineating the temperature decay along the artery and the rewarming by the countercurrent vein.

A developed whole body model by our group (Zhu et al., 2009a) utilizes the simple representation of the Pennes perfusion source term to assess the overall thermal interaction between the tissue and blood in the human body. As shown in Fig. 4.5, a typical human body (male) has a body weight of 81 kg and a volume of 0.074 m^3. The body consists of limbs, torso (internal organs and muscle), neck, and head. The limbs and neck are modeled as cylinders consisting of muscle. Note that the body geometry can be modeled more realistically if one includes a skin layer and a fat layer in each compartment. However, since our objective is to illustrate the principle and feasibility of the developed model, those details are neglected in the sample calculation. The simple geometry results in a body surface area of 1.8 m^2. Applying the Pennes bioheat equation to the whole body yields

$$\rho_t c_t \frac{\partial T_t}{\partial t} = k_t \nabla^2 T_t + q_m''' + \rho_b c_b \omega (T_a - T_t) \tag{4.10}$$

where subscripts t and b refer to tissue and blood, respectively, T_t and T_a are body tissue temperature and blood temperature, respectively, ρ is density, c is specific heat, k_t is thermal conductivity of tissue, q_m''' is the volumetric heat generation rate (W/m^3) due to metabolism, and ω is the local blood

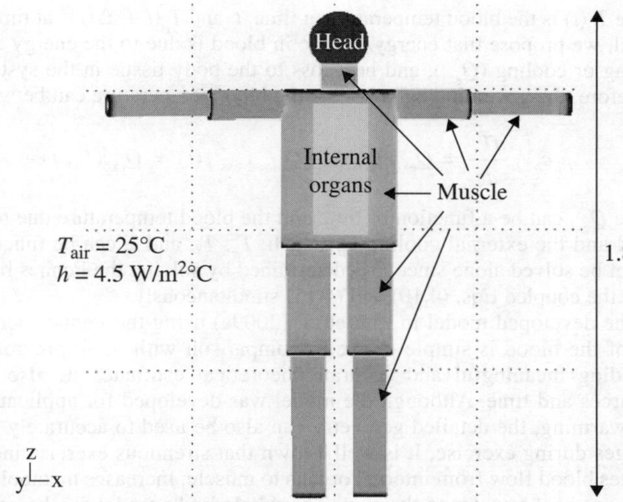

FIGURE 4.5 Schematic diagram of the whole body geometry.

perfusion rate. The above governing equation can be solved once the boundary conditions and initial condition are prescribed. The boundary at the skin surface is modeled as a convection boundary subject to an environment temperature of T_{air} and a convection coefficient of h.

Based on the Pennes bioheat equation, the rate of the total heat loss from the blood to tissue at any time instant is

$$Q_{\text{blood-tissue}} = \iiint_{\text{body volume}} \rho_b c_b \omega (T_a(t) - T_t) dV_{\text{body}} = \rho_b c_b \bar{\omega} (T_a(t) - \bar{T}_t) V_{\text{body}} \tag{4.11}$$

where V_{body} is the body volume, T_a is the blood temperature which may vary with time. Equation (4.11) assumes that both density ρ_b and specific heat c_b of blood are constant. In Eq. (4.11), $\bar{\omega}$ is the average blood perfusion rate defined as

$$\bar{\omega} = \frac{1}{V_{\text{body}}} \iiint_{\text{body volume}} \omega \, dV_{\text{body}} \tag{4.12}$$

In Eq. (4.11), $\bar{T}_t$ is the blood perfusion weighted-average tissue temperature and is defined as

$$\bar{T}_t = \frac{\iiint_{\text{body volume}} \rho_b c_b \omega T_t dV_{\text{body}}}{\rho_b c_b \bar{\omega} V_{\text{body}}} = \frac{\iiint_{\text{body volume}} \omega T_t dV_{\text{body}}}{\bar{\omega} V_{\text{body}}} \tag{4.13}$$

where T_t can be determined by solving the Pennes bioheat equation.

During clinical applications, external heating or cooling of the blood can be implemented to manipulate the body temperature. In the study of Zhu et al. (2009a), the blood in the human body is represented as a lumped system. It is assumed that a typical value of the blood volume of body, V_b, is approximately 5 L. External heating or cooling approaches can be implemented via an intravascular catheter or intravenous fluid infusion. A mathematical expression of the energy absorbed or removed per unit time is determined by the temperature change of the blood, and is written as

$$\rho_b c_b V_b \left[T_a(t + \Delta t) - T_a(t) \right] / \Delta t \approx \rho_b c_b V_b \frac{dT_a}{dt} \tag{4.14}$$

where $T_a(t)$ is the blood temperature at time, t, and $T_a(t + \Delta t)$ is at time $t + \Delta t$. In the mathematical model, we propose that energy change in blood is due to the energy added or removed by external heating or cooling (Q_{ext}), and heat loss to the body tissue in the systemic circulation ($Q_{blood\text{-}tissue}$). Therefore, the governing equation for the blood temperature can be written as

$$\rho_b c_b V_b \frac{dT_a}{dt} = Q_{ext}(T_a, t) - Q_{blood\text{-}tissue}(t) = Q_{ext}(T_a, t) - \rho_b c_b \overline{\omega} V_{body}(T_a - \overline{T}_t) \tag{4.15}$$

where Q_{ext} can be a function of time and the blood temperature due to thermal interaction between blood and the external cooling approach, T_a, T_t, and $\overline{\omega}$ can be functions of time. Equation (4.15) cannot be solved alone since $\overline{T}_t$ is determined by solving the Pennes bioheat equation. One needs to solve the coupled Eqs. (4.10) and (4.15) simultaneously.

The developed model in Zhu et al. (2009a) using the Pennes perfusion term and lumped system of the blood is simple to use in comparison with these previous whole body models while providing meaningful and accurate theoretical estimates. It also requires less computational resources and time. Although the model was developed for applications involving blood cooling or rewarming, the detailed geometry can also be used to accurately predict the body temperature changes during exercise. It is well known that strenuous exercise increases cardiac output, redistributes blood flow from internal organs to muscle, increases metabolism in exercising muscle, and enhances heat transfer to the skin. The whole body model can be easily modified to also include a skin layer and a fat layer in the compartments of the limbs. Further, redistribution of blood flow from the internal organs to the musculature can be modeled as changes of the local blood perfusion rate in the respective compartments and the enhanced skin heat transfer can be adjusted for by inducing evaporation at the skin surface and/or taking off clothes to increase the overall heat transfer coefficient (h). Therefore, one can use the model to accurately delineate important clinical scenarios such as heat stroke, and predict body temperature elevations during heavy exercise and/or heat exposures.

One application of blood cooling involves pumping coolant into the inner tube of a catheter inserted into the femoral vein and advanced to the veno-vera. Once the coolant reaches the catheter, it flows back from the outer layer of the catheter and out of the cooling device. This cooling device has been used in clinical trials in recent years as an effective approach to decrease the temperature of the body for stroke or head injury patients. Based on previous research of this device, the cooling capacity of the device is around –100 W [Q_{ext} in Eq. (4.15)].

Figure 4.6 gives the maximum tissue temperature, the minimum tissue temperature at the skin surface, the volumetric-average body temperature (T_{avg}), and the blood perfusion weighted-average body temperature ($\overline{T}_t$). The difference between the volumetric-average body temperature and the blood perfusion weighted-average body temperature is due to their different definitions. All tissue temperatures decrease almost linearly with time and after 20 minutes, the cooling results in approximately 0.3 to 0.5°C tissue temperature drop. The cooling rate of the skin temperature is smaller (0.2°C/20 min). As shown in Fig. 4.7, the initial cooling rate of the blood temperature in the detailed model is very high (~0.14°C/min), and then it decreases gradually until it is stabilized after approximately 20 minutes. On the other hand, cooling the entire body (the volumetric average body temperature) starts slowly and gradually catches up. It may be due to the inertia of the body mass in responding to the cooling of the blood. Figure 4.7 also illustrates that after the initial cooling rate variation, the stabilized cooling rates of all temperatures approach each other and they are approximately 0.019°C/min or 1.15°C/h. The simulated results demonstrate the feasibility of inducing mild body hypothermia (34°C) within 3 hours using the cooling approach.

This whole body model has been used in predicting temperature elevations in a human body when it is subjected to either heavy exercise or immersed into cold water (Paul et al., 2015). Assessment of heat stroke risks in fire fighters has also been evaluated using this model (Devarakonda et al., 2018; Kalathil et al., 2016). Interestingly, the steady-state temperature field of a human body can be predicted using the whole body model, based on the determination of the overall heat transfer coefficient between the skin surface of the body and the ambient environment (Bartgis et al., 2016;

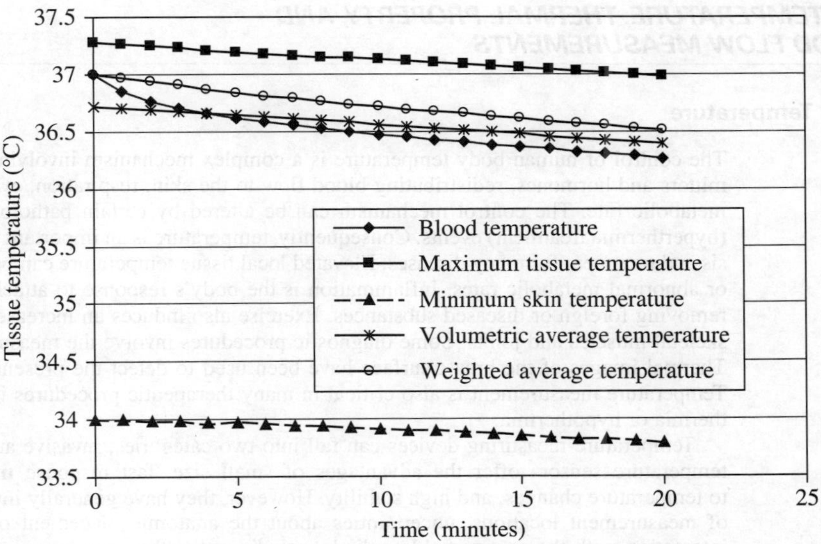

FIGURE 4.6 Temperature decays during the cooling process using the implicit scheme.

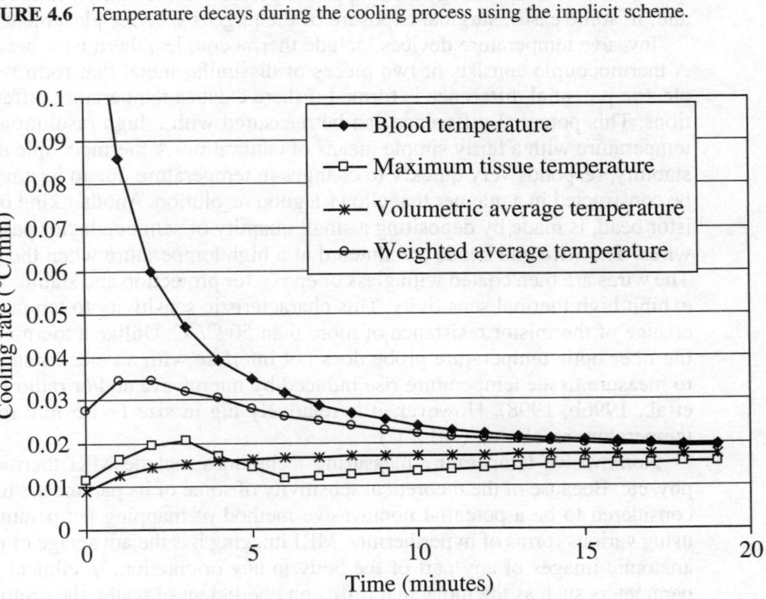

FIGURE 4.7 Induced cooling rates of the blood temperature, the maximum temperature, the volumetric average temperature, and the weighted average temperature.

Vesnovsky et al., 2017). The thermal resistances of clothing layers and convection/radiation are often difficult to evaluate. The whole body model is used to determine the overall heat transfer coefficient during steady state, based on the assumption that a person would dress properly when subject to an ambient environment, to maintain a thermal equilibrium with its environment (Bartgis et al., 2016; Vesnovsky et al., 2017).

4.4 TEMPERATURE, THERMAL PROPERTY, AND BLOOD FLOW MEASUREMENTS

4.4.1 Temperature

The control of human body temperature is a complex mechanism involving release of neurotransmitters and hormones, redistributing blood flow to the skin, respiration, evaporation, and adjusting metabolic rate. The control mechanism can be altered by certain pathologic (fever) and external (hyperthermia treatment) events. Consequently, temperature is an important parameter in the diagnosis and treatment for many diseases. Elevated local tissue temperature can be an indication of excess or abnormal metabolic rates. Inflammation is the body's response to attacks and a mechanism for removing foreign or diseased substances. Exercise also induces an increase in local temperature of skeletal muscles and joints. Some diagnostic procedures involve the measurement of temperatures. Thermal images of the breast surface have been used to detect the presence of malignant tumors. Temperature measurement is also critical in many therapeutic procedures involved in either hyperthermia or hypothermia.

Temperature-measuring devices can fall into two categories, invasive and noninvasive. Invasive temperature sensors offer the advantages of small size, fast response time, extreme sensitivity to temperature changes, and high stability. However, they have generally involved a limited number of measurement locations, uncertainties about the anatomic placement of thermometry devices, interaction with the energy field applied, periodic rather than continuous temperature monitoring, and, in some cases, surgical exposure of the target tissue for placement of the temperature probes.

Invasive temperature devices include thermocouples, thermistor beads, optical fiber sensors, etc. A thermocouple consists of two pieces of dissimilar metal that form two junctions. In the wire, an electric potential difference is formed if there exists a temperature difference between the two junctions. This potential difference can be measured with a high resolution voltmeter and translated to temperature with a fairly simple means of calibration. A thermocouple usually has a good long-term stability, responds very quickly to changes in temperature due to its small thermal capacity, and can be constructed in a manner that allows a good resolution. Another kind of invasive device, the thermistor bead, is made by depositing a small quantity of semiconductor paste onto closely spaced metal wires. The wire and beads are sintered at a high temperature when the material forms a tight bond. The wires are then coated with glass or epoxy for protection and stabilization. The resistors generally exhibit high thermal sensitivity. This characteristic sensitivity to temperature change can result in a change of thermistor resistance of more than 50 Ω/°C. Unlike a thermocouple or a thermistor bead, the fiber optic temperature probe does not interfere with an electromagnetic field. It has been used to measure tissue temperature rise induced by microwave and/or radio frequency (RF) heating (Zhu et al., 1996b, 1998). However, it is relatively big in size (~1.5 mm in diameter) and has a lower temperature resolution (~0.2°C).

Noninvasive temperature-measuring techniques include MRI thermometry, infrared thermography, etc. Because of the theoretical sensitivity of some of its parameters to temperature, MRI has been considered to be a potential noninvasive method of mapping temperature changes during therapies using various forms of hyperthermia. MRI imaging has the advantage of producing three-dimensional anatomic images of any part of the body in any orientation. In clinical practice, MRI characteristic parameters such as the molecular diffusion coefficient of water, the proton spin-lattice (T_1) relaxation time (Parker et al., 1982), and the temperature-dependent proton resonance frequency (PRF) shift have been used to estimate the in vivo temperature distribution in tissues. MRI provides good spatial localization and sufficient temperature sensitivity. At the present time, it also appears to be the most promising modality to conduct basic assessments of heating systems and techniques. The disadvantages of MRI thermometry include limited temporal resolution (i.e., quasireal time), high environmental sensitivity, high material expenditure, and high running costs.

Infrared thermography is based on Planck's distribution law describing the relationship between the emissive power and the temperature of a blackbody surface. The total radiative energy emitted by an object can be found by integrating the Planck equation for all wavelengths. This integration gives the Stefan-Boltzmann law $E(T) = \varepsilon\sigma T^4$. The thermal spectrum as observed by an infrared-sensitive detector can be formed primarily by the emitted light. Hence, the formed thermal image is determined by the local surface temperature and the emissivity of the surface. If the emissivity of the object is known, and no intervening attenuating medium exists, the surface temperature can be quantified.

The major challenge of implementing the approach in biological systems is the unknown emissivity values of skin. It has been shown that normal skin emissivity varies from 0.95 to 0.99, depending on skin tone. When the skin is not a perfect blackbody surface, emission from the surrounding may be incident on the skin and portion of it is reflected. Therefore, the irradiation received by the infrared camera consists of contributions of radiation not only from the skin, but also from the surrounding. Many infrared cameras on the market use the following equation to predict temperature, modified from Bernard et al. (2013):

$$T = \sqrt[4]{\frac{q_{ck}}{\sigma\varepsilon} - \frac{1-\varepsilon}{\varepsilon} T_{amb}^{4}} \tag{4.16}$$

where q_{ck} is the heat flux received by the camera and ε is the emissivity of the skin surface. The ambient temperature T_{amb} affects the reading only when the surface is not a blackbody surface. Figure 4.8 gives the deviation of the temperature reading from that when ε is selected as 1, based on inputs of ε and T_{amb} to the recorded infrared image of human skin using a commercial infrared camera. In a room temperature environment (T_{amb} = 22.5°C), changing ε from 1 to 0.96 results in an uncertainty of 0.5°C. The potential error is more profound when T_{amb} = 8.6°C, with a deviation of 0.83°C (Li et al., 2016). The results from the camera reading are consistent with those predicted by Eq. (4.16).

A numerical simulation of the temperature field of breast (Hu et al., 2004) suggests that image subtraction could be employed to improve the thermal signature of the tumor on the skin surface. Drug-induced vascular constriction in the breast can further enhance the ability of infrared thermography in detecting deep-seated tumor. Qualitative thermography has been successfully used in a wide range of medical applications (Jones, 1998) including cardiovascular surgery (Firorini et al., 1983), breast cancer diagnoses (Gautherie and Gros, 1980; Lapayowker and Revesz, 1980), tumor hyperthermia (Cetas et al., 1980), laser angioplasty, and peripheral venous disease. Clinical studies on patients who had breast thermography demonstrated that an abnormal thermography was associated with an increased risk of breast cancer and a poorer prognosis for the breast cancer

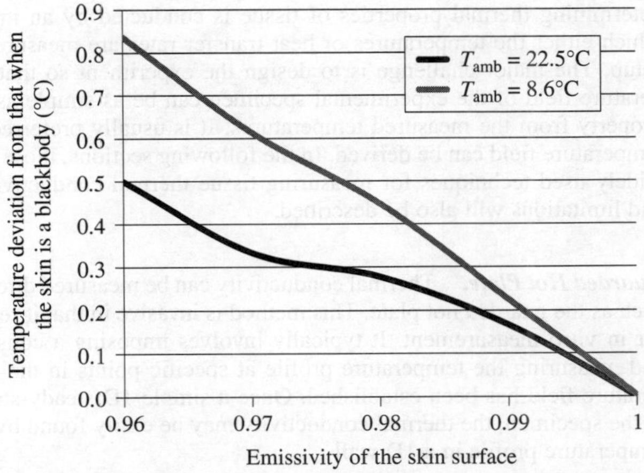

FIGURE 4.8 Effect of skin emissivity and ambient temperature on the temperature reading of a skin location given by the Fluke camera using Eq. (4.16).

patients (Gautherie and Gros, 1980; Head et al., 1993). Infrared tympanic thermometry and temporal thermometry have also been developed and widely used in clinical practice and thermoregulatory research as a simple and rapid device to estimate the body core temperature (Matsukawa et al., 1996; Shibasaki et al., 1998). However, due to uncertainty of the emissivity of tissue surface, large errors may be introduced from the value given by those commercial infrared thermometers, and leading to overestimation or underestimation of actual skin temperature (Li et al., 2016; Vesnovsky et al., 2017).

4.4.2 Thermal Property (Thermal Conductivity and Thermal Diffusivity) Measurements

Knowledge of thermal properties of biological tissues is fundamental to understanding heat transfer processes in biological systems. This knowledge has increased importance in view of the concerns for radiological safety with microwave and ultrasound irradiation, and with the renewed interest in local and regional hyperthermia as a cancer therapy. The availability of a technique capable of accurately characterizing thermal properties of both diseased and normal tissue would greatly improve the predictive ability of theoretical modeling and lead to better diagnostic and therapeutic tools.

The primary requirement in designing an apparatus to measure thermal conductivity and diffusivity is that the total energy supplied should be used to establish the observed nonuniform temperature distribution within the specimen. For accurate measurements, it is important to ensure agreement between the experimental setup and the boundary/initial conditions implemented in the theoretical model. Other structural and environmental factors, such as undesired heat conduction to or from the specimen, convection currents caused by temperature-induced density variations, and thermal radiation, must be minimized if they are not considered in the theoretical model. Biomaterials present additional difficulties. The existing literature on biological heat transfer bears convincing evidence of the complexity of heat transfer processes in living tissue. For example, thermal properties of living tissue differ from those of excised tissue. Clearly the presence of blood perfusion is a major factor in this difference. Relatively large differences in thermal conductivity exist between similar tissues and organs, and variations for the same organ are frequently reported. Such variations suggest the importance of both defining the measurement conditions and establishing a reliable measurement technique.

The thermal property measurement techniques can be categorized as steady-state methods and transient methods. They can also be categorized as invasive and noninvasive techniques. In general, determining thermal properties of tissue is conducted by an inverse heat transfer analysis during which either the temperatures or heat transfer rates are measured in a well-designed experimental setup. The major challenge is to design the experiment so that a theoretical analysis of the temperature field of the experimental specimen can be as simple as possible to determine the thermal property from the measured temperatures. It is usually preferred that an analytical solution of the temperature field can be derived. In the following sections, those principles are illustrated by several widely used techniques for measuring tissue thermal conductivity or diffusivity. Their advantages and limitations will also be described.

Guarded Hot Plate. Thermal conductivity can be measured directly by using steady-state methods, such as the guarded hot plate. This method is invasive in that it requires the excision of the specimen for in vitro measurement. It typically involves imposing a constant heat flux through a specimen and measuring the temperature profile at specific points in the specimen after a steady-state temperature field has been established. Once a simple 1D steady-state temperature field is established in the specimen, the thermal conductivity may be easily found by the expression based on the linear temperature profile in a 1D wall

$$k = \frac{q''L}{T_1 - T_2} \tag{4.17}$$

where q'' is the heat flux passing through the specimen, T_1 and T_2 are temperature values at any two measurement locations in the axial direction (or the direction of the heat flux), and L is the axial distance between these two temperature measurements.

Biological materials typically have moderate thermal conductivities and therefore, require extensive insulation to ensure a unidirectional heat flow in the 1D wall. The contact resistance between the specimen and the plate is also difficult to be minimized. In addition, this method cannot be used to obtain in vivo measurements. Once the tissue specimen is cut from the body, dehydration and temperature-dependent properties may need to be considered. It is also a challenge to accurately measure the thickness of the tissue sample.

Flash Method. The transient flash method, first proposed by Parker et al. (1961), is the current standard for measuring the thermal diffusivity of solids. A schematic diagram of this method is shown in Fig. 4.9. The front face of a thin opaque solid, of uniform thickness, is exposed to a burst of intense radiant energy by either a high-energy flash tube or laser. The method assumes that the burst of energy is absorbed instantaneously by a very thin layer at the surface of the specimen. Adiabatic boundary conditions are assumed on all other surfaces and on the front face during the measurement. The transient temperature at the rear surface is then measured by using a thermocouple or an infrared detector.

The governing equation can be described by the 1D transient heat conduction problem as

$$\begin{gathered}\frac{1}{\alpha}\frac{\partial \Theta}{\partial t} = \frac{\partial^2 \Theta}{\partial x^2}\\ x = 0, \quad \text{and} \quad x = l \quad \frac{\partial \Theta}{\partial x} = 0 \\ t = 0 \begin{cases} \Theta(x, 0) = \dfrac{Q''A}{\rho c(gA)} & for \quad 0 < x \le g \\ \Theta(x, 0) = 0 \quad for & g < x \le l \end{cases}\end{gathered}, \tag{4.18}$$

where $\Theta(x, t)$ is the temperature elevation and equal to $T(x, t) - T(l, 0)$, Q is the absorbed radiant energy per unit area, g is the thickness of the specimen layer that absorbs all the incident radiant energy, l is the sample thickness, ρ is the density of the specimen, c is the specific heat, and α is the thermal diffusivity of the specimen. Solving the governing equation using the method of separation of variables yields

$$\Theta(x, t) = \frac{1}{l}\int_0^l \Theta(x, 0)dx + \frac{2}{l}\left\{\sum_{n=1}^{\infty}\exp\left(-\frac{n^2\pi^2\alpha t}{l^2}\right)\cos\left(\frac{n\pi x}{l}\right)\left[\int_0^l \Theta(x, 0)\cos\left(\frac{n\pi x}{l}\right)dx\right]\right\} \tag{4.19}$$

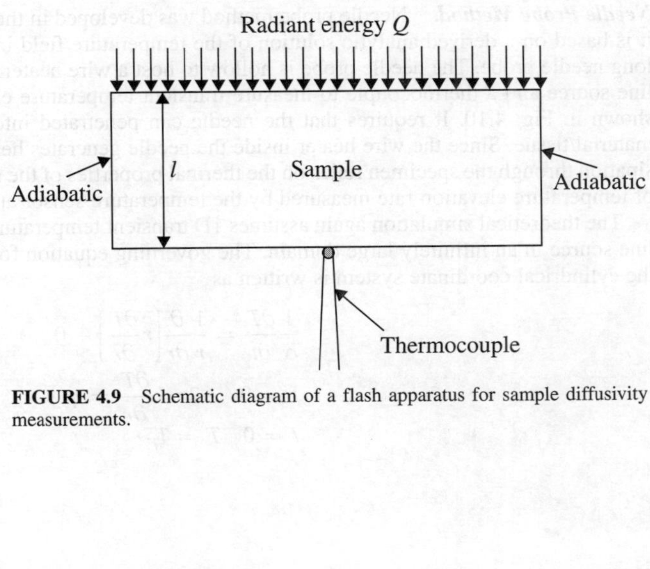

FIGURE 4.9 Schematic diagram of a flash apparatus for sample diffusivity measurements.

The integration in the expression can be derived using the initial condition. After implementing the condition of a very thin layer for energy absorption, i.e., $g \to 0$, one obtains the solution as

$$\Theta(x,t) \approx \frac{Q''}{pcl}\left\{1 + 2\sum_{n=1}^{\infty}\exp\left(\frac{n^2\pi^2\alpha t}{l^2}\right)\cos\left(\frac{n\pi x}{l}\right)\right\}$$
$$\frac{T(x,t) - T(l,0)}{Q''/(\rho cl)} \approx \left\{1 + 2\sum_{n=1}^{\infty}\exp\left(-\frac{n^2\pi^2\alpha t}{l^2}\right)\cos\left(\frac{n\pi x}{l}\right)\right\} \tag{4.20}$$

An analytic expression for the rear surface temperature transient in the 1D temperature field is given by

$$\frac{T(l,t) - T(l,0)}{Q''/(\rho cl)} \approx \left\{1 + 2\sum_{n=1}^{\infty}\exp\left(-\frac{n^2\pi^2\alpha t}{l^2}\right)\cos(n\pi)\right\} \tag{4.21}$$

In theory, the thermal diffusivity α can be calculated from any set of the recorded temperature and time, i.e., $T(l, t_1)$ and t_1. One only needs to substitute the set to Eq. (4.21), and find the root (α) of the equation. Another way to determine the value of the thermal diffusivity of the specimen is to use curve fitting technique to adjust the value of α, until the theoretically predicted temperature transient curve $T(l, t)$ has the best fit to the scattered experimental measurements. In industry, the thermal diffusivity in the direction of heat flow is usually calculated by the expression

$$\alpha = 1.38\frac{l^2}{\pi^2 t_{1/2}} \tag{4.22}$$

where $t_{1/2}$ is the time required for the rear surface to reach half of its maximum temperature elevation, the value 1.38 is derived from Eq. (4.21), and it is the most convenient method to quickly determine α.

The simplicity of the method described above is often offset by the difficulty in satisfying the required adiabatic boundary conditions on both top and bottom surfaces. In order for this 1D heat transfer solution to be valid, the radiant energy incident on the front surfaces is required to be uniform, and the duration of the flash must be sufficiently short compared with the thermal characteristic time of the sample. 1D heat conduction in the x direction also implies uniform thickness of the specimen, which adds challenge to biological specimen. The specimen also has to be considered opaque; thus, all the radiant energy is absorbed within a very thin layer. In addition, it assumes that the sample is homogeneous, isotropic, and opaque, and that the thermal properties of the sample do not vary considerably with temperature.

Needle Probe Method. Needle probe method was developed in the 1990s (Liang et al., 1991), and it is based on a derived analytic solution of the temperature field in tissue/specimen surrounding a long needle probe. The needle probe is hollow to host a wire heater inside to mimic an infinite long line source and a thermocouple to measure transient temperature elevations on the needle surface, shown in Fig. 4.10. It requires that the needle can penetrated into the specimen, preferably soft material/tissue. Since the wire heater inside the needle generates heating at a constant level, its dissipation through the specimen relies on the thermal properties of the specimen, thus affecting the rate of temperature elevation rate measured by the temperature sensor at the needle surface.

The theoretical simulation again assumes 1D transient temperature field surrounding a finite long line source in an infinitely large domain. The governing equation for the temperature field $T(r, t)$ in the cylindrical coordinate system is written as

$$\frac{1}{\alpha}\frac{\partial T}{\partial t} = \frac{1}{r}\frac{\partial}{\partial r}\left(r\frac{\partial T}{\partial r}\right) + 0$$
$$r = 0 \quad -2\pi rk\frac{\partial T}{\partial r} = q' \tag{4.23}$$
$$t = 0 \quad T = T_i$$

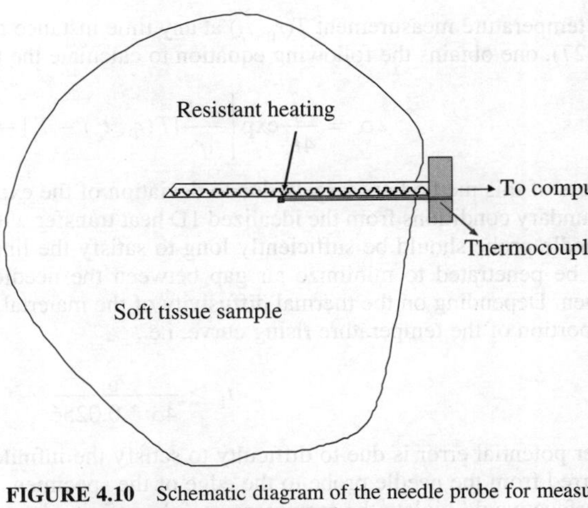

FIGURE 4.10 Schematic diagram of the needle probe for measuring thermal conductivity of a tissue sample.

where q' is the heat transfer rate from the needle probe per unit length of the needle probe, carrying a unit of W/m. The solution for this 1D transient heat conduction problem is given as

$$T - T_i = -\frac{q'}{4\pi k} E_i\left(-\frac{r^2}{4\alpha t}\right) \tag{4.24}$$

where $E_i(-\eta)$ is an exponential integral function defined by

$$E_i(-\eta) = -\int_{\eta}^{\infty} \frac{e^u}{u} du = 0.5772 + \ln \eta + \sum_{n=0}^{\infty} \frac{(-\eta)^n}{n(n!)} \tag{4.25}$$

when η or $r^2/4\alpha t < 0.0256$, the summation portion of Eq. (4.25) can be neglected. The temperature field is then approximated as

$$T - T_i \approx \frac{q'}{4\pi k}\left[\ln\left(\frac{4\alpha t}{r^2}\right) + 0.5772\right] = \frac{q'}{4\pi k} \ln t + \frac{q'}{4\pi k}\left[\ln\left(\frac{4\alpha}{r^2}\right) + 0.5772\right] \tag{4.26}$$

At the needle surface when $r = r_0$, the transient temperature elevation is given as

$$T(r_0, t) - T_i \approx \frac{q'}{4\pi k} \ln t + \frac{q'}{4\pi k}\left[\ln\left(\frac{4\alpha}{r_0^2}\right) + 0.5772\right] \tag{4.27}$$

After plotting the measured temperature above its initial value as a function of $\ln t$, the curve should be linear with a slope equal to $q'/(4\pi k)$. The thermal conductivity can be obtained from the above equation as

$$k = \frac{q'}{4\pi} \frac{d(\ln t)}{dT(r_0, t)} \tag{4.28}$$

This relationship suggests that the faster the temperatures rises, the material is more likely to be poorly conductive. On the other hand, if the material is highly conductive, heat from the needle can be dissipated easily, therefore, resulting in a slower temperature rise at the needle surface. Once the thermal conductivity k is obtained, the thermal diffusivity of the specimen can be calculated based on the temperature measurement $T(r_0, t_c)$ at any time instance t_c, at the location $r = r_0$. Rearranging Eq. (4.27), one obtains the following equation to calculate the thermal diffusivity of the specimen:

$$\alpha = \frac{r_0^2}{4t_c}\exp\left\{\frac{4\pi k}{q'}[T(r_0, t_c) - T_i] - 0.5772\right\} \tag{4.29}$$

Errors of this method are largely due to deviation of the experimental setup, including geometry and boundary conditions from the idealized 1D heat transfer with a line source in an infinite domain. The needle probe should be sufficiently long to satisfy the line source requirement. The specimen should be penetrated to minimize air gap between the needle probe surface and material of the specimen. Depending on the thermal diffusivity of the material, it may take a long time to reach the linear portion of the temperature rising curve, i.e.,

$$t_1 \geq \frac{r_0^2}{4\alpha * 0.0256} \tag{4.30}$$

Another potential error is due to difficulty to satisfy the infinite domain requirement. When heat is transferred from the needle probe to the edge of the specimen, the boundary condition at the specimen surface would violate the requirement of the infinite domain. Therefore, the linear relationship given in Eq. (4.28) would not be valid after a specific time t_2, given by

$$t_2 = \frac{L^2}{4\alpha} \tag{4.31}$$

where L is the minimum distance from the sample boundary to the probe axis. Due to the small thermal diffusivity of biological tissue, it may take some time to reach t_1; however, it may also take a much longer time for the heat to reach the specimen boundary, thus allowing sufficient measurement points for linear curve fitting. Iterations may also be needed due to unknown thermal diffusivity before the measurements. One often has to guess its value to evaluate both t_1 and t_2, and later to readjust the value of α to ensure that only the measurement points in the linear portion of the curve are used for curve fitting.

Temperature Pulse Decay (TPD) Technique. Temperature pulse decay (TPD) technique is based on the approach described and developed by Arkin, Chen, and Holmes (Arkin et al., 1986, 1987). This method needs no insulation, in contrast to some of the methods described above, since testing times are short, usually on the order of seconds. However, the determination of the thermal conductivity or the blood flow rate requires the solution of the transient bioheat transfer equation.

This technique employs a single thermistor serving as both a temperature sensor and a heater. Typically in this technique, either a thermistor is inserted through the lumen of a hypodermic needle, which is in turn inserted into the tissue, or the thermistor is embedded in a glass-fiber-reinforced epoxy shaft. Figure 4.11 shows the structure of a thermistor bead probe embedded in an epoxy shaft and its insertion into tissue. Each thermistor bead probe can consist of one or two small thermistor beads situated at the end or near the middle of the epoxy shaft. The diameter of the finished probe is typically 0.3 mm, and the length can vary as desired. Because the end can be sharpened to a point, it is capable of piercing most tissues with very minimal trauma.

During the experiment, the thermistor bead probe is inserted into the tissue of interest. A short heating pulse of approximately 3 seconds is delivered by the thermistor bead. The pulse heating results in a temperature rise in the area near the tip of the probe. After the pulse heating, the temperature of the probe will decrease. During the pulse heating and its subsequent temperature decay, the temperature at the tip of the probe is measured by the thermistor bead. To determine the thermal conductivity or blood flow rate, a theoretical prediction of the transient temperature profile is needed for the same tissue domain as in the experimental study. Typically, the theoretically predicted temperature profile is obtained by solving a bioheat transfer equation in which the blood flow rate and thermal conductivity have to be given as input to the model. The predicted temperature profile is then compared with the experimental measurements. The values of the blood flow rate and/or thermal conductivity will be adjusted to minimize the square difference between the predicted temperature

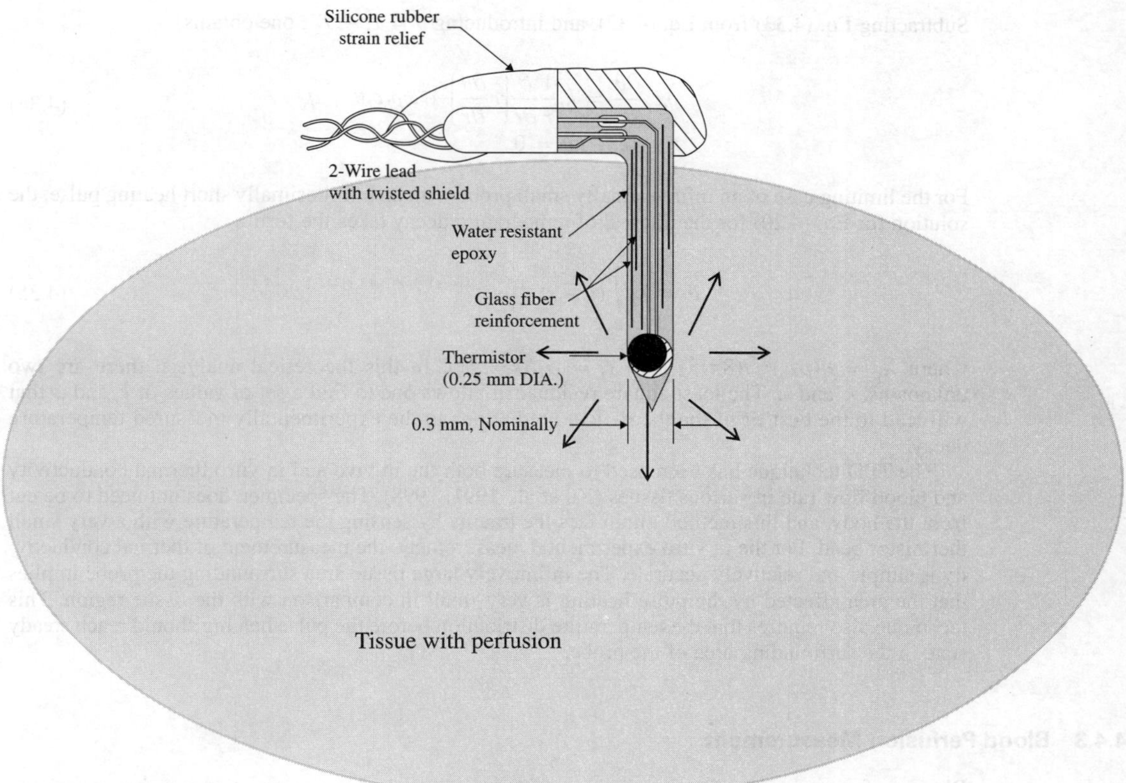

FIGURE 4.11 Sketch of a thermistor bead probe inserted into a tissue region. [*From Xu et al. (1998) with permission.*]

profile and the experimental measurements using the linear-square residual fit. The values for the blood flow rate and thermal conductivity that give the best fit of the experimentally measured temperature profile are the calculated blood flow rate and thermal conductivity of the tissue sample.

Typically, the Pennes bioheat transfer equation is used to predict the temperature transient. It is assumed that the thermistor bead is small enough to be considered a point source inserted into the center of an infinitively large medium. The governing equation and initial condition for this thermal process are described as

$$\rho_t c_t \frac{\partial T_t}{\partial t} = k_t \frac{1}{r}\frac{\partial}{\partial r}\left(r\frac{\partial T_t}{\partial r}\right) + \omega\rho_b c_b(T_a - T_t) + q_p \qquad t = 0, \quad T_t = T_{ss}(r) \tag{4.32}$$

where q_p is the pulse heating deposited locally into the tissue through a very small thermistor bead probe as $q_p = P\,\delta(0)$ for $t \leq t_p$; $q_p = 0$ for $t > t_p$. P is the deposited power, and $\delta(0)$ is the Dirac delta function. Before the measurement, the steady-state temperature distribution $T_{ss}(r)$ in the sample should satisfy the 1D steady-state conduction equation without the pulse heating. The governing equation for $T_{ss}(r)$ is given by

$$0 = k_t \frac{1}{r}\frac{d}{dr}\left(r\frac{dT_{ss}}{dr}\right) + \omega\rho_b c_b(T_a - T_{ss}) \tag{4.33}$$

Subtracting Eq. (4.33) from Eq. (4.32), and introducing $\theta = T_t - T_{ss}$, one obtains

$$\rho_t c_t \frac{\partial \theta}{\partial t} = k_t \frac{1}{r}\frac{\partial}{\partial r}\left(r\frac{\partial \theta}{\partial r}\right) + \omega \rho_b c_b \theta + q_p \qquad (4.34)$$
$$t = 0, \qquad \theta = 0$$

For the limiting case of an infinitesimally small probe with an infinitesimally short heating pulse, the solution for Eq. (4.20) for the interval of temperature decay takes the form

$$\theta = \lambda_2 \int_0^{t_0} (t-s)^{-1.5} e^{-\omega(t-s)} e^{-r^2/[4\lambda_1(t-s)]}\, ds \qquad (4.35)$$

where $\lambda_1 = P(\rho_t c_t)^{0.5}/(8\pi^{1.5})$ and $\lambda_2 = \alpha_t/(k_t^{1.5} t_p^{0.5})$. In this theoretical analysis, there are two unknowns, k_t and ω. The least-square residual fit allows one to find a set of values of k_t and ω that will lead to the best fit of the theoretical predictions to the experimentally measured temperature decay.

The TPD technique has been used to measure both the in vivo and in vitro thermal conductivity and blood flow rate in various tissues (Xu et al., 1991, 1998). The specimen does not need to be cut from the body, and this method minimizes the trauma by sensing the temperature with a very small thermistor bead. For the in vitro experimental measurement, the measurement of thermal conductivity is simple and relatively accurate. The infinitively large tissue area surrounding the probe implies that the area affected by the pulse heating is very small in comparison with the tissue region. This technique also requires that the temperature distribution before the pulse heating should reach steady state in the surrounding area of the probe.

4.4.3 Blood Perfusion Measurement

Blood perfusion rate is defined as the amount of blood supplied to a certain tissue region per minute per 100 g tissue weight. In most of the situation, it is representing the nutrient need in that tissue area. High blood perfusion is also associated with heat dissipation during exercise or thermal stress. In humans, there are several tissue regions, such as kidney, heart, and choriocapillaris in the eye, possessing a high blood perfusion rate. The measured blood perfusion rate in the kidney is approximately 500 mL/min/100 g tissue. In the heart, the blood perfusion rate is about 300 mL/min/100 g which serves for the energy need of pumping the heart. The choriocapillaris in the eyes is a meshed structure within two thin sheets. Its blood perfusion rate is very high and can be as much as 8000 mL/min/100 g tissue. In addition to providing oxygen and other nutrients to the retina, the choriocapillaris also may play a role in stabilizing the temperature environment of the retina and retinal pigment epithelium (RPE) (Aurer and Carpenter, 1980). In addition to its physiological role, blood perfusion measurement is important in theoretical modeling of the temperature distribution during various therapeutic and diagnostic applications.

Radio-Labeled Microsphere Technique. Measurement of blood flow has become an integral part of the physiologic study of humans. While many methods have been utilized in measuring tissue blood flow, the one most often practiced today is dependent on injection of radioactively labeled microspheres. The reason for its overwhelming acceptance is due, in part, to the shortcomings of many of the alternative methods of blood flow determination.

In principle, small particles are uniformly mixed with blood and allowed to circulate freely until they impact in a vessel smaller in diameter than themselves. The tissue or organ is then removed and its radioactivity measured. In such a system, the number of particles impacted in a given tissue is assumed proportional to the volume of particle-containing blood perfusing that tissue. If the number of particles in the tissue sample is determined, and an adequate blood flow reference established, a tissue blood flow can be derived.

Calculating the blood flow rate is straightforward; it is based on the assumption that the number of microspheres in each organ should be directly proportional to blood flow to that organ, e.g.,

$$\frac{\text{Blood flow to organ A}}{\text{Microspheres in organ A}} = \frac{\text{Blood flow to organ B}}{\text{Microspheres in organ B}} = \frac{\text{Cardiac output}}{\text{Total microspheres injected}} \tag{4.36}$$

The cardiac output of the animal is obtained by another independent method.

Like any other experimental method, determination of blood flow by radioactive microspheres is subject to many sources of error, including individual variation among the sample population, the counting accuracy of the total microspheres in the tissue sample by the gamma counter, and the effect of arteriovenous shunting or the migration of the microspheres. Despite all the limitations of this method, the microsphere technique of blood flow determination has become the most powerful method available today and has been used to evaluate the accuracy of other techniques of blood flow measurement.

Doppler Ultrasound. Doppler ultrasound has been widely used to provide qualitative measurements of the average flow velocity in large- to medium-size vessels if the vessel diameter is known. These include the extracranial circulation and peripheral limb vessels. It is also used in an assessment of mapped occlusive disease of the lower extremities. The frequency used for Doppler ultrasound is typically between 1 and 15 MHz. The basis of this method is the Doppler shift, which is the observed difference in frequency between sound waves that are transmitted from simple piezoelectric transducers and those that are received back when both transmitter and receiver are in relative motion. The average frequency shift of the Doppler spectrum is proportional to the average particulate velocity over the cross-sectional area of the sample. When used to measure blood flow, the transducers are stationary and motion is imparted by the flowing blood cells. In this event, red cell velocity V is described by the relationship

$$\delta F/F = (2V/C)\cos\theta \quad \text{or} \quad V = \delta F/F\,(C/2\cos\theta) \tag{4.37}$$

where δF is the frequency change of the emitted wave, C is the mean propagation velocity of ultrasound within tissues (about 1540 m/s), and θ is the angle between the ultrasound beam and the flow velocity. The frequency shift is usually in the audible range and can be detected by an audible pitch variation or can be plotted graphically.

Attenuation of ultrasound increases nearly linearly with frequency in many types of tissue, causing high frequencies to be attenuated more strongly than low frequencies. The depth of penetration of the signal also depends on the density of the fluid; hence sampling of the velocity profile could be inaccurate in situations where this can vary. Determination of absolute flow/tissue mass with this technique has limited potential, since vessel diameter is not accurately measured and volume flow is not recorded. It is not possible, using currently available systems, to accurately measure the angle made by the ultrasonic beam and the velocity vector. Thus, Doppler flow measurements are semiquantitative.

Laser Doppler Flowmetry. Laser Doppler flowmetry (LDF) offers the potential to measure flow in small regional volumes continuously and with repetitive accuracy. It is ideally suited to measure surface flow on skin or mucosa or following surgical exposure. LDF couples the Doppler principle in detecting the frequency shift of laser light imparted by moving red blood vessels in the blood stream. Incident light is carried to the tissue by fiber optic cables, where it is scattered by the moving red blood cells. By sampling all reflected light, the device can calculate flux of red blood cells within the sample volume. Depending on the light frequency, laser light penetrates tissue to a depth of less than approximately 3 mm.

The output from LDF is measured not in easily interpretable units of flow but rather in hertz. It would be ideal to define a single calibration factor that could be used in all tissues to convert laser output to flow in absolute units. Unfortunately, the calibration to determine an absolute flow is limited by the lack of a comparable standard and the lack of preset controlled conditions. This may be due to varying tissue optical properties affected by tissue density (Obeid et al., 1990). Further, LDF signals can be affected by movement of the probe relative to the tissue.

Despite its limitations, LDF continues to find widespread applications in areas of clinical research because of its small probe size, high spatial and temporal resolution, and entire lack of tissue contact if required. It has been suggested that LDF is well suited for comparisons of relative changes in blood flow during different experimental conditions (Smits et al., 1986). It is especially valuable to provide a direct measurement of cutaneous blood flow. In patients with Raynaud's phenomenon, it has been indicated that the abnormal cutaneous blood flow is related to the diminished fibrinolytic activity and increased blood viscosity (Engelhart and Kristensen, 1986). LDF has also been useful for assessing patients with fixed arterial obstructive disease of the lower extremity (Schabauer and Rooke, 1994). Other cutaneous uses of LDF include postoperative monitoring of digit reattachment, free tissue flap, and facial operations (Schabauer and Rooke, 1994). In the noncutaneous application of LDF, it has been reported to measure the retinal blood flow in patients with diabetes mellitus. LDF has also been used to monitor cerebral blood perfusion (Borgos, 1996). It was used to evaluate the brain autoregulation in patients with head injury (Lam et al., 1997).

Temperature Pulse Decay Technique. As described in the section "Temperature Pulse Decay (TPD) Technique," local blood perfusion rate can be derived from the comparison between the theoretically predicted and experimentally measured temperature decay of a thermistor bead probe. The details of the measurement mechanism have been described in that section. The TPD technique has been used to measure the in vivo blood perfusion rates of different physical or physiological conditions in various tissues (Xu et al., 1991, 1998; Zhu et al., 2005). The advantages of this technique are that it is fast and induces little trauma. Using the Pennes bioheat transfer equation, the intrinsic thermal conductivity and blood perfusion rate can be simultaneously measured. In some of the applications, a two-parameter least-square residual fit was first performed to obtain the intrinsic thermal conductivity of the tissue. This calculated value of thermal conductivity was then used to perform a one-parameter curve fit for the TPD measurements to obtain the local blood perfusion rate at the probe location.

The error of blood perfusion measurement using the TPD technique is mainly inherited from the accuracy of the bioheat transfer equation. Theoretical study (Xu et al., 1993) has shown that this measurement is affected by the presence of large blood vessels in the vicinity of the thermistor bead probe. Further, poor curve fitting of the blood perfusion rate occurs if the steady state of the tissue temperature is not established before the heating (Xu et al., 1998). The TPD method can also be used to measure local blood perfusion rate repeatedly, as long as the steady state of the tissue temperature before each pulse heating can be satisfied. In one application (Zhu et al., 2005), a TPD probe has been used to measure real-time blood perfusion rate in prostatic tissue during transurethral RF heating. The results not only confirmed the general trend of increase in blood perfusion rate with rising tissue temperature, but also illustrated the first time that the local blood perfusion increase lagged behind the temperature rise. Simultaneous measurements of temperature and blood perfusion rate at the same tissue location demonstrated coupled relationship between them (Zhu et al., 2005), suggesting that large temperature rise or temperature threshold triggered an increase in local blood perfusion rate, while large blood perfusion rate led to temperature drop. Unfortunately, the local blood perfusion rate would not be measured more frequently than the temperatures in that study, due to time required to establish a steady state before the heating pulse. A typical duration of measuring blood perfusion rate using TPD is more than 1 minute.

4.5 HYPERTHERMIA TREATMENT FOR CANCERS AND TUMORS

4.5.1 Introduction

Within the past three decades, there have been important advances in the use of hyperthermia in a wide variety of therapeutic procedures, especially for cancer treatment. Hyperthermia is used either as a singular therapy or as an adjuvant therapy with radiation and drugs in human malignancy. It has fewer complications and is preferable to more costly and risky surgical treatment

(Dewhirst et al., 1997). The treatment objective of current therapy is to raise tumor temperature higher than 43°C for periods of more than 30 to 60 minutes while keeping temperatures in the surrounding normal tissue below 43°C. It has been suggested that such elevated temperatures may produce a heat-induced cytotoxic response and/or increase the cytotoxic effects of radiation and drugs. Both the direct cell-killing effects of heat and the sensitization of other agents by heat are phenomena strongly dependent on the achieved temperature rise and the heating duration.

One of the problems encountered by physicians is that current hyperthermia technology cannot deliver adequate power to result in effective tumor heating of all sites. The necessity of developing a reliable and accurate predictive ability for planning hyperthermia protocols is obvious. The treatment planning typically requires the determination of the energy absorption distribution in the tumor and normal tissue and the resulting temperature distributions. The heating patterns induced by various hyperthermia apparatus have to be studied to focus the energy on a given region of the body and provide a means for protecting the surrounding normal tissues. Over the past decades, optimization of the thermal dose is possible with known spatial and temporal temperature distribution during the hyperthermia treatment. However, large spatial and temporal variations in temperature are still observed because of the heterogeneity of tissue properties (both normal tissue and tumor), spatial variations in specific absorption rates, and the variations and dynamics of blood flow (Overgaard, 1987). It has been suggested that blood flow in large, thermally unequilibrated vessels is the main cause for temperature nonhomogeneity during hyperthermia treatment, since these large vessels can produce cold tracts in the heated volume. Thus, to heat the tissue and tumor volume effectively and safely, it is critical to experimentally or theoretically monitor the temporal and spatial temperature gradient during the hyperthermia treatment.

4.5.2 Temperature Monitoring during Thermal Treatment

One of the reasons hyperthermia has not yet become widely accepted as a mode of therapy is the lack of noninvasive and inexpensive temperature measurement technology for routine use. Invasive temperature devices have a number of restrictions when applied to temperature monitoring during hyperthermia. These restrictions include small representative tissue sample of the entire tissue and tumor regions, difficulty in inserting the sensor into a deep-seated tumor, and discomfort to patients during the insertion. Because of the problems associated with invasive temperature measurement techniques, there has been a strong demand for noninvasive temperature feedback techniques such as ultrasonic imaging and microwave radiometry imaging (MRI). In addition to their focusing and real-time capabilities, ultrasound-based techniques are capable of providing satisfactory temperature resolution as well as hot-spot localization in soft tissue. MRI was applied as a noninvasive thermometry method, but it has limited temperature resolution (~0.5°C) and spatial resolution (~1 cm) and, therefore, can provide only an estimate of the average temperature over a certain tissue volume. Further, MRI is a costly technique, and therefore, it does not comply with the clinical requirements of treatment monitoring for tissue temperature distribution.

4.5.3 Heating Patten Induced by Hyperthermia Applicators

Ideal Treatment Volume and Temperature Distribution. Heating pattern induced by external devices is defined as the heat energy deposited in the tissue or tumor per second per unit mass [specific absorption rate (SAR)] or per unit volume of tissue (q'''). In optimal treatment planning, it is the temperature rather than the heating pattern that is optimized in the treatment plan. The maximum temperature generally occurs in the tissue region with heat deposition. However, one should note that SAR and temperature distribution may not have the same profile, since temperature distribution can also be affected by the environment or imposed boundary conditions.

The thermal goal of a clinically practical hyperthermia treatment is to maximize the volume of tumor tissue that is raised to the therapeutic temperature. This maximization should be accomplished while keeping the volume of normal tissue at or below some clinically specific temperature level.

There are difficulties to reaching the optimal temperature distribution with the presently available heating devices. Most clinical heating systems have had such fixed power deposition patterns that optimization was limited. In recent years, the cooperation between engineers and clinicians has resulted in a new generation of heating equipment. These heating devices have considerably more flexibility in their ability to deposit power in different patterns that help reach the treatment goal. Further, the ideal temperature distribution may be achieved by manipulating the geometrical consideration or regional blood flow. In most of the transurethral microwave catheters, circulated cold water is installed in the catheter to provide protection to the sensitive prostatic urethra. Manipulation of the flow rate and temperature of the water have been demonstrated to facilitate the achievement of high temperature penetrating deep in the transition zone (Liu et al., 2000). Preheating the large arterial blood to some extent before it enters the treatment region has also been shown to improve the temperature homogeneity in that area.

Currently Used Heating Approaches. It is known that the size and location of the tumor have a significant impact on applicator design and type of heating. Earlier hyperthermia approaches in the 1980s and 1990s included high-energy DC shock (electric conductive heating), RF (alternating current), microwave (electromagnetic wave absorption), ultrasound (sound wave), laser (electromagnetic wave absorption), etc. All the methods require either a wave or a current passing through the tissue and its interaction with molecules in the tissue to generate heating. The wave or current decays as it passes through the tissue, resulting in a heating density diverging from the location where the wave or current is initiated. Collateral thermal damage to healthy tissue may occur if the targeted tissue region is not located very close to the initiation. Actively cooling the healthy tissue region has been shown to be effective to minimize undesired thermal damage. Recent heating methods such as magnetic nanoparticle hyperthermia and laser photothermal therapy are focused on confining heat generation within targeted tumors, thus minimizing collateral thermal damage to healthy tissue. In this section, different heating devices are introduced and their advantages and limitations are described.

In electric cardioversion, high-energy DC shock (Scheinman et al., 1982) has been used as an implanted energy source for the treatment of drug-refractory supraventricular arrhythmias. During the catheter ablation, the peak voltage and current measured at the electrode-tissue interface are typically higher than 1000 V and 40 A, respectively. Although thermal ablation is not an objective of the approach, the high voltage pulse may result in a very high temperature at the electrode surface. Explosive gas formation and a shock wave can occur, which may cause serious complications, including ventricular fibrillation, cardiogenic shock, and cardiac peroration.

Alternating current in the radio frequency range has been investigated as an alternative to shock for heating applicator (Huang et al., 1987; Nath and Haines, 1995; Nath et al., 1994; Wonnell et al., 1992; Zhu and Xu, 1999). Similar to a DC shock, two electrodes or one electrode and a ground pad are needed and local temperature elevations are due to ohmic heating. RF ablation has been successfully used to treat liver neoplasms, solid renal mass, and osteoid osteomas. In recent years, this technique has been applied to destroy brain tissue for the treatment of motor dysfunctions in advanced Parkinson's disease (Kopyov et al., 1997; Linhares and Tasker et al., 2000; Oh et al., 2001; Patel et al., 2003; Su et al., 2002). The current clinical practice of inducing RF lesions in the brain involves implanting a microelectrode-guided electrode and applying RF current to the targeted region, in order to relieve symptoms of the Parkinson's disease in patients whose symptoms cannot be controlled with traditional pharmacological treatment. Clinical evidence suggests that RF ablation has high success rates in patients with colorectal cancer, with only a few unresectable hepatic metastases (<30 mm diameter); in these patients, the 5-year survival rate varies from 14 to 55 percent. A recent study (Zou et al., 2010) using RF for unresectable pancreatic cancer indicated a marked decrease in pain score and improvements in patients. For prostate cancer treatment, local hyperthermia has been considered minimally invasive due to transurethral or transrectal access to the prostate. The effect of RF ablation was examined in another clinical study (Lanuti et al., 2009) for treating inoperable lung cancer and it has shown 78 and 47 percent survival rates after 2 and 4 years, respectively. It has been reported that high-intensity, focused ultrasound has achieved more than 66 to 80 percent success rate in destroying tumors (Chaussy and Thuroff, 2001; Gelet et al., 2001).

RF energy is readily controllable, and the equipment is relatively cheap (Hariharan et al., 2007a). The standard RF generator used in catheter ablation produces an unmodulated sinusoidal wave alternating current at a frequency of 200 to 1000 kHz. Resistive current density is inversely proportional to the square of the distance from the electrode. Thus, resistive heating decreases with the distance from the electrode to the fourth power. Maximal power occurs within a very narrow rim of tissue surrounding the electrodes. The heating typically leads to desiccation of tissue immediately surrounding the catheter electrodes, but diverges and decreases in-between, which can cause broad variations of heating. Improved RF hyperthermia systems have been proposed to reduce the heterogeneity of the RF heating, including implanting a feedback power current system (Astrahan and Norman, 1982; Hartov et al., 1994) and using electrically insulating material around the electrodes (Cosset et al., 1986).

Microwave hyperthermia uses radiative heating produced by high-frequency power. High-frequency electromagnetic waves may be transmitted down an appropriately tuned coaxial cable and then radiated into the surrounding medium by a small antenna. The mechanism of electromagnetic heating from a microwave source is dielectric rather than ohmic. The heating is due to a propagating electromagnetic wave that raises the energy of the dielectric molecules through which the field passes by both conduction and displacement currents. While maintaining alignment with the alternating electric field, neighboring energized dipole molecules collide with each other and the electromagnetic energy is transformed into thermal energy. The main limitation of microwave heating is that the energy is absorbed within a very narrow region around the microwave antenna. Typically, the generated heat decays fast and can be approximated as proportional to $1/r^2$. The highly absorptive nature of the water content of human tissue has limited the penetration of electromagnetic energy to 1 to 2 cm.

Laser photocoagulation is a form of minimally invasive thermotherapy in which laser energy is deposited into a target tissue volume through one or more implanted optical fibers. Laser is used in medicine for incision and explosive ablation of tumors and other tissues, and for blood vessel coagulation in various tissues. Laser light is nearly monochromatic. Most popular lasers utilized in the laboratory include Argon laser (488 nm), pulsed dry laser (585–595 nm), Nd:YAG lasers operating at 1064 nm, and diode lasers operating at 805 nm. Laser-beam power ranges from milliwatts to several watts. Usually the laser energy is focused on a small tissue area of a radius less than 300 μm, resulting in a very high heat flux or volumetric heat generation rate. Because there is minimal penetration of laser energy into the tissue, sufficient energy is delivered to heat tissues surrounding the point of laser contact to beyond 60°C or higher, leading to denaturation and coagulation of biomolecules. Due to the high-temperature elevation in the target tissue, laser photocoagulation may produce vapor, smoke, browning, and char. A char is usually formed when temperature is elevated above 225°C or higher (LeCarpentier et al., 1989; Thomsen, 1991; Torres et al., 1990; Whelan and Wyman, 1999).

In the three primary clinical applications using laser, dermatologists and ophthalmologists are mostly using laser for blood vessel coagulation, and dentists use lasers in both soft and hard tissue ablation. The selection of laser type is largely determined by how deep the targeted region is located in the tissue. Typically, longer wavelength lasers penetrate more deeply into tissue than short wavelength lasers. One example is in laser coagulation of blood vessels in the eyes. Lasers can penetrate the vitreous easily with only minor absorptions (~5 percent) and reach the retina. Conventional treatment for superficial retinal arteries and veins utilizes short wavelength lasers such as Argon laser (527 nm). It will not be suitable for treating deep choroidal feeder vessels (Flower, 2002). Laser energy must penetrate the overlying retinal layer, RPE, and choriocapillaris to reach the targeted choroidal feeder vessels. Previous experimental and theoretical studies have suggested using a near-infrared (NIR) laser such as diode laser at 805 nm wavelength to deliver sufficient laser energy to the choroidal feeder vessels with minimal concomitant retinal and choroidal damage, especially to the sensitive RPE layer (Banerjee et al., 2007; Flower, 2002; Zhu et al., 2008, 2009b).

Similar approaches can be seen in using laser for treatment of port wine stains (PWS), birthmarks due to deep dilated capillaries located superficially in the skin (Jia et al., 2006). The absorption of laser occurs largely due to oxyhemoglobins (HbO_2) and deoxyhemoglobins (Hb) in the blood stream. Short-wavelength lasers, such as pulsed dye laser (PDL) at 577 and 595 nm and potassium titanyl phosphate (KTP) laser at 532 nm strongly absorbed by both oxyhemoglobin and deoxyhemoglobin, have been shown effective to obliterate the blood vessels to improve the skin tone in PWS located less than 1 mm beneath the skin surface (Huikeshoven et al., 2007; Jasim and Handley, 2007). However, for deeply seated PWS, it has been proposed to use Alexandrite 755-nm laser or Nd:YAG laser at 1064 nm, which can penetrate into several millimeters in skin tissue. In addition, coagulation of venous blood with rich deoxyhemoglobins is preferred to use Alexandrite laser since the absorption by Hb at 755-nm wavelength is stronger than the absorption by HbO_2. On the other hand, the Nd:YAG laser at 1064 nm is better for obliteration of arterioles since it is absorbed more by HbO_2 than by Hb. In recent years, it has been proposed to use a dual laser system (short- and long-wavelength lasers) targeting both superficial and deep blood vessels in a combined approach (Izikson et al., 2009). Thermal damage to the epidermis (~60 μm in thickness) may occur even with limited laser energy absorption there. One approach to minimize the thermal damage in epidermis is to use cryogen sprayed on the skin surface before or during laser treatment. Theoretical simulations have been performed to identify suitable cooling parameters for preventing collateral thermal damage while delivering sufficient laser energy to the targeted blood vessels located in the dermis.

In dentistry, both short-wavelength lasers such as Nd:YAG, argon, and diode lasers and long wavelength Er;YAG and Er,Cr;YSGG are used in cutting hard tissue, reshaping gums and implants, and removing debris. Recently, bacterial disinfection in deep dentin area using Er,Cr;YSGG lasers has been proposed for root canal procedures (Zhu et al., 2009b). In addition, simple red lasers at 695 nm emitted from a small probe have been used for diagnosis of caries hidden inside the teeth (Barberia et al, 2008; Chu et al., 2010). Comparing to dermatology and ophthalmology, there are relatively limited studies in dentistry to optimize treatment efficacy when selecting from a variety of lasers. There are also only a few studies to evaluate collateral thermal damages to the tissue surrounding the targeted tooth region.

Unlike the electromagnetic heating devices mentioned above, ultrasound heating is a mechanical hyperthermic technique. The acoustic energy, when absorbed by tissue, can lead to local temperature rise. Modern ultrasound systems use a curved transducer placed on the skin surface, making this the least invasive in the methods. The focal point due to the curvature of the transducer can be adjusted to focus heating mostly on the region of interest. Ultrasound offers many advantages as an energy source for hyperthermia because of its small wavelength and highly controllable power deposition patterns, including penetration depth control in human soft tissue (Hariharan et al., 2007a, 2007b). The depth of the resulting lesion could theoretically be increased or decreased by selecting a lower or higher ultrasound frequency, respectively. It has been shown that scanned focused ultrasound provides the ability to achieve more uniform temperature elevations inside tumors than the electromagnetic applicators. Moros and Fan (1998) have shown that the frequency of 1 MHz is not adequate for treating chest wall recurrences, since it is too penetrating. As for a deep-seated tumor (3 to 6 cm deep), longer penetration depth is achieved by using relatively low frequency (1 MHz) and/or adjusting the acoustic output power of the transducer (Moros et al., 1996). The practical problem associated with ultrasound heating is the risk of overheating the surrounding bone–tissue interface because of the high ultrasound absorption in bone.

Another hyperthermia approach involves microparticles or nanoparticles which can generate heat in tissue when subjected to an alternating magnetic field. Magnetic particle hyperthermia procedure consists of localizing magnetic particles within tumor tissue or tumor vasculature and applying an external alternating magnetic field to agitate the particles (Gilchrist et al., 1957). In this case, magnetic particles function as a heat source, which generates heat due to hysteresis loss, Néel relaxation, Brownian motion, or eddy currents. The employment of nanoparticles smaller than 100 nm is especially advantageous in generating sufficient heat with low magnetic field strength. The heat generated by magnetic particles subject to an alternative magnetic field is suggested to be primarily size-dependent. As the particle size decreases, thermal activation of reorientation processes leads to superparamagnetic (SPM) behavior that is capable of generating impressive levels of heating at low field strengths when the Neel relaxation and Brownian motion are the dominant heating mechanisms (Fortin et al., 2008). The application of nanoparticles in magnetic hyperthermia offers a more effective treatment route than microparticles.

Subsequently, a targeted distribution of temperature elevation can be achieved by manipulating the particle distribution in the tumor and tuning the magnetic field parameters. Compared to most conventional noninvasive heating approaches, this technique is capable of delivering adequate heat to tumor without necessitating heat penetration through the skin surface, thus avoiding the excessive collateral thermal damage along the path of energy penetration if the tumor is deep-seated. In addition to treatment of deep-seated tumor, the employment of nanoparticle smaller than 100 nm is especially advantageous in generating sufficient heating at a lower magnetic field strength. Typically, the particle dosage in the tumor and the magnetic field strength are carefully chosen to achieve the desired temperature elevation. Generally, the usable frequencies are in the range of 0.05 to 1.2 MHz and the field amplitude is controlled lower than 15 kA/m. Previous in vitro and in vivo studies have used a frequency in the hundred kilohertz range (Chan et al., 1993; Hase et al., 1989; Hilger et al., 2001; Jordan et al., 1997; Rand et al., 1981). The studies of heat generation by particles suggest that the heating characteristic of magnetic particles depends strongly on their properties, such as particle size, composition, and microstructure (Chan et al., 1993; Hergt et al., 2004; Hilger et al., 2001; Jordan et al., 1997). In particular, as the particle size decreases, thermal activation of reorientation processes leads to superparamagnetic (*SPM*) behavior that is capable of generating impressive levels of heating at lower field strengths. The spherical nanoparticle of 10 nm diameter is capable of providing a specific loss power (*SLP*) of 211 W/g under a magnetic field of 14 kA/m in amplitude and 300 kHz in frequency. In contrast, particles with diameter of 220 nm only generate an *SLP* of 144 W/g under an identical magnetic field (Hilger et al., 2001). Experimental studies have been performed by Attaluri et al. (2011a, 2011b) on implanted PC3 tumors on mice, although it achieved similar temperature elevations in the tumors under a very low magnetic field strength (3 kA/m) (Attaluri et al., 2011a, 2011b). Magnetic nanoparticle hyperthermia has also been used to treat cancer in the kidney and skin (melanoma). A recent study by us has demonstrated the capability of elevating tumor temperature above 70°C using only 0.1 cc of a commercially available ferrofluid injected to PC3 tumor when it is subjected to a magnetic field strength (LeBrun et al., 2016a, 2016b). All of these studies have shown success in either moderate or complete thermal damage to various tumors using a wide range of strength of magnetic field with a frequency of several hundred kilohertz. Therefore, nanoparticle hyperthermia provides a more effective and clinically safer therapeutic alternative for cancer treatment than microparticles.

The quantification of heat generated by the particles has suggested that the size of the individual particle and properties of the magnetic field (strength and frequency) determine its heating capacity. Hence, given the particle size and magnetic field strength, it is the spatial distribution of the particle dispersed in tissue that affects the resulting temperature elevation. However, it is not clear how the spatial concentration of the particles in the tissue correlates with the particle concentration in the carrier solution before the injection. In nanofluid transport in tissue, the injection strategy as well as interaction between particle and the porous interstitial space may affect the particle distribution. An experimental study by our group has attempted to evaluate how to achieve a spherical shaped nanoparticle distribution in tissue. Figure 4.12 gives two images of nanoparticle distribution in agarose gel (0.2 percent) after a commercially available nanofluid was injected using a syringe pump. The selected injection rate affects significantly the final distribution of the nanofluid. As described in details in Salloum et al. (2008a), the ability of achieving a small spherical particle delivery is the first step to induce uniform temperature elevations in tumors with an irregular shape.

Depending on the amplitude of the magnetic field and particle dosage, the rate of temperature increase at the monitored site was as high as several degrees Celsius per minute. Temperatures up to 71°C were recorded at the tumor center (Hilger et al., 2005). The subsequent work by Johannsen and Jordan (Johannsen et al., 2005a, 2005b; Jordan et al., 2006) focused on testing the magnetic fluid hyperthermia on prostate cancer in human subjects. The histological analysis of the cancerous tissues showed a partial necrosis of the cells after the treatment. Recently, our group performed experimental study on the temperature elevation in rat muscle tissue induced by intramuscular injection of 0.2 cc nanofluid. The elevated temperatures were as high as 45°C and the FWHM (full length at half maximum) of the temperature elevation is 31 mm (Salloum et al., 2008b). All the experimental data have suggested the feasibility of elevating the tumor temperature to the desired level for tissue necrosis. However, in some tumor regions, usually at the tumor periphery, underdosage heating (temperature elevations lower than a critical value) was observed.

Laser photothermal therapy is another approach to maximally confine heat generation to targeted tumor region. It is an approach when metallic (gold) nanoparticles with a size much smaller than the

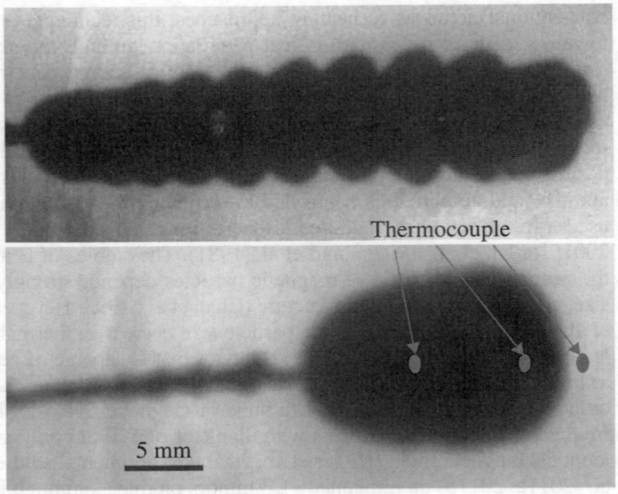

FIGURE 4.12 Two images of nanofluid distribution in agarose gel (0.2%). The injection rate was (A) 5 μL/min and (B) 2.5 μL/min, respectively. The nanofluid can be viewed by the black color in the images.

laser wavelength are exposed to laser irradiation at a specific laser wavelength near its plasmon resonant absorption band to activate and deactivate electrons, leading to dissipating energy. Specifically, laser has both electric and magnetic components, perpendicular to each other and perpendicular to the direction of energy and wave propagations. In the presence of an oscillating electromagnetic field of laser light, the conduction band of electrons of the metallic nanoparticle undergoes a collective coherent resonant oscillation with respect to surface plasmon oscillation. This requires that the natural frequency of the surface plasmon resonance (SPR) matches the frequency of the incident light; this phenomenon is called SPR. The frequency of SPR oscillation depends on the size, shape, surrounding medium, and dielectric constant of the nanoparticles (Huang et al., 2011). The induced surface plasmon oscillations decay either by radiative or nonradiative decay. In radiative decay the absorbed light energy causes phonon emission at the same frequency as the incident light, called Mie or Rayleigh scattering (Mie, 1908). This strong light scattering property of gold nanorods in the NIR region makes them potential candidates for noninvasive imaging techniques in the NIR band. The nonradiative decay occurs via electron-hole recombination. The energy exchange mechanism has two phases: electron–phonon interaction and phonon–phonon interaction. The excited electrons cool off rapidly by energy exchange with the nanoparticles in less than a picosecond, resulting in a hot particle lattice (Link and El-Sayed, 2000). The hot particle lattice exchanges this energy with the surrounding medium within 100 picoseconds via phonon–phonon interaction. The rapid energy exchange and strongly induced heat dissipation are desirable in hyperthermia applications.

The unique and easily tunable optical properties of gold nanoparticles with different shapes and structures such as nanospheres (Halas and West 2003), nanorods (Manuchehrabadi et al., 2012, 2013a, 2013b; Manuchehrabadi and Zhu, 2014), nanocages (Yavuz et al., 2009), nanoprism (Guo et al., 2010), nanowire (Heilmann and Kreibig, 2000), composite nanoparticles with core and shell structure (Kang and Taton, 2005), and nanoparticles with core and assemblies (Westcott et al., 1998) may confine laser energy to targeted tumors. Selecting a laser with appropriate wavelength is equally important. Laser photothermal therapy requires sufficient penetration of the laser energy through the superficial tissue and then adequate accumulation of laser absorption within the targeted tumor region. Among all the wavelengths of available lasers, the NIR range has the advantage of maximal transmissivity in normal tissue over other wavelengths. It has been suggested that an NIR laser with a wavelength of approximately 800 nm may penetrate into normal tissue with minimal laser absorption before reaching the targeted tumor with deposition of gold nanorods. By carefully designing the size, shape, and structure of gold nanoparticles, one can achieve a desired absorption-scattering ratio in the therapeutic optical window (750 to 1100 nm) to maximize laser energy confinement in tumors (Myroshnychenko et al., 2008).

Previous experimental and theoretical studies have shown the effectiveness of laser photothermal therapy in cancer treatment both in tissue cultures and implanted tumors in mice (Manuchehrabadi et al., 2012). Successful treatment outcomes are illustrated by shrinkage of tumors following the therapy, as well as observed tumor cell death in tissue culture (Manuchehrabadi et al., 2013b).

Determination of SAR or Volumetric Heat Generation Rate q'''. SAR is a term normally used to describe heat generation rate per tissue mass. In heat conduction equation or the Pennes bioheat equation, the source term should carry a unit of watt per unit volume of tissue. Strictly speaking, one should convert SAR to q''' to be used in the heat transfer equation. Several methods are used to determine the q''' distribution induced by various heating applicators. The q''' distribution can be directly derived from the Maxwell equation of the electromagnetic field (Camart et al., 2000; Gentill et al., 1995; Ling et al., 1999; Stauffer et al., 1998; Strohbehn, 1984). The electrical field E and magnetic field B are first determined analytically or numerically from the Maxwell equation. The q''' is then calculated by the following equation (Sapozink et al., 1988):

$$q''' = \left(\frac{\sigma}{2\rho}\right)E^2 \tag{4.38}$$

where ρ and σ represent the density and conductivity of the media, respectively. This method is feasible when the derivation of the electromagnetic field is not very difficult. It generally requires a rather large computational resource and a long calculation time, though it is flexible for modeling the applicators and the surrounding media.

Other methods in clinical and engineering applications are experimental determination of the q''' distribution based on the heat conduction equation. The experiment is generally performed on a tissue equivalent phantom gel. The applicability of the q''' distribution measured in the phantom gel to that in tissue depends on the electrical properties of the phantom gel. For energy absorption of ultrasound in tissue, the gel mimics tissue in terms of ultrasonic speed and attenuation/absorption properties. For heat pattern induced by microwave or RF, the applicability requires that the phantom gel mimic the dielectric constant and electrical conductivity of the tissue. The electrical properties of various tissues at different wave frequencies have been studied by Stoy et al. (1982). It has been shown that in addition to the electromagnetic wave frequency, water content of the tissue is the most important factor determining the electrical properties. Thermal properties such as heat capacity and thermal conductivity of the gel are not required if no thermal study is conducted. The ingredients of the gel can be selected to achieve the same electrical characteristics of the tissue for a specific electromagnetic wavelength. As shown in Zhu and Xu (1998), the basic ingredients of the gel used for an RF heating applicator were water, formaldehyde solution, gelatin, and NaCl. Water was used to achieve a similar water content as the tissue. Formaldehyde and gelatin were the solidification agents. NaCl was added to obtain the desired electrical conductivity of tissue at that frequency. The resulted phantom gel was a semitransparent material that permits easy and precise positioning of the temperature sensors during the experimental study.

The simplest experimental approach to determine q''' is measuring the temperature transient at the instant of power on (Wong et al., 1993; Zhu et al., 1996b). In this approach, temperature sensors are placed at different spatial locations within the gel. Before the experiment, the gel is allowed to establish a uniform temperature distribution within the gel. As soon as the initial heating power level is applied, the gel temperature is elevated and the temperatures at all sensor locations are measured and recorded by a computer. The transient temperature field in the gel can be described by the heat conduction equation as follows:

$$\begin{aligned} \rho c \frac{\partial T}{\partial t} &= k\nabla^2 T + q'''(x,y,z) \\ t = 0, \qquad T &= T_{\text{env}} \end{aligned} \tag{4.39}$$

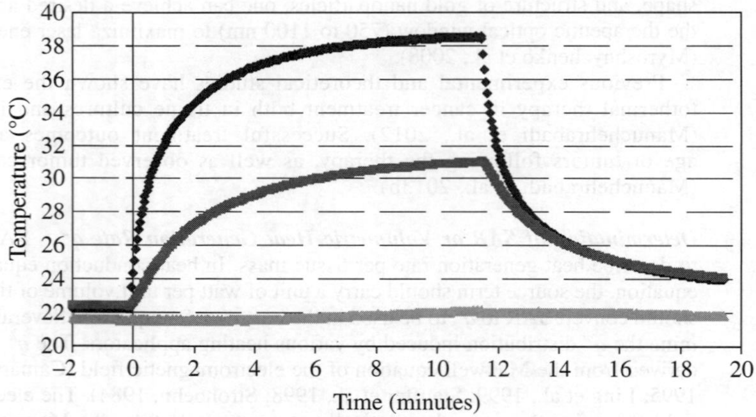

FIGURE 4.13 Initial temperature rises after heating is turned on. Temperatures are measured at three locations in the agarose gel, as shown in Fig. 4.12.

Within a very short period after the heating power is on, heat conduction can be negligible if the phantom gel is allowed to reach equilibration with the environment before the heating. Thus, q''' can be determined by the slope of the initial temperature rise at the specific location (x, y, z), i.e.,

$$q'''(x, y, z) = \rho c \left. \frac{\partial T(x, y, z, t)}{\partial t} \right|_{t=0} \tag{4.40}$$

Since q''' at each spatial location (x, y, z) is a constant during the heating, the temperature rise at each location is expected to increase linearly if heat conduction is negligible. Figure 4.13 gives the measured temperature rises at different radial locations from an injection site of the nanofluid. Note that the temperatures at all three probe locations were very close to each other before the heating. The temperatures increased linearly once the power was on; however, after approximately 60 seconds, the plot became curved and heat conduction within the gel was no longer negligible. For convenience the loose q''' data are generally represented by an analytic expression with several unknown parameters. Then a least-square residual fit of the q''' measurement to the analytical expression is performed to determine the unknown parameters in the expression.

It is simple to determine the q''' distribution from the initial temperature transient. This method is fairly accurate as long as the temperature is uniform before the power is turned on. However, to obtain an accurate expression for the q''' distribution, enough temperature sensors should be placed in the region where the energy is absorbed. In the situation when the SAR decays rapidly in the radial direction because of the superficial penetration of the energy, and it is difficult to place many temperature sensors in the near field, the q''' distribution must be determined by only a few measurements in the near field, which increases the measurement error.

In the experimental study by Zhu et al. (1998), the heating pattern induced by a microwave antenna was quantified by solving the inverse problem of heat conduction in a tissue equivalent gel. In this approach, detailed temperature distribution in the gel is required and predicted by solving a two-dimensional or three-dimensional heat conduction equation in the gel. In the experimental study, all the temperature probes were not required to be placed in the near field of the catheter. Experiments were first performed in the gel to measure the temperature elevation induced by the applicator, as shown in Fig. 4.14. An expression with several unknown parameters was proposed for the q''' distribution. Then, a theoretical heat transfer model was developed with appropriate boundary conditions and initial condition of the experiment to study the temperature distribution in the gel. The values of those unknown parameters in the proposed q''' expression were initially assumed and the temperature field in the gel was calculated by the model. The parameters were then adjusted to minimize the square error of the deviations of the theoretically predicted from the experimentally measured temperatures at all temperature sensor locations.

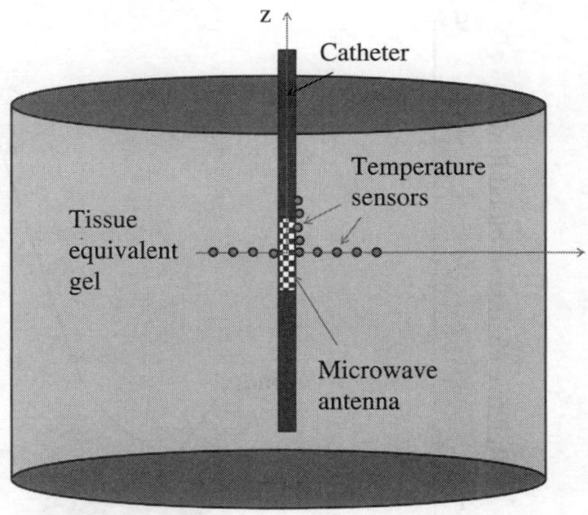

FIGURE 4.14 Schematic diagram of an experimental set up for measuring SARs at various tissue-equivalent phantom locations for microwave-induced heating.

4.5.4 Dynamic Response of Blood Flow to Hyperthermia

As mentioned previously, blood flow plays a profound effect in the temperature field during hyperthermia treatment. Accurately measuring and monitoring blood flow in different tissue regions and at different heating levels are especially crucial to achieve the thermal goal. The distribution of blood flow is quite heterogeneous in the tissue. Blood flow rate may be higher in the skin than in the muscle. Blood flow in the tumor and normal tissue may also be quite different because of different vasculatures. Contrary to the general notion that blood flow is less in tumors than in normal tissues, blood flow in many tumors, particularly in small tumors, is actually greater than that in surrounding normal tissues at normothermic conditions. Even in the same tumor, blood flow generally decreases as the tumor grows larger, owing partially to progressive deterioration of vascular beds and to the rapid growth of tumor cell population relative to vascular bed.

The dynamic responses of the blood flow to hyperthermia in normal tissue and tumors are even more diversified than the blood flow heterogeneity. It is a well-known fact that heat induces a prompt increase in blood flow accompanied by dilation of vessels and an increase in permeability of the vascular wall in normal tissues. The degree of pathophysiological changes in the vascular system in normal tissue is, of course, dependent on the heating temperature, the heating duration, and the heating protocol. Experimental study by Song (1984) has shown how the vasculature changed in the skin and muscle of rodents at different time intervals after hyperthermia for varying heating temperatures at 42° to 45°C. It was shown that the blood flow in the skin increased by a factor of 4 and 6 upon heating at 43°C for 60 and 120 minutes, respectively. At 44°C the skin blood flow was about 12 times the control value within 30 minutes. At high heating temperature, there existed a critical time after which the blood flow decreased because of vasculature damage. This critical time was more quickly reached when the heating temperature was higher. The blood flow increase in the muscle was similar to that observed in the skin layer, a tenfold increase in the blood flow was noticed at the 45°C heating.

An indisputable fact emerging from various experimental data indicates that heat-induced change in the blood flow in some tumors is considerably different from that in normal tissue. As noted in Fig. 4.15, there was a limited increase in blood flow in tumors during the initial heating period (Song, 1984). When the heating was prolonged, the tumor blood flow decreased progressively. The different responses of the normal tissue and tumors suggest the feasibility of selective tumor heating. A relatively small increase in blood flow in tumors favors retention of heat within the tumor volume, and thus causes greater heat damage. On the other hand, a large blood flow increase in the normal tissue by vascular dilation causes tissue cooling and high survival of cells.

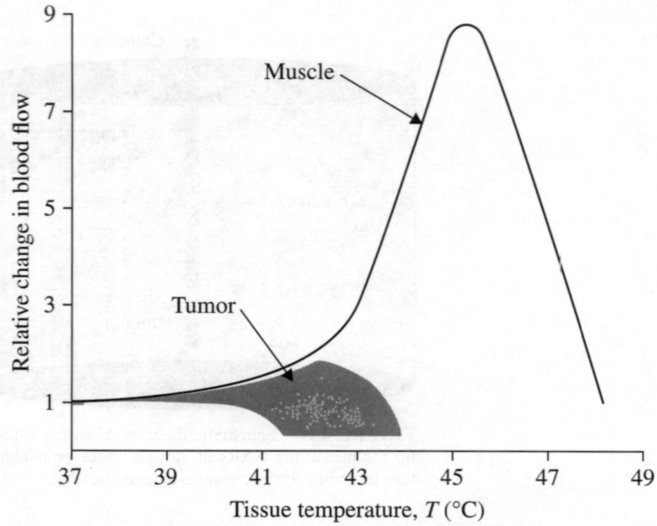

FIGURE 4.15 Temperature-dependent changes in the relative blood perfusion rates for muscle and animal tumors. [*From Song (1984) with permission.*]

Since blood flow is the major route of heat dissipation during hyperthermia, attempts have been made to modify the vascular responses in tumors and normal tissue to heat (Reinhold and Endrich, 1986; Song, 1991). Decreased tumor perfusion may induce changes in the tumor microenvironment, such as reduced pH value and energy supply, thus enhance the thermal cytotoxicity (Gerweck, 1977; Overgaard, 1976; Song et al., 1994). An injection of hydralazine to dogs was reported to decrease the blood flow by 50 percent in the tumor and increase the blood flow in the underlying muscle by a factor of three (Song, 1984). It was demonstrated that the use of vasoactive drugs led to intracellular acidification of the tumor environment (Song et al., 1994). It has been shown that 1 hour after an intravenous or intraperitoneal injection of KB-R8498, the blood flow in the SCK mammary carcinoma tumors of mice was reduced 30 to 60 percent (Griffin et al., 1998; Ohashi et al., 1998). The effect has also been made to induce a blood flow increase in the normal tissue. It was reported that preferentially dilating vessels in normal tissues using vasodilator such as sodium nitroprusside led to shunting of blood away from the tumor, and thus reducing the cooling effect of the blood flow in a tumor during local hyperthermia (Jirtle, 1988; Prescott et al., 1992). Not surprisingly, radiation also altered the response of vasculatures to heat. It was reported that irradiation with 2000 R given 1 hour before heating at 42°C for 30 minutes enhanced the heat-induced vascular damage in the cervical carcinoma of hamsters. Another research showed that hyperthermia of 42°C for 1 hour, given several weeks after irradiation, enhanced the capacity of blood flow increase in skin and muscle (Song, 1984).

It has been increasingly evident that the response of vascular beds to heat in tumors differs considerably from that in normal tissues. The effective clinical use of hyperthermia depends on a careful application of these biological principles emerging from experimental work. More experimental measurements of temperature response are needed for different tumor types at different ages. It is also important to evaluate the applicability of the dynamic response measured in animal to human subjects. Another issue to be addressed is the hyperthermia-induced blood flow change in drug delivery, since the reduced tumor blood flow may decrease the drug delivered to the tumors.

4.5.5 Assessment of Thermal Damage

An optimal heating protocol for a heating experiment can be determined based on the Arrhenius integral or the EM_{43}, an alternative parameter derived from the Arrhenius integral (Dewhirst et al., 2003;

Moritz and Henriques, 1947; Sapareto and Dewey, 1984). The Arrhenius integral (Moritz and Henriques, 1947) can be used to quantitatively assess thermal damage based on measured or simulated temperature history at various tissue locations. Damage is considered to be a unimolecular process. In this process, the native molecules are transformed into a coagulated state, leading to cell death. Damage is quantified as a single dimensionless parameter Ω. This equation is referred to as the Arrhenius integral as follows:

$$\Omega(x, y, z, \tau) = \ln\left|\frac{C(0)}{C(\tau)}\right| = A\int_0^{\tau} \exp\left[-\frac{E_a}{R_u T(x, y, z, t)}\right] dt \tag{4.41}$$

where t is time, C is the concentration of undamaged cells, A is the preexponential factor or frequency factor (1/s), E_a is the activation energy barrier (J/mole), R_u is the universal gas constant (J/mole·K), and $T(x, y, z, t)$ is the absolute tissue temperature at the location (x, y, z). Ω, the extent of damage, is defined as the logarithm of the ratio of the initial concentration of the healthy cells, $C(0)$, to the concentration of the healthy cells remaining after thermal treatment, $C(\tau)$, for a duration of τ. The value of Ω is zero before any thermal therapy, and it increases during heating. Sixty-three percent and 98.2 percent denaturation of protein occurs when $\Omega = 1$ and 4, respectively (LeBrun et al., 2016b). Note that Ω is a function of both tissue location (x, y, z) and heating time τ. Implementing the integral requires knowing of the activation energy and the frequency factor associated with the tissue cells. The values of E_a and A are determined by inverse thermal analyses in matching the model to the data for cell injury and temperature-time history of exposure. The activation energy and frequency factor are related to activation enthalpy and entropy. From the exponential nature of the equation, it suggests that rate damage accumulation will be negligible below certain temperature threshold. Once the threshold value is exceeded, a swift increase in the rate damage accumulation is expected.

The Arrhenius parameters A and E_a are both temperature and cell line/tissue dependent and are typically determined using inverse heat transfer analysis. One previous study of thermal tolerance of various carcinoma cells demonstrated that human prostatic carcinoma cell lines are much easier to be damaged than carcinoma cell lines of other human origins such as colon, breast, lung, and brain under the same mild hyperthermia dosage (Ryu et al., 1996). For example, PC3 cells and RWPE-1 (prostate cells) in the thermal ablation region have frequency factor of is $7 * 10^{17}$ 1/s and the $5.65 * 10^{7}$ 1/s and an activation energy of $1.25 * 10^{5}$ J/mol and $5.88 * 10^{4}$ J/mol, respectively (Rylander et al., 2006). Recently, the Arrhenius integral $\Omega = 4$ is used to design heating time for 100 percent damaging PC3 tumors implanted on mice (LeBrun et al., 2016a). Based on the nanoparticle distribution in a tumor obtained from microCT scans and imported to COMSOL (LeBrun et al., 2016a), one simulates the temperature transients in the tumor, and the heating time of 25 minutes is identified to satisfy the minimal Ω value of 4 over the entire tumor. The Arrhenius damage model is still being used extensively in the field of hyperthermia as a means to predict the probability of damage.

In clinical studies for specific type of cancers and growth stage, it is a common practice to perform experiments at 43°C to determine how long it will take to induce cell damage to a cell of specific type and growth stage. This method is referred to as the cumulative effective minutes at 43°C or CEM_{43}. CEM_{43}, the thermal isoeffective dose, converts the temperature levels and heating duration into an equivalent number of minutes at 43°C to induce the necessary thermal damage. CEM_{43} is widely used to evaluate thermal damage to cells previously studied to understand whether the designed treatment protocols achieve the same thermal dosage. CEM_{43} has been extensively and successfully used in clinical trials to assess the efficacy of heating, despite the fact that the R value has been historically derived from cell cultures and rodents (Nadobny et al., 2015). The proposed method for estimating damage is given as

$$\text{CEM}_{43} \text{ for } T_i = \sum_{j=1}^{n} \Delta t_j R^{T_i(t_j)-43} \tag{4.42}$$

where T_i is the temperature at location i and Δt is the time at T_i. A more general expression of EM43 can be written as

$$\text{CEM}_{43} \text{ for location } i = \int_0^t R^{T_i(t)-43} dt \tag{4.43}$$

The parameter R is referred to the R-value and it represents a constant that is dependent on the temperature range (Dewhirst et al., 2003; Manuchehrabadi et al., 2013b). Similar to the Arrhenius model, R-value is cell line/tissue dependent. Typical R-values for human prostate cancer (PC3) with their temperature ranges can be as follows:

$$R = \begin{cases} 4 & T < 43°\text{C} \\ 2 & 48°\text{C} \geq T \geq 43°\text{C} \\ 1.33 & T > 48°\text{C} \end{cases} \tag{4.44}$$

CEM_{43} method suggests that if temperatures are higher than 43°C, the treatment time decreases. When the tissue temperature is higher than 43°C, the equivalent minutes at 43°C is longer than the actual heating time. For example, if the temperature is maintained at 46°C (R-value of 2) for 20 minutes, i.e., $\Delta t_j = 20$, the equivalent minutes for this time segment will be $20 * 2^{46\text{-}43} = 320$ minutes at 43°C. In other words, the equivalent minutes can be much higher than the actual heating time when the tumor temperature is higher than 43°C. If the calculated number of equivalent minutes is longer than the CEM_{43}, thermal damage is ensured. One study using ultrasound heating determined that the critical thermal dose for liver tissue is $CEM_{43} = 340$ minutes when temperatures are maintained at 54°C (Graham et al., 1999). A recent study by Manuchehrabadi et al. (2013b) has used the approach to estimate the CEM43 in PC3 tumors implanted in mice. The heating is induced by an 808-nm laser with a heating duration of 15 minutes. Based on the measured temperature mapping along two tumor paths in an in vivo experiment, one estimates the EM43 values at all the measurement locations. More than 93 percent of the locations have a CEM43 value longer than 110 minutes. Later the results are compared to histologic analyses and tumor shrinkage studies after the same treatment protocol. The distribution of thermal damage observed in the experiment agrees with the theoretical prediction of the CEM_{43} values.

4.5.6 Theoretical Modeling

In treatment planning, quantitative three-dimensional thermal modeling aids in the identification of power delivery for optimum treatment. Thermal modeling provides the clinician with powerful tools that improve the ability to deliver safe and effective therapy, and permits the identification of critical monitoring sites to assess tumor heating as well as to assure patient safety. Thermal modeling maximizes the information content of (necessarily sparse) invasive thermometry. The empirical temperature expression (if it is possible) can be used to develop an online reference for monitoring tissue temperatures and building a feedback control of the applied power to avoid overheatings in critical tissue areas during the hyperthermia therapy.

Tissue temperature distributions during hyperthermia treatments can be theoretically determined by solving the bioheat transfer equation (continuum model or vascular model), which considers the contributions of heat conduction, blood perfusion, and external heating. In addition to geometrical parameters and thermal properties, the following knowledge must be determined before the simulation. The SAR distribution induced by the external heating device should be determined first. The regional blood perfusion in the tissue and tumor and their dynamic responses to heating are also required. All this information, with appropriate boundary and initial conditions allows one to calculate the temperature distribution of the tissue.

Analytical solution for the temperature field during the hyperthermia treatment is available for certain tissue geometries (Liu et al., 2000; Zhu and Xu, 1999). In most of the situations, temperature field is solved by numerical methods because of the irregular tissue geometry and complicated dynamic response of blood flow to heating (Charny et al., 1987; Chatterjee and Adams, 1994; Clegg and Roamer, 1993; Zhu et al., 2009a, 2009b).

Unfortunately, the distribution of the volumetric heat generation rate in tumors induced by a specific heating method is often nonuniform and unknown. Most tumors are also not represented correctly using simple geometries. These challenges may be addressed by proposing theoretical modeling based on realistic tumor model and volumetric heat generation rate distribution obtained from imaging scans after calibrations. With the advancement of computational and storage resources in the past decade, modeling biotransport in tissue is no longer implemented in simplified geometries such as rectangular columns, cylinders, and spheres. For example, in laser photothermal therapy or laser treatment, traditional approach is to use 1D Beer's law or a modified Beer's law that combines absorption and scattering into a single extinction coefficient to address energy absorption. Currently, energy absorption in tumors by laser can be easily modeled using Monte Carlo simulation that is sufficiently flexible to handle complex geometrical shapes, anisotropic scattering, and nonhomogeneous properties. This method assumes laser as photons emitted from a laser source (Manuchehrabadi et al., 2013a). After a single photon is incident on a tissue surface, the photon can either be specularly reflected or continue to transport inside the tissue. At each step the photon travels, the direction in which it will be heading to and how much energy dissipation due to absorption when the photon interacts with the tissue are determined by probability functions. In addition, photons can interact with tissue via scattering from a particle or tiny tissue structure. During scattering, several probability functions are used to determine which direction the photon will bend from its original path based on an anisotropic factor, as well as the length of the next step of the photon after scattering. After a series of scattering and absorption events inside the tissue, the photons may exhaust their energy to zero or escape from the tissue region. Monte Carlo simulations usually require emitting thousands of photons onto the tissue surface, based on the laser irradiation distribution. This long simulation-intensive process has been shortened significantly due to advancement in computational resources. Any energy dissipation due to absorption in a unit volume element can then be added to calculate the total energy absorption rate by the element to determine the volumetric heat generation rate distribution in tissue, to be used in bioheat transfer simulation.

In magnetic nanoparticle hyperthermia, the available computational resource in recent years makes it possible to import the acquired 3D images of tumor geometries and detailed nanoparticle concentration distribution to commercial software packages for accurate heat transfer simulation. A heat transfer model based on image-generated tumor geometry and volumetric heat generation rate distribution would greatly improve model predicting power and lead to individualized and reliable treatment designs for various tumor sizes and types (LeBrun et al., 2016a). As shown in Fig. 4.16, a prototype

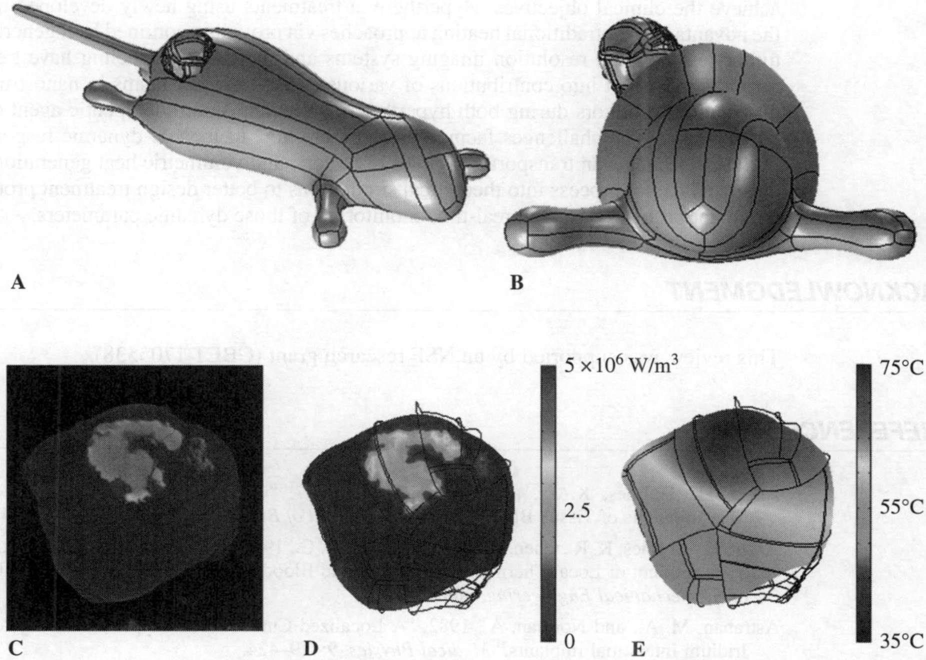

FIGURE 4.16 Generated tumor model embedded in a mouse body from microCT scans (A and B); a slice of microCT image of a tumor with nanoparticle injection (C); generated color contours of volumetric heat generation rate in COMSOL (D); and simulated temperature distribution in the tumor during steady state (E).

of a tumor from about 500 microCT scan slices is generated and mounted on a prototype of a mouse body. Also illustrated in Fig. 4.16 are: an original microCT scan slice of the tumor, an imported volumetric heat generation rate contour to COMSOL, and the resulted steady-state temperature elevation distribution in the tumor (LeBrun et al., 2016a). It is an important advancement to accurately model the details in those geometries and the resulted volumetric heat generation rate distribution, especially when point-to-point comparisons are necessary in some future theoretical simulation applications.

Parametric studies can be performed to evaluate the influence of different parameters, such as heating level, tissue perfusion, and cooling fluid, on the temperature elevation. Extensive parametric studies can be performed quickly and inexpensively so that sensitive (and insensitive) parameters can be identified, systems can be evaluated, and critical experiments can be identified. This is especially important when the parameter is unknown. It is also possible to extract the ideal SAR distribution from the parametric study (Loulou and Scott, 2000) and design an improved heating applicator in future. Knowledge of the expected thermal profiles could be used to guide experimental and clinical studies in using an optimum thermal dose to achieve a desired therapeutic effect. The optimal thermal dose needed in the treatment volume predicted by the theory helps physicians to evaluate the effectiveness of the heating devices and their treatment protocols.

4.6 CONCLUSION

Building on previous efforts to understand fundamental roles played by vasculature on temperature field in biological systems, bioengineers have greatly improved their ability of modeling temperature fields in tissue with high precision for treatment planning with the advancements in computational resources and newly developed imaging tools, which allow accurate description of the tissue geometry and heating source/sink distribution. This greatly enhances the simulation accuracy of heat and mass transfer processes in tissue, which are critical for generating an optimal temperature distribution to achieve the clinical objectives. Hyperthermia treatments using newly developed nanostructures have the advantage over traditional heating approaches via providing confined heat generation in the targeted tumor region. High-resolution imaging systems and multiscale modeling have tremendous potential for gaining insight into contributions of various transport mechanisms in nanostructure transport and distribution in tumors during both hyperthermia treatments and therapeutic agent delivery to targeted tissue region. The challenges facing engineers are how to include dynamic responses of local blood perfusion, changes in transport properties in tumors, and volumetric heat generation rate redistribution during a heating process into theoretical simulations to better design treatment protocols and/or adjust treatment protocol based on real-time monitoring of those dynamic parameters.

ACKNOWLEDGMENT

This review was supported by an NSF research grant (CBET-1705538).

REFERENCES

Arkin, H., Holmes, K. R., and Chen, M. M., 1987, "Computer Based System for Continuous On-line Measurements of Tissue Blood Perfusion," *Journal of Biomedical Engineering*, **9**:38–45.

Arkin, H., Holmes, K. R., Chen, M. M., and Bottje, W. G., 1986, "Thermal Pulse Decay Method for Simultaneous Measurement of Local Thermal Conductivity and Blood Perfusion: A Theoretical Analysis," *ASME Journal of Biomechanical Engineering*, **108**:208–214.

Astrahan, M. A., and Norman, A., 1982, "A Localized Current Field Hyperthermia System for Use with 192 Iridium Interstitial Implants," *Medical Physics*, **9**:419–424.

Attaluri, A., Ma, R., Qiu, Y., Li, W., and Zhu, L., 2011a, "Nanoparticle Distribution and Temperature Elevations in Prostatic Tumors in Mice during Magnetic Nanoparticle Hyperthermia," *International Journal of Hyperthermia*, **27**(5):491–502.

Attaluri, A., Ma, R., and Zhu, L., 2011b, "Using MicroCT Imaging Technique to Quantify Heat Generation Distribution Induced by Magnetic Nanoparticles for Cancer Treatments," *ASME Journal of Heat Transfer*, **133**(1):011003(1–5).

Aurer, C., and Carpenter, D. O., 1980, "Choroidal Blood Flow as a Heat Dissipating Mechanism in the Macula," *American Journal of Ophthalmology*, **89**:641–646.

Baish, J. W., 1994, "Formulation of a Statistical Model of Heat Transfer in Perfused Tissue," *ASME Journal of Biomechanical Engineering*, **116**:521–527.

Banerjee, R. K., Zhu, L., Gopalakrishnan, P., and Kazmierczak, M. J., 2007, "Influence of Laser Parameters on Selective Retinal Treatment Using Single-Phase Heat Transfer Analyses," *Medical Physics*, **34**(5):1828–1841.

Barberia, E., Maroto, M., Arenas, M., and Silva, C. C., 2008, "A Clinical Study of Caries Diagnosis with a Laser Fluorescence System," *Journal of the American Dental Association,* **139**:572–579.

Bartgis, C., LeBrun, A., Ma, R., and Zhu, L., 2016, "Determination of Time of Death in Forensic Science via a 3-D Whole Body Heat Transfer Model," *Journal of Thermal Biology*, **62**:109–115.

Bazett, H. C., 1941, "Temperature Sense in Men," in *Temperature: Its Measurement and Control in Science and Industry*, New York: Reinhold, pp. 489–501.

Bernard, V., Staffa, E., Mornstein, V., and Bourek, A., 2013, "Infrared Camera Assessment of Skin Surface Temperature—Effect of Emissivity," *Physica Medica*, **29**:583–591.

Borgos, J., 1996, "Laser Doppler Monitoring of Cerebral Blood Flow," *Neurological Research*, **18**:251–255.

Brinck, H., and Werner, J., 1994, "Estimation of the Thermal Effect of Blood Flow in a Branching Countercurrent Network Using a Three-dimensional Vascular Model," *ASME Journal of Biomechanical Engineering*, **116**:324–330.

Camart, J. C., Despretz, D., Prevost, B., Sozanski, J. P., Chive, M., and Pribetich, J., 2000, "New 434 MHz Interstitial Hyperthermia System Monitored by Microwave Radiometry: Theoretical and Experimental Results," *International Journal of Hyperthermia*, **16**:95–111.

Cetas, T. C., Conner, W. G., and Manning, M. R., 1980, "Monitoring of Tissue Temperature During Hyperthermia Therapy," *Annals of the New York Academy of Sciences*, **335**:281–297.

Chan, D. C. F., Kirpotin, D. B., and Bunn, P. A., 1993, "Synthesis and Evaluation of Colloidal Magnetic Iron Oxides for the Site-specific Radio Frequency-induced Hyperthermia of Cancer," *Journal of Magnetism and Magnetic Materials,* **122**:374–378.

Charny, C. K., Hagmann, M. J., and Levin, R. L., 1987, "A Whole Body Thermal Model of Man during Hyperthermia," *IEEE Transactions on Biomedical Engineering*, **34**(5):375–387.

Charny, C. K., Weinbaum, S., and Levin, R. L., 1990, "An Evaluation of the Weinbaum-Jiji Bioheat Equation for Normal and Hyperthermic Conditions," *ASME Journal of Biomechanical Engineering*, **112**:80–87.

Chato, J. 1980, "Heat Transfer to Blood Vessels," *ASME Journal of Biomechanical Engineering*, **102**:110–118.

Chatterjee, I., and Adams, R. E., 1994, "Finite Element Thermal Modeling of the Human Body under Hyperthermia Treatment for Cancer," *International Journal of Computer Applications in Technology*, **7**:151–159.

Chaussy, C., and Thuroff, S., 2001, "Results and Side Effects of High-Intensity Focused Ultrasound in Localized Prostate Cancer," *Journal of Endourology,* **15**:437–440.

Chen, M. M., and Holmes, K. R., 1980, "Microvascular Contributions to Tissue Heat Transfer," *Annals of the New York Academy of Science*, **335**:137–150.

Chu, C. H., Lo, E. C. M., and You, D. S. H., 2010, "Clinical Diagnosis of Fissure Caries with Conventional and Laser-Induced Fluorescence Techniques," *Lasers in Medical Science,* **25**:355–362.

Clark, R. S., Kochanek, P. M., Marion, D. W., Schiding, J. K., White, M., Palmer, A. M., and DeKosky, S. T., 1996, "Mild Posttraumatic Hypothermia Reduces Mortality after Severe Controlled Cortical Impact in Rats," *Journal of Cerebral Blood Flow and Metabolism,* **16**(2):253–261.

Clegg, S. T., and R. B. Roemer, 1993, "Reconstruction of Experimental Hyperthermia Temperature Distributions: Application of State and Parameter Estimation," *ASME Journal of Biomechanical Engineering*, **115**:380–388.

Cosset, J. M., Dutreix, J., Haie, C., Mabire, J. P., and Damia, E., 1986, "Technical Aspects of Interstitial Hyperthermia," in *Recent Results in Cancer Research*, Vol. 101, Berlin, Heidelberg: Springer, pp. 56–60.

Crezee, J., and Lagendijk, J. J. W., 1990, "Experimental Verification of Bioheat Transfer Theories: Measurement of Temperature Profiles Around Large Artificial Vessels in Perfused Tissue," *Physics in Medicine and Biology*, **35**(7):905–923.

Crezee, J., Mooibroek, J., Bos, C. K., and Lagendijk, J. J. W., 1991, "Interstitial Heating: Experiments in Artificially Perfused Bovine Tongues," *Physics in Medicine and Biology*, **36**:823–833.

Devarakonda, S., Bulusu, P., Al-Rjoub, M. F., Bhattacharya, A., and Banerjee, R. K., 2018, "Influence of External Head Cooling on the Head, Core Body, and Blood Temperatures Using 3D Whole Body Model," *International Journal of Numerical Methods for Heat and Fluid Flow*, **28**(10):2491–2504.

Dewhirst, M. W., Prosnitz, L., Thrall, D., Prescott, D., Clegg, S., Charles, C., MacFall, J., Rosner, G., Samulski, T., Gillette, E., and LaRue, S., 1997, "Hyperthermia Treatment of Malignant Diseases: Current Status and a View Toward the Future," *Seminars in Oncology*, **24**(6):616–625.

Dewhirst, M. W., Viglianti, B. L., Lora-Michiels, M., Hanson, M., and Hoopes, P. J., 2003, "Basic Principles of Thermal Dosimetry and Thermal Thresholds for Tissue Damage from Hyperthermia," *International Journal of Hyperthermia*, **19**(3):267–294.

Dorr, L. N., and Hynynen, K., 1992, "The Effects of Tissue Heterogeneities and Large Blood Vessels on the Thermal Exposure Induced by Short High-power Ultrasound Pulses," *International Journal of Hyperthermia*, **8**:45–59.

Engelhart, M., and Kristensen, J. K., 1986, "Raynaud's Phenomenon: Blood Supply to Fingers During Indirect Cooling, Evaluated by Laser Doppler Flowmetry," *Clinical Physiology*, **6**:481–488.

Firorini, A., Fumero, R., and Marchesi, R., 1983, "Cardio-surgical Thermography," *Proceedings of SPIE*, **359**:249.

Flower, R. W., 2002, "Optimizing Treatment of Choroidal Neovascularization Feeder Vessels Associated with Age-Related Macular Degeneration," *American Journal of Ophthalmology*, **134**:228–239.

Fortin, J. P., Gazeau, F., and Wilhelm, C., 2008, "Intracellular Heating of Living Cells through Néel Relaxation of Magnetic Nanoparticles," *European Biophysics Journal,* **37**(2):223–228.

Fu, G., 1995, "A Transient 3-D Mathematical Thermal Model for the Clothed Human," Ph.D. Dissertation, Kansas State University.

Gautherie, M., and Gros, C. M., 1980, "Breast Thermography and Cancer Risk Prediction," *Cancer*, **45**(1):51–56.

Gelet, A., Chapelon, J. Y., Bouvier, R., Rouviere, O., Lyonnet, D., and Dubernard, J. M., 2001, "Transrectal High Intensity Focused Ultrasound for the Treatment of Localized Prostate Cancer: Factors Influencing the Outcome," *European Urology*, **40**:124–129.

Gentill, G. B., Lenocini, M., Trembly, B. S., Schweizer, S. E., 1995, "FDTD Electromagnetic and Thermal Analysis of Interstitial Hyperthermic Applicators: Finite-difference Time-domain," *IEEE Transactions on Biomedical Engineering*, **42**(10):973–980.

Gerweck, L. E., 1977, "Modification of Cell Lethality at Elevated Temperatures: the pH Effect," *Radiation Research*, **70**:224–235.

Gilchrist, R. K., Medal, R., Shorey, W. D., Hanselman, R. C., Parrott, J. C., and Taylor, C. B., 1957, "Selective Inductive Heating of Lymph Nodes," *Annals of Surgery*, **146**:596–606.

Graham, S. J., Chen, L., Leitch, M., Peters, R. D., Bronskill, M. J., Foster, F. S., Henkelman, R. M., and Plewes, D. B., 1999, "Quantifying Tissue Damage due to Focused Ultrasound Heating Observed by MRI," *Magnetic Resonance in Medicine*, **41**(2):321–328.

Griffin, R. J., Ogawa, A., Shakil, A., and Song, C. W., 1998, "Local Hyperthermia Treatment of Solid Tumors: Interplay between Thermal Dose and Physiological Parameters," ASME, HTD-Vol. 362, *Advances in Heat and Mass Transfer in Biological Systems*, pp. 67–69.

Guo, Z., Fan, X., Liu, L., Bian, Z., Gu, C., Zhang, Y., Gu, N., Yang, D., and Zhang, J., 2010, "Achieving High-purity Colloidal Gold Nanoprisms and Their Application as Biosensing Platforms," *Journal of Colloid and Interface Science,* **348**(1):29–36.

Halas, N. J., and West, J. L., 2003, "Nanoshell-Mediated Near-Infrared Thermal Therapy of Tumors under Magnetic Resonance Guidance," *Proceedings of the National Academy of Sciences*, **100**(23):13549–13554.

Hariharan, P., Chang, I, Myers, M., and Banerjee, R. K., 2007a, "Radio Frequency (RF) Ablation in a Realistic Reconstructed Hepatic Tissue," *ASME Journal of Biomechanical Engineering*, **129**:354–364.

Hariharan, P., Myers, M. R., and Banerjee, R. K., 2007b, "HIFU Procedures at Moderate Intensities—Effect of Large Blood Vessels," *Physics in Medicine & Biology*, **52**:3493–3513.

Hartov, A., Colacchio, T. A., Hoopes, P. J., and Strohbehn, J. W., 1994, "The Control Problem in Hyperthermia," ASME HTD-Vol. 288, *Advances in Heat and Mass Transfer in Biological Systems*, pp. 119–126.

Hase, M., Sako, M., Fujii, M., Ueda, E., Nagae, T., Shimizu, T., Hirota, S., and Kono, M., 1989, "Experimental Study of Embolohyperthermia for the Treatment of Liver Tumors by Induction Heating to Ferromagnetic Particles Injected into Tumor Tissue," *Nippon Acta Radiologica,* **49**:1171–1173.

He, Q., Zhu, L., and Weinbaum, S., 2003, "Effect of Blood Flow on Thermal Equilibration and Venous Rewarming," *Annals of Biomedical Engineering*. **31**:659–666.

He, Q., Zhu, L., Weinbaum, S., and Lemons, D. E., 2002, "Experimental Measurements of Temperature Variations along Paired Vessels from 200 to 1000 μm In Diameter in Rat Hind Leg," *ASME Journal of Biomedical Engineering*, **124**:656–661.

Head, J. F., Wang, F., and Elliott R. L., 1993, "Breast Thermography Is a Noninvasive Prognostic Procedure That Predicts Tumor Growth Rate in Breast Cancer Patients," *Annals of New York Academy of Sciences*, **698**:153–158.

Heilmann, A., and Kreibig, U., 2000, "Optical Properties of Embedded Metal Nanoparticles at Low Temperatures," *European Physical Journal Applied Physics*, **10**(3):193–202.

Hergt, R., Hiergeist, R., Zeisberger, M., Glockl, G., Weitschies, W., Ramirez, L. P., Hilger, I., and Kaiser, W. A., 2004, "Enhancement of AC-losses of Magnetic Nanoparticles for Heating Applications," *Journal of Magnetism and Magnetic Materials*, **280**:358–368.

Hilger, I., Andra, W., Hergt, R., Hiergeist, R., Schubert, H., and Kaiser, W. A., 2001, "Electromagnetic Heating of Breast Tumors in Interventional Radiology: In Vitro and In Vivo Studies in Human Cadavers and Mice," *Radiology*, **218**:570–575.

Hilger, I., Hergt, R., and Kaiser, W. A., 2005, "Towards Breast Cancer Treatment by Magnetic Heating," *Journal of Magnetism and Magnetic Materials*, **293**:314–319.

Hirsch, L. R., Stafford, R. J., Bankson, J. A., Sershen, S. R., Rivera, B., Price, R. E., Hazle, J. D., and Holmes, K. R., 1997, "Biological Structures and Heat Transfer," in *Report from the Allerton Workshop on the Future of Biothermal Engineering*, pp.14–37.

Hu, L., Gupta, A., Gore, J. P., and Xu, L. X., 2004, "Effect of Forced Convection on the Skin Thermal Expression of Breast Cancer," *Journal of Biomechanical Engineering*, **126**(2):204–211.

Huang, S. K., Bharati, S., Graham, A. R., Lev, M., Marcus, F. I., and Odell, R. C., 1987, "Closed Chest Catheter Desiccation of the Atrioventricular Junction Using Radiofrequency Energy — A New Method of Catheter Ablation," *Journal of the American College of Cardiology*, **9**:349–358.

Huang, X., Jiang, P., and Tanaka, T., 2011, "A Review of Dielectric Polymer Composites with High Thermal Conductivity," *IEEE Electrical Insulation Magazine*, **27**(4):8–16.

Huikeshoven, M., Koster, P. H., de Borgie, C. A., Beek, J. F., van Gemert, M. J., and van der Horst, C. M., 2007, "Redarkening of Port-Wine Stains 10 Years After Pulsed-Dye-Laser Treatment," *New England Journal of Medicine*, **356**(12):1235–1240.

Izikson, L., Nelson, J. S., and Anderson, R. R., 2009, "Treatment of Hypertrophic and Resistant Port Wine Stains with a 755 nm Laser: A Case Series of 20 Patients," *Lasers in Surgery and Medicine*, **41**(6):427–432.

Jamieson, S. W., Kapelanski, D. P., Sakakibara, N., Manecke, G. R., Thistlethwaite, P. A., Kerr, K. M., Channick, R. N., Fedullo, P. F., and Auger, W. R., 2003, "Pulmonary Endarterectomy: Experience and Lessons Learned in 1,500 Cases," *Annals of Thoracic Surgery*, **76**(5):1457–1462.

Jasim, Z. F., and Handley, J. M., 2007, "Treatment of Pulsed Dye Laser Resistant Port Wine Stain Birthmarks," *Journal of American Academy of Dermatology*, **57**(4), 677–682.

Jia, W, Aguilar, G., Verkruysse, W., Franco, W., and Nelson, J. S., 2006, "Improvement of Port Wine Stain Laser Therapy by Skin Preheating Prior to Cryogen Spray Cooling: A Numerical Simulation," *Lasers in Surgery and Medicine*, **38**:155–162.

Jirtle, R. L., 1988, "Chemical Modification of Tumor Blood Flow," *International Journal of Hyperthermia*, **4**:355–371.

Johannsen, M., Gneveckow, U., Eckelt, L., Feussner, A., Waldofner, N., Scholz, R., Deger, S., Wust, P., Loening, S. A., and Jordan A., 2005a, "Clinical Hyperthermia of Prostate Cancer Using Magnetic Nanoparticles: Presentation of a New Interstitial Technique," *International Journal of Hyperthermia*, **21**:637–647.

Johannsen, M., Thiesen, B., Jordan, A., Taymoorian, K., Gneveckow, U., Waldofner, N., Scholz, R., Koch, M., Lein, M., Jung, K., and Loening, S. A., 2005b, "Magnetic Fluid Hyperthermia (MFH) Reduces Prostate Cancer Growth in the Orthotopic Dunning R3327 Rat Model," *Prostate*, **64**:283–292.

Jones, B. F., 1998, "A Reappraisal of the Use of Infrared Thermal Image Analysis in Medicine," *IEEE Transactions on Medical Imaging*, **17**(6):1019–1027.

Jordan, A., Scholz, R., Maier-Hauff, K., Van Landeghem, F. K., Waldoefner, N., Teichgraeber, U., Pinkernelle, J., Bruhn, H., Neumann, F., Thiesen, B., Von Deimling, A., and Felix, R., 2006, "The Effect of Thermotherapy Using Magnetic Nanoparticles on Rat Malignant Glioma," *Journal of Neuro-Oncology*, **78**:7–14.

Jordan, A., Scholz, R., Wust, P., Fahling, H., Krause, J., Wlodarczyk, W., Sander, B., Vogl, T., and Felix, R., 1997, "Effects of Magnetic Fluid Hyperthermia (MFH) on C3H Mammary Carcinoma in Vivo," *International Journal of Hyperthermia*, **13**(6):587–605.

Kalathil, R. T., D'Souza, G. A., Bhattacharya, A., and Banerjee, R. K., 2016, "Uncertainty Analysis of the Core Body Temperature Under Thermal and Physical Stress Using a Three-Dimensional Whole Body Model," *ASME Journal of Heat Transfer*, **139**:031102(1–10).

Kang, Y., and Taton, T. A., 2005, "Controlling Shell Thickness in Core–Shell Gold Nanoparticles via Surface-Templated Adsorption of Block Copolymer Surfactants," *Macromolecules*, **38**(14):6115–6121.

Kopyov, O., Jacques, D., Duma, C., Buckwalter, G., Kopyov, A., Lieberman, A., and Copcutt, B., 1997, "Microelectrode-guided Posteroventral Medial Radiofrequency Pallidotomy for Parkinson's Disease," *Journal of Neurosurgery*, **87**:52–55.

Lam, J. M. K., Hsiang, J. N. K., and Poon, W. S., 1997, "Monitoring of Autoregulation Using Laser Doppler Flowmetry in Patients with Head Injury," *Journal of Neurosurgery*, **86**:438–455.

Lanuti, M., Sharma, A., Digumarthy, S. R., Wright, C. D., Donahue, D. M., Wain, J. C., Mathisen, D. J., and Shepard, A. O., 2009, "Radiofrequency Ablation for Treatment of Medically Inoperable Stage I Non-small Cell Lung Cancer," *Journal of Thoracic and Cardiovascular Surgery*, **137**:160–166.

Lapayowker, M. S., and Revesz, G., 1980, "Thermography and Ultrasound in Detection and Diagnosis of Breast Cancer," *Cancer*, **46**(4 Suppl):933–938.

LeBrun, A., Ma, R., and Zhu, L., 2016a, "MicroCT Image Based Simulation to Design Heating Protocols in Magnetic Nanoparticle Hyperthermia for Cancer Treatment," *Journal of Thermal Biology*, **62**:129–137.

LeBrun, A., Joglekar, T., Bieberich, C., Ma, R., and Zhu, L., 2016b, "Identification of Infusion Strategy for Achieving Repeatable Nanoparticle Distribution and Quantifiable Thermal Dosage in Magnetic Nanoparticle Hyperthermia," *International Journal of Hyperthermia*, **32**(2):132–143.

LeCarpentier, G. L., Motamedi, M., McMath, L. P., Rastegar, S., and Welch, A. J., 1989, "The Effect of Wavelength on Ablation Mechanism During CW Laser Irradiation: Argon Verses Nd:YAG (1.32 μm)," *Proceedings of the 11th Annual IEEE Engineering in Medicine and Biology Society Conference*, pp. 1209–1210.

Lemons, D. E., Chien, S., Crawshaw, L. I., Weinbaum, S., and Jiji, L. M., 1987, "The Significance of Vessel Size and Type in Vascular Heat Transfer," *American Journal of Physiology*, **253**:R128–R135.

Li, Y., LeBrun, A., Topoleski, L. D. T., and Zhu, L., 2016, "Evaluation of Sensitivity and Accuracy of Infrared Thermography for Melanoma Screening," in *Summer Biomechanics, Bioengineering, & Biotransport Conference*, National Harbor, MD. Paper number SB3C-2016-145.

Liang, X. G., Ge, G. X., Zhang, Y. P., and Wang, G. J., 1991, "A Convenient Method of Measuring the Thermal Conductivity of Biological Tissue," *Physics in Medicine and Biology*, **36**:1599–1605.

Ling, J. X., Hand, J. W., and Young, I. R., 1999, "Effect of the SAR Distribution of a Radio Frequency (RF) Coil on the Temperature Field Within a Human Leg: Numerical Studies," ASME HTD-Vol. 363, *Advances in Heat and Mass Transfer in Biotechnology*, pp. 1–7.

Linhares, M. N., and Tasker, R. R., 2000, "Microelectrode-guided Thalamotomy for Parkinson's Disease," *Neurosurgery*, **46**:390–398.

Link, S., and El-Sayed, M. A., 2000, "Shape and Size Dependence of Radiative, Non-radiative and Photothermal Properties of Gold Nanocrystals," *Journal of International Reviews in Physical Chemistry*, **19**(3):409-453.

Liu, J., Zhu, L., and Xu, L. X., 2000, "Studies on the three-dimensional Temperature Transients in the Canine Prostate during Transurethral Microwave Thermal Therapy," *ASME Journal of Biomechanical Engineering*, **122**:372–379.

Loulou, T., and Scott, E. P., 2000, "2-D Thermal Dose Optimization in High Intensity Focused Ultrasound Treatments Using the Adjoint Method," ASME HTD-Vol. 368/BED-Vol. 47, *Advances in Heat and Mass Transfer in Biotechnology*, pp. 67–71.

Manuchehrabadi, N., Attaluri, A., Cai, H., Edziah, R., Lalanne, E., Bieberich, C., Ma, R., Johnson, A. M., and Zhu, L., 2012, "MicroCT Imaging and In Vivo Temperature Elevations in Implanted Prostatic Tumors in Laser Photothermal Therapy Using Gold Nanorods," *Journal of Nanotechnology in Engineering and Medicine*, **3**(2):021003.

Manuchehrabadi, N., Chen, Y., LeBrun, A., Ma, R., and Zhu, L., 2013a, "Computational Simulation of Temperature Elevations in Tumors Using Monte Carlo Method and Comparison to Experimental Measurements in Laser Photothermal Therapy," *Journal of Biomechanical Engineering*, **135**(12):121007.

Manuchehrabadi, N., Toughiri, R., Bieberich, C., Cai, H., Attaluri, A., Edziah, R., Lalanne, E., Johnson, A. M., Ma, R., and Zhu, L., 2013b, "Treatment Efficacy of Laser Photothermal Therapy Using Gold Nanorods," *International Journal of Biomedical Engineering and Technology,* **12**(2):157–176.

Manuchehrabadi, N., and Zhu, L., 2014, "Development of a Computational Simulation Tool to Design a Protocol for Treating Prostate Tumours Using Transurethral Laser Photothermal Therapy," *International Journal of Hyperthermia*, **30**(6):349–361.

Marion, D. W., Leonov, Y., Ginsberg, M., Katz, L. M., Kochanek, P. M., Lechleuthner, A., Nemoto, E. M., Obrist, W., Safar, P., Sterz, F., Tisherman, S. A., White, R. J., Xiao, F., and Zar, H., 1996, "Resuscitative Hypothermia," *Critical Care Medicine*, **24**(2):S81–S89.

Marion, D. W., Penrod, L. E., Kelsey, S. F., Obrist, W. D., Kochanek, P. M., Palmer, A. M., Wisniewski, S. R., and DeKosky, S. T., 1997, "Treatment of Traumatic Brain Injury with Moderate Hypothermia," *New England Journal of Medicine*, **336**:540–546.

Merello, M., Nouzeilles, M. I., Kuzis, G., Cammarota, A., Sabe, L., Betti, O., Starkstein, S., and Leiguarda, R., 1999, "Unilateral Radiofrequency Lesion versus Electrostimulation of Posteroventral Pallidum: A Prospective Randomized Comparison," *Movement Disorders*, **14**:50–56.

Mie, G., 1908, "Beiträge zur Optik Trüber Medien, Speziell Kolloidaler Metallösungen," *Annalen der Physik*, **330**(3):377–445.

Moritz, A. R., and Henriques, F. C., 1947, "Studies of Thermal Injury I: The Conduction of Heat to and through Skin and the Temperature Attained Therein: A Theoretical and an Experimental Investigation," *American Journal of Pathology*, **23**(4):530–549.

Moros, E. G., and Fan, X., 1998, "Model for Ultrasonic Heating of Chest Wall Recurrences," ASME HTD-Vol. 362/BED-Vol. 40, *Advances in Heat and Mass Transfer in Biotechnology*, pp. 27–33.

Moros, E. G., Fan, X., and Straube, W. L., 1996, "Penetration Depth Control with Dual Frequency Ultrasound," ASME HTD-Vol. 337/BED-Vol. 34, *Advances in Heat and Mass Transfer in Biotechnology*, pp. 59–65.

Matsukawa, T., Ozaki, M., Hanagata, K., Iwashita, H., Miyaji, T., and Kumazawa, T., 1996, "A Comparison of Four Infrared Tympanic Thermometers with Tympanic Membrane Temperatures Measured by Thermocouples," *Canadian Journal of Anesthesia*, **43**(12):1224–1228.

Myrhage, R., and Eriksson, E., 1984, "Arrangement of the Vascular Bed in Different Types of Skeletal Muscles,". *Progress in Applied Microcirculation*, **5**:1–14.

Myroshnychenko, V., Rodriguez-Fernandez, J., Pastoriza-Santos, I., Funston, A. M., Novo, C., Mulvaney, P., Liz-Marzan, L. M., and Garcia de Abajo, F. J., 2008, "Modeling the Optical Response of Gold Nanoparticles," *Chemical Society Reviews*, **37**(9):1792–1805.

Nadobny, J., Klopfleisch, R., Brinker, G., and Stoltenburg-Didinger, G., 2015, "Experimental Investigation and Histopathological Identification of Acute Thermal Damage in Skeletal Porcine Muscle in Relation to Whole-Body SAR, Maximum Temperature, and CEM43°C due to RF Irradiation in an MR Body Coil of Birdcage Type at 123 MHz," *International Journal of Hyperthermia*, **31**(4): 409–420.

Nakayama, A., and Kuwahara, F., 2008, "A General Bioheat Transfer Model Based on the Theory of Porous Media," *International Journal of Heat and Mass Transfer*, **51**:3190–3199.

Nath, S., DiMarco, J. P., and Haines, D. E., 1994, "Basic Aspect of Radio frequency Catheter Ablation," *Journal of Cardiovascular Electrophysiology*, **5**:863–876.

Nath, S., and Haines, D. E., 1995, "Biophysics and Pathology of Catheter Energy Delivery System," *Progress in Cardiovascular Diseases*, **37**(4):185–204.

Nussmeier, N. A., 2002, "A Review of Risk Factors for Adverse Neurological Outcome after Cardiac Surgery," *Journal of Extra-corporeal Technology*, **34**:4–10.

Obeid, A. N., Barnett, N. J., Dougherty, G., and Ward, G., 1990, "A Critical Review of Laser Doppler Flowmetry," *Journal of Medical Engineering and Technology*, **14**(5):178–181.

Oh, M. Y., Hodaie, M., Kim, S. H., Alkhani, A., Lang, A. E., and Lozano, A. M., 2001, "Deep Brain Stimulator Electrodes Used for Lesioning: Proof of Principle," *Neurosurgery*, **49**:363–369.

Ohashi, M., Matsui, T., Sekida, T., Idogawa, H., Matsugi, W., Oyama, M., Naruse, K., Kotera, Y., Yoshino, K., Ikeda, Y., and Iuchi, K., 1998, "Anti-tumor Activity of a Novel Tumor Blood Flow Inhibitor, KB-R8498," *Proceedings of the American Association for Cancer Research*, Vol. 39, pp. 312.

Overgaard, J., 1976, "Influence of Extracellular pH on the Viability and Morphology of Tumor Cells Exposed to Hyperthermia," *Journal of National Cancer Institute*, **56**:1243–1250.

Overgaard, J., 1987, "Some Problems Related to the Clinical Use of Thermal Isoeffect Doses," *International Journal of Hyperthermia*, **3**:329–336.

Parker, D. L., Smith, V., Sheldon, P., Crooks, L. E., and Fussell, L., 1982, "Temperature Distribution Measurements in Two-dimensional NMR Imaging," *Medical Physics*, **10**(3):321–325.

Parker, W. J., Jenkins, R. J., Butler, C. P., and Abbott, G. L., 1961, "Flash Method of Determining Thermal Diffusivity, Heat Capacity, and Thermal Conductivity," *Journal of Applied Physics*, **32**:1679–1684.

Patel, N. K., Heywood, P., O'Sullivan, K., McCarter, R., Love, S., and Gill, S. S., 2003, "Unilateral Subthalamotomy in the Treatment of Parkinson's Disease," *Brain*, **126**:1136–1145.

Paul, A. K., Zachariah, S., Zhu, L., and Banerjee, R. K., 2015, "Predicting Core Body Temperature during Cold Water Immersion and Exercise: Application of a Tissue-Blood Interactive Whole Body Model," *Numerical Heat Transfer*, **68**(6):598–618.

Pennes, H. H., 1948, "Analysis of Tissue and Arterial Blood Temperatures in the Resting Human Forearm," *Journal of Applied Physiology*, **1**:93–122.

Prescott, D. M., Samulski, T. V., Dewhirst, M. W., Page, R. L., Thrall, D. E., Dodge, R. K., and Oleson, J. R., 1992, "Use of Nitroprusside to Increase Tissue Temperature During Local Hyperthermia in Normal and Tumor-bearing Dogs," *International Journal of Radiation Oncology, Biology, Physics*, **23**:377–385.

Raaymakers, B. W., Crezee, J., and Lagendijk, J. J. W., 2000, "Modeling Individual Temperature Profiles from an Isolated Perfused Bovine Tongue," *Physics in Medicine and Biology,* **45**:765–780.

Rand, R. W., Snow, H. D., Elliott, D. G., and Snyder, M., 1981, "Thermomagnetic Surgery for Cancer," *Applied Biochemistry and Biotechnology.*, **6**:265–272.

Reinhold, H. S., and Endrich, B., 1986, "Tumor Microcirculation as a Target for Hyperthermia," *International Journal of Hyperthermia*, **2**:111–137.

Reith, J., Jorgensen, H. S., Pedersen, P. M., Nakayama, H., Raaschou, H. O., Jeppesen, L. L., and Olsen, T. S., 1996, "Body Temperature in Acute Stroke: Relation to Stroke Severity, Infarct Size, Mortality, and Outcome," *Lancet,* **347**:422–425.

Roemer, R. B., 1990, "Thermal Dosimetry," in *Thermal Dosimetry and Treatment Planning*, edited by M. Gaytherie, Berlin: Springer, pp. 119–214.

Rylander, M. N., Feng, Y., Zhang, Y., Bass, J., Stafford, R. J., Volgin, A., Hazle, J. D., and Diller, K. R., 2006, "Optimizing Heat Shock Protein Expression Induced by Prostate Cancer Laser Therapy through Predictive Computational Models," *Journal of Biomedical Optics*, **11**(4):041113.

Ryu, S., Brown, S. L., Kim, S. H., Khil, M. S., and Kim, J. H., 1996, "Preferential Radiosensitization of Human Prostatic Carcinoma Cells by Mild Hyperthermia," *International Journal of Radiation Oncology, Biology, Physics*, **34**(1):133–138.

Salloum, M., Ma, R., Weeks, D., and Zhu, L., 2008a, "Controlling Nanoparticle Delivery in Magnetic Nanoparticle Hyperthermia for Cancer Treatment: Experimental Study in Agarose Gel," *International Journal of Hyperthermia*, **24**(4):337–345.

Salloum, M., Ma, R., and Zhu, L., 2008b, "An In-Vivo Experimental Study of the Temperature Elevation in Animal Tissue during Magnetic Nanoparticle Hyperthermia," *International Journal of Hyperthermia*, **24**(7):589–601.

Salloum, M. D., 2005, "A New Transient Bioheat Model of the Human Body and Its Integration to Clothing Models," M.S. Thesis, American University of Beirut.

Sapareto, S. A., and Dewey, W. C., 1984, "Thermal Dose Determination in Cancer Therapy," *International Journal of Radiation Oncology, Biology, Physics,* **10**(6):787–800.

Sapozink, M. D., Cetas, T., Corry, P. M., Egger, M. J., Fessenden, P., and The NCI Hyperthermia Equipment Evaluation Contractors' Group, 1988, "Introduction to Hyperthermia Device Evaluation," *International Journal of Hyperthermia*, **4**:1–15.

Schabauer, A. M. A., and Rooke, T. W., 1994, "Cutaneous Laser Doppler Flowmetry: Applications and Findings," *Mayo Clinic Proceedings*, **69**:564–574.

Scheinman, M. M., Morady, F., Hess, D. S., and Gonzalez, R., 1982, "Catheter-induced Ablation of the Atrioventricular Junction to Control Refractory Supraventricular Arrhythmias," *JAMA*, **248**:851–855.

Shibasaki, M., Kondo, N., Tominaga, H., Aoki, K., Hasegawa, E., Idota, Y., and Moriwaki, T., 1998, "Continuous Measurement of Tympanic Temperature with a New Infrared Method Using an Optical Fiber," *Journal of Applied Physiology*, **85**(3):921–926.

Shrivastava, D., and Vaughan, J. T., 2009, "A Generic Bioheat Transfer Thermal Model for a Perfused Tissue," *Journal of Biomechanical Engineering*, **131**:074506(1–5).

Smith, C. E., 1991, "A Transient Three-Dimensional Model of the Thermal System," Ph.D. Dissertation, Kansas State University.

Smits, G. J., Roman, R. J., and Lombard, J. H., 1986, "Evaluation of Laser-Doppler Flowmetry as a Measure of Tissue Blood Flow," *Journal of Applied Physiology*, **61**(2):666–672.

Song, C. W., 1984, "Effect of Local Hyperthermia on Blood Flow and Microenvironment: A Review," *Cancer Research*, **44**:4721s–4730s.

Song, C. W., 1991, "Role of Blood Flow in Hyperthermia," in *Hyperthermia and Oncology*, M. Urano and E. B. Douple, eds., VSP Publishers, Utrecht, The Netherlands, Vol. 3, pp. 275–315.

Song, C. W., Kim, G. E., Lyons, J. C., Makepeace, C. M., Griffin, R. J., Rao, G. H., and Cragon, E. J. Jr., 1994, "Thermosensitization by Increasing Intracellular Acidity with Amiloride and its Analogs," *International Journal of Radiation Oncology, Biology, Physics*, **30**:1161–1169.

Stauffer, P. R., Rossetto, F., Leoncini, M., and Gentilli, G. B., 1998, "Radiation Patterns of Dual Concentric Conductor Microstrip Antennas for Superficial Hyperthermia," *IEEE Transactions on Biomedical Engineering*, **45**(5):605–613.

Stoy, R. D., Foster, K. R., and Schwan, H. P., 1982, "Dielectric Properties of Mammalian Tissues from 0.1 to 100 MHz: A Summary of Recent Data," *Physics in Medicine and Biology*, **27**:501–513.

Strohbehn, J. W., 1984, "Calculation of Absorbed Power in Tissue for Various Hyperthermia Devices," *Cancer Research* (Suppl) **44**:4781s–4787s.

Su, P. C., Tseng, H-M., Liu, H-M., Yen, R-F., and Liou, H-H., 2002, "Subthalamotomy for Advanced Parkinson's Disease," *Journal of Neurosurgery*, **97**:598–606.

Thomsen, S., 1991, "Pathologic Analysis of Photothermal and Photomechanical Effects of Laser-Tissue Interactions," *Photochemistry and Photobiology*, **53**:825–835.

Torres, J. H., Motamedi, M., and Welch, A. J., 1990, "Disparate Absorption of Argon Laser Radiation by Fibrous Verses Fatty Plaque: Implications for Laser Angioplasty," *Lasers in Surgery and Medicine*, **10**:149–157.

Vesnovsky, O., Li, Y., Topoleski, L. D. T., and Zhu, L., 2017, "Modeling of Differences between Body Core and Forehead Temperatures Measured by Infrared Thermometers," *ASME 2017 Design of Medical Devices Conference*, #DMD2017-3439, April 2017, Minneapolis, MN.

Wagner, K. R., and Zuccarello, M., 2005, "Local Brain Hypothermia for Neuroprotection in Stroke Treatment and Aneurysm Repair," *Neurological Research*, **27**:238–245.

Wang, Y., and Zhu, L., 2007, "Selective Brain Hypothermia Induced by an Interstitial Cooling Device in Human Neck: Theoretical Analyses," *European Journal of Applied Physiology*, **101**(1):31–40.

Wang, Y., Zhu, L., and Rosengart, A. J., 2008, "Targeted Brain Hypothermia Induced by an Interstitial Cooling Device in the Rat Neck: Experimental Study and Model Validation," *International Journal of Heat and Mass Transfer*, **51**:5662–5670.

Wass, C. T., Lanier, W. L., Hofer, R. E., Scheithauer, B. W., and Andrews, A. G., 1995, "Temperature Changes of ≥1°C Alter Functional Neurological Outcome and Histopathology in a Canine Model of Complete Cerebral Ischemia," *Anesthesia,* **83**:325–335.

Weinbaum, S., and Jiji, L. M., 1985, "A New Simplified Bioheat Equation for the Effect of Blood Flow on Local Average Tissue Temperature," *ASME Journal of Biomechanical Engineering*, **107**:131–139.

Weinbaum, S., Jiji, L. M., and Lemons, D. E., 1984, "Theory and Experiment for the Effect of Vascular Microstructure on Surface Tissue Heat Transfer—Part I: Anatomical Foundation and Model Conceptualization," *ASME Journal of Biomechanical Engineering,* **106**:321–330.

Weinbaum, S., Xu, L. X., Zhu, L., and Ekpene, A., 1997, "A New Fundamental Bioheat Equation for Muscle Tissue: Part I—Blood Perfusion Term," *ASME Journal of Biomechanical Engineering*, **119**:278–288.

Westcott, S. L., Oldenburg, S. J., Lee, T. R., and Halas, N. J., 1998, "Formation and Adsorption of Clusters of Gold Nanoparticles onto Functionalized Silica Nanoparticle Surfaces," *Langmuir: the ACS Journal of Surfaces and Colloids*, **14**(19):5396–5401.

Whitmore, R. L., 1968, *Rheology of Circulation*, Pergamon Press, London.

Whelan, W. M., and Wyman, D. R., 1999, "A Model of Tissue Charring During Interstitial Laser Photocoagulation: Estimation of the Char Temperature," ASME HTD-Vol. 363/BED-Vol. 44, *Advances in Heat and Mass Transfer in Biotechnology*, pp. 103–107.

Wissler, E. H., 1985, "Mathematical Simulation of Human Thermal Behavior Using Whole Body Models," in *Heat and Mass Transfer in Medicine and Biology*, Chapter 13, pp. 325–373, New York: Plenum Press.

Wissler, E. H., 1998, "Pennes' 1948 Paper Revisited," *Journal of Applied Physiology*, **85**:35–41.

Wong, T. Z., Jonsson, E., Hoopes, P. J., Trembly, B. S., Heaney, J. A., Douple, E. B., and Coughlin, C. T., 1993, "A Coaxial Microwave Applicator for Transurethral Hyperthermia of the Prostate," *The Prostate*, **22**:125–138.

Wonnell, T. L., Stauffer, P. R., and Langberg, J. J., 1992, "Evaluation of Microwave and Radio Frequency Catheter Ablation in a Myocardium-equivalent Phantom Model," *IEEE Transactions on Biomedical Engineering*, **39**:1086–1095.

Xu, L. X., and Anderson, G. T., 1999, "Techniques for Measuring Blood Flow in the Microvascular Circulation," in *Biofluid Methods and Techniques in Vascular, Cardiovascular, and Pulmonary Systems*, Vol. 4, Chapter 5, Newark, NJ: Gordon and Breach Science Publisher.

Xu, L. X., Chen, M. M., Holmes, K. R., and Arkin, H., 1991, "The Theoretical Evaluation of the Pennes, the Chen-Holmes and the Weinbaum-Jiji Bioheat Transfer Models in the Pig Renal Cortex," ASME WAM, Atlanta, HTD-Vol. 189, pp. 15–22.

Xu, L. X., Chen, M. M., Holmes, K. R., and Arkin, H., 1993, "Theoretical Analysis of the Large Blood Vessel Influence on the Local Tissue Temperature Decay after Pulse Heating," *ASME Journal of Biomechanical Engineering*, **115**:175–179.

Xu, L. X., Zhu, L., and Holmes, K. R., 1998, "Thermoregulation in the Canine Prostate during Transurethral Microwave Hyperthermia, Part I: Temperature Response," *International Journal of Hyperthermia*, **14**(1):29–37.

Yavuz, M. S., Cheng, Y., Chen, J., Cobley, C. M., Zhang, Q., Rycenga, M., Xie, J., Kim, C., Song, K. H., Schwartz, A. G., Wang, L. V., and Xia, Y., 2009, "Gold Nanocages Covered by Smart Polymers for Controlled Release with Near-Infrared Light," *Nature Mater*, **8**(12):935–939.

Zhu, L., Banerjee, R. K., Salloum, M., Bachmann, A. J., and Flower, R. W., 2008, "Temperature Distribution during ICG Dye-enhanced Laser Photocoagulation of Feeder Vessels in Treatment of AMD-related Choroidal Neovascularization (CNV)," *ASME Journal of Biomechanical Engineering*, **130**(3):031010(1–10).

Zhu, L., He, Q., Xu, L. X., and Weinbaum, S., 2002, "A New Fundamental Bioheat Equation for Muscle Tissue: Part II—Temperature of SAV Vessels," *ASME Journal of Biomechanical Engineering*, **124**:121–132.

Zhu, L., Lemons, D. E., and Weinbaum, S., 1995, "A New Approach for Prediction the Enhancement in the Effective Conductivity of Perfused Muscle Tissue Due to Hyperthermia," *Annals of Biomedical Engineering*, **23**:1–12.

Zhu, L., Pang, L., and Xu, L. X., 2005, "Simultaneous Measurements of Local Tissue Temperature and Blood Perfusion Rate in the Canine Prostate during Radio Frequency Thermal Therapy," *Biomechanics and Modeling in Mechanobiology*, **4**(1):1–9.

Zhu, L., Schappeler, T., Cordero-Tumangday, C., and Rosengart, A. J., 2009a, "Thermal Interactions between Blood and Tissue: Development of a Theoretical Approach in Predicting Body Temperature during Blood Cooling/Rewarming," *Advances in Numerical Heat Transfer*, **3**:197–219.

Zhu, L., Tolba, M., Arola, D., Salloum, M., and Meza, F., 2009b, "Evaluation of Effectiveness of Er,Cr:YSGG Laser for Root Canal Disinfection: Theoretical Simulation of Temperature Elevations in Root Dentin," *Journal of Biomechanical Engineering*, **131**(7):071004(1–8).

Zhu, L., Weinbaum, S., and Lemons, D. E., 1996a, "Microvascular Thermal Equilibration in Rat Cremaster Muscle," *Annals of Biomedical Engineering*, **24**:109–123.

Zhu, L., and Xu, L. X., 1999, "Evaluation of the Effectiveness of Transurethral Radio Frequency Hyperthermia in the Canine Prostate: Temperature Distribution Analysis," *ASME Journal of Biomechanical Engineering*, **121**(6):584–590.

Zhu, L., Xu, L. X., and Chencinski, N., 1998, "Quantification of the 3-D Electromagnetic Power Absorption Rate in Tissue During Transurethral Prostatic Microwave Thermotherapy Using Heat Transfer Model," *IEEE Transactions on Biomedical Engineering*, **45**(9):1163–1172.

Zhu, L., Xu, L. X., Yuan, D. Y., and Rudie, E. N., 1996b, "Electromagnetic (EM) Quantification of the Microwave Antenna for the Transurethral Prostatic Thermotherapy," ASME HTD-Vol. 337/BED-Vol. 34, *Advances in Heat and Mass Transfer in Biotechnology*, pp. 17–20.

Zou, Y.-P., Li, W.-M., Zheng, F., Li, F.-C., Huang, H., Du, J.-D., and Liu, H.-R., 2010, "Intraoperative Radiofrequency Ablation Combined with 125 Iodine Seed Implantation for Unresectable Pancreatic Cancer," *World Journal of Gastroenterology*, **16**:5104–5110.

CHAPTER 5

PHYSICAL AND FLOW PROPERTIES OF BLOOD

David Elad and Shmuel Einav
Tel Aviv University, Tel Aviv, Israel

5.1 PHYSIOLOGY OF THE CIRCULATORY SYSTEM

The circulatory transport system is responsible for oxygen and nutrient supply to all body tissues and removal of waste products. The discovery of the circulation of blood in the human body is related to William Harvey (1578–1657). The circulatory system consists of the *heart*—the pump that generates the pressure gradients needed to drive blood to all body tissues, the *blood vessels*—the delivery routes, and the *blood*—the transport medium for the delivered materials. The blood travels continuously through two separate loops; both originate and terminate at the heart. The *pulmonary circulation* carries blood between the heart and the lungs, whereas the *systemic circulation* carries blood between the heart and all other organs and body tissues (Fig. 5.1). In both systems blood is transported in the vascular bed because of a pressure gradient through the following subdivisions: arteries, arterioles, capillaries, venules, and veins. The *cardiac cycle* is composed of the *diastole*, during which the ventricles are filling with blood, and the *systole*, during which the ventricles are actively contracting and pumping blood out of the heart (Martini, 1995; Thibodeau and Patton, 1999).

The total blood volume is unevenly distributed. About 84 percent of the entire blood volume is in the systemic circulation, with 64 percent in the veins, 13 percent in the arteries, and 7 percent in the arterioles and capillaries. The heart contains 7 percent of blood volume and the pulmonary vessels 9 percent. At normal resting activities heart rate of an adult is about 75 beats/min with a stroke volume of typically 70 mL/beat. The *cardiac output*, the amount of blood pumped each minute, is thus 5.25 L/min. It declines with age. During intense exercise, heart rate may increase to 150 beats/min and stroke volume to 130 mL/beat, providing a cardiac output of about 20 L/min. Under normal conditions the distribution of blood flow to the various organs is brain, 14 percent; heart, 4 percent; kidneys, 22 percent; liver, 27 percent; inactive muscles, 15 percent; bones, 5 percent; skin, 6 percent; bronchi, 2 percent. The averaged blood velocity in the aorta (cross-sectional

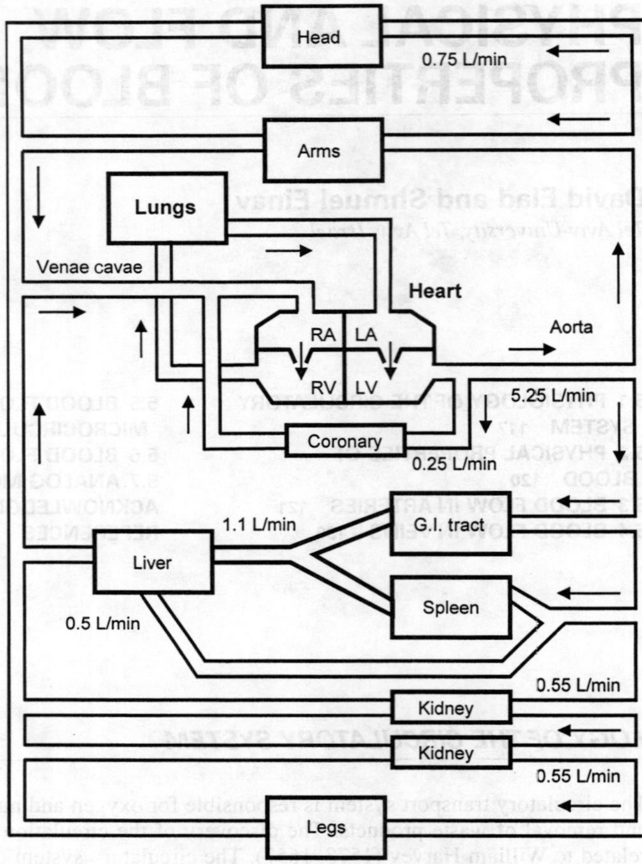

FIGURE 5.1 General organization of the circulatory system with averaged values of normal blood flow to major organs.

area of 2.5 cm^2) is 33 cm/s, while in the capillaries (cross-sectional area of 2500 cm^2) it is about 0.3 mm/s. The blood remains in the capillaries 1 to 3 seconds (Guyton and Hall, 1996; Saladin, 2001).

At normal conditions, the pulsatile pumping of the heart is inducing an arterial pressure that fluctuates between the systolic pressure of 120 mmHg and the diastolic pressure of 80 mmHg (Fig. 5.2). The pressure in the systematic capillaries varies between 35 mmHg near the arterioles to 10 mmHg near the venous end, with a functional average of about 17 mmHg. When blood terminates through the venae cavae into the right atrium of the heart, its pressure is about 0 mmHg. When the heart ejects blood into the aorta, a pressure pulse is transmitted through the arterial system. The traveling velocity of the pressure pulse increases as the vessel's compliance decreases; in the aorta it is 3 to 5 m/s, in the large arteries 7 to 10 m/s, and in small arteries 15 to 35 m/s. Figure 5.3 depicts an example of the variations in the velocity and pressure waves as the pulse wave travels toward peripheral arteries (Caro et al., 1978; Fung, 1984).

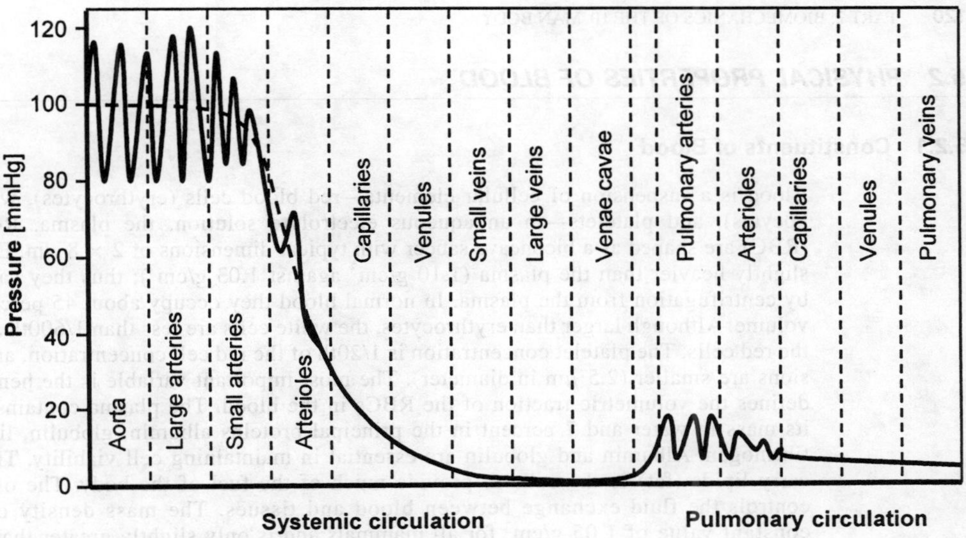

FIGURE 5.2 Variation of blood pressure in the circulatory system.

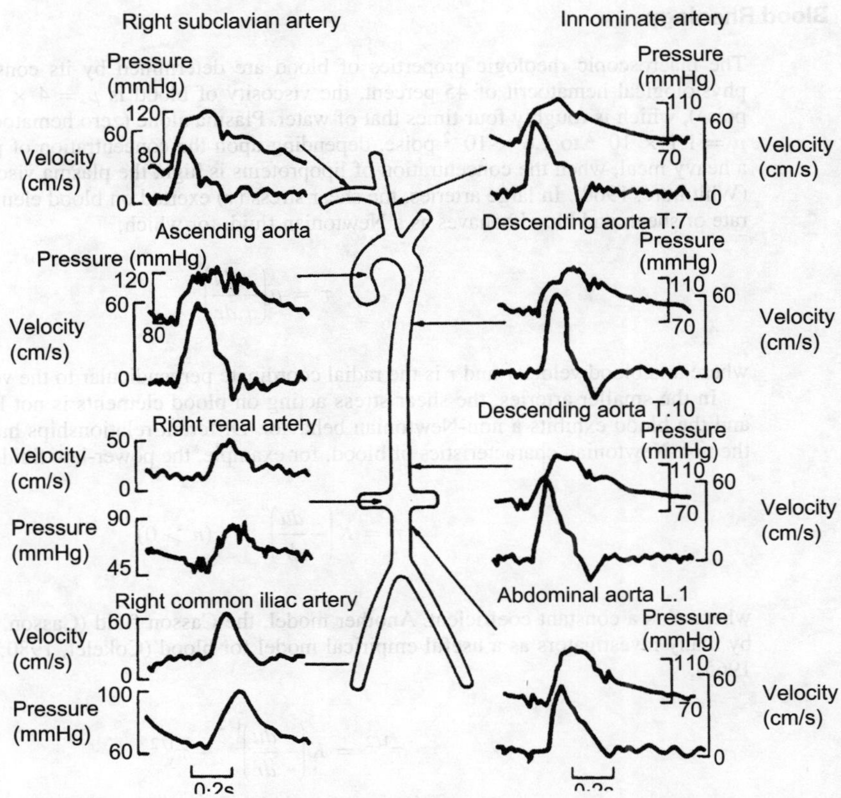

FIGURE 5.3 Pressure and flow waveforms in different arteries of the human arterial tree. [*From Mills et al. (1970) by permission.*]

5.2 PHYSICAL PROPERTIES OF BLOOD

5.2.1 Constituents of Blood

Blood is a suspension of cellular elements—red blood cells (erythrocytes), white cells (leukocytes), and platelets—in an aqueous electrolyte solution, the plasma. Red blood cells (RBC) are shaped as a biconcave saucer with typical dimensions of 2×8 μm. Erythrocytes are slightly heavier than the plasma (1.10 g/cm^3 against 1.03 g/cm^3); thus they can be separated by centrifugation from the plasma. In normal blood they occupy about 45 percent of the total volume. Although larger than erythrocytes, the white cells are less than 1/600th as numerous as the red cells. The platelet concentration is 1/20th of the red cell concentration, and their dimensions are smaller (2.5 μm in diameter). The most important variable is the hematocrit, which defines the volumetric fraction of the RBCs in the blood. The plasma contains 90 percent of its mass in water and 7 percent in the principal proteins albumin, globulin, lipoprotein, and fibrinogen. Albumin and globulin are essential in maintaining cell viability. The lipoproteins carry lipids (fat) to the cells to provide much of the fuel of the body. The osmotic balance controls the fluid exchange between blood and tissues. The mass density of blood has a constant value of 1.05 g/cm^3 for all mammals and is only slightly greater than that of water at room temperature (about 1 g/cm^3).

5.2.2 Blood Rheology

The macroscopic rheologic properties of blood are determined by its constituents. At a normal physiological hematocrit of 45 percent, the viscosity of blood is $\mu = 4 \times 10^{-2}$ dyne $\cdot$ s/cm^2 (or poise), which is roughly four times that of water. Plasma alone (zero hematocrit) has a viscosity of $\mu = 1.1 \times 10^{-2}$ to 1.6×10^{-2} poise, depending upon the concentration of plasma proteins. After a heavy meal, when the concentration of lipoproteins is high, the plasma viscosity is quite elevated (Whitmore, 1968). In large arteries, the shear stress (τ) exerted on blood elements is linear with the rate of shear, and blood behaves as a Newtonian fluid, for which,

$$\tau = \mu\left(-\frac{du}{dr}\right) \tag{5.1}$$

where u is blood velocity and r is the radial coordinate perpendicular to the vessel wall.

In the smaller arteries, the shear stress acting on blood elements is not linear with shear rate, and the blood exhibits a non-Newtonian behavior. Different relationships have been proposed for the non-Newtonian characteristics of blood, for example, the power-law fluid,

$$\tau = K\left(-\frac{du}{dr}\right)^n \quad (n > 0) \tag{5.2}$$

where K is a constant coefficient. Another model, the Casson fluid (Casson, 1959), was proposed by many investigators as a useful empirical model for blood (Cokelet, 1980; Charm and Kurland, 1965),

$$\tau^{1/2} = K\left(-\frac{du}{dr}\right)^{1/2} + \tau_y^{1/2} \tag{5.3}$$

where τ_y is the fluid yield stress.

5.3 BLOOD FLOW IN ARTERIES

5.3.1 Introduction

The aorta and arteries have a low resistance to blood flow compared with the arterioles and capillaries. When the ventricle contracts, a volume of blood is rapidly ejected into the arterial vessels. Since the outflow to the arteriole is relatively slow because of their high resistance to flow, the arteries are inflated to accommodate the extra blood volume. During diastole, the elastic recoil of the arteries forces the blood out into the arterioles. Thus, the elastic properties of the arteries help to convert the pulsatile flow of blood from the heart into a more continuous flow through the rest of the circulation. Hemodynamics is a term used to describe the mechanisms that affect the dynamics of blood circulation.

An accurate model of blood flow in the arteries would include the following realistic features:

1. The flow is pulsatile, with a time history containing major frequency components up to the eighth harmonic of the heart period.
2. The arteries are elastic and tapered tubes.
3. The geometry of the arteries is complex and includes tapered, curved, and branching tubes.
4. In small arteries, the viscosity depends upon vessel radius and shear rate.

Such a complex model has never been accomplished. But each of the features above has been "isolated," and qualitative if not quantitative models have been derived. As is so often the case in the engineering analysis of a complex system, the model derived is a function of the major phenomena one wishes to illustrate.

The general time-dependent governing equations of fluid flow in a straight cylindrical tube are given by the continuity and the Navier-Stokes equations in cylindrical coordinates,

$$\frac{\partial v}{\partial r} + \frac{v}{r} + \frac{\partial u}{\partial z} = 0 \tag{5.4}$$

$$\frac{\partial u}{\partial t} + v\frac{\partial u}{\partial r} + u\frac{\partial u}{\partial z} = F_z - \frac{1}{\rho}\frac{\partial P}{\partial z} + \frac{\mu}{\rho}\left(\frac{\partial^2 u}{\partial r^2} + \frac{1}{r}\frac{\partial u}{\partial r} + \frac{\partial^2 u}{\partial z^2}\right) \tag{5.5}$$

$$\frac{\partial v}{\partial t} + v\frac{\partial v}{\partial r} + u\frac{\partial v}{\partial z} = F_r - \frac{1}{\rho}\frac{\partial P}{\partial r} + \frac{\mu}{\rho}\left(\frac{\partial^2 v}{\partial r^2} + \frac{1}{r}\frac{\partial v}{\partial r} - \frac{v}{r^2} + \frac{\partial^2 v}{\partial z^2}\right) \tag{5.6}$$

Here, u and v are the axial and radial components of the fluid velocity, r and z are the radial and axial coordinates, and ρ and μ are the fluid density and viscosity, respectively. Equations (5.5) and (5.6) are the momentum balance equations in the z and r directions.

5.3.2 Steady Flow

The simplest model of steady laminar flow in a uniform circular cylinder is known as the Hagen-Poiseuille flow. For axisymmetric flow in a circular tube of internal radius R_0 and length l, the boundary conditions are

$$u(r = R_0) = 0 \quad \text{and} \quad \frac{\partial u}{\partial r}(r = 0) = 0 \tag{5.7}$$

For a uniform pressure gradient (ΔP) along a tube, we get the parabolic Poiseuille solution

$$u(r) = -\frac{\Delta P}{4\mu l}\left(R_0^2 - r^2\right) \tag{5.8}$$

The maximal velocity $u_{max} = (R_0)^2\ \Delta P/4\mu l$ is obtained at $r = 0$.

The Poiseuille equation indicates that the pressure gradient ΔP required to produce a volumetric flow $Q = uA$ increases in proportion to Q. Accordingly, the vascular resistance R will be defined as

$$R = \frac{\Delta P}{Q} \tag{5.9}$$

If the flow is measured in cm^3/s and P in dyn/cm^2, the units of R are dyn · s/cm^5. If pressure is measured in mmHg and flow in cm^3/s, resistance is expressed in "peripheral resistance units," or PRU.

The arteries are composed of elastin and collagen fibers and smooth muscles in a complex circumferential organization with a variable helix. Accordingly, the arteries are compliant vessels, and their wall stiffness increases with deformation, as in all other connective tissues. Because of their ability to expand as transmural pressure increases, blood vessels may function to store blood volume under pressure. In this sense, they function as capacitance elements, similar to storage tanks. The linear relationship between the volume V and the pressure defines the capacitance of the storage element, or the vascular capacitance:

$$C = \frac{dV}{dP} \tag{5.10}$$

Note that the capacitance (or compliance) decreases with increasing pressure, and also decreases with age. Veins have a much larger capacitance than arteries and, in fact, are often referred to as capacitance or storage vessels.

Another simple and useful expression is the arterial compliance per unit length, C_u, that can be derived when the tube cross-sectional area A is related to the internal pressure $A = A(P, z)$. For a thin-wall elastic tube (with internal radius R_0 and wall thickness h), which is made of a Hookean material (with Young modulus E), one can obtain the following useful relation,

$$C_u \equiv \frac{dC}{dz} \approx \frac{2\pi R_0^3}{hE} \tag{5.11}$$

5.3.3 Wave Propagation in Arteries

Arterial pulse propagation varies along the circulatory system as a result of the complex geometry and nonuniform structure of the arteries. In order to learn the basic facts of arterial pulse characteristics, we assumed an idealized case of an infinitely long circular elastic tube that contains a homogenous, incompressible, and nonviscous fluid (Fig. 5.4). In order to analyze the velocity of propagation of the arterial pulse, we assume a local perturbation, for example, in the tube cross-sectional area, that propagates along the tube at a constant velocity c.

The one-dimensional equations for conservation of mass and momentum for this idealized case are, respectively (Pedley, 1980; Fung, 1984),

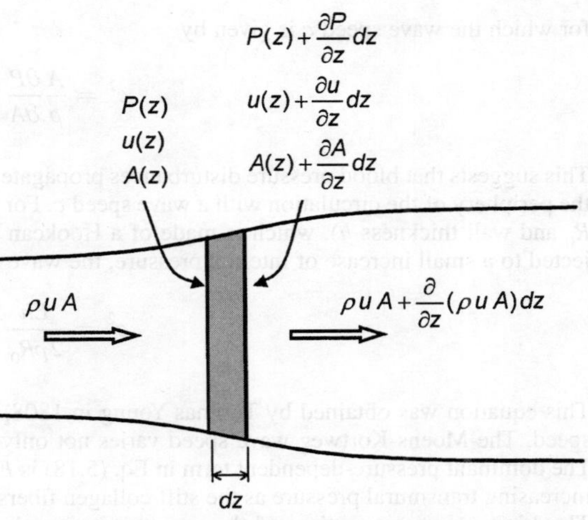

FIGURE 5.4 Cross section of artery showing the change of volume and volume flow.

$$\frac{\partial A}{\partial t} + \frac{\partial}{\partial z}(Au) = 0 \tag{5.12}$$

$$\frac{\partial u}{\partial t} + u\frac{\partial u}{\partial z} + \frac{1}{\rho}\frac{\partial P}{\partial z} = 0 \tag{5.13}$$

where $A(z)$ = tube cross-sectional area
$u(z)$ = uniform axial velocity of blood
$P(z)$ = pressure in the tube
ρ = fluid viscosity
z = axial coordinate
t = time

The elasticity of the tube wall can be prescribed by relationship between the local tube pressure and the cross-sectional area, $P(A)$.

We further assume that the perturbation is small, while the wave length is very large compared with the tube radius. Thus, the nonlinear inertia variables are negligible and the linearized conservation equation of mass and momentum become, respectively,

$$\frac{\partial A}{\partial t} = -A\frac{\partial u}{\partial z} \tag{5.14}$$

$$\frac{\partial u}{\partial t} = -\frac{1}{\rho}\frac{\partial P}{\partial z} \tag{5.15}$$

Next, we differentiate Eq. (5.14) with respect to t and Eq. (5.15) with respect to z, and upon adding the results we obtain the following wave equation:

$$\frac{\partial^2 P}{\partial z^2} = \frac{\rho}{A}\frac{\partial A}{\partial P}\frac{\partial^2 P}{\partial t^2} = c^{-2}\frac{\partial^2 P}{\partial t^2} \tag{5.16}$$

for which the wave speed c is given by

$$c^2 = \frac{A}{\rho}\frac{\partial P}{\partial A} \tag{5.17}$$

This suggests that blood pressure disturbances propagate in a wavelike manner from the heart toward the periphery of the circulation with a wave speed c. For a thin-wall elastic tube (with internal radius R_0 and wall thickness h), which is made of a Hookean material (with Young modulus E) and subjected to a small increase of internal pressure, the wave speed c can be expressed as

$$c^2 = \frac{Eh}{2\rho R_0} \tag{5.18}$$

This equation was obtained by Thomas Young in 1808, and is known as the Moens-Kortweg wave speed. The Moens-Kortweg wave speed varies not only with axial distance but also with pressure. The dominant pressure-dependent term in Eq. (5.18) is E, the modulus of elasticity; it increases with increasing transmural pressure as the stiff collagen fibers bear more of the tension of the artery wall. The high-pressure portion of the pressure wave therefore travels at a higher velocity than the low-pressure portions of the wave, leading to a steepening of the pressure front as it travels from the heart toward the peripheral circulation (Fig. 5.5). Wave speed also varies with age because of the decrease in the elasticity of arteries.

The arteries are not infinitely long, and it is possible for the wave to reflect from the distal end and travel back up the artery to add to new waves emanating from the heart. The sum of all such propagated and reflected waves yields the pressure at each point along the arterial tree. Branching is clearly an important contributor to the measured pressures in the major arteries; there is a partial reflection each time the total cross section of the vessel changes abruptly.

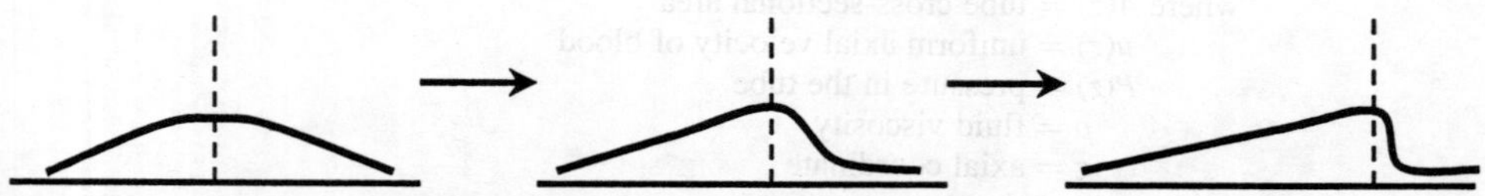

FIGURE 5.5 Steepening of a pressure pulse with distance along an artery.

5.3.4 Pulsatile Flow

Blood flow in the large arteries is driven by the heart, and accordingly it is a pulsating flow. The simplest model for pulsatile flow was developed by Womersley (1955a) for a fully developed oscillatory flow of an incompressible fluid in a rigid, straight circular cylinder. The problem is defined for a sinusoidal pressure gradient composed from sinuses and cosinuses,

$$\frac{\Delta P}{l} = Ke^{i\omega t} \tag{5.19}$$

where the oscillatory frequency is $\omega/2\pi$. Insertion of Eq. (5.19) into Eq. (5.5) yields

$$\frac{\partial^2 u}{\partial r^2} + \frac{1}{r}\frac{\partial u}{\partial r} - \frac{1}{v}\frac{\partial u}{\partial t} = -\frac{K}{\mu}e^{i\omega t} \tag{5.20}$$

The solution is obtained by separation of variables as follows:

$$u(r, t) = W(r) \cdot e^{i\omega t} \tag{5.21}$$

Insertion of Eq. (5.21) into Eq. (5.20) yields the Bessel equation,

$$\frac{d^2W}{dr^2} + \frac{1}{r}\frac{dW}{dr} + \frac{i^3\omega\rho}{\mu}W = -\frac{A}{\mu} \tag{5.22}$$

The solution for Eq. (5.22) is

$$W(r) = \frac{K}{\rho}\frac{1}{i\omega}\left\{1 - \frac{J_0\left(r\sqrt{\frac{\omega}{\nu}} \cdot i^{3/2}\right)}{J_0\left(R\sqrt{\frac{\omega}{\nu}} \cdot i^{3/2}\right)}\right\} \tag{5.23}$$

where J_0 is a Bessel function of order zero of the first kind, $\nu = \mu/\rho$ is the kinematic viscosity, and α is a dimensionless parameter known as the Womersley number and given by

$$\alpha = R_0\sqrt{\frac{\omega}{\nu}} \tag{5.24}$$

When α is large, the velocity profile becomes blunt (Fig. 5.6).

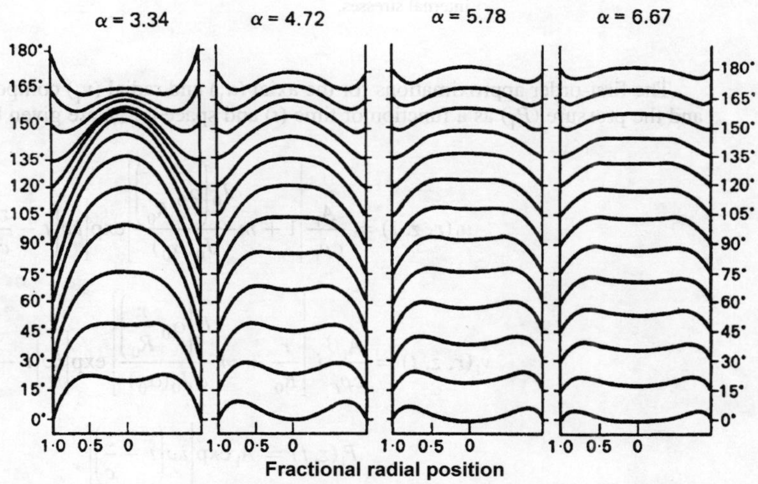

FIGURE 5.6 Theoretical velocity profiles of an oscillating flow resulting from a sinusoidal pressure gradient (cos ωt) in a pipe. α is the Womersley number. Profiles are plotted for intervals of $\Delta\omega t = 15°$. For $\omega t > 180°$, the velocity profiles are of the same form but opposite in sign. [*From Nichols and O'Rourke (1998) by permission.*]

Pulsatile flow in an elastic vessel is very complex, since the tube is able to undergo local deformations in both longitudinal and circumferential directions. The unsteady component of the pulsatile flow is assumed to be induced by propagation of small waves in a pressurized elastic tube. The mathematical approach is based on the classical model for the fluid-structure interaction problem, which describes the dynamic equilibrium between the fluid and the tube thin wall (Womersley, 1955b; Atabek and Lew, 1966). The dynamic equilibrium is expressed by the hydrodynamic equations (Navier-Stokes) for the incompressible fluid flow and the equations of motion for the wall of an elastic tube, which are coupled together by the boundary conditions at the fluid-wall interface. The motion of the liquid is described in a fixed laboratory coordinate system $(\hat{r}, \theta, \hat{z})$, and the dynamic equilibrium of a tube element in its deformed state is expressed in a Lagrangian (material) coordinate system ($\hat{n}$, $\hat{t}$, θ), which is attached to the surface of the tube (Fig. 5.7).

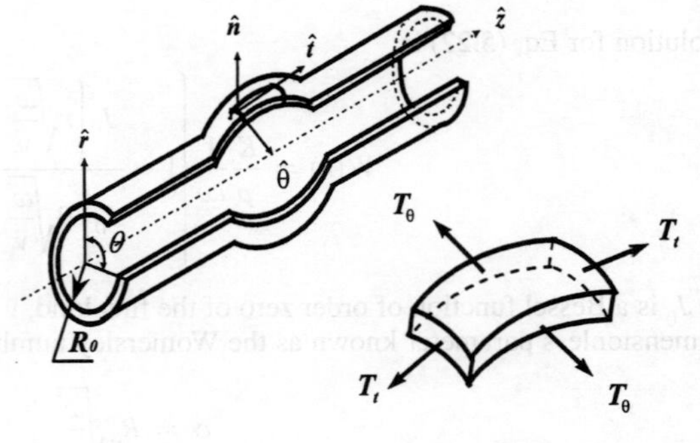

FIGURE 5.7 Mechanics of the arterial wall: (A) axisymmetric wall deformation; (B) element of the tube wall under biaxial loading. The *T*s are longitudinal and circumferential internal stresses.

The first-order approximations for the axial (u_1) and radial (v_1) components of the fluid velocity, and the pressure (P_1) as a function of time (t) and space (r, z), are given by

$$u_1(r, z, t) = \frac{A_1}{c\rho_F}\left[1 + m\frac{J_0\left(\alpha_0 \dfrac{r}{R_0}\right)}{J_0(\alpha_0)}\right]\exp\left[i\omega\left(t - \frac{z}{c}\right)\right] \tag{5.25}$$

$$v_1(r, z, t) = \frac{A_1\beta}{c\rho_F}i\left[\frac{r}{R_0} + m\frac{J_1\left(\alpha_0 \dfrac{r}{R_0}\right)}{\alpha J_0(\alpha_0)}\right]\exp\left[i\omega\left(t - \frac{z}{c}\right)\right] \tag{5.26}$$

$$P_1(z, t) = A_1 \exp\left[i\omega\left(t - \frac{z}{c}\right)\right] \tag{5.27}$$

The dimensionless parameters m, x, k, τ_θ, and F_{10} are related to the material properties and defined as

$$m = \frac{2 + x[2\sigma - (1 - \tau_\theta)]}{x[(1 - \tau_\theta)F_{10} - 2\sigma]} \qquad x = \frac{Eh}{(1 - \sigma^2)R_0\rho_F c^2} \qquad k = \frac{\rho_T h}{\rho_F R_0}$$

$$c = \frac{2 \cdot c_0}{\{(k + 2) + [(k + 2)^2 - 8k(1 - \sigma^2)]^{1/2}\}^{1/2}} \qquad c_0 = \left(\frac{Eh}{2R_0\rho_F}\right)^{1/2} \tag{5.28}$$

$$\tau_\theta = T_{\theta_0}\frac{Eh}{1 - \sigma} \qquad T_{\theta_0} = P_0 R_0 \qquad F_{10} = \frac{2J_1(\alpha_0)}{\alpha_0 J_0(\alpha_0)}$$

$$\alpha = \frac{\omega R_0^2}{c} \qquad \alpha_0^2 = i^3\alpha \qquad \beta = \frac{\omega R_0}{c}$$

where c = wave speed
$\omega = 2\pi\text{HR}/60$ = angular frequency
HR = heart rate
A_1 = input pressure amplitude
J_0 and J_1 = Bessel functions of order 0 and 1 of the first kind
ρ_F and ρ_T = blood and wall densities
R_0 = undisturbed radius of the tube

Excellent recent summaries on pulsatile blood flow may be found in Nichols and O'Rourke (1998) and Zamir (2000).

5.3.5 Turbulence

Turbulence has been shown to exist in large arteries of a living system. It is especially pronounced when the flow rate increases in exercise conditions (Yamaguchi and Parker, 1983). Turbulence is characterized by the appearance of random fluctuations in the flow. The transition to turbulence is a very complex procedure, which schematically can be described by a hierarchy of motions: growth of two-dimensional infinitesimal disturbances to final amplitudes, three-dimensionality of the flow, and a maze of complex nonlinear interactions among the large-amplitude, three-dimensional modes resulting in a final, usually stochastically steady but instantaneously random motion called turbulent flow (Akhavan et al., 1991; Einav and Sokolov, 1993).

In a turbulent flow field, all the dynamic properties (e.g., velocity, pressure, vorticity) are random functions of position and time. One thus looks at the statistical aspects of the flow characteristics (e.g., mean velocity, rms turbulent intensity). These quantities are meaningful if the flow is stochastically random (i.e., its statistics are independent of time) (Nerem and Rumberger, 1976). The time average of any random quantity is given by

$$\bar{f} \equiv \lim_{T\to\infty} \frac{1}{T} \int_0^\infty f(t)\, dt \tag{5.29}$$

One can thus decompose the instantaneous variables u and v as follows:

$$u(x, t) = \bar{U}(x) + u'(x, t) \tag{5.30}$$

$$v(y, t) = \bar{V}(y) + v'(y, t) \tag{5.31}$$

$$P(x, t) = \bar{P}(x) + p'(x, t) \tag{5.32}$$

We assume that u' is a velocity fluctuation in the x direction only and v' in the y direction only. The overbar denotes time average, so that by definition, the averages of u', v', and p' fluctuations are zero (stochastically random), and the partial derivatives in time of the mean quantities $\bar{U}, \bar{V}, \bar{P}$ are zeros (the Reynolds turbulence decomposition approach, according to which velocities and pressures can be decomposed to time-dependent and time-independent components).

By replacing u with $\bar{U} + u'$, etc. in the Navier-Stokes equation and taking time average, it can be shown that for the turbulent case the two-dimensional Navier-Stokes equation in cartesian coordinates becomes

$$\begin{gathered} \rho\bar{U}\frac{\partial \bar{U}}{\partial x} + \rho\bar{V}\frac{\partial \bar{U}}{\partial y} = -\frac{\partial \bar{P}}{\partial x} + \frac{\partial}{\partial y}\left[\mu\frac{\partial \bar{U}}{\partial y} - \rho\overline{u'v'}\right] \\ \frac{\partial \bar{U}}{\partial x} = 0 \rightarrow U = U(y) \qquad \bar{V} = 0 \end{gathered} \tag{5.33}$$

and for the y direction one obtains

$$\frac{\partial}{\partial y}\left(\bar{P} + \rho \overline{v'^2} + \rho g z\right) = 0 \tag{5.34}$$

Integration yields

$$\bar{P} + \rho g z + \rho \overline{v'^2} = \text{constant} \tag{5.35}$$

As v' must vanish near the wall, the values of $P + \rho g z$ will be larger near the wall. That implies that, in a turbulent boundary layer, the pressure does not change hydrostatically (is not height or depth dependent), as is the case of laminar flow. Equation (5.35) implies that the pressure is not a function of y, and thus,

$$\frac{\partial \bar{P}}{\partial x} = \frac{\partial}{\partial y}\left(\mu \frac{d\bar{U}}{dy} - \rho \overline{u'v'}\right) \tag{5.36}$$

Since P is independent of y, integration in y yields

$$\mu \frac{d\bar{U}}{dy} - \rho \overline{u'v'} = y \frac{\partial \bar{P}}{\partial x} + C_1 \tag{5.37}$$

where $C_1 = \tau_0$ is the shear stress near the wall.

We see that in addition to the convective, pressure, and viscous terms, we have an additional term, which is the gradient of the nonlinear term $\rho u'v'$, which represents the average transverse transport of longitudinal momentum due to the turbulent fluctuations. It appears as a pseudostress along with the viscous stress $\mu \partial U/\partial y$, and is called the Reynolds stress. This term is usually large in most turbulent shear flows (Lieber and Giddens, 1988).

5.3.6 Flow in Curved Tubes

The arteries and veins are generally not straight uniform tubes but have some curved structure, especially the aorta, which has a complex three-dimensional curved geometry with multiplanar curvature. To understand the effect of curvature on blood flow, we will discuss the simple case of steady laminar flow in an in-plane curved tube (Fig. 5.8). When a steady fluid flow enters a curved pipe in the horizontal plane, all of its elements are subjected to a centripetal acceleration normal to their original directions and directed toward the bend center. This force is supplied by a pressure gradient in the plane of the bend, which is more or less uniform across the cross section. Hence, all the fluid elements experience approximately the same sideways acceleration, and the faster-moving elements with the greater inertia will thus change their direction less rapidly than the slower-moving ones. The net result is that the faster-moving elements that originally occupy the core fluid near the center of the tube are swept toward the outside of the bend along the diametrical plane, and their place is taken by an inward circumferential motion of the slower moving fluid located near the walls. Consequently, the overall flow field is composed of an outward-skewed axial component on which is superimposed a secondary flow circulation of two counterrotating vortices.

The analytical solution for a fully developed, steady viscous flow in a curved tube of circular cross section was developed by Dean in 1927, who expressed the ratio of centrifugal inertial forces to the viscous forces (analogous to the definition of Reynolds number Re) by the dimensionless Dean number,

$$\text{De} = \text{Re}\sqrt{\frac{r}{R_{\text{curve}}}} \tag{5.38}$$

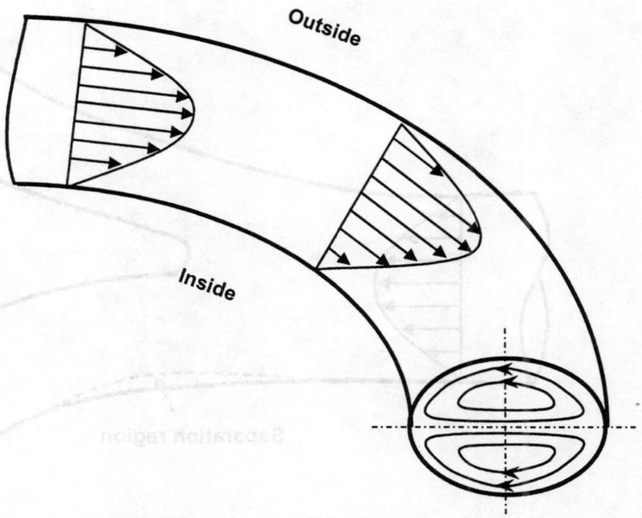

FIGURE 5.8 Schematic description of the skewed axial velocity profile and the secondary motions developed in a laminar flow in a curved tube.

where r is the tube radius and R_{curve} is the radius of curvature. As De increases, the maximal axial velocity is more skewed toward the outer wall. Dean's analytic solutions are limited to small ratios of radius to radius of curvature for which De < 96. However, numerical solutions extended the range up to 5000. Blood flow in the aortic arch is complex and topics such as entry flow from the aortic valve, pulsatile flow, and their influence on wall shear stress have been the subject of numerous experimental and numerical studies (Pedley, 1980; Berger et al., 1983; Chandran, 2001).

5.3.7 Flow in Bifurcating and Branching Systems

The arterial system is a complex asymmetric multigeneration system of branching and bifurcating tubes that distribute blood to all organs and tissues. A simplified arterial bifurcation may be represented by two curved tubes attached to a straight mother tube. Accordingly, the pattern of blood flow downstream of the flow divider (i.e., bifurcating region) is in general similar to flow in curved tubes (Fig. 5.9). Typically, a boundary layer is generated on the inside wall downstream from the flow divider, with the maximum axial velocity just outside the boundary layer. As in flow in curved tubes, the maximal axial velocity is skewed toward the outer curvature, which is the inner wall of the bifurcation.

Comprehensive experimental and computational studies were conducted to explore the pattern of blood flow in a branching vessel, energy losses, and the level of wall shear stress in the branch region (Ku and Giddens, 1987; Pinchak and Ostrach, 1976; Liepsch et al., 1989; Liepsch, 1993; Pedley, 1995; Perktold and Rappitsch, 1995). Of special interest are the carotid bifurcation and the lower extremity bypass graft-to-artery anastomosis whose blockage may induce stroke and walking inability, respectively. A recent review of computational studies of blood flow through bifurcating geometries that may aid the design of carotid endartectomy for stroke prevention and graft-to-artery configuration may be found in Kleinstreuer et al., 2001.

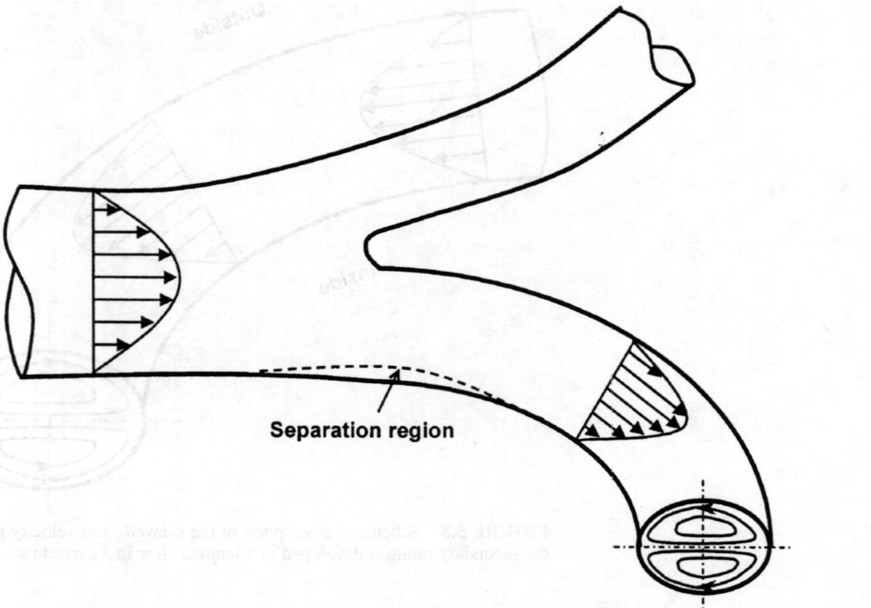

FIGURE 5.9 Qualitative illustration of laminar flow downstream of a bifurcation with a possible region of flow separation, secondary flow, and skewed axial profile.

5.4 BLOOD FLOW IN VEINS

5.4.1 Vein Compliance

The veins are thin-walled tubular structures that may "collapse" (i.e., the cross-sectional area does not maintain its circular shape and becomes less than in the unstressed geometry) when subjected to negative transmural pressures P (internal minus external pressures). Experimental studies (Moreno et al., 1970) demonstrated that the structural performance of veins is similar to that of thin-walled elastic tubes (Fig. 5.10). Three regions may be identified in a vein subjected to a transmural pressure: When $P > 0$, the tube is inflated, its cross section increases and maintains a circular shape; when $P < 0$, the tube cross section collapses first to an ellipse shape; and at a certain negative transmural pressure, a contact is obtained between opposite walls, thereby generating two lumens. Structural analysis of the stability of thin elastic rings and their postbuckling shape (Flaherty et al., 1972), as well as experimental studies (Thiriet et al., 2001) revealed the different complex modes of collapsed cross sections. In order to facilitate at least a one-dimensional fluid flow analysis, it is useful to represent the mechanical characteristics of the vein wall by a "tube law" relationship that locally correlates between the transmural pressure and the vein cross-sectional area.

5.4.2 Flow in Collapsible Tubes

Venous flow is a complex interaction between the compliant structures (veins and surrounding tissues) and the flow of blood. Since venous blood pressure is low, transmural pressure can become negative, thereby resulting in blood flow through a partially collapsed tube. Early studies with a thin-walled elastic tube revealed the relevant experimental evidence (Conrad, 1969). The steady flow rate (Q) through a given length of a uniform collapsible tube depends on two pressure differences selected from among the pressures immediately upstream (P_1), immediately downstream (P_2), and external (P_e) to the collapsible segment (Fig. 5.11). Thus, the pressure-flow relationships in collapsible tubes are more complex than those of rigid tubes, where Q is related to a fixed pressure gradient, and may attain different shapes, depending on which of the pressures (e.g., P_1, P_2, P_e) are held fixed and which are varied. In addition, one should also consider the facts that real veins may be neither uniform nor straight, and that the external pressure is not necessarily uniform along the tube.

The one-dimensional theory for steady incompressible fluid flow in collapsible tubes (when $P - P_e < 0$) was outlined by Shapiro (1977) in a format analogous to that for gas dynamics. The governing equations for the fluid are that for conservation of mass,

$$\frac{\partial A}{\partial t} + \frac{\partial}{\partial z}(Au) = 0 \qquad (5.39)$$

and that for conservation of momentum,

$$\frac{\partial u}{\partial t} + u\frac{\partial u}{\partial z} = -\frac{1}{\rho}\frac{\partial P}{\partial z} \qquad (5.40)$$

where u = velocity
P = pressure in the flowing fluid
ρ = mass density of the fluid
A = tube cross-sectional area
t = time
z = longitudinal distance

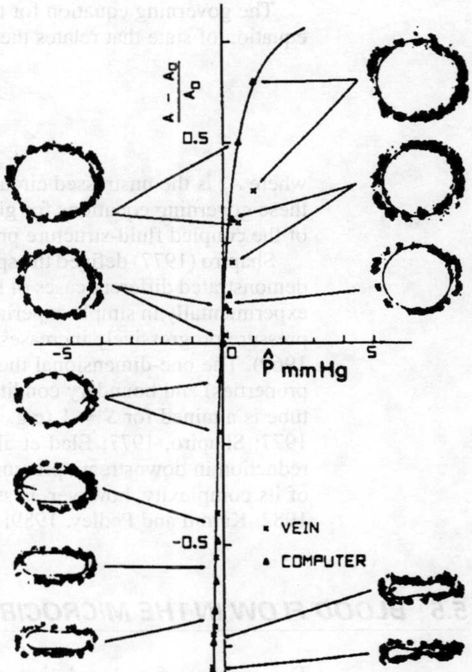

FIGURE 5.10 Relationship between transmural pressure, $P - P_e$, and normalized cross-sectional area, $(A - A_0)/A_0$, of a long segment of inferior vena cava of a dog. The solid line is a computer solution for a latex tube. [*From Moreno et al. (1970) by permission.*]

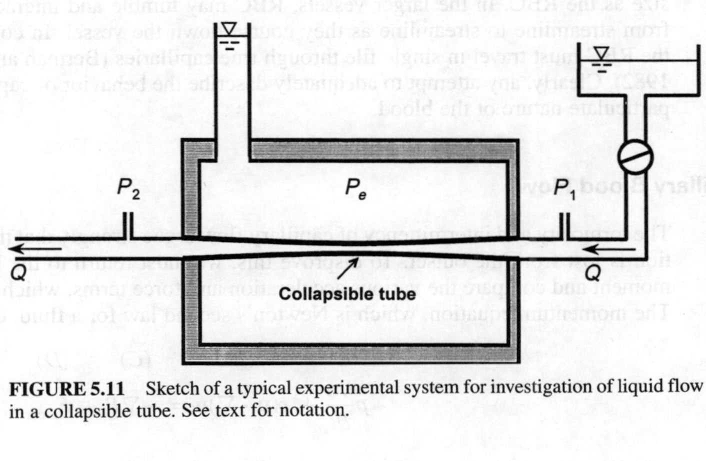

FIGURE 5.11 Sketch of a typical experimental system for investigation of liquid flow in a collapsible tube. See text for notation.

The governing equation for the tube deformation may be given by the tube law, which is also an equation of state that relates the transmural pressure to the local cross-sectional area,

$$P - P_e = K_p \cdot F\left(\frac{A}{A_0}\right) \tag{5.41}$$

where A_0 is the unstressed circular cross section and K_p is the wall stiffness coefficient. Solution of these governing equations for given boundary conditions provides the one-dimensional flow pattern of the coupled fluid-structure problem of fluid flow through a collapsible elastic tube.

Shapiro (1977) defined the speed index, $S = u/c$, similar to the Mach number in gas dynamics, and demonstrated different cases of subcritical ($S < 1$) and supercritical ($S > 1$) flows. It has been shown experimentally in simple experiments with compliant tubes that gradual reduction of the downstream pressure progressively increases the flow rate until a maximal value is reached (Holt, 1969; Conrad, 1969). The one-dimensional theory demonstrates that for a given tube (specific geometry and wall properties) and boundary conditions, the maximal steady flow that can be conveyed in a collapsible tube is attained for $S = 1$ (e.g., when $u = c$) at some position along the tube (Dawson and Elliott, 1977; Shapiro, 1977; Elad et al., 1989). In this case, the flow is said to be "choked" and further reduction in downstream pressure does not affect the flow upstream of the flow-limiting site. Much of its complexity, however, is still unresolved either experimentally or theoretically (Kamm et al., 1982; Kamm and Pedley, 1989; Elad et al., 1992).

5.5 BLOOD FLOW IN THE MICROCIRCULATION

The concept of a closed circuit for the circulation was established by Harvey (1578–1657). The experiments of Hagen (1839) and Poiseuille (1840) were performed in an attempt to elucidate the flow resistance of the human microcirculation. During the past century, major strides have been made in understanding the detailed fluid mechanics of the microcirculation and in depicting a concrete picture of the flow in capillaries and other small vessels.

5.5.1 The Microvascular Bed

We include in the term "microcirculation" those vessels with lumens (internal diameters) that are some modest multiple—say 1 to 10—of the major diameter of the unstressed RBC. This definition includes primarily the arterioles, the capillaries, and the postcapillary venules. The capillaries are of particular interest because they are generally from 6 to 10 μm in diameter, i.e., about the same size as the RBC. In the larger vessels, RBC may tumble and interact with one another and move from streamline to streamline as they course down the vessel. In contrast, in the microcirculation the RBC must travel in single file through true capillaries (Berman and Fuhro, 1969; Berman et al., 1982). Clearly, any attempt to adequately describe the behavior of capillary flow must recognize the particulate nature of the blood.

5.5.2 Capillary Blood Flow

The tortuosity and intermittency of capillary flow argue strongly that the case for an analytic description is lost from the outset. To disprove this, we must return to the Navier-Stokes equations for a moment and compare the various acceleration and force terms, which apply in the microcirculation. The momentum equation, which is Newton's second law for a fluid, can be written as

$$\underset{(A)}{\rho\frac{\partial \mathbf{u}}{\partial t}} + \underset{(B)}{\rho(\mathbf{u}\cdot\nabla)\mathbf{u}} = \underset{(C)}{-\nabla P} + \underset{(D)}{F_{\text{shear}}} \tag{5.42}$$

Since we are analyzing capillaries in which the RBCs are considered solid bodies traveling in a tube and surrounded by a waterlike fluid (plasma), a good representation of the viscous shear forces acting in the fluid phase is the Newtonian flow,

$$F_{\text{shear}} = \mu\nabla^2\mathbf{u} \tag{5.43}$$

We now examine the four terms in the momentum equation from the vantage point of an observer sitting on the erythrocytes. It is an observable fact that most frequently the fluid in the capillary moves at least 10 to 20 vessel diameters before flow ceases, so that a characteristic time for the unsteady term (*A*) is, say, 10 *D*/*U*. The distance over which the velocity varies by *U* is, typically, *D*. (In the gap between the RBC and the wall, this distance is, of course, smaller, but the sense of our argument is not changed.)

Dividing both sides of Eq. (5.42) by ρ, we have the following order-of-magnitude comparisons between the terms:

$$\begin{aligned}\frac{(A)}{(D)} &\approx \frac{U/(10D/U)}{(\nu U/D^2)} = \frac{UD}{10\nu}\\ \frac{(B)}{(D)} &\approx \frac{U^2/D}{(\nu U/D^2)} = \frac{UD}{\nu}\end{aligned} \tag{5.44}$$

The term UD/ν is the well-known Reynolds number. Typical values for human capillaries are $U \approx 500\ \mu$m/s, $D \approx 7\ \mu$m, and $\nu \approx 1.5 \times 10^{-2}$ cm²/s, so that the Reynolds number is about 2×10^{-3}. Clearly, the unsteady (*A*) and convective acceleration (*B*) terms are negligible compared to the viscous forces (Le-Cong and Zweifach, 1979; Einav and Berman, 1988).

This result is most welcome, because it allows us to neglect the acceleration of the fluid as it passes around and between the RBCs, and to establish a continuous balance between the local net pressure force acting on an element of fluid and the viscous stresses acting on the same fluid element. The equation to be solved is therefore

$$\nabla P = \mu\nabla^2\mathbf{u} \tag{5.45}$$

subject to the condition that the fluid velocity is zero at the RBC surface, which is our fixed frame of reference, and *U* at the capillary wall. We must also place boundary conditions on both the pressure and velocity at the tube ends, and specify the actual shape and distribution of the RBCs. This requires some drastic simplifications if we wish to obtain quantitative results, so we assume that all the RBCs have a uniform shape (sphere, disk, ellipse, pancake, etc.) and are spaced at regular intervals. Then the flow, and hence the pressure, will also be subject to the requirement of periodicity, and we can idealize the ends of the capillary as being substantially removed from the region being analyzed. If we specify the relative velocity *U* between the capillary and the RBC, the total pressure drop across the capillary can be computed.

5.5.3 Motion of a Single Cell

For isolated and modestly spaced RBC, the fluid velocities in the vicinity of a red cell is schematically shown in Fig. 5.12. In the gap, the velocity varies from *U* to zero in a distance *h*, whereas in the "bolus" region between the RBC, the same variation is achieved over a distance of *D*/4. If $h < D/4$, as is often observed in vivo, then the viscous shear force is greatest in the gap region and tends to "pull" the RBC along in the direction of relative motion of the wall.

Counteracting this viscous force must be a net pressure, $P_u - P_d$, acting in a direction opposite to the sense of the shear force. This balance of forces is the origin of the parachutelike shape shown in Fig. 5.3 and frequently observed under a microscope.

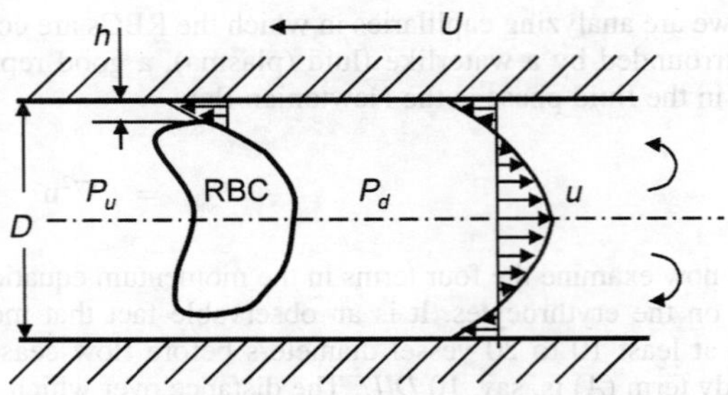

FIGURE 5.12 Diagram of the fluid pressure and velocity near the red blood cell within a capillary.

For $h \ll D/4$, we can approximate the net pressure,

$$(P_u - P_d)\frac{\pi D^2}{4} \approx \left(\mu\frac{U}{h}\right)(\pi D)(2b) \tag{5.46}$$

where $2b$ is the axial extent of the region of the gap. Suppose we use Eq. (5.46) to estimate the pressure drop across a typical capillary. Taking $h = 0.02D$, $b = 0.1D$, $U = 500\ \mu$m/s, $D = 7\ \mu$m, and $\mu = 1.4 \times 10^{-2}$ dyn · s/cm^2, then $P_u - P_d \approx 40$ dyn/cm^2.

5.6 BLOOD FLOW IN THE HEART

5.6.1 Flow in the Heart Ventricles

Under normal physiological conditions, systole and diastole occur in a definite coordination and constitute the *cardiac cycle*. Each cycle is considered to start with the atrial systole. The contraction begins a wave in that part of the right atrium where the orifices of the venae cavae are, and then involves both atria, which have a common musculature. With the cardiac rhythm of 75 contractions per minute, an atrial (auricular) systole lasts 0.1 second. As it ends, the ventricle systole begins, the atria then being in a state of diastole, which lasts 0.7 second. The contraction of the two ventricles occurs simultaneously, and their systole persists for about 0.3 second. After that, ventricular diastole begins and lasts about 0.5 second. One-tenth second before the end of the ventricular diastole, a new atrial systole occurs, and a new cycle of cardiac activity begins. The interconnection and sequence of the atrial and ventricular contractions depend upon where stimulation arises in the heart and how it spreads. Contraction of the ventricular myocardium ejects blood into the aorta and pulmonary arteries.

The heart valves are unidirectional valves, and in normal physiological conditions, blood flows in only one direction in the heart cavities: from the atria into the ventricles, and from the ventricles into the arterial system (Fig. 5.13). The ring-shaped muscle bundles of the atria, which surround the orifices, like a sphincter contract first during atrial systole, constricting these orifices so that blood flows from the atria only in the directions of the ventricles, and does not return into the veins. As the ventricles are relaxed during the atrial systole, and the pressure within them is lower than that in the contracting atria, blood enters them from the atria.

5.6.2 Flow through Heart Valves

The human heart contains four unidirectional valves that are anatomically grouped into two types: the atrioventricular valves and the semilunar valves. The tricuspid and mitral (bicuspid) valves

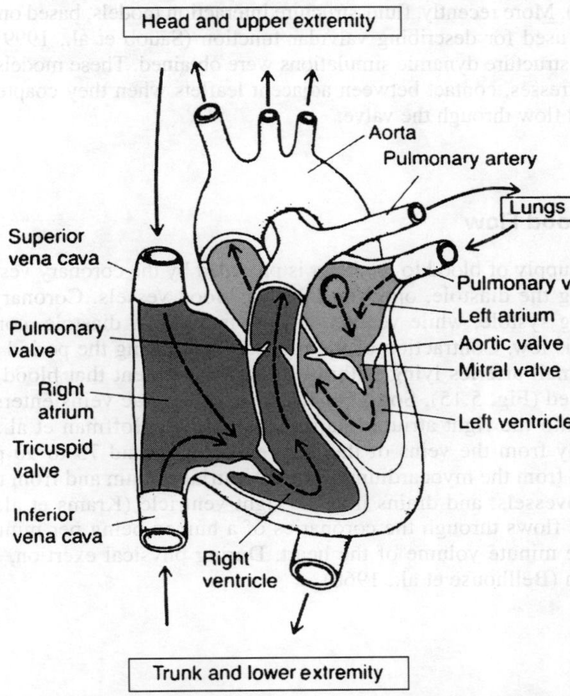

FIGURE 5.13 Structure of the heart and course of blood flow through the heart chambers. [*From Guyton and Hall (1996) by permission.*]

belong to the first type, whereas the pulmonic and aortic valves compose the second. Valves of the same type are not only structurally similar, but also functionally alike. For this reason, conclusions derived from studies on aortic and mitral valves are generally applicable to pulmonic and tricuspid valves, respectively.

One-way passages of blood from the ventricles into the main arteries is due to the heart valves. Though relatively simple in structure, heart valves are in their healthy state remarkably efficient, opening smoothly with little resistance to flow and closing swiftly in response to a small pressure difference with negligible regurgitation. Yet they are essentially passive devices that move in reaction to fluid-dynamical forces imposed upon them.

The motions of heart valves have drawn a considerable amount of attention from physicians and anatomists. One of the major reasons for this interest can be attributed to the frequent diagnosis of valvular incompetence in association with cardiopulmonary dysfunctionings. The first study exploring the nature of valve functioning, by Henderson and Johnson (1912), was a series of simple in vitro experiments, which provided a fairly accurate description of the dynamics of valve closure. Then came the Bellhouse and Bellhouse experiments (1969) and Bellhouse and Talbot (1969) analytical solution, which showed that the forces responsible for valve closure, are directly related to the stagnation pressure of the flow field behind the valve cusps.

Computational fluid dynamics models were developed over the years that include the effects of leaflet motion and its interaction with the flowing blood (Bellhouse et al., 1973; Mazumdar, 1992). Several finite-element structural models for heart valves were also developed in which issues such as material and geometric nonlinearities, leaflet structural dynamics, stent deformation, and leaflet coaptation for closed valve configurations were effectively dealt with (Bluestein and Einav, 1993;

1994). More recently, fluid-structure interaction models, based on the immersed boundary technique, were used for describing valvular function (Sauob et al., 1999). In these models, strong coupled fluid-structure dynamic simulations were obtained. These models allowed for the inclusion of bending stresses, contact between adjacent leaflets when they coapted, and transient three-dimensional blood flow through the valve.

5.6.3 Coronary Blood Flow

The supply of blood to the heart is provided by the coronary vessels (Fig. 5.14), and occurs mainly during the diastole, opposite to other blood vessels. Coronary flow is low and even reversing during systole, while venous outflow is high. In diastole, coronary flow is high while venous flow is low. Contraction of the myocardium during the period of ventricular tension compresses the small arteries lying within it to such an extent that blood flow in the coronaries is sharply reduced (Fig. 5.15). Some blood from the cardiac veins enters the coronary sinus, which empties into the right atrium (Kajiya et al., 1990; Hoffman et al., 1985). The sinus receives blood mainly from the veins of the left ventricle, around 75 to 90 percent. A large amount of blood flows from the myocardium of the interatrial septum and from the right ventricle along numerous microvessels, and drains into the right ventricle (Krams et al., 1989). From 200 to 250 mL of blood flows through the coronaries of a human being per minute, which is about 4 to 6 percent of the minute volume of the heart. During physical exertion, coronary flow may rise to 3 or 4 L/min (Bellhouse et al., 1968).

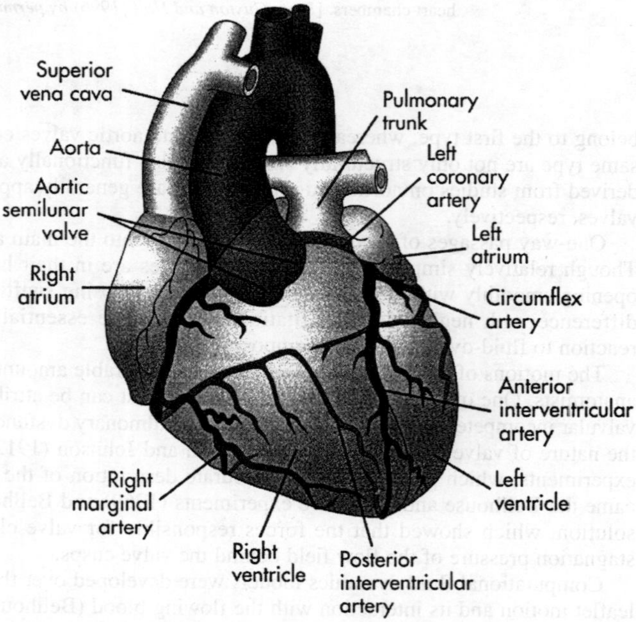

FIGURE 5.14 The arterial coronary circulation from anterior view. Arteries near the anterior surface are darker than those of the posterior surface seen through the heart. [*From Thibodeau and Patton (1999) by permission.*]

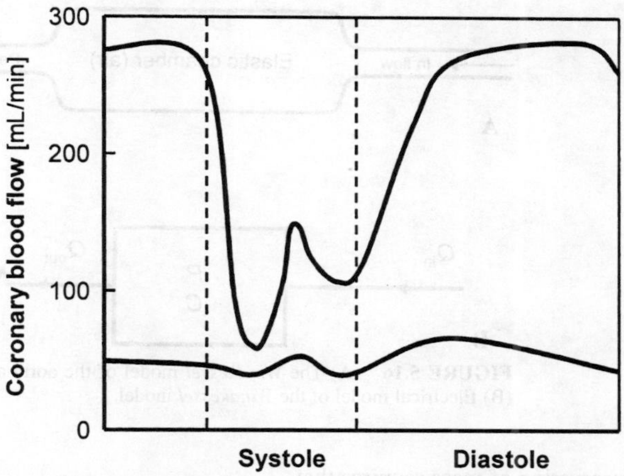

FIGURE 5.15 Blood flow through the coronary arteries: left (top) and right (bottom).

5.7 ANALOG MODELS OF BLOOD FLOW

5.7.1 Introduction

The circulatory system is a complex system of branching compliant tubes, which adjusts itself according to complex controllers. Mechanical and electrical analog models that can be solved analytically were devised to study either single arteries or the whole circulatory subsystem of specific organs (e.g., heart, kidney). Because of the complexity of the human system, there are a multitude of variables, which affect the functions, properties, and response of the circulatory system. Experimentally it is impossible to include all the known variables in a single system. However, analog models can deal with a group of variables at a time, and even make it possible to study the interaction between the variables. For extreme circulatory and physiological situations, it is simply too dangerous to study them experimentally, while the models are immune to studies.

5.7.2 Mechanical Models (Windkessel)

The *Windkessel* (air-cell in German) was suggested by Otto Frank (1899) to represent the cardiovascular system (Fig. 5.16A). In this linear mechanical model, the aorta and large blood vessels are represented by a linear compliant air-cell and the peripheral vessels are replaced by a rigid tube with a linear resistance (Dinnar, 1981; Fung, 1984). Accordingly,

$$V = C \cdot P \qquad \text{and} \qquad Q_{\text{out}} = \frac{P}{R} \tag{5.47}$$

where V, P, and C = volume, pressure, and compliance of the air-cell and are linearly related
Q_{out} = outflow of the air-cell
R = linear resistance of the rigid tube
$P_{venous} = 0$

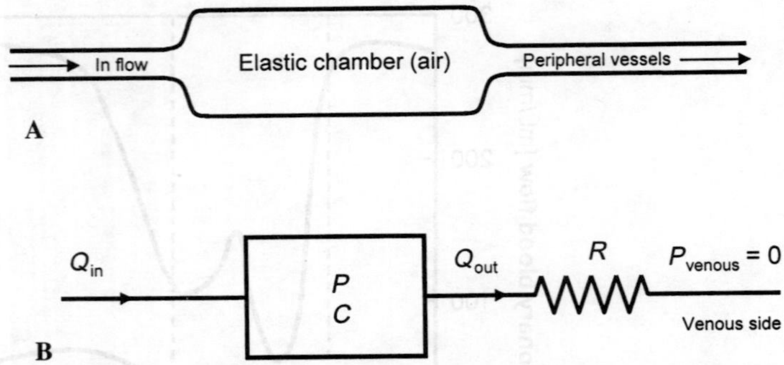

FIGURE 5.16 (A) The *Windkessel* model of the aorta and peripheral circulation. (B) Electrical model of the *Windkessel* model.

Conservation of mass requires that

$$Q_{in} = C\frac{dP}{dt} + \frac{P}{R} \tag{5.48}$$

where Q_{in} is the inflow to the air-cell and represents the cardiac stroke. This governing equation can be solved analytically for a set of given boundary conditions. The scheme of this analog is shown in Fig. 5.16B.

5.7.3 Electrical Models

A realistic model of blood flow in a compliant artery or vein requires a coupled solution of the governing equations for both the fluid and the elastic tube wall along with boundary conditions. These models are known as fluid-structure problems and can be solved by complex numerical techniques. In order to investigate linear approximations of complex blood flow phenomena, electrical analogs, which result in analogous linear differential equations, were developed (Dinnar, 1981). In these models the vessel resistance to blood flow is represented by a resistor R, the tube compliance by a capacitor C, and blood inertia by an inductance L. Assuming that blood flow and pressure are analogous to the electrical current and voltage, respectively, blood flow through a compliant vessel (e.g., artery or vein) may be represented by an electrical scheme (Fig. 5.17). Following Kirchhoff's law for currents, the governing differential equation becomes

$$\frac{d^2P}{dt^2} + RC\frac{dP}{dt} + P = L\frac{dQ}{dt} + RQ \tag{5.49}$$

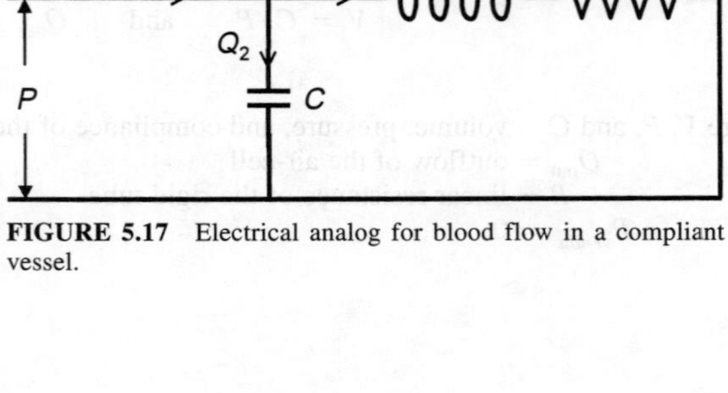

FIGURE 5.17 Electrical analog for blood flow in a compliant vessel.

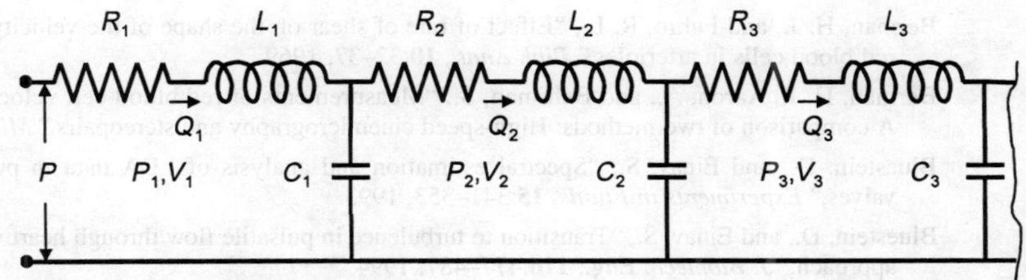

FIGURE 5.18 Lumped-parameter electrical model of a multicompartment arterial segment.

For a system of vessels attached in series (or small units of a nonuniform vessel) a more complicated scheme, composed of a series of compartments whose characteristics are represented by R_i, C_i, and L_i (Fig. 5.18), is used. For this case, Kirchhoff's law applied to each loop will yield

$$P_i - P_{i-1} = R_i Q_i + L_i \frac{dQ}{dt} \tag{5.50}$$

$$P_i = \frac{V_i}{C_i} \tag{5.51}$$

$$Q_i - Q_{i-1} = \frac{dV_i}{dt} \tag{5.52}$$

The problem is reduced to a set of linear differential equations and can be solved for given boundary conditions. The *RCL* characteristics of a given problem may be derived from the known physical properties of blood and blood vessels (Dinnar, 1981; Van der Tweel, 1957). This compartmental approach allowed for computer simulations of complex arterial circuits with clinical applications (McMahon et al., 1971; Clark et al., 1980; Barnea et al., 1990; Olansen et al., 2000; Westerhof and Stergiopulos, 2000; Ripplinger et al., 2001).

ACKNOWLEDGMENT

The authors are thankful to Dr. Uri Zaretsky for his technical assistance.

REFERENCES

Akhavan R. A., Kamm, R. D., and Shapiro, A. H., "An investigation of transition to turbulence in bounded oscillatory Stokes flows—Part 2: Numerical simulations," *J. Fluid Mech.*, **225**:423–444, 1991.

Atabek H. B., and Lew, H. S., "Wave propagation through a viscous incompressible fluid contained in a initially stressed elastic tube," *Biophys. J.*, **6**:481–503, 1966.

Barnea, O., Moore, T. W., and Jaron, D., "Computer simulation of the mechanically-assisted failing canine circulation," *Ann. Biomed. Eng.*, **18**:263–283, 1990.

Bellhouse, B. J., Bellhouse, F. H., and Reid, K. G., "Fluid mechanics of the aortic root with application to coronary flow," *Nature*, **219**:1059–1061, 1968.

Bellhouse, B., and Bellhouse, F., "Fluid mechanics of model normal and stenosed aortic valves," *Circ. Res.*, **25**:693–704, 1969.

Bellhouse, B., and Talbot, L., "Fluid mechanics of the aortic valve," *J. Fluid. Mech.*, **35**:721–735, 1969.

Bellhouse, B. J., Bellhouse, F., Abbott, J. A., and Talbot, L., "Mechanism of valvular incompetence in aortic sinus dilatation," *Cardiovasc. Res.*, **17**:490–494, 1973.

Berger, S. A., Goldsmith, W., and Lewis, E. R., *Introduction to Bioengineering*. Oxford University Press, Oxford, 1996.

Berger, S. A., Talbot, L., and Yao, S., "Flow in curved tubes," *Ann. Rev. Fluid Mech.*, **15**:461–512, 1983.

Berman, H. J., and Fuhro, R. L., "Effect of rate of shear on the shape of the velocity profile and orientation of red blood cells in arterioles," *Bibl. Anat.*, **10**:32–37, 1969.

Berman, H. J., Aaron, A., and Behrman, S., "Measurements of red blood cell velocity in small blood vessels. A comparison of two methods: High-speed cinemicrography and stereopairs." *Microvas. Res.*, **23**:242, 1982.

Bluestein, D., and Einav, S., "Spectral estimation and analysis of LDA data in pulsatile flow through heart valves," *Experiments in Fluids*, **15**:341–353, 1993.

Bluestein, D., and Einav, S., "Transition to turbulence in pulsatile flow through heart valves: A modified stability approach," *J. Biomech. Eng.*, **116**:477–487, 1994.

Caro, C. G., Pedley T. J., Schroter R. C., and Seed, W. A., *The Mechanics of the Circulation*. Oxford University Press, Oxford, 1978.

Casson, M., in *Rheology of Dispersive Systems*, C. C. Mills, ed., Pergamon Press, Oxford, 1959.

Chandran, K. B., "Flow dynamics in the human aorta: Techniques and applications," in *Cardiovascular Techniques*, C. Leondes, ed., CRC Press, Boca Raton, Florida, Chap. 5, 2001.

Charm, S. E., and Kurland, G. S., "Viscometry of human blood for shear rates of 0–100,000 $\sec^{-1}$," *Nature*, **206**:617–618, 1965.

Clark, J. W., Ling, R. Y., Srinivasan, R., Cole, J. S., and Pruett, R. C., "A two-stage identification scheme for the determination of the parameters of a model of left heart and systemic circulation," *IEEE Trans. Biomed. Eng.*, **27**:20–29, 1980.

Cokelet, G. R., "Rheology and hemodynamics," *Ann. Rev. Physiol.*, **42**:311–324, 1980.

Conrad, W. A., "Pressure-flow relationships in collapsible tubes," *IEEE Trans. Biomed. Eng.*, **16**:284–295, 1969.

Dawson, S. V., and Elliott E. A., "Wave-speed limitation on expiratory flow: A unifying concept," *J. Appl. Physiol.*, **43**:498–515, 1977.

Dawson, T. H., *Engineering Design of the Cardiovascular System of Mammals*, Prentice Hall, Englewood Cliffs, N. J., 1991.

Dinnar, U., *Cardiovascular Fluid Dynamics*, CRC Press, Boca Raton, Florida, 1981.

Einav, S., and Berman, H. J., "Fringe mode transmittance laser Doppler microscope anemometer. Its adaptation for measurement in the microcirculation," *J. Biomech. Eng.*, **10**:393–399, 1988.

Einav, S., and Sokolov, M., "An experimental study of pulsatile pipe flow in the transition range," *J. Biomech. Eng.*, **115**:404–411, 1993.

Elad, D., Sahar, M., Avidor, J. M., and Einav, S., "Steady flow through collapsible tubes: Measurement of flow and geometry," *J. Biomech. Eng.*, **114**:84–91, 1992.

Elad, D., Kamm., R. D., and Shapiro, A. H., "Steady compressible flow in collapsible tubes: Application to forced expiration," *J. Fluid. Mech.*, **203**:401–418, 1989.

Flaherty, J. E., Keller, J. B., and Rubinow, S. I., "Post buckling behavior of elastic tubes and rings with opposite sides in contact," *SIAM J. Appl. Math.*, **23**:446–455, 1972.

Frank O. "Die Grundform des Arteriellen Pulses, Z Biol., 37:483–526, 1899. (Translated by Sagawa K., Lie RK., Schaefer J., *J Mol Cell Cardiol.*, 22:253–277, 1990.)

Fung, Y. C., *Biodynamics: Circulation,* Springer-Verlag, New York, 1984.

Guyton, A. C., and Hall J. E., *Textbook of Medical Physiology*, 9th ed., W. B. Saunders, Philadelphia, 1996.

Henderson, Y., and Johnson, F. E., "Two models of closure of the heart valves," *Heart,* **4**:69, 1912.

Hoffman, H. E., Baer, R. W., Hanley, F. L., Messina, L. M., and Grattan, M. T., "Regulation of transmural myocardial blood flow," *J. Biomech. Eng.*, **107**:2–9, 1985.

Holt, J. P., "Flow through collapsible tubes and through in situ veins," *IEEE Trans. Biomed. Eng.*, **16**:274–283, 1969.

Kajiya, F., Klassen, G. A., Spaan, J. A. E., and Hoffman J. I. E., *Coronary Circulation. Basic Mechanism and Clinical Relevance*, Springer, Tokyo, 1990.

Kamm, R. D., "Bioengineering studies of periodic external compression as prophylaxis against deep vein thrombosis—Part I: Numerical studies; Part II: Experimental studies on a stimulated leg," *J. Biomech. Eng.*, **104**:87–95 and 96–104, 1982.

Kamm, R. D., and Pedley, T. J., "Flow in collapsible tubes: A brief review," *J. Biomech. Eng.*, **111**:177–179, 1989.

Kleinstreuer, C., Lei, M., and Archie, J. P., "Hemodynamics simulations and optimal computer-aided designs of branching blood vessels," in *Biofluid Methods in Vascular and Pulmonary Systems,* C. Leondes, ed., CRC Press, Boca Raton, Florida, Chap. 1, 2001.

Krams, R., Sipkema, P., Zegers, J., and Westerhof, N., "Contractility is the main determinant of coronary systolic flow impediment," *Am. J. Physiol.: Heart Circ. Physiol.*, **257**:H1936–H1944, 1989.

Ku, D. N., and Giddens, D. P., "Laser Doppler anemometer measurements of pulsatile flow in a model carotid bifurcation," *J. Biomech.*, **20**:407–421, 1987.

Le-Cong, P., and Zweifach, B. W., "In vivo and in vitro velocity measurements in microvasculature with a laser," *Microvasc. Res.*, **17**:131–141, 1979.

Lieber, B. B., and Giddens, D. P., "Apparent stresses in disturbed pulsatile flow," *J. Biomechanics,* **21**:287–298, 1988.

Liepsch, D., "Fundamental flow studies in models of human arteries," *Front. Med. Biol. Eng.*, **5**:51–55, 1993.

Liepsch, D., Poll, A., Strigberger, J., Sabbah, H. N., and Stein, P. D., "Flow visualization studies in a mold of the normal human aorta and renal arteries," *J. Biomech. Eng.*, **111**:222–227, 1989.

Martini, F. H., *Fundamentals of Anatomy and Physiology*, Prentice Hall, Englewood Cliffs, N. J., 1995.

Mazumdar, J. N., *Biofluid Mechanics*, World Scientific Pub., Singapore, 1992.

McDonald, D. A., "The relation of pulsatile pressure to flow in arteries." *J. Physiol*, **127**:533–552, 1955.

McMahon, T. A., Clark, C., Murthy, V. S., and Shapiro, A. H., "Intra-aortic balloon experiments in a lumped-element hydraulic model of the circulation," *J. Biomech.*, **4**:335–350, 1971.

Mills, C. J., Gabe, I. T., Gault, J. H., Mason, D. T., Ross, J., Braunwald, E., and Shillingford, J. P., "Pressure-flow relationships and vascular impedance in man," *Cardiovasc. Res.*, **4**:405–417, 1970.

Moreno, A. H., Katz, I. A., Gold, L. D., and Reddy, R. V., "Mechanics of distension of dog veins and other very thin-walled tubular structures," *Circ. Res.*, **27**:1069–1080, 1970.

Nerem, R. M., and Rumberger, J. A., "Turbulance in blood flow," *Recent Adv. Eng. Sci.*, **7**:263–272, 1976.

Nichols, W. W., and O'Rourke, M. F., *McDonald's Blood Flow in Arteries: Theoretical, Experimental, and Clinical Principles*, Arnold, London, 1998.

Olansen, J. B., Clark, J. W., Khoury, D., Ghorbel, F., and Bidani, A., "A closed-loop model of the canine cardiovascular system that includes ventricular interaction," *Comput. Biomed. Res.*, **33**:260–295, 2000.

Pedley, T. J., Schroter, R. C., and Sudlow, M. F., "Flow and pressure drop in systems of repeatedly branching tubes," *J. Fluid Mech.*, **46**:365–383, 1971.

Pedley, T. J., *The Fluid Mechanics of Large Blood Vessels*, Cambridge University Press, Cambridge, U.K., 1980.

Pedley, T. J., "High Reynolds number flow in tubes of complex geometry with application to wall shear stress in arteries," *Symp. Soc. Exp. Biol.*, **49**:219–241, 1995.

Perktold, K., and Rappitsch, G., "Computer simulation of local blood flow and vessel mechanics in a compliant carotid artery bifurcation model," *J. Biomech.*, **28**:845–856, 1995.

Pinchak, A. C., and Ostrach, S., "Blood flow in branching vessels," *J. Appl. Physiol.*, **41**:646–658, 1976.

Ripplinger, C. M., Ewert, D. L., and Koenig, S. C., "Toward a new method of analyzing cardiac performance," *Biomed. Sci. Instrum.*, **37**:313–318, 2001.

Saladin, K. S., *Anatomy and Physiology: The Unity of Form and Function*, 2d ed., McGraw-Hill, New York, 2001.

Sauob, S. N., Rosenfeld, M., Elad, D., and Einav, S., "Numerical analysis of blood flow across aortic valve leaflets at several opening angles," *Int. J. Cardiovasc. Med. Sci.*, **2**:153–160, 1999.

Shapiro, A. H., "Steady flow in collapsible tubes," *J. Biomech. Eng.*, **99**:126–147, 1977.

Thibodeau, G. A., and Patton, K. T., *Anatomy and Physiology*. 4th ed., Mosby, St Louis, 1999.

Thiriet, M., Naili, S., Langlet, A., and Ribreau, C., "Flow in thin-walled collapsible tubes," in *Biofluid Methods in Vascular and Pulmonary Systems*, C. Leondes, ed., CRC Press, Boca Raton, Florida, Chap. 10, 2001.

Van der Tweel, L. H., "Some physical aspects of blood pressure pulse wave, and blood pressure measurements," *Am. Heart J.*, **53**:4–22, 1957.

Westerhof, N., and Stergiopulos, N., "Models of the arterial tree," *Stud. Health Technol. Inform.*, **71**:65–77, 2000.

Whitmore, R. L., *Rheology of the Circulation*, Pergamon Press, Oxford, 1968.

Womersley, J. R., "Method for the calculation of velocity, rate of flow and viscous drag in arteries when the pressure gradient is known," *J. Physiol.*, **127**:553–563, 1955a.

Womersley, J. R., "Oscillatory motion of a viscous liquid in a thin-walled elastic tube: I. The linear approximation for long waves," *Philosophical Magazine*, Ser. 7, **46**:199–221, 1955b.

Yamaguchi, T., and Parker K. H., "Spatial characteristics of turbulence in the aorta," *Ann. N. Y. Acad. Sci.*, **404**:370–373, 1983.

Zamir, M., *The Physics of Pulsatile Flow,* Springer, New York, 2000.

CHAPTER 6
RESPIRATORY MECHANICS AND GAS EXCHANGE

James B. Grotberg
University of Michigan, Ann Arbor, Michigan

6.1 ANATOMY

6.1.1 General

As shown in Fig. 6.1, the pulmonary system consists of two lungs; each lung is conical in shape, with an inferior border (or base) that is concave as it overlies the diaphragm and abdominal structures and a superior border (or apex) that is convex and extends above the first rib. The anterior, lateral, and posterior lung surfaces are adjacent to the rib cage, while the medial surface is adjacent to the mediastinum, which contains the heart, great vessels, and esophagus. All of the lung surface is covered by the visceral pleural membrane, while the inside of the chest wall, mediastinum, and diaphragm are covered by the parietal pleural membrane. The two pleural membranes are separated by a thin liquid film (~20 to 40 μm thick) called the pleural fluid which occupies the pleural space, Fig. 6.1. This fluid lubricates the sliding motion between the lung and chest wall, and its pressure distribution determines lung inflation and deflation. Because the air-filled lung is surrounded by the pleural liquid, it experiences a buoyancy force that contributes to the overall force, including lung weight and fluid pressures.[1]

6.1.2 Airway Divisions

The right main bronchus branches from the end of the trachea to the right lung, while the left main bronchus branches to the left. This division of a "parent" airway into two "daughter" airways is called a *bifurcation*. Each level of branching is called a *generation* and is given an integer value n, according to the Weibel symmetric model[2] shown in Table 6.1. The trachea is designated as $n = 0$, the main bronchi, $n = 1$, etc. For a symmetrically bifurcating geometry, then, there would be 2^n airways at each generation level. Generations $0 \leq n \leq 16$ constitute the conducting zone

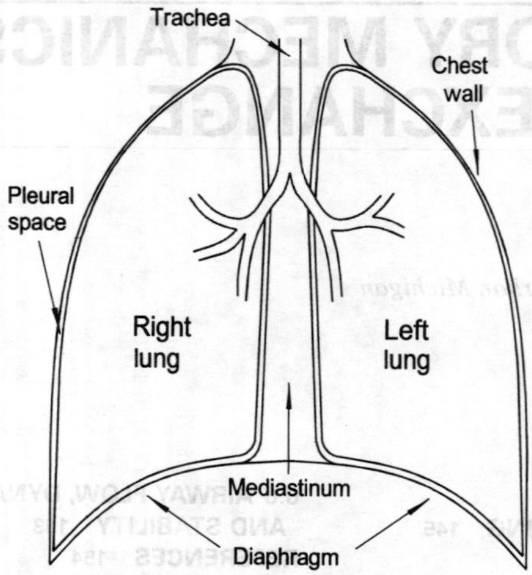

FIGURE 6.1 Sketch of the pulmonary system.

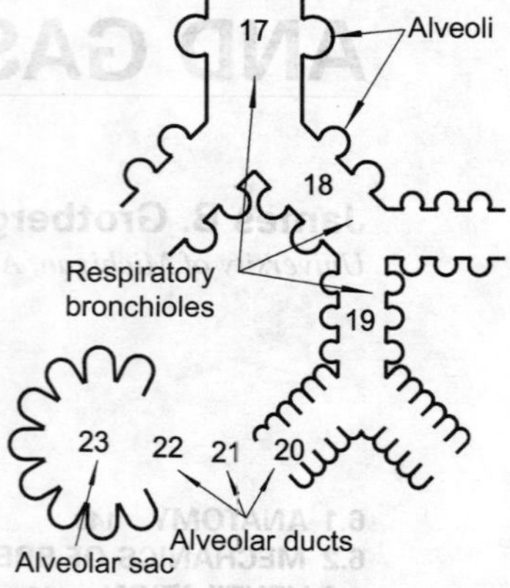

FIGURE 6.2 The respiratory zone of the airway network.

(trachea to terminal bronchiole) whose airways have no alveoli and, hence, do not participate in gas exchange with the pulmonary blood circulation. Each terminal bronchiole enters an acinus or respiratory zone unit for $17 \leq n \leq 23$; see Fig. 6.2. The respiratory bronchioles occupy generations $17 \leq n \leq 19$ and are tubes with partially alveolated surfaces. Generations $20 \leq n \leq 22$ are the alveolar ducts, tubes with totally alveolated surfaces. The alveoli are polyhedral in shape, but, viewed as nearly spherical caps, they each have a diameter of ~200 μm at 3/4 inflation.

6.1.3 Pulmonary Circulation

The pulmonary circulation consists of mixed venous blood entering the pulmonary artery from the right ventricle of the heart. After passing through the pulmonary capillary bed, the blood returns to the left atrium via the pulmonary vein. Flow through portions of the capillary bed that are in ventilated alveolar regions of the lung will discharge CO_2 and absorb O_2. Flows that go to unventilated alveoli will not exchange gas and are called the *shunt flow*. Typical values of pulmonary arterial blood pressures are 20 mmHg systolic/12 mmHg diastolic, about one-sixth the systemic vascular pressures. Because the pulmonary system is a low-pressure system, the vessel walls are much thinner than their systemic counterparts. The pulmonary arterial and venous systems have accompanying divisions, forming a triad with each airway division. The pulmonary capillaries, with a vessel diameter of ~6 μm, form a multivessel mesh surrounding each alveolus and are contained in the alveolar walls. The blood-gas barrier is composed of (starting from the gas side): the alveolar liquid lining, alveolar epithelial cell, basement membrane, and capillary endothelial cell. These combined layers sum to approximately 0.5 to 1.0 μm, in thickness. This is the distance gas must diffuse to enter or leave the blood under normal conditions.

The conducting airways are fed by a second blood supply, the bronchial circulation, which comes from the systemic circulation via the bronchial arteries. Blood returns via the bronchial veins, which empty partly to the systemic veins and partly to the pulmonary veins. The latter case is a circuit that bypasses the lungs entirely and makes the systemic cardiac output slightly larger than the pulmonary cardiac output or lung perfusion $\dot{Q}$.

6.1.4 Lymphatics and Nerves

To maintain homeostasis, the continuous transudation of fluid and solutes from the pulmonary capillary bed into the surrounding interstitium and alveolar space is balanced by lymphatic drainage out of the lung. The lymphatic flow is directed toward the hilum from the pleural surfaces. From lymph nodes in the hilum, the lymph travels to the paratracheal nodes and then eventually into the venous system via the thoracic duct. The lung has nerve fibers from both the vagal nerves (parasympathetic) and the sympathetic nerves. The efferent fibers go to the bronchial musculature and the afferents come from the bronchi and alveoli.

6.2 MECHANICS OF BREATHING

6.2.1 Chest Wall

The rib cage and its muscles form the chest wall, which protects the vital thoracic organs while keeping the lungs inflated. During inspiration, the ribs swing on an axis defined by their articulation with the vertebrae,[3] dashed lines in Fig. 6.3. The result is that upper ribs, such as rib 1, swing forward and up, like a pump handle, increasing the anterior-posterior diameter of the upper chest wall. However, lower ribs swing primarily laterally, like a bucket handle pinned at the spine and sternum. Their motion increases the lateral diameter of the thorax.

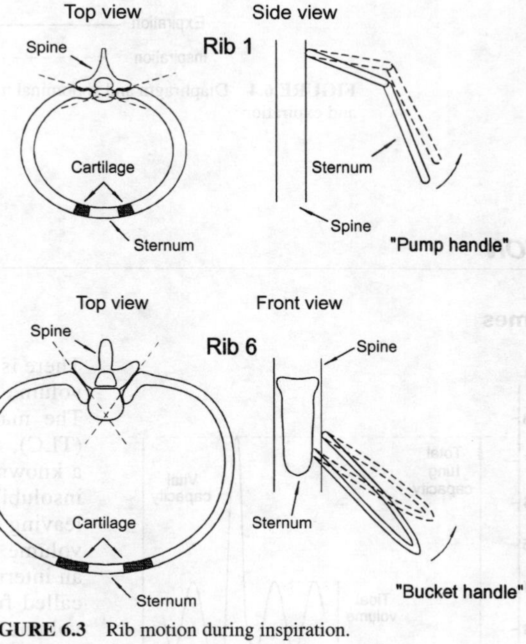

FIGURE 6.3 Rib motion during inspiration.

6.2.2 Muscles of Inspiration and Expiration

The major muscles involved in inspiration and expiration include the diaphragm and the intercostal muscles. During inspiration, the diaphragm contracts, pulling the inferior lung surface (via the pleural fluid) downward, while the external intercostal muscles contract, lifting the ribs; see Fig. 6.4. Expiration is primarily a passive event; the elastic structures simply return to their original, less-stretched, state as the diaphragm and external intercostals relax. At a normal breathing rate of 15 breaths per minute (bpm), inspiration may occupy one-third of the 4-second breathing cycle, while passive expiration occupies the rest, an inspiratory to expiratory time ratio of 1:2. Forceful expiration is accomplished by contraction of the internal intercostal muscles and the abdominal wall muscles that squeeze the abdominal contents hard enough to push them upward. The normal inspiratory to expiratory time ratio can increase with forceful expiration, as may occur during exercise, or decrease with prolonged expiration, as one finds in obstructive airways disease like asthma or emphysema.

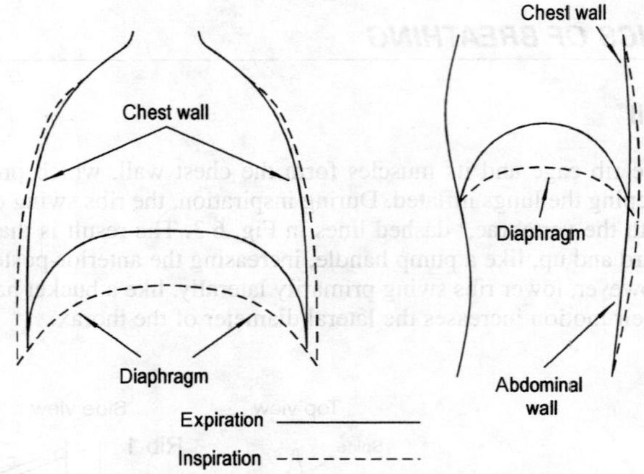

FIGURE 6.4 Diaphragm and abdominal muscles during inspiration and expiration.

6.3 VENTILATION

6.3.1 Lung Volumes

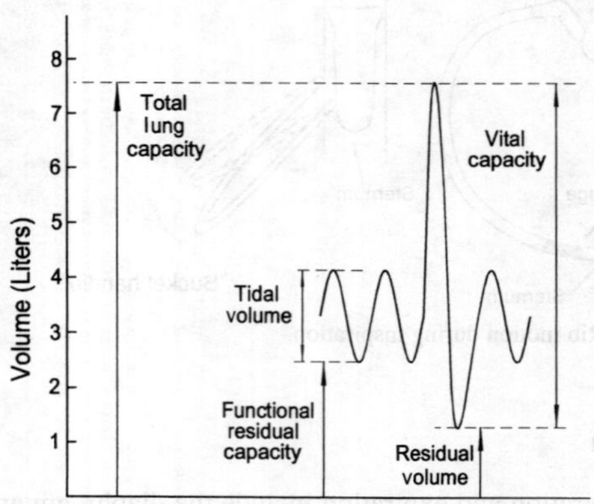

FIGURE 6.5 Lung volumes and definitions.

There is common terminology for different lung volume measurements, as shown in Fig. 6.5. The maximum volume is total lung capacity (TLC), which can be measured by dilution of a known amount of inspired helium gas whose insolubility in tissue and blood prevents it from leaving the air spaces. The minimum is residual volume (RV). Normal ventilation occurs within an intermediate range and has a local minimum called functional residual capacity (FRC). The volume swing from FRC to the end of inspiration is the tidal volume V_T. The vital capacity (VC) is defined by VC = TLC − RV. Within the lung there are also important volume concepts. The anatomic dead space V_D is the summed volume of all conducting airways, measured by the Fowler method, while the physiologic dead space is that portion of the lung that does not transfer CO_2 from the capillaries, measured by the Bohr method. While the methods used to determine these two values are different, normally they yield essentially the same result, approximately 150 cm^3 in an adult male. In some disease states, however, the Bohr method may be affected by abnormalities of the ventilation-perfusion relationship. The alveolar volume V_A, where gas exchange occurs, is the lung volume minus the dead space.

6.3.2 Air Flow and Resistance

A typical V_T of 500 cm^3 at a rate of 15 bpm yields a total ventilation $\dot{V}$ of (0.5 L × 15 breaths/min) = 7.5 L/min. Assuming that air flows in the conducting airways like a plug, for each 500 cm^3 breath inspired the tail 150 cm^3 fills the dead space while the front 350 cm^3 expands the alveoli, where it mixes with the alveolar gas previously retained at FRC. This makes the alveolar ventilation $\dot{V}_A = (0.5 - 0.15)$ L × 15 bpm = 5.25 L/min. The plug flow assumption is not correct, of course, but for resting ventilation it is a useful simplification. It fails, for example, in high-frequency ventilation,[4,5] where the mechanical ventilator can operate at 15 Hz with $V_T \leq 5$ cm^3; i.e., the tidal volumes can be smaller than the dead space. Adequate gas exchange occurs under these circumstances, because of the Taylor dispersion mechanism,[6] which is a coupling of curvilinear, axial velocity profiles with radial diffusion applied to a reversing flow.[7] The properties of airway branching, axial curvature, and flexibility can modify the mechanism considerably.[8,9,10]

The ventilatory flow rate $\dot{\mathbf{V}}$ results from the pressure boundary conditions imposed at the trachea and alveoli. In lung physiology, the flow details are often neglected and simply lumped into a resistance to air flow defined as the ratio of the overall pressure drop $\Delta\mathbf{P}$ to the flow rate; i.e., $\Delta P/\dot{V}$ = Res. A typical value is Res = 0.2 cmH$_2$O-s/L for resting breathing conditions. The appeal of defining airway resistance this way is its analogy to electrical circuit theory and Ohm's law, and other elements such as capacitance (see compliance, below) and inertance may be added.[11,12,13] Then an airway at generation n has its own resistance, Res$_n$, that is in series with its $n - 1$ and $n + 1$ connections but in parallel with the others at n.

The detailed fluid dynamics can be viewed as contributing to either the pressure drop due to kinetic energy changes, ΔP_K, or that due to frictional, viscous, effects, ΔP_F, so that

$$\Delta P = \Delta P_K + \Delta P_F \tag{6.1}$$

For a frictionless system, $\Delta P_F = 0$, Eq. (6.1) becomes the Bernoulli equation, from which we learn that, in general, $\Delta P_K = \frac{1}{2}\,\rho(u^2_{\text{out}} - u^2_{\text{in}})$, where $u_{\text{out}}(u_{\text{in}})$ is the outlet (inlet) velocity. For a given flow rate $\dot{V}$, the average air velocity at generation n is $u_n = \dot{V}/A_n$, where A_n is the total cross-sectional area at generation n. Because $A_0 << A_{23}$, air velocities diminish significantly from the tracheal value to the distal airways. This implies that $\Delta P_K < 0$ for inspiration while $\Delta P_K > 0$ for expiration.

The frictional pressure drop ΔP_F is always positive, but its value depends on the flow regime in each airway generation. For fully developed, laminar tube flow (Poiseuille flow) $\Delta P_F = (128\ \mu L/\pi d^4)\dot{V}$, where μ is the fluid (gas) viscosity, d is the tube diameter, and L is the axial distance. This formula is helpful in understanding some of the general trends for R, like its strong dependence on airway diameter, which can decrease in asthma. Airways are aerodynamically short tubes under many respiratory situations, i.e., not long enough for Poiseuille flow to develop. Then the viscous pressure drop is governed by energy dissipation in a thin boundary layer region near the airway wall where the velocity profile is curvilinear. For this entrance flow, $\Delta P_F \sim \dot{V}^{3/2}$, so resistance now is flow dependent. The local Reynolds number is given by $\text{Re}_n = u_n d_n/\nu$, where $\nu \approx 0.15$ cm^2/s is the kinematic viscosity of air. For $\text{Re}_n \geq 2300$, (see Table 6.1), the flow is turbulent and ΔP_F in those airways has an even stronger dependence on ventilation, $\Delta P_F \sim \dot{V}^{7/4}$ smooth wall, $\sim \dot{V}^2$ rough wall. Expressing these three cases for a single tube (airway) in terms of the friction coefficient, $C_F = \Delta P_F / \frac{1}{2}\rho u^2$. The comparison is shown in Eq. (6.2):

$$\underset{\text{Poiseuille flow}}{C_F = 64\frac{L}{d}\text{Re}^{-1}} \quad \underset{\text{Entrance flow}}{C_F = 6\left(\frac{L}{d}\right)^{1/2}\text{Re}^{-1/2}} \quad \underset{\text{Turbulent flow smooth wall}}{C_F = 0.32\frac{L}{d}\text{Re}^{-1/4}} \quad \underset{\text{Turbulent flow rough wall}}{C_F = k\frac{L}{d}} \tag{6.2}$$

where k depends on the wall roughness; a typical value is $k = 0.04$. Experiments of inspiratory flow with a multigeneration cast of the central airways[14] show that Poiseuille effects dominate for $350 \leq Re_0 \leq 500$, entrance effects for $500 \leq Re_0 \leq 4000$, and rough-walled turbulent effects for $4000 \leq Re_0 \leq 30{,}000$, approximately. C_F tends to be higher during expiration than inspiration.

As shown from measurements in airway models[15] or theories using modifications of the friction coefficients,[16] the vast majority of the pressure drop across the entire lung occurs within the large airways, say $0 \leq n \leq 8$. Thus clinical evaluation of total airway resistance can miss diseases of the small airways whose diameters are less than 2 mm, the so-called silent zone of the network. Pressure drop measurements and models are also important for the design of ventilators and other respiratory assist or therapeutic devices that interface with lung mechanics.

6.3.3 Gas Transport

Transport of O_2, CO_2, anesthetics, toxins, or any other soluble gas occurs by convection, diffusion, and their interplay. The ability of one gas species to diffuse through another is quantified by the molecular diffusivity D for the gas pair. For O_2 diffusing through air, the value of D is $D_{O_2-\text{air}} = 0.22$ cm²/s (at atmospheric pressure and 37°C), whereas for CO_2 the value is less, $D_{CO_2-\text{air}} = 0.17$ cm²/s. A characteristic time for diffusion to provide effective transport of a concentration front over a distance L is $T_d = L^2/D$, where L can be the airway length L_n. By contrast, a characteristic time for convective transport over the same distance is $T_c = L/U$, where $U = u_n$ is the average flow speed of the bulk gas mixture in an airway. The ratio of the two time scales tells us which mechanism, diffusion, or convection, may dominate (i.e., occur in the shortest time) in a given airway situation. This ratio is the Peclet number, $Pe = T_d/T_c = UL/D$, where $Pe >> 1$ indicates convection-dominated transport while $Pe << 1$ indicates diffusion-dominated transport. Table 6.1 shows how Pe_n for O_2 transport varies through the airway tree when $\dot{V} = 500$ cm³/s. Convection dominates in the conducting airways, where negligible O_2 is lost, so the O_2 concentration in these airways on inspiration is essentially the ambient inspired level, normally $P_{IO_2} = 150$ mmHg. At approximately generation 15, where Pe is close to unity and both convection and diffusion are important, the axial concentration gradient in O_2 develops over the next ~0.5 cm in path length to reach the alveolar level ($P_{ACO_2} = 100$ mmHg).

TABLE 6.1 Airway geometry

n generation	Name	2^n number	d_n, diameter, cm	L_n, length, cm	A_n, total cross-sectional area, cm²	V_n, volume of generation, cm³	X_n, distance from carina, cm	Re_n*	Pe_n* (O_2)
0	Trachea		1.80	12.00	2.54	30.50	0	2,362	1,611
1	Main bronchus	1	1.22	4.76	2.33	11.25	4.76	1,745	1,190
2	Lobar bronchus	4	0.83	1.90	2.13	3.97	6.66	1,299	886
3	Segmental bronchus	8	0.56	1.76	2.00	1.52	7.42	933	636
4	Subsegmental bronchus	16	0.45	1.27	2.48	3.46	8.69	605	412
5	Small bronchus	32	0.35	1.07	3.11	3.30	9.76	375	256
10	Small bronchus	1,024	0.13	0.46	13.40	6.21	13.06	32	22
16	Terminal bronchiole	65,536	0.06	0.17	180.00	29.70	14.46	1.11	0.79
17	Respiratory bronchiole	131,072	0.054	0.141	300.00	41.80	14.55	0.60	0.43
20	Alveolar duct	1,048,576	0.045	0.083	1,600.00	139.50	14.77	0.09	0.06
23	Alveolar sac	8,388,608	0.041	0.050	11,800.00	591.00	14.98	0.01	0.01

*Re_n and Pe_n for O_2 transport are evaluated for $\dot{V} = 500$ cm³/s.
Source: Data from Weibel (1963) (Ref. 35).

CO_2 has the reverse gradient during inspiration from its alveolar level ($P_{A_{CO_2}}$ = 40 mmHg) to the ambient level of near zero. During expiration the alveolar levels of both gases are forced out through the airway tree.

Once in the alveoli, gas transport through the alveolar wall and endothelium into the blood (or vice versa) is diffusive transport, which is quantified by the concept of the lung's diffusing capacity. As shown in Fig. 6.6, with wall thickness h, total alveolar membrane surface area A_m, and a gas concentration or partial pressure difference of P_1 (alveolar) – P_2 (blood serum), the mass flow rate across is $\dot{V}_{gas} = A_m D_{gas\text{-}tiss}(P_1 - P_2)/h = D_L(P_1 - P_2)$. $D_{gas\text{-}tiss}$ is the diffusivity of the gas (O_2, CO_2) in tissue and is proportional to solubility/(molecular weight)$^{1/2}$, making $D_{CO_2\text{-}tiss} \sim 20 D_{O_2\text{-}tiss}$ since CO_2 has far greater solubility in tissue. The details of the area, thickness, and diffusivity are lumped into an overall coefficient called the *diffusing capacity* D_L. The diffusion equation can be simplified for transport of carbon monoxide, CO, which is so rapidly taken up by hemoglobin within the red blood cells that the serum P_2 value is essentially zero. Then we find, after rearranging, that the diffusing capacity is given by

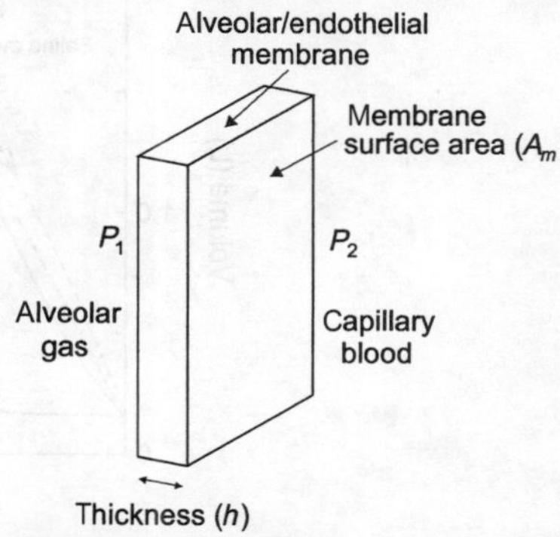

FIGURE 6.6 Diffusion across the alveolar/endothelial membrane.

$$D_L = \frac{\dot{V}_{CO}}{P_{A_{CO}}} \tag{6.3}$$

and there are both single-breath and steady-state methods employed in pulmonary function testing to evaluate D_L by breathing small concentrations of CO. Diseases that thicken the membrane wall, like pulmonary fibrosis, or reduce the available surface area, like emphysema, can cause abnormally low D_L values.

6.4 ELASTICITY

6.4.1 Pressure-Volume Relationship of Isolated Lung

The overall mechanical properties of the isolated lung are demonstrated by its pressure-volume (*P-V*) curve. Lung inflation involves both inflating open alveoli and recruiting those which are initially closed because of liquid plugs or local collapse. Deflation from TLC starts with a relatively homogenous population of inflated alveoli. This irreversible cycling process is partly responsible for the inflation and deflation limbs of the curve being different. Inflation requires higher pressures than deflation for any given volume; see the air-cycled (solid line) curve of Fig. 6.7 adapted from Ref. 17. Irreversible cycling of a system exhibits its hysteresis, and the hatched area within the loop created by the two limbs is called the hysteresis area. The magnitude of the area is the work per cycle required to cycle the lung. The overall slope of the curve, obtained by connecting the endpoints with a straight line, is the total compliance $C_{tot} = \Delta V/\Delta P$, which measures the total volume change obtained for the total pressure increase. Stiffer lungs have lower compliance, for example. Often one

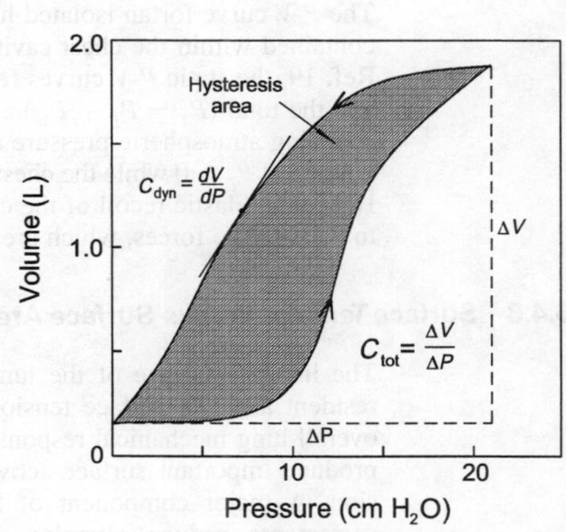

FIGURE 6.7 Air cycling of isolated dog lungs.

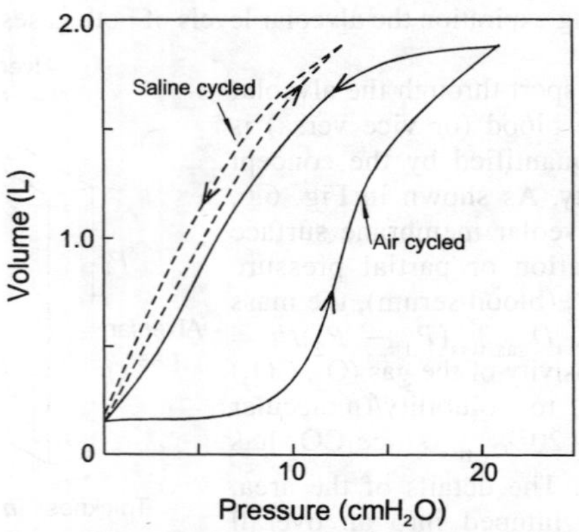

FIGURE 6.8 Saline cycling compared to air cycling.

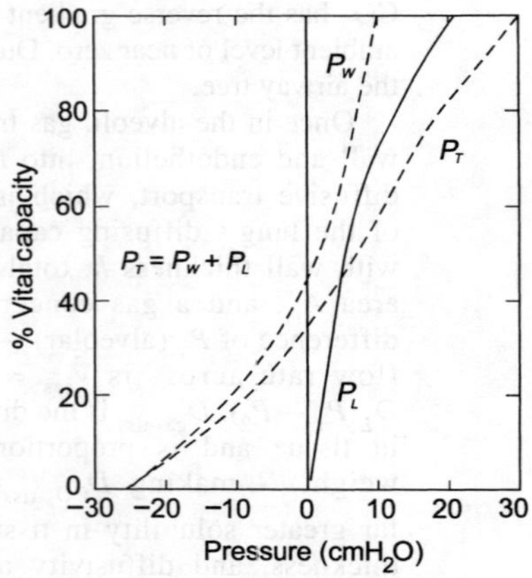

FIGURE 6.9 Pressure-volume curves for lung (P_L), chest wall (P_w), and total respiratory system (P_T).

wants a local measure of compliance, which is the local slope of the *V*(*P*) curve, defined as the dynamic compliance $C_{dyn} = dV/dP$. Other useful parameters are the specific compliance $V^{-1}\, dV/dP$, the elastance $1/C$, and the specific elastance $V\, dP/dV$.

Shown in Fig. 6.8 is the curve for a lung inflated and deflated with saline rather than air. Saline cycling was first noted by Von Neergaard[18] to reduce inflation pressures, as can be seen in the resulting curve that is shifted to the left, because of increased compliance, and has lost almost all of its hysteresis area. Because it removes the air-liquid interface that alveoli normally possess, saline cycling reveals that the surface tension forces exerted by this interface have very significant effects on the lung's mechanical response. Saline cycling allows us to understand the elasticity and hysteresis properties of the lung tissue by removing the surface tension forces and their contributions to hysteresis and compliance.

6.4.2 Pressure-Volume Relationship of the Respiratory System

The *P-V* curve for an isolated lung is only part of the total picture. The intact pulmonary system is contained within the chest cavity, which has its own *P-V* characteristics. In Fig. 6.9 adapted from Ref. 19, the static *P-V* curves for an isolated lung (P_L), a passive chest with no lung contents (P_W), and the total ($P_T = P_L + P_W$) are shown. When $P_T = 0$, the system is in equilibrium with the surrounding atmospheric pressure and the graph indicates that the lung is stretched from its near-zero volume at $P_L = 0$ while the chest cavity is compressed from its higher equilibrium volume at $P_W = 0$. Hence the elastic recoil of the chest wall is pulling outward while the lung tissue is pulling inward to balance the forces, which are in series.

6.4.3 Surface Tension versus Surface Area

The internal surface of the lung is coated with a thin liquid film, which is in contact with the resident air. The surface tension arising at this air-liquid interface has significant effects on the overall lung mechanical response, as shown in Fig. 6.8, when it is removed. Alveolar Type II cells produce important surface-active substances called *surfactants*, which reduce the interfacial tension. A major component of lung surfactant is dipalmitoylphosphatidylcholine (DPPC). Lung surfactants reduce alveolar surface tension from the surfactant-free value for air-water, 70 dyn/cm, to 1 to 5 dyn/cm in the alveoli, depending on the concentration and state of lung inflation. Figure 6.10 shows the relationship between surface tension and surface area for cycling of an air-liquid interface containing lung surfactants. Note that there is a hysteresis area and average slope, or compliance, that characterize the loop and have significant effects on their counterparts in Fig. 6.7.

Insufficient surfactant levels can occur in premature neonates whose alveolar cells are not mature enough to produce sufficient quantities, a condition leading to respiratory distress syndrome, also called hyaline membrane disease.[20] It can also occur in Acute Respiratory Distress Syndrome for adult and pediatric patients.[21] Instilling liquid mixtures, containing either natural or man-made surfactants, directly into airways via the trachea has developed from early work in animal models[22] into an important clinical tool called surfactant replacement therapy. The movement of these liquid boluses through the network relies on several mechanisms, including air-blown liquid plug flow dynamics, gravity, and surface tension and its gradients.[23,24,25] Models show that the instilled surfactant coats the airways which can lead to insufficient delivery to the alveoli.[26,27]

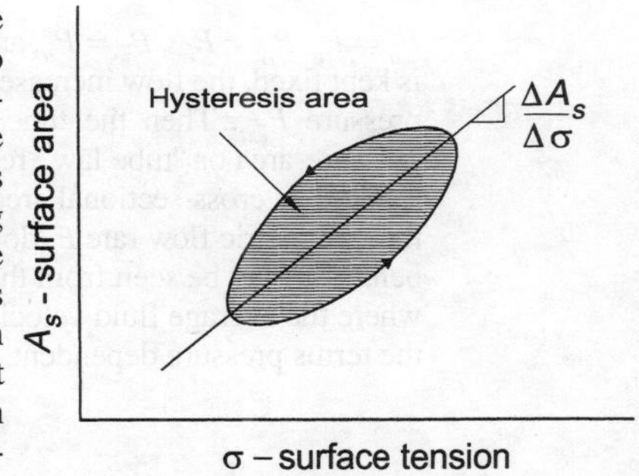

FIGURE 6.10 Surface area A_s versus surface tension σ for a cycled interface containing lung surfactant. There is a hysteresis area and mean slope or compliance to the curve; compare to Fig. 6.7.

6.5 VENTILATION, PERFUSION, AND LIMITS

The lung differs from many other organs in its combination of gas-phase and liquid-phase constituency. Because the densities of these two phases are so different, gravity plays an important role in determining regional lung behavior, both for gas ventilation and for blood perfusion. In an upright adult, the lower lung is compressed by the weight of the upper lung and this puts the lower lung's alveoli on a more compliant portion of their regional *P-V* curve; see Fig. 6.7. Thus inhaled gas tends to be directed preferentially to the lower lung regions, and the regional alveolar ventilation $\dot{V}_A$ decreases in a graded fashion moving upward in the gravity field.

Blood flow $\dot{Q}$ is also preferentially directed toward the lower lung, but for different reasons. The blood pressure in pulmonary arteries, P_a, and veins, P_v, sees a hydrostatic pressure gradient in the upright lung. These vessels are imbedded within the lung's structure, so they are surrounded by alveolar gas pressure, P_A, which is essentially uniform in the gravity field since its density is negligible. Thus there is a region called Zone III in the upper lung where $P_a < P_A$. This difference in pressures squeezes the capillaries essentially shut and there is relatively little pulmonary blood flow there. In the lower lung called Zone I, the hydrostatic effect is large enough to keep $P_a > P_v > P_A$ and blood flow is proportional to the arterial-venous pressure difference, $P_a - P_v$. In between these two zones is Zone II where $P_a > P_A > P_v$. Here there will be some length of the vessel that is neither fully closed nor fully opened. It is partially collapsed into more of a flattened, oval shape. The physics of the flow, called the *vascular waterfall*[28] or *choked flow*[29] or *flow limitation*[30], dictates that $\dot{Q}$ is no longer dependent on the downstream pressure, but is primarily determined by the pressure difference $P_a - P_A$.

Figure 6.11A shows this interesting type of flexible tube configuration and flow limitation phenomena where

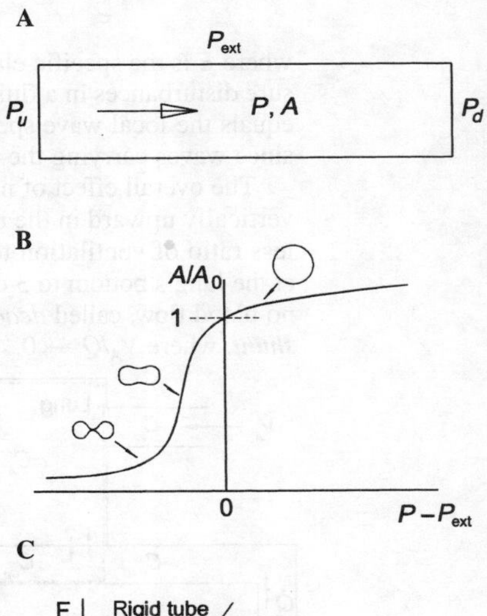

FIGURE 6.11 Choked flow through a flexible tube. (A) Upstream pressure P_u, downstream pressure P_d, external pressure P_{ext}, flow *F*, pressure *P*, cross-sectional area *A*. (B) A/A_0 versus transmural pressure with shapes indicated. (C) Flow versus pressure drop, assuming P_d is decreased and P_u is fixed.

$P_a = P_u$, $P_A = P_{ext}$, $P_v = P_d$, and $\dot{Q} = F$. As downstream pressure P_d is decreased and upstream pressure P_u is kept fixed, the flow increases until the internal pressure of the tube drops somewhat below the external pressure P_{ext}. Then the tube partially collapses, decreasing in cross-sectional area according to its pressure-area or "tube law" relationship *A(P)*, shown in Fig. 6.11B. As P_d is further decreased, the tube reduces its cross-sectional area while the average velocity of the flow increases. However, their product, the volumetric flow rate *F*, does not increase as shown in Fig. 6.11C. A simplified understanding of this behavior may be seen from the conservation of momentum equation for the flow, a Bernoulli equation, where the average fluid velocity *U* is defined as the ratio of flow to cross-sectional area, $U = F/A$, all of the terms pressure dependent.

$$P_{\text{res}} = P + \frac{1}{2}\rho\left(\frac{F(P)}{A(P)}\right)^2 \tag{6.4}$$

where P_{res} = pressure in a far upstream reservoir where fluid velocity is negligibly small
ρ = fluid density

P_{res} is the alveolar air pressure, for example, when applied to limitation of air flow discussed below. Taking the derivative of Eq. (6.4) with respect to *P* and setting the criterion for flow limitation as $dF/dP = 0$ gives

$$U_c = \left(\frac{A}{\rho}\frac{dP}{dA}\right)^{1/2} = \left(\frac{E}{\rho}\right)^{1/2} \tag{6.5}$$

where *E* is the specific elastance of the tube. The quantity $(E/\rho)^{1/2}$ is the "wave speed" of small pressure disturbances in a fluid-filled flexible tube, and flow limitation occurs when the local fluid speed equals the local wave speed. At that point, pressure information can no longer propagate upstream, since waves carrying the new pressure information are all swept downstream.

The overall effect of nonuniform ventilation and perfusion is that both decrease as one progresses vertically upward in the upright lung. But perfusion decreases more rapidly so that the dimensionless ratio of ventilation to perfusion, $\dot{V}_A/\dot{Q}$, decreases upward, and can vary from approximately 0.5 at the lung's bottom to 3 or more at the lung's top.[31] Extremes of this ratio are ventilated regions with no blood flow, called *dead space*, where $\dot{V}_A/\dot{Q} \to \infty$, and perfused regions with no ventilation, called *shunt*, where $\dot{V}_A/\dot{Q} \to 0$.

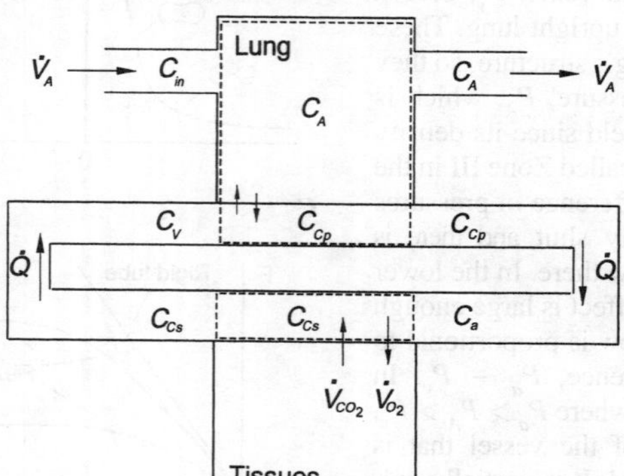

FIGURE 6.12 Schematic for ventilation and perfusion in the lung and tissues. Dashed line indicates control volume for mass balance. Assume instantaneous and homogenous mixing. Subscripts indicate gas concentrations for systemic (*s*) or pulmonary (*p*) end capillary C_c, venous C_v, alveolar C_A, and arterial C_a.

The steady-state gas concentrations within an alveolus reflect the balance of inflow to outflow, as shown in the control volumes (dashed lines) of Fig. 6.12. For CO_2 in the alveolar space, net inflow by perfusion must equal the net outflow by ventilation, $\dot{Q}(C_{vCO_2} - C_{cCO_2}) = \dot{V}_A(C_{ACO_2} - C_{inCO_2})$ where *C* indicates concentration. In the tissue compartment, the CO_2 production rate from cellular metabolism, $\dot{V}_{CO_2}$, is balanced by net inflow versus outflow in the tissues; i.e., $\dot{V}_{CO_2} = \dot{Q}(C_{vCO_2} - C_{cCO_2})$. Noting that $C_{inCO_2} \approx 0$ and combining the two equations, while converting concentrations to partial pressures, leads to the alveolar ventilation equation

$$\dot{V}_A = 8.63\frac{\dot{V}_{CO_2}}{P_{ACO_2}} \tag{6.6}$$

where the constant 8.63 comes from the units conversion. The inverse relationship between alveolar ventilation and alveolar CO_2 is well known clinically. Hyperventilation drops alveolar, and hence arterial, CO_2 levels whereas hypoventilation raises them. Using a similar approach for oxygen consumption $\dot{V}_{O_2}$ and using the results of the CO_2 balance yields the ventilation-perfusion equation

$$\frac{\dot{V}_A}{\dot{Q}} = \frac{8.63R(C_{a_{O_2}} - C_{\bar{V}_{O_2}})}{P_{A_{CO_2}}} \tag{6.7}$$

Equation 6.7 uses the definition of the respiratory exchange ratio, $R = \dot{V}_{CO_2}/\dot{V}_{O_2}$, which usually has a value of $R \approx 0.8$ for $\dot{V}_A/\dot{Q} = 1$. It also replaces the end capillary concentration with the systemic arterial value, $C_{a_{O_2}} = C_{c_{O_2}}$, assuming equilibration. From Eq. (6.7), the extreme limits of $\dot{V}_A/\dot{Q}$, mentioned earlier, may be recognized. Intermediate solutions are more complicated, however, since there are nonlinear relationships between gas partial pressure and gas content or concentration in the blood. Equation 6.7 also demonstrates that higher $\dot{V}_A/\dot{Q}$, as occurs in the upper lung, is consistent with a higher end capillary and alveolar oxygen level. It is often thought that tuberculosis favors the upper lung for this reason.

The $\dot{V}/\dot{Q}$ variation leads to pulmonary venous blood having a mix of contributions from different lung regions. Consequently, there is a difference between the lung-average alveolar $P_{A_{O_2}}$ and the average or systemic arterial $P_{a_{O_2}}$, sometimes called the *A-a* gradient of O_2. An average $P_{A_{O_2}}$, can be derived from the alveolar gas equation,

$$P_{A_{O_2}} = P_{I_{O_2}} - \frac{P_{A_{CO_2}}}{R} + f \tag{6.8}$$

which derives from the mass balance for O_2 in Fig. 6.12. Here $P_{I_{O_2}}$ is the inspired value and f is a small correction normally ignored. Clinically, an arterial sample yields $P_{a_{CO_2}}$, which can be substituted for $P_{A_{CO_2}}$ in Eq. (6.8). The *A-a* gradient becomes abnormally large in several lung diseases that cause increased mismatching of ventilation and perfusion.

6.6 AIRWAY FLOW, DYNAMICS, AND STABILITY

6.6.1 Forced Expiration and Flow Limitation

A common test of lung function consists of measuring flow rate by a spirometer apparatus. When the flow signal is integrated with time, the lung volume is found. Important information is contained in the volume versus time curves. The amount of volume forcefully exhaled with maximum effort in 1 second, FEV1, divided by the maximal volume exhaled or forced vital capacity, FVC, is a dimensionless ratio used to separate restrictive and obstructive lung disease from normal lungs. FEV1/FVC is normally 80 percent or higher, but in obstructed lungs (asthma, emphysema) the patient cannot exhale very much volume in 1 second, so FEV1/FVC drops to diagnostically low levels, say 40 percent. The restricted lung (fibrosis) has smaller than normal FVC, though the FEV1/FVC ratio may fall in the normal range because of the geometric scaling as a smaller lung.

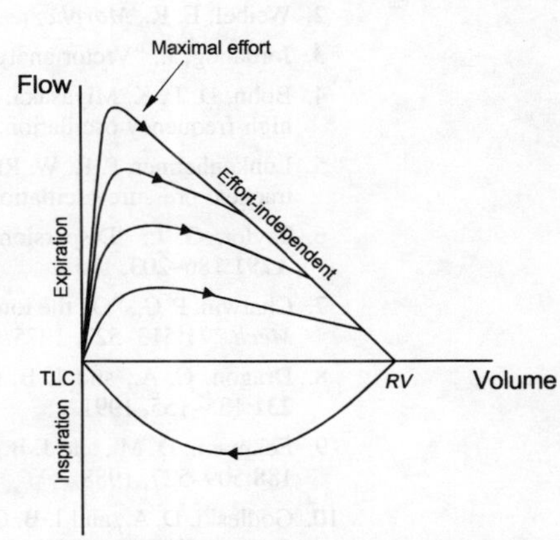

FIGURE 6.13 Flow-volume curves for increasing effort level during expiration, including maximal effort. Note effort-independent portion of curves.

Flow and volume are often plotted against one another as in Fig. 6.13. The flow-volume curves shown are for increasing levels of effort during expiration. The maximal effort curve sets a portion common to all of the curves, the effort-independent region. Expiratory flow limitation is another example of the choked flow phenomenon discussed earlier in the context of blood flow. Similar flow versus driving pressure curves shown in Fig. 6.11 can be extracted from Fig. 6.13 by choosing flows at the same lung volume and measuring the pressure drop at that instant, forming the isovolume pressure-flow curve. Since airway properties and E vary along the network, the most susceptible place for choked flow seems to be the proximal airways. For example, we expect gas speeds prior to choke to be largest at generation $n = 3$ where the total cross-sectional area of the network is minimal; see Table 6.1. So criticality is likely near that generation. An interesting feature during choked flow in airways is the production of flutter oscillations, which are heard as wheezing breath sounds,[32,33,34] so prevalent in asthma and emphysema patients whose maximal flow rates are significantly reduced, in part because E and U_c are reduced.

6.6.2 Airway Closure and Reopening

Most of the dynamics during expiration, so far, have been concerned with the larger airways. Toward the very end of expiration, smaller airways can close off as a result of plug formation from the liquid lining, a capillary instability,[35,36,37] or from the capillary forces pulling shut the collapsible airway,[38] or from some combination of these mechanisms.[39] Surfactants in the airways help to keep them open by both static and dynamic means. The lung volume at which airway closure occurs is called the closing volume, and in young healthy adults it is ~10 percent of VC as measured from a nitrogen washout test. It increases with aging and with some small airway diseases. Reopening of closed airways was mentioned earlier as affecting the shape of the *P-V* curve in early inspiration as the airways are recruited. When the liquid plugs break and the airway snaps open, a crackle sound, or cascade of sounds from multiple airways, can be generated and heard with a stethoscope. Both airway closure and reopening can injure the airway epithelial cells.[40,41,42,43]. Diseases that lead to increased intraairway liquid, such as congestive heart failure, are followed clinically by the extent of lung crackles, as are certain fibrotic conditions that affect airway walls and alveolar tissues.[44,45,46].

REFERENCES

1. Haber, R., J. B. Grotberg, M. R. Glucksberg, G. Miserocchi, D. Venturoli, M. D. Fabbro, and C. M. Waters, "Steady-state pleural fluid flow and pressure and the effects of lung buoyancy," *J. Biomech. Eng.*, **123**:485–492, 2001.
2. Weibel, E. R., *Morphometry of the Human Lung*, New York: Academic Press, p. 151, 1963.
3. Jordanog, J., "Vector analysis of rib movement," *Respir. Physiol.*, **10**:109, 1970.
4. Bohn, D. J., K. Miyasaka, E. B. Marchak, W. K. Thompson, A. B. Froese, and A. C. Bryan, "Ventilation by high-frequency oscillation," *J. Appl. Physiol.*, **48**:710–16, 1980.
5. Lunkenheimer, P. P., W. Rafflenbeul, H. Kellar, I. Frank, H. H. Dickhut, and C. Fuhrmann, "Application of tracheal pressure oscillations as a modification of 'Diffusional Respiration'," *Br. J. Anaesth.*, **44**:627, 1972.
6. Taylor, G. I., "Dispersion of solute matter in solvent flowing through a tube," *Proc. Roy. Soc. Lond.*, **A291**:186–203, 1953.
7. Chatwin, P. C., "On the longitudinal dispersion of passive contaminant in oscillatory flows in tubes," *J. Fluid Mech.*, **71**:513–527, 1975.
8. Dragon, C. A., and J. B. Grotberg, "Oscillatory flow and dispersion in a flexible tube," *J. Fluid Mech.*, **231**:135–155, 1991.
9. Eckmann, D. M., and J. B. Grotberg, "Oscillatory flow and mass transport in a curved tube," *J. Fluid Mech.*, **188**:509–527, 1988.
10. Godleski, D. A., and J. B. Grotberg, "Convection-diffusion interaction for oscillatory flow in a tapered tube," *J. Biomech. Eng.*, **110**:283–291, 1988.
11. Dubois, A. B., A. W. Brody, D. H. Lewis, and B. F. Burgess, "Oscillation mechanics of lungs and chest in man." *J. Appl. Physiol.* **8**:587–594, 1956.

12. Otis, A. B., C. B. McKerrow, R. A. Bartlett, J. Mead, M. B. Mcllroy, N. J. Selverstone, and E. P. Radford, "Mechanical factors in distribution of pulmonary ventilation," *J. Appl. Physiol.*, **8**:427–443, 1956.

13. Suki, B., F. Petak, A. Adamicza, Z. Hantos, and K. R. Lutchen, "Partitioning of airway and lung-tissue properties—comparison of in-situ and open-chest conditions," *J. Appl. Physiol.*, **79**:861–869, 1995.

14. Slutsky, A. S., G. G. Berdine, and J. M. Drazen, "Steady flow in a model of human central airways," *J. Appl. Physiol.*, **49**:417–423, 1980.

15. Isabey, D., and H. K. Chang, "Steady and unsteady pressure-flow relationships in central airways," *J. Appl. Physiol.*, **51**:1338–1348, 1981.

16. Pedley, T. J., R. C. Schroter, and M. F. Sudlow, "The prediction of pressure drop and variation of resistance within the human bronchial airways," *Respir. Physiol.*, **9**:387–405, 1970.

17. Mead, J., J. L. Whittenberger, and E. P. Radford, Jr., "Surface tension as a factor in pulmonary volume-pressure hysteresis," *J. Appl. Physiol.*, **10**:191–196, 1957.

18. Von Neergaard, K., "Neue Auffassungen über einen Grundbegriff der Atemmechanik. Die Retraktionskraft der Lunge, abhängig von der Oberflächenspannung in den Alveolen," *Z. Gesampte Exp. Med.*, **66**:373–394, 1929.

19. Knowles, J. H., S. K. Hong, and H. Rahn, "Possible errors using esophageal balloon in determination of pressure-volume characteristics of the lung and thoracic cage," *J. Appl. Physiol.*, **14**:525–530, 1959.

20. Avery, M. E., and J. Mead, "Surface properties in relation to atelectasis and hyaline membrane disease," *Am. J. Dis. Child.*, **97**:517–523, 1959.

21. Grotberg, J. B., M. Filoche, D. F. Willson, K. Raghavendran, and R. H. Notter, "Did reduced alveolar delivery of surfactant contribute to negative results in adults with acute respiratory distress syndrome?" *Am J Respir Crit Care Med*, **195**(4):538–540, 2017.

22. Enhorning, G., and B. Robertson, "Expansion patterns in premature rabbit lung after tracheal deposition of surfactant," *Acta Path. Micro. Scand. Sect. A—Pathology*, **A79**:682, 1971.

23. Cassidy, K. J., J. L. Bull, M. R. Glucksberg, C. A. Dawson, S. T. Haworth, R. B. Hirschl, N. Gavriely, and J. B. Grotberg, "A rat lung model of instilled liquid transport in the pulmonary airways," *J. Appl. Physiol.*, **90**:1955–1967, 2001.

24. Espinosa, F. F., and R. D. Kamm, "Bolus dispersal through the lungs in surfactant replacement therapy," *J. Appl. Physiol.*, **86**:391–410, 1999.

25. Halpern, D., O. E. Jensen, and J. B. Grotberg, "A theoretical study of surfactant and liquid delivery into the lung," *J. Appl. Physiol.*, **85**:333–352, 1998.

26. Filoche, M., C. F. Tai, and J. B. Grotberg, "Three-dimensional model of surfactant replacement therapy," *Proc Natl Acad Sci U S A* **112**(30):9287–9292, 2015.

27. Kazem,i A., B. Loui, D. Isabey, G. F. Nieman, L. A. Gatto, J. Satalin, S. Baker, J. B. Grotberg, and M. Filoche, "Surfactant delivery in rat lungs: Comparing 3D geometrical simulation model with experimental instillation," *PLOS Comput Biol*, **15**(10):1007408, 2019.

28. Permutt, S., and R. L. Riley, "Hemodynamics of collapsible vessels with tone—vascular waterfall," *J. Appl. Physiol.*, **18**:924, 1963.

29. Shapiro, A. H., "Steady flow in collapsible tubes," *J. Biomech. Eng.*, **99**:126–147, 1977.

30. Lambert, R. K., and T. A. Wilson, "Flow limitation in a collapsible tube," *Journal of Applied Physiology*, **33**:150–153, 1972.

31. West, J. B., "Regional differences in gas exchange in the lung of erect man," *J. Appl. Physiol.*, **17**:893–898, 1962.

32. Gavriely, N., K. B. Kelly, J. B. Grotberg, and S. H. Loring, "Forced expiratory wheezes are a manifestation of airway flow limitation," *J. Appl. Physiol.*, **62**:2398–2403, 1987.

33. Grotberg, J. B., and S. H. Davis, "Fluid-dynamic flapping of a collapsible channel: sound generation and flow limitation," *J. Biomech. Eng.*, **13**:219–230, 1980.

34. Grotberg, J. B., and N. Gavriely, "Flutter in collapsible tubes: a theoretical model of wheezes," *J. Appl. Physiol.*, **66**:2262–2273, 1989.

35. Everett, D. H., and J. M. Haynes, "Model studies of capillary condensation: 1. Cylindrical pore model with zero contact angle," *J. Colloid, Inter. Sci.*, **38**:125–137, 1972.

36. Kamm, R. D., and R. C. Schroter, "Is airway closure caused by a thin liquid instability?" *Respir. Physiol.*, **75**:141–156, 1989.

37. Romano, F., H. Fujioka, M. Muradoglu, and J. B. Grotberg, "Liquid plug formation in an airway closure model," *Phys Rev Fluids*, **4**:093103, 2019.

38. Macklem, P. T., D. F. Proctor, and J. C. Hogg, "The stability of peripheral airways." *Respir. Physiol.* **8**: 191–203, 1970.

39. Halpern, D., J. B. Grotberg, "Surfactant effects on fluid-elastic instabilities of liquid-lined flexible tubes: a model of airway closure," *J Biomech Eng*, **115**(3):271–277, 1993.

40. Huh, D., H. Fujioka, Y. C. Tung, N. Futai, R. Paine, J. B. Grotberg, and S. Takayama, "Acoustically detectable cellular-level lung injury induced by fluid mechanical stresses in microfluidic airway systems," Proc Natl Acad Sci U S A, **104**:18886–18891, 2007.

41. Bilek, A. M., K. C. Dee, and D. P. Gaver, "Mechanisms of surface-tension-induced epithelial cell damage in a model of pulmonary airway reopening," J Appl Physiol, 94(2):770–783, 2003.

42. Muradoglu, M., F. Romano, H. Fujioka, and J. B. Grotberg, "Effects of surfactant on propagation and rupture of a liquid plug in a tube," J Fluid Mech, 872:407–437, 2019. doi: https://doi.org/10.1017/jfm.2019.333.

43. Viola, H., J. Chang, J. R. Grunwell, L. Hecker, R. Tirouvanziam, J. B. Grotberg, and S. Takayama, "Microphysiological systems modeling acute respiratory distress syndrome that capture mechanical force-induced injury-inflammation-repair," APL Bioeng, 3(4):041503, 2019.

44. Alencar, A. M., Z. Hantos, F. Petak, J. Tolnai, T. Asztalos, S. Zapperi, J. S. Andrade, S. V. Buldyrev, H. E. Stanley, and B. Suki, "Scaling behavior in crackle sound during lung inflation," *Phys. Rev. E*, **60**:4659–4663, 1999.

45. Forgacs, P., "Functional basis of pulmonary sounds," *Chest*, **73**:399–405, 1978.

46. Grotberg, J. B., "Crackles and wheezes: agents of injury?" *Ann Am Thorac Soc*, **16**(8):967–969, 2019.

BIBLIOGRAPHY

Fredberg, J. J., N. Wang, D. Stamenovic, and D. E. Ingber, "Micromechanics of the lung: from the parenchyma to the cytoskeleton," *Complexity in Structure and Function of the Lung (Lung Biol. Health Dis. Ser.)*, 99–122, 1998.

Grotberg, J. B., "Respiratory fluid mechanics and transport processes," *Annu. Rev. Biomed. Engr.*, **3**:421–457, 2001.

Kamm, R. D., "Airway wall mechanics," *Annu. Rev. Biomed. Eng.*, **1**:47–72, 1999.

The Lung: Scientific Foundations, R. G. Crystal, and J. B. West, eds., New York: Raven Press, 1991.

West, J. B., *Respiratory Physiology: The Essentials*, 6th ed., Baltimore: Lippincott Williams & Wilkins, 2000.

Grotberg, J. B. and O. E. Jensen, "Biofluid mechanics in flexible tubes," *Ann Rev Fluid Mech*, **36**:121–147, 2004.

Grotberg, J. B., "Respiratory fluid mechanics," *Phys Fluids,* **23**(2):021301-1—0213015, 2011.

CHAPTER 7

BIOMECHANICS OF THE RESPIRATORY MUSCLES

Anat Ratnovsky
Afeka College of Engineering, Tel Aviv, Israel

Pinchas Halpern
Tel Aviv Medical Center, Tel Aviv, Israel, and Sackler School of Medicine, Tel Aviv University, Tel Aviv, Israel

David Elad
Tel Aviv University, Tel Aviv, Israel

7.1 INTRODUCTION

The respiratory tract provides passageways for airflow between environmental air, rich in oxygen, and the gas exchange region within the pulmonary alveoli. Periodic pumping of gas in and out of the lungs is controlled by contractions of the respiratory muscles that rhythmically change the thoracic volume and produce the pressure gradients required for airflow. In this chapter, which is largely based on a recent review in a special issue on respiratory biomechanics (Ratnovsky et al., 2008), we will review techniques for assessment of the biomechanical performance of the respiratory muscles and biomechanical models of chest wall mechanics.

7.2 THE RESPIRATORY MUSCLES

The respiratory muscles are morphologically and functionally skeletal muscles. The group of inspiratory muscles includes the diaphragm, external intercostal, parasternal, sternomastoid, and scalene muscles. The group of expiratory muscles includes the internal intercostal, rectus abdominis, external and internal oblique, and transverse abdominis muscles. During low breathing effort (i.e., at rest) only the inspiratory muscles are active. During high breathing effort (i.e., exercise) the expiratory muscles become active as well.

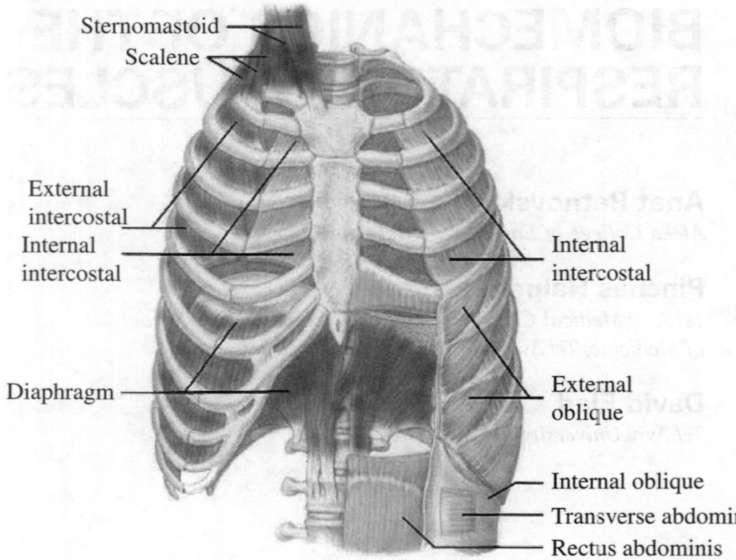

FIGURE 7.1 Schematic description of the anatomy of human respiratory muscles. [*From www.concept2.co.uk/training/breathing.php, with permission.*]

7.2.1 The Diaphragm

The diaphragm, the main muscle of inspiration, is a thin, flat, musculotendinous structure separating the thoracic cavity from the abdominal wall. The muscle fibers of the diaphragm radiate from the central tendon to either the three lumbar vertebral bodies (i.e., crural diaphragm) or the inner surfaces of the lower six ribs (i.e., costal diaphragm) (Fig. 7.1). The tension within the diaphragmatic muscle fibers during contraction generates a caudal force on the central tendon that descends in order to expand the thoracic cavity along its craniocaudal axis. In addition, the costal diaphragm fibers apply a force on the lower six ribs which lifts and rotates them outward (De Troyer, 1997).

7.2.2 The Intercostal Muscles

The intercostal muscles are composed of two thin layers of muscle fibers occupying each of the intercostal spaces. The external intercostal muscle fibers run obliquely downward and ventrally from each rib to the neighboring rib below. The lower insertion of the external intercostal muscles is more distant from the rib's axis of rotation than the upper one (Fig. 7.1), and as a result, contraction of these muscles exerts a larger torque acting on the lower rib which raises the lower rib with respect to the upper one. The net effect of the contraction of these muscles raises the rib cage.

The internal intercostal muscle fibers, on the other hand, run obliquely downward and dorsally from each rib to the neighboring rib below. The lower insertion of these muscles is less distant from the rib's axis of rotation than the upper one, and thus, during their contraction they lower the ribs (De Troyer, 1997).

7.2.3 The Accessory Muscles

The accessory muscles of inspiration include the sternomastoid and scalene muscles. The sternomastoid muscles descend from the mastoid process to the ventral surface of the manubrium sterni and the medial third of the clavicle. The scalene muscles comprise three bundles that run from the transverse processes of the lower five cervical vertebrae to the upper surface of the first two ribs. Contraction of these muscles raises the sternum and the first two ribs and thus assists in expanding the rib cage (Legrand et al., 2003).

7.2.4 The Abdominal Muscles

The four abdominal muscle pairs forming the abdominal wall are the rectus abdominis, external oblique, internal oblique, and transverse abdominis (Fig. 7.1). The rectus abdominis is the most ventral one that runs caudally from the ventral aspect of the sternum and the fifth, sixth, and seventh costal cartilages along the length of the abdominal wall to its insertion into the pubis (De Troyer, 1997). The external oblique is the most superficial that originates from the external surface of the lower eight ribs, well above the costal margin, and covers the lower ribs and intercostal muscles. Its fibers radiate caudally to the iliac crest and inguinal ligament and medially to the linea alba. The internal oblique lies deep to the external oblique. Its fibers arise from the inguinal ligament and iliac crest and insert into the anterolateral surface of the cartilages of the last three ribs and into the linea alba. The transverse abdominis is the deepest muscle of the lateral abdominal wall. Its fibers run circumferentially around the abdominal visceral mass from the inner surface of the lower six ribs, lumbar fascia, iliac crest, and inguinal ligament to the rectus sheath. Contraction of the abdominal muscles pulls the abdominal wall inward, causing the diaphragm to move cranially into the thoracic cavity, and pulls the lower ribs caudally to deflate the rib cage (De Troyer, 1997).

7.3 MECHANICS PERFORMANCE OF RESPIRATORY MUSCLES

All-inclusive function of the respiratory muscles is an important index in diagnosis and follow-up of breathing problems due to respiratory muscle weakness. It can be assessed by employing different techniques, which are based on different measurement protocols.

7.3.1 Global Assessment of Respiratory Muscles Strength

Measurements of maximal inspiratory or expiratory mouth pressures during quasistatic maneuvers are widely used for assessment of the global strength of respiratory muscles (Black and Hyatt, 1969; Chen and Kuo, 1989; Leech et al., 1983; McElvaney et al., 1989; Ratnovsky et al., 1999; Steier et al., 2007; Wilson et al., 1984). The subject inspires or expires through a mouthpiece with an air leak orifice (1.5 to 2 mm) to prevent the contribution of the facial muscles (Black and Hyatt, 1969). Maximal static mouth pressure is measured while performing a maximal inspiratory or expiratory effort against an obstructed airway for at least 1 second. Maximal expiratory mouth pressure is usually measured at lung volumes approaching total lung capacity (TLC), while maximal inspiratory pressure is usually measured near functional residual capacity (FRC) or residual volume (RV). A summary of published values of maximal inspiratory and expiratory mouth pressures is given in Table 7.1.

The ability of respiratory muscles to generate force, like other skeletal muscles, depends on their length and the velocity of contraction (Green and Moxham, 1985; Rochester, 1988). In the respiratory system, force is generally estimated as pressure and their length varies as lung volume changes (Fauroux and Aubertin, 2007). Employment of the interrupter technique, in which the airflow inlet is obstructed during forced expiration or force inspiration maneuvers, allowed measurement of mouth pressures at different lung volumes during maximum inspiratory and expiratory efforts made against different levels of resistance (Agostoni and Fenn, 1960; Cook et al., 1964; Ratnovsky et al., 1999). This is particularly relevant when evaluating hyperinflated patients in whom the geometry of the respiratory muscles changes, and thereby their ability to drive the respiratory pump decreases

TABLE 7.1 Summary of averaged values of maximal mouth pressure of normal subject

		Male				Female			
		P_I (cmH_2O)		P_E (cmH_2O)		P_I (cmH_2O)		P_E (cmH_2O)	
Reference	No. and sex	RV	FRC	FRC	TLC	RV	FRC	FRC	TLC
Cook et al., 1964	37M 11F	124 ± 30	103 ± 20	100 ± 40	190 ± 45	102 ± 20	87 ± 25	57 ± 22	146 ± 30
Black and Hyatt, 1969	120	107 ± 35			208 ± 76	74 ± 30			168 ± 44
Rochester and Arora, 1983	80M 121F	127 ± 28			216 ± 45	91 ± 25			138 ± 39
Wilson et al., 1984	48M 87F	106 ± 31			148 ± 34	73 ± 22			93 ± 17
Chen and Kuo, 1989	80M 80F	104 ± 25	90 ± 25	115 ± 33	132 ± 38	74 ± 21	65 ± 18	75 ± 20	88 ± 25
McElvaney et al., 1989	40M 64F	108 ± 26			173 ± 41	75 ± 24			115 ± 34
Leech et al., 1983	300M 480F	115 ± 35			160 ± 40	70 ± 28			93 ± 33
Nickerson and Keens, 1982	15 M+F	122 ± 8							
Ambrosino et al., 1994	22 M+F	104 ± 28			142 ± 33				
McParland et al., 1992	9 M+F	70–150	70–120	70–200	100–230				
Ratnovsky et al., 1999	6 M+F	89 ± 16	73 ± 14	81 ± 28	109 ± 19				

+/− represents the SD.

(Laghi and Tobin, 2003; Ratnovsky et al., 2006). Measurement of maximal inspiratory and expiratory mouth pressure at different lung volumes in untrained but cooperative subjects revealed a reduction in expiratory muscle strength as lung volume decreases from TLC and in inspiratory muscles as lung volume increases from RV (Ratnovsky et al., 1999).

Measurement of sniff nasal inspiratory pressure is another method to assess the global strength of respiratory muscles. The nasal pressure is measured in an occluded nostril during a maximal sniff performed through the contralateral nostril from FRC. This pressure closely reflects esophageal pressure, and thus, inspiratory muscle strength (Fauroux and Aubertin, 2007; Fitting, 2006; Stefanutti and Fitting, 1999; Steier et al., 2007).

7.3.2 Endurance of the Respiratory Muscles

The ability of a skeletal muscle to endure a task is determined by the force of contraction, the duration of contraction, and the velocity of shortening during contraction. The endurance capacity of respiratory muscles depends on lung volume (which determines muscle length), velocity of muscle shortening, and type of breathing maneuver used in the test (Rochester, 1988). Maximal voluntary ventilation (MVV) is the oldest test of respiratory muscle endurance in which the level of ventilation that can be sustained for 15 minutes or longer is measured. Besides the forces required for reaching this high level of ventilation, this test reflects the ability of the respiratory muscles to reach and sustain the required contractile output (Freedman, 1970).

The two most popular methods to measure respiratory muscle endurance are the resistive and the threshold inspiratory load (Fiz et al., 1998; Hart et al., 2002; Johnson et al., 1997; Martyn et al., 1987; Reiter et al., 2006). The incremental threshold loading is imposed during inspiration through a device with a weighted plunger, which requires development of enough pressure to lift the plunger out of its socket in order to initiate inspiration (Nickerson and Keens, 1982). The endurance is expressed as the time the subject can endure a particular load or as the maximum load tolerated for a specific time (Fiz et al., 1998). In the resistive inspiratory load the subject breathes against a variable inspiratory resistance at which the subject had to generate a percentage of his maximal mouth pressure in order to inspire. Endurance is expressed as the maximal time of sustained breathing against a resistance (Reiter et al., 2006; Wanke et al., 1994). The postinterruption tracing of mouth pressure against time represents an effort sustained (against an obstructed airway) over a length of time and can serve as a pressure-time index of respiratory muscle endurance. The area under this tracing (i.e., the pressure-time integral) represents an energy parameter of the form PT, where P is the mean mouth pressure measure during airway obstruction and T is the time a subject can sustain the obstruction (Ratnovsky et al., 1999). Similar to the strength of respiratory muscles, large dependence on lung volume was found for their endurance. The endurance of expiratory muscles decreased as lung volume decreased from TLC, while the endurance of inspiratory muscles decreased as lung volume increased from RV (Ratnovsky et al., 1999).

7.3.3 Electromyography

Electromyography (EMG) is a technique for evaluating the electrical activity of skeletal muscles at their active state (Luca, 1997). Intramuscular EMG signals are measured by needle electrodes inserted through the skin into the muscle, while surface EMG signals are recorded with surface electrodes that are placed on the skin overlying the muscle of interest. Typically, EMG recordings are obtained using a bipolar electrode configuration with a common ground electrode, which allows canceling unwanted electrical activity from outside of the muscle. The electrical current measured by EMG is usually proportional to the level of muscle activity. Normal range for skeletal muscles is 50 μV to 5 mV for a bandwidth of 20 to 500 Hz (Cohen, 1986).

The raw EMG data resembles a noise signal with a distribution around zero. Therefore, the data must be processed before it can be used for assessing the contractile state of the muscle (Herzog et al., 1994). The data can be processed in the time domain or in the frequency domain. The EMG signal processing in the time domain includes full wave rectification in which only the absolute values of the signal is considered. Then in order to relate the EMG signal to the contractile feature of the muscle it is desired to eliminate the high-frequency content by using any type of low-pass filter that yields the linear envelope of the signal. The root-mean-square (RMS) value of the EMG signal is an excellent indicator of the signal magnitude. RMS values are calculated by summing the squared values of the raw EMG signal, determining the mean of the sum, and taking the square root of the mean

$$\mathrm{RMS} = \sqrt{\frac{1}{T}\int_{t}^{t+T} \mathrm{EMG}^2(t)\,dt} \tag{7.1}$$

The study of EMG signals in the frequency domain has received much attention due to the loss of the high-frequency content of the signal during muscle fatigue (Herzog et al., 1994). Power density spectra of the EMG signal can be obtained by using fast Fourier transformation technique. The most important parameter for analyzing the power density spectrum of the EMG signal is the mean frequency or the centroid frequency, which is defined as the frequency that divides the power of the EMG spectrum into two equal areas.

7.3.4 Electromyography of the Respiratory Muscles

Using EMG for assessment of respiratory muscles performance, in addition to the methods described in the above paragraphs, enables differentiation between different respiratory muscles. The EMG signals can detect abnormal muscle electrical activity that may occur in many diseases and conditions, including muscular dystrophy, inflammation of the muscles, peripheral nerve damage, and myasthenia gravis and other (ATS/ERS, 2002). The EMG of human respiratory muscles has been measured for many years in order to investigate their activity during various respiratory maneuvers and at different lung volumes. Measurements of EMG signals from the diaphragm during inspiration revealed peak values of about 50 μV during quiet breathing and maximal values around 150 μV as inspiration effort increases (Agostoni and Fenn, 1960; Corne et al., 2000; Hawkes et al., 2007; Petit et al., 1960). A similar electrical activity during quiet inspiration was also measured from the parasternal muscle (De Troyer and Sampson, 1982) and from the external intercostals that reached amplitudes of 80 to 100 μV (Hawkes et al., 2007; Maarsingh et al., 2000; Ratnovsky et al., 2003). The EMG activity from the accessory muscle is controversial. Several studies detected activity only at high inspiratory efforts (Costa et al., 1994; Estenne et al., 1998) while other found activity even during quiet breathing which increased as inspiration effort increased (Breslin et al., 1990; Ratnovsky et al., 2003).

Quiet expiration is predominantly the result of passive elastic recoil of the lung and chest wall (Osmond, 1995), and thus the abdominal muscles (i.e., rectus abdominis, external and internal oblique, and transverse abdominis) are not active during quiet breathing. However, as breathing effort increases, EMG signals are observed at the beginning of expiration and they become increasingly noticeable as the expiration proceeds and reaches maximum values of 200 μV (Abraham et al., 2002; Hodges and Gandevia, 2000; Ratnovsky et al., 2003).

The EMG activity of respiratory muscles is also useful for assessing respiratory muscle endurance and fatigue after muscle training or exercise. It is widely accepted that respiratory muscle fatigue is related to the change in the power spectrum of the measured EMG (Rochester, 1988). When a skeletal muscle is in a fatiguing pattern of contraction, the mean frequency in the power spectrum of the EMG is decreased. An additional indicator for muscle fatigue is a reduction in the ratio between the EMG powers in the high-frequency band to that in the low-frequency band (H/L ratio). Using the above frequency analysis of EMG, it has been shown that inspiratory loads higher than 50 percent of maximal diaphragmatic pressure lead to diaphragmatic fatigue (Gross et al., 1979). In addition, an inverse relationship between the inspiratory or expiratory loads and both the mean frequency and the H/L ratio were demonstrated in the diaphragm and rectus abdominis muscles (Badier et al., 1993).

Respiratory muscle fatigue may also be developed in healthy subjects during high-intensity exercise (Johnson et al., 1993; Mador et al., 1993; Verges et al., 2006), which may limit exercise tolerance in both trained and untrained individuals (Sheel et al., 2001). The findings that respiratory muscles training enhances performance in normal subjects support the hypothesis that respiratory muscle fatigue is potentially a limiting factor in intense exercise (Boutellier, 1998; Boutellier and Piwko, 1992). Simultaneous measurement of surface EMG from respiratory muscles (e.g., sternomastoid, external intercostal, rectus abdominis, and external oblique) and the calf muscles demonstrated significantly faster fatigue of the inspiratory muscles (e.g., sternomastoid and external intercostal) than the calf muscles during intense marching on a standard electrically powered treadmill (Perlovitch et al., 2007). Progressive muscle fatigue was associated with the increase of RMS values of the surface EMG data (Krogh-Lund and Jorgensen, 1993; Ohashi, 1993).

7.3.5 Forces of the Respiratory Muscles

The EMG of skeletal muscle provides information on the level of muscle activity during different tasks. Accordingly, several models have been developed for prediction of the forces generated during muscle contraction. The biophysical cross-bridge model of Huxley (Huxley, 1957) is commonly used for understanding the mechanisms of contraction at the molecular level, and to interpret the results of mechanical, thermodynamics, and biochemical experiments on muscles.

The Hill-type muscle model was derived from a classic study of heat production in muscle and became the preferred model for studies of multiple muscle movement systems (Hill, 1938). The model is composed of three elements: the contractile element (representing the contractile muscle fibers), the series elastic component (representing the connective tissue in series with the sarcomeres including the tendon), and the parallel elastic component (representing the parallel connective tissue around the contractile element). The relationship between the force generated by the elastic elements and the change in muscle length is assumed to be exponential, similar to those of connective tissues, while the characteristic equation of the contractile element combines the tension-length and the force-velocity relationships of the muscle with the neural input signal (Winter and Bagley, 1987).

Hill's muscle model was implemented in a study aimed to determine the forces generated by four respiratory muscles from both sides of the chest wall (e.g., sternomastoid, external intercostals, rectus abdominis, and external oblique) during different respiratory maneuvers (Hill, 1938; Ratnovsky et al., 2003; Winter, 1990). The constant parameters for the model were extracted either from the literatures or were measured from cadavers. Linear extrapolation was done to determine the variation in respiratory muscles length at lung volume different than RV, FRC, and TLC during respiration. EMG signal is depicted from the vicinity near the electrode, and it represents the electrical activity of a skeletal muscle with a typical width of 5 cm and length of up to 30 cm. Therefore, for the wide muscles (e.g., external intercostal and external oblique) it was assumed that a muscle unit in the vicinity of the electrodes contributes to the EMG signal. Thus, the total muscle force from these muscles was calculated as the sum of all the parallel units. The averaged forces developed by the abdominal muscles, the sternomastoid muscles, and the fibers of the external intercostal muscles in one intercostal space during low breathing efforts (i.e., expiration from 50 to 60 percent VC to 30 to 40 percent VC or inspiration from 30 to 40 percent VC to 50 to 60 percent VC) were about 10 N, 2 N, and 8 N, respectively. At high respiratory effort (i.e., expiring from 90 to 80 percent VC to RV and inspiring from RV to 80 percent VC) these forces increased to about 40 to 60 N, 12 N, and 30 N, respectively.

The coordinated performance of respiratory muscles from both sides of the chest wall induces its displacement during lung ventilation. Lung ventilation efficacy, therefore, may be influenced from imbalance in the function of the muscles between the two sides. In healthy subjects a highly symmetrical performance both in terms of the value of the forces and the recruitment of the muscles was observed in four respiratory muscles (Ratnovsky et al., 2003).

The same model was also employed to study the forces developed by the external oblique, sternomastoid, and external intercostal muscles in emphysematous patients after a single-lung transplant surgery (Ratnovsky and Elad, 2005). Forces developed by the muscles on the side of the transplanted lung were compared with those of the other side, which has the diseased lung. The averaged values for maximal forces at any breathing effort calculated from the muscles located at the side of the transplanted lung were higher (0.66, 56, and 18 N at low breathing efforts and 7.3, 228, and 22 N at high breathing efforts for the sternomastoid, external intercostal, and external oblique, respectively) than those calculated for muscles on the side of the native (i.e., diseased) lung (0.56, 20.22, and 3 N at low breathing efforts and 5.64, 132, and 6 N at high breathing efforts, respectively).

7.4 MODELS OF CHEST WALL MECHANICS

The human chest wall is a complex structure, and the contribution of its different components to efficient respiration has been the subject of numerous mechanical and mathematical models.

7.4.1 One-Dimensional Chest Wall Model

In early models, the chest wall was simulated as one compartment of the rib cage with a single degree of freedom (Fig. 7.2). It was described as a single cylinder containing three moving, massless bodies that represent the rib cage, the diaphragm, and the abdomen (Primiano, 1982). An electrical analog was used to examine the following limited cases: (1) a very stiff rib cage (as in adult normal breathing) that moves relative to the skeleton as a single unit; (2) a very flaccid rib cage (representing a quadriplegic patient); and (3) Mueller maneuver, which is defined by a complete obstruction of the airway opening, such that lung volume can change only by compressing the gas in the lungs. A pneumatic analog of the inspiratory musculature was used in a quasistatic mechanical model (Fig. 7.3) in order to examine theoretically the forces that act on the rib cage and the influence of lung volume changes on the area of apposition of the diaphragm to the rib cage (Macklem et al., 1983).

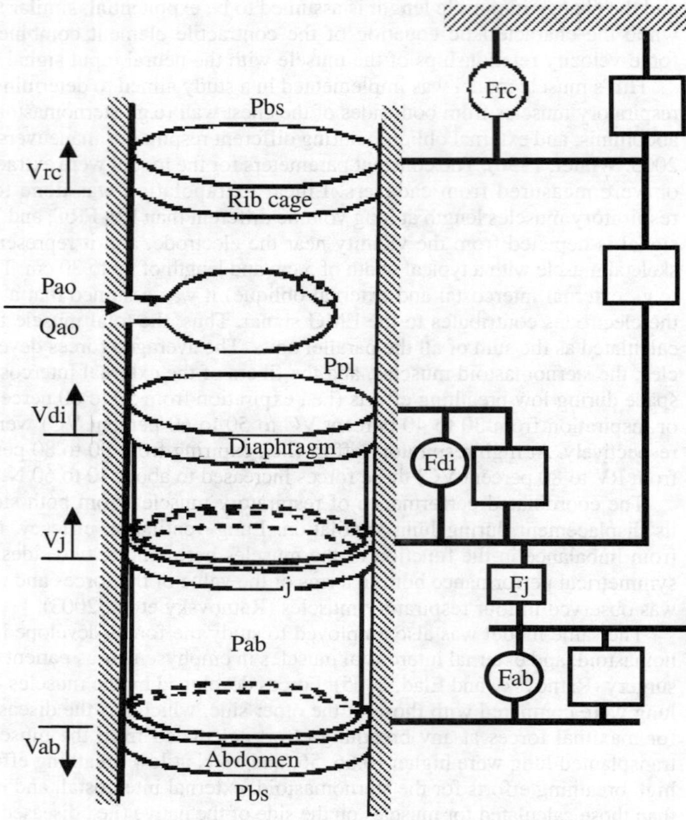

FIGURE 7.2 Mechanical analog of the ventilatory system (chest wall and lungs). The chest wall is modeled as a single cylinder containing three moving massless bodies that represent the rib cage, diaphragm, and abdomen. Circular symbols represent active force produce by contraction respiratory muscles and rectangular symbols represent passive mechanical elements. [*From Primiano (1982), with permission.*]

7.4.2 Two-Dimensional Chest Wall Model

In more advanced models the chest wall was simulated by two compartments separated by the diaphragm (Ben-Haim et al., 1989; Ben-Haim and Saidel, 1989; Ben-Haim and Saidel, 1990; Lichtenstein et al., 1992). The rib cage, diaphragm, and abdomen were simulated as moving membranes attached to a fixed skeleton. Each of the moveable parts was modeled as a membrane that can support a pressure difference without bending. The external surfaces of the ventilatory system were modeled by three membranes associated with the lung-apposed rib cage, the diaphragm-apposed rib cage and the ventral abdominal wall (Fig. 7.4). The quasistatic governing equations of the force balance on each component were solved numerically to study limited cases of stiff and flaccid chest walls, effects of introducing volume displacement in the pleural and abdominal spaces on static lung maneuvers, and the influence of lung abnormalities on the rib cage and diaphragm compliance.

Extension of the single-compartment model of Macklem et al. (1983) was done by separation of the rib cage into two parts, one that is apposing the inner surface to the lung and the other one that is apposing the diaphragm (Ward et al., 1992). In this model three springs represent the elastic

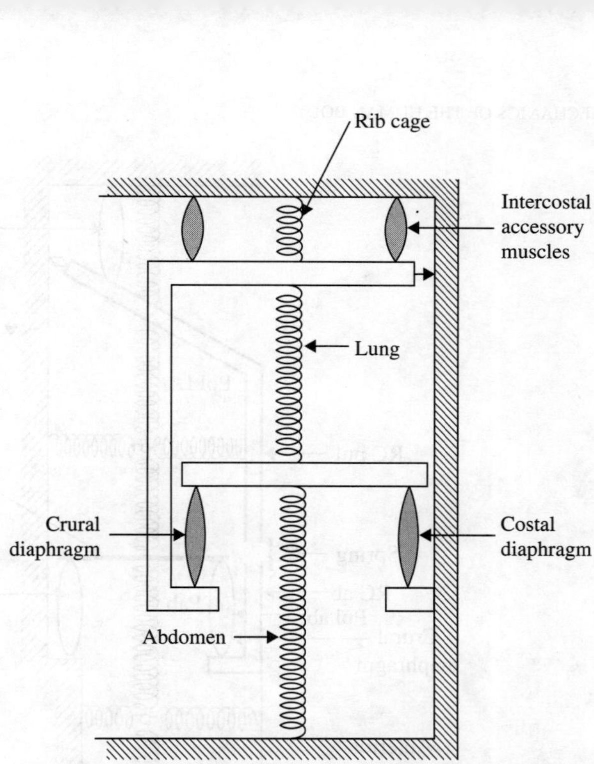

FIGURE 7.3 Mechanical model of inspiratory musculature. Intercostal and accessory muscles are mechanical in parallel with the diaphragm. The springs represent the elastic properties of the rib cage, lung, and abdomen. Bar into which crural and costal fibers insert represents the central tendon of the diaphragm. [*From Macklem et al. (1983), with permission.*]

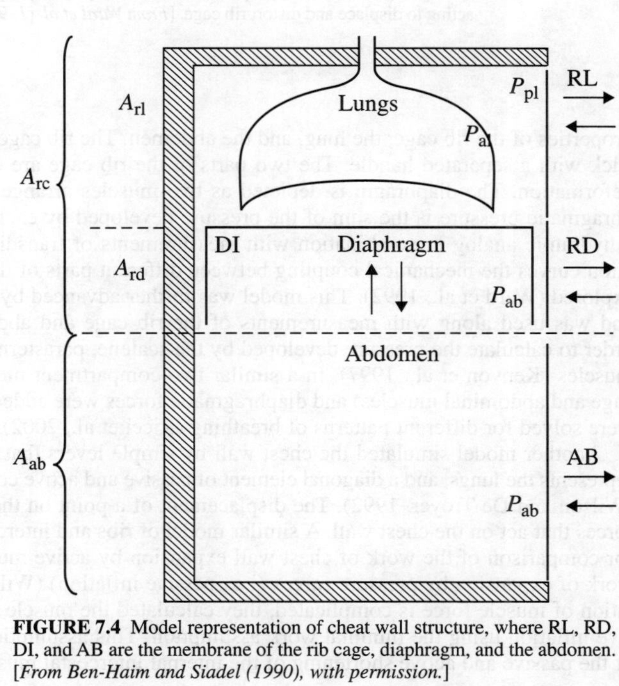

FIGURE 7.4 Model representation of cheat wall structure, where RL, RD, DI, and AB are the membrane of the rib cage, diaphragm, and the abdomen. [*From Ben-Haim and Siadel (1990), with permission.*]

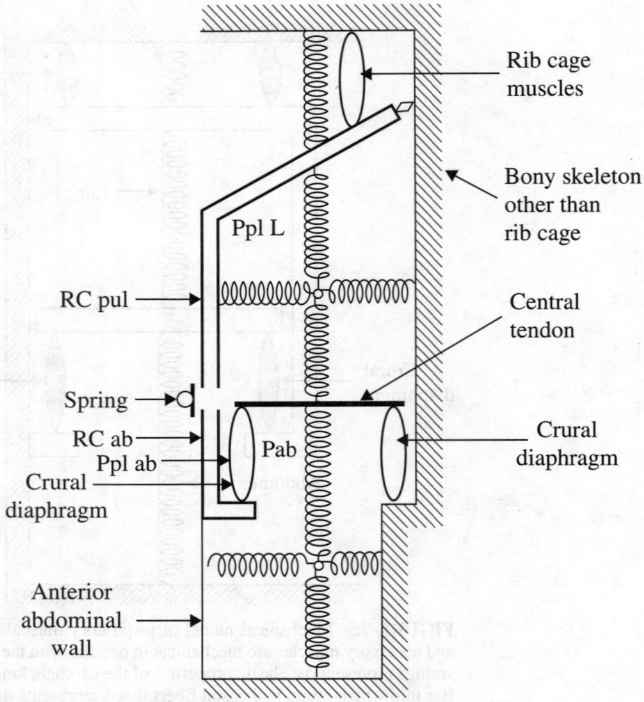

FIGURE 7.5 Mechanical model of the rib cage showing mechanical linkage of rib cage muscles, elastic properties of respiratory system (springs), and agencies acting to displace and distort rib cage. [*From Ward et al. (1992), with permission.*]

properties of the rib cage, the lung, and the abdomen. The rib cage is shaped like an inverted hockey stick with a separated handle. The two parts of the rib cage are connected by a spring that resists deformation. The diaphragm is depicted as two muscles arranged in parallel so that the transdiaphragmatic pressure is the sum of the pressure developed by each of the muscles (Fig. 7.5). Using a hydraulic analog in combination with measurements of transdiaphragmatic pressures and relaxation curves the mechanical coupling between different parts of the rib cage during inspiration was explored (Ward et al., 1992). This model was further advanced by including the abdominal muscles and was used along with measurements of the rib cage and abdomen volume during exercise in order to calculate the pressure developed by the scalene, parasternal intercostals, and sternomastoid muscles (Kenyon et al., 1997). In a similar two-compartment model, extradiaphragmatic (e.g., rib cage and abdominal muscles) and diaphragmatic forces were added in the equilibrium equations and were solved for different patterns of breathing (Ricci et al., 2002).

Another model simulated the chest wall by simple levers that represent the ribs, a cylinder that represents the lungs, and a diagonal element of passive and active components that represents a muscle (Wilson and De Troyer, 1992). The displacement of a point on the chest wall is proportional to the forces that act on the chest wall. A similar model of ribs and intercostal muscles was also developed for comparison of the work of chest wall expansion by active muscles (i.e., active inflation) to the work of expansion by pressure forces (i.e., passive inflation) (Wilson et al., 1999). Since the calculation of muscle force is complicated, they calculated the muscle shortening during active and passive inflation using the minimal work assumption. This assumption was tested with measurements of the passive and active shortening of the internal intercostal muscles in five dogs. The mechanical analogs of all the models described so far have not differentiated between individual groups of respiratory muscles and between the rib cage and the accessory muscles, and thus precluded evaluation of their contribution to respiration.

Recently, a more realistic model of the chest wall has been developed with the objective to evaluate the performance of individual groups of respiratory muscles in terms of the force and the work generated during breathing maneuvers (Ratnovsky et al., 2005). The two-dimensional model in the sagittal plane is composed of stationary and mobile bones and the respiratory muscles (Fig. 7.6). The stationary elements are the bones of the vertebral column, skull, iliac crest, and pelvis, while the rib cage forms the mobile part of the model. The model incorporates three groups of inspiratory muscles (e.g., diaphragm, external intercostal, and sternomastoid) and four groups of

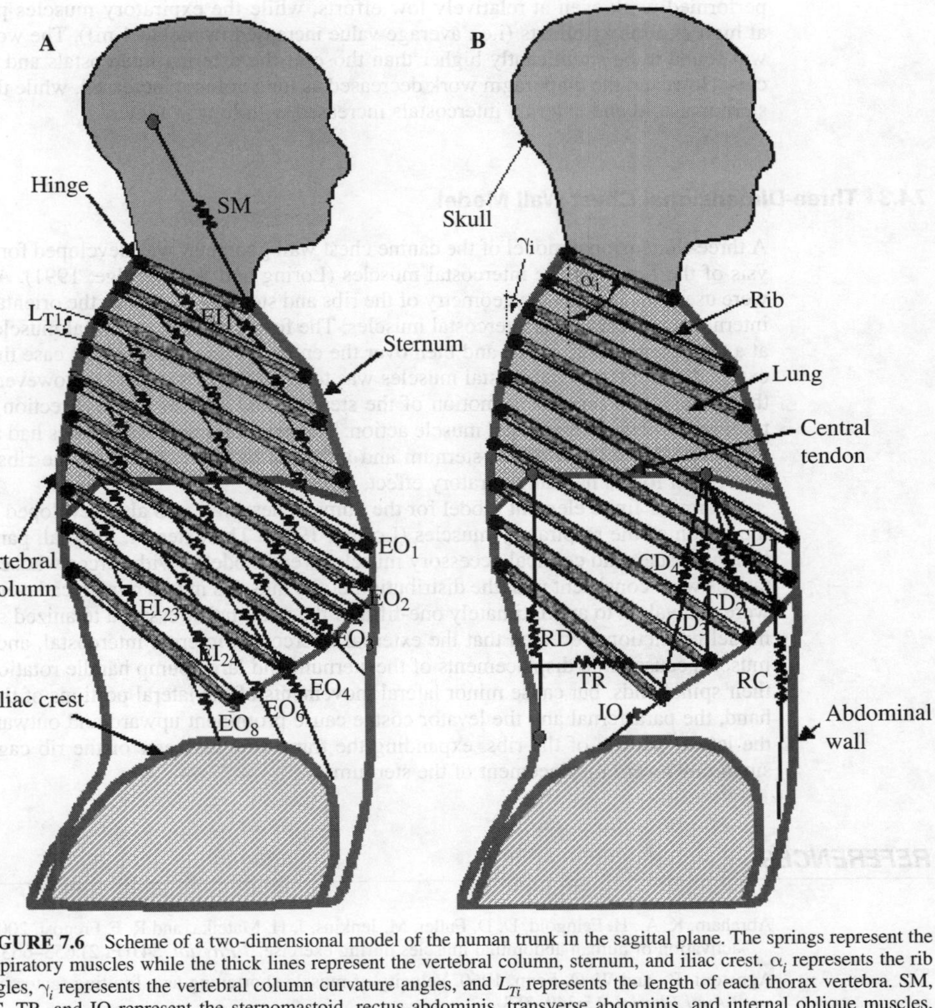

FIGURE 7.6 Scheme of a two-dimensional model of the human trunk in the sagittal plane. The springs represent the respiratory muscles while the thick lines represent the vertebral column, sternum, and iliac crest. α_i represents the rib angles, γ_i represents the vertebral column curvature angles, and L_{Ti} represents the length of each thorax vertebra. SM, RC, TR, and IO represent the sternomastoid, rectus abdominis, transverse abdominis, and internal oblique muscles, respectively. EI_1-EI_{24} represent the external intercostal muscle units and their angle with the horizon. EO_1-EO_6 represent the external oblique muscle units. CD_1, CD_2, CD_3, CD_4, and RD represent the costal fibers and the crural fibers of the diaphragm muscle, respectively. [*From Ratnovsky et al. (2005), with permission.*]

expiratory muscles (e.g., rectus abdominis, external and internal oblique, and transverse abdominis), which act as actuators of the mobile rib cage. The geometry parameters of the model components (e.g., rib length and angle corresponding to the cephacaudal direction, muscle fiber orientation, and muscle length and position) and their variation with lung volumes were derived from the literature (Ratnovsky et al., 2003) and observation of cadavers. Assuming a quasistatic equilibrium at each lung volume sets of force balance equations were constructed (Ratnovsky et al., 2005). The model input parameters were mouth pressure, lung volume, and the forces of the sternomastoid, external intercostals, external oblique, and rectus abdominis that were computed from EMG measurements (Ratnovsky et al., 2003). The instantaneous work done by each of the respiratory muscle during breathing was calculated as the product of the instantaneous force and the corresponding length change at any lung volume. The overall work performed by each of the respiratory muscle during a given breathing phase of inspiration or expiration was calculated from the area under the curve of the instantaneous work (Ratnovsky et al., 2005). The results show that the inspiratory muscles performed work even at relatively low efforts, while the expiratory muscles produced work only at high expiratory efforts (i.e., average value increased from 0 to 1 mJ). The work of the diaphragm was found to be significantly higher than those of the external intercostals and sternomastoid muscles. However, the diaphragm work decreased as lung volume increased, while the work done by the sternomastoid and external intercostals increased with lung volume.

7.4.3 Three-Dimensional Chest Wall Model

A three-dimensional model of the canine chest wall geometry was developed for finite element analysis of the forces of the intercostal muscles (Loring and Woodbridge, 1991). Accurate dimensions were used to construct the geometry of the ribs and sternum as well as the orientation of the external, internal, and parasternal intercostal muscles. The forces of the intercostal muscles were applied first at a single intercostal space and then over the entire rib cage. In the first case the action of both the external and internal intercostal muscles was to draw the ribs together. However, in the second case the result was a prominent motion of the sternum and all ribs in the direction consistent with the traditional view of intercostal muscle action. The external intercostal forces had an inspiratory effect with cephalad motion of the sternum and a "pump-handle" motion of the ribs, while the internal intercostal forces had an expiratory effect.

A similar finite element model for the human chest wall was also developed in order to simulate the action of the respiratory muscles (Loring, 1992). The external, internal, parasternal intercostal, levator costae, and cervical accessory muscles were modeled with forces whose position and orientations were consistent with the distribution of the muscles in two human cadavers. All muscle forces were equivalent to approximately one-fifth of the maximal stress of a tetanized skeletal muscle. The model predictions revealed that the external intercostal, internal intercostal, and cervical accessory muscles cause large displacements of the sternum and large pump handle rotations of the ribs about their spinal ends, but cause minor lateral movements of the lateral portions of the ribs. On the other hand, the parasternal and the levator costae cause prominent upward and outward displacements of the lateral portion of the ribs, expanding the transverse diameter of the rib cage and cause only a small downward displacement of the sternum.

REFERENCES

Abraham, K. A., H. Feingold, D. D. Fuller, M. Jenkins, J. H. Mateika, and R. F. Fregosi. 2002. Respiratory-related activation of human abdominal muscles during exercise. *J Physiol.* **541**(Pt 2):653–663.

Agostoni, E., and W. O. Fenn. 1960. Velocity of muscle shortening as a limiting factor in respiratory air flow. *J Appl Physiol.* **15**:349–353.

Ambrosino, N., C. Opasich, P. Crotti, F. Cobelli, L. Tavazzi, and C. Rampulla. 1994. Breathing pattern, ventilatory drive and respiratory muscle strength in patients with chronic heart failure. *Eur Respir J.* **7**(1):17–22.

ATS/ERS. 2002. ATS/ERS statement on respiratory muscle testing. *Am J Respir Crit Care Med.* **166**(4):518–624.

Badier, M., C. Guillot, F. Lagier-Tessonnier, H. Burnet, and Y. Jammes. 1993. EMG power spectrum of respiratory and skeletal muscles during static contraction in healthy man. *Muscle Nerve.* **16**(6):601–609.

Ben-Haim, S. A., O. Lichtenstein, and G. M. Saidel. 1989. Mechanical analysis of extrapulmonary volume displacements in the thorax and abdomen. *J Appl Physiol.* **67**(5):1785–1790.

Ben-Haim, S. A., and G. M. Saidel. 1989. Chest wall mechanics: effects of acute and chronic lung disease. *J Biomech.* **22**(6–7):559–564.

Ben-Haim, S. A., and G. M. Saidel. 1990. Mathematical model of chest wall mechanics: a phenomenological approach. *Ann Biomed Eng.* **18**(1):37–56.

Black, L. F., and R. E. Hyatt. 1969. Maximal respiratory pressures: normal values and relationship to age and sex. *Am Rev Respir Dis.* **99**(5):696–702.

Boutellier, U., 1998. Respiratory muscle fitness and exercise endurance in healthy humans. *Med Sci Sports Exerc.* **30**(7):1169–1172.

Boutellier, U., and P. Piwko. 1992. The respiratory system as an exercise limiting factor in normal sedentary subjects. *Eur J Appl Physiol Occup Physiol.* **64**(2):145–152.

Breslin, E. H., B. C. Garoutte, V. Kohlman-Carrieri, and B. R. Celli. 1990. Correlations between dyspnea, diaphragm and sternomastoid recruitment during inspiratory resistance breathing in normal subjects. *Chest.* **98**(2):298–302.

Chen, H. I., and C. S. Kuo. 1989. Relationship between respiratory muscle function and age, sex, and other factors. *J Appl Physiol.* **66**(2):943–948.

Cohen, A., 1986. *Biomedical Signal Processing.* CRC Press Inc. Florida. pp. 119–121.

Cook, C. D., J. Mead, and M. M. Orzalesi. 1964. Static volume-pressure characteristics of the respiratory system during maximal efforts. *J Appl Physiol.* **19**:1016–1022.

Corne, S., K. Webster, and M. Younes. 2000. Effects of inspiratory flow on diaphragmatic motor output in normal subjects. *J Appl Physiol.* **89**(2):481–492.

Costa, D., M. Vitti, D. de Oliveira Tosello, and R. P. Costa. 1994. Participation of the sternocleidomastoid muscle on deep inspiration in man. An electromyographic study. *Electromyogr Clin Neurophysiol.* **34**(5):315–320.

De Troyer, A., 1997. The respiratory muscles, In: *The Lung: Scientific Foundation.* Crystal R. G. (ed.), Lippincott Raven. Philadelphia. pp. 1203–1215.

De Troyer, A., and M. G. Sampson. 1982. Activation of the parasternal intercostals during breathing efforts in human subjects. *J Appl Physiol.* **52**(3):524–529.

Estenne, M., E. Derom, and A. De Troyer. 1998. Neck and abdominal muscle activity in patients with severe thoracic scoliosis. *Am J Respir Crit Care Med.* **158**(2):452–457.

Fauroux, B., and G. Aubertin. 2007. Measurement of maximal pressures and the sniff manoeuvre in children. *Paediatr Respir Rev.* **8**(1):90–93.

Fitting, J. W., 2006. Sniff nasal inspiratory pressure: simple or too simple? *Eur Respir J.* **27**(5):881–883.

Fiz, J. A., P. Romero, R. Gomez, M. C. Hernandez, J. Ruiz, J. Izquierdo, R. Coll, and J. Morera. 1998. Indices of respiratory muscle endurance in healthy subjects. *Respiration.* **65**(1):21–27.

Freedman, S., 1970. Sustained maximum voluntary ventilation. *Respir Physiol.* **8**(2):230–244.

Green, M., and J. Moxham. 1985. The respiratory muscles. *Clin Sci (Lond).* **68**(1):1–10.

Gross, D., A. Grassino, W. R. Ross, and P. T. Macklem. 1979. Electromyogram pattern of diaphragmatic fatigue. *J Appl Physiol.* **46**(1):1–7.

Hart, N., P. Hawkins, C. H. Hamnegard, M. Green, J. Moxham, and M. I. Polkey. 2002. A novel clinical test of respiratory muscle endurance. *Eur Respir J.* **19**(2):232–239.

Hawkes, E. Z., A. V. Nowicky, and A. K. McConnell. 2007. Diaphragm and intercostal surface EMG and muscle performance after acute inspiratory muscle loading. *Respir Physiol Neurobiol.* **155**(3):213–219.

Herzog W., A.C.S. Guimaraes, and Y. T. Zhang. 1994. Measuring techniques. In: *Biomechanics of Musculo-Skeletal System.* Nigg B. M., and W. Herzog (eds). Chichester. Wiley. pp. 308–336.

Hill, A. V., 1938. The heat of shortening and the dynamic constants of muscle. *Proc. Roy. Soc.* **126**:136–195.

Hodges, P. W., and S. C. Gandevia. 2000. Changes in intra-abdominal pressure during postural and respiratory activation of the human diaphragm. *J Appl Physiol.* **89**(3):967–976.

Huxley, A. F., 1957. Muscle structure and theories of contraction. *Prog Biophys Biophys Chem.* **7**:255–318.

Johnson, B. D., M. A. Babcock, O. E. Suman, and J. A. Dempsey. 1993. Exercise-induced diaphragmatic fatigue in healthy humans. *J Physiol.* **460**:385–405.

Johnson, P. H., A. J. Cowley, and W. J. Kinnear. 1997. Incremental threshold loading: a standard protocol and establishment of a reference range in naive normal subjects. *Eur Respir J.* **10**(12):2868–2871.

Kenyon, C. M., S. J. Cala, S. Yan, A. Aliverti, G. Scano, R. Duranti, A. Pedotti, and P. T. Macklem. 1997. Rib cage mechanics during quiet breathing and exercise in humans. *J Appl Physiol.* **83**(4):1242–1255.

Krogh-Lund, C., and K. Jorgensen. 1993. Myo-electric fatigue manifestations revisited: power spectrum, conduction velocity, and amplitude of human elbow flexor muscles during isolated and repetitive endurance contractions at 30% maximal voluntary contraction. *Eur J Appl Physiol Occup Physiol.* **66**(2):161–173.

Laghi, F., and M. J. Tobin. 2003. Disorders of the respiratory muscles. *Am J Respir Crit Care Med.* **168**(1):10–48.

Leech, J. A., H. Ghezzo, D. Stevens, and M. R. Becklake. 1983. Respiratory pressures and function in young adults. *Am Rev Respir Dis.* **128**(1):17–23.

Legrand, A., E. Schneider, P. A. Gevenois, and A. De Troyer. 2003. Respiratory effects of the scalene and sternomastoid muscles in humans. *J Appl Physiol.* **94**(4):1467–1472.

Lichtenstein, O., S. A. Ben-Haim, G. M. Saidel, and U. Dinnar. 1992. Role of the diaphragm in chest wall mechanics. *J Appl Physiol.* **72**(2):568–574.

Loring, S. H., 1992. Action of human respiratory muscles inferred from finite element analysis of rib cage. *J Appl Physiol.* **72**(4):1461–1465.

Loring, S. H., and J. A. Woodbridge. 1991. Intercostal muscle action inferred from finite-element analysis. *J Appl Physiol.* **70**(6):2712–2718.

Luca, C. J. D., 1997. The use of surface electromyography in biomechanics. *J Appl Biomech.* **13**:135–163.

Maarsingh, E. J., L. A. van Eykern, A. B. Sprikkelman, M. O. Hoekstra, and W. M. van Aalderen. 2000. Respiratory muscle activity measured with a noninvasive EMG technique: technical aspects and reproducibility. *J Appl Physiol.* **88**(6):1955–1961.

Macklem, P. T., D. M. Macklem, and A. De Troyer. 1983. A model of inspiratory muscle mechanics. *J Appl Physiol.* **55**(2):547–557.

Mador, M. J., U. J. Magalang, A. Rodis, and T. J. Kufel. 1993. Diaphragmatic fatigue after exercise in healthy human subjects. *Am Rev Respir Dis.* **148**(6 Pt 1):1571–1575.

Martyn, J. B., R. H. Moreno, P. D. Pare, and R. L. Pardy. 1987. Measurement of inspiratory muscle performance with incremental threshold loading. *Am Rev Respir Dis.* **135**(4):919–923.

McElvaney, G., S. Blackie, N. J. Morrison, P. G. Wilcox, M. S. Fairbarn, and R. L. Pardy. 1989. Maximal static respiratory pressures in the normal elderly. *Am Rev Respir Dis.* **139**(1):277–281.

McParland, C., B. Krishnan, Y. Wang, and C.G. Gallagher. 1992. Inspiratory muscle weakness and dyspnea in chronic heart failure. *Am Rev Respir Dis.* **146**(2):467–472.

Nickerson, B. G., and T. G. Keens. 1982. Measuring ventilatory muscle endurance in humans as sustainable inspiratory pressure. *J Appl Physiol.* **52**(3):768–772.

Ohashi, J., 1993. Changes in relations between surface electromyogram and fatigue level by repeating fatiguing static contractions. *Ann Physiol Anthropol.* **12**(5):285–296.

Osmond, D., 1995. Functional anatomy of the chest wall. In: *The Thorax, Part A: Physiology*. Roussos C. (ed.) Marcel Dekker Inc. New York. pp. 413–444.

Perlovitch, R., A. Gefen, D. Elad, A. Ratnovsky, M. R. Kramer, and P. Halpern. 2007. Inspiratory muscles experience fatigue faster than the calf muscles during treadmill marching. *Respir Physiol Neurobiol.* **156**(1):61–68.

Petit, J. M., G. Milic-Emili, and L. Delhez. 1960. Role of the diaphragm in breathing in conscious normal man: an electromyographic study. *J Appl Physiol.* **15**:1101–1106.

Primiano, F. P., Jr., 1982. Theoretical analysis of chest wall mechanics. *J Biomech.* **15**(12):919–931.

Ratnovsky, A., and D. Elad. 2005. Anatomical model of the human trunk for analysis of respiratory muscles mechanics. *Respir Physiol Neurobiol.* **148**(3):245–262.

Ratnovsky, A., D. Elad, and P. Halpern. 2008. Mechanics of respiratory muscles. *Respir Phyiol Neurobiol.* Special issue on Respiratory Biomechanics. **163**(1–3):82–89.

Ratnovsky, A., D. Elad, G. Izbicki, and M. R. Kramer. 2006. Mechanics of respiratory muscles in single-lung transplant recipients. *Respiration*. **73**(5):642–650.

Ratnovsky, A., D. Elad, U. Zaretsky, and R. J. Shiner. 1999. A technique for global assessment of respiratory muscle performance at different lung volumes. *Physiol Meas*. **20**(1):37–51.

Ratnovsky, A., M. R. Kramer, and D. Elad. 2005. Breathing power of respiratory muscles in single-lung transplanted emphysematic patients. *Respir Physiol Neurobiol*. **148**(3):263–273.

Ratnovsky, A., U. Zaretsky, R. J. Shiner, and D. Elad. 2003. Integrated approach for in vivo evaluation of respiratory muscles mechanics. *J Biomech*. **36**(12):1771–1784.

Reiter, M., A. Totzauer, I. Werner, W. Koessler, H. Zwick, and T. Wanke. 2006. Evaluation of inspiratory muscle function in a healthy Austrian population—practical aspects. *Respiration*. **73**(5):590–596.

Ricci, S. B., P. Cluzel, A. Constantinescu, and T. Similowski. 2002. Mechanical model of the inspiratory pump. *J Biomech*. **35**(1):139–145.

Rochester, D. F., 1988. Tests of respiratory muscle function. *Clin Chest Med*. **9**(2):249–261.

Rochester, D. F., and N.S. Arora. 1983. Respiratory muscle failure. *Med Clin North Am*. **67**(3):573–597.

Sheel, A. W., P. A. Derchak, B. J. Morgan, D. F. Pegelow, A. J. Jacques, and J. A. Dempsey. 2001. Fatiguing inspiratory muscle work causes reflex reduction in resting leg blood flow in humans. *J Physiol*. **537**(Pt 1): 277–289.

Stefanutti, D., and J. W. Fitting. 1999. Sniff nasal inspiratory pressure. Reference values in Caucasian children. *Am J Respir Crit Care Med*. **159**(1):107–111.

Steier, J., S. Kaul, J. Seymour, C. Jolley, G. Rafferty, W. Man, Y. M. Luo, M. Roughton, M. I. Polkey, and J. Moxham. 2007. The value of multiple tests of respiratory muscle strength. *Thorax*. **62**(11):975–980.

Verges, S., D. Notter, and C. M. Spengler. 2006. Influence of diaphragm and rib cage muscle fatigue on breathing during endurance exercise. *Respir Physiol Neurobiol*. **154**(3):431–442.

Wanke, T., K. Toifl, M. Merkle, D. Formanek, H. Lahrmann, and H. Zwick. 1994. Inspiratory muscle training in patients with Duchenne muscular dystrophy. *Chest*. **105**(2):475–482.

Ward, M. E., J. W. Ward, and P. T. Macklem. 1992. Analysis of human chest wall motion using a two-compartment rib cage model. *J Appl Physiol*. **72**(4):1338–1347.

Wilson, S. H., N. T. Cooke, R. H. Edwards, and S. G. Spiro. 1984. Predicted normal values for maximal respiratory pressures in Caucasian adults and children. *Thorax*. **39**(7):535–538.

Wilson, T. A., M. Angelillo, A. Legrand, and A. de Troyer. 1999. Muscle kinematics for minimal work of breathing. *J Appl Physiol*. **87**(2):554–560.

Wilson, T. A., and A. De Troyer. 1992. Effect of respiratory muscle tension on lung volume. *J Appl Physiol*. **73**(6):2283–2288.

Winter, J. M., 1990. Hill based muscle models: a system engineering perspective, In: *Multiple Muscle Systems Biomechanics and Movement Organization*. Winter, J. M., and S. L. Y. Woo (eds). Springer-Verlag Inc. New York. pp. 69–93.

Winter, J. M., and A. M. Bagley. 1987. Biomechanical modeling of muscle joint system: why it is useful. *IEEE Eng. Med. Biol*. **6**:17–21.

CHAPTER 8

BIOMECHANICS OF HUMAN MOVEMENT

Kurt T. Manal
University of Delaware, Newark, Delaware

Thomas S. Buchanan
University of Delaware, Newark, Delaware

8.1 WHY STUDY HUMAN MOVEMENT?

The biomechanics of human motion is a fascinating field. Who among us has never marveled at the graceful motions of a dancer, or the rapid finger movements of a musician? From the time of Aristotle onward there have been countless books written on the topic of movement in animals and humans. Despite the great minds that have considered the topic, it is just recently that much advancement has been made experimentally. Historically, the study of human movement has been costly and very time consuming. This is because in order to study them, movements are almost always discretized and then analyzed step-by-step, with the size of the steps determined by the speed of the movement (and the questions being asked). Whether it be frames of film from a video camera or digitized samples from an electrogoniometer, most movements are recorded as series of static images which are then reassembled to provide kinematic and kinetic information.

There has been a tremendous growth in the study of human movement in the past two decades due to the low cost of digital data acquisition systems that make possible the storage and analysis of massive amounts of data that are required to accurately characterize complex motion. This growing interest in the study of human movement is coming from five predominate groups.

First, basic scientists are interested in the control of human movement. How the nervous system controls the large number of degrees of freedom necessary to produce smooth, complex movements (or even simple ones!) is poorly understood. The study of the coordination of movement can be compared to the inverse problem faced by the roboticist. The roboticist develops computer programs to produce coordinated movements in a robot. On the other hand, the motor control researcher measures coordinated movements in order to understand what the "neural program" is.

Second, human movements are studied to understand and treat pathologies. For example, gait analysis is often used to help guide the physician contemplating surgery for children with cerebral palsy. The best choice for a tendon transfer or muscle lengthening surgery can be predicted using combinations of movement analysis and biomechanical modeling (e.g., Delp et al., 1996). Gait analysis can also be used to monitor the progression of the disease and the efficacy of the treatment.

Third, the study of human athletic performance has been revolutionized by motion analysis equipment and software that make it possible to readily analyze complex three-dimensional movements. From cricket bowling to figure skating to swimming to pole vaulting, the kinematics and kinetics have been examined with an aim to improve human performance.

Fourth, there is substantial interest in human movement from those studying ergonomics and human factors related to military applications. Both the development of human-machine interfaces for high-tech weapons and the minimization of industrial injuries require knowledge of human kinematics and kinetics.

Finally, the kinematics of human movement has been studied by animators interested in making computer-generated characters move in realistic ways. By recording actors while they perform choreographed dances and movements, it is possible to get complex kinematic data into a computer, which can then be used to animate a computer-generated image.

8.2 FORWARD VERSUS INVERSE DYNAMICS

There are two fundamentally different approaches to studying the biomechanics of human movement: forward dynamics and inverse dynamics. Either can be used to determine joint kinetics (e.g., estimate joint moments during movements).

8.2.1 Forward Dynamics

In a forward dynamics approach to the study of human movement, the input to the system is the neural command (Fig. 8.1). This specifies the level of activation to the muscles. The neural command can be estimated by optimization models (Zajac, 1989; Pandy and Zajac, 1991) or from electromyograms (EMGs). The neural command is the sum of the neuronal signals from the α-motorneurons (that originate in the spinal cord) to the fibers of each muscle. This can be represented by a single value

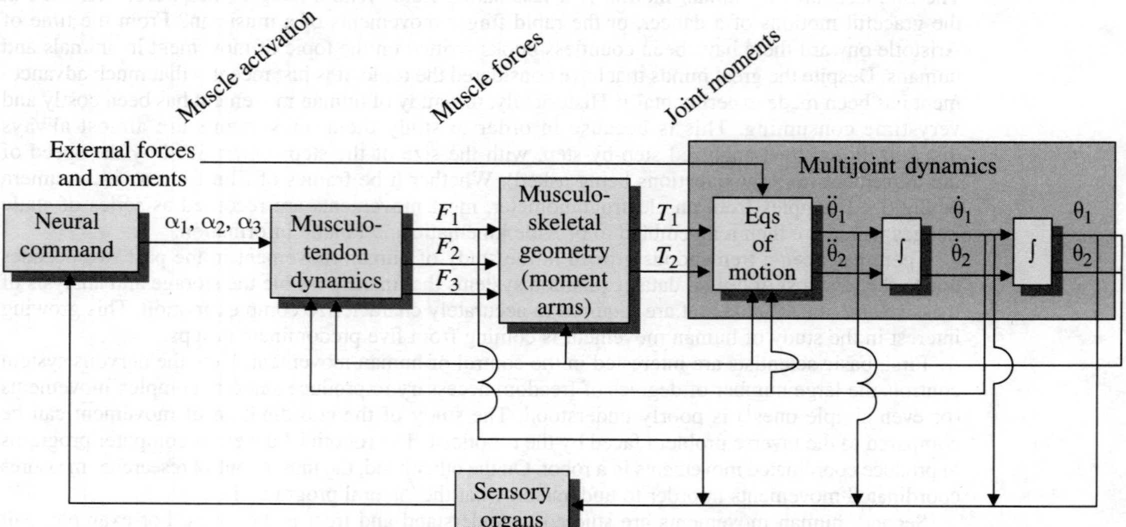

FIGURE 8.1 Forward dynamics approach to studying human movement. This simplified figure depicts the neural command and forces for three muscles and the moments and joint angles for a two-joint system. See text for details.

(at any given time) for each muscle that we will call muscle activation, α_i, and it will be mathematically represented as a value between 0 and 1. Hence, if it is to be estimated from EMGs, additional steps are needed to transform EMGs to muscle activation.

Musculotendon dynamics govern the transformation of muscle activation, α_i, to muscle force, F_i. Once the muscle begins to develop force, the tendon (in series with the muscle) begins to carry load as well. Depending upon the kinetics of the joint, the relative length changes in the tendon and the muscle may be very different. For example, this is certainly the case for a "static contraction." (This commonly used name is an oxymoron, as something cannot *contract*, i.e., shorten, and be *static* at the same time. Hence, the tendon must lengthen as the muscle shortens if the joint is not to move!)

The force in each musculotendonous unit contributes toward the total moment about the joint. The musculoskeletal geometry determines the moment arms of the muscles. (Since muscle force is dependent upon muscle length, i.e., the classic muscle "length-tension curve," there is feedback between joint angle and musculotendon dynamics.) It is important to note that the moment arms of muscles are not constant values, but change as a function of joint angles. Also, one needs to keep in mind the multiple degrees of freedom of each joint, as a muscle may have multiple actions at a joint, depending on its geometry. Finally, it is important to note that the joint moment, T_i, is determined from the sum of the contributions for each muscle. If not all muscles are included in the process, the joint moment will be underestimated. The output of this transformation is a moment for each joint (or, more precisely, each degree of freedom).

From the joint moments, multijoint dynamics can be used to compute the accelerations, velocities, and angles for each joint of interest. On the feedback side, the neural command is influenced by muscle length (via muscle spindles) and tendon force (via Golgi tendon organs). Many other sensory organs play a role in this as well, but these two are generally the most influential.

There are several limitations of the forward dynamics approach. First, it requires estimates of muscle activation. EMG methods have been used to this end, but the high variability in EMG signals has made this difficult, especially during dynamic conditions. Second, the transformation from muscle activation to muscle force is difficult, as it is not completely understood. Most models of this (e.g., Zajac, 1989) are based on phenomenological models derived from A. V. Hill's classic work (Hill, 1938) or the more complex biophysical model of Huxley's (Huxley, 1957; Huxley and Simmons, 1971), such as Zahalack's models (Zahalack, 1986, 2000). One way around the problem of determining force from EMGs is to employ optimization methods to predict muscle forces directly (bypassing these first two limitations). However, the choice of a proper cost function is a matter of great debate. Scientists doing research in human motor control find it surprising that biomechanical engineers replace their entire line of study (and indeed, the entire central nervous system), with a simple, unverified equation. Nevertheless, some cost functions provide reasonable fits of the data when addressing specific questions. Another limitation is that of determining musculoskeletal moment arms. These are difficult to measure in cadavers and even harder to determine with any accuracy in a living person. Finally, joint moments can easily be underestimated. Using forward dynamics, small errors in joint torques can lead to large errors in joint position.

8.2.2 Inverse Dynamics

Inverse dynamics approaches the problem from the opposite end. Here we begin by measuring position and the external forces acting on the body (Fig. 8.2). In gait analysis, for example, the position of tracking targets attached to the segments can be recorded using a camera-based system and the external forces can be recorded using a force platform.

The relative position of tracking targets on adjacent segments is used to calculate joint angles. These data are differentiated to obtain velocities and accelerations.

The accelerations and the information about other forces exerted on the body (e.g., the recordings from a force plate) can be input to the equations of motion to compute the corresponding joint reaction forces and moments.

If the musculoskeletal geometry is included, muscle forces can then be estimated from the joint moments and, from these it may be possible to estimate ligament and joint compressive forces.

As with forward dynamics, inverse dynamics has important limitations. First, in order to estimate joint moments correctly, one must know the inertia of each body segment (this is embedded in the

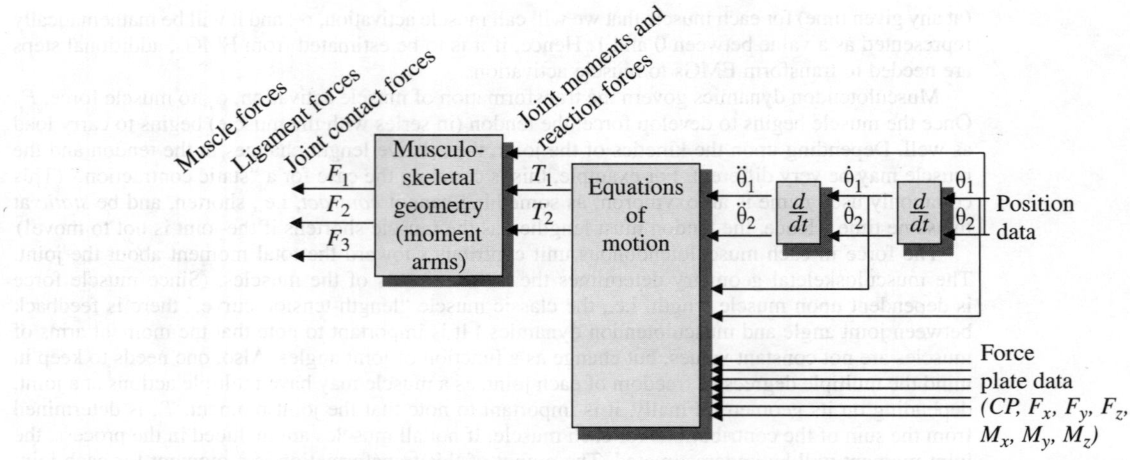

FIGURE 8.2 Inverse dynamics approach to studying human movement. This simplified figure depicts the angular position for two joints, and the forces for three muscles. See text for details.

equations of motion). These parameters are difficult to measure and must be estimated. Typically, they are estimated using established values from cadavers and scaled using simplistic scaling rules, the accuracies of which are rarely verified. Secondly, the resultant joint reaction forces and moments are net values. This is important to keep in mind if an inverse dynamics approach is used to predict muscle forces. For example, if a person activates his hamstrings generating a 30-N·m flexion moment and at the same time activates the quadriceps generating a 25-N·m extension moment, the inverse dynamics method (if it is perfectly accurate) will yield a net knee flexion moment of 5-N·m. Since the actual contribution of the knee flexor muscles was six times greater, this approach is grossly inaccurate and inappropriate for estimating the role of the knee flexors during this task. This is strongly stated because cocontraction of muscles is very common, yet this approach is widely use to estimate muscular contributions. Another limitation of the inverse dynamics approach occurs when one tries to estimate muscle forces. Since there are multiple muscles spanning each joint, the transformation from joint moment to muscle forces yields an infinite number of solutions. Choosing the proper solution requires some sort of optimization analysis, requiring the use of a cost function whose validity is sure to be challenged. Finally, if one wishes to examine muscle activations, there is no current model available that will do this inverse transformation. However, this is rarely the goal of an inverse dynamics analysis.

8.2.3 Comparing Forward and Inverse Dynamics Methods

Given the limitations of each method, which should be used: forward or inverse dynamics? That depends on the question being asked. If one's primary interest is in joint kinematics, it makes more sense to start with a measurement of position as in the inverse dynamics approach. If one is primarily interested in muscle forces, one could argue that forward dynamics has more advantages. For estimating joint moments during movements, inverse dynamics is probably the best bet, depending upon the specific application.

For the remainder of this chapter, we will concentrate on the inverse dynamics approach for the study of human movement. Inverse dynamics are more commonly used than forward dynamics when studying human movement. A forward dynamics approach will be addressed in a subsequent chapter "Biomechanics of the Musculoskeletal System."

8.3 TOOLS FOR MEASURING HUMAN MOVEMENT

In this section, we will discuss three of the more common methods used to collect human movement data: electrogoniometers, electromagnetic tracking devices, and optoelectronic measuring systems. Of these distinctly different measuring tools, optoelectronic systems are the most common registration method, and therefore the majority of this section will focus on video-based motion analysis.

8.3.1 Electrogoniometers

Electrogoniometers are devices that convert joint angle to a voltage. The voltage can be sampled continuously, making electrogoniometers ideal for measuring dynamic movement. There are basically two designs, both of which fall under the category of resistive transducers. These devices, namely, potentiometers and strain gauges, output a voltage related to the angular position of the joint. The voltage is converted to an angle using a manufacturer-supplied scale factor specific to each transducer. The joint angle can be displayed in real time and/or stored on a computer equipped with an analog to digital data acquisition card.

Potentiometers. A potentiometer is nothing more than a variable resistor that is sensitive to changes in angular position. Two arms, one fixed to the outer casing of the potentiometer and the other to the rotating shaft can be used to mount the device to the segments on either side of a joint. The potentiometer is placed over the joint axis of rotation with the arms secured to the segments using medical tape or elasticized wraps. Changes in joint angle will cause the *wiper* (i.e., sliding contact) of the potentiometer to slide across the resistor resulting in an output voltage linearly related to the joint angle. It is important that the potentiometer be placed over the axis of rotation; otherwise, movement of the joint will be restricted. The electrogoniometer is ideally positioned when the rotating shaft of the potentiometer and the joint axis of rotation are aligned. More elaborate mounting methods have been designed to house mutually perpendicular potentiometers in multidegree-of-freedom exoskeletal linkages (e.g., Chao, 1980; Shiavi et al., 1987). These devices are no longer commonly used, but are mentioned for historical purposes since they have played an important role in many previous studies.

Strain Gauges. Strain gauges can also be used to detect changes in joint angular position. An example of a one-degree-of-freedom electrogoniometer is illustrated in Fig. 8.3. Two- and

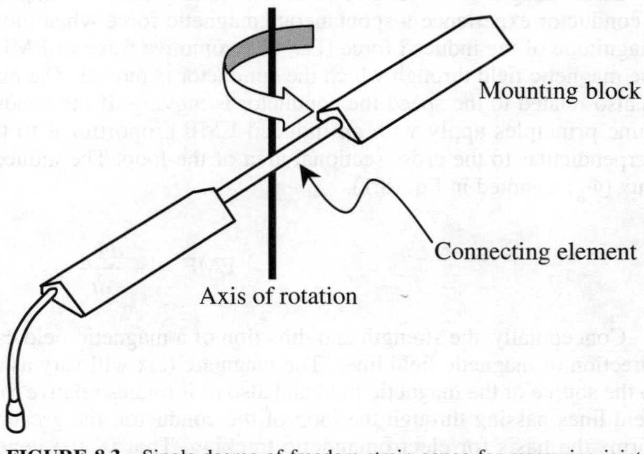

FIGURE 8.3 Single degree of freedom strain gauge for measuring joint angular position. Strain-sensitive wires are fixed to the connecting element between the mounting blocks. The mounting blocks are secured to both segments on either side of a joint. Changes in joint angle are output as a voltage proportional to the amount of rotation about the axis of rotation.

three-degree-of-freedom electrogoniometers of this type are also available. Strain sensitive wires are mounted within a connecting element and electrically connected to form a Wheatstone bridge. Each strain-sensitive wire is, in effect, a resistor and is sensitive to strains in particular directions. Hence, when the electrogoniometer is forced to rotate about the axis of rotation as drawn in Fig. 8.3, the bridge circuitry becomes unbalanced. This "unbalancing" is noted as a change in the output voltage of the bridge and is proportional to the amount of rotation. The design is clever because pure rotation about axes perpendicular to the axis of rotation depicted in Fig. 8.3 will *not* unbalance the bridge. Another interesting and practical characteristic of this device is that it does not have to be positioned over the joint axis of rotation as is the case for rotatory potentiometers. Note, however, that the base of the mounting blocks must lie in the plane of rotation without necessarily being centered over the axis of rotation.

Electrogoniometers of this type can be configured to display joint angles in real time and/or interfaced with a computer for data storage. Additionally, data can be saved to a storage unit (i.e., data logger) strapped to the subject. The data logger is ideal for recording dynamic movements in the field. The stored data can be uploaded to a computer at a later time and converted to joint angles for analysis.

Limitations of Electrogoniometers. There are advantages and disadvantages associated with the use of electrogoniometers. In their favor are ease of use and cost. On the other hand, they are less accurate than other systems used to record movement. In addition, both designs (i.e., potentiometer and strain gauge) require placement over the joint, which may interfere with the natural kinematics due to cumbersome cabling and/or method of attachment. Another drawback of these devices is that while they provide a *relative* measure of joint angular position, the data do not lend themselves to an inverse dynamics analysis in which joint reaction forces and moments are of interest, the computation of which requires knowledge of the absolute positions of the body segments.

8.3.2 Electromagnetic Tracking Systems

Electromagnetic tracking technology originated in the defense industry and has since become widely used in the entertainment industry (e.g., motion pictures, animation, and gaming). The use of electromagnetic tracking has become increasingly popular in the academic environment as evinced by the growing number of research publications using this technology.

Electromagnetic tracking is based on Faraday's law of magnetic induction. That is, electrons in a conductor experience a spontaneous magnetic force when moved through a magnetic field. The magnitude of the induced force (i.e., electromotive force or EMF) is proportional to the strength of the magnetic field through which the conductor is moved. The magnitude of the EMF (i.e., voltage) is also related to the speed the conductor is moving. If the conductor is in the shape of a loop, the same principles apply with an induced EMF proportional to the strength of the magnetic field perpendicular to the cross-sectional area of the loop. The induced EMF is related to the magnetic flux (Φ_B) as noted in Eq. (8.1).

$$\text{EMF} = -\frac{d\Phi_B}{dt} \tag{8.1}$$

Conceptually, the strength and direction of a magnetic field can be thought of as the density and direction of magnetic field lines. The magnetic flux will vary as the conductor moves closer/further to the source of the magnetic field and also as it rotates relative to the magnetic field lines. The more field lines passing through the loop of the conductor, the greater the induced EMF. This principle forms the basis for electromagnetic tracking. That is, the general idea is to move a conducting sensor through a magnetic field and record the induced voltage.

The basic components of an electromagnetic tracking system consist of an active transmitter and passive sensors. The transmitter is stationary and contains three orthogonal coils (i.e., antennae) that are activated in sequence, with only one antenna generating a magnetic field at a time. Interestingly, if the subject (and therefore the sensors attached to the subject) stops moving within the magnetic field, we might think the induced voltage in each sensor would remain constant. However, revisiting Eq. (8.1) shows that this is not the case, because the magnetic flux must change with respect to time or the EMF goes to zero. There are two things that can be controlled to ensure a changing flux: (1) make sure the subject never stops moving or (2) change the strength and direction of the magnetic field. Electromagnetic tracking systems use the latter strategy to ensure the magnetic flux changes. The transmitter not only emits a magnetic field, but also serves as a fixed reference about which position and orientation of each sensor is reported.

Each receiving sensor contains three orthogonal coils used to detect the magnetic field emitted by the transmitter using the principles of magnetic induction. The receiving coils are contained within a 1-in^3 plastic housing for protection and provide a convenient method for attaching the sensor to the subject. The sensors are generally secured using double-sided tape and wrapped with an elasticized band. Proprietary signal processing takes place in real time, compensating for the strength of the earth's magnetic field. Individual coil signals can be used to determine the orientation of the sensor relative to the antenna generating the magnetic field. Each coil within the sensor detects three signals from the transmitter (i.e., one for each antenna of the transmitter) for a total of nine signals. These nine signals suffice to locate the position and orientation of the sensor relative to the transmitter. For example, the receiving coil most parallel to the currently active transmitting antenna will experience the largest EMF, while the more orthogonal the coil, the smaller the induced voltage. Because each coil within a sensor is the same distance from the transmitter, it is possible to determine the distance and orientation of the sensor relative to the currently active antenna by comparing the strength of the induced EMF in each coil to the strength of the emitted magnetic field.

There are two types of electromagnetic tracking systems that are used for the study of human movement. The biggest difference between these systems is that one (e.g., Polhemus Incorporated) uses an AC magnetic field, while the other type (e.g., Ascension Technology Corporation) uses a pulsed DC magnetic field. The precision and accuracy of electromagnetic tracking systems is affected by metallic objects, low-frequency electronic noise, and also by the distance of the sensor from the transmitting antennae. The radius within which precise and accurate data are sampled depends on the particular system and strength of the transmitter. However, when used in an ideal environment, the precision and accuracy of both systems is more than adequate for studying human movement. With proper setup, static accuracy of less than 2 mm RMS and 0.5° RMS for both systems is possible. Real-time data can be sampled at a rate of up to 144 Hz depending on the system, the number of sensors tracked and the type of data communication interface with the computer. These systems do not suffer from line of sight problems typical of optoelectronic systems and are, therefore, ideal for capturing complex movements.

8.3.3 Optical Methods: Camera-Based Systems

The most common method of recording human movement involves "filming" the motion of interest. Historically, images were stored on conventional media such as 16 mm film or on videotape. Today's standard is based on digital technology, bypassing physical media per se, sending the data directly to the computer. Data are commonly sampled between 50 and 240 frames per second, depending on the movement of interest. For example, natural cadence walking is often sampled at a rate of 60 Hz, while running and arm movements tend to be sampled at 100 Hz or faster. There are two types of high-speed video-based systems that are used for studying human movement. The fundamental difference between designs is related to their use of active or passive tracking targets.

Active tracking target systems use infrared light-emitting diodes to indicate the position of the target in space. The diodes are pulsed in order so that only one target is illuminated (i.e., active) at a time. Thus, if a target is not detected by a camera and then suddenly reappears in the camera's field of view, it will automatically be identified based on its order in the pulse sequence. Active target systems are subject to "line of sight" problems common to all optical-based tracking systems. That is, the target must be *seen* by a camera to be detected. Active targets emit a restricted angle of light that may not be detected by the camera if the target rotates relative to the segment to which it is attached.

A limitation of active target systems is that on-board electronics must be strapped to the subject with leads to each of the diodes. These wires, combined with the subject being tethered to the cameras can interfere with certain movements. Tetherless systems (i.e., telemetered systems) are available; however, wires to each diode are still necessary.

In contrast, passive tracking targets merely reflect projected light and do not actively communicate their position in space. It is therefore important that the tracking targets reflect more light than surrounding objects. To promote this, tracking targets are covered with a highly reflective material, most often in the form of retroreflective tape; however, reflective ink or paint can also be used. In addition, a ring of stroboscopic LEDs mounted around the camera lens housing is used to illuminate the tracking targets (see right panel of Fig. 8.4).

FIGURE 8.4 (Left panel) 10- and 25-mm retroreflective tape covered tracking targets. Note how the targets are mounted on lightweight plastic pedestals. The pedestals make it easier to attach the targets to the segment. (Right panel) High-speed digital video camera used to "film" the position of the tracking targets. Note the stroboscopic ring of LEDs around the lens of the camera.

Passive tracking targets typically range between 10 and 40 mm in diameter, with the size of the target usually related to the field of view in which the movement takes place and the accuracy of the experimental setup. There is a trade-off in target size since overly large targets may obscure the detection of other targets, while too small of a target may not reflect sufficient light to be detected by the cameras. A reasonable rule of thumb is that the diameter of the tracking targets should be between 1 and 2 percent of the largest dimension of the calibrated workspace. The workspace may be thought of as the region in which the movement will take place, and is generally defined during a system calibration process (discussed in the subsection "Camera Calibration").

The Role of the Video Camera. The determination of the three-dimensional coordinates of tracking targets from multiple two-dimensional camera views is often taken for granted or treated as a *black box*. In the sections that follow, we will discuss the basic principles of reconstructing three-dimensional target coordinates from multiple camera images. It is advantageous to describe how the process works for a single tracking target prior to discussing how three-dimensional kinematics of segmental motion are calculated.

For the purposes of this discussion, we assume the image plane of our high-speed video camera is a CCD (charge-coupled display) sensor. The image plane may be thought of as the *exposure media* onto which real-world *object-space* is projected. The term *object-space* will be used to describe the *X, Y, Z* inertial reference system in which the tracking targets move. Individual elements of the sensor are arranged in a series of rows and columns, with each element responsible for converting the intensity of light to a voltage such that the greater the intensity of light striking the element, the greater the voltage. This is particularly relevant because the tracking targets should reflect more light than all other objects detected by the camera. The matrix arrangement of light-sensitive elements is illustrated schematically in Fig. 8.5. Note the internal *u, v* coordinate system of the image plane.

Consider the case where a single tracking target is detected by a camera and no other light-reflecting objects are visible. The silver-shaded circle in Fig. 8.5 is used to depict the projection of the target onto the imaging sensor. Clearly, other elements of the sensor would be excited to varying degrees depending on the ambient lighting, but have been turned *off* for the sake of this example. Figure 8.5 is also helpful in depicting the effect of using binary thresholding to suppress background light sources or reflective objects other than the tracking targets. The idea is to suppress all voltages below a user-specified threshold, which has the effect of moving the light-reflective tracking targets to the foreground. This is ideal since we are ultimately concerned with locating the center of a prospective target in *u, v* coordinates and do not want other sources of light affecting the location of the computed center. One method of determining the center of a target is to scan the matrix of light-sensitive elements for transitions in voltage (i.e., edge detection) and fit a circle of best fit to the resulting "edges." While this approach is conceptually straight forward, binary thresholding as described here would eliminate useful information that could otherwise be used to determine the center of the projected target at greater subpixel accuracy. For example, rather than simply treating each element of the sensor as being *on* or *off*, we could use a weighted average of sensor element voltages and a geometric constraint that the active elements form a circle. The center of the target in the image plane is assumed to lie at the center of the circle.

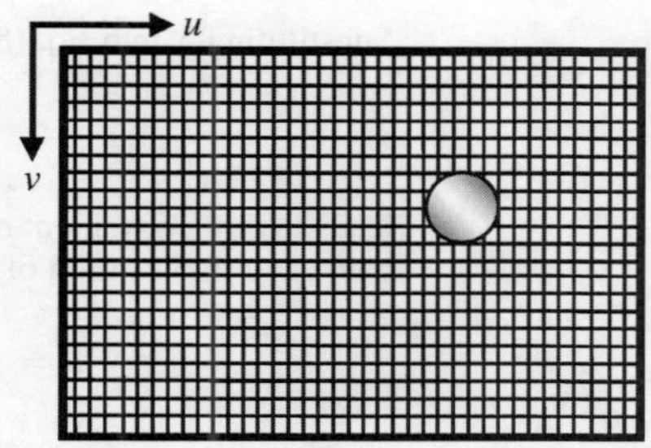

FIGURE 8.5 Schematic representation of the light-sensitive elements of the imaging sensor. The silver circle is the projection of a target onto the image plane. Note the direction of the *u, v* reference axes.

If one were to draw a line from the center of the target in the image plane to the *X, Y,* and *Z* coordinates of the target in object-space, it would be clear that the mapping between these spaces is not unique since all targets lying on this line would map to the same *u, v* coordinates. From this it is evident that the location of a target in object-space cannot be determined using only one camera. This raises a subtle but important distinction regarding the role of the camera in video-based motion analysis. The camera does not actually record the location of a target in object-space, but rather the role of the camera is to define a ray in the direction of the target. When multiple cameras view the same target, the location of the target in object-space is assumed to lie at the intersection of the directed rays from each camera. The cameras must first be calibrated before the intersection of these rays can be calculated.

Camera Calibration. Each camera must be calibrated before it can contribute to locating a target in object-space. Camera calibration defines a *mapping* from three-dimensional object-space into the two-dimensional *u, v* coordinates of the camera. This mapping is expressed in Eq. (8.2) using homogeneous coordinates:

$$\begin{pmatrix} \lambda u \\ \lambda v \\ \lambda \end{pmatrix} = \mathbf{A} \begin{pmatrix} X \\ Y \\ Z \\ 1 \end{pmatrix} \tag{8.2}$$

where λ is a scale factor relating the spaces, u and v are the image plane coordinates of a target, $\mathbf{A}$ is a 3×4 transformation matrix, and *X, Y,* and *Z* are the coordinates of a target in object-space. Expanding the right-hand side of Eq. (8.2) results in the following set of equations:

$$\lambda u = \alpha_{11}X + \alpha_{12}Y + \alpha_{13}Z + \alpha_{14} \tag{8.3}$$

$$\lambda v = \alpha_{21}X + \alpha_{22}Y + \alpha_{23}Z + \alpha_{24} \tag{8.4}$$

$$\lambda = \alpha_{31}X + \alpha_{32}Y + \alpha_{33}Z + \alpha_{34} \tag{8.5}$$

Substituting λ into Eq. (8.3) and (8.4), and introducing the following:

$$\beta_{ij} = \alpha_{ij}/\alpha_{34} \tag{8.6}$$

leads to two convenient expressions relating the coordinates of the center of the target in the image plane and the location of the target in the object-space.

$$u = \beta_{11}X + \beta_{12}Y + \beta_{13}Z + \beta_{14} - u\beta_{31}X - u\beta_{32}Y - u\beta_{33}Z \tag{8.7}$$

$$v = \beta_{21}X + \beta_{22}Y + \beta_{23}Z + \beta_{24} - v\beta_{31}X - v\beta_{32}Y - v\beta_{33}Z \tag{8.8}$$

Note that the *u, v* coordinates of the target are known. Therefore, if the *X, Y,* and *Z* coordinates of the target are also known, we are left with 11 unknowns (i.e., transformation parameters) in two equations. The unknown betas (i.e., β_{ij}) can be determined if the *X, Y,* and *Z* coordinates of at least six *control points* are detected by the camera. That is, each control point provides two equations that can be used to solve for the 11 unknown betas. The term *control point* is used to make clear that the *X, Y,* and *Z* coordinates for these targets are known, having been accurately measured relative to the origin of the object-space. The control points are used solely for the purposes of calibrating the cameras and are removed from the field of view once the cameras have been calibrated. The distribution of the $n \geq 6$ control points must not be colinear and the control points should encompass the volume within which the movement will take place. This volume is often referred to as the *workspace*. One method of defining the workspace is to hang four strings with a number control points attached to each string, as shown in Fig. 8.6.

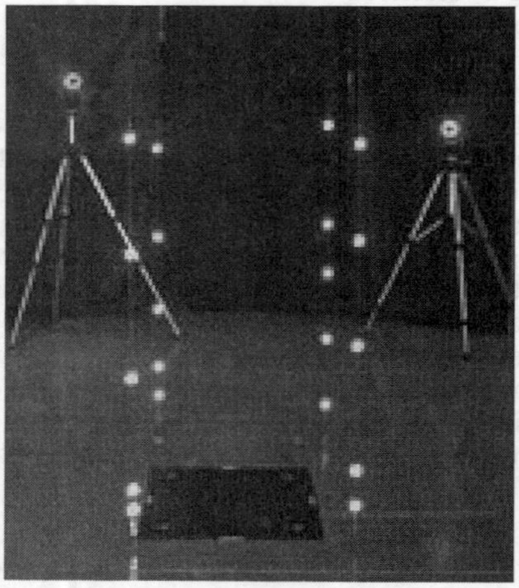

FIGURE 8.6 The *X, Y,* and *Z* coordinates of the control points (i.e., reflective targets) are known relative to the origin of the object-space. Once the cameras have been calibrated, the hanging strings with the control points are removed from the field of view of the cameras. The black rectangle flush with the floor is a force platform (see Sec. 8.4.5).

The direct linear transformation (DLT) proposed by Abdel-Aziz and Karara (1971) is perhaps the most well-known method of calibrating the cameras amongst those conducting video-based motion analysis. The unknown betas for each camera are related to internal and external camera parameters. Examples of internal parameters include the principal distance from the center of the camera lens to the image plane and the *u, v* coordinates of the principal point. (The principal point lies at the intersection of the principal axis and the image plane.) Although the number of internal parameters can vary depending on the accuracy of the geometric representation of the camera, the number of external parameters remains fixed at six. The six external parameters (i.e., 3 position and 3 orientation) describe the relationship between the internal camera coordinate system and the object-space.

Prior to development of the DLT method, the six external parameters were measured manually. This was a painstaking process and subject to errors. The simple act of bumping a camera or repositioning the cameras for a new experimental setup involved remeasuring the external parameters. The DLT greatly facilitated video-based motion analysis, providing a convenient method of solving for the external camera parameters and determining the mapping from object-space to the *u, v* coordinates of the image plane.

This discussion on camera calibration is not meant to be comprehensive. However, it does provide the basic background for understanding how and why cameras are calibrated. Additional terms can be added to the basic 11 parameter DLT model to correct for symmetrical and asymmetrical lens distortions. These errors can be treated, in part, during camera calibration, and may also be accounted for using lens correction maps provided by the manufacturer.

In recent years, the so-called wand or dynamic calibration method has become widely used in place of hanging strings with control points. In a dynamic calibration, two retroreflective targets attached to a wand are moved throughout the entirety of the volume in which the movement will take place. The targets on the wand are not control points per se because their locations in object-space are not known a priori. However, since the coordinates of the two wand targets can be measured with respect to the *u, v* coordinates of each camera and because the distance between targets should remain constant, the cameras can be calibrated in an iterative manner until the length of the wand as detected by the cameras matches the true length of the wand (i.e., distance between targets). Although the length of the wand can be reconstructed very accurately using this method, the direction of the object-space reference axes does not have to be known for determining the length. A static frame with a predefined origin and control points arranged to define the object-space reference axes is placed in the field of view of the "calibrated" cameras to establish the direction of the *X, Y,* and *Z* object-space axes.

Calculating Object-Space Coordinates. Once the cameras have been calibrated and a set of betas for each camera are known, the opposite approach can be used to locate the position of a target in object-space. The term *reconstruction* is often used to describe the process of calculating three-dimensional coordinates from multiple ($n \geq 2$) camera views. Consider the example illustrated in Fig. 8.7, where two cameras have a unique perspective of the same tracking target. The *u, v* coordinates of the target in each camera view are known, as are the betas for both cameras as a result of the calibration. The unknowns in this case are the *X, Y,* and *Z* coordinates of the target in the object-space. Rearranging Eqs. (8.7) and (8.8) and adding two more equations for the second camera leads to the following:

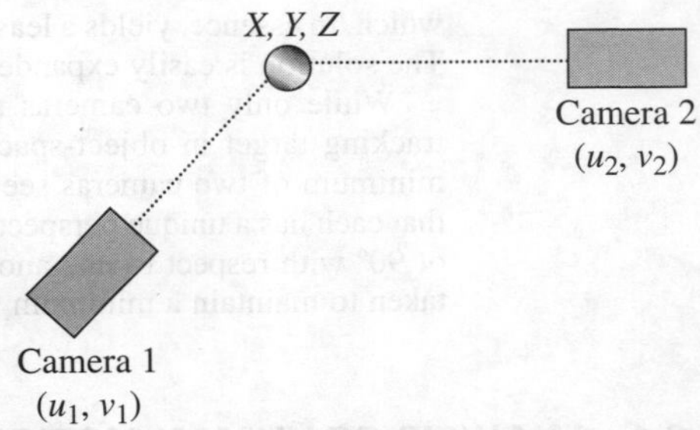

FIGURE 8.7 Cameras 1 and 2 each have a unique perspective of the tracking target in object-space (i.e., silver circle). The *X, Y,* and *Z* coordinates of the target can be calculated using the *u, v* coordinates and the betas determined during calibration.

$$u_1 = \left(\beta'_{11} - u_1\beta'_{31}\right)X + \left(\beta'_{12} - u_1\beta'_{32}\right)Y + \left(\beta'_{13} - u_1\beta'_{33}\right)Z + \beta'_{14} \tag{8.9}$$

$$v_1 = \left(\beta'_{21} - v_1\beta'_{31}\right)X + \left(\beta'_{22} - v_1\beta'_{32}\right)Y + \left(\beta'_{23} - v_1\beta'_{33}\right)Z + \beta'_{24} \tag{8.10}$$

$$u_2 = \left(\beta''_{11} - u_2\beta''_{31}\right)X + \left(\beta''_{12} - u_2\beta''_{32}\right)Y + \left(\beta''_{13} - u_2\beta''_{33}\right)Z + \beta''_{14} \tag{8.11}$$

$$v_2 = \left(\beta''_{21} - v_2\beta''_{31}\right)X + \left(\beta''_{22} - v_2\beta''_{32}\right)Y + \left(\beta''_{23} - v_2\beta''_{33}\right)Z + \beta''_{24} \tag{8.12}$$

where the subscript on *u* and *v* indicates camera 1 or 2, with β'_{ij} and β''_{ij} used to identify the betas for cameras 1 and 2, respectively. We can express Eqs. (8.9) through (8.12) compactly if we let C_{ij} be the terms in parentheses, where *i* indicates row and *j* column [see Eq. (8.13) for an example], and by letting L_i be the combination of the left-hand side and the lone beta on the right-hand side of Eqs. (8.9) through (8.12) [see Eq. (8.14) for an example]. Equation (8.15) reflects this compact notation.

$$C_{11} = \left(\beta'_{11} - u_1\beta'_{31}\right) \tag{8.13}$$

$$L_3 = \left(u_2 - \beta''_{14}\right) \tag{8.14}$$

$$\mathbf{L} = \mathbf{C}\begin{pmatrix} X \\ Y \\ Z \end{pmatrix} \tag{8.15}$$

Since **C** is not a square matrix (it is 4 × 3), the unknown *X*, *Y*, and *Z* coordinates can be solved using the Moore-Penrose generalized inverse, as follows:

$$\begin{pmatrix} X \\ Y \\ Z \end{pmatrix} = (\mathbf{C}^T\mathbf{C})^{-1}\mathbf{C}^T\mathbf{L} \tag{8.16}$$

which, in essence, yields a least-squares solution for the *X*, *Y*, and *Z* coordinates of the tracking target. The solution is easily expanded to account for $n > 2$ cameras.

While only two cameras are necessary to reconstruct the three-dimensional coordinates of a tracking target in object-space, more than two cameras are recommended to help ensure that a minimum of two cameras see the target every point in time. The cameras should be positioned so that each has a unique perspective of the workspace. Ideally the cameras should be placed at an angle of 90° with respect to one another. In practice this may not be possible, and every effort should be taken to maintain a minimum separation angle of at least 60°.

8.4 ANALYSIS OF HUMAN MOTION: AN INVERSE DYNAMICS APPROACH

The inverse dynamics approach is the most commonly used method to solve for unknown joint reaction forces and moments. The analysis begins with the most distal segment, moving upward through the kinematic chain, requiring that all external forces acting on the system are known. A free-body diagram appropriate for a two-dimensional inverse dynamics analysis of the foot and shank is illustrated in Fig. 8.8. This can be expressed mathematically in a generalized form suitable for a two- or three-dimensional analysis of *n* segments.

$$\Sigma M_i = I_i\, d\omega_i / dt \tag{8.17}$$

$$\Sigma F_i = m_i dv_i / dt \tag{8.18}$$

where ΣM_i is the sum of the moments acting on segment *i*, I_i is the inertia tensor for segment *i* about its center of mass (COM), and ω_i is the angular velocity of the segment. Forces acting on segment *i*, mass and linear velocity of the segment correspond to F_i, m_i, and v_i, respectively.

The three types of measurement *tools* described in Sec. 8.3 all provide kinematic data of some form. For example, goniometers provide an estimate of joint angular position, while electromagnetic tracking systems output the relative position and orientation of the sensors attached to the segments. In the case of video-based motion analysis, output data are in the form of target coordinates expressed in the object-space. It is important to note that output from all of these devices contains some degree of error. That is, the sampled signal is actually a combination of "true" signal and "noise." This is an important consideration because the equations of motion contain linear and angular acceleration terms, values that are obtained by numerically differentiating the position data. Differentiating the raw data will have the undesirable effect of magnifying the noise, which can severely compromise the integrity of the results. An excellent discussion of this topic can be found in Winter (1990). The point we wish to make is that the raw data should be treated to reduce or eliminate the amount of contaminating noise before the data are used in subsequent calculations. This process of treating the raw data is commonly referred to as data smoothing.

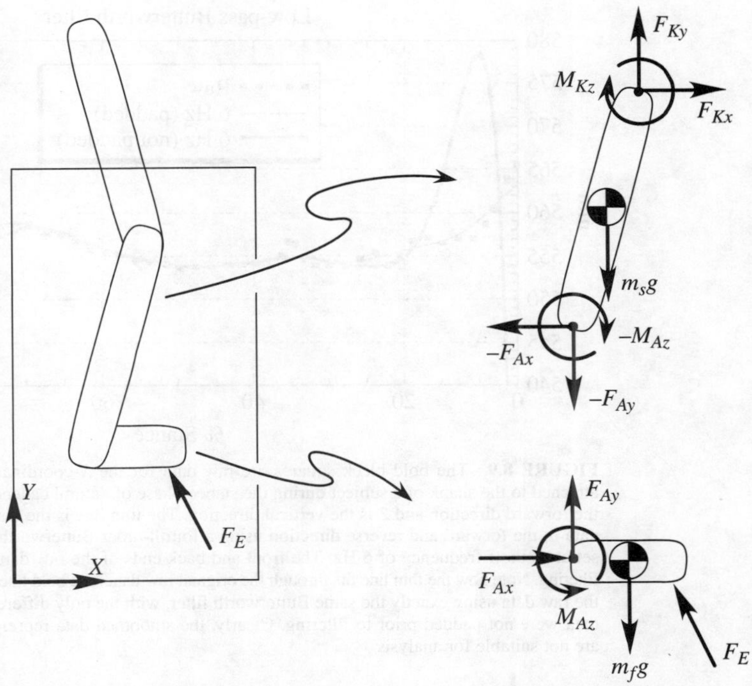

FIGURE 8.8 Two-dimensional FBD of the foot and shank segments. Note how the forces and moment acting at the distal end of the shank are equal in magnitude but opposite in direction compared to the forces and moment acting at the ankle. F and M are used to indicate force and moment, respectively, with A and K used to distinguish between the ankle and knee joints. The foot and shank segments are represented by f and s, while F_E is used to denote the external force acting on the foot.

8.4.1 Data Smoothing

As previously stated, all motion capture data contains some degree of noise. For example, consider the plot in Fig. 8.9. The black dotted line is the trajectory of a tracking target attached to the shank of a subject walking at a natural cadence. The data are limited to the stance phase of gait and have not been treated (i.e., these data are "raw"). The thin line passing through the raw data is a smoothed form of the original signal. The purpose of this section is to introduce several methods that are commonly used in biomechanical studies to smooth motion capture data.

For the purpose of this discussion, consider a single tracking target whose position has been determined using video-based motion analysis. We begin by assuming the data were collected at an adequate sampling rate to prevent aliasing of the signal. The sampling theorem states that the data should be sampled at a rate of at least two times greater than the highest frequency component in the signal being sampled. This minimum rate is commonly described as the Nyquist limit. It is not unreasonable to sample the data at five times the Nyquist limit to ensure the integrity of the data in both the frequency and time domains. Historically, sampling at such a high rate was prohibitive due to constraints on disk space. Storage space, however, is no longer an issue and sampling data well above the Nyquist limit is recommended.

Two general approaches of smoothing data include curve fitting and digital filtering. Both approaches can yield similar results, however, the underlying theory behind each approach is different.

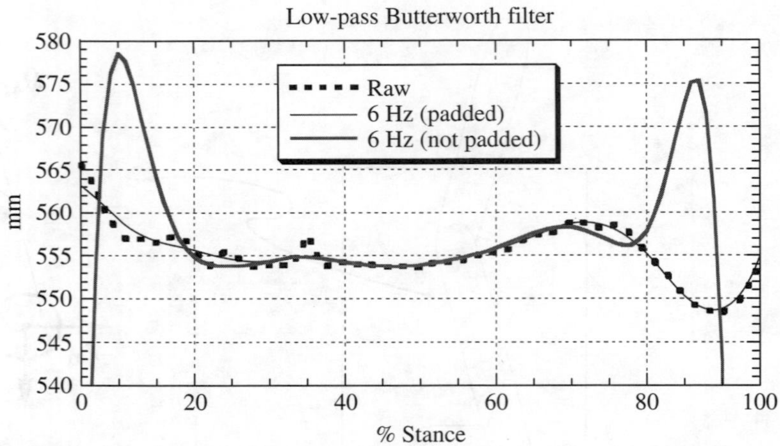

FIGURE 8.9 The bold black squares are raw data for the *X*-coordinate of a tracking target attached to the shank of a subject during the stance phase of natural cadence walking, where *Y* is the forward direction and *Z* is the vertical direction. The thin line is the result of filtering the raw data in the forward and reverse direction using a fourth-order Butterworth low-pass digital filter set at a cutoff frequency of 6 Hz. The front and back ends of the raw data were padded prior to filtering. Note how the thin line fits through the original raw data. The bold line is the result of filtering the raw data using exactly the same Butterworth filter, with the only difference being that the raw data were not padded prior to filtering. Clearly, the smoothed data represented by the bold line are not suitable for analysis.

Curve Fitting. Curve fitting, as the name implies, involves fitting a function or a series of functions through the raw data with a goodness of fit generally based on a least squares difference. For example, polynomial regression and piecewise polynomial approximation are methods of curve fitting, the latter of which is more commonly used when studying human movement. Cubic and quintic splines are the more common of the piecewise approximation methods. These splines require a smoothing parameter be specified to determine how closely the smoothed data fit through the original data points. The goal is to select a smoothing parameter that does not over/under smooth the raw data. In practice, it may be difficult to determine an ideal smoothing parameter. Algorithms have been created in which an ideal smoothing parameter can be determined using a statistical procedure known as generalized cross validation (GCV). The GCVSPL package (Woltring, 1986) is one such program that uses GCV to identify an ideal smoothing parameter for the spline. A description of the GCVSPL package and source code is available for download from the International Society of Biomechanics (1999).

Digital Filtering. Digital filtering is another method that is used to smooth biomechanical data. The concept is based on the fact that any signal, if sampled at an adequate rate can be recreated from a series of sine and cosine waveforms of varying frequency. This principle can be used to reduce the amount of noise, if the frequency content of the noise is known. For the sake of this example we assume the acquired data are contaminated with high-frequency noise. Although a variety of digital filters exist, we focus our attention on the Butterworth filter because it is perhaps the most widely used filter in biomechanics research.

A low-pass Butterworth filter is designed to attenuate frequencies above a specified cutoff frequency, while allowing frequencies below the cutoff to pass through the filter unattenuated. Butterworth filters are not infinitely sharp. The *order* of the filter characterizes the sharpness, or how much the signal is attenuated in the vicinity of the cutoff frequency. The higher the order, the sharper the filter response. Computer implementation of a Butterworth filter is straightforward, which may be in part why it is so widely used. Although we described the role of the Butterworth filter as extracting particular frequencies, the raw signal is actually filtered in the time domain as seen below.

$$Y(t) = a_0X(t) + a_1X(t-1) + a_2X(t-2) + b_1Y(t-1) + b_2Y(t-2) \tag{8.19}$$

where $Y(t)$ and $X(t)$ are the filtered and raw data at time t. The $(t \times 1)$ and $(t \times 2)$ notation is used to indicate data at 1 and 2 samples prior to the current time. Equation (8.19) is for a second-order recursive filter; higher-order filters require additional recursive terms. The a and b coefficients for a Butterworth low-pass filter can be determined using the following equations:

$$\omega_c = \tan\left(\frac{\pi f_c}{f_s}\right) \tag{8.20}$$

$$K_1 = \sqrt{2}\omega_c \tag{8.21}$$

$$K_2 = \omega_c^2 \tag{8.22}$$

$$K_3 = \frac{2a_0}{K_2} \tag{8.23}$$

$$a_0 = a_2 = \frac{K_2}{(1 + K_1 + K_2)} \tag{8.24}$$

$$a_1 = 2a_0 \tag{8.25}$$

$$b_1 = -2a_0 + K_3 \tag{8.26}$$

$$b_2 = 1 - 2a_0 - K_3 \tag{8.27}$$

where f_c and f_s are the cutoff frequency and the sampling frequency expressed in hertz, respectively.

Several practical considerations should be noted when using a Butterworth digital filter. First, we see from Eq. (8.19) that the filtered data at time t are related in a recursive manner to raw and filtered data at times $(t \times 1)$ and $(t \times 2)$. This can cause problems at the beginning of the data set unless the front end of the data is padded with extra data points. The bold line in Fig. (8.9) illustrates the consequence of not padding the data set prior to filtering. Clearly the smoothed data at the beginning (and also at the end!) of the data set are erroneous. Two methods of padding the front end of the data involve reflecting the first n data points (15 or more generally work well for a second-order filter) about data point #1, or simply by collecting more data than is actually needed. It should be noted that this type of digital filter introduces a phase lag in the smoothed signal. The easiest method of correcting for this phase lag is to refilter the already filtered data in the reverse direction. This will shift the data in an equal and opposite direction, realigning the raw and filtered data temporally. Note that filtering the already filtered data in the reverse direction will increase the sharpness of the filter response. If the data are filtered in the reverse direction, it is advisable to pad the back end of the data set for the reasons cited earlier.

The smooth thin line in Fig. 8.9 is the result of filtering the raw data in the forward and reverse directions using a fourth-order, low-pass Butterworth filter set at a cutoff frequency of 6 Hz (note that the front and back ends of the raw data were padded). This raises an interesting question, that is, how do we identify an appropriate cutoff frequency for the filter? There are a number of methods that can be used to help select an appropriate cutoff frequency. An FFT can be used to examine the content of the signal in the frequency domain, or one of several residual analysis methods can be used (Jackson, 1979; Winter, 1990).

8.4.2 Tracking Motion of the Segment and Underlying Bone

We continue with our example of how motion data collected with a video-based tracking system is used in an inverse dynamics analysis. Calculating joint kinetics from the observed kinematics and the external forces acting on the body requires knowledge of how the bones are moving. In this section, we describe how tracking targets attached to the segments can be used to track motion of the underlying bones. We assume the target coordinates have been smoothed using an appropriate method.

The first step in calculating joint and segmental kinematics is to define orthogonal anatomical coordinate systems (ACSs) embedded in each segment. Because it is the kinematics of the underlying bones that are most often of interest, we must define a set of reference axes that are anatomically meaningful for the purposes of describing the motion. An ACS is constructed for each segment in the kinematic chain. Retroreflective targets positioned over anatomical sites (hence the term *anatomical targets*) are used to define the ACS for each segment. Consider the case in the left panel of Fig. 8.10 where anatomical targets are positioned over the malleoli and femoral condyles. These targets are used to define an ACS for the shank (ACS_{shank}). The frontal plane of the shank is defined by fitting a plane through the four anatomical targets. The next step is to define the ankle and knee joint centers, which are assumed to lie midway between the malleoli and femoral condyle targets, respectively. The longitudinal axis of the shank lies in the previously defined plane, originating at the distal joint center (i.e., the ankle joint) and pointing in the direction of the knee joint center. The origin of the ACS_{shank} is set at the COM of the segment. The COM lies along the longitudinal axis, at a location generally determined using anthropometric lookup tables (see Sec. 8.4.4). The unit vector $\mathbf{X}_s$, originating at the COM will be used to define the direction of the longitudinal axis of the

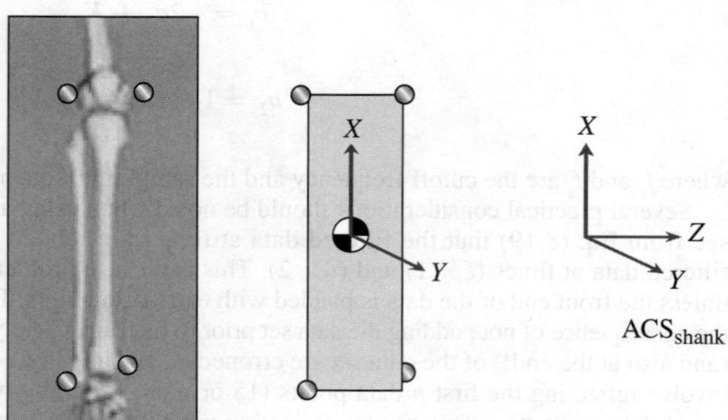

FIGURE 8.10 Retroreflective targets are placed over the medial and lateral malleoli and femoral condyles (see left panel). These anatomical targets are used to define the frontal plane of the shank (see middle panel). The *X* axis projects from the ankle joint center toward the knee joint center. The *Y* axis lies perpendicular to the frontal plane, with the *Z* axis given by the cross product of *X* and *Y*. The orthogonal axes in the right panel represent the ACS_{shank} which is located at the COM of the segment.

ACS_{shank}. An antero-posterior (AP) axis lies perpendicular to the frontal plane of the shank, with a medio-lateral (ML) axis formed by the cross product of the longitudinal and AP axes. Unit vectors $\mathbf{Y}_s$ and $\mathbf{Z}_s$ originating at the COM of the shank are used to define the direction of the AP and ML axes, respectively. The $\mathbf{X}_s$, $\mathbf{Y}_s$, and $\mathbf{Z}_s$ unit vectors are orthonormal by way of construction and form the basis of the ACS_{shank} (see right panel, Fig. 8.10).

A similar approach can be used to construct ACSs for other segments in the kinematic chain given suitable placement of anatomical targets (Cappozzo et al., 1995). Figure 8.11 illustrates ACSs for the shank and thigh without specifying the exact details of how the ACS_{thigh} was constructed.

Although anatomical targets are used to construct the ACSs, and it is motion of the ACSs that is of interest, it is not practical to track motion of the anatomical targets because they are prone to being knocked off, and in many cases pose line of sight problems. The medial malleolus and femoral condyle targets are especially prone to these problems. From a data collection perspective, it is easier to track targets attached to a segment that have been positioned for optimal viewing by the cameras than it is to track targets over anatomical sites. If we define a relationship between the tracking targets and the ACS, we can estimate how the bones are moving by tracking motion of targets on the segment. The easiest way to do this is to construct a set of orthogonal axes using three tracking targets and a series of vector cross products [Eqs. (8.28) through (8.30)]. The resulting orthogonal axes are illustrated in Fig. 8.12. These axes will be referred to as a *local coordinate system*.

$$\mathbf{i} = A - C \tag{8.28}$$

$$\mathbf{j} = (B - C) \times (A - C) \tag{8.29}$$

$$\mathbf{k} = \mathbf{i} \times \mathbf{j} \tag{8.30}$$

where the *X, Y,* and *Z* coordinates of tracking targets *A, B,* and *C* are known in the object-space.

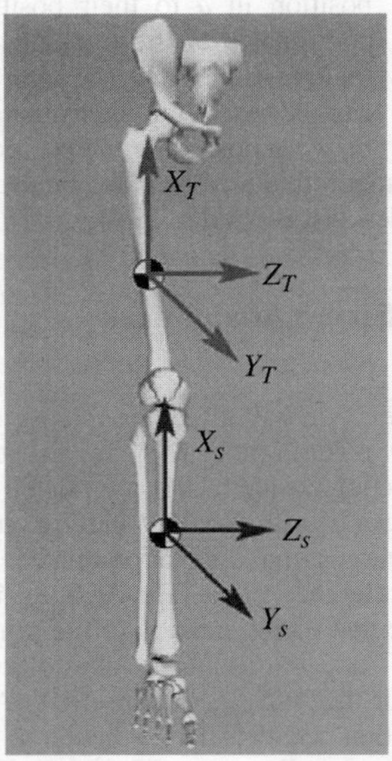

FIGURE 8.11 ACSs for the shank and thigh segments. The ACSs originate at the COM of each segment. Note that changes in the knee angle will cause the relative orientation between the ACS_{shank} and ACS_{thigh} to change.

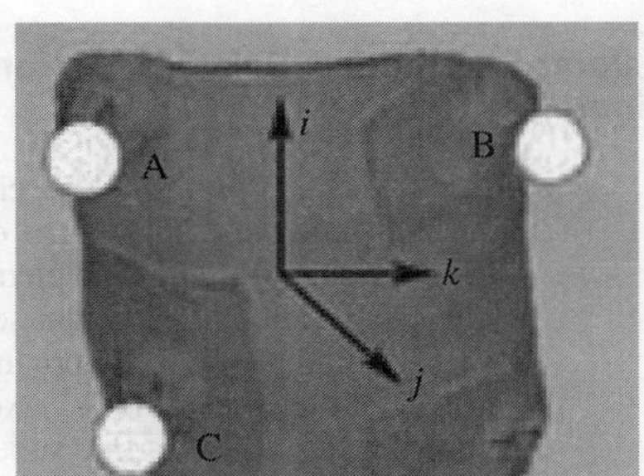

FIGURE 8.12 Three tracking targets A, B, and C are fastened to a contour molded shell. The shell is attached to the segment using an elasticized wrap or some other convenient method. Targets A, B, and C are used to construct an orthogonal local coordinate system as per Eqs. (8.28) through (8.30). The origin of the local coordinate system has been drawn in the middle of the figure for convenience.

The relative position and orientation of the local coordinate system and the ACS can be represented as a translation vector relating their origins and a rotation matrix of direction cosines. Moreover, the relative position and orientation between the local coordinate system and the ACS should not change if we assume the segment is rigid. This relationship can be used to estimate the position and orientation of the ACS at any point in time by tracking motion of targets attached to the segment. This idea is easily expanded to multiple segments and forms the basis for comparing relative motion between adjacent bones (i.e., ACSs).

Constructing a local coordinate system for the purposes of estimating motion of the ACS is a straightforward and convenient method. However, the position and orientation of the local coordinate system is generally sensitive to errors in the coordinates of the tracking targets, and therefore, the estimated position and orientation of the ACS will also be affected. For this reason, it is generally advantageous to use more than three targets per segment and a least squares method to track motion of the segment and underlying bone. The singular value decomposition (SVD) method has been used to this end with good success (Soderkvist & Wedin, 1993; Cheze et al., 1995). The SVD method *maps* all of the tracking targets ($n \geq 3$) from position a to position b using a least squares approximation. This is illustrated schematically in Fig. 8.13 and represented algebraically in Eq. (8.31).

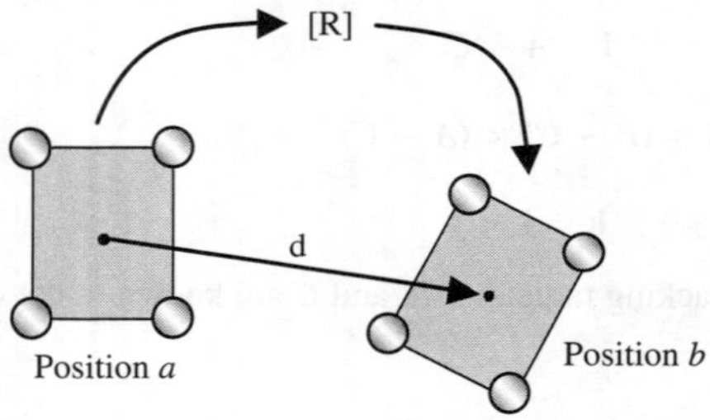

FIGURE 8.13 Least squares mapping of the tracking targets from position a to position b. **R** is a 3 × 3 rotation matrix and **d** is a displacement vector.

$$\min \sum_{i=1}^{n} \left\| R a_i + \mathbf{d} - b_i \right\|^2 \tag{8.31}$$

where n represents the number of targets attached to the segment, with a_i and b_i used to indicate the object-space coordinates of the individual tracking targets. R is a 3 × 3 rotation matrix, while **d** is a displacement vector that, when combined with R, maps all targets in a least squares sense from their position in a to their position in b. Because the coordinates of the tracking targets are also known relative to the ACS, the same least squares approach can be used to determine how the ACS moved between position a and position b. Note that although this example maps the targets on the same segment, this idea can also be used to determine relative kinematics between adjacent segments (cf. Soderkvist & Wedin, 1993).

8.4.3 Joint Kinematics: Relative Motion between Adjacent Anatomical Coordinate Systems

It is clear from Fig. 8.11 that changing the knee angle will affect the relative orientation between the ACS_{shank} and the ACS_{thigh}. The orientation at any point in time can be represented by a 3 × 3 matrix of direction cosines. The nine elements of the direction cosine matrix are related to an ordered sequence of rotations about a particular set of axes. This can be visualized by starting out with the ACS_{shank} and ACS_{thigh} initially aligned, moving the ACS_{shank} into its final orientation relative to the ACS_{thigh} by rotating about the Z, Y', and X'' axes of a moving reference frame. The ACS_{shank} is the moving reference in our example. The prime superscripts indicate that the orientation of the primed axes is related to a previous rotation. The first rotation in the Z, Y', and X'' sequence takes place about the ML axis of the ACS_{thigh} (or equivalently about the Z axis of the ACS_{shank} because both ACSs are aligned at the onset!). The Y' axis about which the second rotation occurs is perpendicular to both the ML axis of the thigh and the longitudinal axis of the shank. This mutually perpendicular axis is often called the line of nodes (or floating axis in joint coordinate system terminology). The line of nodes is formed by the vector cross product of the ML axis of the thigh and the longitudinal axis of the shank. The final r otation takes place about the longitudinal axis of the shank (i.e., X''). Note the double superscript indicating the orientation of the longitudinal axis has been influenced by two previous rotations about the Z and Y' axes. These ordered rotations are known as Euler Z, Y', and X'' angles. The

Euler angles described here are commonly reported in biomechanical studies (e.g., Grood and Suntay, 1983) because the rotations take place about clinically meaningful axes corresponding to joint flexion-extension (Z), abduction-adduction (Y'), and internal-external rotation (X''). The Z, Y', and X'' sequence of rotations is expressed using matrix notation in Eq. (8.32), with the elements of the individual matrices shown in Eq. (8.33).

$$\mathbf{R} = [R_z][R_{y'}][R_{x''}] \tag{8.32}$$

$$R_{x''} = \begin{bmatrix} 1 & 0 & 0 \\ 0 & \cos\psi & -\sin\psi \\ 0 & \sin\psi & \cos\psi \end{bmatrix} \quad R_{y'} = \begin{bmatrix} \cos\theta & 0 & \sin\theta \\ 0 & 1 & 0 \\ -\sin\theta & 0 & \cos\theta \end{bmatrix} \quad R_z = \begin{bmatrix} \cos\phi & -\sin\phi & 0 \\ \sin\phi & \cos\phi & 0 \\ 0 & 0 & 1 \end{bmatrix} \tag{8.33}$$

where ϕ, θ, and φ are the Euler angles about the Z, Y', and X'' axes, respectively. Expanding Eq. (8.33) using the matrices from Eq. (8.33) leads to the rotation matrix **R** in Eq. (8.34).

$$\mathbf{R} = \begin{bmatrix} \cos(\phi)\cos(\theta) & \cos(\phi)\sin(\theta)\sin(\psi) - \sin(\phi)\cos(\psi) & \cos(\phi)\sin(\theta)\cos(\psi) + \sin(\phi)\sin(\psi) \\ \sin(\phi)\cos(\theta) & \sin(\phi)\sin(\theta)\sin(\psi) + \cos(\phi)\cos(\psi) & \sin(\phi)\sin(\theta)\cos(\psi) - \cos(\phi)\sin(\psi) \\ -\sin(\theta) & \cos(\theta)\sin(\psi) & \cos(\theta)\cos(\psi) \end{bmatrix} \tag{8.34}$$

It is easy to show that a different sequence of rotations can be used to move the $\text{ACS}_{\text{shank}}$ from its initially aligned position to its final orientation relative to the $\text{ACS}_{\text{thigh}}$. Because matrix multiplication is not commutative in general, the terms of **R** in Eq. (8.34) will differ depending on the sequence of rotations selected. Equations (8.35) through (8.37) can be used to determine the Euler angles for this particular sequence of rotations:

$$\phi = \arctan\left(\frac{r_{21}}{r_{11}}\right) \tag{8.35}$$

$$\theta = \arctan\left(\frac{-r_{31}}{\sqrt{r_{11}{}^2 + r_{21}{}^2}}\right) \tag{8.36}$$

$$\psi = \arctan\left(\frac{r_{32}}{r_{33}}\right) \tag{8.37}$$

where r_{ij} is the element in the ith row and jth column of matrix **R**.

The methods outlined above can also be used to calculate segmental kinematics. For example, rather than calculating the relative orientation between the shank and thigh at time 1, we can use Euler angles to determine the relative orientation between the $\text{ACS}_{\text{shank}}$ at times 1 and 2.

8.4.4 Body Segment Parameters

Reexamining Eqs. (8.17) and (8.18), we see that estimates for mass (m) and the inertia tensor (I) for each segment are required to determine the right-hand side of the equations. Several other terms, including the location of the center of mass and the distances from the distal and proximal joint centers to the COM, are embedded in the left-hand side of Eq. (8.18). The term *body segment parameters* (BSP) is used to describe this collection of anthropometric information.

There are essentially two approaches that are used for estimating BSP values. The more exact approach is to measure the BSP values experimentally. In practice, this is rarely done because the process is tedious, subject to error, and certainly not practical to perform for every subject. Because the BSP values are difficult to measure accurately, they are generally estimated using anthropometric lookup tables and/or regression equations (e.g., Dempster, 1955; Winter, 1990; Zatsiorsky and Seluyanov, 1985).

For the case of a two-dimensional analysis, when motion is assumed planar, the moment of inertia in Eq. (8.18) takes on a single value. In the case of a three-dimensional analysis, I becomes a 3×3 inertia tensor. The main diagonal of the inertia tensor is constant and the off-diagonal elements vanish when the principal axis of inertia is aligned with the axes of the ACS. The diagonal matrix in Eq. (8.38) reflects this alignment and is the form used in Eq. (8.18) for a three-dimensional analysis in which the moments are expressed in the ACS of the segment.

$$\mathrm{I} = \begin{bmatrix} I_{xx} & 0 & 0 \\ 0 & I_{yy} & 0 \\ 0 & 0 & I_{zz} \end{bmatrix} \tag{8.38}$$

If we assume that each segment is a homogeneous solid of known geometry, we can use standard formulas for calculating mass moment of inertia about the *X, Y,* and *Z* axes.

8.4.5 Force Transducers

The role of a force transducer is to record external forces acting on the body. Force plates used in gait and postural studies to measure ground reaction forces are perhaps the most familiar type of force transducer used in biomechanics. A force platform is sensitive to the load a subject applies to the plate, with the plate exerting an equal and opposite load on the subject (hence the term *ground reaction forces*). Although we will limit our discussion to force plates, we wish to point out that other types of force transducers are used in the study of human movement. For example, multiaxial load cells are used to investigate the motor control of arm movements (e.g., Buchanan et al., 1993, 1998).

Commercially available force platforms use one of the two different measuring principles to determine the applied load. The first type of force plates use strain gauge technology to indirectly measure the force applied to the plate (e.g., AMTI and Bertec), while the second type uses piezoelectric quartz (e.g., Kistler). Piezoelectric materials produce an electrical charge directly proportional to the magnitude of the applied load. In this section, we focus on how the output of a force platform is used in an inverse dynamics analysis, without considering how the forces and moments detected by the plate are calculated.

Force platforms are used to resolve the load a subject applies to the ground. These forces and moments are measured about *X, Y,* and *Z* axes specific to the force platform. In general, the orientation of the force platform axes will differ from the orientation of the reference axes of the object-space. This is illustrated schematically in Fig. 8.14. Thus, it is necessary that the ground reaction forces be transformed into the appropriate reference system before they are used in subsequent calculations. For example, the ground reaction forces acting on the foot should be transformed into the foot coordinate system, if ankle joint forces and moments are expressed in an anatomically meaningful reference system (i.e., about axes of the $\mathrm{ACS}_{\mathrm{foot}}$).

Another variable that must be considered is the location of the external force acting on the system. For the case of a subject stepping on a force platform, the location of the applied load is assumed to act at the center of pressure (COP). The term is aptly named since the subject really applies a distributed pressure to the top surface of the force plate that is treated as an equivalent point force. As with the forces and moments, the location of the COP in the force platform system should be transformed into the appropriate reference system. Other devices such as pressure insoles and mats can measure pressure distributions, but are not suitable for three-dimensional motion analysis because they do not provide a complete 6∞ of freedom history of the applied load. If the data from

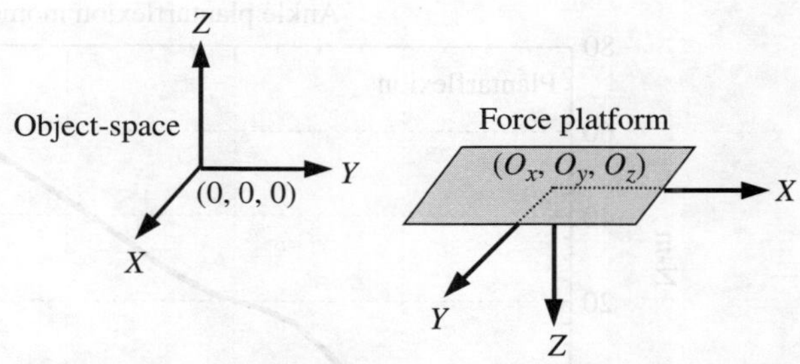

FIGURE 8.14 Relationship between the reference axes of the force platform and the reference axes of the object-space. In general, the reference axes will not be aligned. The force platform is located at a distance O_x, O_y, O_z from the origin of the object-space.

a force platform are used in an inverse dynamics analysis, the data must be synchronized with the kinematic observations. Generally, analog data sampled from a force platform are collected at an integer multiple of the video collection rate.

8.4.6 Example: Results from an Inverse Dynamics Analysis

We close this section by presenting several examples of joint kinematic and kinetic data calculated using the methods outlined above. The ground reaction forces for a subject walking at a natural cadence are illustrated in Fig. 8.15. The vertical component of the ground reaction force (GRF) is by far the largest, with the peak AP component of the GRF next largest in magnitude. Notice how the AP force component has both a negative phase and a positive phase corresponding to *braking* and *propulsive* phases during stance. The first "hump" of the vertical component of the GRF corresponds to a deceleration of the whole body COM during weight acceptance (note how this corresponds with the AP braking force). The second "hump" in the vertical component of the GRF and the positive phase of the AP force component accelerate the body COM upward and forward as the subject prepares for push-off at the end of stance.

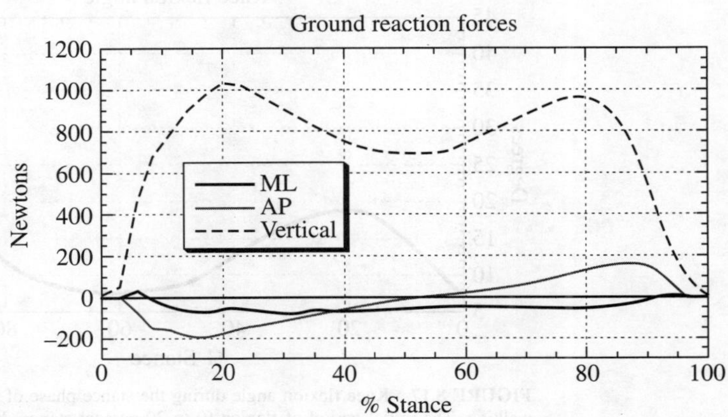

FIGURE 8.15 Ground reaction forces during the stance phase of natural cadence walking. The stance phase begins at foot strike and ends when the foot leaves the ground. ML = medio-lateral, AP = antero-posterior.

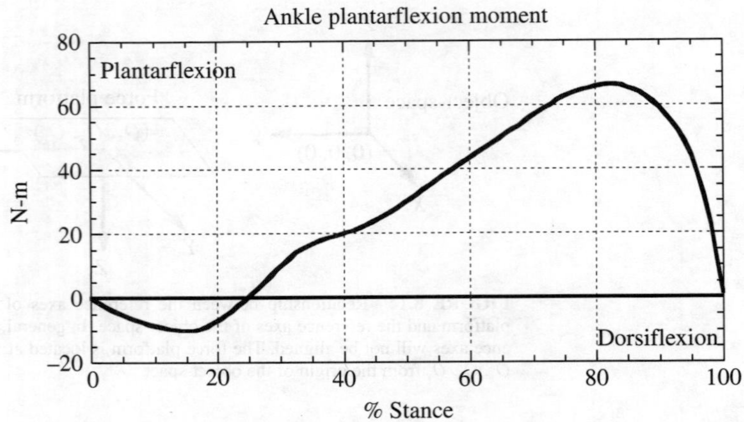

FIGURE 8.16 Sagittal plane ankle moment during the stance phase of natural cadence walking. Notice the small dorsiflexion moment during the first 20 percent of stance. This prevents the foot from "slapping" the ground shortly after contact. The large plantarflexion moment during the latter half of stance helps propel the body upward and forward.

The curve in Fig. 8.16 is the sagittal plane ankle moment that was calculated using the data from the force platform and Eqs. (8.17) and (8.18). At the ankle, we see a small dorsiflexion moment shortly after contact. This moment prevents the foot from "slapping" down during initial contact with the ground (i.e., the dorsiflexion moment "pulls" the toes toward the shank). As the subject moves into the latter half of stance, a sizable plantarflexion moment is generated as a main contributor to the body's forward progression. This increase in plantarflexion moment is due to the gastrocnemius and soleus muscles contracting, essentially "pushing" the foot into the ground.

Also toward the end of the stance phase, the knee joint flexion angle increases in preparation for push-off. (Think what would happen if the knee did not flex as the leg begins to swing.) The weight acceptance period shortly after initial contact is mediated, in part, by the knee joint, which undergoes a brief period of flexion (Fig. 8.17). During this initial period of stance, the knee acts as a

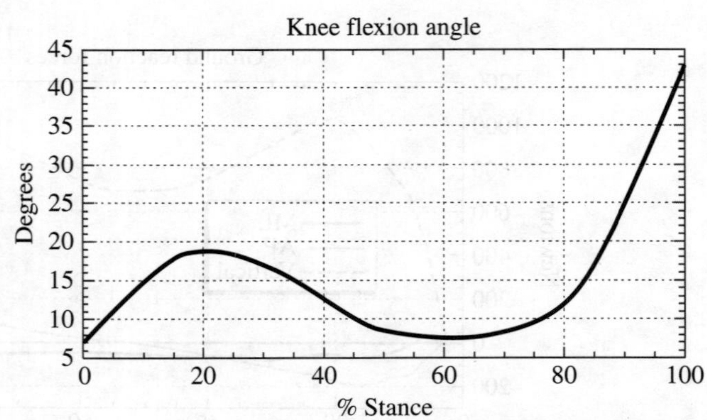

FIGURE 8.17 Knee flexion angle during the stance phase of natural cadence walking. The initial period of flexion (0 to 20 percent stance) helps absorb the shock of impact when the foot hits the ground. A second period of flexion begins at approximately 70 percent of stance, increasing rapidly in preparation for the swing phase.

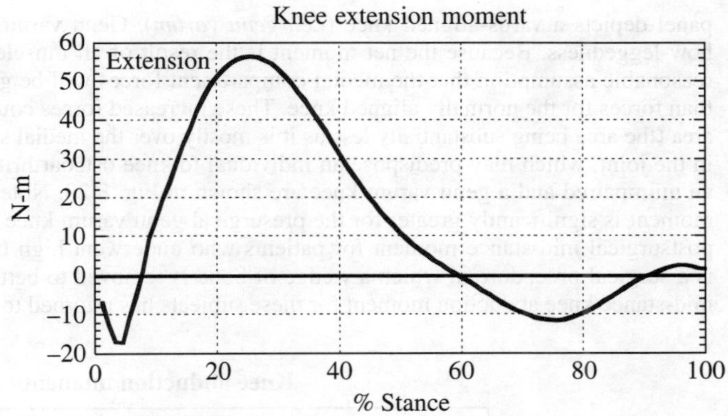

FIGURE 8.18 Knee extension moment during the stance phase of natural cadence walking. The net extension moment reveals that the quadriceps muscles are the dominant group during stance. The initial small flexion moment is caused by the vertical ground reaction force when the foot hits the ground.

spring, resisting the force of impact. Hence, in Fig. 8.18 we see that a substantial knee extension moment is generated by the quadriceps muscle group to control knee flexion during this time.

Reporting the results of an inverse dynamics analysis in graphical form as we have done here demonstrates the interdependence of the kinematic and kinetic variables. The figures are helpful when communicating with an athlete or trainer in breaking down a movement pattern to determine how performance might be improved. Inverse dynamics is also a valuable tool that is used to plan surgical treatment and assess the outcome. For example, consider the case in Fig. 8.19. The right

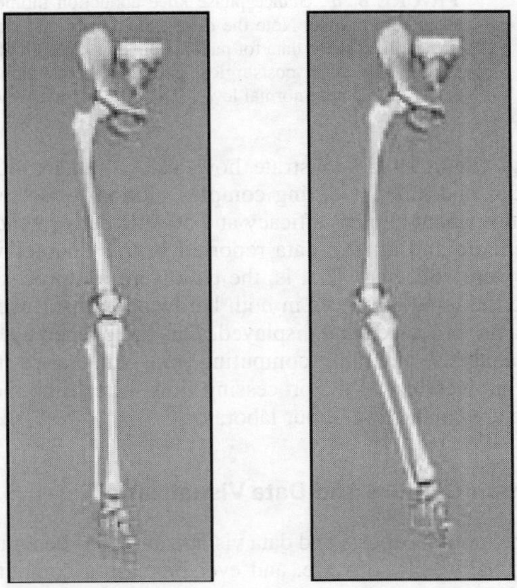

FIGURE 8.19 Examples of a normally aligned (right panel) and a genu varum (left panel) knee. A larger abduction moment and reduced joint contact area for the genu varum knee will lead to higher than normal stresses during stance.

panel depicts a varus-aligned knee (i.e., *genu varum*). Genu varum is more commonly known as bow-leggedness. Because the net moment is the result of all muscles acting about the joint, it is a reasonable assumption that the medial compartment forces will be greater for the genu varum knee than forces for the normally aligned knee. These increased forces coupled with reduced joint contact area (the area being substantially less as it is mostly over the medial side) will lead to greater stresses in the joint, which may predispose an individual to knee osteoarthritis. The abduction moments for an unimpaired and a genu varum knee are shown in Fig. 8.20. Note how the mid-stance abduction moment is significantly greater for the presurgical genu varum knee. The dashed line is the average postsurgical mid-stance moment for patients who underwent high tibial osteotomy surgery, which is a surgical procedure in which a wedge of bone is removed to better align the joint. Note that the mid-stance knee abduction moment for these subjects has returned to near normal following surgery.

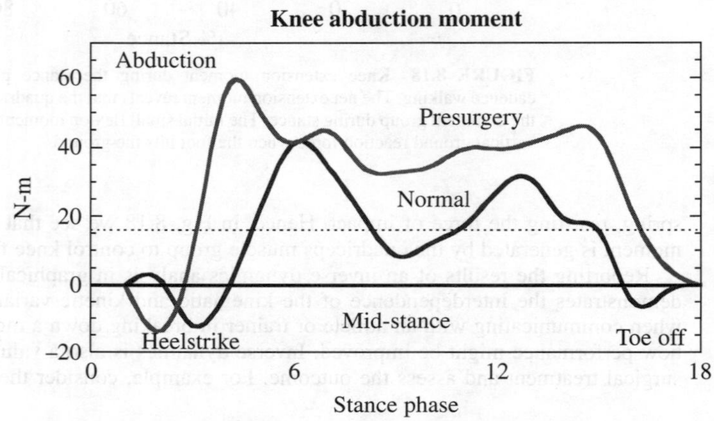

FIGURE 8.20 Stance phase knee abduction moment for a normally aligned and a genu varum knee. Note the difference during mid-stance. The dashed grey line is the postsurgical mean data for patients undergoing high tibial osteotomy to correct the genu varum. The mean postsurgical mid-stance abduction moment (mean = 16 N·m) has returned to a near normal level. [*Data taken from* Weidenhielm et al. (1995).]

These examples demonstrate how, using human movement analysis, we can calculate the kinematics and kinetics during complex motions and how these, in turn, can be used to provide information about clinical efficacy and athletic performance.

Kinematic and kinetic data reported in this chapter were calculated after the movements of interest were collected. That is, the data were postprocessed. The study of human movement is a dynamic field and advances in both hardware and software are providing new possibilities for the way data are processed and displayed. This has opened up exciting new applications for video-based motion analysis, including computing joint kinematics in real time. In the following section we provide an overview of the processing flow in realtime motion analysis and present an example of work we are conducting in our laboratory.

8.4.7 Real-Time Motion Capture and Data Visualization

Real-time motion capture and data visualization has become a reality in recent years due to improvements in hardware, software, and ever increasing computing power. It is now possible to view a recorded motions and resulting kinematics at almost exactly the same time the movement was performed. There are numerous advantages of real-time data capture and visualization for those in the entertainment industry, researchers, and clinicians. Animators and directors benefit because they can decide if movements were done as the scene had intended rather than waiting hours or days only to find out there was a problem and the scene needs to be reshot. Researchers are using real-time information from motion capture to provide patients with visual feedback on how they are performing a task. Movement patterns can be modified using visual guidance by showing the patient their pattern (e.g., knee angle) and how it compares to a target pattern. This allows the patient to visualize how to change their movement pattern to match a desired trajectory. Clinicians are using real-time motion capture to immerse patients in virtual environments providing a more stimulating exercise and rehabilitation experience.

Processing Flow for Real-Time Motion Capture. Latency is the key to the "realness" of real-time motion capture. For our purposes latency is the time difference between the initiation of a movement and an accurate characterization of the movement as determined by the motion capture system. A great deal happens between the time a marker is registered by a CCD sensor and the calculation of three-dimensional kinematics. Not surprisingly, many factors affect latency including the number of cameras being used, the number of markers that are tracked and of obviously the processing speed of the CPU. It is helpful to understand the data processing flow from the image sensor to desktop display when considering latency in the context of real-time motion capture. Although specific details may vary from system to system, our goal in this section is to provide an overview of the processing flow and describe how each step adds to the total latency. The steps involved for a passive marker system can be summarized as follows:

1. Light-emitting diodes on the face of a camera illuminate retroreflective tracking markers in the camera's field of view. The diodes are strobed to coincide with the opening of the camera's shutter. Light is reflected back off each marker through the camera lens and excites a portion of the CCD imaging sensor. The exposure time is related to the sampling frequency of the camera and for some systems the exposure time can be set by the user. For our purposes we will assume the exposure time is approximately 1 ms at sampling rates typically used when recording human movement.
2. After exposure, the sensor is scanned and circle fitted to compute the center point of each marker imaged by the sensor. The time required to do so is approximately 1/maximum frame rate. For example, a camera that can sample up to 500 fps would require 2 ms to scan the sensor and circle fit the data.
3. The two-dimensional camera coordinates (u, v) for each marker are packaged and sent to the data acquisition computer via Ethernet. This is done very efficiently requiring approximately 1 ms for the number of markers typical of human movement studies (i.e., <40 markers).
4. The data acquisition software must now reconstruct the three-dimensional X, Y, and Z coordinates for each marker and assign the coordinates to a model being tracking. Correct assignment is imperative for accurate model tracking and the time required for this depends on the number of cameras and markers used. This may take anywhere from 1 to 5 ms. The position and orientation of the model has now been computed and the data can be sent to another process (i.e., rendered to screen or sent to third party software).

The processing flow outlined in steps 1 to 4, and the times required for each step are approximate values. To accurately determine true latency requires access to low-level system architecture. Qualisys Inc. has reported latency figures for their 6 camera Oqus system tracking 36 markers at 160 fps. The total latency was 6 ms, which corresponds to a delay of 1 video frame. A delay of 1 to 2 video frames is a realistic goal for modern motion capture systems. It is important to note that this delay is at the level of the motion capture system and does not include additional processing time associated with rendering to the screen or processing in third party software for visualization. This can add a significant layer of delay (10 to 30 ms) to the overall latency depending on how the real-time data are used.

Real-Time Feedback: A Gait Retraining Example. The knee flexes during the initial portion of stance and helps absorb the impact our body experiences with every step. Normal peak knee flexion during this time varies from person to person, but is generally between 15° and 25° for healthy adults

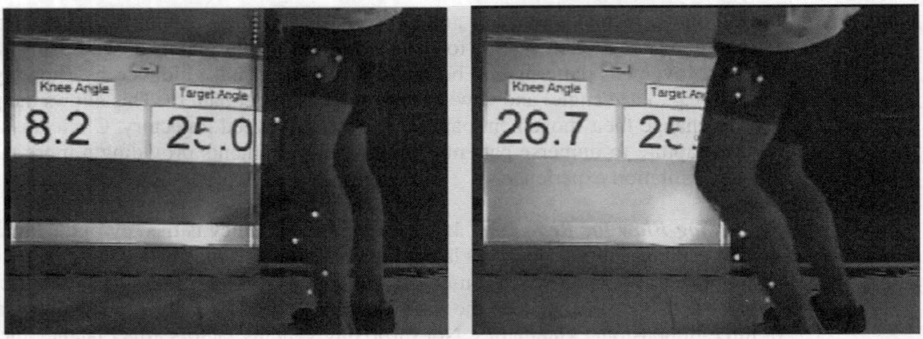

FIGURE 8.21 The subject in this example walks with a stiff knee gait. His peak knee flexion angle during weight acceptance is less than 10°. This is re-created during standing (left panel) and provides the subject with a kinesthetic sense of the flexion angle. The subject is encouraged to flex his knee to 25° (right panel). The real-time knee flexion angle (26.7°) is displayed and the subject can modify his flexion angle accordingly. The screen is updated every 30 ms.

(i.e., first peak in Fig. 8.17). Individuals who do not flex sufficiently during weight acceptance may be at greater risk for developing tibial stress fractures. The real-time capabilities of the Qualisys system can be used to help guide a patient on how they should adjust their pattern to match a target. An example of this is shown in Fig. 8.21. The subject walks with a stiff knee gait and flexes less than 10° during weight acceptance. This is re-created while standing to give the subject visual feedback regarding the flexion angle. In the right panel the subject is encouraged to practice flexing his knee to 25°. Although this early phase of retraining is done while standing, it provides the subject with a kinesthetic awareness of his knee positioning. Once the subject can achieve the desired angle without visual guidance (i.e., numbers being displayed) he then practices walking so that the knee flexion during weight acceptance is within a prescribed range. Performance can be monitored in real time and used to direct changes that need to be made to achieve the desired target angle.

8.5 CONCLUDING REMARKS

In this chapter we have examined forward and inverse dynamics approaches to the study of human motion. We have outlined the steps involved when using the inverse approach to studying movement with a particular focus on human gait. This is perhaps the most commonly used method for examining joint kinetics. The forward or direct dynamics approach requires that one start with knowledge of the neural command signal, the muscle forces, or, perhaps, the joint torques. These are then used to compute kinematics.

Before concluding, a brief word might be said for hybrid approaches that combine both forward and inverse dynamics approaches to meet in the middle. These methods record both the neural command signal (i.e., the EMG) and the joint position information using standard motion analysis methods as described in Sec. 8.4. The EMG is processed so as to determine muscle forces, which are then summed together to yield joint moments. These same joint moments can also be computed from the inverse dynamics. This provides a means by which to calibrate the EMG to muscle force relationships. This method has been shown to work well with gait studies (Bessier, 2000) and has great potential for studying altered muscle function associated with pathological gait, which cannot be readily examined using optimization techniques.

The biomechanics of human movement is growing field, spanning many disciplines. As new techniques are developed and shared across these disciplines, the field will continue to grow, allowing us to peer deeper into the mechanics of movement.

REFERENCES

Abdel-Aziz, Y. I., and Karara, H. M. (1971) Direct linear transformation from comparator coordinates into object-space coordinates. *Close-Range Photogrammetry*. American Society of Photogrammetry, Falls Church, Virginia.

Bessier, T. F. (2000) Examination of neuromuscular and biomechanical mechanisms of non-contact knee ligament injuries. Doctoral dissertation, University of Western Australia.

Buchanan, T. S., Delp, S. L., and Solbeck, J. A. (1998) Muscular resistance to varus and valgus loads at the elbow. *Journal of Biomechanical Engineering.* **120**(5):634–639.

Buchanan, T. S., Moniz, M. J., Dewald, J. P., and Zev Rymer, W. (1993) Estimation of muscle forces about the wrist joint during isometric tasks using an EMG coefficient method. *Journal of Biomechanics.* **26**:547–560.

Cappozzo, A., Catani, F., Della Croce, U., and Leardini, A. (1995) Position and orientation in space of bones during movement: anatomical frame definition and determination. *Clinical Biomechanics.* **10**(4):171–178.

Chao, E. Y. S. (1980) Justification of triaxial goniometer for the measurement of joint rotation. *Journal of Biomechanics.* **13**:989–1006.

Cheze, L., Fregly, B. J., and Dimnet, J. (1995) A solidification procedure to facilitate kinematic analyses based on video system data. *Journal of Biomechanics.* **28**(7):879–884.

Delp, S. L., Arnold, A. S., Speers, R. A., and Moore, C. A. (1996) Hamstrings and psoas lengths during normal and crouch gait: implications for muscle-tendon surgery. *Journal of Orthopaedic Research.* **14**:144–151.

Dempster, W. T. (1955) Space Requirements of the Seated Operator Geometrical, Kinematic, and Mechanical Aspects of the Body with Special Reference to the Limbs. *Technical Report (55-159) (AD 87892)*. Wright Air Development Center, Air Research and Development Command, Wright-Patterson Air Force Base, OH.

Grood, E. S., and Suntay, W. J. (1983) A joint coordinate system for the clinical description of three-dimensional motions: application to the knee. *Journal of Biomechanical Engineering.* **105:**136–144.

Hill, A. V. (1938) The heat of shortening and the dynamic constants of muscle. *Proceedings of the Royal Society of London Series B.* **126:**136–195.

Huxley, A. F. (1957) Muscle structure and theories of contraction. *Progress in Biophysical Chemistry.* **7**:255–318.

Huxley, A. F., and Simmons R. M. (1971) Proposed mechanism of force generation in striated muscle. *Nature.* **233**:533–538.

International Society of Biomechanics, (1999) *ISB software sources*, http://isb.ri.ccf.org/software.

Jackson, K. M. (1979) Fitting of mathematical functions to biomechanical data. *IEEE Transactions on Biomedical Engineering* BME. **26**(2):122–124.

Pandy, M. G., and Zajac, F. E. (1991) Optimal muscular coordination strategies for jumping. *Journal of Biomechanics.* **24**:1–10.

Shiavi, R., Limbird, T., Frazer, M., Stivers, K., Strauss, A., and Abramovitz J. (1987) Helical motion analysis of the knee—I. Methodology for studying kinematics during locomotion. *Journal of Biomechanics.* **20**(5):459–469.

Soderkvist, I., and Wedin, P. (1993) Determining the movements of the skeleton using well-configured markers. *Journal of Biomechanics.* **26**(12):1473–1477.

Weidenhielm, L., Svensson, O. K., and Brostrom, L-A. (1995) Change of adduction moment about the hip, knee and ankle joints after high tibial osteotomy in osteoarthrosis of the knee. *Clinical Biomechanics.* **7**:177–180.

Winter, D. A. (1990) *Biomechanics and Motor Control of Human Movement.* 2 ed. New York: John Wiley & Sons, Inc.

Woltring, H. J. (1986) A FORTRAN package for generalized, cross-validatory spline smoothing and differentiation. *Advances in Engineering Software.* **8**(2):104–113.

Zahalak, G. I. (1986) A comparison of the mechanical behavior of the cat soleus muscle with a distribution-moment model. *Journal of Biomechanical Engineering.* **108**:131–140.

Zahalak, G. I. (2000) The two-state cross-bridge model of muscle is an asymptotic limit of multi-state models. *Journal of Theoretical Biology.* **204**:67–82.

Zajac, F. E. (1989) Muscle and tendon: properties, models, scaling and application to the biomechanics of motor control. In: Bourne, J. R. (ed.), *Critical Reviews in Biomedical Engineering.* **17**, CRC Press, pp. 359–411.

Zatsiorsky, V., and Seluyanov, V. (1985) Estimation of the mass and inertia characteristics of the human body by means of the best predictive regression equations. In: Winter, D., Norman, R., Wells, R., Hayes, K., and Patla, A. (eds.), *Biomechanics IX-B.* Champaign, IL: Human Kinetics Publisher, pp. 233–239.

CHAPTER 9
BIOMECHANICS OF THE MUSCULOSKELETAL SYSTEM

Marcus G. Pandy
University of Melbourne, Melbourne, Australia

Ronald E. Barr
University of Texas, Austin, Texas

9.1 INTRODUCTION

As the nervous system plans and regulates movement, it does so by taking into account the mechanical properties of the muscles, the mass and inertial properties of the body segments, and the external forces arising from contact with the environment. These interactions can be represented schematically as in Fig. 9.1, which suggests that the various elements of the neuromusculoskeletal system can be compartmentalized and modeled independently.

Muscles provide the forces needed to make movement possible; they transmit their forces to tendons, whose forces in turn cause rotation of the bones about the joints. Muscles, however, are not simple force generators: the force developed by a muscle depends not only on the level of neural excitation provided by the central nervous system (CNS), but also on the length and speed at which the muscle is contracting. Thus, muscles are the interface between the neuromuscular and musculoskeletal systems, and knowledge of their force-producing properties is crucial for understanding how these two systems interact to produce coordinated movement.

In this chapter, we review the structure and properties of the neuromusculoskeletal system, and show how the various components of this system can be idealized and described in mathematical terms. Section 9.2 begins with an overview of the mechanical properties of muscle, tendon, ligament, and cartilage. In Secs. 9.3 and 9.4, we focus on the structure of the body-segmental (skeletal) system, emphasizing how musculoskeletal geometry (i.e., muscle moment arms) converts linear actuation (musculotendon forces) into rotary (joint) motion. How motor output from the CNS is converted to muscle activation and ultimately muscle force is described in Sec. 9.5. Section 9.6 presents two methods commonly used to determine musculoskeletal loading during human movement.

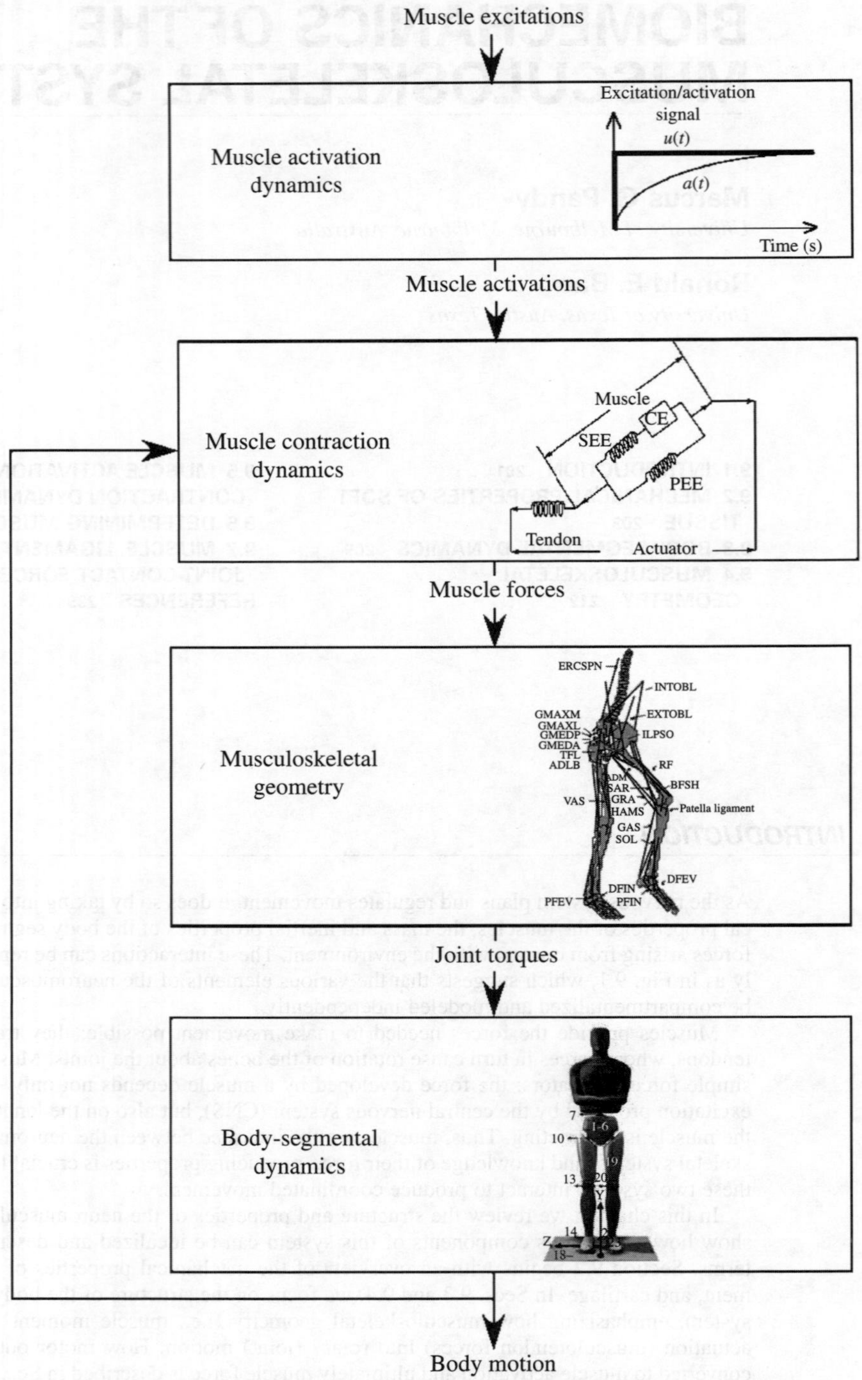

FIGURE 9.1 Schematic diagram showing how the human neuromusculoskeletal system can be compartmentalized for modeling purposes.

Representative results of muscle, ligament, and joint-contact loading incurred during exercise and daily activities like walking and running are given in Sec. 9.7.

9.2 MECHANICAL PROPERTIES OF SOFT TISSUE

We focus our description of the mechanical properties of soft tissue on muscle, tendon, ligament, and cartilage. The structure and properties of bone are treated elsewhere in this volume.

9.2.1 Muscle

Gross Structure. Muscles are molecular machines that convert chemical energy into force. Individual muscle fibers are connected together by three levels of collagenous tissue: endomysium, which surrounds individual muscle fibers; perimysium, which collects bundles of fibers into fascicles; and epimysium, which encloses the entire muscle belly (Fig. 9.2A). This connective tissue matrix connects muscle fibers to tendon and ultimately to bone.

Whole muscles are composed of groups of muscle fibers, which vary from 1 to 400 mm in length and from 10 to 60 μm in diameter. Muscle fibers, in turn, are composed of groups of myofibrils (Fig. 9.2B), and each myofibril is a series of sarcomeres added end to end (Fig. 9.2C). The sarcomere is both the structural and functional unit of skeletal muscle. During contraction, the sarcomeres are shortened to about 70 percent of their uncontracted, resting length. Electron microscopy and biochemical analysis have shown that each sarcomere contains two types of filaments: thick filaments, composed of myosin, and thin filaments, containing actin (Fig. 9.2D). Near the center of the sarcomere, thin filaments overlap with thick filaments to form the AI zone (Fig. 9.2E).

In sections. "Force-Length Property" and "Force-Velocity Property," the force-length and force-velocity properties of muscle are assumed to be scaled-up versions of the properties of muscle fibers, which in turn are assumed to be scaled-up versions of properties of sarcomeres.

Force-Length Property. The steady-state property of muscle is defined by its isometric force-length curve, which is obtained when activation and fiber length are both held constant. When a muscle is held isometric and is fully activated, it develops a steady force. The difference in force developed when the muscle is activated and when the muscle is passive is called the active muscle force (Fig. 9.3A). The region where active muscle force is generated is (nominally) $0.5l_o^M < l^M < 1.5l_o^M$, where l_o^M is the length at which active muscle force peaks; that is, $F^M = F_o^M$ when $l^M = l_o^M$; F_o^M is called muscle fiber resting length or *optimal muscle fiber length* and l_o^M is the maximum isometric force developed by the muscle (Zajac, 1989). In Fig. 9.3A, passive muscle tissue bears no force at length l_o^M. The force-length property of muscle tissue that is less than fully activated can be considered to be a scaled down version of the one that is fully activated (Fig. 9.3B). Muscle tissue can be less than fully activated when some or all of its fibers are less than fully activated.

The shape of the active force-length curve (Fig. 9.3) is explained by the experimental observation that active muscle force varies with the amount of overlap between the thick and thin filaments within a sarcomere (see also the section "Mechanism of Muscle Contraction" under Sec. 9.5.2). The muscle force-striation spacing curve given in Fig. 9.3C shows that there is minimal overlap of the thick and thin filaments at a sarcomere length of 3.5 μm, whereas at a length of about 2.0 μm there is maximum overlap between the cross-bridges. As sarcomere length decreases to 1.5 μm, the filaments slide farther over one another, and the amount of filament overlap again decreases. Thus, muscle force varies with sarcomere length because of the change in the number of potential cross-bridge attachments formed.

Force-Velocity Property. When a constant load is applied to a fully activated muscle, the muscle will shorten (concentric contraction) if the applied load is less than the maximum isometric force developed by the muscle for the length at which the muscle is initially contracting. If the applied

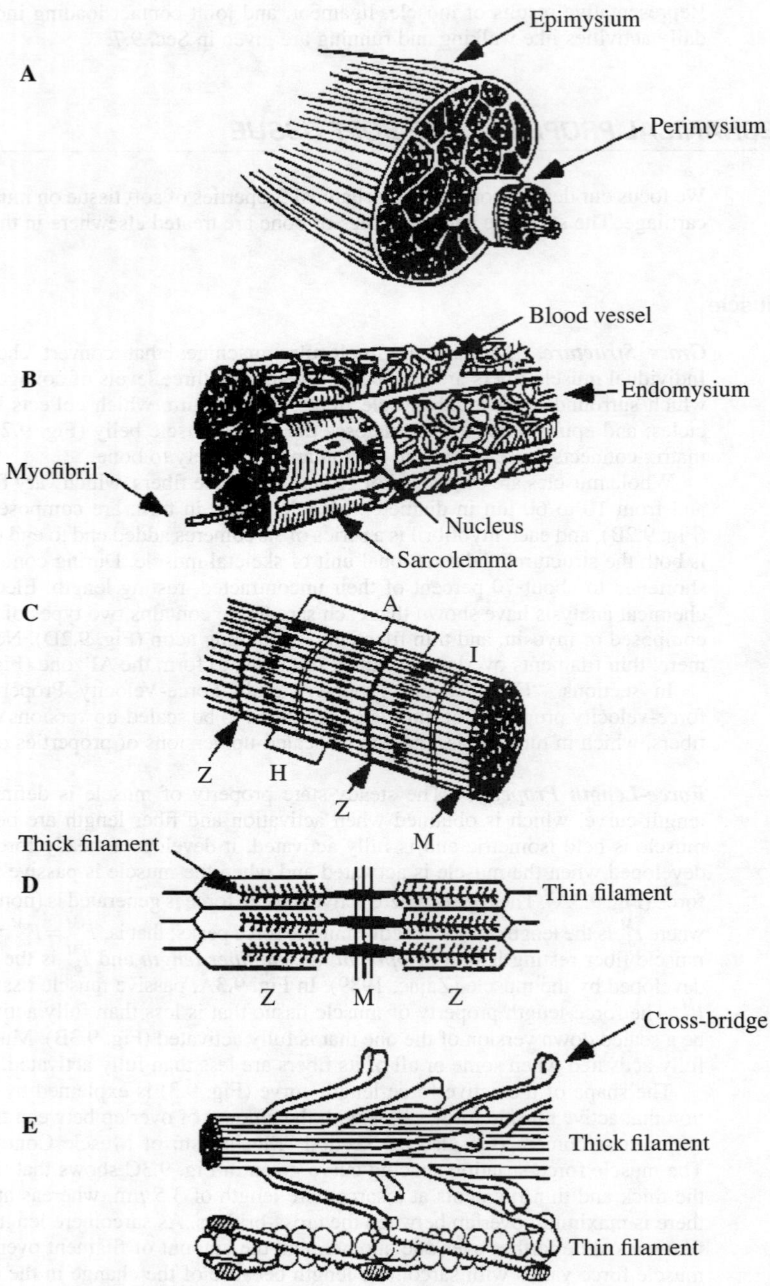

FIGURE 9.2 Structural organization of skeletal muscle from macro to micro level. Whole muscle (A), bundles of myofibrils (B), single myofibril (*c*), sarcomere (D), and thick (myosin) filament and thin (actin) filament (E). All symbols are defined in the text. [*Modified from Enoka (1994).*]

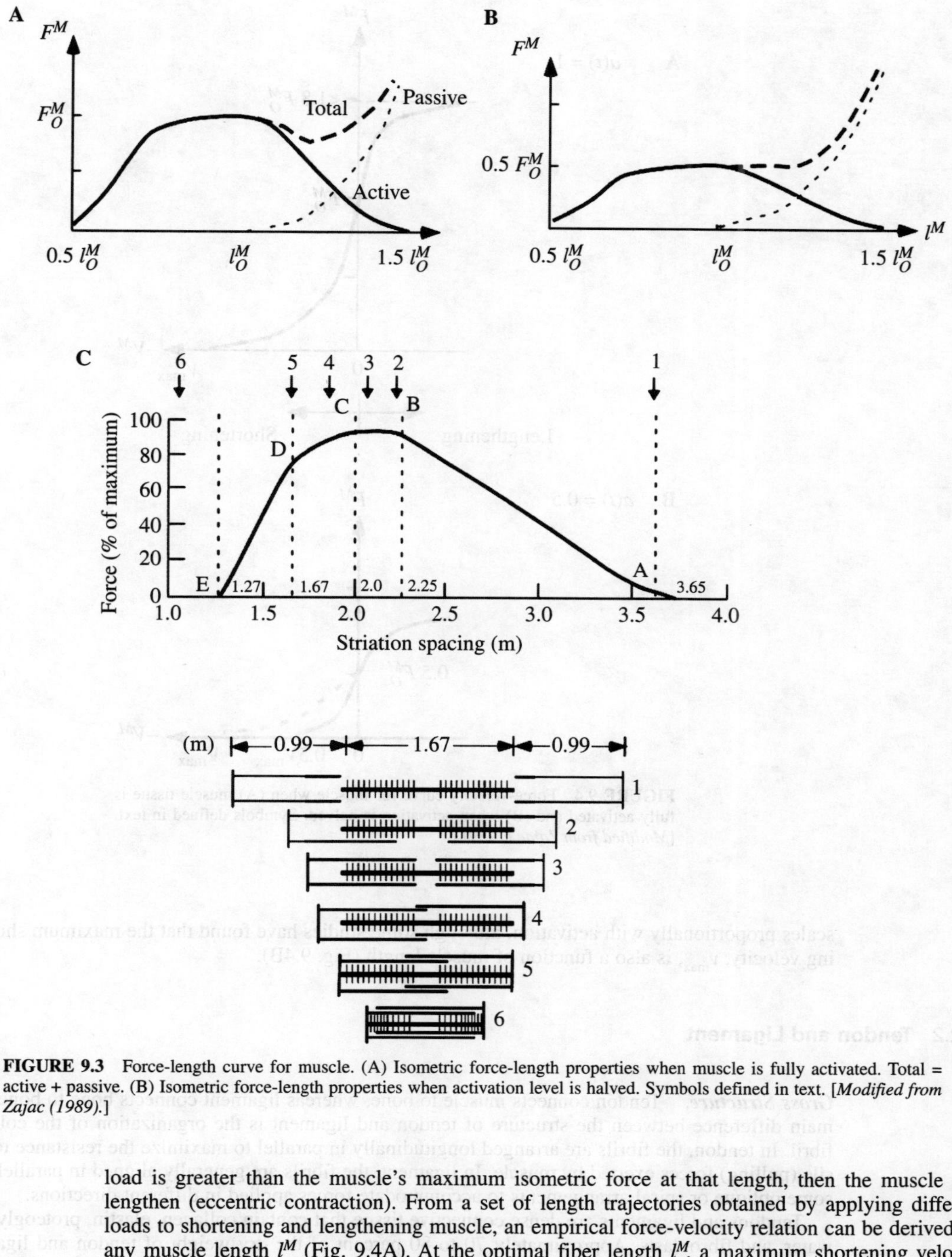

FIGURE 9.3 Force-length curve for muscle. (A) Isometric force-length properties when muscle is fully activated. Total = active + passive. (B) Isometric force-length properties when activation level is halved. Symbols defined in text. [*Modified from Zajac (1989).*]

load is greater than the muscle's maximum isometric force at that length, then the muscle will lengthen (eccentric contraction). From a set of length trajectories obtained by applying different loads to shortening and lengthening muscle, an empirical force-velocity relation can be derived for any muscle length l^M (Fig. 9.4A). At the optimal fiber length l_o^M, a maximum shortening velocity v_{max}, can be defined such that the muscle tissue cannot resist any load even when it is fully activated (Fig. 9.4A). As with the force-length curve, it is commonly assumed that the force-velocity relation

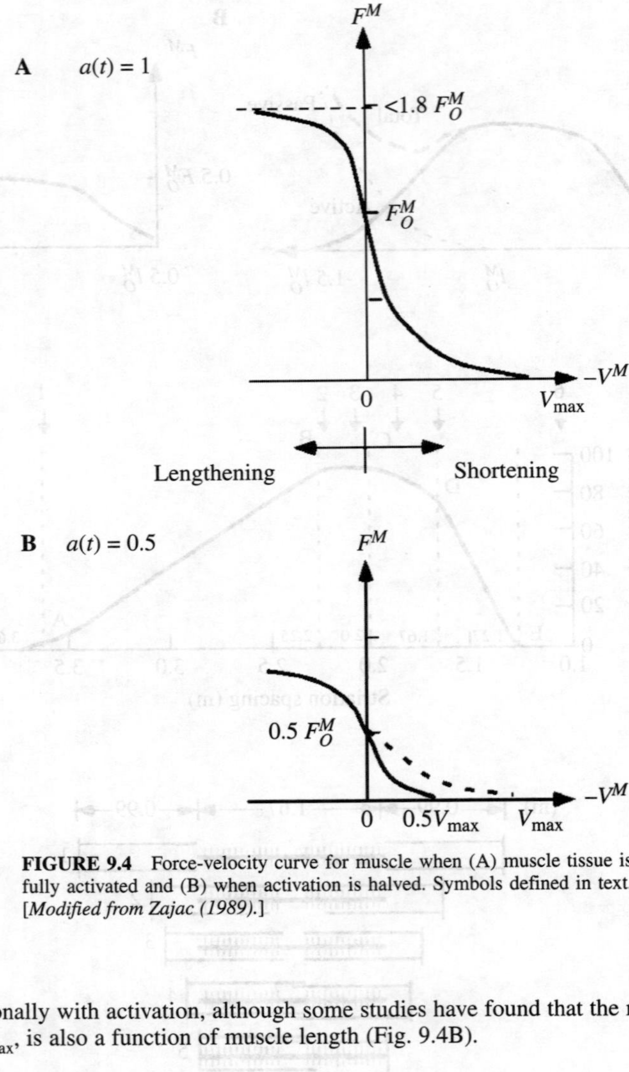

FIGURE 9.4 Force-velocity curve for muscle when (A) muscle tissue is fully activated and (B) when activation is halved. Symbols defined in text. [*Modified from Zajac (1989).*]

scales proportionally with activation, although some studies have found that the maximum shortening velocity, v_{max}, is also a function of muscle length (Fig. 9.4B).

9.2.2 Tendon and Ligament

Gross Structure. Tendon connects muscle to bone, whereas ligament connects bone to bone. The main difference between the structure of tendon and ligament is the organization of the collagen fibril. In tendon, the fibrils are arranged longitudinally in parallel to maximize the resistance to tensile (pulling) forces exerted by muscle. In ligament, the fibrils are generally aligned in parallel with some oblique or spiral arrangements to accommodate forces applied in different directions.

Tendons and ligaments are dense connective tissue that contain collagen, elastin, proteoglycans, water, and fibroblasts. Approximately 70 to 80 percent of the dry weight of tendon and ligament consists of Type I collagen, which is a fibrous protein. Whole tendon is comprised of bundles of fascicles, each made up in turn of bundles of fibrils (Fig. 9.5). The collagen fibril is the basic

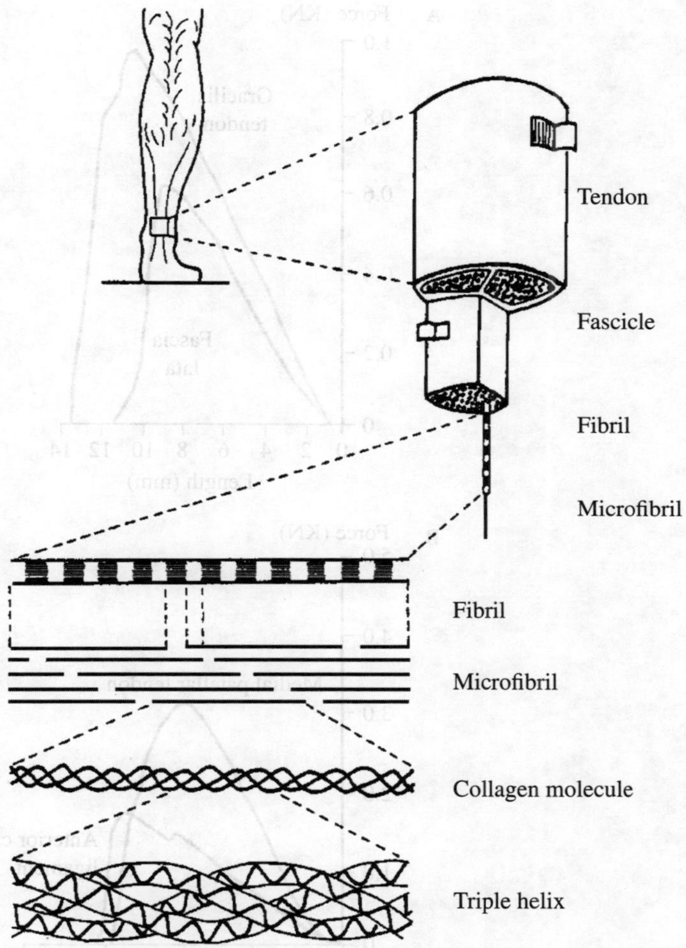

FIGURE 9.5 Structural organization of tendon or ligament from macro to micro level. [*Modified from Enoka (1994).*]

load-bearing unit of tendon and ligament. The fibril consists of bundles of microfibrils held together by biochemical bonds (called cross-links) between the collagen molecules. Because these cross-links bind the microfibrils together, the number and state of the cross-links are thought to have a significant effect on the strength of the connective tissue.

Stress-Strain Property. When a tensile force is applied to tendon or ligament at its resting length, the tissue stretches. Figure 9.6 shows the force-length curves for three different muscle tendons and one knee ligament found in humans. These data show that the medial patellar tendon is much stronger than either the gracilis or fascia lata tendons. Interestingly, the anterior cruciate ligament is also stronger than the gracilis and fascia lata tendons, and is slightly more compliant as well.

Force-length curves can be normalized to subtract out the effects of geometry; thus, force can be normalized by dividing by the cross-sectional area of a tissue, while length can be normalized by dividing by the initial length of the tendon or ligament. The resulting stress-strain curve displays three characteristic regions: the toe region, the linear region, and the failure region (Fig. 9.7). The toe

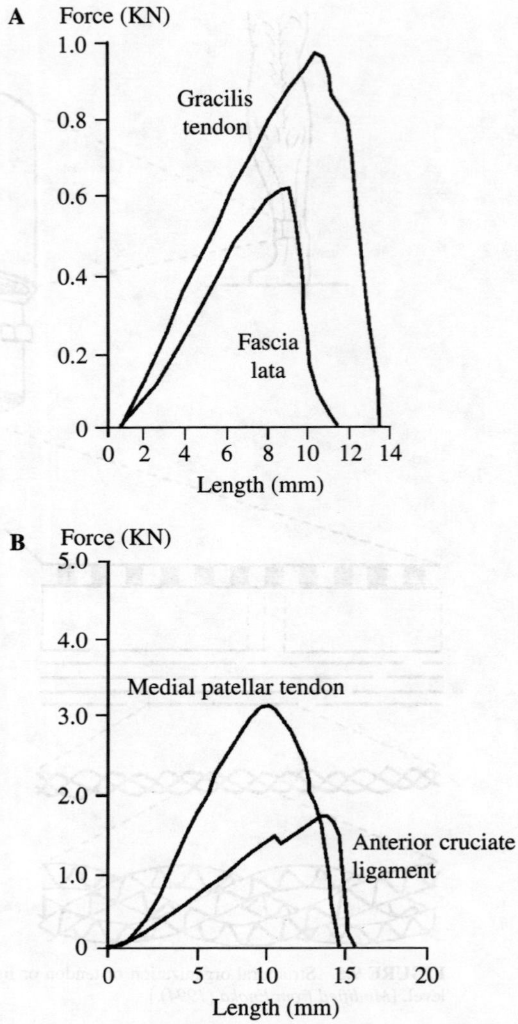

FIGURE 9.6 Force-length curves for human medial patellar tendon, gracilis tendon, fascia lata tendon, and the anterior cruciate ligament.

region corresponds to the initial part of the stress-strain curve and describes the mechanical behavior of the collagen fibers as they are being stretched and straightened from the initial, resting zig-zag pattern. The linear region describes the elastic behavior of the tissue, and the slope of the curve in this region represents the elastic modulus of the tendon or ligament. The failure region describes plastic changes undergone by the tissue, where a small number of fibrils first rupture, followed by ultimate failure of the whole tissue.

9.2.3 Articular Cartilage

Articular cartilage is a white, dense, connective tissue, which appears as a layer anywhere from 1 to 5 mm thick on the bony articulating ends of a diarthrodial joint. Cartilage is multiphasic, nonlinearly

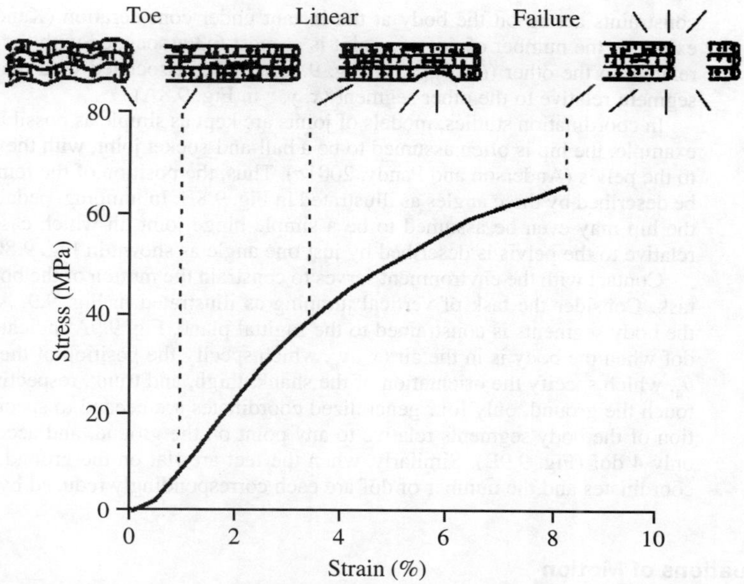

FIGURE 9.7 Idealized stress-strain curve for tendon or ligament. [*Modified from Butler et al. (1978).*]

permeable, and viscoelastic. It consists of two phases: a solid organic matrix, composed predominantly of collagen fibrils and proteoglycan macromolecules, and a movable interstitial fluid phase, composed primarily of water. The ratio by wet weight of these two phases is approximately 4:1, with water accounting for roughly 80 percent of the total mass.

In mathematical models of healthy human joints, cartilage is often represented as a single-phase, elastic material with homogeneous and isotropic properties. This approximation is valid, provided only the short-term response of the tissue is of interest; when cartilage is loaded for 1 to 5 seconds, its response is more-or-less elastic (Hayes and Bodine, 1978; Hori and Mockros, 1976). In the long term, however, say more than 1 minute, the response of the tissue is dominated by the nonlinear, viscoelastic properties of creep and stress relaxation (Hayes and Mockros, 1971; Mow et al., 1984).

Kempson (1980) performed uniaxial compression tests on an isolated cylinder of cartilage. Values of the elastic (Young's) modulus for articular cartilage of the human knee ranged from $E = 8.4$ to $E = 15.4$ MPa when measured 0.2 second after application of the force. Hori and Mockros (1976) estimated the values of elastic modulus and Poisson's ratio at 1 second of loading by conducting torsion and confined compression tests on cartilage of the human tibia. The elastic modulus of normal cartilage was reported to lie in the range $E = 5.6$ to $E = 10.2$ MPa, and that of degenerate cartilage in the range $E = 1.4$ to $E = 9.3$ MPa. Poisson's ratio for normal and degenerate cartilage was also found to lie in the range $\nu = 0.42$ to $\nu = 0.49$.

9.3. BODY-SEGMENTAL DYNAMICS

9.3.1 Generalized Coordinates and Degrees of Freedom

The minimum number of coordinates needed to specify the position and orientation of a body in space is the set of generalized coordinates for the body. The number of degrees of freedom (dof) of the body is equal to the number of generalized coordinates minus the number of kinematic constraints acting on the body at the instant under consideration (Kane and Levinson, 1985). For example, the number of dof of a joint is at most 6:3 associated with the orientation of one segment relative to the other (θ_1, θ_2, θ_3 in Fig. 9.8A), and 3 associated with the position of a point on one segment relative to the other segment (x, y, z in Fig. 9.8A).

In coordination studies, models of joints are kept as simple as possible. In studies of walking, for example, the hip is often assumed to be a ball-and-socket joint, with the femur only rotating relative to the pelvis (Anderson and Pandy, 2001*a*). Thus, the position of the femur relative to the pelvis can be described by three angles as illustrated in Fig. 9.8B. In jumping, pedaling, and rising from a chair, the hip may even be assumed to be a simple hinge joint, in which case the position of the femur relative to the pelvis is described by just one angle as shown in Fig. 9.8C.

Contact with the environment serves to constrain the motion of the body segments during a motor task. Consider the task of vertical jumping as illustrated in Fig. 9.9. Assuming that movement of the body segments is constrained to the sagittal plane, Fig. 9.9A indicates that the motor task has 6 dof when the body is in the air (x_p, y_p, which specify the position of the metatarsals plus, θ_1, θ_2, θ_3, θ_4, which specify the orientation of the shank, thigh, and trunk, respectively). When the metatarsals touch the ground, only four generalized coordinates are needed to specify the position and orientation of the body segments relative to any point on the ground, and accordingly, the motor task has only 4 dof (Fig. 9.9B). Similarly, when the feet are flat on the ground, the number of generalized coordinates and the number of dof are each correspondingly reduced by 1 (Fig. 9.9C).

9.3.2 Equations of Motion

Once a set of generalized coordinates has been specified and a kinematic model of the motor task has been defined, the governing equations of motion for the motor task can be written. The number of dynamical equations of motion is equal to the number of dof of the motor task; thus, if the number of dof changes during a motor task (see Fig. 9.9), so too will the structure of the equations of motion.

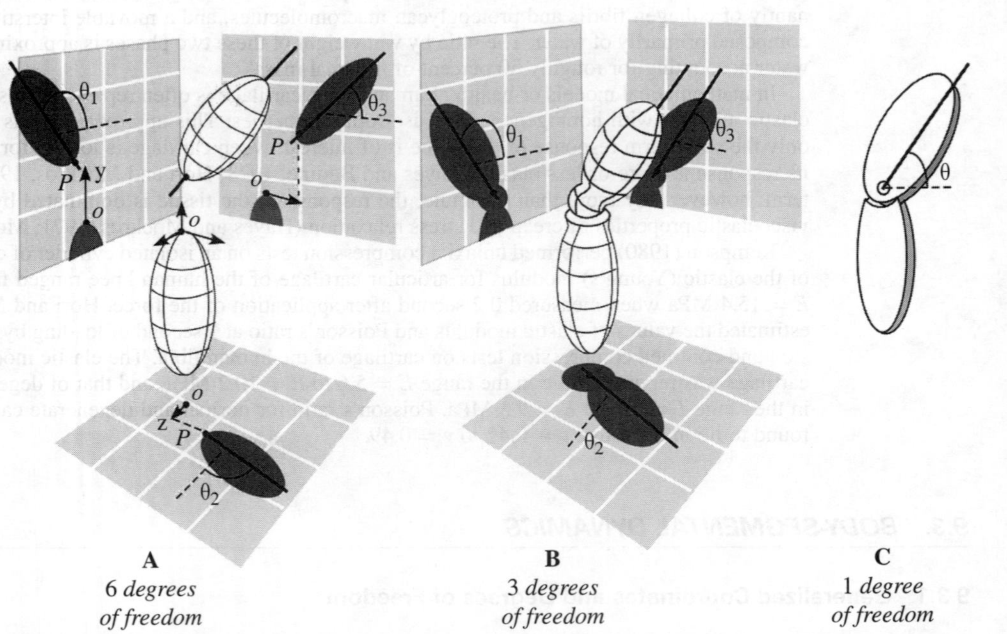

FIGURE 9.8 Number of degrees of freedom (dof) of a joint. See text for explanation. [*Modified from Zajac and Gordon (1989).*]

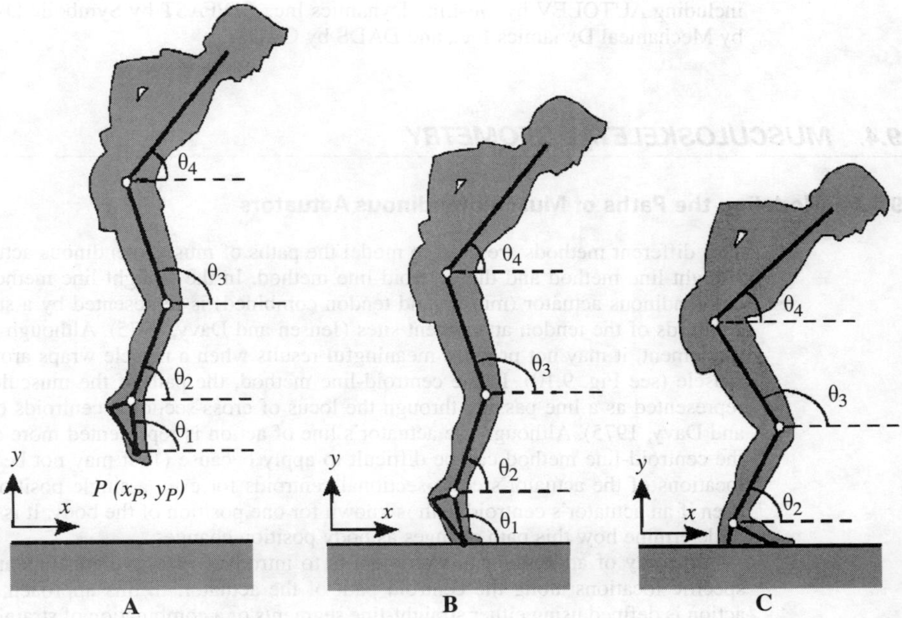

FIGURE 9.9 Number of dofs of a motor task such as landing from a vertical jump. See text for explanation. [*Modified from Zajac and Gordon (1989).*]

Different methods are available to derive the dynamical equations of motion for a motor task. In the Newton-Euler method (Pandy and Berme, 1988), free-body diagrams are constructed to show the external forces and torques acting on each body segment. The relationships between forces and linear accelerations of the centers of mass of the segments are written using Newton's second law ($\Sigma \boldsymbol{F} = \mathrm{m}\boldsymbol{a}$), and the relationships between torques and angular accelerations of the segments are written using Euler's equation ($\Sigma \boldsymbol{T} = \mathrm{I}\alpha$).

The Newton-Euler method is well suited to a recursive formulation of the kinematic and dynamic equations of motion (Pandy and Berme, 1988); however, its main disadvantage is that all of the intersegmental forces must be eliminated before the governing equations of motion can be formed. In an alternative formulation of the dynamical equations of motion, Kane's method (Kane and Levinson, 1985), which is also referred to as Lagrange's form of D'Alembert's principle, makes explicit use of the fact that constraint forces do not contribute directly to the governing equations of motion. It has been shown that Kane's formulation of the dynamical equations of motion is computationally more efficient than its counterpart, the Newton-Euler method (Kane and Levinson, 1983).

The governing equations of motion for any multijoint system can be expressed as

$$\boldsymbol{M}(\boldsymbol{q})\ddot{\boldsymbol{q}} + \boldsymbol{C}(\boldsymbol{q})\dot{\boldsymbol{q}}^2 + \boldsymbol{G}(\boldsymbol{q}) + \boldsymbol{R}(\boldsymbol{q})\boldsymbol{F}^{\mathrm{MT}} + \boldsymbol{E}(\boldsymbol{q},\dot{\boldsymbol{q}}) = \boldsymbol{0} \tag{9.1}$$

where q, $\dot{q}$, and $\ddot{q}$ are vectors of the generalized coordinates, velocities, and accelerations, respectively; $\boldsymbol{M}(\boldsymbol{q})$ is the system mass matrix and $\mathrm{M}(\boldsymbol{q})\ddot{q}$ is a vector of inertial forces and torques; $\boldsymbol{C}(\boldsymbol{q})\dot{\boldsymbol{q}}^2$ is a vector of centrifugal and Coriolis forces and torques; $\boldsymbol{G}(\boldsymbol{q})$ is a vector of gravitational forces and torques; $\mathrm{R}(\boldsymbol{q})$ is the matrix of muscle moment arms (see Sec. 9.4.3), $\boldsymbol{F}^{\mathrm{MT}}$ is a vector of musculotendon forces, and $\boldsymbol{R}(\boldsymbol{q})\boldsymbol{F}^{\mathrm{MT}}$ is a vector of musculotendon torques; and $\boldsymbol{E}(\boldsymbol{q},\dot{\boldsymbol{q}})$ is a vector of external forces and torques applied to the body by the environment.

If the number of dof of the motor task is greater than, say, 4, a computer is needed to obtain Eq. (9.1) explicitly. A number of commercial software packages are available for this purpose including AUTOLEV by On-Line Dynamics Inc., SD/FAST by Symbolic Dynamics Inc., ADAMS by Mechanical Dynamics Inc., and DADS by CADSI.

9.4. MUSCULOSKELETAL GEOMETRY

9.4.1 Modeling the Paths of Musculotendinous Actuators

Two different methods are used to model the paths of musculotendinous actuators in the body: the straight-line method and the centroid-line method. In the straight-line method, the path of a musculotendinous actuator (muscle and tendon combined) is represented by a straight line joining the centroids of the tendon attachment sites (Jensen and Davy, 1975). Although this method is easy to implement, it may not produce meaningful results when a muscle wraps around a bone or another muscle (see Fig. 9.10). In the centroid-line method, the path of the musculotendinous actuator is represented as a line passing through the locus of cross-sectional centroids of the actuator (Jensen and Davy, 1975). Although the actuator's line of action is represented more accurately in this way, the centroid-line method can be difficult to apply because (1) it may not be possible to obtain the locations of the actuator's cross-sectional centroids for even a single position of the body and (2) even if an actuator's centroid path is known for one position of the body, it is practically impossible to determine how this path changes as body position changes.

One way of addressing this problem is to introduce effective attachment sites or via points at specific locations along the centroid path of the actuator. In this approach, the actuator's line of action is defined using either straight-line segments or a combination of straight-line and curved-line segments between each set of via points (Brand et al., 1982; Delp et al., 1990). The via points remain fixed relative to the bones even as the joints move, and muscle wrapping is taken into account by making the via points active or inactive depending on the configuration of the joint. This method works quite well when a muscle spans a 1 dof hinge joint, but it can lead to discontinuities in the calculated values of moment arms when joints have more than 1 rotational dof (Fig. 9.10).

9.4.2 Obstacle-Set Method

An alternate approach, called the Obstacle-set method, idealizes each musculotendinous actuator as a frictionless elastic band that can slide freely over the bones and other actuators as the configuration of the joint changes (Garner and Pandy, 2000). The musculotendinous path is defined by a series of straight-line and curved-line segments joined together by via points, which may or may not be fixed relative to the bones.

To illustrate this method, consider the example shown in Fig. 9.11, where the path of the actuator is constrained by a single obstacle, which is fixed to bone A. (An *obstacle* is defined as any regular-shaped rigid body that is used to model the shape of a constraining anatomical structure such as a bone or another muscle.) The actuator's path is defined by the positions of the five fixed via points and the positions of the two obstacle via points. (A *fixed via point* remains fixed in a bone reference frame and is always active; an *obstacle via point* is not fixed in any reference frame, but is constrained to move on the surface of an underlying obstacle.) Via points P_1 and P_2 are fixed to bone A, while S_1, S_2, and S_3 are fixed to bone B. For a given configuration of the joint, the paths of all segments of the muscle are known, except those between the bounding-fixed via points, P_2 and S_3. The path of the actuator is known once the positions of the obstacle via points Q and T have been found.

Figure 9.12 shows a computational algorithm that can be used to model the centroid path of a musculotendinous actuator for a given configuration of the joints in the body. There are four steps in the computational algorithm. Given the relative positions of the bones, the locations of all fixed via points are known and can be expressed in the obstacle reference frame (Fig. 9.12, Step 1). The locations of the remaining via points in the actuator's path, the obstacle via points, can be calculated using one or more of the four different obstacle sets given in Apps. C through F in Garner and Pandy

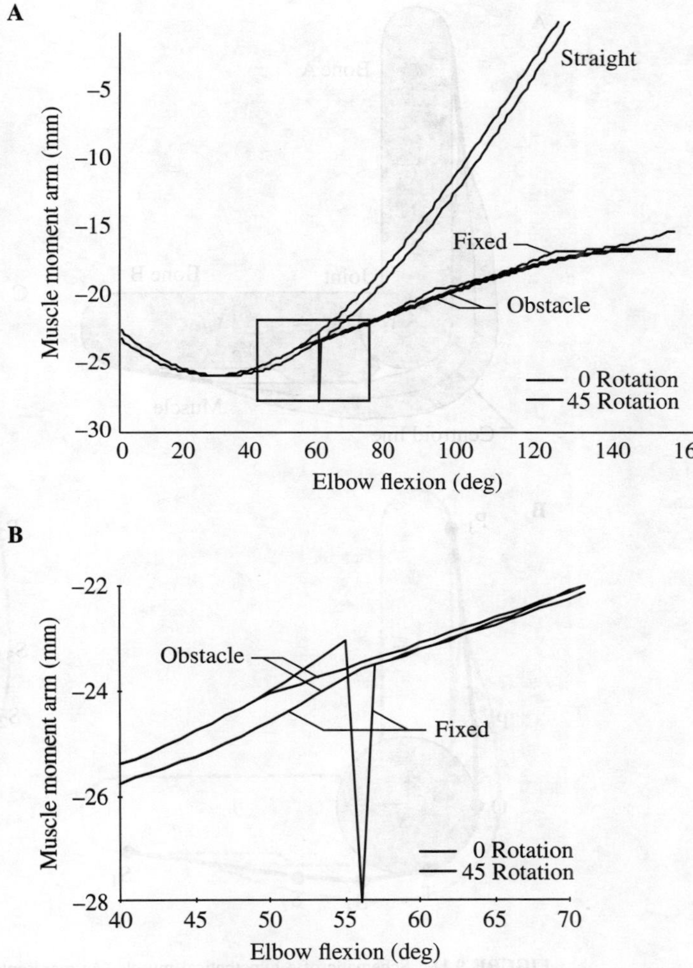

FIGURE 9.10 Comparison of moment arms for the long head of triceps obtained using the straight-line model (straight), fixed-via-point model (fixed), and the obstacle-set model (obstacle). For each model, the moment arms were calculated over the full range of elbow flexion, with the humerus positioned alongside the torso in neutral rotation (solid lines) and in 45° internal rotation (dotted lines). Bottom: Expanded scale of the graph above, where the moment arms obtained using the fixed-via-point and obstacle-set models are shown near the elbow flexion angle where the muscle first begins to wrap around the obstacle (cylinder) placed at the elbow [see part (A)]. The fixed-via-point model produces a discontinuity in moment arm when the shoulder is rotated 45° internally (fixed, dotted line). [*Modified from Garner and Pandy (2000).*]

(2000) (Fig. 9.12, Step 2). Once the locations of the obstacle via points are known, a check is made to determine whether any of these points should be inactive (Fig. 9.12, Step 3). If an obstacle via point should be inactive, it is removed from the actuator's path and the locations of the remaining obstacle via points are then recomputed (Fig. 9.12, repeat Steps 2 and 3). Finally, the lengths of the segments between all of the active via points along the actuator's path are computed (Fig. 9.12, Step 4).

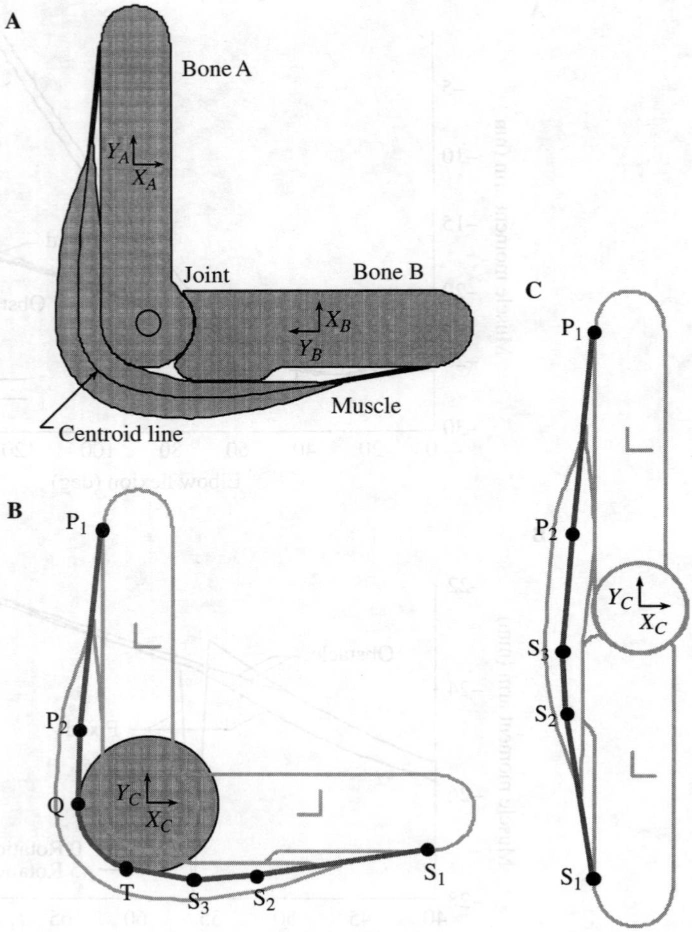

FIGURE 9.11 Schematic of a hypothetical muscle (A) represented by the obstacle-set model (B and C). The muscle spans a single joint that connects bones A and B. Reference frames attached to the bones are used to describe the position and orientation of the bones relative to each other. At certain joint configurations, the muscle contacts the bones and causes the centroid path of the muscle to deviate from a straight line (A). The muscle path is modeled using a total of seven via points: five of these are fixed via points (P_1, P_2, S_1, S_2, S_3); the remaining two are obstacle via points (Q, T) which move relative to the bones and the obstacle. Points P_1 and S_1 are the origin and insertion of the muscle. Points P_2 and S_3 are bounding-fixed via points. The obstacle is shown as a shaded circle, which represents the cross section of a sphere or cylinder. An obstacle reference frame positions and orients the obstacle relative to the bones. The obstacle is made larger than the cross sections of the bones in order to account for the thickness of the muscle belly. The obstacle set is defined by the obstacle, the four via points (P_2, Q, T, S_3), and the segments of the muscle path between the via points P_2 and S_3. At some joint configurations, the muscle path can lose contact with the obstacle, and the obstacle via points then become inactive (C). See Garner and Pandy (2000) for details of the obstacle-set method. [*Modified from Garner and Pandy (2000).*]

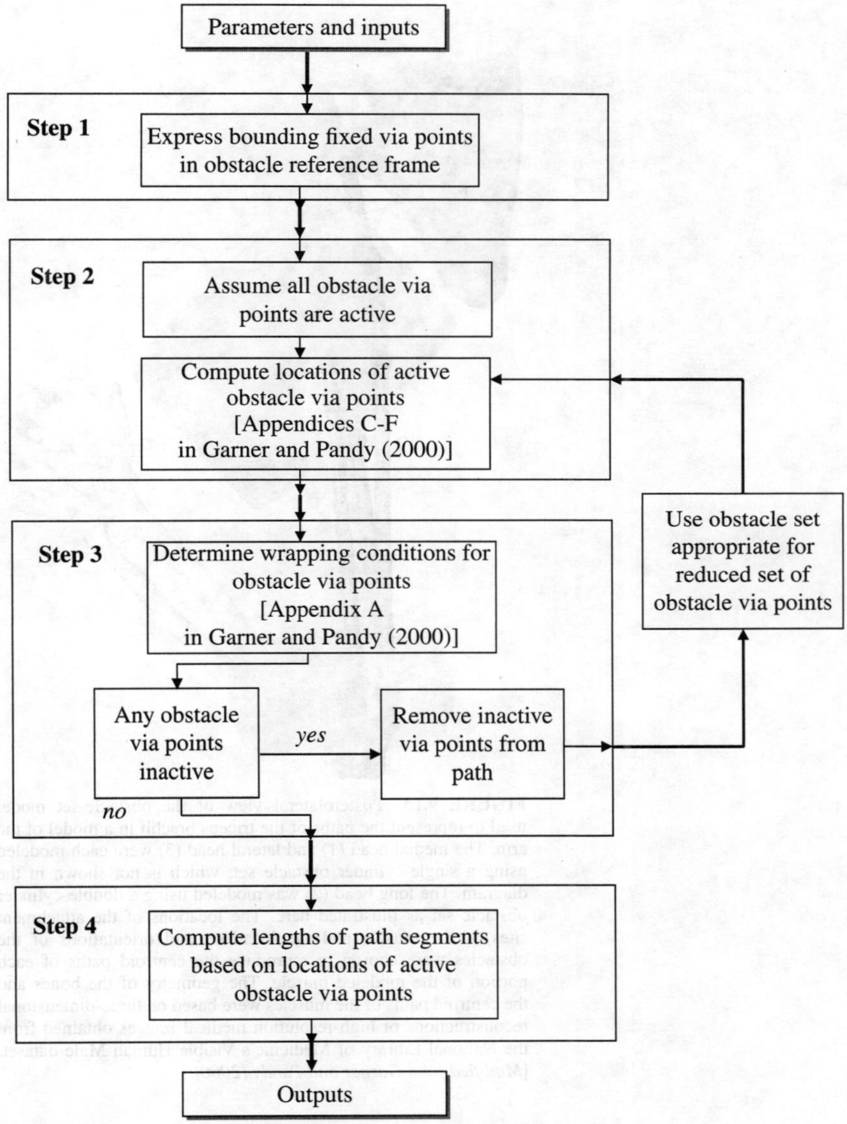

FIGURE 9.12 Flowchart of the obstacle-set algorithm. See text for details.

The computational algorithm shown in Fig. 9.12 was used to model the paths of the triceps brachii muscle in the arm (Garner and Pandy, 2000). The muscle was separated into three segments: the medial, lateral, and long heads (Fig. 9.13). The medial head [Fig. 9.13(1)] and lateral head [Fig. 9.13(3)] were each modeled using a single-cylinder obstacle set (not shown in Fig. 9.13). The long head [Fig. 9.13(2)] was modeled using a double-cylinder obstacle set as illustrated. The locations of the attachment sites of each muscle segment and the locations and orientations of the obstacles were chosen to reproduce the centroid paths of each head as accurately as possible. The geometry of the bones and the centroid paths of the muscle segments were obtained from 3D

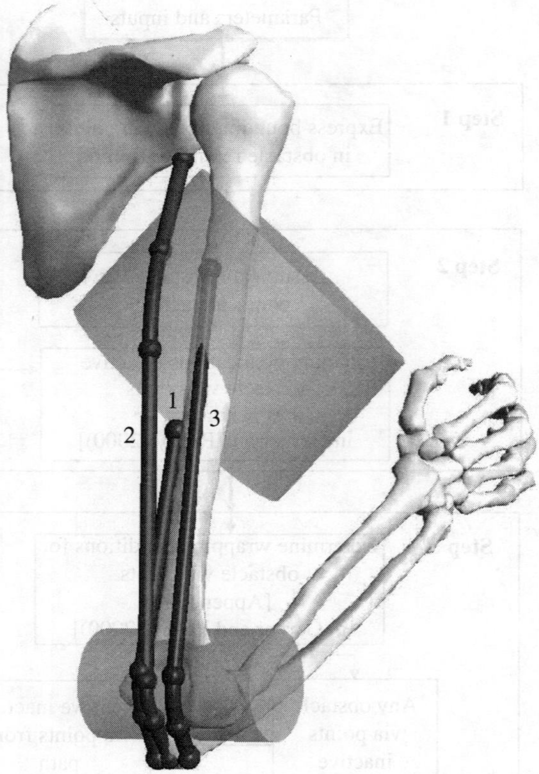

FIGURE 9.13 Posterolateral view of the obstacle-set model used to represent the paths of the triceps brachii in a model of the arm. The medial head (1) and lateral head (3) were each modeled using a single-cylinder obstacle set, which is not shown in the diagram. The long head (2) was modeled using a double-cylinder obstacle set as illustrated here. The locations of the attachment sites of the muscle and the locations and orientations of the obstacles were chosen to reproduce the centroid paths of each portion of the modeled muscle. The geometry of the bones and the centroid paths of the muscles were based on three-dimensional reconstructions of high-resolution medical images obtained from the National Library of Medicine's Visible Human Male dataset. [*Modified from Garner and Pandy (2000).*]

reconstructions of high-resolution medical images obtained from the National Library of Medicine's Visible Human Male dataset (Garner and Pandy, 2001). Because the path of a muscle is not improperly constrained by contact with neighboring muscles and bones, the Obstacle-set method produces not only accurate estimates of muscle moment arms, but also smooth moment arm-joint angle curves as illustrated in Fig. 9.10.

9.4.3 Muscle Moment Arms

Muscles develop forces and cause rotation of the bones about a joint. The tendency of a musculotendinous actuator to rotate a bone about a joint is described by the actuator's moment arm. Two

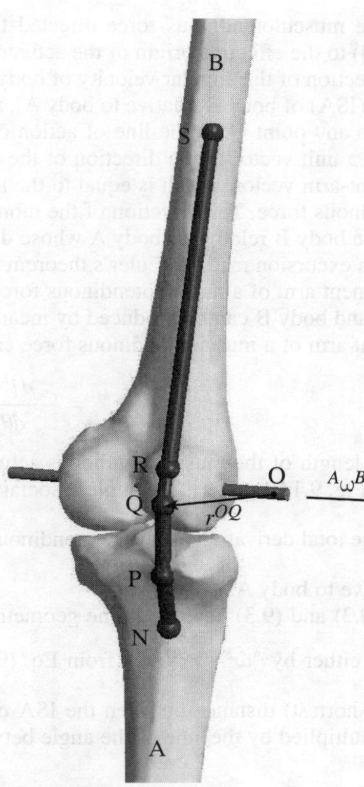

FIGURE 9.14 Two bodies, A and B, shown articulating at a joint. Body A is fixed in an inertial reference frame, and body B moves relative to it. The path of a generic muscle is represented by the origin S on B, the insertion N on A, and three intermediate via points P, Q, and R. Q and R are via points arising from contact of the muscle path with body B. Via point P arises from contact of the muscle path with body A. The ISA of B relative to A is defined by the angular velocity vector of B in A (ω). [*Modified from Pandy (1999).*]

methods are commonly used to measure the moment arm of an actuator—the geometric method and the tendon excursion method.

In the geometric method, a finite center of rotation is found using x-rays, computed tomography, or magnetic resonance imaging, and the moment arm is found by measuring the perpendicular distance from the joint center to the line of action of the muscle (Jensen and Davy, 1975). In the tendon excursion method, the change in length of the musculotendinous actuator is measured as a function of the joint angle, and the moment arm is obtained by evaluating the slope of the actuator-length versus joint-angle curve over the full range of joint movement (An et al., 1983).

Consider two body segments, A and B, which articulate at a joint (Fig. 9.14). By considering the instantaneous power delivered by a musculotendinous actuator to body B, it can be shown that the moment arm of the actuator can be written as (Pandy, 1999):

$$r^M = ({}^A\hat{\omega}^B \cdot r^{OQ} x \hat{F}^M)\,{}^A\hat{\omega}^B \qquad (9.2)$$

where $\boldsymbol{F}^M$ is the musculotendinous force directed from the effective insertion of the actuator on body B (point Q) to the effective origin of the actuator on body A (point P), ${}^A\hat{\omega}^B$ is a unit vector that specifies the direction of the angular velocity of body B in body A [i.e., parallel to the instantaneous axis of rotation (ISA) of body B relative to body A], $\boldsymbol{r}^{OQ}$ is a position vector directed from any point O on the ISA to any point Q on the line of action of the actuator between its origin and insertion sites, and $\hat{\boldsymbol{F}}^M$ is a unit vector in the direction of the actuator force $\boldsymbol{F}^M$ (see Fig. 9.14). In Eq. (9.2), $\boldsymbol{r}^M$ is the moment-arm vector, which is equal to the *moment* of the musculotendinous force per unit of musculotendinous force. The direction of the moment-arm vector is along the instantaneous axis of rotation of the body B relative to body A whose direction is described by the unit vector ${}^A\hat{\omega}^B$.

In the tendon excursion method, Euler's theorem on rotation is used to define an equivalent relation for the moment arm of a musculotendinous force. Thus, if every change in the relative orientation of body A and body B can be produced by means of a simple rotation of B in A about the ISA, then the moment arm of a musculotendinous force can also be written as (Pandy, 1999)

$$\boldsymbol{r}^M = -\frac{dl^M}{d\theta}\,{}^A\hat{\omega}^B \tag{9.3}$$

where l^M is the length of the musculotendinous actuator between the effective origin and insertion sites (P to Q in Fig. 9.14), and θ is the angle associated with the simple rotation of body B about the ISA. $\frac{dl^M}{d\theta}$ is the total derivative of musculotendinous length with respect to the angle of rotation θ, of body B relative to body A.

Equations (9.2) and (9.3) have the same geometric interpretation: the moment arm of a muscle force r^M, given either by ${}^A\hat{\omega}^B \cdot \boldsymbol{r}^{OQ} x \hat{\boldsymbol{F}}^M$ from Eq. (9.2) or by $\frac{dl^M}{d\theta}$ from Eq. (9.3), is equal to the perpendicular (shortest) distance between the ISA of B relative to A and the line of action of the muscle force, multiplied by the sine of the angle between these two lines (Pandy, 1999).

9.5. MUSCLE ACTIVATION AND CONTRACTION DYNAMICS

9.5.1 Muscle Activation Dynamics

Neural Excitation of Muscle. Voluntary contraction of human muscle initiates in the frontal motor cortex of the brain, where impulses from large pyramidal cells travel downward through corticospinal tracts that lead out to peripheral muscles. These impulses from the motor cortex are called action potentials and each impulse is associated with a single motor neuron. The principal structure of a motor neuron is shown in Fig. 9.15. The action potential initiates in the cell body, or soma, and travels down a long efferent trunk, called the axon, at a rate of about 80 to 120 m/s. The action potential waveform is the result of a voltage depolarization-repolarization phenomenon across the neuron cell membrane. The membrane ionic potential at rest is disturbed by a surrounding stimulus, and Na^+ ions are allowed to momentarily rush inside. An active transport mechanism, called the Na^+-K^+ pump, quickly returns the transmembrane potential to rest. This sequence of events, which lasts about 1 ms, stimulates a succession of nerve impulses or wave that eventually reaches muscle tissue. When the impulse reaches the muscle, it conducts over muscle tissue as a motor unit action potential (MUAP). Motor unit action potentials can have a variety of general shapes (Fang et al., 1997), as depicted in Fig. 9.16.

The connecting site between the motor neuron and the muscle is called the neuromuscular junction. One motor neuron can have branches to many muscle fibers, and these together are called a motor unit. When the nerve impulse reaches the end of the nerve fiber, a neurotransmitter called acetylcholine is released into the motor end plate of the muscle. This in turn causes the release of Ca^{++} ions deep into the muscle fiber. The presence of Ca^{++} ions causes cross-bridges to be formed

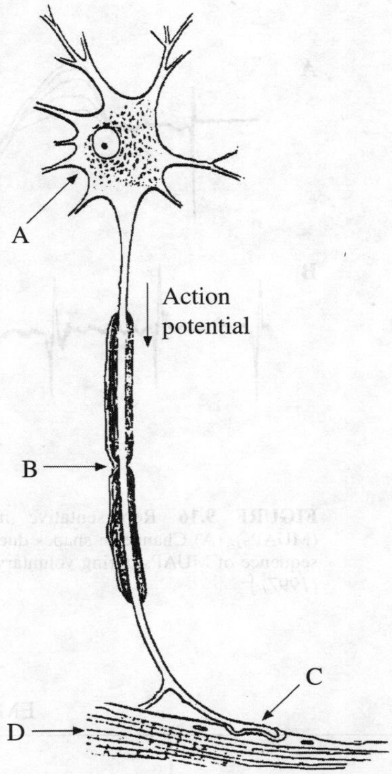

FIGURE 9.15 Motor neuron. (A) cell body, (B) axon, (C) neuromuscular junction, and (D) muscle fiber. The action potential travels downward, from the cell body toward the neuromuscular junction.

between actin and myosin filaments in the sarcomeres. The actin filaments slide inward along the myosin filaments, causing the muscle fiber to contract.

In addition to cortical motor neurons, control of the musculoskeletal system also relies on afferent receptors or sensory neurons that carry information from the periphery to the brain or spinal cord. The simplest nerve pathways lead directly from sensory neurons to motor neurons, and are known as reflex arcs. One such example is the withdrawal reflex. When skin receptors sense something is hot or sharp (pinprick), a sensory impulse is sent to the spinal cord where an interneuron integrates the information, and relays it to a motor neuron. The motor neuron in turn transmits a signal to the appropriate flexor muscle, which contracts and thus completes the reflex loop.

Muscle Electromyography. While motor unit action potentials form the cellular origin for muscle activation, they are normally not observable in routine clinical applications. The electromyogram (EMG) is the primary tool to study muscle activation in clinical and research settings using both surface and indwelling electrodes (Basmajian and DeLuca, 1985). The electromyogram is the summation of all motor unit action potentials at a given location during muscle contraction. Hence it represents a "gross" measure of the strength of a muscle contraction, since the number of muscle fibers contracting is directly related to the number of motor units firing.

The EMG appears as a random series of bursts that represent periods of muscle contraction and relaxation. Figure 9.17 shows a series of EMG bursts. The EMG signal is acquired using both

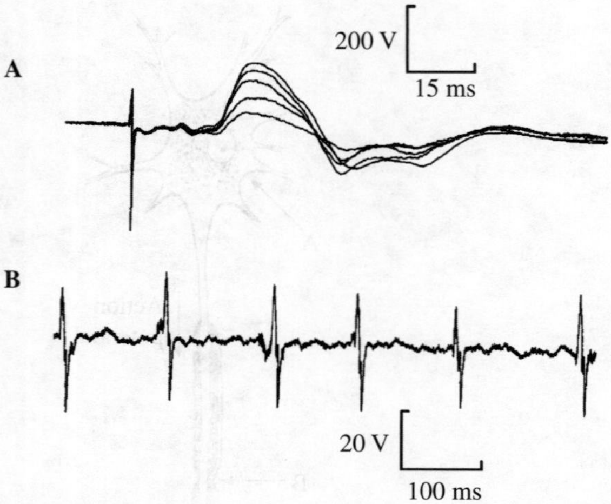

FIGURE 9.16 Representative motor unit action potentials (MUAPs). (A) Change in shapes due to increase in stimulation, (B) sequence of MUAPs during voluntary contraction. [*From Fang et al. (1997).*]

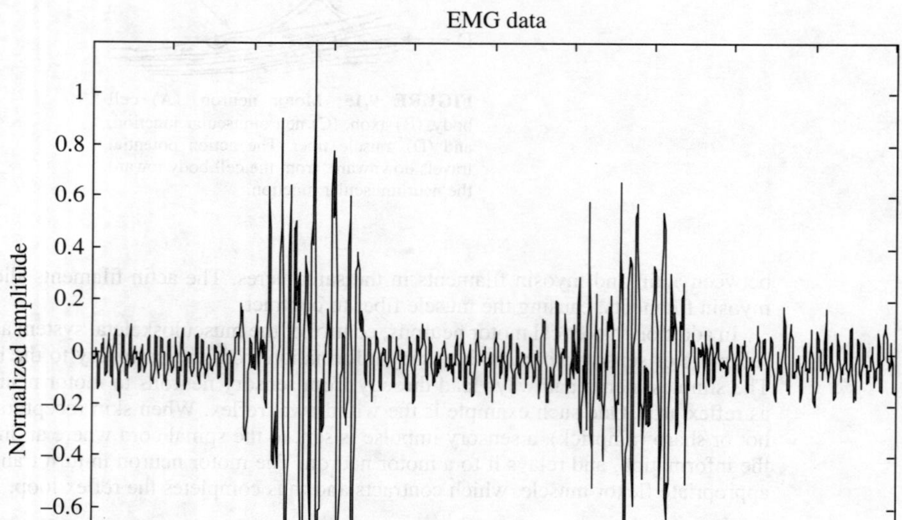

FIGURE 9.17 Two representative EMG bursts from the biceps muscle during an elbow flexion maneuver.

invasive and noninvasive techniques. In invasive detection, a needle or fine wire is inserted directly into the muscle to a depth of several centimeters. In noninvasive techniques, also known as surface electromyography, a recording electrode is pasted onto the skin approximately halfway between the muscle's origin and insertion sites. In either case, due to the low voltage of the EMG signal (100 μV to several millivolts), some amplification of the signal is needed leading into the digital data collection system. In addition, to reduce unwanted noise in the signal, an analog filter with pass band of 20 to 500 Hz should be used. This necessitates a typical digital sampling rate of 1000 Hz. Subsequent reduction of noise in the EMG signal can be handled computationally using digital filtering (Barr and Chan, 1986). A set of 16 recommendations for EMG acquisition and processing has been presented by DeLuca (1997).

The EMG is analyzed in both the amplitude and frequency domains. For amplitude analysis, the most common processing technique is to compute a running root-mean-square (RMS) of the signal. Over a short observational period T, the RMS of the signal $x(t)$ can be expressed as

$$\text{EMG}_{\text{RMS}} = \sqrt{\frac{1}{T} \int [x(t)]^2 di} \tag{9.5}$$

In discrete form, over N contiguous samples, the RMS can be expressed as

$$\text{EMG}_{\text{RMS}} = \sqrt{\frac{1}{N} \sum_{i=1}^{N} [x_{\text{i}}(t)]^2} \tag{9.6}$$

An alternative, but similar, approach to EMG amplitude analysis is to rectify and then integrate the signal over the short period T (called integrated EMG or IEMG). This approach has the advantage in that a simple electronic circuit can be used and no numerical computation is necessary. In either case, the objective is to obtain an estimation of the underlying muscle contraction force, which is roughly proportional to the EMG_{RMS} or IEMG. In recent efforts to use the EMG signal as a myoelectric control signal (Evans et al., 1994), a three-stage digital processing approach has arisen and is illustrated in Fig. 9.18. The process consists of (a) band pass filtering (20 to 200 Hz) the signal, (b) full wave rectification, and (c) low pass filtering (10-Hz cut-off) to produce a smooth signal.

In the frequency domain, the most common tool is to apply a fast Fourier transform (FFT) to the EMG signal. A typical result is shown in Fig. 9.19. One can see that most of the power in the signal is confined to the 20- to 200-Hz range, and that the center frequency or mean power point is typically below 100 Hz. One use of EMG frequency analysis is in the study of muscle fatigue. It has been shown that as the muscle fatigues, the median power frequency of the EMG shifts downward (Bigland-Ritchie et al., 1983).

Modeling Activation Dynamics. As noted in the section "Neural Excitation of Muscle," muscle cannot activate or relax instantaneously. The delay between excitation and activation (or the development of muscle force) is due mainly to the time taken for calcium pumped out of the sarcoplasmic reticulum to travel down the T-tubule system and bind to troponin (Ebashi and Endo, 1968). This delay is often modeled as a first-order process (Pandy et al., 1992; Zajac, 1989):

$$\dot{a}^m = (1/\tau_{rise})(u^2 - ua^m) + (1/\tau_{fall})(u - a^m); \qquad u = u(t); \quad a^m = a^m(t) \tag{9.6}$$

where u represents the net neural drive to muscle and a^m the activation level. Other forms of this relation are also possible; for example, an equation that is linear in the control u has been used to simulate jumping (Pandy et al., 1990) as well as pedaling (Raasch et al., 1997). Implicit in the formulation of Eq. (9.6) is the assumption that muscle activation depends only on a single variable u. Other models assume that a depends on two inputs, u_1 and u_2 say, which represent the separate effects of recruitment and stimulation frequency (Hatze, 1978). In simulations of multijoint movement, whether or not both recruitment and stimulation frequency are incorporated in a model of excitation-contraction (activation) dynamics is probably not as important as the values assumed for the time constants, τ_{rise} and τ_{fall}. Values of these constants range from 12 to 20 ms for rise time, τ_{rise},

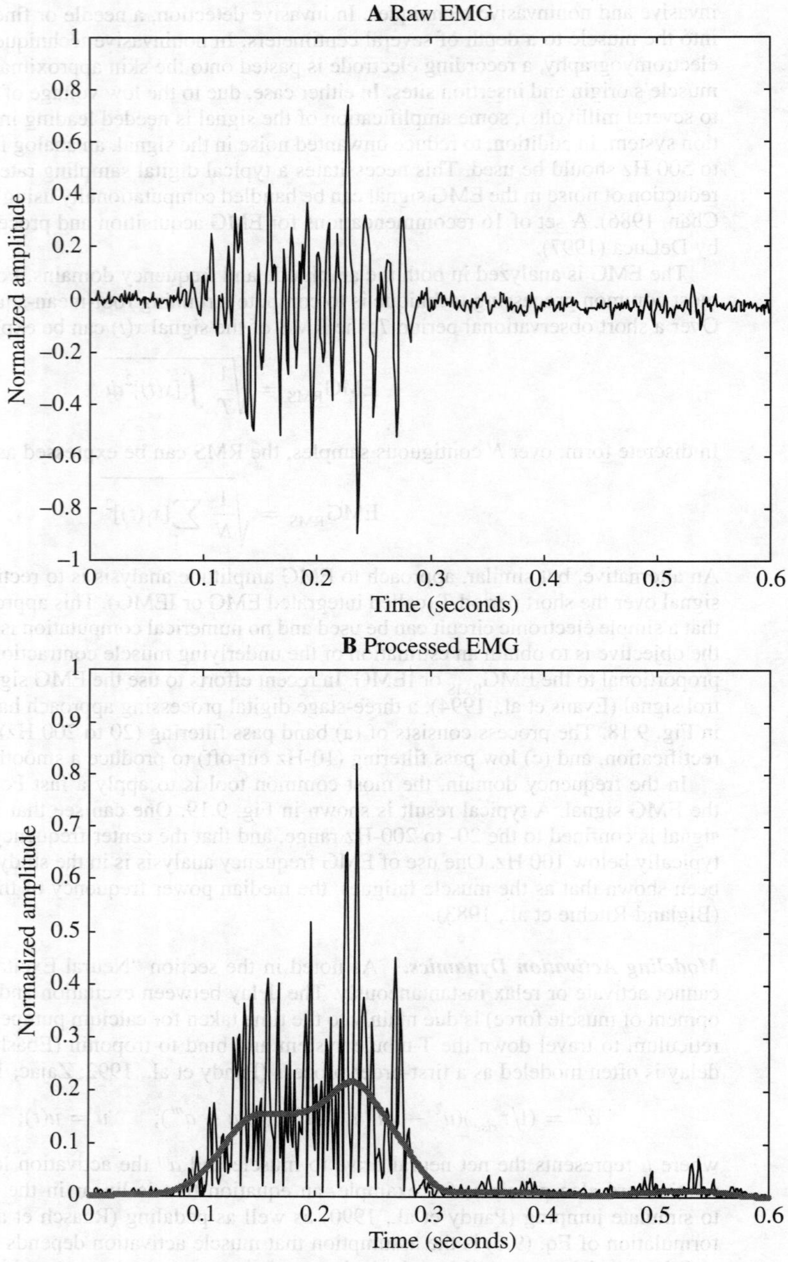

FIGURE 9.18 A method for processing EMG data for a myoelectric control signal. (A) The raw EMG data, and (B) the signal after being rectified and low pass filtered (10-Hz cut-off).

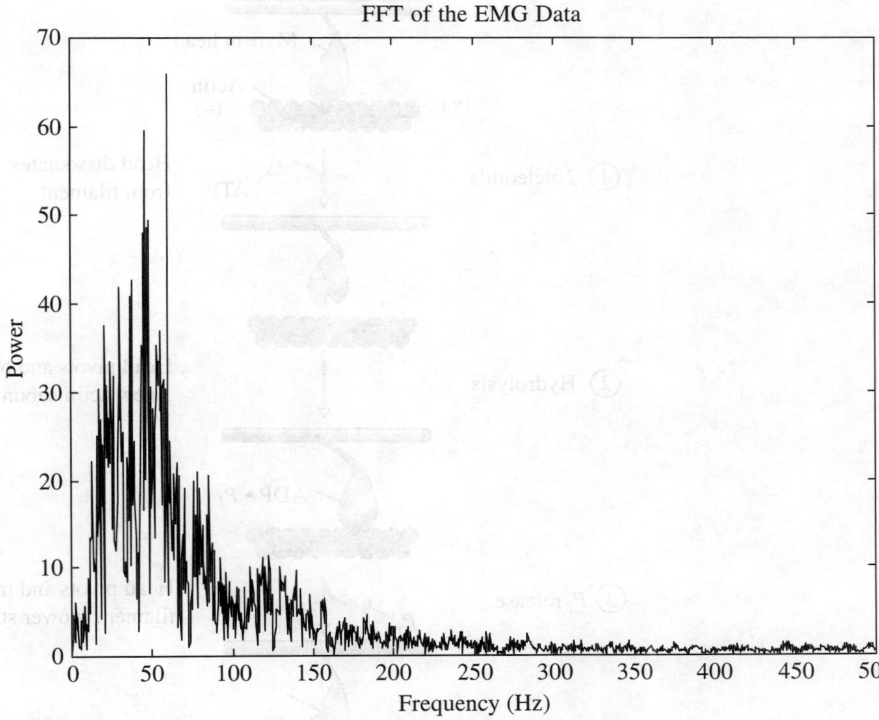

FIGURE 9.19 The fast Fourier transform (FFT) of an EMG sample. Most of the signal power is in the 20- to 200-Hz range.

and from 24 to 200 ms for relaxation time, τ_{fall} (Pandy, 2001). Changes in the values of τ_{rise} and τ_{fall} within the ranges indicated can have a significant effect on predictions of movement coordination.

9.5.2 Muscle Contraction Dynamics

Mechanism of Muscle Contraction. Our understanding of how a muscle develops force is based on the sliding-filament theory of contraction. This theory, formulated by A. F. Huxley in 1957, proposes that a muscle shortens or lengthens because the thick and thin filaments slide past each other without the filaments themselves changing length (Huxley, 1957). The central tenet of the theory is that adenosine triphosphate (ATP) dependent interactions between thick filaments (myosin proteins) and thin filaments (actin proteins) generate a force that causes the thin filaments to slide past the thick filaments. The force is generated by the myosin heads of thick filaments, which form cross-bridges to actin thin filaments in the AI zone, where the two filaments overlap (see Fig. 9.2E). Subsequent structural changes in these cross-bridges cause the myosin heads to "walk" along an actin filament. The sliding-filament theory correctly predicts that the force of contraction is proportional to the amount of overlap between the thick and thin filaments (see Fig. 9.3).

To understand the mechanism of muscle contraction, consider Fig. 9.20, which shows the various steps involved in the interaction between one myosin head and a thin filament, also often referred to as the cross-bridge cycle. In the absence of ATP, a myosin head binds tightly to an actin filament in a "rigor" state. When ATP binds (Step 1), it opens the cleft in the myosin head, which weakens the interaction with the actin filament. The myosin head then reacts with ATP (Step 2), causing a

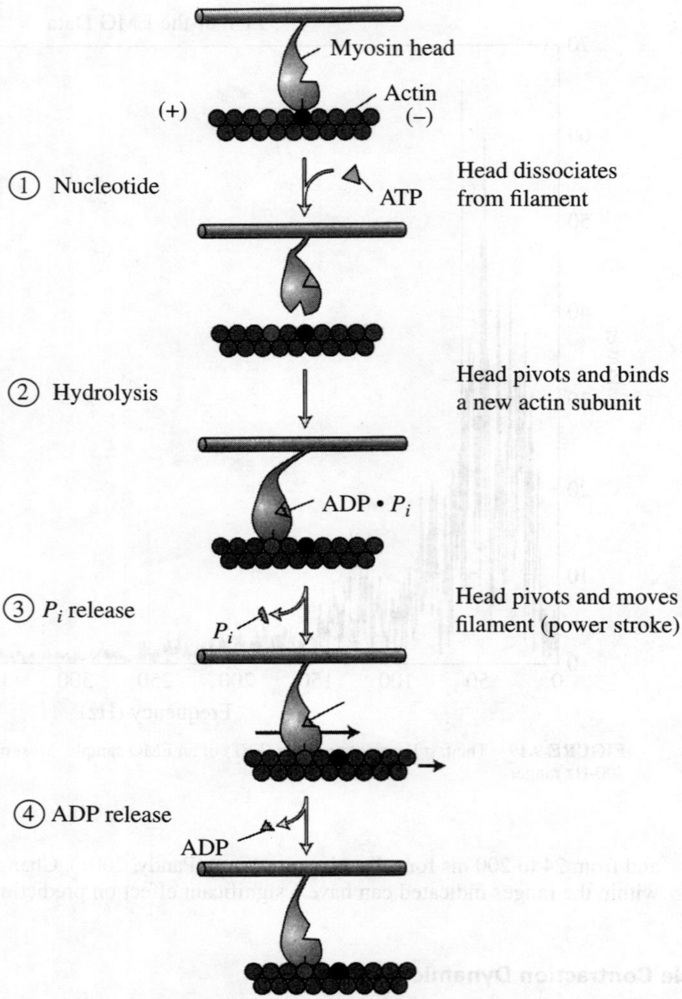

FIGURE 9.20 Schematic diagram illustrating the mechanism of force development in muscle. [*Modified from Lodish et al. (2000).*]

structural change in the head that moves it to a new position, closer to the end of the actin filament or Z disk, where it then rebinds to the filament. Phosphate is then released from the ATP-binding pocket on the myosin head (Step 3), and the head then undergoes a second structural change, called the power stroke, which restores myosin to its rigor state. Because the myosin head is bound to the actin filament, this second structural change exerts a force that causes the myosin head to move the actin filament (Fig. 9.20).

Modeling Contraction Dynamics. A. F. Huxley developed a mechanistic model to explain the structural changes at the sarcomere level that were seen under the electron microscope in the late 1940s and early 1950s. Because of its complexity, however, this (cross-bridge) model is rarely, if ever, used in studies of coordination. Instead, an empirical model, proposed by A. V. Hill, is used

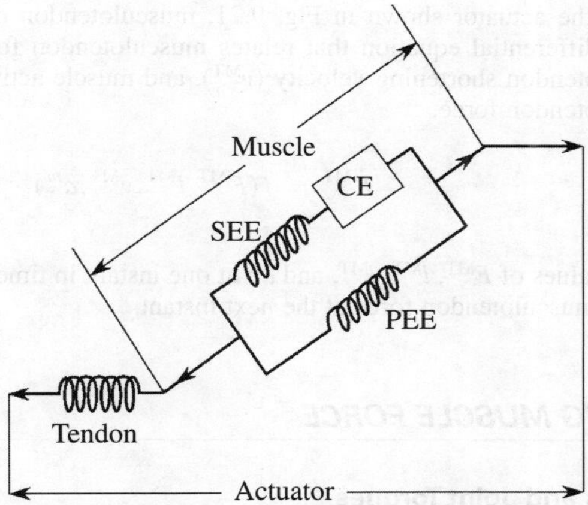

FIGURE 9.21 Schematic diagram of a model commonly used to simulate musculotendon actuation. Each musculotendon actuator is represented as a three-element muscle in series with an elastic tendon. The mechanical behavior of muscle is described by a Hill-type contractile element (CE) that models muscle's force-length-velocity property, a series-elastic element (SEE) that models muscle's active stiffness, and a parallel-elastic element (PEE) that models muscle's passive stiffness. The instantaneous length of the actuator is determined by the length of the muscle, the length of the tendon, and the pennation angle of the muscle. In this model the width of the muscle is assumed to remain constant as muscle length changes. [*Modified from Zajac (1989) and Pandy et al. (1990).*]

in virtually all models of movement to account for the force-length and force-velocity properties of muscle (Hill, 1938) (Fig. 9.21).

In a Hill-type model, muscle's force producing properties are described by four parameters (Zajac, 1989): muscle's peak isometric force (F_o^m) and its corresponding fiber length (l_o^m) and pennation angle (α), and the intrinsic shortening velocity of muscle (v_{max}). F_o^m is usually obtained by multiplying muscle's physiological cross-sectional area by a generic value of specific tension. Values of optimal muscle fiber length, l_o^m, and α, the angle at which muscle fibers insert on tendon when the fibers are at their optimal length, are almost always based on data obtained from cadaver dissections (Ward et al., 2009). v_{max} is often assumed to be muscle-independent; for example, simulations of jumping (Anderson and Pandy, 1999; Pandy et al., 1990), pedaling (Raasch et al., 1997), and walking (Anderson and Pandy, 2001a) assume a value of $v_{max} = 10\ s^{-1}$ for all muscles, which models the summed effect of slow, intermediate, and fast fibers (Zajac, 1989). Very few studies have examined the sensitivity of model simulations to changes in v_{max}, even though a change in the value of this parameter has been found to affect performance nearly as much as a change in the value of F_o^m (Pandy, 1990).

Tendon is usually represented as elastic (Anderson and Pandy, 1993; Pandy et al., 1990). Even though force varies nonlinearly with a change in length as tendon is stretched from its resting length, l_s^T (see Fig. 9.5), a linear force-length curve is sometimes used (Anderson and Pandy, 1993). This simplification will overestimate the amount of strain energy stored in tendon, but the effect on actuator performance is not likely to be significant, because tendon force is small in the region where the force-length curve is nonlinear. Values of the four muscle parameters plus tendon rest length for a number of musculotendinous actuators in the human arm and leg can be found in Garner and Pandy (2001) and Anderson and Pandy (1999), respectively.

For the actuator shown in Fig. 9.21, musculotendon dynamics is described by a single, nonlinear, differential equation that relates musculotendon force (F^{MT}), musculotendon length (l^{MT}), musculotendon shortening velocity (v^{MT}), and muscle activation (a^m) to the time rate of change in musculotendon force:

$$\dot{F}^{\mathrm{MT}} = f(F^{\mathrm{MT}}, l^{\mathrm{MT}}, v^{\mathrm{MT}}, a^m) \qquad 0 \le a^m \le 1 \tag{9.7}$$

Given values of F^{MT}, l^{MT}, l^{MT}, and a^m at one instant in time, Eq. (9.7) can be integrated numerically to find musculotendon force at the next instant.

9.6. DETERMINING MUSCLE FORCE

9.6.1 Muscle Forces and Joint Torques

The torque of a musculotendinous force is equal to the magnitude of the actuator force F^{MT}, multiplied by the moment arm of the actuator r^{MT}. Thus, the torque exerted by actuator i about joint j is

$$T_j^{MT} = r_i^{MT} F_i^{MT} \tag{9.8}$$

where r_i^{MT} can be found using either Eq. (9.2) or (9.3). For a system with m actuators and n joints, the above relation can be expressed in matrix form [see also Eq. (9.1)]:

$$\begin{bmatrix} T_1^{MT} \\ T_2^{MT} \\ \cdot \\ T_n^{MT} \end{bmatrix} = \begin{bmatrix} r_{11} & r_{12} & \cdot & r_{1m} \\ r_{21} & r_{22} & \cdot & r_{2m} \\ \cdot & \cdot & \cdot & \cdot \\ r_{n1} & r_{n2} & \cdot & r_{nm} \end{bmatrix} \begin{bmatrix} F_1^{MT} \\ F_2^{MT} \\ \cdot \\ F_m^{MT} \end{bmatrix} \tag{9.9}$$

where r_{11} is the moment arm of the actuator force F_1^{MT} that exerts a torque T_1^{MT} about joint 1, etc.

9.6.2 Indeterminate Problem in Biomechanics

Both agonist and antagonist muscles contribute (unequally) to the net torque developed about a joint. In fact, for any given joint in the body, there are many more muscles crossing the joint than there are dof prescribing joint movement. The knee, for example, has at most 6 dof, yet there are at least 14 muscles which actuate this joint. One consequence of this arrangement is that the force developed by each muscle cannot be determined uniquely. Specifically, there are more unknown musculotendinous actuator forces than net actuator torques exerted about the knee; that is, $m > m$ in Eq. (9.9), which means that the matrix of muscle moment arms is not square and therefore not invertible. This is the so-called indeterminate problem in biomechanics, and virtually all attempts to solve it are based on the application of optimization theory (see also Chap. 8).

9.6.3 Inverse-Dynamics Method

In the inverse-dynamics method, noninvasive measurements of body motions (position, velocity, and acceleration of each segment) and external forces are used as inputs in Eq. (9.1) to calculate the net actuator torques exerted about each joint (see Fig. 9.22). This is a determinate problem because

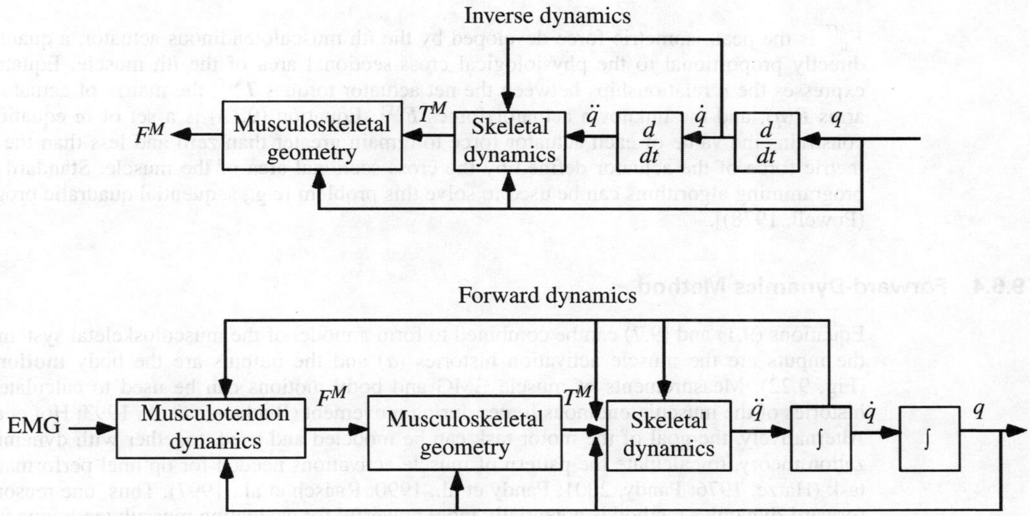

FIGURE 9.22 Comparison of the forward- and inverse-dynamics methods for determining muscle forces during movement. Top: Body motions are the inputs and muscle forces are the outputs in inverse dynamics. Thus, measurements of body motions are used to calculate the net muscle torques exerted about the joints, from which muscle forces are determined using static optimization. Bottom: Muscle excitations are the inputs and body motions are the outputs in forward dynamics. Muscle force (F^M) is an intermediate product (i.e., output of the model for musculotendon dynamics).

the number of net actuator torques is equal to the number of equations of motion of the system. Specifically, from Eq. (9.1), we can write

$$\boldsymbol{T}^{MT}(\boldsymbol{q}) = -\left\{\boldsymbol{M}(\boldsymbol{q})\,\ddot{\boldsymbol{q}} + \boldsymbol{C}(\boldsymbol{q})\,\dot{\boldsymbol{q}}^2 + \boldsymbol{G}(\boldsymbol{q}) + \boldsymbol{E}(\boldsymbol{q},\dot{\boldsymbol{q}})\right\} \tag{9.10}$$

where Eq. (9.9) has been used to replace $\boldsymbol{R}(\boldsymbol{q})\boldsymbol{F}^{\text{MT}}$ with $\boldsymbol{T}^{\text{MT}}(\boldsymbol{q})$ in Eq. (9.1). The right-hand side of Eq. (9.10) can be evaluated using noninvasive measurements of body motions $(\boldsymbol{q},\dot{\boldsymbol{q}},\ddot{\boldsymbol{q}})$ and external forces $\boldsymbol{E}(\boldsymbol{q},\dot{\boldsymbol{q}})$. This means that all quantities on the left-hand side of Eq. (9.9) are known. The matrix of actuator moment arms on the right-hand side of Eq. (9.9) can also be evaluated if the origin and insertion sites of each musculotendinous actuator and the relative positions of the body segments are known at each instant during the movement (Sec. 9.4).

However, Eq. (9.9) cannot be solved for the m actuator forces because $m > n$ (i.e., the matrix of actuator moment arms is nonsquare). Static optimization theory is usually used to solve this indeterminate problem (Crowninshield and Brand, 1981; Hardt, 1978; Seireg and Arvikar, 1973). Here, a cost function is hypothesized, and an optimal set of actuator forces is found subject to the equality constraints defined by Eq. (9.9) plus additional inequality constraints that bound the values of the actuator forces. If, for example, actuator stress is to be minimized, then the static optimization problem can be stated as follows (Crowninshield and Brand, 1981; Seireg and Arvikar, 1973): Find the set of actuator forces which minimizes the sum of the squares of actuator stresses:

$$J = \sum_{i=1}^{m}\left(F_i^{MT}/F_{oi}^{MT}\right)^2 \tag{9.11}$$

subject to the equality constraints

$$\boldsymbol{T}^{\text{MT}} = \boldsymbol{R}(\boldsymbol{q})\,\boldsymbol{F}^{\text{MT}}, \tag{9.12}$$

and the inequality constraints

$$\boldsymbol{0} \le \boldsymbol{F}^{\text{MT}} \le \boldsymbol{F}_o^{\text{MT}}. \tag{9.13}$$

F_{oi}^{MT} is the peak isometric force developed by the ith musculotendinous actuator, a quantity that is directly proportional to the physiological cross-sectional area of the ith muscle. Equation (9.12) expresses the n relationships between the net actuator torques $\boldsymbol{T}^{MT}$, the matrix of actuator moment arms $\boldsymbol{R}(\boldsymbol{q})$, and the unknown actuator forces $\boldsymbol{F}^{MT}$. Equation (9.13) is a set of m equations which constrains the value of each actuator force to remain greater than zero and less than the peak isometric force of the actuator defined by the cross-sectional area of the muscle. Standard nonlinear programming algorithms can be used to solve this problem [e.g., sequential quadratic programming (Powell, 1978)].

9.6.4 Forward-Dynamics Method

Equations (9.1) and (9.7) can be combined to form a model of the musculoskeletal system in which the inputs are the muscle activation histories ($\boldsymbol{a}$) and the outputs are the body **motions** $(\boldsymbol{q},\dot{\boldsymbol{q}},\ddot{\boldsymbol{q}})$ (Fig. 9.22). Measurements of muscle EMG and body motions can be used to calculate the time histories of the musculotendinous forces during movement (Buchanan et al., 1993; Hof et al., 1987). Alternatively, the goal of the motor task can be modeled and used, together with dynamic optimization theory, to calculate the pattern of muscle activations needed for optimal performance of the task (Hatze, 1976; Pandy, 2001; Pandy et al., 1990; Raasch et al., 1997). Thus, one reason why the forward-dynamics method is potentially more powerful for evaluating musculotendinous forces than the inverse-dynamics method is that the optimization is performed over a complete cycle of the task, not just at one instant at a time.

If we consider once again the example of minimizing muscle stress (Sec. 9.6.3), an analogous dynamic optimization problem may be posed as follows: Find the time histories of all actuator forces which minimize the sum of the squares of actuator stresses:

$$J = \int_0^{t_f} \sum_{i=1}^{m} \left(F_i^{MT} / F_{oi}^{MT}\right)^2 \tag{9.14}$$

subject to the equality constraints given by the dynamical equations of motion [Eqs. (9.7) and (9.1), respectively]:

$$\dot{F}^{MT} = f(F^{MT}, l^{MT}, v^{MT}, a^m) \quad 0 \le a^m \le 1$$

and

$$\boldsymbol{M}(\boldsymbol{q})\ddot{\boldsymbol{q}} + \boldsymbol{C}(\boldsymbol{q})\dot{\boldsymbol{q}}^2 + \boldsymbol{G}(\boldsymbol{q}) + \boldsymbol{R}(\boldsymbol{q})\boldsymbol{F}^{MT} + \boldsymbol{E}(\boldsymbol{q},\dot{\boldsymbol{q}}) = 0 \text{ the initial states of the system,}$$

$$\boldsymbol{x}(0) = \boldsymbol{x}_o \qquad \underline{x} = \left\{\boldsymbol{q}, \dot{\boldsymbol{q}}, \boldsymbol{F}^{MT}\right\} \tag{9.15}$$

and any terminal and/or path constraints that must be satisfied additionally. The dynamic optimization problem formulated above is a two-point, boundary-value problem, which is often difficult to solve, particularly when the dimension of the system is large (i.e., when the system has many dof and many muscles).

A better approach involves parameterizing the input muscle activations (or controls) and converting the dynamic optimization problem into a parameter optimization problem (Pandy et al., 1992). The procedure is as follows. First, an initial guess is assumed for the control variables $\boldsymbol{a}$. The system dynamical equations [Eqs. (9.7) and (9.1)] are then integrated forward in time to evaluate the cost function in Eq. (9.14). Derivatives of the cost function and constraints are then calculated and used to find a new set of controls which improves the values of the cost function and the constraints in the next iteration (see Fig. 9.23). The computational algorithm shown in Fig. 9.23 has been used to find the optimal controls for vertical jumping (Anderson and Pandy, 1999), rising from a chair (Pandy et al., 1995), pedaling (Fregly and Zajac, 1996), and walking (Anderson and Pandy, 2001a).

If accurate measurements of body motions and external forces are available, then inverse dynamics should be used to determine musculotendinous forces during movement, because this method is

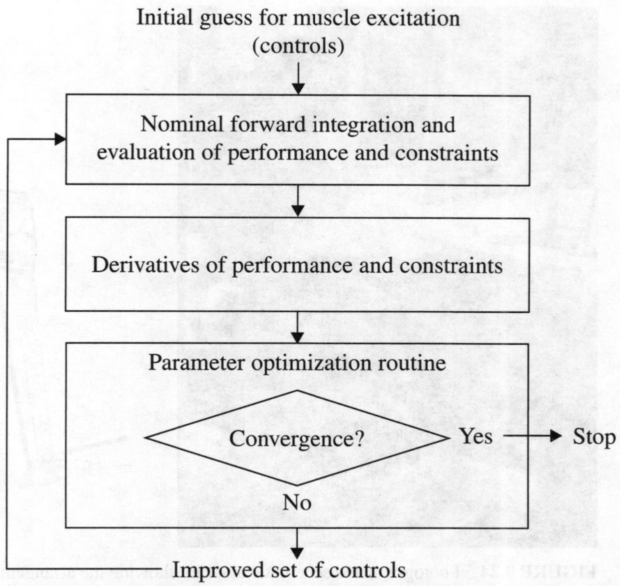

FIGURE 9.23 Computational algorithm used to solve dynamic optimization problems in human movement studies. The algorithm computes the muscle excitations (controls) needed to produce optimal performance (e.g., maximum jump height). The optimal controls are found using parameter optimization. See text for details.

much less expensive computationally. If, instead, the goal is to study how changes in body structure affect function and performance of a motor task, then the forward-dynamics method is preferred, for measurements of body motions and external forces are a priori not available in this instance.

9.7 MUSCLE, LIGAMENT, AND JOINT-CONTACT FORCES

Because muscle, ligament, and joint-contact forces cannot be measured noninvasively in vivo, estimates of these quantities have been obtained by combining mathematical models with either the inverse-dynamics or the forward-dynamics approach (Sec. 9.6). Below we review the levels of musculoskeletal loading incurred in the lower-limb during rehabilitation exercises, such as isokinetic knee extension, as well as during daily activity such as gait.

9.7.1 Knee Extension Exercise

The strength of the quadriceps muscle group can be demonstrated by performing an isometric knee-extension exercise. Here, the subject is seated comfortably in a Cybex or Biodex dynamometer with the torso and thigh strapped firmly to the seat. The hip is flexed to 60°, and the leg is strapped to the arm of the machine, which can either be fixed or allowed to rotate at a constant angular velocity (see Fig. 9.24). Locking the machine arm in place allows the muscles crossing the knee to contract isometrically, because the knee angle is then held fixed. Under these conditions, the quadriceps muscles can exert up to 9500 N when fully activated. As shown in Fig. 9.25, peak isometric force is developed with the knee bent to 90°, and decreases as the knee is moved toward extension (Fig. 9.25,

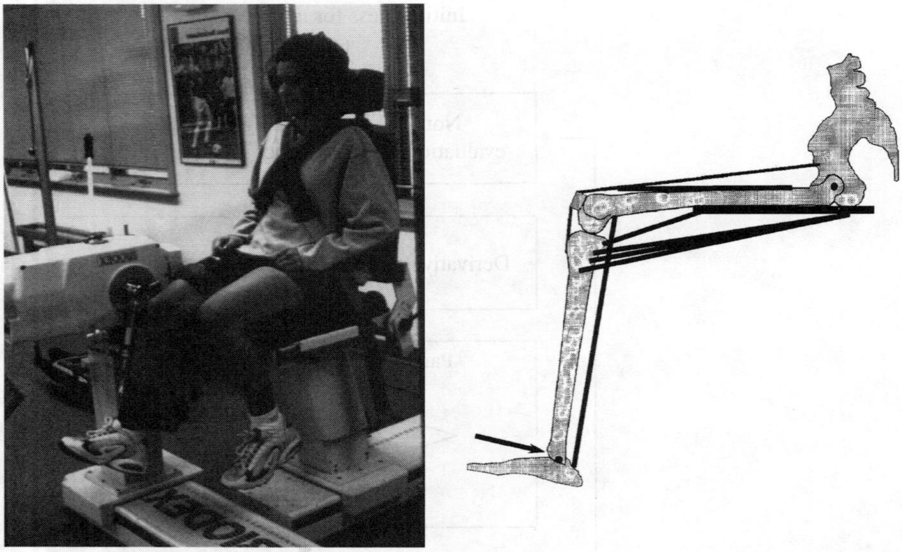

FIGURE 9.24 Photograph and schematic diagram showing the arrangement commonly used when people perform a knee-extension exercise on a Biodex or Cybex dynamometer. Notice that the strap fixed on the machine arm is attached distally (near the ankle) on the subject's leg.

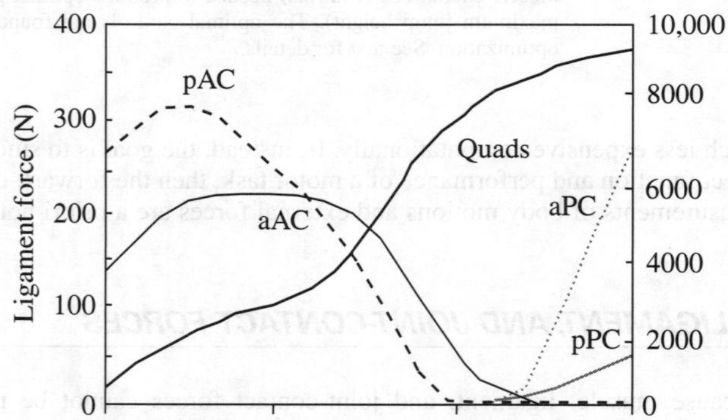

FIGURE 9.25 Muscle and knee-ligament forces incurred during a maximum isometric knee-extension exercise. The results were obtained from a 2D mathematical model of the knee joint, assuming the quadriceps muscles are fully activated and there is no cocontraction in the flexor muscles of the knee (Shelburne and Pandy, 1997). The thick solid line represents the resultant force acting in the quadriceps tendon. The thin lines are the forces transmitted to the cruciate ligaments (aAC, black solid line; pAC, black dashed line; aPC, gray dashed line; pPC, gray solid line). The forces in the collateral ligaments are nearly zero. [*Modified from Shelburne and Pandy (1997).*]

Quads). Quadriceps force decreases as knee-flexion angle decreases because the muscle moves down the ascending limb of its force-length as the knee extends (see Fig. 9.3).

Quadriceps force increases monotonically from full extension and 90° of flexion, but the forces borne by the cruciate ligaments of the knee do not (Fig. 9.25, ACL). Calculations obtained from a

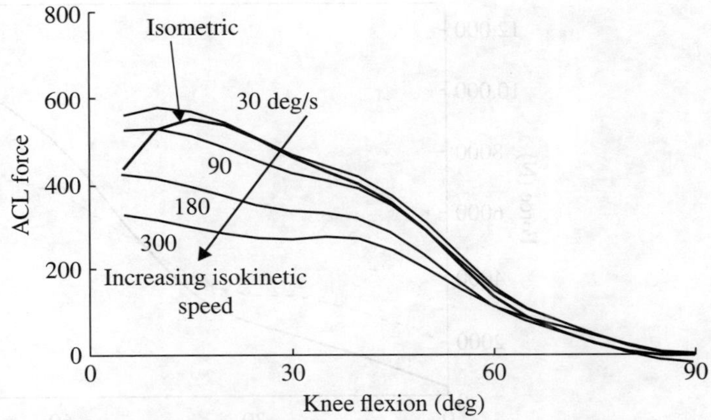

FIGURE 9.26 Resultant force in the ACL for isometric (thick line) and isokinetic (30, 90, 180, and 300 deg/s) knee-extension exercises. The results were obtained from a two-dimensional model of the knee joint, assuming the quadriceps are fully activated and there is no cocontraction in the flexor muscles of the knee (Serpas et al., 2002). The model results show that exercises in the studied speed range can reduce the force in the ACL by as much as one-half. [*Modified from Serpas et al. (2002).*]

mathematical model of the knee (Pandy and Sasaki, 1998; Pandy and Shelburne, 1997; Shelburne and Pandy, 1997) indicate that the ACL is loaded from full extension to 80° of flexion during knee-extension exercise. The model calculations also show that the resultant force in the ACL reaches 500 N at 20° of flexion, which is lower than the maximum strength of the human ACL (2000 N) (Noyes and Grood, 1976).

The calculations show further that load sharing within a ligament is not uniform. For example, the force borne by the anteromedial bundle of the ACL (aAC) increases from full extension to 20° of flexion, where peak force occurs, and aAC force then decreases as the knee flexion increases (Fig. 9.25, aAC). The changing distribution of force within the ACL suggests that single-stranded reconstructions may not adequately meet the functional requirements of the natural ligament.

For isokinetic exercise, in which the knee is made to move at a constant angular velocity, quadriceps force decreases as knee-extension speed increases. As the knee extends more quickly, quadriceps force decreases because the muscle shortens more quickly, and, from the force-velocity property, an increase in shortening velocity leads to less muscle force (see Fig. 9.4). As a result, ACL force also decreases as knee-extension speed increases (Fig. 9.26), because of the drop in shear force applied to the leg by the quadriceps (via the patellar tendon) (Serpas et al., 2002).

The forces exerted between the femur and patella and between femur and tibia depend mainly on the geometry of the muscles that cross the knee. For maximum isometric extension, peak forces transmitted to the patellofemoral and tibiofemoral joints are around 11,000 and 6500 N, respectively (i.e., 15.7 and 9.3 times body weight, respectively) (Fig. 9.27). As the knee moves faster during isokinetic extension exercise, joint-contact forces decrease in direct proportion to the drop in quadriceps force (Yanagawa et al., 2002).

The results of Figs. 9.25 to 9.27 have significant implications for the design of exercise regimens aimed at protecting injured or newly reconstructed knee ligaments. For maximum, isolated contractions of the quadriceps, Fig. 9.25 shows that the ACL is loaded at all flexion angles less than 80°. Quadriceps-strengthening exercises should therefore be limited to flexion angles greater than 80° if the ACL is to be protected from load. In this region, however, very high contact forces can be applied to the patella (Fig. 9.27), so limiting this exercise to large flexion angles may result in patellofemoral pain. This scenario, known as the "paradox of exercise," is the reason why surgeons and physical therapists now prescribe so-called closed-chain exercises, such as squatting, for strengthening the quadriceps muscles subsequent to ACL reconstruction.

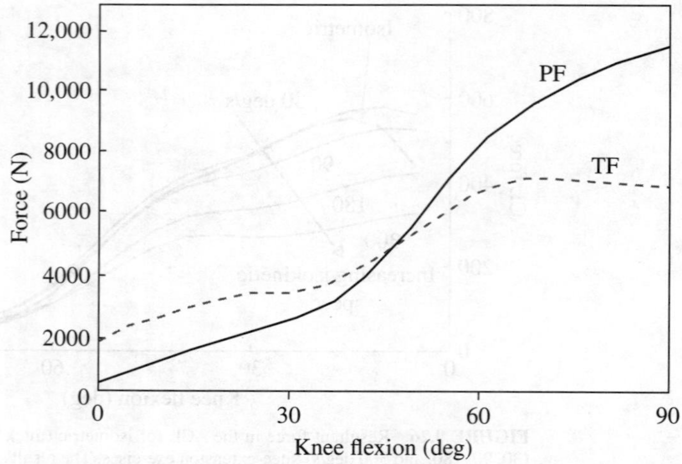

FIGURE 9.27 Resultant forces acting between the femur and patella (PF) and between the femur and tibia (TF) during maximum isometric knee-extension exercise. See Figure 9.25 for details.

9.7.2 Walking

Muscle and joint loading are much lower during walking than during knee-extension exercise. Various studies have used inverse-dynamics or static optimization (Crowninshield and Brand, 1981; Glitsch and Baumann, 1997; Hardt, 1978) and forward-dynamics or dynamic optimization (Anderson and Pandy, 2001a; Davy and Audu, 1987; Yamaguchi and Zajac, 1990) to estimate muscle forces during normal gait. There is general agreement in the results obtained from these modeling studies.

Analysis of a dynamic optimization solution has shown that the hip, knee, and ankle extensors are the prime movers of the lower limb during normal walking. Specifically, gluteus maximus and vasti provide support against gravity during initial stance; gluteus medius provides the majority of support during midstance; and soleus and gastrocnemius support and simultaneously propel the body forward during terminal stance (also known as push-off) (Anderson and Pandy, 2001a).

The plantarflexors generate the largest forces of all the muscles in the leg during normal gait. Soleus and gastrocnemius, combined, produce peak forces of roughly 3000 N (or four times body weight) during the push-off phase (Fig. 9.28, SOL and GAS prior to OHS). By comparison, the hip extensors, gluteus maximus and gluteus medius combined, produce peak forces that are slightly less (around 2500 N or 3.5 times body weight during initial stance) (Fig. 9.28, GMAXL, GMAXM, GMEDP, and GMEDA near OTO). Finally, the quadriceps, vasti and rectus femoris combined, develop peak forces that are barely two times body weight near the transition from double support to single support (Fig. 9.28, VAS and RF at OTO).

Muscles dominate the forces transmitted to the bones for most activities of daily living. Thus, the loading histories applied at the ankle, knee, and hip are in close correspondence with the predicted actions of the muscles that cross each of these joints (Fig. 9.29). For example, the peak force transmitted by the ankle is considerably higher than the peak forces transmitted by the hip or knee, which is consistent with the finding that the ankle plantarflexors develop the largest forces during normal gait (compare joint-contact force at ankle in Fig. 9.29 with forces produced by SOL and GAS in Fig. 9.28). Similarly, peak hip-contact force is around four times body weight near OTO, which results from the actions of the hip extensors, gluteus maximus, and gluteus medius, at this time (compare joint-contact force at hip in Fig. 9.29 with forces developed by GMAXL, GMAXM, GMEDP, and GMEDA in Fig. 9.28).

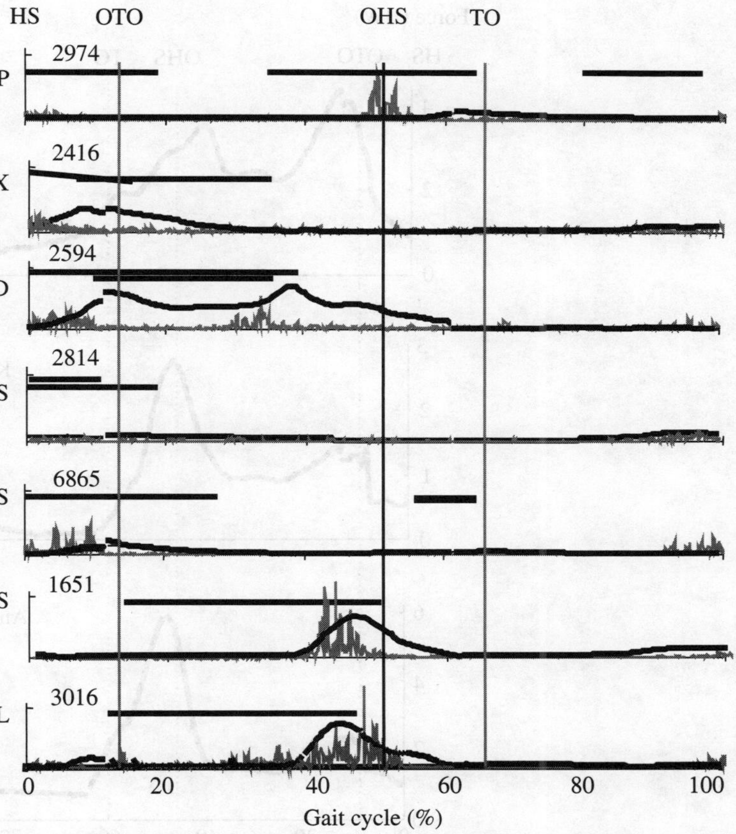

FIGURE 9.28 Forces generated by muscles spanning the hip, knee, and ankle (heavy black lines) during normal walking over level ground. The muscle forces were found by solving a dynamic optimization problem that minimized the amount of metabolic energy consumed by the muscles in the body per meter walked. In the model used to simulate gait, the body was represented as a 10-segment, 23-dof articulated linkage, and was actuated by 54 musculotendinous units (Anderson, and Pandy 1999; Anderson and Pandy, 2001a; Anderson and Pandy, 2001b). The time scale is represented as a percentage of the gait cycle. The gray wavy lines are EMG data recorded from one subject, and are given to show that the timing of the muscle-force development is consistent with the measured EMG activity of the muscles. The following gait cycle landmarks are demarcated by thin vertical lines: opposite toe-off (OTO), opposite heel-strike (OHS), toe-off (TO), and heel-strike (HS). The muscle-force plots are scaled to each muscle's maximum isometric strength (e.g., peak isometric strength in vasti is 6865 N). Muscle abbreviations are as follows: erector spinae (ERSP), gluteus maximus (GMAX), gluteus medius (GMED), hamstrings (HAMS), vasti (VAS), gastrocnemius (GAS), and soleus (SOL). [*Modified from Anderson and Pandy (2001b).*]

During walking, the peak articular contact force transmitted by the tibiofemoral joint at the knee is less than three times body weight. This level of joint loading is much lower than that estimated for knee-extension exercise, where forces approaching 10 times body weight have been predicted to act between the femur and tibia (Fig. 9.27). During the single-support portion of stance, where only a single foot is in contact with the ground, the center of mass of the body passes medial to the center of pressure of the foot. This results in an adduction moment exerted at the knee (Morrison, 1970). The magnitude of the knee adduction moment varies among individuals, with a mean value of around

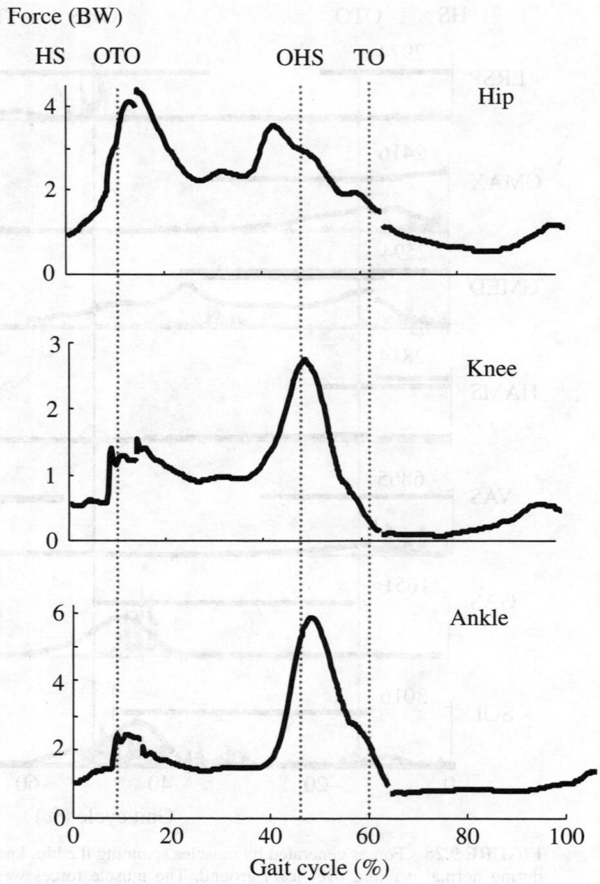

FIGURE 9.29 Joint contact forces acting at the hip, knee, and ankle during gait. The results were obtained by solving a dynamic optimization problem for normal walking (see Figure 9.28 for details). [*Modified from Anderson and Pandy (2001b).*]

3.2 percent of body weight times height (Hurwitz et al., 1998). The adduction moment is large enough that it would open the tibiofemoral joint on the lateral side, if it were not resisted by some internally generated abduction moment (Schipplein and Andriacchi, 1991), which is produced by the muscles and ligaments that span the knee. The quadriceps and gastrocnemius muscles generate most of the supporting abduction moment (Fig. 9.30), with a peak at contralateral toe off generated by the quadriceps, and a second peak at contralateral heel strike generated by the gastrocnemius (Shelburne et al., 2006). Ligaments also contribute to this abduction moment, during early- and mid-stance, when the quadriceps and gastrocnemius muscles are not active (Fig. 9.30). The knee adduction moment results in an articular contact force at the tibiofemoral joint that is shared unevenly between the medial and lateral joint compartments, at the points of contact between the femoral condyles and the tibial plateau (Fig. 9.31). The medial compartment supports most of the load (up to a peak of 2.4 times body weight), with the lateral compartment supporting far less (only 0.8 times body weight) (Shelburne et al., 2006).

The tension calculated in the ACL during walking is shown in Fig. 9.32. The peak value is 303 N, which is less than the 500 N predicted for knee-extension exercise (Fig. 9.25, aAC and pAC).

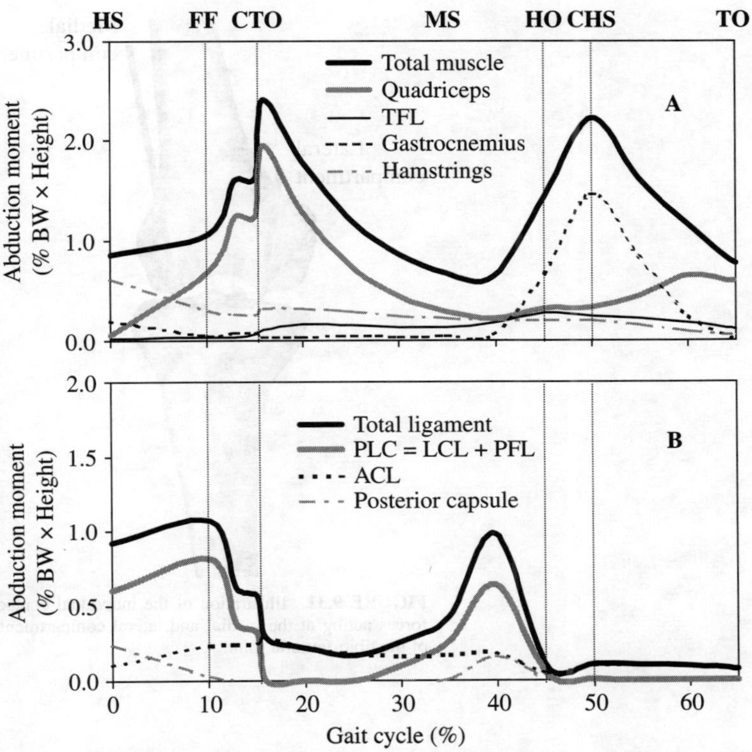

FIGURE 9.30 Contributions of individual muscles (A) and ligaments (B) to the total knee abduction moment during normal walking. [*Modified from Shelburne et al. (2006).*]

The ACL acts to resist anterior translation of the tibia relative to the femur, and so it is loaded whenever the total shear force acting on the tibia is directed anteriorly. The components of the tibial shear force are shown in Fig. 9.33. The large peak in ACL force at contralateral toe off is caused by contraction of the quadriceps muscles, and their resulting pull on the patellar tendon. In later stance, anterior shear forces produced by the quadriceps and gastrocnemius muscles are balanced by a posterior shear force produced by the ground reaction force (Fig. 9.33), resulting in a relatively small ACL force for this period of the stride.

Injuries to the ACL are common and often result in rupture of the ligament, producing an ACL-deficient (ACLD) knee. In the ACLD knee, the total anterior shear force acting on the tibia is reduced, from a peak of 262 N in the intact knee, to only 128 N in an ACLD knee (Shelburne et al., 2004b). This reduction in total anterior shear arises mainly from a reduction in the shear force induced by the quadriceps muscles acting via the patellar tendon. In the ACLD knee, the ACL no longer acts to resist anterior translation of the tibia, and so tension in the patellar tendon can translate the tibia to a more anterior location, relative to the femur, than it occupies in the intact knee. This anterior translation reduces the angle between the tibia and the patellar ligament, and causes a concomitant reduction in quadriceps shear force (Shelburne et al., 2004b; Fig. 9.34). The smaller anterior shear force in the ACLD knee is then supported by the other, remaining ligaments, with the vast majority borne by the medial collateral ligament.

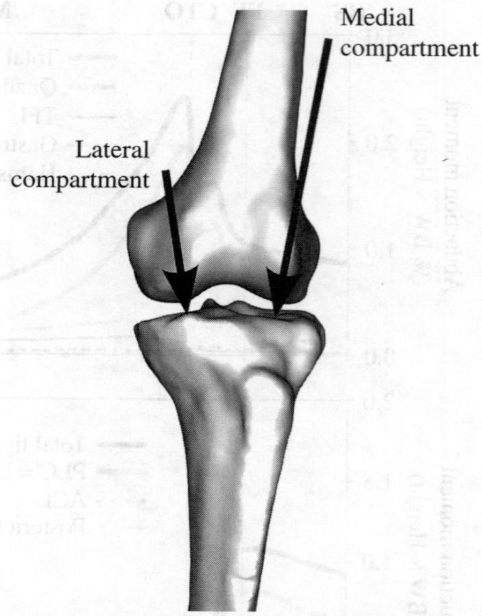

FIGURE 9.31 Illustration of the individual contact forces acting at the medial and lateral compartments of the tibio-femoral joint.

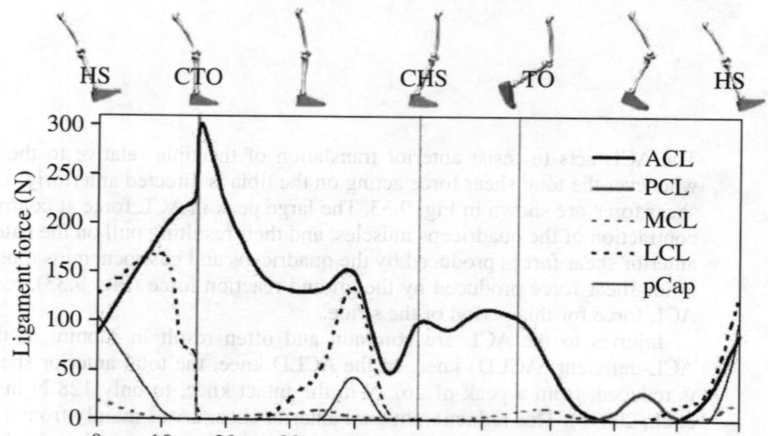

FIGURE 9.32 Forces transmitted to the anterior (ACL) and posterior (PCL) cruciate ligaments, the medial (MCL) and lateral (LCL) collateral ligaments, and the posterior capsule (pCap) of the knee during normal walking. Events of the stride shown above the figure are: heel strike (HS), contralateral toe-off (CTO), contralateral heel strike (CHS), and toe-off (TO). [*Modified from Shelburne et al. (2004a).*]

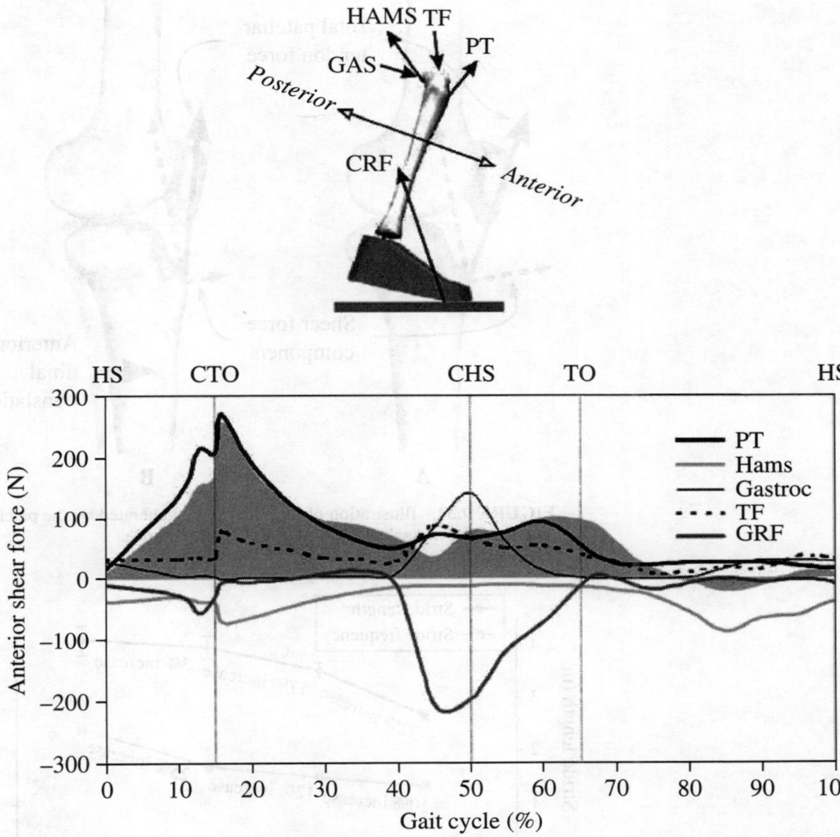

FIGURE 9.33 Shear forces acting on the lower leg (shank and foot) during normal walking. The shaded region shows the total shear force borne by the knee ligaments of the model, while the lines show shear forces exerted by the patellar tendon (PT), hamstrings muscles (Hams), gastrocnemius muscle (Gastroc), tensor fascia lata muscle (TF), and the ground reaction force (GRF). Events of the stride shown above the figure are: heel strike (HS), contralateral toe-off (CTO), contralateral heel strike (CHS), and toe-off (TO). [*Modified from Shelburne et al. (2004a).*]

9.7.3 Running

As running speed progresses from slow to fast, stride length increases more quickly in magnitude than stride frequency; beyond 7.0 m/s, however, the opposite trend occurs as stride frequency then increases very quickly (Fig. 9.35). Thus, faster running is initially achieved by increasing stride length at a greater rate than stride frequency, but eventually a threshold is reached and a shift in strategy occurs so that the progression to maximum running speed is achieved by increasing stride frequency at a greater rate than stride length. By developing a computational model of running, it has been found that the ankle plantarflexor muscles are primarily responsible for this muscular strategy shift (Dorn et al., 2012). Specifically, for running speeds up to 7 m/s, the ankle plantarflexors (i.e., the gastrocnemius and soleus muscles) provide a significant contribution to vertical support and hence increases in stride length. For speeds beyond 7 m/s, these muscles shorten at relatively high

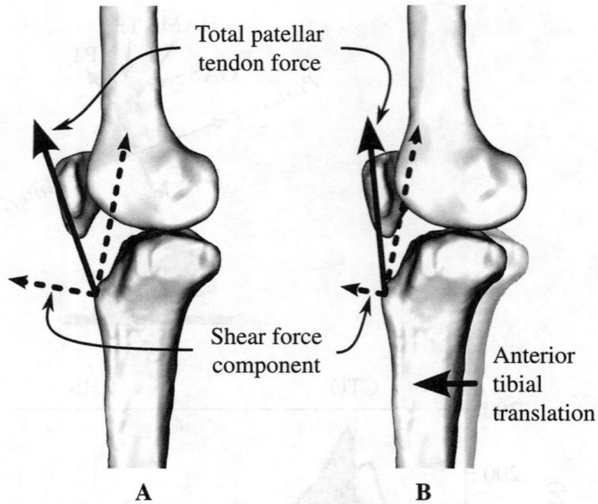

FIGURE 9.34 Illustration of the shear force generated by the patellar tendon in the normal (A) and ACL-deficient (B) knee.

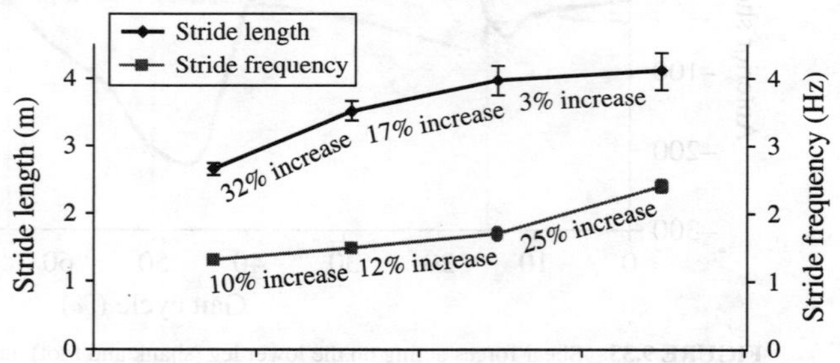

FIGURE 9.35 Dependence of running speed on stride length and stride frequency. [*Modified from Dorn et al. (2012).*]

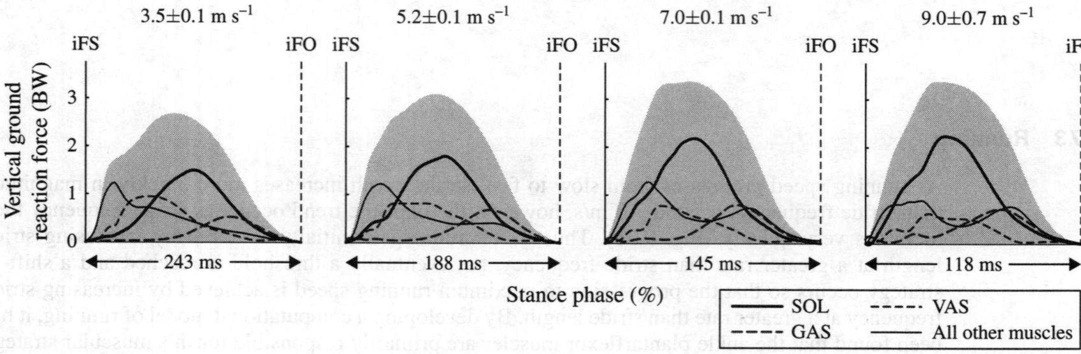

FIGURE 9.36 Contributions of the lower limb muscles to vertical support at different running speeds. The ankle plantarflexors, soleus and gastrocnemius, contribute most substantially to support at all running speeds; their contributions increase as running speed increases up to 7 m/s but then remain relatively unchanged as speed increases further. [*Modified from Dorn et al. (2012).*]

velocities and have less time to generate the forces needed for vertical support. Indeed, the contribution of the ankle plantarflexors to vertical support remains approximately the same at running speeds beyond 7 m/s as their contribution at slower running speeds (Fig. 9.36). Thus, running speed is progressed to maximum-effort sprinting by having the hip flexors and extensors (i.e., the iliopsoas, gluteus maximus, and hamstring muscles) accelerate the hip and knee joints more vigorously during swing, thereby increasing stride frequency. These findings offer insight into the strategies used by the lower-limb muscles to maximize running performance. The function of the ankle plantarflexor muscles appears to be critical, and it could be theorized that a key difference between elite and subelite sprinting athletes relates to the rate at which these muscles produce maximum force. Compared to their subelite counterparts, elite sprinters may have the capacity to produce maximum force from the ankle plantarflexors in a much shorter period of time, thus allowing them to reach higher running speeds before needing to shift from an ankle-dominant strategy to a hip-dominant strategy.

One consequence of the switch to a hip-dominant strategy as running speed approaches maximum sprinting is that the magnitudes of the forces acting about the hip and knee joints during the terminal swing phase of the stride cycle become very high. High "external" hip flexor and knee extensor torques are produced, which are primarily opposed by the hamstring muscles. It is therefore not surprising that the majority of hamstring muscle strain-type injuries occur when running at maximal or close to maximal speeds (Schache et al., 2012).

REFERENCES

An, K. N., Ueba, Y., Chao, E. Y., et al. (1983). Tendon excursion and moment arm of index finger muscles. *Journal of Biomechanics*. **16**:419–425.

Anderson, F. C., and Pandy, M. G. (1993). Storage and utilization of elastic strain energy during jumping. *Journal of Biomechanics*. **26**:1413–1427.

Anderson, F. C., and Pandy, M. G. (1999). A dynamic optimization solution for vertical jumping in three dimensions. *Computer Methods in Biomechanics and Biomedical Engineering*. **2**:201–231.

Anderson, F. C., and Pandy, M. G. (2001a). Dynamic optimization of human walking. *Journal of Biomechanical Engineering*.

Anderson, F. C., and Pandy, M. G. (2001b). Static and dynamic optimization solutions for gait are practically equivalent. *Journal of Biomechanics*. **34**:153–161.

Barr, R., and Chan, E. (1986). Design and implementation of digital filters for biomedical signal processing. *Journal of Electrophysiological Techniques*. **13**:73–93.

Basmajian, J., and DeLuca, C. (1985). *Muscles Alive: Their Function Revealed by Electromyography*. Williams and Wilkens, Baltimore.

Bigland-Ritchie, R., Johansson, R., Lippold, O., et al. (1983). Changes in motor neuron firing rates during sustained maximal voluntary contractions. *Journal of Physiology*. **340**:335–346.

Brand, R. A., Crowninshield, R. D., Wittstock, C. E., et al. (1982). A model of lower extremity muscular anatomy. *Journal of Biomechanical Engineering*. **104**: 304–310.

Buchanan, T. S., Moniz, M. J., Dewald, J. P., and Rymer, W. Z. (1993). Estimation of muscle forces about the wrist joint during isometric tasks using an EMG coefficient method. *Journal of Biomechanics*. **26**:547–560.

Butler, D. L., Grood, E. S., Noyes, F. R., and Zernicke, R. F. (1978). Biomechanics of ligaments and tendons. *Exercise and Sport Sciences Reviews*. **6**:125–181.

Crowninshield, R. D., and Brand, R. A. (1981). A physiologically based criterion of muscle force prediction in locomotion. *Journal of Biomechanics*. **14**:793–801.

Davy, D. T., and Audu, M. L. (1987). A dynamic optimization technique for predicting muscle forces in the swing phase of gait. *Journal of Biomechanics*. **20**:187–201.

Delp, S. L., Loan, J. P., Hoy, M. G., Zajac, F. E., Topp, E. L., and Rosen, J. M. (1990). An interactive graphics-based model of the lower extremity to study orthopaedic surgical procedures. *IEEE Transactions on Biomedical Engineering*. **37**:757–767.

DeLuca, C. (1997). The use of surface electromyography in biomechanics. *Journal of Applied Biomechanics.* **13**:135–163.

Dorn, T. W., Schache, A. G., and Pandy, M. G. (2012). Muscular strategy shift in human running: dependence of running speed on hip and ankle muscle performance. *Journal of Experimental Biology.* **215**:1944–1956.

Ebashi, S., and Endo, M. (1968). Calcium ion and muscle contraction. *Progress in Biophysics and Molecular Biology.* **18**:125–183.

Enoka, R. M. (1994). *Neuromechanical Basis of Kinesiology,* 2nd ed. Human Kinetics, New York.

Evans, H., Pan, Z., Parker, P., and Scott, R. (1994). Signal processing for proportional myoelectric control. *IEEE Transactions on Biomedical Engineering.* **41**:207–211.

Fang, J., Shahani, B., and Graupe, D. (1997). Motor unit number estimation by spatial-temporal summation of single motor unit potential. *Muscle and Nerve.* **20**:461–468.

Fregly, B. J., and Zajac, F. E. (1996). A state-space analysis of mechanical energy generation, absorption, and transfer during pedaling. *Journal of Biomechanics.* **29**:81–90.

Garner, B. A., and Pandy, M. G. (2000). The obstacle-set method for representing muscle paths in musculoskeletal models. *Computer Methods in Biomechanics and Biomedical Engineering.* **3**:1–30.

Garner, B. A., and Pandy, M. G. (2001). Musculoskeletal model of the human arm based on the Visible Human Male dataset. *Computer Methods in Biomechanics and Biomedical Engineering.* **4**:93–126.

Glitsch, U., and Baumann, W. (1997). The three-dimensional determination of internal loads in the lower extremity. *Journal of Biomechanics.* **30**:1123–1131.

Hardt, D. E. (1978). Determining muscle forces in the leg during human walking: an application and evaluation of optimization methods. *Journal of Biomechanical Engineering.* **100**:72–78.

Hatze, H. (1976). The complete optimization of human motion. *Mathematical Biosciences.* **28**:99–135.

Hatze, H. (1978). A general myocybernetic control model of skeletal muscle. *Biological Cybernetics.* **28**:143–157.

Hayes, W. C., and Bodine, A. J. (1978). Flow-independent viscoelastic properties of articular cartilage matrix. *Journal of Biomechanics.* **11**:407–419.

Hayes, W. C., and Mockros, L. F. (1971). Viscoelastic properties of human articular cartilage. *Journal of Applied Physiology.* **31**:562–568.

Hill, A. V. (1938). The heat of shortening and the dynamic constants of muscle. *Proceedings of the Royal Society (London)*, Series B. **126**:136–195.

Hof, A. L., Pronk, C. A. N., and van Best, J. A. (1987). Comparison between EMG to force processing and kinetic analysis for the calf muscle moment in walking and stepping. *Journal of Biomechanics.* **20**:167–178.

Hori, R. Y., and Mockros, L. F. (1976). Indention tests of human articular cartilage. *Journal of Applied Physiology.* **31**:562–568.

Hurwitz, D. E., Sumner, D. R., Andriacchi, T. P., and Sugar, D. A. (1998). Dynamic knee loads during gait predict proximal tibial bone distribution. *Journal of Biomechanics.* **31**:423–430.

Huxley, A. F. (1957). Muscle structure and theories of contraction. *Progress in Biophysics and Biophysical Chemistry.* **7**:255–318.

Jensen, R. H., and Davy, D. T. (1975). An investigation of muscle lines of action about the hip: a centroid line approach vs the straight line approach. *Journal of Biomechanics.* **8**:103–110.

Kane, T. R., and Levinson, D. A. (1983). The use of Kane's dynamical equations in robotics. *The International Journal of Robotics Research.* **2**:3–21.

Kane, T. R., and Levison, D. A. (1985). *Dynamics: Theory and Applications*. McGraw-Hill, New York.

Kempson, G. E. (1980). *The Joints and Synovial Fluid*, vol. 2. Academic Press, Chapter 5, pp. 177–238.

Lodish, H., Berk, A., Zipursky, S. L., et al. (2000). *Molecular Cell Biology*, 4th ed. W.H. Freeman and Company, New York.

Morrison, J. B. (1970). The mechanics of the knee joint in relation to normal walking. *Journal of Biomechanics.* **3**:51–61.

Mow, V. C., Holmes, M. H., Lai, and W. M. (1984). Fluid transport and mechanical properties of articular cartilage: a review. *Journal of Biomechanics.* **17**:377–394.

Noyes, F. R., and Grood, E. S. (1976). The strength of the anterior cruciate ligament in humans and rhesus monkeys. *Journal of Bone and Joint Surgery.* **58-A**:1074–1082.

Pandy, M. G. (1990). An analytical framework for quantifying muscular action during human movement. In: Winters, J. M., and Woo, S. L-Y. (eds.): *Multiple Muscle Systems—Biomechanics and Movement Organization*, Springer-Verlag, New York, pp. 653–662.

Pandy, M. G. (1999). Moment arm of a muscle force. *Exercise and Sport Sciences Reviews*. **27**:79–118.

Pandy, M. G. (2001). Computer modeling and simulation of human movement. *Annual Review of Biomedical Engineering*. **3**:245–273.

Pandy, M. G., Anderson, F. C., and Hull, D. G. (1992). A parameter optimization approach for the optimal control of large-scale musculoskeletal systems. *Journal of Biomechanical Engineering*. **114**:450–460.

Pandy, M. G., and Berme, N. (1988). A numerical method for simulating the dynamics of human walking. *Journal of Biomechanics*. **21**:1043–1051.

Pandy, M. G., Garner, B. A., and Anderson, F. C. (1995). Optimal control of non-ballistic muscular movements: a constraint-based performance criterion for rising from a chair. *Journal of Biomechanical Engineering*. **117**:15–26.

Pandy, M. G., and Sasaki, K. (1998). A three-dimensional musculoskeletal model of the human knee joint. Part II: Analysis of ligament function. *Computer Methods in Biomechanics and Biomedical Engineering*. **1**:265–283.

Pandy, M. G., and Shelburne, K. B. (1997). Dependence of cruciate-ligament loading on muscle forces and external load. *Journal of Biomechanics*. **30**:1015–1024.

Pandy, M. G., and Zajac, F. E. (1991). Optimal muscular coordination strategies for jumping. *Journal of Biomechanics*. **24**:1–10.

Pandy, M. G., Zajac, F. E., Sim, E., and Levine, W. S. (1990). An optimal control model for maximum-height human jumping. *Journal of Biomechanics*. **23**:1185–1198.

Pflum, M. A., Shelburne, K. B., Torry, M. R., Decker, M. J., and Pandy, M. G. (2004). Model prediction of anterior cruciate ligament force during drop-landings. *Medicine and Science in Sports and Exercise*. **36**:1949–1958.

Powell, M. J. D. (1978). A fast algorithm for nonlinearly constrained optimization calculations. In: Matson, G. A. (ed.): *Numerical Analysis: Lecture Notes in Mathematics*, Springer-Verlag, vol. 630, pp. 144–157.

Raasch, C. C., Zajac, F. E., Ma, B., and Levine, W. S. (1997). Muscle coordination of maximum-speed pedaling. *Journal of Biomechanics*. **6**:595–602.

Schache, A. G., Blanch, P. D., Brown, N. A., and Pandy, M. G. (2012). Mechanics of the human hamstring muscles during sprinting. *Medicine and Science in Sports and Exercise*. **44**:647–658.

Schipplein, O. D., and Andriacchi, T. P. (1991) Interaction between active and passive knee stabilizers during level walking. *Journal of Orthopaedic Research*. **9**:113–119.

Seireg, A., and Arvikar, R. J. (1973). A mathematical model for evaluation of forces in the lower extremities of the musculoskeletal system. *Journal of Biomechanics*. **6**:313–326.

Serpas, F., Yanagawa, T., and Pandy, M. G. (2002). Forward-dynamics simulation of anterior cruciate ligament forces developed during isokinetic dynamometry. *Computer Methods in Biomechanics and Biomedical Engineering*. **5**(1):33–43.

Shelburne, K. B., and Pandy, M. G. (1997). A musculoskeletal model of the knee for evaluating ligament forces during isometric contractions. *Journal of Biomechanics*. **30**:163–176.

Shelburne, K. B., and Pandy, M. G. (1998). Determinants of cruciate-ligament loading during rehabilitation exercise. *Clinical Biomechanics*. **13**:403–413.

Shelburne, K. B., Pandy, M. G., Anderson, F. C., and Torry, M. R. (2004a). Pattern of anterior cruciate ligament force in normal walking. *Journal of Biomechanics*. **37**:797–805.

Shelburne, K. B., Pandy, M. G., and Torry, M. R. (2004b). Comparison of shear forces and ligament loading in the healthy and ACL-deficient knee during gait. *Journal of Biomechanics*. **37**:313–319.

Shelburne, K. B., Torry, M. R., and Pandy, M. G. (2006). Contributions of muscles, ligaments, and the ground reaction force to tibiofemoral joint loading during normal gait. *Journal of Orthopaedic Research*. **24**:1983:1990.

Ward, S. R., Eng, C. M., Smallwood, L. H., and Lieber, R.L. (2009). Are current measurements of lower extremity muscle architecture accurate? *Clinical Orthopaedics and Related Research*. **467**:1074–1082.

Yamaguchi, G. T., and Zajac, F. E. (1990). Restoring unassisted natural gait to paraplegics via functional neuromuscular stimulation: a computer simulation study. *IEEE Transactions on Biomedical Engineering*. **37**:886–902.

Yanagawa, T., Shelburne, K. B., Serpas, F., and Pandy, M. G. (2002). Effect of hamstrings muscle action on stability of the ACL-deficient knee in isokinetic extension exercise. *Clinical Biomechanics*. **17**: 705-712.

Zajac, F. E. (1989). Muscle and tendon: properties, models, scaling, and application to biomechanics and motor control. In: Bourne, J. R. (ed.): *CRC Critical Reviews in Biomedical Engineering*, CRC Press, Boca Raton, vol. 19, pp. 359–411.

Zajac, F. E., and Gordon, M. E. (1989). Determining muscle's force and action in multi-articular movement. *Exercise and Sport Sciences Reviews*. **17**:187–230.

CHAPTER 10
BONE MECHANICS

Tony M. Keaveny
University of California, San Francisco, California, and
University of California, Berkeley, California

Elise F. Morgan
University of California, Berkeley, California

Oscar C. Yeh
University of California, Berkeley, California

10.1 INTRODUCTION

Bone is a complex tissue that is continually being torn down and replaced by biological remodeling. As the main constituent in whole bones (which as organs contain other tissues such as bone marrow, nerves, and blood vessels), the two types of bone tissue—cortical and trabecular bone—have the functional task of withstanding substantial stress during the course of locomotion and strenuous activities such as lifting heavy weights or fast running. Since bones are loaded both cyclically and statically, fatigue and creep responses are important aspects of their mechanical behavior. Indeed, there is evidence that a primary stimulus for bone remodeling is the repair of damage that accumulates from habitual cyclic loading.[1,2] With aging, however, the balance between bone loss and gain is disrupted, and bone deteriorates, leading to a variety of devastating clinical problems. In modern populations, fractures from osteoporosis are becoming increasingly common, the spine, hip, and wrist being the primary sites. Implantation of orthopedic prostheses for conditions such as disc degeneration and osteoarthritis require strong bone for optimal fixation, a difficult requirement for sites such as the aged spine or hip, where bone strength can be greatly compromised. The goal of this chapter is to summarize the highlights of what is known about the mechanical behavior of bone as a material. With a focus on the behavior of human bone, we review the mechanics of cortical bone, trabecular bone, and trabecular tissue material. Rather than attempt to provide an encyclopedic review of the literature, our intent is to provide a focused summary that will be most useful as input for biomechanical analyses of whole bone and bone-implant systems.

10.2 COMPOSITION OF BONE

At the nanometer scale, bone tissue is composed of inorganic and organic phases and water. On a weight basis, bone is approximately 60 percent inorganic, 30 percent organic, and 10 percent water,[3] whereas on a volume basis, these proportions are about 40 percent, 35 percent, and 25 percent, respectively. The inorganic phase of bone is a ceramic crystalline-type mineral that is an impure form of naturally occurring calcium phosphate, most often referred to as *hydroxyapatite*: $Ca_{10}(PO_4)_6(OH)_2$.[4] Bone hydroxyapatite is not pure hydroxyapatite because the tiny apatite crystals (2- to 5-nm-thick $\times$15-nm-wide $\times$ 20- to 50-nm-long plates) contain impurities such as potassium, magnesium, strontium, and sodium (in place of the calcium ions), carbonate (in place of the phosphate ions), and chloride or fluoride (in place of the hydroxyl ions). The organic phase of bone consists primarily of type I collagen (90 percent by weight), some other minor collagen types (III and VI), and a variety of noncollagenous proteins such as osteocalcin, osteonectin, osteopontin, and bone sialoprotein.[5] The collagen molecules are arranged in parallel with each other head to tail with a gap or "hole zone" of approximately 40 nm between each molecule.[6] Mineralization begins in the hole zones and extends into other intermolecular spaces, resulting in a mineralized fibril. The three-dimensional arrangement of collagen molecules within a fibril is not well understood. However, collagen fibrils in bone range from 20 to 40 nm in diameter, suggesting that there are 200 to 800 collagen molecules in the cross section of a fibril.

10.3 BONE AS A HIERARCHICAL COMPOSITE MATERIAL

At the micron scale and above, bone tissue is a hierarchical composite (Fig. 10.1). At the lowest level ($\approx$0.1-μm scale), it is a composite of mineralized collagen fibrils. At the next level (1- to 10-μm scale), these fibrils can be arranged in two forms, either as stacked thin sheets called *lamellae* (about 7 μm thick) that contain unidirectional fibrils in alternating angles between layers or as a block of randomly oriented *woven* fibrils. Lamellar bone is most common in adult humans, whereas woven bone is found in situations of rapid growth, such as in children and large animals, as well as during the initial stages of fracture healing.

Lamellar bone is found in different types of histological structures at the millimeter scale. Primary lamellar bone is new tissue that consists of large concentric rings of lamellae that circle the outer 2 to 3 μm of diaphyses similar to growth rings on a tree. The most common type of cortical bone in adult humans is osteonal or Haversian bone, where about 10 to 15 lamellae are arranged in concentric cylinders about a central Haversian canal, a vascular channel about 50 μm in diameter that contains blood vessel capillaries, nerves, and a variety of bone cells (Fig. 10.2*A*). The substructures of concentric lamellae, including the Haversian canal, is termed an *osteon*, which has a diameter of about 200 μm and lengths of 1 to 3 μm. Volkmann's canals are about the same diameter as Haversian canals but run transverse to the diaphyseal axis, providing a radial path for blood flow within the bone. Osteons represent the main discretizing unit of human adult cortical bone and are continually being torn down and replaced by the bone remodeling process. Over time, the osteon can be completely removed, leaving behind a resorption cavity that is then filled in by a new osteon. Typically, there are about 13 Haversian canals per square millimeter of adult human cortical bone. Since mineralization of a new osteon is a slow process that can take months, at any point in time there is a large distribution of degree of mineralization of osteons in any whole-bone cross section. A *cement line*,

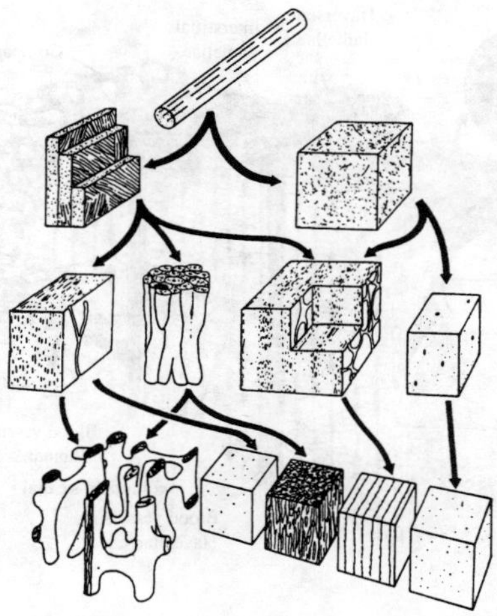

FIGURE 10.1 The four levels of bone microstructure, from the level of mineralized collagen fibrils to cortical and trabecular bone. It is generally assumed that at the former level, all bone is equal, although there may be subtle differences in the nature of the lamellar architecture and degree of mineralization between cortical and trabecular bone. (*Adapted from Ref. 7.*)

which is a thin layer of calcified mucopolysaccharides with very little collagen and low mineral content,[8] remains around the perimeter of each newly formed osteon. The cement line is thought to represent a weak interface between the osteon and the surrounding interstitial bone.[9] These weak interfaces are thought to improve the fatigue properties of cortical bone by providing avenues for dissipation of energy during crack propagation.[8]

The bone matrix that comprises lamellar and woven bone contains another level of porosity on the order of 5 to 10 μm that is associated with the bone cells (see Fig. 10.2A, B, C). Osteocytes, the most common type of bone cell, are surrounded by a thin layer of extracellular fluid within small ellipsoidal holes (5 μm minor diameter, 7 to 8 μm major diameter) called *lacunae*, of which there are about 25,000 per μm^3 in bone tissue. The lacunae are generally arranged along the interfaces between lamellae. However, the lacunae also have a lower-scale porosity associated with them. Each osteocyte has dendritic processes that extend from the cell through tiny channels ($\approx$0.5 μm diameter, 3 to 7 μm long) called *canaliculi* to meet at cellular gap junctions with the processes of surrounding cells.* There are about 50 to 100 canaliculi per single lacuna and about 1 million per mm^3 of bone.

At the highest hierarchical level (1 to 5 mm), there are two types of bone: cortical bone, which comes as tightly packed lamellar, Haversian, or woven bone; and trabecular bone, which comes as a highly porous cellular solid. In the latter, the lamellae are arranged in less well-organized "packets" to form a network of rods and plates about 100 to 300 μm thick interspersed with large marrow spaces. Many common biological materials, such as wood and cork, are cellular solids.[10]

The distinction between cortical and trabecular bone is most easily made based on porosity. Cortical bone can be defined as bone tissue that has a porosity P of less than about 30 percent or, equivalently, a volume fraction V_f of greater than about 0.70 ($V_f = 1 - P$). Volume fraction is the ratio of the volume of actual bone tissue to the bulk volume of the specimen. In the field of bone mechanics, porosity measures usually ignore the presence of lacunae and canaliculi. Porosity of adult

*Gap junctions are arrays of small pores in the cell membrane that make connections between the interiors of neighboring cells, allowing direct passage of small molecules such as ions from one cell to another.

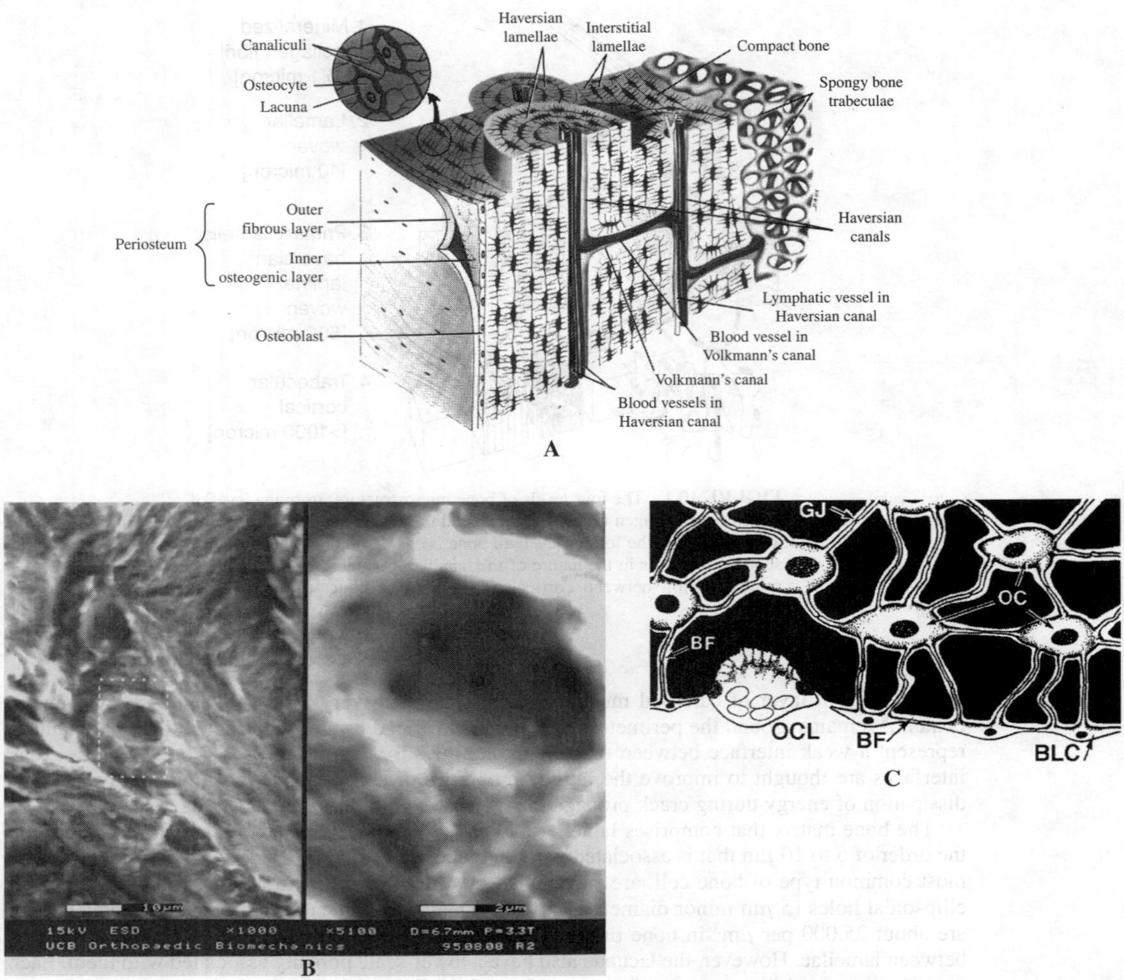

FIGURE 10.2 (A) Diagram of a sector of the shaft of a long bone showing the different types of cortical bone, trabecular bone, and the various channels. (*From Figure 5–1d of Ref. 11.*) (B) Environmental scanning electron micrograph of a fracture surface of a piece of cortical bone showing a fractured lacuna at low (*left*) and high (*right*) magnifications. Note the elliptical shape of the lacuna and the multiple smaller canaliculi. (C) A schematic depicting the interconnection of osteocytes (OC) via the cell processes that extend along the canaliculi and meet at gap junctions (GJ). Bone-lining cells (dormant osteoblasts, BLC) lie on each exposed bone surface, where osteoclasts (OCL) can be found removing bone as part of the ongoing remodeling process. A thin layer of bone fluid (BF) surrounds the cells and their processes.

human femoral cortical bone, for example, can vary from as low as 5 percent at age 20 up to almost 30 percent above age 80.[12] Porosity of trabecular bone can vary from 70 percent in the femoral neck[13] up to about 95 percent in the elderly spine.[14]

Two other common measures of bone density in biomechanical studies are termed *tissue* and *apparent densities*. Tissue density ρ_{tiss} is defined as the ratio of mass to volume of the actual bone tissue. It is similar for cortical and trabecular bone, varies little in adult humans, and is about 2.0 g/cm^3. Apparent density ρ_{app} is defined as the ratio of the mass of bone tissue to the bulk volume of the specimen, including the volume associated with the vascular channels and higher-level porosity. Volume fraction, tissue density, and apparent densities are related as follows:

$$\rho_{app} = \rho_{tiss} V_f$$

Typically, mean values of apparent density of hydrated cortical bone are about 1.85 g/cm^3, and this does not vary much across anatomic sites or species. By contrast, the average apparent density of trabecular bone depends very much on anatomic site. It is as low as 0.10 g/cm^3 for the spine,[15] about 0.30 g/cm^3 for the human tibia,[16] and up to about 0.60 g/cm^3 for the load-bearing portions of the proximal femur.[13] After skeletal maturity (around ages 25 to 30), trabecular bone density decreases steadily with aging, at a rate of about 6 percent per decade.[17]

Spatially, the relatively high porosity of trabecular bone is in the form of a network of interconnected pores filled with bone marrow. The trabecular tissue forms an irregular lattice of small rods and plates that are called *trabeculae* (Fig. 10.3). Typical thicknesses of individual trabeculae are in the range 100 to 300 μm, and typical intertrabecular spacing is on the order of 500 to 1500 μm.[18] The spatial arrangement of the trabeculae is referred to as the *trabecular architecture*. Architectural type varies across anatomic site and with age. Bone from the human vertebral body tends to be more rodlike, whereas bone from the bovine proximal tibia consists almost entirely of plates. As age

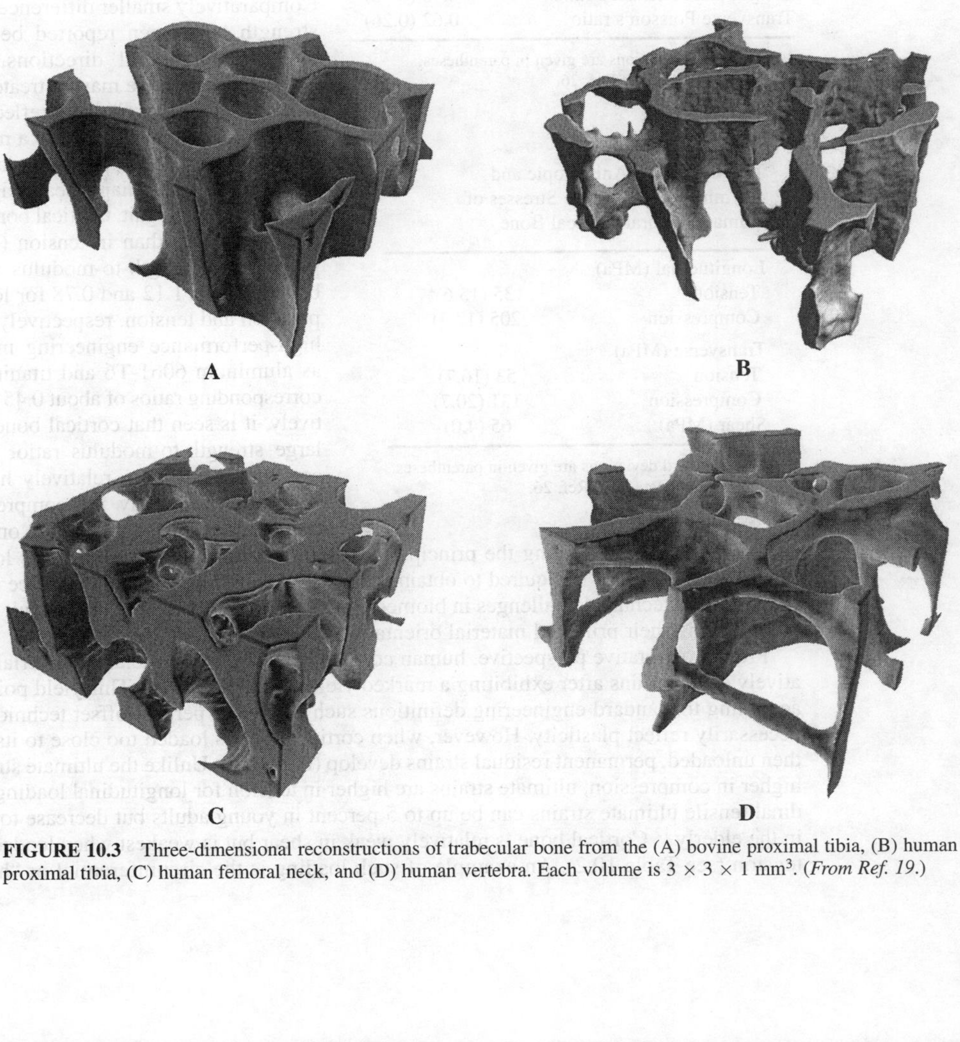

FIGURE 10.3 Three-dimensional reconstructions of trabecular bone from the (A) bovine proximal tibia, (B) human proximal tibia, (C) human femoral neck, and (D) human vertebra. Each volume is 3 × 3 × 1 mm^3. (*From Ref. 19.*)

increases and volume fraction decreases, the architecture becomes increasingly rodlike, and these rods become progressively thin and can be perforated. Quantification of trabecular architecture with the intent of understanding its role in the mechanical behavior of trabecular bone has been the subject of intense research. In addition to calculating trabecular thickness, spacing, and surface-to-volume ratio, stereological and three-dimensional methods may be used to determine the mean orientation (main grain axis) of the trabeculae, connectivity, and the degree of anisotropy.[20] While earlier studies used two-dimensional sections of trabecular bone to perform these architectural analyses,[21,22] more recent investigations use three-dimensional reconstructions generated by microcomputed tomography and other high-resolution imaging techniques.[19,23–25]

10.4 MECHANICAL PROPERTIES OF CORTICAL BONE

TABLE 10.1 Anisotropic Elastic Properties of Human Femoral Cortical Bone

Longitudinal modulus (MPa)	17,900 (3,900)*
Transverse modulus (MPa)	10,100 (2,400)
Shear modulus (MPa)	3,300 (400)
Longitudinal Poisson's ratio	0.40 (0.16)
Transverse Poisson's ratio	0.62 (0.26)

*Standard deviations are given in parentheses.
Source: Data from Ref. 26.

TABLE 10.2 Anisotropic and Asymmetrical Ultimate Stresses of Human Femoral Cortical Bone

Longitudinal (MPa)	
Tension	135 (15.6)*
Compression	205 (17.3)
Transverse (MPa)	
Tension	53 (10.7)
Compression	131 (20.7)
Shear (MPa)	65 (4.0)

*Standard deviations are given in parentheses.
Source: Data from Ref. 26.

Reflecting the anisotropy of its microstructure, the elastic and strength properties of human cortical bone are anisotropic. Cortical bone is both stronger and stiffer when loaded longitudinally along the diaphyseal axis compared with the radial or circumferential "transverse" directions (Table 10.1). Comparatively smaller differences in modulus and strength have been reported between the radial and circumferential directions, indicating that human cortical bone may be treated as transversely isotropic. This is probably a reflection of its evolutionary adaptation to produce a material that most efficiently resists the largely uniaxial stresses that develop along the diaphyseal axis during habitual activities such as gait. Cortical bone is also stronger in compression than in tension (Table 10.2). The percentage strength-to-modulus ratio for cortical bone is about 1.12 and 0.78 for longitudinal compression and tension, respectively. Compared with high-performance engineering metal alloys such as aluminum 6061-T6 and titanium 6Al-4V with corresponding ratios of about 0.45 and 0.73, respectively, it is seen that cortical bone has a relatively large strength-to-modulus ratio. In this sense, it can be considered a relatively high-performance material, particularly for compression. It should be noted that these properties only pertain to its behavior when loaded along the principal material direction. If the specimen is loaded oblique to this, a transformation is required to obtain the material constants. This consequence of the anisotropy can introduce technical challenges in biomechanical testing since it is often difficult to machine bone specimens in their principal material orientations.

From a qualitative perspective, human cortical bone is a linearly elastic material that fails at relatively small strains after exhibiting a marked yield point (Fig. 10.4). This yield point is determined according to standard engineering definitions such as the 0.2 percent offset technique and does not necessarily reflect plasticity. However, when cortical bone is loaded too close to its yield point and then unloaded, permanent residual strains develop (Fig. 10.5). Unlike the ultimate stresses, which are higher in compression, ultimate strains are higher in tension for longitudinal loading. These longitudinal tensile ultimate strains can be up to 5 percent in young adults but decrease to about 1 percent in the elderly.[12] Cortical bone is relatively weak in shear but is weakest when loaded transversely in tension (see Table 10.2). An example of such loading is the circumferential or "hoop" stress that

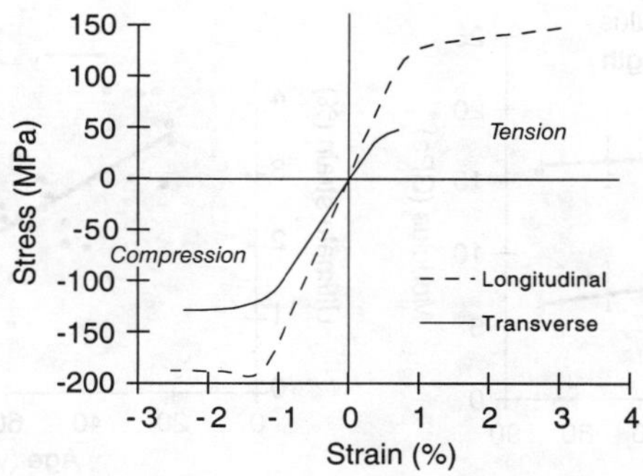

FIGURE 10.4 Typical stress-strain behavior for human cortical bone. The bone is stiffer in the longitudinal direction, indicative of its elastic anisotropy. It is also stronger in compression than in tension, indicative of its strength asymmetry (modulus is the same in tension and compression). (*From Ref. 10.*)

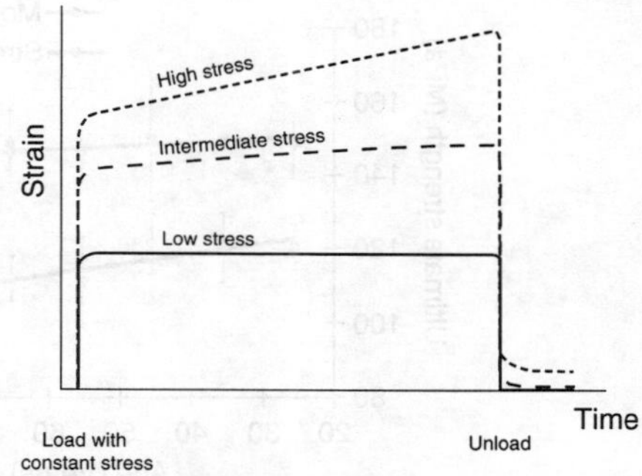

FIGURE 10.5 Creep response of cortical bone for three different stress levels. When a low stress is applied to the bone, the strain remains constant over time, and there is no permanent deformation after unloading. For stresses just below yield, strains increase with time at a constant rate, and a small permanent deformation exists after unloading. As the magnitude of the stress is increased, the rate of creep increases, and a larger permanent deformation exists after unloading. (*From Ref. 27.*)

can develop when large intramedullary tapered implants such as uncemented hip stems are impacted too far into the diaphysis.

While it is often appropriate to assume average properties for cortical bone, as shown in Tables 10.1 and 10.2, it may be necessary in some cases to account for the heterogeneity that can arise from variations in microstructural parameters such as porosity and percentage mineralization. Both modulus and ultimate stress can halve when porosity is increased from 5 to 30 percent[12,28] (Fig. 10.6A). Small increases in percentage mineralization cause large increases in both modulus and strength (see Fig. 10.6B), and while this parameter does not vary much in adult humans,[12] it can vary substantially across species.[29]

Aging also affects the mechanical properties of cortical bone. Tensile ultimate stress decreases at a rate of approximately 2 percent per decade[30] (Fig. 10.7A). Perhaps most important, tensile ultimate strain decreases by about 10 percent of its "young" value per decade, from a high of almost

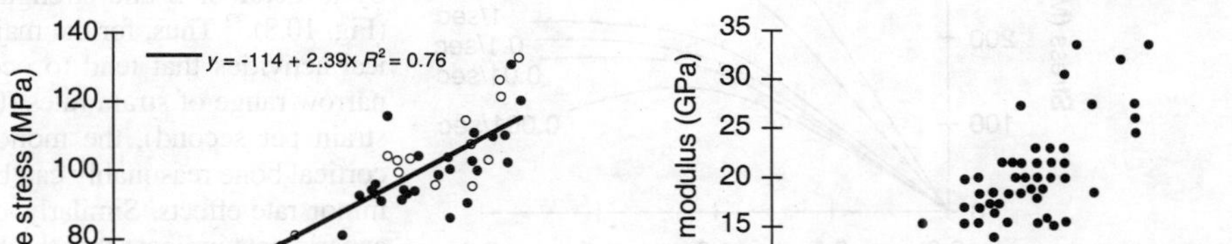

A **B**

FIGURE 10.6 (A) Dependence of the ultimate tensile stress of human cortical bone on volume fraction (expressed as a percentage). Ages of the specimens were in the range 20 to 100 years. (*From Ref. 12.*) (B) Modulus versus calcium content (in mg/g of dehydrated bone tissue) for cortical bone taken from 18 different species. (*From Ref. 29.*)

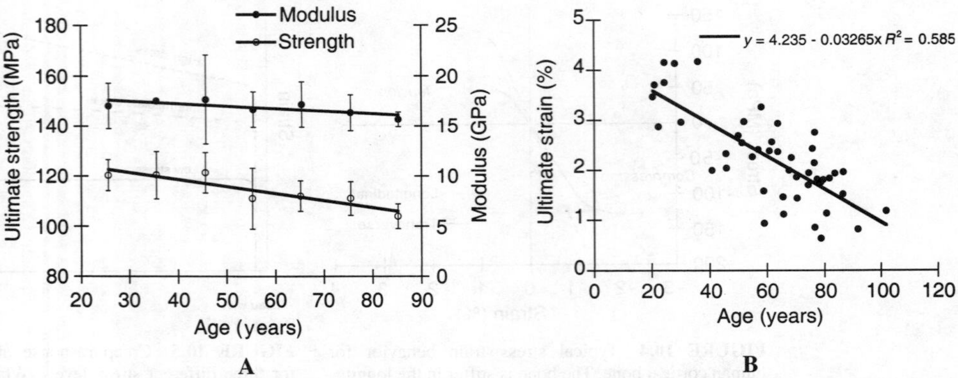

FIGURE 10.7 Reductions of human cortical bone mechanical properties with age. (A) Modulus is not reduced much, if at all, whereas strength is reduced more, at a rate of about 2 percent per decade. (*From Ref. 30.*) (B) Ultimate strain decreases markedly with age, at a rate of about 10 percent of its young value per decade. (*From Ref. 12.*)

5 percent strain at ages 20 to 30 years to a low of less than 1 percent strain above age 80 years[12] (see Fig. 10.7B). Thus the energy to fracture, given by the total area under the stress-strain curve before fracture, is much less for old bone than for younger bone. As discussed below, fracture mechanics studies also show a decrease in the fracture toughness with aging. For these reasons, old cortical bone is more brittle than young bone. It is not currently clear if this age-related brittleness arises from hypermineralization or collagen changes, although it appears that the latter is more plausible, since mineralization does not change much in adult humans with aging.[12] Many of these age-related changes in mechanical properties are to be expected, since porosity increases with age. However, there are concurrent changes in other aspects of the tissue microstructure and composition such that porosity is not simply a surrogate measure of age. For example, although strength and ductility clearly decrease with age in adults, there is controversy over whether elastic modulus changes with age.[12,30,31]

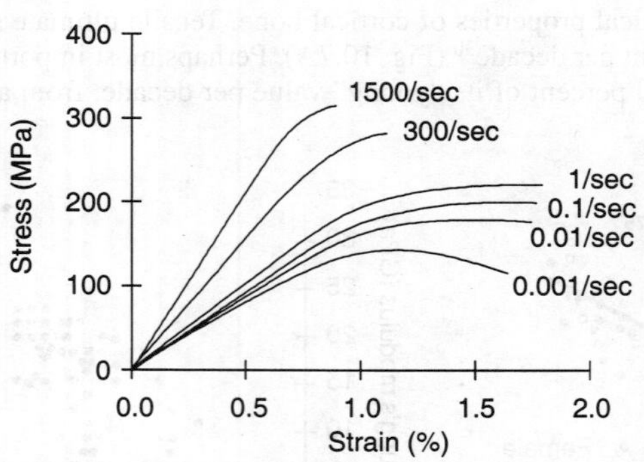

FIGURE 10.8 Strain-rate sensitivity of cortical bone for longitudinal tensile loading. Typically, modulus and strength increase only by factors 2 and 3, respectively, as the loading rate is increased by 6 orders of magnitude. The higher strain rates shown here may occur in vehicular accidents or gunshot wounds. (*Data from Ref. 32.*)

Although cortical bone is viscoelastic, the effect of loading rate on modulus and strength is only moderate. Over a 6 orders of magnitude increase in strain rate, modulus only changes by a factor of 2 and strength by a factor of 3 (Fig. 10.8).[32] Thus, for the majority of physiological activities that tend to occur in a relatively narrow range of strain rates (0.01 to 1.0 percent strain per second), the monotonic response of cortical bone reasonably can be assumed to have minor rate effects. Similarly, dynamic sinusoidal experiments indicate that the loss tangent attains a broad minimum (0.01 to 0.02) over the range of physiological frequencies.[33,34] These values, which are lower than those for polymers by a factor of 10, indicate that significant mechanical damping does not occur within this frequency range. Clearly, in extraordinary situations such as high-speed trauma, strength properties can increase by a factor of 2 to 3, and this should be recognized. Additionally, it has been found that loading rate has a significant effect on the accumulation of damage within the tissue. Slower loading rates produce higher numbers of acoustic emission events, but these events are of lower amplitude than those emitted at faster rates.[35]

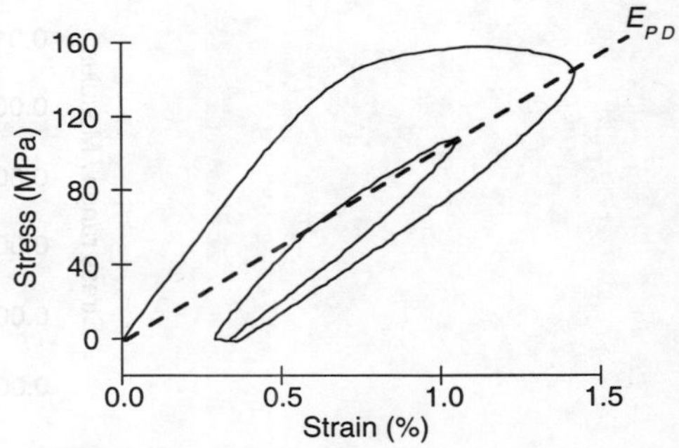

FIGURE 10.9 Comparison of loading and reloading tensile stress-strain curves for human cortical bone. On reloading, the modulus is similar to that for initial loading, but it is quickly reduced to a value that is close to the *perfect damage modulus*, the secant modulus at the unloading point. Substantial residual strains are evident even after a 1- to 2-minute hold between loading cycles. (*Data from Ref. 38.*)

Multiaxial failure properties of cortical bone are not well understood, although it is clear that simple isotropic and symmetrical criteria such as the von Mises are not capable of describing the multiaxial strength properties of this tissue. The Tsai-Wu criterion, commonly used for fiber-reinforced composite materials, has been applied to cortical bone using both transversely isotropic[36] and orthotropic[37] treatments. The transversely isotropic case works quite well for axial-shear-loading configurations,[36] but neither this case nor the orthotropic one has been validated across the full range of multiaxial stresses. Regardless, this criterion accounts for the difference in tensile and compressive strengths, as well as the low shear strength with respect to the tensile strength, and in this sense is the most suitable criterion currently available.

Cortical bone exhibits mechanical property degradations characteristic of a damaging material. When cortical bone is loaded beyond its yield point, unloaded, and reloaded, its modulus is reduced[39,40] (Fig. 10.9). This evidence of mechanical damage does not occur for metals for which the reloading modulus after yield is the same as the initial modulus. Studies using acoustic emissions to monitor structural changes in the tissue during monotonic loading to failure support the idea that the postyield behavior of cortical bone is damage-related.[41,42] Fatigue loading can also induce modulus reductions, and these reductions are accompanied by increases in energy dissipation per cycle.[43,44] Similar to engineering composites, the secant modulus exhibits a gradual reduction in stiffness until the final 5 percent of fatigue life, at which point the stiffness declines sharply until complete fracture.[44] However, there may be a load threshold below which this fatigue damage does not occur.[45] Cortical bone has a greater resistance to fatigue failure in compression than in tension, and the effect of mean strain on fatigue life is negligible.[43,46] For strain amplitude controlled tests, the following life prediction has been reported for human femoral cortical bone[43]:

$$N_f = (2.94 \times 10^{-9})\Delta\varepsilon^{-5.342} \quad n = 68$$

where N_f is the number of cycles to failure, and $\Delta\varepsilon$ is the applied strain amplitude. The standard error of the estimate for this regression[43] on the log-transformed data is 0.4085. Interestingly, creep appears to be an intrinsic component of the fatigue behavior. With increasing numbers of cycles, increasing creep strains can be observed.[44] When fatigue and creep behaviors are expressed as functions of stress/modulus versus time to failure, fatigue life is independent of frequency (0.2- to 2.0-Hz range), and substantial similarities appear between the fatigue and creep behaviors[46,47] (Fig. 10.10).

Microscopy techniques have established the presence of histological damage in cortical bone in vivo. Collectively termed *microdamage*, the patterns of damage include longitudinal and transverse microcracks, diffuse damage, and cross-hatched shear band patterns. It appears that histological damage increases with age[48,49] and is more pronounced in women.[49,50] These correlations have fueled a large body of research attempting to determine a relationship between mechanical property degradations and microdamage. True cause-and-effect relationships have not been established and have been controversial. The ability to detect microdamage at a high enough resolution, as well as to quantify it unambiguously, has been proposed as a confounding factor.

Damage may have direct biological consequences since the underlying cells will undergo structural damage as the surrounding bone matrix permanently deforms and sustains microdamage. This cellular damage may induce a biological response, perhaps prompting the bone cells to repair the subtle matrix damage. This is an important point when interpreting fatigue or creep properties because it should be realized that no biological healing can occur during in vitro experiments. Thus

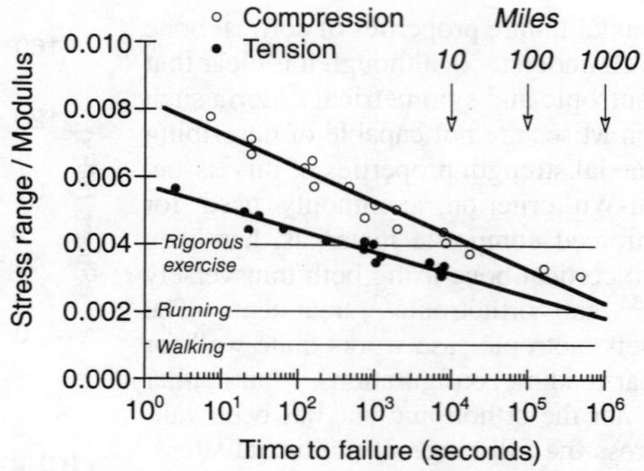

FIGURE 10.10 Fatigue and creep behaviors of human cortical bone versus time to failure. For fatigue loading, the ordinate on this graph can be converted to number of cycles by multiplying the time to failure by the frequency, which is typically one cycle per second for normal walking. Note that both creep and fatigue resistance are lower in tension, consistent with monotonic behavior. *(Data from Refs. 43 and 47.)*

the preceding fatigue characteristics are best considered as lower bounds on the in vivo fatigue life (see Fig. 10.10). It is unlikely that high-cycle (low-stress) fatigue failure occurs in vivo since the resulting fatigue damage would be healed biologically before large enough cracks could develop that would cause overt fracture of the bone. However, it should also be noted that the increase in porosity associated with the initial stages of the bone remodeling process may actually weaken the bone tissue even as the process attempts to strengthen it.

Fracture mechanics has been applied to cortical bone to determine its resistance to crack initiation and propagation. Various experimental techniques involving single-edge-notch (SEN), center-notched-cylindrical (CNC), and compact-tension (CT) specimens have been used to measure critical stress intensity factor K_c and critical energy release rate G_c. Size requirements of standard fracture toughness tests cannot be strictly met due to limitations on the size of available human tissue. Therefore, experimentally determined values of fracture toughness depend on specimen geometry and do not reflect a true material property. Additionally, plane-strain conditions and the associated relationships between K_c and G_c cannot be assumed. Theoretical developments[51] and tests on larger bones (see Ref. 52 for review), such as bovine tibiae, have been used to determine correction factors that are used to account for specimen geometry. Comparisons of reported values should be made with care because some studies do not attempt to correct for specimen geometry but rather report values in a comparative sense only consistent with the specific study.

Average values for K_c and G_c range from 2 to 6 $MNm^{-3/2}$ and 50 to over 1000 N/m, respectively, for specimens oriented such that the crack propagated along the longitudinal axis of the long bone (Table 10.3). These values are similar, for example, to those of polystyrene. This orientation has been

TABLE 10.3 Fracture Toughness Values per Anatomic Site for Human Cortical Bone

	G_{Ic} (N/m)		G_{IIc} (N/m)	
Anatomic site	Mean	SD	Mean	SD
Femoral neck	1,128	344	5,642	1,272
Femoral shaft	706	288	1,817	1,090
Tibial shaft	816	327	5,570	1,749

Source: Data from Ref. 51.

found to be the weaker in terms of crack resistance relative to the transverse orientation (ratio of 1:1.75 for bovine bone[52]). Fracture toughness decreases with age in the diaphyses of long bones[31,53] at a rate of 4.1 percent per decade in the femoral shaft.[31] Fracture toughness in mode II loading can be greater by as much as fivefold than that in mode I.[51,54] The most significant factors that are correlated with fracture toughness are age and a variety of porosity-related measures (including apparent density, water content, and osteon density).[53,54]

A number of studies have developed micromechanical models for the elastic and strength properties of cortical bone. This work has been motivated by observations that changes in the mechanical properties with age and disease are accompanied by alterations in the tissue microstructure.[55] While it is generally agreed on that bone behaves mechanically as a composite material, the complex hierarchy of composite structure has led to disagreements over which scale or scales are most relevant for a particular aspect of the mechanical behavior. For instance, ultrastructural models have focused on the role of the mineral phase as reinforcement for the collagen matrix,[56,57] whereas macrostructural models have treated the Haversian systems as fibers embedded in a matrix of cement lines and interstitial lamellae.[58–60] On an intermediate scale, the individual mineralized collagen fibers have been modeled as reinforcement for the noncollagenous mineralized matrix.[61,62] Still another class of models has used a hierarchical approach to synthesize two or more of these different length scales.[63–65] These modeling efforts rely extensively on accurate information regarding the constituent and interface properties. Obtaining this information has proven challenging not only because of the extremely small scale involved but also because, unlike the case with engineering composites, isolating the different phases of bone tissue often involves processes that may alter the properties being measured.[66] Recent studies using nanoindentation,[67,68] for example, have begun to address the issue of scale by providing the ability to measure the elastic modulus and microhardness of various microstructures within cortical tissue. Thus efforts are ongoing to develop micromechanical constitutive models for cortical bone.

It is also of keen interest to determine the role of mechanical stimuli on bone cells and the interaction between cell biology and bone mechanical properties. Biological processes that are active throughout an individual's lifetime can alter the bone tissue on many scales. It has often been suggested that osteocytes act as sensors of mechanical loading and initiators of the bone-adaptation processes.[69–72] Whether these processes add or remove bone, or whether they are activated at all, is thought to depend on the level of mechanical loading[73] and on the presence or absence of tissue damage.[1,2] Many studies have suggested that strain or strain rate is the appropriate measure of mechanical stimulus,[74–76] although others have used stress or strain energy.[77,78] In addition, other characteristics of the mechanical loading, such as mode, direction, frequency, duration, and distribution, have also been identified as important. Using this collective empirical evidence, several theories of mechanical adaptation have been proposed (see Ref. 79 for a comprehensive treatment of this topic). When applied to finite-element models of whole bones, some of these theories have been able to predict the density pattern of the trabecular bone in the proximal femur[80,81] and the loss of bone in the regions surrounding a hip implant.[82] This remains an area of active research since experimentally validated mechanobiological constitutive relations of the remodeling process have yet to be developed.

10.5 MECHANICAL PROPERTIES OF TRABECULAR BONE

Although trabecular bone—also referred to as *cancellous* or *spongy bone*—is nonlinearly elastic even at small strains,[83] it is most often modeled as linearly elastic until yielding. It yields in compression at strains of approximately 1 percent, after which it can sustain large deformations (up to 50 percent strain) while still maintaining its load-carrying capacity. Thus trabecular bone can absorb substantial energy on mechanical failure. A heterogeneous porous cellular solid, trabecular bone has anisotropic mechanical properties that depend on the porosity of the specimen as well as the architectural arrangement of the individual trabeculae. Its apparent (whole-specimen) level properties also depend on the tissue-level material properties of the individual trabeculae. An overwhelming portion

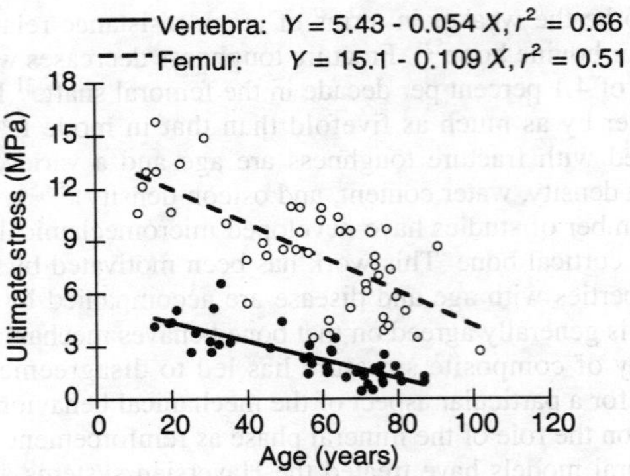

FIGURE 10.11 Dependence of ultimate stress on age for trabecular bone from the human vertebra and femur. For both anatomic sites, strength decreases approximately 10 percent per decade. (*Data from Refs. 17 and 84.*)

of trabecular bone mechanics research has been devoted to improving our understanding of the relative contributions and interplay of porosity, architecture, and tissue properties in the apparent level properties.

The elastic and strength properties of trabecular bone display substantial heterogeneity with respect to donor age and health, anatomic site, loading direction (with respect to the principal orientation of the trabeculae), and loading mode. Both modulus and strength decrease with age, falling approximately 10 percent per decade[17,85] (Fig. 10.11). Pathologies such as osteoporosis, osteoarthritis, and bone cancer are also known to affect mechanical properties.[86,87] Young's modulus can vary 100-fold within a single epiphysis[88] and threefold depending on loading direction.[89–92] Typically, the modulus of human trabecular bone is in the range 10 to 3000 MPa depending on the preceding factors; strength, which is linearly and strongly correlated with modulus,[13,88,89] is generally 2 orders of magnitude lower than modulus and is usually in the range 0.1 to 30 MPa.

In compression, the anisotropy of trabecular bone strength increases with age[85] and decreasing density (Fig. 10.12). The strength also depends on loading mode, being highest in compression and lowest in shear.[93,94] Ratios of compressive to tensile strength and compressive to shear strength are not constant but rather depend on modulus[94] and density (see Fig. 10.12). Both modulus and strength depend heavily on apparent density, yet these relationships vary for different types of trabecular bone because of the anatomic site-, age-, and disease-related variations in trabecular architecture. Linear and power-law relationships* can be used to describe the dependence of modulus and compressive strength on apparent density (Tables 10.4 and 10.5), with typical coefficients of determination (r^2 values) in the range 0.5 to 0.9.

Interestingly, the failure (yield and ultimate) strains of human trabecular bone have only a weak dependence, if any, on apparent density and modulus.[13,15,85, 95–98] A recent study designed to test for intersite differences found that yield strains were approximately uniform within anatomic sites, with standard deviations on the order of one-tenth the mean value, but mean values could vary across sites[13] (Fig. 10.13). Thus, for analysis purposes, yield strains can be considered constant within sites but heterogeneous across sites. Regardless of anatomic site, however, yield stains are higher in compression than in tension.[13] Ultimate strains are typically in the range of 1.0 to 2.5 percent. Evidence from experiment on bovine bone indicates that yield strains are also isotropic[99,100] despite substantial anisotropy of modulus and strength.

*Differences in the predictive power between the various linear and power laws are usually negligible within a single anatomic site because the range of apparent density exhibited by trabecular bone is less than 1 order of magnitude.

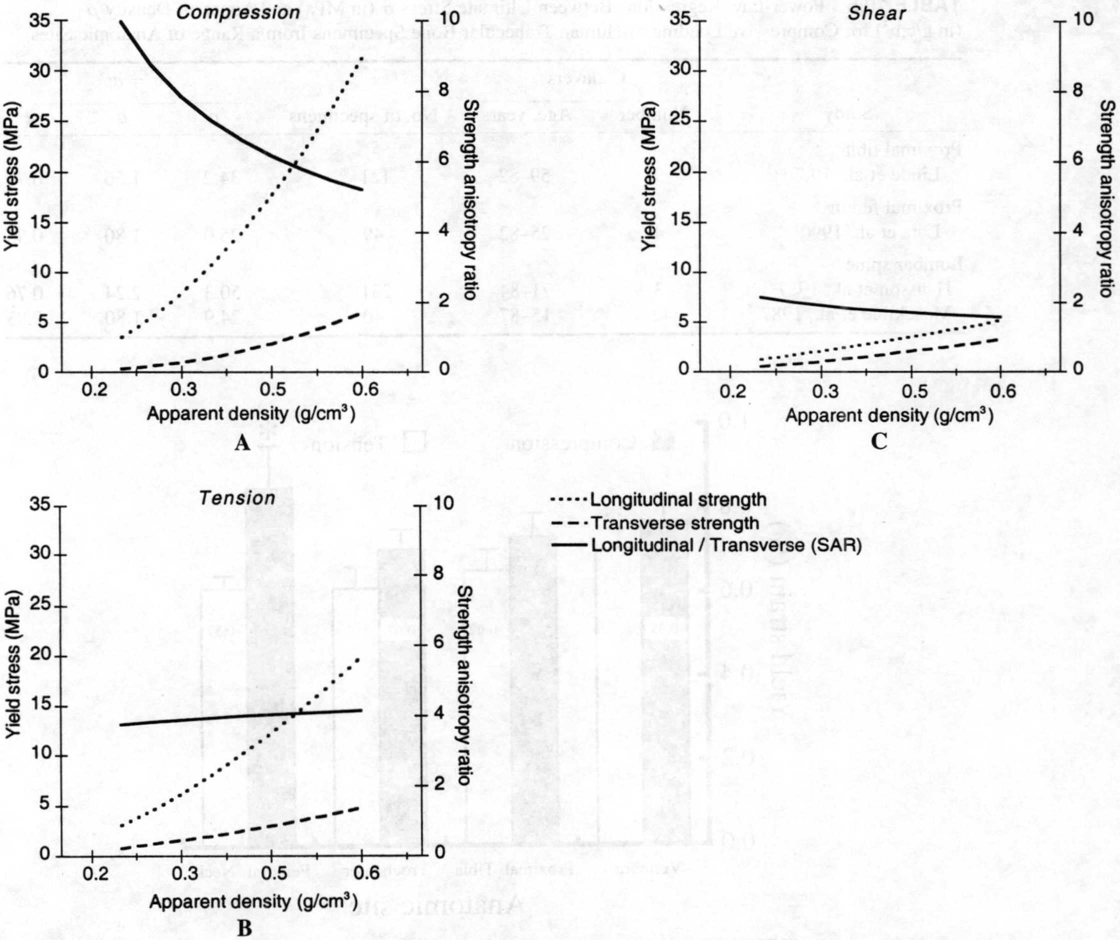

FIGURE 10.12 Dependence of yield stress in (A) compression, (B) tension, and (C) torsion on apparent density for bovine tibial trabecular bone specimens oriented both longitudinally (along) and transverse to the principal trabecular orientation. Overall, strength is greatest in compression and least in shear. In compression, the strength-anisotropy ratio [SAR = (longitudinal strength)/(transverse strength)] increases with decreasing density. (*Data from Ref. 101.*)

TABLE 10.4 Power-Law Regressions Between Modulus E (in MPa) and Apparent Density ρ (in g/cm^3) for Human Trabecular Bone Specimens from a Range of Anatomic Sites

	Cadavers			$\sigma = a\rho^b$		
Study	Number	Age, years	No. of specimens	a	b	r^2
Vertebra (T_{10}–L_5)	25	20–90	61	4,730	1.56	0.73
Proximal tibia	16	40–85	31	15,490	1.93	0.84
Femoral greater trochanter	21	49–101	23	15,010	2.18	0.82
Femoral neck	23	57–101	27	6,850	1.49	0.85

Source: Data from Ref. 13.

TABLE 10.5 Power-Law Regressions Between Ultimate Stress σ (in MPa) and Apparent Density ρ (in g/cm^3) for Compressive Loading of Human Trabecular Bone Specimens from a Range of Anatomic Sites

Study	Cadavers		No. of specimens	$\sigma = a\rho^b$		
	Number	Age, years		a	b	r^2
Proximal tibia						
Linde et al., 1989[102]	9	59–82	121	34.2	1.56	0.79
Proximal femur						
Lotz et al., 1990[103]	4	25–82	49	25.0	1.80	0.93
Lumbar spine						
Hansson et al., 1987[95]	3	71–84	231	50.3	2.24	0.76
Mosekilde et al., 1987[85]	42	15–87	40	24.9	1.80	0.83

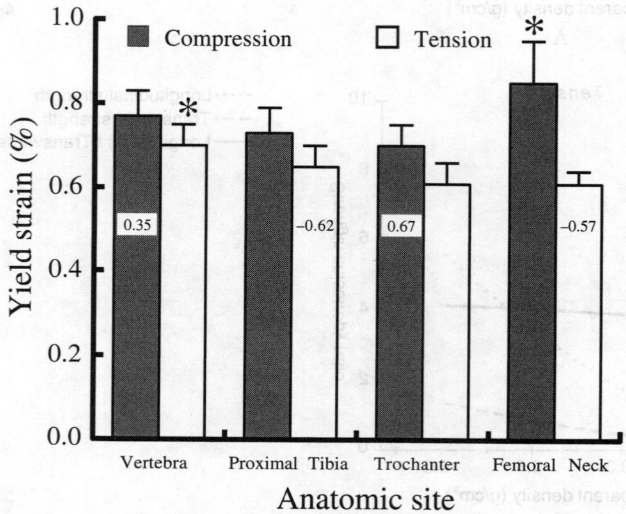

FIGURE 10.13 Mean yield strain per anatomic site in both compression and tension. Error bars indicate 1 standard deviation. Yield strain is only weakly dependent on apparent density for four of the groups, as indicated by the Pearson correlation coefficient r in the bar. Compressive yield strains are higher than tensile yield strains for each anatomic site. Intrasite scatter is on the order of one-tenth the mean values. (*From Ref. 13.*)

The advent of high-resolution finite-element modeling[104] has led to enormous progress in determining elastic stiffness matrices, multiaxial failure behavior, and as will be seen later, trabecular tissue properties. Finite-element models of individual specimens, developed using microcomputed tomography[105,106] and other types of microscopic imaging,[20,107] have been used to compute the full set of elastic constants for specimens from multiple anatomic sites. Results indicate that trabecular bone can be considered orthotropic[108,109] or, in some cases, transversely orthotropic.[110] Poisson's ratios, which are difficult to measure experimentally for trabecular bone, range from 0.03 to 0.60.[25,109]

Given the complexity of in vivo loading conditions, there is a need to develop a multiaxial failure criterion for trabecular bone. Results have been reported for bovine bone only.[93,111,112] These studies indicate that the von Mises criterion does not work well and that expression of the criterion in terms of strain (or nondimensional measures of stress divided by modulus) greatly simplifies the mathematical form of the criterion since it eliminates the dependence of the criterion on specimen density.

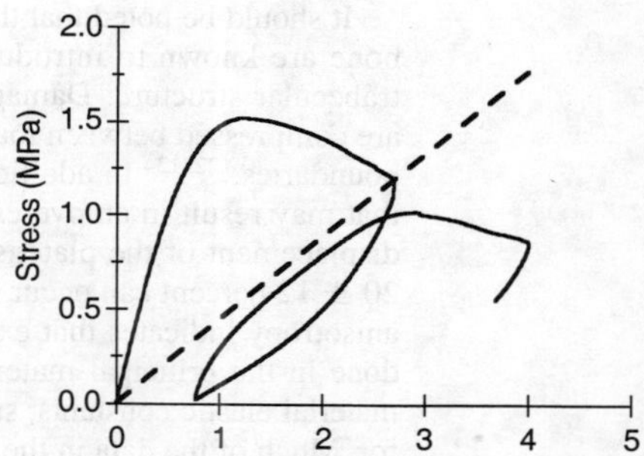

FIGURE 10.14 Compressive load-unload-reload behavior of human vertebral trabecular bone. Similar to cortical bone tested in tension, an initial overload causes residual strains and a reloading curve whose modulus quickly reduces from a value similar to the intact modulus to a value similar to the perfect damage modulus. (*From Ref. 114.*)

Criteria such as the Tsai-Wu criterion have only a limited ability to describe multiaxial failure of trabecular bone for arbitrary stress states. Coupling between normal strengths in different directions (longitudinal versus transverse, for example) appears to be minimal.[113] At present, it is recommended for multiaxial failure analysis that the tensile-compressive-shear-strength asymmetry be recognized, as well as the strength anisotropy. If properties are not available for a specific site under analysis, failure strains should be used from sites that have a similar density range and architecture.

When trabecular bone is loaded in compression beyond its elastic range, unloaded, and reloaded, it displays loss of stiffness and development of permanent strains[114] (Fig. 10.14). In particular, it reloads with an initial modulus close to its intact Young's modulus but then quickly loses stiffness. The residual modulus is statistically similar to the perfect-damage modulus (a secant modulus from the origin to the point of unloading). In general, the reloading stress-strain curve tends to reload back toward the extrapolated envelope of the original curve. Phenomenologically, trabecular bone therefore exhibits elements of both plasticity and damage. The magnitudes of stiffness loss $\%\Delta E$ and residual strain $\varepsilon_{\mathrm{RESDIUAL}}$ for human vertebral trabecular bone are highly correlated with the applied strain $\varepsilon_{\mathrm{TOTAL}}$ (all expressed in percent) in the initial overload:

$$\varepsilon_{\mathrm{RESIDUAL}} = -0.046 + 0.104\varepsilon_{\mathrm{TOTAL}} + 0.073\varepsilon^2_{\mathrm{TOTAL}} \qquad r^2 = 0.96$$

$$\%\Delta E = 178 - \frac{496}{\varepsilon_{\mathrm{TOTAL}} + 2.58} \qquad r^2 = 0.94$$

Also, at any given strain, modulus on reloading is reduced more than strength:

$$\%\Delta S = 17.1 + 19.1\varepsilon_{\mathrm{TOTAL}} - 149\rho_{\mathrm{APP}} \qquad r^2 = 0.62$$

where $\%\Delta S$ is the percentage change in strength, and ρ_{APP} is the apparent density. These relations are for applied strains on the order of 1 to 5 percent only; residual behavior for much greater applied strains has not yet been reported. The percent modulus reductions and residual strains do not depend on volume fraction because similar trends have been reported for bovine bone, which is much more dense and platelike.[115,116] Furthermore, the trabecular behavior is qualitatively similar to that for cortical bone loaded in tension.[39,117] This suggests that the dominant physical mechanisms for damage behavior act at the nanometer scale of the collagen and hydroxyapatite.

Regarding time-dependent behavior, trabecular bone is only slightly viscoelastic when tested in vitro, with both compressive strength and modulus being related to strain rate raised to a power of 0.06.[27,118] The stiffening effect of marrow is negligible except at very high strain rates (10 strains/s), although there is evidence that the constraining effects of a cortical shell may allow hydraulic stiffening of whole bones in vivo under dynamic loads.[119] Minor stress relaxation has been shown to occur[120] and depends on the applied strain level,[121] indicating that human trabecular bone is nonlinearly viscoelastic. Little else is known about its time-dependent properties, including creep and fatigue for human bone. Fatigue and creep studies on bovine bone have revealed the following power law relations between compressive normalized stress (stress divided by modulus, expressed in percent) and time to failure (frequency for fatigue loading was 2 Hz):

Fatigue: $$t_f = 1.71 \times 10^{-24}(\Delta\sigma/E_o)^{-11.56} \qquad r^2 = 0.77$$

Creep: $$t_f = 9.66 \times 10^{-33}(\sigma/E_o)^{-16.18} \qquad r^2 = 0.83$$

Failure in these experiments was defined by a 10 percent reduction in secant modulus compared with the initial Young's modulus.

It should be noted that the in vitro mechanical test methods most often used to date on trabecular bone are known to introduce substantial errors in the data as a result of the porous anisotropic trabecular structure. Damage preferentially occurs at the ends of machined specimens when they are compressed between loading platens due to disruption of the trabecular network at the specimen boundaries.[122–124] In addition, friction at the platen-specimen interface creates a triaxial stress state that may result in an overestimation of modulus.[122,123,125] If strains are computed from the relative displacement of the platens, substantial systematic and random errors in modulus on the order of 20 ± 12 percent can occur.[126] Strength and failure strain data are also affected.[127,128] The trabecular anisotropy indicates that experimental measurements of the orthotropic elastic constants should be done in the principal material coordinate system. Since off-axis moduli are functions of multiple material elastic constants, substantial errors can be introduced from misalignment[129] if not corrected for. Much of the data in the literature have been obtained in various types of off-axis configurations, since specimens are often machined along anatomic rather than material axes. The difficulty in interpreting these off-axis measurements is heightened when intersite and interstudy comparisons are attempted. For all these reasons, and since the in vitro test boundary conditions rarely replicate those in vivo, interpretation and application of available data must be done with care.

An important development for structural analysis of whole bones is the use of quantitative computed tomography (QCT) to generate anatomically detailed models of whole bone[130–135] or bone-implant[136,137] systems. At the basis of such technology is the ability to use QCT to noninvasively predict the apparent density and mechanical properties of trabecular bone. Some studies have reported excellent predictions ($r^2 \geq 0.75$) of modulus and strength from QCT density information for various anatomic sites.[89,96,103,138] Since the mechanical properties depend on volume fraction and architecture, it is important to use such relations only for the sites for which they were developed; otherwise, substantial errors can occur. Also, since QCT data do not describe any anisotropic properties of the bone, trabecular bone is usually assumed to be isotropic in whole-bone and bone-implant analyses. Typically, in such structural analyses, cortical bone properties are not assigned from QCT since it does not have the resolution to discern the subtle variations in porosity and mineralization that cause variations in cortical properties. In these cases, analysts typically assign average properties, sometimes transversely isotropic, to the cortical bone.

10.6 MECHANICAL PROPERTIES OF TRABECULAR TISSUE MATERIAL

While most biomechanical applications at the organ level require knowledge of material properties at the scales described earlier, there is also substantial interest in the material properties of trabecular tissue because this information may provide additional insight into diseases such as osteoporosis and drug treatments designed to counter such pathologies. Disease- or drug-related changes could be most obvious at the tissue rather than apparent or whole-bone level, yet only recently have researchers begun to explore this hypothesis. This is so primarily because the irregular shape and small size of individual trabecula present great difficulties in measuring the tissue material properties.

Most of the investigations of trabecular tissue properties have addressed elastic behavior. Some of the earlier experimental studies concluded that the trabecular tissue has a modulus on the order of 1 to 10 GPa.[139–142] Later studies using combinations of computer modeling of the whole specimen and experimental measures of the apparent modulus have resulted in a wide range of estimated values for the effective modulus of the tissue (Table 10.6) such that the issue became controversial. However, studies using ultrasound have concluded that values for elastic modulus are about 20 percent lower than for cortical tissue.[143,144] This has been supported by results from more recent nanoindentation studies.[67,68,145] The combined computer-experiment studies that successfully eliminated end artifacts in the experimental protocols also found modulus values more typical of cortical bone than the much lower values from the earlier studies.[146] Thus an overall consensus is emerging that the elastic modulus of trabecular tissue is similar to, and perhaps slightly lower than, that of cortical bone.[150] Regarding failure behavior, it appears from the results of combined computational-experimental

TABLE 10.6 Trabecular Tissue Moduli Using a Variety of Experimental and Computational Techniques

Study	Testing method	Anatomic site	No. of specimens	Tissue modulus (GPa) Mean	SD
Ashman and Rho, 1988[143]	Ultrasound	Human femur	53	13.0	1.5
Rho et al., 1993[144]	Ultrasound	Human tibia	20	14.8	1.4
	Microtensile			10.4	3.5
Rho et al., 1997[67]	Nanoindentation	Human vertebra	2	13.4	2.0
Zysset et al., 1998[148]	Nanoindentation	Human femoral neck	8	11.4	5.6
Hou et al., 1998[149]	FEM	Human vertebra	28	5.7	1.6
Ladd et al., 1998[150]	FEM	Human vertebra	5	6.6	1.0
Turner et al., 1999[145]	Nanoindentation	Human distal femur	1	18.1	1.7
	Ultrasound			17.5	1.1
Niebur et al., 2000[146]	FEM	Bovine tibia	7	18.7	3.4

studies that the yield strains for trabecular tissue are similar to those for cortical bone, being higher in compression than in tension.[149] Experimental studies on machined microbeams have shown that the fatigue strength of trabecular tissue is lower than that of cortical tissue.[151]

10.7 CONCLUDING REMARKS

The field of bone mechanics has evolved to a very sophisticated level where mechanical properties of cortical and trabecular bone are available for many anatomic sites. Studies have also reported on the effects of bone density, aging, and disease on these properties, enabling researchers to perform highly detailed specimen-specific analyses on whole bone and bone-implant systems. We have reviewed here much of that literature. Our focus was on data for human bone, although we reported bovine data when no other reliable data were available. One important theme in bone mechanics is to account for the substantial heterogeneity in bone properties that can occur for both cortical and trabecular bone, particularly for the latter. The heterogeneity results from aging, disease, and natural interindividual biological variation and thus occurs longitudinally and cross-sectionally in populations. The heterogeneity also exists spatially within bones. Successful structural analysis depends on appreciation of this heterogeneity so that appropriate material properties are used for the analysis at hand. Improved understanding of the micromechanics and damage behaviors of bone is also leading to unique insight into mechanisms of disease and their treatment as well as biological remodeling and tissue engineering. While a number of excellent texts are available for more detailed study of these topics and many of those presented here,[19,79,152,153] it is hoped that this review will provide a concise basis for practical engineering analysis of bone.

ACKNOWLEDGMENTS

Support is gratefully acknowledged from NIH (AR41481, AR43784), NSF (BES-9625030), and The Miller Institute for Basic Research in Science, Berkeley, Calif.

REFERENCES

1. Burr, D. B., Forwood, M. R., Fyhrie, D. P., Martin, R. B., Schaffler, M. B., and Turner, C. H. (1997), Bone microdamage and skeletal fragility in osteoporotic and stress fractures, *J. Bone Miner. Res.* **12**(1):6–15.

2. Burr, D. B., Martin, R. B., Schaffler, M. B., and Radin, E. L. (1985), Bone remodeling in response to in vivo fatigue microdamage, *J. Biomech.* **18**(3):189–200.
3. Gong, J. K., Arnold, J. S., and Cohn, S. H. (1964), Composition of trabecular and cortical bone, *Anat. Rec.* **149**:325–332.
4. Lowenstam, H. A., and Weiner, S. (1989), *On Biomineralization*, Oxford University Press, New York.
5. Herring, G. (1972), The organic matrix of bone, in G. Bourne (ed.), *The Biochemistry and Physiology of Bone*, 2d ed., Vol. 1, pp. 127–189, Academic Press, New York.
6. Hodge, A. J., and Petruska, J. A. (1963), Recent studies with the electron microscope on ordered aggregates of the tropocollagen molecule, in G. N. Ramachandran (ed.) *Aspects of Protein Structure*, Academic Press, London, pp. 289–300.
7. Wainwright, S., Gosline, J., and Biggs, W. (1976), *Mechanical Design in Organisms*, Halsted Press, New York.
8. Burr, D. B., Schaffler, M. B., and Frederickson, R. G. (1988), Composition of the cement line and its possible mechanical role as a local interface in human compact bone, *J. Biomech.* **21**(11):939–945.
9. Lakes, R., and Saha, S. (1979), Cement line motion in bone, *Science* **204**(4392):501–503.
10. Gibson, L. J., and Ashby, M. F. (1997), *Cellular Solids: Structures & Properties*, 2d ed., Pergamon Press, Oxford, U.K.
11. Tortora, G. (1983), *Principles of Human Anatomy,* 3d ed., Harper & Row, New York.
12. McCalden, R. W., McGeough, J. A., Barker, M. B., and Court-Brown, C. M. (1993), Age-related changes in the tensile properties of cortical bone: The relative importance of changes in porosity, mineralization, and microstructure, *J. Bone Joint Surg.* **75A**(8):1193–1205.
13. Morgan, E. F., and Keaveny, T. M., (2001), Dependence of yield strain of human trabecular bone on anatomic site, *J. Biomech.* **34**(5):569–577.
14. Snyder, B. D., Piazza, S., Edwards, W. T., and Hayes, W. C. (1993), Role of trabecular morphology in the etiology of age-related vertebral fractures, *Calcif. Tissue Int.* **53S**(1):S14–S22.
15. Kopperdahl, D. L., and Keaveny, T. M. (1998), Yield strain behavior of trabecular bone, *J. Biomech.* **31**(7):601–608.
16. Linde, F., Hvid, I., and Pongsoipetch, B. (1989), Energy absorptive properties of human trabecular bone specimens during axial compression, *J. Orthop. Res.* **7**(3):432–439.
17. McCalden, R. W., McGeough, J. A., and Court-Brown, C. M. (1997), Age-related changes in the compressive strength of cancellous bone: The relative importance of changes in density and trabecular architecture, *J. Bone Joint Surg.* **79A**(3):421–427.
18. Hildebrand, T., Laib, A., Müller, R., Dequeker, J., and Rüegsegger, P. (1999), Direct three-dimensional morphometric analysis of human cancellous bone: Microstructural data from spine, femur, iliac crest, and calcaneus, *J. Bone Miner. Res.* **14**(7):1167–1174.
19. Cowin, S. (2001), *Bone Mechanics Handbook*, 2d ed., CRC Press, Boca Raton, Fla.
20. Odgaard, A. (1997), Three-dimensional methods for quantification of cancellous bone architecture, *Bone* **20**(4):315–328.
21. Mosekilde, L. (1989), Sex differences in age-related loss of vertebral trabecular bone mass and structure: Biomechanical consequences, *Bone* **10**(6):425–432.
22. Whitehouse, W. J. (1974), The quantitative morphology of anisotropic trabecular bone, *J. Microsc.*, **2**:153–168.
23. Goldstein, S. A., Goulet, R., and McCubbrey, D. (1993), Measurement and significance of three-dimensional architecture to the mechanical integrity of trabecular bone, *Calcif. Tissue Int.* **53S**(1):S127–S133.
24. Majumdar, S., Kothari, M., Augat, P., Newitt, D. C., Link, T. M., Lin, J. C., Lang, T., Lu, Y., and Genant, H. K. (1998), High-resolution magnetic resonance imaging: Three-dimensional trabecular bone architecture and biomechanical properties, *Bone* **22**(5):445–454.
25. Ulrich, D., Van Rietbergen, B., Laib, A., and Rueegsegger, P. (1999), The ability of three-dimensional structural indices to reflect mechanical aspects of trabecular bone, *Bone* **25**(1):55–60.
26. Reilly, D. T., and Burstein, A. H. (1975), The elastic and ultimate properties of compact bone tissue, *J. Biomech.* **8**:393–405.
27. Carter, D. R., and Hayes, W. C. (1977), The compressive behavior of bone as a two-phase porous structure, *J. Bone Joint Surg.* **59A**:954–962.

28. Schaffler, M. B., and Burr, D. B., (1988), Stiffness of compact bone: Effects of porosity and density, *J. Biomech.* **21**(1):13–16.

29. Currey, J. D. (1988), The effect of porosity and mineral content on the Young's modulus of elasticity of compact bone, *J. Biomech.* **21**(2):131–139.

30. Burstein, A. H., Reilly, D. T., and Martens, M. (1976), Aging of bone tissue: Mechanical properties, *J. Bone Joint Surg.* **58A**(1):82–86.

31. Zioupos, P., and Currey, J. D. (1998), Changes in the stiffness, strength, and toughness of human cortical bone with age, *Bone* **22**(1):57–66.

32. McElhaney, J. H., and Byars, E. F. (1965), Dynamic response of biological materials, in *Proc. Amer. Soc. Mech. Eng.*, ASME 65-WA/HUF-9:8, Chicago.

33. Lakes, R. S. (1982), Dynamical study of couple stress effects in human compact bone, *J. Biomech. Eng.* **104**(1):6–11.

34. Lakes, R. S., Katz, J. L., and Sternstein, S. S. (1979), Viscoelastic properties of wet cortical bone: I. Torsional and biaxial studies, *J. Biomech.* **12**(9):657–678.

35. Fischer, R. A., Arms, S. W., Pope, M. H., and Seligson, D. (1986), Analysis of the effect of using two different strain rates on the acoustic emission in bone, *J. Biomech.* **19**(2):119–127.

36. Cezayirlioglu, H., Bahniuk, E., Davy, D. T., and Heiple, K. G. (1985), Anisotropic yield behavior of bone under combined axial force and torque, *J. Biomech.* **18**(1):61–69.

37. Cowin, S. C. (1989), *Bone Mechanics*, CRC Press, Boca Raton, Fla.

38. Fondrk, M. T. (1989), An experimental and analytical investigation into the nonlinear constitutive equations of cortical bone, Ph.D. thesis, Case Western Reserve University, Cleveland.

39. Courtney, A. C., Hayes, W. C., and Gibson, L. J. (1996), Age-related differences in post-yield damage in human cortical bone: Experiment and model, *J. Biomech.* **29**(11):1463–1471.

40. Fondrk, M. T., Bahniuk, E. H., and Davy, D. T. (1999), A damage model for nonlinear tensile behavior of cortical bone, *J. Biomech. Eng.* **121**:533–541.

41. Wright, T. M., Vosburgh, F., and Burstein, A. H. (1981), Permanent deformation of compact bone monitored by acoustic emission, *J. Biomech.* **14**(6):405–409.

42. Zioupos, P., Currey, J. D., and Sedman, A. J. (1994), An examination of the micromechanics of failure of bone and antler by acoustic emission tests and laser scanning confocal microscopy, *Med. Eng. Phys.* **16**(3):203–212.

43. Carter, D. R., Caler, W. E., Spengler, D. M., and Frankel, V. H. (1981), Fatigue behavior of adult cortical bone: The influence of mean strain and strain range, *Acta Orthop. Scand.* **52**(5):481–490.

44. Pattin, C. A., Caler, W. E., and Carter, D. R. (1996), Cyclic mechanical property degradation during fatigue loading of cortical bone, *J. Biomech.* **29**(1):69–79.

45. Schaffler, M. B., Radin, E. L., and Burr, D. B. (1990), Long-term fatigue behavior of compact bone at low strain magnitude and rate, *Bone* **11**(5):321–326.

46. Carter, D. R., Caler, W. E., Spengler, D. M., and Frankel, V. H. (1981), Uniaxial fatigue of human cortical bone: The influence of tissue physical characteristics, *J. Biomech.* **14**(7):461–470.

47. Caler, W. E., and Carter, D. R. (1989), Bone creep-fatigue damage accumulation, *J. Biomech.* **22**(6–7):625–635.

48. Frost, H. M. (1960), Presence of microscopic cracks in vivo in bone, *Bull. Henry Ford Hosp.* **8**:27–35.

49. Schaffler, M. B., Choi, K., and Milgrom, C. (1995), Aging and matrix microdamage accumulation in human compact bone, *Bone* **17**(6):521–525.

50. Norman, T. L., and Wang, Z. (1997), Microdamage of human cortical bone: Incidence and morphology in long bones, *Bone* **20**(4):375–379.

51. Brown, C. U., Yeni, Y. N., and Norman, T. L. (2000), Fracture toughness is dependent on bone location: A study of the femoral neck, femoral shaft, and the tibial shaft, *J. Biomed. Mater. Res.* **49**(3):380–389.

52. Melvin, J. W. (1993), Fracture mechanics of bone, *J. Biomech. Eng.* **115**(4B):549–554.

53. Yeni, Y. N., Brown, C. U., and Norman, T. L. (1998), Influence of bone composition and apparent density on fracture toughness of the human femur and tibia, *Bone* **22**(1):79–84.

54. Yeni, Y. N., Brown, C. U., Wang, Z., and Norman, T. L. (1997), The influence of bone morphology on fracture toughness of the human femur and tibia, *Bone* **21**(5):453–459.

55. Landis, W. J. (1995), The strength of a calcified tissue depends in part on the molecular structure and organization of its constituent mineral crystals in their organic matrix, *Bone* **16**(5):533–544.
56. Katz, J. L. (1971), Hard tissue as a composite material: I. Bounds on the elastic behavior, *J. Biomech.* **4**(5):455–473.
57. Mammone, J. F., and Hudson, S. M. (1993), Micromechanics of bone strength and fracture, *J. Biomech.* **26**(4–5):439–446.
58. Gottesman, T., and Hashin, Z. (1980), Analysis of viscoelastic behaviour of bones on the basis of microstructure, *J. Biomech.* **13**(2):89–96.
59. Katz, J. L. (1981), Composite material models for cortical bone, in S. C. Cowin (ed.), *Mechanical Properties of Bone: Proceedings of the Joint ASME-ASCE Applied Mechanics, Fluids Engineering, and Bioengineering Conference, Boulder, Colorado, June 22–24, 1981*, Vol. 45, pp. 171–184, American Society of Mechanical Engineers, New York.
60. Krajcinovic, D., Trafimow, J., and Sumarac, D. (1987), Simple constitutive model for cortical bone, *J. Biomech.* **20**(8):779–784.
61. Braidotti, P., Branca, F. P., and Stagni, L. (1997), Scanning electron microscopy of human cortical bone failure surfaces, *J. Biomech.* **30**(2):155–162.
62. Pidaparti, R. M., Chandran, A., Takano, Y., and Turner, C. H. (1996), Bone mineral lies mainly outside collagen fibrils: Predictions of a composite model for osteonal bone, *J. Biomech.* **29**(7):909–916.
63. Akiva, U., Wagner, H. D., and Weiner, S. (1998), Modelling the three-dimensional elastic constants of parallel-fibred and lamellar bone, *J. Mater. Sci.* **33**(6):1497–1509.
64. Sasaki, N., Ikawa, T., and Fukuda, A. (1991), Orientation of mineral in bovine bone and the anisotropic mechanical properties of plexiform bone, *J. Biomech.* **24**(1):57–61.
65. Wagner, H. D., and Weiner, S. (1992), On the relationship between the microstructure of bone and its mechanical stiffness, *J. Biomech.* **25**(11):1311–1320.
66. McCutchen, C. W. (1975), Do mineral crystals stiffen bone by straitjacketing its collagen? *J. Theor. Biol.* **51**(1):51–58.
67. Rho, J. Y., Tsui, T. Y., and Pharr, G. M. (1997), Elastic properties of human cortical and trabecular lamellar bone measured by nanoindentation, *Biomaterials* **18**(20):1325–1330.
68. Zysset, P. K., Guo, X. E., Hoffler, C. E., Moore, K. E., and Goldstein, S. A. (1999), Elastic modulus and hardness of cortical and trabecular bone lamellae measured by nanoindentation in the human femur, *J. Biomech.* **32**(10):1005–1012.
69. Cowin, S. C., Moss-Salentijn, L., and Moss, M. L. (1991), Candidates for the mechanosensory system in bone, *J. Biomech. Eng.* **113**(2):191–197.
70. Lanyon, L. E. (1993), Osteocytes, strain detection, bone modeling and remodeling, *Calcif. Tissue Int.* **53**(Suppl. 1):S102–S106; see also Discussion, pp. S106–S107.
71. Marotti, G., Ferretti, M., Muglia, M. A., Palumbo, C., and Palazzini, S. (1992), A quantitative evaluation of osteoblast-osteocyte relationships on growing endosteal surface of rabbit tibiae, *Bone* **13**(5):363–368.
72. Mullender, M. G., and Huiskes, R. (1995), Proposal for the regulatory mechanism of Wolff's law, *J. Orthop. Res.* **13**(4):503–512.
73. Frost, H. M. (1987), Bone "mass" and the "mechanostat": A proposal, *Anat. Rec.* **219**(1):1–9.
74. Biewener, A. A., Thomason, J., Goodship, A., and Lanyon, L. E. (1983), Bone stress in the horse forelimb during locomotion at different gaits: A comparison of two experimental methods, *J. Biomech.* **16**(8):565–576.
75. Lanyon, L. E. (1984), Functional strain as a determinant for bone remodeling, *Calcif. Tissue Int.* **36**(Suppl. 1):S56–S61.
76. Turner, C. H., Owan, I., and Takano, Y. (1995), Mechanotransduction in bone: Role of strain rate, *Am. J. Physiol.* **269**(3 Pt. 1):E438–E442.
77. Fyhrie, D. P., and Carter, D. R. (1986), A unifying principle relating stress to trabecular bone morphology, *J. Orthop. Res.* **4**(3):304–317.
78. Weinans, H., Huiskes, R., and Grootenboer, H. J. (1992), The behavior of adaptive bone-remodeling simulation models, *J. Biomech.* **25**(12):1425–1441.
79. Martin, R. B., and Burr, D. B. (1989), *Structure, Function, and Adaptation of Compact Bone*, Raven Press, New York.

80. Carter, D. R., Orr, T. E., and Fyhrie, D. P. (1989), Relationships between loading history and femoral cancellous bone architecture, *J. Biomech.* **22**(3):231–244.

81. Mullender, M. G., Huiskes, R., and Weinans, H. (1994), A physiological approach to the simulation of bone remodeling as a self-organizational control process, *J. Biomech.* **27**(11):1389–1394.

82. Huiskes, R., Weinans, H., and van Rietbergen, R. (1992), The relationship between stress shielding and bone resorption around total hip stems and the effects of flexible materials, *Clin. Orthop.* **274**:124–134.

83. Morgan, E. F., Yeh, O. C., Chang, W. C., and Keaveny, T. M. (2001), Non-linear behavior of trabecular bone at small strains, *J. Biomech. Eng.* **123**(1):1–9.

84. Mosekilde, L., and Mosekilde, L. (1986), Normal vertebral body size and compressive strength: Relations to age and to vertebral and iliac trabecular bone compressive strength, *Bone* **7**:207–212.

85. Mosekilde, L., Mosekilde, L., and Danielsen, C. C. (1987), Biomechanical competence of vertebral trabecular bone in relation to ash density and age in normal individuals, *Bone* **8**(2):79–85.

86. Hipp, J. A., Rosenberg, A. E., and Hayes, W. C. (1992), Mechanical properties of trabecular bone within and adjacent to osseous metastases, *J. Bone Miner. Res.* **7**(10):1165–1171.

87. Pugh, J. W., Radin, E. L., and Rose, R. M. (1974), Quantitative studies of human subchondral cancellous bone: Its relationship to the state of its overlying cartilage, *J. Bone Joint Surg.* **56A**(2):313–321.

88. Goldstein, S. A., Wilson, D. L., Sonstegard, D. A., and Matthews, L. S. (1983), The mechanical properties of human tibial trabecular bone as a function of metaphyseal location, *J. Biomech.* **16**(12):965–969.

89. Ciarelli, M. J., Goldstein, S. A., Kuhn, J. L., Cody, D. D., and Brown, M. B. (1991), Evaluation of orthogonal mechanical properties and density of human trabecular bone from the major metaphyseal regions with materials testing and computed tomography, *J. Orthop. Res.* **9**(5):674–682.

90. Goulet, R. W., Goldstein, S. A., Ciarelli, M. J., Kuhn, J. L., Brown, M. B., and Feldkamp, L. A. (1994), The relationship between the structural and orthogonal compressive properties of trabecular bone, *J. Biomech.* **27**(4):375–389.

91. Linde, F., Pongsoipetch, B., Frich, L. H., and Hvid, I. (1990), Three-axial strain controlled testing applied to bone specimens from the proximal tibial epiphysis, *J. Biomech.* **23**(11):1167–1172.

92. Townsend, P. R., Raux, P., Rose, R. M., Miegel, R. E., and Radin, E. L. (1975), The distribution and anisotropy of the stiffness of cancellous bone in the human patella, *J. Biomech.* **8**(6):363–367.

93. Ford, C. M., and Keaveny, T. M. (1996), The dependence of shear failure properties of bovine tibial trabecular bone on apparent density and trabecular orientation, *J. Biomech.* **29**:1309–1317.

94. Keaveny, T. M., Wachtel, E. F., Ford, C. M., and Hayes, W. C. (1994), Differences between the tensile and compressive strengths of bovine tibial trabecular bone depend on modulus, *J. Biomech.* **27**:1137–1146.

95. Hansson, T. H., Keller, T. S., and Panjabi, M. M. (1987), A study of the compressive properties of lumbar vertebral trabeculae: Effects of tissue characteristics, *Spine* **12**(1):56–62.

96. Hvid, I., Bentzen, S. M., Linde, F., Mosekilde, L., and Pongsoipetch, B. (1989), X-ray quantitative computed tomography: The relations to physical properties of proximal tibial trabecular bone specimens, *J. Biomech.* **22**(8–9):837–844.

97. Hvid, I., Jensen, N. C., Bunger, C., Solund, K., and Djurhuus, J. C. (1985), Bone mineral assay: Its relation to the mechanical strength of cancellous bone, *Eng. Med.* **14**:79–83.

98. Rohl, L., Larsen, E., Linde, F., Odgaard, A., and Jorgensen, J. (1991), Tensile and compressive properties of cancellous bone, *J. Biomech.* **24**(12):1143–1149.

99. Chang, W. C. W., Christensen, T. M., Pinilla, T. P., and Keaveny, T. M. (1999), Isotropy of uniaxial yield strains for bovine trabecular bone, *J. Orthop. Res.* **17**:582–585.

100. Turner, C. H. (1989), Yield behavior of bovine cancellous bone, *J. Biomech. Eng.* **111**(3):256–260.

101. Keaveny, T. M., Wachtel, E. F., Zadesky, S. P., and Arramon, Y. P. (1999), Application of the Tsai-Wu quadratic multiaxial failure criterion to bovine trabecular bone, *J. Biomech. Eng.* **121**:99–107.

102. Linde, F., and Hvid, I. (1989), The effect of constraint on the mechanical behaviour of trabecular bone specimens, *J. Biomech.* **22**(5):485–490.

103. Lotz, J. C., Gerhart, T. N., and Hayes, W. C. (1990), Mechanical properties of trabecular bone from the proximal femur: A quantitative CT study, *J. Comput. Assist. Tomogr.* **14**(1):107–114.

104. Van Rietbergen, B., Weinans, H., Huiskes, R., and Odgaard, A. (1995), A new method to determine trabecular bone elastic properties and loading using micromechanical finite element models, *J. Biomech.* **28**(1):69–81.
105. Kinney, J. H., Lane, N. E., and Haupt, D. L. (1995), In vivo three-dimensional microscopy of trabecular bone, *J. Bone Miner. Res.* **10**(2):264–270.
106. Kuhn, J. L., Goldstein, S. A., Feldkamp, L. A., Goulet, R. W., and Jesion, G. (1990), Evaluation of a micro-computed tomography system to study trabecular bone structure, *J. Orthop. Res.* **8**(6):833–842.
107. Beck, J. D., Canfield, B. L., Haddock, S. M., Chen, T. J. H., Kothari, M., and Keaveny, T. M. (1997), Three-dimensional imaging of trabecular bone using the computer numerically controlled milling technique, *Bone* **21**:281–287.
108. Yang, G., Kabel, J., Van Rietbergen, B., Odgaard, A., Huiskes, R., and Cowin, S. (1999), The anisotropic Hooke's law for cancellous bone and wood, *J. Elasticity* **53**:125–146.
109. Zysset, P. K., Goulet, R. W., and Hollister, S. J. (1998), A global relationship between trabecular bone morphology and homogenized elastic properties, *J. Biomech. Eng.* **120**(5):640–646.
110. Odgaard, A., Kabel, J., an Rietbergen, B., Dalstra, M., and Huiskes, R. (1997), Fabric and elastic principal directions of cancellous bone are closely related, *J. Biomech.* **30**(5):487–495.
111. Fenech, C. M., and Keaveny, T. M. (1999), A cellular solid criterion for predicting the axial-shear failure properties of trabecular bone, *J. Biomech. Eng.* **121**:414–422.
112. Stone, J. L., Beaupre, G. S., and Hayes, W. C. (1983), Multiaxial strength characteristics of trabecular bone, *J. Biomech.* **16**(9):743–752.
113. Niebur, G. L., and Keaveny, T. M. (2001), Trabecular bone exhibits multiple failure surfaces in biaxial loading, *Trans. Orthop. Res. Soc.* **26**:517.
114. Keaveny, T. M., Wachtel, E. F., and Kopperdahl, D. L. (1999), Mechanical behavior of human trabecular bone after overloading, *J. Orthop. Res.* **17**:346–353.
115. Keaveny, T. M., Wachtel, E. F., Guo, X. E., and Hayes, W. C. (1994), Mechanical behavior of damaged trabecular bone, *J. Biomech.* **27**(11):1309–1318.
116. Zysset, P. K., and Curnier, A. (1996), A 3D damage model for trabecular bone based on fabric tensors, *J. Biomech.* **29**(12):1549–1558.
117. Fondrk, M., Bahniuk, E., Davy, D. T., and Michaels, C. (1988), Some viscoplastic characteristics of bovine and human cortical bone, *J. Biomech.* **21**(8):623–630.
118. Linde, F., Norgaard, P., Hvid, I., Odgaard, A., and Soballe, K. (1991), Mechanical properties of trabecular bone: Dependency on strain rate, *J. Biomech.* **24**(9):803–809.
119. Ochoa, J. A., Sanders, A. P., Kiesler, T. W., Heck, D. A., Toombs, J. P., Brandt, K. D., and Hillberry, B. M. (1997), In vivo observations of hydraulic stiffening in the canine femoral head, *J. Biomech. Eng.* **119**(1):103–108.
120. Zilch, H., Rohlmann, A., Bergmann, G., and Kolbel, R. (1980), Material properties of femoral cancellous bone in axial loading: II. Time dependent properties, *Arch. Orthop. Trauma Surg.* **97**(4):257–262.
121. Deligianni, D. D., Maris, A., and Missirlis, Y. F. (1994), Stress relaxation behaviour of trabecular bone specimens, *J. Biomech.* **27**(12):1469–1476.
122. Linde, F., Hvid, I., and Madsen, F. (1992), The effect of specimen geometry on the mechanical behaviour of trabecular bone specimens, *J. Biomech.* **25**:359–368.
123. Odgaard, A., and Linde, F. (1991), The underestimation of Young's modulus in compressive testing of cancellous bone specimens, *J. Biomech.* **24**(8):691–698.
124. Zhu, M., Keller, T. S., and Spengler, D. M. (1994), Effects of specimen load-bearing and free surface layers on the compressive mechanical properties of cellular materials, *J. Biomech.* **27**(1):57–66.
125. Keaveny, T. M., Borchers, R. E., Gibson, L. J., and Hayes, W. C. (1993), Theoretical analysis of the experimental artifact in trabecular bone compressive modulus, *J. Biomech.* **26**(4–5):599–607.
126. Keaveny, T. M., Pinilla, T. P., Crawford, R. P., Kopperdahl, D. L., and Lou, A (1997), Systematic and random errors in compression testing of trabecular bone, *J. Orthop. Res.* **15**:101–110.
127. Keaveny, T. M., Borchers, R. E., Gibson, L. J., and Hayes, W. C. (1993), Trabecular bone modulus and strength can depend on specimen geometry, *J. Biomech.* **26**:991–1000.
128. Keaveny, T. M., Guo, X. E., Wachtel, E. F., McMahon, T. A., and Hayes, W. C. (1994), Trabecular bone exhibits fully linear elastic behavior and yields at low strains, *J. Biomech.* **27**(9):1127–1136.

129. Turner, C. H., and Cowin, S. C. (1988), Errors introduced by off-axis measurements of the elastic properties of bone, *J. Biomech.* **110**:213–214.

130. Cody, D. D., Gross, G. J., Hou, F. J., Spencer, H. J., Goldstein, S. A., and Fyhrie, D. P. (1999), Femoral strength is better predicted by finite element models than QCT and DXA, *J. Biomech.* **32**(10):1013–1020.

131. Keyak, J. H., Meagher, J. M., Skinner, H. B., and Mote, C. D., Jr. (1990), Automated three-dimensional finite element modelling of bone: A new method, *J. Biomed. Eng.* **12**(5):389–397.

132. Keyak, J. H., Rossi, S. A., Jones, K. A., and Skinner, H. B. (1998), Prediction of femoral fracture load using automated finite element modeling, *J. Biomech.* **31**:125–133.

133. Keyak, J. H., and Skinner, H. B. (1992), Three-dimensional finite element modelling of bone: Effects of element size, *J. Biomed. Eng.* **14**(6):483–489.

134. Lotz, J. C., Cheal, E. J., and Hayes, W. C. (1991), Fracture prediction for the proximal femur using finite element models: I. Linear analysis, *J. Biomech. Eng.* **113**(4):353–360.

135. Lotz, J. C., Cheal, E. J., and Hayes, W. C. (1991), Fracture prediction for the proximal femur using finite element models: II. Nonlinear analysis, *J. Biomech. Eng.* **113**(4):361–365.

136. Cheal, E. J., Spector, M., and Hayes, W. C. (1992), Role of loads and prosthesis material properties on the mechanics of the proximal femur after total hip arthroplasty, *J. Orthop. Res.* **10**(3):405–422.

137. Keaveny, T. M., and Bartel, D. L. (1995), Mechanical consequences of bone ingrowth in a hip prosthesis inserted without cement, *J. Bone Joint Surg.* **77A**:911–923.

138. Kopperdahl, D. L., and Keaveny, T. M. (2002), Quantitative computed tomography estimates of the mechanical properties of human vertebral trabecular bone, *J. Orthop. Res.* (in press).

139. Choi, K., Kuhn, J. L., Ciarelli, M. J., and Goldstein, S. A. (1990), The elastic moduli of human subchondral, trabecular, and cortical bone tissue and the size-dependency of cortical bone modulus, *J. Biomech.* **23**(11):1103–1113.

140. Kuhn, J. L., Goldstein, S. A., Choi, K., London, M., Feldkamp, L. A., and Matthews, L. S. (1989), Comparison of the trabecular and cortical tissue moduli from human iliac crests, *J. Orthop. Res.* **7**(6):876–884.

141. Mente, P. L., and Lewis, J. L. (1989), Experimental method for the measurement of the elastic modulus of trabecular bone tissue, *J. Orthop. Res.* **7**(3):456–461.

142. Ryan, S. D., and Williams, J. L. (1989), Tensile testing of rodlike trabeculae excised from bovine femoral bone, *J. Biomech.* **22**(4):351–355.

143. Ashman, R. B., and Rho, J. Y. (1988), Elastic modulus of trabecular bone material, *J. Biomech.* **21**(3):177–181.

144. Rho, J. Y., Ashman, R. B., and Turner, C. H. (1993), Young's modulus of trabecular and cortical bone material: Ultrasonic and microtensile measurements, *J. Biomech.* **26**:111–119.

145. Turner, C. H., Rho, J., Takano, Y., Tsui, T. Y., and Pharr, G. M. (1999), The elastic properties of trabecular and cortical bone tissues are similar: Results from two microscopic measurement techniques, *J. Biomech.* **32**(4):437–441.

146. Niebur, G. L., Feldstein, M. J., Yuen, J. C., Chen, T. J., and Keaveny, T. M. (2000), High-resolution finite element models with tissue strength asymmetry accurately predict failure of trabecular bone, *J. Biomech.* **33**:1575–1583.

147. Guo, X. E., and Goldstein, S. A. (1997), Is trabecular bone tissue different from cortical bone tissue? *Forma* **12**:185–196.

148. Zysset, P. K., Guo, X. E., Hoffler, C. E., Moore, K. E., and Goldstein, S. A. (1998), Mechanical properties of human trabecular bone lamellae quantified by nanoindentation, *Technol. Health Care* **6**(5–6):429–432.

149. Hou, F. J., Lang, S. M., Hoshaw, S. J., Reimann, D. A., and Fyhrie, D. P. (1998), Human vertebral body apparent and hard tissue stiffness, *J. Biomech.* **31**(11):1009–1015.

150. Ladd, A. J., Kinney, J. H., Haupt, D. L., and Goldstein, S. A. (1998), Finite-element modeling of trabecular bone: Comparison with mechanical testing and determination of tissue modulus, *J. Orthop. Res.* **16**(5):622–628.

151. Choi, K., and Goldstein, S. A. (1992), A comparison of the fatigue behavior of human trabecular and cortical bone tissue, *J. Biomech.* **25**(12):1371–1381.

152. Currey, J. (1984), *The Mechanical Adaptations of Bones*, Princeton University Press, Princeton, N.J.

153. Martin, R., Burr, D., and Sharkey, N. (1998), *Skeletal Tissue Mechanics*, Springer-Verlag, New York.

CHAPTER 11
BIOMECHANICS OF THE FOOT AND KNEE

Paul Grimshaw
University of Adelaide, Adelaide, Australia

Chris Jones
Independent Researcher, Adelaide, Australia

Merilyn Lock
University of South Australia, Adelaide, Australia

11.1 INTRODUCTION

The objective of this chapter is to introduce the basic biomechanics of the lower limb and more detailed biomechanics of the knee joint. The following sections provide an overview of the foot and ankle joints including their impact on the knee, followed by a description of knee joint biomechanics with an emphasis on the knee joint ligaments. This chapter also discusses injury to the anterior cruciate ligament, the impact on knee joint biomechanics, and associated long-term outcomes. The authors propose a contemporary and critical view of knee joint biomechanics.

11.2 THE FOOT AND THE LOWER EXTREMITY

The foot consists of numerous anatomical structures including over 30 joints (Fig. 11.1). Three of the major joints in the foot are the ankle (talocrural), subtalar, and midtarsal or transverse joints.

Figures 11.2 and 11.3 show the sagittal and transverse plane motion of the lower extremity during the gait cycle (heel strike of one foot to heel strike of the same foot) and during stance (contact with the ground) and swing (no contact with the ground) throughout normal walking. However, it is important to note that in walking there are periods of double (both feet on the ground) and single (one foot on the ground) support.

The ankle joint (Fig. 11.4) consists of the talar trochlear surfaces of the distal tibia and fibula. The axis of this joint is the major axis of free foot motion, which is formed by the articulation of the talus with the tibial and fibular malleoli. As a result of the obliquity of the ankle joint axes of rotation if the foot is raised from the floor, plantar flexion will cause the foot to move laterally. When the foot is weight-bearing, plantar and dorsiflexion can only be achieved if there is rotation of the tibia and

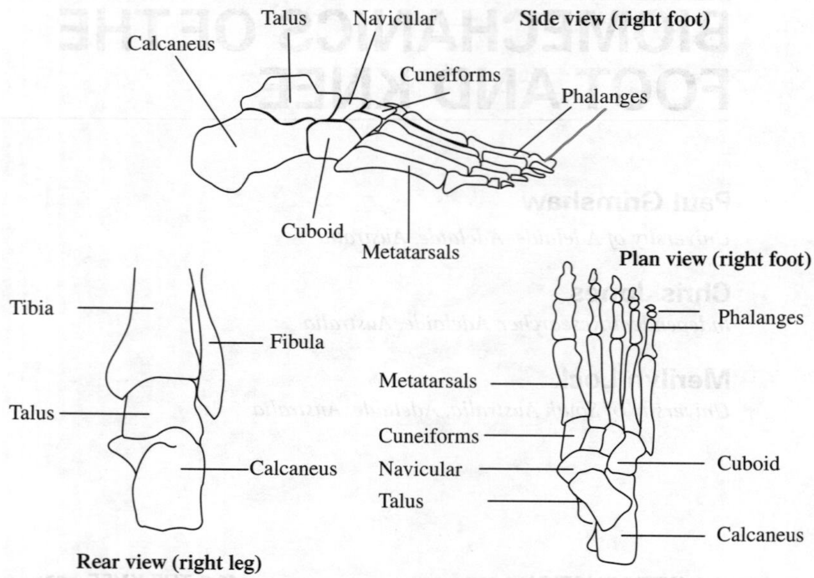

FIGURE 11.1 The major anatomical structures of the foot. [*Adapted from the work of Wells and Luttgens (1976).*]

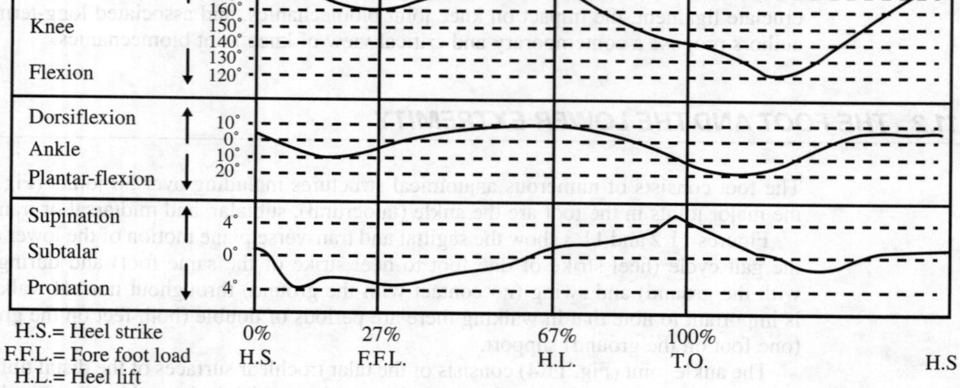

FIGURE 11.2 Sagittal plane motion of the lower extremity during the gait cycle. [*Adapted from the work of Root et al. (1977).*]

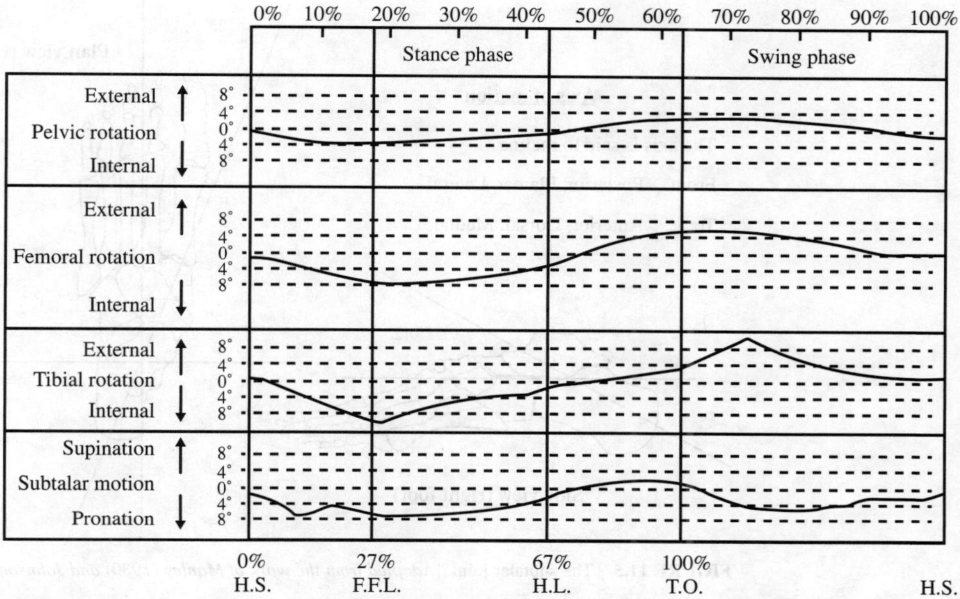

FIGURE 11.3 Transverse plane motion of the lower extremity during the gait cycle. [*Adapted from the work of Root et al. (1977).*]

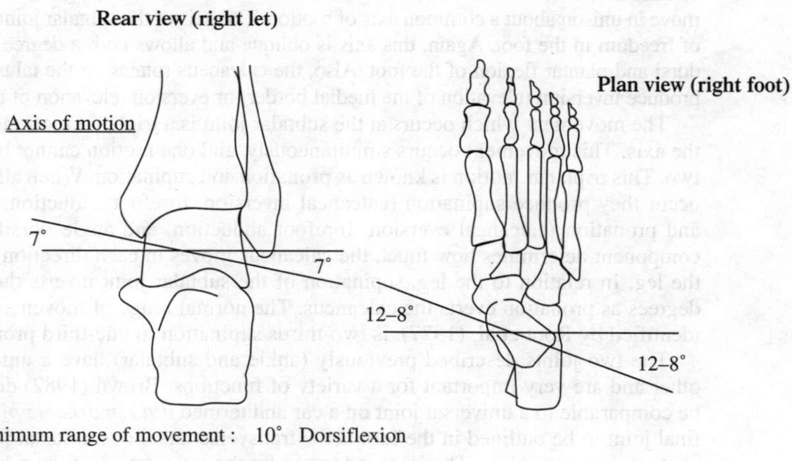

FIGURE 11.4 The ankle joint. [*Adapted from the work of Manley (1980) and Johnson (1981).*]

fibula. Normally, there is an insignificant degree of frontal or transverse plane motion when the foot is not allowed to dorsi/plantar flex. The foot abducts during dorsiflexion and adducts during plantarflexion. This transverse movement of the foot dampens the effect upon transverse leg rotation. The ankle joint rotation forces the subtalar and midtarsal joints into more supination during propulsion. Thus, not all transverse rotation of the leg, which is associated with locomotion, is reflected into the foot, some is absorbed by opposite rotation at the ankle as it moves through dorsiflexion during the stance phase (Johnson, 1981; Manley, 1980; Root et al., 1977).

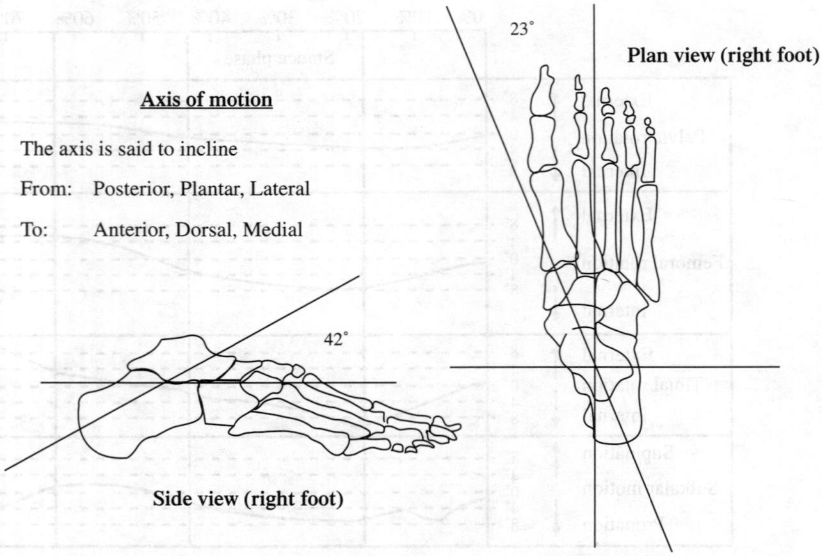

FIGURE 11.5 The subtalar joint. [*Adapted from the work of Manley (1980) and Johnson (1981).*]

The subtalar joint (Fig. 11.5) is composed of three articulations between the proximal surface of the calcaneus and the distal surface of the talus. Within the normal range of motion, the three articulations move in unison about a common axis of motion. The axis of the subtalar joint is the second critical degree of freedom in the foot. Again, this axis is oblique and allows both a degree of abduction-adduction and dorsi and plantar flexion of the foot. Also, the calcaneus rotates on the talus about the foot's midline to produce inversion (elevation of the medial border) or eversion (elevation of the lateral border).

The movement which occurs at the subtalar joint is a triplanar motion because of the obliquity of the axis. This movement occurs simultaneously, and one motion cannot be present without the other two. This triplanar motion is known as pronation and supination. When all of the subtalar movements occur they produce supination (calcaneal inversion, forefoot adduction, and ankle plantar flexion) and pronation (calcaneal eversion, forefoot abduction, and ankle dorsiflexion). The frontal plane component determines how much the calcaneus moves in each direction relative to the long axis of the leg. In relation to the leg, supination of the subtalar joint inverts the calcaneus twice as many degrees as pronation everts the calcaneus. The normal range of movement of these two motions, as identified by Root et al. (1977), is two-thirds supination to one-third pronation.

The two joints described previously (ankle and subtalar) have a unique relationship with each other and are very important for a variety of functions. Brown (1982) described the relationship to be comparable to a universal joint on a car and termed it *a remarkable piece of Bioengineering*. The final joint to be outlined in the foot is the transverse tarsal or midtarsal joint (sometimes referred to as the transverse joint). The joint is formed by the articulation of the talus on the navicular and the calcaneus on the cuboid. Figure 11.6 illustrates this joint in more detail. The midtarsal joint consists of two joints which act as a functional unit about two common axes. The two joints are known as the talonavicular and the calcaneocuboid joints. Each axis of motion allows the movements of pronation and supination but because they are each angled in relation to the three body planes, the movements are the triplane motions of supination and pronation.

The relatively large talar surface, which articulates with the adjacent surface of the navicular, allows inversion and eversion of the foot to occur at the talonavicular joint. The longitudinal axis, therefore, allows inversion/eversion of the forefoot with pronation/supination, while the free motion available at the calcaneocuboid joint is limited mainly to adduction and abduction. Hence, the oblique axis allows major degrees of adduction/abduction and dorsi/plantar flexion, with the

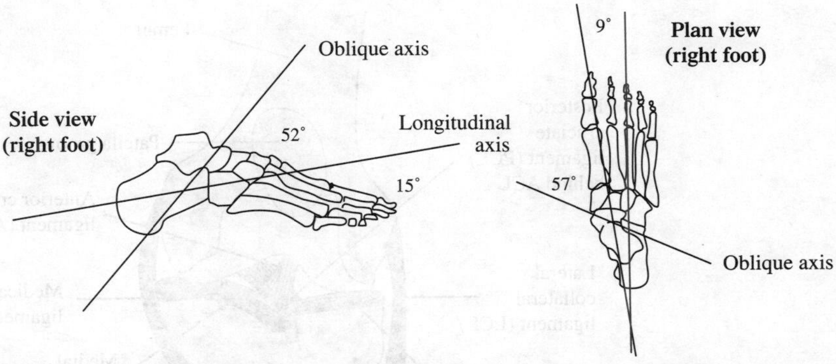

FIGURE 11.6 The midtarsal joint. [*Adapted from the work of Manley (1980) and Johnson (1981).*]

TABLE 11.1 Lower Extremity Movement during the Walking Gait Cycle

Gait phase	**Stance phase**			**Swing Phase**		
Limb Component						
Lower limb (tibia/fibula)	Internal rotation	External (outward) rotation		Internal (inward) rotation		
Ankle joint	Plantar flexion	Dorsi-flexion	Plantar flexion	Dorsi-flexion		
Subtalar joint	Pronation	Supination		Pronation		
Midtarsal joint	Free motion	Increasingly restricted		Free motion		
Gait cycle (%)	**0**	**20**	**40**	**60**	**80**	**100**
heel strike	**flat foot**	**mid stance**		**toe off**	**heel strike**	

Source: Adapted from Manley (1980).

movements of pronation and supination. With the two joint axes, the foot can perform wide ranges of movement in each plane. The advantage of the biaxial arrangement is that the foot can invert/evert with no clinically significant motion occurring in the other two planes.

As the midtarsal joint is comprised of these two minor joints, any movement in the talus or calcaneus will affect the transverse tarsal axis. In the pronated foot the axes of the talonavicular and calcaneocuboid joints are parallel to one another, allowing relatively free tarsal motion. By comparison, in the supinated foot the two axes are divergent, thus the transverse tarsal motion is restricted, and the foot is stable (Johnson, 1981, Manley, 1980; Root et al. 1977). In normal locomotion (walking and running) the body requires a flexible foot to accommodate the large variations in the external environment (mobile adapter) and then to be a rigid lever in order to push off the ground. Pronation unlocks the foot for mobile adaption while supination locks the foot for propulsion.

Pronation and supination have a unique relationship with the other structures of the lower extremity such as the knee and hip and during the stance phase the lower limb has internal rotation (inward) initially while the foot is pronating and then external rotation (outward) while it is supinating. During the swing phase the lower limb is internally rotating. Table 11.1 helps to illustrate this relationship.

11.3 THE KNEE

As a result of the relative incongruency of the articulating surfaces of the femur and tibia, other structures must play a crucial role in stabilizing the knee joint and also determining, to a major extent, its passive motion characteristics. By far the most important of these structures are the ligaments

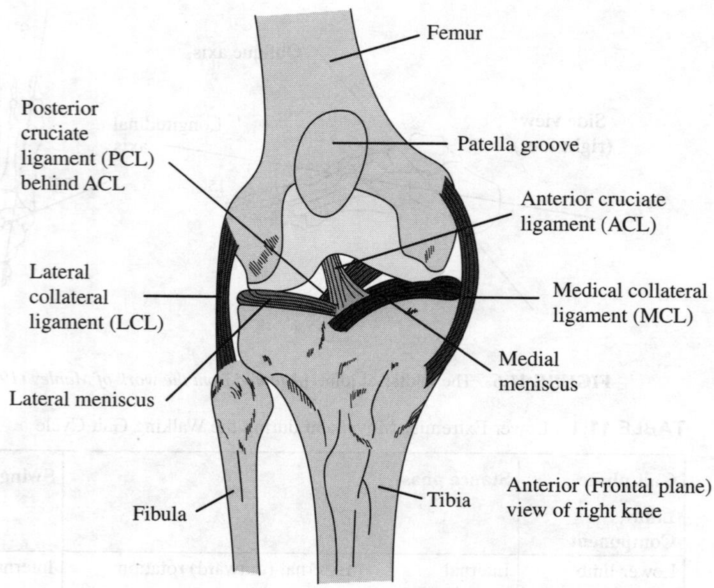

FIGURE 11.7 The ACL, PCL, MCL, and LCL human knee ligaments.

of the knee joint, which primarily are as follows: the anterior cruciate ligament (ACL), posterior cruciate ligament (PCL), medial collateral ligament (MCL), and lateral collateral ligament (LCL); an additional important ligament termed the *anterolateral ligament* (ALL) has also been confirmed (Claes et al. 2013). In a knee with sound ligaments, problems of joint stability rarely arise, but even quite modest ligamentous injuries can lead to significant degrees of functional impairment. Following injury, knee joint assessment techniques are carried out in an attempt to define the precise mechanical damage, in order to guide the clinician toward the most appropriate treatment regimen. Ligament structure and function is therefore one of the most important topics in today's orthopedic and biomechanical evaluations of the knee joint. However, despite a large amount of experimental data, conflicting opinion still exists on the precise function of individual ligaments, in particular the ACL. This chapter describes the basic ligamentous biomechanics and some current issues, which are necessary for a full understanding of the techniques used in the assessment of human knee joint instability. Figure 11.7 illustrates the location of the ACL, PCL, MCL, and LCL.

11.3.1 Knee Ligaments

Ligaments consist predominantly of type I collagen fibers arranged in a parallel orientation so that they require little or no realignment during stretch (Table 11.2).

Water accounts for the largest percentage of weight (technically mass) and volume in all tissues (60 to 80 percent), while collagen is the major solid component. On a fat-free, dry-weight basis the percentage of collagen in ligaments is 75 to 80 percent. Elastin, another protein, with stiffness significantly lower than that of collagen, also exists in ligaments but in much smaller quantities. The other major solid component of soft tissues is proteoglycans, which are noncollagenous macromolecules interwoven with collagen fibers and elastin. These contribute minimally to the tissues' elasticity but because of their enormous size, play a significant role in the time- and history-dependent viscoelastic properties in ligaments (Rosenberg, 1975). The structure of ligaments is described precisely by Viidik (1990) as a complex integration of various levels of helical organization. Three left-handed helices form the type I molecule. Five

TABLE 11.2 The Constituents of Soft Tissue

Tissue	% Total weight of water	% Fat-free dry weight		
		Collagen	Elastin	Proteoglycons
Ligament				
Cruciate	65–70	75–80	<5	2.5–3.0
Collateral	65–70	75–80	<5	1.0–1.5
Articular cartilage	70–80	60–65	Trace	10–15

Source: Adapted from Woo et al. (1976).

quartered staggered rows of these molecules are in turn assembled into a left-handed super-super helix called the microfibril. On the next level a large number of microfibrils are organized into a fibril, which appears as a right-handed super-super helix (with a diameter over 500 nm). On the following levels (fibers and fiber bundles, diameter 1 to 10 and up to 100 μm, respectively) no such helicality is found. Finally, on the fascicle level, helicality or irregular deviation only exists in specific ligaments.

11.3.2 Knee Biomechanical Function

The primary function of ligaments is to control joint displacement and therefore they must carry very large muscle and joint forces with minimal deformation. The parallel-fibered organization is uniquely designed to connect bone to bone. Joint ligaments are the strongest soft tissue structures in the human body and their strength (50 to 100 N/mm^2) is derived primarily from the two sources previously described: the type I collagen fibers and the parallel fiber arrangement. The microstructure of ligaments is stabilized by the conversion of axial stresses to lateral compression and changes in helical pitches, brought about by tensile loading. In the relaxed tissue a planar waviness is described by the collagen substance interaction. This wavy pattern is then straightened when a small tensile load is placed on the tissue. The waviness is different immediately after the release of the tension and eventually returns to the original pattern after a short resting period. Rupture of the whole ligament occurs most often in several steps in rapid sequence. The weakest point in the bone-ligament-bone unit, when tested along the major ligament fiber direction, is at the bone insertion. The ligament itself fails first only when tested with a joint angle allowing only some of the fiber bundles to take the load simultaneously.

Several questions regarding ligaments still remain, for example: is there a resting tension in a ligament, and what is the physiological working range of a ligament? A resting tension in ligaments must exist because of the tension derived from the resting muscle; however, the working range of a ligament is technically difficult to measure in an intact joint. The general biological rule, however, allows for a safety factor of at least two for ligaments and three for tendons. The ligaments of the knee are minimally strained during flexion without external loads and a delicate equilibrium is present with only a small ligament force. Large strains occur with internal and external loads and anterior and posterior forces that are even far below normal physiological loads. Hence, it appears unlikely that ligaments alone can counteract these forces, and other structures such as the muscles must be of major importance in protecting ligaments. Ligaments are nonlinear, viscoelastic materials with properties that vary with the direction of loading and the age and gender of the individual. The mechanical properties of ligaments are many and varied and have been researched by many groups over the last 30+ years. The following sections present a description of some of the prominent early research that have contributed to the understanding of the mechanical properties of knee ligaments.

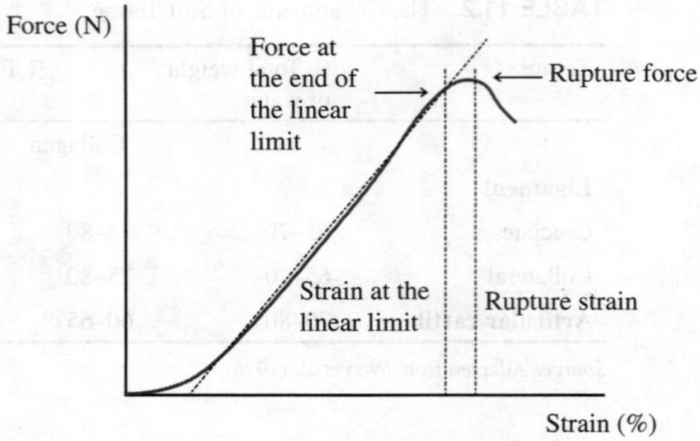

FIGURE 11.8 Force-strain diagram of a test for tensile strength on a typical human knee ligament such as the ACL.

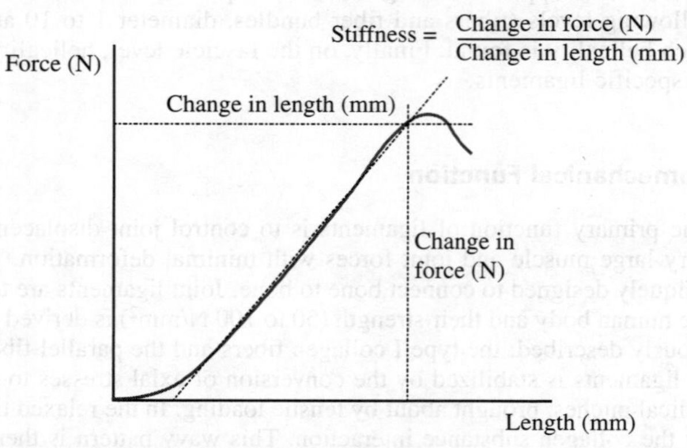

FIGURE 11.9 Definition of ligament stiffness.

11.3.3 Knee Ligament Mechanical Properties

Ligament ruptures tend to occur at ligamentous insertion points and are rarely intraligamentous. Hence, tests for rupture strength are not performed solely on the ligaments but must include their bony attachments. Rupture strength is determined by a test for tensile strength in which a force-strain diagram is graphed. The maximum of the curve is defined as the rupture strength (Fig. 11.8).

A force at the linear limit of the curve indicates the load at which stress is reversible without causing damage to the ligament. Higher forces lead first to rupture of the individual ligament structures and finally to total rupture. The strains measured at the linear limit and at the rupture force provide a measure of the extensibility of the ligament. In order to avoid the problems of calculating the Young's modulus of elasticity, many researchers have introduced the term *stiffness*. The stiffness is described by the gradient of the force deformation graph of the tensile test. Stiffness characterizes the biomechanical properties in a similar way to the Young's modulus but dispenses with the complicated determination of cross-sectional area. Figure 11.9 illustrates the stiffness variable in more detail.

The bulk of the more important early work on the mechanical properties of ligaments has been carried out primarily in four centers: *University of Western Ontario, University of Ulm,*

Ohio State University, and *University of California*. The following paragraphs outline data from each of these centers in turn.

University of Western Ontario, Canada. Kennedy et al. (1976) calculated the ultimate failure strengths of human medial collateral and anterior and posterior cruciate ligaments at two different loading rates (22.5 and 50 cm/min) using an Instron tensile testing machine. The results demonstrated that the PCL was significantly stronger than the MCL and ACL. At ultimate failure the ligaments were intact macroscopically but electron microscopy revealed that widespread disruption of the collagen fibrils may be responsible for the clinical instability present in seemingly intact ligaments. The results of the work showed that the PCL was almost twice as strong as the ACL and MCL at both strain rates. The ACL and MCL had equal strengths at both loading rates. Knee ligament injuries normally occur at fast loading rates and exact loading rates for knee ligament ruptures have not been determined. However, in this experimental work it is believed that the more rapid rate used (50 cm/min) may approach the rates experienced in the practical injury situation. It is important to note that the experimental results from this study only represent the effect of a unidirectional tensile force and are therefore not applicable to most injury situations. However, one of the more interesting possibilities is that the rarity of PCL disruption may be partly explained by its much greater strength, while conversely, the more frequent disruption of the ACL may be in part attributed to its relative weakness. Many researchers have shown that in "other animal species," ligaments have viscoelastic properties. The work of Kennedy et al. (1976) confirmed that human ligaments behave similarly, absorbing more energy and requiring more force to rupture as the loading rate is increased.

University of Ulm, West Germany. Claes (1983) conducted an investigation into the biomechanical properties of human knee ligaments. Previously, investigations into the biomechanical behavior of ligaments were carried out using measurements of the absolute or relative changes in length of the ligaments as a criterion for the stress exerted on them. Due to the lack of homogeneity of the ligaments, the irregular ligamentous cross sections and the likelihood that there is no linear correlation between the tensile force and the extension of the ligament, this study adopted a different technique. Twenty cadaveric knees were used with the ligaments and capsule left intact. Special strain gauge measuring cells were then sewn onto the collateral ligaments of the knee. The small width of the measuring cells allowed precise measurement of the various proportions of the broad MCL.

A plastic distal femur was cast into a clamping device and the free-to-move portion of the tibia was turned with a motor between 0° and 135° of knee flexion at a constant rotational velocity. The study examined the effects of flexion and allowed a valgus-varus moment of up to 4000 N·mm to be applied. The results from the measuring cells were then plotted as a function of the flexion angle. The three measuring cells located on the MCL showed different results. In extension, the forces and strains were greatest on the posterior (rear) aspect of the ligament, with the lowest values recorded on the anterior (front) aspect. As flexion increased, the tensile forces and strains decreased anteriorly and increased posteriorly. Force measurements under flexion in the neutral position (no valgus or varus loading) showed a tensile force of 20 N between 0° and 25°, which was carried largely by the anterior aspect of the ligament. The tensile forces were at a minimum between 25° and 80°, but then increased in the neutral position to a maximum of 135°. An additional valgus moment increased the tensile forces in all positions of the ligament to about three times the regular load. In this case the ventral portion carried the majority of the load. The LCL was affected by tensile forces in extension, which decreased with an increasing angle of flexion reaching zero at 40° of knee flexion. A varus moment increased the tensile force in the ligament to a maximum of about 70° of flexion. The strains measured were not proportional to the forces and revealed that during pure flexion the highest strains were around 5 percent. Under valgus and varus loading of 4000 N·mm the strains increased, but no value greater than 10 percent was recorded.

Since the forces acting on the ligament and the resulting strains are not proportional, no quantitative statement of the individual ligament load can be made. In this experiment, values greater than 40 N were never observed in the collateral ligaments under any flexion condition. Under varus and valgus and rotational loading the tensile forces on the ligaments increased until the ligaments finally

TABLE 11.3 Ligament Rupture Forces (N)

	Collateral ligaments		Cruciate ligaments	
	Medial mean (SD)	Lateral mean (SD)	Anterior mean (SD)	Posterior mean (SD)
Kennedy et al. (1976)	477 (34)		482 (28)	940 (48)
Noyes and Grood (1976)			Young: 1730 (660) Old: 734 (266)	
Trent et al. (1976)	526 (na)	384 (na)	633 (na)	571 (na)
Noyes (1977)			475 (na)	927 (na)
Piziali et al. (1980)			350–620	1315–1745
Tremblay et al. (1980)			530 (na)	670 (na)
Claes (1983)	654.2 (151.9)	354 (139.2)		

SD = standard deviation; na = information not available.

ruptured. Table 11.3 indicates the rupture loads of the ligaments from the work of Claes (1983) and the work of some other authors.

This early literature suggests that the rupture load of the PCL lies in the range 571 to 1745 N. The corresponding values for the ACL are in the range 350 to 734 N. The values for the MCL vary by as much as those for the cruciate ligaments with the average values being quoted as between 477 and 654 N. It is clear from the various sources of research that the weakest ligament of the knee is the LCL with a range of 354 to 384 N. The study by Claes (1983) further determined the rupture strengths of the MCL and LCL. A tensile test machine was adapted and used for the experiment at a test velocity of 5 cm/min on 10 fresh cadaveric knees. The rupture forces of the MCL were significantly higher (average value 654 ± 151.9 N) than those for the LCL (average value 354 ± 139.2 N). The stiffness of the MCL was found to be 93.9 N/mm and that for the LCL was 47.4 N/mm. In all cases rupture occurred at the site of ligament insertion. Rupture strains (Table 11.4) show "no notable differences" between ligament types. The published values are between 18.1 and 30.8 percent. However, Noyes and Grood (1976) quoted values of 44.3 percent for the young ACL, with the force at the linear limit averaging about 80 percent of the rupture force and the strain at the linear limit being about 65 percent of the rupture strain of the ligaments.

Important differences in stiffness values in different ligaments are demonstrated by the research presented in Table 11.4. The stiffness of the cruciate ligaments is about twice as high as that of the collaterals and no significant difference between the cruciate ligaments can be determined from this original literature. This work determined the viscoelastic properties of the ligaments by characterizing the dependence of the material on time and/or load velocity. It is known that an increase in load velocity for ligaments tends to increase stiffness, the modulus of elasticity, and the rupture strength together with the reduction of strains. The results showed that knee ligaments have viscoelastic properties and as a result the ligaments can store deformation energy under dynamic load and release it in phases of relief. Such ligaments are then in a position to reduce peak loads and absorb impacts to the knee joint.

Later work at the University of Ulm, West Germany, determined further mechanical properties from the ACL and PCL. Using the same experimental approach as the earlier work the ACL was divided into one anterior and one posterior part, whereas the PCL mostly showed three parts: anterior, middle, and posterior. The results showed that the posterior part of the PCL experienced moduli of between 240 and 490 MPa. The result of the PCL and the entire range of the ACL were found to be between 86 and 156 MPa. The large cross sections of the cruciate ligaments (ACL 26 mm^2 and

TABLE 11.4 Mechanical Characteristics of In Vitro Knee Ligaments

	Collateral ligaments		Cruciate ligaments	
	Medial	Lateral	Anterior	Posterior
Rupture strain (%)				
Kennedy et al. (1976)	23.0 ± 24.0		30.8 ± 23.0	28.3 ± 19.0
Claes (1983)	18.15 ± 3.48	20.89 ± 7.55		
Noyes and Grood (1976)			Young: 44.3 ± 85.0 Old: 30.8	28.3
Force at the linear limit (N)				
Kennedy et al. (1976)	463 ± 32.0		402 ± 28.0	813 ± 51.0
Claes (1983)	538 ± 164.9	258 ± 133.0		
Noyes and Grood (1976)			Young: 1170 ± 750.0 Old: 622 ± 283.0	
Noyes (1977)			396.5	801.0
Tremblay et al. (1980)			470.0	
Strain at the linear limit (%)				
Kennedy et al. (1976)	19.6 ± 1.7		29.9 ± 2.0	20.7 ± 1.9
Claes (1983)	9.0 ± 1.79	10.4 ± 3.54		
Noyes and Grood (1976)			Young: 25.5 ± 8.1 Old: 21.9 ± 6.9	
Noyes (1977)			22.9	20.7
Tremblay et al. (1980)			25.0	30.0
Stiffness of the human knee ligaments (N/mm)				
Tremblay et al. (1980)	72	62	141	183
Claes (1983)	93.9 ± 20.6	47.4 ± 12.6		
Noyes and Grood (1976)			Young: 129 ± 39 Old: 182 ± 56	

TABLE 11.5 The Mechanical Properties of the Knee Ligaments

	MCL	LCL	ACL	ACL young:	PCL
Rupture force (N)	427–654	354–384	482–734	1734–2,450	571–1745
Rupture strain (%)	18.15–23	20.89	30.0–44.3		28.2
Stiffness (N/mm)	72–93.9	47.4–62	129–141		183

ACL = anterior cruciate ligament; LCL = lateral collateral ligament; MCL = medial collateral ligament; PCL = posterior cruciate ligament.

PCL 46 mm^2) compared to the collateral ligaments (MCL 15 mm^2 and LCL 11 mm^2) explain their higher stiffness as well as higher rupture force. An alignment of the collagen fibrils along the tensile direction (i.e., the start of the linear part of the stress-strain curve) was observed for the cruciate ligaments and the LCL at about 50 N of tensile force. The MCL reached this point at around 15 N of load. In conclusion, it was stated that the mechanical properties of the knee ligaments do not vary in a very large range except in the ventral part of the MCL.

Ohio State University, Columbus, Ohio. Meglan et al. (1986) measured the ACL strain by implanting 0.6-mm diameter liquid metal strain gauges in unembalmed cadavers. Four gauges were used: one in the anterior part, one in the posterior part, and two in the intermediate part of the ligament. The testing frame used in this work involved fixing the femur rigidly while the tibia was firmly attached to a six-component load cell. An electrogoniometer was then connected between the tibial and femoral frames. Anterior and posterior forces, valgus-varus moments, and internal-external rotations were applied to the knee when the knee was flexed at 0°, 30°, 45°, 60°, and 90°. An anterior force caused all the gauges to lengthen, while a posterior force either caused all of them to shorten relative to their unloaded length or had no effect. All four gauges behaved similarly, although the actual amount of length change varied. This would be expected if the ACL was the primary restraint to anterior subluxation of the tibia relative to the femur. This was true for all flexion angles. One conclusion of the work was that maximum effect of the moment occurred when the knee was flexed between 45° and 60°. This would agree with the general clinical opinion for ACL rupture. The results showed that although ACL length changes consistently across the ligament when loaded, the strain in the anterior portion of the ligament is less than the posterior aspect. This difference can be explained by the fact that the posterior fibers are shorter than the anterior ones when unloaded. Ligament length increased when anterior-posterior, valgus-varus moments or internal-external rotations were applied. The largest increase in length for a prescribed load occurred when the knee was flexed at 45° or 60°.

University of California, La Jolla, California. Woo et al. (1987) determined important and accurate data on the structural properties of the normal femur-ACL-tibia complex (FATC). In this study a new testing apparatus was developed. The tibia and femur were both fixed into cylinders. The tibial side was mounted on a shaft supported by bearings, which allowed axial tibial rotation. Accurate alignment in the coronal and sagittal plane for both femoral and tibial cylinders could also be achieved. Thus, the applied tensile load could be aligned with respect to the axes of the ACL and/or the tibia at all angles of knee flexion. The apparatus was then mounted in the Instron tensile testing machine and linear bearings permitted ease of load alignment for anterior-posterior and medial-lateral translations. Five pairs of cadaveric knees (22 to 44 years) were tested at 30° of flexion. Half of the specimens were tested with the tensile load applied along the axis of the tibia, while the remaining half were tested aligning the axis of the ligament. All soft tissue structures around the joint, excluding the ACL, were removed. A preload of 2.5 N was then applied to the FATC followed by cycling 10 times between 0 and 2 mm of deformation, and finally to failure at a rate of 200 mm/min. The load deformation curve, ultimate load, and linear stiffness were recorded, and the failure mode of the FATC noted. The results showed that the linear stiffness for the specimens tested along the tibial axis ranged between 150 ± 9 and 122 ± 19 N/mm. The ultimate load showed a similar trend to these stiffness values with loads ranging between 1750 ± 194 and 1256 ± 214 N. The tibial axis group failed mostly by the ligament peeling off at the femoral attachment site, while midsubstance tear was most common for the ACL axis group. For the younger donors (<25 years old), the data showed a higher ultimate load (2450 N) than that of the 1730 N found by Noyes and Grood (1976). Finally, it was concluded that the direction of loading is an important parameter for accurate FATC assessment and therefore should always be considered in any qualitative or quantitative study.

Summary. Measured strain values for ligaments range from 12 to over 50 percent. These variations are partly due to age, species, and type of specimens studied. However, the following are probably more important and realistic causes of these large variations:

1. Error in cross-sectional area measurements.
2. Clamping of test specimens, resulting in premature failures.
3. Poor length-width ratio for uniform stress during testing.

4. Poor techniques in measuring tissue strain.
5. Improper testing environments (temperature, pH, and drying of specimens).

The viscoelastic effects of the four ligaments that predominantly contribute to knee joint stability ranged from 14.1 to 19.6 percent relaxation decrease in the applied preload and 3.7 to 5.1 percent recovery following a decrease in maximum load. Table 11.5 summarizes the rupture force, rupture strain, and stiffness values of the four ligaments of the knee in more detail. Clearly the strongest of the four ligaments is the PCL with rupture force values reaching 1745 N. The MCL and LCL are considerably weaker than the ACL. The rupture strain is similar in all ligaments except the ACL, which is able to deform to a greater extent before rupture occurs. However, this capability is limited due to the fact that the ultimate rupture force is considerably lower, thus producing a lower stiffness value. Stiffness values show as expected that the PCL has the greatest stiffness value. However, the ACL has values which are significantly greater than both the MCL and LCL. These values would tend to agree with the current clinical opinion as to the strengths of various ligaments of the knee joint.

The ACL is most vulnerable to injury between 40° and 60° of knee flexion with an additional internal rotation. Also, more often than not, the application of the tensile load does not correspond to the ligament axis but acts along the tibial axis. In this situation the ligament is most vulnerable to trauma. The PCL is very rarely ruptured, likely largely due to its particular size and ultimate failure capabilities. Valgus-varus deformation did not significantly affect the loads in the ACL or PCL but caused a threefold increase of loads acting on the MCL and LCL. Internal-external rotations introduced significant increases in the loads acting in the MCL and LCL. Also, it is important to note that knee ligaments, particularly the MCL, are likely to rupture at certain sites within the ligament. For example, in extension a rupture of the posterior aspect of the MCL is most likely to occur, while in flexion it is the anterior aspect of the ligament that is the weakest. Finally, the quadriceps femoris muscle group has been shown to significantly increase the strain in the ACL, MCL, and LCL during the first 30° of flexion. This would tend to increase the chance of ligament rupture in this position; however, the value of the increase was only in the region of 2 percent. The posterior femoral muscles (or hamstrings) showed no obvious effect on ligament strain at any angle of flexion.

11.3.4 Knee Measurement: Applied Displacement versus Applied Loading Techniques

This section addresses itself to the question of whether there is any difference in the measuring techniques that apply load and measure displacement, or those that apply displacement and measure resistive force. Butler et al. (1980) was the first group that proposed that accurate qualitative and quantitative assessment can only be achieved by applying a fixed displacement and measuring the resistive load. Ligaments limit motion of the joint by the development of a restraining force when stretched. The total restraining force is the sum of the individual ligament forces in the absence of muscle, weight bearing, and other similar forces. Controlling joint displacement controls the amount of ligament stretch and hence its force. Reproducing the displacement reproduces the force in each ligament. By contrast, other studies have examined ligament function by measuring the joint displacement resulting from the application of a known load after a ligament has been cut. This does not parallel the clinical (Lachman or anterior drawer) test, which aims to assess the degree and type of injury from observed laxities. However, the amount of joint laxity depends upon the magnitude of the applied load and the complex interaction among all the ligaments present. When a ligament is cut or injured, the interaction changes, causing an increase in laxity which depends on both the loss of the restraining force in the cut ligament and the change in interaction of the remaining ligaments. This does not directly indicate the function of the cut or injured ligament. Indeed, the increase in laxity after the cut or injury is due to the action of the remaining ligaments acting in a new relationship to each other.

Both primary and secondary restraints to joint deformation are offered by ligaments and capsular structures. For example, it has been shown that during anterior drawer of the tibia, 86 percent of the restraint is offered by the ACL. However, if the ACL is ruptured or severely strained, secondary restraints to the force are provided by the iliotibial tract (24.8 percent), midmedial (22.3 percent) and midlateral capsule (20.8 percent), MCL (16.3 percent), and LCL (12.4 percent). In addition, it has also been shown that the cutting order of the various ligaments affects the stability of the joint. Change the order of the ligament sectioning and a resulting change in the stiffness of the joint occurs. This would indicate that the ligaments behave in different combinations, which are dependent upon the intact or partially intact structures of the joint. The combination of ligamentous arrangement following injury must be infinite, and any testing method that is dependent on the cutting or injury order of the ligaments cannot possibly provide an accurate assessment of individual ligamentous contribution. Since applying displacement and measuring resistive force provides an outline of individual ligamentous contribution (by subtracting the results from the intact or uninjured knee), it is therefore independent of cutting or injury order.

11.3.5 A Modern Conceptualization of Knee Joint Biomechanics

The contribution of the ACL to the biomechanics of the knee has been a major focus of researchers, due at least in part to the prevalence of ACL injuries as well as the debilitating consequences of ACL deficiency. Technological developments in methods have been applied to produce greater understanding of the role the ACL plays in normal function of the knee. There is a vast literature dealing with the biomechanics of the ACL relating to its normal function, to its deficiency following injury, and to its reconstruction after injury. As an example, Bates et al. (2015) performed a meta-analysis of a series of studies investigating the kinematics of the knee in the ACL-intact, ACL-deficient, and ACL-reconstructed states. The studies included in the Bates et al. (2015) paper followed a test-retest sequence, where the knee was loaded and the displacement measured, for example, before and after transection of the ligament. The authors showed that when knees were loaded with an anterior tibial force, the principal resultant movement measured was anterior tibial translation. Deficiency of the ACL was presented as a large increase in anterior translation, as found by Butler et al. (1980) and many other researchers, showing the substantial role of the ACL in resisting anterior force and restraining anterior translation. The characteristic increase in anterior translation is the basis of the Lachman test (Torg et al. 1976), a clinical test of ACL function using a manual application of an anterior force.

When an internal tibial torque is applied, the principal resultant movement produced is internal tibial rotation. Studies examined by Bates et al. (2015) found an increase in internal rotation on application of internal torque to ACL-deficient knees, showing another function of the ACL in restraining internal rotation. This is in keeping with other studies not included in the paper, such as Wroble et al. (1993) and Lipke et al. (1981). However, a role for the ACL in restraining internal rotation is not a universal conclusion. Other researchers did not find increased rotation with internal torque in the ACL-deficient condition (Lane et al., 1994; Wünschel et al., 2010), leading to some uncertainty in the function of the ACL in this context. The Bates et al. (2015) study shows that application of anterior force in the ACL-intact state also led to internal rotation, which persisted in the deficient state. Fukubayashi et al. (1982) also found such rotation, and found that restricting rotation led to a decrease in translation, and further, that transecting the ACL led to an abolition of rotation, which contradicted the results included in the Bates et al. (2015) paper. This brief survey shows that the biomechanics of the ACL are far from clear-cut.

Understanding the biomechanics of the knee in relation to the ACL in normal and injured knees stands to have important clinical consequences. Untreated rupture of the ACL tends to lead to instability, meniscal damage, and accelerated osteoarthritis. It is presumed that instability causes the accelerated osteoarthritis through imposition of unusual and excessive forces on the joint surface [e.g., Kaiser et al. (2016)], that is, curved brackets. Primary repair, where the ligament fragment ends are sutured together, has historically resulted in failure (Vavken and Murray, 2011). Surgical reconstruction of the ligament is a popular choice of treatment, where the damaged ligament is replaced by a graft typically taken from the patient's own patellar ligament or hamstring tendons (Kraeutler et al., 2017). The goals of ACL reconstruction are, through replacement of the ACL, to reduce instability and preserve long-term joint structure; the latter is commonly articulated as mediated through restoration of normal biomechanics of the knee [e.g., Dodds et al. (2014) and Herfat et al. (2012)]. Unfortunately, the results of reconstruction have not met initial expectations. Although stability is in general improved, ACL reconstruction patients still have an increased risk of accelerated osteoarthritis.

To return to the Bates et al. (2015) paper, the studies included in the meta-analysis also tested knees after ACL reconstruction. Although ACL reconstruction reduced anterior tibial translation on anterior force from ACL-deficient levels, ACL-reconstructed knees showed greater translation. Despite this increase in laxity, ACL-reconstructed knees showed a decrease in internal rotation in response to anterior force. This decrease in internal rotation on anterior force has also been shown by studies not included in the Bates et al. (2015) paper, for example, by Yoo et al. (2005), who concluded that internal rotation had been overconstrained.

Considering the lack of clarity around the biomechanics of the ACL-intact and ACL-reconstructed knees, and importantly the differences between them, and the lack of success in preventing accelerated degeneration, we can review the hypothesis central to this goal—*Hypothesis 1: Restoration of normal biomechanics prevents accelerated joint degeneration*. But there is a fundamental issue with this hypothesis: what is "normal biomechanics?"—not simply biomechanical variables, but a biomechanical state that normalizes stresses and protects the joint surfaces. An answer in terms of "that which is consistent with normal joint structure" is currently not available to us, as this is part of the background theory we are trying to prove (Schick Jr and Vaughn, 2014). To consider normal biomechanics as simply that displayed by the ACL-intact knee is only useful until we try to delve a little deeper and say exactly what we mean by that. If the hypothesis is scientific, we should be able to test it, so it follows that we should be able to (1) describe precisely how the knee should behave, and (2) have a means to establish that it behaves like that. Given the common usage of the term "normal biomechanics" [e.g., normal biomechanics of the ACL (Carter et al. 1997) and of the knee (Centeno et al. 2015)], the remainder of this section will deal with the conceptual issues inherent in trying to define just what that means.

In addressing Hypothesis 1, how exactly would we know that normal biomechanics has been restored after reconstruction? In a clinical setting we could start by applying a force to estimate the resultant displacement, and compare the ACL-reconstructed state with the ACL-intact state (i.e., using the uninjured side)—for example, anterior tibial translation through the Lachman test and perhaps internal rotation via the pivot shift test (Fetto and Marshall, 1979)—but what of the rest of biomechanics? Differences have also been found in external as well as internal rotation (Nordt et al., 1999), but also (the much harder to measure) contact area (Kaiser et al., 2016); should these be included? Should variables be measured in nonweight-bearing on the clinical couch, or given gait differences found in rotation, such as those found by Asaeda et al. (2017), should gait-related variables be included? Beyond kinematic variables, torque and power during gait may also be significant (Devita et al., 1998). In fleshing out what we mean by normal biomechanics we are attempting to move normal biomechanics from the abstract realm to the concrete, and we need a complete (or complete enough) description, not just examples. A thought experiment might seem straightforward—measure a suite of variables, cut the ACL, replace it with a graft, and remeasure those variables; within a level of tolerance, we could establish that pre- and postreconstruction variables were similar enough to call the ensemble "normal," and measure the progress of joint degeneration. In a thought experiment this might be satisfactory but considering all of the parameters of biomechanics that researchers make available to us (not to mention those not yet, or little, discovered), the aim of replicating all biomechanical variables would be a practical impossibility, and might not actually be necessary. After all, the school of bounded rationality holds that even successful human decision making is based on less than a full complement of information (Simon, 1979).

It is probable that at least some of the variables are redundant, either not of relevance to joint degeneration or due to correlations with other relevant variables, to the point that a subset of the total would be complete enough for our purposes. Assuming that we could create an exact match on that reduced suite of variables consistent with normal patterns of variation, could we be sure that we were measuring the right variables, i.e., that we had selected the variables that play a causative role in early degeneration? Anterior tibial translation and internal rotation may be obvious candidates, but does an excess of these lead to advanced degeneration? To focus on these obvious variables may be an example of the availability heuristic (Tversky and Kahneman, 1974), where we focus on variables that come more easily to mind and risk errors by ignoring less obvious but possibly more material information. Biomechanics is a rich and expansive field, and a conveniently workable subset of variables might not be informative enough for our purposes. To get to a meaningful subset of descriptor variables requires an understanding of the relationship between the biomechanical variables and joint degeneration, and although we are not at that point yet, we are no doubt closer to it than before, and with further research will get closer still.

If we could isolate the subset of biomechanical variables necessary to replicate to protect the knee, we should then give some thought as to what level of tolerance is required when judging that a variable is close enough to a target value. A measure of statistical significance will not help us, as statistical significance does not consider biological significance. Wroble et al. (1993) concluded that their finding of an increase in internal rotation in ACL-deficient knees was "clinically unimportant," but how is such a conclusion reached? Is there a linear relation between deviation from the normal value and speed of degeneration, so that the closer to normal the better the outcome? Or is any degree of deviation intolerable, and a millimeter or degree difference the beginning of the end of the joint? Accordingly, we could tighten our levels of tolerance, in so making it harder to achieve "normality," and to continue to reduce our tolerance until no knee could show normal biomechanics. Researchers have not yet reached consensus about how an ACL-deficient knee behaves, let alone what (specifically) about that behavior leads to accelerated degeneration. A 3-mm difference between knees in anterior tibial translation is considered normal, based on measurements in normal knees (Daniel et al., 1985). Assuming abnormal anterior tibial translation causes accelerated degeneration, how do we know how much can be tolerated? A more useful hypothesis linking biomechanics and degeneration would put forward a picture of a functional relationship, such that a deviation of X mm or degrees in Y direction causes Z degeneration. To allow a certain tolerance in anterior tibial translation as normal suggests understanding of a relationship that is not yet understood.

The practical difficulties attendant on the use of "normal biomechanics" in Hypothesis 1, in the context of ACL reconstruction but applicable to corrective treatment of any joint injury, leave the hypothesis useful in the abstract only. The concept of "normal biomechanics" as the basis of a hypothesis is too abstract to be fully empirically tested, and more specific hypotheses around explicit biomechanical variables are required to predict joint degeneration, but our knowledge is not yet sufficient. Without any way to precisely and meaningfully determine the normal condition, these hypotheses cannot be tested. If we cannot create normal biomechanics, how could we find disconfirmatory evidence, or even confirmatory evidence for that matter? We need to define normal biomechanics in a meaningful way, and currently we lack that meaning.

Given that initial disruption to the joint biomechanics is implicit in Hypothesis 1, it makes sense to also state its obverse—*Hypothesis 2: Abnormal joint biomechanics causes accelerated joint degeneration.* Hypothesis 2 has greater scope (Schick Jr and Vaughn, 2014) and can be applied to predict degeneration in other joints and other circumstances where biomechanics has been disrupted, and surgical restoration has not been attempted. Is Hypothesis 2 an improvement? After all, abnormal biomechanics is much more readily made concrete, for example, a marked increase in anterior tibial translation, or an overconstrained knee with a tendency toward external rotation. With traumatic ACL ruptures, there is the risk of a post hoc fallacy that injury precedes, and therefore causes, accelerated degeneration. Although normal biomechanics (in its abstract form) represents a narrow band of possible biomechanical values, the range of abnormal values is vast and may not meaningfully fill one "abnormal" picture. Is an internally rotated, underconstrained knee any different to an externally rotated, overconstrained knee, given that both are "abnormal"? Is a knee with 10-mm anterior tibial translation really worse off than one with 5 mm?

What we know about biomechanics, impressive as it is, should not mask what we do not know. We are ignorant of what "normal biomechanics of the knee" means because that simple-looking concept contains a vast amount of information, only some of which we possess. Vitek and Jackson (2008) contrast knowledge-based and ignorance-based worldviews. A knowledge-based worldview focuses on what is known, confident that we know what we need to, and any gaps will be closed with the application of time and effort. An ignorance-based worldview takes account of knowledge gaps and is less confident about our chances of filling them: "knowledge will always be dwarfed by what we do not, should not, and cannot ever know." We conclude that "normal biomechanics" as a concrete and complete ensemble of knowledge as a basis for treatment prescription is something we cannot ever know. While it is one thing to agree on certain features, including compatibility with long-term joint health, this is spectating on the results of years of development. To build up a biomechanical picture as an endpoint to a journey that starts with abnormality, such that we can be confident of long-term success, is currently beyond our reach. If we do not know our target, we cannot understand the consequences of not reaching our target. While the goal of reducing instability is sound, avoiding giving way and related further incidents of trauma to the knee, or even simply returning the patient to normal functional activities [e.g., Ott et al. (2003)], the goal of restoring biomechanics and thus preventing accelerated degeneration seems more hope than hypothesis.

11.4 CONCLUDING REMARKS

This overview of joint biomechanics has hopefully conveyed enough detail to tell an interesting story of foot and knee function, but then again only enough, to draw a picture that is both complicated and complex but without too much in the way of imposition.

Joint biomechanics are complicated. Function of the foot depends on the coordinated action of the ankle, subtalar and midtarsal joints, whose multiplanar actions convert torque between the leg and the foot much like a universal joint. Knee joint movement and stability is dependent on the mechanical properties of ligaments, but even a limited account of a subset of ligaments shows that these properties vary between ligaments as well as between testing conditions. Viscoelastic effects lead to differences based on loading rate, and anatomical structure determines that properties of the ligaments depend on the portion of the ligament under investigation and the direction of the applied load (whether applied tension is in line with the ligament or with the limb, or the physiological movement imposed).

Measurement of properties of ligaments is also affected by what other structures are intact or cut. The interactions of intact ligaments present a dimension of complexity to our picture, which is relevant not just to laboratory investigations but also to the effect on joints of ligament injuries. This is shown in sharp relief in attempts to replace the anterior cruciate ligament after rupture. Failure to avoid early osteoarthritis suggests an inability to mimic the function of the original ligament, and stacking up the vast amounts of what we know against this result points to the significance of what we do not—perhaps cannot ever—know.

But rather than dwell on these knowledge gaps, perhaps it is fitting to reflect on the material given to us to study, and admire instead what clearly are *remarkable pieces of bioengineering*.

REFERENCES

Asaeda, M., Deie, M., Fujita, N., Kono, Y., Terai, C., Kuwahara, W., Watanabe, H., Kimura, H., Adachi, N., Sunagawa, T., and Ochi, M. (2017), Gender differences in the restoration of knee joint biomechanics during gait after anterior cruciate ligament reconstruction, *The Knee,* **24**(2):280–288.

Bates, N. A., Myer, G. D., Shearn, J. T., and Hewett, T. E. (2015), Anterior cruciate ligament biomechanics during robotic and mechanical simulations of physiologic and clinical motion tasks: A systematic review and meta-analysis, *Clinical Biomechanics,* **30**(1):1–13.

Brown, B. (1982), Pronation, *Running Review Magazine*, March 1982.

Butler, D. L., Noyes, F. R., and Grood, E. S. (1980), Ligamentous restraints to anterior-posterior drawer in the human knee. A biomechanical study, *Journal of Bone & Joint Surgery—American Volume,* **62**(2):259–270.

Carter, N. D., Jenkinson, T. R., Wilson, D., Jones, D. W., and Torode, A. S. (1997), Joint position sense and rehabilitation in the anterior cruciate ligament deficient knee, *British Journal of Sports Medicine,* **31**(3):209–212.

Centeno, C. J., Pitts, J., Al-Sayegh, H., and Freeman, M. D. (2015), Anterior cruciate ligament tears treated with percutaneous injection of autologous bone marrow nucleated cells: A case series, *Journal of Pain Research,* **8**:437–447.

Claes, L. (1983), Biomechanical properties of human ligaments, *Aktuelle Probleme in Chirurgie und Orthopadie,* **25**:12–19.

Claes, S., Vereecke, E., Maes, M., Victor, J., Verdonk, P., and Bellemans, J. (2013), Anatomy of the anterolateral ligament of the knee, *Journal of Anatomy,* **223**(4):321–328.

Daniel, D. M., Stone, M. L., Sachs, R., and Malcom, L. (1985), Instrumented measurement of anterior knee laxity in patients with acute anterior cruciate ligament disruption, *American Journal of Sports Medicine,* **13**(6):401–407.

Devita, P., Hortobagyi, T., and Barrier, J. (1998), Gait biomechanics are not normal after anterior cruciate ligament reconstruction and accelerated rehabilitation, *Medicine & Science in Sports & Exercise,* **30**(10):1481–1488.

Dodds, A. L., Halewood, C., Gupte, C. M., Williams, A., and Amis, A. A. (2014), The anterolateral ligament anatomy, length changes and association with the Segond fracture, *Bone & Joint Journal,* **96**(3):325–331.

Fetto, J. F., and Marshall, J. L. (1979), Injury to the anterior cruciate ligament producing the pivot-shift sign, *Journal of Bone & Joint Surgery—American Volume,* **61**(5):710–714.

Fukubayashi, T., Torzilli, P. A., Sherman, M. F., and Warren, R. F. (1982), An in vitro biomechanical evaluation of anterior-posterior motion of the knee. Tibial displacement, rotation, and torque, *Journal of Bone & Joint Surgery—American Volume,* **64**(2):258–264.

Herfat, S. T., Boguszewski, D. V., Nesbitt, R. J., and Shearn, J. T. (2012), Effect of perturbing a simulated motion on knee and anterior cruciate ligament kinetics, *Journal of Biomechanical Engineering,* **134**(10): 104504–104504.

Johnson, G. R. (1981), Ankle, in Dowson, D., and Wright, V., eds., *Introduction to the Biomechanics of Joints and Joint Replacement*, London: Wiley-Blackwell.

Kaiser, J., Vignos, M. F., Liu, F., Kijowski, R., and Thelen, D. G. (2016), American Society of Biomechanics Clinical Biomechanics Award 2015: MRI assessments of cartilage mechanics, morphology and composition following reconstruction of the cnterior cruciate ligament, *Clinical Biomechanics,* **34**(2016):38–44.

Kennedy, J. C., Hawkins, R. J., Willis, R. B., and Danylchuck, K. D. (1976), Tension studies of human knee ligaments. Yield point, ultimate failure, and disruption of the cruciate and tibial collateral ligaments, *Journal of Bone & Joint Surgery—American Volume,* **58**(3):350–355.

Kraeutler, M. J., Wolsky, R. M., Vidal, A. F., and Bravman, J. T. (2017), Anatomy and biomechanics of the native and reconstructed anterior cruciate ligament: Surgical implications, *Journal of Bone & Joint Surgery—American Volume,* **99**(5):438–445.

Lane, J. G., Irby, S. E., Kaufman, K., Rangger, C., and Daniel, D. M. (1994), The anterior cruciate ligament in controlling axial rotation: An evaluation of its effect, *The American Journal of Sports Medicine,* **22**(2): 289–293.

Lipke, J. M., Janecki, C. J., Nelson, C. L., McLeod, P., Thompson, C., Thompson, J., and Haynes, D. W. (1981), The role of incompetence of the anterior cruciate and lateral ligaments in anterolateral and anteromedial instability. A biomechanical study of cadaver knees, *Journal of Bone & Joint Surgery—American Volume,* **63**(6):954–960.

Manley, M. T. (1980), Biomechanics of the foot, in Helfet, A. J., and Gruebel Lee, D. M., eds., *Disorders of the Foot*, London: Lippincott Williams & Wilkins.

Meglan, D., Berme, N., Zuelzer, W., and Colvin, J. (1986), Direct measurement of anterior cruciate ligament lengthening due to external loads, in *ESB Workshop: Biomechanics of Human Knee Ligaments*, University of Ulm, June 1986, pp. 32–33.

Nordt, W. E., Lotfi, P., Plotkin, E., and Williamson, B. (1999) The in vivo assessment of tibial motion in the transverse plane in anterior cruciate ligament-reconstructed knees, *The American Journal of Sports Medicine,* **27**(5): 611-616.

Noyes, F. (1977), Functional properties of knee ligaments and alterations induced by immobilization: A correlative biomechanical and histological study in primates, *Clinical Orthopaedics and Related Research,* **1977**(123):210–242.

Noyes, F. R., and Grood, E. S. (1976), The strength of the anterior cruciate ligament in humans and Rhesus monkeys, *Journal of Bone & Joint Surgery—American Volume,* **58**(8):1074–1082.

Ott, S. M., Ireland, M. L., Ballantyne, B. T., Willson, J. D., and Davis, I. S. M. (2003), Comparison of outcomes between males and females after anterior cruciate ligament reconstruction, *Knee Surgery, Sports Traumatology, Arthroscopy,* **11**(2):75–80.

Piziali, R. L., Rastegar, J., Nagel, D. A., and Schurman, D. J. (1980), The contribution of the cruciate ligaments to the load-displacement characteristics of the human knee joint, *Journal of Biomechanical Engineering,* **102**(4):277–283.

Root, M. L., Orien, W. P., and Weed, J. H. (1977), *Normal and Abnormal Function of the Foot,* Los Angeles: Clinical Biomechanics Corp.

Rosenberg, L. (1975), Dynamics of connective tissue macromolecules, in Burleigh, P. M. C., and Poole, A. R., eds., *Symposium on Dynamics of Connective Tissue Macromolecules (1974: Cambridge),* New York: Elsevier, pp. 105–128.

Schick Jr, T., and Vaughn, L. (2014), *How to Think about Weird Things: Critical Thinking for a New Age,* 7th ed., New York: McGraw-Hill.

Simon, H. A. (1979), Rational decision making in business organizations, *The American Economic Review,* **69**(4):493–513.

Torg, J. S., Conrad, W., and Kalen, V. (1976), Clinical I diagnosis of anterior cruciate ligament instability in the athlete, *American Journal of Sports Medicine,* **4**(2):84–93.

Tremblay, G., Laurin, C., and Drovin, G. (1980), The challenge of prosthetic cruciate ligament replacement, *Clinical Orthopaedics and Related Research,* **147**:88–92.

Trent, P., Walker, P., and Wolf, B. (1976). Ligament length patterns, strength, and rotational axes of the knee joint, *Clinical Orthopaedics and Related Research,* **117**:263–270.

Tversky, A., and Kahneman, D. (1974), Judgment under uncertainty: Heuristics and biases, *Science,* **185**(4157):1124–1131.

Vavken, P. M. D. M., and Murray, M. M. M. D. (2011), The potential for primary repair of the ACL, *Sports Medicine & Arthroscopy Review,* **19**(1):44–49.

Viidik, A. (1990), Structure and function of normal and healing tendons and ligaments, in *Biomechanics of Diarthrodial Joints*, New York: Springer, pp. 243–238.

Vitek, B., and Jackson, W. (2008), Taking ingnorance seriously, in Vitek, B., and Jackson, W., eds., *The Virtues of Ignorance: Complexity, Sustainability, and the Limits of Knowledge*, Lexington: University Press of Kentucky.

Wells, K. F., and Luttgens, K. (1976), *Kinesiology : Scientific Basis of Human Motion,* 6th ed., Philadelphia, PA: Saunders.

Woo, S. L. Y., Akeson, W. H., and Jemmott, G. F. (1976), Measurements of nonhomogeneous, directional mechanical properties of articular cartilage in tension, *Journal of Biomechanics,* **9**(12):785–791.

Woo, S. L. Y., Hollis, J. M., Roux, R. D., Gomez, M. A., Inoue, M., Kleiner, J. B., and Akeson, W. H. (1987), Effects of knee flexion on the structural properties of the rabbit femur-anterior cruciate ligament-tibia complex (FATC), *Journal of Biomechanics,* **20**(6):557–563.

Wroble, R. R., Grood, E. S., Cummings, J. S., Henderson, J. M., and Noyes, F. R. (1993), The role of the lateral extraarticular restraints in the anterior cruciate ligament-deficient knee, *American Journal of Sports Medicine,* **21**(2):257–263.

Wünschel, M., Müller, O., Lo, J., Obloh, C., and Wülker, N. (2010), The anterior cruciate ligament provides resistance to externally applied anterior tibial force but not to internal rotational torque during simulated weight-bearing flexion, *Arthroscopy: The Journal of Arthroscopic & Related Surgery,* **26**(11):1520–1527.

Yoo, J. D., Papannagari, R., Park, S. E., DeFrate, L. E., Gill, T. J., and Li, G. (2005), The effect of anterior cruciate ligament reconstruction on knee joint kinematics under simulated muscle loads, *American Journal of Sports Medicine,* **33**(2):240–246.

CHAPTER 12
FINITE-ELEMENT ANALYSIS

Michael D. Nowak
University of Hartford, West Hartford, Connecticut

12.1 INTRODUCTION

In the realm of biomedical engineering, computer modeling in general and finite-element modeling in particular are powerful means of understanding the body and the adaptations that may be made to it. Using the appropriate inputs, a better understanding of the interrelation of the components of the body can be achieved. In addition, the effects of surgical procedures and material replacement can be evaluated without large numbers of physical trials. The "what if" and iterative aspects of computer modeling can save a great deal of time and money, especially as compared with multiple bench testing or series of live trials.

In attempting to understand the human body, much can be learned from material and fluids testing and cadaveric examination. These processes do not, in general, determine the relative forces and interactions between structures. They are also neither able to determine the stresses within hard or soft tissue, nor the patterns of flow due to the interaction of red blood cells within the vascular system.

Every aspect of the human body and devices to aid or replace function fall within the realm of computer modeling. These models range from the more obvious arenas based on orthopedic and vascular surgery to trauma from accident (Huang et al., 1999) to the workings of the middle ear (Ferris and Prendergast, 2000).

There are an increasing number of journals that include articles using finite-element analysis (FEA) in evaluation of the body and implants. These range from the journals dedicated to the engineering evaluation of the body (such as *The Journal of Biomechanics* and *The Journal of Biomechanical Engineering)* to those associated with surgical and other specialties (such as *The Journal of Orthopaedic Research, The Journal of Prosthetic Dentistry*, and *The Journal of Vascular Surgery*).

As with any use of FEA results, the practitioner must have some understanding of the actual structure to determine if the model is valid. One prime example of error when overlooking the end use in the FEA realm is that of the femoral component of hip implants. If one only examines loading patterns, the best implant would be placed on the exterior of the femoral bone, since the bone transfers load along its outer material. Doing so in reality would lead to failure because the nutrient supply to the bone would be compromised, and the bone would resorb (bone mass would be lost).

This chapter gives an overview of the requirements and uses of FEA and similar codes for biomedical engineering analysis. The examples that will be used refer to FEA, but the techniques will be the same for other systems, such as finite difference and computational fluid dynamics. The literature cited in this chapter gives a flavor of the breadth of information available and the studies being undertaken. This listing is far from exhaustive because of the large number of ongoing efforts. Numerous search engines are available to find abstracts relating to the subjects touched on in this chapter.

A large number of software packages and a wide range of computational power are used in FEA of the human body, ranging from basic personal computer (PC) programs and simplified constructs to high-powered nonlinear codes and models that require extensive central processing unit (CPU) time on supercomputers. Most of the examples in this chapter will be those run on desktop PCs.

The remainder of this chapter focuses on three basic concerns of a useful finite-element model: the geometry, the material properties, and the boundary conditions.

12.2 GEOMETRIC CONCERNS

12.2.1 Two Dimensions versus Three Dimensions

The very first question is two-dimensional versus three-dimensional. While the human body is three-dimensional (3D), many situations lend themselves to a successful two-dimensional (2D) analysis.

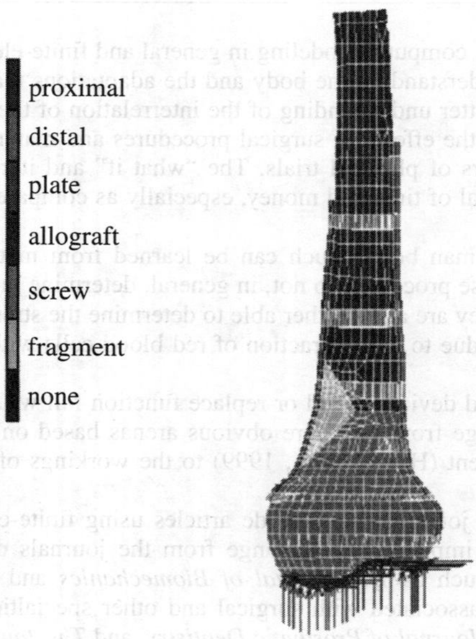

FIGURE 12.1 Two-dimensional distal femur with plate, screws, and bone allograft. A fracture with butterfly bone separation is shown (butterfly bone segment is the light-colored triangle on the left). The plate is shown at the right, with screws through overdrilled holes on the near side and full attachment to the cortical bone on the left side. The additional bone graft is on the far left of the bone.

First approximations for implants (such as the hip) may include 2D analysis. If the leg is in midstance (not stair climbing), the loading pattern is 2D. The head and proximal end of the femur are placed in compression and bending, but there is minimal out-of-plane loading. Long bone fracture fixation may require the use of a plate and screws, such as noted in Fig. 12.1. Since the plate is axial and not expected to be subjected to off-axis motion, a 2D model reasonably models the system. Loading for this model is single-leg stance, so the weight is almost directly above the section shown (at approximately 10 degrees to vertical). There is no torque applied to the femur at this point in walking. If one wishes to examine the full walking cycle or a position in early or late stance where the leg is bent forward or backward, a 3D analysis would be better suited (Chu et al., 2000; Kurtz et al., 1998).

The analysis of dental implants follows a similar pattern. For simple biting, the loading on a tooth is basically 2D in nature. An implant using an isotropic material such as metal may also be evaluated in 2D (Maurer et al., 1999), whereas a composite implant in general will require a 3D analysis to include the out-of-plane material properties (Augereau et al., 1998; Merz et al., 2000).

Many examinations of single ligament or tendon behavior may also be considered 2D. For example, the carpal arch or the wrist (noted in cases of carpal tunnel syndrome) may be modeled in 2D (Nowak and Cherry, 1995). Multiple attachment sites or changes in orientation would necessitate a shift to 3D.

In the cardiovascular realm, due to symmetry, the evaluation of single aortic valve leaflets may be considered 2D for a first approximation (de Hart et al., 2000). The full pattern of valve motion or flow in the proximal aorta would require a 3D analysis (de Hart et al., 1998; Grande et al., 2000).

Fluid boundary layer separation at vascular bifurcations or curves (as found in the carotid and coronary arteries) may be considered 2D if evaluating centerline flow (Steinman and Ethier, 1994). Along this plane, the secondary flows brought on by the vessel cross-sectional curvature will not affect the flow patterns. These models may be used to evaluate boundary layer separation in the carotid artery, the coronaries, and graft anastomoses.

12.2.2 Model Detail

In addition to the number of dimensions is the detail of the model. As with 2D versus 3D models, detail varies with area of interest. If you are examining a plate along a long bone, the bone surface may be considered smooth. If you are assuming complete integration of the screw threads into the bone, this interface may not include the screw teeth (but rather a "welded" interface). Braces and orthotics (if precast) may also be considered smooth and of uniform thickness. Thermoformed materials (such as ankle-foot orthotics) may be considered of a uniform thickness to start, although the heavily curved sections are generally thinner. Large joints, such as the knee, hip, and shoulder may also be considered smooth, although they may have a complex 2D shape.

Bones such as the spine require varying levels of detail, depending on the analysis of interest. A general model examining fixation of the spine via a rod or clamps would not require fine detail of vertebral geometries. A fracture model of the spinous processes would require a greater level of detail.

Joints such as the ankle and wrist consist of many small bones, and their surfaces must be determined accurately. This may be done via cadaveric examination or noninvasive means. The cadaveric system generally consists of the following (or a modification): The ligaments and tendons are stained to display the attachments (insertions) into the bones; the construct is then embedded in Plexiglas, and sequential pictures or scans are taken as the construct is either sliced or milled. Slices on the order of a fraction of a millimeter are needed to fully describe the surfaces of wrist carpal bones. Noninvasive measures, such as modern high-sensitivity computed tomographic (CT) scans, may also be able to record geometries at the required level of detail.

Internal bone and soft tissue structures may generally be considered uniform. A separation should be made with bone to distinguish the hard cortical layer from the spongier cancellous material, but it is generally not required to model the cell structure of bone. If one is interested in specifically modeling the head of the femur in great detail, the trabecular architecture may be required. These arches provide a function similar to that of buttresses and flying buttresses in churches. While work continues in detailed FEA studies of these structural alignments down to the micron level, this is not required if one only seeks to determine the general behavior of the entire structure.

Similar approximations may be made in the biofluids realm. Since the size and orientation of vessels vary from person to person, a simple geometry is a good first step. The evaluation of bifurcations can be taken to the next level of complexity by varying the angle of the outlet sides. Cadaveric studies are helpful in determining general population data. As mentioned earlier, CT studies lend exact data for a single subject or a small group of subjects [such as the abdominal aortic aneurysm work of Raghavan et al. (2000)].

12.3 MATERIAL PROPERTIES

Hard tissue should be modeled as orthotropic, even when using 2D analysis. The differences in properties are on the order of those seen in wood, with the parallel-to-the-grain direction (vertical along the tree trunk) being the stiffest. Basic mechanical properties can be found in Fung's text on biomechanics (1996). As can be seen, isotropic modeling will produce significant deviation from expected clinical results. Most FEA codes allow orthotropic material properties in 2D or 3D. This being stated, it must also be noted that since people vary widely in shape and size, material properties may have standard deviations of 30 percent or more. Once a determination of what material properties are going to be used is made, it may be beneficial to vary these parameters to ensure that changes of properties within the standards will not significantly alter the findings.

Distinction must be made between cortical and cancellous bone structures. The harder cortical outer layer carries the bulk of the loading in bones. Although one should not neglect the cancellous bone, it must be recalled that during femoral implant procedures for hip implants, the cancellous canal is reamed out to the cortical shell prior to fitting the metal implant.

Joint articular cartilage is a particular area of concern when producing an FEA model. Work continues on fully describing the mechanical behavior of these low-friction cushioning structures that allow us to move our joints freely. As a first approximation, it is generally assumed that these surfaces are hard and frictionless. If the purpose of the model is to investigate general bone behavior away from the joint, this will be a reasonable approximation. To isolate the cartilage properties, one should perform a data search of the current literature. Of course, implant modeling will not require this information because the cartilage surface is generally removed.

When evaluating intact joints, after the articular cartilage has been modeled, one is forced to examine the synovial fluid. This material is a major component to the nearly frictionless nature of joints. Long molecular chains and lubricants interact to reduce friction to levels far below that of the best human-made materials. At a normal stress of 500 kPa, a sample of a normal joint with synovial fluid has a friction coefficient of 0.0026, whereas a Teflon-coated surface presents coefficients in the range of 0.05 to 0.1 (Fung, 1996). In addition, the articular cartilage reduces friction by exuding more synovial fluid as load increases, effectively moving the articular surfaces further apart. When the load is reduced, the fluid is reabsorbed by the articular materials.

Implants require their own careful study as pertains to the implant-bone interface. If an uncemented implant is to be investigated, the question is one of how much bone integration is expected. If one examines the typical implant, e.g., the femoral component of a hip implant or the tibial component of a knee implant, one will see that a portion of the surface is designed for bone ingrowth through the use of either a beaded or wire-mesh style of surface. These surfaces do not cover the entire implant, so it should not be assumed that the entire implant will be fixed to the bone after healing. Cemented implants are expected to have a better seal with the bone, but two additional points must be made. First, the material properties of bone cement must be included. These are isotropic and are similar to the acrylic grout that is the primary component of bone cement. This brings up the second point, which is that bone cement is not an actual cement that bonds with a surface but rather a tightfitting grout. As a first approximation, this bonding may be considered a rigid linkage, but it must be recalled that failure may occur by bone separation from the implant (separation from the bone is less likely as the bone cement infiltrates the pores in the bone).

Ligaments and tendons may be modeled as nonlinear springs or bundles of tissue. In the simplest case, one may successfully model a ligament or tendon as one or more springs. The nonlinear behavior is unfortunately evident as low force levels for ligaments and tendons. The low force segment of their behavior, where much of the motion occurs, is nonlinear (forming a toe or J in the stress-strain curve) due to straightening of collagen fibers of different lengths and orientations (Nowak, 1993; Nowak and Logan, 1991). The upper elastic range is quasi linear. As multifiber materials, ligaments and tendons do not fail all at once but rather through a series of single-fiber microfailures. If one is interested in evaluating behavior in the permanent deformation region, this ropelike behavior must be accounted for.

Dental implants are also nonisotropic in nature, as are many of the implant materials, especially composite-reinforced materials (Nowak et al., 1999). Fiber-reinforced composites generally require a 3D model for analysis, and the properties must be applied using a local coordinate system. This is so because the composites are generally wrapped around a post, and the lengthwise properties no longer run simply in one direction. Choosing a local coordinate system around curves will allow the modeler to keep the high-modulus direction along the cords of the reinforcements.

Although skin is an anisotropic material having different properties in each direction, Bischoff et al. (2000) have presented an interesting model as a second step beyond isotropic material selection.

They used an anisotropic stress loading on the material and achieved a more anisotropic material response. While an anisotropic, nonlinear elastic-plastic model would be best to model skin, the preceding may be used as an intermediate step in FEA.

Vascular flow models (i.e., arterial, venous, and cardiac) and airways models have to be concerned with vessel wall elasticity. As a first step, a rigid wall may be useful when investigating simply the flow patterns. As one progresses toward a more realistic model, elastic properties (e.g., radial, circumferential, and axial) may be required. Texts such as that by Fung (1996) present some of these properties. Another issue is that of tissue tethering. Most mechanical property evaluations have used material removed from its surrounding tissue. Vascular tissue is intimately connected with its surrounding tissue, which may reduce the elastic component slightly. Commercial silicone tubing is a reasonable material on which to model vessel walls if one is evaluating the material as isotropic. If one varies vessel compliance (elasticity) from rigid to that of thin-walled silicone tubing (and beyond), one can achieve a reasonable cross section of possible flow patterns. This is of particular importance when evaluating pulsatile flows. The downside to adding vessel compliance is the dramatic increase in computational time. Steinman and Ethier (1994) evaluated an end-to-side anastomosis pulsatile flow model in two dimensions with either a rigid or elastic wall. The computational time on a workstation was 3 to 4 hours for the rigid model versus 78 hours for the same model when elastic walls were included.

The next topic when discussing material behavior in vascular flows is the nonlinear flow material itself (blood). As a first approximation, a Newtonian fluid (water) may be used to model blood. This is generally the first material used when evaluating flows by bench testing. Flows in the larger arteries and veins, such as the carotid artery, may be successfully evaluated in this manner. Whole-blood viscosity is 0.035 cP, with a density just slightly above that of water (Fung, 1996). This model is reasonable for larger vessels because the solid components of blood do not interact enough to greatly vary the results. The flow in the boundary layer near the vessel walls tends to have fewer red cells in the large vessels because the particles tend to shift toward the higher-velocity core flow. Smaller diameter vessels, such as the coronaries, will demonstrate greater deviation from Newtonian flow as the red blood cells become a dominant factor in the flow. These flows are best modeled as a combination of Bingham material and power-law flow. The flow is often modeled as a Casson's flow, including a plug-like flow in the vessel core and a combination of the preceding two flows nearer the wall. A finite shear stress is required for flow to exist, and then the viscosity changes as a power-law fit to the shear rate. At higher shear rates, this tends to become a straight line and would be well modeled as Newtonian. Capillary flows should not be modeled as Newtonian or power-law flows because they are much more complex. The normal red blood cell is larger than the diameter of a capillary and must be "forced" through the vessel by deforming the cell in either a balloon-like form or a so-called slipper-zipper form that forces the cell along one side of the vessel.

The decision to "accurately" model blood flow becomes difficult when evaluating the red blood cell component. Although the red blood cell begins as the biconcave form seen in most anatomy and physiology texts, it deforms under the shears seen in flow. The cell becomes elongated (looking much like a football), and the cell membrane slides in a tank-treading motion (Sutera et al., 1989). The interior of the cell is also a viscoelastic fluid, making the modeling of this system difficult. While the preceding is correct for normal red blood cells, disease states, such as sickle cell anemia, modify the mechanical structure of the cell membrane, which in turn alters the flow characteristics of the blood.

12.4 BOUNDARY CONDITIONS

The final important area of FEA is that of boundary conditions. What are the loadings and constraints of the systems? For hard and soft tissues, these include loading sites and multiple attachments. For biofluids, these include pressures, velocities, and pulsatile conditions.

The primary concern when evaluating hard tissues is to determine how many ligament and tendon attachments are required. For example, the wrist is made up of a vast network of ligaments but only a few major ones (An et al., 1991). In a two-dimensional model of the wrist or even in a 3D model, a reasonably accurate model may be produced by only adding a few ligament attachments per carpal bone. Ligament attachment sites may also be approximated as a first step, although point attachments such as might be made by a single spring are cause for concern.

As noted in Sec. 12.2, a 3D model of a joint will be more accurate than a 2D model. If one is evaluating a long bone model in isolation, it must be decided whether the joint area is of importance and whether the model is to be constructed for static or dynamic evaluation. In a static case, if one is concerned with structures away from the articular cartilage, a simple loading or constraint system may be used successfully to represent the joint. A fully dynamic model or one that examines the joint itself will require a more complex 3D model with fixed constraints and loadings further from the joint surfaces.

Soft tissue analysis requires an evaluation of insertion geometries and paths for complete evaluation. As tendons travel from muscle to bone they often travel through sheaths and are partially constrained. While these issues are generally not of importance to general modeling of bone interactions and muscle forces, they may be needed if the desired result is a clinically accurate model of a given tendon.

Blood flow requires a knowledge of both the velocity and pressure conditions and the time-based changes in these parameters. While venous flow is basically steady state, it is readily apparent that arterial flow is pulsatile. Even in arterial flows, a mean flow is considered reasonable as a first modeling mechanism. Higher and lower steady flow velocities and pressures begin to produce a fuller picture of behavior. In the more complex models, a fully pulsatile flow is desirable, although generally at a large computational expense (hence the use of supercomputers for many of these models). As noted in Sec. 12.3, vessel wall behavior is an important boundary condition for blood flow.

Airways flow has a boundary condition of diffusion only at the terminal level within the alveolar sacs. While air is moved in and out in the upper respiratory system, diffusion is the means by which material is shifted near the lung-blood interfaces. A flow model of the lower respiratory system should be such that air does not physically move in and out of the alveolar sacs.

12.5 CASE STUDIES AND REVIEWS

Ankle Foot Orthotic. The first study is an evaluation of an ankle-foot orthosis (AFO) or brace such as is used for patients with "drop foot" (Abu-Hasaballah et al., 1997). Although the orthosis is made of lightweight thermoplastic, many patients still find it heavy and uncomfortable, especially in the summer when the orthosis may become sweat covered.

A 3D model with appropriate geometries and material properties was developed from a physical brace (Fig. 12.2). After verifying the model by comparison to actual AFO behavior, a series of design modifications was made, by element removal, to reduce weight while retaining structural integrity. Figure 12.3 presents one of the final versions, with segments along the calf removed. The weight reduction was approximately 30 percent, and the large openings along the calf would reduce sweat buildup in this region.

It should be noted that a single AFO cost $200 or more, so FEA is an inexpensive means by which many design changes may be evaluated before any actual brace has to be built. Computational times were reasonably low, from a few minutes to a few hours on a PC.

Carotid Blood Flow. As a second example of the process that may be followed when modeling the human body with FEA, let us consider blood flow through the carotid artery. This is the main blood supply to the brain (through the internal carotid artery) and is the site of stenoses. Plaque formation (atherosclerosis) narrows the common carotid artery at the origin of the external carotid artery (which flows toward the face) until blood flow is reduced to the brain.

To first evaluate this flow, many simplifications will be made to reduce the opportunities for error in modeling. Each model result should be evaluated based on available bench and clinical data prior to adding the next level of complexity. These checks may also be used to determine which simplifications do not affect the relevant results.

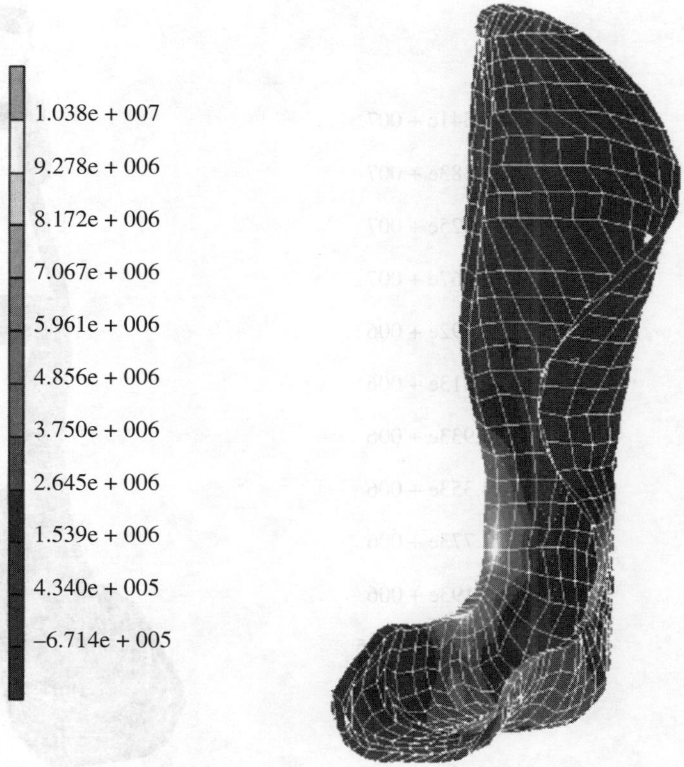

FIGURE 12.2 Finite-element model of an isentropic ankle-foot orthosis demonstrating high-stress regions near inner ankle. The material is thermoplastic.

As a first approximation of geometry, a Y bifurcation using straight rigid tubing may be used. The blood may be modeled as a Newtonian fluid without particles. As boundary conditions, the inlet flow may either be considered Poiseuille or uniform across the tube (if a sufficient entry length is included to produce a fully developed flow profile). Steady flow will be used for this model.

The next sequence in modeling will be to improve the geometry. The bulb shape of the carotid sinus will be added, as well as the geometry of the external carotid inlet. For this second model, a Y shape may still be used, or a more anatomically correct angle may be used. Liquid and inlet conditions will be maintained from the first model, and the vessel walls will remain rigid. Differences in flow behavior may be apparent between these first two models.

Once the second model is functional, we will turn our attention to the material in the flow. A combination of Bingham and power-law fluid will be used to better model the non-Newtonian characteristics of whole blood. RBCs will not be added for this model because the fluid is now a reasonable approximation of large-vessel flow. We will still use steady flow in this model.

Once the third version solves smoothly, pulsatile flow will be added. As a first step, a sinusoidal flow pattern will be added to the constant-flow conditions. Subsequent modifications will add user-defined patterns resembling the actual pulse forms found in the human carotid.

The fourth generation of the model will seek to include the nonrigid vessel wall properties. As a first step, the walls will include varying amounts of elasticity, such as might be found in silicone tubing.

The viscoelastic behavior of actual arterial wall may be investigated during the final model or two in the process.

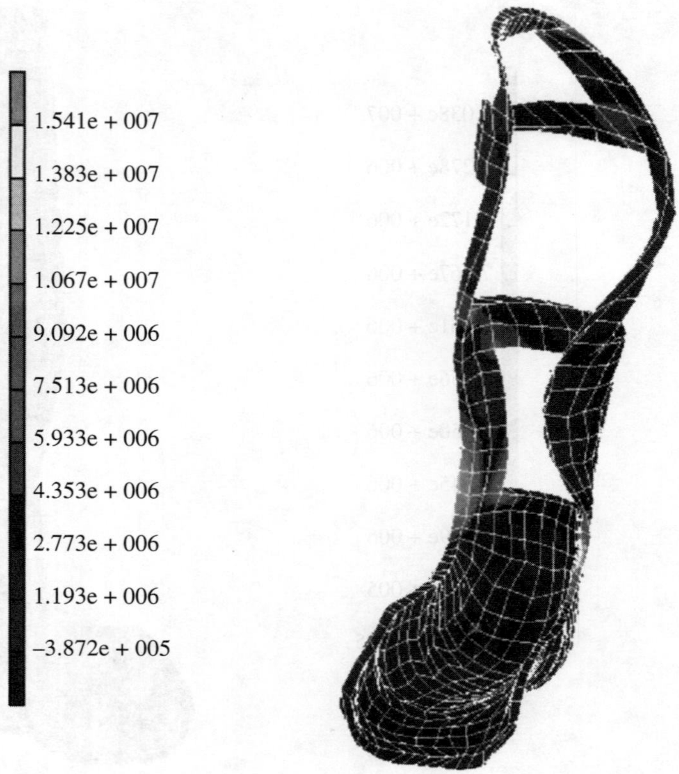

FIGURE 12.3 Ankle-foot orthosis optimized manually to reduce material in regions of low stress. Total weight reduction is approximately 30 percent.

The fifth version of the model will now seek to address the issues of the red blood cells. Using software allowing for the addition of user-defined particles, rigid disks may first be used. After success with this version, deformable cells may be used to better approximate red blood cells.

At each point in the process (each generation of the model), the user should compare the findings with those of available bench and clinical studies, along with the results from previous model versions. Little change from previous models may suggest either that there is no need for a more complex model or that all the modifications have not been taken account of.

It should also be noted that varying the simpler models may encompass the behavior of more complex models. For example, varying the static flow parameters may account for many of the behavior modifications seen in the pulsatile model. For similar reasons, varying the elastic properties of the vessel wall may encompass behavioral changes brought about by viscoelastic modeling at a great savings of computational time and power.

Acromion Bone. A good example of the linkage of the engineer to the clinician can be found in a masters of engineering project (de Oliveira, 2017). A model of the acromion bone was developed to evaluate drilled holes used in reconstruction. The clinical issue was to determine the best (and worst) locations to drill holes to prevent bone fracture (Dyrna et al., 2018). These may fail under load, such as due to a fall. The engineer used mechanical bone testing to determine mechanical properties and various measuring systems to determine geometries. The results of an intact FEA specimen were then matched to cadaveric testing, and the model adjusted until convergence. Loading was adjusted to model the most common fall orientations seen clinically. Then various hole specifications were

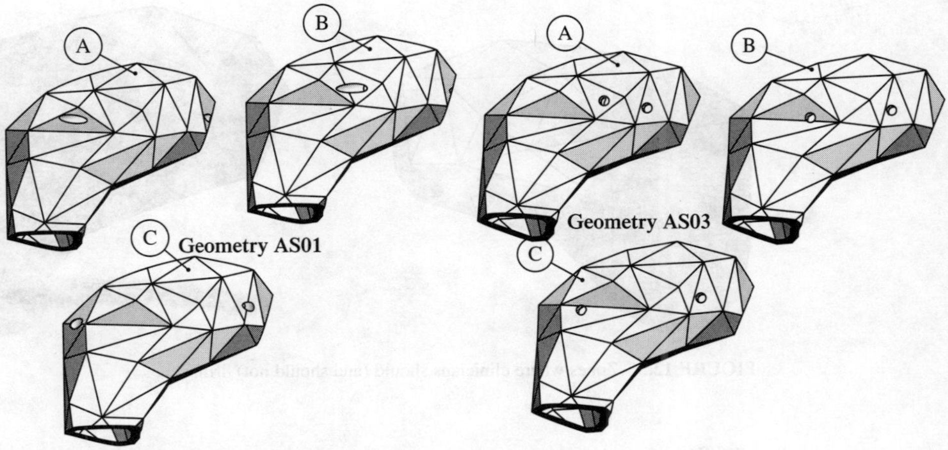

FIGURE 12.4A 0.24-mm diameter holes in a model acromion bone.

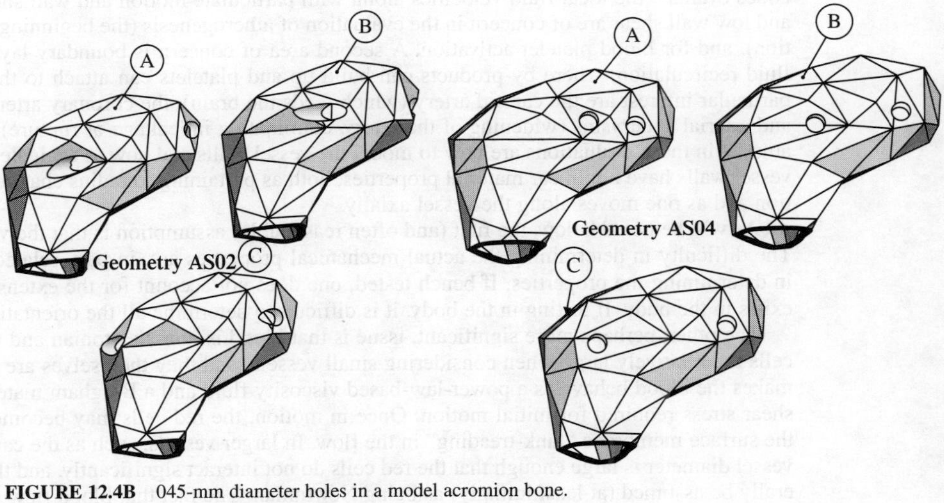

FIGURE 12.4B 045-mm diameter holes in a model acromion bone.

examined (two hole sizes, and six configurations each, Figs. 12.4*A* and 12.4*B*). Regions of "go/no go" were developed (Fig. 12.5). This information was then used by the clinicians to determine the sites of holes for reconstruction. As an aside, it should be noted that the student is a civil engineer, who was basically evaluating a structure.

12.5.1 Other Areas of Computer Modeling

In addition to orthopedic-based research noted above, modeling research is being performed in all aspects of biomedicine. Following are a few examples pertaining to some of the major arenas of current research. Of particular interest are the idealizations that must be made to keep both computational and general modeling times within reason. In many cases, these idealizations have been shown to present findings very close to those seen clinically.

FIGURE 12.5 Zones where clinicians should (and should not) drill.

Arterial Studies. Numerous recent papers have sought to evaluate the behavior of blood in arteries utilizing computational fluid dynamics (CFD). Analogous to solid finite-element modeling, these codes evaluate the local fluid velocities along with particulate motion and wall shear profiles. High and low wall shear are of concern in the evaluation of atherogenesis (the beginning of plaque formation), and for blood platelet activation. A second area of concern is boundary layer separation and fluid recirculation, where by-products can build up and platelets can attach to the vessel wall. Of particular interest are the carotid artery (which feeds the brain), the coronary arteries (to the heart), and arterial aneurysms (widening of the artery, culminating in leakage or rupture). The major areas at issue in these evaluations are how to model the vessel walls and how to evaluate the blood. Blood vessel walls have nonlinear material properties, both as pertaining to radius changes at a given location and as one moves along the vessel axially.

As will be noted below, the first (and often reasonable) assumption is that the vessel is isotropic. The difficulty in determining the actual mechanical properties are, in part, related to the difficulty in determining the properties. If bench tested, one does not account for the extensive tethering that exists in the body. If testing in the body, it is difficult to determine all the orientational properties.

The other, perhaps more significant, issue is that blood is non-Newtonian and pulsatile. The red cells are relatively large when considering small vessels, and they themselves are deformable. This makes the blood behave as a power-law-based viscosity fluid and a Bingham material, with a finite shear stress required for initial motion. Once in motion, the red cells may become elongated, with the surface membrane "tank-treading" in the flow. In larger vessels, such as the carotid or aorta, the vessel diameter is large enough that the red cells do not interact significantly, and the flows can generally be assumed (at least initially) as being Newtonian. The fact that blood flow in most instances is pulsatile (although some new heart assist devices utilize steady flow with no apparent ill effects) makes computer modeling difficult. On the other hand, it should be pointed out that the elasticity of the arterial walls partially damps out the effects of the pulsatile flow.

Carotid Artery. First, it should be noted that "old" averaged models remain valid. Many recent studies utilize subject-specific 3D geometries. Bressloff (2007) recently utilized an averaged carotid geometry developed in the 1980s to evaluate the need for using an entire pulse cycle.

Most recent studies have utilized rigid walls in their studies. Birchall et al. (2006) evaluated wall shear in stenosed (narrowed) carotid vessels, with atherosclerotic plaque geometries derived from magnetic resonance images. Glor et al. (2004) compared MRI to ultrasound for 3D imaging for computational fluid dynamics, and suggested (while using Newtonian pulsatile flow) that MRI is more accurate, although more expensive. Tambasco and Sreinman (2003) utilized deformable red cell equivalents and pulsatile conditions to simulate stenosed vessel bifurcations (branches). Box et al. (2005) utilized a carotid model averaged from 49 healthy subjects and non-Newtonian blood flow to evaluate wall shear (it should be noted that a cell-free layer clinically exists adjacent to the wall).

Coronary Artery. Giannoglou et al. (2005) averaged 83 3D geometries for their CFD model of the left coronary artery tree, using rigid walls and non-Newtonian averaged flow conditions, noted adverse pressure and shear gradients near bifurcations. Papafaklis et al. (2007) utilized biplane angiography and ultrasound of atherosclerotic coronaries to produce their models, which noted the correlation of low shear to plaque thickness.

The author has not touched upon the realm of heart valve replacement. This is an area where the solid and fluid computer models intersect. Utilizing similar techniques to those noted above for arterial studies (Birchall et al., 2006; Box et al., 2005; Bressloff, 2007; Glor et al., 2004; Giannoglou et al., 2005; Papafaklis et al., 2007; Tambasco and Sreinman, 2003), it is convenient to model new valve designs prior to initial bench testing, and to compare them to earlier valves as well as native (intact) valves.

Coronary Artery Disease. The issues and directions of CFD for the coronary arteries were reviewed by Zhang et al. (2014). Among other findings, it was noted that patient-specific geometries are becoming more prevalent in research, but they are limited by imaging accuracy. This is particularly important for the smaller diameter coronary arteries. Wall shear stresses are areas of clinical interest and many papers seek to evaluate this, as these are directly related to coronary artery disease. There remains much work to be done in the realm of blood-wall interactions, and the effects of heart motion on the coronary arteries.

Arterial Grafts. Many studies utilize CFD to evaluate the replacement of arteries. As a transition from the coronary flow models above to graft analysis, an example of this work is the study by Frauenfelder et al. (2007a). This study utilized a pulsatile Newtonian flow with rigid walls, based on two subjects with coronary bypass grafts, and evaluated flow velocities and wall shear near the anastomoses (joinings of the native and graft arteries). O'Brien et al. (2005) utilized CFD to evaluate a new design for arterial grafts in the mid leg (near the knee) using a rigid wall, Newtonian pulsatile model to evaluate wall shear and regions of recirculation.

Arterial Stents. In recent years, the insertion of stents has become popular to maintain patency in stenosed coronary arteries after dilation. Stents are also used to bypass aneurysms in arteries without having to resort to replacing the vessel segment with a graft. While the author will not enter the debate as to their effectiveness, it should be noted that many CFD papers have been published evaluating stents.

Strut design is critical to its proper function and has been the subject of many studies. The general topic of stent design remains an area of study, as does the effect on local blood motion and wall shear. Seo et al. (2005) evaluated stent wire size using a pulsatile, non-Newtonian fluid and rigid walls. LaDisa Jr. et al. (2005) utilized a Newtonian pulsatile model to evaluate strut mesh geometries. Papaioannou et al. (2007) utilized a rigid wall model with pulsatile Newtonian flow in their evaluation of wall shear, and validated their model with a bench-top system. Frauenfelder et al. (2007b) evaluated an abdominal aortic aneurysm model based on CT scans with Newtonian pulsatile flow and deformable walls, validated the steady-flow model, and examined both the stent and the surrounding walls. Chen et al. (2005) used biplane cine angiography to produce coronary models for hemodynamic modeling of stents.

Vascular Assist Devices. Another classic example of computer modeling is for vascular assist devices. These include ventricular assist devices (VADs) and pumps for extracorporeal membrane oxygenation (ECMO) to temporarily replace the lungs. Many of these devices are either centrifugal, axial (screw-style), or positive displacement (typically with a diaphragm). Virtually all recent cardiac assist devices have been developed using CFD. In 2011, Fraser et al. (2011) described various ventricular assist devices, including centrifugal, axial flow, and positive displacement pumps. These systems continue to evolve, and analysis assists in the design of not only the devices themselves but also the cannulae attaching them to the patient and their location. The authors point out the critical need for validation, especially due to the number of input options. The idealizations used (such as Newtonian fluid) are also to be considered. The authors also note that adding the computational time may be a consideration (especially for unsteady flow). Recent literature has many examples of CFD for ventricular assist devices of the above types.

Aortic Valve Replacement. The recent interest in transcatheter aortic valve replacement (TAVR), along with further developments for traditional aortic valve replacement, is another rich area of CFD analysis. As with the other heart-related examples above, their literature has numerous articles on the subject. A 2018 article by Rotman et al. discussed many of the challenges for the understanding of TAVRs (Rotman et al., 2018). Specifically, they note: "Among the advantages of computational models: (i) once established, it allows analysis of the results in extremely high spatial and temporal resolution, (ii) it allows analysis of more parameters than in an equivalent experimental setup, without interfering with the measurements, (iii) it allows investigation of more complex models and various scenarios while simultaneously considering more factors, and (iv) isolation of any of the input parameters and performing sensitivity analyses are relatively easy and cost-effective as compared to equivalent costly experiments." This nicely sums up the advantages noted for CFD analysis. As noted for the other examples, the model must be fully verified, and the limitations of the model must be understood to make use of the system.

Skin. Due to its bidirectional mechanical properties and (obvious) importance, an increasing number of FEA studies are investigating skin biomechanics. Of particular interest is the issue of skin deterioration of damage. These evaluations include both the skin surface and subdural tissue layers. Some authors have investigated skin in general, while others evaluated specific regions. Hendricks et al. (2003) used an isotropic nonlinear 2D model to evaluate the effect of suction on skin. Kuroda and Akimoto (2005) used a 2D linear, elastic, isotropic model to evaluate the stresses caused by various sizes of ulcerations to investigate the growth of ulcers.

Working from the top down, the following studies give a brief overview of the areas being investigated via FEA. To evaluate the effect of high-and low-frequency vibration, Wu et al. (2007) produced a model of a fingertip including the nail, bone, and skin. While the other structures were assumed to be linear and elastic, the skin and subcutaneous tissue was modeled as a nonlinear elastic and viscoelastic 2D material. Linder-Ganz et al. (2007) used MRI data to construct a FEA model to evaluate stresses in subdermal tissue (just below the skin) while sitting, under weight-bearing and nonweight-bearing conditions. Finally, to the foot, Erdemir et al. (2005) utilized a 2D model taken during maximum pressure of stance to evaluate the effects of various shoe sole materials on the reduction of local plantar pressures. This FEA model used a hyperelastic strain energy function for the foot's soft tissue.

Prosthetic Stump Skin. A subset of skin FEA evaluation is that of the anatomic stump remaining in limb prostheses. When replacing a portion of a limb, especially the leg, great care must be taken so that the local soft tissue does not deteriorate. Much of this work focuses on the local soft tissue stresses. Portnoy et al. (2007) validated a FEA model by matching their studies with sensors in the sock normally placed between the limb and prosthesis, along with devices monitoring indentation in to the stump. Goh et al. (2005) produced a FEA model of a below-the-knee residual limb which included bone and soft tissue, both modeled as linear, elastic, isotropic, and homogeneous materials. They also validated their model via sensors built into the prosthesis. A third study in this brief review, by Jia et al. (2005), investigated stresses during walking. This study utilized isotropic, linear material properties, and further simplified the model by assuming the knee motion to be hinge like. Actual knee motion includes the revolving and sliding of the instantaneous center of rotation but, as noted before, simplifications of this sort are very useful in early studies (and often are adequate for significant advances in the field).

Dental. A final review area the author would like to present is that of dental FEA. The realm of implants and tooth behavior is of particular interest considering the number and variety of implants and procedures available today. The complexity of tooth interaction both with its neighbors and underlying bones and ligaments is well suited for FEA. Many studies evaluate implanted teeth and dental bridges. In one study, Lin et al. (2003) evaluated the stresses between a prosthetic tooth and its abutting native teeth. This 3D study utilized CT scanned geometries and isotropic material properties for the prosthesis and the native tooth enamel, dentin, and pulp. No attaching structures (bone, ligament) were evaluated in this study. A study by Magne et al. (2002) evaluated a 2D model of partial dentures, between two abutment native teeth, which included the periodontal membrane and supporting bone. The cortical and cancellous bone, ligament, enamel, and dentin were assumed to be isotropic. A number of implant materials, ranging from gold to fiber-reinforced composites, were evaluated. A final example paper from Holberg et al. (2005) utilized a 3D FEA model to evaluate the consequences of corrective facial surgery, including the jaw. Their simulations were based upon patient-specific scanned images, and utilized isotropic properties for soft tissue modeling.

12.5.2 Case Studies Conclusions

From the brief outline above, it can be seen that FEA and CFD are being used in all aspects of medicine to great advantage. While touching on a few areas of significant interest, there is no area of the body or function that does not lend itself to computer modeling. The major issues when comparing the various models include how far to accept the simplifications. While a linear, 2D, steady or static, isotropic model can still be quite useful, most studies incorporate at least some nonlinearity. The bulk of the fluid models evaluate pulsatile flow, and many include the non-Newtonian behavior of blood. Solid models often use isotropic material properties, while the issue of 2D versus 3D seems to be on a case-by-case basis. As with all modeling, the bottom line is to be able to produce a validated model that will successfully mimic or evaluate the clinical situation.

As can be seen from these examples, multiple generations of modeling are often used to evaluate all the aspects of biological systems. Many simplifications are made initially to determine a first-generation solution. The number of subsequent model generations will vary, depending on the sophistication of results desired. At this point in time it is perhaps unlikely that all nonlinear parameters of the human body can be included in an FEA model, mainly due to the fact that all properties are not yet known. Comparison with bench and clinical findings will demonstrate, however, that similar behavioral results are possible.

The researcher should not be overly concerned with the minutiae of the model parameters. Considering the variances between people, an overview covering most of the noted effects should be the goal. The purpose of the models is to examine system behavior when changes are made, such as the effects of geometric and material modifications. Although the actual behavior may not be exact, the variances due to changes in the model may well mimic those of the device or human system.

12.6 CONCLUSIONS

The main points to be taken from this chapter are that many simplifications must be made initially when evaluating human-related structures with FEA, but this may not be a major problem. Each of the three main areas (geometry, material properties, and boundary conditions) is of equal importance and should be considered separately. Depending on the detail of the construct modeled, many geometric components may be simplified. Care should be taken when using isentropic models for solids, but even these may be used for general evaluations of tissue regions. Soft tissues are difficult to fully model without the use of nonlinear properties. Newtonian flows are reasonable for large-vessel flows (such as the aorta or carotid artery) as long as the aspects of flows have been shown not to be affected by the particular components. Boundary conditions may begin with steady-state values, but dynamic components will add the complexities of the true system.

In closing, a computer model of portions of the human body or an added component may be as simple or complex as the user desires. One should use properties to be found in this and other sources and always confirm findings with clinical or bench values. The future is unlimited in this field as we learn more about the body and seek to best aid or replace its many functions.

REFERENCES

Abu-Hasaballah, K. S., Nowak, M. D., and Cooper, P. S. (1997), Enhanced solid ankle-foot orthosis design: Real-time contact pressures evaluation and finite element analysis, *1997 Adv. Bioeng.* pp. 285–286.

An, K.-N., Berger, R. A., and Cooney, W. P. (eds.) (1991), *Biomechanics of the Wrist Joint*, Springer-Verlag, New York.

Augereau, D., Pierrisnard, L., Renault, P., and Barquins, M. (1998), Prosthetic restoration after coronoradicular resection: Mechanical behavior of the distal root remaining and surrounding tissue, *J. Prosthet. Dent.* **80**:467–473.

Birchall, D., Zaman, A., Hacker, J., Davies, G., and Mendlow, D. (2006), Analysis of haemodynamic disturbance in the atherosclerotic carotid artery using computational fluid dynamics, *Eur. Radiol.* **16**:1074–1083.

Bischoff, J. E., Arruda, E. M., and Grosh, K. (2000), Finite element modeling of human skin using an isotropic, nonlinear elastic constitutive model, *J. Biomech.* **33**:645–652.

Box, F. M. A., van der Geest, R. J., Rutten, M. C. M., and Reiber, J. H. C. (2005), The influence of flow, vessel diameter, and non-Newtonian blood viscosity on the wall shear stress in a carotid bifurcation model for unsteady flow, *Invest. Radiol.* **40**(5):277–294.

Bressloff, N. W. (2007), Parametric geometry exploration of the human carotid artery bifurcation, *J. Biomech.* **40**:2483–2491.

Chen, M. C. Y., Lu, P., Chen, J. S. Y., and Hwang, N. H. C. (2005), Computational hemodynamics of an implanted coronary stent based on three-dimensional cine angiography reconstruction, *ASAIO J.* **51**(4):313–320.

Chu, Y. H., Elias, J. J., Duda, G. N., Frassica, F. J., and Chao, E. Y. S. (2000), Stress and micromotion in the taper lock joint of a modular segmental bone replacement prosthesis, *J. Biomech.* **33**:1175–1179.

de Hart, J., Cacciola, G., Schreurs, P. J. G., and Peters, G. W. M. (1998), A three-dimensional analysis of a fiber-reinforced aortic valve prosthesis, *J. Biomech.* **31**:629–638.

de Hart, J., Peters, G. W. M., Schreurs, P. J. G., and Baaijens, F. P. T. (2000), A two-dimensional fluid-structure interaction model of the aortic valve, *J. Biomech.* **32**:1079–1088.

de Oliveira, C. C. T. (2017), *Structural Analysis of Repairing Process of Acromioclavicular Joint Injury that Requires a Drilled Hole*, Masters of Engineering Project, University of Hartford, West Hartford, Connecticut.

Dyrna, F., de Oliveira, C. C. T., Nowak, M., Voss, A., Obopilwe, E., Braun, S., Pauzenberger, L., Imhoff, A. B., Mazzocca, A. D., and Beitzel, K. (2018), Risk of fracture of the acromion depends on size and orientation of acromial bone tunnels when performing acromioclavicular reconstruction, *Knee Surg. Sports Traum. Arth.* **26**(1):275–284.

Erdemir, A., Saucerman, J. J., Lemmon, D., Loppnow, B., Turso, B., Ulbrecht, J. S., and Cavanagh, P. R. (2005), Local plantar pressure relief in therapeutic footwear: Design guidelines from finite element models, *J. Biomech.* **38**:1798–1806.

Ferris, P., and Prendergast, P. J. (2000), Middle-ear dynamics before and after ossicular replacement, *J. Biomech.* **33**:581–590.

Fraser, K. H., Taskin, M. E., Griffith, B. P., and Wu, Z. J. (2011), The use of computational fluid dynamics in the development of ventricular assist devices, *Med. Eng. Phy.* **33**:263–280.

Frauenfelder, T., Boutsianis, E., Schertler, T., Husmann., L., Leschka, S., Poulikakos, D., Marincek, B., and Alkadhi, H. (2007a), Flow and wall shear stress in end-to-side and side-to-side anastomosis of venous coronary artery bypass graft, *Biomed. Eng. On-Line* **6**:35.

Frauenfelder, T., Lotfey, M., Boehm, T., and Wildermuth, S. (2007b), Computational fluid dynamics: Hemodynamic changes in abdominal aortic aneurysm after stent-graft implantation, *Cardiovasc. Intervent. Radiol.* **29**:613–623.

Fung, Y. C. (1996), *Biomechanics: Mechanical Properties of Living Tissues*, 2d ed., Springer-Verlag, New York.

Giannoglou, G. D., Soulis, J. V., Farmakis, T. M., Giannakoulas, G. A., Parcharidis, G. E., and Louridas, G. E. (2005), Wall pressure gradient in normal left coronary artery tree, *Med. Eng. Physics* **27**:455–464.

Glor, F. P., Ariff, B., Hughes, A. D., Crowe, L. A., Verdonck, P. R., Barratt, D. C., Thom, S. A. McG., Firmin, D. N., and Xu, X. Y. (2004), Image-based carotid flow reconstruction: A comparison between MRI and ultrasound, *Physiol. Meas.* **25**:1495–1509.

Goh, J. C. H., Lee, P. V. S., Toh, S. L., and Ooi, C. K. (2005), Development of an integrated CAD-FEA process for below-knee prosthetic sockets, *Clin. Biomech.* **20**:623–629.

Grande, K. J., Cochran, R. P., Reinhall, P. G., and Kunzelman, K. S. (2000), Mechanisms of aortic valve incompetence: Finite element modeling of aortic root dilation, *Ann. Thorac. Surg.* **69**:1851–1857.

Hendricks, F. M., Brokken, D., van Eemeren, J. T. W. M., Oomens, C. W. J., Baaijens, F. P. T., and Horsten, J. B. A. M. (2003), A numerical-experimental method to characterize the nonlinear mechanical behavior of human skin, *Skin Res. Tech.* **9**:274–283.

Holberg, C., Heine, A-K., Geis, P., Schwenzer, K., and Rudzki-Janson, I. (2005), Three-dimensional soft tissue prediction using finite elements, *J. Orofacial Orthop.* **66**:122–134.

Huang, H. M., Lee, M. C., Chiu, W. T., Chen, C. T., and Lee, S. Y. (1999). Three-dimensional finite element analysis of subdural hematoma, *J. Trauma* **47**:538–544.

Jia, X., Zhang, M., Li X., and Lee, W. C. C. (2005), A quasi-dynamic nonlinear finite element model to investigate prosthetic interface stresses during walking for trans-tibial amputees, *Clin. Biomech.* **20**:630–635.

Klinnert, J., Nowak, M., and Lewis, C. (1994), Addition of a medial allograft to stabilize supracondylar femur fractures, 1994 *Adv. Bioeng.* pp. 193–194.

Kuroda, S., and Akimoto, M. (2005), Finite element analysis of undermining of pressure ulcer with a simple cylinder model, *J. Nippon Med. Sch.* **72**:174–178.

Kurtz, S. M., Ochoa, J. A., White, C. V., Srivastav, S., and Cournoyer, J. (1998), Backside nonconformity and locking restraints affect liner/shell load transfer mechanisms and relative motion in modular acetabular components for total hip replacement, *J. Biomech.* **31**:431–437.

LaDisa, J. F., Jr., Olson, L. E., Guler, I., Hettrick, D. A., Kersten, J. R., Warltier, D. C., and Pagel, P. S. (2005), Circumferential vascular deformation after stent implantation alters wall shear stress evaluated with time-dependent 3D computational fluid dynamics models, *J. Appl. Physiol.* **98**:947–957.

Lin, C-L., Lee, H-E., Wang, C-H., and Chang K-H. (2003), Integration of CT, CAD system and finite element method to investigate interfacial stresses of resin-bonded prosthesis, *Comp. Methods and Programs in Biomed.* **72**:55–64.

Linder-Ganz, E., Shabshin, N., Itzchak, Y., and Gefen, A. (2007), Assessment of mechanical conditions in subdermal tissues during sitting: A combined experimental-MRI and finite element approach, *J. Biomech.* **40**:1443–1454.

Magne, P., Perakis, N., Belser, U. S., and Krejci, I. (2002), Stress distribution of inlay-anchored adhesive fixed partial dentures: A finite element analysis of the influence of restorative materials and abutment preparation design, *J. Prosth. Dent.* **87**:516–527.

Maurer, P., Holwig, S., and Schubert, J. (1999), Finite-element analysis of different screw diameters in the sagittal split osteotomy of the mandible, *J. Craniomaxillofac. Surg.* **27**:365–372.

Merz, B. R., Hunenbaart, S., and Belser, U. C. (2000), Mechanics of the implant-abutment connection: An 8-degree taper compared to a butt joint connection, *Int. J. Oral Maxillofac. Implants* **15**:519–526.

Nowak, M. D. (1993), Linear versus nonlinear material modeling of the scapholunate ligament of the human wrist, in H. D. Held, C. A. Brebbia, R. D. Ciskowski, H. Power (eds), *Computational Biomedicine*, pp. 215–222, Computational Mechanics Publications, Boston.

Nowak, M. D., and Cherry, A. C. (1995), Nonlinear finite element modeling of the distal carpal arch, *1995 Adv Bioeng.* pp. 321–322.

Nowak, M. D., Haser, K., and Golberg, A. J. (1999), Finite element analysis of fiber composite dental bridges: The effect of length/depth ratio and load application method, *1999 Adv. Bioeng.* pp. 249–250.

Nowak, M. D., and Logan, S. E. (1991), Distinguishing biomechanical properties of intrinsic and extrinsic human wrist ligaments, *J. Biomech. Eng.* **113**:85–93.

O'Brien, T. P., Grace, P., Walsh, M., Burke, P., and McGloughlni, T. (2005), Computational investigations of a new prosthetic femoral-popliteal bypass graft design, *J Vasc. Surg.* **42**(6):1169–1175.

Papafaklis, M. I., Bourantas, C. V., Theodorakis, P. E., Katsouras, C. S., Fotiadis, D. I., and Michalis, L. K. (2007), Association of endothelial shear stress with plaque thickness in a real three-dimensional left main coronary artery bifurcation model, *Int. J. Cariol.* **115**:276–278.

Papaioannou, T. G., Christofidis, C. C., Mathioulakis, D. S., and Stefanadis, C. I. (2007), A novel design of a noncylindric stent with beneficial effects of flow characteristics: An experimental and numerical flow study in an axisymmetric arterial model with sequential mild stenosis, *Artif. Org.* **31**:627–638.

Portnoy, S., Yarnitzky, G., Yizhar, Z., Kristal, A., Oppenheim, U., Siev-Ner, I., and Gefen, A. (2007), Real-time patient-specific finite element analysis of internal stresses in the soft tissues of a residual limb: A new tool for prosthetic fitting, *Ann. Biomed. Eng.* **35**:120–135.

Raghavan, M. L., Vorp, D. A., Federle, M. P., Makaroun, M. S., and Webster, M. W. (2000), Wall stress distribution on three-dimensionally reconstructed models of human abdominal aortic aneurysm, *J. Vasc. Surg.* **31**:760–769.

Rotman, O. M., Bianchi, M., Ghosh, R. P., Kovarovic, B., and Bluestein, D. (2018), Principles of TAVR valve design, modelling, and testing, *Exp. Rev. Med. Dev.* **15**(11):771–791.

Seo, T., Schachter, L. G., and Barakat, A. I. (2005), Computational study of fluid mechanical disturbance induced by endovascular stents, *Ann. Biomed. Eng.* **33**:444–456.

Steinman, D. A., and Ethier, C. R. (1994), The effect of wall distensibility on flow in a two-dimensional end-to-side anastomosis, *J. Biomech. Eng.* **116**:294–301.

Sutera, S. P., Pierre, P. R., and Zahalak, G. I. (1989), Deduction of intrinsic mechanical properties of the erythrocyte membrane from observations of tank-treading in the rheoscope, *Biorheology.* **26**:177–197.

Tambasco, M., and Sreinman, D. A. (2003), Path dependent hemodynamics of the stenosed carotid bifurcation, *Ann. Biomed. Eng.* **31**:1054–1065.

Wu, J. Z., Welcome, D. E., Krajnak, K., and Dong, R. G. (2007), Finite element analysis of the penetrations of shear and normal vibrations into the soft tissue in a fingertip, *Med. Eng. Phys.* **29**:718–727.

Zhang, J-M., Zhong, L., Su, B., Wan, M., Yap, J. S., Tham, J. P. L., Chua, L. P., Ghista, D. N., and Tan, R. S. (2014), Perspective on CFD studies of coronary artery disease lesions and hemodynamics: A review, *Int. J. Numer. Method Biomed. Eng.* **30**(6):659–680.

CHAPTER 13
VIBRATION, MECHANICAL SHOCK, AND IMPACT

Anthony J. Brammer
University of Connecticut Health, Farmington, Connecticut

Donald R. Peterson
Northern Illinois University, DeKalb, Illinois

13.1 INTRODUCTION

Time-varying forces and accelerations occur in daily life, and are commonly experienced, for example, in an elevator and in aircraft, railway trains, and automobiles. All of these situations involve motion of the whole body transmitted through a seat, or from the floor in the case of a standing person, where the human response is commonly related to the relative motion of body parts, organs, and tissues. The vibration, shocks, and impacts become of consequence when activities are impaired (e.g., writing and drinking on a train, or motion sickness), or health is threatened (e.g., a motor vehicle crash). Equally important are exposures involving a localized part of the body, such as the hand and arm (e.g., when operating a hand tool), or the head (e.g., impacts causing skull fracture or concussion).

In this chapter, methods for characterizing human response to vibration, shock, and impact are considered in order to prescribe appropriate countermeasures. The methods involve data from experiments on humans, animals, and cadavers, and predictions using biodynamic models and manikins. Criteria for estimating the occurrence of health effects and injury are summarized, together with methods for mitigating the effects of potentially harmful exposures. There is an extensive literature on the effects of vibration, shocks, and impacts on humans (Brammer, 2010; Griffin, 1990; Krajnak, 2018; Mansfield, 2005; Nahum and Melvin., 2002; Yoganandan et al., 2015).

13.1.1 Definitions and Characterization of Vibration, Mechanical Shock, and Impact

Vibration and Mechanical Shock. *Vibration* is a time-varying disturbance of a mechanical, or biological, system from an equilibrium condition for which the long-term average of the motion will tend to zero, and on which may be superimposed either translations or rotations, or both. The mechanical forces may be distributed, or concentrated over a small area of the body, and may be applied at an angle to the surface (e.g., tangential or normal). Vibration may contain random or deterministic components, or both; they may also vary with time (i.e., be nonstationary). Deterministic vibration may contain harmonically related components, or pure tones (with sinusoidal time dependence), and may form "shocks." A mechanical *shock* is a nonperiodic disturbance characterized by suddenness and severity with, for the human body, the maximum forces being reached within a few tenths of a second, and a total duration of up to about a second. An *impact* occurs when the body, or body part, collides with an object. When considering injury potential, the shape of the object in contact with, or impacting, the body is important, as is the posture. In addition, for hand tools, both the compressive (grip) and thrust (feed) forces employed to perform the manual task need to be considered.

Although vibration, shock, and impact may be expressed by the *displacement* of a reference point from its equilibrium position (after subtracting translational and rotational motion), they are more commonly described by the *velocity* or *acceleration*, which are the first and second time derivatives of the displacement.

Vibration Magnitude. The magnitude of vibration is characterized by second, and higher even-order mean values, as the net motion expressed by a simple, long-term time average will be zero. For an acceleration that varies with time t, as $a(t)$, the higher-order mean values are calculated from:

$$a_{\text{RM}} = \left[\frac{1}{T}\int_0^T [a(t)]^m\,dt\right]^{1/r} \tag{13.1}$$

where the integration is performed for a time T, and m and r are constants describing the moment and root of the function. By far the most common metric used to express the magnitude of whole-body or hand-transmitted vibration is the *root mean square* (RMS) acceleration a_{RMS}, which is obtained from Eq. (13.1) with $m = r = 2$; i.e.,

$$a_{\text{RMS}} = \left[\frac{1}{T}\int_0^T [a(t)]^2\,dt\right]^{1/2} \tag{13.2}$$

Other metrics used to express the magnitude of vibration and shock include the *root mean quad* (RMQ) acceleration a_{RMQ}, with $m = r = 4$ (and higher even orders, such as the *root mean sex* (RMX) acceleration a_{RMX}, with $m = r = 6$).

The RMS value of a continuous random vibration with a Gaussian amplitude distribution corresponds to the magnitude of the 68th percentile of the amplitudes in the waveform. The higher-order means correspond more closely to the peak value of the waveform, with the RMQ corresponding to the 81st percentile and the RMX to the 88th percentile of this amplitude distribution. The relationships between these metrics depend on the amplitude distribution of the waveform, wherein they find application to characterize the magnitude of shocks entering, and objects impacting, the body (Brammer et al., 2010). This can be inferred from the following example, where the RMS value corresponds to 0.707 of the amplitude of a sinusoidal waveform, while the RMQ value corresponds to 0.7825 of the amplitude.

EXAMPLE 13.1 *Calculate the RMS and RMQ accelerations of a pure-tone (single-frequency) vibration of amplitude A and angular frequency ω.*

Answer: *The time history (i.e., waveform) of a pure-tone vibration of amplitude A can be expressed as a(t) = A sin ωt, so that, from Eq. (13.2):*

$$a_{\text{RMS}} = \left[\frac{1}{T}\int_0^T [A\sin(\omega t)]^2\,dt\right]^{1/2} \quad \text{or} \quad a_{\text{RMS}} = \left[\frac{A^2}{2T}\int_0^T [1-\cos(2\omega t)]\,dt\right]^{1/2}$$

Let us integrate for one period of the waveform, so that $T = 2\pi/\omega$ (any complete number of periods will give the same result). Then:

$$a_{\text{RMS}} = \frac{A}{\sqrt{2}} = 0.707A$$

From Eq. (13.1):

$$a_{\text{RMQ}} = \left[\frac{1}{T}\int_0^T [A\sin(\omega t)]^4\,dt\right]^{1/4} \quad \text{or} \quad a_{\text{RMQ}} = \left[\frac{A^4}{4T}\int_0^T [1-\cos(2\omega t)]^2\,dt\right]^{1/4}$$

$$a_{\text{RMQ}} = \left[\frac{A^4}{4T}\int_0^T \left[\frac{3}{2} - 2\cos(2\omega t) - \frac{1}{2}\cos(4\omega t)\right] dt\right]^{1/4}$$

Again, integrating for one period of the waveform:

$$a_{\text{RMQ}} = \left[\frac{3A^4}{8}\right]^{1/4} = 0.7825A$$

Equinoxious Frequency Contours. Human response to vibration, shock, and impact depends on the frequency content of the stimulus, as well as the magnitude. This may be conveniently introduced electronically, by filtering the time history of the stimulus signal, and has led to the specification of vibration magnitudes at different frequencies with an equal probability of causing a given human response or injury, so defining an *equinoxious frequency contour*. The concept, while almost universally employed, is strictly only applicable to linear systems. The biomechanic and biodynamic responses of the human body to external forces and accelerations commonly depend nonlinearly on the magnitude of the stimulus, and so any equinoxious frequency contour can be expected to apply only to a limited range of vibration, shock, or impact magnitudes.

Equinoxious frequency contours may be estimated from epidemiological studies of health effects, or from the response of human subjects, animals, cadavers, or biodynamic models to the stimuli of interest. Human subjects cannot be subjected to injurious accelerations and forces for ethical reasons, and so little direct information is available from this source. Some information has been obtained from studies of accidents, though in most cases the input acceleration-time histories are poorly known.

Frequency Weighting. The inverse frequency contour (i.e., reciprocal) to an equinoxious contour should be applied to a stimulus containing many frequencies to produce an overall magnitude that appropriately combines the contributions from each frequency. The frequency weightings most commonly employed for whole-body and hand-transmitted vibration are shown in Fig. 13.1 (ISO 2631-1, 1997; ISO 5349-1, 2001). The range of frequencies is from 0.5 to 80 Hz for whole-body vibration, and from 5.6 to 1400 Hz for vibration entering the hand. A frequency weighting for shocks may also be derived from a biodynamic model (see "Dynamic Response Index (DRI)" in Sec. 13.3.1).

Vibration Exposure. Health disturbances and injuries are related to the magnitude of the stimulus, its frequency content, and its duration. A generalized expression for exposure may be written:

$$E(a_w, T)_{m,r} = \left[\int_0^T [F(a_w(t))]^m\,dt\right]^{1/r} \tag{13.3}$$

where $E(a_w, T)_{m,r}$ is the exposure occurring during a time T to a stimulus function that has been frequency weighted to equate the hazard at different frequencies, $F(a_w(t))$. In general, $F(a_w(t))$ may be expected to be a nonlinear function of the frequency-weighted acceleration-time history $a_w(t)$.

Within this family of exposure functions, usually only those with *even* integer values of m are of interest. A commonly used function is the so-called *energy-equivalent* vibration exposure for which $F(a_w(t)) = a_w(t)$ and $m = r = 2$:

$$E(a_w, T)_{2,2} = \left[\int_0^T [a_w(t)]^2\,dt\right]^{1/2} \tag{13.4}$$

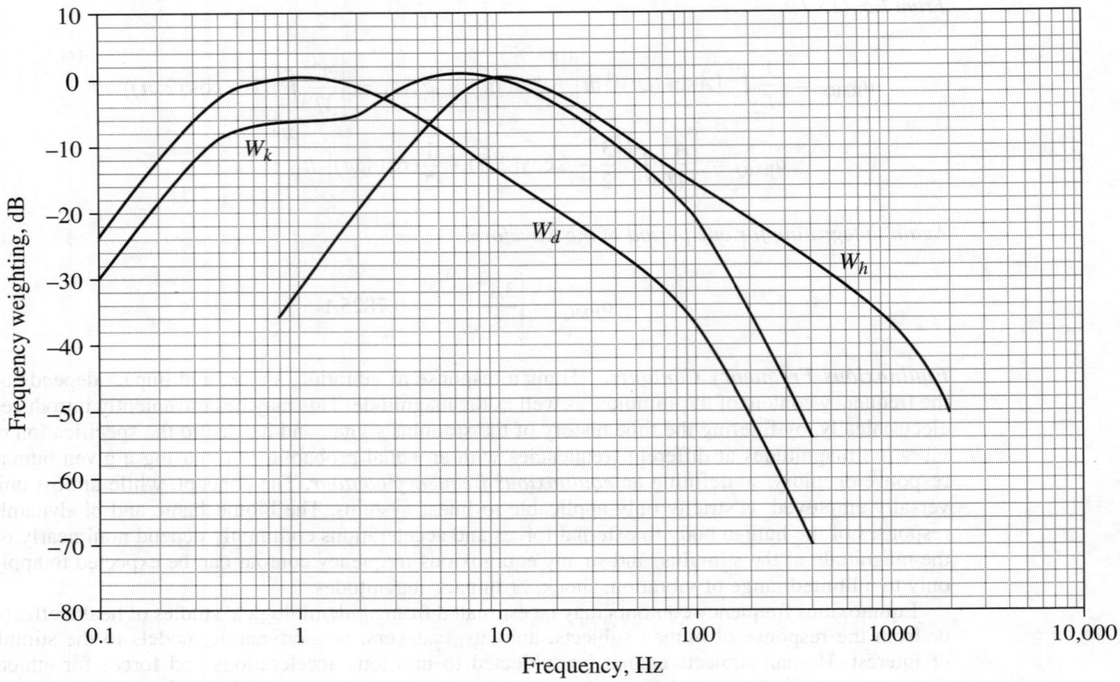

FIGURE 13.1 Frequency weightings for whole-body (W_k and W_d) and hand-transmitted (W_h) vibration. W_k and W_d are for the z direction and x and y directions, respectively, and are applicable to seated and standing persons (see Fig. 13.2). W_h is for all directions of vibration entering the hand. The filters are applied to acceleration-time histories $a(t)$. *(ISO 2631-1, 1997; ISO 5349-1, 2001.)*

For an exposure continuing throughout a working day, $T = T_{(8)} = 28{,}800$ s, and Eq. (13.4) can be written [using Eq. (13.2)]:

$$E(a_w, T)_{2,2} = T_{(8)}^{1/2}\left[\frac{1}{T_{(8)}}\int_0^{T_{(8)}} [a_w(t)]^2\, dt\right]^{1/2} = T_{(8)}^{1/2} a_{\mathrm{RMS}(8)} \tag{13.5}$$

where $a_{\mathrm{RMS}(8)}$ is the 8-hour, energy-equivalent, frequency-weighted RMS acceleration.

A second function, used for exposure to whole-body vibration, is the *vibration dose value*, VDV, for which $F(a_w(t)) = a_w(t)$ and $m = r = 4$. The function is thus:

$$\mathrm{VDV} = E(a_w, T)_{4,4} = \left[\int_0^T (a_w(t))^4\, dt\right]^{1/4} \tag{13.6}$$

which is more influenced by the large amplitudes in a fluctuating vibration than the energy-equivalent exposure. A related function, the *severity index* for which $F(a_w(t)) = a_w(t)$, $m = 2.5$, and $r = 1$, is used for the assessment of head impact, though it cannot be applied to continuous acceleration-time histories owing to the value of m (see "Survivable Shocks and Impacts" under Sec. 13.4.1).

13.1.2 Human Response to Vibration, Mechanical Shock, and Impact

Mechanical damage can occur at large vibration magnitudes, which are usually associated with exposure to shocks, and to objects impacting the body (e.g., bone fracture, brain injury, organ hemorrhage, and tearing or crushing of soft tissues). At moderate magnitudes there can be physiological effects leading to chronic injury, such as to the spine, and disorders affecting the hands. At all magnitudes above the threshold for perception there can be behavioral responses ranging from discomfort to interference with tasks involving visual or manual activities.

Injury from Vibration. *Whole-Body Vibration.* Small animals (e.g., mice and dogs) have been killed by intense vibration lasting only a few minutes (see Griffin, 1990). The internal injuries observed on postmortem examination (commonly heart and lung damage, and gastrointestinal bleeding) are consistent with the organs beating against each other and the rib cage, and suggest a *resonance* motion of the heart, and lungs, on their suspensions. In humans, these organ suspension resonances are at frequencies between 3 and 8 Hz.

Chronic exposure to whole-body vibration may result in an increased risk of low back pain, sciatic pain, and prolapsed or herniated lumbar disks compared to control groups not exposed to vibration (Seidel, 2005). These injuries occur predominantly in crane operators, tractor drivers, and drivers in the transportation industry (Bovenzi, 2010; Bovenzi and Hulshof, 1998). However, it is difficult to differentiate between the roles of whole-body vibration and ergonomic risk factors, such as posture, in the development of these disorders (Bovenzi et al., 2006).

Hand-Transmitted Vibration. Chronic injuries may be produced when the hand is exposed to vibration. Symptoms of numbness or paresthesia in the fingers or hands are common. Reduced grip strength and muscle weakness may also be experienced, and episodic finger blanching, often called colloquially "white fingers," "white hand," or "dead hand," may occur in occupational groups (e.g., operators of pneumatic drills, grinders, chipping hammers, riveting guns, and chain saws). The blood vessel, nerve, and muscle disorders associated with regular use of hand-held power tools are termed the *hand-arm vibration syndrome* (HAVS) (Taylor, 1988). An exposure-response relationship has been derived for the onset of finger blanching (Brammer, 1986). Attention has also been drawn to the influence of vibration on task performance and on the manual control of objects (Griffin, 1990; Martin and Adamo, 2001).

Repeated flexing of the wrist can injure the tendons, tendon sheaths, muscles, ligaments, joints, and nerves of the hand and forearm (Peterson and Cherniack, 2001). These *repetitive strain injuries* occur in occupations involving repeated hand-wrist deviations (e.g., keyboard and computer operators) and vibration, and frequently involve nerve compression at the wrist (e.g., *carpal tunnel syndrome*) (Cherniack, 1999; Cherniack et al., 2008).

Injury from Shock and Impact. Physiological responses to shocks and objects impacting the body include those discussed for whole-body vibration. For small contact areas, the injuries are often related to the elastic and tensile limits of tissue (Haut, 2002). The responses are critically dependent on the magnitude, direction, and time history of the acceleration and forces entering the body, the posture, and on the nature of any body supports or restraints (e.g., seat belt or helmet) (Brammer, 2010).

Vertical Shocks. Exposure to single shocks applied to a seated person directed from the seat pan toward the head ("headward") has been studied in connection with the development of aircraft ejection seats, from which the conditions for spinal injury and vertebral fractures have been documented (Anon., 1950; Eiband, 1959). Exposure to intense *repeated* vertical shocks is experienced in some off-the-road vehicles, high-speed boats, and high-performance military aircraft, where spinal injury has also been reported. A headward shock with acceleration in excess of $g = 9.81\ \text{m/s}^2$ (the acceleration of gravity) is likely to be accompanied by a downward ("tailward") impact, when the mass of the torso returns to being supported by the seat.

Horizontal Shocks. Exposure to rapid decelerations in the horizontal direction has been extensively studied in connection with motor vehicle and aircraft crashes ("spineward" deceleration) (Yoganandan et al., 2015). Accident statistics indicate that serious injuries to the occupants of motor vehicles involved in frontal collisions are most commonly to the head, neck, and torso, including the abdomen (AGARD-AR-330, 1997).

Injuries to the head usually involve diffuse or focal brain lesions either with or, commonly, without skull fracture. The former consists of brain swelling, concussion, and *diffuse axonal injury*, that is, mechanical disruption of nerve fibers; the latter consists of localized internal bleeding and death of brain tissue. The injuries result from both rotational and translational accelerations, where the former induces relative motion between the brain and skull while the latter produces a pressure wave within the skull with compression initially at the site of impact ("coup" and "contrecoup").

The most common neck injury is caused by rearward flexion and forward extension ("whiplash"), which may result in dislocation or fracture of the cervical vertebrae, and compression of the spinal cord.

13.2 PHYSICAL MEASUREMENTS

The complexity of a living organism, and its ability to modify its mechanical properties (e.g., in response to mechanical or physiological demands or muscle tension), necessitates the careful design of experiments. There is a large variability in response between individuals. Also, the direct attachment of vibration and shock sensors to soft tissues produces a mechanical load that influences tissue motion. With appropriate measurement methods and instrumentation (Mansfield, 2005; ISO 8041-1, 2017), mechanical responses to vibration can be determined for tissues, body segments, and the whole body.

13.2.1 Methods and Apparatus

Tissue Vibration. Noncontact methods are preferred for measuring the surface motion of tissues. Laser vibrometers are commercially available with sufficient bandwidth and resolution for most studies. A direct mass load on the skin, together with the skin's elasticity, forms a mechanical low-pass filter (see "Simple Lumped Models" in Sec. 13.3.1). If a device is to be mounted directly on the skin, it must be of low weight (e.g., <3 g) and possess a comparatively large attachment area (e.g., >5 cm^2), in order for vibration to be recorded without attenuation of the motion at 80 Hz. An upper frequency limit of 200 Hz is theoretically achievable (−3 dB) with a transducer and skin mount weighing 3 g and an attachment area of 1.8 cm^2 (Brammer, 2010).

The measurement of hand-transmitted vibration requires a bandwidth extending to at least 1400 Hz, which is unobtainable by localized, skin-mounted transducers. Miniature accelerometers attached to wood or metal disk-like mounts, which are held onto the skin surface by straps, have been used to record the motion of the wrist and arm. When used to measure the total transmission of vibration from the hand (i.e., the vector sum of orthogonal components—see "Orientation of Sensors" below), the so-called adapters are found to replicate the motion sensed by a 3D laser vibrometer up to a frequency of about 150 Hz (Xu et al., 2015). A distributed sensor, such as a pressure-sensitive lightweight film, would permit the motion of a large skin area to be monitored with acceptable mass loading, and could respond to vibration at higher frequencies.

Interface between Body and Vibrating Surface. Devices have been developed to measure the motion of the interface between the skin and a source of vibration in contact with the body, such as a vehicle seat pan or tool handle. The former consists of a flexible disk of rubber-like material thickened at the center, where an accelerometer is mounted. The dimensions have been standardized (ISO 7096, 1982). To record motion of the interface between the hand and a vibrating surface, the transducer mount commonly consists of a thin plate to which a miniature accelerometer is attached, which is held against the vibrating surface by the palm, or by one or more fingers (ISO 5349-2, 2001). Devices have also been developed for when gloves are worn (Asaki et al., 2014; Kudernatsch et al., 2014; ISO 10819, 2013; Xu et al., 2019). Such interface mounts are suitable for measuring the component of vibration normal to the skin surface but may not be suitable for recording motion along the interface. In addition, the energy entering the hands will be influenced by the compressive force with which the hand holds a vibrating handle (e.g., the combined grip and thrust forces exerted by the hand when operating a power tool) (Aldien et al., 2006). This has led to the development of combined accelerometer and force sensor mounts: the frequency response of one such palm mount extends to more than 1 kHz for motion normal to the skin surface (Peterson et al., 2008).

Structures in Contact with the Body. The vibration of structures in contact with the body, such as seats and tool handles, is conveniently measured by accelerometers rigidly attached to a structural element. Accelerometers are designed to respond to the vibration in a given direction and may be grouped to record simultaneously accelerations in three orthogonal directions. They are commercially available in a wide range of sizes and sensitivities, and may be attached by screws, straps, or adhesives to the structure of interest (ISO 5349-2, 2001; Mansfield, 2005).

Orientation of Sensors. Tissue-, interface-, and structure-mounted sensors may be aligned as closely as possible with the axes of a *biodynamic coordinate system* (see Fig. 13.2), even though these may have inaccessible origins that are anatomical sites within the body. In practice, transducers that sense motion in one spatial direction are commonly oriented to record the component accelerations defined by the *basicentric coordinate systems* shown in Fig. 13.2 (ISO 2631-1, 1997; ISO 5349-1, 2001), which have origins at the interface between the body and the vibrating surface. The location of accelerometers to record the handle vibration of specific power tools is described in an international standard (ISO 5349-2, 2001).

Errors in Shock and Impact Measurement. Care must be taken when accelerometers employing piezoelectric elements are used to measure large-magnitude shocks and impacts, as they are subject to internal crystalline changes that result in dc shifts in the output voltage. After signal conditioning, the effects are frequently evidenced as transient changes in the baseline of acceleration-time histories and as artificially elevated accelerations at low frequencies that increase as frequency decreases (Griffin, 1990). Results containing such shifts should be considered erroneous. This limitation of piezoelectric transducers may be overcome by mounting the sensor on a mechanical low-pass filter (see "Simple Lumped Models" in Sec. 13.3.1), which is, in turn, attached to the structure of interest. Such filters possess a resilient element that serves to reduce the transmission of vibration at high frequencies (Mansfield, 2005). The filter cutoff frequency is selected to be above the maximum vibration frequency of interest but below the internal mechanical resonance frequency of the accelerometer.

Data Recording. The signal produced by vibration, shock, and impact sensors is first conditioned to remove bias voltages or other signals required for the device to function, and then amplified and buffered for output to a digital data acquisition system. It should possess low-pass, antialiasing filters (with cutoff frequency typically one-half the sampling frequency), and an analog-to-digital (A/D) converter with sufficient dynamic range (commonly 16 bits). The data acquisition system should be capable of recording time histories at sampling frequencies of at least 2800 Hz for hand-transmitted vibration, or 160 Hz for whole-body vibration, *per vibration component and measurement site* (e.g., palm and wrist, or seat surface and seat back).

13.2.2 Small-Amplitude Response of the Human Body

Tissue Properties. The properties of human tissues when the body is considered a linear, passive mechanical system are summarized in Table 13.1 (Brammer, 2010; Gomez et al., 2002). The values shown for soft tissues are typical of muscle tissue, while those for bone depend on the structure of the specific bone. Cortical bone is the dominant constituent of the long bones (e.g., femur, tibia), while trabecular bone, which is more elastic and energy absorbent, is the dominant constituent of the vertebrae (Gomez et al., 2002). The shear viscosity and bulk elasticity of soft tissue are from a model for the response in vivo of a human thigh to the vibration of a small-diameter piston (von Gierke et al., 1952). The nonlinear mechanical properties of biological tissues have been studied extensively in vitro, including deviations from Hooke's law (Fung, 1993; Haut, 2002).

Mechanical Impedance of Muscle Tissue. The (input) *mechanical impedance* is the complex ratio between the dynamic force applied to the body and the velocity at the interface where vibration enters the body. The real and imaginary parts of the mechanical impedance of human muscle in vivo are shown as a function of frequency in Fig. 13.3 (von Gierke et al., 1952). In this diagram the measured

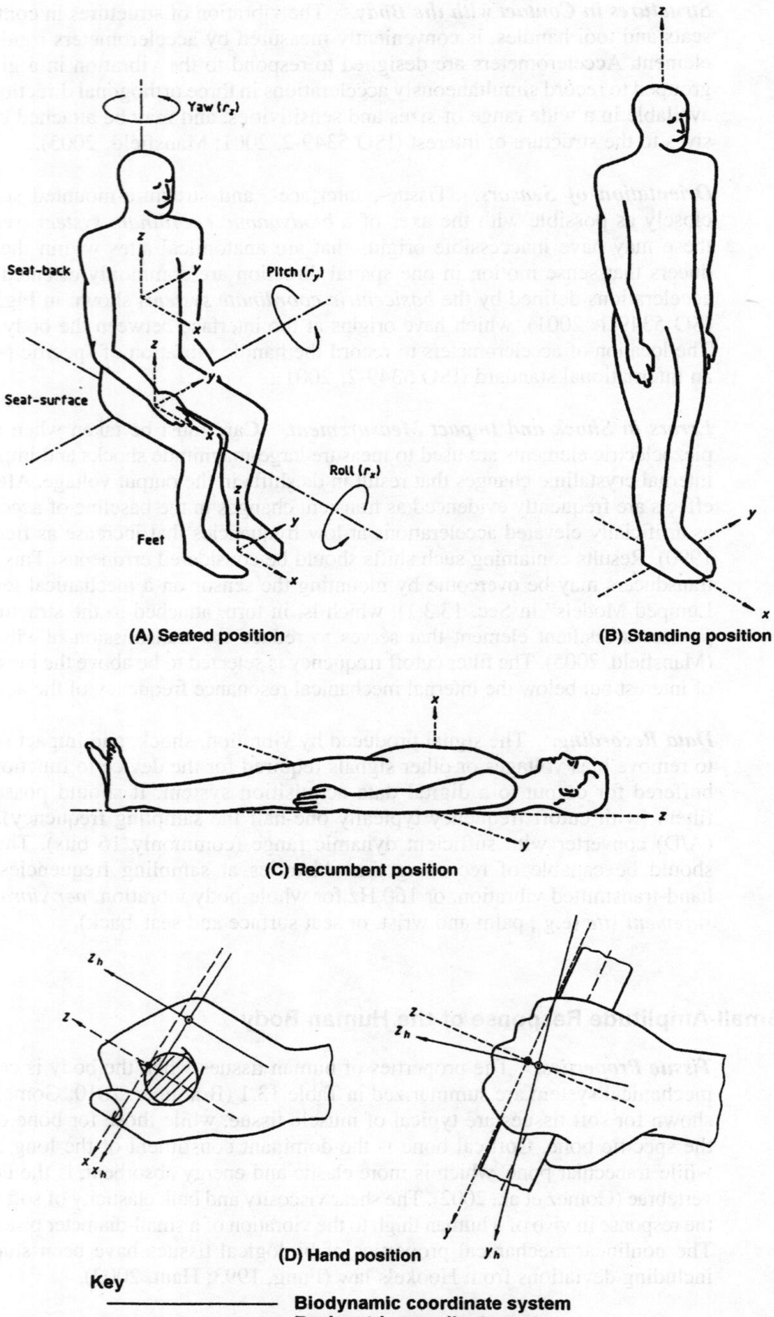

FIGURE 13.2 Basicentric coordinate axes for translational (x, y, and z) and rotational (r_x, r_y, and r_z) whole-body vibration, and basicentric (filled circles and dashed lines) and biodynamic (open circles and continuous lines) axes for hand-transmitted vibration. The biodynamic coordinate axes for the hand are x_h, y_h, and z_h. (*ISO 2631-1, 1997; ISO 5349-1, 2001.*)

TABLE 13.1 Typical Physical Properties of Human Tissues at Frequencies Less than 100 kHz

Property	Soft tissues	Bone (wet)	Bone (dry)
Density, kg/m^3	1–1.2 × 10^3	1.9–2.3 × 10^3	1.9 × 10^3
Young's modulus, Pa	7.5 × 10^3	1.6–2.3 × 10^{10}	1.8 × 10^{10}
Shear modulus,* Pa	2.5 × 10^3†	2.9–3.4 × 10^9	7.1 × 10^9
Bulk modulus, Pa	2.6 × 10^9†		1.3 × 10^{10}
Shear viscosity, Pa · s			
Sound velocity, m/s	1.5–1.6 × 10^3	3.4 × 10^3	
Acoustic impedance, Pa · s/m	1.7 × 10^6	6 × 10^6	6 × 10^6
Tensile strength, Pa			
Cortical bone		1.3–1.6 × 10^8	1.8 × 10^8
Compressive strength, Pa			
Cortical bone		1.5–2.1 × 10^8	
Trabecular bone (vertebrae)		0.4–7.7 × 10^6	
Shear strength, Pa			
Cortical bone		7.0–8.1 × 10^7	

*Lamé constant.
†From soft tissue model (von Gierke et al., 1952).
Source: After Brammer (2010) and Gomez et al. (2002).

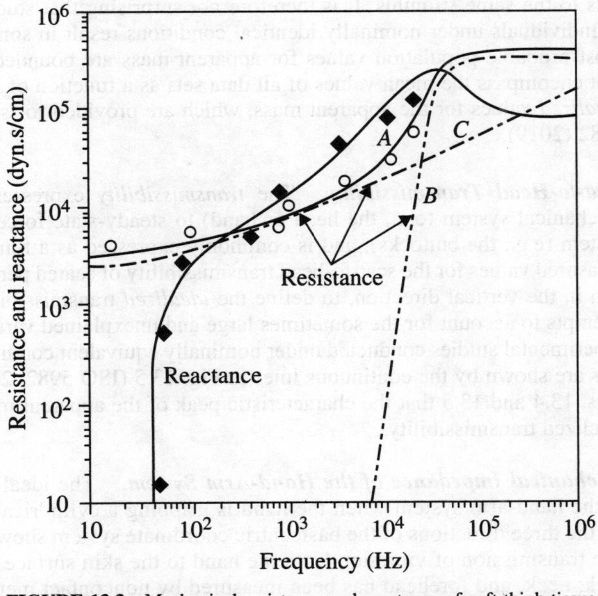

FIGURE 13.3 Mechanical resistance and reactance of soft thigh tissue (2 cm in diameter) in vivo from 10 Hz to 1 MHz. The measured values (open circles—resistance; diamonds—reactance) are compared with the calculated resistance and reactance of a 2-cm-diameter sphere vibrating in a viscous, elastic compressible medium with properties similar to soft human tissue (continuous lines, curves A). The resistance is also shown for the sphere vibrating in a frictionless compressible fluid (acoustic compression wave, curve B) and an incompressible viscous fluid (curve C). (*von Gierke et al., 1952.*)

resistance (open circles) and reactance (diamonds) are compared with the predictions of a model, from which some tissue properties may be derived (see Table 13.1). It should be noted that the mechanical stiffness and resistance of soft tissues approximately triple in magnitude when the static compression of the surface increases by a factor of three. The relationship, however, is not linear.

Apparent Mass of Seated Persons. The *apparent mass* is often used to describe the response of the body at the point of stimulation rather than the mechanical impedance, and is the complex ratio between the dynamic force applied to the body and the acceleration at the interface where vibration enters the body. It is commonly expressed as a function of frequency, and is equal to the static weight of a person in the limiting case of zero frequency when the legs are supported to move in unison with the torso. The influence of posture, muscle tension, and stimulus magnitude on the apparent mass of seated persons, in the vertical direction, is shown for four subjects in Fig. 13.4 (Fairley and Griffin, 1989). The column of graphs to the left of the diagram shows the modulus of the apparent mass measured with a comfortable, "normal," upright posture and muscle tension (labeled N), with this posture but an erect torso and the shoulders held back (E), with all muscles in the upper body tensed (T), and, finally, with the subject leaning backward to rest against a rigid backrest (B). The largest variation in apparent mass between these conditions was associated with tensing the back muscles, which clearly increased the frequency of the characteristic peak in the response (at around 5 Hz). In some subjects the frequency of this peak could be changed by a factor of 2 by muscle tension. A variation in the apparent mass could also be induced by changing the stimulus magnitude, as is shown for four RMS accelerations (0.25, 0.5, 1.0, and 2.0 m/s^2) to the right of Fig. 13.4. Within this range of stimulus magnitudes, the frequency of the characteristic peak in the apparent mass was found to decrease with increasing stimulus magnitude, for each subject.

Even casual inspection of Fig. 13.4 reveals the large differences in response between individuals to the same stimulus. It is therefore not surprising that studies conducted on different groups of individuals under nominally identical conditions result in somewhat different mean values. The most probable population values for apparent mass are bounded by upper and lower limit curves that encompass the mean values of all data sets as a function of frequency. These define a range of *idealized* values for the apparent mass, which are provided for seated and standing persons in ISO 5982 (2019).

Seat-to-Head Transmissibility. The *transmissibility* expresses the response of one part of a mechanical system (e.g., the head or hand) to steady-state forced vibration of another part of the system (e.g., the buttocks), and is commonly expressed as a function of frequency. A synthesis of measured values for the seat-to-head transmissibility of seated persons has been performed for vibration in the vertical direction, to define the *idealized* transmissibility. The idealized transmissibility attempts to account for the sometimes large and unexplained variations in the results from different experimental studies conducted under nominally equivalent conditions. The results of one such analysis are shown by the continuous lines in Fig. 13.5 (ISO 5982, 2019). It can be seen by comparing Figs. 13.4 and 13.5 that the characteristic peak of the apparent mass remains in the modulus of the idealized transmissibility.

Mechanical Impedance of the Hand-Arm System. The idealized mechanical input impedance of the hand-arm system when the hand is gripping a cylindrical or oval handle has been derived for the three directions of the basicentric coordinate system shown in Fig. 13.2 (ISO 10068, 2012). The transmission of vibration from the hand to the skin surface at the wrist, upper arm, shoulder, back, neck, and forehead has been measured by noncontact methods or an adapter whose performance has been verified by comparison with the motion sensed by a laser vibrometer (Xu et al., 2017). Little vibration is transmitted to any of these locations at frequencies above 100 Hz, and the transmissibility to most is not unlike that of a low-pass mechanical filter with peak response between 7 and 25 Hz (see "Simple Lumped Models" in Sec. 13.3.1). When gripping a handle, the maximum total transmissibility from the handle to the wrist is close to two and occurs at a frequency of ~20 Hz. The corresponding values for the upper arm are 1.5 at ~9 Hz, and 0.5 at ~8 Hz for the shoulder.

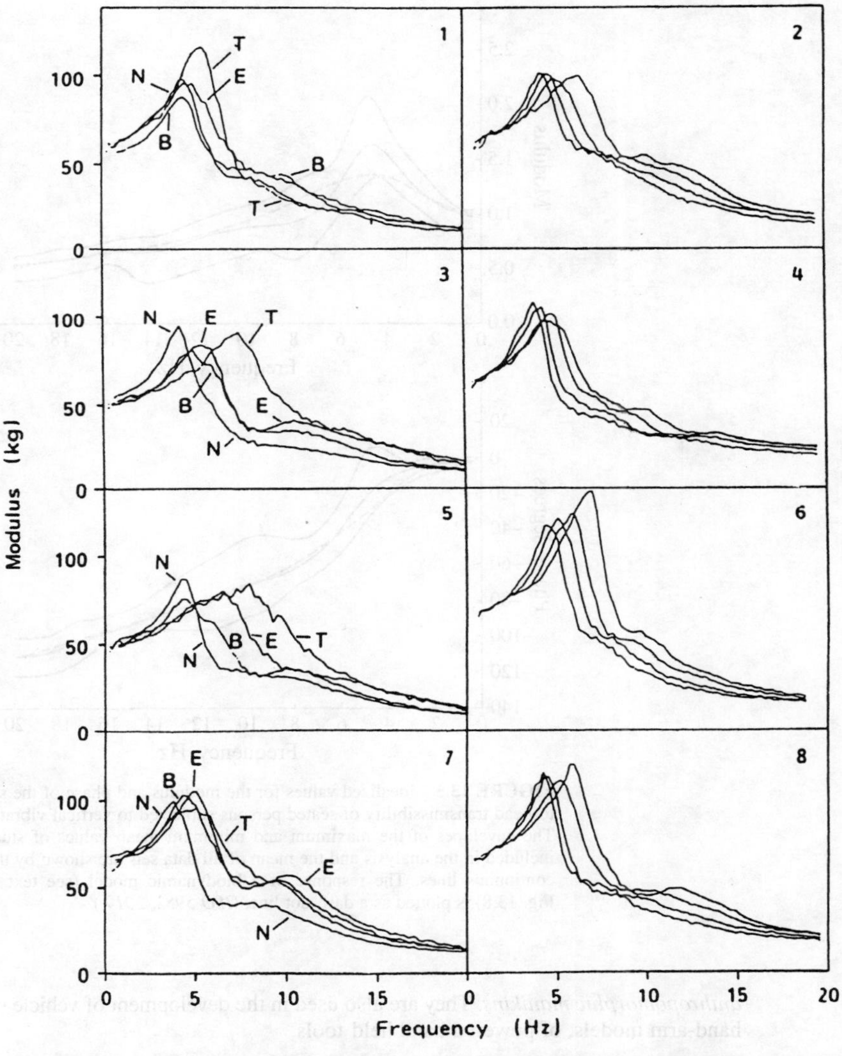

FIGURE 13.4 Effect of posture (N—normal; E—erect; B—with backrest), muscle tension (T—tensed muscles), and stimulus magnitude (0.25, 0.5, 1.0, and 2.0 m/s^2) on the apparent mass of a seated person for four subjects (see text for explanation). (*Fairley and Griffin, 1989.*)

13.3 MODELS AND HUMAN SURROGATES

Knowledge of tolerable limits for exposure to vibration, shock, and impact is essential for maintaining health and performance in the many environments in which humans are subjected to dynamic forces and accelerations. As already noted, humans cannot be subjected to injurious stimuli for ethical reasons, and so little direct information is available from this source. In these circumstances, the simulation of human response to potentially life-threatening dynamic forces and accelerations is desirable, and is commonly undertaken using *biodynamic models*, and *anthropometric* or

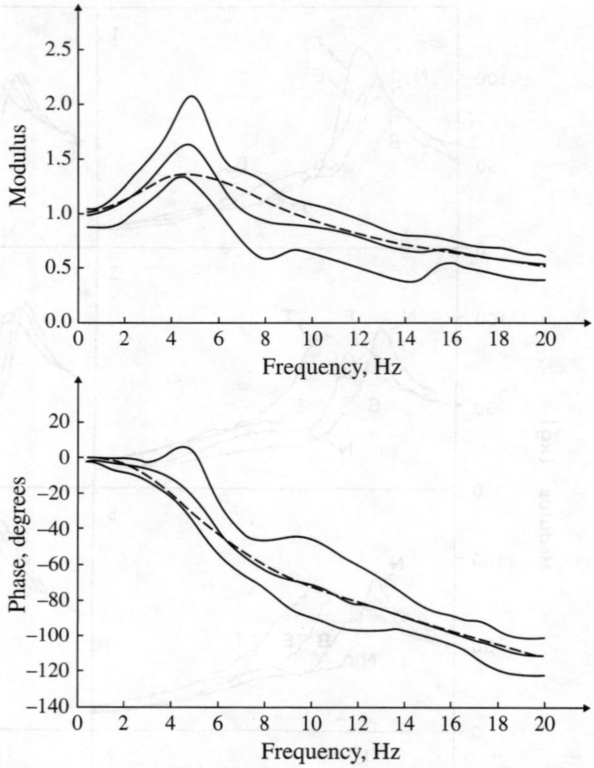

FIGURE 13.5 Idealized values for the modulus and phase of the seat-to-head transmissibility of seated persons subjected to vertical vibration. The envelopes of the maximum and minimum mean values of studies included in the analysis and the mean of all data sets are shown by thick continuous lines. The response of a biodynamic model (see text and Fig. 13.8) is plotted as a dash-dot line. (*ISO 5982, 2019.*)

anthropomorphic manikins. They are also used in the development of vehicle seats and, in the case of hand-arm models, of powered hand held tools.

13.3.1 Biodynamic Models

Simple Lumped Models. At frequencies up to several hundred hertz, the biodynamic response of the human body can be represented theoretically by point masses, springs, and dampers, which constitute the elements of *lumped* biodynamic models (von Gierke, 1970). The simplest one-dimensional model consists of a mass supported by a spring and damper, as sketched in Fig. 13.6, where the system is excited at its base. The equation of motion of a mass m when a spring with stiffness k and damper with resistance proportional to velocity, c, are base driven with a displacement $x_0(t)$ is:

$$ma_1(t) + c(\dot{x}_1(t) - \dot{x}_0(t)) + k(x_1(t) - x_0(t)) = 0 \qquad (13.7)$$

where the displacement of the mass is $x_1(t)$, its acceleration is $a_1(t)$, and differentiation with respect to time is shown by dots.

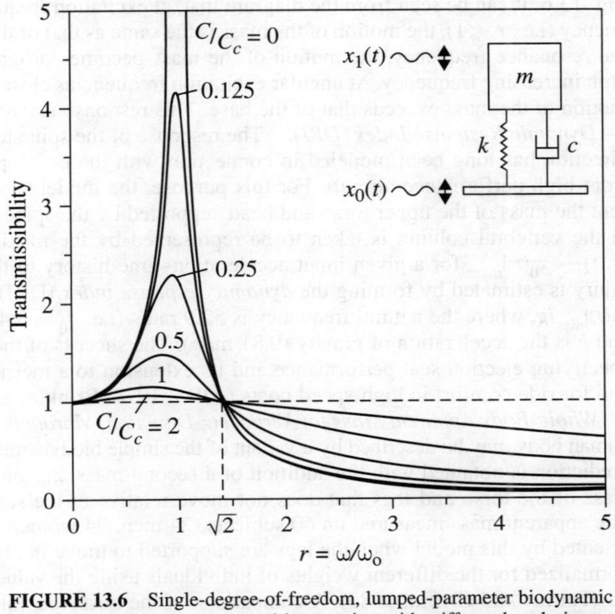

FIGURE 13.6 Single-degree-of-freedom, lumped-parameter biodynamic model. The mass m is supported by a spring with stiffness k and viscous damper with resistance c. The transmissibility of motion to the mass is shown as a function of the frequency ratio r (= ω/ω_0) when the base is subjected to a displacement $x_0(t)$. *(After Griffin, 1990.)*

For this simple mechanical system, the apparent mass may be expressed as a function of frequency by (Griffin, 1990):

$$M(\omega) = \frac{m(k + i\omega c)}{k - \omega^2 m + i\omega c} \tag{13.8}$$

where ω is the angular frequency (= $2\pi f$), $i = (-1)^{1/2}$, and the transmissibility from the base to the mass is

$$H(\omega) = \frac{k + i\omega c}{k - \omega^2 m + i\omega c} \tag{13.9}$$

The modulus of the transmissibility may then be written

$$|H(\omega)| = \left[\frac{1 + (2\xi r)^2}{(1 - r^2)^2 + (2\xi r)^2}\right]^{1/2} \tag{13.10}$$

where r is the ratio of the angular excitation frequency to the angular *resonance frequency* of the system, ω/ω_0, and

$$\omega_0 = 2\pi f_0 = \left(\frac{k}{m}\right)^{1/2} \tag{13.11}$$

In Eq. (13.10), the damping is expressed in terms of the damping ratio $\xi = c/c_c$, where c_c is the critical viscous damping coefficient [$=2(mk)^{1/2}$]. The transmissibility of the system is plotted as a function of the ratio of the angular excitation frequency to the natural (resonance) frequency in

Fig. 13.6. It can be seen from the diagram that, at excitation frequencies less than the resonance frequency (i.e., $r \ll 1$), the motion of the mass is the same as that of the base. At frequencies greater than the resonance frequency, the motion of the mass becomes progressively less than that of the base with increasing frequency. At angular excitation frequencies close to the resonance frequency ω_0, the motion of the mass exceeds that of the base. This response is that of a *low-pass mechanical filter*.

Dynamic Response Index (DRI). The response of the spine to shocks in the vertical (headward) direction has long been modeled in connection with the development of ejection seats for escape from high-performance aircraft. For this purpose, the model shown in Fig. 13.6 is taken to represent the mass of the upper torso and head supported by the spine (the spring). The maximum stress in the vertebral column is taken to be represented by the maximum displacement of the spring, $|x_1(t) - x_0(t)|_{max}$, for a given input acceleration–time history to the model. The potential for spinal injury is estimated by forming the *dynamic response index* (DRI), which is defined as $(\omega_0)^2|x_1(t) - x_0(t)|_{max}/g$, where the natural frequency is 52.9 rad/s (i.e., $f_0 = 8.42$ Hz), the damping ratio is 0.224, and g is the acceleration of gravity (9.81 m/s^2). The success of the model has led to its adoption for specifying ejection seat performance and its extension to a metric for exposure to repeated shocks and for ride comfort in high-speed boats (Allen, 1978; Brinkley et al., 1990; Payne, 1976).

Whole-Body Apparent Mass for Vertical (z-Direction) Vibration. The apparent mass of the seated human body may be described by a variant of the simple biodynamic model of Fig. 13.6. A satisfactory prediction is obtained with the addition of a second mass, m_0, on the seat platform to represent the mass of the torso and legs that does not move relative to the seat (i.e., to the base of the model). The apparent mass measured on 60 subjects (24 men, 24 women, and 12 children) can be well represented by this model when the legs are supported to move in phase with the seat, and the data are normalized for the different weights of individuals using the value of apparent mass recorded at 0.5 Hz (Fairley and Griffin, 1989). A comparison of the observed values for the magnitude, and phase, of the normalized apparent mass (continuous lines) and the predicted values (dashed lines) is shown in Fig. 13.7. To obtain this agreement, the natural angular frequency of the model is 31.4 rad/s (i.e., $f_0 = 5$ Hz), and the damping ratio is 0.475. These values differ considerably from those of the DRI model (see above), reflecting the stimulus magnitude dependent, nonlinear response of the human body to vibration.

Whole-Body Impedance, Apparent Mass, and Transmissibility for Vertical (z-direction) Vibration. A model has been developed to predict idealized values for the input impedance, apparent mass, *and* transmissibility of the seated human body when subjected to vertical vibration. The model, shown in Fig. 13.8, comprises elements forming three of the models sketched in Fig. 13.6 (ISO 5982, 2019). It contains elements similar to those used to predict apparent mass on the left-hand side of the diagram with, in addition, two basic models in series to the right of the diagram (i.e., one on top of the other), in order to represent "head" motion (i.e., motion of mass m_2). The model predictions for the transmissibility from the seat to the head are shown by the dashed lines in Fig. 13.5, and should be compared with the target mean values. While the model meets the considerable challenge of predicting three biodynamic responses with one set of model values, the parameters of the model do not possess precise anatomical correlates, a common failing of simple lumped models, and the predictions are applicable only to a limited range of stimulus magnitudes.

Multielement, Finite-Element (FE), and Neural Network Models. More complex mathematical models have been developed to incorporate more realistic descriptions of individual body parts and to predict the motion of one body part relative to another.

Hand-Arm Lumped Parameter Models. Four- and five-degree-of-freedom models have been developed to predict the input impedance or apparent mass of the hand-arm system in three orthogonal directions related to the basicentric system in Fig. 13.2 (Dong et al., 2013; ISO 10068, 2012). They contain four or five of the simple models sketched in Fig. 13.6, respectively, for each of the three orthogonal directions. The one-degree-of-freedom models are arranged as shown in Fig. 13.9, and include those with subscripts 1–4 in the four-degree-of-freedom model and 0–4 in the five-degree-of-freedom model.

The simple models represent the upper arm and shoulder (subscript 0), the palm, wrist, and forearm (subscript 1), the fingers (subscript 2), and the soft tissue directly driven by the source of

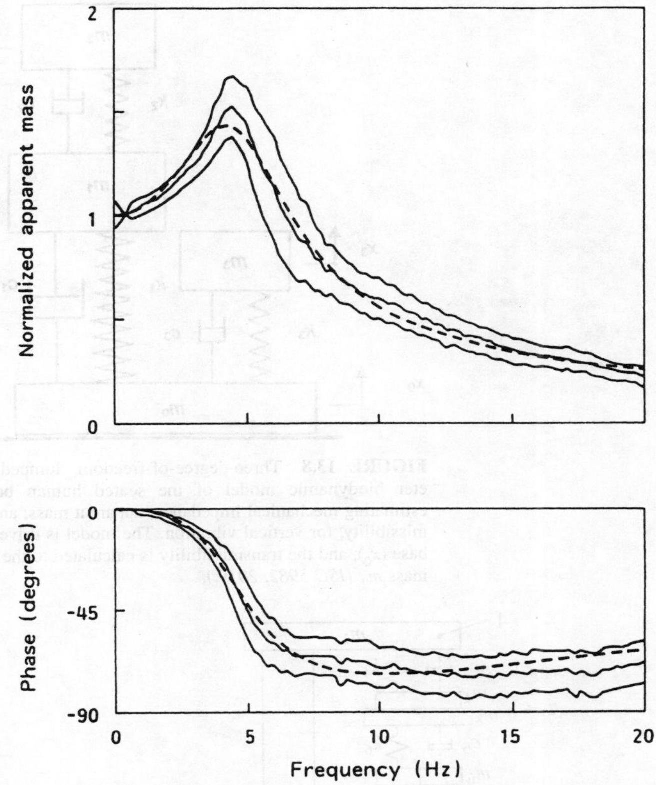

FIGURE 13.7 Comparison between predicted and observed apparent mass. The mean, normalized apparent masses of 60 subjects, ±1 standard deviation, are shown by the continuous lines, and the predictions of a single-degree-of-freedom, lumped parameter biodynamic model by the dashed line. (*Fairley and Griffin, 1989.*)

vibration (subscript 3 for the palm and subscript 4 for the fingers). Both four- and five-degree-of-freedom models adequately predict the impedance or apparent mass, with the five-degree-of-freedom model improving the prediction of phase at the palm in the x_h direction at low frequencies (see Fig. 13.2). The transmission of vibration from the source (i.e., handle) to mass m_1, and to mass m_0, predicted by the five-degree-of-freedom model corresponds well with the measured transmissibility to the wrist and upper arm, respectively. A seven degree-of-freedom model for the hand-arm system has been developed to assess the performance of vibration-reducing gloves (Dong et al., 2013). This model is shown in Fig. 13.9, and includes elements to represent, separately, the palmar and finger work surfaces and resilient materials (identified by subscripts 5 and 6, respectively) and the inner lining of the glove in contact with the hand (subscripts 7 and 8).

Whole-Body Models. Of the many multielement models that have been developed, the *MAthematical DYnamical MOdel* (MADYMO), in its many forms, is most widely used with another, the *Articulated Total Body* (ATB) model, more associated with the dynamics of manikins (see "Anthropometric Manikins," Sec. 13.3.2). A prime driver of model development has been the avoidance of injury to automobile occupants in frontal and side collisions (Yang et al., 2006). The multielement models typically employ a combination of rigid bodies, joints, springs,

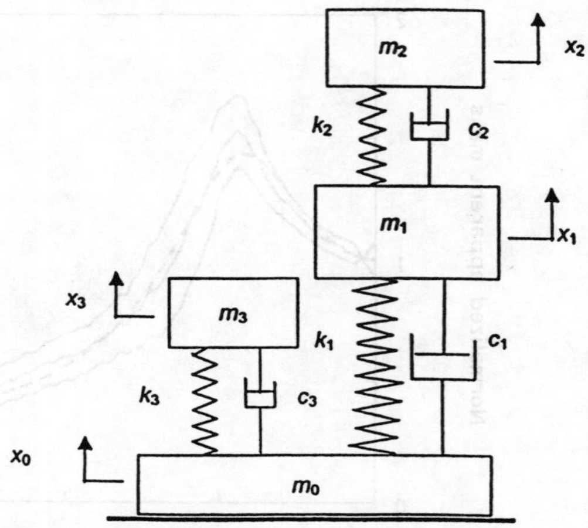

FIGURE 13.8 Three-degree-of-freedom, lumped-parameter biodynamic model of the seated human body for estimating mechanical impedance, apparent mass, and transmissibility, for vertical vibration. The model is driven at the base (x_0), and the transmissibility is calculated to the "head," mass m_2. *(ISO 5982, 2019.)*.

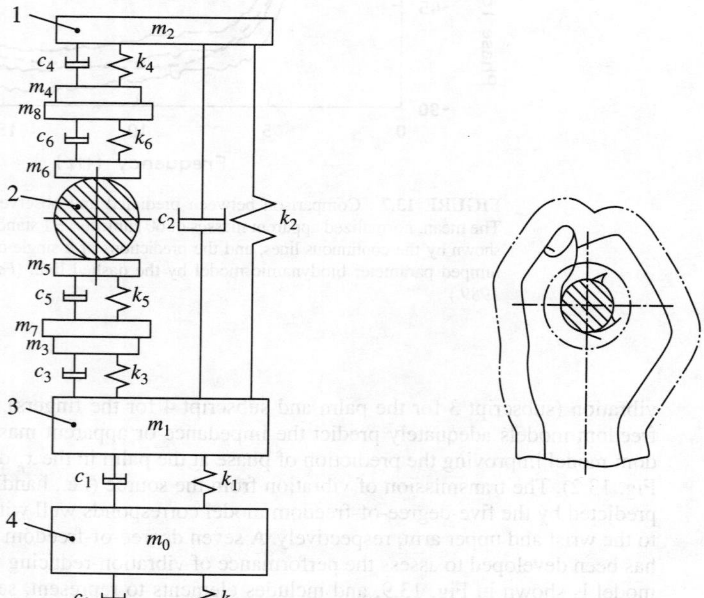

FIGURE 13.9 Seven-degree-of-freedom, lumped-parameter biodynamic model of the hand wearing a vibration-reducing glove, for estimating the transmissibility of gloves (see Fig. 13.14). Without glove elements (subscripts 5 to 8), the model becomes a five-degree-of-freedom model of the hand-arm system for estimating mechanical impedance, apparent mass, and transmissibility. Key: 1-fingers; 2-handle; 3-palm, wrist and forearm; 4-upper arm and shoulder; 5-upper body. (*ISO 10068, 2012.*)

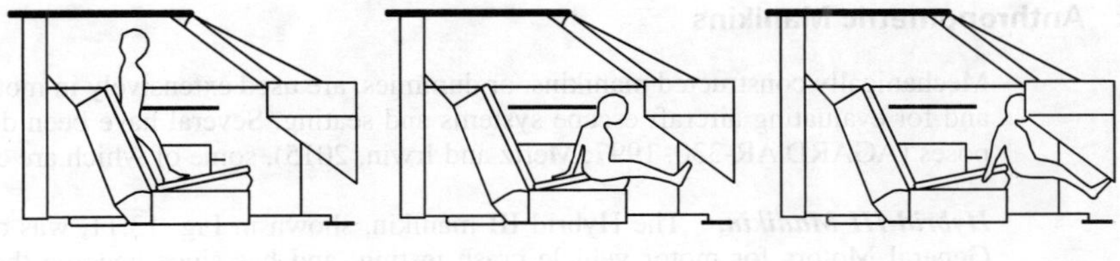

FIGURE 13.10 Articulated total body (ATB) model prediction for the response of an unrestrained standing child to panic braking in an automobile at 500 and 600 ms after commencing braking. (von Gierke, 1997.)

and dampers to represent the human, or manikin, and set up and solve numerically the equations of motion for the system. The applied forces and torques on these components are established by different routines for contact with external surfaces, the effect of gravity and body restraints. The connections between the rigid bodies commonly possess elastic and resistive properties based on measurements on human joints. The environment to be simulated may include seats, seat belts, and air bags. The models may include advanced harness systems and wind forces to model seat ejection from aircraft and can also describe aircraft crash. An example of the use of these models to predict human response in crash-likesituations is shown in Fig. 13.10 (von Gierke, 1997). In this diagram, the motion of an unrestrained child standing on the front seat of an automobile is shown in response to panic braking. The output of the model has been calculated at the onset of braking and after 500 and 600 ms. It can be seen from the diagram that the model predicts the child will slide down and forward along the seat until its head impacts the dashboard of the vehicle.

Finite-Element (FE) Models. The detailed response of selected parts of the body and the environment being simulated (e.g., head and neck, spine, and vehicle seating) have been modeled by using finite elements (FEs). In the MADYMO model, the FEs can interact with the multibody model elements. The many FE and composite models developed for body subsystems subjected to rapid horizontal deceleration have been summarized by Yang et al. (2006). An example of the predictions of a head and neck model for rotation of the head and neck during rapid horizontal deceleration compared with human responses is shown in Fig. 13.13 (RTO-MP-20, 1999). FE models have also been constructed for the whole body to predict the injury potential of vertebral compression from exposure to vibration (Seidel, 2005). One family of models includes anatomically based adaptations for posture, body mass, and body mass index, and accounts for the nonlinearity of responses to whole-body vibration by constructing models applicable to different ranges of acceleration magnitudes (Schust et al., 2015). The models are applicable, in principle, to peak accelerations of less than 9.81 m/s^2, and have been used to assess the health risks of vibration exposures, including shocks, experienced by professional drivers (e.g., bus-, tractor-, and forklift-drivers).

Artificial Neural Network Models. The response of the spine to vertical accelerations has also been modeled by an artificial neural network (Nicol et al., 1997), which permits the magnitude-dependent (i.e., nonlinear) characteristics of the human body to be included (see, for example, panels 2, 4, 6, and 8 of Fig. 13.4). The parameters of the network were established by "training" the model using repeated shocks, which were applied to a seated person with back unsupported in the headward direction, with peak amplitudes from –20 to 40 m/s^2 (ISO 2631-5., 2004). Since a neural network model has no predictive power beyond its "training," the applicability of the model is restricted to shocks and impacts in this direction and with this range of accelerations.

13.3.2 Anthropometric Manikins

Mechanically constructed manikins, or dummies, are used extensively in motor vehicle crash testing and for evaluating aircraft escape systems and seating. Several have been developed for these purposes (AGARD AR-330, 1997; Mertz and Irwin, 2015), some of which are commercially available.

Hybrid III Manikin. The Hybrid III manikin, shown in Fig. 13.11, was originally developed by General Motors for motor vehicle crash testing, and has since become the de facto standard for simulating the response of motor vehicle occupants to frontal collisions and for tests of occupant safety restraint systems. The manikin approximates the size, shape, and mass of the 50th percentile North American adult male, and consists of metal parts to provide structural strength and define the overall geometry. This "skeleton" is covered with foam and an external vinyl skin to produce the desired shape. The manikin possesses a rubber lumbar spine, curved to mimic a sitting posture. The head, neck, chest, and leg responses are designed to simulate the following human responses during rapid deceleration: head acceleration resulting from forehead and side-of-the-head impacts;

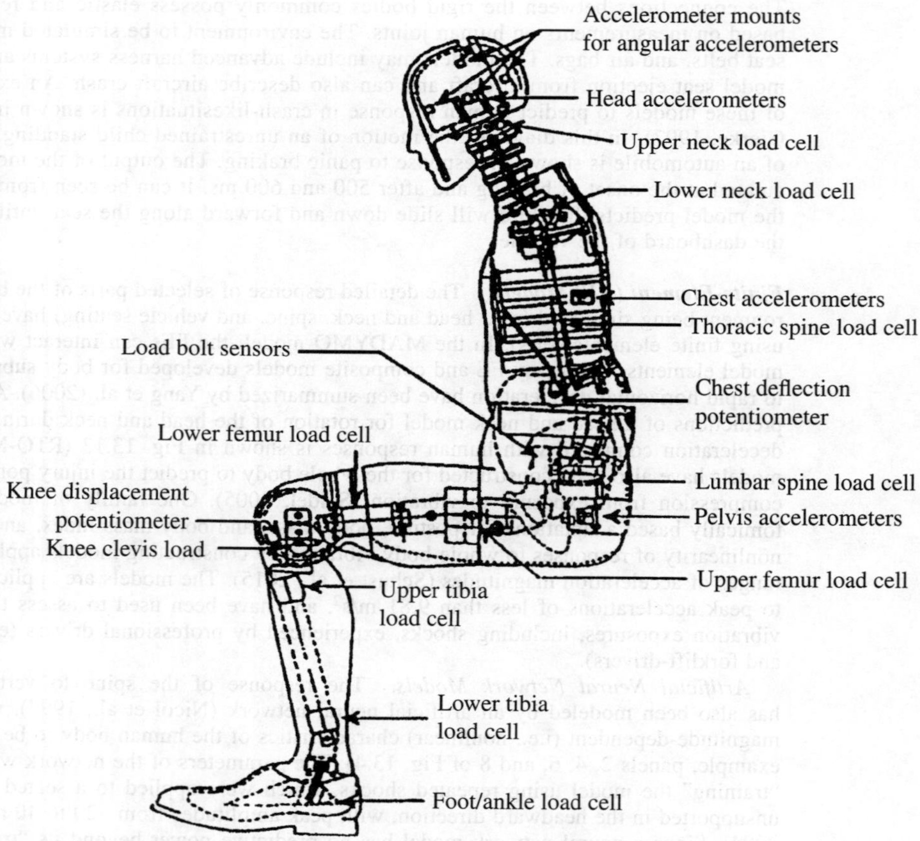

FIGURE 13.11 Hybrid III anthropometric dummy designed for use in motor-vehicle frontal crash tests, showing elements of construction and sensors. (*AGARD-AR-330, 1997.*)

fore-and-aft, and lateral, bending of the neck; deflection of the chest to distributed forces on the sternum; and impacts to the knee (Mertz and Irwin, 2015). The instrumentation required to record these responses is shown in Fig. 13.11. Hybrid III dummies are now available for small (fifth percentile) adult females, and large (95th percentile) adult males, as well as for infants and children. A related *side impact dummy* (SID) has been developed for the U.S. National Highway Traffic Safety Administration (NHTSA), for crash tests involving impacts on the sides of motor vehicles.

ADAM. ADAM (Advanced Dynamic Anthropomorphic Manikin) is a fully instrumented manikin primarily used in the development of aircraft ejection systems. Its overall design is conceptually similar to that of the Hybrid III dummy (see Fig. 13.11), in that ADAM replicates human body segments, surface contours, and weight. In addition to a metal skeleton, the manikin possesses a sandwich skin construction of sheet vinyl separated by foamed vinyl to mimic the response of human soft tissue. ADAM also attempts to replicate human joint motion and the response of the spine to vertical accelerations for both small-amplitude vibration and large impacts. The spine consists of a mechanical spring-damper system, which is mounted within the torso.

13.3.3 Biodynamic Fidelity of Human Surrogates

Animals, cadavers, manikins, and computer models have been used to predict human responses to potentially injurious or life-threatening stimuli. To evaluate the biofidelity of the surrogate or model, it is necessary to identify the response characteristics that are most relevant (Griffin, 2001). For biodynamic responses, the time histories of the acceleration, velocity, displacement, and forces provide the most meaningful comparisons, though point-by-point comparisons can be misleading if the system response to the stimulus of interest is extremely nonlinear. In these circumstances, evaluating peak values in the time history, impulses calculated from the acceleration or contact forces, or energy absorption may be more appropriate.

Manikins and Biodynamic Models. The current state of the art is illustrated in Figs. 13.12 and 13.13, where several biodynamic parameters of the response of the human head and neck to rapid horizontal decelerations are compared. The comparisons are between the responses of human volunteers, the limits of which are shown by dotted lines, with those of the Hybrid III manikin at the same deceleration (Fig. 13.12), and with those of a three-dimensional head and neck for a MADYMO computer model (Fig. 13.13) (RTO-MP-20, 1999).

While the Hybrid III manikin can reproduce some human responses, the head and neck system does not introduce appropriate head rotation lag (see neck angle versus head angle in Fig. 13.12C) or torque at the occipital condyles joint [see moment of force OC joint versus time (Fig. 13.12E)]. Note, however, that the linear acceleration of the center of gravity of the head is well reproduced by the manikin, except for the peak acceleration at 100 ms [see response of head acceleration versus time (Fig. 13.12F)]. In contrast, the three-dimensional head and neck biodynamic model can be seen to reproduce most human responses when active muscle behavior is included (the continuous lines in Fig. 13.13). In this computer model, the neck muscles are represented by simple cords between anatomical attachment points on the head and the base of the neck.

Animals. Employing the results of experiments with animals to predict biodynamic responses in humans introduces uncertainties associated with interspecies differences such as the size of body parts and organs, which influence resonance frequencies. For this reason, most animal research on the limit of exposure to rapid horizontal deceleration and to vertical acceleration, which commonly involves shock and impact, has employed mammals of roughly similar size and mass to humans (i.e., pigs and chimpanzees). Research on pathophysiological mechanisms is less subject to concerns with different body size, and more with the biological equivalence of the systems being studied.

Cadavers. Human cadavers have also been used for experiments involving potentially injurious stimuli, and in particular to relate skull fracture to frontal head impact. Such studies resulted in the

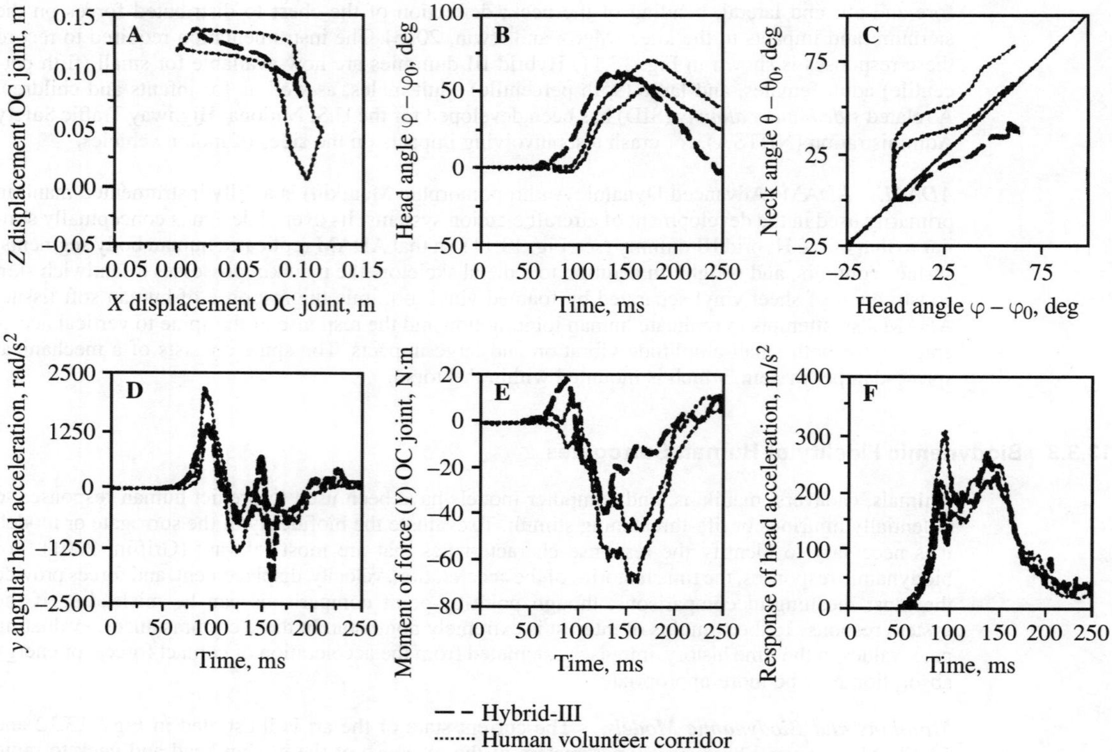

FIGURE 13.12 Response of human volunteers and the Hybrid III head and neck to 15 *g* spineward deceleration. The range of responses from human subjects is shown by the dotted lines, and the response of the manikin by the dashed lines (see text for explanation of the motions plotted). *(RTO-MP-20, 1999.)*

formulation of the Wayne State concussion tolerance curve, which has been widely used to define survivable head impacts in motor vehicle collisions (Prasad, 2015). Cadavers lack appropriate mechanical properties for tissues and muscle tension. The latter is important for obtaining realistic human responses, as can be seen from Fig. 13.13 by comparing the results with and without active muscle behavior.

13.4 COUNTERMEASURES

Reducing the effects of vibration, shock, and impact on humans is effected in several ways: (1) by isolation, to reduce the transmission of dynamic forces and accelerations to the body; (2) by personal protective equipment, to distribute the dynamic forces over as large a surface area as possible and provide vibration isolation, and absorption; and (3) by redesign, to reduce the source's vibration intensity. These subjects are considered after summarizing the occurrence of health effects from exposure to vibration, shock, and impact, which establishes the performance required of ameliorative measures.

13.4.1 Occurrence of Health Effects and Injury

There is extensive literature on the occurrence of health effects and injury from exposure to vibration, shock, and impact, which serves as the basis for the present discussion. Estimates of exposures

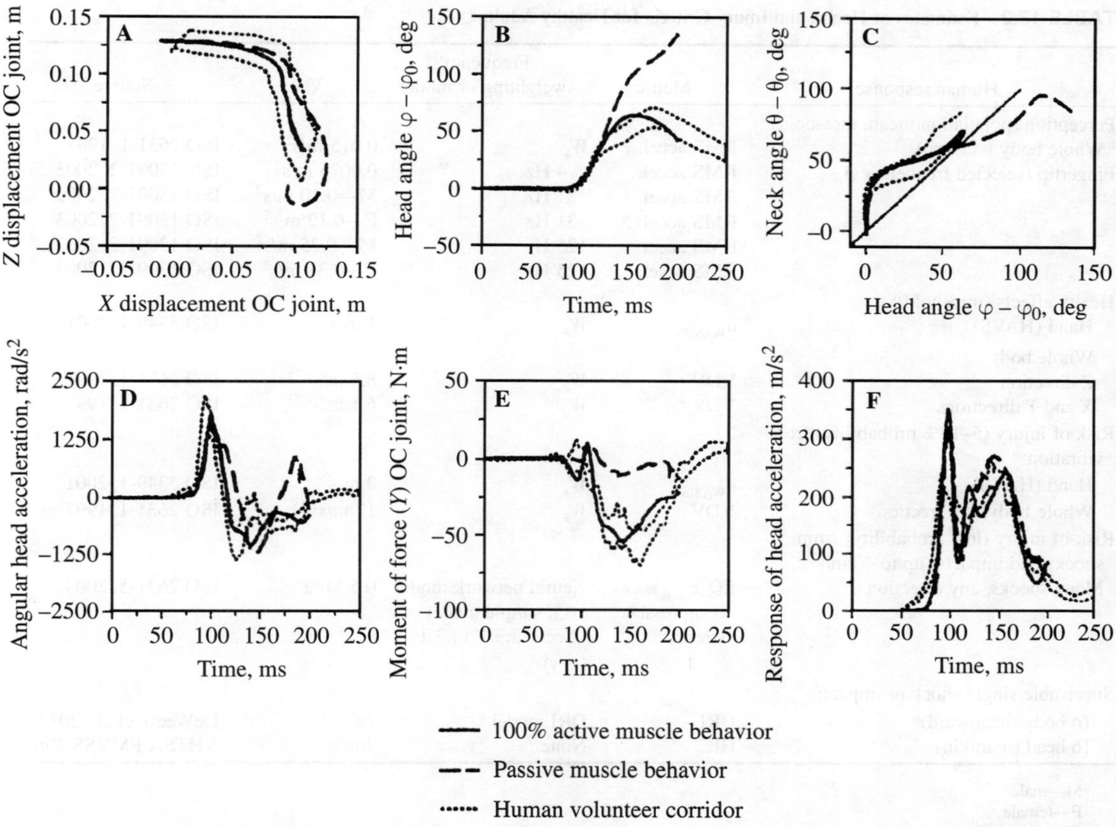

FIGURE 13.13 Response of human volunteers and the 3D MADYMO model of the head and neck to spineward decelerations. The range of responses from human subjects is shown by the dotted lines, and the response of the model with passive and active muscles is shown by the dashed and continuous lines, respectively (see text for explanation of the motions plotted). (*RTO-MP-20, 1999.*)

necessary for common human responses and health effects are summarized in Table 13.2 for healthy adults; the interested reader is directed to the references given in the table for more complete information.

Included in Table 13.2 are the metric used for assessing the exposure, the frequency or weighting of the stimulus, or model, and a *representative* value for the response or health effect under consideration. As already noted, there are large variations between individuals in response, and susceptibility, to vibration, shock, and impact.

Vibration Perception. The perception of vibration depends on the body site and on the stimulus frequency. The thresholds in Table 13.2 are typical of those for healthy adults, and are expressed as instantaneous RMS accelerations [i.e., with $T \approx 1$ s in Eq. (13.2)]. The value for whole-body vibration is given in terms of a frequency-weighted acceleration, and so is applicable to vibration at frequencies from 1 to 80 Hz. The values for hand-transmitted vibration are for sinusoidal stimuli applied to the fingertips of males (M) and females (F) at the specified frequencies.

Thresholds for Health Effects. Thresholds for the onset of health effects have been estimated for regular, near-daily exposure to hand-transmitted and to whole-body vibration. The metrics

TABLE 13.2 Estimates of Health and Injury Criteria for Healthy Adults

Human response	Metric	Frequency, weighting or model	Value	Source
Perception (population mean, threshold):				
Whole body (vertical)	RMS accel.	W_k	0.015 m/s^2	ISO 2631-1, 1997
Fingertip (selected frequencies)	RMS accel.	4 Hz	0.0075 m/s^2	ISO 13091-2, 2003
	RMS accel.	31 Hz	M—0.10 m/s^2	ISO 13091-2, 2003
	RMS accel.	31 Hz	F—0.12 m/s^2	ISO 13091-2, 2003
	RMS accel.	125 Hz	M—0.25 m/s^2	ISO 13091-2, 2003
	RMS accel.	125 Hz	F—0.32 m/s^2	ISO 13091-2, 2003
Health effects (threshold):				
Hand (HAVS)	$a_{\text{WAS(8)}}$	W_h	1 m/s^2	ISO 5349-1, 2001
Whole body				
Z direction	VDV	W_k	8.5 m/s$^{1.75}$	ISO 2631-1, 1997
X and *Y* directions	VDV	W_d	6.1 m/s$^{1.75}$	ISO 2631-1, 1997
Risk of injury (5–10% probability) from vibration:				
Hand (HAVS)	$a_{\text{WAS(8)}}$	W_h	3 m/s^2	ISO 5349-1, 2001
Whole-body, *Z* (direction)	VDV	W_k	17 m/s$^{1.75}$	ISO 2631-1, 1997
Risk of injury (low probability) from shocks and impacts (up to 40 m/s^2):				
Many shocks, any direction	$E(\sum a_{\text{peak}})6.6 \Rightarrow$ compressive stress	Neural network model (*z*); simple model of Secs.13.3.1 13.3.1 (*x*, *y*)	0.5 MPa	ISO 2631-5, 2004
Survivable single shock or impact:				
To body (headward)*	DRI	DRI model	18	DeWeese et al., 2015
To head (manikin)	HIC	None	700	NHTSA FMVSS 208†

M—male
F—female
*When body is restrained.
†U.S. National Highway Traffic Safety Administration Federal Motor Vehicle Safety Standard 208.

employed, however, differ. For hand-transmitted vibration, the assessment is in terms of the magnitude of the 8 h, energy-equivalent, frequency-weighted, RMS, vector acceleration sum, $a_{\text{WAS(8)}}$. This metric employs values of the RMS component accelerations averaged over 8 h [i.e., $T = 28{,}800$ s in Eq. (13.2)] which have been frequency-weighted using W_h in Fig. 13.1. The components are determined for each of the directions of the basicentric, or biodynamic, coordinate system shown in Fig. 13.2, $a_{x,\text{RMS(8)}}$, $a_{y,\text{RMS(8)}}$, and $a_{z,\text{RMS(8)}}$, respectively. Thus:

$$a_{\text{WAS(8)}} = \left[a^2_{x,\text{RMS(8)}} + a^2_{y,\text{RMS(8)}} + a^3_{2,\text{RMS(8)}}\right]^{1/2} \tag{13.12}$$

A reduction in the metric will occur for a given acceleration magnitude if the duration of the exposure is reduced, as is illustrated by the following example (see also "Vibration Exposure" in Sec. 13.1.1).

EXAMPLE 13.2 *A worker uses a percussive rock drill for 3 h daily. Measurement of the handle vibration indicates a frequency-weighted RMS acceleration of 18 m/s^2 along the drill axis, and a frequency-weighted RMS acceleration of 5 m/s^2 perpendicular to this axis. Estimate the 8-hour daily exposure.*

Answer: *From the (limited) available information, we obtain the following approximate values:*

$$a_{z,\text{RMS(3)}} = 18 \quad a_{x,\text{RMS(3)}} = a_{y,\text{ RMS(3)}} = 5$$

So $$a_{\text{WAS}(3)} = (5^2 + 5^2 + 18^2)^{1/2} = 19.3$$

Now an exposure for 3 h ($T_{(3)}$) can be expressed as an equivalent 8-h exposure using Eq. (13.5):

$$a_{\text{WAS}(8)} = a_{\text{WAS}(3)}\left(\frac{T_{(3)}}{T_{(8)}}\right)^{1/2}$$

so that $$a_{\text{WAS}(8)} = 19.3\left(\frac{10{,}800}{28{,}800}\right)^{1/2}$$

$$a_{\text{WAS}(8)} = 11.8 \text{ m/s}^2$$

The assessment of whole-body vibration employs the VDV averaged over 8 h [i.e., $T = 28{,}800$ s in Eq. (13.6)], with frequency weighting W_k for vertical vibration and frequency weighting W_d for horizontal vibration. It is believed that the higher-order metrics, as recommended here, better represent the hazard presented by motion containing transient events, particularly when these become small-magnitude shocks or impacts. The most appropriate metric, however, remains a subject for research.

Risk of Injury. Exposures to vibration magnitudes between the threshold for perception and that for health effects commonly occur in daily life. Near-daily exposures to values of $a_{\text{WAS}(8)}$ and VDV in excess of those estimated to result in 5 to 10 percent injury in Table 13.2 occur in numerous occupations (involving some 8 million persons in the United States) and lead to the symptoms described in Sec. 13.1.2.

The risk of injury from multiple shocks and impacts to the spine is estimated for the most commonly affected bony vertebral endplates (lumbar spine) by the method described by Morrison et al. (1997). The method requires biodynamic models that predict peak accelerations of the lumbar vertebrae in the *x*, *y*, and *z* directions for a seated person in response to shocks entering from the seat (see Fig. 13.2); a model for accumulating exposure to repeated shocks to form a dose; and an injury risk model based on the cumulative probability of fatigue failure. A recurrent neural-network model is employed for motion in the *z* direction, with simple, one-degree-of-freedom models used for the *x* and *y* directions (see Sec. 13.3.1). The acceleration dose is constructed, separately, from the output of the biodynamic models using Eq. (13.3) with $F(a_w(t))$ representing the peak acceleration of the shock or impact that compresses the spine, and the peak acceleration in either direction for the *x* and *y* components, and $m = r = 6$. The combined acceleration dose is converted into an equivalent *static* compressive stress, which is interpreted for fatigue failure of the vertebral end plates taking into account the reducing strength of vertebrae with age. The value in Table 13.2 is the daily dose below which there is a "low probability of a health effect" in a working lifetime (ISO 2631-5, 2004).

The range of applicability of the neural network model is restricted to peak compressive accelerations of –20 to 40 m/s^2. This restriction is of limited practical consequence. Larger accelerations occur infrequently outside military operations (e.g., shocks experienced in high-speed boats), when they may be assessed by survivability criteria (see "Survivable Shocks and Impacts" below). For shocks smaller than 5 m/s^2, the FE whole-body models described by Schust et al. (2015) have been shown to predict the risk of developing sciatic pain (Bovenzi et al., 2015), which is associated with degenerative processes in the lumbar spine.

Survivable Shocks and Impacts. Estimates for *survivable* exposures to single impacts and shocks are given for both headward acceleration and spineward deceleration in Table 13.2. For headward acceleration, experience with nonfatal ejections from military aircraft suggests that a DRI of 18 is associated with a 5 to 10 percent probability of spinal injury among healthy, *young* males who are restrained in their seats. For spineward deceleration, the estimate is based on the *head injury criterion* (HIC), which was developed from the severity index (see "Vibration Exposure" in Sec. 13.1.1). The metric is defined as:

$$\text{HIC} = \left\{(t_2 - t_1)\left[\frac{1}{(t_2 - t_1)}\int_{t_1}^{t_2} a(t)\,dt\right]^{2.5}\right\}_{\max} \qquad (13.13)$$

where t_1 and t_2 are the times between which the HIC attains its maximum value and $a(t)$ is measured at the location of the center of gravity of the head (in units of gravity). The HIC is applied to instrumented crash test dummies; its ability to rank order, by magnitude, the severity of injuries in humans has been questioned. The time interval $(t_2 - t_1)$ is the duration of contact with the aircraft interior in aviation regulations, which require the HIC to be ≤1000 (DeWeese et al., 2015). For motor vehicles, the maximum value allowable by the NHTSA in frontal collisions is listed in Table 13.2. In this case the time interval $(t_2 - t_1)$ for calculating the HIC is 15 ms (Prasad, 2015). Survivable injuries to the neck and chest, and fracture limits for the pelvis, patella, and femur in frontal and side impacts have also been determined for manikins (Mertz and Irwin, 2015).

The HIC does not take into account head rotations, which are believed to be a primary source of brain injury (Newman, 2015).

13.4.2 Protection against Whole-Body Vibration

Vibration Isolation. Excessive whole-body vibration is most commonly encountered in transportation systems, where it predominantly affects seated persons. In consequence, an effective remedial measure is to reduce the vertical component of vibration transmitted through seats (and, where applicable, vehicle suspension systems), by means of low-pass mechanical filters. The transmissibility of a vibration-isolated seat or vehicle suspension (neglecting tire flexure) can be modeled in the vertical direction by the mechanical system shown in Fig. 13.6. For a vibration-isolated seat, the spring and damper represent mechanical elements supporting the seat pan and person, which are represented by a single mass m. For a vehicle suspension, the mechanical elements support the passenger compartment. With this model, it is evident that the vibration transmitted to the body will be reduced at frequencies above the resonance frequency of the mechanical system defined by the spring, damper, and total supported mass [i.e., for $r > \sqrt{2}$ in Fig. 13.6 and Eq. (13.10)]. The frequency weighting W_k (Fig. 13.1) suggests that effective vibration isolation for humans will require a resonance frequency of ~2 Hz or less. The low resonance frequency can be achieved by using a soft coiled spring, or an air spring, and a viscous damper. Vehicle suspensions with these properties are commonly employed. So-called *suspension seats* are commercially available, but are limited to applications in which the vertical displacement of the seat pan that results from the spring deflection is acceptable. A situation can be created in which the ability to control a vehicle is impaired by the position, or motion, of the driver sitting on the vibration-isolated seat relative to the (nonisolated) controls.

Active Vibration Reduction. An *active vibration control system* consists of one or more hydraulic or electrodynamic actuators, vibration sensors, and an electronic controller designed to maintain the seat pan stationary irrespective of the motion of the seat support. Such a control system must be capable of reproducing the vehicle motion at the seat support, which will commonly possess large displacement at low frequencies, and supply a phase-inverted version to the seat pan to counteract the vehicle motion in real time. This imposes a challenging performance requirement for the control system and vibration actuator(s). Also, the control system must possess safety interlocks to ensure it does not erroneously generate harmful vibration at the seat pan. While active control systems have been employed commercially to adjust the static stiffness or damping of vehicle suspensions, to improve the ride comfort on different road surfaces, there are few commercial active seat suspensions.

13.4.3 Protection against Hand-Transmitted Vibration

Vibration-Isolated Tool Handles. Vibration isolation systems have been applied to a range of powered hand tools, often with dramatic consequences. For example, the introduction of vibration-isolated handles to gasoline-powered chain saws has significantly reduced the incidence of HAVS among professional saw operators. Unfortunately, such systems are not provided for the handles of all consumer-grade chain saws. The principle is the same as that described for whole-body vibration isolation, but in this case the angular resonance frequency can be ~350 rad/s (i.e., $f_0 \approx 55$ Hz) and still effectively reduce chain-saw vibration. The higher resonance frequency results in a static deflection of the saw tip relative to the handles that, with skill, does not impede the utility of the tool.

Tool Redesign. Some hand and power tools have been redesigned to reduce the vibration at the handles. Many are now commercially available (Linqvist, 1986). The most effective designs counteract the dynamic imbalance forces at the source—for example, a two-cylinder chain saw with 180° opposed cylinders and synchronous firing. A second example is a pneumatic chisel in which the compressed air drives both a cylindrical piston into the chisel (and workpiece) and an opposing counterbalancing piston; both are returned to their original positions by springs. A third is a rotary grinder in which the rotational imbalance introduced by the grinding wheel and motor is removed by a *dynamic balancer*. The dynamic balancer consists of a cylindrical enclosure, attached to the motor spindle, containing small ball bearings that are free to move and self-adjust with axial rotation of the cylinder to positions on the walls that result in the least radial vibration—the desired condition.

Gloves. The principle of vibration isolation has been applied to gloves, and so-called *antivibration* gloves are commercially available. Such gloves satisfy the requirements of an international standard (ISO 10819, 2013), which only specifies performance in the z_h direction (see Fig. 13.2). The transmissibility will depend on the direction of the vibration relative to the glove surface (e.g., compression or shear), and may be predicted by biodynamic models for the three coordinate directions when appropriate values for glove components are introduced (see Fig. 13.9). The predicted transmission of vibration to the fingers, and to the palm, in the z_h direction is shown in Fig. 13.14 for a glove containing a resilient element between the outer and inner surfaces (ISO 10068, 2012).

It can be seen that the transmissibility is predicted to be close to unity at frequencies below approximately 30 Hz at the palm and 100 Hz at the fingers. A reduction in vibration at the palm of the hand is expected at frequencies above 30 Hz, while a peak in the transmissibility at the fingers (i.e., amplification of source vibration) is predicted at frequencies above 100 Hz before the transmissibility decreases with increasing frequency. An extremely soft spring is required to obtain this performance because of the small dynamic mass of the hand and is achieved by an air spring formed from small air bladders sewn into the palm, fingers, and thumb of the glove. The reduction in frequency-weighted acceleration at the hand (obtained using W_h in Fig. 13.1) will depend also on the frequency spectrum of the vibrating power tool, tool handle, or work piece held in the hand. An overall reduction in the total frequency-weighted acceleration at the palm of the hand (i.e., combining all vibration components) of, typically, 0 to 15 percent can be achieved by vibration-reducing gloves, some of which do not satisfy the requirements of ISO 10819 (2013) (Dong et al., 2014).

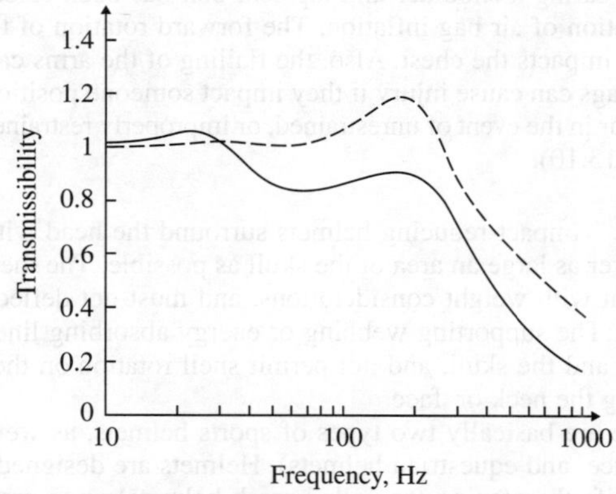

FIGURE 13.14 Transmissibility of a vibration-reducing glove at the fingers (dashed line) and at the palm of the hand (continuous line) in the z_h direction predicted by the lumped parameter biodynamic model shown in Fig. 13.9. (*ISO 10068, 2012.*)

13.4.4 Protection against Mechanical Shocks and Impacts

Protection against potentially injurious shocks and impacts is obtained by distributing the dynamic forces over as large a surface area of the body as possible and transferring the residual forces preferably to the pelvic region of the skeleton (though not through the vertebral column). Modifying the impact-time history to involve smaller peak forces lasting for a longer time is usually beneficial. Progressive crumpling of the passenger cabin floor and any forward structural members while absorbing horizontal crash forces, as well as extension of a seat's rear legs, are all used for this purpose.

Seat Belts and Harnesses. For seated persons, lap belts, or combined lap and shoulder harnesses, are used to distribute shock loads, and are routinely installed in automobiles and passenger aircraft. In addition, the belts hold the body against the seat, which serves to strengthen the restrained areas. Combined lap and shoulder harnesses are preferable to lap belts alone for forward-facing passengers, as the latter permit the upper body to flail in the event of a spineward deceleration, such as occurs in motor vehicle and many aircraft crashes. Harnesses with broader belt materials can be expected to produce lower pressures on the body and consequently less soft tissue injury. For headward accelerations the static deformation of the seat cushion is important, with the goal being to spread the load uniformly and comfortably over as large an area of the buttocks and thighs as possible.

An improvement in performance can be obtained by pretensioning the restraint harness before the shock is experienced by the occupants of the automobile or aircraft (e.g., by means of an actuator triggered by a deceleration sensor mounted close to the point of impact). The resulting increase in shock duration experienced by the seated persons permits the maximum load to be reduced (Kent and Forman, 2015).

Air Bags. Although originally conceived as an alternative to seat belts and harnesses, air bags are now recognized to provide most benefit when used with passive restraints, which define the position of the body. The device used in automobiles consists, in principle, of one or more crash sensors (accelerometers) that detect rapid decelerations, and a controller that processes the data and initiates a pyrotechnic reaction to generate gas. The gas inflates a porous fabric bag between the decelerating vehicle structure and the occupant within about 25 to 50 ms, to distribute the shock and impact forces over a large surface of the body.

An example of the use of a MADYMO model to simulate air bag inflation and occupant response to the frontal collision of an automobile is shown in Fig. 13.15. In this diagram, the response of a person wearing a shoulder and lap seat belt has been calculated at 25-ms time intervals following the initiation of air bag inflation. The forward rotation of the head is clearly visible and is arrested before it impacts the chest. Also, the flailing of the arms can be seen.

Air bags can cause injury if they impact someone positioned close to the point of inflation, which may occur in the event of unrestrained, or improperly restrained, vehicle occupants (e.g., small children; see Fig. 13.10).

Helmets. Impact-reducing helmets surround the head with a rigid shell to distribute the dynamic forces over as large an area of the skull as possible. The shell of a helmet must be as stiff as possible consistent with weight considerations, and must not deflect sufficiently on impact for it to contact the head. The supporting webbing or energy absorbing liner must maintain the separation between the shell and the skull, and not permit shell rotation on the head, to avoid the edges of the helmet impacting the neck or face.

There are basically two types of sports helmets, as well as special purpose helmets (e.g., military, police, and equestrian helmets). Helmets are designed either to withstand a single impact that may be life threatening (so-called crash helmets) or to provide protection from concussion caused by multiple smaller impacts (e.g., sports helmets for football, ice hockey). Special purpose helmets typically include additional characteristics such as resistance to penetration by pointed or other shaped objects, depending on the application. Some helmets emphasize the smoothness of the outer surface of the shell, or even provide an outer "skin" that can slide on the shell, in an attempt to reduce

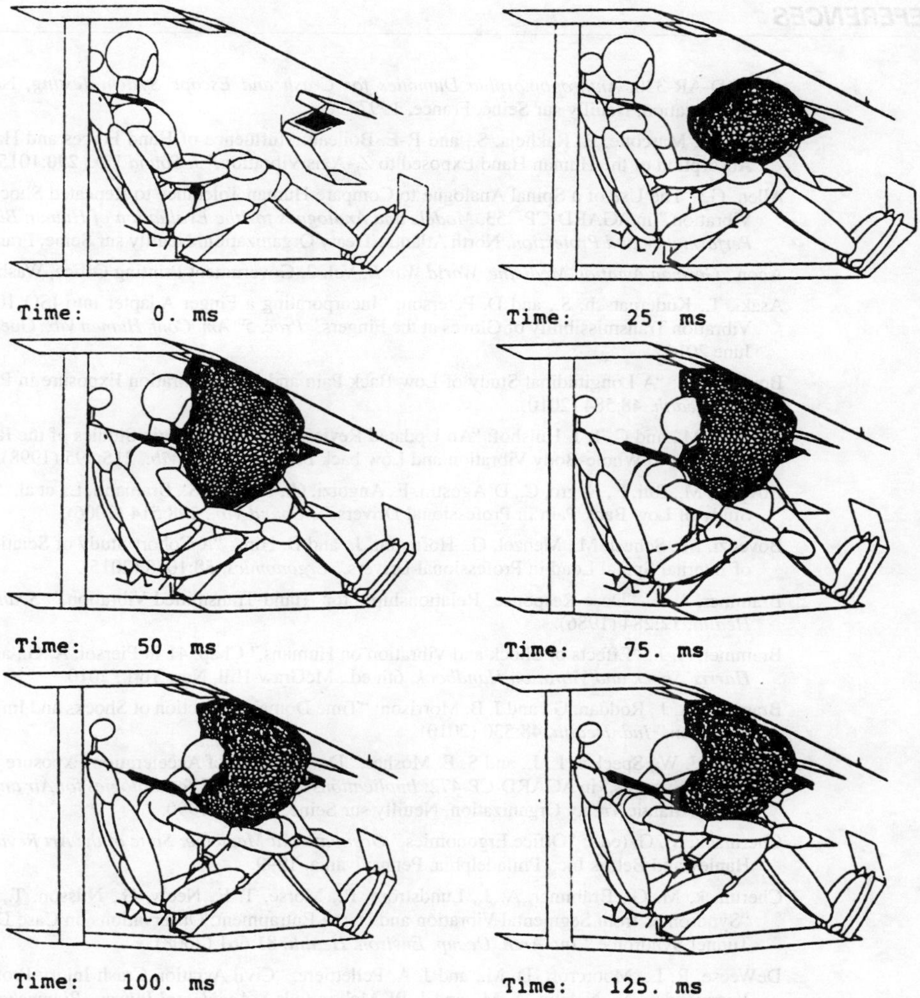

FIGURE 13.15 MADYMO simulation of the response of a person wearing a shoulder and lap seat belt to the inflation of an air bag in a frontal motor vehicle collision. The model predicts the body position every 25 ms after the collision. Note the time for the air bag to inflate (between 25 and 50 ms), the rotation of the head, the flailing of the arms, and the bending of the floor. (*AGARD-AR-330, 1997.*)

injuries from head rotation. Crushable foams (e.g., polystyrene bead foams) are commonly used for liners designed to withstand a single impact, and resilient rubber-like foams for liners designed for multiple impacts. Deformable plastic structures conceptually reminiscent of stacked egg cartons have found application in liners for some military helmets (Newman, 2015).

Most practical helmet designs are a compromise between impact protection and other considerations (e.g., bulk and weight, visibility, comfort, ability to communicate). Their efficacy has been demonstrated repeatedly by experiment and accident statistics.

REFERENCES

AGARD-AR-330, *Anthropomorphic Dummies for Crash and Escape System Testing*, North Atlantic Treaty Organization, Neuilly sur Seine, France, 1997.

Aldien, Y., Marcotte, P., Rakheja, S., and P.-E. Boileau: "Influence of Hand Forces and Handle Size on Power Absorption of the Human Hand Exposed to Z_h-Axis Vibration," *J. Sound Vib.*, **290**:1015 (2006).

Allen, G.: "The Use of a Spinal Analogue to Compare Human Tolerance to Repeated Shocks with Tolerance to Vibration," in AGARD-CP-253, *Models and Analogues for the Evaluation of Human Biodynamic Response, Performance and Protection*, North Atlantic Treaty Organization, Neuilly sur Seine, France, 1978.

Anon., *German Aviation Medicine, World War II*, Vol. 2, Government Printing Office, Washington, D. C., 1950.

Asaki, T., Kudernatsch, S., and D. Peterson: "Incorporating a Finger Adapter into ISO 10819 to Measure the Vibration Transmissibility of Gloves at the Fingers," *Proc. 5th Am. Conf. Human Vib.*, Guelph, Ontario, Canada, June 2014.

Bovenzi, M.: "A Longitudinal Study of Low Back Pain and Daily Vibration Exposure in Professional Drivers," *Ind. Health,* **48**:584 (2010).

Bovenzi, M., and C. T. J. Hulshof: "An Updated Review of Epidemiologic Studies of the Relationship Between Exposure to Whole-Body Vibration and Low back Pain," *J. Sound Vib.*, **215**:595 (1998).

Bovenzi, M., Rui, F., Negro, C., D'Agostin, F., Angotzi, G., Bianchi, S., Bramanti, L., et al.: "An Epidemiological Study of Low Back Pain in Professional Drivers," *J Sound Vib.*, **298**:514 (2006).

Bovenzi, M., Schust, M., Menzel, G., Hofmann, J., and B. Hinz: "A Cohort Study of Sciatic Pain and Measures of Internal Spinal Load in Professional Drivers," *Ergonomics,* **58**:1088 (2015).

Brammer, A. J.: "Dose-Response Relationships for Hand-Transmitted Vibration," *Scand. J. Work Environ. Health*, **12**:284 (1986).

Brammer, A. J.: "Effects of Shock and Vibration on Humans," Chap. 41 in Piersol, A. G., and T. L. Paez (eds.): *Harris' Shock and Vibration Handbook*, 6th ed., McGraw-Hill, New York, 2010.

Brammer, A. J., Roddan, G., and J. B. Morrison: "Time Domain Detection of Shocks and Impacts in Whole-Body Vibration," *Ind. Health*, **48**:530 (2010).

Brinkley, J. W., Specker, L. J., and S. E. Mosher: "Development of Acceleration Exposure Limits for Advanced Escape Systems," in AGARD-CP-472: *Implications of Advanced Technologies for Air and Spacecraft Escape*, North Atlantic Treaty Organization, Neuilly sur Seine, France, 1990.

Cherniack, M. G. (ed.): "Office Ergonomics," *Occupational Medicine: State of the Art Reviews*, Vol. **14**, Issue 1, Hanley and Belfus Inc., Philadelphia, Pennsylvania. 1999.

Cherniack, M. G., Brammer, A. J., Lundström, R., Morse, T. F., Neely, G., Nilsson, T., Peterson, D., et al.: "Syndromes from Segmental Vibration and Nerve Entrapment: Observations on Case Definitions for Carpal Tunnel Syndrome," *Int. Arch. Occup. Environ. Health*, **81**:661 (2008).

DeWeese, R. L., Moorcroft, D. M., and J. A. Pellettiere: "Civil Aviation Crash Injury Protection," Chap. 28 in Yoganandan, N., Nahum, A. M., and J. W. Melvin (eds.), *Accidental Injury—Biomechanics and Prevention*, 3rd ed., Springer, New York, 2015.

Dong, R. G., Welcome, D. E., McDowell, T. W., and J. Z. Wu: "Modeling the Biodynamic Responses Distributed at the Fingers and Palm of the Hand in Three Orthogonal Directions," *J. Sound Vib.*, **332**:1125 (2013).

Dong, R. G., Welcome, D. E., Peterson, D. R., Xu, X. S., McDowell, T. W., Warren, C., Asaki, T., et al.: "Tool-Specific Performance of Vibration-Reducing Gloves for Attenuating Palm-Transmitted Vibrations in Three Orthogonal Directions," *Int. J. Industrial Ergonomics*, **44**:827 (2014).

Eiband, A. M.: "*Human Tolerance to Rapidly Applied Accelerations: A Summary of the Literature*," NASA Memo 5-19-59E, National Aeronautics and Space Administration, Washington, D.C., 1959.

Fairley, T. E., and M. J., Griffin: "The Apparent Mass of the Seated Human Body: Vertical Vibration," *J. Biomechanics*, **22**:81 (1989).

Fung, Y. C.: *Biomechanics—Mechanical Properties of Living Tissues,* 2nd ed., Springer-Verlag, New York, 1993.

Gomez, M. A., and A. M. Nahum: "Biomechanics of Bone," Chap. 10 in Nahum, A. M., and J. W. Melvin (eds.), *Accidental Injury—Biomechanics and Prevention*, 2nd ed., Springer-Verlag, New York, 2002.

Griffin, M. J.: *Handbook of Human Vibration,* Academic Press, London, 1990.

Griffin, M. J.: "The Validation of Biodynamic Models," *Clinical Biomechanics, Supplement* 1, 16:S81 (2001).

Haut, R. C.: "Biomechanics of Soft Tissue," Chap. 11 in Nahum, A. M., and J. W. Melvin (eds.): *Accidental Injury—iomechanics and Prevention*, 2nd ed. Springer-Verlag, New York, 2002.

ISO 2631-1, *Mechanical Vibration and Shock—Evaluation of Human Exposure to Whole Body Vibration—Part 1: General Requirements*, 2nd ed., International Organization for Standardization, Geneva, 1997.

ISO 2631-5, *Mechanical Vibration and Shock—Evaluation of Human Exposure to Whole Body Vibration—Part 5: Method for Evaluation of Vibration Containing Multiple Shocks*, International Organization for Standardization, Geneva, 2004.

ISO 5349-1, *Mechanical Vibration—Measurement and Evaluation of Human Exposure to Hand-Transmitted Vibration—Part 1: General Guidelines*, International Organization for Standardization, Geneva, 2001.

ISO 5349-2, *Mechanical Vibration—Measurement and Evaluation of Human Exposure to Hand-Transmitted Vibration—Part 2: Practical Guidance for Measurement at the Workplace*, International Organization for Standardization, Geneva, 2001.

ISO 5982, *Mechanical Vibration and Shock—Range of Idealized Values to Characterize Human Biodynamic Response under Whole-Body Vibration*, 3rd ed., International Organization for Standardization, Geneva, 2019.

ISO 7096, *Earth Moving Machinery—Operator Seat—Measurement of Transmitted Vibration*, International Organization for Standardization, Geneva, 1982.

ISO 8041-1, *Human Response to Vibration—Measuring Instrumentation—Part 1: General Purpose Vibration Meters*, International Organization for Standardization, Geneva, 2017.

ISO 10068, *Mechanical Vibration and Shock—Mechanical Impedance of the Human Hand-Arm System at the Driving-Point*, 2nd ed., International Organization for Standardization, Geneva, 2012.

ISO 10819, *Mechanical Vibration and Shock—Hand-Arm Vibration—Method for the Measurement and Evaluation of the Vibration Transmissibility of Gloves at the Palm of the Hand*, 2nd ed., International Organization for Standardization, Geneva, 2013.

ISO 13091-2, *Mechanical Vibration—Vibrotactile Perception Thresholds for the Assessment of Nerve Dysfunction—Part 2: Analysis and Interpretation of Measurements at the Fingertips*, International Organization for Standardization, Geneva, 2003.

Kent, R. W., and J. Forman: "Restraint System Biomechanics," Chap. 5 in Yoganandan, N., Nahum, A. M., and J. W. Melvin (eds.), *Accidental Injury—Biomechanics and Prevention*, 3rd ed., Springer, New York, 2015.

Krajnak, K.: "Health Effects Associated with Occupational Exposure to Hand-Arm or Whole-Body Vibration," *J. Toxicology & Environ. Health, Part B: Critical Rev.*, **21**:320 (2018).

Kudernatsch, S., Asaki, T. and D. Peterson: "Design of a Hand-Mounted Palm and Finger Adapter System to Measure Palm and Finger Forces and Vibration Exposures," *Proc. 5th Am. Conf. Human Vib.*, Guelph, Ontario, Canada, June 2014.

Linqvist, B. (ed.): *Ergonomic Tools in Our Time*, Atlas-Copco, Stockholm, Sweden, 1986.

Mansfield, N. J.: *Human Response to Vibration*, CRC Press, Boca Raton, 2005.

Martin, B. J., and D. Adamo: "Effects of Vibration on Human Systems: A Neurophysiological Perspective," *Can. Acoust. Assoc. J.*, **29**:3, 10 (2001).

Mertz, H. J., and A. L. Irwin: "Anthropomorphic Test Devices and Injury Risk Assessments," Chap. 4 in Yoganandan, N., Nahum, A. M., and J. W. Melvin (eds.), *Accidental Injury—Biomechanics and Prevention*, 3rd ed., Springer, New York, 2015.

Morrison, J. B., Martin, S. H., Robinson, D. G., Roddan, G., Nicol, J. J., Springer, M. J-N., Cameron, J., et al.: "Development of a Comprehensive Method of Health Hazard Assessment for Exposure to Repeated Mechanical Shocks," *J. Low Freq. Noise Vib. Active Cont.*, **16**:245 (1997).

Nahum, A. M., and J. W. Melvin (eds.): *Accidental Injury—Biomechanics and Prevention*, 2nd ed. Springer-Verlag, New York, 2002.

Newman, J. A.: "Design and Testing of Sports Helmets: Biomechanical and Practical Considerations," Chap. 25 in Yoganandan, N., Nahum, A. M., and J. W. Melvin (eds.), *Accidental Injury—Biomechanics and Prevention*, 3rd ed., Springer, New York, 2015.

Nicol, J., Morrison, J., Roddan, G., and A. Rawicz: "Modeling the Dynamic Response of the Human Spine to Shock and Vibration Using a Recurrent Neural Network," *Heavy Vehicle Systems*, Special Series, *Int. J. Vehicle Design*, **4**:145 (1997).

Payne, P. R., "*On Quantizing Ride Comfort and Allowable Accelerations*," Paper 76-873, AIAA/SNAME Advanced Marine Vehicles Conf., Arlington, Va., American Institute of Aeronautics and Astronautics, New York, 1976.

Peterson, D. R., and M. G. Cherniack: "Repetitive Impact from Manual Hammering: Physiological Effects on the Hand-Arm System," *Can. Acoust. Assoc. J.* **29**:3; 12 (2001).

Peterson, D. R., Brammer, A. J., and M. G. Cherniack: "Exposure Monitoring System for Day-Long Vibration and Palm Force Measurements," *Int. J. Industrial Ergonomics*, **38**:676 (2008).

Prasad, P.: "Injury Criteria and Motor Vehicle Regulations," Chap. 27 in Yoganandan, N., Nahum, A. M., and J. W. Melvin (eds.), *Accidental Injury—Biomechanics and Prevention*, 3rd ed., Springer, New York, 2015.

RTO-MP-20, *Models for Aircrew Safety Assessment: Uses, Limitations and Requirements,* North Atlantic Treaty Organization, Neuilly sur Seine, France, 1999.

Schust, M., Menzel, G., Hofmann, J., Forta, N., Pinto, I., Hinz, B., and M. Bovenzi: "Measures of Internal Lumber Load in Professional Drivers: The Use of a Whole-Body Finite Element Model for the Evaluation of Adverse Health Effects of Multi-Axis Vibration," *Ergonomics,* **58**:1191 (2015).

Seidel, H.: "On the Relationship between Whole-Body Vibration Exposure and Spinal Health Risk," *Ind. Health*, **43**:361 (2005).

Taylor, W.: "Biological Effects of the Hand-Arm Vibration Syndrome: Historical Perspective and Current Research," *J. Acoust. Soc. Am.*, **83**:415 (1988).

von Gierke, H. E.: "Biodynamic Models and their Application," *J. Acoust. Soc. Am.* **50**:1397 (1970).

von Gierke, H. E.: "Effects of Vibration and Shock on People," Chap. 145 in Crocker, M. (ed.), *Encyclopedia of Acoustics*, Academic Press, New York, 1997.

von Gierke, H. E., Oestreicher, H. L., Franke, E. K., Parrach, H. O., and W. W. von Wittern: "Physics of Vibrations in Living Tissues," *J. Appl. Physiol.*, **4**:886 (1952).

Xu, X. S., Dong, R. G., Welcome, D. E., Warren, C., and T. W. McDowell: "An Examination of an Adapter Method for Measuring the Vibration Transmitted to the Human Arms," *Measurement*, **73**:318 (2015).

Xu, X. S., Dong, R. G., Welcome, D. E., Warren, C., McDowell, T. W., and J. Z. Wu: "Vibrations Transmitted from Human Hands to Upper Arm, Shoulder, Back, Neck, and Head," *Int. J. Industrial Ergonomics*, **62**:1 (2017).

Xu, X. S., Welcome, D. E., Warren, C. M., McDowell, T. W., and R. G. Dong: "Development of Finger Adapter Method for Testing and Evaluating Vibration-Reducing Gloves and Materials," *Measurement* **137**:362 (2019).

Yang, K. H., Hu, J., White, N. A., and A. I. King: "Development of Numerical Models for Injury Biomechanics Research: A Review of 50 Years of Publications in the Stapp Car Crash Conference," *Stapp. Car Crash J.*, **50**:429 (2006).

Yoganandan, N., Nahum, A. M., and J. W. Melvin (eds.): *Accidental Injury—Biomechanics and Prevention*, 3rd ed., Springer, New York, 2015.

CHAPTER 14

ELECTROMYOGRAPHY AS A TOOL TO ESTIMATE MUSCLE FORCES

Qi Shao and Thomas S. Buchanan
University of Delaware, Newark, Delaware

14.1 INTRODUCTION: HOW TO ESTIMATE MUSCLE FORCES

Knowledge of internal muscle forces during movements is of great importance for understanding human neuromuscular control strategies, developing better rehabilitation regimens, and improving the design of prosthesis for patients with neurological disorders. However, the human neuromusculoskeletal system is complicated and different muscles are finely coordinated to accomplish various tasks, which makes their study difficult.

Unfortunately, in vivo muscle force measurement is invasive and only practical in very few cases. Additionally, the musculoskeletal system is indeterminate, having more muscles than necessary for a unique solution. For this reason, optimization techniques have been employed to predict muscle forces using a variety of cost functions. Linear optimization techniques were first used for numerical convenience (Seireg and Arvikar, 1973; Crowninshield, 1978). These linear cost functions were found to be insufficient, so nonlinear cost functions have been developed, assuming one constant underlying neuromuscular control strategy during movement (Pedotti et al., 1978; Crowninshield and Brand, 1981; Dul et al., 1984; Li et al., 1999). Pedotti et al. (1978) used a sum of individual muscle forces and normalized muscle forces as their nonlinear cost function. Crowninshield and Brand (1981) utilized muscle endurance as a nonlinear cost function to mathematically predict individual muscle forces. Muscle endurance was described by a sum of muscle stresses to the third power. Dul et al. (1984) developed a nonlinear optimization algorithm based on minimizing muscle fatigue, which took into account maximal muscle force and composition of slow and fast twitch fibers. Li et al. (1999) found that the number of degrees of freedom involved in their optimization played an important role in prediction of the recruitment of antagonistic muscles rather than the selection of a particular cost function. They concluded that a properly formulated inverse dynamics optimization should balance the knee joint in three orthogonal planes. Other studies using forward dynamics simulation optimize muscle excitation patterns to reproduce coordinated movements and estimate muscle forces (Neptune et al., 2001; Thelen and Anderson, 2006). In these studies, the cost function was the error between measured and simulated joint kinematics and ground reaction forces.

Unfortunately, the linear cost functions described above have been shown to have difficulty predicting cocontraction and recorded muscle activation patterns, and cannot account for different recruitment patterns during various tasks (Herzog and Leonard, 1991; Buchanan and Shreeve, 1996). The dynamics-simulation-based cost functions have limitations because they do not account for the differences in neural control strategies that may be employed by different people. They generally ignore cocontractions, which is a commonly used strategy when learning a new task or when injured.

Electromyography (EMG) is the study of the electrical signal recorded by electrodes over or inside muscles. An EMG signal includes real-time information about the electrical activity of a specific muscle—which is related to muscle force—and has been studied for over 50 years. The relationship between EMG and muscle force has been studied during isometric contractions and dynamic contractions. It has been reported to be linear (Lippold, 1952; Bouisset and Goubel, 1971; Moritani and deVries, 1978) and slightly nonlinear (Heckathorne and Childress, 1981; Woods and Bigland-Ritchie, 1983) during isometric contractions. For dynamic contractions, the change of muscle force has been found to be also dependent on the change of muscle fiber length (Gordon et al., 1966) and fiber velocity (Edman, 1978; Edman, 1979), so the relationship between the amplitude of EMG and the force output should be modeled more comprehensively.

Based on the research of muscle force-EMG relationship, different EMG-driven biomechanical models have been developed to estimate muscle forces (De Duca and Forrest, 1973; Hof and Van den Berg, 1981; Buchanan et al., 1993; Thelen et al., 1994; Lloyd and Buchanan, 1996; Lloyd and Besier, 2003; Buchanan et al., 2004; Buchanan et al., 2005). Since these models determine muscle forces based on recorded EMG data, they can account for different muscle activation patterns and may predict muscle force more accurately (especially when studying different neural control strategies) than other methods.

14.2 THE EMG SIGNAL

14.2.1 How EMG Is Generated

The EMG signal is a complex, time-varying biopotential waveform, which is emanated by the muscle underneath the electrode. It includes information about muscle activity and has been used as a primary tool to study muscle function. Clinicians can diagnose problems in the neuromuscular system by analyzing the onset/offset of EMG signal, or the peak amplitude of EMG signal; biomechanists can use the EMG signal as an input to estimate muscle force; neurophysiologists can use the EMG signal to identify different mechanisms of motor control and learning. In this section we will introduce how muscle force is generated and EMG signal is detected (Enoka, 2002).

In human skeletal muscle, the muscle fibers do not contract individually; instead, they act as small groups in concert. A single smallest controllable muscular unit is named a motor unit. A motor unit is composed of a single motor neuron, the multiple branches of its axon, and the muscle fibers that the motor neuron innervates (Fig. 14.1). Voluntary contraction of a motor unit initiates from an action potential (an all-or-none electrical impulse that is issued by a cell if the input to the cell exceeds its threshold) sent out from the central nervous system (CNS), and travels down the axon to the muscle fibers. When the impulse of action potential reaches the muscle fibers, it activates all the fibers in the motor unit almost simultaneously.

A motor neuron is an efferent neuron that transmits the output signal (action potential) from the CNS to skeletal muscle. There are two main kinds of motor neurons: upper motor neurons and lower motor neurons. An upper motor neuron resides in the motor region of cerebral cortex or the brain stem, and extends its axon down the spinal cord to the lower motor neuron. The lower motor neuron then sends its axon out through the ventral root of the spinal cord, and the axon is bundled together into peripheral nerves that reach the target muscle. When the axon reaches the muscle, it splits into

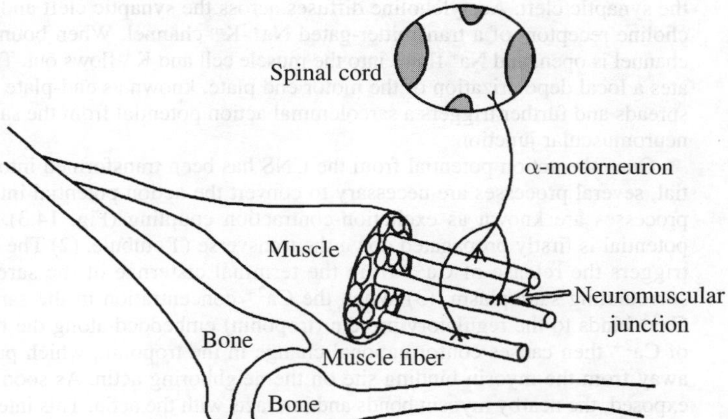

FIGURE 14.1 Scheme of a motor unit, which is a single α-motorneuron and its associated muscle fibers.

many terminal branches, and each axonal branch innervates only one muscle fiber. A single muscle fiber is innervated by only one motor neuron, but a single motor neuron can innervate more than one muscle fiber, varying from 9 (e.g., extrinsic eye muscles) to 2000 (e.g., gastrocnemius) muscle fibers (Feinstein et al., 1955).

The synapse or junction between the axon of a motor neuron and a muscle fiber is known as a neuromuscular junction, sometimes referred to as a motor end plate (Fig. 14.2). There is a narrow synaptic cleft between the presynaptic membrane (axon) and the postsynaptic membrane (muscle fiber membrane). When an action potential arrives at the presynaptic terminal, it triggers synaptic vesicular fusion to the terminal neuron membrane and releases neurotransmitter (acetylcholine) into

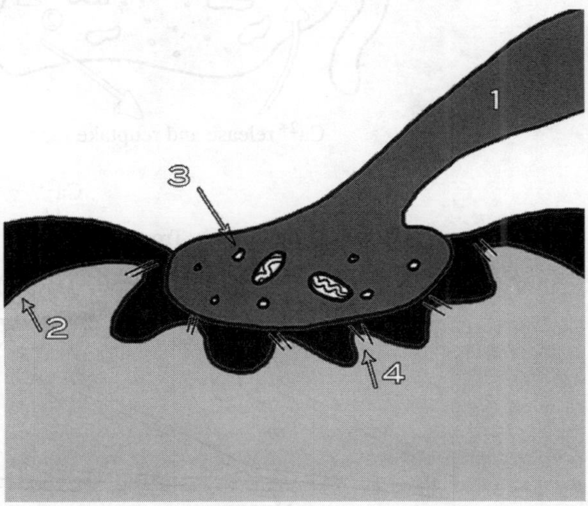

FIGURE 14.2 Neuromuscular junction (closer view): (1) presynaptic terminal; (2) sarcolemma; (3) synaptic vesicles; and (4) acetylcholine receptors.

the synaptic cleft. Acetylcholine diffuses across the synaptic cleft and binds to the nicotinic acetylcholine receptors of a transmitter-gated Na^+-K^+ channel. When bounded by the acetylcholine, the channel is open, and Na^+ flows into the muscle cell and K^+ flows out. The flow of Na^+ and K^+ generates a local depolarization of the motor end plate, known as end-plate potential. This depolarization spreads and further triggers a sarcolemmal action potential from the sarcolemma in the region of the neuromuscular junction.

Once the action potential from the CNS has been transformed into a sarcolemmal action potential, several processes are necessary to convert the action potential into a muscle fiber force. These processes are known as excitation-contraction coupling (Fig. 14.3). (1) The sarcolemmal action potential is firstly propagated down the transverse (T) tubule. (2) The T-tubule action potential then triggers the release of Ca^{2+} from the terminal cisternae of the sarcoplasmic reticulum into the surrounding sarcoplasm. (3) When the Ca^{2+} concentration in the sarcoplasm reaches a threshold, Ca^{2+} binds to the regulatory protein (troponin) embedded along the thin filament. (4) The binding of Ca^{2+} then causes conformational change in the troponin, which pulls the attached tropomyosin away from the myosin-binding site on the neighboring actin. As soon as the myosin-binding site is exposed, the nearby myosin bonds and interacts with the actin. This interaction of actin and myosin to generate force is referred to as cross-bridge cycle. The thick and thin filaments slide relative to each other and exert a force on the cytoskeleton during this cycle. The release of energy by ATP hydrolysis powers this cycling process. After the action potential ends, Ca^{2+} is removed by active transport into the sarcoplasmic reticulum. The tropomyosin is then restored to block the myosin-binding site, the contraction then ends and muscle fiber relaxes.

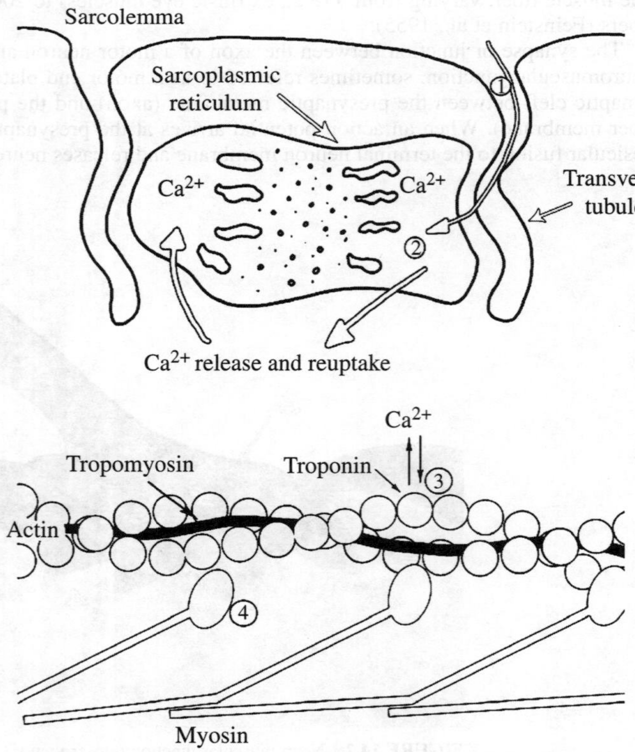

FIGURE 14.3 The four steps in excitation-contraction coupling (see text for details). [*Adapted and modified from Fitts and Metzger (1993).*]

Motor unit force can be explained as a consequence of the cycling of many cross-bridges following the innervation. Since the stimulus to a motor unit is typically a superposition of several action potentials, a motor unit rarely generates an individual twitch in response to a single action potential. Instead, these superposed action potentials result in overlapping twitch responses, which is known as tetanus. When the stimulating frequency at which the action potentials are sent to the motor unit is small, the tetanus has an irregular force profile. With the increase of the stimulating frequency, the tetanus is changed to a smooth plateau and has a greater force output. The stimulating frequency can determine both the magnitude and the shape of the motor unit force profile. Thus, a muscle can increase its force output by either recruiting more motor units or increasing firing rate.

Electrodes can be used to detect the electrical waveform over a muscle fiber when an action potential propagates along the muscle fiber, and this waveform is referred to as muscle fiber action potential. Motor unit action potential (MUAP) is defined as the detected waveform consisting of the spatiotemporal summation of individual muscle fiber action potentials originating from muscle fibers in the vicinity of a given electrode or electrode pair. Motor unit action potential train (MUAPT) is defined as the repetitive sequence of MUAPs from a given motor unit (Winter et al., 1980).

14.2.2 Different Types of Electrodes

The electrodes used to measure EMG are of a wide variety of types and structures. They must be positioned close enough to the muscle of interest to pick up the electrical signal. Surface electrode, percutaneous (needle and wire) electrode are the electrodes usually used (Basmajian and De Luca, 1985).

Surface electrodes detect the electrical signal on the skin surface outside the muscle of interest (Fig. 14.4). They are convenient to use and give the subject little discomfort. The detected signal

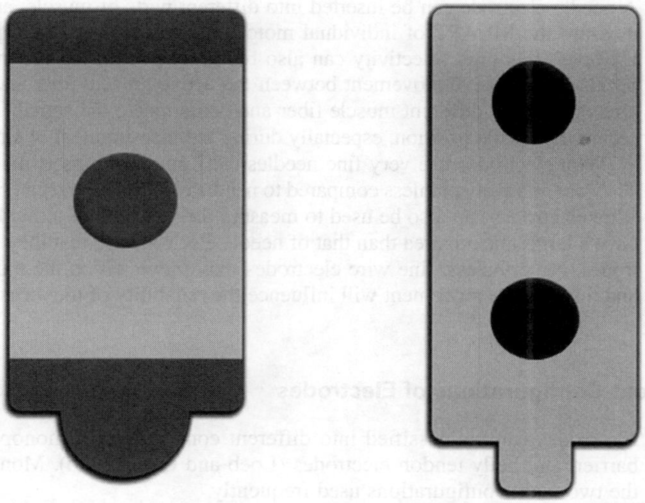

FIGURE 14.4 Monopolar and bipolar surface electrodes.

is a summation of the MUAPTs from all active motor units within its pickup area. Muscle fibers are randomly scattered throughout the cross section of the muscle, therefore the signal represents a substantial part of the muscle of interest (De Luca, 1997). As a drawback, surface electrodes can only be used to study the EMG of superficial muscles and cannot be used for deep muscles.

Two kinds of surface electrodes with different electrode-skin interfaces are commonly in use: dry electrodes and gelled electrodes. Dry electrodes directly contact the skin, and a preamplifier circuitry at the electrode site is usually used. This preamplifier system can convert the high impedance of the skin to low impedance output of the amplifier, and reduce motion artifact (Hagemann et al., 1985). Dry electrodes are often used during motion analysis for the suppression of motion artifact. Gelled electrodes use an electrolytic gel or paste as a chemical interface between the skin and electrodes. The electrode-electrolyte interface can reduce the electrode-skin impedance and improve signal quality under static conditions, but it also leads to significant increases in signal artifact when mechanically perturbed (e.g., limb movement, impact during heel strike), especially when the skin is wet after perspiration (Roy et al., 2007).

Abrasion of the skin is necessary for removing the dead tissue of the skin and its protective oils, which helps lower the electrical impedance and improve the quality of the collected signal (Tam and Webster, 1977). A poor contact between the electrode and the skin would introduce additional noise, so adhesive strips or tapes are usually used to secure the contact (Roy et al., 2007).

When a surface electrode is placed too far from the active motor units, the amplitude of the electrical signal will be very low because of the quick attenuation throughout the tissue. The EMG signal from deep muscles and adjacent muscles also interfere with the EMG of the muscle of interest, and this interference is referred to as cross-talk. It is, therefore, necessary to put surface electrodes at a proper position, where the cross-talk noise can be reduced and the EMG signal represents the muscle of interest with a higher signal-to-noise ratio. There are established standards for placing electrodes on different muscles (e.g., Zipp, 1982, for surface electrodes and Perotto and Delagi, 1994, for intramuscular recordings). The placement of surface electrodes can be easily performed by a person after little training.

Percutaneous electrodes are invasive and can cause discomfort or pain, but they can be used to measure the activity of deep muscles and the action potential of a single muscle fiber or motor unit.

Needle electrodes are inserted directly into the muscle of interest to measure the electrical activity. Various needle electrodes are available for different measurement purposes, such as the monopolar needle electrode, multipolar needle electrode, concentric needle electrode, and macroneedle electrode. A needle electrode can be inserted into different parts of muscle, and the high selectivity allows it to measure the MUAPT of individual motor unit or even the action potential of a single muscle fiber. However, this high selectivity can also be a problem during the measurement of single-fiber EMG, because the relative movement between the active muscle fiber and electrode may locate the pickup area in a totally different muscle fiber and contaminate the signal. Therefore, care should be taken to secure the needle position, especially during the measurement of single-fiber EMG.

Wire electrodes use very fine needles (~27 gauge) to insert the wires into the muscle of interest. They are relatively painless compared to needle electrodes, and can be easily implanted and withdrawn. Wire electrodes can also be used to measure the MUAPT of individual motor unit, and they generally have a larger pickup area than that of needle electrodes so that they are not as selective as needle electrodes. Nevertheless, fine wire electrodes may move within the muscle during a muscle contraction, and this relative movement will influence the reliability of the measured signal.

14.2.3 Different Configurations of Electrodes

Electrodes can be classified into different configurations: monopolar, bipolar, tripolar, multipolar, barrier, and belly tendon electrodes (Loeb and Gans, 1986). Monopolar and bipolar electrodes are the two main configurations used frequently.

In monopolar configuration, the electrical activity of a muscle is acquired by placing one detection electrode in the pickup area, and another reference electrode in a place that is electrically quiet or a place that has minimal physiological and anatomical association with the detection electrode. Therefore, a monopolar electrode has a single recording point, and the signal is collected with respect to a remote reference point. This configuration is often used in clinical applications because of its relative simplicity. Monopolar surface electrodes detect a summation of all the electrical signals in the vicinity of the detection surface and may introduce cross-talk noises from other adjacent or deep muscle tissues. This leads to the further development of bipolar electrodes to counteract the cross-talk noise.

Bipolar electrodes have two detection electrodes at two recording points in the pickup area, and another reference electrode is used at a remote position similar to that of monopolar configuration.

The two signals detected at the two different positions are then passed through a differential amplifier at the electrode site, which treats each signal equally and amplifies the difference between the two signals. Through this method, the components common in the two signals (mostly noises) are suppressed. Since the electrochemical events in muscle contraction are localized, the electrical signals emanated from the muscle of interest are different on the two recording positions, and thus can be kept after passing through the differential amplifier. The noises from a more distant source (the cross-talk of other muscles, A/C power devices, electromagnetic devices, etc.) are detected with similar amplitudes at both recording positions, and they are treated as correlated signal contents common to both sites and subtracted prior to being amplified. This way, bipolar electrodes can theoretically eliminate the noises from distant sources, and they have been used more with the technical development of electronics amplifiers.

14.2.4 Selection of Different Electrodes

We have introduced many different types and structures of electrodes above. The selection of the electrodes depends on the practical condition and specific aim.

Surface electrodes are most often used to measure the EMG of superficial large muscles. They are noninvasive and convenient to use. The data collection can be operated by a person with little training. Hence surface electrodes are the most popular in a laboratory environment. The bipolar configuration is recommended to reduce the noises from cross-talk or other distant sources. However, surface electrodes cannot be used for deep muscles, and it is also difficult to use them on small muscles, because the cross-talk from adjacent muscles would severely contaminate the signal (Robertson, 2004).

Needle and fine wire electrodes must be used to accurately measure the EMG of deep muscles, small muscles, individual motor units, or muscle fibers. They are invasive and should be used by a person with special training for inserting these indwelling electrodes. The implementation of needle and wire electrodes will increase the time and expense of data collection, and may also influence the subject's movement pattern because of the pain (especially for needle electrodes).

14.2.5 Electronics of the Electrode System

The observable EMG signal initiates from the superposed action potentials of motor units and passes through muscle and skin tissues, electrode-skin interface, amplifier, and recorder. These mediums act as different filters changing the amplitude and frequency of the original signal, as shown in Fig. 14.5 (Basmajian and De Luca, 1985).

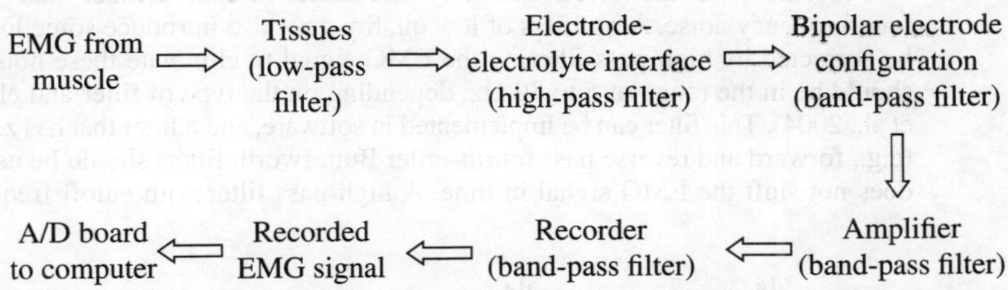

FIGURE 14.5 Block diagram of how the electrical signal is transferred in a typical EMG system of gelled electrode. Note the EMG from muscle refers to the electrical signals emanated from the muscle of interest. [*Adapted from Basmajian and De Luca (1985).*]

During the acquisition procedure of EMG, electronic noises are introduced to the signal by different sources. They include the environmental noise from surrounding electromagnetic devices (such as computers, power supplies, and power cords), transducer noise from the electrode-skin contact, electrical noise introduced by electronic components, and motion artifact introduced by the movement of electrodes.

14.3 PROCESSING THE EMG SIGNAL

The EMG signal detected by electrodes is a complicated signal, which is affected by the timing and intensity of muscle contraction, the recording positions of electrodes, the quality of the contact between electrodes and skin, the electrode and amplifier properties, the lab environment, etc. Here we will introduce various procedures that can be used to analyze and interpret the EMG signal for different purposes.

14.3.1 Rectification

The EMG signal comprises positive and negative phases that fluctuate about a central line of zero voltage (isoelectric line). Direct averaging the signal will not provide any useful information because of the fluctuation about zero value. Thus, rectification is a necessary process for data analysis by taking the absolute value of the EMG signal, that is, inverting the negative phases (Fig. 14.6).

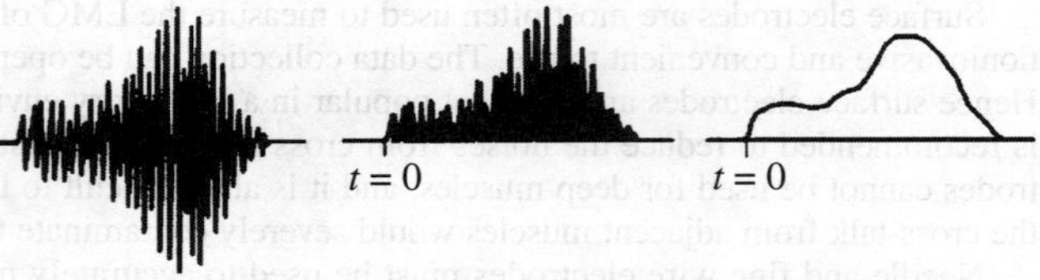

FIGURE 14.6 Rectification and filtering of raw EMG. [*Adapted from Buchanan et al. (2004).*]

14.3.2 Smoothing

The rectified signal still shows an irregular pattern due to different types of noises, so smoothing should then be implemented to remove unwanted noises and get the desired information about muscle activity (Fig. 14.7). High-pass filter and low-pass filter are two typical approaches to reduce the low-frequency and high-frequency contents of the noise.

Movement of the electrodes may introduce motion artifact that is composed mostly of low-frequency noise. Amplifiers of low quality may also introduce some low-frequency noise. It can be corrected by high-pass filtering the EMG signal to eliminate these noises. The cutoff frequency should be in the range of 5 to 30 Hz, depending on the type of filter and electrodes used (Buchanan et al., 2004). This filter can be implemented in software, and a filter that has zero-phase delay properties (e.g., forward and reverse pass fourth-order Butterworth filter) should be used, such that the filtering does not shift the EMG signal in time. A high-pass filter with cutoff frequency of 5 to 30 Hz will

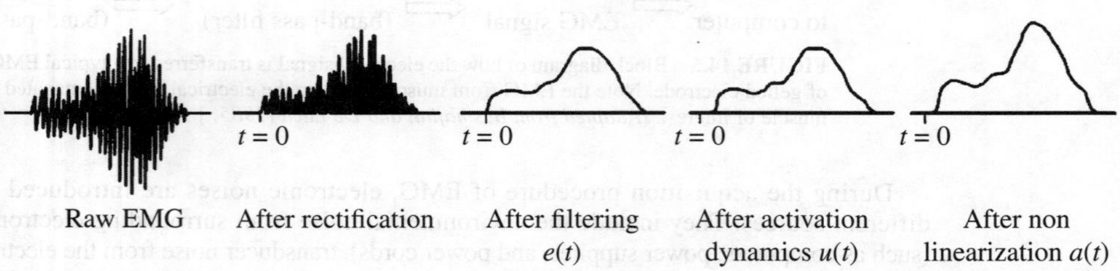

FIGURE 14.7 Muscle activation dynamics: transformation from EMG to muscle activation. [*Adapted from Buchanan et al. (2004).*]

usually preserve the important contents in the EMG signal. Only the information relative to the firing rates of active motor units, in the range of 5 to 25 Hz for most muscles (Enoka, 2002), is disregarded. However, this information is not of great importance for most applications.

After the EMG is high-pass-filtered, the processed signal still has many sharp peaks. The power spectrum from surface EMG signal shows that the majority of the signal power is at frequencies below 350 Hz (Wakeling and Rozitis, 2004). The rest of the high-frequency contents are mostly noises, which may be generated by surrounding electromagnetic devices, and poor electrode-skin contact (Cram and Garber, 1986). A low-pass filter can then be applied to eliminate the high-frequency noises. The cutoff frequency is usually chosen close to 500 Hz (De Luca, 1997). The filter should also have zero-phase delay properties (e.g., forward and reverse pass fourth-order Butterworth filter).

If the EMG signal will be used to estimate muscle force, more high-frequency contents of the signal should be eliminated, because muscle naturally acts as a filter and we want this to be characterized in the EMG-force transformation. That is, although the electrical signal that passes through the muscle has frequency components over 100 Hz, the force that the muscle generates is of much lower frequencies (e.g., muscle force profiles are smoother than raw EMG profiles). In muscles there are many mechanisms that cause this filtering; for example, calcium dynamics, finite amount of time for transmission of muscle action potentials along the muscle, and muscle and tendon viscoelasticity. Thus, in order for the EMG signal to be correlated with the muscle force, it is important to filter out the high-frequency components with a lower cutoff frequency. The range of 3 to 10 Hz is typical for the cutoff frequency in the EMG-force transformation (Buchanan et al., 2004).

14.3.3 Different Approaches to Analyze EMG

After the unwanted noises are removed from the EMG signal, different approaches may then be used to analyze the signal.

Three parameters are commonly calculated in the time domain to provide useful measurement of EMG signal amplitude: root-mean-squared (RMS) value, mean integrated rectified value, and average rectified value (De Luca and Vandyk, 1975). RMS value represents the signal power during voluntary contractions, and thus is recommended above the other two parameters (De Luca, 1997).

The power density spectrum of EMG signal is commonly used to analyze the EMG in the frequency domain. A fast Fourier transform can be used to obtain the power density spectrum of the signal. Mean frequency, median frequency, and bandwidth of the spectrum are the three main parameters used to provide useful measurement of the spectral properties of the signal. The power spectrum of EMG signal is typically a skewed bell-shaped curve, and the majority of the signal power lies between 50 and 150 Hz (Wakeling and Rozitis, 2004). The power spectrum of the EMG signal will be changed during the progression of muscle fatigue, and this spectrum modification property can be used in the study of muscle fatigue. The median frequency of the power spectrum is often used as a fatigue index as a measure of muscle fatigue.

All of the above approaches are implemented to analyze the contraction of a muscle. Meanwhile, the EMG signal can also be decomposed into individual MUAPTs, which can help researchers to study motor unit properties and behavior (Stashuk, 2001).

14.4 *EMG-DRIVEN MODELS TO ESTIMATE MUSCLE FORCES*

EMG-driven models use EMG and joint kinematics, recorded during a range of static and dynamic trials, as input to estimate individual muscle forces and joint moments (Lloyd and Besier, 2003; Buchanan et al., 2004; Buchanan et al., 2005). Given appropriate anatomical and physiological data, these models can be applied to any joint, such as the elbow joint (Manal et al., 2002), the knee joint (Lloyd and Besier, 2003), and the ankle joint (Buchanan et al., 2005).

This overall model is composed of four main parts: (1) anatomical model, (2) muscle activation dynamics model, (3) muscle contraction dynamics model, and (4) model of calibration process. Here we will discuss the details involved in each of these steps for an ankle and knee model as an example.

14.4.1 Anatomical Model

The first step requires that we decide which joints and muscles will be included and how their parameters will be obtained. For this lower limb model, a popular anatomical model is that developed using SIMM (Musculographics Inc.) (Delp et al., 1990, and extended by Lloyd and Buchanan, 1996). This model includes 12 musculotendon actuators, represented as line elements that wrap around bone segments or other muscles. These are the rectus femoris (RF), vastus lateralis (VL), vastus intermedius (VI), vastus medialis (VM), medial gastrocnemius (MG), lateral gastrocnemius (LG), semimembranosus (SM), semitendinosus (ST), biceps femoris long (BFL) head, biceps femoris short (BFS) head, tibialis anterior (TA), and soleus (Sol). Joint kinematics will be used as input for this anatomical model to determine individual muscle tendon lengths and moment arms.

14.4.2 Muscle Activation Dynamics Model

The magnitudes of the EMG signals will change as the neural command calls for increased or decreased muscular effort. Nevertheless, it is difficult to compare the absolute magnitude of an EMG signal from one muscle to that of another because the magnitudes of the signals can vary depending on many factors such as the gain of the amplifiers, the types of electrodes used, and the placements of the electrodes. Thus, in order to use the EMG signals in a neuromusculoskeletal model, we must first transform them into muscle activation. The muscle activation dynamics model transforms raw EMG to muscle activation, and the whole process is shown in Fig. 14.7.

Firstly, the raw EMGs are high-pass-filtered using a forward and reverse pass fourth-order Butterworth filter to remove movement artifact, then full wave rectified, normalized by peak rectified EMG values obtained from maximum voluntary contraction (MVC) trials, and then low-pass-filtered using a forward and reverse pass fourth-order Butterworth filter to account for the natural filtering property of muscle.

After rectifying, normalizing, and filtering the raw EMG data, activation dynamics needs to be used to characterize the time varying features of EMG. Muscle twitch response can be well represented by a critically damped linear second-order differential system (Milner-Brown et al., 1973). This type of response has been the basis for the differential equations to determine neural activation, $u(t)$, from the rectified, normalized, and filtered EMG input, $e(t)$.

$$u(t) = \mathrm{M}\frac{de^2(t)}{dt^2} + \mathrm{B}\frac{de(t)}{dt} + \mathrm{K}e(t) \tag{14.1}$$

where M, B, and K are the constants that define the second-order differential system.

This differential equation can be expressed in discrete form by using backward differences (Thelen et al., 1994; Lloyd and Buchanan, 1996).

$$u(t) = \alpha \cdot e(t-d) - \beta_1 \cdot u(t-1) - \beta_2 \cdot u(t-2) \tag{14.2}$$

where d is the electromechanical delay, and α, β_1, and β_2 are the coefficients that define the second-order dynamics. To realize a positive stable solution of Eq. (14.1), a set of constraints are employed.

$$\begin{aligned} \beta_1 &= \gamma_1 + \gamma_2 \\ \beta_2 &= \gamma_1 \times \gamma_2 \\ |\gamma_1| &< 1 \\ |\gamma_2| &< 1 \end{aligned} \tag{14.3}$$

This equation can be seen as a recursive filter, where the neural activation depends not only on the current level of neural activation but also on its recent history. This filter should have unit gain so that neural activation does not exceed 1, and to ensure this, the following condition must be satisfied.

$$\alpha - \beta_1 - \beta_2 = 1 \tag{14.4}$$

There is a nonlinear relationship between stimulation frequency and force for single motor units (Woods and Bigland-Ritchie, 1983), and this nonlinearity can be offset by other factors such as the recruitment of small motor units at low force levels and larger ones at higher levels (i.e., the size principle). Muscle activation can be expressed as a function of neural activation, *u(t)*, using a logarithmic function instead of a power function for low values and a linear function for high values (Manal and Buchanan, 2003).

$$\begin{aligned} a(t) &= d\ln(c \cdot u(t) + 1) \qquad 0 \le u(t) <\sim 0.3 \\ a(t) &= m \cdot u(t) + b \qquad 0.3 \le u(t) < 1 \end{aligned} \tag{14.5}$$

where *u(t)* is the neural activation and *a(t)* is the muscle activation. The coefficients *c*, *d*, *m*, and *b* can be solved and reduced to a single parameter, *A*. Then the parameter *A* is used to characterize the curvature of the relationship. It varies from 0.0 to approximately 0.12.

14.4.3 Muscle Contraction Dynamics Model

A modified Hill-type muscle model can then be used to calculate individual muscle forces. The muscle-tendon unit is modeled as a muscle fiber in series with a tendon. The muscle fiber also has a contractile element in parallel with an elastic element and a damping element, as shown in Fig. 14.8. Pennation angle (φ) is the angle between the lines of action of the tendons and the muscle fiber. l_m is the muscle fiber length, l_t is the total length of the tendons (each one is half of the length), and l_{mt} is the musculotendon length. The force produced by the tendon is represented as F^t. The muscle fiber produces the total muscle force (F^m), and comprises three parallel elements. The contractile element produces the active force depending on muscle activation, fiber length, and fiber velocity. The elastic element gives the passive force (F_P) depending on muscle fiber length. The damping element is quantified by damping factor b_m. The general form of the equations for the muscle-tendon force (*F*) was given by

$$F = F^t = F_{\max}\left[\tilde{F}_A(\tilde{l}_m) \cdot \tilde{F}_V(\tilde{v}_m) \cdot a(t) + \tilde{F}_P(\tilde{l}_m) + b_m \cdot \tilde{v}_m\right] \cdot \cos(\varphi) \tag{14.6}$$

where $F_{\max}$ is the maximum isometric muscle force, $\tilde{l}_m$ is the normalized muscle fiber length, $\tilde{v}_m$ is the normalized muscle fiber velocity, and *a(t)* is the muscle activation. $\tilde{F}_A(\tilde{l}_m)$ represents the

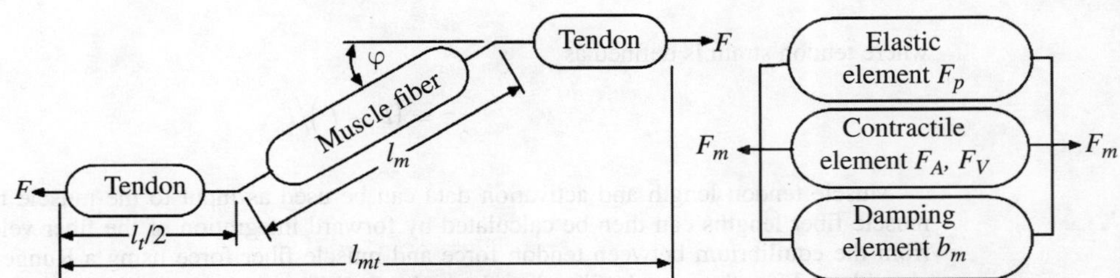

FIGURE 14.8 Hill-type muscle model.

force-length relationship (Gordon et al., 1966), $\tilde{F}_V(\tilde{v}_m)$ represents the force-velocity relationship (Hill, 1938; Zajac, 1989; Epstein and Herzog, 1998), and $\tilde{F}_P(\tilde{l}_m)$ represents the passive elastic force-length relationship (Schutte, 1992), and b_m is the damping factor (Schutte et al., 1993). These parameters are normalized to the maximum isometric muscle force, optimal fiber length (l_o^m), and maximum muscle contraction velocity (v_{max}).

Pennation angle ($\varphi(t)$) changed with instantaneous muscle fiber length by assuming that muscle has constant thickness and volume as it contracts (Scott and Winter, 1991). A typical equation to calculate pennation angle, $\varphi(t)$ is

$$\varphi(t) = \sin^{-1}\left(\frac{l_o^m \sin\varphi_o}{l^m(t)}\right) \tag{14.7}$$

where $l^m(t)$ is the muscle fiber length at time t, and φ_o is the pennation angle at muscle optimal fiber length l_o^m.

The contractile element's force-length relationship $\tilde{F}_A(\tilde{l}_m)$ is a curve created by a cubic spline interpolation of the points on the force-length curve defined by Gordon et al. (1966). Huijing (1996) has shown that optimal fiber lengths increase as activation decreases, an observation which has also been reported by Guimaraes et al. (1994). This coupling relationship between muscle activation and optimal fiber length can be incorporated into the muscle model (Lloyd and Besier, 2003) as

$$l_o^m(t) = l_o^m(\lambda(1 - a(t)) + 1) \tag{14.8}$$

where λ is the percentage change in optimal fiber length, and $l_o^m(t)$ is the optimal fiber length at time t.

The passive elastic force-length function $\tilde{F}_P(\tilde{l}_m)$ is given by an exponential relationship that is described by Schutte (1992).

$$\tilde{F}_P(\tilde{l}_m) = \frac{e^{10(\tilde{l}_m - 1)}}{e^5} \tag{14.9}$$

The force-velocity relationship $\tilde{F}_V(\tilde{v}_m)$ and damping element can be used based on that employed by Schutte et al. (1993). The damping element accounts for the intrinsic damping characteristics of muscles, and improves the stability of the model.

Tendon force varies with tendon strain ε only when tendon length l^t is greater than tendon slack length l_s^t; otherwise the tendon force is zero. Subsequently the normalized tendon force, $\tilde{F}^t$, is given by (Zajac, 1989)

$$\begin{aligned} &\tilde{F}^t = 0 && \varepsilon \le 0 \\ &\tilde{F}^t = 1480.3\varepsilon^2 && 0 < \varepsilon < 0.0127 \\ &\tilde{F}^t = 37.5\varepsilon - 0.2375 && \varepsilon \ge 0.0127 \end{aligned} \tag{14.10}$$

where tendon strain is defined as

$$\varepsilon = \left(l^t - l_s^t\right)/l_s^t \tag{14.11}$$

Muscle tendon length and activation data can be used as input to the muscle model, and then muscle fiber lengths can then be calculated by forward integration of the fiber velocities obtained from the equilibrium between tendon force and muscle fiber force using a Runge-Kutta-Fehlberg algorithm. After the muscle fiber lengths and velocities are determined, the muscle force can be calculated through Eq. (14.6). Once individual muscle forces are estimated, they are multiplied by muscle moment arms and summed to determine total joint moments.

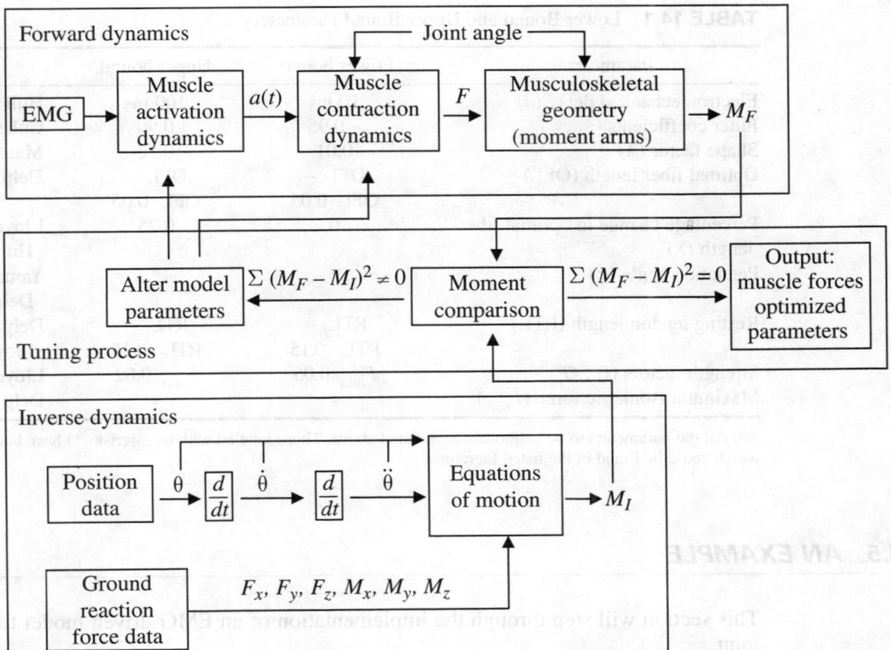

FIGURE 14.9 Theoretical flow of the hybrid forward-inverse dynamics model. Legend: EMG = electromyograms; $a(t)$ = muscle activation; F = muscle force; M_F = joint moment calculated from forward dynamics; M_I = joint moment calculated from inverse dynamics; θ (and derivatives) = joint angle, joint angular velocity, joint angular acceleration; $F_x, F_y, F_z, M_x, M_y, M_z$ = ground reaction forces and moments in all three directions. In this model, M_F was used as a reference baseline, and we used a tuning process to optimize the parameters of forward dynamics model such that M_F matches M_I.

14.4.4 Model of Calibration Process

This model uses a hybrid forward-inverse dynamics approach, which assumes that the forward dynamic joint moments estimated from the EMG-driven model should equal the joint moments estimated from inverse dynamics, as shown in Fig. 14.9. A tuning process can then be used to calibrate the model and obtain a set of model parameters for each subject to accurately estimate the knee joint moments during five different calibration trials. Calibration tasks should be chosen to encompass a wide range of contractile conditions. Simulated annealing (Goffe et al., 1994) is an often-used optimization method to alter model parameters to minimize the difference between forward dynamic joint moments and inverse dynamic joint moments. Simulated parallel annealing within a neighborhood (SPAN) can also be used on clusters to improve the computational speed (Higginson et al., 2005). The initial values of l_s^t and l_o^m for each muscle is necessary and can be obtained from Yamaguchi et al. (1990), and constrained to change within ±15 percent and ±5 percent of their initial values, respectively. The ranges of γ_1, γ_2, and A were described before, and the range of d should be approximately 10 to 100 ms (Hull and Hawkins, 1990). Strength factors can be set to be within approximately 0.5 to 2.0, and the $F_{\max}$ for each muscle can also be obtained from Yamaguchi et al. (1990). The initial values for γ_1, γ_2, d, A, and strength factors can be set to be the average of their upper and lower limits (Table 14.1).

This EMG-driven knee model can account for different activation strategies and produce joint moments similar to inverse dynamic joint moments during different tasks. It can be verified that once the parameters are tuned, the model can then be used to predict joint moments of new tasks with new muscle activation patterns.

TABLE 14.1 Lower Bound and Upper Bound Parameters

Parameter	Lower bound	Upper bound	Reference
Electromechanical delay (d)	10 ms	100 ms	Hull and Hawkins (1990)
Filter coefficients (γ_1, γ_2)	−0.95	0.90	Cohen (2004)
Shape factor (A)	0.01	0.12	Manal and Buchaan (2003)
Optimal fiber length (OFL)	OFL − OFL·0.05	OFL + OFL·0.05	Delp et al. (1990)
Percentage change in optimal fiber length (λ)	0	0.25	Lloyd and Besier (2003), Huijing (1996)
Pennation angle (φ)	*	*	Yamaguchi et al. (1990), Delp et al. (1990)
Resting tendon length (RTL)	RTL_i − $RTL_i \cdot 0.15$	RTL_i − $RTL_i \cdot 0.15$	Delp et al. (1990), Lloyd and Buchanan (1996)
Strength factors (G_f, G_e)	$F_{max} \cdot 0.05$	$F_{max} \cdot 0.02$	Lloyd and Besier (2003)
Maximum isometric force (F_{max})	*	*	Delp et al. (1990)

All the parameters to be calibrated were listed above. Those labeled with an asterisk (*) have been fixed at a specific value, which could be found in the listed literature.

14.5 AN EXAMPLE

This section will step through the implementation of an EMG-driven model for the ankle and knee joint.

In this example, we will include the major muscles across the ankle and knee: RF, VL, VI, VM, MG, LG, SM, ST, BFL, BFS, Sol, and TA. EMGs from the major muscles, joint positions, and force plate data have been collected from three walking trials on two young healthy subjects. Maximum voluntary contraction trials were also collected for normalization of EMG. The raw EMG are firstly high-pass-filtered using a forward and reverse pass fourth-order Butterworth filter (cutoff frequency 50 Hz), then full wave rectified, normalized by peak rectified EMG values obtained from MVC trials, and then low-pass-filtered using a forward and reverse pass fourth-order Butterworth filter (cutoff frequency 6 Hz). The ankle joint of subject #1 and the knee joint of subject #2 are illustrated as an example.

The EMG-driven models are calibrated using one walking trial of the subjects, focusing on the stance phase of gait. The calibrated models are then employed to predict the other walking trials, which could verify the predictable ability of the model.

The coefficients of determination (R^2) between the joint moments estimated using forward dynamics and inverse dynamics, and the associated normalized root-mean-square (RMS) error (normalized to peak-to-peak joint moment) for all calibration trials and prediction trials of both subjects, can then be calculated (Tables 14.2 and 14.3).

Once the models are *calibrated*, joint moments can be *predicted* from new data based on novel tasks not used in the calibration process. The joint moment predicted using forward dynamics matched the joint moment determined using inverse dynamics for both trials (Fig. 14.10A,

TABLE 14.2 Statistical Results of Calibration and Prediction on the Ankle Joint of the Walking Trials of Subject #1

Subject		Trial	R^2 value	RMS error (N·m)	Normalized RMS error (%)
1	Calibration	1	0.935	9.61	6.30
	Prediction	2~3 (Mean value (SD))	0.939 (0.021)	8.98 (2.78)	6.20 (2.13)

TABLE 14.3 Statistical Results of Calibration and Prediction on the Knee Joint of the Walking Trials of Subject #2

Subject		Trial	R^2 value	RMS error (N·m)	Normalized RMS error (%)
1	Calibration	1	0.928	7.42	6.30
	Prediction	2~3 (Mean value (SD))	0.908 (0.008)	9.98 (1.21)	8.39 (1.00)

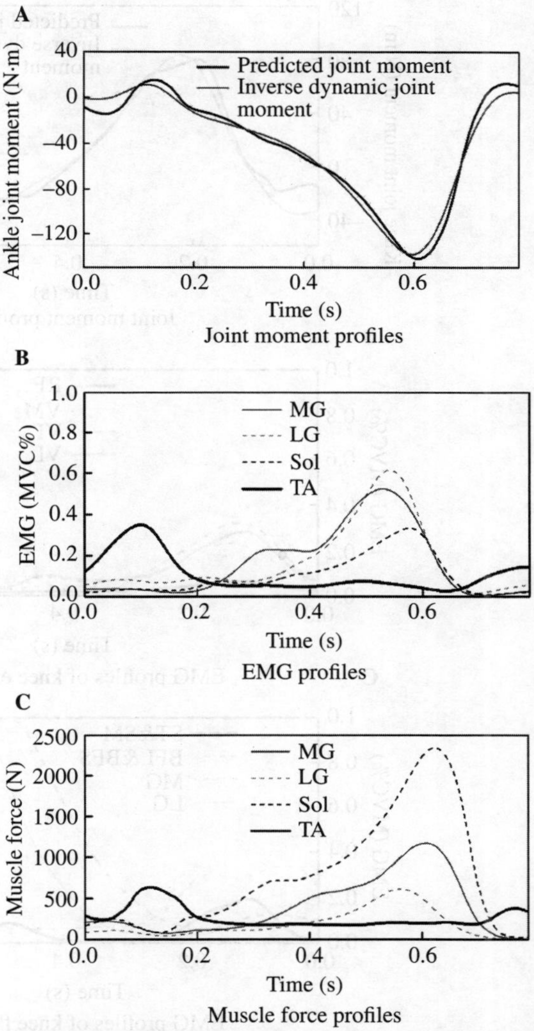

FIGURE 14.10 Predicted results of the ankle joint on trial 2 of a young healthy subject after tuning the model using data from trial 1. (Positive joint moment indicates dorsiflexion. The data started from heel strike to toe-off.)

Table 14.2). The EMG profile and muscle force profile of the prediction trial on the ankle joint of subject #1 shows the onset/offset of the dorsiflexor and plantarflexors, corresponding to the ankle joint moment patterns (Fig. 14.10B, 14.10C).

The forward dynamics joint moment matches the inverse dynamics joint moment for both trials (Fig. 14.11A, Table 14.3). The EMG profile and muscle force profile of the prediction trial on the knee joint of subject #1 showed the onset/offset of the knee flexors and extensors, corresponding to the ankle joint moment patterns (Fig. 14.11B, 14.11C, 14.11D, 14.11E).

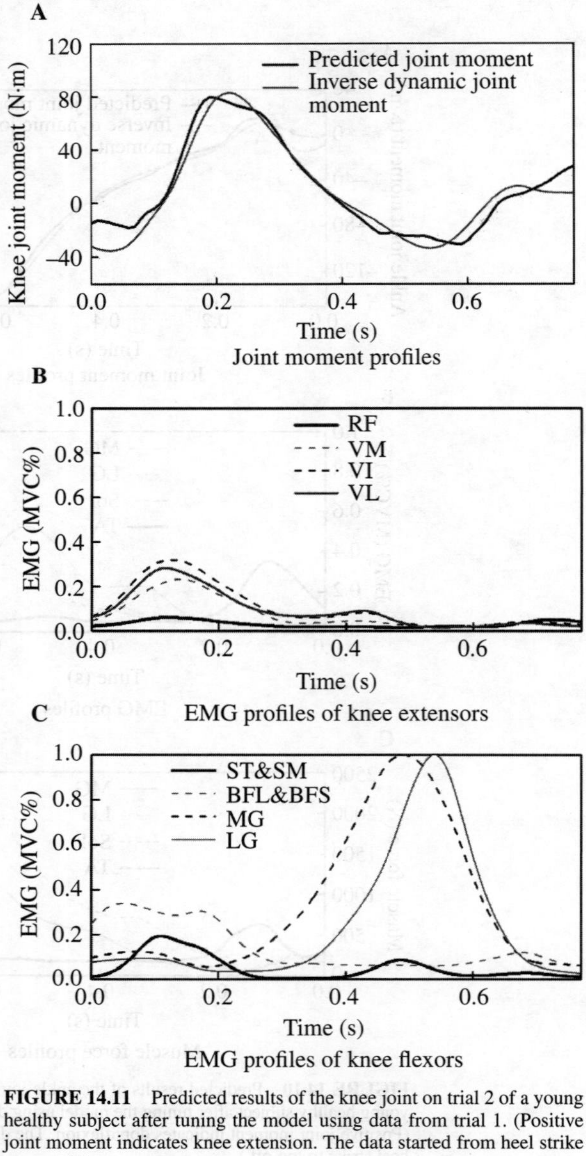

FIGURE 14.11 Predicted results of the knee joint on trial 2 of a young healthy subject after tuning the model using data from trial 1. (Positive joint moment indicates knee extension. The data started from heel strike to toe-off.)

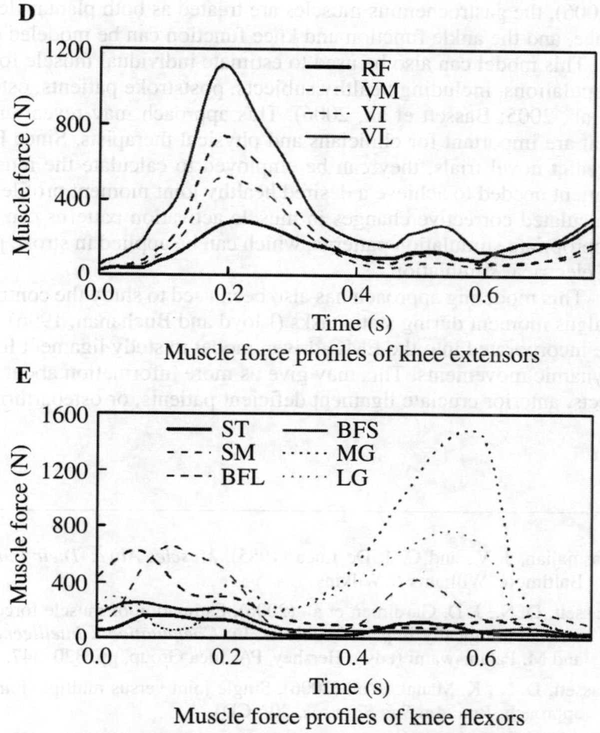

FIGURE 14.11 Predicted results of the knee joint on trial 2 of a young healthy subject after tuning the model using data from trial 1. (Positive joint moment indicates knee extension. The data started from heel strike to toe off.) (*Continued*)

The results show that once the parameters are calibrated (e.g., the model is tuned), the model can then be used to predict the joint moments of new tasks with new muscle activation patterns. This provides confidence that the calibrated model parameters are anatomically and physiologically representative of each specific subject, which makes the model an alternative way to estimate muscle forces.

14.6 LIMITATIONS AND FUTURE DEVELOPMENT OF EMG-DRIVEN MODELS

There are several assumptions and limitations of this approach. First, although model parameters are tuned for each subject, the models do not account for differences in musculoskeletal size. In the future, a subject-specific musculoskeletal models may be developed based on a subject's MRI, X-ray, or ultrasound images. Parameters that would be measured include the bone structure, musculotendon length, pennation angle, moment arm, etc. Second, although the gastrocnemius's length changes at the knee are accounted for in the above formulation, the model is essentially single-joint. This specific example does not attempt to balance the moments at the knee as well as the ankle, and a multijoint model combining both the ankle and knee may be included for more detailed gait studies involving other muscles. However, this can be remedied. In the multijoint model of Bassett et al.

(2006), the gastrocnemius muscles are treated as both plantar flexors of the ankle and flexors of the knee, and the ankle function and knee function can be modeled simultaneously.

This model can also be used to estimate individual muscle forces and joint moments of different populations, including healthy subjects, poststroke patients, osteoarthritis patients, etc. (Buchanan et al., 2005; Bassett et al., 2006). This approach may reveal underlying neuromuscular principles that are important for clinicians and physical therapists. Since EMG-driven models can be used to predict novel trials, they can be employed to calculate the muscle activation patterns for a stroke patient needed to achieve a desired healthy joint moment profile (Shao and Buchanan, 2006). These calculated corrective changes in muscle activation patterns can be used as reference data to derive appropriate stimulation patterns, which can be applied in stroke patients' gait training with functional electrical stimulation.

This modeling approach has also been used to study the contribution of soft tissues to knee varus/valgus moment during static tasks (Lloyd and Buchanan, 1996). In the future, a ligament model can be incorporated into the EMG-driven model to study ligament forces and joint contact forces during dynamic movements. This may give us more information about the knee mechanics of healthy subjects, anterior cruciate ligament deficient patients, or osteoarthritis patients.

REFERENCES

Basmajian, J. V., and C. J. De Luca (1985), *Muscles Alive: Their Functions Revealed by Electromyography.* Baltimore, Williams & Wilkins.

Bassett, D. N., J. D. Gardinier, et al. (2006), Estimation of muscle forces about the ankle during gait in healthy and neurologically impaired subjects. In: *Computational Intelligence for Movement Sciences*. Begg, R. K. and M. Palaniswami (eds.). Hershey, PA, Idea Group, pp. 320–347.

Bassett, D. N., K. Manal, et al. (2006), Single joint versus multiple joint modeling using a hybrid EMG-driven approach. *Proc Am Soc Biomech,* 30, (CD).

Bouisset, S., and F. Goubel (1971), Interdependence of relations between integrated EMG and diverse biomechanical quantities in normal voluntary movements. *Act Nerv Super (Praha),* **13**(1):23–31.

Buchanan, T. S., D. G. Lloyd, et al. (2004), Neuromusculoskeletal modeling: estimation of muscle forces and joint moments and movements from measurements of neural command. *J Appl Biomech*, **20**(4):367–395.

Buchanan, T. S., D. G. Lloyd, et al. (2005), Estimation of muscle forces and joint moments using a forward-inverse dynamics model. *Med Sci Sports Exerc*, **37**(11):1911–1916.

Buchanan, T. S., M. J. Moniz, et al. (1993), Estimation of muscle forces about the wrist joint during isometric tasks using an EMG coefficient method. *J Biomech*, **26**(4–5):547–560.

Buchanan, T. S., and D. A. Shreeve (1996), An evaluation of optimization techniques for the prediction of muscle activation patterns during isometric tasks. *J Biomech Eng,* **118**(4):565–574.

Cram, J. R., and A. Garber (1986), The relationship between narrow and wide bandwidth filter settings during an EMG scanning procedure. *Biofeedback and Self-Regulation*, **11**(2):105–114.

Crowninshield, R. D. (1978), Use of optimization techniques to predict muscle forces. *J Biomech Eng-Trans Asme*, **100**(2):88–92.

Crowninshield, R. D., and R. A. Brand (1981), A physiologically based criterion of muscle force prediction in locomotion. *J Biomech*, **14**(11):793–801.

De Duca, C. J., and W. J. Forrest (1973), Force analysis of individual muscles acting simultaneously on the shoulder joint during isometric abduction. *J Biomech,* **6**(4):385–393.

De Luca, C. J. (1997), The use of surface electromyography in biomechanics. *J Appl Biomech,* **13**(2):135–163.

De Luca, C. J., and E. J. Vandyk (1975), Derivation of some parameters of myoelectric signals recorded during sustained constant force isometric contractions. *Biophys J*, **15**(12):1167–1180.

Delp, S. L., J. P. Loan, et al. (1990), An interactive graphics-based model of the lower extremity to study orthopaedic surgical procedures. *IEEE Trans Biomed Eng,* **37**(8):757–767.

Dul, J., G. E. Johnson, et al. (1984), Muscular synergism .2. A minimum-fatigue criterion for load sharing between synergistic muscles. *J Biomech,* **17**(9):675–684.

Edman, K. A. (1978), Maximum velocity of shortening in relation to sarcomere length and degree of activation of frog muscle fibres [proceedings]. *J Physiol,* **278**:9P–10P.

Edman, K. A. (1979), The velocity of unloaded shortening and its relation to sarcomere length and isometric force in vertebrate muscle fibres. *J Physiol,* **291**:143–159.

Enoka, R. M. (2002). *Neuromechanics of Human Movement*. Champaign, IL, Human Kinetics.

Epstein, M., and W. Herzog (1998), *Theoretical Models of Skeletal Muscle*. New York, Wiley.

Feinstein, B., B. Lindegard, et al. (1955), Morphologic studies of motor units in normal human muscles. *Acta Anat (Basel),* **23**(2):127–142.

Fitts, R. H., and J. M. Metzger. (1993), Mechanisms of muscular fatigue. *In Medicine and Sport Science; Principle of Exercise Biochemistry.* New York, Karger, **27**:248–268.

Goffe, W. L., G. D. Ferrier, et al. (1994), Global optimization of statistical functions with simulated annealing. *J Econometr,* **60**(1–2):65–99.

Gordon, A. M., A. F. Huxley, et al. (1966), The variation in isometric tension with sarcomere length in vertebrate muscle fibres. *J Physiol,* **184**(1):170–192.

Guimaraes, A. C., W. Herzog, et al. (1994), Effects of muscle length on the EMG-force relationship of the cat soleus muscle studied using non-periodic stimulation of ventral root filaments. *J Exp Biol,* **193**:49–64.

Hagemann, B., G. Luhede, et al. (1985), Improved active electrodes for recording bioelectric signals in work physiology. *Eur J Appl Physiol Occup Physiol,* **54**(1):95–98.

Heckathorne, C. W., and D. S. Childress (1981), Relationships of the surface electromyogram to the force, length, velocity, and contraction rate of the cineplastic human biceps. *Am J Phys Med,* **60**(1):1–19.

Herzog, W., and T. R. Leonard (1991), Validation of optimization models that estimate the forces exerted by synergistic muscles. *J Biomech,* **24**:31–39.

Higginson, J. S., R. R. Neptune, et al. (2005), Simulated parallel annealing within a neighborhood for optimization of biomechanical systems. *J Biomech,* **38**(9):1938–1942.

Hill, A. V. (1938), The heat of shortening and the dynamic constants of muscle. *Proc R Soc B,* **126**(843):136–195.

Hof, A. L., and J. Van den Berg (1981), EMG to force processing II: estimation of parameters of the Hill muscle model for the human triceps surae by means of a calfergometer. *J Biomech,* **14**(11):759–770.

Huijing, P. A. (1996), Important experimental factors for skeletal muscle modelling: non-linear changes of muscle length force characteristics as a function of degree of activity. *Eur J Morphol,* **34**(1):47–54.

Hull, M. L., and D. Hawkins (1990), Analysis of muscular work in multisegmental movements: application to cycling. In: *Multiple Muscle Systems: Biomechanics and Movement Organization*. Winters, J. M., and S. L.-Y. Woo (eds.). New York, Springer, pp. 621–638.

Li, G., K. R. Kaufman, et al. (1999), Prediction of antagonistic muscle forces using inverse dynamic optimization during flexion extension of the knee. *J Biomech Eng-Trans Asme,* **121**(3):316–322.

Lippold, O. C. (1952), The relation between integrated action potentials in a human muscle and its isometric tension. *J Physiol,* **117**(4):492–499.

Lloyd, D. G., and T. F. Besier (2003), An EMG-driven musculoskeletal model to estimate muscle forces and knee joint moments in vivo. *J Biomech,* **36**(6):765–776.

Lloyd, D. G., and T. S. Buchanan (1996), A model of load sharing between muscles and soft tissues at the human knee during static tasks. *J Biomech Eng,* **118**(3):367–376.

Loeb, G. E., and C. Gans (1986), *Electromyography for Experimentalists*. Chicago, University of Chicago Press.

Manal, K., R. V. Gonzalez, et al. (2002), A real-time EMG-driven virtual arm. *Comput Biol Med,* **32**(1):25–36.

Manal K., and T. S. Buchanan. (2003). A one-parameter neural activation to muscle activation model: estimating isometric joint moments from electromyograms. *J Biomech,* **36**(8):1197–1202.

Milner-Brown, H. S., R. B. Stein, et al. (1973), Changes in firing rate of human motor units during linearly changing voluntary contractions. *J Physiol,* **230**(2):371–390.

Moritani, T., and H. A. deVries (1978), Reexamination of the relationship between the surface integrated electromyogram (IEMG) and force of isometric contraction. *Am J Phys Med,* **57**(6):263–277.

Neptune, R. R., S. A. Kautz, et al. (2001), Contributions of the individual ankle plantar flexors to support, forward progression and swing initiation during walking. *J Biomech,* **34**(11):1387–1398.

Pedotti, A., V. V. Krishnan, et al. (1978), Optimization of muscle-force sequencing in human locomotion. *Math Biosci,* **38**(1–2):57–76.

Perotto, A., and E. F. Delagi (1994), *Anatomical Guide for the Electromyographer: The Limbs and Trunk.* Springfield, Ill., Charles C. Thomas.

Robertson, D. G. E. (2004), *Research Methods in Biomechanics*. Champaign, IL, Human Kinetics.

Roy, S. H., G. De Luca, et al. (2007), Electro-mechanical stability of surface EMG sensors. *Med Biol Eng Comput,* **45**(5):447–457.

Schutte, L. M. (1992), *Using Musculoskeletal Models to Explore Strategies for Improving Performance in Electrical Stimulation-Induced Leg Cycle Ergometry*. Ph.D. thesis, Stanford University.

Schutte, L. M., M. M. Rodgers, et al. (1993), Improving the efficacy of electrical stimulation induced leg cycle ergometry: an analysis based on a dynamic musculoskeletal model. *IEEE Trans Rehabil Eng,* **1**(2):109–125.

Scott, S. H., and D. A. Winter (1991), A comparison of three muscle pennation assumptions and their effect on isometric and isotonic force. *J Biomech,* **24**(2):163–167.

Seireg, A., and R. J. Arvikar (1973), A mathematical model for evaluation of forces in lower extremities of the musculo-skeletal system. *J Biomech,* **6**(3):313–326.

Shao, Q., and T. S. Buchanan (2006), Estimation of corrective changes in muscle activation patterns for post-stroke patients, *Proc ASME Summer Bioeng Conf,* paper #151962.

Stashuk, D. (2001), EMG signal decomposition: how can it be accomplished and used? *J Electromyogr Kinesiol,* **11**(3):151–173.

Tam, H. W., and J. G. Webster (1977), Minimizing electrode motion artifact by skin abrasion. *IEEE Trans Biomed Eng,* **24**(2):134–139.

Thelen, D. G., and F. C. Anderson (2006), Using computed muscle control to generate forward dynamic simulations of human walking from experimental data. *J Biomech,* **39**(6):1107–1115.

Thelen, D. G., A. B. Schultz, et al. (1994), Identification of dynamic myoelectric signal-to-force models during isometric lumbar muscle contractions. *J Biomech,* **27**(7):907–919.

Wakeling, J. M., and A. I. Rozitis (2004), Spectral properties of myoelectric signals from different motor units in the leg extensor muscles. *J Exp Biol,* **207**(Pt 14):2519–2528.

Winter, D. A., G. Rau, et al. (1980), Units, Terms and Standards in the Reporting of EMG Research. International Society of Electrophysiological Kinesiology.

Woods, J. J., and B. Bigland-Ritchie (1983), Linear and non-linear surface EMG/force relationships in human muscles. An anatomical/functional argument for the existence of both. *Am J Phys Med,* **62**(6):287–299.

Yamaguchi, G. T., A. G.-U. Sawa, et al. (1990). A survey of human musculotendon actuator parameters. In: *Multiple Muscle Systems: Biomechanics and Movement Organization.* Winters, J. M., and S. L.-Y. Woo (eds.). New York, Springer, pp. 717–773.

Zajac, F. E. (1989), Muscle and tendon: properties, models, scaling, and application to biomechanics and motor control. *Crit Rev Biomed Eng,* **17**(4):359–411.

Zipp, P. (1982), Recommendations for the standardization of lead positions in surface electromyography. *Eur J Appl Physiol Occup Physiol,* **50**(1):41–54.

P · A · R · T · 3

BIOMATERIALS

CHAPTER 15
POLYMERIC BIOMATERIALS

Christopher Batich
University of Florida, Gainesville, Florida

Patrick Leamy
LifeLink Foundation, Tampa, Florida

Bradley Jay Willenberg
University of Central Florida, Orlando, Florida

15.1 INTRODUCTION

Polymers are the newest and broadest class of materials compared to metals and ceramics. Hence, they have the largest range of properties and options for using in biomedical applications. They are large molecules synthesized from smaller molecules, called monomers. Most polymers are organic compounds with carbon as the base element. Plastics are polymers that are rigid solids at room temperature and generally contain additional additives. Some common plastics used in biomedical applications are polymethyl methacrylate (PMMA) for intraocular lenses, braided polyethylene terephthalate (PET) for vascular grafts, and ultrahigh-molecular-weight polyethylene for the articulating surfaces of orthopedic implants. Polymers, and biopolymers, encompass a much broader spectrum than plastics alone. Biopolymers can include synthetic polymers and natural polymers such as proteins, polysaccharides, and polynucleotides, but sometimes biopolymers are only considered to be polymers derived from natural sources such as cellulose. This chapter covers only the most commonly used examples in each class but will provide references to more extensive sources.

Many useful polymers are water soluble and used as solutions. Hyaluronic acid is a naturally occurring high-molecular-weight polymer found in connective tissues and is used to protect the iris and cornea during ophthalmic surgery. Polyvinyl pyrrolidinone is a synthetic polymer used as a binder or additive in 25 percent of all pharmaceuticals.[1] Hydrogels are another class of polymer that has many biomedical applications. Hydrogels are polymers that swell in water but retain their overall shape. They are therefore soft and moist, and mimic many natural tissues. The most well-known hydrogel series is poly(hydroxyethyl methacrylate) (PHEMA) and PHEMA copolymers which are used in soft contact lenses.

Gelling polymers are hydrogels that can be formed in situ using chemical or physical bonding of polymers in solution. Alginates, for instance, are acidic polysaccharides that can be cross-linked using divalent cations such as calcium. Other examples of gelling polymers are the poloxamers that can gel with an increase in temperature. Alginates are widely used in cell immobilization, and poloxamers as coatings to prevent postsurgical adhesions.

Elastomers are low-modulus polymers that can reversibly stretch to many times (some over 500 percent) their original size. Silicones and polyurethanes are common elastomeric biopolymers.

Polyurethane is used as a coating for pacemaker leads and for angioplasty balloons. Silicones are used for a variety of catheters, soft contact lenses, and foldable intraocular lenses.

This chapter begins with an overview of polymer science topics, including synthesis, structure, and mechanical properties. The remainder of the chapter will discuss individual polymers, including their applications and properties. The polymers are presented in the following order: water-soluble polymers, gelling polymers, hydrogels, elastomers, and finally rigid polymers. These five categories are roughly ordered from low to high modulus (i.e., high to low compliance). Water-soluble polymers in solution do not have an elastic modulus since they are fluids, so these are presented first. In fact, most polymers do not have a true elastic modulus since they are viscoelastic and exhibit solid and viscous mechanical behavior, depending on the polymer structure, strain rate, and temperature.

Natural tissues are continuously repaired and remodeled to adjust to changes in the physiologic environment. No current synthetic biomaterial or biopolymer can mimic these properties effectively. Consequently, the ideal biomaterial or biopolymer performs the desired function, then eventually disappears, and is replaced by natural tissue. Therefore, degradable polymers are of great interest to the biomedical engineering community. Polylactides and their copolymers are currently used as bone screws and sutures since they have good mechanical properties and degrade by hydrolysis so that they can, under optimum conditions, be replaced by natural tissue.

In addition to classification as water-soluble polymers, gelling polymers, hydrogels, elastomers, and rigid polymers, polymers can also be classified as biostable or degradable. Biostable polymers are nontoxic in vivo and do not degrade significantly even over many years. Polymers can degrade by simple chemical means or under the action of enzymes. For the purposes of this chapter, resorbable polymers such as polylactide are those that degrade by simple chemical means and biodegradable are those that degrade with the help of enzymes. Most natural polymers (proteins, polysaccharides, and polynucleotides) are biodegradable, while most synthetic degradable polymers are resorbable. The most common degradation reactions for resorbable polymers are hydrolysis and oxidation.

15.2 POLYMER SCIENCE

15.2.1 Polymer Synthesis and Structure

Polymers are frequently classified by their synthesis mechanism as either step-growth or chain-growth polymers. Step-growth polymers are formed by stepwise reactions between functional groups. Linear polymers are formed when each monomer has two functional groups (functionality = 2). The second type of polymerization is chain-growth polymerization where monomers are added one at a time to a small number of actively growing polymer chains.

Most polymerization techniques yield polymers with a distribution of polymer molecular weights. Polymer molecular weight is of great interest since it affects mechanical, solution, and melt properties of the polymer. The number average molecular weight M_n averages the molecular weight over the number of molecules (the "mean"), while the weight average molecular weight M_w averages over the weight of each polymer chain. Equations 15.1 and 15.2 define M_w and M_n. Figure 15.1

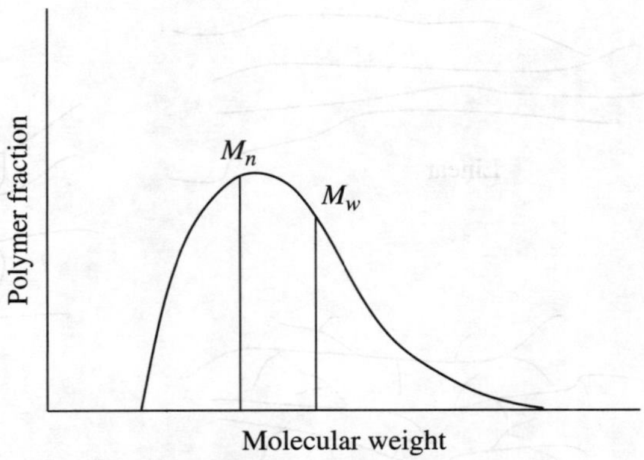

FIGURE 15.1 Typical polymer molecular weight distribution.

shows a schematic diagram for a polymer molecular weight distribution, where N_i is the number of polymer chains with molecular weight M_i.

$$M_n = \frac{\sum N_i M_i}{\sum N_i} \tag{15.1}$$

$$M_w = \frac{\sum N_i M_i^2}{\sum N_i M_i} \tag{15.2}$$

The polymerization mechanism is a useful classification because it indicates the likely low-molecular-weight contaminants present. Chain-growth polymers frequently contain unreacted monomers, while step-growth polymers often have low-molecular-weight oligomers (short chains). These low-molecular-weight species are more mobile or soluble than polymers and hence more likely to have physiologic effects. For instance, the monomer of PMMA causes a lowering of blood pressure and has been associated with life-threatening consequences when present (e.g., in some bone cements). Furthermore, the same polymer can be prepared by both mechanisms, leading to different impurities. For instance, polylactide is usually prepared by a chain-growth mechanism involving ring opening of a cyclic dimer (lactide) rather than the condensation of lactic acid.

As with all materials, a polymer's properties can be predicted and explained by understanding the polymer structure on the atomic, microscopic, and macroscopic scale. Polymers can be roughly classified into two different groups: thermoplastic and thermoset. Thermoplastic polymers are made of individual polymer chains which are held together by relatively weak van der Waals and dipole-dipole forces. Thermoplastic polymers can be processed into useful products by melt processing, namely, injection molding and extrusion. They can also be dissolved in solvents and cast to form films and other devices. Although they often degrade or denature before melting, most proteins and polysaccharides can be considered thermoplastics since they are made of individual chains and can be dissolved in solvents. Additionally, thermoplastics can be linear or branched leading to different mechanical properties.

Thermosetting polymers contain cross-links between polymer chains. Cross-links are covalent bonds between chains and can be formed using monomers with functionalities of greater than two during synthesis. Some polyurethanes and many silicones are formed using monomers with functionalities greater than 2. Cross-links can also be created after the polymer is formed. An example of this is vulcanization that was discovered by Charles Goodyear in 1839 to toughen natural rubber.

Vulcanization uses sulfur as a cross-linking agent. Thermosets are, in essence, one giant molecule since all the polymer chains are connected through the cross-links. Thermosets cannot be melted after they are formed and cannot be dissolved in solvents. Depending on the cross-link

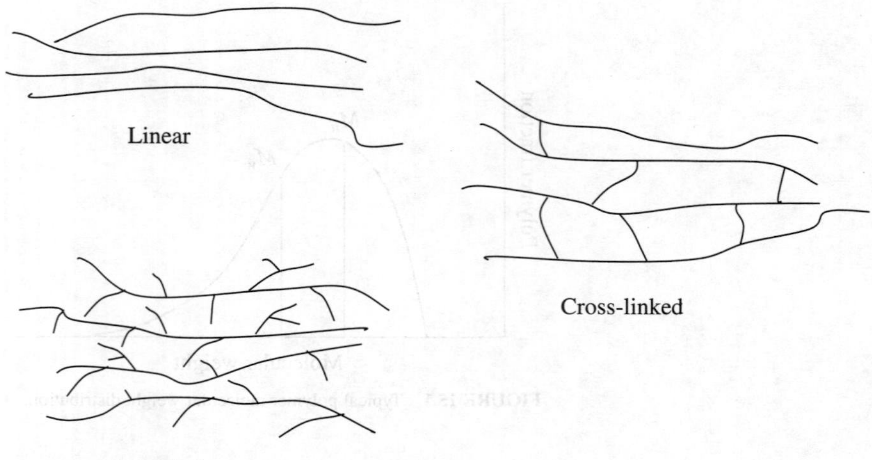

FIGURE 15.2 Schematic diagram showing different polymer structures.

density, thermosets can swell in certain solvents. When a cross-linked polymer solidifies or gels, it usually has some linear or unconnected polymer present, which sometimes can be extracted after implantation. Figure 15.2 shows a schematic diagram for linear, branched, and cross-linked polymers.

Polymers in the solid state have varying degrees of crystallinity. No polymer is truly 100 percent crystalline, but some are purely amorphous. Figure 15.3 is a simple model depicting a crystalline polymer. Polymer chains folding over themselves form crystalline regions. Amorphous regions of disordered polymer connect the crystals. Polymer chains are packed tighter in crystalline regions leading to higher intermolecular forces. This means that mechanical properties such as modulus and strength increase with crystallinity. Ductility decreases with crystallinity since polymer chains have less room to slide past each other.

The primary requirement for crystallinity is an ordered repeating chain structure. This is why stereoregular polymers are often crystalline and their irregular counterparts are amorphous. Stereoregular polymers have an ordered stereostructure: either isotactic or syndiotactic. Isotactic polymers have the same configuration at each stereocenter, while configuration alternates for syndiotactic polymers (see Fig. 15.4). Atactic polymers have no pattern to their stereostructure. Polypropylene (PP) is a classic example of a polymer whose crystallinity and properties change drastically depending on stereostructure. Syndiotactic and isotactic PP have a high degree of crystallinity, while atactic PP is completely amorphous. Isotactic PP has excellent strength and flexibility due to this regular structure and makes excellent sutures. The atactic PP is a weak, gum-like material. Recent advances in polymer synthesis have made available new polymers with well-controlled tacticity based on olefins. It is likely that they will find use as biomaterials in the future.

Crystallinity plays a large role in the physical behavior of polymers. The amorphous regions play perhaps an even greater role. Some amorphous polymers such as PMMA are stiff and hard plastics at room temperature, while polymers such as polybutadiene are soft and flexible at room temperature. If PMMA is heated to 105°C, it will soften, and its modulus will be reduced by orders of magnitude. If polybutadiene is cooled to –73°C, it will become stiff and hard. The temperature at which this hard to soft transformation takes place is called the glass transition temperature T_g.

Differential thermal analysis (DTA) or a similar technique called differential scanning calorimetry (DSC) can be used to determine the temperature at which phase transitions such as glass transition temperature and melting temperature T_m occur. DTA involves heating a polymer sample along with a standard that has no phase transitions in the temperature range of interest. The ambient temperature is increased at a regular rate and the difference in temperature between the polymer and the standard measured. The glass transition is endothermic; therefore, the polymer sample will be

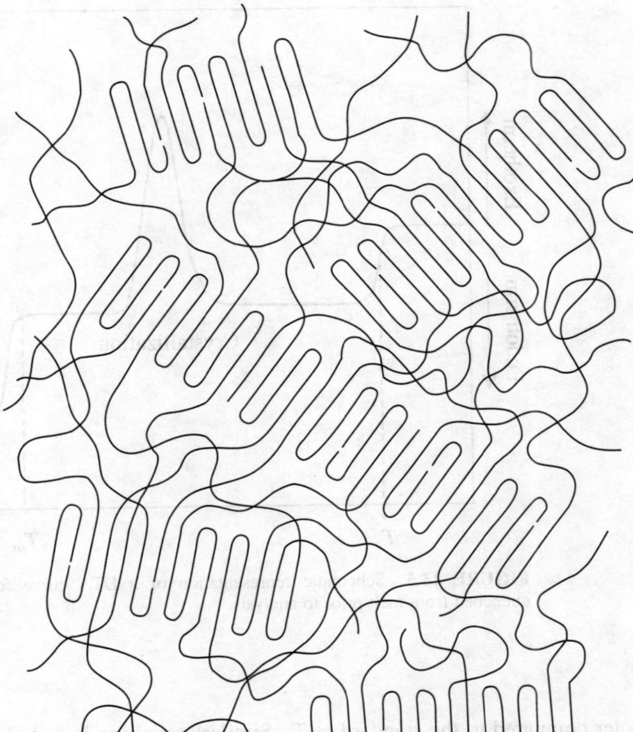

FIGURE 15.3 Simple model showing crystalline and amorphous polymer regions. [*Reproduced from Fundamental Principles of Polymeric Materials, Stephen L. Rosen (ed.). New York: Wiley, 1993, p. 43.*][88]

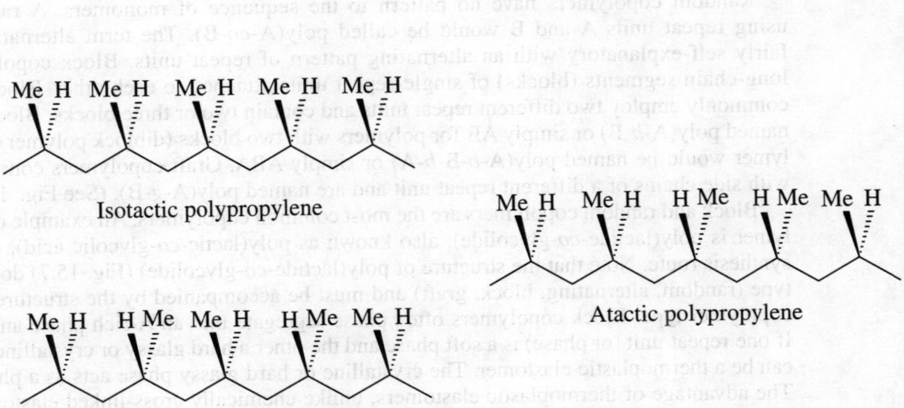

FIGURE 15.4 Stereoisomerism in polypropylene: Me=CH_3.

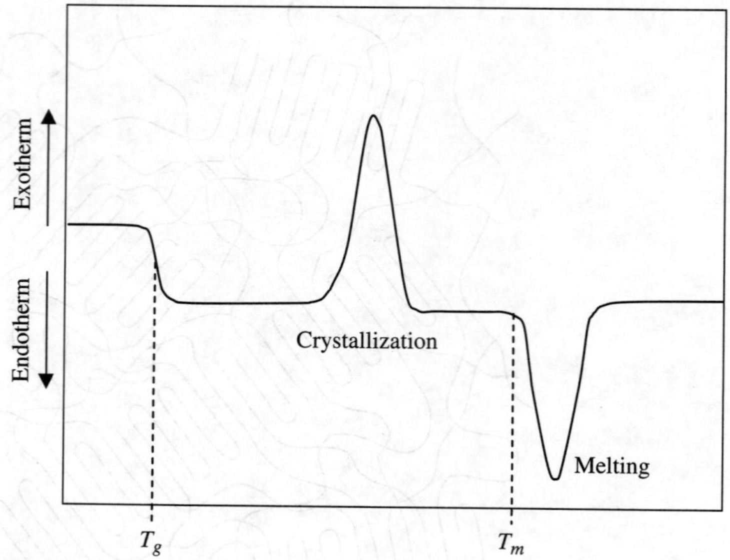

FIGURE 15.5 Schematic representation of a DTA curve for crystalline polymer quenched from melt prior to analysis.

cooler compared to the standard at T_g. Similarly, melting is endothermic and will be detected as a negative temperature compared to the standard. If the polymer was quenched from melt prior to DTA analysis, it may be amorphous even though it has the potential to crystallize. In this case, the sample will crystallize during the DTA run at a temperature between the T_g and T_m. Figure 15.5 shows a schematic DTA curve for a crystalline polymer quenched for melt. A polymer that does not crystallize would show a glass transition only and the crystallization and melting peaks would be absent. These measurements can be made to identify an unknown plastic, or to aid in the synthesis of new polymers with desired changes in mechanical properties at certain temperatures.

Random copolymers have no pattern to the sequence of monomers. A random copolymer using repeat units A and B would be called poly(A-*co*-B). The term alternating copolymer is fairly self-explanatory with an alternating pattern of repeat units. Block copolymers consist of long-chain segments (blocks) of single-repeat units attached to each other. Block polymers most commonly employ two different repeat units and contain two or three blocks. Block copolymers are named poly(A-*b*-B) or simply AB for polymers with two blocks (diblock polymer). A triblock copolymer would be named poly(A-*b*-B-*b*-A) or simply ABA. Graft copolymers consist of a backbone with side chains of a different repeat unit and are named poly(A-*g*-B). (See Fig. 15.6.)

Block and random copolymers are the most common copolymers. An example of a random copolymer is poly(lactide-*co*-glycolide), also known as poly(lactic-*co*-glycolic acid), depending on the synthesis route. Note that the structure of poly(lactide-*co*-glycolide) (Fig. 15.7) does not specify the type (random, alternating, block, graft) and must be accompanied by the structure name to specify copolymer type. Block copolymers often phase segregate into an A-rich phase and a B-rich phase. If one repeat unit (or phase) is a soft phase and the other a hard glassy or crystalline phase, the result can be a thermoplastic elastomer. The crystalline or hard glassy phase acts as a physical cross-link. The advantage of thermoplastic elastomers, unlike chemically cross-linked elastomers, is that they can be melt or solution processed. Many polyurethanes are thermoplastic elastomers. They consist of soft segments, either a polyester or polyether, bonded to hard segments. The hard segments are ordinarily synthesized by polymerizing diisocyanates with glycols.

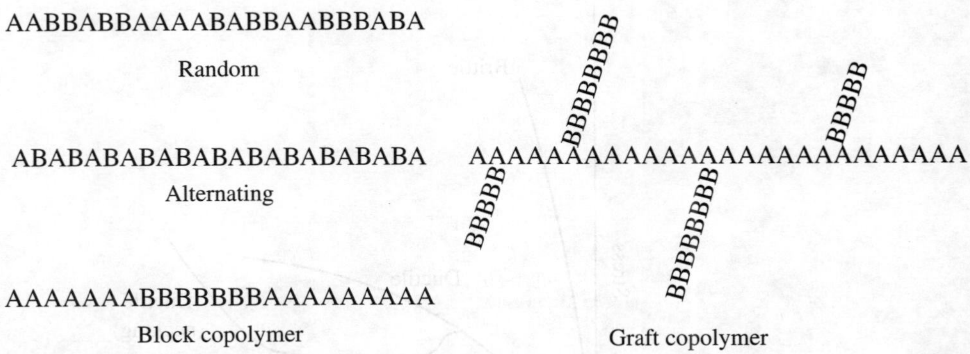

FIGURE 15.6 Schematic diagram showing classes of copolymer.

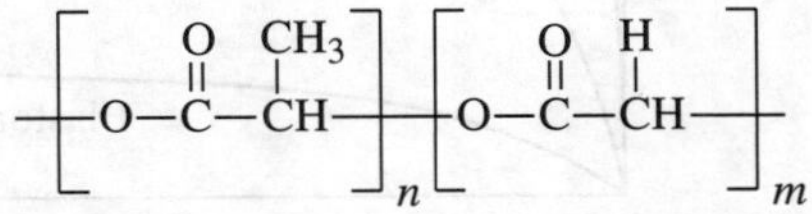

FIGURE 15.7 Poly(lactide-*co*-glycolide) chemical structure.

Similarly, thermoplastic hydrogels can be synthesized by using a hydrophilic A block and a hydrophobic B block. Poly(ethylene oxide-*b*-lactide) (PEO-*b*-PLA) are biodegradable hydrogel polymers which are being developed for drug delivery applications.[2–5] PEO is a water-soluble polymer that promotes swelling in water, and PLA is a hard degradable polymer that acts as a physical cross-linker.

15.2.2 Polymer Mechanical Properties

Solid polymer mechanical properties can be classified into three categories: brittle, ductile, and elastomeric (see Fig. 15.8). Brittle polymers such as PMMA are polymers with a T_g much higher than room temperature. These polymers have a high modulus and high ultimate tensile strength, but low ductility and toughness. Ductile polymers are semicrystalline polymers such as polyethylene and PTFE that have a T_g below room temperature for the amorphous polymer content. The crystals lend strength, but the rubbery amorphous regions offer toughness. These polymers have lower strength and modulus, but greater toughness than brittle polymers. Elastomers have low moduli since they have T_g well below room temperature, but they can return to their original shape following high extensions since cross-links prevent significant polymer chain translations.

Mechanical properties of polymers, unlike other engineering materials, are highly strain rate and temperature dependent. Modulus increases with increasing strain rate and decreasing temperature (see Fig. 15.9 for schematic diagram). The strain rate dependence for mechanical properties shows that polymers exhibit viscous behavior in addition to solid or elastic behavior.

For an elastic solid, stress σ is a linear function of the applied strain ε and there is no strain rate dependence. Elastic modulus E is the slope of the stress versus strain curve. An elastic material can be modeled as a spring, while viscous materials can be modeled as a dashpot. For a fluid (viscous material), stress is proportional to strain rate ($d\varepsilon/dt$) and unrelated to strain. Viscosity η is the slope of the stress versus strain rate curve. Figure 15.10 shows the stress/strain relationship for elastic solids and the stress/strain-rate relationships for viscous liquids.

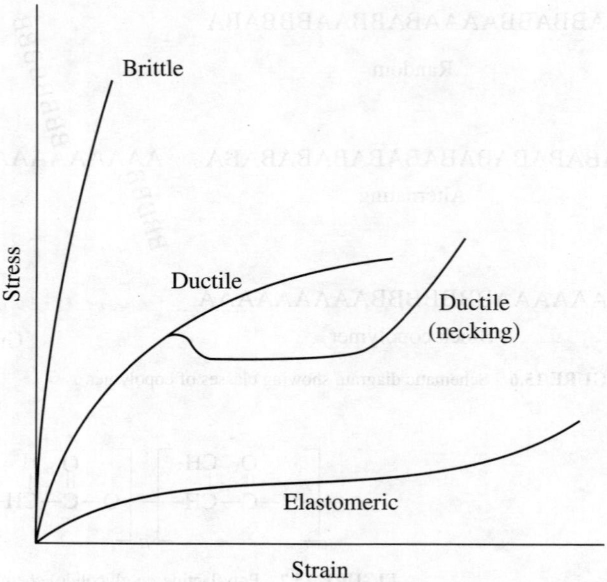

FIGURE 15.8 Mechanical behavior of polymers. [*Reproduced from Encyclopedia of Materials Science and Engineering, M. B. Bever (ed.). Cambridge, MA: MIT Press, 1986, p. 2917.*][89]

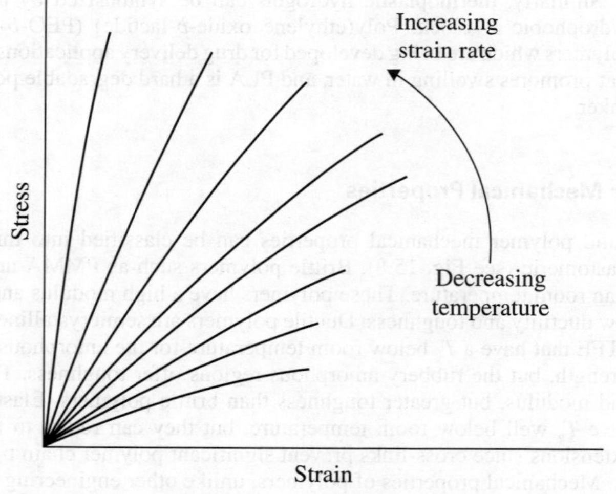

FIGURE 15.9 Schematic diagram showing strain rate and temperature dependence of polymer mechanical properties. [*Reproduced from Encyclopedia of Materials Science and Engineering. M. B. Bever (ed.). Cambridge, MA: MIT Press, 1986, p. 2917.*][89]

Polymers can exhibit both viscous and solid mechanical behavior; this phenomenon is called viscoelasticity. For a given polymer, the degree of viscous behavior depends on temperature. Below T_g, polymers will behave more or less as elastic solids with very little viscous behavior. Above T_g, polymers exhibit viscoelastic behavior until they reach their melting temperature, where they behave as liquids.

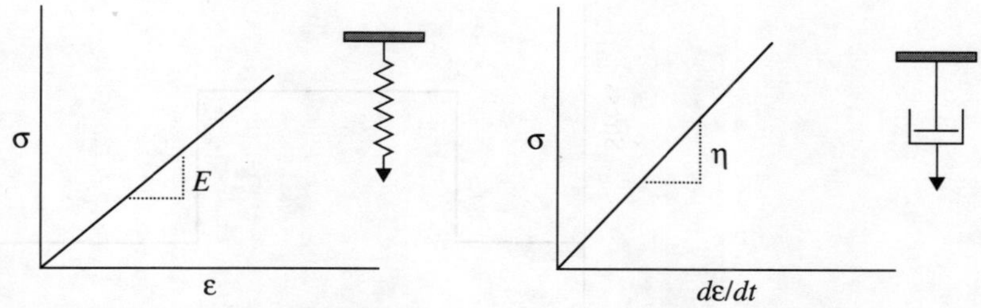

FIGURE 15.10 Stress/strain relationship for elastic solids and the stress/strain-rate relationships for viscous liquids.

When designing with polymers it is important to keep in mind that many polymers deform over time when they are under a continuous load. This deformation with time of loading is called creep. Ideal elastic solids do not creep since strain (deformation) is proportional to stress and there is no time dependence. Viscous materials (liquids) deform at a constant rate with a constant applied stress. Equation (15.3) describes the strain in a viscous material under constant load or stress σ.

$$\sigma = \eta \frac{d\varepsilon}{dt} \tag{15.3}$$

$$\int_0^{\varepsilon} d\varepsilon = \frac{\sigma}{\eta} \int_0^{t} dt \tag{15.4}$$

$$\varepsilon = \frac{\sigma}{\eta} t \tag{15.5}$$

Figure 15.11 shows the strain with time of constant stress for a viscous and elastic material. The stress is applied at t_i and removed at t_f. The elastic model shows an instantaneous deformation when stress is applied at t_i, a constant deformation with time, and then returns to its original length when the load is removed. Therefore, the elastic solid does not creep. The viscous (dashpot) model deforms continuously (creeps) from t_i to t_f and remains permanently deformed after removal of load.

Adding spring and dashpot models in series and parallel creates viscoelastic models. Several models have been proposed. Figure 15.12 shows the creep behavior for three viscoelastic models. Stress relaxation is a similar phenomenon and is defined as a reduction in stress during a constant deformation. One example of stress relaxation is the use of plastic washers between a nut and bolt. After the screw is secured, the washer deformation is constant, but the stress in the washer diminishes with time (stress relaxation) and the screw is more likely to loosen with time.

Therefore, creep and stress relaxation should be accounted for when designing with polymers. The strain rate for a given application must also be known since modulus, ductility, and strength are strain rate dependent.

15.3 SPECIFIC POLYMERS

15.3.1 Water-Soluble Polymers

Water-soluble polymers are used for a variety of applications. They can be adsorbed or covalently bound to surfaces to make them more hydrophilic, less thrombogenic, and more lubricious. They can be used as protective coatings to prevent damage during surgery. Hyaluronic acid solutions are used in ophthalmic surgery to prevent damage to the cornea and iris. They can be cross-linked to form hydrogels for soft tissue replacement and for drug delivery applications. There are numerous water-soluble biopolymers. The polymers discussed below are some of the more common and useful examples.

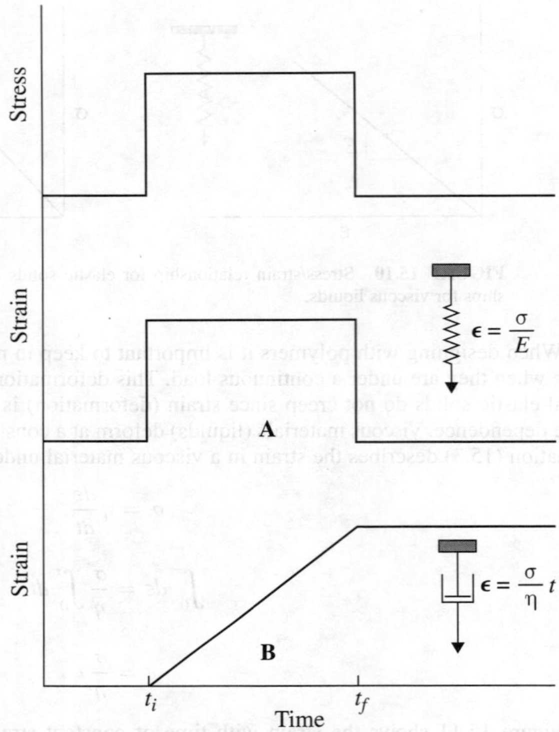

FIGURE 15.11 Response of elastic model (A) and viscous model (B) to a constant stress applied from t_i to t_f *[Reproduced from Encyclopedia of Materials Science and Engineering, M. B. Bever (ed.). Cambridge, MA: MIT Press, 1986, p. 2919.]*[90]

Poly(N-vinyl-pyrrolidinone). Degradation: Biostable. Poly(*N*-vinyl-pyrrolidinone) (Fig. 15.13) is a widely used water-soluble polymer. Like dextran, it has been used as a plasma volume expander to replace lost blood in mass casualty situations. PVP can also be used as a detoxifying agent since many toxic compounds form nontoxic complexes with PVP, which the kidneys eventually excrete. PVP is also used extensively as a binder in the pharmaceutical industry.

Polyethylene Glycol. Degradation: Biostable. Polyethylene glycol (PEG) (Fig. 15.14), also known as polyethylene oxide (PEO), is used primarily to make hydrophobic surfaces more hydrophilic. These hydrophilic coatings are known to drastically reduce bacterial adhesion to substrates, making the surfaces antimicrobial.[6–8] PEO can also be coated or grafted onto the surfaces of microparticles to aid in colloidal stability.[9–11] Microparticles for drug delivery applications are quickly recognized and cleared from circulation by the reticuloendothelial system (RES). PEO coatings help particles elude the RES, thereby increasing their residence time in the circulation.[12–15]

Hyaluronic Acid. Degradation: Biodegradable. Hyaluronic acid (HA) (Fig. 15.15) is a very lubricious, high-molecular-weight, and water-soluble polymer found in connective tissue and the synovial fluid that cushions the joints. HA is also found in the vitreous and aqueous humors of the eye. Solutions are injected in the eye during intraocular lens surgery to protect the cornea and the

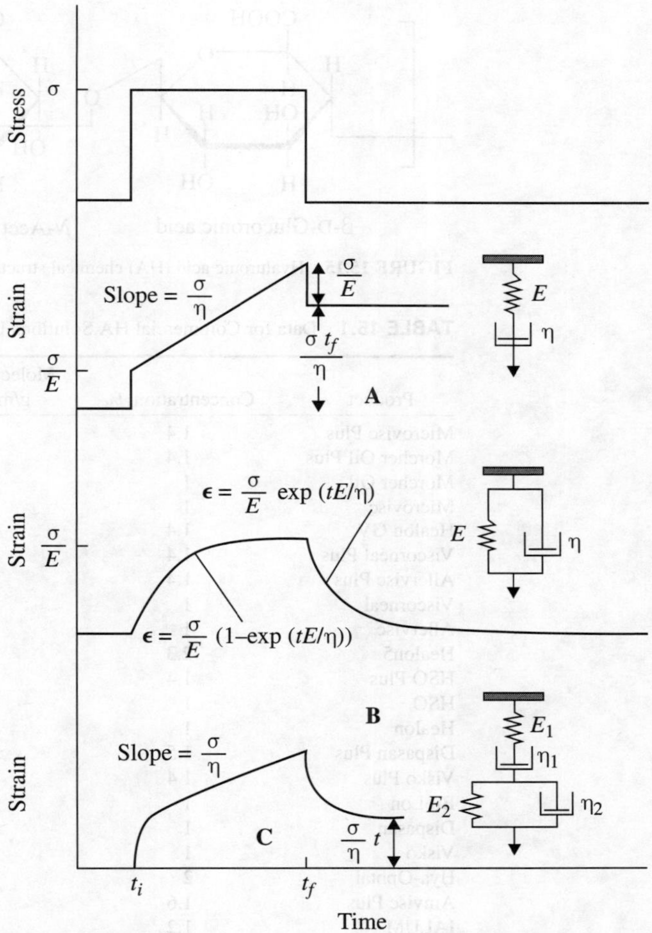

FIGURE 15.12 Creep response for (A) Maxwell model, (B) Voight-Kelvin model, and (C) four-parameter model for constant stress applied at t_i and removed at t_f.

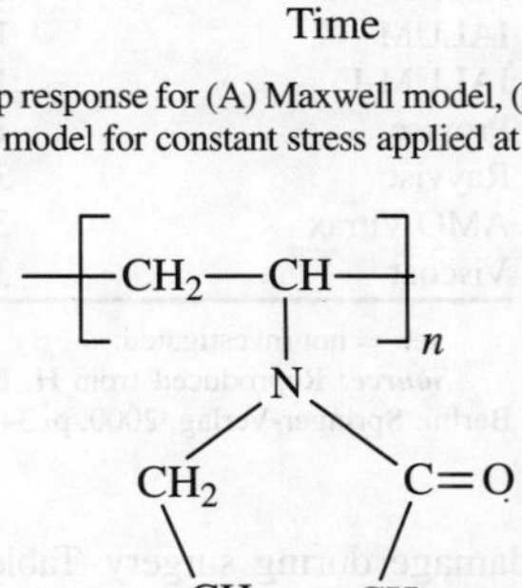

FIGURE 15.13 Poly(*N*-vinyl-pyrrolidinone) chemical structure.

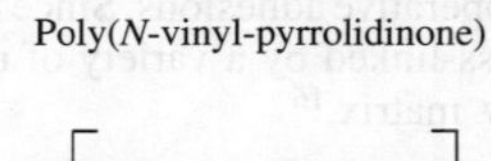

FIGURE 15.14 Polyethylene glycol (PEG) chemical structure.

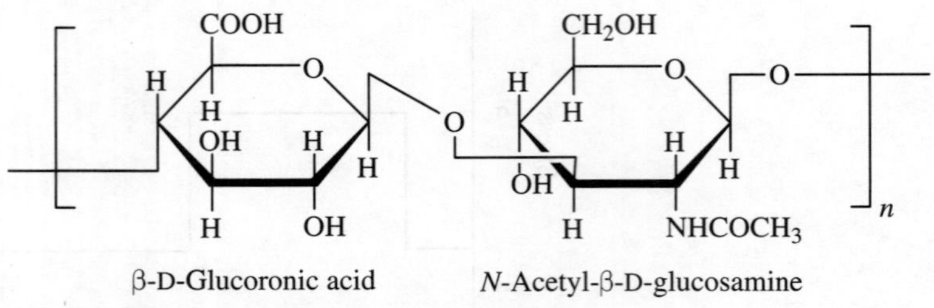

FIGURE 15.15 Hyaluronic acid (HA) chemical structure.

TABLE 15.1 Data for Commercial HA Solutions Used in Opthalmic Surgery

Product	Concentration, %	Molecular weight, g/mol × 10^6	Viscosity, mPa · s
Microvisc Plus	1.4	7.9	n.i.*
Morcher Oil Plus	1.4	7.9	1×10^6
Morcher Oil	1	6.1	1×10^6
Microvisc	1	5	n.i.
Healon GV	1.4	5	2×10^6
Viscorneal Plus	1.4	5	500,000
Allervisc Plus	1.4	5	500,000
Viscorneal	1	5	200,000
Allervisc	1	5	200,000
Healon5	2.3	4	7×10^6
HSO Plus	1.4	4	4.8×10^6
HSO	1	4	1×10^6
Healon	1	4	200,000
Dispasan Plus	1.5	>3	2.5×10^6
Visko Plus	1.4	3	500,000
BioLon	1	3	115,000
Dispasan	1	>2	35,000
Visko	1	2	300,000
Hya-Ophtal	2	2	n.i.
Amvisc Plus	1.6	1.5	60,000
IALUM	1.2	1.2	10,000
IALUM-F	1.8	1.2	22,000
Provisc	1	>1.1	50,000
Rayvisc	3	0.8	50,000
AMO Vitrax	3	0.5	40,000
Viscoat	3	>0.5	ca. 40,000

*n.i. = not investigated.

Source: Reproduced from H. B. Dick and O. Schwenn, *Viscoelastics in Ophthalmic Surgery.* Berlin: Springer-Verlag, 2000, p. 34.[92]

iris from damage during surgery. Table 15.1 shows data on HA concentration, molecular weight, and viscosity for some commercially available HA solutions. HA is currently being investigated to prevent postoperative adhesions. Since HA has many functional groups (OH, carboxylate, acetamido), it can be cross-linked by a variety of reagents. Therefore, HA may have applications as a hydrogel drug delivery matrix.[16]

Dextran. Degradation: Biodegradable. Dextran is a simple water-soluble polysaccharide manufactured by *Leuconostoc mesenteroides* and *L. dextranicum* (Lactobacteriaceae). Its structure is shown as a linear polymer, but some branching occurs at the three remaining OH groups (Fig. 15.16).

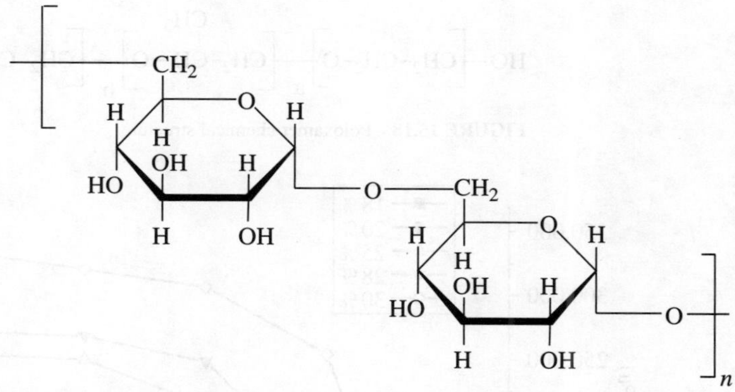

FIGURE 15.16 Dextran chemical structure.

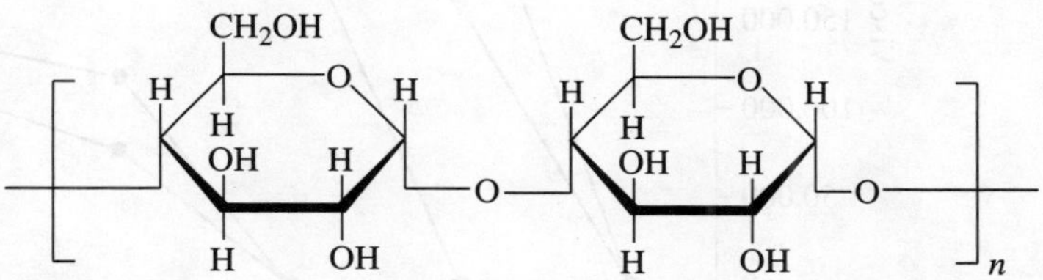

FIGURE 15.17 Amylose: Poly(1, 4'-α-D-glucopyranose) chemical structure.

The native form of dextran has a high molecular weight near 5×10^8 g/mol. Dextran is depolymerized to yield a variety of molecular weights depending on the application. Similar to polyvinyl pyrrolidinone, dextran solutions can be used as a blood plasma extender for mass casualty situations. Dextran of between 50,000 and 100,000 g/mol is used for this application. Like many of the water-soluble polymers, cross-linked dextran can be used as a drug delivery matrix in whole or microsphere form. Dextran-coated magnetite (Fe_3O_4) nanoparticles are finding use as a magnetic resonance imaging (MRI) contrast agent. The dextran adsorbs onto the particle surfaces and provides a steric barrier to prevent agglomeration of the nanoparticles.

Starch. Degradation: Biodegradable. Starch is the primary source of carbohydrate in the human diet. Starch is composed of two monosaccharides: amylose and amylopectin (Fig. 15.17). Amylose is a linear polymer that varies in molecular weight between 100,000 and 500,000 g/mol. Amylopectin is similar to amylose, having the same backbone structure, but with 4 percent branching. Starch is insoluble in water but can be made soluble by treating with dilute HCl. Soluble starch has similar properties to dextran and therefore has similar applications.

15.3.2 Gelling Polymers

Gelling polymers are polymers in solution that transform into relatively rigid network structures with a change in temperature or by addition of ionic cross-linking agents. This class of polymers is useful because hydrogels can be formed at mild conditions. These polymers can therefore be used for cell immobilization and for injectable materials that gel in vivo. They are also used as coatings for drug tablets to control release in vivo.

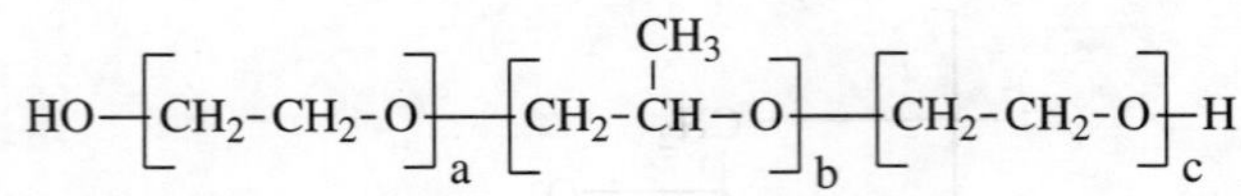

FIGURE 15.18 Poloxamer chemical structure.

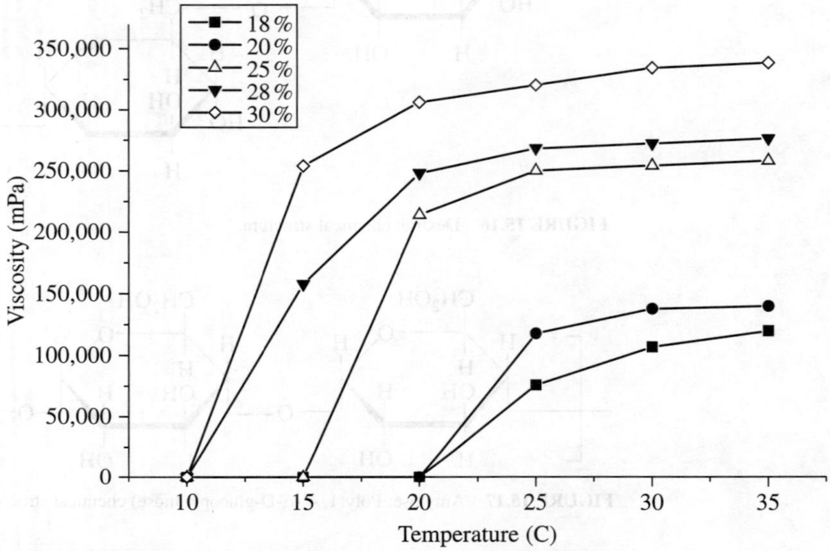

FIGURE 15.19 Viscosity of poloxamer solutions as a function of temperature and polymer concentration. [*Reproduced from L. E. Reeve. "Poloxamers: Their Chemistry and Applications," in Handbook of Biodegradable Polymers, A. J. Domb, J. K. Kost, and D. M. Wiseman (eds.). London: Harwood Academic Publishers, 1997, p. 235.*][91]

Poloxamers. Degradation: Biostable. Poloxamers consist of two polyethylene oxide (PEO) blocks attached on both sides of a polypropylene oxide (PPO) block (Fig. 15.18). The polymers are water soluble but increasing the temperature or concentration can lead to gel formation. The gelling properties are a function of the polypropylene content and the block lengths. Figure 15.19 shows the viscosity as a function of temperature for poloxamer 407. For a given concentration of poloxamer, the viscosity increases by several orders of magnitude at a transition temperature. The transition temperature decreases as polymer concentration increases.

The unique gelling properties of poloxamers make them useful as a coating to prevent postsurgical adhesions. They can be applied as a liquid since they gel at body temperature to provide a strong barrier for prevention of adhesions. Similarly, poloxamers are being investigated for use as an injectable drug depot. Drug can be mixed with an aqueous poloxamer solution that thermally gels in the body and provides a matrix for sustained release. Another research area for poloxamers is for coating hydrophobic polymer microspheres. The PPO block adsorbs to the hydrophobic microsphere, while the PEO blocks extend into the solution and provide steric repulsion to prevent coagulation. The PEO blocks also prolong circulation after intravenous injection, since the hydrophilic PEO retards removal by the reticuloendothelial system.

Alginate. Degradation: Slow or Nondegradable. As the structure in Fig. 15.20 shows, alginate is a copolymer of guluronic and mannuronic acids. Alginate is a natural polysaccharide that is readily cross-linked using divalent or trivalent cations. Cross-linking occurs between acid groups of adjacent mannuronic acid units. Ca^{++} is commonly used as a cross-linking agent. The sodium salt of alginate

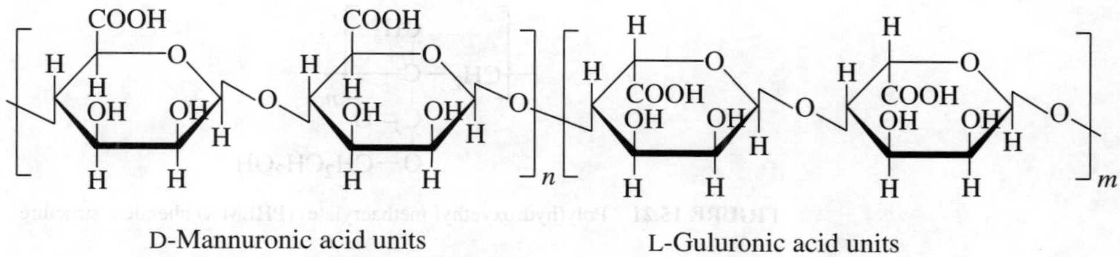

FIGURE 15.20 Alginate chemical structure.

(sodium alginate) is used rather than the plain alginate, since the acidic alginate can be harmful to cells and tissues.

Since cross-linking is chemically mild and easily accomplished, calcium cross-linked alginate is commonly used for cell immobilization. Cells are immobilized to prevent immune response in vivo and to prevent cells from traveling from the desired location in vivo. Immobilization is most often accomplished by adding cells to a sodium alginate solution, followed by dripping the solution into a calcium chloride solution to cross-link the alginate and entrap cells.

Gelatin. Degradation: Biodegradable. Gelatin is a protein prepared by hydrolyzing type I collagen using aqueous acids or bases. Collagen is discussed further in the section on hydrogels. Hydrolysis involves disruption of the collagen tertiary triple helix structure and reduction of molecular weight to yield gelatin that is soluble in warm water. Following hydrolysis, gelatin is purified and dried to yield a powder. Contrary to the poloxamers, gelatin solutions (>0.5 weight percent) gel with a reduction in temperature. Gelatin gels melt between 23 and 30°C and gelatin solutions set around 2 to 5°C lower than the melting point. Gelatin is used as a tablet coating or capsule materials as an enteric coating to control the release rate of drugs. Gelatin sponges are similar to collagen sponges and are used as hemostatic agents.

Fibrin. Degradation: Biodegradable. Fibrin is the monomer formed from fibrinogen in the blood when a clot is formed. It is a protein that first polymerizes and then cross-links during clot formation and has been isolated and used as a biological adhesive and matrix for tissue engineering. The gel formation involves mixing fibrinogen with the gelling enzyme (thrombin) and a second calcium-containing solution. Speed of gelation is controlled by concentrations. Biodegradation occurs fairly rapidly due to natural enzymatic activity (fibrinolysis) resulting from plasmin in tissue. Fibrin is used as a soft tissue adhesive and is used in tissue scaffolds.

15.3.3 Hydrogels

Hydrogels are materials that swell when placed in aqueous environments but maintain their overall shape. Hydrogels can be formed by cross-linking nearly any water-soluble polymer. Many natural materials such as collagen and chitosan (derived from chitin) absorb significant amounts of water and can be considered to be hydrogels. Hydrogels are compliant since the polymer chains have high mobilities due to the presence of water. Hydrogel mechanical properties are dependent on water content. Modulus and yield strength decrease with water content, while elongation tends to increase. Hydrogels are lubricious due to their hydrophilic nature. Hydrogels resist protein absorption and microbial attack due to their hydrophilicity and dynamic structure.

Poly(hydroxyethyl methacrylate). Degradation: biostable. Poly(hydroxyethyl methacrylate) (PHEMA) is a hydrogel generally cross-linked with ethylene glycol dimethacrylate (which is normally present as a contaminant in the monomer) (Fig. 15.21). PHEMA's hydrogel properties such as resistance to protein adsorption and lubricity make it an ideal material for contact lenses. Hydrated

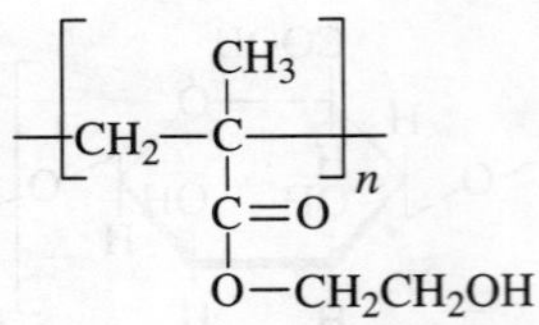

FIGURE 15.21 Poly(hydroxyethyl methacrylate) (PHEMA) chemical structure.

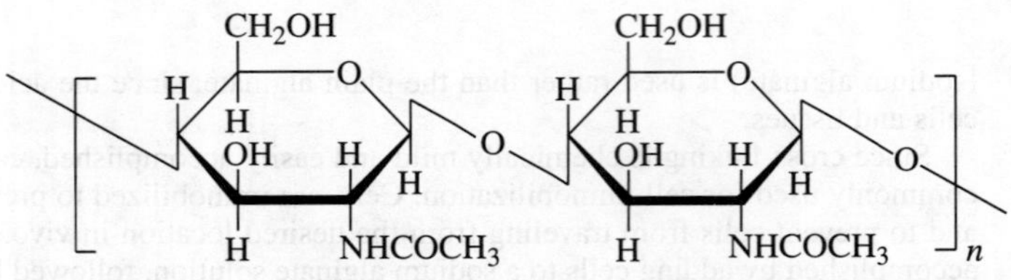

FIGURE 15.22 Chitin: Poly(1, 4'-β-*N*-acetyl-2-amino-2-deoxy-D-glucopyranose) chemical structure.

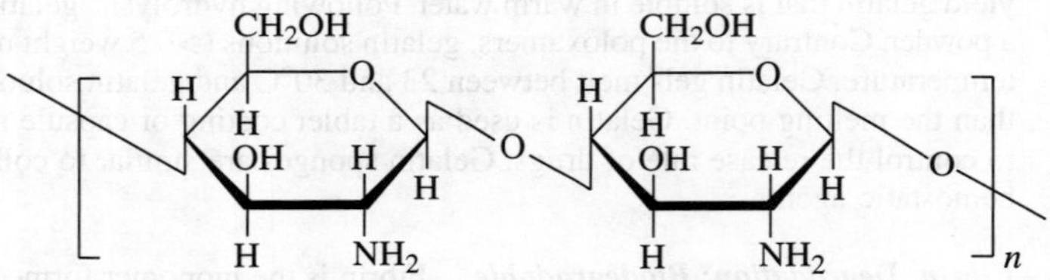

FIGURE 15.23 Chitosan: Poly(1, 4'-β-2-amino-2-deoxy-D-glucopyranose) chemical structure.

PHEMA gels have good oxygen permeability, which is necessary for the health of the cornea. PHEMA is copolymerized with polyacrylic acid (PAA) or poly-(*N*-vinyl pyrrolidinone) to increase its water absorbing capability.

Chitosan. Degradation: Biodegradable. Chitin is a polysaccharide that is the major component of the shells of insects and shellfish (Fig. 15.22). Chitosan is deacetylated chitin (Fig. 15.23). Deacetylation is accomplished using basic solutions at elevated temperatures. Chitin is not 100 percent acetylated and chitosan is not 100 percent deacetylated. The degree of acetylation has a large influence on properties, in particular solubility. Chitin is difficult to use as a biomaterial since it is difficult to process. It cannot be melt-processed and is insoluble in most aqueous solutions and organic solutions. It is soluble only in strong acid solutions. Chitosan, on the other hand, is soluble in dilute organic acids; acetic acid is most commonly used. Chitosan has a positive charge due to the primary amines in its structure. The positive charge is significant because most tissues are negatively charged. Chitosan has been used for artificial skin, sutures, and a drug delivery matrix.[16]

Chitosan absorbs a significant amount of water when placed in aqueous solutions. Equilibrium water content of 48 percent was determined by immersing chitosan films in deionized water. Tensile testing on these wet films resulted in an ultimate tensile stress of approximately 1600 psi with 70 percent elongation at break.[17]

TABLE 15.2 Medical Applications of Collagen

Specialty	Application
Cardiology	Heart valves
Dermatology	Soft tissue augmentation
Dentistry	Oral wounds
	Biocoating for dental implants
	Support for hydroxyapatite
	Periodontal attachment
General surgery	Hemostasis
	Hernia repair
	IV cuffs
	Wound repair
	Suture
Neurosurgery	Nerve repair
	Nerve conduits
Oncology	Embolization
Orthopedic	Bone repair
	Cartilage reconstruction
	Tendon and ligament repair
Ophthalmology	Corneal graft
	Tape or retinal attachment
	Eye shield
Plastic surgery	Skin replacement
Urology	Dialysis membrane
	Sphincter repair
Vascular	Vessel replacement
	Angioplasty
Other	Biocoatings
	Drug delivery
	Cell culture
	Organ replacement
	Skin test

Source: Reproduced from F. H. Silver and A. K. Garg, "Collagen characterization, processing, and medical applications," in *Handbook of Biodegradable Polymers*, A. J. Domb, J. Kost, and D. M. Wiseman, (eds.). London: Harwood Academic Publishers, 1997, Chap. 17, p. 336.[18]

Collagen. Degradation: Biodegradable. Collagen is the major structural protein in animals and exists in sheet and fibrillar form. Collagen fibrils consist of a triple helix of three protein chains. Type I collagen is a fibrillar form of collagen that makes up 25 percent of the protein mass of the human body. Due to its prevalence and ability to be separated from tissues, type 1 collagen is most often used in medical devices. Collagen fibrils are strong and biodegradable, and collagen is hemostatic, making it useful in a variety of applications. Table 15.2 shows many of the applications for collagen. Collagen is usually obtained from bovine corium, the lower layer of bovine hide. Bovine collagen is nonimmunogenic for most people, but immune response may be triggered in those with allergies to beef.[18]

Both water-soluble and water-insoluble collagen can be extracted from animal tissues. Water-soluble collagen can be extracted from collagen using salt solutions, organic acids, or a combination of organic acids and proteases. Proteases break down cross-links and nonhelical ends, yielding more soluble collagen than acid alone or the salt solutions. Water-soluble collagen finds little use in preparation of materials and devices since it quickly resorbs in the moist environment of the body. Water-insoluble collagen, however, is routinely used in the manufacture of medical devices. Water-insoluble collagen is ground and purified to yield a powder that can be later processed into materials and devices. Collagen cannot be melt-processed and is, therefore, processed by evaporating water from collagen suspensions. Insoluble collagen disperses well at pH between 2 and 4. Evaporating 1 percent suspensions forms collagen films. Freezing suspensions followed by lyophilizing (freeze drying) forms sponges. Ice crystals form during freezing, which results in porosity after water is removed during lyophilizing. Freezing temperature controls ice crystal size and 14-μm pores result from freezing at −80°C and 100-μm pores at −30°C. Fibers and tubes are formed by extruding collagen suspensions into aqueous solutions buffered at pH 7.5.[18]

Collagen absorbs water readily in the moist environment of the body and degrades rapidly; therefore, devices are often cross-linked or chemically modified to make them less hydrophilic and to reduce degradation. Viswanadham and Kramer showed that the water content of untreated collagen hollow fibers (15 to 20 μm thick, 400 μm outer diameter) is a function of humidity. The absorbed water plasticizes collagen, lowering both the modulus and yield strength. Table 15.3 summarizes these results. Cross-linking the fibers using UV radiation increased the modulus of the fibers.[19]

Albumin. Degradation: Biodegradable. Albumin is a globular, or soluble, protein making up 50 percent of the protein content of plasma in humans. It has a molecular weight of 66,200 and contains 17 disulfide bridges.[20] Numerous carboxylate and amino (lysyl) groups are available for cross-linking reactions providing for a very broad range of mechanical behavior. Heating is also an effective cross-linking method, as seen in ovalbumin (egg white cooking). This affords another gelling mechanism and is finding increasing use in laser welding of tissue, where bond strengths of 0.1 MPa have been achieved.[21] As with collagen, the most common cross-linking agent used is glutaraldehyde, and toxic by-products are of concern. Careful cleaning and neutralization with glycine wash have provided biocompatible albumin and collagen structures in a wide variety of strengths up to tough, very slowly degradable solids. It should be noted that albumin and collagen solidification is generally different than that of fibrin, which gels by a normal biological mechanism. The glutaraldehyde methods yield a variety of nonbiologic solids with highly variable mechanical properties. This has led to an extensive literature, and very wide range of properties for collagen and albumin structures which are used for tissue substitutes and drug delivery vehicles.

Oxidized Cellulose. Degradation: Resorbable. Oxidized cellulose is one of the fastest degrading polymers at physiologic pH. It is classified as resorbable since it degrades without the help of

TABLE 15.3 Water Absorption and Its Effect on Modulus (E) and Yield Strength of Collagen Hollow Fibers[19]

Humidity, %	Water absorption, g/100 g collagen
wet	240
90	50
80	25
60	17
30	10
Humidity, %	**Yield stress, psi**
Wet	3,000
90	5,200
66	13,000
36	19,000
8	24,000
Humidity	**E, ksi***
Wet	44
90	450
75	750
8	970

*1 ksi = 1000 psi

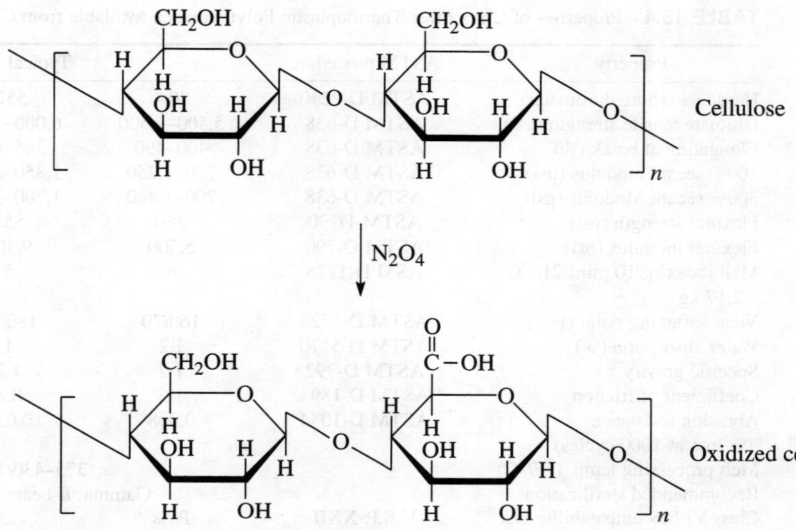

FIGURE 15.24 Cellulose and oxidized cellulose chemical structure.

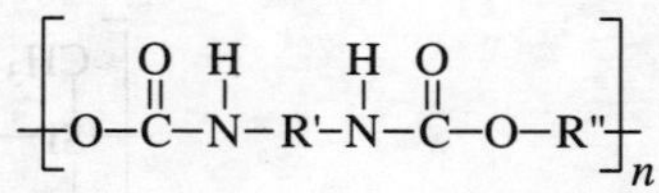

FIGURE 15.25 Polyurethane chemical structure.

enzymes. It is relatively stable at neutral pH, but above pH 7 it degrades. Oxidized cellulose disappears completely in 21 days when placed in phosphate buffered saline (PBS). Similarly, it dissolves 80 percent after 2 weeks in vivo.

Cellulose is oxidized using nitrogen tetroxide (N_2O_4) (Fig. 15.24). Commercially available oxidized cellulose contains between 0.6 and 0.93 carboxylic acid groups per glucose unit, which corresponds to between 16 and 24 weight percent carboxylic acid.[22]

Oxidized cellulose is used as a degradable hemostatic agent. The acid groups promote clotting when placed in wounds. Furthermore, oxidized cellulose swells with fluid to mechanically close damaged vessels. Oxidized cellulose sheets are placed between damaged tissues following surgery to prevent postsurgical adhesions. The sheets separate tissue during healing and dissolve in a few weeks after healing occurs.[22]

15.3.4 Elastomers

Silicones and polyurethanes are the two main classes of elastomers used for in vivo applications. Both are versatile polymers with a wide range of mechanical properties. Polyurethanes tend to be stiffer and stronger than silicones, while silicones are more stable and have the advantage of being oxygen permeable. Polyurethanes are more versatile from a processing standpoint since many polyurethanes are thermoplastics, while silicones rely on covalent cross-linking and are therefore thermosets.

Polyurethane Elastomers. Degradation: Biostable or Slow Resorption. The above repeat unit in Fig. 15.25 can describe most polyurethanes. Polyurethanes are a versatile class of block copolymers consisting of a "hard block" (R′) and a "soft block" (R″). The hard block is a glassy polymer (T_g above room temperature) often synthesized by polymerizing diisocyanates with glycols. R″ is a low

TABLE 15.4 Properties of Chronoflex Thermoplastic Polyurethanes Available from CardioTech[24]

Property	ASTM procedure	Typical values		
		80A	55D	75D
Hardness (shore durometer)	ASTM D-2240	80A	55D	75D
Ultimate tensile strength (psi)	ASTM D-638	5,500–6,500	6,000–7,500	7,000–8,000
Elongation at break (%)	ASTM D-638	400–490	365–440	255–320
100% secant modulus (psi)	ASTM D-638	770–1,250	1,850–2,200	5,300–5,700
300% secant Modulus (psi)	ASTM D-638	700–1,400	1,700–2,000	2,700–3,200
Flexural strength (psi)	ASTM-D790	350	550	10,000
Flexural modulus (psi)	ASTM D-790	5,500	9,300	300,000
Melt index (g/10 min) 210°C 2.17 kg	ASM D-1238	8	5	3
Vicat softening point (F/C)	ASTM D-1525	160/70	180/80	–
Water absorption (%)	ASTM D-5170	1.2	1	0.8
Specific gravity	ASTM D-792	1.2	1.2	1.2
Coefficient of friction	ASTM D-1894	1.5	0.8	0.64
Abrasion resistance (% loss at 1000 cycles)	ASTM D-1044	0.008	0.035	0.053
Melt processing temp. (°F/°C)			375–430/190–220	
Recommended sterilization			Gamma; E-beam; ethylene oxide	
Class VI biocompatability test	U.S.P. XXII	Pass	Pass	Pass

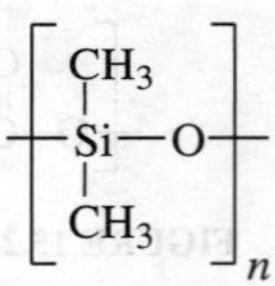

FIGURE 15.26 Poly(dimethyl siloxane) chemical structure.

T_g (T_g << room temperature) polyester or polyether. Polyurethanes with polyester soft blocks are degradable, while those with polyether blocks degrade very slowly. Polyurethanes are usually elastomers since hard and soft blocks are present. Rubbers of different hardness or durometer can be prepared by varying the ratio of R′ to R″. Covalently cross-linked polymers can be prepared by using monomers with functionalities greater than 2. But the most useful polyurethanes for medical applications are the thermoplastic elastomers since these can be melt processed or solution cast. Polyurethanes have good fatigue strength and blood compatibility and are used for pacemaker lead insulation, vascular grafts, and ventricular assist device/artificial heart membranes.[23] Table 15.4 shows properties of thermoplastic polyurethane elastomers available from CardioTech International Inc.[24] These values are for the Chronoflex C series of polymers.

Silicone Elastomers (Polysiloxanes). Degradation: Biostable. Silicone elastomers are cross-linked derivatives of poly(dimethyl siloxane) (PDMS) (Fig. 15.26). Polysiloxane liquids with functional endgroups such as OH or sidegroups such as $CH{=}CH_2$ can be molded at room temperature and cross-linked to form elastomers using various cross-linking agents. Silicone elastomer kits consisting of the polysiloxane precursor liquids and cross-linking agents are commercially available from corporations such as GE Bayer Silicones (Table 15.5). Silicones cross-linked at room temperature are called room-temperature vulcanized (RTV) elastomers and those requiring elevated temperatures are called heat-cured silicone elastomers.

Silicones are more flexible and of lower strength than polyurethanes. But they are more chemically stable and are used for artificial finger joints, blood vessels, heart valves, breast implants, outer ears, and chin and nose implants. Silicones have high oxygen permeability and are used for membrane oxygenators and soft contact lenses.[25]

TABLE 15.5 Mechanical Properties for Cured Silicone

Product	Shore hardness	Tensile strength, psi	Elongation at break, %	Tear strength, lb/in
Silopren HV 3/322	30A	800	600	86
Silopren HV 3/822	80A	1,300	400	142
Silopren HV 4/311	35A	1,000	600	57
Silopren HV 4/811	80A	1,450	400	114
Silopren LSR 4020	22A	940	1,000	86
Silopren LSR 4070	70A	1,300	400	114

Source: Available from GE Bayer Silicones[82]

TABLE 15.6 Literature Values for Physical Properties of Bioinert Plastics

Material	Specific gravity	Tensile strength, psi	Elastic modulus, ksi	T_g, C	T_m, C
Cellulose acetate	1.22–1.34[a]	1,900–9,000[a]	580[b]		230[b]
Polyether ether ketone (PEEK)	1.30[e]	14,000[e]	508[e]	143[e]	343[e]
Nylon 6,6	1.13–1.15[a]	11,000†–13,700*,[a] 230†–500[a]	230*–550[a]	50[c]	255–265[a]
Poly(methyl methacrylate)	1.17–1.20[a]	7,000–10,500[a]	325–470[a]	85–105[a]	Amorphous
Nylon 6	1.12–1.14[a]	6,000†–24,000[a] 100†–247[a]	380*–464[a]	40–52[c]	210–220[a]
Poly(ethylene terephthalate)	1.30–1.38[a]	8,200–8,700[a]	280–435[a]	62–77[c]	220–267[a]
Poly (vinyl chloride)	1.39–1.43[b]	7200[d]	363[d]	75–85[b]	120–210[b]
Polypropylene	0.90–0.91[a]	4,500–6,000[a]	165–225[a]	–20[a]	160–175[a]
High density polyethylene	0.95–0.97[a]	3,200–4,500[a]	155–158[a]	–125[c]	130–137[a]
Poly(tetrafluoroethylene)	2.14–2.20[a]	3,000–5,000[a]	58–80[a]	–80, 126[c]	327[a]
Perfluorinated ethylene-propylene	2.12–2.17[a]	2,700–3,100[a]	50[a]	–90, 70[c]	275[a]

*Tested at 0.2 percent moisture content.
†Tested after conditioning at 50 percent relative humidity.
Source:
[a]Data from *Modern Plastics Encyclopedia*. McGraw-Hill 1999.[93]
[b]Data from *Encyclopedia of Polymer Science and Engineering,* 2d ed. New York: John Wiley and Sons, 1985.[26]
[c]Data from *Polymer Handbook,* 3rd ed. New York: John Wiley and Sons, 1989.[94]
[d]Data from *Encyclopedia of Materials Engineering*. Cambridge, MA: MIT Press, 1986.[95]
[e]Data from Victrex plastics, UK product literature.[96]

15.3.5 Rigid Polymers

Most biostable, rigid polymers are commodity plastics developed for nonmedical applications. Due to their chemical stability and nontoxic nature, many commodity plastics have been used for implantable materials. The following section on rigid polymers is separated into biostable and resorbable materials. Table 15.6 is at the end of the section on biostable materials and contains mechanical property data for these polymers. Table 15.6 is roughly ordered by elastic modulus. Polymers such as the nylons and poly(ethylene terephthalate) slowly degrade by hydrolysis of the polymer backbone. But they are considered biostable since a significant decrease in properties takes years.

Most rigid degradable polymers degrade without the aid of enzymes and are therefore resorbable. Table 15.7 is at the end of the section on resorbable polymers and shows mechanical property data for these polymers.

Cellulose. Degradation: Biostable. Cellulose is a partially crystalline polysaccharide and is the chief constituent of plant fiber (Fig. 15.27). Cotton is the purest natural form of cellulose containing 90 percent cellulose. Cellulose decomposes before melting and therefore cannot be melt processed.

TABLE 15.7 Physical Properties for Degradable Polyesters

Material	Tensile strength, psi	Elastic modulus, ksi	T_g, C	T_m, C
Polyglycolide*	10,000	1,000	35–40	225–230
Poly (L-lactide)*	8,000–12,000	600	60–65	173–178
50/50 Poly(DL-lactide-*co*-glycolide)*	6,000–8,000	400	45–50	Amorphous
Poly (DL-Lactide)*	4,000–6,000	400	55–60	Amorphous
Polycaprolactone*	3,000–5,000	50	−65–0	58–63
Poly(3HB)†	5,800	500	4	177
Poly(3HB-*co*-20%3HV)†	4,600	170	−1	145
Poly(4HB)†	15,100	22	−50	60
Poly(3HB-*co*-16%4HB)†	3,800	Not meas.	−8	152

*Data from Birmingham polymers product literature.[97]
†Data from *Biopolymers, Volume 4, Polyesters III—Applications and Commercial Products*, Chapter 4: "Applications of PHAs in Medicine and Pharmacy." Page 96. Authors: Simon F. Williams and David P. Martin. Editors Yoshiharu Doi, Alexander Steinbuchel.

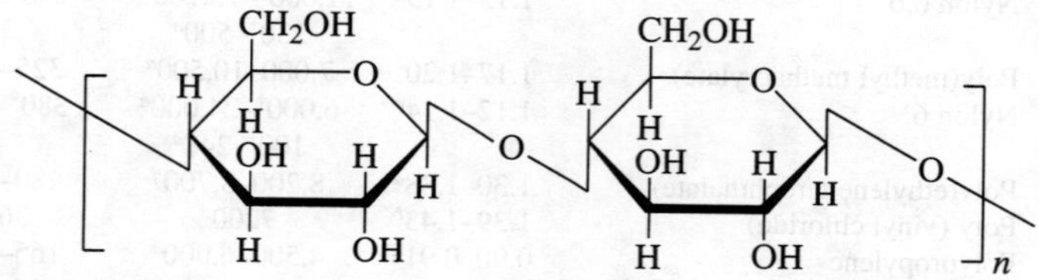

FIGURE 15.27 Cellulose: Poly(1, 4'-β-D-glucopyranose) chemical structure.

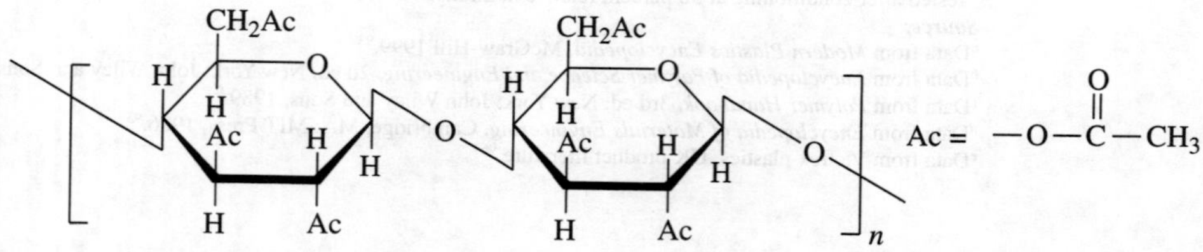

FIGURE 15.28 Cellulose acetate chemical structure.

It is insoluble in organics and water and can only be dissolved in strong basic solutions. Regenerated cellulose, also known as rayon, is cellulose that has been precipitated from a basic solution. Cellulose is used in bandages and sutures. Cuprophan is cellulose precipitated from copper hydroxide solutions to form hemodialysis membranes.

Cellulose Acetate. Degradation: Biostable. Cellulose acetate is a modified cellulose that can be melt processed (Fig. 15.28). Cellulose acetate membranes are used for hemodialysis.

Nylon 6,6. Degradation: Slow Resorption. Poly(hexamethylene diadipamide) is also known as nylon 6,6 since its repeat unit has two 6 carbon sequences per repeat unit (Fig. 15.29). Nylon is tough, abrasion resistant, and has a low coefficient of friction, making it a popular suture material.[26] Nylon 6,6 is hydrophilic and absorbs water when placed in tissues or in humid environments (9 to 11 percent water when fully saturated[27]). Absorbed water acts as a plasticizer, increasing the ductility

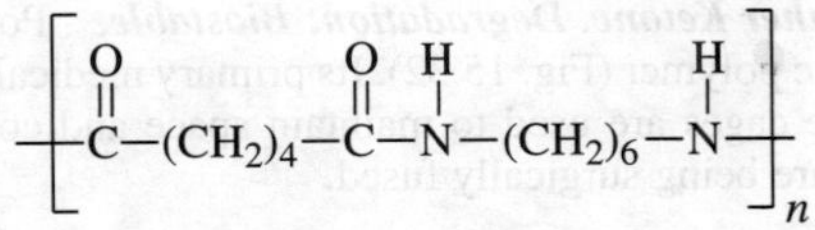

FIGURE 15.29 Poly(hexamethylene adipimide): Nylon 6,6 chemical structure.

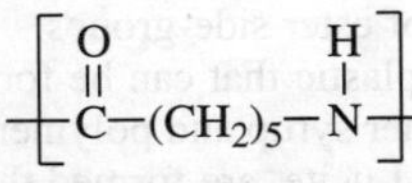

FIGURE 15.30 Poly(caprolactam): Nylon 6 chemical structure.

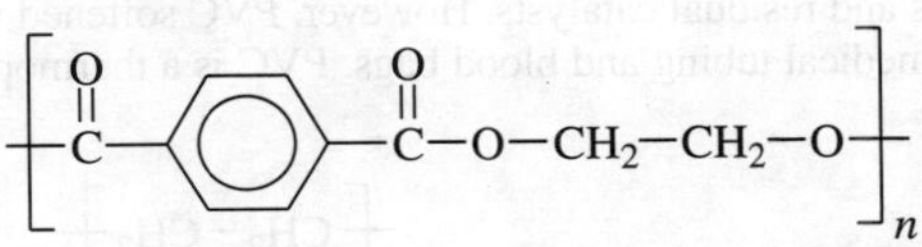

FIGURE 15.31 Poly(ethylene terephthalate) (PET) chemical structure.

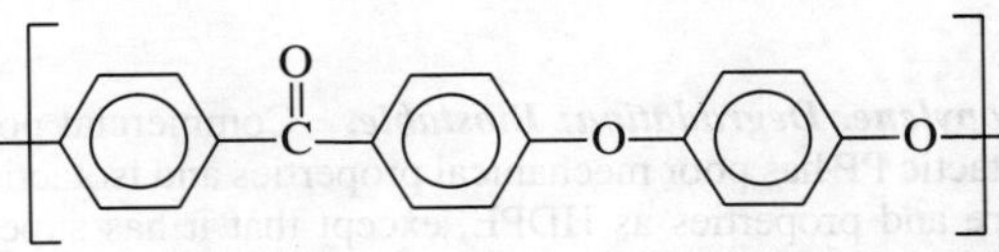

FIGURE 15.32 Polyether ether ketone (PEEK) chemical structure.

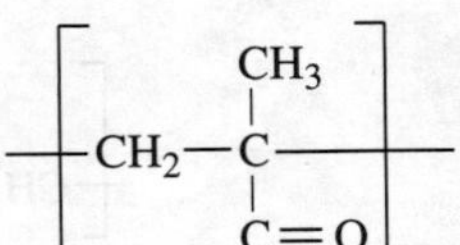

FIGURE 15.33 Poly(methyl methacrylate) (PMMA) chemical structure.

and reducing the modulus of nylon 6,6. Nylon resorbs at a very slow rate. Nylon 6,6 implanted in dogs lost 25 percent of its tensile strength after 89 days and 83 percent after 725 days.[28]

Nylon 6: Poly(caprolactam). Degradation: Slow Resorption. Nylon 6 has similar properties to nylon 6,6, the primary difference being that nylon 6 has a lower melting temperature and is more moisture sensitive (Fig. 15.30).

Poly(ethylene terephthalate). Degradation: Very Slow Resorption. Poly(ethylene terephthalate) (PET), also known simply as polyester or Dacron®, is a rigid semicrystalline thermoplastic polymer (Fig. 15.31). It is widely used as a material for woven large diameter vascular grafts. PET is usually considered to be stable, but it undergoes very slow resorption in vivo.

Polyether Ether Ketone. Degradation: Biostable. Polyether ether ketone (PEEK) is a strong, rigid thermoplastic polymer (Fig. 15.32). Its primary medical is as a material for vertebral interbody fusion cages. These cages are used to maintain space and contain bone graft materials between vertebral bodies that are being surgically fused.

Poly(methyl methacrylate). Degradation: Biostable. Poly(methyl methacrylate) (PMMA) (Fig. 15.33) is an amorphous polymer with a high T_g (approximately 100°C). PMMA is a stiff, hard, and transparent material with a refractive index of 1.5, and is therefore used for intraocular lenses and hard contact lenses as well as bone cement. PMMA is very biostable, but less so than PTFE due to possible hydrolysis of ester side-groups.

PMMA is a thermoplastic that can be formed by injection molding or extrusion. Casting monomer or monomer/polymer syrup and polymerizing can also form PMMA. PMMA plates, commonly known as Plexiglass or Lucite, are formed this way.

Polyvinyl Chloride. Degradation: Biostable. Polyvinyl chloride (PVC) (Fig. 15.34) is a rigid glassy polymer that is not used in vivo because it causes a large inflammatory response probably due to metal stabilizers and residual catalysts. However, PVC softened with plasticizers such as dioctyl phthalate is used for medical tubing and blood bags. PVC is a thermoplastic and can be melt processed.

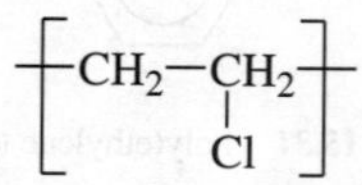

FIGURE 15.34 Polyvinyl chloride (PVC) chemical structure.

Polypropylene. Degradation: Biostable. Commercial polypropylene (PP) is isotactic (Fig. 15.35) since atactic PP has poor mechanical properties and isotactic is difficult to synthesize. PP has similar structure and properties as HDPE, except that it has superior flex fatigue properties and a higher melting point. Polypropylene is commonly used for nondegradable sutures. Like PE, polypropylene can be melt processed.[25]

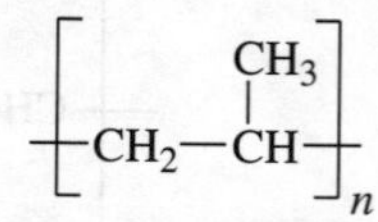

FIGURE 15.35 Polypropylene (PP) chemical structure.

Polyethylene. Degradation: Biostable. Polyethylene (PE) is a flexible polymer with a T_g of around −125°C (Fig. 15.36). It is available in three different forms: low density (LDPE), linear low density (LLDPE), and high density (HDPE). LDPE and LLDPE are typically not used in vivo since they cannot be autoclaved. HDPE can be autoclaved and is used in tubing for drains and as a catheter material. Ultrahigh-molecular-weight polyethylene (UHMWPE) has a high molecular weight ($\approx 2 \times 10^6$ g/mol) and is used for the articulating surfaces of knee and hip prosthesis. UHMWPE, like all PE, has a low coefficient of friction, but is very hard and abrasion resistant.[29]

With the exception of UHMWPE, PE can be melt-processed. UHMWPE has a high melting point and, like PTFE, is formed by pressing and sintering of powders.

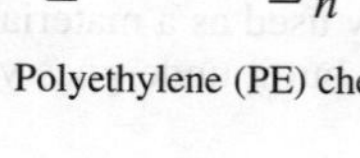

FIGURE 15.36 Polyethylene (PE) chemical structure.

Polytetrafluoroethylene. Degradation: Very Biostable. Polytetrafluoroethylene (PTFE: Teflon™, Fluorel™) (Fig. 15.37) is best known for its excellent chemical stability and low coefficient of friction. Expanded PTFE (ePTFE) contains microporosity created by stretching PTFE film and is used in small-diameter vascular grafts and for artificial heart valve sewing rings (e.g., Gore-tex®).

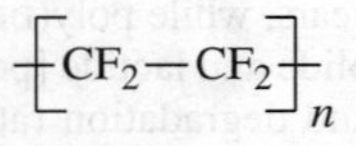

FIGURE 15.37 Polytetrafluoroethylene (PTFE: Teflon™, Fluorel™) chemical structure.

PTFE is highly crystalline (92 to 98 percent) and degrades near its melting temperature of 327°C; therefore, it cannot be melt processed even though it is a thermoplastic. Due to the inability to melt process, PTFE is formed by pressing PTFE powder followed by heating to sinter the powder, or it is heated and pressed simultaneously (pressure sintered).[26]

Perfluorinated Ethylene-Propylene Polymer. Degradation: Biostable. Perfluorinated ethylene-propylene polymer (FEP) is a copolymer of tetrafluoroethylene (TFE) and hexafluoropropylene (HFP) (Fig. 15.38). FEP has similar properties to PTFE, but its lower melting temperature of 275°C allows it to be melt processed.[26]

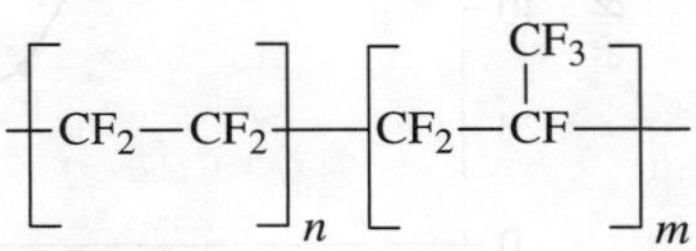

FIGURE 15.38 Perfluorinated ethylene-Propylene polymer (FEP) chemical structure.

Polylactide, Polyglycolide, and Copolymers. Degradation: Resorbable. Polylactide and polyglycolide (also known as polylactic acid and polyglycolic acid) are the most widely used synthetic degradable biopolymers. They are popular since they have good mechanical properties and degrade to nontoxic metabolites: glycolic or lactic acid. Polylactide, polyglycolide, and copolymers of the two find clinical use in degradable sutures and orthopedic pins and screws. Recent research has focused on their use as a drug delivery matrix since sustained release of drugs can be achieved as the materials degrade. Drug delivery matrices include monoliths and microspheres. Microspheres are routinely prepared by dissolution of polymer and drug in chloroform (or dichloromethane), suspension in aqueous polyvinyl alcohol (to form an oil in water emulsion), and evaporation to form drug-entrapped microspheres or nanospheres. Stirring speed and polymer/drug concentration in the oil phase (chloroform or dichloromethane solution) are the primary controls of sphere size.

Polylactide differs from polyglycolide in that R is a methyl group (CH_3) for polylactide and a hydrogen for polyglycolide (Fig. 15.39). Polylactide and polyglycolide are usually synthesized from lactide and glycolide cyclic monomers using initiators such as stannous 2-ethyl hexanoate (stannous octoate).

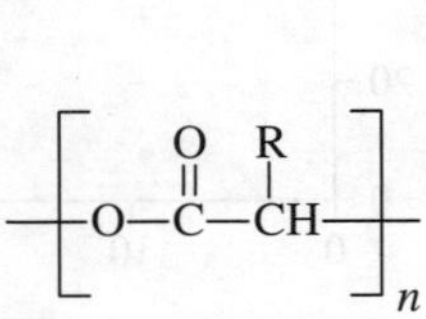

FIGURE 15.39 Polylactide and polyglycolide chemical structures.

Like polypropylene, the stereochemistry of the repeat unit has a large effect on the structure and properties of polylactide. Poly(DL-lactide) is atactic, meaning it has no regular stereostructure and as a result is mainly amorphous. Poly(D-lactide) and poly(L-lactide) are isotactic and consequently are up to 50 percent crystalline depending on processing conditions. Poly(D-lactide) is seldom used commercially since D-lactic acid (degradation product of D-lactide) does not occur naturally in the human body, while L-lactic acid is a common metabolite. Poly(L-lactide) has a higher modulus and tensile strength than the amorphous poly(DL-lactide). Similarly, the crystalline poly(L-lactide) degrades completely in vivo in 20 months to 5 years, while poly(DL-lactide) degrades much faster, in 6 to 17 weeks.[30]

Copolymers of glycolide and lactide [poly (lactide-*co*-glycolide)] are amorphous and have similar mechanical properties and degradation rates as poly(DL-lactide). Pure polyglycolide is very strong and stiff, yet has similar degradation as the poly(DL-lactides) and the lactide/glycolide copolymers. Polyglycolide is highly crystalline, with crystallinities between 35 and 70 percent.[30] Figures 15.40 and 15.41 show degradation rates for polyglycolide and poly(L-lactide).

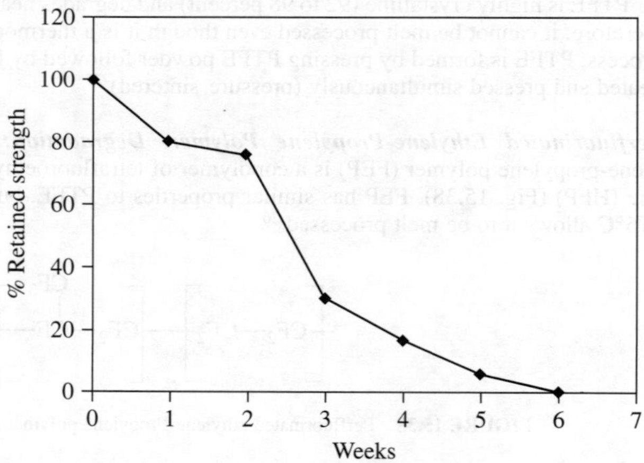

FIGURE 15.40 In vitro degradation of polyglycolide. Retained tensile strength versus time. [*Reproduced from D. E. Perrin and J. P. English, "Polyglycolide and polylactide," in Handbook of Biodegradable Polymers, A. J. Domb, J. K. Kost, and D. M. Wiseman (eds.). London: Harwood Academic Publishers, 1997, p. 12.*][30]

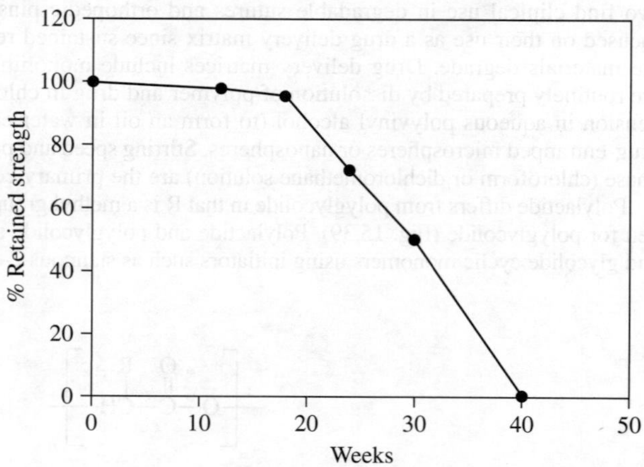

FIGURE 15.41 In vitro degradation of poly(L-lactide). Retained tensile strength versus time. [*Reproduced from D. E. Perrin and J. P. English, "Polyglycolide and polylactide," in Handbook of Biodegradable Polymers, A. J. Domb, J. K. Kost, and D. M. Wiseman (eds.). London: Harwood Academic Publishers, 1997, p. 12.*][30]

Polylactide, polyglycolide, and poly(lactide-*co*-glycolide) are often called polylactic acid, polyglycolic acid, and poly(lactic-*co*-glycolic acid) since their structures can be deduced by the direct condensation of lactic and glycolic acid. Though it is rare, synthesis of polylactic and glycolic acids can be achieved by direct condensation, but this results in low-molecular-weight polymer (on the order of 2000 g/mol), with poor mechanical properties but increased degradation rates.

Polycaprolactone. Degradation: Resorbable. Polycaprolactone (PCL) is a biodegradable, semicrystalline polyester that is synthesized from caprolactone using stannous octoate in a similar manner to polylactide or polyglycolide (Fig. 15.42). PCL has a very low modulus of around 50 KSI since it has a low T_g of –60°C. PCL degrades very slowly, and, therefore, it is usually not used as a homopolymer. Caprolactone, however, is copolymerized with glycolide to make a flexible suture material (trade name MONOCRYL).[31]

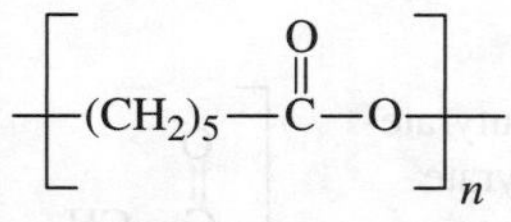

FIGURE 15.42 Polycaprolactone chemical structure.

Polyhydroxyalkanoates. Degradation: Resorbable. Polyhydroxyalkanoates (PHAs) are another class of thermoplastic degradable polyesters like polylactide, polyglycolide, and polycaprolactone. Materials with properties ranging from elastomers to strong, rigid polymers can be produced. PHAs are widely studied in the scientific literature but are just beginning to be commercialized for use in medical devices. Figure 15.43 shows the structure of PHAs, which can vary widely. The alkyl group within the polymer chain $[CH_2]_x$ typically contains 1 to 4 CH_2 groups. R is most commonly a short-chain alkyl group such as methyl (CH_3) or ethyl (CH_2CH_3). A variety of different mechanical properties and degradation rates can be achieved by varying x and R. The ranges of degradation rates, mechanical properties, and applications for PHAs are similar to polylactide, polyglycolide, and their copolymers.[32]

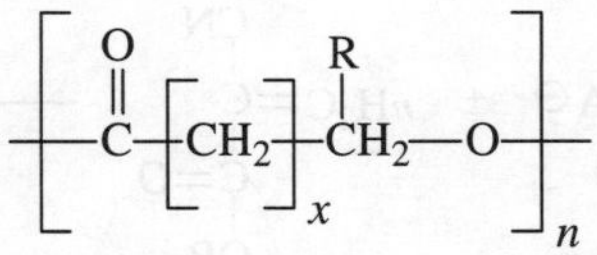

FIGURE 15.43 Polyhydroxyalkanoate chemical structure.

PHAs are produced in nature by many different microorganisms, which use them for energy storage. Tepha (Cambridge, MA) has isolated the DNA sequences responsible for production of PHAs in bacteria and has developed methods to produce PHAs with tailored chemistry and properties by fermentation using transgenic bacteria. Tepha received FDA clearance for a suture made from poly-4-hydroxybutyrate [poly(4HB)] in February 2007. Figure 15.44 shows some PHAs that have been studied in the literature. Table 15.7 shows physical properties for PHAs compared to polylactide, polyglycolide, and their copolymers.

Poly(alkylcyanoacrylates). Degradation: Resorbable. Cyanoacrylates are reactive monomers initiated by nearly any anion to form a rigid polymer. The only anions that *cannot* initiate polymerization are the conjugate bases of strong acids (e.g., Cl^-, NO_3^-, SO_4^{2-}). The reactive nature of cyanoacrylate monomers makes them useful adhesives. OH^- from adsorbed water is believed to initiate polymerization in many applications. R in Fig. 15.45 represents an alkyl chain. Methyl cyanoacrylate (R = CH_3) is found in commercial adhesives for nonmedical applications. Butyl cyanoacrylate is FDA approved and is used as an injectable glue for repair of arteriovenous malformations.

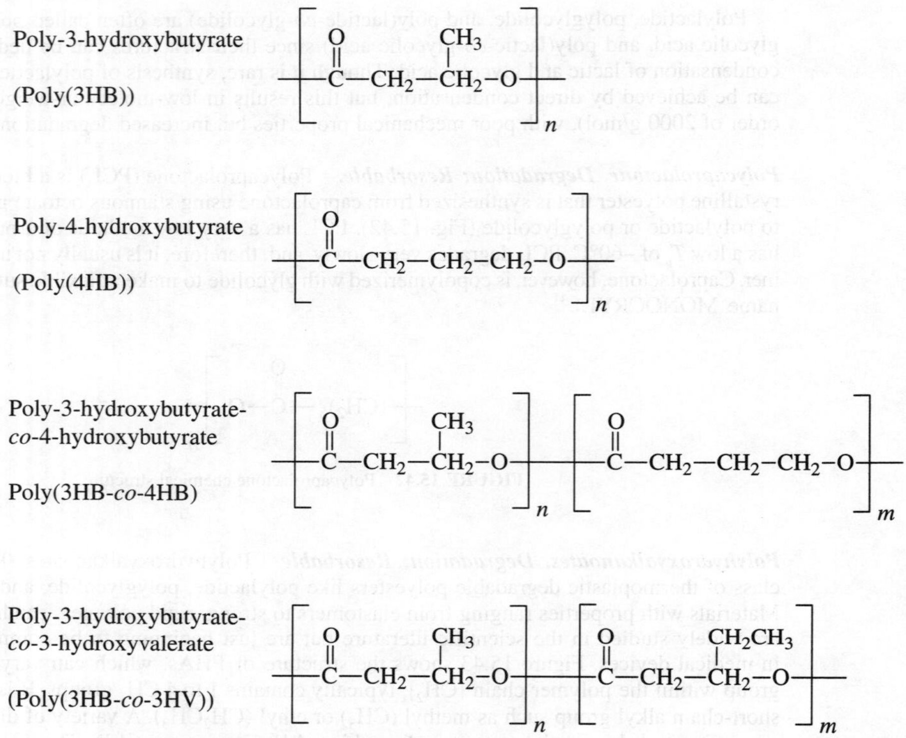

FIGURE 15.44 Chemical structures of different PHAs.

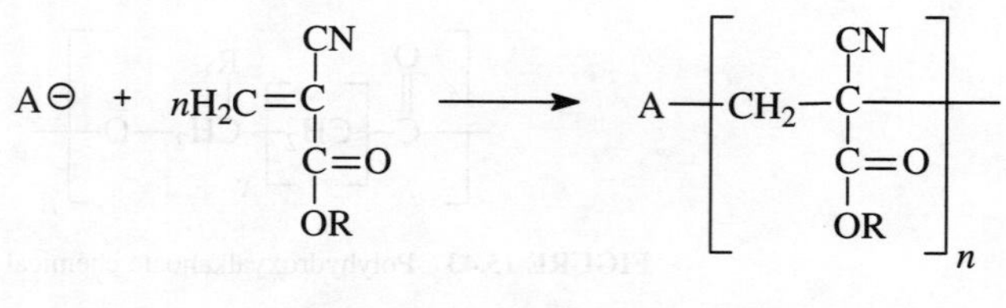

FIGURE 15.45 Polycyanoacrylate chemical structure.

Micro- and nanospheres can also be prepared by dispersion and emulsion polymerization and loaded with drugs for drug delivery applications.

Degradation is slow at neutral or acidic conditions, but above pH 7 polycyanoacrylates degrade faster. Formaldehyde is one of the degradation products (especially for methyl cyanoacrylate); therefore there is some question as to the safety of polycyanoacrylates.[33–35] Degradation rates decrease with increasing alkyl chain length (R) since hydrophobicity increases with alkyl chain length. Degradation occurs at the polymer surface; therefore surface degradation rates are highly surface area dependent. For example, poly(ethyl cyanoacrylate) microspheres[36] degrade completely in PBS (pH 7.4) in 4 to 20 hours, depending on polymerization conditions. Smaller-sized poly(methyl cyanoacrylate) nanospheres degrade completely in 20 minutes in PBS at pH 7.4 and 1 hour in fetal calf serum.[37] The longer alkyl chain poly(isobutyl cyanoacrylate) and poly(isohexyl cyanoacrylate) nanospheres take over 24 hours to degrade completely.[37] Larger poly(ethyl cyanoacrylate) particles, near 100 μm in size, take weeks to degrade completely at pH = 7.4 due to their small surface area compared to micro- and nanospheres.[34]

15.4 BIOCOMPATIBILITY CONSIDERATIONS

No discussion of biomaterials would be proper nor complete without a short consideration of biocompatibility. Biocompatibility is a widely used, yet imprecisely defined term intended to describe the body's response to a biomaterial. Implanted and blood-contacting biomaterials have received considerable attention in this regard. In the case of implanted biomaterials, determination of biocompatibility is synonymous with the evaluation of inflammatory and immune reactions generated in response to a biomaterial. A critical point that cannot be overstated is that there is not a blanket approval of a biomaterial as biocompatible; rather, approvals are for specific materials for specific uses, in specific applications and/or within specific devices. When considering the biocompatibility of a biomaterial, the operant phrase is, "it depends…." It (biocompatibility) depends on the following[38,39]:

- Material type and composition.
- Size, morphology, architecture, and microstructure.
- Degradation and bioabsorbtion modes and by-products/products.
- Release of leachable materials (not degradation related).
- Mechanical properties.
- Surface properties such as surface energy and roughness.
- Post implantation proteinaceous coating composition.
- Material bioactivity (immunological).
- Anatomic site conditions, specifics, demands, and requirements.

Hence, biocompatibility is evaluated on a case-by-case basis.

Over the years, important generalizations informed by numerous studies of the biological responses to implanted materials have been developed around biocompatibility. A widely shared viewpoint is that a biocompatible material will elicit a so-called "foreign body reaction (FBR)" that is "mild" and "uncomplicated" rather than stimulate unintended, antigenically driven immune responses against the implant directly, a leachant or a degradation product.[40–43] For biostable (nonabsorbable) materials, this FBR would ultimately resolve in the formation of an essentially avascular, thin (50 to 200 μm)[44] collagenous envelope around—but not adhered to—the implanted biomaterial, ostensibly sequestering it from the body at some level both physically and immunogenically.[40–42] Further, the overall response would also be limited in time and completed rather quickly, lasting ideally for no more than a few weeks.[41] In the case of resorbable or biodegradable biomaterials, the ultimate resolution is complete bioabsorbtion of the implanted biomaterial. However, depending on material characteristics such as the rate of bioabsorbtion (i.e., in vivo degradation or clearance rate: days-years depending largely on the material composition), collagenous encapsulation can occur around such implanted biomaterials as well.[45,46] Implicit in the above is that the implanted "biocompatible" biomaterial induces minimal to no alterations in the wound-healing program typical for the otherwise healthy/normal tissue in question. Consequently, the implant site ideally becomes quiescent as rapidly as possible and the implanted biomaterial becomes essentially ignored by the body for all intents and purposes.[47,48]

Defining and evaluating biocompatibility are becoming increasingly complex, however, as more and more biomaterials are designed to be "bioactive" and intentionally stimulate and/or modulate cells and processes involved in, for example, the inflammatory and immune response(s)/cascades to implanted materials. Moving forward, thorough evaluations of the bioactivity of materials in terms of the character of the inflammatory and wound healing responses (e.g., cytokines, cell populations, and cell polarizations) will likely be central to biocompatibility determinations.[40,42]

Currently of particular interest is the development of implanted biomaterials (both biostable and bioabsorbable) that tune these aforementioned biological response(s) upon implantation to facilitate rapid in vivo vascularization and tissue integration. This rapid vascularization in and around implanted biomaterial systems is particularly important when biomaterials serve as delivery systems and/or scaffolds for transplanted cells, which require oxygen and nutrients to survive.[49,50] Therefore, biocompatibility will continue to have a "living" definition determined by a set of questions and guidelines to be asked and applied to specific applications of biomaterials and devices.

15.5 A NOTE ON TISSUE ENGINEERING APPLICATIONS

As mentioned in the introductory section of this chapter, no polymer can fully replace the functions of healthy tissue. Hence, the best outcome is often to have the polymer undergo biodegradation/resorption and replacement by appropriate tissue. Tissue engineering (TE), a subset of regenerative medicine, is a field involving multiple disciplines that aims to restore physiologic function(s) through regeneration or replacement of cells, tissues, and organs that have been lost and/or damaged.[51] Over the past decades, advances in TE have generated excitement around TE-based alternatives for organ transplantation and reconstructive surgery. Two general areas are included in this approach: immunoisolation and regeneration scaffolds.

Immunoisolation serves to isolate foreign cells from the host immunological environment while allowing nutrients and product to pass through the membrane. Since antibodies are above 100,000 Da molecular weight, and cells of the immune system are large, many of the membranes used for this have a molecular weight cutoff of about 50,000 Da. The main target of immunoisolation strategies is treatment of type 1 diabetes, which requires insulin supplementation (insulin molecular weight is 5808 Da). However, there has only been ambiguous progress toward a working implantable insulin production/delivery system. The polymers used for such devices are film forming, slow degrading (e.g., alginate/polylysine "layer-by-layer" structures), or nondegradable materials similar to those used in dialysis membranes (e.g., polyacrylates). More recent and successful applications have been in the area of biotechnology.[52]

The main focus of the TE field has been on regeneration scaffolds, and this area is very active with clinical products in large-scale use. It is commonly posited that tissue scaffolds help target cells to form and integrate tissue(s) of interest, ultimately resulting in functional recovery. Tissue scaffolds can therefore be described as a three-dimensional (3D), "open" systems comprised of biomaterials possessing at least two of the following features: (1) maintains space, geometry, or architecture, (2) delivers and/or reposits biologics of interest (cells, factors, ligands, receptors, drugs, etc.), (3) stimulates and integrates with growing cells and tissues, and (4) blocks the advance of elements adverse to regeneration (e.g., deleterious cytokines or scar forming cells).[51,53,54]

Scaffolds act as habitats wherein cells can take up residence and carry out various life processes (differentiation, metabolism, mitosis, etc.); essential tissue scaffold features are well articulated in several texts and are summarized below.[39,51,53,55] Conventionally, scaffolds should possess highly porous microstructures with large surface/volume ratios; the pores should be sized for the application, and an interconnected pore structure (sponge-like) is usually regarded as beneficial. Degradability is typically required, and ideally, degradation rates are tailored to match the rate of developing "neotissue."[53] Furthermore, scaffold materials and potential products generated from biodegradation should not be toxic, particularly to those cells and tissues of interest.[39,51,53,55] Scaffolds are also often required to maintain form, provide physiologically matched mechanical properties, and encourage adhesion, growth, migration, differentiation, and/or phenotypic function of target cells.[39,51,53,55] Scaffolds should also likely facilitate rapid in vivo vascularization and approximate the key target tissue extracellular matrix physicochemical properties critical to functional recovery.

Degradable polymers are commonly used in TE strategies and include the previously discussed polymers as well as others such as small intestine submucosa (SIS).[56] This material, similar to the composition of natural sausage casing, is typically derived from the intestinal extracellular matrix of pigs and has been used in over a million human patients for multiple applications. Other natural materials are used (fibrin glue, collagen, alginate, etc.) as well as most of the degradable materials mentioned earlier in this chapter. In particular, most work using synthetic biomaterials has involved polylactic acid and copolymers with glycolic acid. The main differences involved for this application include surface modification for selective cell attachment, controlled release of signal molecules (usually proteins), and geometry (e.g., foams, fibers, and patches).

Foams, fibers, mats, and gels are commonplace scaffold morphologies found in TE applications.[57] Foams (random or structured) can be produced simply through lyophilization, phase separation, gas foaming, and particle leaching methods. These methods can be used individually or in combination. Fibers can be formed and then further processed into woven and nonwoven mats, and polymer polymerization and aggregation methods are frequently used to prepare gels. Choosing the proper tissue scaffold morphology is considered vital and often depends on the primary goal of the TE venture, i.e., the tissue-specific biological aims of the scaffold.

Although outside the scope of this chapter, it is important to note much effort has gone into investigating alternative approaches using decellularized scaffolds derived from allogeneic or xenogeneic sources as matrices for seeding with stem cells. Works on the heart,[58] lung,[59] bladder,[60] kidney,[61–64] liver, [65,66] and pancreas[67] have been described in the literature to date. Additionally, commercial product exists for skin, nerve,[68] and bone tissue regeneration.[69] Recent reviews list dozens of other commercially available materials and are incomplete.[70] While these decellularized systems are appropriate for a number of applications, a number of issues remain including immune responses to foreign proteins and glycosylations, and removal or denaturation of matrix proteins by the extraction process. Especially for complex tissues, as opposed to the more simple geometry most often available, removal of such potentially immunogenic proteins may be a significant barrier to overcome. There are many books and research groups focused on TE, and most physicians feel that this area has great promise for the future.

15.6 POLYMER STERILIZATION PROCESS SELECTION

Implantable medical devices are required to be sterile for patient safety and to meet regulatory requirements. For ethical reasons and to ensure consistent results, biomaterials implanted in animals for research should also be sterile. Similarly, biomaterials used in cell culture systems are ideally sterile to prevent microbial contamination of the media, which of course will influence the cellular activity and health.

Sterilization processes including chemical, radiation, and heat sterilization generally have some impact on biopolymer chemical structure and properties, which depending on the sterilization method and material may include chain scission (molecular weight reduction), cross-linking, oxidation, and/or covalent bonding of the sterilant to the polymer. These chemical changes have the potential to influence the polymer physical properties and cellular response in vitro or in vivo. Sterilization, especially heat sterilization such as dry heat and moist heat (steam), may also impact physical structure such as crystallinity and implant shape (because of phase transformations), which may influence physical properties and device design. Since sterilization influences the biomaterial structure and properties, sterilization process selection and the impact of sterilization should be carefully considered and studied for translational research and as part of product development when using biopolymers. Sterilization of drug delivery systems composed of polymers and drugs further complicates sterilization since the method must be compatible with both the drug and the delivery matrix.[71]

See definitions in Sec. 15.6.1 for sterilization-related terms. Sterility is the state of being free from viable microorganisms. This definition implies that sterilization processes must be capable of inactivating resistant microorganisms including bacterial endospores (often referred to simply as *spores*). High-level disinfection is similar to sterilization except that high-level disinfection is capable of inactivating bacterial endospores but only when they exist in relatively low quantities. For liquid chemical disinfectants such as glutaraldehyde, hydrogen peroxide, or peracetic acid, sterilization may be achieved by using a longer exposure time than is required for high-level disinfection. Table 15.8 shows examples for sterilization methods and different levels of disinfection; the table was designed for medical instrumentation, but the same principles and processes are used for biomaterials and medical devices intended for implantation.

Terminal sterilization involves sterilizing materials or products after packaging within a sterile barrier. This form of sterilization is often preferred by the pharmaceutical and medical device industry since after sterilization the sterility is conveniently maintained by the sterile barrier package, which may be a pouch or tray sealed prior to sterilization. On the other hand, if sterilization occurs prior to packaging the sterility must be maintained by handling the product in a controlled (aseptic) environment to prevent recontamination.

For commercial medical devices, sterilization validation is required to ensure a low probability of a nonsterile product unit following sterilization. Since sterilization is based on statistical probabilities for microbial inactivation, absolute statements about the sterility of a given product unit after sterilization cannot be made. Instead a probability of a unit being nonsterile termed the *sterility assurance level* (SAL) is established as part of sterilization validation. For implantable medical devices, regulatory agencies recommend an SAL is 10^{-6}, which is a one in a million probability of a nonsterile unit after sterilization.[72]

15.6.1 Sterilization Definitions[73]

Sterility State of being free from viable microorganisms.

Sterility assurance level (SAL) Probability of a single viable microorganism occurring on an item after sterilization. The term *SAL* takes a quantitative value, generally 10^{-6} or 10^{-3}. When applying this quantitative value to assurance of sterility, a SAL of 10^{-6} has a lower value but provides a greater assurance of sterility than a SAL of 10^{-3}.

Sterilization Validated process used to render product free from viable microorganisms.

Sterile barrier system Minimum package that prevents ingress of microorganisms and allows aseptic presentation of product at the point of use.

Terminal sterilization Process whereby product is sterilized within its sterile barrier system.

15.6.2 Sterilization Methods

Sterilization methods are often divided into two main categories: chemical methods where a chemical sterilant is applied as a liquid, gas, or vapor and physical methods such as filtration, radiation, and heat. In this section, the more common sterilization methods are described including their mechanism of action and potential impacts on different biopolymers.

Table 15.9 shows general compatibility guidelines for common medical device polymers and sterilization methods. The table is a rough guide; the specific polymer characteristics and intended application will influence which sterilization method and sterilization process parameters are ultimately suitable.

Sterile Filtration. Sterile filtration in an aseptic environment is a convenient method to sterilize polymer solutions using 0.22 micron or smaller filters. Viscous solutions such as hyaluronic acid may be difficult to sterilize by sterile filtration and these solutions are often steam-sterilized, although this results in a reduction in molecular weight and viscosity.[74] Sterile filtration is not a terminal sterilization method; therefore, the filling operation must be performed in a controlled (aseptic) environment.

Liquid Chemical Sterilization. Liquid chemical sterilization is easy to apply and does not require complex machinery; therefore, it is convenient for sterilization in a research environment.

TABLE 15.8 Overview of Common Sterilization and Disinfection Methods

Process	Level of microbial inactivation	Method	Examples (with processing times)	Health care application (examples)
Sterilization	Destroys all microorganisms, including bacterial spores	High temperature	Steam (~40 min), dry heat (1-6 hr depending on temperature)	Heat-tolerant critical (surgical instruments) and semicritical patient care items
		Low temperature	Ethylene oxide gas (~15 hr), hydrogen peroxide gas plasma (28–52 min), ozone (~4 hr), hydrogen peroxide vapour (55 min)	Heat-sensitive critical and semi-critical patient care items
		Liquid immersion in chemical sterilants	Chemical sterilants: >2% glutaraldehyde (~10 hr); 1.12% glutaraldehyde with 1.93% phenol (12 hr); 7.35% hydrogen peroxide with 0.23% peracetic acid (3 hr); 8.3% hydrogen peroxide and 7.0% peracetic acid (5 hr); 7.5% hydrogen peroxide (6 hr); 1.0% hydrogen peroxide with 0.08% peracetic acid (8 hr); ≥0.2% peracetic acid (12 min at 50–56°C)	Heat-sensitive critical and semi-critical patient care items that can be immersed
High-level disinfection (HLD)	Destroys all micro-organisms except high numbers of bacterial spores	Heat automated	Pasteurization (65–77°C, 30 min)	Heat-sensitive semicritical items (e.g., Respiratory therapy equipment)
		Liquid immersion	Chemical sterilants/HLDs: ≥2% glutaraldehyde (20–45 min); 0.55% orthophthalaldehyde (12 min); 1.12% glutaraldehyde with 1.93% phenol (20 min); 7.35% hydrogen peroxide with 0.23% peracetic acid (15 min); 7.5% hydrogen peroxide (30 min); 1% hydrogen peroxide with 0.08% peracetic acid (25 min); 400–450 ppm chlorine (10 min); 2.0% hydrogen peroxide (8 min); 3.4% glutaraldehyde with 26% isopropanol (10 min)	Heat-sensitive semicritical items (e.g., GI endoscopes, bronchoscopes, endocavity probes)
Intermediate-level disinfection	Destroys vegetative bacteria, mycobacteria, most viruses, most fungi but not bacterial spores	Liquid contact	EPA-registered hospital disinfectant with label claim regarding tuberculocidal activity (e.g., Chlorine-based products, phenolics, improved hydrogen peroxide exposure times at least 1 min)	Noncritical patient care item (blood pressure cuff) or surface with visible blood.
Low-level disinfection	Destroys vegetative bacteria, some fungi and viruses but not mycobacteria or spores	Liquid contact	EPA-registered hospital disinfectant with no label claim regarding tuberculocidal activity (e.g., Chlorine-based products, phenolics, improved hydrogen peroxide, quaternary ammonium compounds-exposure times at least 1 minute) or 70–90% alcohol.	Noncritical patient care item (blood pressure cuff) or surface (bedside table) with no visible blood.

Source: Reproduced from Rutala, W.A., and Weber D. J., "Disinfection and sterilization: An overview." *American Journal of Infection Control*, **41**(5):S2-S5 (2013).[99]

TABLE 15.9 General Compatibility Guidelines for Common Medical Device Plastics and Sterilization Methods

Polymer	Polymer abbreviation	Steam	Dry heat	Ethylene oxide	Gamma radiation	Electron Beam
Polyolefins						
High-density polyethylene	HDPD	Poor	Poor	Good	Good	Good
Low-density polyethylene	LDPE	Poor	Poor	Good	Good	Good
Ultrahigh molecular weight polyethylene	UHMWPE	Poor	Poor	Good	Good	Good
Polypropylene[a]	PP	Good	Fair	Good	Fair	Fair
Polypropylene copolymers	PP copolymers	Good	Fair	Good	Fair	Fair
Cyclo olefin copolymer	COC	Fair	Fair	Good	Good	Good
Polyvinyl Chloride						
PVC plasticised[a,b]	PVC	Fair	Fair	Good	Good	Good
PVC unplasticised[a,b]	PVC	Poor	Poor	Good	Fair	Fair
Polystyrene/styrenics						
Polystyrene	PS	Poor	Poor	Good	Good	Good
Acrylonitrile butadiene styrene	ABS	Poor	Poor	Good	Good	Good
Styrene acrylonitrile	SAN	Poor	Poor	Good	Good	Good
Acrylonytrile styrene acrylate	ASA	Poor	Poor	Good	Good	Good
Methyl methacrylate acrylonitrile butadiene styrene	MABS	Poor	Poor	Good	Good	Good
Styrene butadiene copolymer	SBC	Poor	Poor	Good	Good	Good
Acrylics[a,b]		Poor	Poor	Good	Good	Good
Polycarbonates[a,b]		Fair	Fair	Good	Good	Good
High heat polycarbonates[a,b]		Good	Good	Good	Good	Good
Polyurethanes		Poor	Poor	Good	Good	Good
Acetals		Good	Good	Good	Poor	Poor
Polyamides						
Nylon 6, Nylon 66		Fair	Fair	Good	Fair	Fair
Aromatic		Good	Good	Good	Good	Good
Nylon 12, 10, 6/12		Poor	Poor	Good	Fair	Fair
Polyesters						
Polybutylene terephthalate	PBT	Fair	Fair	Good	Good	Good
Polyethylene terephthalate	PET	Poor	Poor	Good	Good	Good
Copolyesters		Poor	Poor	Good	Good	Good
High-temperature thermoplastics						
Polysulfones	PS	Good	Good	Good	Good	Good
Polyphenylene sulphide	PPS	Good	Good	Good	Good	Good
Liquid crystal polymer	LCP	Good	Good	Good	Good	Good
Polyether imide	PEI	Fair	Fair	Good	Good	Good
Polyamide imide	PAI	Fair	Fair	Good	Good	Good

TABLE 15.9 General Compatibility Guidelines for Common Medical Device Plastics and Sterilization Methods (*Continued*)

Polymer	Polymer abbreviation	Steam	Dry heat	Ethylene oxide	Gamma radiation	Electron Beam
Polyether ether ketone	PEEK	Good	Good	Good	Good	Good
Fluoropolymers						
Polytetrafluoroethylene	PTEE	Fair	Fair	Good	Poor	Poor
Fluorinated ethylene propylene	FEP	Good	Good	Good	Fair	Fair
Perfluoroalkoxy alkane	PFA	Good	Good	Good	Good	Good
Ethylene chlorotrifluoroethylene	ECTFE	Good	Good	Good	Good	Good
Ethylene tetrafluoroethylene	ETFE	Good	Good	Good	Good	Good
Polyvinyl fluoride	PVF	Good	Good	Good	Good	Good
Polyvinylidene fluoride	PVF2	Good	Good	Good	Good	Good
Elastomers						
Silicones		Good	Good	Good	Good	Good
Thermoplastic	TPU	Poor	Fair	Good	Good	Good
Thermoplastic copolyester elastomer	TPC	Poor	Good	Good	Good	Good
Thermoplastic polyamide elastomer	TPA	Poor	Poor	Good	Good	Good
Thermoplastic styrenic elastomer	TPS	Poor	Poor	Good	Good	Good
Thermoplastic olefin elastomer	TPO	Poor	Fair	Good	Good	Good
Biopolymers						
Poly-L-lactide (Poly-L-lactic acid)	PLLA	Fair	Good	Good	Good	Good
Poly-DL-lactide (Poly-DL-lactic acid)	PLA	Poor	Fair	Good	Good	Good
Polyhydroxybutyrate	PHB	Poor	Poor	Good	Fair	Fair
Polyglycolide (Polyglycolic acid)	PGA	Good	Good	Good	Good	Good
Poly lactide-co-glycolic acid	PLGA	Poor	Poor	Good	Fair	Fair
Polycaprolactone	PCL	Fair	Good	Good	Good	Good
Thermosets		Good	Good	Good	Good	Good

[a]Radiation grade should be considered for gamma and ebeam sterilization.
[b]PVC, acrylics, and PC require corrective tint to compensate for discoloration.
Source: Reproduced from Sastri, V. R., *Plastics in Medical Devices: Properties, Requirements, and Applications.*[100]

One disadvantage is that it is not a terminal sterilization method and if performed in industry it requires significant environmental controls and aseptic process validations to ensure the product is not recontaminated following sterilization. Common liquid chemical sterilants are aqueous peroxides such as hydrogen peroxide and peracetic acid, and aldehydes such as glutaraldehyde and formaldehyde. Peroxides inactivate microorganisms by oxidizing proteins, cell wall components, and DNA, which inactivates enzymes, interferes with cell transport, and prevents replication.[75,76] Aldehydes inactivate microorganisms by cross-linking proteins, especially those in the cell wall, thereby interfering with cell transport and other cell functions.[76]

Aldehydes are more toxic than peroxides and peroxides break down into relatively harmless compounds (water and oxygen for hydrogen peroxide, and acetic acid and oxygen for peracetic acid);[76] therefore, sterilization with peroxides is often preferable over aldehydes. Aldehydes covalently link to proteins and other natural polymers that contain primary amines like chitosan by cross-linking,

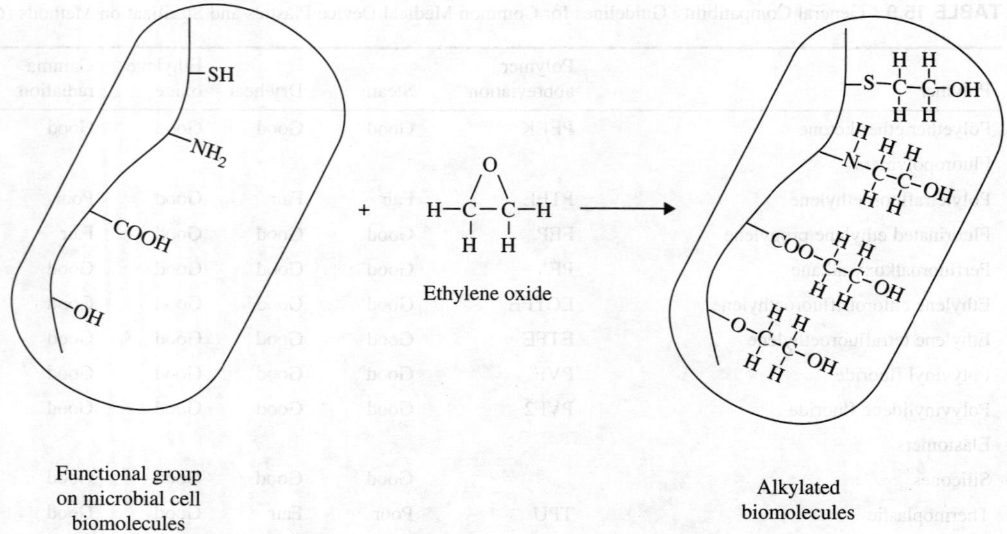

FIGURE 15.46 Reaction of EO with reactive chemical groups within microorganisms.

which adds a foreign molecule and changes the material physical properties. Therefore, many natural polymers should not be sterilized with aldehydes unless cross-linking is beneficial for applications requiring enhanced mechanical properties or structural integrity. Peroxides affect the chemical structure of natural polymers to some degree and the effects of sterilization with peroxides should be considered and studied when using peroxides for natural polymer sterilization.[77,78]

Liquid chemical sterilization is generally compatible with biostable plastics and many elastomers since they are relatively nonreactive and are not degraded by water with short-term exposure. Resorbable polymers such as the degradable polyesters and polyhydroxyalkanoates may degrade during and after liquid chemical sterilization since they degrade by hydrolysis.[79]

Ethylene Oxide (EO) Sterilization. Ethylene oxide (EO) is the most common gas sterilant used for industrial sterilization. Ethylene oxide alkylates hydroxyl, primary amine, sulfhydryl, and carboxylic acid groups on different molecules within the microbial cell including DNA, proteins, and polysaccharides (see Fig. 15.46). The primary mechanism of action for EO is thought to be preventing microbial replication by altering microbial DNA, but alteration of proteins and other molecules within the cell may also contribute to inactivation.[80]

EO sterilization is typically a terminal sterilization where products are packaged in breathable sterile barrier packaging such as Tyvek®. Since EO sterilization involves evacuating the product prior to EO gas exposure, EO can only be applied to dry materials.

Typical ethylene oxide cycles are performed within the following parameter ranges:[79]

- Temperature: 30 to 65°C
- Humidity: 40 to 80 percent RH
- Ethylene oxide exposure time: 3 to 6 hours

The ethylene oxide cycle may last up to 2 days since the cycle includes evacuation and humidification prior to ethylene oxide exposure and several evacuation and air wash cycles to remove EO from the chamber. Several days of heated aeration are often required following the cycle to reduce toxic EO residuals within the biomaterial.

EO is known to be compatible with a wide range of polymers. However, cycle temperature, aeration temperature, and EO cycle humidity may need to be adjusted for temperature- and humidity-sensitive materials like degradable polymers. Toxic EO residuals include ethylene oxide, ethylene glycol, and ethylene chlorohydrin. Ethylene glycol results from the reaction of EO and water; therefore, hygroscopic materials are susceptible to ethylene glycol residuals that are difficult to remove by aeration. Similarly, chlorides react with EO to form ethylene chlorohydrin which is also difficult to remove by aeration; therefore, chlorides should be limited in the processing of biomaterials that are EO sterilized or they should be reduced by washing prior to EO exposure.[81]

Vaporous Hydrogen Peroxide (VHP) and Vaporous Peracetic Acid (VPA) Sterilization. Vaporous hydrogen peroxide and peracetic acid sterilization processes are performed at room temperature or slightly above room temperature and involve placing the biomaterial or device in a chamber, evacuating the chamber and introducing an aqueous vapor of hydrogen peroxide or peracetic acid into the chamber. The mechanism of inactivation is the same as for liquid chemical sterilization using the same sterilants. Vaporous sterilization may be performed as terminal sterilization since it is compatible with breathable sterile barrier packaging such as Tyvek. Similar to ethylene oxide, VHP and VPA are performed using one or more evacuation in preparation for the sterilant vapor and one or more evacuation to reduce sterilant levels in the product. Because of the evacuation, hydrated polymers are not suitable for VHP and VPA. The product is exposed to water in the form of vapor but since it is not immersed in water, the vaporous form may be preferable for resorbable polymers. Cellulose is known to absorb hydrogen peroxide sterilant, degrade sterilant, and may be difficult to aerate; therefore, sterilization of cellulose or the use of paper packaging is not recommended.[82] Other natural polymers such as collagen may pose similar challenges to VHP and VPA, although the authors of this chapter did not find any scientific studies on compatibility of natural polymers with VHP or VPA sterilization.

Steam (Moist Heat) and Dry Heat Sterilization. Sterilization using heat is a very consistent and reliable form of sterilization, although many plastics (rigid polymers) are not compatible since their dimensional stability may be compromised if the plastics are subject to phase transitions such as glass transitions and melting during the sterilization cycle. Steam sterilization can lower the molecular weight of polymers like polyesters that are susceptible to hydrolytic degradation.[83]

Table 15.10 shows temperatures for inactivation of different heat-resistant bacteria showing typical sterilization temperatures of 121°C for moist heat and 170°C for dry heat. Moist heat requires lower temperatures because of the improved heat transfer properties of steam over air. Aqueous polymer solutions and hydrogels are often sterilized by moist heat, although this mode

TABLE 15.10 Times Required for Lethal Effect on Bacterial Spores by Thermal Exposure[80]

	Moist heat time (min)			Dry heat time (min)		
Organism	100°C	110°C	121°C	120°C	140°C	170°C
B. anthracis	5–15	–	–	–	180	–
C. botulinum	330	90	10	120	60	15
C. welchii	5–10	–	–	50	5	–
C. Tetani	5–15	–	–	–	15	–
Soil bacilli	>1020	120	6	–	–	15

Source: "Table 9" in Avis, K. E., "Sterilization," in *Theory and Practice of Industrial Pharmacy*, 2nd ed., Lachman, Leiberman, and Kanig (eds.). Lea and Febiger, Philadelphia. **1976**, pp. 567–585.[101]

TABLE 15.11 Radiation Penetration for Different Forms of Ionizing Radiation[80]

Radiation type	Source or energy	ᵃUseful Penetration (cm) Irradiating from one side	Irradiating from both sides
Y rays	Co^{60}	10.2	40.6
X-rays	50 KeV	<0.1	~0.5
	10 MeV	12.7	61.0
EBeam (Cathode rays)	1 MeV	~0.3	~0.8
		1.8	4.3
		3.8	8.6
B rays	Sr^{90}	<0.1	~0.3

ᵃThe dose received at any one point will exceed 60% of that at points of maximum intensity.

of sterilization may degrade the polymer molecular weight.[74,84] Dry products are packaged in breathable Tyvek or paper packaging for steam sterilization and in nylon pouches for dry heat sterilization.

Radiation Sterilization. Radiation sterilization involves the application of ionizing radiation (gamma rays, x-rays, or high-energy electrons) to inactivate microorganisms. Radiation sterilization is a bulk sterilization since the radiation can pass through materials and is typically a terminal sterilization method as it is compatible with a wide variety of sterile barrier packaging. Radiation sterilization requires specialized equipment or use of a radioisotope (Cobalt 60 for gamma); therefore, it often requires a third-party sterilizer.

Ionizing radiation inactivates microorganisms by alterations to DNA and other biomolecules within microorganisms because of the initial ionizing event and from subsequent reactions with free radicals that form the initial ionizing event.[85]

For a given polymer, the penetration depth into the material is proportional to the electron density, which is roughly proportional to the mass density.[85] Radiation penetration profiles into polymers, water, and food are therefore similar. Gamma rays and high-energy x-rays penetrate deeper into materials than high-energy electrons used in terminal sterilization (see Table 15.11).

Polymers may undergo chain scission (and resulting molecular weight reduction) and/or cross-linking during and after irradiation. Both chain scission and cross-linking often occur simultaneously and which degradation mechanism dominates depends on the chemical structure. Cross-linking generally dominates in polymers with carbon–carbon backbones that have one or more hydrogen attached to each carbon. Scission dominates when hydrogen is not attached to the carbons in the backbone; such is the case with PTFE. Aromatic polymers such as PET and polystyrene are generally less affected by irradiation than nonaromatic polymers.[80]

Free radicals in the polymer may cause degradation during post-irradiation storage; therefore, the impact of storage after irradiation should be taken into account.[86] Oxidation during irradiation and with storage is known to occur especially for polyethylene; therefore, these materials are often packaged in nitrogen or other inert gasses prior to irradiation.[87]

ACKNOWLEDGMENTS

The authors would like to acknowledge Alicia Willenberg, MS and Mona Doshi, PhD for their significant efforts helping to review and edit this chapter.

REFERENCES

1. *GFedia of Polymer Science and Engineering*, Vol. 17. New York: Wiley, 1985, pp. 198–257.
2. Chen, X. H., McCarthy, S. P., and Gross, R. A., "Synthesis and characterization of L-lactide-ethylene oxide multiblock copolymers." *Macromolecules*, **30**(15):4295–4301 (1997).
3. Hu, D. S.-G., and Liu, H.-J., "Structural analysis and degradation behavior in polyethylene glycol/poly(L-lactide) copolymers." *Journal of Applied Polymer Science*, **51**(3):473-482 (1994).
4. Yamaoka, T., Takahashi, Y., Ohta, T., Miyamoto, M., Murakami, A., and Kimura, Y., "Synthesis and properties of multiblock copolymers consisting of poly(L-lactic acid) and poly(oxypropylene-co-oxyethylene) prepared by direct polycondensation." *Journal of Polymer Science Part a-Polymer Chemistry*, **37** (10):1513–1521 (1999).
5. Youxin, L., and Kissel, T., "Synthesis and properties of biodegradable ABA triblock copolymers consisting of poly(L-lactic acid) or poly (L-lactic-co-glycolic acid) A-blocks attached to central poly (oxyethylene) B-blocks." *Journal of Controlled Release* **27**(3):247–257 (1993).
6. Park, K. D., Kim, Y. S., Han, D. K., Kim, Y. H., Lee, E. H. B., Suh, H., and Choi, K. S., "Bacterial adhesion on PEG modified polyurethane surfaces." *Biomaterials*, **19**(7–9):851–859 (1998).
7. Razatos, A., Ong, Y. L., Boulay, F., Elbert, D. L., Hubbell, J. A., Sharma, M. M., and Georgiou, G., "Force measurements between bacteria and poly(ethylene glycol)-coated surfaces." *Langmuir*, **16**(24):9155–9158 (2000).
8. Vigo, T. L., and Leonas, K. K., "Antimicrobial activity of fabrics containing crosslinked polyethylene glycols." *Textile Chemist & Colorist & American Dyestuff Reporter*, **1**(1): 42-46 (1999).
9. Guo, Y. Q., and Hui, S. W., "Poly(ethylene glycol)-conjugated surfactants promote or inhibit aggregation of phospholipids." *Biochimica Et Biophysica Acta-Biomembranes*, **1323**(2):185–194 (1997).
10. Slepushkin, V. A., Simões, S., Dazin, P., Newman, M. S., Guo, L. S., de Lima, M. C. P., and Düzgüneş, N.,"Sterically stabilized pH-sensitive liposomes intracellular delivery of aqueous contents and prolonged circulation in vivo." *Journal of Biological Chemistry*, **272**(4):2382–2388 (1997).
11. Woodle, M. C., Newman, M. S., and Cohen, J. A., "Sterically stabilized liposomes - physical and biological properties." *Journal of Drug Targeting*, **2**(5):397–403 (1994).
12. Dunn, S. E., Brindley, A., Davis, S. S., Davies, M. C., and Illum, L., "Polystyrene-poly(ethylene glycol) (PS-PEG2000) particles as model systems for site-specific drug-delivery. 2. The effect of peg surface-density on the in vitro cell-interaction and in vivo biodistribution." *Pharmaceutical Research*, **11**(7):1016–1022 (1994).
13. Maruyama, K., Takahashi, N., Tagawa, T., Nagaike, K., and Iwatsuru, M., "Immunoliposomes bearing polyethyleneglycol-coupled Fab' fragment show prolonged circulation time and high extravasation into targeted solid tumors in vivo." *FEBS Letters*, **413**(1):177–180 (1997).
14. Verrecchia, T., Spenlehauer, G., Bazile, D. V., Murry-Brelier, A., Archimbaud, Y., and Veillard, M., "Non-stealth (poly(lactic acid/albumin)) and stealth (poly(lactic acid-polyethylene glycol)) nanoparticles as injectable drug carriers." *Journal of Controlled Release*, **36**(1):49–61 (1995).
15. Vittaz, M., Bazile, D., Spenlehauer, G., Verrecchia, T., Veillard, M., Puisieux, F., and Labarre, D., "Effect of PEO surface density on long-circulating PLA-PEO nanoparticles which are very low complement activators." *Biomaterials*, **17**(16):1575–1581 (1996).
16. Kost, J., and Goldbart, R., "Natural and modified polysaccharides," in *Handbook of Biodegradable Polymers*, Domb, A. J., Kost, J., and Wiseman, M. W. (eds.). London: Harwood Academic Publishers, 1997, pp. 282–286.
17. Qurashi, M. T., Blair, H. S., and Allen, S. J., Studies on modified chitosan membranes. 1. Preparation and characterization. *Journal of Applied Polymer Science*, 46(2):255–261 (1992).
18. Silver, F. H., and Garg, A. K., "Collagen: characterization, processing, and medical applications," in *Handbook of Biodegradable Polymers*, Domb, A. J., Kost, J., and Wiseman, M. W. (eds.). London: Harwood Academic Publishers, 1997, pp. 319–346.
19. Viswanadham, R. K., and Kramer, E. J., "Elastic properties of reconstituted collagen hollow fiber membranes." *Journal of Materials Science*, **11**(7):1254–1262 (1976).
20. Mathews, C., and Holde, K. *Biochemistry*. San Francisco: Benjamin Publishing, 1990.

21. Chivers, R. A., "In vitro tissue welding using albumin solder: bond strengths and bonding temperatures." *International Journal of Adhesion and Adhesives*, **20**(3):179–187.

22. Stillwell, R. L., Marks, M. G., Saferstein, L., and Wiseman, D. M., "Oxidized cellulose: chemistry, processing, and medical applications," in *Handbook of Biodegradable Polymers*, Domb, A. J., Kost, J., and Wiseman, M. W. (eds.). London: Harwood Academic Publishers, 1997, pp. 291–306.

23. Ratner, B. D., Hoffman, A. S., Schoen, F. J., and Lemons, J. E. (eds.), *Biomaterials Science: An Introduction to Materials in Medicine*. New York: Academic Press, 1996, p. 60.

24. Szycher, M., *Encyclopedia of Biomaterials and Biomedical Engineering*. Wnek, G. E., and Bowlin, G. L. (eds). CRC Press, 2008, pp. 2208–2214.

25. Ratner, B. D., Hoffman, A. S., Schoen, F. J., and Lemons, J. E. (eds.), *Biomaterials Science: An Introduction to Materials in Medicine*. New York: Academic Press, 1996, p. 59.

26. *Encyclopedia of Polymer Science and Engineering*, Vol. 11. New York: Wiley, 1985.

27. Ratner, B. D., Hoffman, A. S., Schoen, F. J., and Lemons, J. E. (eds.), *Biomaterials Science: An Introduction to Materials in Medicine*. New York: Academic Press, 1996, p. 247.

28. Zaikov, G. E., "Quantitative aspects of polymer degradation in the living body." *Journal of Macromolecular Science—Reviews in Macromolecular Chemistry and Physics*, **C25**(4):551–597 (1985).

29. Ratner, B. D., Hoffman, A. S., Schoen, F. J., and Lemons, J. E. (eds.), *Biomaterials Science: An Introduction to Materials in Medicine*. New York: Academic Press, 1996, p. 58.

30. Perrin, D. E., and English, J. P. "Polyglycolide and polylactide," in *Handbook of Biodegradable Polymers*, Domb, A. J., Kost, J., and Wiseman, M. W. (eds.). London: Harwood Academic Publishers, 1997, pp. 2–27.

31. Perrin, D. E., and English, J. P., "Polycaprolactone," in *Handbook of Biodegradable Polymers*, Domb, A. J., Kost, J., and Wiseman, M. W. (eds.). London: Harwood Academic Publishers, 1997, pp. 63–77.

32. Williams, S. F., and Martin, D. P., in *Polyesters III—Applications and Commercial Products*, Doi, Y., and Stenbucher, A. (eds.). New York: Wiley, 2002, pp. 91–120.

33. Leonard, F., Kulkarni, R. K., Brandes, G., Nelson, J., and Cameron, J. J., "Synthesis and degradation of poly(alkyl α-cyanoacrylates)." *Journal of Applied Polymer Science*, **10**(2):259–272 (1966).

34. Vezin, W. R., and Florence, A. T., "In vitro heterogeneous degradation of poly(n-alkyl α-cyanoacrylates)." *Journal of Biomedical Materials Research*, 14(2):93–106 (1980).

35. Wade, C. W. R., and Leonard, F., "Degradation of poly(methyl 2-cyanoacrylates)." *Journal of Biomedical Materials Research*, **6**(3):215–220 (1972).

36. Tuncel, A., Cicek, H., Hayran, M., and Piskin, E., "Monosize poly(ethylcyanoacrylate) microspheres—preparation and degradation properties." *Journal of Biomedical Materials Research*, **29**(6):721–728 (1995).

37. Müller, R H., Lherm, C., Herbert, J., and Couvreur, P., "In vitro model for the degradation of alkylcyanoacrylate nanoparticles." *Biomaterials*, 11(8):590–595 (1990).

38. Babensee, J. E., Anderson, J. M., McIntire, L. V., and Mikos, A. G., "Host response to tissue engineered devices." *Advanced Drug Delivery Reviews*, **33**(1–2):111–139 (1998).

39. Kohane, D. S., and Langer, R., "Polymeric biomaterials in tissue engineering." *Pediatric Research*, 63(5):487–491 (2008).

40. Anderson, J. M., et al., "Host reactions to biomaterials and their evaluation," in *Biomaterials*, Ratner, B. D., Hoffman, A. S., Schoen, F. J, and Lemons, J. E., (eds.). London: Elsevier, 2004, pp. 293–354.

41. Anderson, J. M., "Inflammatory and immune responses to tissue engineered devices," in *Tissue Engineering*, Fisher, J. D., Mikos, A. G., and Bronzino, J. D., (eds.). Boca Raton, FL: CRC Press, 2007.

42. Anderson, J. M., Rodriguez, A., and Chang, D. T., "Foreign body reaction to biomaterials." *Seminars in Immunology*, **20**(2):86–100 (2008).

43. Ratner, B. D., "Biocompatibility of implant materials," in *Host Response to Biomaterials*, Badylak, S. F., (ed.). London: Elsevier, 2015, pp. 37–41.

44. Ratner, B. D., "Reducing capsular thickness and enhancing angiogenesis around implant drug release systems." *Journal of Controlled Release*, 78(1–3):211–218 (2002).

45. Della Rocca, D. G., Willenberg, B. J., Qi, Y. F., Simmons, C. S., Rubiano, A., Ferreira, L. F., Huo, T., Petersen, J. W., Ruchaya, P. J., Wate, P. S., Wise, E. A., Handberga, E. M., Cogle, C. R., Batich, C. D., Byrne, B. J., and Pepine, C. J., "An injectable capillary-like microstructured alginate hydrogel improves left ventricular function after myocardial infarction in rats." *International Journal of Cardiology*, 220:149–154 (2016).

46. Bosak, A., Kwan, M. W. C., Willenberg, A., Perle, K. M. D. L., Weinstein, D., Hines, R. B., Schultz, G. S., Ross, E. A., and Willenberg, B. J., "Capillary alginate gel (Capgel™) for the treatment of full-thickness dermal wounds in a hypoxic mouse model." *International Journal of Polymeric Materials and Polymeric Biomaterials*, **68**(18):1108–1117 (2019).

47. U.S. FDA, Genrally recognizedas safe, at: https://www.fda.gov/Food/IngredientsPackagingLabeling/GRAS/. Accessed on April 2, 2019.

48. U.S. FDA, Food additive status list, at: https://www.fda.gov/Food/IngredientsPackagingLabeling/FoodAdditivesIngredients/ucm091048.htm. Accessed on April 2, 2019.

49. Vlahos, A. E., Cober, N., and Sefton, M. V., "Modular tissue engineering for the vascularization of subcutaneously transplanted pancreatic islets." *Proceedings of the National Academy of Sciences of the United States of America*, **114**(35):9337–9342 (2017).

50. Weaver, J. D., Headen, D. M., Aquart, J., Johnson, C. T., Shea, L. D., Shirwan, H., and Garcia, A. J., "Vasculogenic hydrogel enhances islet survival, engraftment, and function in leading extrahepatic sites." *Science Advances*, 3(6):e1700184 (2017).

51. Langer, R., and Vacanti, J. P., "Tissue engineering." *Science*, **260**(5110):920–926 (1993).

52. Chang, T. M. S. "Cell encapsulation technology and therapeutics," in *Tissue Engineering*, Kühtreiber, W. M., Lanza, R. P., and Chick, W. L., (eds.). Boston, MA: Birkhauser Publisher, 1999.

53. Ma, P. X., "Scaffolds for tissue fabrication." *Materials Today*, **7**(5):30–40 (2004).

54. Mooney, D. J., and Langer, R. S., "Engineering biomaterials for tissue engineering: The 10-100 micron size scale," in *The Biomedical Engineering Handbook*, Bronzine, J. D. (ed.), Boca Raton, FL: CRC Press, 1995, pp. 1609–1618.

55. Langer, R., and Peppas, N. A., "Advances in biomaterials, drug delivery, and bionanotechnology." *Aiche Journal*, **49**(12):2990–3006 (2003).

56. Badylak, S. F., "Regenerative medicine and developmental biology: the role of the extracellular matrix." *Anatomical Record Part B:The New Anatomist*, 287(1):36–41 (2005).

57. Atala, A., and Lanza, R. (eds.), *Methods of Tissue Engineering*. San Diego, CA: Academic Press, 2001.

58. Ott, H. C., Matthiesen, T. S., Goh, S. K., Black, L. D., Kren, S. M., Netoff, T. I., and Taylor, D. A., "Perfusion-decellularized matrix: using nature's platform to engineer a bioartificial heart." *Nature Medicine*, **14**(2): 213–221 (2008).

59. Ott, H. C., Clippinger, B., Conrad, C., Schuetz, C., Pomerantseva, I., Ikonomou, L., Kotton, D., and Vacanti, J. P., "Regeneration and orthotopic transplantation of a bioartificial lung." *Nature Medicine*, 16(8):927–933 (2010).

60. Song, L. J., Murphy, S. V., Yang, B., Xu, Y. M., Zhang, Y. Y., and Atala, A., "Bladder acellular matrix and its application in bladder augmentation." *Tissue Engineering Part B-Reviews*, **20**(2):163–172 (2014).

61. Ross, E. A., Abrahamson, D. R., St. John, P., Clapp, W. L., Williams, M. J., Terada, N., Hamazaki, T., Ellison, G. W., and Batich, C. D., "Mouse stem cells seeded into decellularized rat kidney scaffolds endothelialize and remodel basement membranes." *Organogenesis*, **8**(2):49–55 (2012).

62. Ross, E. A., Williams, M. J., Hamazaki, T., Terada, N., Clapp, W. L., Adin, C., Ellison, G. W., Jorgensen, M., and Batich, C. D., "Embryonic stem cells proliferate and differentiate when seeded into kidney scaffolds." *Journal of the American Society of Nephrology*, **20**(11):2338–2347 (2009).

63. Song, J. J., Guyette, J. P., Gilpin, S. E., Gonzalez, G., Vacanti, J. P., and Ott, H. C., "Regeneration and experimental orthotopic transplantation of a bioengineered kidney." *Nature Medicine*, **19**(5):646–651 (2013).

64. Willenberg, B. J., Oca-Cossio, J., Cai, Y., Brown, A. R., Clapp, W. L., Abrahamson, D. R., Terada, N., Ellison, G. W., Mathews, C. E., Batich, C. D., and Ross, E. A., "Repurposed biological scaffolds: kidney to pancreas." *Organogenesis*, **11**(2):47–57 (2015).

65. Shupe, T., Williams, M., Brown, A., Willenberg, B., and Petersen, B. E., "Method for the decellularization of intact rat liver." *Organogenesis*, **6**(2):34–136 (2010).

66. Mazza, G., Rombouts, K., Hall, A. R., Urbani, L., Luong, T. V., Al-Akkad, W., Longato, L., Brown, D., Maghsoudlou, P., Dhillon, A. P., Fuller, B., Davidson, B., Moore, K., Dhar, D., De Coppi, P., Malago, M., and Pinzani, M., "Decellularized human liver as a natural 3D-scaffold for liver bioengineering and transplantation." *Scientific Reports*, **5**:13079 (2015).

67. Goh, S. K., Bertera, S., Olsen, P., Candiello, J. E., Halfter, W., Uechi, G., Balasubramani, M., Johnson, S. A., Sicari, B. M., Kollar, E., Badylak, S. F., and Banerjee, I., "Perfusion-decellularized pancreas as a natural 3D scaffold for pancreatic tissue and whole organ engineering." *Biomaterials*, **34**(28):6760–6772 (2013).

68. Neubauer, D., Graham, J. B., and Muir, D., "Chondroitinase treatment increases the effective length of acellular nerve grafts." *Experimental Neurology*, **207**(1):163–170 (2007).

69. Miyazaki, M., Tsumura, H., Wang, J. C., and Alanay, A., "An update on bone substitutes for spinal fusion." *European Spine Journal*, **18**(6):783–799 (2009).

70. Scarritt, M., Murdock, M., and Badylak, S. F., "Biologic scaffolds composed of extracellular matrix for regenerative medicine," in *Principles of Regenerative Medicine*, 3rd ed., Atala, A., Lanza, R. P., Mikos, A. G., and Nerem, R. (eds.). Academic Press, 2019, pp. 613–626.

71. Lambert, B. J., Mendelson, T. A., and Craven, M. D., "Radiation and ethylene oxide terminal sterilization experiences with drug eluting stent products." *Aaps Pharmscitech*, **12**(4):1116–1126 (2011).

72. FDA guidance: Submission and review of sterility information in premarket notification (510(k)). Submissions for devices labeled as sterile guidance for industry and Food and Drug Administration Staff. 2016.

73. ANSI/AAMI/ISO TIR11139:2006. Sterilization of healthcare products—Vocabulary.

74. Swann, D. A., Kuo, J. W., and Pinsky, V., U.S. Patent No. 5,621,093. Wahsington, CD: U.S. Patent and Trademark Office, 1997.

75. Finnegan, M., Linley, E., Denyer, S. P., McDonnell, G., Simons, C., and Maillard, J. Y., "Mode of action of hydrogen peroxide and other oxidizing agents: differences between liquid and gas forms." *Journal of Antimicrobial Chemotherapy*, **65**(10):2108–2115 (2010).

76. McDonnell, G., and Russell, A. D., "Antiseptics and disinfectants: activity, action, and resistance." *Clinical Microbiology Reviews*, **12**(1):147–179 (2010).

77. Hodde, J., Janis, A., Ernst, D., Zopf, D., Sherman, D., and Johnson, C., "Effects of sterilization on an extracellular matrix scaffold: Part I. Composition and matrix architecture." *Journal of Materials Science—Materials in Medicine*, **18**(4):537–543 (2007).

78. Hodde, J., Janis, A., and Hiles, M., "Effects of sterilization on an extracellular matrix scaffold: Part II. Bioactivity and matrix interaction." *Journal of Materials Science—Materials in Medicine*, 18(4):545–550 (2007).

79. Dai, Z., Ronholm, J., Tian, Y. P., Sethi, B., and Cao, X. D., "Sterilization techniques for biodegradable scaffolds in tissue engineering applications." *Journal of Tissue Engineering*, **7**: 2041731416648810 (2016).

80. Dempsey, D. J., and Thirucote, R. R., "Sterilization of medical devices: a review." *Journal of Biomaterials Applications*, **3**(3):454–523 (1989).

81. Mendes, G. C. C., Brandao, T. R. S., and Silva, C. L. M., "Ethylene oxide sterilization of medical devices: a review." *American Journal of Infection Control*, **35**(9):574–581 (2007).

82. Silicone Elastomers Brochure. *GE Bayer AG. Momentive Performance Materials*. Waterford, NY, 2013.

83. Nair, P. D., "Currently practised sterilization methods: some inadvertent consequences." *Journal of Biomaterials Applications*, **10**(2):121–135 (1995).

84. Jarry, C., Chaput, C., Chenite, A., Renaud, M. A., Buschmann, M., and Leroux, J. C., "Effects of steam sterilization on thermogelling chitosan-based gels." *Journal of Biomedical Materials Research*, **58**(1):127–135 (2001).

85. Fairand, B. P., *Radiation Sterilization for Health Care Products: X-Ray, Gamma, and Electron Beam*. CRC Press, 2001.

86. ISO 11137-1:2006, *Sterilization of Health Care Products: Radiation Part 1: Requirements for Development, Validation and Routine Control of a Sterilization Process for Medical Devices*.

87. Streicher, R. M., "Influence of ionizing irradiation in air and nitrogen for sterilization of surgical grade polyethylene for implants." *Radiation Physics and Chemistry*, **31**(4–6):693–698 (1988).

88. *Fundamental Principles of Polymeric Materials*, Stephen L. Rosen (ed.). New York: Wiley, 1993, p. 43.

89. *Encyclopedia of Materials Science and Engineering*, Bever, M. B. (ed.). Cambridge, MA: MIT Press, 1986, p. 2917.

90. *Encyclopedia of Materials Science and Engineering*, Bever, M. B. (ed.). Cambridge, MA: MIT Press, 1986, p. 2919.

91. Reeve, L. E., "Poloxamers: their chemistry and applications," in *Handbook of Biodegradable Polymers*, Domb, A. J., Kost, J. K., and Wiseman, D. M. (eds.). London: Harwood Academic Publishers, 1997, p. 235.

92. Dick, H. B., and Schwenn, O. *Viscoelastics in Ophthalmic Surgery*. Berlin: Springer-Verlag, 2000, p. 34.
93. *Modern Plastics Encyclopedia*. McGraw-Hill, 1999.
94. *Polymer Handbook*, 3rd ed. Brandrup, J., and Immergut, H. (eds.), New York: John Wiley and Sons, 1989.
95. *Encyclopedia of Materials Engineering*. Cambridge, MA: MIT Press, 1986.
96. Victrex Polymer Solutions. *Material Properties Guide*. Lancashire, UK.
97. http://www.absorbables.com/technical/properties.html.
98. Williams, S. F., and Martin, D. P., "Applications of PHAs in medicine and pharmacy," in *Biopolymers, Vol 4, Polyesters III—Applications and Commercial Products*, Chapter 4, Doi, Y., and Steinbuchel, A. (eds). Wiley-Blackwell, Hoboken, NJ 2005, p. 96.
99. Rutala, W. A., and Weber, D. J., "Disinfection and sterilization: an overview." *American Journal of Infection Control*, **41**(5):S2–S5 (2013).
100. Sastri, V. R., *Plastics in Medical Devices: Properties, Requirements, and Applications*, 2nd ed. Elesevier, Amsterdam, Holland, 2013, pp. 1–305.
101. Avis, K. E., "Sterilization," in *Theory and Practice of Industrial Pharmacy*, 2nd ed., Lachman, L., Lieberman, H. A., and Kanig, J. L., (eds.). Lea and Febiger, Philadelphia. 1976, pp. 567–585.

CHAPTER 16
BIOMEDICAL COMPOSITES

Arif Iftekhar
University of Minnesota, Minneapolis, Minnesota

16.1 INTRODUCTION

A common debate about the definition of composite materials among composite engineers and materials scientists continues to this day. More recently, biomedical engineers have used the term *composite* prolifically for newly developed biomaterials, and it might be argued that not every usage of the term *composite* for a biomaterial would satisfy the traditional composite engineer, who is used to thinking in terms of fibers, matrices, and laminates. That said, defining composites a certain way in this chapter is not meant to preclude its use outside this definition.

The difficulty lies, on the one hand, in the depth of the material to which the definition refers. Practically everything is a composite material in some sense, except for pure elements. For example, a common piece of metal is a composite (polycrystal) of many grains (or single crystals). Thus alloys, ceramics, steels, etc., would be considered composites if the definition refers to the microstructure. However, if it is the macrostructure that concerns us, then we get the traditional treatment of composites as a *materials system* of different macroconstituents.[1]

On the other hand, there is also a question in this definition regarding how these macroconstituents are brought together and for what purpose. For instance, thin coatings on a material do not make it a typical composite, and the same could be said about adding resin-extending fillers to plastics, although the constituents exist at the macrostructure. Furthermore, a structure that is assembled with components made of different materials does not qualify it to be a composite. Thus a pacemaker lead that has a metallic core and a polymeric sheath would not be considered a composite in the strict sense, whereas a catheter tube polymer reinforced with embedded braided metal wires would. In addition, foams and porous coatings on materials will not be considered composites in this discussion.

The following is an operational definition for the purpose of this chapter:

> A *composite material* consists of two or more physically and/or chemically distinct, suitably arranged or distributed materials with an interface separating them. It has characteristics that are not depicted by any of the components in isolation, these specific characteristics being the purpose of combining the materials.

Composite materials have a bulk phase, which is continuous, called the *matrix*, and one or more dispersed, noncontinuous phases, called the *reinforcement*, which usually has superior mechanical or thermal properties to the matrix. The region between the two can be simply a surface, called an *interface*, or a third phase, called an *interphase*. An example of the latter is a layer of coupling agent coated on glass fibers that facilitates adhesion of the glass to the matrix polymer.

The essence of the concept of composites is this: the bulk phase accepts the load over a large surface area and transfers it to the reinforcement phase, which, being different, changes the mechanical properties of the composite suitably, whether it is strength, stiffness, toughness, or fatigue resistance. For instance, in structural polymer composites, the reinforcement is much stiffer than the matrix, making the composite several times stiffer than the bulk polymer and resulting in a reduction in bulk strain on deformation, as seen in Fig. 16.1. The significance here lies in the fact that there are numerous matrix materials and as many reinforcement types that can be combined in countless ways to produce just the desired properties.

The concept of composite materials is ancient: to combine different materials to produce a new material with performance and efficiency unattainable by the individual constituents. An example is adding straw to mud for building stronger mud walls. Some more recent examples, but before engineered materials became prominent, are steel rods in concrete, cement, and asphalt mixed with sand, fiberglass in resin, etc. In nature, examples abound: a palm leaf, cellulose fibers in a lignin matrix (wood), collagen fibers in an apatite matrix (bone), etc.

Most research in engineered composite materials has been done since the mid-1960s. Today, given the most efficient design of, say, an aerospace structure, a boat, or a motor, we can make a composite material that meets or exceeds the performance requirements. The benefits are mostly in weight and cost, measured in terms of ratios such as stiffness/weight, strength/weight, etc. Advances in biomedical composites have been focused on the design of dental and orthopedic implants, which are mainly structural applications. However, tremendous stiffness and strength improvement is not always the concern in the design of biomedical composites and even less so for large weight savings. Other concerns, such as biocompatibility, precise property matching, mimicking natural structures, etc., can become more important, yet these too are areas where composites offer much promise in device design. Engineers and materials scientists who are used to working with traditional materials such as metal alloys, ceramics, and plastics are increasingly challenged to design with composites that have different physical characteristics, mechanical behaviors, and processing methods.

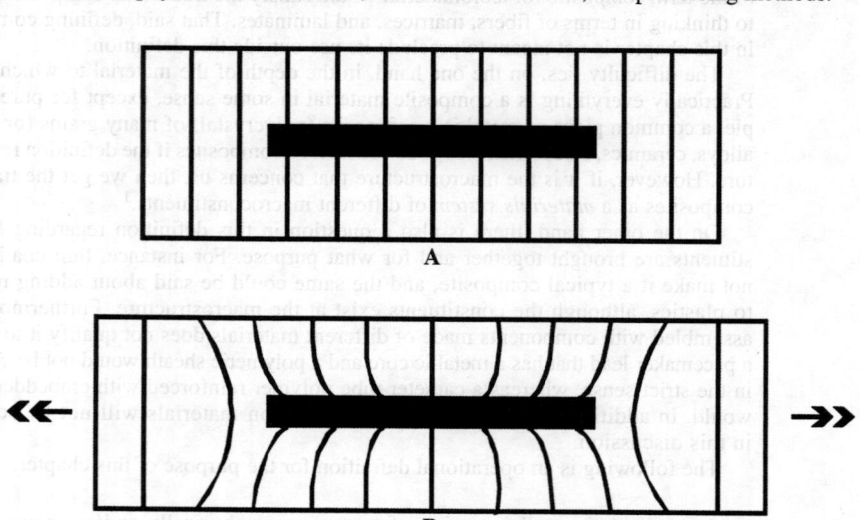

FIGURE 16.1 High-modulus fiber opposes strain around it in a low-modulus matrix. (A) Before deformation; (B) after deformation. Arrows indicate force direction. (*Adapted from Ref. 1.*)

In the design of composite problem solutions, particularly load-bearing implants, it is important to base the design on a firm theoretical understanding of composites to avoid creating new problems while trying to solve an existing one. Three factors need to be considered rationally: material selection for the bulk and reinforcement phases, internal and external structure of the device, and a suitable processing method.[2]

16.2 CLASSIFICATION

The factors that most contribute to the engineering performance of the composite include[1]

1. Materials that make up the individual components
2. Quantity, form, and arrangement of the components
3. Interaction between the components

Of these, the reinforcement system in a composite material strongly determines the properties achievable in a composite. It is thus convenient and common to classify composites according to the characteristics of the reinforcement. These can include the shape, size, orientation, composition, distribution, and manner of incorporation of the reinforcement. For the purposes of a discussion of biomedical composites, this results in two broad groups, namely, fiber-reinforced and particle-reinforced composites. Figure 16.2 shows further divisions within these groups.

Composite materials can also be broadly classified based simply on the matrix material used. This is often done more for processing than for performance purposes. Thus there are polymer-matrix composites (PMCs), ceramic-matrix composites (CMCs), or metal-matrix composites (MMCs). The last type is an advanced composite uncommon in biomedical applications and is mostly used for high-temperature applications.

16.3 CONSTITUENTS

16.3.1 Matrices

The matrix in a composite is the continuous bulk phase that envelopes the reinforcement phase either completely or partially. It serves several important functions.[1] It holds the fibers or particles in place, and in oriented composites, it maintains the preferred direction of fibers. The matrix transfers the applied load to the reinforcement and redistributes the stress. When used with brittle fibers, the matrix helps increase fracture toughness because it is typically of a lower stiffness material and can tolerate greater elongation and shear forces than the reinforcement. The matrix also determines the environmental durability of the composite by resisting chemical, hygroscopic, and thermal stresses and protecting the reinforcement from these stresses. The matrix also greatly influences the processing characteristics of a composite.

Common matrices in biomedical composites are listed in Table 16.1. In nonmedical applications, thermosets make up the bulk of the matrix materials, particularly in structural and aerospace applications, where high stiffness and temperature resistance are very important requirements. In most medical applications, however, thermoplastics are the matrix materials of choice due to their nonreactive nature, processing flexibility, and generally greater toughness. Also, thermosets are nondegradable, whereas some thermoplastics can be designed to be biodegradable. Instead of using off-the-shelf materials, new matrices are constantly being developed for medical applications that have designed reactivity, flexibility, and strength. Resorbable matrices are useful when a composite is not permanently needed once implanted, but it is challenging to design a stiff reinforcing material that

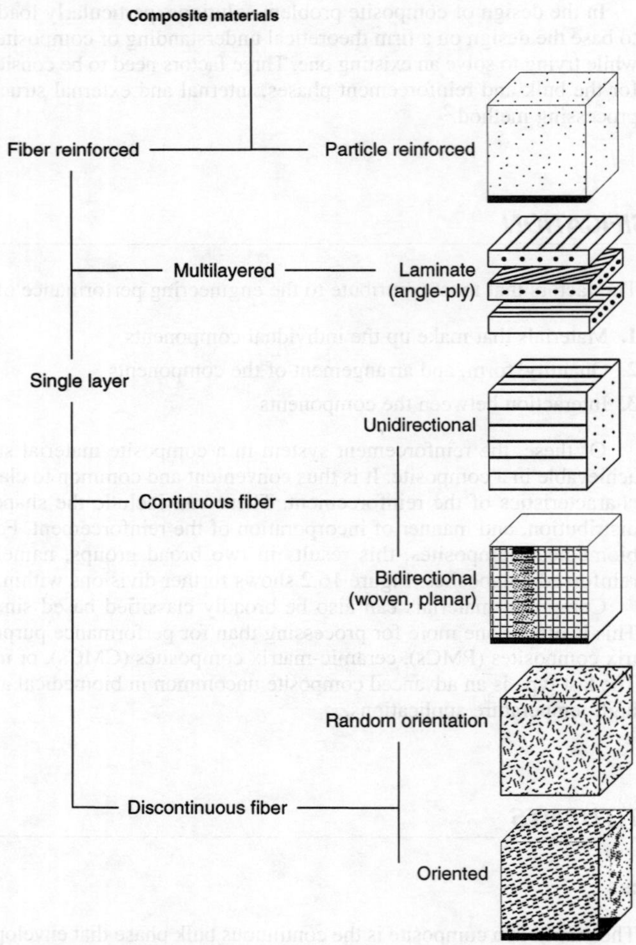

FIGURE 16.2 Classification of composite materials.

has a comparable degradation rate to such matrices. Ceramic matrices are used for their compressive properties and bioactive possibilities but suffer from poor fracture toughness.

16.3.2 Fibers

A great majority of materials is stronger and stiffer in the fibrous form than in any other form. This explains the emphasis on using fibers in composite materials design, particularly in structural applications, where they are the principal load-carrying component. Fibers have a very high aspect ratio of length to diameter compared with particles and whiskers, and the smaller the diameter, the greater is the strength of the fiber due to a reduction in surface flaws. Many properties of a composite are determined by the length, orientation, and volume fraction of fibers of a given type.

Fibers are often manufactured as continuous filaments, with diameters in the range of 5 to 50 μm, and then they are arranged to produce tows, yarns, strands, rovings, mats, etc. These are

TABLE 16.1 Constituents of Biomedical Composites

Matrix	Fibers	Particles
Thermosets	*Polymers*	*Inorganic*
Epoxy	Aromatic polyamides (aramids)	Glass
Polyacrylates	UHMWPE	Alumina
Polymethacrylates	Polyesters	*Organic*
Polyesters	Polyolefins	Polyacrylate
Silicones	PTFE	Polymethacrylate
Thermoplastics	*Resorbable polymers*	
Polyolefins (PP, PE)	Polylactide, and its copolymers with polyglycolide	
UHMWPE	Collagen	
Polycarbonate	Silk	
Polysulfones	*Inorganic*	
Poly(ether ketones)	Carbon	
Polyesters	Glass	
Inorganic	Hydroxyapatite	
Hydroxyapatite	Tricalcium phosphate	
Glass ceramics		
Calcium carbonate ceramics		
Calcium phosphate ceramics		
Carbon		
Steel		
Titanium		
Resorbable polymers		
Polylactide, polyglycolide and their copolymers		
Polydioxanone		
Poly(hydroxy butyrate)		
Alginate		
Chitosan		
Collagen		

used to fabricate continuous-fiber composites, often for large structural applications. Filaments can be chopped to form short fibers ranging in length from 3 to 50 mm that are used to make discontinuous or short-fiber composites, more commonly for low-cost applications or small intricate parts. Whiskers are fibers made of single crystals with very small diameters around 10 μm, but their aspect ratio is high (>100). They have very high strengths but also high manufacturing cost.[3] Compared with continuous-fiber composites, short-fiber composites are less efficient in the use of fibers and in achieving a desired orientation, but they are also less limited in design and processing possibilities and can come very close to achieving their theoretical strength.[1]

Both continuous and short fibers can be oriented in one, two, or three dimensions, resulting in unidirectional, planar, and random reinforcement systems. The volume fraction of fibers oriented in a given direction strongly affects the physical properties of a composite in that direction. Unidirectional and planar reinforced composites exhibit anisotropy; i.e., their properties vary depending on the axis of measurement. The third composite type is isotropic, having equal properties in all directions. As mentioned earlier, it is difficult to orient short fibers, particularly in mold-filling processes, and the resulting composites tend to be isotropic. Laminate composites are a type of fiber-reinforced composite consisting of anisotropic layers or plies bonded together that can differ in relative fiber orientation and volume fraction. This allows high-fiber-volume fractions and three-dimensional orientation not achievable in isotropic short-fiber composites.

Table 16.1 lists some fibers common in biomedical composites. There are many naturally occurring fibers, such as cotton, flax, collagen, jute, wood, hemp, hair, wool, silk, etc., but these have extremely varying properties and present many processing challenges. Among these, collagen fibers have been successfully utilized in tissue engineering of skin and ligament. Borosilicate glass fiber is ubiquitous in the composites industry but not common in biomedical composites, where, instead, adsorbable bioglass fibers made from calcium phosphate have found some applications. Carbon fiber is as strong as glass fiber but is several times stiffer owing to its fine structure of axially aligned graphite crystallites and is also lighter than glass. It is used extensively to make high-strength lightweight composites in prosthetic structural components, where the fatigue resistance of carbon-fiber composites is also an advantage.[4] Carbon fibers tend to be brittle and are anisotropic, particularly in their thermal properties. They also add electrical conductivity to a composite, which can have corrosive effects next to metallic implants. Among polymers, highly oriented aramid fibers such as Kevlar are used in orthopedic applications because of their high resistance to impact fracture. However, Kevlar has very poor compressive properties, making it unsuitable for bending applications, and it is difficult to process due to its strong cut-through resistance. Teflon and polyester (Dacron) fibers are used to make vascular prostheses that are flexible. Polylactide and polyglycolide and their copolymers are used to make fiber composites in which adsorbability is more important than mechanical properties.

16.3.3 Particles

Particles can be added to a matrix to improve mechanical properties such as toughness and hardness. Other properties, such as dimensional stability, electrical insulation, and thermal conductivity, can also be controlled effectively by particles, especially when added to polymer matrices. Particulate reinforcement is randomly distributed in a matrix, resulting in isotropic composites. Particles can either strengthen or weaken a matrix, depending on its shape, stiffness, and bonding strength with the matrix. Spherical particles are less effective than platelet- or flakelike particles in adding stiffness. Hard particles in a low-modulus polymer increase stiffness, whereas compliant particles such as silicone rubber, when added to a stiff polymer matrix, result in a softer composite. Fillers are nonreinforcing particles such as carbon black and glass microspheres that are added more for economic and not performance purposes.

Particulate reinforcement in biomedical composites is used widely for ceramic matrices in dental and bone-analogue applications. The most common such particle form is hydroxyapatite, a natural component of bone where it exists in a composite structure with collagen. Hydroxyapatite particles have very poor mechanical properties and may serve more as a bioactive than reinforcement component.

16.3.4 Interface

The transfer and distribution of stresses from the matrix to the fibers or particles occur through the interface separating them. The area at the interface and the strength of the interfacial bond greatly affect the final composite properties and long-term property retention.[1] A low interfacial area denotes poor wetting of the fiber with the matrix material. Wetting can be enhanced by processing methods in which there is greater pressure (metal matrices) or lower-viscosity flow (polymer matrices). When mechanical coupling is not sufficient, coupling agents are often used to coat fibers to improve chemical compatibility with the matrix.

Interfacial shear strength determines the fiber-matrix debonding process and thus the sequence and relative magnitude of the different failure mechanisms in a composite. Strong interfaces common in polymer matrix composites make ductile matrices very stiff but also lower the fracture toughness. Weak interfaces in ceramic matrix composites make brittle matrices tough by promoting matrix crack but also lower strength and stiffness.[5]

16.4 PROCESSING

16.4.1 Polymer-Matrix Composites

Continuous-fiber composites can be made in a variety of ways, such as manual layup of laminates, filament winding, pultrusion, and resin transfer molding. Manual layup involves stacking preimpregnated (or prepreg) tapes and sheets of parallel-fiber filaments held together by thermoplastic resin or partially cured thermoset resin, followed by autoclaving. This is not very expensive and not suitable for small medical implants. Like layup, filament winding allows for high-fiber-volume fraction and control of properties but is limited to tubular shapes, and the fibers cannot be oriented along the axis of the component. Pultrusion is ideal for very stiff composite rods and beams and can be used for making orthodontic archwires. Resin transfer molding allows very complex shapes and short cycle times but requires expert design of preforms and molds. Compression molding is another method suitable for both thermosets and thermoplastics.

Short-fiber thermoplastic composites are typically injection molded, which allows rapid, high-volume, and economical production but requires expensive tooling. The fiber length and volume fraction are limited by this method, and fiber orientation and distribution are difficult to control.

16.4.2 Ceramic-Matrix Composites

Ceramic-matrix composites are manufactured commonly by either pressing methods or infiltration methods. In the former, the reinforcement is mixed with a powder of the matrix, which is densified by hot pressing or hot isotactic pressing (HIP). Near-zero porosity can be achieved, but the simultaneous high pressure and temperature can degrade fibers or result in a strong interfacial bond that may reduce fracture toughness. In infiltration methods, a sintered fibrous or particulate preform is filled by the matrix by such methods as chemical vapor deposition, glass melt infiltration, and preceramic polymer or sol infiltration. Alumina-glass dental composites are made by this method. This method has the advantage of complex shape capability, low pressure, and flexible fiber architecture. Disadvantages are high matrix porosity (>10 percent) and long fabrication cycles. Particulate reinforcement can also be used through tape-casting and slip-casting the initial preform.

16.5 PHYSICAL PROPERTIES

Composite materials can be designed to have a wide range of physical and biochemical properties, making it important to develop predictive models to aid in designing with the many complex variables that face the composites engineer. Although these models tend to be complicated due to the microstructure of composites, it is important to resist the temptation to treat a composite as a black box with gross properties because this macroscopic approach does not have the predictive power crucial for failure analysis. There have been three general approaches to predicting the basic mechanical properties of a composite[3,5]:

1. Mechanics of materials models
2. Theory of elasticity models
3. Semiempirical models

16.5.1 Mechanics of Materials Models

The mechanics of materials model uses simple analytical equations to arrive at effective properties of a composite, using simplifying assumptions about the stress and strain distribution in a representative volume element of the composite. This approach results in the common rule of mixtures equations for composites, where properties are relative to the volume fraction of the fibers and matrix.

Physical properties such as density are easily calculated by the following equations:

$$V_f + V_m + V_v = 1 \tag{16.1}$$

$$\rho_c = \rho_f V_f + \rho_m V_m \tag{16.2}$$

where V_f, V_m, and V_v are the volume fractions of the fiber, matrix, and voids, respectively, and similarly, ρ_c, ρ_f, and ρ_m are densities of the composite, fiber, and matrix.

The rule of mixtures is useful in roughly estimating upper and lower bounds of mechanical properties of an oriented fibrous composite, where the matrix is istropic and the fiber orthotropic, with coordinate 1 the principal fiber direction and coordinate 2 transverse to it. For the upper bound, the Voight model is used (Fig. 16.3), where it is assumed that the strain is the same in the fiber and matrix. For the lower bound, the Reuss model is used, where the stress is assumed to be the same. This gives the following equations for composite moduli:

$$E_{1c} = E_{1f} V_f + E_m V_m \tag{16.3}$$

$$\frac{1}{E_{2c}} = \frac{V_f}{E_{2f}} + \frac{V_m}{E_m} \tag{16.4}$$

$$\frac{1}{G_{12c}} = \frac{V_f}{G_{12f}} + \frac{V_m}{G_m} \tag{16.5}$$

where E and G are the Young's modulus and shear modulus, respectively. The equations for transverse modulus and shear modulus are known as the inverse law of mixtures. Some fibers, such as carbon, have different properties along their longitudinal and transverse axes that the preceding equations can take into account.

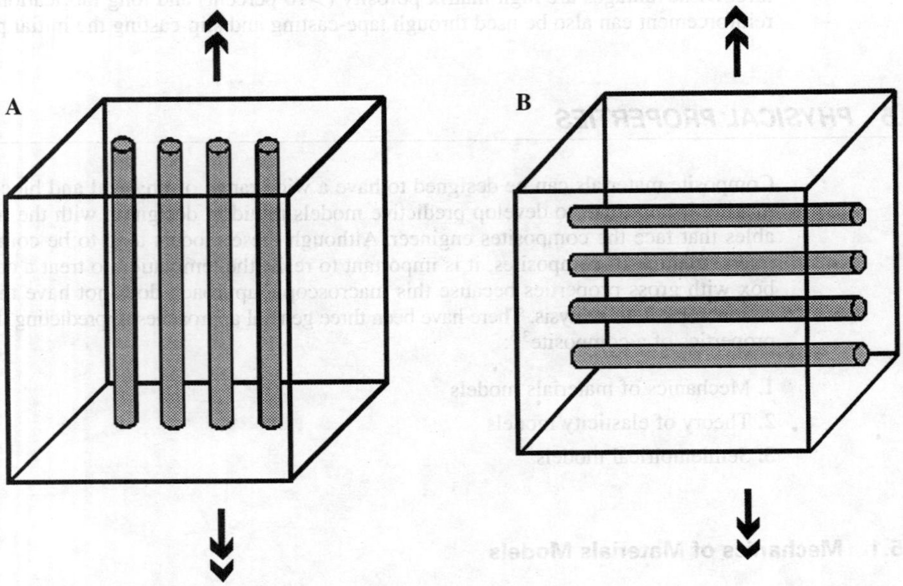

FIGURE 16.3 Composite stress models: (A) Voight or isostrain; (B) Reuss or isostress. Arrows indicate tension force direction.

The rule of mixtures equations have several drawbacks. The isostrain assumption in the Voight model implies strain compatibility between the phases, which is very unlikely because of different Poisson's contractions of the phases. The isostress assumption in the Reuss model is also unrealistic since the fibers cannot be treated as a sheet. Despite this, these equations are often adequate to predict experimental results in unidirectional composites. A basic limitation of the rule of mixtures occurs when the matrix material yields, and the stress becomes constant in the matrix while continuing to increase in the fiber.

The ultimate tensile strength of a fibrous composite σ_c^* depends on whether failure is fiber-dominated or matrix-dominated. The latter is common when V_f is small. One result of such treatment is

$$\sigma_c^* = \frac{\sigma_m}{E_m} E_{1f} V_f + \sigma_m^* V_m \tag{16.6}$$

where σ_m^* is the fracture strength of the matrix.

Other results from this simple analytical approach for orthotropic composites are

$$\alpha_{1c} = \frac{E_{1f}\alpha_{1f}V_f + E_m\alpha_m V_m}{E_{1f}V_f + E_m V_m} \tag{16.7}$$

$$C_c = \frac{1}{\rho_c}(\rho_f C_f V_f + \rho_m C_m V_m) \tag{16.8}$$

$$K_{1c} = K_f V_f + K_m V_m \tag{16.9}$$

where α is the coefficient of thermal expansion, C is the specific heat, and K is the thermal conductivity. The coefficient of hygroscopic expansion β can be found by substituting α with β above. These results are for the longitudinal directions only.

16.5.2 Theory of Elasticity Models

In this approach, no assumptions are made about the stress and strain distributions per unit volume. The specific fiber-packing geometry is taken into account, as is the difference in Poisson's ratio between the fiber and matrix phases. The equations of elasticity are to be satisfied at every point in the composite, and numerical solutions generally are required for the complex geometries of the representative volume elements. Such a treatment provides for tighter upper and lower bounds on the elastic properties than estimated by the rule of mixtures, as is described in the references used in this section.

One illustrative result for the longitudinal Young's modulus is

$$E_{1c} = \frac{[2(\nu_f - \nu_m)^2 E_f V_f E_m V_m]}{\left\{E_m V_m\left(1 - \nu_f - 2\nu_f^2\right) + E_f\left[V_f\left(1 - \nu_m - 2\nu_m^2\right) + (1 - \nu_m)\right]\right\}} + E_m + (E_f - E_m)V_f \tag{16.10}$$

where ν_f and ν_m are the Poisson's ratios of the fiber and matrix, respectively. Very small differences in the Poisson's ratios of the phases cause such equations to be simplified to the rule of mixtures.

16.5.3 Semiempirical Models

Curve-fitting parameters are used in semiempirical and generalized equations to predict experimental results. The most common model was developed by Halpin and Tsai, and it has been modified for aligned discontinuous fiber composites to produce such results as the following for the longitudinal modulus:

$$\frac{E_{1c}}{E_m} = \frac{1 + \xi\eta V_f}{1 - \eta V_f} \tag{16.11}$$

where
$$\eta = \frac{E_{1f}/E_m - 1}{E_{1f}/E_m + \eta} \tag{16.12}$$

and the Halpin-Tsai curve-fitting parameter is assumed to be $\xi = 2L/d$, where L is the length and d the diameter of the fiber. The expression can be simply substituted to also obtain E_{2c} and G_{12} using experimental values for ξ.

For two-dimensional randomly oriented fibers in a composite, approximating theory of elasticity equations with experimental results yielded this equation for the planar isotropic composite stiffness and shear modulus in terms of the longitudinal and transverse moduli of an identical but aligned composite system with fibers of the same aspect ratio:

$$E_c = 3/8 E_1 + 5/8 E_2 \tag{16.13}$$

$$G_c = 1/8 E_1 + 1/4 E_2 \tag{16.14}$$

For a three-dimensional random orientation of fibers, a slightly different equation is proposed for the isotropic tensile modulus:

$$E_c = 1/5 E_1 + 4/5 E_2 \tag{16.15}$$

The stiffness of particulate composites can be predicted depending on the shape of the particles.[6] For a dilute concentration of rigid spherical particles, the composite stiffness is approximated by

$$E_c = \frac{5(E_p - E_m)V_p}{3 + 2E_p/E_m} + E_m \tag{16.16}$$

where E_p and V_p are the stiffness and volume fraction of particles, respectively.

It is important to note that any model for composite behavior requires experimental validation and may prove to be quite inaccurate for not taking into account many irregularities typical in composite design and processing. In addition, these results are usually valid for static and short-term loading.

16.6 FRACTURE AND FATIGUE FAILURE

Failure of fiber-reinforced composites is generally preceded by an accumulation of different types of internal damage that slowly or catastrophically renders a composite structure unsafe. The damage can be process-induced, such as nonuniform curing control of a dental resin, or it can be service-induced, such as undesired water absorption. Fiber breaking, fiber bridging, fiber pullout, matrix cracking, and interface debonding are the failure mechanisms common in all composites, but the sequence and interaction of these mechanisms depend on the type of loading and the properties of the constituents, as well as on the interfacial shear strength (Fig. 16.4). Various fracture mechanics theories are available for failure analysis of composites, among them the maximum stress theory and the maximum strain theory described in more detail in Ref. 5.

Energy absorption and crack deflection during fracture lead to increased toughness of the composite. The two most important energy-absorbing failure mechanisms in a fiber-reinforced composite are debonding at the fiber-matrix interface and fiber pullout. If the interface bonds relatively easily, the crack propagation is interrupted by the debonding process, and instead of moving through the fiber, the crack is deflected along the fiber surface, allowing the fiber to carry higher

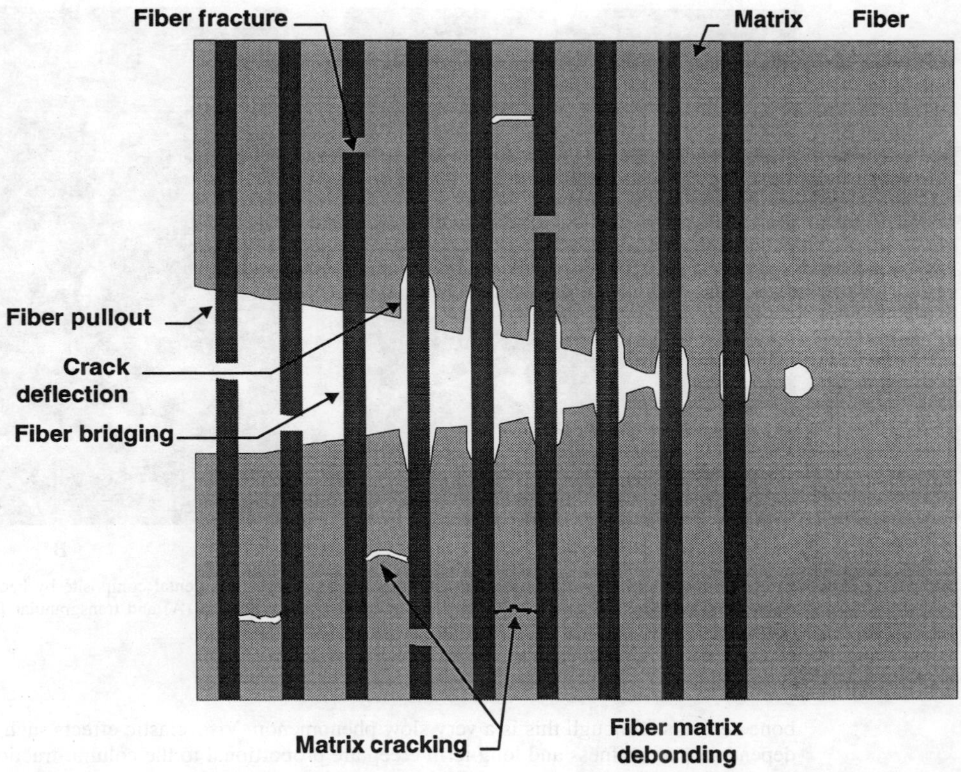

FIGURE 16.4 Failure mechanisms in a unidirectional fiber composite. (*Adapted from Ref. 3.*)

loads. Fiber pullout occurs because fibers do not all break at the crack plane but at random locations away from this plane. If the pullout occurs against high frictional forces or shear stresses at the interface, there maybe a significant increase in fracture toughness.[3] The same holds true for particulate reinforcements, although here crack deflection is more common than bridging and pullout due to the smaller aspect ratio. In an alumina-glass composite, as shown in Fig. 16.5, indentation cracks in the glass matrix are deflected around the angular alumina granules in (A) but not as much in (B), where the cracks propagate more through the granules, indicating a stronger interface but more likely lower toughness. In laminate composites, delamination loads between the layers from in-plane shear loads are a common failure mechanism, initiating at the free edge of the plate or a hole, e.g., where screws would go in a carbon-reinforced bone plate.

Long-term durability of composites is a challenging and still developing area of study. Unlike many metallic biomaterials, the static strength of most load-bearing composite materials does not correlate well with their long-term performance, especially under cyclic loading. The reasons for this include fatigue damage, matrix creep, and stress relaxation, as well as environmental effects at the implant site.[2] Fatigue damage and implant life are difficult to predict, unlike for metals, which have a distinct endurance stress limit below which the material can be loaded an infinite number of times without failure. Many composites do not exhibit an endurance limit. In addition, the loads on implants are highly variable both in direction and magnitude and between patients, and the most damaging loads may occur randomly as a result of accidents. Water absorption in polymer matrices can cause swelling and have a plasticizing effect, which is problematic in dental composites and

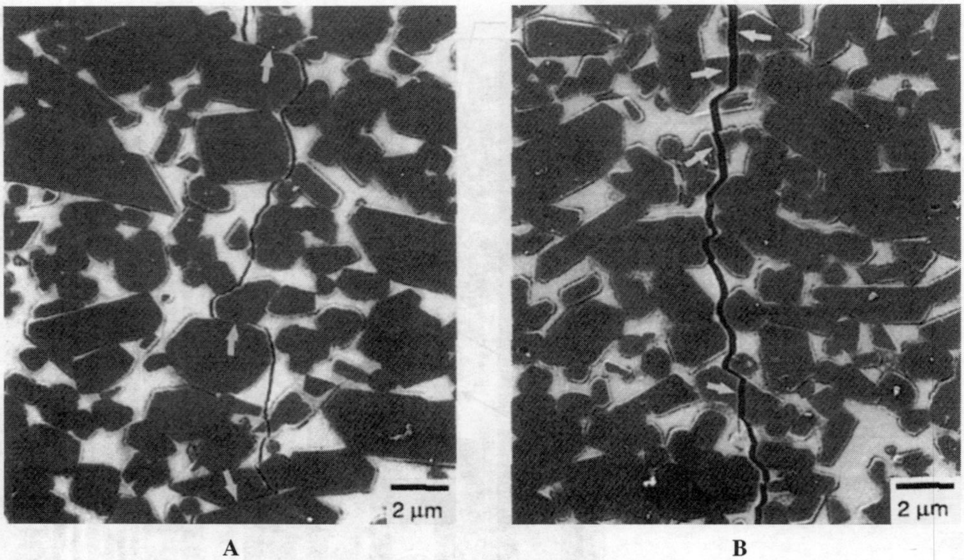

FIGURE 16.5 Surface traces of indentation cracks in alumina-glass dental composite by backscattered scanning electron microscopy (SEM). Grain bridging sites are near the arrows in (A) and transgranular fracture sites in (B). (*From Ref. 21.*)

bone cements, although this is a very slow phenomenon. Visocelastic effects such as the strain-rate dependence of stiffness and long-term creep are proportional to the column fraction of matrix such that highly reinforced continuous-fiber composites are less prone than short-fiber composites.

16.7 BIOLOGIC RESPONSE

In designing biomedical composites and predicting their performance, several issues must be considered regarding the biological response. As the number of constituent materials in a composite increases, so can the variations in the host response. Additional tests are necessary to establish that while the individual materials may be by themselves biocompatible, their specific composition, arrangement, and interaction are also biocompatible. This has implications for both the flexibility of design and obtaining regulatory approval. The potential of composite design to obtain the desired set of properties can be restricted by being conservative in the choice and number of materials used. Even if all the materials used may be approved by the Food and Drug Administration (FDA), their particular combination in a composite may require additional approval.

Materials can elicit a different host response in the bulk form than in the fibrous or particulate form. For instance, UHMWPE, as in an acetabular cup of a hip prosthesis, is generally biocompatible, whereas its fibrous form, as in a finely woven fabric, has been shown to produce a different, more adverse reaction. Furthermore, when the discontinuous phase is particles, whiskers, platelets, or microspheres with dimensions on a cellular scale, the inflammatory response can include their ingestion by immune cells and transport to other parts of the body. This can be accompanied by the release of enzymes that can adversely affect the performance of the composite, such as by altering the degradation kinetics of a biodegradable composite.[7] The composite can be designed in such a way that the fibers or particles are not exposed to the host, but this is challenging because it involves elimination of all voids at the fiber-matrix or particle-matrix interface during processing. In addition, friction in a moving part, such as in orthopedic or dental composites, can cause abrasion of the matrix and produce new voids at the interface, exposing the reinforcing material to the host.

The interaction of materials at the interface is integral to composite performance, and this can be affected by the tissue response in various ways, such as filling and swelling of interfacial voids with fluid and fibrous tissue, altering the interfacial adhesion strength between matrix and reinforcement, and delamination of laminate composites. Such effects can lead to failure of a composite, particularly in structural applications.

Thermosetting polymers, although uncommon in biomedical implants, may contain unreacted monomer and cross-linking agents, particularly in laminated composites made from prepreg layers. In both thermosetting and thermoplastic polymer composites, the sizing applied to glass and carbon fibers is another compound that may be present, and some residual solvents may also leach from the matrix if they are not completely removed during processing. These trace amounts may not be an issue if the application is external to the body, as in prosthetic limbs.

16.8 BIOMEDICAL APPLICATIONS

The use of composite materials in biomedical implants and devices is illustrated by the following examples of structural applications.

16.8.1 Orthopedic

Composite materials have found wide use in orthopedic applications, as summarized by Evans,[2] particularly in bone fixation plates, hip joint replacement, bone cement, and bone grafts. In total hip replacement, common materials for the femoral-stem component such as 316L stainless steel, Co-Cr alloys, and Ti-6A1-4V titanium alloy have very high stiffness compared with the bone they replace. Cortical bone has a stiffness of 15 GPa and tensile strength of 90 MPa.[8] Corresponding values for titanium are 110 GPa and 800 MPa, which are clearly very high. This produces adverse bone remodeling and stress shielding, which over the long term leads to reduction in bone mass and implant loosening, specially in the proximal region. Fiber composites can be tailored to match the specific mechanical properties of the adjacent bone. Carbon-fiber composites in PEEK or polysulfone matrices can be fabricated with stiffness in the range 1 to 170 GPa and tensile strength from 70 to 900 MPa.[9] Examples are press-fit femoral stems made from laminated unidirectional carbon fibers in PEEK, polysulfone, liquid crystalline polymer (LCP),[10] and polyetherimide (PEI).[11] These composites are difficult to fabricate and have not had very encouraging durability, but they continue to be developed for the inherent advantages of tailorability, flexibility, noncorrosiveness, and radiolucency.[12] Problems with biocompatibility due to particulate carbon debris from these composites have been addressed by polishing and coating with hydroxyapatite (Fig. 16.6) or carbon-titanium alloy.[13]

For fracture fixation, a fully resorbable bone plate is desirable to avoid the need for a second operation to remove the implant after healing. This in the form of a tailored low-stiffness composite also avoids the problem of stress shielding described earlier. The rate of degradation must be controlled to maintain the mechanical properties such that strength loss in the implant mirrors strength increase in the healing. In addition, the degradation by-products must be nontoxic. A summary of the design of adsorbable fixation devices is provided by Pietrzak.[14] Examples of composite bone plates include laminated continuous carbon fiber in a polylactide (PLA) matrix, which is partially adsorbable, and calcium-phosphate glass fibers also in PLA, which is fully resorbable.[15] Continuous poly (L-lactide) fibers in a PLA matrix also produced a fully resorbable composite.[16] These composites, however, did not have adequate mechanical properties and degraded quite rapidly. Nonresorbable carbon-epoxy bone plates with sufficient strength and fatigue properties are available from such manufacturers as Orthodesign, Ltd.

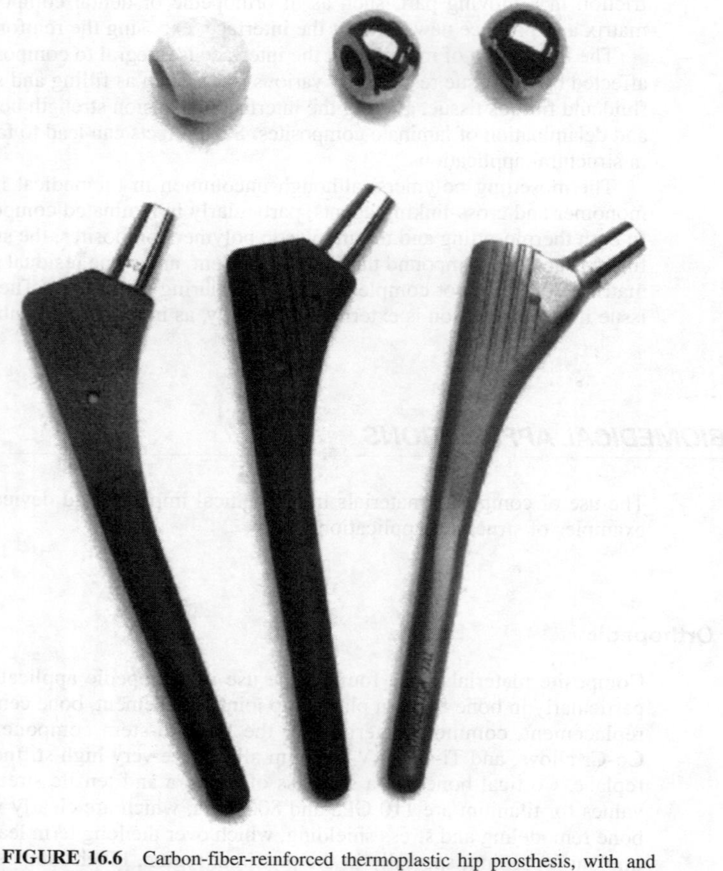

FIGURE 16.6 Carbon-fiber-reinforced thermoplastic hip prosthesis, with and without hydroxyapatite coating, shown alongside conventional titanium equivalent. (*Courtesy of Orthodesign, Ltd., Christchurch, U.K.*)

Bone cements used to fill the void and improve adhesion between implants and the host bone tissue have been reinforced with various fibers to prevent loosening and enhance shear strength. The typical bone cement is PMMA powder mixed with a methacrylate-type monomer that is polymerized during fixation. Low volume fractions of graphite, carbon, and Kevlar fibers have been added to PMMA matrices to increase fatigue life and reduce creep deformation.[17]

16.8.2 Dental

Composites have been by far the most successful in dental applications by meeting several stringent design requirements difficult to achieve with homogeneous materials such as ceramics and metal alloys. Whether it is preparation of crowns, repair of cavities, or entire tooth replacement, the product needs to be aesthetically matched in color and translucence with other teeth and retain its gloss. It must match the hardness of the opposing tooth and be resistant to wear or fatigue fracture. It must be dimensionally stable and withstand the largely varying thermal stresses in the mouth. It also has to have short processing time and near-net shape. Particulate composites used to repair cavities have a polymer resin matrix filled with stiff inorganic or organic inclusions. The resin monomer is typically a methacrylate or a urethane dimethacrylate ester derivative such as bis-GMA cured on site by cross-linkers, ultraviolet light (UV), or light-emitting diodes. The stiff filler particles that increase strength and impart wear resistance can be glass ceramics, calcium silicate, calcium fluoride, crystalline quartz, and silicon nitride whiskers. These are usually silane treated or fused with silica particles to improve retention in the matrix, especially in stress-bearing restorations and to reduce water absorption. The filler can be from 50 to 80 percent by volume of the composite and have varying sizes from 20 nm to 50 μm. In a microfilled dental resin, fused silica particles 20 to 40 nm in size can be incorporated to modest volume fractions up to 40 percent to produce a composite that is translucent and can be polished to a high gloss but not mechanically strong enough for posterior teeth and difficult to handle because of low viscosity. Hybrid dental resins have particle sizes of different orders of magnitude from around 0.1 to around 10 μm, allowing for higher filler volume, up to 80 percent and higher viscosity for easier handling, as well as lower water absorption compared with microfilled resins. Commercial dental composite resins have polymerization shrinkages varying from 1.6 to 2.5 percent,[18] followed by water absorption of up to 1.5 percent,[19] causing dimensional changes. They also have poor adhesion to dentin,[20] making it important to use bonding agents to prevent fitting and leakage problems.

All-ceramic dental composites are used for stress-bearing restorations of dental crowns and bridges. Fracture toughness is a very important concern and is addressed by designing crack deflection and bridging mechanisms into the composite. A common type is the alumina-glass composite known as In-Ceram, in which a skeleton of alumina particles is slip cast and sintered, followed by melt infiltration of glass into the porous core. The composition in one example is 75 percent by volume α-alumina particles of average 3 μm size and 25 percent glass.[21] Thermal expansion mismatch between the alumina and glass was shown not to affect fracture toughness significantly. Recent development of aqueous tape-casting of the alumina core has made it easier to conform the composite to a tooth model.[22] The composite can be many times harder than the enamel of the opposing teeth and can thus wear them out. They are coated with either alkali aluminosilicate dental porcelains or calcium phosphate composites to reduce the surface hardness.[23]

Another application of dental composites is orthodontic archwires.[24] One example is a unidirectional pultruded S2-glass-reinforced dimethacrylate thermoset resin.[25] Depending on the yarn of glass fiber used, the fiber volume fraction varied from 32 to 74 percent. The strength and modulus were comparable with those of titanium wires. Orthodontic brackets were also made from composites with a polyethylene matrix reinforced with ceramic hydroxyapatite particles,[26] resulting in isotropic properties and good adhesion to enamel.

16.8.3 External Prosthetics and Orthotics

Traditional prosthetic and orthotic materials such as wood, aluminum, and leather have been largely replaced by high-performance composites and thermoplastics.[27] The requirements of low weight, durability, size reduction, safety, and energy conservation have made fiber-reinforced plastics very attractive in this area. This is one application where traditional composites design and manufacturing, particularly using thermosets, are common because the products are structural and external to the body. For transtibial (TT) and transfemoral (TF) prostheses, composites have been used for the socket-frame component that interfaces with the residual limb and transmits the load and for the shank component that supports the load over the ground. TT and TF prostheses have a target weight limit of 1 and 2 kg, respectively, which makes carbon-fiber-reinforced (CFR) composites ideal. Socket frames in the ISNY system have been made from carbon fiber tape and acrylic resin produced by laminate layup. The matrix used is a blend of rigid and flexible methyl methacrylate resins for tailoring the stiffness of the socket. CFR epoxy tubing has been used to replace stainless steel in artificial arms. Satin-weave carbon-fiber cloth in epoxy prepreg has been used to make the shank of the Endolite TF prosthesis. Hybrid composites for the shank with carbon and nylon fibers in polyester resins had better impact resistance than just carbon- or nylon-only composites. Using thermoplastics, CFR Nylon 6,6 made easily by injection molding has excellent vibration-damping characteristics important for shock absorption. However, the part will need to be heavier because a simple analysis reveals that the wall thickness of a tubular molding in 30 percent discontinuous CFR Nylon 6,6 needs to be seven times that in 60 percent continuous CFR epoxy at constant tube radius. This can be overcome by using more advanced thermoplastics such as PEEK and longer fibers in injection molding. For the prosthetic foot unit, various composites have been used with the objective of storing energy and returning it during motion. The Flex-Foot unit has a long CFR epoxy composite beam that stores flexural energy along the entire length of the prosthesis rather than just the foot unit and is tailored to the individual patient characteristics and activity level. In the Carbon Copy 2 foot, the keel is made of a posterior Kevlar-reinforced nylon block and anterior CFR plastic leaf springs, providing two-stage resistance to flexion. Finally, a nylon-reinforced silicone elastomer has been used to make a durable cover for the flexible foam that encases the prosthesis. In the area of orthotics designed to support injured tissue, composites find use in new bandage-form splinting materials replacing the old cotton fabric and plaster of paris method. These are commonly laminated fiberglass or polyester knitted fabrics in partially cured polyurethane matrices. Besides strength, they have the advantages of better x-ray transmission and lower water adsorption. However, these casts also produce more dust during sawing and are harder to remove.

16.8.4 Soft-Tissue Engineering

Cross-linked hydrogel networks are suitable as a scaffold for skin regeneration due to their high water content and barrier properties, but they have poor mechanical properties. The tensile strength and break point of the hydrogel poly(2-hydroxyethyl methacrylate) (pHEMA) were dramatically enhanced by reinforcing it with Spandex and gauze fibers, resulting in gels that withstood greater forces before tearing. In cartilage repair, where high compressive and shear properties are desirable, low-density linear polyethylene was melt coated onto a woven three-dimensional fabric of UHMWPE fibers to produce a composite that had compressive behavior approximating that of natural cartilage.[28] Fibrous poly(glycolic acid) (PGA) felts and poly(lactide-*co*-glycolide) (PLGA) fibers have been used as surfaces and scaffolds for cartilage cell growth, where the cells produce the bulk matrix when implanted at the site of the cartilage defect. The fiber diameter, interfiber distance, and biodegradation rate were important parameters that affected the quality of the neocartilage formed from such constructs. In the area of vascular grafts, woven-fiber tubes made from polyester (Dacron) have high permeability during implantation, resulting in severe blood leakage through the graft walls. To avoid the lengthy preclotting time needed to overcome this leakage problem, various impermeable materials are coated on such grafts to form a composite, where the matrix functions as the sealant rather than the load bearer. For example, alginate and gelatin have been used to thoroughly wet Dacron fibers and seal the vascular prosthesis, and over time they are biodegraded. For hemodialysis vascular access, where the graft has to be resilient to frequent needle puncture, a technique employed in the DIASTAT graft involves PTFE fibers sandwiched between layers of porous expanded PTFE. The fibers are pushed aside where the needle enters, and after needle withdrawal, the fibers create a baffle effect to reduce leaking blood velocity and improve resealing.[29]

REFERENCES

1. M. M. Schwartz, *Composite Materials Handbook*, 2d ed. New York: McGraw-Hill, 1992.
2. S. L. Evans and P. J. Gregson, "Composite technology in load-bearing orthopaedic implants," *Biomaterials* **19**:1329–1342 (1998).
3. P. K. Mallick, *Composites Engineering Handbook*. New York: Marcel Dekker, 1997.
4. D. L. Wise, *Human Biomaterials Applications*. Totowa, N. J.: Humana Press, 1996.
5. E. E. Gdoutos, K. Pilakoutas, and C. A. Rodopoulos, *Failure Analysis of Industrial Composite Materials*. New York: McGraw-Hill, 2000.

6. R. Christensen, *Mechanics of Composite Materials*. New York: Wiley, 1979.

7. B. D. Ratner, *Biomaterials Science: An Introduction to Materials in Medicine*. San Diego: Academic Press, 1996.

8. J. Katz, "Orthopedic applications," in *Biomaterials Science*, B. D. Ratner (ed.). San Diego: Academic Press, 1966, pp. 335–346.

9. H. Yildiz, S. K. Ha, and F. K. Chang, "Composite hip prosthesis design: 1. Analysis," *Journal of Biomedical Materials Research* **39**:92–101 (1998).

10. J. Kettunen, E. A. Makelaa, H. Miettinen, et al., "Mechanical properties and strength retention of carbon fiber-reinforced liquid crystalline polymer (LCP/CF) composite: An experimental study on rabbits," *Biomaterials* **19**:1219–1228 (1998).

11. R. De Santis, L. Ambrosio, and L. Nicolais, "Polymer-based composite hip prostheses," *Journal of Inorganic Biochemistry* **79**:97–102 (2000).

12. S. Srinivasan, J. R. de Andrade, S. B. Biggers, Jr., and R. A. Latour, Jr., "Structural response and relative strength of a laminated composite hip prosthesis: Effects of functional activity," *Biomaterials* **21**:1929–1940 (2000).

13. L. Bacakova, V. Start, O. Kofronova, and V. Lisa, "Polishing and coating carbon fiber-reinforced carbon composites with a carbon-titanium layer enhances adhesion and growth of osteoblastlike MG63 cells and vascular smooth muscle cells in vitro," *Journal of Biomedical Materials Research* **54**:567–578 (2001).

14. W. S. Pietrzak, "Principles of development and use of absorbable internal fixation," *Tissue Engineering* **6**:425–433 (2000).

15. H. Alexander, "Composites," in *Biomaterials Science*, B. D. Ratner (ed.). San Diego: Academic Press, 1996, pp. 94–105.

16. M. Dauner, H. Planck, L. Caramaro, et al., "Resorbable continuous-fiber reinforced polymers for osteosynthesis," *Journal of Materials Science: Materials in Medicine* **9**:173–179 (1998).

17. A. Kelly, R. W. Cahn, and M. B. Bever, *Concise Encyclopedia of Composite Materials*, Revised Edition. New York: Pergamon Press, 1994.

18. W. D. Cook, M. Forrest, and A. A. Goodwin, "A simple method for the measurement of polymerization shrinkage in dental composites," *Dental Materials* **15**:447–449 (1999).

19. M. W. Beatty, M. L. Swartz, B. K. Moore, et al., "Effect of microfiller fraction and silane treatment on resin composite properties," *Journal of Biomedical Materials Research* **40**:12–23 (1998).

20. J. W. Nicholson, "Adhesive dental materials: A review," *International Journal of Adhesion and Adhesives* **18**:229–236 (1998).

21. W. D. Wolf, K. J. Vaidya, and L. Falter Francis, "Mechanical properties and failure analysis of alumina-glass dental composites," *Journal of the American Ceramic Society* **79**:1769–1776 (1996).

22. D. J. Kim, M. H. Lee, and C. E. Kim, "Mechanical properties of tape-cast alumina-glass dental composites," *Journal of the American Ceramic Society* **82**:3167–3172 (1999).

23. L. F. Francis, K. J. Vaidya, H. Y. Huang, and W. D. Wolf, "Design and processing of ceramic-based analogs to the dental crown," *Materials Science and Engineering [C]* **3**:63–74 (1995).

24. R. P. Kusy, "A review of contemporary archwires: Their properties and characteristics," *Angle Orthodontist* **67**:197–207 (1997).

25. D. W. Fallis and R. P. Kusy, "Variation in flexural properties of photo-pultruded composite archwires: Analyses of round and rectangular profiles," *Journal of Materials Science: Materials in Medicine* **11**:683–693 (2000).

26. M. Wang, C. Berry, M. Braden, and W. Bonfield, "Young's and shear moduli of ceramic particle filled polyethylene," *Journal of Materials Science: Materials in Medicine* **9**:621–624 (1998).

27. R. Hanak and E. S. Hoffman, "Specification and fabrication details for the ISNY above-knee socket system," *Orthotics and Prosthetics* **40**:38–42 (1986).

28. B. Seal and A. Panitch, "Polymeric biomaterials for tissue and organ regeneration," *Materials Science and Engineering [R]* **262**:1–84 (2001).

29. J. M. Lohr, K. V. James, A. T. Hearn, and S. A. Ogden, "Lessons learned from the DIASTAT vascular access graft," *American Journal of Surgery* **172**:205–209 (1996).

CHAPTER 17
BIOCERAMICS

Eric J. Madsen and David H. Kohn
University of Michigan, Ann Arbor, Michigan

17.1 INTRODUCTION

The clinical goal when using ceramic biomaterials, as with any biomaterial, is to replace lost tissue structure and/or function. The rationale for using ceramics in medicine and dentistry was initially based upon the relative biological inertness of ceramic materials compared to metals. However, in the past 30 years, emphasis has shifted toward the use of bioactive ceramics, materials that elicit normal tissue formation and also form an intimate bond with tissue through partial dissolution of the material surface. Bioceramics are also used in conjunction with biological therapies, where the ceramic delivers cells, proteins, and/or genes, with an end-goal of regenerating functional tissue.

Ceramic biomaterials are processed to yield one of four types of surfaces and associated mechanisms of tissue attachment (Kohn and Ducheyne, 1992): (1) fully dense, relatively inert crystalline ceramics that attach to tissue by either a press fit, tissue growth onto a roughened surface, or via a grouting agent; (2) porous, relatively inert ceramics, where tissue grows into the pores, creating a mechanical attachment between the implant and tissue; (3) fully dense, surface reactive ceramics, which attach to tissue via a chemical bond; and (4) resorbable ceramics that integrate with tissue and eventually are replaced by new or existing host tissue. Ceramics may therefore be classified by their macroscopic surface characteristics (smooth, fully dense, roughened, or porous) or their chemical stability (inert, surface reactive, or bulk reactive/resorbable). The integration of biological (i.e., inductive) agents with ceramics further expands the clinical potential of these materials.

Relatively inert ceramics elicit minimal tissue response and lead to a thin layer of fibrous tissue adjacent to the ceramic surface. Surface-active ceramics are partially soluble, resulting in ion exchange and the potential to lead a direct chemical bond with tissue. Bulk bioactive ceramics are fully resorbable, have greater solubility than surface-active ceramics, and may be replaced by an equivalent volume of regenerated tissue. The relative level of bioactivity mediates the thickness of the interfacial zone between the biomaterial surface and host tissue (Fig. 17.1). There are no standardized measures of "reactivity," but the most common are pH changes, ion solubility, tissue reaction, and assays for cell function.

Five main ceramics are used for musculoskeletal reconstruction and regeneration: carbon (Christel et al., 1987; More et al., 2004), alumina (Al_2O_3) (Kohn and Ducheyne, 1992; Popat and

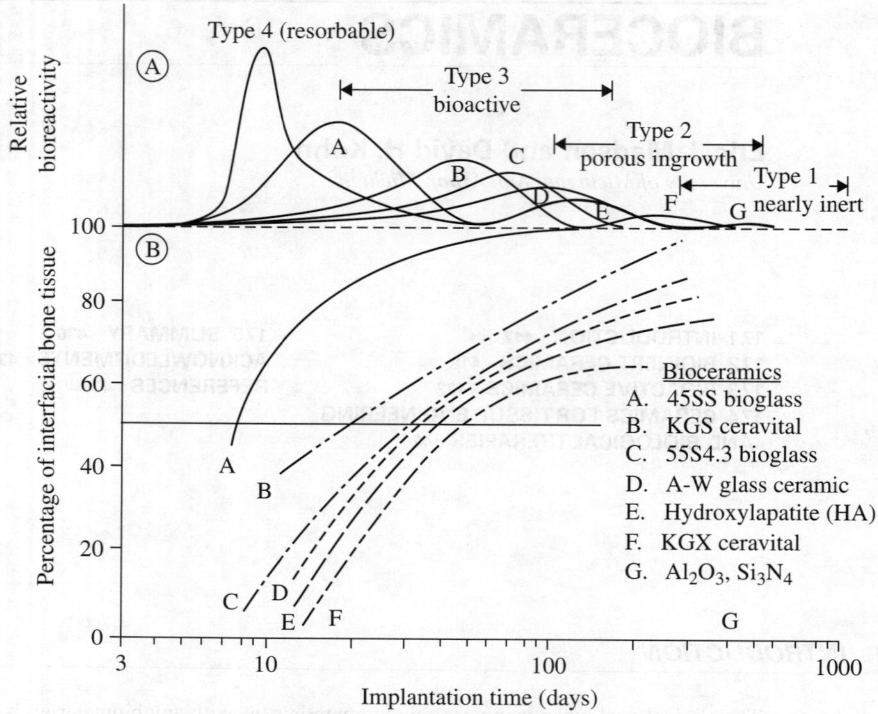

FIGURE 17.1 Bioactivity spectra for selected bioceramics: (A) relative magnitudes and rates of bioactivity, (B) time dependence of bone formation at bioceramic surface and ceramic/bone bonding. [*From Hench and Best (2013), with permission.*]

Desai, 2013), zirconia (ZrO_2) (Cales and Stefani, 1995; Kohn and Ducheyne, 1992), bioactive glasses and glass ceramics (Ducheyne, 1985; Hench and Best, 2013; Kohn and Ducheyne, 1992), and calcium phosphates (Kohn and Ducheyne, 1992; Van Raemdonck et al., 1984).

In this chapter, three types of bioceramics (bioinert, surface bioactive, and bulk bioactive) are discussed, with a focus on musculoskeletal and dental applications. A materials science approach is taken to address design issues of importance to a biomedical engineer; the processing-structure-composition-property synergy is discussed for each material, then properties important to the design and clinical success of each class of bioceramic are presented. Within the framework of discussing the processing-composition-structure synergy, issues of material selection, service conditions, fabrication routes, and characterization methodologies are discussed.

17.2 BIOINERT CERAMICS

Ceramics are fully oxidized materials and are therefore chemically stable and less likely to elicit an adverse biological response than metals, which only oxidize at their surface. Three types of "inert" ceramics are of interest in musculoskeletal applications: carbon, alumina, and zirconia.

17.2.1 Carbon

The benign biological reaction to carbon-based materials, along with the similarity in stiffness and strength between carbon and bone, made carbon a candidate material for musculoskeletal reconstruction almost 50 years ago (Bokros et al., 1972). Carbon has a hexagonal crystal structure that is formed by covalent bonds. Graphite has a planar hexagonal array structure, with a crystal size of approximately 1000Å (Bokros, 1978). The carbon-carbon bond energy within the planes is large (114 kcal/mol), whereas the bond between the planes is weak (4 kcal/mol) (Hench and Ethridge, 1982). Therefore, carbon derives its strength from the strong in-plane bonds, whereas the weak bonding between the planes results in a low modulus, near that of bone (Bokros, 1978).

Isotropic carbon, on the other hand, has no preferred crystal orientation and therefore possesses isotropic material properties. Pyrolytic carbons are formed by the deposition of carbon from a fluidized bed onto a substrate. The fluidized bed is formed from pyrolysis of hydrocarbon gas (Hench and Ethridge, 1982). Low-temperature isotropic (LTI) carbons are formed at temperatures below 1500°C. LTI pyrolytic carbon possesses good wear resistance and incorporation of silicon can further increase wear resistance (Bokros, 1978). Vitreous carbon is a fine-grained polycrystalline material formed by slow heating of a polymer. Upon heating, the more volatile components diffuse from the structure and only carbon remains (Hench and Ethridge, 1982). Properties of all three forms of carbon are summarized in Table 17.1.

Deposition of LTI coatings onto metal substrates is limited by the brittleness of the coatings. Carbon may also be vapor deposited onto a substrate by the evaporation of carbon atoms from a high-temperature source and subsequent condensation onto a low-temperature substrate (Hench and Ethridge, 1982). Vapor-deposited coatings are approximately 1 μm thick, allowing properties of the substrate to be retained. Diamond-like carbon (DLC) coatings also improve fixation to bone (Koistinen et al., 2005; Reikeras et al., 2004) and wear resistance (Allen et al., 2001). Carbon-based thin films are produced from solid carbon or liquid/gaseous hydrocarbon sources, using ion beam or plasma deposition techniques, and have properties intermediate to those of graphite and diamond (Allen et al., 2001).

With the advent of nanotechnology, interest in carbon has been rekindled, in the form of carbon nanotubes (CNTs). CNTs have been proposed as scaffolds to support osteoconductivity (Zanello et al., 2006) and as a second phase in polymer scaffolds (Shi et al., 2006). CNTs can guide the spatial deposition of mineral in hydrogels (Cancian et al., 2016). CNTs have also been combined with hydroxyapatite (HA) and collagen to make composites. CNT/collagen/HA composites exhibit increased stiffness, mesenchymal stem cell (MSC) proliferation, spreading, osteogenic gene expression, and bone formation (Jing et al., 2017). Despite these many uses, there are concerns about toxicity. Several mechanisms of toxicity have been proposed, including trace metals generating reactive oxygen species, membrane rupture, and disruption of biochemical processes. Smaller sized CNTs are especially toxic due to increased surface area. The toxic effects are greatest when the CNTs are dispersed or in suspension, and minimized when bound to a substrate (Newman et al., 2013).

17.2.2 Alumina

High density, high purity, and polycrystalline alumina is used for femoral stems, femoral heads, acetabular components, and dental implants (Boutin et al., 1988; Hannouche et al., 2011; Heimke et al., 2002; Kohn and Ducheyne, 1992; Nizard et al., 2008; Popat and Desai, 2013; Tateiwa et al., 2008). Ion-modified and nanostructured Al_2O_3 have been synthesized to increase strength and bioactivity (Webster et al., 2000; Zreiqat et al., 1999). In addition to chemical stability another attribute of alumina is wear resistance. A main motivation for using alumina in orthopedic surgery is to increase tribological properties, and many total hip replacements are now designed as modular devices—that is, an alumina femoral head is press-fit onto the neck of a metal femoral stem.

High-purity alumina powder is isostatically compacted and shaped. Sintering at 1600 to 1800°C transforms a preform into a dense polycrystalline solid having a grain size less than 5 μm

TABLE 17.1 Physical and Mechanical Properties of Bioceramics

Material	Porosity, %	Density, mg/m³	Modulus, GPa	Compressive strength, MPa	Tensile strength, MPa	Flexural strength, MPa	K_{Ic} ($MPa \cdot m^{1/2}$)
Graphite (isotropic)	7	1.8	25	–	–	140	–
	12	1.8	20–24	65–95	24–30	45–55	–
	16–20	1.6–1.85	6–13.4	18–58	8–19	14–27	–
	30	1.55	7.1	–	–	–	–
	–	0.1–0.5	–	2.5–30	–	–	–
Pyrolytic graphite, LTI	2.7	2.19	28–41	–	–	–	–
	–	1.3–2	17–28	900	200	340–520	–
	–	1.7–2.2	17–28	–	–	270–550	–
Glassy (vitreous) carbon	–	1.4–1.6	–	–	–	70–205	–
	–	1.45–1.5	24–28	700	70–200	150–200	–
	–	1.38–1.4	23–29	–	–	190–255	–
	≤50	<1.1	7–32	50–330	13–52	–	–
Bioactive ceramics and	–	–	–	–	56–83	–	–
Glass ceramics	–	2.8	–	500	–	100–150	–
	31–76	0.65–1.86	2.2–21.8	–	–	4–35	–
Hydroxyapatite	0.1–3	3.05–3.15	7–13	350–450	38–48	100–120	–
	10	2.7	–	–	–	–	–
	30	–	–	120–170	–	–	–
	40	–	–	60–120	–	15–35	–
	2.8–19.4	2.55–3.07	44–48	310–510	–	60–115	–
	2.5–26.5	–	55–110	≤800	–	50–115	–
Tetracalcium- phosphate	Dense	3.1	–	120–200	–	–	–
Tricalcium phosphate	Dense	3.14	30–120	120	–	15–120	–
Other calcium phosphates	Dense	2.8–3.1	–	70–170	–	–	–
Al_2O_3	0	3.93–3.95	380–400	4000–5000	350	400–500	5–6
	25	2.8–3.0	150	500	–	70	–
	35	–	–	200	–	55	–
	50–75	–	–	80	–	6–11.4	–
ZrO_2, stabilized	0	4.9–5.6	150–200	1750	–	150–900	4–12
(~3% Y_2O_3)	1.5	5.75	210–240	–	–	280–450	–
	5	–	150–200	–	–	50–500	–
	28	3.9–4.1	–	<400	–	50–65	–

Source: Modified from Kohn and Ducheyne (1992), with permission.

(Boutin et al., 1988). Single crystals (sapphire) may be grown by feeding powder onto a seed and allowing build up.

The mechanical properties of alumina are a function of purity, grain size, grain size distribution, porosity, and inclusions (Boutin et al., 1988; Dorre and Dawihl, 1980; Kohn and Ducheyne, 1992) (Table 17.1). The elastic modulus of dense alumina is two- to fourfold greater than that of metals used in bone and joint reconstruction. Both grain size (d) and porosity (P, $0 \leq P \leq 1$) affect strength

(σ) via power law and exponential relations, respectively [Eqs. (17.1) and (17.2)], where σ_0 is the strength of the dense ceramic, *A*, *n*, and *B* are material constants, experimentally determined, and *n* is approximately 0.5.

$$\sigma = Ad^{-n} \tag{17.1}$$

$$\sigma_P = \sigma_0 \, e^{-BP} \tag{17.2}$$

Decreasing the grain size of Al_2O_3 from 7 to 4 μm increases strength by approximately 20 percent (Dorre and Dawihl, 1980). It is now possible to fabricate alumina with grain sizes approximately 1 μm increasing strength further. Wear in alumina-alumina bearing couples can be 10 times less than in metal-polyethylene systems (Hannouche et al., 2011; Lusty et al., 2007).

The major limitation of alumina is its low fracture toughness. As a consequence, alumina is sensitive to stress concentrations and overloading. Retrieved alumina total hip replacements exhibit damage caused by fatigue, impact, or overload (Walter and Lang, 1986).

17.2.3 Zirconia

Yttrium oxide partially stabilized zirconia (YPSZ) is an alternative to alumina, and there are approximately 500,000 zirconia components in clinical use (Mantripragada et al., 2013). YPSZ has a higher toughness than alumina, since it can be transformation toughened, and is used in bulk form or as a coating (Filiaggi et al., 1996).

At room temperature, pure zirconia has a monoclinic crystal symmetry. Upon heating, it transforms to a tetragonal phase at approximately 1000 to 1100°C, and then to a cubic phase at approximately 2000°C (Fig. 17.2). A partially reversible volumetric shrinkage (density increase) of 3 to 10 percent occurs during the monoclinic to tetragonal transformation (Christel et al., 1989). The volumetric changes resulting from the phase transformations can lead to residual stresses and cracking. Because of the large volume reduction, pure zirconia cannot be sintered. However, sintering and phase transformations can be controlled via the addition of stabilizing oxides. Yttrium oxide (Y_2O_3) stabilizes the tetragonal phase such that upon cooling the tetragonal crystals are maintained in a metastable state and do not transform back to a monoclinic structure. The tetragonal to monoclinic transformation and volume change are also prevented by neighboring grains inducing compressive stresses on one another (Christel et al., 1989).

The modulus of partially stabilized zirconia is approximately half that of alumina, while the bending strength and fracture toughness are two to three times greater (Table 17.1). The strength and toughness result from transformation toughening, where crack nucleation and propagation lead to locally elevated stresses and energy in the tetragonal crystals surrounding the crack tip (Fig. 17.3). The elevated energy induces the metastable tetragonal grains to locally transform into monoclinic grains. Since the monoclinic grains are larger than the tetragonal grains, there is a local volume increase, compressive stresses are induced, more energy is needed to advance the crack, and crack blunting occurs.

The wear rate of YPSZ on UHMWPE is variable, but can be less than the wear rate of alumina on UHMWPE (Chen et al., 2016). Wear resistance is a function of grain size, surface roughness and residual compressive stresses induced by the phase transformation. The increased mechanical and tribological properties of zirconia may allow for smaller diameter femoral heads to be used in comparison to alumina.

Partially stabilized zirconia is typically shaped by cold isostatic pressing and then densified by sintering. The material is usually presintered until 95 percent dense and then HIP-ed to remove residual porosity (Christel et al., 1989). Sintering can be performed without inducing grain growth, and final grain sizes can be less than 1 μm.

Zirconia has seen increasing use in dentistry as a material for crown restorations, bridges, and onlays/inlays. CAD/CAM systems that can mill such restorations from a ceramic block make zirconia attractive compared to full cast metal and porcelain fused to metal restorations that require

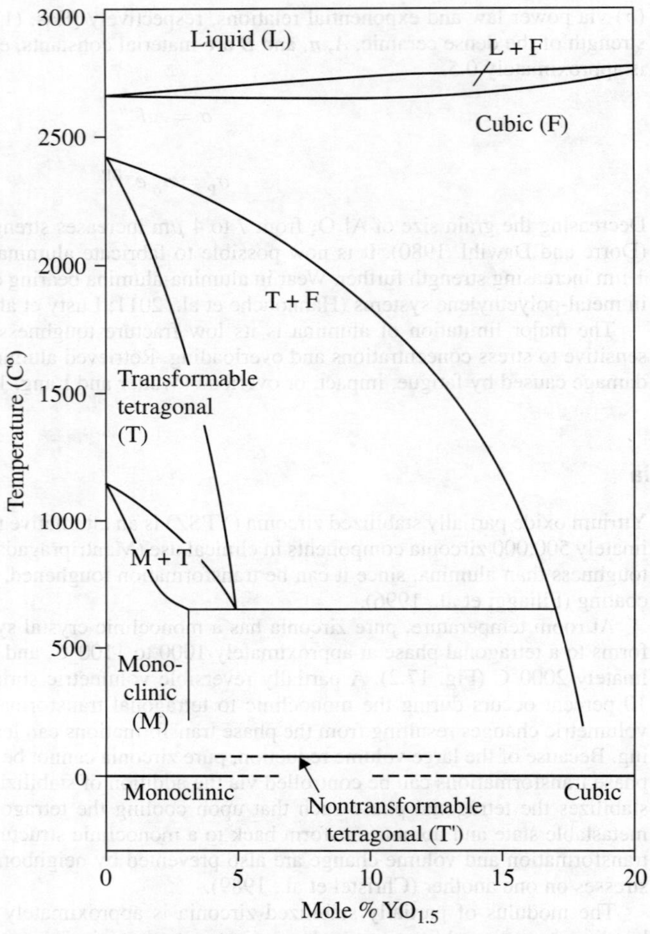

FIGURE 17.2 Schematic phase diagram of the ZrO_2–Y_2O_3 system. [*From Cales and Stefani (1995), with permission.*]

time-consuming casting techniques to fabricate (Bona et al., 2015). Zirconia dental implants have also received much attention as an alternative to titanium due to improved aesthetics. Despite good osseointegration, zirconia implants have increased risk of fracture, although there is a lack of long-term clinical studies (Cionca et al., 2017).

17.2.4 Critical Properties of Bioinert Ceramics

Properties of bioinert ceramics important for their long-term clinical function include stiffness, strength, toughness, wear resistance, and biological response. Stiffness represents a gauge of the mechanical interaction between an implant and surrounding tissue. Stiffness is a determinant of the magnitude and distribution of stresses at a biomaterial/tissue interface, and dictates the potential for stress shielding. Load-bearing biomaterials must also be designed to ensure that they maintain their structural integrity—that is, designed to be fail-safe at stresses above peak in-service stresses for a

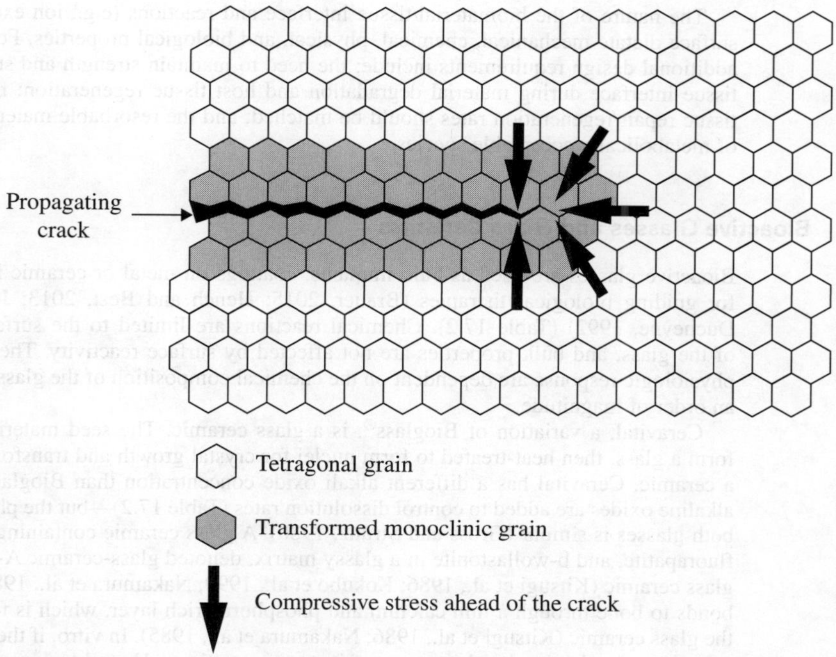

FIGURE 17.3 Schematic of microstructure in yttria partially stabilized zirconia (YPSZ) bioceramic undergoing transformation toughening at a crack tip. [*From Miller et al. (1981), with permission.*]

lifetime greater than the expected service life of the prosthesis. Thus, the static (tensile, compressive, and flexural strength), dynamic (high cycle fatigue), and toughness properties of ceramics, in physiological media, under a multitude of loading conditions and rates must be well-characterized.

Although knowledge of these properties is an important aspect of bioceramic design, the mechanical integrity of a bioceramic is also dependent on its processing, size, and shape. Failure of ceramics usually initiates at a critical defect, at a stress level that depends on the geometry of the defect. To account for these variables and minimize the probability of failure, fracture mechanics and statistical distributions are used to predict failure probability at different load levels (Soltesz and Richter, 1984).

17.3 BIOACTIVE CERAMICS

The concept of bioactivity originated with bioactive glasses via the hypothesis that the biocompatibility of an implant is optimal if it elicits the formation of normal tissues at its surface, and if it establishes a contiguous interface capable of supporting the loads which occur at the site of implantation (Hench et al., 1972). Three classes of ceramics may fulfill these requirements: bioactive glasses and glass ceramics, calcium phosphate ceramics, and composites of gasses and ceramics. Incorporation of inductive factors into each of these ceramics may enhance bioactivity. These different classes of ceramics (and biological constituents) are used in a variety of applications, including bulk implants (surface active), coatings on metal or ceramic implants (surface active), permanent bone augmentation devices/scaffold materials (surface active), temporary scaffolds for tissue engineering (surface or bulk active), fillers in cements or scaffolds (surface or bulk active), and drug delivery vehicles (bulk active).

The nature of the biomaterial/tissue interface and reactions (e.g., ion exchange) at the ceramic surface dictate mechanical, chemical, physical, and biological properties. For resorbable materials, additional design requirements include: the need to maintain strength and stability of the material/tissue interface during material degradation and host tissue regeneration; material resorption and tissue repair/regeneration rates should be matched; and the resorbable material should consist only of metabolically acceptable species.

17.3.1 Bioactive Glasses and Glass Ceramics

Bioactive glasses are used as bulk implants, coatings on metal or ceramic implants, and scaffolds for guiding biological therapies (Brauer, 2015; Hench and Best, 2013; Jones, 2015; Kohn and Ducheyne, 1992) (Table 17.2). Chemical reactions are limited to the surface (~300 to 500 μm) of the glass, and bulk properties are not affected by surface reactivity. The degree of activity and physiologic response are dependent on the chemical composition of the glass, and may vary by over an order of magnitude.

Ceravital, a variation of Bioglass®, is a glass ceramic. The seed material is quench melted to form a glass, then heat-treated to form nuclei for crystal growth and transformation from a glass to a ceramic. Ceravital has a different alkali oxide concentration than Bioglass®—small amounts of alkaline oxides are added to control dissolution rates (Table 17.2)—but the physiological response to both glasses is similar (Gross and Strunz, 1980). A glass ceramic containing crystalline oxyapatite, fluorapatite, and b-wollastonite in a glassy matrix, denoted glass-ceramic A-W, is another bioactive glass ceramic (Kitsugi et al., 1986; Kokubo et al., 1990; Nakamura et al., 1985). A-W glass-ceramic bonds to bone through a thin calcium and phosphorus-rich layer, which is formed at the surface of the glass ceramic (Kitsugi et al., 1986; Nakamura et al., 1985). In vitro, if the physiological environment is correctly simulated in terms of ion concentration, pH, and temperature, this layer consists of small carbonated HA crystallites with a defective structure, and the composition and structural characteristics are similar to those of bone (Kokubu et al., 1990).

Glass and glass-ceramics interact with the physiological microenvironment because ceramics are susceptible to surface changes in an aqueous media. Lower valence ions segregate to surfaces and grain boundaries, leading to concentration gradients and ion exchange. These reactions are dependent on the local pH and can be biologically beneficial or adverse.

When placed in physiological media, bioactive glasses leach Na^+ ions, and subsequently K^+, Ca^{2+}, P^{5+}, Si^{4+}, and Si-OH. These ionic species are replaced with H_3O^+ ions from the media through an ion exchange reaction which produces a silica-rich gel surface layer. The depletion of H^+/H_3O^+ ions in solution causes a pH increase, which further drives dissolution of the glass surface. The high surface area silica-rich surface gel chelates calcium and phosphate ions, and a Ca-P-rich,

TABLE 17.2 Composition (weight percent) of Bioactive Glasses and Glass Ceramics

Material	45S5 Bioglass	45S5-F Bioglass	45S5-B5 Bioglass	52S4.6 Bioglass	Ceravital	Stabilized ceravital	A-W Glass ceramic
SiO_2	45.0	45.0	45.0	52.0	40–50	40–50	34.2
P_2O_5	6.0	6.0	6.0	6.0	10–15	7.5–12.0	16.3
CaO	24.5	12.3	24.5	21.0	30–35	25–30	44.9
Na_2O	24.5	24.5	24.5	21.0	5–10	3.5–7.5	–
B_2O_3	–	–	5.0	–	–	–	–
CaF_2	–	12.3	–	–	–	–	0.5
K_2O	–	–	–	–	0.5-3.0	0.5–2.0	–
MgO	–	–	–	–	2.5-5.0	1.0–2.5	4.6
Al_2O_3	–	–	–	–	–	5.0–15.0	–
TiO_2	–	–	–	–	–	1.0–5.0	–
Ta_2O_5	–	–	–	–	–	5.0–15.0	–

Source: From Kohn and Ducheyne (1992), with permission.

amorphous apatite layer forms on top of the silica-rich layer. The amorphous Ca-P layer eventually crystallizes and CO_3^{2-} substitutes for OH^- in the apatite lattice, leading to the formation of carbonated apatite. Bioactive glasses have also been prepared with added strontium, and Sr-doped glass downregulates RANKL (receptor activator of nuclear factor kappa-B ligand) while upregulating OPG (osteoprotegerin), demonstrating the potential to modulate both bone resorption and formation (Fiorilli et al., 2018).

In parallel with these physical/chemical-mediated reactions, in an in vivo setting, proteins adsorb/desorb from the silica gel and carbonate layers. The bioactive surface and preferential protein adsorption can enhance attachment, differentiation, and proliferation of osteoblasts and secretion of an extracellular matrix (ECM). Crystallization of carbonated apatite within an ordered collagen matrix leads to an interfacial bond.

The rate of change of the glass surface, R, is quantified as the sum of the reaction rates of each stage of the reaction (Hench and Best, 2013):

$$R = -k_1 t^{0.5} - k_2 t^{1.0} + k_3 t^{1.0} + k_4 t^y + k_5 t^z \tag{17.3}$$

where k_i is the rate constant for each stage i and represents, respectively, the rate of exchange between alkali cations in glass and H^+/H_3O^+ in solution (k_1), interfacial SiO_2 network dissolution (k_2), repolymerization of SiO_2 (k_3), carbonate precipitation and growth (k_4), and other precipitation reactions (k_5). Using these rates, the following design criterion may be established: the kinetics of each stage, especially stage 4, should match the rate of biomineralization in vivo. For $R >>$ in vivo rates, resorption will occur, whereas if $R <<$ in vivo rates, the glass will be nonbioactive (Hench and Best, 2013).

The degree of activity and physiological response (e.g., rates of formation of the Ca-P surface and glass/tissue bond) therefore depend on the glass composition and time, and are mediated by the biomaterial, solution, and cells. The dependence of reactivity and rate of bond formation on glass composition is defined by the ratio of network former to network modifier: $SiO_2/[CaO + Na_2O + K_2O]$ (Hench and Clark, 1982). The higher this ratio, the less soluble the glass, and the slower the rate of bone formation. A SiO_2-Na_2O-CaO ternary diagram (Fig. 17.4) is useful to quantify the relationship between composition and biological response (Hench and Best, 2013). The diagram may be divided into three zones: zone A—bioactive bone bonding: glasses are characterized by CaO/P_2O_5 ratios > 5 and $SiO_2/[CaO + Na_2O] < 2$; zone B—nearly inert: bone bonding does not occur (only fibrous tissue formation occurs), because the SiO_2 content is too high and reactivity is too low—these high SiO_2 glasses develop only a surface hydration layer or too dense of a silica-rich layer to enable further dissolution and ion exchange; zone C—resorbable glasses: no bone bonding occurs because reactivity is too high and SiO_2 undergoes rapid selective alkali ion exchange with protons or H_3O^+, leading to a thick but porous unprotected SiO_2-rich film that dissociates at a high rate.

The level of bioactivity is related to bone formation via an index of bioactivity I_B, which is related to the amount of time it takes for 50 percent of the interface to be bonded (Hench and Best, 2013):

$$I_B = 100/t_{0.5BB} \tag{17.4}$$

The compositional dependence of the biological response may be understood by iso-I_B contours superposed onto the ternary diagram (Fig. 17.4). The cohesion strength of the glass/tissue interface will be a function of surface area, thickness, and stiffness of the interfacial zone, and is optimum for $I_B \sim 4$ (Hench and Best, 2013).

17.3.2 Calcium-Phosphate Ceramics

Among the calcium phosphates (Ca-P), the apatites, defined by the chemical formula $M_{10}(XO_4)_6Z_2$, are most relevant to biomaterials. Apatites form a range of solid solutions as a result of ion substitution at the M^{2+}, XO_4^{3-}, or Z^- sites. The M^{2+} species is typically a bivalent metallic cation, such as Ca^{2+} or Sr^{2+}, the XO_4^{3-} species is typically PO_4^{3-}, and the monovalent Z^- ions are usually OH^- or F^- (Van Raemdonck et al., 1984). More complex ionic structures may also exist. For example,

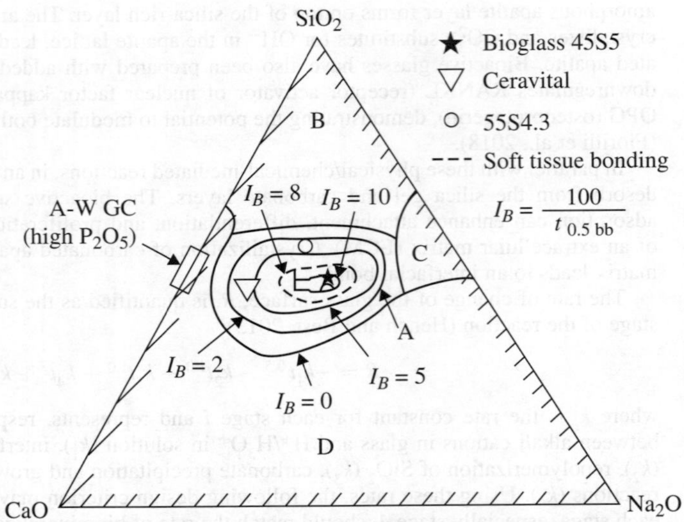

FIGURE 17.4 Ternary diagram (SiO_2-Na_2O-CaO, at fixed 6 percent P_2O5) showing the compositional dependence (in weight percent) of bone bonding and fibrous tissue bonding to the surfaces of bioactive glasses and glass ceramics: zone A: bioactive bone bonding ceramics; zone B: nearly inert ceramics—bone bonding does not occur at the ceramic surface, only fibrous tissue formation occurs; zone C: resorbable ceramics—no bone bonding occurs because reactivity is too high; IB = index of bioactivity for bioceramics in zone A. [*From Hench and Best (2013), with permission.*]

replacing the two monovalent Z^- ions with a bivalent ion, such as CO_3^{2-}, results in the preservation of charge neutrality, but one anionic position becomes vacant. The M^{2+} positions may also have vacancies; in this case, charge neutrality is maintained by vacancies at the Z^- positions or by substitution of trivalent PO_4^{3-} ions with bivalent ions (Shin et al., 2007).

The most common apatite used in medicine and dentistry is hydroxyapatite, $Ca_{10}(PO_4)_6(OH)_2$ (Fig. 17.5). Hydroxyapatite has ideal weight percents of: 39.9 percent Ca, 18.5 percent P, and 3.38 percent OH and an ideal Ca/P ratio of 1.67. The crystal structure and crystallization behavior of HA are affected by ionic substitutions.

The impetus for using synthetic HA as a biomaterial stems from the hypothesis that a material similar to the mineral phase in bone and teeth will have superior binding to mineralized tissues and is therefore advantageous for replacing these tissues. Additional advantages include elastic properties similar to bone, control of in vivo degradation rates through control of material properties, and the potential for ceramic to function as a barrier when coated onto a metal.

Most synthetic hydroxyapatites contain substitutions for the PO_4^{3-} and/or OH^- groups and vary from the ideal stoichiometry and Ca/P ratios. Oxyhydroxyapatite, tricalcium phosphate, tetracalcium phosphate, and octocalcium phosphate have all been detected in commercially available apatite implants (Table 17.3) (Segvich et al., 2008a).

Synthetic apatites are processed via hydrolysis, hydrothermal synthesis and exchange, sol-gel techniques, wet chemistry, and conversion of natural bone and coral (Koeneman et al., 1990). Differences in the structure, chemistry, and composition arise from differences in processing techniques, time, temperature, and atmosphere. Understanding the processing-composition-structure-processing synergy for calcium phosphates is therefore critical to understanding the in vivo function of these materials. For example, at temperatures above 1050°C, HA decomposes into β-TCP and tetracalcium phosphate (Van Raemdonck et al., 1984), and at temperatures above 1350°C, β-TCP transforms into β-TCP.

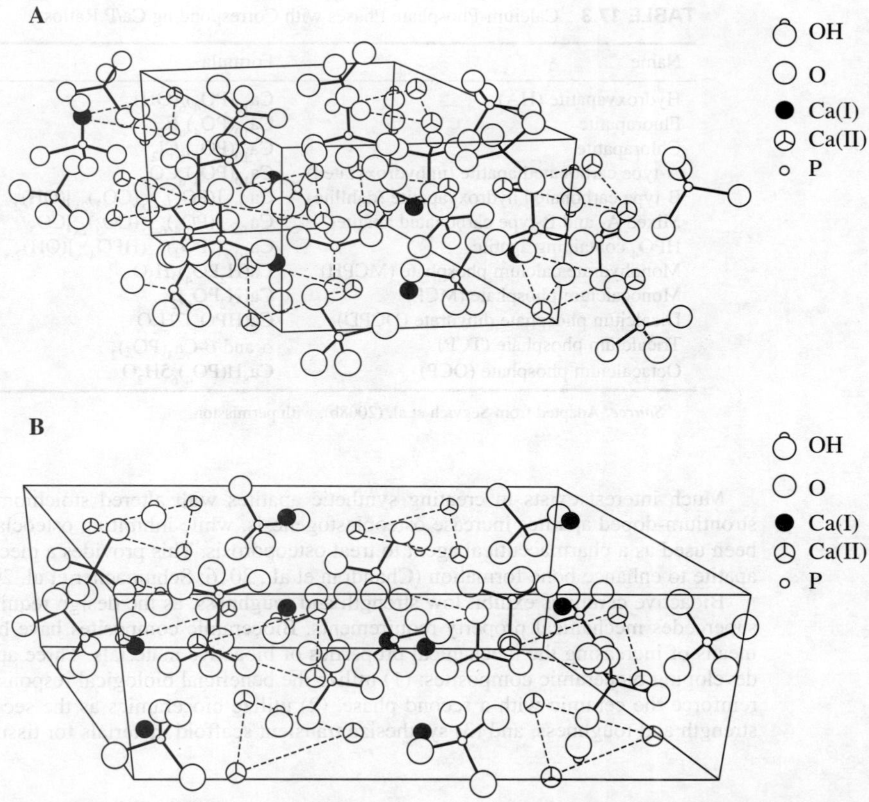

FIGURE 17.5 Schematic of hydroxyapatite crystal structure: (A) hexagonal, (B) monoclinic. [*From Kohn and Ducheyne (1992), with permission.*]

Bone bonding to calcium phosphates occurs by osteoblasts secreting a mineralized matrix at the ceramic surface, resulting in a narrow, amorphous electron-dense band approximately 3 to 5 μm thick. Collagen bundles form between this zone and cells. Bone mineral crystals nucleate within this amorphous zone in the form of an octocalcium phosphate precursor phase and undergo a conversion to HA. As the healing site matures, the bonding zone shrinks to approximately 0.05 to 0.2 μm, and bone attaches through a thin epitaxial layer as the growing bone crystals align with apatite crystals of the material (de Bruijn et al., 1995).

Calcium phosphates are used as coatings on dense and porous implants to accelerate fixation to tissue (Ducheyne et al., 1980; Kohn and Ducheyne, 1992; Ong and Chan 2017; Oonishi et al., 1994). Bond strength to bone, solubility, and in vivo function vary, suggesting a window of material variability in parallel with a window of biological variability.

Processing techniques used to bond Ca-P powders to substrates include plasma and thermal-spraying, sintering, ion-beam and other sputter techniques, electrophoretic deposition, sol-gel techniques, pulsed laser deposition, and chemical vapor deposition (Chai et al., 1998; de Groot et al., 1987; Ducheyne et al., 1990; Garcia et al., 1998; Wolke et al., 1994). Different structures and compositions result from different processing approaches, and modulate biological reactions. For example, increased Ca/P ratios, fluorine and carbonate content, and crystallinity lead to greater stability. Ca/P ratios in the range 1.5 to 1.67 yield the most beneficial tissue response.

TABLE 17.3 Calcium-Phosphate Phases with Corresponding Ca/P Ratios

Name	Formula	Ca/P ratio
Hydroxyapatite (HA)	$Ca_{10}(PO_4)_6(OH)_2$	1.67
Fluorapatite	$Ca_{10}(PO_4)_6F_2$	1.67
Chlorapatite	$Ca_{10}(PO_4)_6Cl_2$	1.67
A-type carbonated apatite (unhydroxylated)	$Ca_{10}(PO_4)_6CO_3$	1.67
B-type carbonated hydroxyapatite (dahllite)	$Ca_{10-x}[(PO_4)_{6-2x}(CO_3)_{2x}](OH)_2$	≥1.67
Mixed A- and B-type carbonated apatites	$Ca_{10-x}[(PO_4)_{6-2x}(CO_3)_{2x}]CO_3$	≥1.67
HPO_4 containing apatite	$Ca_{10-x}[(PO_4)_{6-x}(HPO_4)_x](OH)_{2-x}$	≤1.67
Monohydrate calcium phosphate (MCPH)	$Ca(H_2PO_4)_2H_2O$	0.50
Monocalcium phosphate (MCP)	$Ca(H_2PO_4)_2$	0.50
Dicalcium phosphate dihydrate (DCPD)	$Ca(HPO_4)2H_2O$	1.00
Tricalcium phosphate (TCP)	α and β-$Ca_3(PO_4)_2$	1.50
Octacalcium phosphate (OCP)	$Ca_8H(PO_4)_65H_2O$	1.33

Source: Adapted from Segvich et al. (2008b), with permission.

Much interest exists in creating synthetic apatites with altered stoichiometries. For example, strontium-doped apatites increase osteoblastogenesis, while inhibiting osteoclastogenesis, and have been used as a pharmaceutical agent to treat osteoporosis. This provides a mechanism for strontium apatite to enhance bone formation (Chandran et al., 2016; Schumacher et al. 2016).

Bioactive ceramics exhibit low strength and toughness, as the design requirement of bioactivity supercedes mechanical property requirements. Bioceramic composites have been synthesized as a means of increasing the mechanical properties of bioactive materials. Three approaches are used in developing bioceramic composites: (1) utilize the beneficial biological response to bioceramics, but reinforce the ceramic with a second phase, (2) utilize bioceramics as the second phase to achieve strength and toughness, and (3) synthesize transient scaffold materials for tissue (re)generation.

17.3.3 Critical Properties of Bioactive Ceramics

Important needs in bioactive ceramics research and development include characterization of the processing-composition-structure-property synergy, characterization of in vivo function, and establishing predictive relationships between in vitro and in vivo outcomes. Understanding reactions at the ceramic surface and increasing ceramic/tissue bond strength depend on (1) characterization of surface activity, including surface analysis, biochemistry, and ion transport, (2) physical-chemistry, pertaining to strength and degradation, stability of the tissue/ceramic interface, and tissue resorption, and (3) biomechanics, as related to strength, stiffness, design, wear, and tissue remodeling.

Physical/chemical properties that are important to characterize and relate to biological response include powder particle size and shape, pore size, shape and distribution, specific surface area, phases present, crystal structure and size, grain size, density, coating thickness, hardness, and surface roughness (Table 17.4).

An additional factor that should be considered in evaluating chemical stability and surface activity of bioceramics is the aqueous microenvironment. The type and concentration of electrolytes in solution and the presence of proteins or cells influence how the ceramic surface changes. A solution with constituents, concentrations, and pH equivalent to human plasma most accurately reproduces surface changes observed in vivo, whereas standard buffers do not reproduce these changes (Kokubo et al., 1990).

Surface analyses can be accomplished with solution chemical methods, such as atomic absorption spectroscopy; physical methods, such as x-ray diffraction (XRD), electron microprobe analysis (EMP), energy dispersive x-ray analysis (EDXA), Fourier transform infrared spectroscopy (FTIR); and surface sensitive methods, such as AES, x-ray photoelectron spectroscopy (XPS), and secondary ions mass spectroscopy (SIMS) (Fig. 17.6).

TABLE 17.4 Physical and Chemical Properties Important to Function of Calcium-Phosphate Bioceramics

Material parameter(s)	Functional and biological relevance	Technique(s) to characterize
Particle size, shape, distribution	Strength	Sifting, quantitative stereology
Pore size, shape, distribution	Strength, bioreactivity	Stereology, SEM
Specific surface area	Dissolution, precipitation reactions	BET
Phases	Dissolution, protein adsorption	XRD, FTIR
Crystal structure, grain size density	Strength, toughness, protein adsorption	Optical microscopy, SEM, TEM
Composition	Solubility	AES, XPS
Chemical stability, surface activity	Solubility, dissolution, cell adhesion	XPS, ionic flux, zeta potential
Thickness, hardness, roughness	Cell, protein adsorption	SEM, nanoindentation, profilometry

AES = auger electron spectroscopy; BET = Brunauer-Emmett-Teller theory; FTIR = Fourier-transform infrared spectroscopy; SEM = scanning electron microscopy; TEM = transmission electron microscopy; XPS = x-ray photoelectron spectroscopy; XRD = x-ray diffraction.

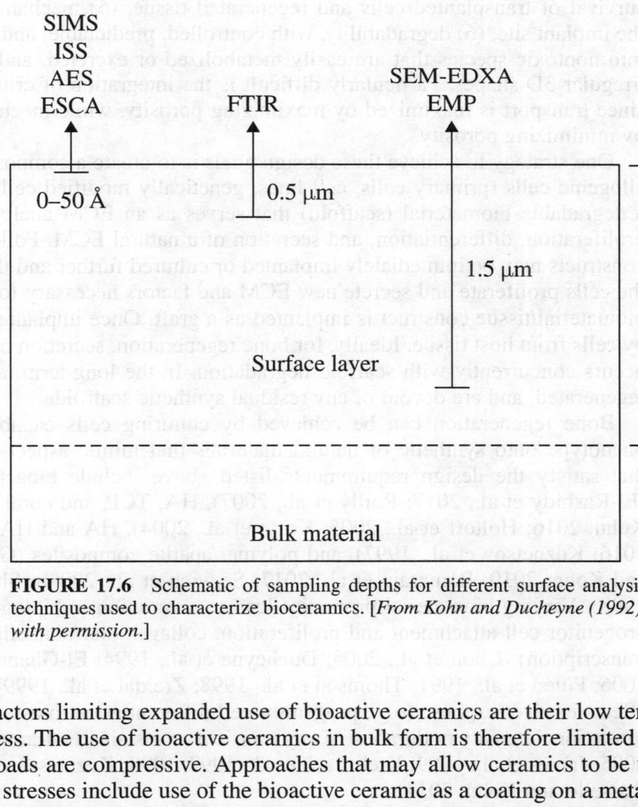

FIGURE 17.6 Schematic of sampling depths for different surface analysis techniques used to characterize bioceramics. [*From Kohn and Ducheyne (1992), with permission.*]

The major factors limiting expanded use of bioactive ceramics are their low tensile strength and fracture toughness. The use of bioactive ceramics in bulk form is therefore limited to applications in which service loads are compressive. Approaches that may allow ceramics to be used in sites subjected to tensile stresses include use of the bioactive ceramic as a coating on a metal or ceramic substrate, strengthening the ceramic via crystallization or nanotechnology, and reinforcing the ceramic with a second phase (Ducheyne et al., 1980; Gross et al., 1981; Kitsugi et al., 1986; Li et al., 1995; Siddiqui et al., 2018; Zhao et al., 2018).

No matter which of these strategies is used, the ceramic must be stable, both chemically and mechanically, until it fulfills its intended function(s). The property requirements depend upon the application. For example, if a metallic total hip prosthesis is to be fixed to bone by coating the stem with a Ca-P coating, then the ceramic/metal bond must remain intact throughout the service-life of the prosthesis. However, if the coating will be used on a porous coated prosthesis to accelerate bone ingrowth into the pores of the metal, then the ceramic/metal bond need only be stable until tissue ingrowth is achieved. A number of interfacial bond tests are available, including pull-out, lap-shear, 3 and 4 point bending, double cantilever beam, double torsion, indentation, scratch tests, and interfacial fracture toughness tests.

17.4 CERAMICS FOR TISSUE ENGINEERING AND BIOLOGICAL THERAPIES

An ideal tissue substitute would possess the biological advantages of an autograft and supply advantages of an allograft, but alleviate the complications each of these grafts is subject to. Such a construct would also satisfy design requirements of (1) biocompatibility, (2) osteoconductivity—it should provide an appropriate environment for attachment, proliferation, and function of osteoblasts or their progenitors, leading to secretion of a new bone ECM, (3) ability to incorporate osteoinductive factors to direct and enhance new bone growth, (4) ingrowth of vascular tissue to ensure survival of transplanted cells and regenerated tissue, (5) mechanical integrity to support loads at the implant site, (6) degradability, with controlled, predictable, and reproducible rate of degradation into nontoxic species that are easily metabolized or excreted, and (7) being easily processed into irregular 3D shapes. Particularly difficult is the integration of criteria (4) and (5) into one design, since transport is maximized by maximizing porosity, while mechanical properties are maximized by minimizing porosity.

One strategy to achieve these design goals is to create a composite graft in which autogenous or allogenic cells (primary cells, cell lines, genetically modified cells, or stem cells) are seeded into a degradable biomaterial (scaffold) that serves as an ECM analogue and supports cell adhesion, proliferation, differentiation, and secretion of a natural ECM. Following cell-seeding, cell/scaffold constructs may be immediately implanted or cultured further and then implanted. In the latter case, the cells proliferate and secrete new ECM and factors necessary for tissue growth, in vitro, and the biomaterial/tissue construct is implanted as a graft. Once implanted, the scaffold is also populated by cells from host tissue. Ideally, for bone regeneration, secretion of a calcified ECM by osteoblasts occurs concurrently with scaffold degradation. In the long-term, a functional ECM and tissue are regenerated, and are devoid of any residual synthetic scaffold.

Bone regeneration can be achieved by culturing cells capable of expressing the osteoblast phenotype onto synthetic or natural materials that mimic aspects of natural ECMs. Bioceramics that satisfy the design requirements listed above include bioactive glasses and glass ceramics (El-Rashidy et al., 2017; Reilly et al., 2007), HA, TCP, and coral (Bouler et al., 2017; Denry and Kuhn, 2016; Holtorf et al., 2005; Kruyt et al., 2004), HA and HA/TCP + collagen (Cholas et al., 2016; Kuznetsov et al., 1997), and polymer/apatite composites (Guillaume et al., 2017; Ramaraju and Kohn, 2019; Ramaraju et al., 2017; Segvich et al., 2008b; Shin et al., 2007; Thomson et al., 1998). Varying biomaterial properties lead to a variation in biological outcome (e.g., osteoblast or progenitor cell attachment and proliferation, collagen and noncollagenous protein synthesis, RNA transcription) (Chou et al., 2005; Ducheyne et al., 1994; El-Ghannam et al., 1997; Leonova et al., 2006; Puleo et al., 1991; Thomson et al., 1998; Zreiqat et al., 1999). The nature of the scaffold also affects in vivo response (e.g., progenitor cell differentiation to osteoblasts, amount and rate of bone formation, intensity or duration of any transient or sustained inflammatory response) (Hartman et al., 2005; James et al., 1999; Krebsbach et al., 1997, 1998; Kuznetsov et al., 1997; Ohgushi et al., 1990; Rossello and Kohn, 2014).

17.4.1 Biomimetic Ceramics

Biomimetic materials, or man-made materials that mimic select aspects of biology, are hypothesized to lead to a superior biological response. Compared to synthetic materials, natural biominerals reflect a remarkable level of control in their composition, size, shape, and organization at all levels of hierarchy (Lowenstein and Weiner, 1989). A biomimetic mineral surface could therefore promote preferential absorption of proteins that regulate adhesion of osteogenic precursors and cell-mediated biomineralization. The rationale for using biomimetic mineralization as a material design strategy is based on the mechanisms of biomineralization (Lowenstein and Weiner, 1989; Mann and Ozin, 1996) and bioactive material function (Sec. 17.3). Bioactive ceramics bond to bone through a layer of bone-like apatite, which forms on the surfaces of these materials in vivo, and is characterized by a carbonate-containing apatite with small crystallites and defective structure (Combes and Rey, 2002; Kokubo and Takadama, 2006; Nakamura et al., 1985). This type of apatite is not observed at the interface between nonbioactive materials and bone and it has been suggested, but not universally agreed upon, that nonbioactive materials do not exhibit surface-dependent cell differentiation (Ohgushi and Caplan, 1999). It is therefore hypothesized that a requirement for a biomaterial to bond to bone is the formation of a biologically active bone-like apatite layer (Ducheyne, 1987; Kokubo and Takadama, 2006; Nakamura et al., 1985).

A bone-like apatite layer can be formed in vitro at STP conditions (Bunker et al., 1994; Kokubo and Yamaguichi, 2019; Murphy et al., 2000; Shin et al., 2007, 2017; Wen et al., 1997), providing a strategy to control the in vivo response to a biomaterial. The basis for synthesizing bone-like mineral in a biomimetic fashion lies in the observation that in nature, organisms use macromolecules to control mineral nucleation and growth (Bunker et al., 1994; Weiner, 1986). Macromolecules usually contain functional groups that are negatively charged at the crystallization pH (Weiner, 1986), enabling them to chelate ions present in the surrounding media which stimulate crystal nucleation (Bunker et al., 1994). The key requirement is to chemically modify a substrate to induce heterogeneous nucleation of mineral from a solution (Bunker et al., 1994). Biomimetic processes are guided by the pH and ionic concentration of the microenvironment, and conditions conducive to heterogeneous nucleation will support epitaxial growth of mineral (Fig. 17.7).

Surface functionalization may be achieved via hydrolysis, grafting, self-assembled monolayers, irradiation, or alkaline treatment (Hanawa et al., 1998; Kokubo and Yamaguichi, 2019; Murphy et al., 2000; Shin et al., 2007; Tanahashi et al., 1995; Wu et al., 1997; Yamamoto et al., 1997). This biomimetic strategy has been used with metals to accelerate osseointegration (Campbell et al.,

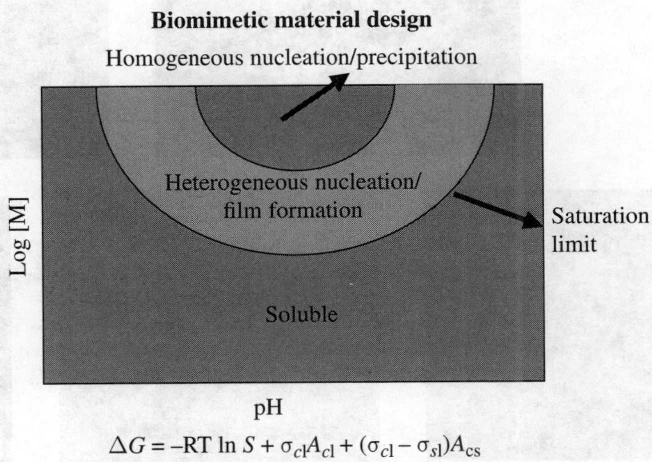

$$\Delta G = -RT \ln S + \sigma_{cl}A_{cl} + (\sigma_{cl} - \sigma_{sl})A_{cs}$$

FIGURE 17.7 Schematic of a design space for biomimetic mineralization of materials. Variations in ionic concentration and pH modulate mineral nucleation. Heterogenous nucleation of mineral onto a substrate is the thermodynamically driven design goal. The free energy for crystal nucleation (ΔG) is a function of the degree of solution supersaturation (S), temperature (T), crystal interfacial energy (σ), and crystal surface area (A). Subscripts c, s, and l denote interfaces involving the crystal, solid substrate, and liquid, respectively.

1996; Hanawa et al., 1998; Kohn, 1998; Kokubo and Yamaguichi, 2016; Wen et al., 1997) as well as glasses, ceramics, and polymers (Chou et al., 2005; Du et al., 1999; Hong et al., 2008; Kamei et al., 1997; Murphy et al., 2000; Segvich et al., 2008b; Shin et al., 2007; Taguchi et al., 1999; Tanahashi et al., 1995; Wu et al., 1997; Yamamoto et al., 1997).

As an example of this biomimetic strategy, porous polyester scaffolds incubated in a simulated body fluid (SBF, a supersaturated salt solution with a composition and ionic concentrations approximating those of plasma) exhibit coordinated surface functionalization, nucleation, and growth of a continuous bone-like apatite layer on the polymer surfaces and within the pores (Fig. 17.8) after relatively short incubation times (Murphy et al., 2000; Segvich et al., 2008b; Shin et al., 2007). FTIR analyses confirm the nature of the bone-like mineral, and ability to control mineral composition via controlling the ionic activity product (IP) of the SBF (Fig. 17.9). As IP increases, more mineral grows on the scaffold pore surfaces, but the apatite is less crystalline and the Ca/P molar ratio decreases. Since mineral composition and structure affect cell function, the IP of the mineralization solution is an important modulator of both material properties and biological outcomes. Mineralization of the polymer substrate also results in a fivefold increase in compressive modulus, without a significant reduction in scaffold porosity (Murphy et al., 2000). The increase in mechanical properties with the addition of only a thin sheath of mineral is important in light of the competing design requirements of transport and mechanics, which frequently may only be balanced by choosing an intermediate porosity.

The self-assembly of mineral within the pores of a polymer scaffold enhances cell adhesion, proliferation, and osteogenic differentiation, as well as modulates cytoskeletal organization and

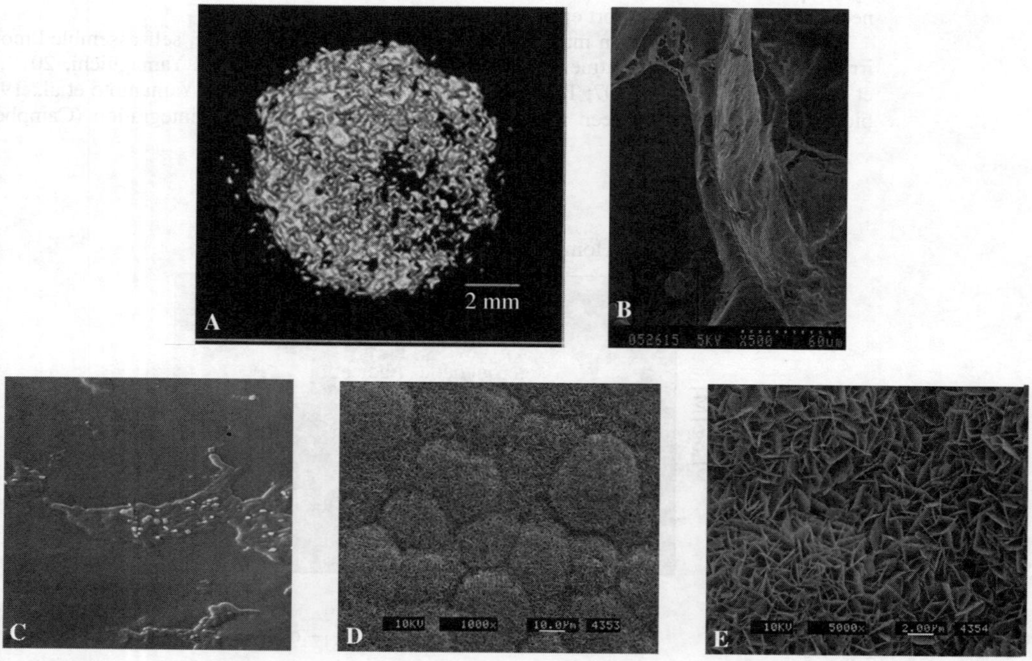

FIGURE 17.8 Images of 85:15 polylactide/glycolide scaffolds incubated in a simulated body fluid (SBF). (A) Microcomputed tomography image of whole scaffold showing mineralization through the thickness of the scaffold; (B) localized SEM image of a scaffold cross-section, showing mineralization of a pore wall; (C) SEM image of mineral nucleation on hydrolyzed PLGA; (D) SEM image of continuous mineral grown on the PLGA—a conglomerated granular structure with needle-shaped precipitates is visible; (E) higher magnification SEM image of elongated platelike hexagonal crystals extending out of the plane of the granular structure. [(A), *From Segvich et al. (2008a), with permission;* (B), *from Murphy et al., (2000), with permission;* (D),(E), *from Hong et al. 2008, with permission.*]

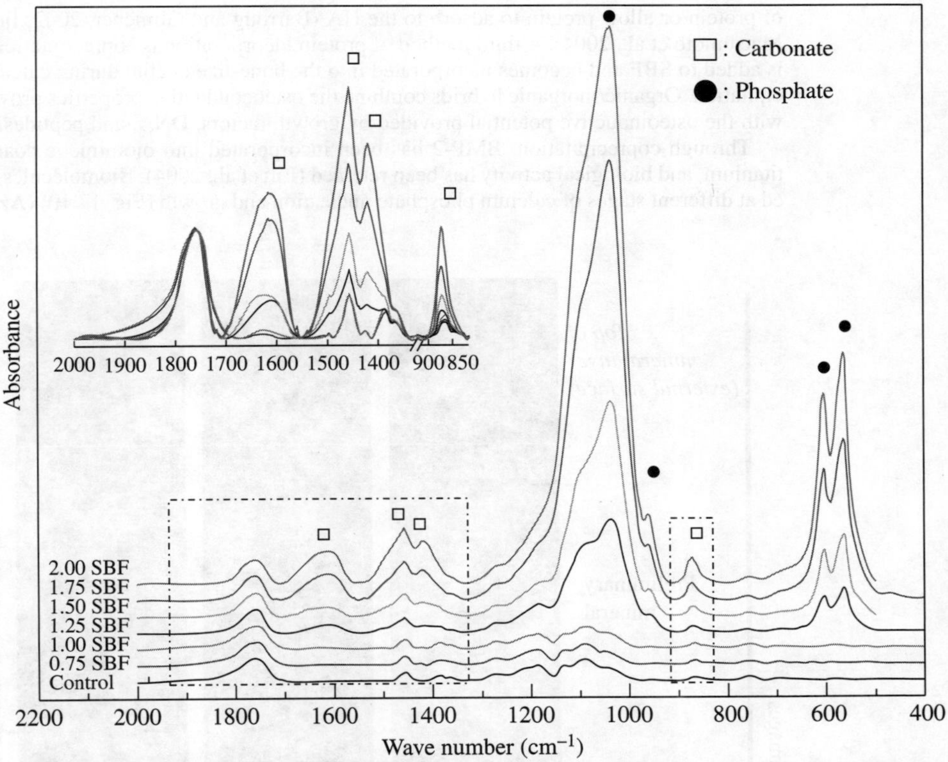

FIGURE 17.9 FTIR spectra of the mineralized pore surfaces of 85:15 PLGA scaffolds incubated in simulated body fluids (SBFs) of varying ionic activity products (IP) for 16 days. Inset = bands within the boxes stacked and enlarged to better show changes in CO_3^{2-}. Band intensities of phosphate and carbonate increased with increasing IP. [*From Shin et al. (2007), with permission.*]

cell motility in vitro (Leonova et al., 2006; Rossello and Kohn, 2014). When progenitor cells are transplanted on these materials, a larger and more spatially uniform volume of bone is regenerated, compared to unmineralized templates (Rossello and Kohn, 2014). An additional benefit of biomimetic processing (room temperature, atmospheric pressure) is that growth factors and plasmid DNA can be incorporated into the mineral without concern for denaturing (Fig. 17.10) (Luong et al., 2006, 2009, 2012; Segvich et al., 2008b). Biomineralized materials can serve as a platform for conductive, inductive, and cell transplantation approaches to regeneration, and fulfill the majority of the design requirements outlined earlier.

17.4.2 Inorganic/Organic Hybrid Biomimetics

Mineral-organic hybrids consisting of bone-like apatites combined with inductive factors can increase cell proliferation, differentiation, and bone formation. The method of combining inorganic mineral with organic factors can influence the release profile and, therefore, influence the response of cells. The most basic method of incorporating proteins into ceramics is adsorption, where the factor is loosely bound to the ceramic surface by submersion or pipetting. A second way of incorporating protein with apatite is to create microcarriers that allow HA crystals to form in the presence of protein or allow protein to adsorb to the HA (Barroug and Glimcher, 2002; Ijntema et al., 1994; Matsumoto et al., 2004). A third method of protein incorporation is coprecipitation, in which protein is added to SBF and becomes incorporated into the bone-like apatite during calcium-phosphate precipitation. Organic/inorganic hybrids combine the osteoconductive properties provided by the apatite with the osteoinductive potential provided by growth factors, DNA, and peptides.

Through coprecipitation, BMP-2 has been incorporated into biomimetic coatings deposited on titanium, and biological activity has been retained (Liu et al., 2004). Biomolecules can be incorporated at different stages of calcium phosphate nucleation and growth (Fig. 17.10) (Azevedo et al., 2005;

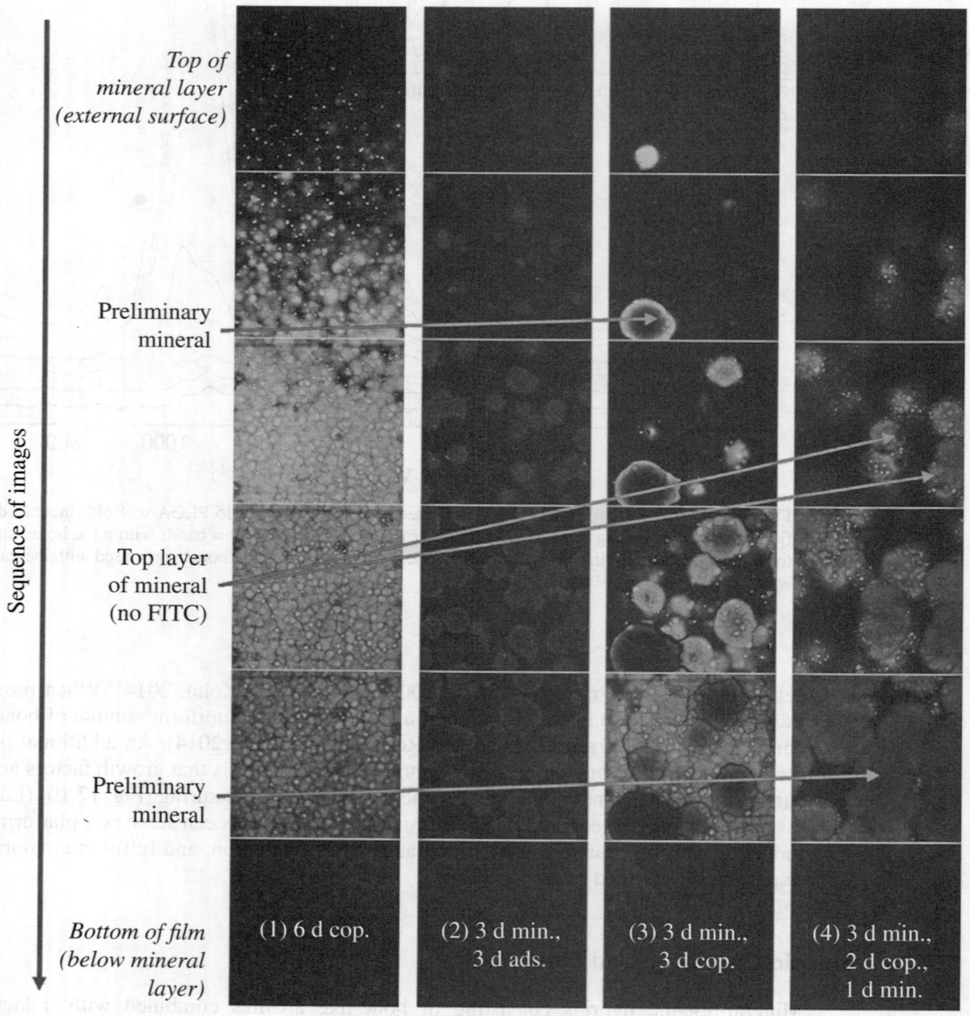

FIGURE 17.10 Images through the thickness of a mineral layer containing FITC-labeled BSA taken using confocal microscopy. Spatial distribution of the protein through the thickness of the mineral is exhibited for the following protein incorporation techniques: (1) 6 days of mineral/BSA coprecipitation; (2) 3 days of mineralization followed by 3 days of protein adsorption; (3) 3 days of mineralization followed by 3 days of mineral/BSA coprecipitation; (4) 3 days of mineralization, followed by 2 days of mineral/BSA coprecipitation, followed by 1 day of mineralization. [*From Luong et al. (2006), with permission from Elsevier.*]

Luong et al., 2006), enabling spatial localization of the biomolecule through the apatite thickness, and controlling its release. With spatial localization, there is also the potential for delivery of multiple biomolecules.

Techniques used to incorporate growth factors into bone-like mineral can also be used to incorporate genes. One of the most common methods of gene delivery is to encapsulate DNA within a Ca-P precipitate (Jordan et al., 1996). This method protects DNA from degradation and encourages cellular uptake, but DNA is released in a burst. By utilizing coprecipitation to incorporate plasmid DNA into a biomimetic apatite layer, more sustained release can be achieved (Luong et al., 2009). The mineral increases substrate stiffness, which also enhances cellular uptake of plasmid DNA (Kong et al., 2005).

Following coprecipitation, the release of biological factors and resultant biological responses are influenced by many variables, including the concentration of the factor, the expression of the receptors that are affected by the presence of the factor, the physical characteristics of the delivery substrate and mineral/organic coating, and the site of implantation. Release kinetics can be controlled via diffusion of the biological factor, dissolution/degradation of the carrier, and/or osmotic effects. For delivery systems based on coprecipitation of a biological molecule with a biomineral, the dissolution mechanisms of mineral are the most important.

Mineral dissolution is controlled by factors associated with the solution (pH, saturation), bulk solid (solubility, chemical composition), and surface (adsorbed ions, phases). The apatite that is typically formed from a supersaturated ionic solution is carbonated (Shin et al., 2007). The presence of carbonate in an apatite lattice influences crystallinity and solubility (McElderry et al., 2013). The dissolution rate of carbonated HA depends on pH, and occurs with the protonation of the carbonate or phosphate group to form either carbonic acid or phosphoric acid (Hankermeyer et al., 2002).

Proteins simply adsorbed to an apatite surface are released in a burst, with most of the protein released within the first 6 hours. In comparison, less than 1 percent of the protein incorporated within bone-like apatite is released after 5 days (Liu et al., 2001). With coprecipitation, a sustained release occurs because protein is incorporated within the apatite matrix, rather than just a superficial association (Liu et al., 2001). The affinity a protein has for apatite influences the dissolution rate of the mineral and, therefore, the release rate. Since protein release is proportional to apatite dissolution, the possibility of temporally controlling the release profile, as well as developing multifactor delivery systems is possible due the ability to spatially localize the protein within the biomimetically nucleated mineral (Luong et al., 2006, 2012).

In addition to controlling cell function via biomolecular incorporation within apatite, another strategy is to present biomolecules on a biomimetic surface. While the objective of coprecipitation is to control spatial and temporal release of biomolecules, the objective of presenting peptides with conformational specificity on a material surface is to recruit a population of cells that can initiate the early stages of bone regeneration. Proteins, growth factors, and peptides have been ionically or covalently attached to biomaterial surfaces to increase cell adhesion, and ultimately, the amount of tissue regeneration. Proteins are prone to degradation and can change conformation because they possess domains with varying hydrophobicities. On the other hand, peptides can mimic the same response as a protein while being smaller, cheaper, and less susceptible to degradation. Peptides have a greater potential for controlling initial biological activity, because they can contain specific target amino acid sequences and can permit control of hydrophilic properties through sequence design (Ladner et al., 2004).

Identification of cell recognition sequences has motivated the development of bioactive materials that can recruit cells to adhere to a material surface via specific integrin-mediated bonding. One peptide sequence that interacts with a variety of cell adhesion receptors is the RGD (Arg-Gly-Asp) sequence. Other peptide sequences have been designed to mimic sections of the ECM proteins: bone sialoprotein, osteopontin, fibronectin, statherin, elastin, and osteonectin (Fujisawa et al., 1997; Gilbert et al., 2000; Simionescu et al., 2005). Peptide sequences with preferential affinity to HA and bone-like mineral have been discovered using phage display libraries (Segvich et al., 2009).

Non specific adsorption of peptides onto the surface of bioceramics can be a simple but sufficient method for inducing a biological reaction. An excellent example of this is the P15 peptide, a collagen-derived peptide that supports bone formation when adsorbed onto HA. Pepgen-P15 is a commercially available product that consists of P15 peptide adsorbed onto bovine-derived bone particles (Gomar et al., 2007). RGD peptides have also been adsorbed onto HA, but reduced cell adhesion due to competing interactions with serum proteins such as fibronectins (Hennessy et al., 2008).

The lack of affinity of many of these peptides to apatite results in poor adsorption or nonoptimal orientation, the development of more effective ways to functionalize ceramic surfaces. One strategy is to use chemical cross-linking to covalently couple the active domains of the peptide onto the ceramic surface. For example, silane agents can react with hydroxyl groups on the surface of zirconia to functionalize the surface with chemically active groups such as amines, carboxylates, or alkyl halides. Subsequently, proteins and peptides can be coupled via amino and carboxyl groups with the aid of cross-linking agents (Fernandez-Garcia et al., 2015).

Covalent coupling is not effective for calcium-phosphate ceramics such as hydroxyapatite due to their ionic nature. Another strategy is to use peptide sequences with preferential affinity for apatite. Polyglutamate sequences have high affinity for HA via electrostatic binding due to their strong negative charge and are found in naturally occurring bone-binding proteins such as osteonectin (Fujisawa et al., 1997). Phage display, a high throughput screening technique, has been used to identify peptides with strong affinity for apatite. These peptides include the VTKHLNQISQSY (VTK) sequence, which has preferential affinity for the biomimetic carbonated apatite found in bone-like mineral (BLM) versus highly crystalline stoichiometric HA (Segvich et al., 2009) and SVSVGMKPSPRP (Roy et al., 2008).

While these mineral-binding sequences have no inherent cell-binding capabilities, they can be coupled to cell-binding sequences. For example, the sequence EEEEEEEPRGDT contains both polyglutamate and RGD, and increases osteoblast attachment and differentiation on mineral substrates (Fujisawa et al., 1997; Itoh et al., 2002). Collagen-derived peptide DGEA has also been combined with polyglutamate, resulting in nine times greater loading onto allograft and significantly increased peptide density (Culpepper et al., 2013). The VTK peptide was coupled to a mesenchymal stem cell–binding peptide DPIYALSWSGMA (DPI) and the dual-peptide DPI-VTK-enhanced attachment of MSCs to mineralized scaffolds (Ramaraju et al., 2017). Interestingly, this dual peptide retains its high affinity for hydroxyapatite despite containing no net charge. DPI-VTK mediates both the magnitude and specificity of MSC attachment to biomimetic apatite (Ramaraju et al., 2017). When adsorbed onto three-dimensional mineralized scaffolds and seeded with iPS-MSCs, DPI-VTK increased bone and vasculature formation in vivo (Ramaraju and Kohn, 2019).

Hydroxyapatite nanoparticles are another application of inorganic/organic hybrid materials. Different preparation methodologies have been used, including chemical precipitation, emulsions, electrospraying, vapor deposition, and hydrothermal methods (Haider et al., 2017). Bioactive molecules can be incorporated into nanoparticles through encapsulation, coprecipitation, and surface adsorption (Munir et al., 2018; Xie et al., 2010). Growth factors such as BMP-2 have been incorporated into these particles for controlled delivery (Xie et al., 2010). Another potential application of nanoparticles is a controlled release system for antibiotics for the treatment of bone infections (Munir et al., 2018). HA nanoparticles have also been used to fabricate larger and more complex constructs such as microspheres (Bi et al., 2019).

17.5 SUMMARY

Bioceramics have a long clinical history, especially in skeletal reconstruction and regeneration. Bioceramics are classified as relatively inert (a minimal tissue response is elicited and a layer of fibrous tissue forms adjacent to the implant), surface active (partially soluble, resulting in surface ion exchange with the microenvironment and leading to a direct chemical bond with tissue), and bulk bioactive (fully resorbable, with the potential to be completely replaced with de novo tissue). Ceramics are processed via conventional materials science strategies, as well as strategies inspired by nature. The biomimetic approaches discussed in Sec. 17.4, along with all other strategies to reproduce the design rules of biological systems, do not completely mimic nature. Instead, just selected biological aspects are mimicked. However, if the selected biomimicry is rationally designed into biomaterial, then the biological system will be able to respond in a more controlled, predictable, and efficient manner, providing an exciting new arena for biomaterials research and development.

ACKNOWLEDGMENTS

Parts of the authors' research discussed in this chapter were supported by NIH/NIDCR R01 DE 026116 and F30 DE 028465.

REFERENCES

Allen, M., Myer, B., Rushton, N., *J. Biomed. Mater. Res. (Appl. Biomat.)* **58**:319–328, 2001.

Azevedo, H. S., Leonor, I. B., Alves, C. M., Reis, R. L., *Mat. Sci. Eng. C.—Bio. S.* **25**:169, 2005.

Barroug, A., Glimcher, M. J., *J. Orthop. Res.* **20**:274, 2002.

Bi, Y., Lin, Z., Deng, S., *Mater. Sci. Eng. C* **100**:576–583, 2019.

Bokros J. C., *Trans. Biomed. Mater. Res. Symp.* **2**:32–36, 1978.

Bokros J. C., LaGrange, L. D., Schoen, G. J., In: *Chemistry and Physics of Carbon*, Vol. 9, Walker, P. L., (ed.), New York, Dekker, pp. 103–171, 1972.

Bona, A. D., Pecho, O. E., Alessandretti, R. *Materials (Basel).* **8**:4978–4991, 2015.

Bouler, J. M., Pilet, P., Gauthier, O., Verron, E. *Acta Biomater.* **53**:1–12, 2017.

Boutin, P., Christel, P., Dorlot, J. M., Meunier, A., de Roquancourt, A., Blanquaert, D., Herman, S., Sedel, L., Witvoet, J., *J. Biomed. Mater. Res.* **22**:1203–1232, 1988.

Brauer, D. S. *Angew. Chem. Int.* **54**:4160–4181, 2015.

Bunker, B. C., Rieke, P. C., Tarasevich, B. J., Campbell, A. A., Fryxell, G. E., Graff, G. L., Song, L., Liu, J., Virden, J. W., McVay, G. L. *Science.* **264**:48–55, 1994.

Cales, B., Stefani, Y., In: *Biomedical Engineering Handbook*, Bronzino, J. D., (ed.), Boca Raton, FL, CRC Press, pp. 415–452, 1995.

Campbell, A. A., Fryxell, G. E., Linehan, J. C., Graff, G. L., *J. Biomed. Mater. Res.* **32**:111–118, 1996.

Cancian, G., Tozzi, G., Hussain, A. A. B., De Mori, A., Roldo, M. *J. Mater. Sci. Mater. Med.* **27**:1–10 (2016).

Chandran, .S. Suresh Babu, S., Hari Krishnan, V. S., Varma, H. K., John, A. *J. Biomater. Appl.* **31**:499–509, 2016.

Chai, C. S., Gross, K. A., Ben-Nissan, B., *Biomaterials.* **19**:2291–2296, 1998.

Chen, Y. W., Moussi, J., Drury, J. L., Wataha, J. C. *Expert Rev. Med. Devices.* **13**:945–963, 2016.

Cholas, R., Kunjalukkal Padmanabhan, S., Gervaso, F., Udayan, G., Monaco, G., Sannino, A., Licciulli, A. *Mater. Sci. Eng. C Mater. Biol. Appl.* **63**:499–505, 2016.

Chou, Y. F., Huang, W., Dunn, J. C. Y., Miller, T. A., Wu, B. M., *Biomaterials.* **26**:285–295, 2005.

Christel, P., Meunier, A., Heller, M., Torre, J. P., Peille, C. N., *J. Biomed. Mater. Res.* **23**:45–61, 1989.

Christel, P., Meunier, A., Leclercq, S., Bouquet, P., Buttazzoni, B., *J. Biomed. Mater. Res.: Appl. Biomat.* **21**(A2):191–218, 1987.

Cionca, N., Hashim, D., Mombelli, A. *Periodontology 2000.* **73:**241–258, 2017.

Combes, C., Rey, C., *Biomaterials.* **23**:2817–2823, 2002.

Culpepper, B. K., Bonvallet, P. P., Reddy, M. S., Ponnazhagan, S., Bellis, S. L. *Biomaterials.* **34**:1506–1513, 2013.

de Bruijn, J. D., van Blitterswijk, C. A., Davies, J. E., *J. Biomed. Mater. Res.* **29**: 89–99, 1995.

de Groot, K., Geesink, R. G. T., Klein, C. P. A. T., Serekian, P., *J. Biomed. Mater. Res.* **21**:1375–1381, 1987.

Denry, I., Kuhn, L. T. *Dent. Mater.* **32**:43–53, 2016.

Dorre, E., Dawihl, W., In: *Mechanical Properties of Biomaterials*, Hastings, G. W., Williams, D. F., (eds.), New York, Wiley, pp. 113–127, 1980.

Du, C., Cui, F. Z., Zhu, X. D., de Groot, K., *J. Biomed. Mater. Res.* **44**:407–415, 1999.

Ducheyne, P., *J. Biomed. Mater. Res.* **19**:273–291, 1985.

Ducheyne, P., *J. Biomed. Mater. Res.: Appl. Biomat.* **21**(A2):219–236, 1987.

Ducheyne, P., Hench, L. L., Kagan, A., II, Martens, M., Bursens, A., Mulier, J. C., *J. Biomed. Mater. Res.* **14**:225–237, 1980.

Ducheyne, P., Radin, S., Heughebaert, M., Heughebaert, J. C., *Biomat.* **11**:244–254, 1990.

Ducheyne, P., El-Ghannam, A., Shapiro, I., *J. Cell Biochem.* **56**:162–167, 1994.

El-Ghannam, A., Ducheyne, P., Shapiro, I. M., *J. Biomed. Mater. Res.* **36**:167–180, 1997.

El-Rashidy, A. A., Roether, J. A., Harhaus, L., Kneser, U., Boccaccini, A. R. *Acta Biomater.* **62**:1–28, 2017.

Fernandez-Garcia, E., et al., *J. Dent.* **43**:1162–1174, 2015.

Filiaggi, M. J., Pilliar, R. M., Yakubovich, R., Shapiro, G., *J. Biomed. Mater. Res. (Appl. Biomat.)* **33**:225–238, 1996.

Fiorilli, S., et al. *Materials (Basel).* **11**, 2018.

Fujisawa, R., Mizuno, M., Nodasaka, Y., Kuboki, Y., *Matrix Biol.* **16**:21, 1997.

Garcia, F., Arias, J. L., Mayor, B., Pou, J., Rehman, I., Knowles, J., Best, S., Leon, B., Perez-Amor, M., Bonfield, W., *J. Biomed. Mater. Res. (Appl. Biomat.)* **43**:69–76, 1998.

Gilbert, M., Shaw, W. J., Long, J. R., Nelson, K., Drobny, G. P., Giachelli, C. M., Stayton, P. S., *J. Biol. Chem.* **275**:16213, 2000.

Gomar, F., Orozco, R., Villar, J. L., Arrizabalaga, F., *Int. Orthop.* **31**:93–99, 2007.

Gross, U., Brandes, J., Strunz, V., Bab, I., Sela, J., *J. Biomed. Mater. Res.* **15**:291–305, 1981.

Gross, U., Strunz, V., *J. Biomed. Mater. Res.* **14**:607–618, 1980.

Guillaume, O., Geven, M. A., Sprecher, C. M., Stadelmann, V. A., Grijpma, D. W., Tang, T. T., Qin, L., Lai, Y., Alini, M., de Bruijn, J. D., Yuan, H., Richards, R. G., Eglin, D. *Acta Biomater.* **54**:386–398, 2017.

Haider, A., Haider, S., Han, S. S., Kang, I. K. *RSC Adv.* **7**:7442–7458, 2017.

Hanawa, T., Kon, M., Ukai, H., Murakami, K., Miyamoto, Y., Asaoka, K., *J. Biomed. Mater. Res.* **41**:227–236, 1998.

Hankermeyer, C. R., Ohashi, K. L., Delaney, D. C., Ross, J., Constantz, B. R., *Biomaterials* **23**:743, 2002.

Hannouche, D., Zaoui, A., Zadegan, F., Sedel, L., Nizard, R. *Int. Orthop.* **35**:207–213, 2011.

Hartman, E. H. M, Vehof, J. W. M., Spauwen, P. H. M., Jansen, J. A., *Biomaterials* **26**:1829–1835, 2005.

Heimke, G., Leyen, S., Willmann, G. *Biomaterials.* **23**:1539–1551, 2002.

Hench, L. L., Best, S. M. In: *Biomaterials Science: An Introduction to Materials in Medicine*. 3rd ed., Ratner, B. D., Hoffman, A. S., Schoen, F. J., Lemons, J. E. (eds.), London, Elsevier Academic Press, pp. 128–151, 2013.

Hench, L. L, Clark, A. E., In: *Biocompatibility of Orthopaedic Implants*, Vol. II, Williams, D. F. (ed.), Boca Raton, FL, CRC Press, pp. 129–170, 1982.

Hench, L. L., Ethridge, E. C., *Biomaterials An Interfacial Approach*, New York, Academic Press, 1982.

Hench, L. L., Splinter, R. J., Allen, W. C., Greenlee, T. K., Jr., *J. Biomed. Mater. Res. Symp.* **2**:117–141, 1972.

Hennessy, K. M., Pollot, B. E., Clem, W. C., et al. *Biomaterials.* **30**(10):1898–1909, 2008.

Holtorf, H. L., Sheffield, T. L., Ambrose, C. G., Jansen, J. A., Mikos, A. G., *Ann. Biomed. Eng.* **33**:1238–1248, 2005.

Hong, S. I., Lee, K. H., Outslay, M. E., Kohn, D. H., *J. Mater. Res.* 23:478–485, 2008.

Ijntema, K., Heuvelsland, W. J. M., Dirix, C., Sam, A. P., *Int. J. Pharm.* **112**:215, 1994.

Itoh, D., et al. *J. Biomed. Mater. Res.* **62**:292–298, 2002.

James, K., Levene, H., Parson, J. R., Kohn, J., *Biomaterials* **20**:2203–2212, 1999.

Jing, Z., et al. *Ann. Biomed. Eng.* **45**:2075–2087, 2017.

Jones, J. R. *Acta Biomater.* **Suppl**:S53–S82, 2015.

Jordan, M., Schallhorn, A., Wurm, F. M., *Nucleic. Acids Res.* **24**:596, 1996.

Kamei, S., Tomita, N., Tamai, S., Kato, K., Ikada, Y., *J. Biomed. Mater. Res.* **37**:384–393, 1997.

Kitsugi, T., Yamamuro, T., Nakamura, T., Higashi, S., Kakutani, Y., Hyakuna, K., Ito, S., Kokubo, T., Takagi, M., Shibuya, T., *J. Biomed. Mater. Res.* **20**:1295–1307, 1986.

Koeneman, J., Lemons, J., Ducheyne, P., Lacefield, W., Magee, F., Calahan, T., Kay, J., *J. Appl. Biomat.* **1**:79–90, 1990.

Kohn, D. H., *Curr. Opin. Solid State Mater. Sci.* **3**:309–316, 1998.

Kohn, D. H., Ducheyne, P., Materials for bone, joint and cartilage replacement, In: *Medical and Dental Materials*, Williams, D. F. (ed.), VCH Verlagsgesellschaft, FRG, pp. 29–109, 1992.

Koistinen, A., Santavirta, S. S., Kroger, H., Lappalainen, R., *Biomaterials* **26**:5687–5694, 2005.

Kokubo, T., Ito, S., Huang, Z. T., Hayashi, T., Sakka, S., Kitsugi, T., Yamamuro, T., *J. Biomed. Mater. Res.* **24**:331–343, 1990.

Kokubo, T., Takadama, H., *Biomaterials* **27**:2907–2915, 2006.

Kokubo, T., Yamaguichi, S. *Acta Biomater.* **44**:16–30, 2016.

Kokubo, T., Yamaguichi, S. *J. Biomed. Mater. Res. A* **107**:968–977, 2019.

Kong, H. J., Liu, J. D., Riddle, K., Matsumoto, T., Leach, K., Mooney, D. J., *Nat. Mater.* **4**:460, 2005.

Krebsbach, P. H., Kuznetsov, S. A., Satomura, K., Emmons, R. V. B., Rowe, D. W., Gehron-Robey, P., *Transplantation* **63**:1059–1069, 1997.

Krebsbach, P. H., Mankani, M. H., Satomura, K., Kuznetsov, S. A., Gehron-Robey, P., *Transplantation* **66**:1272–1278, 1998.

Kruyt, M. C., Dhert, W. J. A., Yuan, H., Wilson, C. E., van Blitterswijk, C. A., Verbout, A. J., de Bruijn, J. D., *J. Orthop. Res.* **22**:544–551, 2004.

Kuznetsov, S. A., Krebsbach, P. H., Satomura, K., Kerr, J., Riminucci, M., Benayahu, D., Gehron-Robey, P., *J. Bone Min. Res.* **12**:1335–1347, 1997.

Ladner, R. C., Sato, A. K., Gorzelany, J., de Souza, M., *Drug Discov. Today* **9**:525, 2004.

Leonova, E. V., Pennington, K. E., Krebsbach, P. H., Kohn, D. H., *J. Biomed. Mater. Res. Part A.* **79A**:263–270, 2006.

Li, J., Fartash, B., Hermansson, L., *Biomaterials* **16**:417–422, 1995.

Liu, Y. L., Hunziker, E. B., Layrolle, P., de Bruijn, J. D., de Groot, K., *Tissue Eng.* **10**:101–108, 2004.

Liu, Y. L., Layrolle, P., de Bruijn, J., van Blitterswijk, C., de Groot, K., *J. Biomed. Mater. Res.* **57**:327, 2001.

Lowenstein, H. A., Weiner, S., *On Biomineralization*, Oxford University Press, Oxford, 1989.

Luong, L. N., Hong, S. I., Patel, R. J., Outslay, M. E., Kohn, D. H., *Biomaterials.* **27**:1175–1186, 2006.

Luong, L. N., McFalls, K. M., Kohn, D. H. *Biomaterials.* **30**:6996–7004, 2009.

Luong, L. N., Ramaswamy, J., Kohn, D. H. *Biomaterials.* **33**:283–294, 2012.

Lusty, P. J., Watson, A., Tuke, M. A., Walter, W. L., Walter, W. K., Zicat, B., *J. Bone Joint Surg.* **89B**:1158–1164, 2007.

Mann, S., Ozin, G. A., *Nature.* **382**:313–318, 1996.

Mantripragada, V. P., Lecka-Czernik, B., Ebraheim, N. A., Jayasuriya, A. C. *J. Biomed. Mater. Res. A.* **101**:3349–3364, 2013.

Matsumoto, T., Okazaki, M., Inoue, M., Yamaguchi, S., Kusunose, T., Toyonaga, T., Hamada, Y., Takahashi, J., *Biomaterials.* **25**:3807, 2004.

McElderry, J. D., Zhu, P., Mroue, K. H., Xu, J., Pavan, B., Fang, M., Zhao, G., McNerny, E., Kohn, D. H., Franceschi, R. T., Banaszak Holl, M. M., Tecklenburg, M. M., Ramamoorthy, A., Morris, M. D. *J. Solid State Chem.* **206**:192–198, 2013.

Miller, R. A., Smialek, R. G., Garlick, In: *Advances in Ceramics,* Vol. 3, *Science and Technology of Zirconia*, Westerville, OH, American Ceramic Society, p. 241, 1981.

More, R. B., Haubold, A. D., Bokros, J. C. Pyrolytic carbon for long-term medical implants. In: *Biomaterials Science: An Introduction to Materials in Medicine*, 2nd ed., Ratner, B. D., Hoffman, A. S., Schoen, F. J., Lemons, J. E. (eds.), Elsevier Academic Press, London, pp. 171–180, 2004.

Munir, M. U., et al. *Int. J. Pharm.* **544:**112–120, 2018.

Murphy, W. L., Kohn, D. H., Mooney, D. J. *J. Biomed. Mater. Res.* **50**:50–58, 2000.

Nakamura, T., Yamamuro, T., Higashi, S., Kokubo, T., Ito, S., *J. Biomed. Mater. Res.* **19**:685–698, 1985.

Newman, P., Minett, A., Ellis-Behnke, R., Zreiqat, H. *Nanomed. Nanotechnol. Biol. Med.* **9**:1139–1158. 2013.

Nizard, R., Pourreyron, D., Raould, A., Hannouche, D., Sedel, L., *Clin. Orthop. Rel. Res.* **466**:317–323, 2008.

Ohgushi, H., Caplan, A. I., *J. Biomed. Mater. Res. (Appl. Biomat.)* **48**:913–927, 1999.

Ohgushi, H., Okumura, M., Tamai, S., Shors, E. C., Caplan, A. I., *J. Biomed. Mater. Res.* **24**:1563–1570, 1990.

Ong, J. L., Chan, D. C. N. *Crit. Rev. Biomed. Eng.* **45**:411–451, 2017.

Oonishi, H., Noda, T., Ito, S., Kohda, A., Ishimaru, H., Yamamoto, M., Tsuji, E., *J. Appl. Biomat.* **5**:23–37, 1994.

Popat, K. C., Desai, T. A. Alumina, In: *Biomaterials Science: An Introduction to Materials in Medicine*, 3rd ed., Ratner, B. D., Hoffman, A. S., Schoen, F. J., Lemons, J. E. (eds.), Elsevier Academic Press, London, pp. 162–166, 2013.

Puleo, D. A., Holleran, L. A., Doremus, R. H., Bizios, R., *J. Biomed. Mater. Res.* **25**:711–723, 1991.

Ramaraju, H., Miller, S. J., Kohn, D. H. *Biomaterials.* **134**:1–12, 2017.

Ramaraju, H., Kohn, D. H. *Adv. Healthcare Mater.* **1801356**:1–11, 2019.

Reikeras, O., Johansson, C. B., Sundfeldt, M., *J. Long Term Effects of Med. Impl.* **14**:443–454, 2004.

Reilly, G. C., Radin, S., Chen, A. T., Dycheyne, P., *Biomaterials.* **28**:4091–4097, 2007.

Rossello, R. A., Kohn, D. H. *J. Tissue Sci. Eng.* **S1**:005, 2014.

Roy, M. D., Stanley, S. K., Amis, E. J., Becker, M. L. *Adv. Mater.* **20**:1830–1836, 2008.

Schumacher, M., et al. **37**:184–194, 2016.

Segvich, S. J., Luong, L. N., Kohn, D. H. Biomimetic approaches to synthesize mineral and mineral/ organic biomaterials. In: *Biomaterials and Biomedical Engineering*, Ahmed, W., Ali, N., Öchsner, A. (eds.), Trans Tech Publications, UK, 2008a.

Segvich, S. J., Smith, H. C., Luong, L. N., Kohn, D. H., *J. Biomed. Mater. Res., Part B,* **84B**:340–349, 2008b.

Segvich, S. J., Smith, H. C., Kohn, D. H. *Biomaterials.* **30**:1287–1298, 2009.

Shi, X., Hudson, J. L., Spicer, P. P., Tour, J. M., Krishnamoorti, R., Mikos, A. G., *Biomacromolecules.* **7**:2237–2242, 2006.

Shin, K., Acri, T., Geary, S., Salem, A. K. *Tissue Eng. Part A.* **19–20**:1169–1180, 2017.

Shin, K., Jayasuriya, A. C., Kohn, D. H., *J. Biomed. Mater. Res. Part A,* **83A**:1076–1086, 2007.

Siddiqui, H. A., Pickering, K. L., Mucalo, M. R. *Materials.* **11**:E1813, 2018.

Simionescu, A., Philips, K., Vyavahare, N., *Biochem. Biophys. Res. Commun.* **334**:524–532, 2005.

Soltesz, U., Richter, H., In: *Metal and Ceramic Biomaterials Volume II Strength and Surface*, Ducheyne, P., Hastings, G. W., (eds.), Boca Raton, FL, CRC Press pp. 23–61, 1984.

Taguchi, T., Shiraogawa, M., Kishida, A., Arashi, M., *J. Biomater. Sci. Polymer Edn.* **10**:19–31, 1999.

Tanahashi, M., Yao, T., Kokubo, T., Minoda, T., Miyamoto, T., Nakamura, T., Yamamuro, T., *J. Biomed. Mater. Res.* **29**:349–357, 1995.

Tateiwa, T., Clarke, I. C., Williams, P. A., Garino, J., Manaka, M., Shishido, T., Yamamoto, K., Imakiire, A. *Am. J. Orthop.* **37**:E26–E31, 2008.

Thomson, R. C., Yaszemski, M. J., Powers, J. M., Mikos, A. G., *Biomaterials.* **19**:1935–1943, 1998.

Van Raemdonck, W., Ducheyne, P., De Meester, P., In: *Metal and Ceramic Biomaterials Volume II Strength and Surface*, Ducheyne, P., Hastings, G. W., (eds.), Boca Raton, FL, CRC Press, pp. 143–166, 1984.

Walter, A., Lang, W., In: *Biomedical Materials*—Mater. Res. Soc. Symp. Proc. Vol. 55, Williams, J. M., Nichols, M. F., Zingg, W., (eds.), Pittsburgh, PA, Materials Research Society, pp. 181–190, 1986.

Webster, T. J., Ergun, C., Doremus, R. H., Siegel, R. W., Bizios, R., *J. Biomed. Mater. Res.* **51**:475–483, 2000.

Weiner, S., *CRC Crit. Rev. Biochem.* **20**:365–408, 1986.

Wen, H. B., de Wijn, J. R., Cui, F. Z., de Groot, K., *J. Biomed. Mater. Res.* **35**:93–99, 1997.

Wolke, J. G. C., van Dijk, K., Schaeken, H. G., de Groot, K., Jansen, J. A., *J. Biomed. Mater. Res.* **28**:1477–1484, 1994.

Wu, W., Zhuang, H., Nancollas, G. H., *J. Biomed. Mater. Res.* **35**:93–99, 1997.

Xie, G., Sun, J., Zhong, G., Liu, C., Wei, J. *J. Mater. Sci. Mater. Med.* **21**:1875–1880, 2010.

Yamamoto, M., Kato, K., Ikada, Y., *J. Biomed. Mater. Res.* **37**:29–36, 1997.

Zanello, L. P., Zhao, B., Hu, H., Haddon, R. C., *Nano Letters.* **6**:562–567, 2006.

Zhao, X., Yang, J., Xin, H., Wang, X., Zhang, L., He, F., Liu, Q., Zhang, W. *Mater. Sci. Eng. C Mater. Biol. Appl.* **91**:135–145, 2018.

Zreiqat, H., Evans, P., Howlett, C. R., *J. Biomed. Mater. Res.* **44**:389–396, 1999.

CHAPTER 18
CARDIOVASCULAR BIOMATERIALS

Shrirang V. Ranade
Genentech Inc., a member of the Roche Group, South San Francisco, California

Crystal Anderson-Cunanan
Boston Scientific Corporation, Marlborough, Massachusetts

Michael N. Helmus
Medical Devices, Drug Delivery, and Nanotechnology, Worcester, Massachusetts

Dedicated to the memory of Roger Snyder (1939–2016), who was the lead author of the original 2003 chapter and its 2009 update. Roger was a colleague, friend, mentor, researcher, and visionary.[a]

18.1 INTRODUCTION

Numerous definitions for *biomaterials* have been proposed. One of the more inclusive is "any substance (other than a drug) or combination of substances synthetic or natural in origin, which can be used for any period of time, as a whole or part of a system which treats, augments, or replaces tissue, organ, or function of the body," proposed by a Biomaterials Consensus Committee meeting at the NIH [1]. This definition must be expanded because biomaterials are currently being utilized as drug delivery coatings and scaffolds for tissue-engineered tissue and organs. Coronary stents are available that use coatings to release bioactive agents that prevent hyperplastic reactions (excessive tissue formation). Completely adsorbable scaffolds for tissue-engineered devices (hybrids of synthetic or biologic scaffolds and living cells and tissue for vessels, heart valves, and myocardium) can result in new organs without a trace of the original biomaterial.

[a]Helmus, M. N. and Tenney, B. (2016), In Memoriam—Roger Snyder, 1939–2016. *J. Biomed. Mater. Res.* **104**:1579–1580.

The cardiovascular system consists of the heart and all the blood vessels. Cardiovascular biomaterials may contact blood (both arterial and venous), vascular endothelial cells, fibroblasts, and myocardium, as well as a number of other cells and extracellular matrix that make up all biological tissue. This chapter will consider a wide range of biomaterials that interact with the heart, blood, and blood vessels.

Biomaterials used in the cardiovascular system are susceptible to a number of failure modes. Like all materials, mechanical failure is possible, particularly in implants. Although typical loads are low (as compared to orthopedic implants, for example), implant times are expected to exceed 10 years. At a typical heart rate of 90 beats a minute, 10 years of use would require more than 470 million cycles.

Thrombosis is a unique failure mode for cardiovascular biomaterials. The resulting clots may occlude the device or may occlude small blood vessels resulting in heart attacks, strokes, paralysis, failures of other organs, etc. On the other hand, devices can also damage blood cells. Hemolysis can diminish the oxygen-carrying capacity of the blood. Hemolysis can occur as a reaction to the material or its degradation products or as a result of shear due to the relative motion between the material surface and the blood.

Cardiovascular biomaterials are also in contact with other tissues. Another common failure mode of these devices is excessive growth of the tissues surrounding the device. This can be caused by reaction to the material (the natural encapsulation reaction to any foreign body), stresses on surrounding tissues caused by the device, or reaction to material degradation products. Vascular grafts (in particular, smaller-diameter grafts) are subject to anastomotic hyperplasia, which reduces the diameter of the graft at the anastomosis. A similar hyperplastic response occurs around endovascular stents used to keep vessels open after angioplasty or as a de novo treatment. Mechanical heart valves can fail if tissue grows into the space occupied by the moving disc. Nonliving replacement valves can become a nidus for infection, providing sessile bacteria with sequestered hiding places. Finally, tissue surrounding a device can die. As in hemolysis, this can be the result of reaction with the material or its degradation products or due to glutaraldehyde residuals leaching from the device.

Biomaterials that have been used in the cardiovascular system include processed biological substances, metals, and polymers (see Table 18.1 for typical materials and applications). Materials of biologic origin include structures such as pericardia, arteries, veins, and heart valves. Devices can also include biological substances, for example, coatings, such as collagen and heparin. Acellular materials such as porcine small intestinal submucosa (SIS) are in clinical evaluations.

Metals such as titanium, stainless steel, nitinol, and cobalt-chrome alloys are used in many devices. Generally, these are metals with passive surfaces, or surfaces that can be passivated. Silver has been used as a coating designed to resist infection. Glassy carbons have also been used as coatings to render surfaces thromboresistant. Pyrolytic carbon structures or coatings on graphite have been utilized in the fabrication of bileaflet heart valves. These are the most popular mechanical valves in use today. Recently, more radioopaque alloys have been utilized, e.g., PtCr alloys. Biodegradable magnesium alloys for stents and temporary devices such as bone plates and components are being evaluated with this alloy.

Polymeric materials that have been used in the cardiovascular system include polytetrafluorethylene, polyethylene terephthalate, polyurethane, polyvinyl chloride, etc. Textiles based on polytetrafluorethylene and polyethylene terephthalate are used extensively as fabrics for repair of vasculature and larger vessel replacement, greater than 6 mm in diameter. Stent-grafts are hybrid stent and grafts placed by catheter to treat aortic aneurysms nonsurgically and are fabricated of the same metallic alloys used in stents with textiles similar to those used in vascular grafts. Table 18.1 lists many of the biomaterials currently used in the cardiovascular system.

Biomaterials are used throughout the cardiovascular system in both temporary and permanent devices. Cardiovascular devices can be considered as temporary or permanent and internal or external. These categories are useful in determining the type of testing required.

Temporary external devices range from simple tubing (for bypass or hemodialysis) to more complicated devices such as oxygenators, arterial filters, and hemodialysis equipment. For purposes of this chapter, we will consider devices that contact blood only as external devices. Temporary internal

TABLE 18.1 Cardiovascular Biomaterials

Material	Applications
Hydrogels	
Hydrocolloids, hydroxyethyl-methacrylate, poly(acrylamide), poly(ethylene oxide), poly(vinyl alcohol), poly(vinyl-pyrrolidone)	Slippery coatings for catheters, vascular sealants, antiadhesives, thromboresistant coatings, endovascular paving, and drug delivery coatings
Elastomers	
Latex rubber, poly(amide) elast, poly(ester) elast, poly(olefin) elast, poly(urethanes), poly(vinyl chloride), silicones, styrene-butadiene copolymers	Central Venus catheters, intraaortic balloon pump balloons (polyurethanes), artificial heart bladders (polyurethanes), carrier for drug delivery coatings, insulators for pacemaker leads, vascular grafts (e.g., biostable polyurethanes), heart valve components (nonstructural), and extracorporeal tubing
Plastics	
Acrylics, cyanoacrylates, fluorocarbons, ethylene tetrafluoroethylene, ethylene-chloro-trifluoroethylene, fluorinated ethylene propylene, poly(tetra fluoroethylene), poly(vinylidene fluoride), poly(amides), poly(carbonates), poly(esters), poly(methyl pentene), poly(ethylene), poly(propylene), poly(urethane), poly(vinyl chloride)	Housings for extracorporeal devices [acrylics, poly(carbonates), poly(methyl pentane)], catheters, angioplasty balloons, sutures, vascular grafts (polyester textiles, expanded PTFE), medical tubing, oxygenator, and hemodialysis membranes
Engineering plastics and thermoset	
Epoxies, poly(acetals), poly(etherketones), poly(imides), poly(methyl methacrylate), poly(olefin) high, crystallinity, poly(sulfones)	Structural components for bioprosthetic heart valves [poly(acetals)], artificial heart housings, catheter components, and two-part systems for adhesives (e.g., epoxies)
Bioadsorbables	
Poly(amino acids), poly(anhydrides), polycarbonate and polycaprolactone 2-ureido-4 [1H]-pyrimidinones, poly (caprolactones), poly(lactic/glycolic) acid copolymers, poly(hydroxybutyrates), poly(orthoesters), tyrosine-derived polycarbonates	Sutures, biodegradable stents, scaffolds for tissue engineering, nanoparticles for treatment of blood vessels to prevent restenosis, and drug delivery coatings
Biologically derived materials	
Bovine vessels, bovine pericardium, porcine heart valve, porcine pericardium, human umbilical vein, human heart, decellularized tissue (e.g., porcine SIS, porcine urinary bladder matrix), tissue engineered/bioreactor grown tissue, e.g., smooth muscle cell type 1 collagen	Vascular patches and grafts, pericardial substitute, heart valves, and scaffolds for tissue engineering
Bioderived macromolecules	
Albumin, alginate, cellulose acetates, cuprammonium cellulose, chitosans, collagen, fibrin, elastin, gelatin, hyaluronic acid, phospholipids, silk, polyhydroxyalkanoate	Vascular graft coatings, hemodialysis membranes, experimental coatings, lubricious coatings (e.g., hyaluronic acid), controlled release coatings, scaffolds for tissue engineering, tissue sealants, antiadhesives, nanoparticles for intravascular drug delivery, thromboresistant coatings, and sutures
Passive coatings	
Albumin, alkyl chains, fluorocarbons, hydrogels, silica-free silicones, silicone oils	Biocompatibility, thromboresistance, lubricious coatings for catheters, cannulas, needles
Bioactive coatings	
Anticoagulants, e.g., heparin and hirudin, antimicrobials, cell adhesion peptides, cell adhesion proteins, metal oxide coatings (e.g., titania, zirconia), negative surface charge, plasma-polymerized coating, thrombolytics	Anti inflammatory, antithrombotic, injection resistance, enhanced cell adhesion, enhanced soft tissue and vascular healing, and recruitment of regenerative cells
Tissue adhesives	
Cyanoacrylates, fibrin, molluscan glue, PEG-based systems	Microsurgery for anastomosing vessels, vascular graft coating, enhancement of cell adhesion

(*Continued*)

TABLE 18.1 Cardiovascular Biomaterials (*Continued*)

Material	Applications
Metals and metallic alloys	
Cobalt chrome alloys, gold alloys, mercury amalgams, nickel chrome alloys, nitinol alloys (shape memory and super elastic), stainless steels, tantalum, titanium and titanium alloys	Guide wires; mechanical heart valve housings and struts, biologic heart valve and Tavi stents, vascular stents, vena cava umbrellas, artificial heart housings, pacemaker leads, leads for implantable electrical stimulators, surgical staples, superelastic properties of some nickel titanium formulations, shape memory properties of some Ni titanium formulations, and radio opaque markers
Ceramics, inorganics, and glasses	
Bioactive glasses, bioactive glass/ceramics, high-density alumina, hydroxyapatite, single crystal alumina, zirconia	Hermetic seals for pacemakers, enhanced cell adhesion, limited vascular applications, and experimental heart valve components
Carbons	
Pyrolytic (low-temperature isotropic) carbon, ultralow temperature isotropic carbon, pyrolyzed polymers for carbon-carbon composites, pyrolyzed fibers for fiber composites	Heart valves, coatings, fibers for carbon-fiber reinforced plastics or carbon-carbon composites
Composites	
Carbon-fiber-based: epoxy, poly(ether ketones), poly(imide), poly(sulfone), radioopacifiers ($BaSO_4$, $BaCl_2$, TiO_2) blended into: poly(olefins), poly(urethanes), silicones	Heart valve housing and struts and stents, housings for artificial heart, composites to control torque and steering of catheters, radioopaque fillers in polymers to identify location on x-ray

devices include a wide range of catheters used for diagnostics and treatment. These also include guidewires and introducers for use with catheters and cannulae for use in bypass circuits. An embolic filter to capture debris after carotid stenting is a newer interventional device.

Many left ventricular assist devices (LVADs) are chronic devices[b] that have drivelines or power lines that exit the skin to connect with the external power source. Vascular grafts and patches, as well as heart valves, are among the oldest examples of permanent cardiovascular implants. More recent examples of permanent internal devices include pacemakers, defibrillators, stents, LVADs, and artificial hearts.

New biomaterials have recently been developed and entering clinical use in medical devices, carriers for drug delivery and biologics, and synthetic and biologic scaffolds for tissue engineering/regenerative medicine. It is important to note that in the current clinical environment there is a strong focus on acute success driven by TAVI and the ability of patients to recover very quickly compared to surgical placement. However, one must be careful to note that the chronic outcomes could be disappointing and needs to be followed.

There are new processing techniques that have become or are becoming important methodology for producing biomaterials products, including electro spinning and 3D printing/additive manufacturing. It is important to remember that these are processing methods that have their own processing aids and additives, as is the case in any processing technique. The biomaterials are a tool in the production of these products. As with any manufacturing process, all products need to be evaluated for biocompatibility and durability, which can be profoundly affected by processing. It is also important to note that there are significant differences in the additive manufacturing process for the class of material: polymeric/plastic, biopolymer, metals, and ceramics. There has been more progress

[b]It might be argued that this is not a permanent external device, but more of a bridge to recovery or a bridge to transplant. It would be considered permanent based on ISO definition of >90 days use in terms of biocompatibility.

of the use of PEEK in orthopedic devices [2] but limited for vascular applications. As described by Ventola [3], "The three most commonly used 3D printer technologies in medical applications are: selective laser sintering (SLS), thermal inkjet (TIJ) printing, and fused deposition modeling (FDM)." Additionally, bioprinting deposits "bioink," i.e., biologically derived molecules suitable for processing that contain living cells or tissue. These printed structures can be further differentiated into the desired tissue or organ by direct implantation or by further cell growth in a bioreactor and is receiving strong attention for cardiovascular use.

Drug-eluting devices are representative of combination devices that have the potential to create potent new therapies by using the best properties of drug-device, biologic-device, or drug-biologic combinations. The U.S. Food and Drug Administration (FDA)'s Office of Combination Products (OCP) has broad responsibilities covering the regulatory life cycle of these combination products and will determine which center has primary regulatory responsibility [4, 5]. For example, the drug-eluting stent (DES) is primarily regulated by the Center for Devices and Radiological Health, but the Center for Drug Evaluation and Research has secondary responsibility for the analysis of drug content and compounding and manufacturing requirements.

DES have been a common therapy in coronary artery disease and are being evaluated in peripheral and specific organ applications. The field has moved through biostable coatings, biodegradable coatings, biodegradable stents, coating-free stents, and bare metal stents [6]. Newer therapies for drug-coated balloons for peripheral and coronary applications are just moving into the clinic. The drug may be coated directly on the surface of the balloon with a carrier or the drug can be placed in an excipient/carrier coated on the angioplasty balloon. Many use carriers (known as excipients), which are soluble agents and macromolecules such as polysorbate, sorbitol, hydrophilic urea, and polyethylene glycol 8000 [7].

Biomaterials for use as scaffolds for tissue engineering and carriers (excipients) for pluripotent cells like mesenchymal stem cells have become critically important for bioreactor grown tissue and in situ repair [8]. Scaffolds can be made from synthetic polymers, with a strong focus on biodegradables, or biological polymers, such as extracellular matrix materials that have a strong capability to adhere cells via cell adhesion peptides like RGD. The American Society for Testing and Materials (ASTM) standards for scaffolds are useful documents and, in some cases, necessary for FDA submissions.

More recently, animal-derived mucosal-like tissues, e.g., porcine small intestinal submucosa (SIS) and urinary bladder matrix (UBM), have regenerative capabilities [9]. These tissues are being evaluated in new applications such as heart valves. Any claims made on tissue regeneration are likely to be regulated as a biologic investigational new drug (IND).

Most of the applications for emergent nanoparticles have been for imaging and drug delivery [10] and are regulated as a pharmaceutical. These particles can be fabricated from biodegradables like polylactide/glycolide or albumin, hydrogels like polyethylene glycol (PEG), and magnetic materials like magnetite. Pharmaceutical use of nanoparticles will be regulated as a pharmaceutic. These require not only the local and systemic toxicology to be evaluated but also ADME (adsorption, distribution, metabolism, and excretion) of the drug and nanoparticle [11]. There is an example of a magnetic nanoparticle therapy regulated as a medical device to enhance delivery of thrombolytic drugs through clots [12].

Magnetic particle targeting methodology is evolving and allows precise delivery within organs, e.g., the arterial lesions [13], for drug delivery and/or precise energy delivery by localized heat, electric, or magnetic fields. Magnetite nanoparticles typically have demonstrated inherent biocompatibility. Translation into the clinic will dramatically increase over the next decade [14].

There continue to be many unknowns about the potential safety effects of nanomaterials, particularly nanoparticulates. These effects relate to their uptake in the reticuloendothelial system (e.g., lung, spleen, and liver), the ability to cross cell membranes, the potential to induce necrotic cell death or apoptosis, and the ability to interact at the level of cellular receptors [15].

Recent cardiovascular pre market approvals (PMAs) have been focused on bioabsorbable and DESs, and less invasively placed heart valves based on bovine or porcine bioprosthetic tissue.

18.2 MATERIALS

18.2.1 Metals

Metals are utilized for applications requiring high strength and/or endurance, such as structural components of heart valves, endovascular stents, and stent-graft combinations. Commonly used alloys include austenitic stainless steels (SS), cobalt-chrome (Co-Cr) alloys including molybdenum-based alloys, tantalum (Ta), and titanium (Ti) and its alloys. Elgiloy, a cobalt-nickel-chrome-iron alloy, has been used in fine wire devices such as self-expanding endovascular stents. The shape memory or superelastic properties of nickel-titanium alloys are also used in both coronary and heart valve stents. Drug-eluting polymer coatings have become an important design feature of coronary stents. These will be discussed in Sec. 18.2.3.

Noble metals such as platinum-iridium are also utilized in implantable pacemaker and cardioverter defibrillator electrodes. In addition to the noble metals, stainless steel and tantalum can also be used in sensing (non pacing) electrodes. Stainless steel has also been used as wire braids and reinforcements in catheters, particularly in high-pressure catheters such as those used for radiopaque dye injection. Enhanced radiopacity of metal alloys is a desired property for stents. Platinum-alloyed stainless steel has been developed to utilize the desired properties of stainless steel but with enhanced visibility during angiograms [16].

18.2.2 Carbons and Ceramics

Carbons and glassy carbons have been widely used as heart-valve components, particularly as pyrolytic carbon in the leaflets and housings of mechanical valves [17]. These materials demonstrate good biocompatibility and thromboresistance, as well as high lubricity and resistance to wear, in this application. Graphite is used as the substrate for many of the pyrolytic carbon coatings. The pyrolytic coatings impart strength and durability. The use of a graphite substrate reduces residual stresses that become significant in thick pyrolytic coatings. The substrate has the potential to act as a barrier to crack propagation within the pyrolytic coating. Low-temperature isotropic (LTI) coatings can be used to coat more heat-sensitive polymeric substrates. Sapphires have also been utilized as bearings in high-rpm implantable rotary blood pumps.

Ceramics have had limited application in cardiovascular devices except for hermetic seals on pacemakers and for insulation in radioablation catheters. Potentially, bioactive ceramics and glasses could have uses for enhanced cell and tissue adhesion. Recently, hydroxyapatite is being investigated as a nanoporous stent coating [18]. Experimental heart valves have been fabricated from ceramics such as single-crystal sapphire leaflets for heart valves. Ceramic coatings of heart-valve components to improve their wear properties, particularly by chemical vapor deposition methods, for example, diamond-like coatings (DLCs), are another potential application. The vapor-deposited coatings like DLC are also utilized in the impellers of left ventricular assist systems.

18.2.3 Polymers

In the early 1900s Carrel pioneered the use of vein grafts, which were used to close arterial defects [19]. However, the supply of these materials was limited. Long-term results were not promising, with many of the grafts developing aneurysms. In the early 1900s, solid wall tubes of glass, methyl methacrylate, and various metals were tried. These were largely unsuccessful due to thrombosis and anastomotic aneurysms.

During World War II and the Korean War, great progress was made in vascular surgery. Based on observations of sutures placed in the aorta, a textile was shown to have the ability to retain a fibrin layer, which then organized into a fibrous tissue layer. A number of materials were tested. Selection of these materials was based upon two criteria: (1) minimal tissue reactivity and (2) availability in a textile form.

Materials such as polyvinyl alcohol, polyamide, polyacrylonitrile, polyethylene terephthalate, and polytetrafluorethylene (PTFE) were all tried. When these textile tubes were implanted in the aorta, there was little clinical difference among the materials. Most of the differences in results were due to the different textile structures used. However, biostability and availability of commercial yarns did depend upon the polymer chosen.

Polyvinyl alcohol was soon abandoned due to excessive ruptures. Polyamide and polyacrylonitrile were discovered to be biodegradable, although it took 12 to 24 months to occur. Thus, polyethylene terephthalate (polyester) and PTFE became the polymers of choice. Both materials have demonstrated their longevity as an implant [20].

The PTFE textile graft is no longer commercially available. In general, the handling characteristics of that device were not as good as the polyester textile because commercially available PTFE fibers were larger in diameter than polyester fibers.

Clinical results are excellent when the devices are implanted in a high-flow, large-diameter arteries such as the aorta. However, patency rates decrease significantly when these devices are implanted below the aortic bifurcation. Thus, other materials and structures have been investigated for low-flow, small-diameter arteries.

In the mid-1970s, PTFE in a different form was introduced. Expanded PTFE is formed by compressing PTFE with a carrier medium and extruding the mixture. This is termed as a *paste extrusion,* since PTFE is not a thermosetting polymer. The resultant extrudate is then heated to near the glass transition temperature and stretched. Finally, the stretched material is sintered at a higher temperature. The resulting structure is microscopically porous with transverse plates of PTFE joined by thin PTFE fibers. This form of PTFE was indicated for use in smaller arteries with lower flow rates. However, the long-term patency results obtained with this vascular graft is not significantly higher than that obtained with a polyester textile. Another form of a PTFE vascular graft incorporates carbon particles in the inner 20 to 25 percent of the wall [21]. This graft showed improved patency rates at 24 months, but this difference disappeared by 36 months [22]. Recently, a heparin-coated expanded PTFE (ePTFE) vascular prosthesis has become available with potentially enhanced thromboresistance [23]. It is important to note that the blood response to traditional ePTFE is highly influenced by the air/PTFE interface. PTFE is hydrophobic and air is retained in the pores unless specific methods such as vacuum, hydrostatic pressure, or alcohol replacement of the air is utilized [24]. For use as a scaffold for tissue engineering it may be important to consider the role air plays on blood protein denaturation and its impact on pro inflammatory vs. a pro healing environment.

Polyester and PTFE textiles, as well as expanded PTFE are available as flat sheets. The textile materials are available as knits, weaves, and felts. These materials are used for patches and suture buttresses.

Silicone is a rubber-like polymer. It is normally cross-linked in a mold or during extrusion. The most common silicone used is room temperature vulcanizing (or RTV) silicone. In general, tissue does not adhere to silicone. The first commercially viable heart valve used a peroxide-heat-cured silicone ball in a cage. However, when first used, these silicone balls absorbed lipids and swelled, causing premature failure of the valves due to processing issues. These problems were corrected and until recently small numbers of these valves were still implanted. It is not uncommon that explants are recovered 30 years after implantations showing no degradation, minor wear, and only discoloration of the silicone ball [25]. In current cardiovascular devices, it may be used as percutaneous drivelines. Many of the silicones currently used in catheters and implant applications are platinum-cured RTV systems.

In 1992, the FDA banned breast implants with silicone-gel-filled silicone shells, following reports of women claiming that the implants had caused an autoimmune response. Saline-filled implants remained available. This had two impacts. First, manufacturers removed several commercial materials from the market. Second, silicone was perceived as a material that was perhaps unsuitable for long-term implant. After studies failed to establish a link between silicone-gel-filled implants, the FDA approved the use of these breast implants in 2006. Manufacturers of materials focused specifically for the biomedical market have established themselves. Silicones continue their long history of cardiovascular use for central venous lines, heart-valve sewing rings, and the drug delivery matrices for steroid-releasing pacemaker leads. There is an evolving concern of lymphoma development in porous silicone breast implants [26] but originally did not appear to be of concern for smooth-surfaced implants. The FDA recently released a notice indicating that there is concern for all breast implants including smooth surfaces.[c]

Polymers for DES. The vast majority of percutaneous coronary interventions involve the implantation of a DES [27, 28]. Treatment with DES has become the standard of care for prevention of restenosis after coronary angioplasty because they provide superior clinical outcomes in inhibiting acute recoil, negative remodeling, and neointimal hyperplasia with a single medical device [29]. Drug-eluting polymer coatings have become an important design feature of coronary stents. Elution of antiproliferative agents has been shown to prevent neointimal growth and inhibit restenosis. Innovation has resulted in previously unused polymer systems being used as an implantable component of stents including thermoplastic triblock elastomers [poly(styrene-*b*-isobutylene-*b*-styrene)] containing paclitaxel as nanoparticles [30] and butyl methacrylate/polyvinyl acetate mixtures with sirolimus with a butyl methacrylate membrane. Newer systems that have entered clinical use include a copolymer of vinylidene fluoride and hexafluoro propylene and a blend of polyvinyl pyrrolidinone and a proprietary hydrophobic and hydrophilic polymer described by the manufacturer as C19 and C10 [29, 30, 31, 32].

Currently, there are *seven* major commercially successful DES cleared for marketing by FDA for the treatment of patients with CAD: the sirolimus-eluting stent CYPHER®, the paclitaxel-eluting stents TAXUS® Express® and the thinner-strut version TAXUS® Liberté®, the zotarolimus-eluting stents Endeavor® and Resolute®, and the everolimus-eluting stent Xience V® and Promus® (the Xience V and Promus are essentially the same DES product sold under different trade names). Several other DES have received approval from regulatory bodies in Europe (CE Mark) and marketed in Europe, Latin America, and Asia-Pacific countries. Table 18.2 shows the details of drug-eluting polymer-coated stents [30].

Synthetic bioadsorbable materials have had a wide application as suture materials, although they have not generally been used in vascular anastomoses. They are being investigated for scaffolds for tissue-engineered heart valves and blood vessels. They are also being investigated as drug-release coatings on vascular prostheses and stents (to prevent thrombosis, infection, and excessive tissue formation) and as nanoparticles to deliver drugs to prevent restenosis. Bioadsorbable coatings forming drug-eluting layers on metal stents have been commercialized successfully; Table 18.3 shows details of stents that are being studied with bioadsorbable drug-eluting coatings.

Recently, stents made completely from synthetic bioadsorbable materials (both metals and polymers) have been investigated and have shown early promise of safety and efficacy. There is tremendous interest in the possibility of attaining success with a fully adsorbable DES as evidenced by the large number of on-going projects and studies. There are several reviews in the literature of the various polymer stents that have been studied in human trials worldwide, and it is apparent that other than a few examples the predominant technology being applied is based on PLGA [33, 34]. However, it should also be noted that the design and materials performance requirements from a fully adsorbable system place a potentially overwhelming burden on the materials technologies currently available and only underline the limitations due to structural and mechanical challenges (strut thickness), crimping and deployment limitations, and their inability to deal with hard calcified lesions. This has to be balanced overall with the need to have faster resorption times. Ideally, the material should maintain structural function beyond the period of revascularization and then accelerate in terms of resorption, thus providing function followed by a faster resorption process. This inherent conflicting requirement is the fundamental challenge to achieving the "holy grail" of a fully adsorbable DES and work continues in this area. Reva's polycarbonate tyrosine bioadsorbable stent has been CE Marked in Europe.[d]

[c] https://www.fda.gov/MedicalDevices/Safety/LetterstoHealthCareProviders/ucm630863.htm?utm_campaign=FDA%20MedWatch%20Notice%20-%20Breast%20Implants%3A%20Letter%20to%20Health%20Care%20Providers&utm_medium=email&utm_source=Eloqua

[d] https://globenewswire.com/news-release/2018/02/26/1387381/0/en/REVA-Announces-CE-Mark-and-First-Implant-of-the-Fantom-Encore-Bioresorbable-Scaffold.html

TABLE 18.2 Biostable Polymers for Drug Delivery Matrix for U.S.-cleared DES Products

Stent	Company	Polymer matrix
Cypher	Cordis (J&J)	Poly (ethylene-co-vinyl acetate) (PEVA) + Poly (*n*-butyl methacrylate) (PBMA)
Taxus/ Taxus Liberte	Boston Scientific	Poly (styrene-b-isobutylene-b-styrene) (SIBS)
Xience V/Promus	Abbott/Boston Scientific	Poly (vinylidene fluoride-co-hexafluoropropylene) (PVDF-HFP)
Endeavor	Medtronic	Methacrylated phosphorylcholine-based (PC) (cross-linked)
Resolute	Medtronic	Poly (butyl methacrylate-co-vinyl acetate) ("C10") + Poly (hexyl methacrylate-co-vinyl pyrrolidone-co-vinyl acetate) ("C19") + Poly (vinyl pyrrolidone) (PVP)

Source: Adapted from Ref. 30.

TABLE 18.3 Survey of Bioabsorbable Polymer Coatings for Nondegradable DES in Various Stages of Clinical Development

DES	Company	Polymer-drug coating	Regulatory status
BioMatrix	Biosensors	PLA-Biolimus A-9	CE, OUS
DESyne	Elixir	PLA-Novolimus	CE
Ultimaster	Terumo	PLA-PCL-Sirolimus	CE
Nobori	Terumo	PLA-Biolimus A-9	CE
Supralimus	Sahajanand	PLGA-Sirolimus	CE
Infinnium	Sahajanand	PLGA-Paclitaxel	CE
Genous	OrbusNeich	SynBiosys-Sirolimus, anti-CD34	FIH
NEVO	Cordis (J&J)	PLGA-Sirolimus; PLGA-paclitaxel	FIH*
JACTAX	Labcoat (BSC)	PLA-Paclitaxel	FIH*
Sparrow	CadioMind (Biosensors)	SynBiosys-Sirolimus	FIH
BioMime	Meril Life Sciences	PLGA/PLLA-Sirolimus	CE
Abrax	Rotis Vacsular	PLGA-Sirolimus	CE
Excel	JW Medical	PLA-Sirolimus	China
Yukon	Translumina Therapeutics	Microporous SS-Sirolimus-Resomer with shellac topcoat	CE
Synergy	Boston Scientific	PLGA-Everolimus	CE
Orsiro	Biotronik	PLLA-Sirolimus; SiC	CE
RENatural	Cardionovum	PLLA-Sirolimus	FIH

* = Discontinued development.
Source: Adapted from Ref. 30.

18.2.4 Biological Materials

Materials of biological origin are used as cardiovascular devices and as coatings. Most of the devices commercially available rely on collagen as the structural material. Collagen is a macromolecule that exists as a triple helical structure of several amino acids. Cells express procollagen; the ends of the procollagen molecule are enzymatically trimmed, allowing the trimmed helical strands to self-assemble into the collagen molecule. Twenty-eight different types of collagen have been identified [35, 36], with Types I and III predominant in cardiovascular structures and Type IV as part of the basement membrane underlying endothelial cells.

Collagen can be cross-linked by a number of techniques to improve its structural integrity and biostability. An early example of this is the tanning of skin to make leather. The use of formaldehyde to preserve biological samples is another example.

In 1969, porcine aortic valves were cross-linked with glutaraldehyde and used to replace human aortic valves. Glutaraldehyde cross-linking was shown to yield a more biostable structure than cross-linking with formaldehyde [41]. These valves have been very successful in older patients and do not require the anticoagulation regimen needed for mechanical heart valves. Significant effort has been made to reduce the calcification of bioprosthetic heart valves, both porcine aortic valve prostheses and bovine pericardial valve prostheses [37]. Calcification and degradation mechanisms limit the use of these devices in young patients and children. Reduction of calcification entails modification of the surface, for example, binding amino oleic acid, or treatments with alcohols and surfactants to remove lipids and other agents that can be a nidus for calcification [38, 39]. A recent meta-analysis of published series that included clinical data on structural valve deterioration (SVD) for at least 10 years follow-up determined that the absence of an anti calcification treatment in the process, regardless of the type of tissue used in the valve, was associated with higher SVD risk [40]. The use of bioprosthetic valves in patients under 60 years of age is increasing and will continue to increase with the development of new treatments to reduce calcification and with the development of minimally invasive methods for valve replacement. Cross-linked bovine arteries and human umbilical veins have been used as vascular replacements. Cross-linked pericardium has also been used as a patch material, primarily between the myocardium and the pericardia, sac to prevent adhesions.

Biological materials can also be used as coatings. Textile vascular grafts are porous and must be sealed (preclotted) prior to use. Research suggests that a four-step procedure, including a final coat with heparinized blood, can improve patency results. However, surgeons typically take nonheparinized blood and coat the graft in one or two applications. Precoated grafts are commercially available [41]. Cross-linked collagen and gelatin (a soluble form of collagen) as well as cross-linked albumin can be used to seal porous materials. The rate of degradation of the coating will depend upon the material chosen, as well as the degree of cross-linking. Alginates are being evaluated as an injectable into heart muscle for CHF therapy [42].

Significant effort is now focusing on tissue-engineered vessels and heart valves. Given the complexity of a heart valve, the most logical choice is to start with an existing animal tissue heart valve and decellularize it to reduce its antigenicity [43]. Clinical experience with such decellularized animal valves began in 2001 and multiple approaches have been tried since that time. Despite beginning with a functional valve, these decellularized xenogeneic valves ultimately failed from immune-mediated reactions [44]. Due to the issues with immunogenicity, the field has begun to focus more on creating synthetic scaffolds from various polymeric materials, using such techniques as dip molding, spraying, or electrospinning [45]. The hope then is that these synthetic scaffolds will repopulate with cells in vivo, regenerating a living human tissue valve. Termed *endogenous tissue restoration* (ERT), some success with biodegradable polyurethane scaffolds has been achieved in children for pulmonary valve replacement [27].

The history of this effort for tissue-engineered vascular grafts is found in the seeding or culturing of endothelium on synthetic vascular prostheses. The clinical outcomes did not justify continued development. However, new technology allows vascular tissue to be formed on scaffolds of either synthetic or adsorbable materials. The awareness that endothelium alone was not suitable has led to the evolution of techniques to recreate the vascular tissue utilizing multiple cell types [46, 47]. This approach utilizes the cell types expected in final structure, for example, endothelium, smooth muscle cells, and fibroblasts, or pluripotent cells such as stem cells. There had been some efforts at decellularizing vessels and heart valves to remove soluble proteins and cellular material to create vessels that would not require cross-linking [48]. It was observed that this was an ideal substrate for reendothelialization. Recently this approach has been used to decellularize a rat heart and recellularize with cardiac and endothelial cells to recreate a potentially functional heart [49].

Devices combining external and internal components, such as LVADs, need a means of communicating and/or supplying power across the skin. Drivelines can be wrapped in textile. However, the epithelial cells at the device–tissue interface will attempt to encapsulate the percutaneous device, forming a pocket that often becomes infected. Using a device seeded with autologous fibroblasts has been demonstrated to decrease the risk of such infections [50]. Epithelial cells will not penetrate a fibroblast to device seal.

Using biologic materials in a device requires additional controls and testing. Materials of biological origin must be certified as coming from disease-free animals and tested for assay, viruses, mycoplasma, endotoxins, and sterility. In addition, shipping and storage for a product that may degrade will require special consideration.

18.3 TESTING

The testing program for any medical device can be divided into five phases: (1) biocompatibility, (2) short-term bench (or in vitro) tests, (3) long-term bench tests, (4) animal (or in vivo) studies, and (5) human clinical studies [51, 52]. For each of these five phases, the type of device and length of time it will be used must be considered in developing test protocols.

18.3.1 Biocompatibility

The sterilized device and by default the materials of which it is constructed need to meet basic biocompatibility requirements, generally as defined by the ISO 10993 standards, to be nontoxic, nonthrombogenic, noncarcinogenic, nonantigenic, and nonmutagenic [52]. ISO 10993-1 has moved to "Evaluation and testing within a risk management process" [53]. This process should generally begin with assessing materials, the manufacturing processes, the clinical use, and the frequency and duration of exposure. This assessment may identify biomaterial-based risks, e.g., chemical toxicity, biological response—including manufacturing and processing, that could alter the physicochemical characteristics of the device. Potential risks should be addressed and include knowledge gaps to be evaluated by testing. A context is given for interpretation in the appropriate benefit-risk context.

The Guidance for Industry [54] issued by FDA in 2016 tabulates the tests required to demonstrate biocompatibility. These tables are based on an International Organization for Standardization (ISO) Document ISO-10993 [53]. For implant devices contacting blood for more than 30 days, the following tests are required: cytotoxicity, sensitization, irritation or intracutaneous reactivity, acute system toxicity, subchronic toxicity, genotoxicity, implantation, and hemocompatibility. For devices in contact with blood for less than 24 hours, subchronic toxicity and genotoxicity are not required. The international standard also has a category for devices that are in use for between 24 hours and 30 days. This standard does not require the subchronic toxicity testing. The FDA may require this type of testing, however. The tests required for implanted cardiovascular devices that do not contact blood require the same type of testing program except for the hemocompatibility requirement and for the implantation tests for devices in use for less than 24 hours.

The tests for external devices contacting blood are also the same as for implanted devices, although implantation tests are noted as "may be applicable." For long-term devices, external or implants, chronic toxicity and carcinogenicity testing may also be required.

Biocompatibility will be affected by surface contamination. Surface contamination can occur as a result of processing. Process aids, cleaning agents, finger oils, etc., can all have an impact on compatibility. Residues can also result from sterilization. Residual sterilant (EO or glutaraldehyde) or sterilant by-products (such as ECH), modification of the material surface from radiation, and toxic debris from microbes can impact biocompatibility. Materials such as solvents, plasticizers, unreacted monomers, and low-molecular-weight polymers can diffuse from polymers. Certain cleaning or thermal processes can accelerate diffusion.

Therefore, all samples for biocompatibility testing should be from completed devices, which have seen the complete process, including sterilization (usually termed finished goods in industry). If there is a chance that contaminants could continue to diffuse from the material, testing samples after long-term storage should be considered.

Many manufacturers can provide biocompatibility data either in their literature or as an FDA master file. Often material manufacturers will advertise that a material meets Class VI biocompatibility requirements. Class VI requirements are an old set of tests published in the U.S. Pharmacopeia and were developed for testing food packaging. They are similar to the cytotoxicity, acute toxicity, and subchronic toxicity tests. However, the data provided by a materials manufacturer are on samples that have not seen the processing and storage of the device. The data is simply an indication that the material can pass the initial set of biocompatibility tests if processed appropriately.

There are a wide variety of tests in the literature addressing these various requirements. Protocols for many of these tests have been issued as ISO standards. ASTM has also developed protocols for demonstrating biocompatibility. Since these standard protocols are recognized by many regulatory agencies, their use will often aid in the device approval process.

Collaborating with a laboratory that specializes in these types of tests and is familiar with the regulatory requirements will generally produce the best data to demonstrate biocompatibility.

18.3.2 Special Risks Associated with the Use of Materials of Animal Origin

The use of animal tissues or animal-derived materials in a medical device should only be done after careful consideration of non tissue-based alternatives. Using animal tissues or derivatives in a medical device introduces special risks that are unique to the use of animal tissues. Additional precautions must be taken when using animal tissues, so this should only be done when a performance characteristic is required that is not available from non animal-based materials. In heart valves, for example, the use of animal tissues for the leaflet of the valve is justified, as synthetic materials have not yet been developed that can provide the same degree of flexibility and durability as animal tissues. For coatings, however, a synthetic hydrogel may be entirely suitable, and carries less risk associated with it than a collagen or fibrin coating.

The considerations of the special risks associated with the use of animal tissues and derivatives are spelled out in a series of regulatory standards called the ISO 22442 series [55, 56]. This series of standards was developed after several cases of patient harm occurred with the use of biologically sourced materials. These European standards, and parallel regulations in the United States, Japan, Australia, and other countries, require the manufacturer to consider the potential special risks associated with the use of animal tissues and materials, and introduce controls and safeguards to reduce the potential risks to levels as low as possible. These unique risks include contamination by bacteria, moulds, yeasts, viruses, prions, parasites, or other materials that could result in undesired pyrogenic, immunological, or toxicological reactions.

Close attention must be given to the source of the material, including the animal species, tissue type, source country, region, and herd, and selecting suppliers that can document the proper breeding, raising, and feeding of animals used to supply the starting material for the device. Every animal must be inspected by a trained veterinarian and certified to be fit for human consumption before tissues can be harvested from the animal. Traceability from the finished device back to the farms that supplied the animals that contributed to the tissues used must be maintained in the event of an outbreak. Only in cases where especially rigorous processes are used (e.g., tallow derivatives, charcoal, and amino acids), can processing provide adequate safeguards from the threat of transmissible spongiform encephalopathies (TSEs). Constant vigilance must be maintained to ensure adequate control of microbial levels, and processes must be validated for their ability to inactivate viruses. Only in exceptional circumstances can high-risk neural tissues be used for medical devices, and lower risk tissues must be harvested and processed in such a way as to avoid the potential for cross-contamination with higher risk tissues.

Tissues must be processed in defined and validated processes, within validated timeframes and under controlled packing, shipping, and storage conditions. Oftentimes special chemical sterilization procedures must be used when other, more robust, sterilization methods would adversely affect the mechanical properties of the tissue. Finally, the shelf life of the finished product must be demonstrated with time, using methods specifically developed for tissue so that any untoward effects of storage can be detected.

18.3.3 Short-Term Bench Testing

Short-term bench (in vitro) testing includes material identification, surface characterization, mechanical properties, etc. Material identification tests characterize the bulk properties of the material. Tests chosen depend upon the type of material. Chemical formula, molecular weight, degree of crystallinity, melting or softening point, and degree of cross-linking may all be important to characterize a polymer. Composition, grain size, and contamination levels may define metallic materials. Composition, molecular weight, cross-linking, shrinkage temperature, and purity may define materials of a biological origin.

Surface properties will affect the reaction between the material and tissue. Material composition at the surface may differ from the bulk composition. Coatings, either deliberately applied or as contaminates, will modify the biological response. Chemical extraction studies, perhaps performed as part of the development of the cleaning process, could identify any inadvertent contamination. The coating should have an identification test. The geometry of the surface, such as surface roughness, will also modify this response. The dimensions of the surface roughness can be measured microscopically. For smaller features, scanning electron microscopy or atomic force microscopy can be utilized to characterize the surface roughness.

Mechanical properties of the material will determine if a device will suffer an early failure. Tensile strength and elastic modulus can be measured by a simple tensile test. If the device could be subjected to impact loading, an impact type test can be performed. Tear tests are important for materials in sheets such as fabrics and films. This is particularly true for tear-sensitive materials such as silicone.

ASTM has published numerous protocols for mechanical tests and for operating test equipment.

18.3.4 Long-Term Bench Testing

For long-term devices, endurance (or fatigue) testing is required. In general, simple tensile or bending tests can be performed on the basic material. Frequently, however, the device itself is tested in some simulated loading condition. Such a test includes the effects of processing, sterilization, and shelf life on the material. It also allows the designer to calculate reliability. There are test and reliability standards for some cardiovascular devices. Vascular grafts, heart valves, stents, and left-ventricular assist devices, among others, have reliability requirements and recommendations for the types of tests that can be employed. However, since there is a wide variation in these types of devices, tests that fit the device must be developed.

Materials can be tested in tension, compression, or bending. Using the material in a sheet form, biaxial loading can be applied. For larger stress or strain ranges (and thus a lower number of cycles), the same equipment used to test for material strength can be used. However, for smaller loads and higher numbers of cycles, specialized equipment is required to complete the tests in a reasonable time. Loading devices using rotating camshafts will apply fixed strain ranges. Fixed stress ranges can be applied using pressure-actuated devices. For very small stress or strain loads approaching the endurance limit, electronic mechanisms similar to those used to drive audio speakers can be used to drive a material at very high speeds.

If one plots a variable such as stress range or strain range versus number of cycles, the resulting curve will approach a limit known as the *endurance limit*. Below this limit, the number of cycles that a material can withstand is theoretically infinite. Above this limit, the number of cycles that a material can withstand under a variable load can be calculated from Miner's rule:

$$\frac{n_1}{N_1} + \frac{n_2}{N_2} + \frac{n_3}{N_3} + \cdots \frac{n_k}{N_k} = 1$$

where, n_1 through n_k are the number of cycles for a given load, N_1 through N_k are the total number of cycles to failure under each load, and k is the total number of different loads. Thus, if the stresses on a device can be calculated, the fatigue life of a device can be estimated.

However, regulatory agencies prefer that the life of a device, or its reliability, be measured rather than calculated. Therefore, it is common practice to perform reliability testing on the device, as it will be used in a patient. Although it is usually not possible to use blood or other biological fluid in a long-term test setup, due to the difficulty in preserving the fluid, if the environment will affect the material, then a reasonable substitute must be found. In general, buffered saline at body temperature has been accepted as a substitute test media.

Since cardiovascular devices, particularly implants, are expected to function for multiple years, tests to demonstrate reliability must be accelerated. At the same time, the test setup should apply loads that are as close to the actual usage as possible. Although some forms of degradation can be accelerated by an increase in temperature, it is common practice to test materials and devices at normal body temperature. If environmental temperature is increased to accelerate the testing, internal temperatures of materials with glass transition points must remain below these transition points. Thus, increasing the cyclic rate normally accelerates reliability tests.

The upper limit of this type of acceleration is determined by several factors. First, the normal range of load and motion must be duplicated. For larger device parts, such as heart-valve discs, inertia will limit the cyclic rate. Second, any increase in temperature due to accelerating bending must not change the material. Finally, the rate of loading must not affect, either negatively or positively, the amount of creep (or viscoelastic deformation) experienced by the material in actual use.

Reliability can be calculated by several methods. One method used in other industries (such as the automotive industry) is to test 12 samples to the proposed life of the device. If all 12 samples survive then the sample size is adequate to demonstrate a reasonable risk of failure using a binomial model. To determine failure modes, the stress or strain on the device can be increased by 10 percent for 10 percent of the proposed life of the device. If there are no failures at 110 percent of the proposed life, the stress or strain range is increased another 10 percent. This stair-step method continues until a failure mode is demonstrated.

A more common method for medical devices is to run the life test until failure occurs. Then an exponential model can be used to calculate the percent survivability. Using a chi-square distribution, limits of confidence on this calculation can be established. These calculations assume that a failure is equally likely to occur at any time. If that assumption is unreasonable (e.g., if there are a number of early failures), it may be necessary to use a Weibull model to calculate the mean time to failure. This statistical model requires the determination of two parameters and is much more difficult to apply to a test that some devices survived. In the heart valve industry lifetime prediction based on SN or damage-tolerant approaches has been traditionally used. These methods require fatigue testing and ability to predict crack growth [17, 52, 57].

Another long-term bench test required for these devices is shelf life. Some cardiovascular biomaterials can degrade during long-term storage. Thus, typical devices, having seen the standard process, are packaged and aged before testing. Generally, increasing the temperature of the storage conditions can accelerate aging. As a general rule, it is accepted that the rate of degradation doubles for every 10°C increase in temperature [58]. This is generally acceptable for most materials; however, regulatory agencies may be reluctant to review test data on tissue-based heart valves that have undergone accelerated aging, since elevated temperatures can affect the tissue components. If you plan to include accelerated aging in your device testing program, it would be prudent to review this decision with your regulatory agency(ies) to ensure that the data will be accepted. Durability testing on bioprosthetic heart valves is intensive, expensive, and time consuming. Some test labs also include variations in humidity in the protocol and may include a short period of low-temperature storage. Products that have been packaged and aged can then be tested to determine if they still meet the performance criteria (including biocompatibility). At the same time, similarly aged units can be tested for sterility, thus demonstrating that the packaging material and packaging process also yield the appropriate shelf life.

Polymeric and biologic-based devices may also need to be evaluated on the basis of the biostability of the materials. This could include hydrolytic and enzymatic stability, requiring a combination of testing that examines hydrolytic stability under simulated physiologic stresses as well as evaluation in animals. Stress tends to accelerate many of these degradation mechanisms, and materials that look stable under static conditions may not perform well when stressed. Soft grades of poly(ether urethane) are an example of a material than can undergo oxidative degradation when stressed due to the presence of oxidative enzymes present in biologic systems.

18.3.5 Animal Studies

There are few standard protocols for animal studies. Each study is typically designed to account for the function and dimensions of the device. There are two approaches to developing a protocol. First, one could use a model of the condition being treated to demonstrate the function of the device. For example, vascular grafts can be implanted as replacements for arterial segments. The second approach is to design a test that will demonstrate the functioning of the device, but not treat an abnormal condition. For example, a left-ventricular assist device can be implanted in normal animals. The protocol would then consist of operating the device and monitoring the effect of the device on the blood. In addition, the effect of the biological environment on the device could be documented.

The first step in developing an appropriate protocol is to determine the purpose of the test. Is the purpose to demonstrate the functionality of the device, to demonstrate that the device is effective in treating a medical condition, or to test long-term biocompatibility and biostability of the device? The purpose of the test and the proposed use of the device (i.e., biological environment and length of use) will determine the model and length of time required for the test.

If the device can be miniaturized, or if nonfunctioning devices are appropriate for the purpose of the test, then smaller animals can be used. Of course, the life span of the animal must be adequate for the implant time required. Additionally, miniaturized devices will not replicate the forces in larger devices and durability may not be adequately assessed. If, however, the purpose of the test requires a full-sized functioning device, a larger animal model will have to be selected.

18.4 MATERIAL PROCESSING AND DEVICE DESIGN

Processing methods can have a major impact upon the success or failure of a cardiovascular biomaterial. As described previously, surface features (either deliberately introduced or as the result of machining or tool imperfections), residues (from cleaning, handling, or sterilization), or process aids (either as surface residues or as bulk material diffusing from the biomaterial) can change the biological results. For tissue-based devices, prolonged exposure of the tissue to conditions which could support microbial growth (e.g., open bottle of saline) can lead to microbial colonization of the tissue or device, resulting in tissue degradation, elevated bioburden and pyrogens, and potentially a nonsterile device. See Ref. 27 for a thorough review of processing considerations for tissue-based products.

Fatigue life is critical in many of the applications for which metallic alloys are used. Processing and joining methods can significantly affect crack initiation, thus decreasing fatigue life. Surface scratches, bubbles, and inclusions can significantly increase local stresses. Extruded, molded, and cast metals can have internal stresses “frozen in” as the material cools and solidifies. These stresses will add to the stresses caused by external forces and decrease the fatigue life of the material. Internal stresses will cause some materials, such as polycarbonate, to be more susceptible to stress crazing in the presence of solvents.

Surfaces of structures subject to a high load and/or high multiples of cycles should be highly polished. Metals with internal stresses should be annealed. Appropriate cleaning materials should be selected in order to avoid etching or damaging the surface.

There are three methods currently used to decrease thrombosis: (1) use of a smooth surface to prevent thrombi from adhering, (2) use of a rough surface (usually a fiber-like surface) to encourage the formation of a neointima, and (3) use of a coating to prevent coagulation or platelet adherence. All of these methods have been used in cardiovascular medical devices, with varying degrees of success.

As a general rule, the slower the flow of blood, the more likely thrombi will form. Conversely, areas of high shear and turbulence can result in platelet damage and activation, resulting in thrombus formation. Thus, the design of a device should avoid areas of stasis, low flow, high shear, and turbulence.

A suitable surface must be either smooth, avoiding any small features that might cause micro eddies in the flow, or of sufficient roughness so as to allow the resulting coagulation products to securely anchor to the surface.

The thickness of the resulting layer is limited by the need to provide nutrients to the underlying tissue. Without the formation of blood vessels, this is generally about 0.7 mm. Should the material itself cause the formation of a thicker layer or should parts of the underlying structure move or constrict the tissue, the tissue will die. If this occurs continuously, the tissue will calcify or the underlying biomaterial will remain unhealed.

Cleanliness of a material will also affect the biologic outcome. All processing aids should be completely removed. This includes any surfactant used in the preliminary cleaning steps. Surfactants can cause cell lysis or pyrogenic reactions. Solvents can diffuse into plastics and diffuse out slowly after implantation causing a local toxic reaction. Some plastics may retain low-molecular-weight polymer, or even monomers from their formation. These can also be toxic to cells. These may also leach out slowly after implantation. Plasticizers (used to keep some polymers pliable) can also damage blood components. The oxidation by-products of some metals can also be locally toxic.

Thus, it is important to establish a processing method prior to final evaluation of a cardiovascular biomaterial for use in a medical device.

REFERENCES

1. Williams, D. F. (1987). *Definitions in biomaterials: Proceedings of a consensus conference of the European Society for Biomaterials*, Chester, England, March 3–5, 1986, D. F. Williams (ed.). New York: Elsevier.
2. McGilvray, K. C., J. Easley, H. B. Seim, D. Regan, S. H. Berven, W. K. Hsu, T. E. Mroz, and C. M. Puttlitz (2018). "Bony in-growth potential of 3D-printed porous titanium alloy: A direct comparison of interbody cage materials in an in vivo ovine lumbar fusion model." *The Spine Journal*, **18**(7):1250–1260.
3. Ventola, C. L. (2014). "Medical applications for 3D printing: Current and projected uses." *P & T: A Peer-Reviewed Journal for Formulary Management*, **39**(10):704–711.
4. Helmus, M. N., D. F. Gibbons, and D. Cebon (2008). "Biocompatibility: Meeting a key functional requirement of next-generation medical devices." *Toxicologic Pathology*, **36**(1):70–80.
5. FDA. "Combination products." Accessed 2019, https://www.fda.gov/combinationproducts/default.htm
6. Chandrasekhar, J., K. Martin, and R. Mehran (2016). "Role of coronary drug-eluting stents in current clinical Practice." *Clinical Pharmacist*, 8(11):1–29.
7. "Materials Database" accessed 2019, https://matdata-s.asminternational.org/mmd/index.aspx
8. Mao, A. S. and D. J. Mooney (2015). "Regenerative medicine: Current therapies and future directions." *Proceedings of the National Academy of Sciences of the United States of America*, **112**(47):14452–14459.
9. Londono, R. and S. F. Badylak (2016). "Biomaterials from decellularized tissues," in *Biomaterials from Nature for Advanced Devices and Therapies*. Neves, N. M. and Rei, R. L. (eds.), Hoboken, NJ:Wiley, pp. 190–210.
10. Anselmo, A. C. and S. Mitragotri (2016). "Nanoparticles in the clinic." *Bioengineering & Translational Medicine*, **1**(1):10–29.
11. Brand, W., Noorlander, C. W., Giannakou C., et al. (2017). "Nanomedicinal products: A survey on specific toxicity and side effects." *International Journal of Nanomedicine*, **12**:6107–6129.
12. "Pulse therapeutics." Accessed 2019, https://euphratesvascular.com/#pulse
13. Chorny, M., Fishbein, I., Yellen, B. B., et al. (2010). "Targeting stents with local delivery of paclitaxel-loaded magnetic nanoparticles using uniform fields." *Proceedings of the National Academy of Sciences*, **107**(18):8346–8351.
14. Weinberg, I., Mair, L. O., Jafari, S., et al. (2018). "Image-guided placement of magnetic neuroparticles as a potential high-resolution brain-machine interface," in *Brain-Computer Interface and Dynamical Brain States*, Larrivee, D. (ed.), London, UK:Intechopen, pp. 141–155.
15. Helmus, M. N., D. F. Gibbons, and D. Cebon (2008). "Biocompatibility: Meeting a key functional requirement of next-generation medical devices." *Toxicologic Pathology*, **36**(1):70–80.

16. Craig, C. H., Radisch, H. R., Trozera, T.A., et al. (2003). "Development of a platinum-enhanced radiopaque stainless steel (PERSS). Stainless steels for medical and surgical applications." in *Symposium on Stainless Steels for Medical and Surgical Applications*. Winters, G. L. and Nutt M. J. (eds.), West Conshohocken, PA: ASTM International. STP 1438: pp. 28–38.
17. Ritchie, R. O. (1996). "Fatigue and fracture of pyrolytic carbon: A damage-tolerant approach to structural integrity and life prediction in 'ceramic' heart valve prostheses." *Journal of Heart Valve Disease*, **5**(Suppl 1): S9–S31.
18. Van Beusekom, H. M., Peters, I., Kerver, W., et al. (2007). "Hydroxyapatite coating eluting low dose sirolimus shows less delayed healing but equal efficacy to Cypher in porcine coronary arteries." *Circulation*, **116**:TT-777-c.
19. Campbell, P. A., McGeachie, J. K., and Prendergast, F. J. (1981). "Vein grafts for arterial repair: Their success and reasons for failure." *Annals of the Royal College of Surgeons of England*, **63**(4):257–260.
20. Guidoin, R. G., Snyder, R. W., Awad, J. A., et al. (1992). "Biostability of vascular prostheses," in *Cardiovascular Biomaterials*, Hastings, G. W. (ed.), London: Springer, pp. 143–172.
21. Tenney, B., W., Catron, D., Goldfarb, and R. Snyder (1984). *Testing of Filled PTFE Vascular Prostheses Using Panel Grafts*. Paper presented at the Second World Congress on Biomaterials, Washington, DC.
22. Kapfer, X., W. Meichelboeck, and F. M. Groegler (2006). "Comparison of carbon-impregnated and standard ePTFE prostheses in extra-anatomical anterior tibial artery bypass: A prospective randomized multicenter study." *European Journal of Vascular and Endovascular Surgery*, **32**(2):155–168.
23. Battaglia, G., R. Tringale, and V. Monaca (2006). "Retrospective comparison of a heparin bonded ePTFE graft and saphenous vein for infragenicular bypass: Implications for standard treatment protocol." *Journal of Cardiovascular Surgery*, **47**(1):41–47.
24. Ritter, E. F., R. D. Vann, C. Wyble, W. J. Barwick, and B. Klitzman (1989). "Hydrostatic pressure reduces thrombogenicity of polytetrafluoroethylene vascular grafts." *American Journal of Physiology-Heart and Circulatory Physiology*, **257**(4):H1076–H1081.
25. Tarzia, V., T. Bottio, L. Testolin, and G. Gerosa (2007). "Extended (31 years) durability of a Starr-Edwards prosthesis in mitral position." *Interactive CardioVascular and Thoracic Surgery*, **6**(4):570–571.
26. Clemens, M. W., M. B. Nava, N. Rocco, and R. N. Miranda (2017). Understanding rare adverse sequelae of breast implants: Anaplastic large-cell lymphoma, late seromas, and double capsules. *Gland Surgery*, **6**(2):169–184.
27. Serruys P. W., Miyazaki, Y., Katsikis, A., et al. (2017). "Restorative valve therapy by endogenous tissue restoration: Tomorrow's world? Reflection on the EuroPCR 2017 session on endogenous tissue restoration." *EuroIntervention*, **13**(AA):AA68–AA77.
28. Wessely, R. (2010). "New drug-eluting stent concepts." *Nature Reviews Cardiology*, **7**(4):194–203.
29. Ranade, S. V. and K. Udipi (2016). "Drug delivery coatings for coronary stents," in Glocker, D. and Ranade, S. V. (eds.), *Medical Coatings and Deposition Technologies.* Salem, MA: Scrivener Wiley.
30. Ranade, S. V., R. E. Richard, and M. N. Helmus (2005). "Styrenic block copolymers for biomaterial and drug delivery applications." *Acta Biomaterialia*, **1**(1):137–144.
31. Daemen, J. and P. W. Serruys (2007). "Drug-eluting stent update 2007." *Circulation*, **116**(3):316–328.
32. Udipi, K., MELDER, R. J., CHEN, M., et al. (2007). "The next generation endeavor resolute stent: Role of the BioLinx™ Polymer System." *EuroIntervention*, **3**(1):137–139.
33. Ang, H. Y., H. Bulluck, P. Wong, S. S. Venkatraman, Y. Huang, and N. Foin (2017). "Bioresorbable stents: Current and upcoming bioresorbable technologies." *International Journal of Cardiology*, **228**:931–939.
34. Zhu, Y., Yang, K., Cheng, R., et al. (2017). "The current status of biodegradable stent to treat benign luminal disease." *Materials Today*, **20**(9):516–529.
35. Collagen. Retrieved from http://en.wikipedia.org/wiki/Collagen.
36. Prockop, D. J. and K. I. Kivirikko (1995). "Collagens: Molecular biology, diseases, and potentials for therapy." *Annual Review of Biochemistry*, **64**(1):403–434.
37. Helmus, M. N. and C. M. Cunanan (2011). "Mechanical and bioprosthetic heart valves," in *Biomaterials for Artificial Organs*, Lysaght, M. and Webster, T. J. (eds.), Woodhead, pp. 113–162.
38. Carpentier, A. F., S. Carpentier, C. M. Cunanan, L. Quintero, M. N. Helmus, C. Loshbaugh, and H. C. Sarner (2007). USA Patent No. 7,214,344.
39. Schoen, F. J. and R. J. Levy (1999). "Tissue heart valves: Current challenges and future research perspectives." *Journal of Biomedical Materials Research*, **47**(4):439–465.

40. Wang, M., A. P. Furnary, H.-F. Li, and G. L. Grunkemeier (2017). "Bioprosthetic aortic valve durability: A meta-regression of published studies." *Annals of Thoracic Surgery*, **104**(3):1080–1087.

41. Greisler, H. P. (1991). *New Biologic and Synthetic Vascular Prostheses*. Austin, TX: Landes.

42. Mann, D. L., R. J. Lee, A. J. Coats, et al. (2016). "One-year follow-up results from AUGMENT-HF: A multicentre randomized controlled clinical trial of the efficacy of left ventricular augmentation with Algisyl in the treatment of heart failure." *European Journal of Heart Failure*, **18**(3):314–325.

43. Crapo, P. M., T. W. Gilbert, and S. F. Badylak (2011). "An overview of tissue and whole organ decellularization processes." *Biomaterials*, **32**(12):3233–3243.

44. Naso, F. and A. Gandaglia (2018). "Different approaches to heart valve decellularization: A comprehensive overview of the past 30 years." *Xenotransplantation*, **25**(1):e12354.

45. Nachlas, A. L. Y., S. Li, and M. E. Davis (2017). "Developing a clinically relevant tissue engineered heart valve—A review of current approaches." *Advanced Healthcare Materials*, **6**(24):1700918.

46. Helmus, M. N. (1998). "Introduction/general perspective. Frontiers of industrial research, International Society for Applied Cardiovascular Biology (Abstract)." *Cardiovascular Pathology*, **7**(5):281.

47. Helmus, M. N. (1999). From Bioprosthetic Tissue Engineered Constructs for Heart Valve Replacement. Paper presented at the *First International Symposium, Tissue Engineering for Heart Valve Bioprostheses, Satellite Symposium of the World Symposium on Heart Valve Disease*, Westminster, London.

48. Malone, J. M., K. Brendel, R. C. Duhamel, and R. L. Reinert (1984). "Detergent-extracted small-diameter vascular prostheses." *Journal of Vascular Surgery*, **1**(1):181–191.

49. Ott, H. C., Matthiesen, T. S., Goh, S. K., et al. (2008). "Perfusion-decellularized matrix: Using nature's platform to engineer a bioartificial heart." *Nature Medicine*, **14**:213.

50. Gesler, W., Smith, R., DeDecker, P. G., et al. (2004). "Updated feasibility trial experience with the Viaderm percutaneous access device." *ASAIO Journal*, **50**(4):349–353.

51. Van Recum, A. F. (1998). *Handbook of Biomaterials Evaluation: Scientific, Technical and Clinical Testing of Implant Materials*. Philadelphia, PA: Taylor & Francis.

52. Helmus, M. N. (2003). *Biomaterials in the Design and Reliability of Medical Devices*. Georgetown, TX: Landes Bioscience.

53. ISO 10993-1:2018. Biological evaluation of medical devices—Part 1: Evaluation and testing within a risk management process (p. 41): ISO Technical Committee: ISO/TC 194 Biological and clinical evaluation of medical devices.

54. FDA. (2016). Use of International Standard ISO 10993-1, "Biological evaluation of medical devices—Part 1: Evaluation and testing within a risk management process."

55. ISO 22442-1:2015. Medical devices utilizing animal tissues and their derivatives—Part 1: Application of risk management: ISO/TC 194/SC 1 Tissue product safety.

56. ISO 22442-3:2007. Medical devices utilizing animal tissues and their derivatives—Part 3: Validation of the elimination and/or inactivation of viruses and transmissible spongiform encephalopathy (TSE) agents (p. 22).

57. Kafesjian, R. and P. Schmidt (1995). "Life analysis and testing," *Short Course, Evaluation and Testing of Cardiovascular Devices*. Cenitos, CA: Society for Biomaterials.

58. ASTM F1980-16 (2016). *Standard Guide for Accelerated Aging of Sterile Barrier Systems for Medical Devices*. West Conshohocken, PA: ASTM International.

CHAPTER 19
DENTAL BIOMATERIALS

Roya Zandparsa
Tufts University School of Dental Medicine, Boston, Massachusetts

19.1 INTRODUCTION: HISTORY OF DENTAL MATERIALS

Gold was one of the first dental materials known; its use has been traced to circa 500 B.C. Its durability and lack of corrosion make it one of the best restorative materials available. Gold foils were used in Italy for tooth filling in A.D. 1500. At the same time, wax was used for taking impressions of the teeth. The impressions were poured with plaster. The plaster models were used as a replica for making the artificial teeth using ivory or human bones which were fixed in place with low melting temperature metals. Around the 1700s in France, other materials like lead and tin were also used as fillings to replace the missing part of the teeth structure.

The first dental porcelain which was used for making complete dentures and individual teeth was introduced at the end of 1700s. One of the major benefits of ceramic as a dental restorative material was the resemblance to natural dentition.

The first traditional (low-copper) lathe-cut amalgam was introduced by G. V. Black in the 1890s. At the same time, other dental materials like plaster, gutta percha, gold alloys, denture teeth, and zinc oxychloride cement were developed and appeared in market. All the materials and techniques revolutionized dentistry and made it possible to create better and more accurate fitting restorations.

Since the nineteenth century, other dental materials like high-copper amalgam, polymers, including composite resins, elastic impression materials, base metal alloys, orthodontic wires, bonding agents, glass ionomer, and polycarboxylate cements were also developed, which enhanced treatment possibilities.

Every year new versions of dental materials with better properties are developed and introduced to practitioners. Among them are all-ceramic restorations, better quality composite resin and bonding agents, flowable composites and sealants, resin-modified glass ionomers and resin cements, compomers, more accurate impression materials, and many more.[1]

Biomaterials are used in orthopedics, cardiovascular surgery, and plastic surgery. In dentistry they occur in all areas of prosthodontics, periodontics, orthodontics, endodontics, implantology, and restorative dentistry. Their use may be temporary, that is, less than 60 minutes; short (<30 days); or longstanding (>30 days). Biomaterials that result in few biological reactions are classified as biocompatible. Most reactions from dental materials are allergies with symptoms from the skin and oral tissues.[2,3]

The science of dental materials studies the composition and properties of materials and the way they interact with the environment. The selection of materials for any given application can thus be undertaken with confidence and sound judgment. Dentists spend much of their professional career handling materials. The success or failure of many treatments depend on the correct selection of materials and their manipulation. Dental biomaterials are the natural tissues or synthetic products that are used to restore or replace decayed, damaged, fractured, or missing teeth. Natural dental tissues include enamel, dentin, cementum, bone, and other intraoral tissues. The major synthetic dental material groups are metals, ceramics, and polymers, including composite structures (Table 19.1).[4]

TABLE 19.1 Three Basic Materials Used in Dentistry with Some of Their Applications

Metals	Alloys	Components of dentures, orthodontic wires, cast restorations
Ceramics	Crystalline ceramics	Al_2O_3, SiO_2
	Glasses	Dental porcelain
	Inorganic salts	Gypsum product, dental cements
Polymers	Rigid	Denture bases, direct filling
	Elastomers	Impression materials

19.2 METALS

In the last 25 years, alloys used in dentistry have become more complex. There are many choices from different global companies. Today's alloys have as their most abundant element a number of metals, including gold, palladium, platinum, silver, nickel, cobalt, chromium, and titanium. The metallurgy of each of these alloy systems is generally complex and demanding of the laboratory and the dentist. The proper selection and manipulation of these alloys is imperative if dental prostheses are to perform well with longevity. In their molten state, metals dissolve to various degrees in one another which allows them to form alloys in their solid state.[5,6]

19.2.1 Clinically Important Properties of Dental Alloys

Dentists and laboratory technicians should always select alloys based on their properties, not their cost. Some alloy properties that must be considered are reviewed in this section.[6]

19.2.2 Corrosion

The corrosion of an alloy is the key to the success of a prosthesis. For metals and alloys, corrosion is always accompanied by a release of elements and a flow of current. All alloys corrode to some extent intraorally, but alloys vary significantly in this regard. Corrosion can lead to poor esthetics, compromise of physical properties, or increased biological irritation.[7] Corrosion is complex and impossible to predict based simply on the composition of the alloy. The presence of multiple phases or high percentages of nonnoble elements does, however, increase the risk of corrosion.[7–9] In dental metallurgy, the seven elements that are recognized as noble are gold, platinum, palladium, iridium, rhodium, osmium, and ruthenium. Corrosion of alloys may be clinically visible if it is severe, but more often the release of elements continues for months or years at low levels and is not visible to the eye.[7,10] Corrosion is clearly related to biocompatibility, but the relationships between them are complex and difficult to predict.[9] All alloys should be tested in vitro and in vivo for their biological effects such as biocompatibility.[7]

19.2.3 Alloys Available in Dentistry Today

Today many alloys are common to several different types of restoration: full-cast restoration, ceramometal restorations, and removable appliances framework. Before 1975, specific restorations were limited to specific alloys.[7]

High-Noble Alloys. High-noble alloys have, by definition, at least 40 weight percent gold and 60 weight percent noble elements in their composition. Gold-platinum alloys are highnoble alloys that may be used for full-cast or ceramo-metal applications. They may contain zinc or silver as hardeners and are often multiple-phase alloys. These alloys may or may not contain silver but almost always contain tin, indium, rhodium, iridium, osmium, or gallium as oxide-forming elements to promote the bonding with porcelain.[7]

Noble Alloys. Noble alloys are precious metals that are resistant to tarnish. This excludes silver by definition. They have no stipulated gold content but must contain at least 25 weight percent noble metal. This is a very diverse group of alloys which includes gold and palladium.[7]

Base-Metal Alloys. Base-metal alloys do not contain precious metals to impart their corrosion resistance. They contain less than 25 weight percent noble metal according to the ADA classification. But in practice, most contain no noble metal; these alloys include nickel, cobalt, chromium, and berlium.[7]

19.2.4 Trends for Tomorrow

Although it is difficult to predict, several trends are likely for dental alloys. The trend toward "metal-free" dentistry and associated use of all-ceramic restorations has received much promotion in recent years. Although all-ceramic restorations are clearly advantageous in some clinical applications and can provide excellent esthetics, they currently are not a viable replacement for all the ceramometal restorations.[7]

The vast majority of tooth-colored restorations are still ceramometal restorations that[11] have proven long-term clinical records that are still not available for any all-ceramic system. All-ceramic systems require the removal of significantly more tooth structure and are susceptible to fracture, especially in posterior teeth or in fixed partial denture applications due to fatigue.[12–14] If properly constructed by a qualified laboratory technologist, the traditional ceramometal restoration can yield excellent esthetic results. Finally, the claims of superior biocompatibility of all-ceramic materials are often not proven but assumed based on tests with traditional ceramic materials.[7]

A relatively recent development has been the use of a sintered metal composite as a metallic substructure for ceramometal restorations (Captek).[15] These composites consist of a sintered high-noble alloy sponge infiltrated with an almost pure gold alloy. The result is a composite between two gold alloys that is not cast, but fired onto a special refractory die. The porcelain does not bond to an oxide layer in these systems but presumably bonds mechanically to a micro rough gold surface. Any stress concentrations at the ceramometal interface are presumably relieved by the excellent ductility of the gold. The esthetics of these ceramometal restorations is good because the yellow color of the metal is more like that of dentin than other alloys. Several companies make gold composite systems. Although these systems might be an alternative to cast metal, ceramometal, or all-ceramic single unit restorations but there is not enough long-term data available on them yet.[7]

Some researchers claim that the number of periodontal pathogens around the restorations made using these alloy system are reduced but more clinical research need to be done regarding this claim.[7]

There have always been some controversies about the biological safety of metals that may leach from alloys. Manufacturers are trying to develop new alloys to eliminate this problem. Any material, to some degree, releases elements. The question is, how safe are they? There are some assessments that can be done clinically to test the compatibility of the patient with any materials, but they are not approved yet. It would be more relevant and advantageous to find some way to test and investigate these materials for their allergic or chronic low-dose effects. The practitioner must always try to decide whether questions about biological safety are founded in fact or hyperbole.[7]

19.3 CERAMICS

Teeth are complex organs of the human body and consist of several component tissues, both hard and soft. The tooth is subject to many damaging influences. Restorative dentistry concerns itself with repairing damaged teeth and their supporting structures. Aesthetics are today of paramount concern, and the only medical material that in any way provides a durable and satisfactory solution to the aesthetic repair of teeth is ceramic.[16]

19.3.1 Historic Perspectives: Ceramics as a Restorative Material

Although routine use of ceramics in restorative dentistry is a recent phenomenon, the desire for a durable and esthetic material is ancient. Most cultures through the centuries have acknowledged teeth as an integral facial structure for health, youth, beauty, and dignity. Teeth have routinely been designated with an equally powerful, if occasionally perverse, role in cultures where dentitions were purposely mutilated as inspired by vanity, fashion, and mystical and religious beliefs. Therefore, it has been almost universal that unexpected loss of tooth structure and, particularly, missing anterior teeth create physical and functional problems and often psychologic and social disturbances as well. During the eighteenth century, artificial teeth were made of human teeth, animal teeth carved to the size and shape of human teeth, ivory, bone, or mineral (porcelain) teeth. Other than for costly human teeth that were scarce, the selection of artificial tooth materials was based on their mechanical versatility and biologic stability. Animal teeth were unstable toward the "corrosive agents" in saliva, and elephant ivory and bone contained pores that easily stained. Hippopotamus ivory appears to have been more desirable than other esthetic dental substitutes. John Greenwood carved teeth from hippopotamus ivory for at least one of the four sets of complete dentures he fabricated for George Washington.[17,18] Mineral teeth or porcelain dentures greatly accelerated an end to the practice of transplanting freshly extracted human teeth and supplanted the use of animal products. Feldspathic dental porcelains were adapted from European triaxial whiteware formulations (clay-quartz-feldspar), nearly coincident with their development. After decades of effort, Europeans mastered the manufacture of fine translucent porcelains, comparable to porcelains of the Chinese, by the 1720s. The use of feldspar, to replace lime (calcium oxide) as a flux, and high firing temperatures were both critical developments in fine European porcelain.[19] Around 1774, a Parisian apothecary Alexis Duchateau, with assistance of a Parisian dentist Nicholas Dubois de Chemant, made the first successful porcelain dentures at the Guerhard porcelain factory, replacing the stained and malodorous ivory prostheses of Duchateau.[17,18] Dubois de Chemant continually improved porcelain formulations and fabricated porcelain dentures as part of his practice.[17,18] While in England, Dubois de Chemant procured supplies from collaborations with Josiah Wedgwood during the formative years of the famous porcelain manufacturing concern that currently bears his name. In 1808, Giuseppangelo Fonzi formed individual porcelain teeth that contained embedded platinum pins. Fonzi called these teeth "terrametallic incorruptibles" and their esthetic and mechanical versatility provided a major advance in prosthetic dentistry. In 1723, Pierre Fauchard described the enameling of metal denture bases. Fauchard was credited with recognizing the potential of porcelain enamels and initiating research with porcelains to imitate color of teeth and gingival tissues.[17,20]

19.3.2 Mechanical Versatility and Esthetics

Improvements in translucency and color of dental porcelains were realized through developments that ranged from the formulations of Elias Wildman in 1838 to vacuum firing in 1949.[21] Glass inlays were introduced by Herbst in 1882 with crushed glass frit fired in molds made of plaster and asbestos.[20] In 1885, Logan resolved the retention problem encountered between porcelain crowns and posts that were commonly made of wood by fusing the porcelain to a platinum post (termed a Richmond crown). These platinum post crowns represented the first innovative use of a ceramometal system.[20] In 1886, Land introduced the first fused feldspathic porcelain inlays and crowns by combining burnished platinum foil as a substructure with the high controlled heat of a gas furnace.[17,20] The all-ceramic crown system, despite its esthetic advantages, failed to gain widespread popularity until the introduction of alumina as a reinforcing phase in dental porcelain. A noteworthy development occurred in the 1950s with the addition of leucite to porcelain formulations that elevated the coefficient of thermal expansion to allow their fusion to certain gold alloys to form complete crowns and fixed partial dentures (FPDs). Refinements in ceramometal systems dominated dental ceramics research during the past 35 years which resulted in improved alloys, porcelain-metal bonding, and porcelains. In 1980, a "shrink-free" all-ceramic crown system[22] (Cerestore, Coors Biomedical, Lakewood, Colo) and a castable glass-ceramic crown system[23] (Dicer, Dentsply/York Division, York, Penn) were introduced. They provided additional flexibility for achieving esthetic results, introduced advanced ceramics with innovative processing methods, and stimulated a renewed interest in all-ceramic prostheses.[17]

For dental use ceramics are composed of metal oxides and half-metals. Silicium dioxide, Al_2O_3, K_2O, MgO, CaO, and B_2O_3 are the most frequently used oxides.[24,25] In production of crowns and veneers, feldspathic ceramic (a mixture of feldspar, quartz, and kaolin) has been the most usual ceramic. The latest feldspathic materials have been reinforced with Al_2O_3 (i.e., Hi-Ceram, Vita) and fibers of Zr (Mirage). Glass-ceramic materials are also used, as leucite-reinforced feldpathic ceramics (IPS Empress) or tetrasilic micaglass (Dicor). In recent years glass-infiltrated core mixtures (In-Ceram) have been introduced. Variants of these materials like high-density alumina core (Procera), ceramics for CAD-CAM system (Cerec), and ZrO_2 with YO (Denzir) have also been introduced. Ceramic-fused-to-metal is usually produced with SiO_2 and contains oxides from Na, K, Ca, Al, B, and Zn. The colors of ceramics are made by the addition of oxides of Fe, Ni, Cu, Ti, Mn, Co, Sn, Zr, and Ti.[24]

Most dental materials have relatively low fracture toughness values ranging from 0.9 to 4.0 MPa. For toughening the materials, three mechanisms have been described: (1) increasing plasticity, (2) dissipation of strain energy through the introduction of microcracks, and (3) inducing phase changes. Each of these mechanisms can increase toughness by a factor of three or more.[26] Although fatigue is the most dominant mechanism responsible for the failure of ceramics, the possibilities of stress corrosion, hydrogen embrittlement, liquid-metal embrittlement (creep fatigue), and creep should also be considered. Rob Ritchie described the damage-tolerant approach to lifetime predictions and associated test methods for small cracks and compared them with other methods, including standard fatigue tests and fatigue crack growth analysis for long cracks. For enhancing the fatigue resistance of materials four mechanisms have been described: (1) crack deflection and meandering, (2) zone shielding, (3) contact shielding, and (4) combinations of these mechanisms. Rob Ritchie recommended that materials should be chosen according to the ability of their microstructures to make the cracks meander during applied loading. Since mechanisms which reduce crack initiation may not reduce crack growth, and vice versa, materials should be designed to retard crack initiation and then incorporate crack growth blockers to enhance lifetime performance further. Chemical factors, plasticity, and microstructure have been identified as the three major variables which control interfacial toughness. Rob Ritchie proposed a novel concept of intentionally placing defects along the interfacial region as a method of diverting crack paths and increasing the interfacial toughness.[26]

There have been many investigations about crack-resistant or crack-tolerant designs in dental ceramic engineering. Some crack-resistant materials like zirconia and alumina cores have been introduced to market, and both have been used by practitioners.

Some models have also been proposed for crack-tolerant designs which will arrest cracks or slow down their propagation rates. A layered ceramic technique has been proposed and it seems to have potential since different layers can be designed to have different properties that produce crack blunting.[27]

Natural tooth consists of two distinct materials: enamel with approximately 65 GPa Young's modulus and dentin with approximately 20 GPa Young's modulus. They are bonded by dentin-enamel junction (DEJ). In dental crown restorations, Young's modulus of the ceramic crown material is typically 65 to 300 GPa, while that of the cement is 2 to 13 GPa. Hence, there is a tensile stress concentration in the crown at the interface between the crown and the cement. In contrast, in nature, DEJ provides a graded interface between enamel and dentin. Due to the complex structure of actual dental restorations, flat multilayered structures (with equivalent elastic properties) are often used to study contact-induced damage in dental multilayers. Huang et al.[28] proposed using a bioinspired functionally graded material layer to reduce the stress in the dental crown restoration structures. These include the modulus mapping of the cross section of natural tooth by using nanoindentation technique and finite element simulation to obtain optimal design for actual dental crown structures. Unlike existing dental crown restorations that give rise to high stress concentration, the functionally graded layers (between crown materials and the joins that attach them to dentin) are shown to promote significant reductions in stress and improvements in the critical crack size. This technique also provides new insights into the design of functionally graded crown architecture that can increase the durability of future dental restorations.[28]

Textured ceramics also seem to discourage crack formation. Different surface treatments such as sandblasting may also be used to reduce the formation and the growth of cracks. It is very difficult and challenging to form ceramics into different shapes using a high-temperature process. Some processes are available for custom operations, such as hot-isostatic-pressing (HIP) and computer-aided design/computer-integrated machining (CAD/CAM). HIP seems to be very promising for creating standard shapes but not for custom prosthesis. The advantage of ceramic blocks used in CAD/CAM system is that they are defect free. But it is difficult to get an optimum esthetic result using these blocks compared to a traditional ceramic fabrication technology in which a laboratory technician places and characterizes the dental porcelain layer by layer.[27]

Even though CAD/CAM has been available commercially to create low-cost chairside all-ceramic restorations in a short time, but due to the high cost of the equipment, training needs, and problems with marginal fit and esthetic, CAD/CAM still has not replaced the traditional technique. Researchers have been working on developing a dental ceramic system which would have a higher esthetic, lower cost, more resistance to fatigue and crack formation, and better ability to bond. These newer innovations are still to come.[27]

19.3.3 Dental CAD/CAM Technology

Bioceramics have rapidly been adopted in dental restorations for implants, bridges, inlays, onlays, and all-ceramic crowns.[29] Structurally, dental bioceramics cover a wide spectrum of glass ceramics, reinforced porcelains, zirconias, aluminas, fiber-reinforced ceramic composites, and multilayered ceramic structures.[29,30] Bioceramics in dental restorations are essentially oxide-based glass-ceramic systems and other traditional ceramic materials. The materials cover mica-containing glass ceramics, feldspar- and leucite-containing porcelains, glass-infiltrated alumina, and yttria-stabilized tetragonal zirconia.[17,29] With increasing interest in improving the esthetic quality of restorations, a wide variety of ceramic structures and their composites have also been developed. These include the ceramic whisker-reinforced composites[31,32] and the damage-resistant brittle-coating bilayer or trilayer structures.[29,33] During the last two decades, dental CAD/CAM technology has been used to replace the laborious and time-consuming, conventional lost-wax technique for efficient fabrication of restorations. This technology enables dentists to produce complex shapes of ceramic prostheses under the computer-controlled manufacturing conditions directly from the simply shaped blocks of materials within 1 hour.[34] However, dental CAD/CAM systems utilize abrasive machining processes, in which the machining damage is potentially induced, resulting in the reduction of the strength of ceramic prostheses and the need for final finishing in oral conditions using a dental handpiece and diamond burs. It is expected that a ceramic restoration should have a high longevity. However, wear and fatigue damage is often observed to cause the failures of bioceramic prostheses in their performance. With the CAD/CAM systems, restorations can be produced quicker, which eliminates the need for temporary restorations. Moreover, with CAD/CAM, making prostheses with consistent quality become possible.[34] Dental CAD/CAM technology consists of digital image generation, data acquisition, computer-assisted milling systems, and tooling systems.[34]

Currently, there are two major CAD/CAM systems, one for machinable bioceramics, the other one for the difficult to machine materials. In the first system, the computer-assisted milling process can be used to machine the machinable ceramics directly from their blanks (Fig. 19.1).[35] In the second

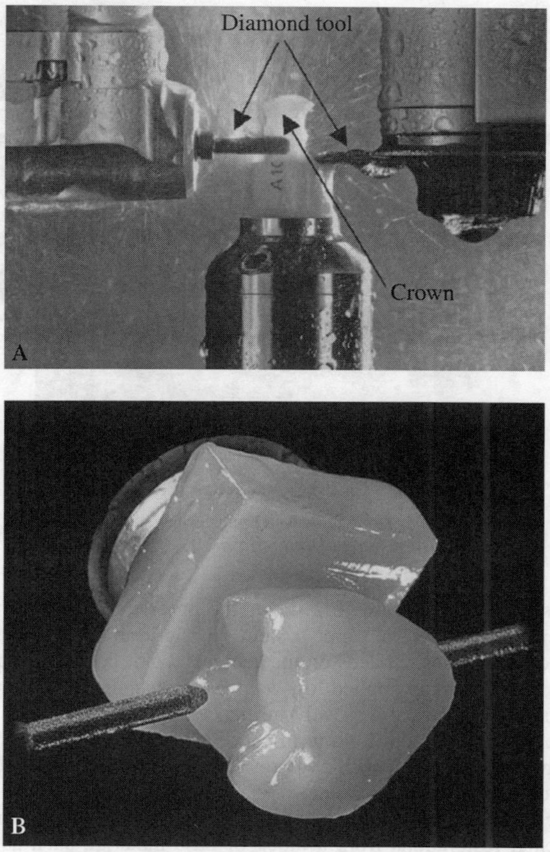

FIGURE 19.1 (A) The computer-aided milling system in a Cerec system,[35] and (B) the machined crown from a blank using the Cerec system.[35] *(Photo courtesy Sirona Dental Systems.)*

system, the milling process is firstly conducted from the presintered blanks of the difficult-to-machine ceramics, and then the sintering is followed to harden the ceramic prostheses considering the compensation for shrinkage during sintering in a special high-temperature furnace.[35–38] In the computer-aided design of prostheses, there are two digital image generation systems for data acquisition. The three-dimensional, noncontact, optical/laser scanning systems are more widely applied in

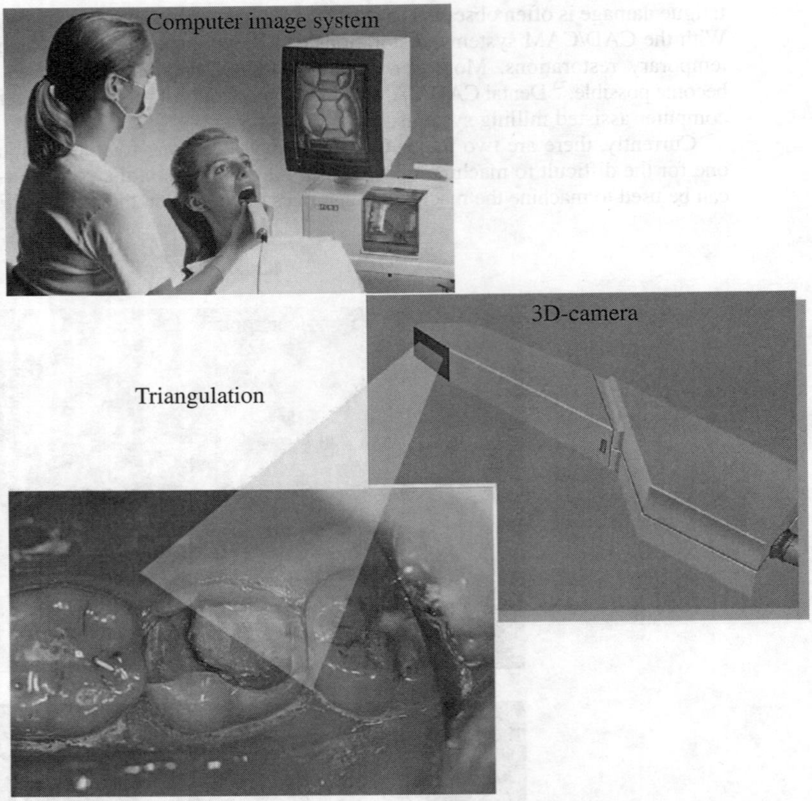

FIGURE 19.2 Computer-aided optical triangulation system for data acquisition in a Cerec system.[35] (*Photo courtesy Sirona Dental Systems.*)

dentistry.[29,34,35,38] Figure 19.2 shows the proprietary optical three-dimensional measurement system used in the commercial Cerec system.[35] Long-term success of single and multiple unit fixed prosthodontic restorations depends on the accuracy of fit between restoration and prepared tooth structure.[39] With the commonly applied lost-wax-casting technique in the production of metal castings or frameworks, their accuracy is greatly influenced by the dimensional properties of investment and casting alloy. The quality and long-term success of cast restorations also can be impaired and affected by casting imperfections such as porosities or impurities, poor solder joints, and underdimensioned or nonhomogeneous metal frameworks. With the aid of x-ray defectography, it was possible to demonstrate that roughly a third of all cast restorations exhibit manufacture-related deficiencies. Milling of dental restorations from a block of base material, such as metal, ceramic, or resin, is proposed as an alternative for fabricating restorations. This technology promises results of greater accuracy and structural homogeneity. With quality as the objective, the significant advantage in using milling technology lies in the fact that cold working of rolled structures and ceramic materials will always yield homogenous material structures. To produce milled restorations with accurate fit, digitization of the prepared tooth surface and converting the data into control signals for computer-assisted milling is required. Since the shapes of prepared teeth and dental restorations cannot be described with regular geometric methods due to their unlimited number of degrees of freedom, CAD/CAM technology has encountered numerous problems. Therefore, when using current CAD/CAM technology, data acquisition has to be performed with digital mechanical scanning of the cast parts or by point-based optical systems. High-speed data acquisition with the aid of complex free-form surface geometry has so far been an unsolved problem. In addition, problems arise in the generation of customized occlusal surfaces. Some techniques, with varying amounts of effort, enable the creation of occlusal surfaces by transferring digitized data obtained from measurements of a reference denture or from recordings of mandibular joint movements, which is a time-consuming process with considerable variations in precision.[39]

CAD/CAM technology holds promise for being an important technology to fabricate dental restorations in the future. Assuming continued improvements, we will hope to be able to achieve a consistent quality and precision and to be less labor intense and less expensive than conventional techniques. The quality and the speed of intraoral imaging of the CAD/CAM process still need improvement.[39]

19.4 POLYMER MATERIALS

Polymers have a major role in most areas of dentistry. Their distinctive properties allow a range of clinical applications not possible with other types of materials. The most widely used impression materials (alginates, polyethers, polysulfides, and silicones) are polymers. A polymeric matrix with particulate ceramic filler (quartz) is the most commonly used restorative material. Additional applications include denture base, denture teeth, dentin/ceramic/metal bonding systems, cements, dies, provisional crowns, endodontic fillings, tissue conditioners, and pit and fissure sealants. However, the primary use of polymers in term of quantity is in the construction of complete dentures and the tissue-bearing portions of removable partial dentures (RPDs).[40]

To manufacture removable complete or partial dentures, or veneers for crowns and fixed partial dentures (FPDs), polymer-based materials are used. Complete crowns may also be produced with monomers in a polymerization process in which the material is loaded by ceramic particles and fibers.[24,41] Various materials have been used for the production of prostheses: (poly)acrylic acid esters, (poly)substituted acrylic acid esters, (poly)vinyl esters, polystyrene, rubber-modified (poly)metacrylic esters, polycarbonates, polysulfones, and mixtures of the above-mentioned polymers.[24,42] Polyacetal is a polymer made from formaldehyde and used to make tooth-colored brackets in RPDs. Polyurethane has also been applied for the production of dentures. (Poly)methyl methacrylate (PMMA) is the most common polymer used to make removable complete and RPDs. These dentures are made of prepolymerized particles of PMMA, a monomer system with one or more oligo- or polyfunctional methacrylates and an initiator system such as benzoyl peroxide. PMMA contains phthalates, stabilizers, and antioxidants. And dentures made of acrylates are polymerized by free radicals either by heat or by chemicals.[24,43] Many efforts have been made to improve the tensile bond strength of PMMA dentures by, for example, the addition of polyethylene with a very high molecular weight.[24,44] Until now it has not been possible to evolve better materials replacing the extensive clinical use of PMMA for denture production.[24]

19.5 COMPOSITES

Despite the rich history associated with development of dental composites (Fig. 19.3)[27] and their prominent position in dentistry today, their future is even more promising for other reasons. Nonshrink prototypes will reach the market in the short term, solving some of the problems related to premature bonding system stresses. This will also reduce internal porosity that may have contributed to higher than desired water absorption. More attention is being focused on silanes since they have never been optimized or well controlled to produce potentially excellent interphase bonding. Filler technologies, which directly affect most composite properties, including wear resistance, now include more and more nanofiller use. Nanofillers permit substantially smaller interparticle distances and shelter the resin matrix from wear.[27,45]

Nanofillers also have a better esthetic outcomes. The technology has been moving toward not only developing a higher esthetic composite but also a better light curing system which has a consistent and deeper depth of curing, reaching the poorly accessible areas in a shorter time since the majority of the reaction and shrinkage happens literally in few seconds. Researchers and manufacturers are

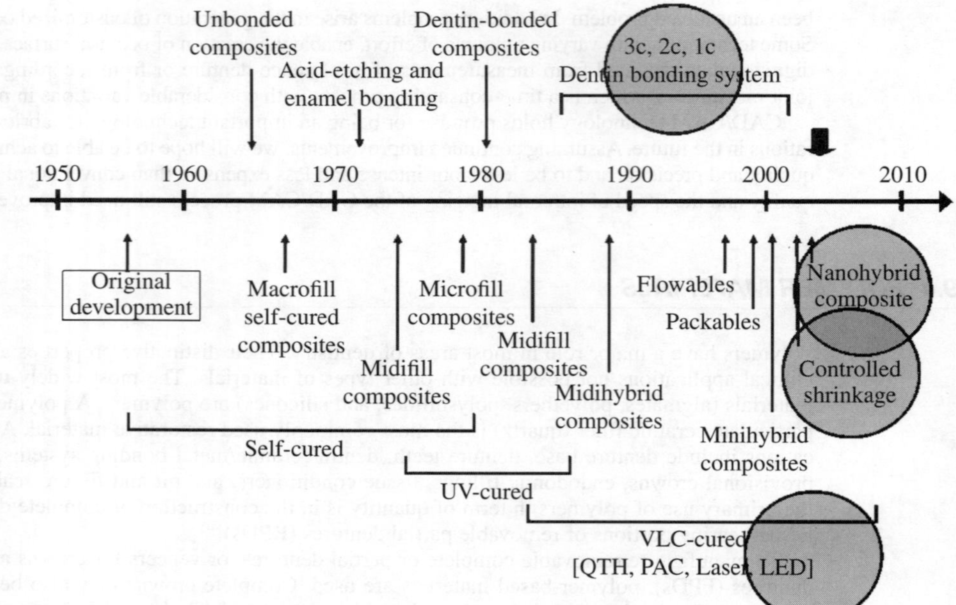

FIGURE 19.3 Simple chronology of the development of dental composites based on their filler technologies and textures in comparison to curing systems and available bonding system technologies.[27]

continuously trying to overcome the inherent physical, mechanical, and chemical nature of the composites which are coefficient of thermal expansion problem and polymerization shrinkage. Composites consist of a polymer matrix [bisphenol-A-glycidyldimethacrylate (BIS-GMA) or similar monomers] and inorganic filler (quartz). The polymerization shrinkage can be controlled with adjustments in filler levels or monomer combinations in some degree.[27]

Some stresses get released during composites and bonding agents polymerization. These stresses can lead to some damage like interfacial failures (between composite and tooth, bonding agent and composite, or even between matrix and filler). They can cause separation or porosity which can reduce the fracture resistance and increase the water absorption. By managing shrinkage the properties of composites will improve substantially.[27]

Low shrinkage or no shrinkage composites have already been demonstrated as prototypes using varying chemical approaches. In this particular case, prototypes utilized ring-opening reactions typical of epoxy systems to compensate for the double-bond reaction shrinkage.[27,46,47]

19.5.1 Visible-Light Curing

Before 1960, chemically cured composites were used by practitioners exclusively. Few years later light curing system [first, ultraviolet (UV) light and later visible light curing (VLC)] became very popular. VLC has many advantages over UV light but has its own shortcomings as well. Many factors like fluctuations in line voltage, problems with light reflectors and filters, nonuniform fiberoptic transport depth of cure, composite shade, thickness of the material, accessibility, light angulations, and distance between light and material affect proper curing with VLC which has led to variable outcomes. By contrast, chemically cured systems polymerize much more uniformly throughout the entire composite. Researchers came out with a newer VLC such as light emitting diode (LED) system. This system has many advantages over the older version of VLC units which are quartztungsten-halogen (QTH) types. The majority of the practitioners started using the LED system and it seems to solve some of the problems we faced with the VLC machines. Although LED units have fewer parts, do not require fans, are much more lightweight and often portable most are rechargeable battery operated but still the depth of cure and access remain an issue.[27]

19.6 DENTAL IMPLANTS

Replacement of missing tooth structure has been challenging. A long-term goal of dentistry was the ability to anchor a foreign material into the jaw to replace an entire tooth. The use of implants in medicine like total hip joint replacement and other prostheses have a long-term clinical success and are routine today. The use of dental implants in dentistry requires the optimization of several important variables to enhance the chances of success, including appropriate material selection and design, an understanding and evaluation of the biological interaction at the interface between the implant and the tissue, careful and controlled surgical techniques, collaboration between various specialties to optimize patient selection, implant design, size, and surface, and follow-up care.[48]

There have been three basic designs of dental implants. The endosseous implant was preceded by the subperiosteal and transosteal implants. The most successful and frequently used implant design is the endosseous type. These implants are submerged and integrated within the bone of the mandible or maxilla. The success of the endosseous dental implants depends on the formation of a tight junction or interface between the bone and the implant which is formed by the growth of new bone. This bonding has been called osseointegration because it represents an integration of the implant surface with new bone.[1]

Dental implants have been manufactured in a wide variety of different shapes and materials. Dental implants have been made from many different materials, such as platinum, silver, steel, cobalt alloys, and titanium, acrylic, carbon, sapphire, porcelain, alumina, zirconia, and calcium phosphate compounds.[1]

19.6.1 Dental Implant Materials

Metals. Metals and alloys most commonly are used for dental implants. Surgical-grade stainless steel and cobalt-chromium alloys initially were used because of their acceptable physical properties, relatively good corrosion resistance, and biocompatibility. These materials also had a history of use as medical implants, primarily in orthopedic surgery. Titanium is the most commonly used metal for dental implants due to its greater corrosion resistance and tissue compatibility. Commercial pure titanium has become one of the materials of choice because of its predictable interaction with the biological environment. Titanium has a modulus of elasticity about one-half that of stainless steel or cobalt-chromium alloys. This is still 5 to 10 times higher than bone. Design of the dental implants is also important in distributing stress correctly. Titanium oxidizes (passivates) readily on contact with air or tissue fluids. The oxide surface does release titanium ions at a low rate into electrolytes such as blood or saliva. Elevated levels of titanium as well as stainless steel and cobalt-chromium alloys have been found in tissue surrounding implants and in major organs. Although some questions remain to be answered, the long-term clinical applications of these alloys in orthopedic and dental implants suggest that these levels have not been demonstrated to have significant associated sequelae other than the allergic reaction related to nickel.[48]

Ceramics. Because of their outstanding biocompatibility and inert behavior, ceramics are logical materials for dental implants.[48] In this case, bone is replaced with similar composition. Because bone is composed of a calcium phosphate ceramic, hydroxyapatite, it would seem most reasonable to replace it with a synthetic hydroxyapatite. The problem is that as a pure ceramic, which also contains protein, hydroxyapatite is brittle and cannot support the same types of forces as bone or a metallic implant. This has led to the development of metallic implants which may contain calcium phosphate coatings.[1]

Polymers and Composites. The application of polymers and composites continues to expand. Polymers have been fabricated in porous and solid forms for tissue attachment and replacement augmentation. The use of polymeric implants in dentistry is still in the research stage.[48]

19.6.2 Computer-Aided Navigation in Dental Implantology

Computer-assisted navigation systems are widespread in neurosurgery, orthopedics, ear, nose, and throat surgery.[49–52] In the field of oral and maxillofacial surgery, navigation technology is particularly applied with success in arthroscopy of the temporomandibular joint, in the surgical treatment of posttraumatic deformities of the zygomatic bone, in orthognathic surgery, and for distractions, osteotomies, tumor surgery, punctures, biopsies, and removal of foreign bodies.[49] Currently, a clear trend in the use of computer-assisted navigation in dental implantology can be observed. Navigation systems are developed for research purposes and for use by commercial companies which provide hardware and software to position dental implants. A substantial advantage of navigation is precise preoperative planning, which is optimized by taking into consideration prosthetic and functional aspects. This is of crucial importance to avoid an unfavorable mechanical load, which can lead to peri-implant bone loss and thus an early loss of implants.[49–53] Furthermore, navigation systems improve intraoperative safety, because damage to critical anatomic structures such as nerves or neighboring teeth can be avoided.[49–55] The accuracy attainable with computer-aided navigation systems has been examined in several studies and found to be sufficient.[49–55]

The work flow consists of getting all vital information from the patient's anatomy using a CT scan or a cone beam scan. The conversed scan data is the three-dimensional representation of the patient's anatomy and provides all the vital information needed to plan the implants placement. The final treatment planning transform into a customized drill guide which will link the planning to the actual surgery, and it will help the surgeon to place the implants more accurately. The computer-aided surgical guide indicates the angle, position, and depth of the implants in the preoperative plan and can be placed on the bone or on the mucosa and guides the drill in the planned position during the surgery (Fig. 19.4).[56]

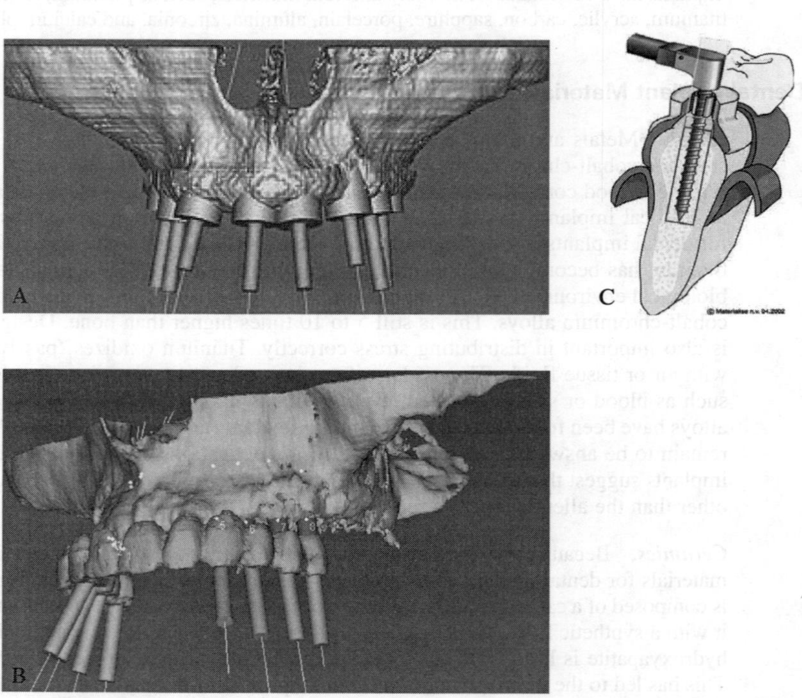

FIGURE 19.4 Navigator system for CT-guided dental implant surgery. (A) The 3D is calculated and implants are planned. (B) The relation of the implants to the bone and the planned restoration is shown. (C) The SurgiGuide is placed on the bone surface for which it was created, and guides the drill.[56] (*SurgiGuide system, photos courtesy of Materialise Dental Inc.*)

Computer-aided navigation in dental implantology is a promising technology, which has been successfully tested in routine clinical application. Computer-aided navigation can substantially contribute to an increase in quality and intraoperative safety for the placement of implants.[49]

19.7 MATERIALS SCIENCE: BIOLOGICAL ASPECTS

Biological aspects of dental materials have received scientific interest ever since they were used in patients. However, during the first half of the last century, these aspects were apparently not considered to be very important; for example, standards (specifications) for dental materials which were developed in the 1920s covered only technical properties, not biological aspects. The same was true for materials used in medical applications.[57]

Materials science toxicology was based on an interfaculty agreement between the Colleges of Dentistry and Pharmacy of the University of Tennessee. And it was devoted to the study of the toxicity of biomaterials, their ingredients, their interaction with drugs, and to safety and standardization aspects which caused merging materials science and pharmacology/toxicology. In 1997, a full standard on the preclinical evaluation of biocompatibility of medical devices used in dentistry and test methods for dental materials was finalized (International Organization for Standardization).[57]

In line with the attempts to elucidate the mechanisms, research proceeded from cellular toxic to subtoxic effects. One example is mutagenicity. Some components of dental materials, such as TEGDMA or BADGE, may interfere with DNA which can be transferred to future cell generations. Other research concentrated on the influence of dental materials and their constituents on inflammation mediators.[58,59] This approach seems very interesting to us, because it may show a direct biochemical link between the parameters measured in vitro and clinical effects (inflammation) in vivo. Other groups concentrated on phospholipids and glutathione,[60] on estrogenic effects,[61] or on heat-shock proteins.[62] Thus, the influence of materials on cell metabolism has become a topic of research.[57]

A look into current textbooks of dental materials shows that the biological aspects have become an indispensable part of materials science during the last century. The scope of biological aspects of dental materials will further be widened. Activities will no longer be restricted to adverse effects, but will extend to "positive" interactions with the living tissue, for example, incorporation of signal molecules into materials to stimulate dentin apposition or bone formation.[63] The concept of a biomaterial, which in every application must be inert, should be abandoned in lieu of an active interaction with cell metabolism. Research on biological aspects of dental materials was a result of the interdisciplinary approaches of dentists with other disciplines like pharmaceutical science, toxicology, chemistry, and biology. Even more, it has been shown that the basic problems, strategies for their solution, and the single methods are very similar for biomaterials with both dental and medical applications, which again shows that dentistry is an integral part of the medical scene.[57]

19.8 BIOCOMPATIBILITY OF DENTAL RESTORATIVE MATERIALS

Ideally, a dental material that is to be used in the oral cavity should be harmless to all oral tissues, gingiva, mucosa, pulp, and bone. Furthermore, it should contain no toxic, leachable, or diffusible substance that can be absorbed into the circulatory system, causing systemic toxic responses, including teratogenic or carcinogenic effects. The material also should be free of agents that could elicit sensitization or an allergic response in a sensitized patient. Rarely, unintended side effects may be caused by dental restorative materials as a result of toxic, irritative, or allergic reactions. They may be local and/or systemic. Local reactions involve the gingiva, mucosal tissues, pulp, and hard tooth tissues, including excessive wear on opposing teeth from restorative materials or inflammation and gum recession due to the faulty or irritating restorations or calculus. Systemic reactions are expressed generally as allergic skin reactions. Side effects may be classified as acute or chronic. The oral environment is especially hostile for dental restorative materials. Saliva has corrosive properties (chloride ion) and bacteria are ever present. This environment demands appropriate biological tests and standards for evaluating any material that is developed and intended to be used in the mouth. These tests and standards have been developed in the past 10 to 15 years, and they serve as the basis for recommending any dental restorative material.[64,65]

Soderholm stated that dentists should emphasize on factors such as biocompatibility, mechanical and physicochemical properties, esthetic, handling characteristics, and cost effectiveness in selecting of any dental restorative material. Of these properties, biocompatibility of the material should be of greatest importance, while the other properties are of variable significance for different situations.[27]

Until a few years ago, almost all national and international dental standards and testing programs focused entirely on mechanical, physical, and chemical properties. The mechanical, physical, and chemical requirements set forth in the specifications for dental materials have been mainly based on published clinical studies and clinical use of the materials. At present time, dental materials standards require biological testing as well. Today, the science of dental materials encompasses a knowledge and appreciation of certain biological considerations associated with the selection and use of materials designed for use in the oral cavity.[66]

In accordance with existing standards, all dental materials should pass primary tests (screening to indicate cellular response), secondary tests (evaluating tissue responses), and usage tests in animals before being evaluated clinically in humans. Testing programs for dental materials are based on specifications or standards established by national standards organizations such as the American National Standards Institute (ANSI) or International Standards Organization (ISO). The oldest and largest of these programs has been operated continuously by the American Dental Association (ADA) since the late 1920s. Initial, secondary, and usage tests, described in ADA/ANSI specification #41 have been reviewed by Craig.[67] Summary of biocompatibility considerations of some of dental restorative materials is shown in Table 19.2.[64–77]

TABLE 19.2 Summary of Biocompatibility Considerations of Dental Restorative Materials[64–77]

Restorative materials	Biocompatibility consideration
Dental amalgam	- No adverse pulpal responses from mercury - Corrosion may limit marginal leakage, but in the long term may lead to breakdown of marginal integrity, especially with low-copper amalgams - Innocuous to gingival tissues - Lichenoid reasons reported - Thermal conduction to pulp
Polymers including composites	- Few documented systemic adverse effects and very little research on systemic biocompatibility - Associated with many organic compounds, the effects of which are not known - Incomplete polymerization leading to degradation, leaching, and imperfect bonding - Predisposed to polymerization shrinkage - Associated with adverse local pulpal and dentin reactions, development of recurrent caries, and pain - May increase plaque adhesion and elevate level of dental disease - Lichenoid reactions reported
Cast alloys	- Inert; sensitivities are rare - Rare allergic reactions to metals such as Ni, Cr, Co, Pd
Ceramics	- No known reactions except wear on opposing dentition and restoration - No long-term data on biocompatibility

A higher level of posttreatment reactions to dental materials has been studied and reported by the Europeans. Most of the clinical trials are short term and they do not report the problems that may occur 10 to 40 years later. For example, composites are considered safe and practitioners have been using them for a long period of time. But there are some concerns regarding the matrix part of composites which may go under degradation and alter receptivity toward biofilms and increase the wear rate. More research and investigation should be devoted to this area to ensure that composites are biologically safe.[27]

19.9 BIOMATERIALS EVOLUTION: ATTACHMENT OF BIOMATERIALS TO TISSUE

Dental treatment often involves the placement of restorative materials or prepared tooth substrates. They are usually fixed in place by mechanical retention within undercuts in the tissue prepared by dental instruments or by friction between them. The introduction of an adhesive should improve the results. The attachment of biomaterials to tissues and organs is very important in the application of devices to support natural organ function. There are significant differences between most biomaterials applications and restorative dentistry, as they are usually implanted deep in tissue and they are not constantly exposed to bacteria. Infection by microorganism is a severe complication within the mouth. The impermeable acid-resistant enamel protects dentin and pulp from the invading microorganisms. Once dentin is exposed, pulp becomes exposed via the dentinal tubules. Exposed dentin cannot resist caries. The restorative materials should ideally heal the exposed dentin. But in most situations, the tissues can heal themselves. The healing is initiated by the bleeding and blood coagulation. Obviously, dentin does not have blood vessels so that there is no opportunity for the dentin to heal in this way. In exposed dentin, the caries become established because of a lack of wound healing, and sometimes tertiary dentin is formed as a reaction to external insult such as caries.[78]

Also it is not possible to connect artificial materials to natural tissues (including tooth substrates). It has been argued that adhesive technology should provide the option of better dental treatments. Initially, loss of tissue needs to be minimized during the treatment. Nakabayashi has developed new technologies which give tooth substrates pseudowound-healing characteristics; these could revolutionize dental treatments. The interface between the tooth and restorative materials has always been a susceptible area. The introduction of adhesive technology to dentistry was an important step in addressing these difficulties.[79] The initial attempt at adhesion concentrated on enamel was first reported by Buoncore in 1955.[80] Bonding to dentin is much more complicated. In 1982, Nakabayashi[81] prepared hybridized dentin in the subsurface layer in order to achieve adhesion. The binding mechanism was not simple. The hybridization of polymers with dentin has many advantages but it is not predictable. There are beneficial effects with respect to the incidence of recurrent caries, postoperative hypersensitivity, and reducing the need for the replacement of restorations. If the hybridized layer is impermeable to various chemical stimuli, it could protect dentin and pulp in the same manner as enamel.[82] Nakabayashi prepared the hybridized layer in the dentin subsurface, conditioned with an aqueous solution of 10 percent citric acid and 3 percent ferric chloride which removes the smear layer, and diffusion into the dentin of 5 percent 4-methacryloyloxyethyl trimellitate anhydride (4-META) dissolved in methyl methacrylate (MMA) which are polymerized by tri-*n*-butylborane (TBB) in the presence of polymethyl methacrylate powder.[79] Chemical characterization of the hybrid, to differentiate it from the cured copolymer and from the dentin, revealed that it resisted demineralization by HCl and degradation by NaOCl. Soaking bonded specimens in HCl and then in NaOCl mimics the process seen in dental caries and can be postulated that the hybrid could inhibit recurrent caries. A further important point about soaking bonded specimens in NaOCl is confirmation of the absence of residual demineralized dentin resulting from incomplete impregnation of the polymer into the demineralized layer. This information is important with respect to the longevity of the bond. It was found that the hydroxyapatite crystals encapsulated with the copolymers in the hybridized dentin could resist demineralization with HCl, whereas those crystals in the contiguous intact dentin were demineralized, suggesting that the hybridized dentin is impermeable to HCl.[82]

The hybridized dental tissue, together with impermeable and acid-resistant artificial enamel, could resolve many current problems in dentistry. Dental biomaterials may then eliminate many defects in dental hard tissue and rejuvenate their function.[79]

19.10 NANOTECHNOLOGY IN DENTISTRY

Nanotechnology is engineering of molecularly precise structures. These are the molecular machines of typically 0.1 μm or smaller than that. The prefix "nano" means ten to the minus ninth power 10^{-9}, or one billionth. The nanoscale is about a 1000 times smaller than micro, which is about 1\80,000 of the diameter of a human hair. It is expected that nanotechnology will be developed at several levels: materials, devices, and systems. At present, the nanomaterials level is the most advanced both in scientific knowledge and in commercial applications. To appreciate nanodentistry we have to have a background in nanotechnology and nanomedicine. Nanotechnology aims to manipulate and control particles to create novel structures with unique properties and promises advances in medicine and dentistry. The growing interest in the future of medical applications of nanotechnology is leading to the emergence of a new field called nanomedicine. With nanodentistry, it is possible to maintain a comprehensive oral health care by involving the use of nanomaterials, biotechnology, and ultimately dental nanorobotics. Nanorobots induce oral analgesia, desensitize tooth, manipulate the tissue to realign and straighten irregular set of teeth, and improve durability of teeth. They also can be used for preventive, restorative, and curative procedures.[83,84]

19.10.1 Major Tooth Repair

Many techniques have been proposed for tooth repair using tissue engineering procedures. Some of them will replace the whole tooth which includes all the mineral and cellular components.[85,86]

19.10.2 Nanorobotic Dentifrice (Dentifrobots)

We are hoping that dentifrobots would be able to recognize and destroy all the patogenes that causes tooth caries. They will be delivered by either mouthwash or toothpaste so that they could fight plaque formation, halitosis, and even calculus.[85,87]

19.10.3 Dentin Hypersensitivity

Many patients have been suffering from dentinal hypersensitivity. The goal is to come up with some dental nanorobots that would be able to target the exposed dentinal tubules and block them so patients would not feel any sensitivity.[85,87]

19.10.4 Orthodontic Nanorobots

Moving teeth always has been challenging. There have been always some problems associated with realign and straighten irregular set of teeth rapidly and painlessly. We are hoping that we would be able to move and straighten teeth in a matter of minutes to hours using orthodontic nanorobots.[85,87]

19.10.5 Tooth Durability and Appearance

Tooth durability and appearance may be improved by replacing enamel layers with covalently bonded artificial materials such as sapphire[88] or diamond,[89] which are 100 times harder than natural enamel or contemporary ceramic veneers, as well as good biocompatibility. Like enamel, sapphire is somewhat susceptible to acid corrosion, but sapphire can be manufactured in virtually any color,[90] offering interesting cosmetic alternative. Pure sapphire and diamond are brittle and prone to fracture if sufficient shear forces are imposed, but they can be made more fracture resistant as part of a nanostructure composite material that possibly includes embedded carbon nanotubes.[85,87]

Nanocomposites are the new restorative nanomaterial which increase tooth durability. They manufactured by nonagglomerated discrete nanoparticles that are homogeneously distributed in resins or coatings to produce nanocomposites. The nanofiller includes an aluminosilicate powder with a mean particle size of about 80 nm and a 1:4 ratio of alumina to silica. The nanofiller has a refractive index of 1.508; it has superior hardness, modulus of elasticity, translucency, esthetic appeal, excellent color density, high polish, and 50 percent reduction in filling shrinkage. They are superior to conventional composites and blend with a natural tooth structure much better.[27,87,91,92]

Strength alone does not explain the relationship of filler to wear resistance. Intraoral wear occurs via several different mechanisms, but most occlusal wear is caused by proximately 0.1-m-diameter abrasive particles that exist within food that are suspected to be silica.[93] The matrix part of all composites are subjected to wear. Manufacturers suggested a microprotection process. They are trying to design a composite so that the filler would cover and protect the matrix from contacting abrasive food particles. This phenomenon has been seen in some of the available dental composites today such as microfills, microhybrids, and now in nanohybrids. We are hoping that nanocomposite will be the composite of choice in the near future.[27]

Nanofillers are not all the same. A variety of nanofillers have already been demonstrated. 3M uses sol-gel technology to produce tiny nanospheres they call nanomers.[94] These can be agglomerated into nanoclusters, and either the spheres or clusters can become filler particles for composite formulations. 3M ESPE Filtek Supreme[95] uses primarily nanoclusters in combination with submicron fillers to produce a hybrid. Pentron has had excellent success with Simile utilizing POSS technology borrowed from Hybrid Plastics.[96] In this case, molecular-sized silicate cages are produced from silane and functionalized for coreaction with matrix monomers. This technology has great potential that is still being explored. Still others have designed nanoscale fillers using tantalum nanoparticles.[97,98]

19.10.6 Nanoimpression

Impression material is available with nanotechnology application. Nanofillers are integrated in the vinylpolysiloxanes, producing a unique addition siloxane impression material. This material has better flow, improved hydrophilic properties, better model pouring, and enhanced detail precision.[87,91]

19.10.7 Nanoanesthesia

One of the most common procedures in dentistry is the injection of local anesthesia, which can involve long procedure, patient discomfort, and many associated complications. To induce oral anesthesia in the era of nanodentistry, a colloidal suspension containing millions of active analgesic micron-sized dental robots will be instilled on the patient's gingiva. After contacting the surface of the tooth or mucosa, the ambulating nanorobots reach the pulp via the gingival sulcus, lamina propria, and dentinal tubules. Once installed in the pulp, the analgesic dental robots may be commanded by the dentist to shut down all sensitivity in any particular tooth that requires treatment. After completion of oral procedure, the dentist orders the nanorobots to restore all sensation, to relinquish control of nerve traffic, and to egress from the tooth by similar pathways used for ingress.[85,87]

19.10.8 Tissue Engineering

True biological biomaterials are ones that lead to natural tissue restoration. Tissue engineering approaches often rely on synthetic scaffolds that are generally resorbable as a means of managing tissue development.[27]

In 2003, Nakashima and Reddi presented an excellent summary of tissue engineering for dentistry and the role of bone morphogenic proteins (BMPs).[99] There is a significant potential in the orofacial complex for fracture healing, bone augmentation, TMJ cartilage repair or regeneration, pulpal repair, periodontal ligament regeneration, and osseointegration for implants.[100–102] Regenerative treatments require the three key elements: an extracellular matrix scaffold (which can be synthetic), progenitor/stem cells, and inductive morphogenetic signals. The oral cavity has special advantages over other parts of the body for tissue engineering due to its ease of access and observation. The signaling processes that control the development of discrete dental morphologies for incisors, canines, premolars, and molars are not clear yet. Successful bioengineering of recognizable tooth structures has been reported using cells from dissociated porcine third molar tooth buds seeded on biodegradable polymer scaffolds that were grown in rat hosts for 20 to 30 weeks.[103] Successful bioengineering has demonstrated that mature tooth structures form single-cell suspensions of 4-day postnatal cultured rat tooth bud cells on polylactic acid scaffolds grown as implants in the omenta of adult rat hosts over 12 weeks.[104] Murine teeth have been produced recently using stem-cell-based engineering techniques.[105] The developmental capacity of embryonic stem cells (ESCs) and the tissue repair potential for adult stem cells (ASCs) make their use truly exciting.[106] The transplantation of dental pulp stem cells may be used to repair bone or regenerate teeth in the near future. The issue of histocompatibility can be avoided by using patient's own stem cells which has been shown in regeneration experiments conducted in animal models. However, significant technical hurdles still exist. Scaffolds, cells, and signals have been combined without much elegant control until relatively recently. The same lithography and printing techniques discussed for ceramics are also available to lay down scaffolds, cells, and signals in a well-controlled three-dimensional architecture.[107] Printing is a special tissue engineering tool for the future. Numerous surfaces of nonbiological materials such as implants could benefit by pretreatment (preintegration) with those tissues that would normally result from healing or osseointegration. This has already been evaluated with existing implant systems, and it may eliminate the long healing process and could make a much more biologically and physiologically stable, immediately loaded implant.[27,102]

Titanium is a well-known bone repairing material and it has been used widely in orthopaedics and dentistry. Titanium has a high fractural strength, ductility, and weight-to-strength ratio. But it suffers from the lack of bioactivity, and does not support cell adhesion and growth well. Apatite coatings are known to be bioactive and to bond to the bone. Several techniques were used in the past to produce an apatite coating on titanium. Those coatings suffer from thickness nonuniformity, poor adhesion, and low mechanical strength. In addition, a stable porous structure is required to support the nutrients transport through the cell growth. It was shown that using a biomimetic approach such as a slow growth of nanostructured apatite film from the simulated body fluid resulted in formation of a strongly adherent and a uniform nanoporous layer. The layer was found to be built of 60-nm crystallites which possess a stable nanoporous structure and bioactivity.[108,109]

Natural bone surface quite often contains features that are about 100 nm across. It has been demonstrated that by creating nano-sized features on the surface of the hip or knee prosthesis, one could reduce the chances of rejection as well as to stimulate the production of osteoblasts. The osteoblasts are the cells responsible for the growth and formation of the bone matrix and are found on the advancing surface of the developing bone.[110,111,109]

Nanostructural, hydroxyapatite, and other calcium phosphates-related materials have been studied as implant materials in orthopaedics and dentistry due to their excellent soft and/or hard tissue attachment, biocompatibility, and ease of formation.[112]

A real bone is a nanocomposite material, composed of hydroxyapatite crystallites in the organic matrix, which is mainly composed of collagen. The bone is mechanically tough but at the same time can recover from a mechanical damage. The actual nanoscale mechanism which leads to this useful combination of properties is still debated. An artificial hybrid material was prepared from 15- to 18-nm ceramic nanoparticles and poly (methyl methacrylate) copolymer. Using tribology approach (interacting surfaces in relative motion), a viscoelastic behavior (healing) of the human teeth was demonstrated. An investigated hybrid material, deposited as a coating on the tooth surface, improved scratch resistance, as well as possessed a healing behavior similar to that of the tooth.[109,110,113]

19.10.9 Future Directions

Today, the trends of oral health have been changing to more preventive intervention than a curative and restorative procedure. Nanodentistry will give a new visionary to comprehensive oral health care and has a strong potential to revolutionize dentists to diagnose and to treat diseases in the near future. It opens up new ways for vast, abundant research work. Nanotechnology will change dentistry, health care, and human life more profoundly than other developments.[87,114]

Nanomaterials are at the leading edge of the rapidly developing field of nanotechnology. Their unique properties make these materials superior and indispensable in many areas of human activity. At present, the nanomaterials level is the most advanced both in scientific knowledge and in commercial applications. In medicine, the majority of commercial nanoparticle applications are geared toward drug delivery. In biosciences, nanoparticles are replacing organic dyes in the applications that require high photo-stability as well as high multiplexing capabilities. There are some developments in directing and remotely controlling the functions of nanoprobes, for example, driving magnetic nanoparticles to the tumor and making them either to release the drug load or just heating them in order to destroy the surrounding tissue. The major trend in further development of nanomaterials is to make them multifunctional and controllable by external signals or by local environment, thus essentially turning them into nanodevices.[87,109,110]

REFERENCES

1. Ferracane, J. L., *Materials in Dentistry: Principles and Applications*, 2nd ed., Pennsylvania: Lippincott Williams & Wilkins Philadelphia, 2001.
2. Lygre, H., Prosthodontic biomaterials and adverse reactions: a critical review of the clinical and research literature. *Acta Odontol. Scand.* **60**:1–9, 2002.
3. Szycher, M., *Szycher's Dictionary of Biomaterials and Medical Devices*. Lancaster: Technomic Co.; pp. 21–2, 1992.
4. McCabe, J. F. and Walls, A. W. G., *Applied Dental Materials.* Blackwell Science, Blackwell Publishing Ltd, Oxford, U.K, p. 1, 1999.
5. Craig, R. G., *Restorative Dental Materials,* 10th ed., St. Louis: Mosby, p. 383, 1997.
6. Wataha, J. C., Alloys for prosthodontic restorations. *J. Prosthet. Dent.* **87**:351–363, 2002.
7. Johansson, B. I., Lemons, J. E., and Hao, S. Q., Corrosion of dental copper, nickel, and gold alloys in artificial saliva and saline solutions. *Dent. Mater.* **5**:324–328, 1989.
8. Wataha, J. C., and Lockwood, P. E., Release of elements from dental casting alloys into cell-culture medium over 10 months. *Dent. Mater.* **14**:158–163, 1998.
9. Wataha, J. C., Biocompatibility of dental casting alloys: a review. *J. Prosthet. Dent.* **83**:223–234, 2000.
10. Wataha, J. C., Lockwood, P. E., Nelson, S. K., and Bouillaguet, S., Long-term cytotoxicity of dental casting alloys. *Int. J. Prosthodont.* **12**:242–248, 1999.
11. Giordano, R. A., Dental ceramic restorative systems. *Compendium* **17**:779–782, 784–786 passim; quiz 794, 1996.
12. Anusavice, K. J., and Zhang, N. Z., Chemical durability of Dicor and lithia-based glass-ceramics. *Dent. Mater.* **13**:13–19, 1997.
13. Anusavice, K. J., Recent developments in restorative dental ceramics. *J. Am. Dent. Assoc.* **124**:72–74, 76–78, 80–84, 1993.
14. Deany, I. L., Recent advances in ceramics for dentistry. *Crit. Rev. Oral Biol. Med.* **7**:134–143, 1996.
15. Nathanson, D., and Shoher, I., Initial evaluations of a gold composite alloy restorative system (Captek); Captek: an advanced gold composite alloy coping. *Lab. Digest* Spring:4–6, 1998.
16. Jedynakiewicz, N. M., Ceramics in Dentistry; School of Dentistry, The University of Liverpool, Liverpool, U.K. Encyclopedia of Biomaterials and Biomedical Engineering, March 2006.
17. Kelly, R. J., Nishimura, I., and Campbell, S. D., Ceramics in dentistry: historical roots and current perspectives. *J. Prosthet. Dent.* **75**:18–32, 1996.

18. Ring, M. E., *Dentistry, An Illustrated History*. New York: H. N. Abrams, pp. 160–181, 193–211, 1985.
19. Kingery, W. D., and Vaudiver, P. B., *Ceramic Masterpieces. Art, structure, technology*. New York: The Free Press, pp. 7–36, 1986.
20. Jones, D. W., Development of dental ceramics. *Dent. Clin. North Am.* **29**:621–644, 1985.
21. Southan, D. E., Dental porcelain. In: *Scientific Aspects of Dental Materials*. van Fraunhofer, J. A., (ed.). London: Butterworths, pp. 277–279, 1975.
22. Sozio, R. B., and Riley, E. J., The shrink-free ceramic crown. *J. Prosthet. Dent.* **49**:182–189, 1983.
23. Malament, K. A., The cast-glass ceramic restoration. *J. Prosthet. Dent.* **57**:674–683, 1987.
24. Lygre, H., Prosthodontic biomaterials and adverse reactions: a critical review of the clinical and research literature. *Acta Odontol. Scand.* **60**:1–9, 2002.
25. Craig, R. G. (ed.), Dental materials. *Properties & Manipulation,* 6th ed., St. Louis: Mosby, p. 222, 1996.
26. Anusavice, K. J., and de Rijk, W. G., Performance of dental biomaterials: conference report. *Dent. Mater.* **6**:69–72, January, 1990.
27. Bayne, S. C., Dental biomaterials: where are we and where are we going? *J. Dent. Educ,* **69**(5):571–583, 2005.
28. Huang, M., Rahbar, N., Wang, R., Thompson, V., Rekow,-D., and Soboyejo, W. O., Bioinspired design of dental multilayers. *Mater. Sci. Eng.* **A464**:315–320, 2007.
29. **Yin, L., Song, X. F., Song, Y. L., Huang, T., and Li, J.,** An overview of in vitro abrasive finishing and CAD/CAM of bioceramics in restorative dentistry. *Int. J. Mach. Tools Manuf.* **46**:1013–1026, 2006.
30. Kelly, J. R., Ceramics in restorative and prosthetic dentistry. *Mater. Sci.* **27**:443–468, 1997.
31. Xu, H. H. K., and Quinn, J. B., Whisker-reinforced bioactive composites containing calcium phosphate cement fillers: effects of filler ratio and surface treatments on mechanical properties. *J. Biomed. Mater. Res.* **57**:165–174, 2001.
32. Xu, H. H. K., Schumacher, G. E., Eichmiller, F. C., Peterson, R. C., Antonucci, J. M., and Mueller, H. J., Continuous-fiber preform reinforcement of dental resin composite restorations. *Dent. Mater.* **19**:523–530, 2003.
33. Lawn, B. R., Deng, Y., Lloyd, I. K., Janal, M. N., Rekow, E. D., and Thompson, V. P., Materials design of ceramic-based layer structures for crowns, *J. Dent. Res.* **81**(6): 433–438, 2002.
34. Rekow, E. D., Erdman, A. G., Riley, D. R., and Klamecki, B., CAD/CAM for dental restorations some of the current challenges. *Biomed. Eng.* **38**(4):318–414, 1991.
35. Cerec Dental CAD/CAM Systems, at: www.sirona.com.
36. Celay CAD/CAM systems, at: www.vita-in-ceram-de. http://www.vita-vip.com.
37. CYNOVAD, The New Player with Deep Roots in Dental CAD/CAM, at: www.cynovad.com.
38. M ESPE LavaTM All-Ceramic System, Technical Product Profile, Dental Products, 3M Center, St. Paul, MN, USA.
39. Willer, J., Rossbach, A., Weber, H.-P., Computer-assisted milling of dental restorations using a new CAD/CAM data acquisition system. *J. Prosthet. Dent.* **80**:346–353, 1998.
40. O'Brien, W. J., *Dental Materials and Their Selection*, 3rd ed., Hanover Park, Illinois: Quintessence Publishing Co, Inc., 2002.
41. Notice in CRA newsletter. *Clin. Res. Assoc.* **21**(5): 1997.
42. International Standard. ISO 1567. Dentistry. Denture base polymers. The International Organization for Standardization; 1988. p. 1.
43. Ruyter, I. E., and Oysaed, H., Analysis and characterization of dental polymers. *CRC Crit. Rev. Biocompat.* **4**:247–279, 1988.
44. Carlos, N. B., and Harrison, A., The effect of untreated UHMWPE beads on some properties of acrylic resin denture base materials. *J. Dent.* **25**:59–64, 1997.
45. Bayne, S. C., Taylor, D. F., and Heymann, H. O., Protection hypothesis for composite wear. *Dent. Mater.* **8**:305–309, 1992.
46. Eick, J. D., Kostoryz, E. L., Rozzi, S. M., Jacobs, D. W., Oxman, J. D., Chappelow, C. C., Glaros, A. G., and Yourtee, D. M. In vitro biocompatibility of oxirane/polyol dental composites with promising esthetic physical properties. *Dent. Mater.* **18**:413–421, 2002.

47. Guggenberger, R., and Weinmann, W., Exploring beyond methacrylates. *Am. J. Dent.* **13**:82D–84D, 2000.

48. Ralph, W. P., and Keith Moore, B., *Elements of Dental Materials*, 5th ed., Philadelphia: W. B. Saunders Co., pp. 274–278, 1995.

49. Ewers, R., Schicho, K., Truppe, M., Seemann, R., Reichwein, A., Figl, M., and Wagner, A., Computer-aided navigation in dental implantology: 7 years of clinical experience. *J. Oral Maxillofac. Surg.* **62**:329–334, 2004.

50. Kelly, P. J., State of the art and future directions of minimally invasive stereotactic neurosurgery. *Cancer Control* **2**:287, 1995.

51. Freysinger, W., Gunkel, A. R., Pototschnig, C., Thumfart, W. F., and Truppe, M. J. *New Developments in 3D Endonasal and Frontobasal Endoscopic Sinus Surgery*. Paris, France: Kugler Publications, 1995.

52. Thumfart, W. F., Freysinger, W., and Gunkel, A. R., 3D image-guided surgery on the example of the 5,300-year-old Innsbruck Iceman. Acta Otolaryngol. **117**:131, 1997.

53. Hobkirk, J. A., and Havthoulas, T. K., The influence of mandibular deformation, implant numbers, and loading position on detected forces in abutments supporting fixed implant superstructures. *J. Prosthet. Dent.* **80**:169, 1998.

54. Birkfellner, W., Solar, P., Gahleitner, A., Huber, K., Kainberger, F., Kettenbach, J., Homolka, P., Diemling, M., Watzek, G., and Bergmann, H., In-vitro assessment of a registration protocol for image guided implant dentistry. *Clin. Oral Implants Res.* **12**:69, 2001.

55. Wagner, A., Wanschitz, F., Birkfellner, W., Zauza, K., Klug, C., Schicho, K., Kainberger, F., Czerny, C., Bergmann, H., and Ewers, R., Computer-aided placement of endosseous oral implants in patients after ablative tumour surgery: assessment of accuracy. *Clin. Oral Implants Res.* **14**:340, 2003.

56. SurgiGuide system at: www.SimPlant@materialise.com.

57. Schmalz, G., Materials science: biological aspects. *J. Dent. Res.* **81**(10):660–663, 2002.

58. Schmalz, G., Schuster, U., and Schweiklm, H., Influence of metals on IL-6 release in vitro. *Biomaterials* **19**:1689–1694, 1998.

59. Schmalz, G., Schweikl, H., and Hiller, K. A., Release of prostaglandin E2, IL-6 and IL-8 from human oral epithelial culture models after exposure to compounds of dental materials. *Eur. J. Oral Sci.* **108**:442–448, 2000.

60. Engelmann, J., Leyhausen, G., Leibfritz, D., and Geurtsen, W., Metabolic effects of dental resin components in vitro detected by NMR spectroscopy. *J. Dent. Res.* **80**:869–875, 2001.

61. Hashimoto, Y., and Nakamura, M., Estrogenic activity of dental materials and bisphenol-A-related chemicals in vitro. *Dent. Mater. J.* **19**:245–262, 2000.

62. Noda, M., Wataha, J. C., Kaga, M., Lockwood, P. E., Volkmann, K. R., and Sano, H., Components of dentinal adhesives modulate heat shock protein 72 expression in heat-stressed THP-1 human monocytes at sublethal concentrations. *J. Dent. Res.* **81**:265–269, 2002.

63. Decup, F., Six, N., Palmier, B., Buch, D., Lasfargues, J. J., Salih, E., and Goldberg, M., Bone sialoprotein-induced reparative dentinogenesis in the pulp of rat's molar. *Clin. Oral Investig.* **4**:110–119, 2000.

64. Stanley, H. R., *Toxicity Testing of Dental Materials*. Boca Raton, FL: CRC Press, Inc., 1985.

65. Mjör, I. A., Current Restorative Materials: Recent Developments and Future Needs. Prepared for Committee to Coordinate Environmental Health and Related Programs, PHS, DHHS, 1991.

66. Kenneth, J., *Anusavice, Phillips' Science of Dental Materials,* 11th ed., Saint Louis, Missouri: W. B. Saunders Co., pp. 171–202, 2003.

67. Craig, R. G., Biocompatibility testing of dental materials. In: *Restorative Dental Materials,* Craig, R. G. (ed.). St. Louis: C. V. Mosby, pp. 149–187, 1989.

68. Roulet, J. F., and Herder, S., Ceramic inlays: an alternative for esthetic restorations in posterior teeth. *Today's FDA* **2**(6):1C–6C, 1990.

69. Council on Dental Materials, Instruments and Equipment, Biological effects of nickel-containing dental alloys. *JADA* **104**:501–505, 1982.

70. Lamster, I. B., Kalfus, D. I., Steigerwald, P. J., and Chasens, A. I., Rapid loss of alveolar bone associated with nonprecious alloy crowns in two patients with nickel hypersensitivity. *J. Periodontol.* **58**:486–492, 1987.

71. De Melo, J. F., Gjerdet, N. R., and Erichsen, E. S., Metal release from cobalt-chromium partial dentures in the mouth. *Acta Odontol. Scand.* **41**:71–74, 1983.

72. Norman, R. D., A Review of Metals Used in Dentistry. Prepared for Committee to Coordinate Environmental Health and Related Progratns, PHS, DHHS, 1991.

73. Bayne, S. C., Taylor, D. F., Wilder, A. D., Heymann, H. O., and Tangen, C. M., Clinical longevity of ten posterior composite materials based on wear. *J. Dent. Res.* **70**(A):244, Abs 630, 1991.

74. Caughman, W. F., Caughman, G. B., Dominy, W. T., and Schuster, G. S., Glass ionomer and composite resin cements: effects on oral cells. *J. Prosthet. Dent.* **69**:513–521, 1990.

75. Stanley, H. R., Pulpal response to ionomer cements—biological characteristics. *JADA* **120**:25–29, 1990.

76. Bolewska, J., Holmstrup, P., Miller-Madsen, B., Kenrad, B., and Danscher, G., Amalgam associated mercury accumulations in normal oral mucosa, oral mucosal lesions of lichen planus and contact lesions associated with amalgam. *J. Oral Pathol. Med.* **10**(1):39–42, 1990.

77. Holmstrup, P., Reactions of the oral mucosa related to silver amalgam: a review. *J. Oral Pathol. Med.* **20**(1):1–7, 1991.

78. Nakabayashi, N., Dental biomaterials and the healing of dental tissue. *Biomaterials* **24**:2437–2439, 2003.

79. Nakabayashi, N., and Iwasaki, Y., *Biomaterials: Evolution, Materials Science and Application. Page 70-71 Institute of Biomaterials and Bioengineering*. Tokyo Medical and Dental University, Kanda, Tokyo 101-0061, Japan.

80. Buonocore, M. G., A simple method of increasing the adhesion of acrylic filling materials to enamel surfaces. *J. Dent. Res.* **34**:849–853, 1955.

81. Nakabayashi, N., Kojima, K., and Masuhara, E., The promotion of adhesion by the infiltration of monomers into tooth substrates. *J. Biomed. Mater Res.* **16**:265–273, 1982.

82. Nakabayashi, N., and Pashley, D. H., *Hybridization of Dental Hard Tissues*. Tokyo, Chicago, Berlin: Quintessence Publishing Co. Ltd., 1998.

83. Feynman, R., There's plenty of room at the bottom. *Science* **254**:1300–1301, 1991.

84. Feynman, R. P., There's plenty of room at the bottom. *Eng. Sci. Feb.* **23**:22–36, 1960.

85. Frietas, R. A., Nanodentistry. *JADA* **131**:1559–1569, 2000.

86. Somerman, M. J., Ouyang, H. J., Berry, J. E., Saygin, N. E., Strayhorn, C. L., D'Errico, J. A., Hullinger, T., and Giannobile, W. V., Evolution of periodontal regeneration: from the roots' point of view. *J. Periodont. Res.* **34**(7):420–424, 1999.

87. Saravanakumar, R., and Vijaylakshmi, R., Nanotechnology in dentistry. *Ind. J. Dent. Res.* **17**(2):62–65, 2006.

88. Fartash, B., Tangerud, T., Silness, J., and Arvidson, K., Rehabilitation of mandibular edentulism by single crystal sapphire implants and overdentures: 3–12 year results in 86 patients—a dual center international study. *Clin. Oral Implants Res.* **7**(3):220–229, 1996.

89. Reifman, E. M., Diamond teeth. In: *Nanotechnology: Molecular Speculations on Global Abundance*. Crandall, B. C., (ed.). Cambridge, Mass.: MIT Press, pp. 81–66, 1996.

90. Freitas, R. A., Jr., Nanomedicine. Vol. 1. Basic capabilities. Georgetown, Texas: Landes Bioscience, 1999. Available at: www.nanomedicine.com. Accessed on Sept. 26, 2000.

91. Jhaveri, H. M., and Balaji, P. R., Nanotechnology. The future of dentistry a review. *Jr. I. Prosthetic.* **5**:15–17, 2005.

92. Bayne, S. C., Heymann, H. O., and Swift, E. J., Jr., Update on dental composite restorations. *J. Am. Dent. Assoc.* **125**(6):687–701, 1994.

93. Bayne, S. C., Thompson, J. Y., and Taylor, D. F., Dental materials (Chap. 4). In: *Sturdevant's Art and Science of Operative Dentistry,* 4th ed., Roberson, T. M., (ed.). St. Louis: Mosby, pp. 135–236, 2001.

94. Mitra, S. B., Wu, D., and Holmes, B. N., An application of nanotechnology in advanced dental materials. *J. Am. Dent. Assoc.* **34**:1382–1390, 2003.

95. 3M ESPE. *Filtek Supreme Universal Restorative System Technical Product Profile.* St. Paul, MN, p. 8, 2002.

96. Hybrid plastics. At: www.hybridplastics.com/Accessed on Oct. 28, 2004.

97. Chan, D. C., Titus, H. W., Chung, K. Y., Dixon, H., Wellinghoff, S. T., and Rawls, H. R., Radiopacity of tantalum oxide nanoparticle filled resins. *Dent. Mater.* **15**:219–222, 1999.

98. Furman, B., Rawls, H. R., Wellinghoff, S., Dixon, H., Lankford, J., and Nicolella, D., Metal-oxide nanoparticles for the reinforcement of dental restorative resins. *Crit. Rev. Biomed. Eng.* **28**:439–443, 2000.

99. Nakashima, M., and Reddi, A. H., The application of bone morphogenic proteins to dental tissue engineering. *Nature Biotech.* **21**:1025–1032, 2003.

100. Jin, Q. M., Zhao, S. A., Berry, J. E., Somerman, M. J., and Giannobile, W. V., Cementum engineering with three-dimensional polymer scaffolds. *J. Biomed. Mater. Res.* **67A**:54–60, 2003.

101. Seo, B. M., Miura, M., Gronthos, S., Bartold, P. M., Batouli, S., Brahim, J., Young, M., Robey, P. G., Wang, C. Y., and Shi, S., Investigation of multipotent postnatal stem cells from human periodontal ligament. *Lancet* **364**:149–155, 2004.

102. Yamada, Y., Ueda, M., Naiki, T., and Nagasaka, T., Tissue-engineered injectable bone regeneration for osseointegrated dental implants. *Clin. Oral Impl. Res.* **15**:589–597, 2004.

103. Young, C. S., Terada, S., Vacanti, J. P., Honda, M., Bartlett, J. D., and Yelick, P. C., Tissue engineering of complex tooth structures on biodegradable polymer scaffolds. *J. Dent. Res.* **81**:695–700, 2002.

104. Duailibi, M. T., Dualilibi, S. E., Young, C. S., Bartlett, J. D., Vacanti, J. P., and Yelick, P. C., Bioengineered teeth from cultured rat tooth bud cells. *J. Dent. Res.* **83**:523–528, 2004.

105. Ohazama, A., Modino, S. A. C., Miletich, I., and Sharpe, P. T., Stem cell-based tissue engineering of murine teeth. *J. Dent. Res.* **83**:518–522, 2004.

106. Krebsbach, P. H., and Robey, P. G., Dental and skeletal stem cells: potential cellular therapeutics for craniofacial regeneration. *J. Dent. Educ.* **66**:766–773, 2002.

107. Roth, E. A., Xu, T., Das, M., Gregory, C., Hickman, J. J., and Boland, T., Inkjet printing for high-throughput cell patterning. *Biomaterials* **25**:3707–3715, 2004.

108. Ma, J., Wong, H., Kong, L. B., and Peng, K. W., Biomimetic processing of nanocrystallite bioactive apatite coating on titanium. *Nanotechnology* **14**:619–623, 2003.

109. Salata, O. V., Applications of nanoparticles in biology and medicine. *J. Nanobiotechnol.* **2**:3, 2004.

110. Salata, O. V., Review applications of nanoparticles in biology and medicine. *J. Nanobiotechnol.* **2**:3, 2004.

111. Gutwein, L. G., and Webster, T. J., Affects of alumina and titania nanoparticulates on bone cell function. *American Ceramic Society 26th Annual Meeting Conference Proceedings 2003*.

112. Hu, J., Russell, J. J., Ben-Nissan, B., and Vago, R., Production and analysis of hydroxyapatite derived from Australian corals via hydrothermal process. *J. Mater. Sci. Lett.* **20**:85, 2001.

113. de la Isla, A., Brostow, W., Bujard, B., Estevez, M., Rodriguez, J. R., Vargas, S., and Castano, V. M., Nanohybrid scratch resistant coating for teeth and bone viscoelasticity manifested in tribology. *Mat. Resr. Innovat.* **7**:110–114, 2003.

114. Scheyler, T. L. Nanodentistry fact or fiction. *JADA* **131**:1567–1568, 2000.

CHAPTER 20
ORTHOPEDIC BIOMATERIALS

Michele J. Grimm
Michigan State University, East Lansing, Michigan

20.1 INTRODUCTION

Before the circulation of blood was discovered by Harvey in 1628 (Lee, 2000), before Vesalius systematically documented the anatomy of the human body in 1543 (Venzmer, 1968), the structural function of the skeletal system was understood. Bone protected organs such as the brain and provided the frame on which the soft tissues of the body were formed. Based on this basic understanding, the first medical interventions to replace bone—removed due to damage or underlying injury—were seen at least as far back as the time of the Aztecs, who are known to have used gold and silver to replace pieces of the skull following craniotomies (Sanan and Haines, 1997). The fact that bone was a living material that could heal itself was documented over 5000 years ago, when the ancient Egyptians recorded techniques for setting fractures on papyrus (Peltier, 1990), and this knowledge has led to interventions designed to manipulate the fracture healing properties of the tissue.

Our greater understanding of the overall physiology of bone did not develop until much more recent history. The complex and important role of the cellular component of bone, though only a small fraction of the overall material volume, is still being investigated. While the general properties of bone, ligament, tendon, and cartilage have been well characterized over the past century, knowledge of how these properties can be best mimicked or taken advantage of to promote tissue healing remains in its infancy.

Orthopedic tissues are affected by both the stresses that they experience, on a daily basis or as a result of trauma, and disease processes. Many of these injuries or pathologies require medical intervention that may be assisted through the use of engineered materials. The science behind the selection of these materials has moved from the realm of trial and error to one based on scientific theory and understanding. This chapter will give a brief overview of the natural orthopedic biomaterials—bone, cartilage, tendon, and ligament—before proceeding on to a discussion of the historical development and current technology in engineered biomaterials for orthopedic applications.

20.2 NATURAL MATERIALS

20.2.1 Bone

Bone has a diverse set of physiological roles, ranging from the obvious structural support and protection to maintenance of calcium homeostasis and hematopoiesis, the production of red blood cells by the bone marrow. As such, both the material characteristics and the cellular characteristics of bone must be understood in order to fully appreciate the complexity of the tissue. However, to initiate this understanding, it is easier to examine the material and cellular components of bone separately at first.

Bone's Material Components. From a structural standpoint, bone is essentially a composite of organic and inorganic components—namely collagen and hydroxyapatite. Collagen is a protein with a high tensile strength and viscoelastic properties, while hydroxyapatite is a calcium phosphate compound with properties similar to that of a ceramic. Hydroxyapatite crystals, needle-like structures with a size on the order of an angstrom, are imbedded in the sides of long collagen fibers. The collagen fibers are then arranged in sheets as parallel structures, which in turn are layered in concentric circles with the collagen fiber orientation varying between layers. The dimension about which these concentric layers of composite, or lamellae, are formed depends on the type of bone involved.

Cortical bone, or compact bone, is the dense form of the tissue that is generally called to mind when an image of "bone" is produced. It is found on the outer surface of all bones and comprises the majority of the shaft (or diaphysis) of long bones, such as the femur. Two basic forms of cortical bone exist in humans: osteonal and lamellar. Lamellar bone is formed when the concentric layers of collagen-mineral composite are wrapped around the inner (endosteal) or outer (periosteal) surfaces of a whole bone structure. Osteonal bone involves a more complex microstructure, with the composite layers wrapped in concentric circles about a vascular or Haversian canal (Fig. 20.1). A group of these lamellae with its central Haversian canal form an osteon, the diameter of which can range from 150 to 250 μm for secondary (or remodeled) osteons, while primary osteons tend to be smaller. The axis of the osteon is generally oriented along the direction of primary loading in a bone.

Trabecular bone is formed through a different arrangement of lamellae. An individual trabeculum is a tube of wrapped lamellae on the order of 150 to 300 μm in diameter. Trabeculae can also form in the shape of plates, which have a slightly larger dimension but are again formed by parallel layers

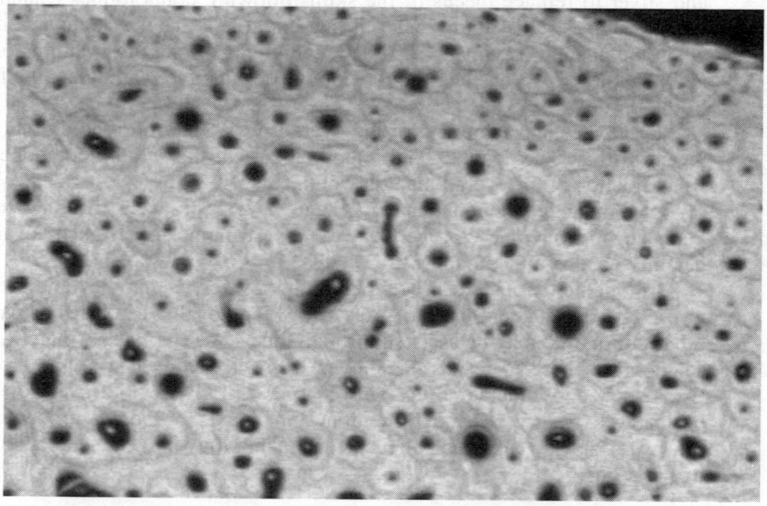

FIGURE 20.1 Scanning acoustic microscopy image of cortical bone from a human femur. Note the circular arrangement of the lamellae around the central Haversian canal.

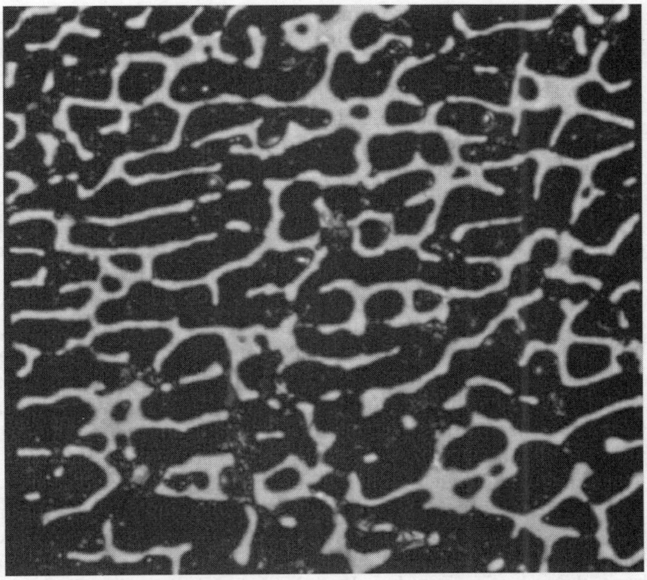

FIGURE 20.2 Scanning acoustic microscopy image of vertebral trabecular bone from a young individual. The vertical beams and the horizontal struts form a three-dimensional network to maximize the mechanical properties while minimizing weight.

TABLE 20.1 Representative Properties of Cortical and Trabecular Bone

Cortical bone	Compressive strength (MPa)	131–224	longitudinal
		106–133	transverse
	Tensile strength (MPa)	80–172	longitudinal
		51–56	transverse
	Shear strength (MPa)	53–70	
	Elastic modulus (GPa)	11–20	longitudinal
Trabecular bone	Tissue compressive strength (MPa)	0.5–50	
	Tissue elastic modulus (MPa)	5–150	
	Material elastic modulus (GPa)	1–11	

Sources: Cowin (1989), Hayes and Bouxsein (1997), An (2000).

of the collagen-mineral composite. The trabecular plates, beams, and struts are arranged into a three-dimensional structure that mimics the internal skeleton of a modern skyscraper (Fig. 20.2). The beams and plates are generally arranged in the direction of primary loading, while the struts provide supporting structures in an off-axis direction in order to minimize buckling. Healthy trabecular bone is "designed" to have an improved strength-to-weight ratio compared to cortical bone—it can carry a substantial amount of load without contributing added weight to the body. It is found at the ends of long bones, in the metaphyseal and epiphyseal regions, as well as the inner portions of bones such as the vertebrae of the spine, the carpal bones of the wrist, and the flat bones of the ribs and skull.

The mechanical and material properties of bone have been extensively characterized, and representative properties are listed in Table 20.1. The structural and material properties of cortical bone are approximately equal, due to the low porosity. However, as the porosity and arrangement of trabecular bone play an important role in the structural properties of this phase, the material modulus may be up to three orders of magnitude higher than structural modulus. It must be noted, however, that unlike traditional engineering materials, the properties of bone are not constant. The strength, modulus, and density can vary between individuals, between anatomic locations, and as a result of age or disease processes. Variations in the properties of bone may be a function of changes in either the structure of the tissue (e.g., how many trabeculae are present and how they are arranged)—or the material of the tissue (e.g., the properties of the collagen-mineral composite itself). In healthy tissue, the material of bone changes very little, with the mineral density fairly constant at a level of 1.8 to 1.9 g/cc (Kaplan et al., 1994) and the mineral to collagen ratio set to about 1:1 by volume. Disease processes, such as osteomalacia or osteogenesis imperfecta, can affect the collagen or mineral components of bone, and as such have a profound effect on the underlying properties of the tissue.

The structural properties of bone, even at the microscopic level, can also vary due to anatomic location (which can be seen as a design variation), age, or disease. A prime example of this is the loss of trabecular bone seen in all individuals after the age of 35 and exacerbated by osteoporosis. It has been shown that in the vertebrae, for example, osteoporosis results in the selective resorption of the horizontal, supporting trabeculae. The trabecular bone, which makes up all but a small fraction of the volume of the vertebral centrum, is weakened as each of the load-bearing beams is then characterized by a larger characteristic length. Based on Euler's theories on buckling, these trabeculae will be more susceptible to buckling—and hence failure—at lower loads. Figure 20.3 shows examples of buckled trabeculae in an image of vertebral trabecular bone from a 75-year-old.

Finally, the properties of a whole bone will be affected by the amounts of trabecular and cortical bone present and their geometric arrangement. As will be discussed below, bone is a living tissue that can adapt to its loading environment. The loss of cross-sectional area in the diaphysis of a long bone, the reduction in trabecular volume fraction, or the change in shape of a bone will all affect a bone's overall properties and likelihood of fracture.

Bone's Living Components. Like liver, kidney, and muscle, bone is a living tissue that responds to its physiologic environment. Two basic processes take place in bone as it responds to physiological

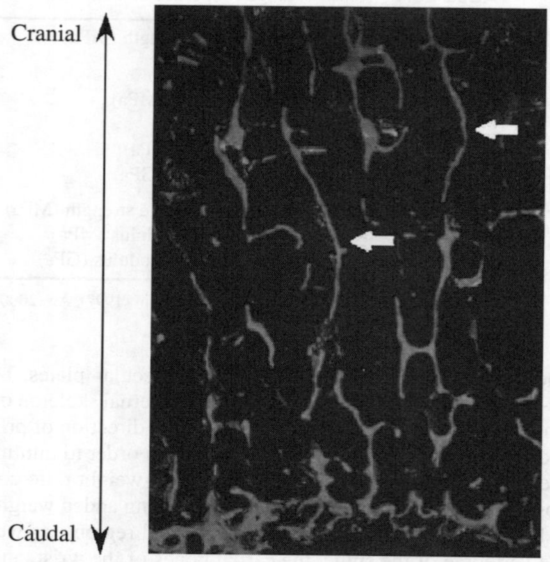

FIGURE 20.3 Scanning acoustic microscopy image of vertebral trabecular bone from a 75-year-old male. The arrows indicate the location of trabeculae that have begun to buckle under the supero-inferiorly (craniocaudally) directed physiologic load due to a loss of supporting struts.

demands. Bone modeling occurs primarily in children and young adults and results in bone growth—both in length and in cross-sectional area. The growth of bones through the addition of material to the endosteum or periosteum, which is the result of the modeling process, can also continue throughout life. Bone remodeling involves the removal, and, in general, replacement of bone. This process allows for the continual recycling of bone, and in healthy tissue it prevents the accumulation of microcracks that could lead to fatigue failure of the structure. The same general processes are seen in fracture healing.

The cellular component of bone consists of three cell types: osteoblasts, osteoclasts, and osteocytes. Osteoblasts are the cells in bone that will lay down new collagen matrix, which is then mineralized to form the lamellae of bone. Osteoclasts remove bone during the normal remodeling process, which is then replaced through osteoblastic activity. Osteoclasts also act to remove bone due to changes in the loading environment. This response in bone, which has tremendous implications in implant design and use, is discussed in the section "Wolff's Law." Osteocytes are the general cells of bone, acting as communication systems from one location in bone to another. Connected through cellular processes in the canaliculi of osteonal bone, osteocytes are thought to act as transducers that sense the mechanical and chemical environment around bone and then relay this information to the osteoclasts and osteoblasts in order to illicit the necessary cellular response.

Wolff's Law. Developed in 1892 by Professor Wolff (Wolff, 1892), this theory of bone behavior remains the governing principle behind our understanding of bone physiology. After observing that the structural orientation in the head and neck of the femur resembled the principal stress trajectories of a Cullman crane (a mechanical structure with a similar shape and loading pattern), Wolff hypothesized that bone develops in response to the loading environment that it experiences. Through the last 115 years, this hypothesis has been reinforced through empirical and experimental data. Thus, bones which are not loaded sufficiently will lose tissue mass, while bones that are loaded at a greater level than their previous history will add bone in order to reduce the stress experienced. This response does require a time-averaged response—a single day spent in bed or lifting weights will not change the structure of bone. However extended periods in a hypogravity environment, such as the International Space Station, will result in bone loss, and therefore a reduction in whole bone strength. In loading-related bone remodeling, the changes in bone mass are due to increases or decreases in the structural arrangement of bone, not a change in the amount of mineral per unit volume of collagen at the material level.

Mechanobiology of Bone. Mechanobiology—the study of how mechanical forces, including at the microlevel, affect cell function and tissue development—has only been recognized as its own field of study in the past few decades. New experimental techniques have permitted biomedical engineers to move beyond Professor Wolff's empirical observations to study the actual molecular mechanisms that underlie bone's response to its mechanical environment. It is important to consider the cell in combination with the extracellular matrix (ECM) when working to understand how forces are transmitted to and are transduced by the cells (Eyckmans et al., 2011). The stiffness of the ECM, which can be affected by calcification, for instance, will impact how forces are transmitted to the osteocytes, which then signal the osteoblasts and osteoclasts to affect the tissue-level response. These latter cells also experience and transduce information from their mechanical environment. The osteocytes will also respond to stresses caused by fluid flow within the canaliculi and lacunae. Thus, the cellular response of bone in growth, remodeling, and healing processes is a complicated one—involving multiple sensing cells, multiple modes of stress, and a myriad of biochemical signals (Giorgi et al., 2016). The basic process of mechanotransduction involves four steps: mechanoreception (sensing the force); biochemical coupling (conversion of the force into a biochemical response); transmission of the biochemical signal to other cellular or molecular structures; and a response from the effector cell (Duncan and Turner, 1995).

The study of the complete response of bone to its mechanical environment is still an area that demands significant research. However, some basic mechanisms have been identified:

- Osteocytes and osteoblasts respond directly to mechanical stimulation by expressing or releasing various compounds, including matrix proteins, growth factors, prostaglandins, and NO (Liedert et al., 2005).

- Integrins, which are transmembrane receptors that transduce signals from the ECM to the intracellular components and vice versa, are one of the subcellular structures that have been shown to sense and respond to changes in the mechanical environment of bone cells. There are numerous integrins found in osteoblasts that have been found to affect bone formation. For example, binding of integrins to ligands induces a set of complex biochemical cascades involving signaling proteins and enzyme activation that results in differentiation of progenitor cells into osteoblasts as well as collagen synthesis (Marie et al., 2014). Integrin activity can be affected by the presence of growth factors, such as transforming growth factor-β (TGF-β). Thus, the presence, activation, and interaction of various transmembrane receptors will contribute to the overall bone formation process.
- Cadherins, which are molecules that create cell-cell adhesion and thus connect the response of adjacent cells, have also been found to play a role in both osteoblast differentiation and function. They have been shown to modulate intercellular signaling that is mediated by cell-cell contact (Marie et al., 2014).
- Activation of transduction pathways, including integrins, cadherins, ion channels, hormone receptors, and others, can result in gene expression that regulates cell division and matrix synthesis (Liedert et al., 2005). As the cells and matrix respond, the mechanical environment surrounding the cells changes, which can then either support homeostasis or drive remodeling processes forward.

The key takeaway regarding bone mechanobiology is that, despite its outward appearance, bone is an extremely complex, living tissue. The cellular processes are highly integrated, interdependent, and affecting/affected by the extracellular matrix. A basic understanding of this concept is imperative to engineering effective systems that interface with bone—though the details may still take decades to fully tease out.

20.2.2 Cartilage

From an orthopedic material viewpoint, the type of cartilage of interest is articular cartilage—located at the bearing surfaces of the joints. Cartilage provides a covering surface on the ends of bones that meet to form an articulation, such as the femur and tibia at the knee. It acts to provide a smooth, low-friction bearing surface, as well as to absorb some of the energy transferred through the joints during normal activities.

Cartilage is a soft tissue composed of a proteoglycan matrix reinforced with collagen. The orientation of the collagen varies through the thickness of the structure, with fibers oriented perpendicular to the articular surface at the deepest level (furthest from the point of joint contact) and parallel to the surface in the uppermost region (Mankin et al., 1994). Sixty-five to eighty percent of the total tissue weight is due to the water contained within the tissue matrix (Mankin et al., 1994). Cartilage is predominantly loaded in compression and is viscoelastic in nature. Under initial loading, the water within the proteoglycan matrix is extruded, and the stiffness of the material is a function of the tissue permeability. In fact, the fluid pressure within the matrix supports approximately 20 times more load than the underlying material during physiological loading (Mankin et al., 1994). Under extended, noncyclic loading, the collagen and proteoglycan matrix will determine the material behavior after the water has been forced from the tissue. Table 20.2 shows representative values for cartilage properties.

The low-friction environment provided by healthy cartilage as an articulating surface is also due to the fluid that is forced from the structure under compressive loading. As the tissue is loaded in compression, the water released from the proteoglycan matrix provides fluid film lubrication between the two surfaces. During the unloading portion of a motion cycle, the cartilage resorbs a portion of the water, returning it to the matrix.

The principal cell in cartilage is the chondrocyte. Responsible for matrix production during growth and maintenance of the matrix in mature tissue, chondrocytes occupy only about 10 percent of the overall tissue volume (Mankin et al., 1994). Due to the avascular nature of articular cartilage, the provision of metabolites to the cells is assumed to occur via diffusion from the synovial fluid or, to a lesser extent, the underlying bone (Mankin et al., 1994). However, the lack of blood supply severely diminishes the ability of cartilage to heal once it has been damaged.

TABLE 20.2 Representative Properties for Human Articular Cartilage Taken from the Lateral Condyle of the Femur

Property	Value
Poisson's ratio	0.10
Compressive modulus	0.70 MPa
Permeability coefficient	1.18×10^{-15} m^4/Ns

Source: Mankin et al. (1994).

The mechanobiology of cartilage has been less studied than that of bone—perhaps because intervening to promote bone healing has been successful even based on empirical observations, while cartilage repair and healing remains a mystery. Perhaps because of this challenge, better understanding of the cellular and molecular responses that occur in healthy and pathological cartilage are needed. It is known that in pathologic conditions, such as osteoarthritis, the anabolic (formation) and catabolic (removal) activities are not in homeostasis (Sanchez-Adams et al., 2014). In healthy cartilage, as in healthy bone, physical activity supports the maintenance of cartilage. However, in osteoarthritis, an interaction of mechanical factors and changes in biological behavior are believed to affect the progression of the disease. The pericellular matrix (PCM) in articular cartilage, which is biomechanically and biochemically distinct from the ECM, has been found to modulate the strains that the chondrocytes experience within the varying layers of the structure (Sanchez-Adams et al., 2014). Like bone cells, chondrocytes respond to changes and cyclic variations in mechanical loading through the production of various ECM molecules, including proteoglycans, collagens, and proteins. Mechanotransduction by chondrocytes is due to opening and closing of mechanosensitive ion channels, integrin signaling, and primary cilia (Sanchez-Adams et al., 2014). In pathological conditions, the production of molecules and enzymes that enhance catabolic events has been found. Inflammatory pathways have also been shown to affect the normal activity of chondrocytes, which negatively affects their response to the mechanical environment (Sanchez-Adams et al., 2014).

20.2.3 Ligaments and Tendons

Although different structures with different physiological functions, ligaments and tendons are often examined together due to their similar, tensile loading patterns. Ligaments connect bones to each other across a joint, while tendons attach muscles to bone and provide the anchor necessary for muscles to cause movement. Each is composed of a combination of collagen and elastin fibers, arranged primarily in parallel along the axis of loading. However, in the unloaded state, the fibers are slightly crimped. Therefore, initial tensile loading of the structure acts only to straighten out the component fibers—resulting in a region of low stiffness. Once the fibers have been completely straightened, the individual fiber stiffness dictates the overall structural stiffness. The resulting load-deformation curve (Fig. 20.4) exhibits a characteristic low stiffness, toe region followed by a region of increasing stiffness. If loading continues, failure of individual fibers within the structure will result in decreasing overall stiffness followed by rupture.

Table 20.3 shows typical values for the tensile properties of ligament and tendon. Tendon tends to be slightly stiffer than ligament, due to the higher concentration of collagen. Both tissues are highly viscoelastic and will fail at lower extensions when loaded at high rates. This behavior explains why a slow stretch will not injure a tendon or ligament, while a rapid motion may result in rupture. The properties of both types of tissue vary based on anatomic location, indicating that the properties develop to match the normal physiologic demands.

Tendons tend to be avascular if they are surrounded by a tendon sheath to direct passage around a sharp prominence of bone, such as is seen in the flexor tendons of the hand. However, the remaining tendons tend to have a reasonable blood supply through surrounding connective tissue (Woo et al., 1994). Ligaments have a very limited blood supply through the insertion sites. In all cases, tendons

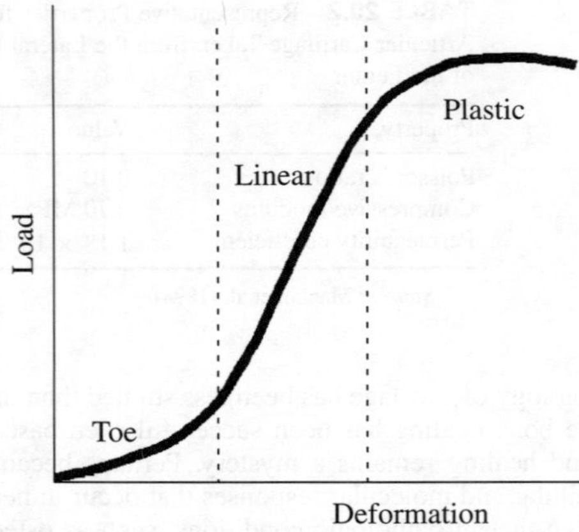

FIGURE 20.4 Schematic diagram of a loading curve for ligament and tendon, showing an initial toe region (fiber straightening), followed by a region of increased stiffness (elastic deformation of collagen), and finally plastic deformation and failure (fiber rupture).

TABLE 20.3 Representative Properties of Human Tendon and Ligament under Tensile Loading

Tissue	Property	Value
Tendon	Elastic modulus (GPa)	1.2–1.8
	Ultimate strength (MPa)	50–105
	Ultimate strain (%)	9–35
	Energy absorbed during elastic deformation	4–10% per cycle
Ligament	Tangent modulus (MPa)	150–294
	Ultimate strength (MPa)	38

Sources: Woo et al. (1994, 2006).

and ligaments have a small population of cells (fibroblasts) within the collagen and elastin fibers. The vascular supply that does exist is necessary for the maintenance of tissue properties. Periods of immobilization, such as occur when a limb is casted, result in a decrease in both stiffness and strength in ligaments. The ligament substance can recover in a period of time approximately equal to that of immobilization. However, the strength of the insertion has been seen to reach only 80 to 90 percent of its original strength after 12 months of recovery following 9 weeks of nonweight bearing (Woo et al., 1994).

Compared to bone and even cartilage, the study of tendon and ligament mechanobiology is in its infancy. For ligaments, researchers are beginning to characterize the various types of stem cells found in different regions of key ligaments, as these are key to tissue healing processes (Chen et al., 2018). For tendon, it has been established that homeostasis is maintained through the regulation of ECM turnover, which is governed through the balance of collagen production and the production of matrix degrading enzymes (Killian et al., 2012). Significant attention has been paid recently to the changes in expression of scleraxis, a transcription factor necessary for tenocyte differentiation and tendon development (Nichols et al., 2018), and TGF-b (Mehdizadeh et al., 2018) under different loading conditions and their role in mechanotransduction. These and other biochemical factors are thought to play a role in the complex response of the tendon to loading and unloading conditions during development, homeostasis, and healing (Killian et al., 2012).

20.2.4 Autografts and Allografts

In many cases, natural tissues can be used to replace damaged or diseased tissue structures. Natural tissue that is obtained from an individual and will be implanted into the same person is termed an autograft. If the donor is a different individual, the material is referred to as an allograft. Bone grafts, used to fill bony defects or replace whole sections of bone, can range from morselized bone fragments to an intact hemipelvis. The larger the graft, the more likely the need to obtain it through a tissue bank as opposed to the patient himself. Soft tissue grafts are more likely to be autologous in nature. The use of a portion of the patellar tendon to replace a ruptured anterior cruciate ligament is one example. Tissue grafts face unique problems in terms of viability, tissue matching, and damage to the donor site (for autografts and allografts from living donors) that are not seen with artificial materials.

20.3 ENGINEERED MATERIALS

Treatment of many orthopedic injuries or pathologies includes the introduction of an engineered material to replace a portion of tissue or augment the structure to assist in healing. These interventions may be permanent or temporary in nature. For the selection of any material for biomedical applications, both the function of the implant and the material's biocompatibility must be considered. The general concerns of corrosion, leaching, absorption, and mutagenicity must be addressed for orthopedic biomaterials as they are for other applications. The following sections provide a brief history of the selection of various material types for orthopedic implant use. The material considerations are discussed, including biocompatibility issues that are specific to orthopedic tissue replacement. However, while the clinical success of an implant depends not only on the material choice but also on the overall implant design, clinical studies into implant efficacy have not generally been included.

20.3.1 Hard Tissue

The most common applications of biomaterials for the replacement or augmentation of bone are used to treat injuries, particularly fractures. A much smaller proportion of implants are used in the treatment of bony diseases, such as replacing bone resected due to osteosarcoma. Total joint replacement, such as the hip, knee, or shoulder, can be used to treat both bony fractures and joint disease.

Stress Shielding. Beyond the traditional biocompatibility issues, hard tissue biomaterials must also be designed to minimize a phenomenon known as stress-shielding. Due to the response of bone remodeling to the loading environment, as described by Wolff's law, it is important to maintain the stress levels in bone as close to their preimplant state as possible. When an implant is oriented parallel to the main loading direction of a bone, such as in a bone plate or a hip stem, the engineered material takes a portion of the load—which then reduces the load, and as a result the stress, in the remaining bone. When the implant and bone are sufficiently well bonded, it can be assumed that the materials deform to the same extent and therefore experience the same strain. In this isostrain condition, the stress in one of the components of a two-phase composite can be calculated from the equation:

$$\sigma_1 = \frac{E_1 F}{E_1 A_1 + E_2 A_2} \tag{20.1}$$

where F is the total load on the structure, and E and A are the Young's modulus and cross-sectional area of each of the components. Thus, the fraction of the load carried by each material, and the resulting stress, is related to its Young's modulus and cross-sectional area as compared to those of the other components of the composite structure. The stiffer materials in the composite will carry a greater proportion of the load per unit cross-sectional area.

If bone in its natural state is compared to bone with a parallel implant, the effect of this intervention on the stress in the bone, and therefore its remodeling response, can be estimated from Eq. (20.1). The applied load can be assumed to be the same pre- and postimplant, which yields the following equations for the stress in the bone in the two configurations:

Pre implant ($E_{\text{implant}} = 0$; $A_{\text{implant}} = 0$)

$$\sigma_{\text{bone}} = \frac{E_{\text{bone}} F}{E_{\text{bone}} A_{\text{bone}}} = \frac{F}{A_{\text{bone}}} \tag{20.2a}$$

Post implant

$$\sigma_{\text{bone}} = \frac{E_{\text{bone}} F}{E_{\text{bone}} A_{\text{bone}} + E_{\text{implant}} A_{\text{implant}}} \tag{20.2b}$$

Thus, the amount of the stress reduction in bone when an implant is included is dependent on the modulus and area of the implant. Implants with a higher modulus and a larger cross-sectional area will shield the bone from a greater proportion of its normal, physiological stress, resulting in bone loss according to Wolff's law.

An ideal implant would match the modulus of bone and occupy no greater cross-sectional area than the tissue replaced while meeting all of the other design requirements of the implant. As such a constraint cannot generally be met by current materials or designs, it is necessary to construct an implant that will minimize, if not entirely eliminate, stress-shielding.

Nondegradable Metals for Bone Applications. Due to the structural role of bone, metals—with their high strength and modulus (Table 20.4)—are an obvious choice for replacement or augmentation of the tissue. The first metals implanted into the body for bony replacement were used in prehistoric times in a nonstructural role to replace cranial defects (Sanan and Haines, 1997). Gold, though of lower modulus than most metals, proved to be a suitable selection for this application due to its lack of reactivity within the body. Structural augmentation of bone using metals to assist fracture healing began in the nineteenth century, when common materials such as silver wires, iron nails, and galvanized steel plates were used to hold fragments of bone together (Peltier, 1990). In the case of metals susceptible to oxidation, such as steel and iron, corrosion led to premature mechanical failure and severe tissue reactions. In 1912, Sherman developed a steel alloy that contained vanadium and chromium (Sherman, 1912), providing it with higher strength and ductility than the previously used tool steels or crucible steels. Studies on cytotoxicity that began in the 1920s (Zierold, 1924) and the 1930s (Jones and Lieberman, 1936) led to a reduction in the types of metals used in implants, focusing attention on gold, lead, aluminum, and specific formulations of steels (Peltier, 1990).

TABLE 20.4 Summary of Properties of Metals Currently Used in Hard Tissue Implants, in Comparison with Bone

Material	Elastic modulus, GPa	Compressive strength, MPa	Tensile strength, MPa
Stainless steel (316L)	200	505–860	485
Cast Co-Cr-Mo	200	655	
Wrought CoNiCrMo	200	600–1790	
Titanium alloy (Ti6Al4V)	110	860	1000
Porous tantalum (structural)	0.37–2.2	4–12.7	63
Cortical bone	11–20	106–224	51–172
Trabecular bone (structural)	0.005–0.150	0.5–50	7.6

Note: Properties of porous materials, including cortical bone, trabecular bone, and porous tantalum, vary significantly with porosity.

Sources: Cowin (1989), Havelin et al. (1995), Hayes and Bouxsein (1997), ASTM-F136 (1998), ASTM-F562 (2000), Zardiackas et al. (2001), Shimko et al. (2005).

The first metallic implant for a hip replacement was introduced in 1940 and was constructed of Vitallium, a form of cobalt-chromium alloy (Rang, 2000). Along with stainless steel, this became a standard metal for large joint replacement and internal fracture fixation. Both materials showed good biocompatibility and excellent structural properties. The choice between the two often depended on the individual opinions of the designing physician, as they balanced biocompatibility and mechanical performance. Multiple medical grades of stainless steel were developed and standardized, including the most common formulation in use today—316L (containing iron, chromium, nickel, molybdenum, and manganese in decreasing concentrations, with additional trace elements). In addition to the cast alloy that is Vitallium (Co-30Cr-6Mb), a wrought alloy was also introduced (Co-20Cr-10Ni-15Tu) that possesses improved tensile strength and ductility (Brettle et al., 1971).

One of the keys to the chemical biocompatibility of stainless steel and cobalt chromium was the formation of a passivation layer in vivo, thus minimizing the amount of corrosion that occurs to the implant. However, as indicated in Table 20.4, while the strength of these two metals reduced the chance for failure within the implant, their elastic moduli are an order of magnitude higher than seen in healthy, cortical bone. This resulted in the occurrence of stress shielding and concomitant bone loss in many patients with large implants.

In the 1940s, the aerospace industry introduced titanium and its alloys into the market. The high strength-to-weight ratio and comparatively low modulus attracted the attention of surgeons and implant designers. Titanium also proved to be chemically biocompatible, forming its passivation layer in air before implantation—thus further reducing the chemical reactions occurring at the implant interface. Despite the higher cost of the bulk material and the difficulty in machining titanium, due to its tendency to seize when in contact with other metals, titanium alloys have proven to be an effective choice for large joint replacement and some techniques of fracture fixation, including compression plates. The most common titanium alloy used in orthopedic surgery is T318 (Ti-6Al-4V). The strength of the alloy is greater than that of pure titanium, and it maintains its good biocompatibility (Brettle et al., 1971). Titanium has been shown to promote good bone apposition to its surface when it is implanted, and porous surfaces have proven to be receptive to bone ingrowth. Neither of these features is as apparent in ferrous or cobalt-based alloys.

A more recent metal to hit the orthopedic market is tantalum, marketed by Zimmer as Trabecular Metal. The benefit to tantalum is the ability to form it into porous foams with a structure on the order of trabecular bone, providing a scaffold that is optimum for bone ingrowth. The mechanical properties of this novel metal depend on its porosity and structure, but are sufficient to provide mechanical support during the period of bony integration (Shimko et al., 2005; Zardiackas et al., 2001). Bone ingrowth into the porous structure after 4 weeks of implantation into cortical bone provided stronger fixation than observed in many other porous structures and progressed to fill over 60 percent of the pores by 16 weeks of implantation (Bobyn et al., 1999). In addition to its strong mechanical attributes, both in terms of initial stability and bony fixation, tantalum has been shown to be virtually inert, provoking a minimal tissue response (Black, 1994). This combination of properties has led to the development of tantalum structures for the backing of acetabular cups and spinal fusion cages. Trabecular Metal has been used clinically to supplement fixation in total knee and total hip arthroplasties when substantial bone loss had occurred (Meneghini et al., 2008; Rose et al., 2006). It also shows promise as a means to repair tendon insertions (Reach et al., 2007). It has most recently been demonstrated to be successful in reconstructive surgery involving significant bony defects (Burastero et al., 2018). The applications of this unique and biocompatible material are most likely in the initial stages, with many more opportunities still to be developed and validated.

In addition to bulk implants, metals have been used to form the ingrowth surface for total joint replacements. The design goal of these implants, which use a porous surface on all or part of the bone-contacting portion of the implant, is to better transfer the load from the implant through to the bone. Various companies have developed porous surface systems based on sintered particles, sintered wires, or rough, plasma sprayed surfaces. The common goal in these systems is to produce a pore size into which bone will grow and become firmly fixed. Due to the substantially increased surface area of the metal in these implants, corrosion becomes a point of increased concern. In addition, it is necessary to maintain a strong bond between the porous surface and the underlying, bulk metal in order to allow full load transfer to occur.

TABLE 20.5 Summary of Mechanical Properties of Some Ceramics Used in Orthopedic Applications

Material	Elastic modulus, GPa	Compressive strength, MPa	Tensile strength, MPa
Alumina	380	4500	270
Zirconia	100–250	1200–5200	115–711
Dense calcium phosphate	40–117	294	
Bioglass	63		Bulk: 100 – 200 Fiber: 617–1625

Note: Calcium phosphate properties vary depending on formulation (e.g., tricalcium phosphate vs. hydroxyapatite). Bioactive glass properties vary as a function of composition and structure, with fibers possessing higher tensile strength than bulk material.

Sources: Boutin et al. (1988), Park and Lakes (1992), Pirhonen et al. (2006), Gautam et al. (2016).

Biodegradable Metals. One of the commonly accepted characteristics of metallic, biomedical implants is that they are not biodegradable. This has some benefits, as the materials selected (which are corrosion resistant) can be assumed to maintain their mechanical and structural properties over an extended period of implantation. However, the continued presence of an implant can result in complications, and efforts have been made to develop materials that combine the load-bearing capabilities of metals with the ability for controlled degradation to avoid the need for a second removal surgery. The main biodegradable metals are magnesium, iron, and zinc, with zinc demonstrating a mid-range degradation rate (between 4 and 6 months) as well as fully bioresorbable degradation products (Bowen et al., 2013; Su et al., 2018). Due to the relatively low mechanical properties of zinc, its primary use has been in vascular implants rather than in load-bearing implants for orthopedic applications. However, the possibility of alloying it with other metals (Su et al., 2018) or developing degradable zinc-based metal matrix composites, such as with hydroxyapatite (Yang et al., 2018), open up the possibilities for advancement of biodegradable metals for use in orthopedics.

Ceramics for Bone Applications. As bone is a composite consisting essentially of ceramic and polymeric components, and due to the essential inertness of many ceramics, this class of materials was looked to in order to find truly biocompatible materials for structural applications. However, the brittle nature and low tensile strength of ceramics have led to some concerns regarding the fracture behavior of these materials, while the high modulus again raises the specter of stress shielding for implants with large geometries (Table 20.5).

Ceramics, particularly alumina, were first introduced as structural, orthopedic biomaterials in the late 1960s (Boutin, 1972). However, limitations in processing technology and lack of quality control led to materials with higher than desired levels of impurities and imperfections, including high porosity levels. These defects caused a further reduction in the strength of ceramics in tensile or shear loading, resulting in premature failure in a number of clinical cases (Holmer and Nielsen, 1993; Peiro et al., 1991).

Processing techniques for ceramics improved by 1977, resulting in smaller and less variable grain sizes. As processing technologies improved, the true chemical biocompatibility of these materials caused them to be reexamined for use in orthopedic applications. Alumina and zirconia have become the most popular ceramics for use in total joint replacement. Zirconia was introduced in an attempt to further reduce the risks of component fracture and wear particle production (Jazwari et al., 1998). In general, the low tensile strength of both materials has precluded their use in structures subjected to substantial bending, such as the femoral stem of a total hip replacement. However, highly polished ceramics have shown good success as articulating components in total joint arthroplasty—with articulation against either a polymer or another ceramic both possible. Implants constructed predominantly of ceramics, particularly for total knee replacement, are currently being investigated. These designs are particularly useful in patients with demonstrated metal sensitivities, which often precludes the use of a standard implant design. The clinical outcomes for ceramic-on-ceramic implants appeared to be promising initially (Murphy et al., 2006), but further follow-up has restricted this success in total hip implants to those with large (>28 mm) femoral head diameters (Sedrakyan et al., 2014). Thus, material selection and mechanical design must be considered concurrently when evaluating implants. It is interesting to note that new types of side effects are being reported—such as audible squeaking or clicking in total hip replacements with total ceramic bearings (Keurentjes et al., 2008).

Bioactive Ceramics. On the opposite end of the spectrum to the ceramics investigated for their inert nature are a group of ceramic materials that are designed to induce a reaction from the surrounding tissue. These bioactive materials take advantage of the tissue's cellular physiology and structural component materials to induce bone remodeling, growth, and integration into the implant. An ideal bioactive ceramic would actually spur bone growth adjacent to the implant, promote integration of the bone with the implant structure, and gradually biodegrade as healthy bone tissue replaces the artificial structure. Two general categories of bioactive ceramics have been developed: calcium-based ceramics, such as calcium phosphate, calcium sulfate, and hydroxyapatite; and bioglasses, mineral-rich structures that can be tailored to optimize the tissue response. Bioactive materials such as these can have either osteo*inductive* or osteo*conductive* properties. The former refers to the ability of a material to trigger bone cell differentiation and remodeling in locations where bone cell proliferation and healing would not normally occur (such as a large defect), while the latter defines a material that promotes bony ingrowth and vascularization, allowing for integration and remodeling to take place.

Calcium-based composites rely on their similarity to the mineral component of natural bone—hydroxyapatite (HA). The theory behind their use is that the body will see these materials as tissues that need to be remodeled, allowing them to be integrated with and then replaced by bone. Tricalcium phosphate [TCP—$Ca_3(PO_4)_2$], calcium sulfate (plaster of Paris—$CaSO_4$), and hydroxyapatite [$Ca_{10}(PO_4)_6(OH)_2$] are all currently being used to fill bony deflects and stimulate or direct bone formation. Calcium sulfate has been used for over a century due to its ready availability and biocompatibility (Taylor and Rorabeck, 1999). The crystal size (nanometers) of biological HA is much smaller than can be produced in synthetic versions of the material (Cooke, 1992); however, it has still been shown to be more osteoconductive in nature than TCP (Klein et al., 1983).

TCP, calcium sulfate, and HA can be inserted into a defect in the cortical or trabecular bone in the form of pellets or particles. The high surface-to-volume ratios of these implants, used in areas where immediate structural support is maintained through remaining bone or fracture fixation, allows for more rapid integration and remodeling of the material. The calcium sulfate formulation has been shown to resorb in only 6 to 8 weeks (Ladd and Pliam, 1999).

Less frequently, blocks of calcium-based ceramics are used to replace large segments of bone that have been resected due to injury or disease. These implants have not proven to become fully replaced by living bone, but serve as a continued structural support that is integrated with the surrounding bone surface. The blocks can be made porous, to mimic the structure of trabecular bone, and this has been shown to increase bone ingrowth into the material. One brand of porous hydroxyapatite has been manufactured from the tricalcium phosphate laid down by marine coral (Ladd and Pliam, 1999) and has been shown to possess substantial osteoconductive properties, filling over 50 percent of the porosity volume with bone within 3 months (White, 1986). Hydroxyapatite has also been combined with polymethylmethacrylate (PMMA) bone cement (see below) with the goal of inducing bone growth into the cement through the remodeling of these small particles of calcium-based ceramic. Ceramic bone grafts can be augmented with biological molecules designed to increase their osteoinductive nature, including transforming growth factor β (TGF-β) and bone morphogenic protein (BMP) (Ladd and Pliam, 1999). These materials then begin to bridge the gap to tissue engineering.

One of the newest techniques for applying a calcium-based material to assist with fracture fixation is through the injection of a viscous "cement" that then fully hardens in vivo. Norian SRS (Skeletal Replacement System), an injectable, calcium phosphate material, was introduced in 1995 (Constantz et al., 1995). It has been shown to reduce the immobilization time required during fracture fixation (Kopylov et al., 1999), as it carries a portion of the load during bone healing. After

12 hours in vivo, Norian has cured to between 85 and 95 percent of its ultimate properties, with a final compressive strength of 55 MPa (Constantz et al., 1995). Successful clinical applications have included the reduction and stabilization of unstable or intra-articular radial fractures (Kopylov et al., 1999; Yetkinler et al., 1999), complex calcaneal fractures (Schildhauer et al., 2000), vertebral compression fractures (Bai et al., 1999), and the augmentation of hip screw fixation of unstable fractures in the intertrochanteric region of the femur (Elder et al., 2000). Calcium sulfate injectables were developed in the early 2000s to increase the resorption rate and prevent possible complications from long-term persistence of the injected ceramic and have undergone several revisions to promote improved clinical outcomes (Yu et al., 2009). Cerament, an injectable and moldable ceramic composed of hydroxyapatite and calcium sulfate that has drug-eluting properties, has also been used clinically with success for filling voids in bones and treatment of vertebral compression fractions (Iundusi et al., 2015; Rauschmann et al., 2010). Additional formulations of injectable ceramics are also been developed in order to optimize properties for particular orthopedic applications, including glass polyalkenoate cements (Khader et al., 2017).

In addition to its use in bulk form, ceramics can be coated onto metallic implants to improve fixation and biocompatibility. This has been happening for several years with calcium-based ceramics, and research is currently being conducted on nanostructured bioinert ceramics for coatings, including diamond (Amaral et al., 2007). Hydroxyapatite-coated titanium has shown firm fixation to bone in implant conditions, both in mechanically stable and mechanically unstable conditions (Soballe et al., 1999), with the fixation occurring at a faster rate than in implants where the porous coating is manufactured from titanium itself (Kotzki et al., 1994). HA coatings degrade with time and are replaced with natural bone, allowing close apposition with the underlying implant material. Clinical studies have shown that the inclusion of the additional material layer does not promote increased wear or osteolysis in a properly designed implant (Capello et al., 1998). The bioactive ceramics can be applied through plasma spraying, creating a rough or porous surface approximately 50 μm thick (Cooke, 1992). Laser ablation is a newer coating technology, which can produce coatings that are less than 5 μm thick and have improved mechanical properties (Cléries et al., 2000). In addition to their role in improving implant fixation, coatings have the benefit of minimizing metallic contact with the physiologic environment. Coatings can also be used to deliver various pharmaceutical agents to the tissue surrounding the implant in an attempt to minimize infection (Radin et al., 1997) or improve bone healing (Duan et al., 2005). New ideas are being put forward to combine calcium phosphate with bioactive molecules, including bone morphogenic protein and extracellular matrix molecules such as collagen, in order to improve the osteoinductive properties of the coating (Zhang et al., 2014). While cemented implants or metallic, porous coatings are still most frequently used for total joint replacement, a substantial amount of research is being directed at coating systems. Clinical assessment of these materials and designs has shown disparate results, with some of the variations in outcomes likely due to variations in surgical technique and patient factors (Zhang et al., 2014). There is continued interest in these coatings as a way to improve patient outcomes, and therefore research is expected to continue.

Bioglass was introduced to the scientific world in the late 1960s by Dr. Hench. This glass-ceramic, which was produced in several forms containing varied proportions of SiO, Na_2O, CaO, P_2O_3, CaF_2, and B_2O_3, was designed to interact with the normal physiology of bone in order to allow strong bone bonding (Ducheyne, 1985). Initial work by Greenspan and Hench (1976) indicated that an alumina implant coated with bioglass showed substantially improved attachment to bone and new bone formation when implanted in rats compared to alumina-only controls. The bonding mechanism was found to depend on the composition of the glass, and that has sparked the development of other variations of glass-ceramics. These include Ceravital [which contains K_2O and MgO in place of CaF_2 and B_2O_3 (Ducheyne, 1985)] and a form containing apatite and wollastonite known as Cerabone A-W (Nishio et al., 2001). The particular composition and manufacturing technique of bioactive glasses can be manipulated to develop systems that are best adapted to their proposed application (Saravanapavan et al., 2004).

Glass-ceramics have low tensile strength and fracture toughness, limiting their use in bulk form to applications subject to purely compressive loading. Attempts have been made to use these materials as part of composite structures in order to increase their application. The most common method is to coat a ceramic or metallic implant with the glass in order to create an osteoinductive surface. The coating may be applied in a pure layer of glass or as an enamel coating with imbedded glass particles (Ducheyne, 1985). For the enamel systems, it is important to ensure that the components of the enamel do not interfere with the bone formation process (Ducheyne, 1985). The glass coating is still a brittle material and must be handled with care—any substantial impact may lead to failure of the entire coating system.

Glass composites have also been investigated using stainless steel fibers (50 to 200 μm thick) to reinforce the glass-ceramic (Ducheyne and Hench, 1982). The goal of these composites follows that of other fiber-reinforced materials—to increase their resistance to fracture by blunting crack growth and introducing a residual, compressive stress within the material (Ducheyne, 1985). This procedure was found to make the material significantly more ductile and stronger, thus reducing its tendency to fail catastrophically. In addition, the elastic modulus was reduced from that of the pure glass (Ducheyne, 1985), bringing it closer to the ideal properties for bony replacement.

The potential uses for bioactive glasses and glass-ceramics have been increasing in recent years. Initially, the low tensile strength limited their application to that of a material for filling bony defects, along the lines of a bone graft (Ladd and Pliam, 1999; Pavek et al., 1994), reconstruction of the ossicular bones (Hughes et al., 1987), spine reconstruction (Yamamuro and Shimizu, 1994), and dental reconstruction (Kudo et al., 1990; Yukna et al., 2001). However, their unique features are expanding their application. Their ability to regulate gene expression is being exploited to develop designer scaffolds for tissue engineering and tissue regrowth (Eldesoqi et al., 2014; Jell and Stevens, 2006). Utilizing the material to improve the interface with artificial ligaments has also been the subject of preclinical research (Li et al., 2012). They have even been used as a system to minimize dental sensitivity when applied through a toothpaste (Lee et al., 2007).

Polymers for Bone Applications. Until recently, the only polymer used to replace or augment bone itself (as opposed to the articulating surfaces, which are actually cartilage replacement) was polymethylmethacrylate (PMMA), or bone cement. This material was introduced to the world of orthopedics in 1951 (Rang, 2000), became widely used in the 1960s, and provided good clinical success at maintaining the fixation of a total joint implant within a medullary canal. Bone cement does not act as an adhesive, but rather as a space filler. It fills the void left between the stem of an implant and the endosteum of the bone, interdigitating with both the implant and the natural surfaces. This minimizes the need for an exact fit between the implant and the bone, required with press-fit implants, and provides an immediate source of fixation. This is in contrast to porous-coated implants that require several weeks for bone to grow into the implant surface. Bone cement has been used for almost 70 years with little change in its composition and is still the preferred fixation method for some implants—particularly those to be used in patients with poor bone quality. Three negative factors affect the use of bone cement. First, it polymerizes in vivo through an exothermic reaction that elevates the temperature of the surrounding tissues. The effect of this high temperature on cells has not been fully established and is thought to depend in part on the volume of cement used (Leeson and Lippitt, 1993). Some more recent research looking at in vitro results indicates that despite this exothermic effect, the effects on the cell-implant interaction may not be as pronounced as previously thought (Verrier et al., 2012). However, this study also used small volumes of the acrylic cement. Second, it can deteriorate through fatigue and biological processes, resulting in the production of wear debris. These particles of cement can cause osteolysis (bone loss) of the femoral bone or enter the articulating region, promoting third-body wear in either of the articular components. This latter process would then further exacerbate any debris-related bone loss. Finally, the cement provides an additional material and an additional interface (bone-cement-implant vs. bone-implant) at which macroscopic failure can occur. This can result in a reduced life span for the implant.

In the 1990s, researchers and clinicians began to look at polymers for fracture fixation. This work built upon the idea of epoxy-carbon fiber composite plates, introduced in the previous decade (Ali et al., 1990). While they do not possess the same mechanical strength seen in the metals traditionally used for bone plates and screws (Table 20.6), they do have some properties that may outweigh this lack of strength. First, the bone plates are less stiff—resulting in reduced stress shielding and less bone loss compared with traditional plates. Second, the polymers can be designed to degrade

TABLE 20.6 Characteristic Properties of Polymers Used in Orthopedic Implant Applications

Material property	Young's modulus, GPa	Tensile strength, MPa	Compressive strength, MPa	Elongation, %
UHMWPE	0.4–1.2	44	15.2–24.8 MPa	400–500
PMMA bone cement	1.35	45.5	89.6 MPa	4.6
PLA	0.64–4.0	11.4–72		1.8–3.7
PLGA		45		
PGA	6.5	57		0.7

Note: Properties of the PLGA copolymer depend significantly on composition.
Sources: Dumbleton and Black (1975), Engelberg and Kohn (1991), Agrawal et al. (1995).

with time, allowing the healing bone to eventually take over the entire load-bearing role while avoiding a second surgery for plate removal. While the fixed constructs (bone + plate) are generally stronger during the initial healing when a metal plate is used, the loss of bone due to the higher stress shielding of stainless steel causes a substantial reduction in bone strength at extended time points (Hanafusa et al., 1995). Degradable plates and screws are typically constructed of poly(lactide-co-glycolide) [PLGA], poly(L-lactide) [PLA], or polyglycolic acid [PGA]. The polymer matrix can be augmented with hydroxyapatite to improve the mechanical strength or bonding with bone (Furukawa et al., 2000; Hasirci et al., 2000). Clinical results with these new constructs appear promising for certain applications, such as malleolar fractures (Bostman et al., 1987) and craniofacial reconstruction (Peltoniemi et al., 2002). They are also becoming very popular in the development of scaffolds for tissue engineering of bone (Ifkovits and Burdick, 2007).

Tissue-Engineered Bone Replacements. The phrase tissue engineering has been applied to bone for a wide range of developments. Interventions can be as straightforward as delivery of osteoinductive factors, such as TGF-β and BMP, to the surrounding tissue through a porous scaffold. The more complicated designs include cultured bone cells within a three-dimensional matrix. Due to bone's hard tissue nature, both hard (ceramic) and soft (polymer) scaffolds are being investigated for this application (Burg et al., 2000; Temenoff and Mikos, 2000a). In general, all of the calcium-based ceramics and the degradable polymers—including natural collagen—have been the subject of research interest for this application. Some polymers may need to be reinforced to provide adequate mechanical stability (Burg et al., 2000; Hutmacher et al., 2007). These scaffolds have been seeded with chondrocytes, periosteal osteoblasts, and marrow progenitor cells in order to determine the best cell type to promote osteogenesis when implanted into a defect site (Burg et al., 2000). Advancements in processing and manufacturing of scaffold materials may also address some of the challenges that have been seen to date (Narayanan et al., 2016; Turnbull et al., 2018). These studies are still experimental in nature and have not yet been applied in the clinical arena. However, clinicians have already begun to anticipate the first uses for such a technology, especially in such low load bearing areas as craniofacial reconstruction (Moreau et al., 2007). One of the fundamental challenges for all 3D tissue-engineered structures is provision of adequate blood supply through the development of an integrated capillary network—when this "holy grail" is eventually discovered, true applications of tissue engineering are finally likely to be practical.

20.3.2 Soft Tissue

As with bone, replacement or augmentation of orthopedic soft tissues can be used to treat injury or disease-based degradation to the original tissue. Osteoarthritis—characterized by degradation of the articular cartilage that progresses to the bony surfaces themselves—is one of the most common pathologies experienced by the aging population, with up to 20 percent of the aging population showing signs of degenerative joint disease (DJD) (Felson et al., 2000). Ligament damage is generally the result of injury, often (though not exclusively) caused by athletic activity. Many ligaments are designed with redundant systems—the failure of a single ligament need not result in complete instability in a joint. One of the first questions that must be asked following ligament damage is whether a repair is needed, or if (given the activity level of the individual) conservative treatment and bracing will provide the needed support to the joint. Tendons are damaged much less frequently than other orthopedic soft tissues, and are not the site of common, implant-based repair. Thus, they will not be addressed in this section.

Polymers for Cartilage Replacement. Given the relatively low stiffness of cartilage, and the need for low coefficients of friction, polymers have been the principal material of choice for replacement of articulating joint surfaces, or at least one of the surfaces of an articulating joint. Replacement of large joints, such as the hip, knee, and shoulder, are generally designed with a metal or ceramic component articulating against a polymer surface. For smaller joints, such as those of the fingers, polymeric pieces have been used as spacers and hinges.

Silicone, polyethylene, and polyolefin have all been used as a flexible hinge to replace a joint of the hand damaged through injury or arthritis. The most widely accepted implant for this application was designed by Swanson in the 1960s and continues to be used today (Chung et al., 2017; Linscheid, 2000). Constructed of Silastic, a form of silicone rubber, it achieves fixation through the planned formation of a fibrous capsule around the implant. Such capsular formation is a standard response to implanted structures in the body, but in many cases, it has been determined to be contra-indicated for optimal implant performance. In the case of Swanson's joint replacement, the implant is designed to move within the medullary canal of the connected bones, promoting an enhanced fibrous capsule formation. This fixation avoids the problems seen in the hand with screw fixation or porous coatings designed to promote bony ingrowth (Linscheid, 2000).

Beyond the traditional biocompatibility concerns, which include the effects of leaching and absorption, the greatest obstacle to the use of polymers in the role of articulating surfaces has been wear. The cyclic motion of an opposing implant component or bone against the polymer may produce substantial amounts of wear debris that can then precipitate bone loss and implant failure.

When Charnley introduced his low-friction arthroplasty in the late 1950s, he originally selected Teflon (PTFE—polytetrafluoroethylene) for the acetabular component. However, within a few years, he realized that while it possessed a very low coefficient of friction, its wear resistance was poor (Charnley, 1970). While the observations made on these implants provided substantial information regarding wear processes for plastics in vivo, it was obvious that another material was required. A "filled" Teflon (given the name Fluorosint) was investigated, in which glass fibers or synthetic mica were added in order to improve the wear resistance of the artificial joint. While laboratory tests, using a water lubricant, showed that the newly formulated material had a 20-fold reduction in wear, clinical studies showed that the filled Teflon suffered wear at the same rate as the pure version. The clinical picture was worsened, however, as it was discovered that the particles used in the new formulation acted as an abrasive against the stainless steel femoral head (Charnley, 1970). This difference emphasizes the need to conduct laboratory tests in conditions that mimic the physiologic environment as closely as possible before progressing to animal and human trials. Charnley hypothesized that the difference in results was due to the action of the extracellular fluids on the Teflon, preventing the formation of a protective surface layer (Charnley, 1970).

After the failure of Teflon, high-density polyethylene (HDP) was investigated as a bearing material. It was shown to be substantially more resistant to wear than PTFE, although the particles produced by the wear that was still expected to occur were a concern of Charnley's back in 1970 (Charnley, 1970). The creep behavior of HDP under compressive loading was also a concern, as this would alter the shape of the articulating surfaces. New or modified materials were thus investigated. In order to counter the problem of creep, Delrin 150 was introduced and used clinically in Europe. This is a high-viscosity, extruded polymer that is biocompatible, significantly harder than HDP, and resistant to creep—a property that is extremely important for sites such as the tibia (Fister et al., 1985). Polyester was also examined in the early 1970s for use as the bearing surface in implants with modular femoral components. However, wear proved to be the downfall of these materials as well (Clarke, 1992; Havelin et al., 1986; Sudmann et al., 1983). Similarly, composites of carbon fiber-reinforced PE were also developed for use as a joint surface with the goal of reducing wear. It proved to be as biocompatible as polyethylene alone (Tetik et al., 1974). However, while the laboratory studies showed improved wear resistance, clinical results proved to be substantially worse (Busanelli et al., 1996; Clarke, 1992).

Today, the density of polyethylene has been increased further from that first used by Charnley, and joint bearings are now typically constructed from ultrahigh molecular weight polyethylene (UHMWPE). The material has proven to provide good articulation, with the main concern being long-term wear. The problem with wear is not only the mechanical impingement that can occur as a result of a change in the articulating surface geometry, but more importantly the effect of wear debris on the surrounding tissue. Bone, as a living material, is affected by inflammatory processes. The body reacts to the presence of foreign debris by triggering the immune system, in an attempt to rid the body of this unwanted material. Phagocytotic processes are thus set in motion that eventually produces chemicals that adversely affect the surrounding bone. This process of osteolysis, and the resulting loss of bone, is a principal cause of implant failure in the absence of infection. Substantial efforts are still underway to develop an implant system that minimizes the production of wear debris and protects the surrounding tissue.

Metals and Ceramics for Cartilage Replacement. Due to the problems encountered with wear debris from the polymeric components of large joint implants, a number of designs have appeared that utilize highly polished, hard materials on both articulating surfaces. Both ceramic-ceramic and metal-metal designs have been shown to produce substantially reduced volumes of wear (Boutin et al., 1988; Schmalzried et al., 1996; Wagner and Wagner, 2000); however, in both cases, the particles are substantially smaller than those produced from a metal or ceramic articulating against polyethylene (Boutin et al., 1988; Shahgaldi et al., 1995; Soh et al., 1996). In fact, the number of particles produced per step is about the same for cobalt-chromium articulating with either UHMWPE or itself (Wagner and Wagner, 2000). Research into the effect of these smaller wear particles is ongoing, and no definitive answers have been developed (Wooley, 2014). Despite questions that still deserve to be addressed, hard-bearing implants for total joint replacement have gained increasing amounts of interest, especially for application in younger patients for whom the lifetime accumulation of wear debris is of greater concern.

The initial designs for hard-bearing surfaces may have been abandoned in part due to the high-frictional torques and early failures that were caused by problems in both implant design and material processing (Amstutz and Grigoris, 1996; Boutin et al., 1988). Second-generation metal-on-metal and ceramic-on-ceramic bearings generally have similar coefficients of friction to joints with UHMWPE components (Table 20.7). They have proved to be clinically feasible, and initial studies indicated good medium-term survival rates (Boutin et al., 1988; Dorr et al., 2000; Murphy et al., 2006; Wagner and Wagner, 2000). However, longer-term follow-up has demonstrated that large head (>36 mm) metal-on-metal total hip arthroplasty implants have a higher failure and

TABLE 20.7 Coefficients of Friction for Sample Material Combinations Used in Total-Hip Replacement

Material combination	Coefficient of friction
Cartilage/Cartilage	0.002
CoCr/UHMWPE	0.094
Zirconia/UHMWPE	0.09 – 0.11
Alumina/UHMWPE	0.08 – 0.12
CoCr/CoCr	0.12
Alumina/Alumina	0.05 – 0.1

Note: UHMWPE, ultrahigh-molecular weight polyethylene; CoCr, cobalt-chromium alloy.

Sources: Park and Lakes (1992), Streicher et al. (1992).

revision rate than standard ceramic or metal on polymer articulations and that metal-on-metal hip resurfacing systems require close adherence to the patient selection criteria in order to maximize success (van Lingen et al., 2016). For ceramic-on-ceramic, higher failure rates were found with small head (≤28 mm) implants, but larger head implants showed longer-term success—though the benefit over metal on polyethylene implants decreased after 2 years (Sedrakyan et al., 2014). In small joint replacement, components manufactured from pyrolitic carbon—a material proven to have exceptional biocompatibility—have also shown good preliminary results in clinical trials but may have greater occurrence of implant dislocations than the silicone standard (Chung et al., 2009; Cook et al., 1999; Parker et al., 2007). The take-away message for all of these material development scenarios is that close monitoring of clinical outcomes is key—what looks promising in the laboratory may not translate to actual improvements in the field.

Tissue-Engineered Cartilage Replacements. The ideal replacement material would be one that would mimic all of the functions of the original tissue, including those attributed to the cellular components. Artificial biomaterials cannot meet this goal. However, the new technologies of tissue engineering have opened the door to the development of living replacement tissues that can be "manufactured" in the laboratory. Thus, these are not allografts or autografts, with their inherent problems, but materials that can either be banked for use when necessary or grown to meet the needs of a particular individual. As the majority of past interventions for replacement of cartilage (e.g., not part of a total joint replacement) have not proved to be successful, tissue engineered cartilage holds great promise.

The premise behind an engineered tissue is to manufacture a scaffold, from a biocompatible and possibly biodegradable material, and then to seed this material with appropriate cells. The scaffold supports the cells, allowing them to grow, proliferate, and become integrated with the surrounding, healthy tissue. In the case of cartilage, chondrocytes must be harvested and allowed to reproduce in the laboratory in order to provide the required number of cells. These can be taken from healthy cartilage (articular cartilage or the epiphysis) or isolated as more primitive cells that can be directed to differentiate into the desired form (mesenchymal stem cells or bone marrow stromal cells) (Suh and Fu, 2000a). The choice of scaffold is equally challenging, with the goal being to match the property of the normal cartilage matrix. In the case of cartilage, research is being conducted into the construction and application of scaffolds based on collagen, polyglycolic acid (PGA) and poly-(L-lactic) acid (PLLA) (both alone and as copolymers), hyaluronic acid, and polysaccharide-based hydrogels (Suh and Fu, 2000a; Suh and Matthew, 2000b; Temenoff and Mikos, 2000b; Yang et al., 2017). A three-dimensional scaffold is required in order to prevent the chondrocytes from dedifferentiating and losing some of their needed properties (Temenoff and Mikos, 2000a). Three-dimensional bioprinting, including with cell-laden hydrogels or bioinks, holds promise in developing engineered constructs with variations in the tissue structure and properties that mimic the normal cartilage zones of cartilage structure (You et al., 2017). Similar research is being undertaken to develop tissue engineered menisci (Schoenfeld et al., 2007). Injectable materials that can deliver chondrocytes to the area of interest without an invasive surgery are also being investigated (Peretti et al., 2006). Fibrinogen and thrombin can be combined in vivo to provide the necessary stability to the cells (Temenoff and Mikos, 2000b). All of this research is in its infancy and has not progressed past animal studies, but it promises great advances during the next decades.

Polymers and Ceramics for Ligament Replacement and Augmentation. The most frequently damaged ligament is the anterior cruciate (ACL), located in the knee. Therefore, much of the work that has been done on ligament repair, replacement, and augmentation has examined this anatomic location. However, the knowledge gained through decades of work on the ACL can be transferred to other sites in the body, as long as new designs undergo appropriate, application-specific testing.

Four schools of thought exist when it comes to repair of damaged ligaments:

1. If sufficient joint stability exists, do nothing and allow collateral structures to maintain the mechanical function of the joint.
2. Utilize autologous structures to replace the damaged ligament, such as a section of the patellar tendon for the ACL.

3. Provide a bridge that the damaged structure or implanted replacement (allograft or autograft) can use as it heals. This augmentation device also carries a significant portion of the tensile load until the ligament has healed sufficiently.
4. Replace the ligament completely with an artificial material or allograft material.

Much of the debate in this field comes from the healing behavior of ligaments. Because they possess a minimal vascular supply, ligaments heal and remodel slowly. During this healing process, they are not able to carry the normal amount of tensile load. However, ligaments—like bone—also require regular, cyclic loading beyond some threshold value in order to regain and maintain their mechanical properties. Most initial repairs of the ACL involve autograft tissue, taken from the patellar tendon, the ilio-tibial band, or other similar tissues (Schepsis and Greenleaf, 1990). However, donor site morbidity and the occasional failure of these grafts has driven the need for the development of other implant options. For the artificial augmentation or replacement implants, polymeric fabrics have become the material of choice.

The goals for a ligament prosthesis or augmentation device must be to provide the necessary mechanical stability to the joint without premature degradation or failure. Table 20.8 provides a summary of mechanical properties for a number of synthetic grafts in comparison with normal ACL tissue.

At the beginning of the twentieth century, silk was applied as the first artificial material for ACL replacement (Alwyn-Smith, 1918); however, these implants failed within a few months of implantation. Use of synthetic materials for this application was virtually abandoned until the 1970s, when UHMWPE rods were introduced (Schepsis and Greenleaf, 1990). This design, along with the Proplast rod of propylene copolymer, had a short life span before fracture or elongation of the prosthesis occurred (Ahlfeld et al., 1987; Schepsis and Greenleaf, 1990). Carbon fiber was investigated as a potential material for prosthetic ligaments (Jenkins, 1978, 1985); however, its brittle nature and tendency to fail became more problematic than the benefits of the biodegradable nature of the fibers. The fibers were then coated with PLA in order to improve the handling in the OR as well as prevent failure in vivo (Alexander et al., 1981), but they have not gained wide use. PTFE ligaments have been seen in clinical studies to provide higher levels of patient satisfaction than the Proplast structures (Ahlfeld et al., 1987); however, the failure rate is still higher than desirable (Schepsis and Greenleaf, 1990). The most recent material additions to the field of prosthetic ligaments have been Dacron (nylon), a polyethylene braid, and polyethylene terephthalate (PET); results using these implants are mixed (Chen et al., 2015; Schepsis and Greenleaf, 1990). Despite their promise in terms of mechanical stability and long-term outcomes, artificial ligaments have proven to be controversial. There have been substantial numbers of cases reported in which the artificial material produced a synovitis—inflammation of the synovial fluid in the joint—or failed completely (Christel and Djian, 1994). While they have gained acceptance for revision surgery for chronically unstable knees—such as may result from failure of a graft—many clinicians believe that prosthetic ligaments have not yet met the performance of autografts for primary repairs. Results from China (Chen et al., 2015) contend that short- and middle-term follow-up of PET ligaments and some polyester ligaments show promise for primary ligament replacement, both for the ACL and other anatomical locations.

TABLE 20.8 Representative Properties for Normal ACL and Devices Designed to Replace the Ligament or Augment Healing of an Allograft or Autograft

Material	Yield force, N	Stiffness, kN/m
Normal ACL	1750	182
GoreTex prosthesis	5000	320
Polypropylene LAD	1500–1730	330

Note: LAD, ligament augmentation device.
Source: Schepsis and Greenleaf (1990).

Thus, this area is still in need of research in the area of biomaterials, preclinical testing, and clinical evaluation.

The advent of ligament augmentation devices (LADs) was the result of the observation that autografts or allografts experienced a period of decreased mechanical strength and stiffness soon after implantation (Kumar and Maffulli, 1999). This degradation results from the natural remodeling process that takes place in order to fully integrate the biological structure into its new surroundings. One implant designed to minimize the chance of failure for the healing graft is constructed of diamond-braided polypropylene (Kumar and Maffulli, 1999). Other designs have included PLA-coated carbon fiber (Strum and Larson, 1985), knitted Dacron (Pinar and Gillquist, 1989), and polydioxanone (Puddu et al., 1993). Despite expectations based on laboratory studies, clinical results have not shown an improvement in outcomes when LADs have been used to supplement the biological reconstruction of the ACL (Kumar and Maffulli, 1999). There is concern that an LAD will stress-shield a healing ligament graft (Schepsis and Greenleaf, 1990), therefore reducing its mechanical properties and increasing the likelihood of graft failure.

The state-of-the-art in ligament replacement remains the application of autografts and allografts. The use of artificial materials in this application is in its relative adolescence compared to fracture fixation and total joint replacement. While artificial structures for total ligament replacement or graft augmentation have not been fully optimized to date, they have proven to be effective in secondary repair situations—where a primary graft has failed—or cases of chronic instability. Future developments in materials, particularly composites, may produce a structure that can meet the mechanical and fixation requirements for ligament replacement with improved clinical outcomes. Artificial biological ligaments (engineered from a xenograft) (Wang et al., 2008) and tissue engineered constructs (Cooper et al., 2007) may also provide a solution in the future where purely artificial materials have failed.

20.4 CONCLUSION

Orthopedic injuries and pathologies are among the most common medical conditions. While fractures are no longer an anticipated part of a child's medical history, over 6.2 million fractures occur each year in the U.S. population (Taylor and Rorabeck, 1999) and fracture numbers seem to be increasing as the population ages (Amin et al., 2014). Osteoarthritis affects one in five individuals over the age of 70 (Felson et al., 2000). These and other conditions—including rheumatoid arthritis, osteosarcoma, and ligament tears—often require an intervention that includes the replacement of some portion of tissue. For most of these applications, autografts and allografts have proven problematic based primarily on material availability. Artificial materials have shown tremendous success in a number of applications, particularly total joint replacement, but are not without their downsides, including long-term biocompatibility and survivability issues. As is the case in many areas of tissue and organ replacement, the future of tissue engineering holds great promise. If orthopedic surgeons are able to replace diseased or damaged tissue with a material that will immediately take over the original structural and mechanical function, while it becomes completely integrated with the natural tissue with time, the current gap between natural and engineered materials may be bridged. Until the time when tissue engineering of complex, structural tissues is perfected, the need for the continued development, refinement, and investigation of artificial materials for orthopedic applications continues. The material selected plays a large role in the overall success of an implant design—as past failures have so dramatically shown. However, a poor result with a material cannot be divorced from the implant design itself. Boutin provided good evidence of this in his historical discussion of alumina acetabular components—in which loosening rates were reduced from 26 to 0.5 percent based on the position of the stabilizing pegs alone (Boutin et al., 1988). Thus, materials should not be deleted from the database of potential choices until it is determined if a failure was due to material selection or mechanical design. It is also important to have a thorough understanding of the underlying physiological processes in orthopedic tissues, in both normal and pathological conditions, so that implants of any type can be designed to be optimally integrated into the body from a mechanical and biological standpoint. The combined efforts of materials scientists, tissue physiologists, biomechanists, clinicians, and others will continue to offer developments in the field of orthopedic tissue replacement and enhancement—a discipline that already dates back thousands of years.

REFERENCES

Agrawal, C. M., G. G. Niederauer, and K. A. Athanasiou (1995). Fabrication and characterization of Pla-Pga orthopedic implants. *Tissue Eng.* **1**(3):241–252.

Ahlfeld, S. K., R. L. Larson, and H. R. Collins (1987). Anterior cruciate reconstruction in the chronically unstable knee using an expanded polytetrafluoroethylene (Ptfe) prosthetic ligament. *Am. J. Sports Med.* **15**(4):326–330.

Alexander, H., J. R. Parsons, I. D. Strauchler, and E. Al (1981). Canine patellar tendon replacement with a polylactic acid polymer-filamentous carbon tissue scaffold. *Orthop. Rev.* **10**:41–51.

Ali, M. S., T. A. French, G. W. Hastings, T. Rae, N. Rushton, E. R. Ross, and C. H. Wynn-Jones (1990). Carbon fibre composite bone plates: development, evaluation, and early clinical experience. *J. Bone Joint Surg. Br.* **72**(4):586–591.

Alwyn-Smith, S. (1918). The diagnosis and treatment of injuries to the crucial ligaments. *Br. J. Surg.* **6**:176.

Amaral, M., A. G. Dias, P. S. Gomes, M. A. Lopes, R. F. Silva, J. Santos, and M. H. Fernandes (2007). Nanocrystalline diamond: in vitro biocompatibility assessment by Mg63 and human bone marrow cells cultures. *J. Biomed. Mater. Res. A* **17**:17.

Amin, S., Achenbach, S.J., Atkinson, E.J., Khosla, S., and Melton, L.J. (2014). "Trends in Fracture Incidence: A Population-Based Study Over 20 Years." J Bone Miner Res 29(3):581-589.

Amstutz, H. C. and P. Grigoris (1996). Metal on metal bearings in hip arthroplasty. *Clin. Orthop. Relat. Res.* **329S**:11–34.

An, Y. H. (2000). Mechanical properties of bone. Y. H. An and R. A. Draugn (eds.). *Mechanical Testing of Bone and the Bone-Implant Interface*. CRC Press, Boca Raton, FL, pp. 41–63.

ASTM-F136 (1998). Standard specification for wrought Titanium-6 Aluminum-4 Vanadium Eli (Extra Low Interstitial) Alloy (UNS R56401) for surgical implant applications. W. Conshohocken, PA: American Society for Testing and Materials.

ASTM-F562 (2000). Standard specification for wrought cobalt-35 nickel-20 chromium-10 molybdenum alloy for surgical implant applications. W. Conshohocken, PA: American Society for Testing and Materials.

Bai, B., L. M. Jazrawi, F. J. Kummer, and J. M. Spivak (1999). The use of an injectable, biodegradable calcium phosphate bone substitute for the prophylactic augmentation of osteoporotic vertebrae and the management of vertebral compression fractures. *Spine* **24**(15):1521–1526.

Black, J. (1994). Biological performance of tantalum. *Clin. Mater.* **16**(3):167–173.

Bobyn, J. D., K. K. Toh, S. A. Hacking, M. Tanzer, and J. J. Krygier (1999). Tissue response to porous tantalum acetabular cups: a canine model. *J. Arthroplasty* **14**(3):347–354.

Bostman, O., S. Vainionpaa, E., Hirvensalo, A. Makela, K. Vihtonen, P. Tormala, and P. Rokkanen (1987). Biodegradable internal fixation for malleolar fractures. A prospective randomised trial. *J. Bone Joint Surg. Br.* **69**(4):615–619.

Boutin, P. (1972). Arthroplastie totale de la hanche par prostheses en aluminine fritte. *Rev. Chir. Orthop.* **58**:230–246.

Boutin, P., P. Christel, J. -M. Dorlot, A. Meunier, A. De Roquancourt, D. Blanquaert, S. Herman, L. Sedel, and J. Witvoet (1988). The use of dense alumina-alumina ceramic combination in total hip replacement. *J. Biomed. Mater. Res.* **22**:1203–1232.

Bowen, P. K., J. Drelich, and J. Goldman (2013). Zinc exhibits ideal physiological corrosion behavior for bioabsorbable stents. *Adv. Mater.* **25**(18):2577–2582.

Brettle, J., A. N. Huges, and B. A. Jordan (1971). Metallurgical aspects of surgical implant materials. *Injury* **2**(3):225–234.

Burastero, G., L. Cavagnaro, F. Chiarlone, M. Alessio-Mazzola, G. Carrega, and L. Felli (2018). The use of tantalum metaphyseal cones for the management of severe bone defects in septic knee revision. *J. Arthroplasty.* **33**(12):3739–3745.

Burg, K. J., S. Porter, and J. F. Kellam (2000). Biomaterial developments for bone tissue engineering. *Biomaterials* **21**(23):2347–2359.

Busanelli, L., S. Squarzoni, L. Brizio, D. Tigani, and A. Sudanese (1996). Wear in carbon fiber-reinforced polyethylene (Poly-Two) knee prostheses. *Chir. Organi. Mov.* **81**(3):263–267.

Capello, W. N., J. A. D'Antonio, M. T. Manley, and J. R. Feinberg (1998). Hydroxyapatite in total hip arthroplasty.

Clinical results and critical issues. *Clin. Orthop. Relat. Res.* **355**(355):200–211.

Chambers, P. A., R. A. Loukota, and A. S. High (2007). Vascularisation of Norian CRS bone cement and its replacement by autologous bone when used for orbital reconstruction. *Br. J. Oral Maxillofacial Surg.***45**(1):77–78.

Charnley, J. (1970). Total hip replacement by low-friction arthroplasty. *Clin. Orthop. Relat. Res.* **72**:7–21.

Chen, B., J. Zhang, D. Nie, G. Zhao, F. H. Fu, and J. H. C. Wang (2018). Characterization of the structure of rabbit anterior cruciate ligament and its stem/progenitor cells. *J. Cell Biochem.* doi: 10.1002/jcb.28019.

Chen, T., J. Jiang, and S. Chen (2015). Status and headway of the clinical application of artificial ligaments. *Asia Pac. J. Sports Med. Arthrosc. Rehabil. Technol.* **2**(1):15–26.

Christel, P., and P. Djian (1994). Recent advances in adult hip joint surgery. *Curr. Opin. Rheumatol.* **6**(2):161–171.

Chung, K.C., A. N. Ram, and M. J. Shauver (2009). Outcomes of pyrolytic carbon arthroplasty for the proximal interphalangeal joint. *Plast. Reconstr. Surg.* **123**(5):1521–1532.

Chung, K. C., S. V. Kotsis, P. B. Burns, F. D. Burke, E. F. S. Wilgis, D. A. Fox, and H. M. Kim (2017). Seven year outcomes of the silicone arthroplasty in rheumatoid arthritis (sar) prospective cohort study. *Arthritis Care Res.* **69**(7): 973–981.

Clarke, I. C. (1992). Role of ceramic implants. Design and clinical success with total hip prosthetic ceramic-to-ceramic bearings. *Clin. Orthop. Relat. Res.* **282**(282):19–30.

Clèries, L., E. Martìnez, J. M. Fern·Ndez-Pradas, G. Sardin, J. Esteve, and J. L. Morenza (2000). Mechanical properties of calcium phosphate coatings deposited by laser ablation. *Biomaterials* **21**(9):967–971.

Constantz, B. R., I. C. Ison, M. T. Fulmer, R. D. Poser, S. T. Smith, M. Vanwagoner, J. Ross, S. A. Goldstein, J. B. Jupiter, and D. I. Rosenthal (1995). Skeletal repair by in situ formation of the mineral phase of bone. *Science* **267**:1796–1799.

Cook, S. D., R. D. Beckenbaugh, J. Redondo, L. S. Popich, J. J. Klawitter, and R. L. Linscheid (1999). Long-term follow-up of pyrolytic carbon metacarpophalangeal implants. *J. Bone Joint Surg. Am.* **81**(5):635–648.

Cooke, F. W. (1992). Ceramics in orthopaedic surgery. *Clin. Orthop. Relat. Res.* **16**(276):135–146.

Cooper, J. A., Jr., J. S. Sahota, W. J. Gorum, IInd, J. Carter, S. B. Doty, and C. T. Laurencin (2007). Biomimetic tissue-engineered anterior cruciate ligament replacement. *Proc. Natl. Acad. Sci. USA* **104**(9):3049–3054.

Cowin, S. C. (1989). Mechanical properties of cortical bone. *Structure and Function of Cortical Bone.* CRC Press, Boca Raton, FL, pp. 97–127.

Dorr, L. D., Z. Wan, D. B. Longjohn, B. Dubois, and R. Murken (2000). Total hip arthroplasty with use of the metasul metal-on-metal articulation. Four to seven-year results. *J. Bone Joint Surg. Am.* **82**(6):789–798.

Duan, K., Y. Fan, and R. Wang (2005). Electrolytic deposition of calcium etidronate drug coating on titanium substrate. *J. Biomed. Mater. Res. B Appl. Biomater.* **72**(1):43–51.

Ducheyne, P. (1985). Bioglass coatings and bioglass composites as implant materials. *J. Biomed. Mater. Res.* **19**:273–291.

Ducheyne, P., and L. L. Hench (1982). The processing and static mechanical properties of metal fibre reinforced bioglass. *J. Mater. Sci.* **17**:595–606.

Dumbleton, J., and D. Black, (1975). An Introduction to *Orthopaedic Materials*. Springfield, III, Charles C. Thomas.

Duncan, R., and C. Turner (1995). Mechanotransduction and the functional response of bone to mechanical strain. *Calcif. Tissue Int.* **57**(5):344–358.

Elder, S., E. Frankenburg, J. Goulet, D. Yetkinler, R. Poser, and S. Goldstein (2000). Biomechanical evaluation of calcium phosphate cement-augmented fixation of unstable intertrochanteric fractures. *J. Orthop. Trauma* **14**(6):386–393.

Engelberg, I. and J. Kohn (1991). Physicomechanical properties of degradable polymers used in medical applications: a comparative study. *Biomaterials* **12**:292–304.

Eldesoqi, K., D. Henrich, A. M. El-Kady, M. S. Arbid, B. M. Abd El-Hady, I. Marzi, and C. Seebach (2014). Safety evaluation of a bioglass-polylactic acid composite scaffold seeded with progenitor cells in a rat skull critical-size bone defect. *PLoS One* **9**(2):e87642.

Eyckmans, J., T. Boudou, X. Yu, and C. S. Chen (2011). A Hitchhiker's guide to mechanobiology. *Dev. Cell.* **21**(1):35–47.

Felson, D. T., R. C. Lawrence, P. A. Dieppe, R. Hirsch, C. G. Helmick, J. M. Jordan, R. S. Kington, et al. (2000). Osteoarthritis: new insights. Part 1: the disease and its risk factors. *Ann. Intern. Med.* **133**(8):635–646.

Fister, J. S., V. A. Memoli, J. O. Galante, W. Rostoker, and R. M. Urban (1985). Biocompatibility of Delrin 150: a creep-resistant polymer for total joint prostheses. *J. Biomed. Mater. Res.* **19**:519–533.

Furukawa, T., Y. Matsusue, T. Yasunaga, Y. Nakagawa, Y. Shikinami, M. Okuno, and T. Nakamura (2000). Bone bonding ability of a new biodegradable composite for internal fixation of bone fractures. *Clin. Orthop. Relat. Res.* **379**(379):247–258.

Gautam, C., J. Joyner, A. Gautam, J. Rao, and R. Vajtai (2016). Zirconia-based dental ceramics: structure, mechanical properties, biocompatibility, and applications. *Dalton Trans.* **45**(48):19194–19215.

Giorgi, M., S. W. Verbruggen, and D. Lacroix (2016). In silico bone mechanobiology: modeling a multifaceted biological system. *Wiley Interdiscipl. Rev. Syst. Biol. Med.* **8**(6):485–505.

Greenspan, D. C., and L. Hench (1976). Chemical and mechanical behavior of bioglass-coated alumina. *J. Biomed. Mater. Res. Symp.* **7**:503–509.

Hanafusa, S., Y. Matsusue, T. Yasunaga, T. Yamamuro, M. Oka, Y. Shikinami, and Y. Ikada (1995). Biodegradable plate fixation of rabbit femoral shaft osteotomies. A comparative study. *Clin. Orthop. Relat. Res.* **315**(315):262–271.

Hasirci, V., K. U. Lewandrowski, S. P. Bondre, J. D. Gresser, D. J. Trantolo, and D. L. Wise (2000). High strength bioresorbable bone plates: preparation, mechanical properties and in vitro analysis. *Biomed. Mater. Eng.* **10**(1):19–29.

Havelin, L. I., B. Espehaug, S. E. Vollset, and L. B. Engesaeter (1995). The effect of the type of cement on early revision of Charnley total hip prostheses. A review of eight thousand five hundred and seventy-nine primary arthroplasties from the Norwegian arthroplasty register. *J. Bone Joint Surg. Am.* **77**(10):1543–1550.

Havelin, L. I., N. R. Gjerdet, O. D. Lunde, M. Rait, and E. Sudmann (1986). Wear of the Christiansen hip prosthesis. *Acta Orthop. Scand.* **57**(5):419–422.

Hayes, W. C., and M. L. Bouxsein, (1997). Biomechanics of cortical and trabecular bone: implications for assessment of fracture risk. In: V. C. Mow and W. C. Hayes (eds.). *Basic Orthopaedic Biomechanics*. Philadelphia, Pa., Lippincott-Raven.

Holmer, P., and P. T. Nielsen (1993). Fracture of ceramic femoral heads in total hip arthroplasty. *J. Arthroplasty* **8**(6):567–571.

Hughes, M. S., S. M. Handley, and J. G. Miller (1987). *Nearly Local Kramers-Kronig Relations Applied to Porous Epoxy.* Ultrasonics Symposium, IEEE.

Hutmacher, D. W., J. T. Schantz, C. X. Lam, K. C. Tan, and T. C. Lim (2007). State of the art and future directions of scaffold-based bone engineering from a biomaterials perspective. *J. Tissue Eng. Regen. Med.* **1**(4):245–260.

Ifkovits, J. L., and J. A. Burdick (2007). Review: photopolymerizable and degradable biomaterials for tissue engineering applications. *Tissue Eng.* **13**(10):2369–2385.

Iundusi, R., E. Gasbarra, M. D'Arienzo, A. Piccioli, and U. Tarantino (2015). Augmentation of tibial plateau fractures with an injectable bone substitute: CERAMENT™. Three-year follow-up from a prospective study. *BMC Musculoskelet Disord.* **16**:115.

Jazwari, L. M., F. J. Kummer, and P. E. Dicesare (1998). Alternative bearing surfaces for total joint arthroplasty. *J. Am. Acad. Orthop. Surg.* **6**(4):198–203.

Jell, G., and M. M. Stevens (2006). Gene activation by bioactive glasses. *J. Mater. Sci. Mater. Med.* **17**(11):997–1002.

Jenkins, D. H. R. (1978). The repair of cruciate ligaments with flexible carbon fibre. A longer term study of the induction of new ligaments and of the fate of the implanted carbon. *J Bone Joint Surg. Br.* **60**-B(4):520–522.

Jenkins, D. H. R. (1985). Ligament induction by filamentous carbon fiber. *Clin. Orthop. Relat. Res.* **196**:88–89.

Jones, L., and B. A. Lieberman (1936). Interaction of bone and various metals. *AMA Arch. Surg.* **32**: 990–1006.

Kaplan, F. S., W. C. Hayes, T. M. Keaveny, A. L. Boskey, T. A. Einhorn, and J. P. Ianotti, (1994). Form and function of bone. In: S. R. Simon (ed.). *Orthopaedic Basic Science*. American Academy of Orthopaedic Surgeons, Chicago.

Keurentjes, J. C., R. M. Kuipers, D. J. Wever, and B. W. Schreurs (2008). High incidence of squeaking in THAs with alumina ceramic-on-ceramic bearings. *Clin. Orthop. Relat. Res.* **26**:26.

Khader, B. A., S. A. F. Peel, and M. R. Towler (2017). An injectable glass polyalkenoate cement engineered for fracture fixation and stabilization. *J. Funct. Biomater.* **8**(3):25–44.

Killian, M. L., L. Cavinatto, L. M. Galatz, and S. Thomopoulos (2012). The role of mechanobiology in tendon healing. *J. Shoulder Elbow Surg.* **21**(2):228–237.

Klein, C. P. A. T., A. A. Driessen, K. De Groot, and A. Van Den Hoof (1983). Biodegradation behavior of various calcium phosphate materials in bone tissue. *J. Biomed. Mater. Res.* **17**:769.

Kopylov, P., K. Runnqvist, K. Jonsson, and P. Aspenberg (1999). Norian SRS versus external fixation in redisplaced distal radial fractures. A randomized study in 40 patients. *Acta Orthop. Scand.* **70**(1):1–5.

Kotzki, P. O., D. Buyck, D. Hans, E. Thomas, F. Bonnel, F. Favier, P. J. Meunier, and M. Rossi. (1994). Influence of fat on ultrasound measurements in the os calcis. *Calcif. Tissue Int.* **54**:91–95.

Kudo, K., M. Miyasawa, Y. Fujioka, T. Kamegai, H. Nakano, Y. Seino, F. Ishikawa, T. Shioyama, and K. Ishibashi (1990). Clinical application of dental implant with root of coated bioglass: short-term results. *Oral Surg. Oral Med. Oral Pathol.* **70**(1):18–23.

Kumar, K., and N. Maffulli (1999). The ligament augmentation device: an historical perspective. *Arthroscopy* **15**(4):422–432.

Ladd, A. L., and N. B. Pliam (1999). Use of bone-graft substitutes in distal radius fractures. *J. Am. Acad. Orthop. Surg.* **7**(5):279–290.

Lee, B. S., S. H. Kang, Y. L. Wang, F. H. Lin, and C. P. Lin (2007). In vitro study of dentinal tubule occlusion with sol-gel DP-bioglass for treatment of dentin hypersensitivity. *Dent. Mater. J.* **26**(1):52–61.

Lee, H. S. J. (2000). *Dates in Cardiology: A Chronological Record of Progress in Cardiology Over the Last Millennium.* Parthenon Publishing Group, New York.

Leeson, M. C., and S. B. Lippitt (1993). Thermal aspects of the use of polymethylmethacrylate in large metaphyseal defects in bone. A clinical review and laboratory study. *Clin. Orthop. Relat. Res.* **295**(295):239–245.

Li, H., S. Chen, Y. Wu, J. Jiang, Y. Ge, K. Gao, P. Zhang, and L. Wu (2012). Enhancement of the osseointegration of a polyethylene terephthalate artificial ligament graft in a bone tunnel using 58S bioglass. *Int. Orthop.* **36:**191–197.

Liedert, A., D. Kaspar, P. Augat, A. Ignatius, and L. Claes (2005). Mechanobiology of bone tissue and bone cells. In: A. Kamkin and I. Kiseleva (eds.). *Mechanosensitivity in Cells and Tissues*. Academia, Moscow.

Linscheid, R. L. (2000). Implant arthroplasty of the hand: retrospective and prospective conditions. *J. Hand Surg.* **25A**(5):796–816.

Mankin, H. J., V. C. Mow, J. A. Buckwalter, J. P. Ianotti, and A. Ratcliffe (1994). Form and function of articular cartilage. In: S. R. Simon (ed.). *Orthopaedic Basic Science*. American Academy of Orthopaedic Surgeons, Chicago.

Marie, P. J., E. Haÿ, and Z. Saidak (2014). Integrin and cadherin signaling in bone: role and potential therapeutic targets. *Trends Endocrinol. Metab.* **25**(11):567–575.

Mehdizadeh, A., B. S. Gardiner, M. Lavagnino, and D. W. Smith (2018). Effect of collagen length distribution and timing for repair on the active TGF-β concentration in tendon. *Connect. Tissue Res.* **59**(5):396–409.

Meneghini, R. M., D. G. Lewallen, and A. D. Hanssen (2008). Use of porous tantalum metaphyseal cones for severe tibial bone loss during revision total knee replacement. *J. Bone Joint Surg. Am.* **90**(1):78–84.

Moreau, J. L., J. F. Caccamese, D. P. Coletti, J. J. Sauk, and J. P. Fisher (2007). Tissue engineering solutions for cleft palates. *J. Oral Maxillofac. Surg.* **65**(12):2503–2511.

Murphy, S. B., T. M. Ecker, and M. Tannast (2006). Two- to nine-year clinical results of alumina ceramic-on-ceramic THA. *Clin. Orthop. Relat. Res.* **453**:97–102.

Narayanan, G., V. N. Vernekar, E. L. Kuyinu, and C. T. Laurencin (2016). Poly (lactic acid)-based biomaterials for orthopaedic regenerative engineering. *Adv. Drug Deliv. Rev.* **107:**247–276.

Nichols, A. E. C., R. E. Settlage, S. R. Werre, and L. A. Dahlgren (2018). Novel roles for scleraxis in regulating adult tenocyte function. *BMC Cell Biol.* **19**(1):14.

Nishio, K., M. Neo, H. Akiyama, Y. Okada, T. Kokubo, and T. Nakamura (2001). Effects of apatite and wollastonite containing glass-ceramic powder and two types of alumina powder in composites on osteoblastic differentiation of bone marrow cells. *J. Biomed. Mater. Res.* **55**(2):164–176.

Park, J. B., and R. S. Lakes (1992). *Biomaterials: An Introduction.* Plenum Press, New York.

Parker, W. L., M. Rizzo, S. L. Moran, K. B. Hormel, and R. D. Beckenbaugh (2007). Preliminary results of nonconstrained pyrolytic carbon arthroplasty for metacarpophalangeal joint arthritis. *J. Hand Surg. Am.* **32**(10): 1496–1505.

Pavek, V., Z. Novak, Z. Strnad, D. Kudrnova, and B. Navratilova (1994). Clinical application of bioactive glass-ceramic Bas-O for filling cyst cavities in stomatology. *Biomaterials* **15**(5):353–358.

Peiro, A., J. Pardo, R. Navarrete, L. Rodriguez-Alonso, and F. Martos (1991). Fracture of the ceramic head in total hip arthroplasty. Report of two cases. *J. Arthroplasty* **6**(4):371–374.

Peltier, L. F. (1990). *Fractures: A History and Iconography of Their Treatment.* Norman Publishing, San Francisco.

Peltoniemi, H., N. Ashammakhi, R. Kontio, T. Waris, A. Salo, C. Lindqvist, K. Gratz, and R. Suuronen (2002). The use of bioabsorbable osteofixation devices in craniomaxillofacial surgery. *Oral Surg. Oral Med. Oral Pathol. Oral Radiol. Endod.* **94**(1):5–14.

Peretti, G. M., J. W. Xu, L. J. Bonassar, C. H. Kirchhoff, M. J. Yaremchuk, and M. A. Randolph (2006). Review of injectable cartilage engineering using fibrin gel in mice and swine models. *Tissue Eng.* **12**(5):1151–1168.

Pinar, H. and J. Gillquist (1989). Dacron augmentation of a free patellar tendon graft: a biomechanical study. *Arthroscopy* **5**:328–330.

Pirhonen, E., L. Moimas, and M. Brink (2006). Mechanical properties of bioactive glass 9-93 fibres. *Acta Biomaterialia* **2**(1):103–107.

Puddu, G., M. Cipolla, G. Cerullo, V. Franco, and E. Gianni, (1993). Anterior cruciate ligament reconstruction and augmentation with PDS graft. *Clin. Sports Med.* **12**:13–24.

Radin, S., J. T. Campbell, P. Ducheyne, and J. M. Cuckler (1997). Calcium phosphate ceramic coatings as carriers of vancomycin. *Biomaterials* **18**(11):777–782.

Rang, M. (2000). *The Story of Orthopaedics.* W.B. Saunders Co, Philadelphia.

Rauschmann, M., T. Vogl, A. Verheyden, R. Pflugmacher, T. Werba, S. Schmidt, and J. Hierholzer (2010). Bioceramic vertebral augmentation with a calcium sulphate/hydroxyapatite composite (Cerament^{TM} SpineSupport) in vertebral compression fractions due to osteoporosis. *Eur. Spine. J.* **19**(6):887–892.

Reach, J. S., Jr., I. D. Dickey, M. E. Zobitz, J. E. Adams, S. P. Scully, and D. G. Lewallen (2007). Direct tendon attachment and healing to porous tantalum: an experimental animal study. *J Bone Joint Surg. Am.* **89**(5):1000–1009.

Rose, P. S., M. Halasy, R. T. Trousdale, A. D. Hanssen, F. H. Sim, D. J. Berry, and D. G. Lewallen (2006). Preliminary results of tantalum acetabular components for THA after pelvic radiation. *Clin. Orthop. Relat. Res.* **453**:195–198.

Sanan, A., and S. J. Haines (1997). Repairing holes in the head: a history of cranioplasty. *Neurosurgery* **40**(3): 588–603.

Sanchez-Adams, J., H. A. Leddy, A. L. McNulty, C. J. O'Conor, and F. Guilak (2014). The mechanobiology of articular cartilage: bearing the burden of osteoarthritis. *Curr. Rheumatol. Rep.* **16**(10):451–465.

Saravanapavan, P., J. R. Jones, S. Verrier, R. Beilby, V. J. Shirtliff, L. L. Hench, and J. M. Polak (2004). Binary CaO-SiO(2) gel-glasses for biomedical applications. *Biomed. Mater. Eng.* **14**(4):467–486.

Schepsis, A. A., and J. Greenleaf (1990). Prosthetic materials for anterior cruciate ligament reconstruction. *Orthop. Rev.* **19**(11):984–991.

Schildhauer, T. A., T. W. Bauer, C. Josten, and G. Muhr (2000). Open reduction and augmentation of internal fixation with an injectable skeletal cement for the treatment of complex calcaneal fractures. *J. Orthop. Trauma* **14**(5):309–317.

Schmalzried, T. P., E. S. Szuszczewicz, K. H. Akizuki, T. D. Petersen, and H. C. Amstutz (1996). Factors correlating with long term survival of McKee-Farrar total hip prostheses. *Clin. Orthop. Relat. Res.* **329**(329 suppl):S48–S59.

Schoenfeld, A. J., W. J. Landis, and D. B. Kay (2007). Tissue-engineered meniscal constructs. *Am. J. Orthop.* **36**(11):614–620.

Sedrakyan, A., S. Graves, B. Bordini, M. Pons, L. Havelin, S. Mehle, E. Paxton, T. Barber, and G. Cafri (2014). Comparative effectiveness of ceramic-on-ceramic implants in stemmed hip replacement: a multinational study of six national and regional registries. *J. Bone Joint Surg. Am.* **96**(S1):34–41.

Shahgaldi, B. F., F. W. Heatley, A. Dewar, and B. Corrin (1995). In vivo corrosion of cobalt-chromium and titanium wear particles. *J. Bone Joint Surg. Br.* **77**(6):962–966.

Sherman, W. D. (1912). Vanadium steel plates and screws. *Surg. Gynecol. Obstetrics* **14**:629.

Shimko, D. A. V. F. Shimko, E. A. Sander, K. F. Dickson, and E. A. Nauman (2005). Effect of porosity on the fluid flow characteristics and mechanical properties of Tantalum scaffolds. *J. Biomed. Mater. Res. B Appl. Biomater.* **73**(2):315–324.

Soballe, K., K. Overgaard, E. S. Hansen, H. Brokstedt-Rasmussen, M. Lind, and C. Bunger (1999). A review of ceramic coatings for implant fixation. *J. Long Term Effects of Med. Implants* **9**(1–2):131–151.

Soh, E. W., G., W. Blunn, M. E. Wait, and E. Al (1996). *Size and shape of metal particles from metal-on-metal total hip replacements*. Transactions of the Orthopaedic Research Society.

Streicher, R. M., M. Senlitsch, and R. Schön (1992). Articulation of ceramic surfaces against polyethylene. In: A. Ravaglioli and A. Krajewsk (eds.). *Bioceramics and the Human Body*. Elsevier Applied Science, New York pp. 118–123.

Strum, G. M., and R. L. Larson (1985). Clinical experience and early results of carbon fiber augmentation of anterior cruciate reconstruction of the knee. *Clin. Orthop. Relat. Res.* **196**:124–138.

Su, Y., I. Cocerill, Y. Wang, Y.-X. Qin, L. Chang, Y. Zheng, and D. Zhu (2018). Zinc-based biomaterials in regeneration and therapy. *Trends Biotech.* doi:10.1016/j.tibtech.2018.10.009

Sudmann, E., L. I. Havelin, O. D. Lunde, and M. Rait (1983). The Charnley versus the Christiansen total hip arthroplasty. *Acta Orthop. Scand.* **54**:545–552.

Suh, J.-K., and F. H. Fu (2000a). Application of tissue engineering to cartilage repair. *Gene Therapy and Tissue Engineering in Orthopaedic and Sports Medicine*. Birkäuser, Boston.

Suh, J. K., and H. W. Matthew (2000b). Application of chitosan-based polysaccharide biomaterials in cartilage tissue engineering: a review. *Biomaterials* **21**(24):2589–2598.

Taylor, J. W., and C. H. Rorabeck (1999). Hip revision arthroplasty. Approach to the femoral side. *Clin. Orthop. Relat. Res.* **369**(369):208–222.

Temenoff, J. S., and A. G. Mikos (2000a). Injectable biodegradable materials for orthopedic tissue engineering. *Biomaterials* **21**(23):2405–2412.

Temenoff, J. S., and A. G. Mikos (2000b). Review: tissue engineering for regeneration of articular cartilage. *Biomaterials* **21**(5):431–440.

Tetik, R. D., J. O. Galante, and W. Rostoker (1974). A wear resistant material for total joint replacement—tissue biocompatibility of an ultra-high molecular weight (UHMW) polyethylene-graphite composite. *J. Biomed. Mater. Res.* **8**:231–250.

Turnbull, G., J. Clarke, F. Picard, P. Riches, L. Jia, F. Han, B. Li, and W. Shu (2018). 3D bioactive composite scaffolds for bone tissue engineering. *Bioact. Mats.* **3**:278–314.

van Lingen, C. P., L. M. Zagra, H. B. Etterna, and C. C. Verheyen (2016). Sequelae of large-head metal-on-metal hip arthroplasties: current status and future prospects. *EFORT Open Rev.* **1**(10). https://doi.org/10.1302/2058-5241.1.160014

Venzmer, G. (1968). *Five Thousand Years of Medicine*. Taplinger Publishing Co. New York.

Verrier, S., L. Hughes, A. Alves, M. Peroglio, M. Alini, and A. Boger (2012). Evaluation of the in vitro cell-material interactions and in vivo osteo-integration of a spinal acrylic bone cement. *Eur. Spine J.* **21** (Suppl 6):S800–S809.

Wagner, M., and H. Wagner (2000). Medium-term results of a modern metal-on-metal system in total hip replacement. *Clin. Orthop. Relat. Res.* **379**:123–133.

Wang, K., L. Zhu, D. Cai, C. Zeng, H. Lu, G. Xu, X. Guo, S. Lin, and S. Cheng (2008). Artificial biological ligament: its making, testing, and experimental study on animals. *Microsurgery* **28**(1):44–53.

White, D. N. (1986). The acoustic characteristics of skull. In: J. F. Greenleaf (ed.). *Tissue Characterization with Ultrasound.* CRC Press, Inc., Boca Raton, FL. pp. 2–39.

Wolff, J. (1892). *Das Gesetz der Transformation der Knochen.* A. Hirchwald, Berlin.

Woo, S. L., S. D. Abramowitch, R. Kilger, and R. Liang (2006). Biomechanics of knee ligaments: injury, healing, and repair. *J. Biomech.* **39**(1):1–20.

Woo, S. L.-Y., K.-N. An, S. P. Arnoczky, J. S. Wayne, D. C. Fithian, and B. S. Myers (1994). Anatomy, biology, and biomechanics of tendon, ligament, and meniscus. In: S. R. Simon (ed.). *Orthopaedic Basic Science*. American Academy of Orthopaedic Surgeons, Chicago.

Wooley, P. H. (2014). How has the introduction of new bearing surfaces altered the biological reactions to byproducts of wear and modularity? *Clin. Orthop. Relat. Res.* **472:**3699–3708.

Yamamuro, T., and K. Shimizu (1994). Clinical application of aw glass ceramic prosthesis in spinal surgery. *Nippon Seikeigeka Gakkai Zasshi* **68**(7):505–515.

Yang, H., X. Qu, W. Lin, C. Wang, D. Zhu, K. Dai, and Y. Zheng (2018). In vitro and in vivo studies on zinc-hydroxyapatite composites as novel biodegradable metal matrix composite for orthopedic applications. *Acta Biomat.* **71**:200–214.

Yang, J., Y. S. Zhang, K. Yue, and A. Khademhosseini (2017). Cell-laden hydrogels for osteochondral and cartilage tissue engineering. *Acta Biomater.* **57**:1–25.

Yetkinler, D. N., A. L. Ladd, R. D. Poser, B. R. Constantz, and D. Carter (1999). Biomechanical evaluation of fixation of intra-articular fractures of the distal part of the radius in cadavera: Kirschner wires compared with calcium-phosphate bone cement. *J. Bone Joint Surg. Am.* **81**(3):391–399.

You, F., B. F. Eame, and X. Chen (2017). Application of extrusion-based hydrogel bioprinting for cartilage tissue engineering. *Int. J. Molec. Sci.* **18:**1597–1622.

Yu, B., K. Han, H. Ma, C., Zhang, J. Su, J. Zhao, J. Li, Y. Bai, and H. Tang (2009). Treatment of tibial plateau fractures with high strength injectable calcium sulphate. *Int. Orthop.* **33:**1127–1133.

Yukna, R. A., G. H. Evans, M. B. Aichelmann-Reidy, and E. T. Mayer (2001). Clinical comparison of bioactive glass bone replacement graft material and expanded polytetrafluoroethylene barrier membrane in treating human mandibular molar class II furcations. *J. Periodontol.* **72**(2): 125–133.

Zardiackas, L. D., D. E. Parsell, L. D. Dillon, D. W. Mitchell, L. A. Nunnery, and R. Poggie (2001). Structure, metallurgy, and mechanical properties of a porous tantalum foam. *J. Biomed. Mater. Res.* **58**(2):180–187.

Zhang, B. G. X., D. E. Myers, G. G. Wallace, M. Brandt, and P. F. M. Choong (2014). Bioactive coatings for orthopaedic implants - recent trends in development of implant coatings. *Int. J. Molec. Sci.* **15**:11878–11921.

Zierold, A. A. (1924). Reaction of bone to various metals. *AMA Arch. Surg.* **9**:365–412.

CHAPTER 21
BIOMATERIALS TO PROMOTE TISSUE REGENERATION

Nancy J. Meilander
National Institute of Standards and Technology, Gaithersburg, Maryland

Hyunjung Lee
Georgia Institute of Technology, Atlanta, Georgia

Ravi V. Bellamkonda
Georgia Institute of Technology/Emory University, Atlanta, Georgia

21.1 BACKGROUND

Historically, biomaterial implants have been designed to replace a specific function, usually mechanical, and were considered "ideal" if they elicited little or no response in vivo. For instance, synthetic vascular grafts have typically been made of inert materials such as expanded polytetrafluoroethylene (Teflon) with the necessary mechanical strength to support the forces created by pulsatile blood flow. Likewise, materials for orthopedic screws and plates for bone fixation were usually metals, chosen for their mechanical strength. However, synthetic small-diameter vascular grafts fail by thrombosis, and orthopedic implants can weaken existing bone due to stress shielding or fail due to implant loosening. In addition, most surface modification approaches to improve integration of the implant with the host tissue have not been very successful over the last 20 years. These failures demonstrate that synthetic materials alone cannot fully replace all of the functions (structural, mechanical, biochemical, metabolic, etc.) that the original tissue provided.

Due to new understanding from a molecular biology perspective, it is clear that most tissue has two categories of components: (1) structural and (2) biochemical. The field of tissue engineering considers both of these components in the design of implants to promote regeneration and facilitate better integration of implants. The field of tissue engineering has been fast growing at a compound annual rate (1995 to 2001) of 16 percent and more than 70 companies are there with a combined annual expenditure over \$600 million. The net capital value of post IPO companies ($n = 16$, Jan 1st, 2001) is \$2.6 billion and the cumulative investment since 1990 now is over \$3.5 billion (Lysaght and Reyes, 2001). Tissue-engineered skin products (Apligraf from Organogenesis, Transcyte from Smith & Nephew) and bioengineered cartilage (Carticel from Genzyme) are examples of commercially available treatments.

TABLE 21.1 Parameters to Optimize Biomaterials for Tissue Regeneration

Structural components	Biochemical components
Physical properties	Immobilized signals
Shape	ECM proteins
Size	Adhesive peptides
Pore features	Growth factors
Three-dimensionality	
Surface topography	Diffusible signals
	One-component system
Mechanical properties	Two-component system
Reinforced composites	Gene delivery
Mechanical loading	
Electrical stimuli	Living component
	Cell seeding
Chemical properties	Differentiated cells
Hydrophilicity	Scaffold prevascularization
Charge	Cells for neuroregeneration
Biodegradation	Combination therapy
	Stem cells
	Commercial, cell-based products

Using the tissue engineering strategy, materials designed for tissue regeneration attempt to control the physiological response to the implanted biomaterial by mimicking the structural and biochemical components of natural tissue. A variety of techniques have been implemented in this approach to the design of regenerative biomaterials, as listed in Table 21.1. Tissue engineers typically use synthetic or natural biomaterials to achieve the "structure" design parameters. The design space in optimizing the "structural" parameters includes the physical, mechanical, and chemical characteristics of the material. The "biochemical" parameters are incorporated via immobilized signals, diffusible chemoattractive agents, or living cells. The critical factors that promote tissue growth in vivo can be determined by examining environments that stimulate tissue generation and regeneration in the body, such as those found during development, tissue remodeling, and wound healing. By providing similar cues, regenerative materials can function in a supportive role, aiding the biological processes when necessary, rather than permanently replacing a lost function. The materials discussed in this chapter are listed in Table 21.2.

21.2 STRUCTURAL COMPONENT

In order to properly guide tissue regeneration, a biomaterial ought to satisfy the structural requirements of the native tissue. For each type of tissue and application, the implant must be designed with the physical architecture and appropriate mechanical and chemical properties to help retain implant function. Table 21.3 provides examples of approaches that utilize these properties for tissue regeneration.

21.2.1 Physical Properties

In tissue regeneration, both natural and synthetic materials contribute to the spectrum of physical properties displayed in biomaterials today. Collagen, a naturally occurring, bioresorbable protein, is commonly used as a scaffold for tissue regeneration. The most frequently used collagen is type I collagen, and type IV is also used with tissue-engineered scaffolds. However, natural materials like collagen can only provide a limited range of properties, and they may be immunogenic (Rubin et al., 1965; Madsen and Mooney, 2000). Synthetic materials, such as the biodegradable aliphatic polyesters: poly(L-lactic acid) (PLLA), poly(D,L-lactic acid) (PDLLA), poly(glycolic acid) (PGA), and poly(lactide-co-glycolide) copolymers (PLGA), can be formed to provide a range of physical properties and degradation behaviors and may therefore offer greater flexibility. These materials are often

TABLE 21.2 Materials Discussed in This Chapter

Material
Agarose
Alginate
Calcium phosphate
Cellulose
Chitosan
Collagen I, IV
Collagen-glycosaminoglycan, chitosan linked
Dextran
Dicalcium phosphate dihydrate
Expanded polytetrafluoroethylene
Fibrin
Fluorinated ethylene propylene
Gelatin
Gelfoam matrices
Glod
Hyaluronic acid
Hydroxyethyl methacrylate-methyl methacrylate
Hydroxyapatite
Matrigel
Nanophase alumina
Poly-4-hydroxybutyrate
Poly(acrylonitrile-co-vinyl chloride)
Polyanhydrides
Polycarbonate
Polycaprolactone
Polydimethylsiloxane
Poly(D-L-lactic acid)
Polyester
Poly(ethylene glycol)
Polyethylene
Poly(fluoroacetate)
Poly(glycolic acid)
Poly(L-lactic acid)
Poly(L-lactide-co-6-caprolactone)
Poly(lactide-glycolide)
Polylysine
Poly(methyl methacrylate)
Poly *N*-(2-hydroxypropyl)-methacrylamide
Polyorthoesters
Polypropylene
Poly(propylene fumarate)
Polypyrrole
Polystyrene
Poly(styrenesulfonate)
Polyurethane
Polyvinyl alcohol
Quartz
Silica
Titanium
Tricalcium phosphate
Vinylidene fluoride-trifluoroethylene copolymer

produced in a less expensive, more reproducible manner relative to natural materials. However, processing often involves the use of high temperatures or harsh organic solvents that may preclude the incorporation of sensitive proteins or nucleic acids. Also, residual solvent in the final product may detrimentally affect the in vivo response to the material. Consequently, while evaluating the physical properties including shape, size, porosity, three-dimensionality, and surface topography, other innate characteristics of the materials also need to be considered.

Shape. The overall shape of a biomaterial implant is often dictated by the application. Polymers and natural materials have been formed into thin films to facilitate the growth of cells in vitro and in vivo. PLGA films (Giordano et al., 1997; Lu et al., 1998) have been used for culturing epithelium cells; collagen for hepatocytes (Fassett et al., 2006), fibroblasts and endothelial cells (Tiller et al., 2001); collagen-coated polyactide films for human keratinocytes (Shved et al., 2007); PLLA films with an apatite/collagen coating for osteoblastlike cells (Chen et al., 2005); polycaprolactone films with ECM component coating for vein endothelial cells (Pankajakshan et al., 2007); polydimethylsiloxane with fibronectin coating for cardiomyocytes (Feinberg et al., 2007); and PLGA polymers for ocular tissues (Huhtala et al., 2007).

Other shapes such as wraps, foams, or conduit forms also have been applied. For perivascular treatment of intimal hyperplasia in blood vessels, alginate hydrogels containing PLGA-drug-delivery systems were fabricated into perivascular wraps (Edelman et al., 2000). For orbital implants in a minipig animal study, hydroxyapatite and porous polyethylene wrapping were used with acellular dermis to extend fibrovascular ingrowth in orbital implants. Twelve weeks after surgery, harvested implants showed complete fibrovascularization (Thakker et al., 2004). In the nervous system, polymeric degradable rods made of PDLLA foams mixed with poly(ethylene oxide)-block-poly(D,L-lactide) (PELA) (Maquet et al., 2001) and porous chitosan nerve conduits (Cheng et al., 2007) have been used for spinal cord regeneration in rats, and porous conduits of PLGA, PLLA (Widmer et al., 1998)

TABLE 21.3 Examples of Structural Techniques for Designing Regenerative Biomaterials

Design parameter	Biomaterial	Application	References
Physical properties			
Shape	PLGA thin film	Retinal pigment epithelium sheets	Giordano et al., 1997
	Gelatin microcarriers	Human retinal epithelial implantation	Stover et al., 2005
Size	PGA fibers	SMC transplantation	Eiselt et al., 1998
	Agar substrate	Spheroid growth in 3D	Folkman and Hochberg 1973
Pore features	Hydroxyapatite	3D pore network formation	Jun et al., 2007
	PDLLA-PELA with longitudinal pores	Nerve regeneration	Maquet et al., 2001
Three-dimensionality	Alginate beads	3D hepatocyte culture	Selden et al., 1999
	Agarose hydrogels	3D neuron culture	Balgude et al., 2001
Surface topography	Textured polyurethane	BAEC spreading	Goodman et al., 1996
	Aligned submicron-PAN-MA fibers	Nerve regeneration	Kim et al., 2008
Mechanical properties			
Reinforced composites	PLGA with hydroxyapatite	Bone regeneration	Devin et al., 1996
	PPF with PLGA	Bone regeneration	Hasirci et al., 2002
Mechanical loading	PGA/poly-4-hydroxybutyrate	Vascular grafts	Hoerstrup et al., 2001
	Agarose	Chondrocyte differentiation	Elder et al., 2000
Electrical stimuli	PP-HA and PP/PSS bilayer films	Implant vascularization	Collier et al., 2000
	Polypyrrole	Enhanced neurite extension	Schmidt et al., 1997
Chemical properties			
Hydrophilicity	PLGA with varying hydrophilicity	Fibroblast adhesion	Khang et al., 1999
	Silica films with PEG	Inhibit cell adhesion	Alcantar et al., 2000
Charge	PLLA and PLGA with polylysine	Increase chondrocyte attachment	Sittinger et al., 1996
	Agarose hydrogel with chitosan	Induce neurite extension	Dillon et al., 2000
Biodegradation	PLA and PLGA with e-beam radiation	Adjustable degradation rates	Leonard et al., 2009
	MMP sensitive hydrogel	Adjustable degradation rates	Kraehenbuehl et al., 2008

or poly(L-lactide-co-6-caprolactone) (Giardino et al., 1999) have been fabricated to facilitate regeneration of peripheral nerves (Evans et al., 1999a). To form tubular shapes for applications such as intestinal tissue engineering, PLGA copolymers have been made into porous films, formed into tubular structures, and implanted in vivo to develop tubular fibrovascular tissue (Mooney et al., 1994). Another example of tubes are biotubes, vascularlike tubular tissues consisting of autologous tissues. They are made by embedding polymeric rods such as poly(ethylene), poly(fluoroacetate), poly(methyl methacrylate), poly(urethane), poly(vinyl chloride), and silicone (Nakayama et al., 2004). Tissues with complex three-dimensional (3D) shapes require a more sophisticated technique to fabricate appropriately shaped implants. One study produced a dome-shaped bone formation in a rabbit calvarial defect using PLLA-tricalcium phosphate (TCP) matrices (Lee et al., 2001). For joint repair, the specific 3D shapes of the metacarpal-phalangeal pieces have been replicated with PLLA and PLGA using a lamination technique to precisely control the profile (Mikos et al., 1993). Another technique, rapid prototyping, manufactures 3D object layer-by-layer by reading data from computer-aided design (CAD) drawings. The scaffolds can be built with micrometer-sized detail, allowing the tissue-engineered construct to be customized for each patient (Peltola et al., 2008). These studies illustrate the variety of methods available to create almost any desired shape.

In addition to large, continuous shapes, smaller discontinuous materials have also been used for tissue regeneration, either for delivery of growth factors or as a scaffold to culture and transport cells to diseased or injured areas. To act as a drug or gene delivery system, microparticles, nanoparticles, and microtubes are used as carriers. For example, poly(ethylene glycol) (PEG)-PLGA microparticles were loaded with transforming growth factor-β1 (TGF-β1) to increase the proliferation of rat marrow stromal cells (Peter et al., 2000) and PLGA nanoparticles loaded with methylprednisolone were implanted into the contused spinal cord in rats (Chvatal et al., 2008). When designed as cell scaffolds, microcarriers made of collagen have been used to culture human chondrocytes (Frondoza et al., 1996), and fibrin microbeads for transporting fibroblasts (Gorodetsky et al., 1999) and skin epidermal and dermal cell-seeded PLLA microspheres (LaFrance and Armstrong 1999) have been used for skin wound-healing applications. Glass and collagen-coated dextran microspheres have been used to transplant cells for neuroregeneration (Borlongan et al., 1998; Saporta et al., 1997). Also for neuroregeneration, PC12 cells have been microencapsulated in 75:25 hydroxyethyl methacrylate-methyl methacrylate copolymers (Vallbacka et al., 2001). Gelatin microcarriers were used to implant human retinal pigment epithelial cells into the brain for Parkinson's disease and showed improvement in motor symptoms in patients (Stover et al., 2005). Small particles are also advantageous because, unlike large implants, these are usually injectable by needles.

Size. The overall size of an implant is important, especially with respect to the diffusion of oxygen and nutrients within the implant. It is essential for regenerating tissue to have access to the appropriate nutrients as well as a method of waste removal, and the oxygen supply is often the limiting factor. Cells typically require an oxygen partial pressure P_{O_2} of 1 to 3 mmHg for basic cellular metabolism (Hunter et al., 1999). Due to the capillary P_{O_2} and the oxygen diffusion coefficient in tissue, cells are usually found no more than 50 μm from a capillary in vivo (Guyton and Hall, 1996b). When biomaterial scaffolds have a thickness significantly greater than 100 μm, oxygen deficits may occur, depending on the diffusive properties of the scaffold. When PLLA sponges infiltrated with polyvinyl alcohol (PVA) were formed into 1-mm-thick samples for the seeding and delivery of hepatocytes, the cells on the interior of the sponges necrosed in vivo (Mooney et al., 1995), probably because the oxygen and nutrient demands of the cells exceeded the supply. Another study seeded smooth muscle cells (SMCs) onto PGA fibers for transplantation into rats. After 18 days, viable SMCs were found at the edges of the implant, but cells more than 100 μm into the implant did not survive (Eiselt et al., 1998). Consequently, if a cellular implant is sufficiently large, it will require enhanced oxygen transport, perhaps via an internal blood supply, to support the cells deep within the implant.

Blood vessels naturally invade foreign materials as part of the wound healing response, so macroporous scaffolds will eventually vascularize. However, this process is lengthy, taking over 3 weeks even for relatively small (5 mm) PLLA scaffolds (Voigt et al., 1999). The distance that blood vessels can penetrate into the scaffold and the distance of the seeded or ingrown cells from blood vessels can be just as important, if not more so, than the overall size of scaffold. To avoid the development of a necrotic core, implant size should be based on the diffusive properties of the material as well as the metabolic needs of the cells. Multicell spheroids cultured in soft agar enlarged until they reached a critical size, after which they ceased to expand. Although the critical size ranged from 2.4 to 4.0 mm, the first cells to necrose were greater than 150 to 200 μm from the surface, probably due to the limitation of oxygen diffusion (Folkman and Hochberg, 1973). In this study, the allowable distance between the viable cells within the spheroids and the nutrient/oxygen source was larger than the typical in vivo distance between cells and blood vessels (50 μm), most likely due to the diffusive properties of the agar and the density and metabolism of the cells. Nevertheless, diffusion alone was not sufficient to sustain cells deep within the spheroids. To overcome limitations such as this, a biochemical stimulus to enhance nutrient influx to promote ingrowth of cells and vascularization of scaffolds can be included in the material, as discussed in Sec. 21.3.

Pore Features. A biomaterial for tissue regeneration must be porous enough to allow cells to invade the material, with ample surface area for an appropriate quantity of cells to adhere and proliferate. By controlling pore features, permeability affecting the diffusion of nutrients in and waste out of the scaffold as well as influencing the pressure fields within the construct also can be engineered. Studies have shown that creating pores in polycarbonate and polyester membranes enhanced

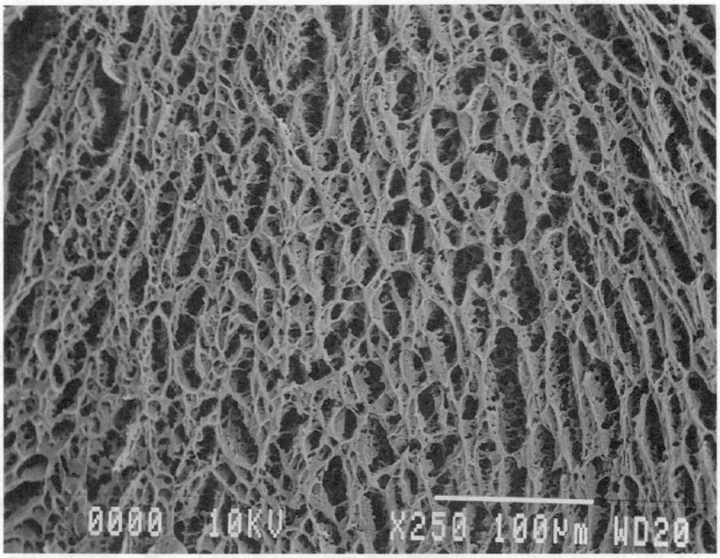

FIGURE 21.1 Scanning electron micrograph showing the porosity of a critical-point-dried 1.5% (wt/vol) agarose hydrogel (bar = 100 μm).

corneal epithelial tissue migration (Steele et al., 2000), and the introduction of pores into PLGA foams increased rat hepatocyte adhesion (Ranucci and Moghe, 1999). In addition, the surface area for cell attachment is correlated with the porosity of the polymer, so highly porous PLGA foams have the advantage of increased available surface area to support cellular attachment and growth (Zheng et al., 1998). Pore features such as porogen type, pore size, and interpore distance affect endothelial cell growth on PLGA but not on PLLA (Narayan and Venkatraman 2008). The porosity of a biomaterial also affects the diffusion of oxygen and nutrients within the scaffold, as well as the rate of neovascularization (Eiselt et al., 1998). Larger pores in the biomaterial may allow for improved mass transport and neovascularization (Zhang and Ma, 2000). In addition, pore shape can be adjusted to enhance tissue regeneration. Biodegradable PDLLA-PELA foams have been made with longitudinally oriented pores to facilitate spinal cord regeneration (Maquet et al., 2001).

Often, a specific pore size enhances cellular activity, and the optimal pore diameter depends on the cell type. In one set of studies, the nominal pore size of porous polycarbonate membranes affected epithelial tissue migration (Steele et al., 2000) and the formation of a continuous basement membrane (Evans et al., 1999b). Likewise, when the average pore radius of agarose hydrogels (see Fig. 21.1) was below a critical threshold, neurite extension from rat embryonic striatal cells and embryonic chick dorsal root ganglia (DRG) was inhibited (Bellamkonda et al., 1995; Dillon et al., 1998). Also, cellulose membranes with 0.2 μm pores were unable to support cell ingrowth, but when the pore size was increased to 8 μm, cells were able to invade the membranes (Padera and Colton, 1996). The effect of pore size varies with cell type; in the case of smooth muscle cells, cell density was significantly higher with small villi feature but pore size did not affect cell density (Lee et al., 2008). Interestingly, rat hepatocyte attachment to 3D PLGA foams of varying porosity showed no preference for any given porosity. However, when protein secretion was evaluated, cells cultured on foams with supracellular-sized (67 μm) pores had a significantly increased secretion of albumin, as compared to cells on foams with intermediate- (17 μm) or subcellular- (3 μm) sized pores. This effect may have been due to increased cell-cell contacts in the scaffolds with supracellular-sized pores (Ranucci and Moghe, 1999). These results indicate that pore size and shape should be optimized for each application; in addition, more than one fundamental parameter needs to be used to determine the best morphology.

Since the optimum pore size depends on the application, it is important to have control over the porosity of materials. Novel methods of fabricating a porous matrix include using a 3D paraffin mold to create a spherical pore network (Ma and Choi, 2001); utilizing sugar particles, discs, and fibers to produce a variety of controlled porous PLLA structures (Zhang and Ma, 2000); and using high-pressure gas foaming in combination with particulate leaching to create porous scaffolds from PLGA copolymers without the use of organic solvents (Murphy and Mooney, 1999). The porosity of PLGA-PEG blends, fabricated by solvent casting and particulate leaching methods, was significantly dependent on the initial salt fraction as well as the ratio of PLGA to PEG (Wake et al., 1996). Similarly, the porosity of collagen-chitosan matrices was controlled by changing the component ratios, with increased amounts of chitosan resulting in smaller pores. As the chitosan concentration increased, proliferation of a human hemopoietic cell line decreased, perhaps due to the smaller pore size. Notably, cell viability remained unchanged (Tan et al., 2001). These collagen-chitosan matrices may be suitable for applications such as cell encapsulation where it is desirable for cells to remain viable but not highly proliferative so they do not overcrowd the scaffold. Porous polyurethanes made by salt leaching and thermally induced phase separation (Heijkants et al., 2008) allows for the ability to independently control porosity, pore size, and interconnectivity without the use of toxic materials. Rapid prototyping (RP) is a recent technique for fabricating layer-by-layer a 3D structure with pore networks in CAD fashion (Jun et al., 2007), allowing pore features to be designed by computer-aided drawing. However, RP cannot be used for smaller pore sizes that can be achieved with traditional methods, and it is limited by which materials can be used. Even with a thorough, controlled design of initial porosity, as described in these studies, processes including fibrous encapsulation, scaffold degradation, cellular ingrowth, and extracellular matrix (ECM) production must be considered because they may alter the scaffold pore features after implantation.

Three-Dimensionality. Since tissues in vivo are generally 3D constructs, cells cultured in 3D substrates are more likely to reflect in vivo scenarios. Culturing cells in vitro on two-dimensional (2D) substrates rather than in three dimensions has been shown to affect cell phenotype. Hepatocytes cultured in alginate beads (400 μm diameter) secreted more albumin, fibrinogen, α-1-antitrypsin, α-1-acid glycoprotein, and prothrombin than a similar cell density in a 2D monolayer culture. Moreover, the levels produced by the cells on the alginate beads approached those of normal hepatocytes in vivo, perhaps because the 3D cell architecture mimicked that found in vivo (Selden et al., 1999). Primary human chondrocytes cultured on 2D substrates transitioned to a "fibroblastoid" cell phenotype. When cultured on 3D collagen microcarriers, they reverted back to the original chondrocytic phenotype (Frondoza et al., 1996). Similarly, when neurons were cultured on 2D agarose cultures, they did not adhere and grow. However, when embedded in 3D agarose hydrogels with the identical chemistry, the neurons were viable and extended long processes (Balgude et al., 2001). Photomicrographs of growth cones extending from primary neurons illustrate the difference between the growth cone morphology on 2D tissue culture substrates and the 3D morphology in agarose hydrogel (Fig. 21.2). These examples show that cell phenotype, morphology, and differentiation depend on the dimensionality of the culture conditions.

But it is still difficult to know the clear differences of molecular and cellular mechanism under 2D and 3D culture systems. The differences could be the result of interactions between integrins and receptors, signaling events, and different compositions of extracellular matrix (ECM) proteins (Keely et al., 2007). Under the 2D culture system, the surface coated with various ECM proteins confers rigidity to the cells, which is a major difference between 3D and 2D. This difference of matrix stiffness caused a different level and distribution of focal adhesion and resulted in cellular response and signaling regulation in tumors (Paszek et al., 2005). In some applications, a 3D model more closely approximates the condition. Breast epithelial cells required a floating 3D collagen gels for tubulogenensis. The results showed that breast epithelial cells respond to the rigidity and density of 3D collagen matrix by ROCK-mediated contractility (Wozniak et al., 2003).

In spite of this fact, many in vitro studies related to cell migration and proliferation have been performed on 2D tissue culture substrates due to the relative simplicity of these experiments. Some groups have performed transmigration assays (Gosiewska et al., 2001) and proliferation assays (Chu et al., 1995; Tan et al., 2001) with 3D cultures. However, imaging and analyzing 3D cultures is difficult, as

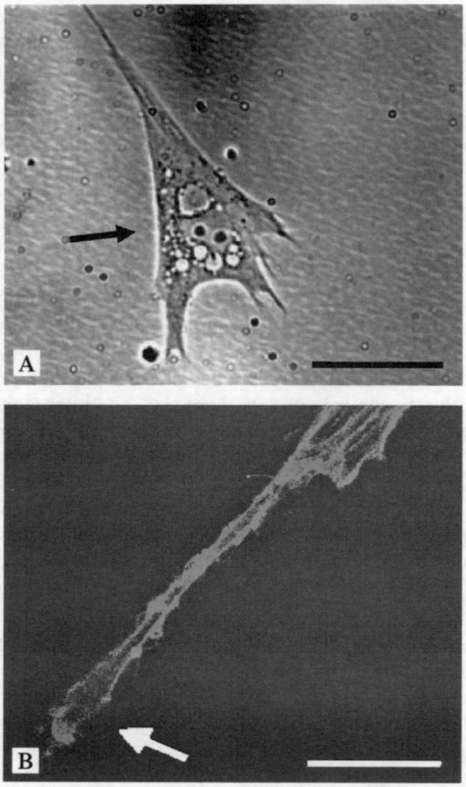

FIGURE 21.2 Images of growth cones (*arrows*) extending from embryonic chick dorsal root ganglia in vitro: (A) growth cone morphology on 2D substrates is typically flat and extended (image captured via light microscopy); (B) in 3D agarose hydrogel cultures, growth cones exhibit a 3D ellipsoidal shape (image is one optical slice through a 3D growth cone captured via confocal microscopy) (bar = 25 μm).

cells cannot be manipulated or imaged as easily as those on 2D substrates. Live imaging of cells cultured in 3D scaffolds via light microscopy is challenging because the thickness of the 3D culture and light scatter problems caused by the material's nontransparent nature.

In addition, techniques such as immunostaining require adaptation for 3D cultures in vitro. Often, when in vitro experiments are performed using 3D scaffolds, the cultures are either fixed and sectioned prior to staining (Gosiewska et al., 2001; Schreiber et al., 1999), or stained in situ and then sectioned for analysis (Attawia et al., 1995; Chu et al., 1995; Holy et al., 2000). A method for staining PLGA scaffolds in situ and then performing a histological analysis has been published (Holy and Yakubovich, 2000). Immunostaining of neuritis and growth cones is not so straightforward. Three-dimensional cultures of primary neurons in agarose hydrogels can be imaged via light microscopy because the hydrogels are transparent and the cell density is low (Dillon et al., 2000). Multiphoton laser-scanning microscopy has been studied for high-resolution imaging of live tissue (Provenzano et al., 2006; Zipfel et al., 2003). The combination of multiphoton excitation and second harmonic generation provides convenient excitation of intrinsic fluorophores without exogenous stains ex vivo. While culturing in 3D substrates can be useful in maintaining normal phenotypes, significant challenges with cultures, qualitative visualization, and assays still remain.

Surface Topography. Modifying the surface topography and surface roughness of a material is another approach to enhance interactions between the implant and the tissue. When the topography of the subendothelial extracellular matrix was replicated with biomedical polyurethane, bovine aortic endothelial cells (BAECs) spread more rapidly and appeared more like cells in a native environment, as compared with cells on nontextured polyurethane (Goodman et al., 1996). To determine the effect of surface roughness on bone augmentation, smooth and grit-blasted (textured) titanium cylinders were implanted in rabbits. Although both types of surfaces resulted in similar amounts of trabecular bone formation, the grit-blasted titanium had a larger area of bone directly contacting the implant (Lundgren et al., 1999). As these studies illustrate, cells sometimes prefer a textured surface to a smooth surface, perhaps due to the increased surface area available for cell attachment and tissue integration.

Grooves have also been used to adjust the surface topography of materials. By creating microgrooves on tissue culture polystyrene, a significantly higher number of rat dermal fibroblasts attached onto and aligned actin filaments with 1-μm-wide grooves relative to smooth surfaces and surfaces with grooves greater than 2 μm width (Walboomers et al., 2000). Similarly, chick embryo cerebral neurons and their processes have been shown to follow micron- but not nanometer-scale grooves faithfully in vitro (Clark et al., 1990; Clark et al., 1991). *Xenopus* spinal cord neurons cultured on microgrooved quartz extended neurites parallel to the grooves, regardless of groove dimensions, but rat hippocampal neurons extended neurites parallel to deep, wide grooves and perpendicular to shallow, narrow grooves (Rajnicek et al., 1997). The topography of the luminal surface affected the regeneration when polymeric guidance channels were used for rat sciatic nerve regeneration (Guenard et al., 1991), and submicro-printed patterns in PMMA guided adult mouse sympathetic and sensory ganglia (Johansson et al., 2006). Only channels with a smooth inner surface produced a discrete nerve cable with microfascicles consisting of myelinated axons (Aebischer et al., 1990). Electrospun nanofibers also provide aligned topography to cell outgrowth and regeneration. Our laboratory and others (Corey et al., 2007) demonstrated that dorsal root ganglia processes and Schwann cells on aligned nano-PLLA fibers extended in the direction of fiber alignment. Also, aligned submicron-poly(acrylonitrile-co-methylacrylate) (PAN-MA) scaffolds enhanced regeneration across large gaps (17 mm) in the rodent sciatic nerve injury model (Kim et al., 2008). Due to the critical influence of surface topography on tissue organization and response, topography should be considered when designing regenerative biomaterials.

21.2.2 Mechanical Properties

Biomaterials to regenerate load-bearing tissues, including bone, cartilage, and blood vessels, have obvious requirements for mechanical properties such as modulus of elasticity, tensile and shear strength, and compliance. For instance, biodegradable bone cement designed to aid in the repair of broken bones or to fill bone voids must have mechanical properties similar to those of the native bone until the bone heals (Peter et al., 1998a). For such implants, composite reinforced materials may be necessary to achieve the desired mechanical properties. Moreover, in the regeneration of soft tissue such as cartilage, the development of the appropriate mechanical properties may be critically dependent upon the mechanical conditioning imposed in vitro.

Mechanical properties are also important for other applications where mechanical strength is not the primary function. One such application is electrodes for stimulation or recording in the brain. Silicon microelectrodes inevitably seem to elicit astroglial scar due to mechanical mismatch with the host neural tissue and lack of integration between the implant and the brain tissue (Maynard et al., 2000) and chronic injury caused by micromotion around the electrode (Lee et al., 2005), and then this fibrous scarring can lead to electrode failure (Williams et al., 1999). Soft tissues like the nervous system should not be overlooked when considering mechanical properties.

Reinforced Composites. Bone regeneration and fixation require strong materials, so applicable biomaterials must have the strength to sustain the mechanical loads experienced in bone. However, many materials with desirable physical and chemical properties, such as biodegradable polymers, are often unable to provide this strength by themselves. Furthermore, adjusting physical parameters to enhance tissue ingrowth, such as by increasing the pore size, leads to a further decrease in the mechanical strength (Ma and Choi, 2001). By combining two different materials, reinforced composites with the joint properties of both materials can be fabricated.

PLLA, PGA, and PLGA are common scaffolds for a number of tissue-regeneration applications, including bone regeneration, and are biodegradable and FDA approved for certain applications. The Bioscrew, a PLLA screw, has been found to perform comparably to metal screws as a fixation device for patellar tendon autografts. Moreover, the Bioscrew is completely degradable and has the ability to compress slightly and conform to its surroundings when inserted into bone (Barber et al., 2000).

Reinforcing techniques via the addition of mineral and ceramic components have been developed to strengthen these and other materials for load-bearing applications. Hydroxyapatite (HA), a mineral component found in bone, is commonly used to reinforce polymers for bone regeneration because it can enhance mechanical properties as well as provide osteoinductive properties. Absorbable, high-strength composites of PLLA reinforced with HA are being considered for fixation devices in bone. These composite rods have an initial bending strength exceeding that of human cortical bone and have promoted greater bone contact and better bone integration than PLLA without HA in a rabbit bone defect model (Furukawa et al., 2000). PLGA has also been strengthened with HA to form PLGA-HA composites with an elastic modulus and yield strength similar to that of cancellous bone (Devin et al., 1996). Short HA fibers have been used to reinforce PLGA and produce stronger composite foams for bone regeneration (Thomson et al., 1998). Based on these and other studies, it can be concluded that HA incorporated into biodegradable polymers can increase the strength of the composite to a level useful for orthopedic implants.

The bioactive ceramic β-tricalcium phosphate (β-TCP) has also been used to develop composite materials for bone regeneration. Poly(propylene fumarate) (PPF) has been strengthened by incorporating β-TCP to result in a biodegradable composite material with sufficient mechanical strength to temporarily replace trabecular bone (Yaszemski et al., 1996). It is notable that the mechanical properties of the composite actually increased during degradation, maintaining a compressive strength of at least 5 MPa and a compressive modulus greater than 50 MPa for 3 (Peter et al., 1998b) to 12 (Yaszemski et al., 1996) weeks, depending on the composition. PPF also can be applied to reinforce polymers. PPF cross-linked with a mixture of *N*-vinylpyrrolidone and ethyleneglycol dimethacrylate reinforced PLGA bone plates with higher flexural modulus and compressive strength (Hasirci et al., 2002). Materials that maintain their mechanical strength in this manner are useful for tissue regeneration, as they allow a gradual, smoother "replacement" of the temporary biomaterial with the host matrix and cells. If the mechanical properties of a biomaterial decrease very rapidly, it may be beneficial to overengineer the initial implant to compensate for the loss.

Reinforcements are used for nonpolymeric materials as well. Hydroxyapatite coatings on titanium bone fixtures increased contact between the native bone and the implant, as well as provided a greater shear and antitorque strength (Meffert, 1999). Microporous calcium phosphate ceramics (CPC; 75 percent HA and 25 percent β-TCP) generally have weak mechanical properties under compression. When the pores were filled with calcium phosphate cement consisting of β-TCP and dicalcium phosphate dihydrate, the mechanical strength of the ceramic improved without compromising the bone healing and regeneration process (Frayssinet et al., 2000). CPC with absorbable polyglactin meshes showed a threefold increase of strength and 150-fold increase of work-of-fracture. The mesh can be dissolved, after which interconnected cylindrical macropores were formed and supported the adhesion, spreading, proliferation, and viability of osteoblastlike cells in vitro (Xu and Simon 2004). By reinforcing available materials with components that provide strength as well as osteoinductive properties, bone regeneration can be enhanced.

Mechanical Conditioning. Tissue regeneration has been shown to benefit from external mechanical stimuli. One study demonstrated that constant mechanical tension elongated the axon bundles of synapsed primary embryonic rat cortical neurons in vitro (Smith et al., 2001). Moreover, certain tissues require mechanical loads for the generation of proper cell phenotypes. When in vitro culture conditions emulate in vivo loading, native cell phenotypes can be maintained.

Blood vessels in vivo are mechanically loaded by the pulsatile flow of the bloodstream. To simulate these conditions, tissue-engineered blood vessels are often grown under pulsatile flow conditions.

Tissue-engineered arteries grown in vitro under pulsatile flow appeared more similar to native arteries than vessels not cultured under flow (Niklason et al., 1999), and cell-seeded vascular grafts cultured under pulsatile flow demonstrated superior mechanical strength relative to static control grafts (Hoerstrup et al., 2001). Phenotype of vascular smooth muscle cells was manipulated by mechanical stretch, which stimulated RhoA. RhoA signaling pathways manipulate cell phenotype and cytoplasmic organization, migration, proliferation, and contraction (Halka et al., 2008). Thus, in vitro cultures of blood vessels benefit from mechanical conditioning similar to the in vivo mechanical loading.

Cartilage is another tissue that experiences mechanical loads in vivo. To engineer cartilage, mechanical stimuli have been applied to help the cells express a similar phenotype as native cartilage. Explants of healthy cartilage respond to compressive loads and in particular to the release of those loads. The release of a static compressive load stimulated the chondrocytes, and continuous dynamic loading was able to stimulate or inhibit the biosynthesis of proteins, depending on the amplitude and frequency of the compression (Sah et al., 1989; Steinmeyer and Knue, 1997). This behavior of native cartilage extends to chondrocytes cultured in vitro. Chondrocytes cultured on agarose disks were evaluated under static and dynamic compression. Dynamic compression resulted in an increase in proteoglycan and protein synthesis with time, whereas little change in synthesis was seen with static compression (Buschmann et al., 1995; Lee and Bader, 1997). Likewise, cyclic loading was able to stimulate chick mesenchymal stem cells cultured on agarose hydrogels to differentiate into chondrocytes, making them useful for cartilage regeneration applications (Elder et al., 2000). The chondrogenesis depended on the frequency and duration of the cyclic compressive load, indicating the similarity between these constructs and native cartilage (Elder et al., 2001). Multiaxial loading combined the application of 5 percent compression and 5 percent shear to chondrocyte cultures in vitro (Waldman et al., 2007). ECM accumulation such as collagen and proteoglycan, and mechanical properties such as compression modulus and shear modulus significantly increased compared to static controls. These and other studies have established the importance of mechanical stimulation for chondrocytes and offer a possible approach to enhance cartilage generation in vitro and regeneration in vivo.

Electrical Stimuli. Electrically active materials have also been used to encourage tissue growth. The use of piezoelectric materials made of vinylidene fluoride-trifluoroethylene copolymer, P(VDF-TrFE), enhanced peripheral nerve regeneration in vivo (Fine et al., 1991), and when PC12 cells were cultured on oxidized polypyrrole, the application of an electrical stimulus resulted in enhanced neurite extension (Schmidt et al., 1997), as shown in Fig. 21.3. Implant vascularization was enhanced when bilayer films of polypyrrole/hyaluronic acid (PP-HA) and polypyrrole/poly(styrenesulfonate) (PP/PSS) were implanted subcutaneously (Collier et al., 2000). These types of electrical stimuli can be used in conjunction with a biomaterial to promote tissue regrowth.

21.2.3 Chemical Properties

The chemistry of a material affects the interactions that occur between the implant and its surrounding environment, including protein adsorption, cellular response, and bioresorption. In particular, the hydrophilicity, charge, and degradability of the material can impact tissue regeneration.

Hydrophilicity. One aspect of material chemistry that affects cell behavior is the hydrophilicity of the biomaterial. Most mammalian cells are anchorage dependent and only viable when attached to a substrate in a receptor-mediated fashion. Since they have no receptors for most synthetic biomaterials, cells will not attach to bare materials in a receptor-mediated manner. However, protein adsorption onto biomaterials results in a surface permissible for cell attachment with moderate hydrophilicity (20° to 40° water contact angle) (Van Wachem et al., 1985). It has been shown that moderately hydrophilic surfaces, in the presence of serum proteins, often support greater cell attachment on polycarbonate (Chang et al., 1999) and PLGA (Khang et al., 1999), spreading on the glass (Webb et al., 1998), and normal phenotypes on alkylthiol monolayers (McClary et al., 2000) relative to hydrophobic or highly hydrophilic surfaces. Focal contacts and stress fibers in cells on

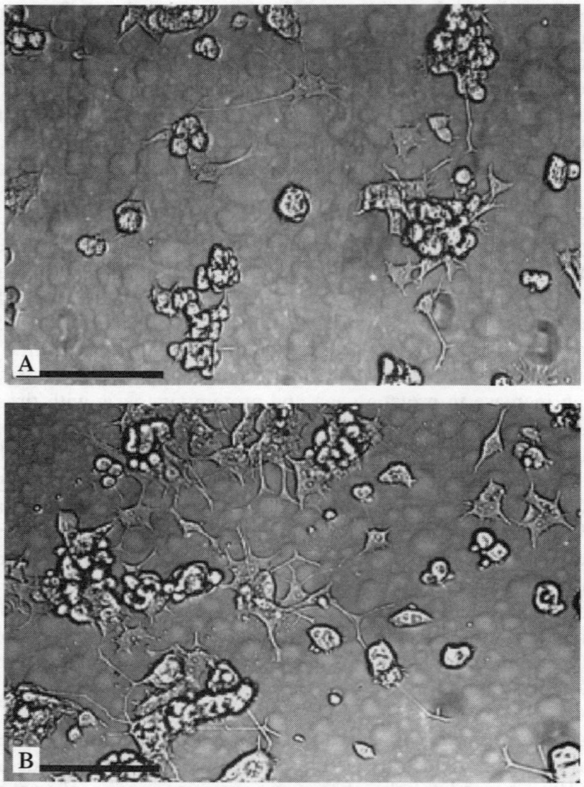

FIGURE 21.3 PC12 cell differentiation on polypyrrole (PP) without (A) and with (B) application of an electric potential. PC12 cells were grown on PP for 24 h in the presence of nerve growth factor and then exposed to electrical stimulation (100 mV) across the polymer film (B). Images were acquired 24 h after stimulation. Cells grown for 48 h but not subjected to electrical stimulation are shown for comparison (A) (bar = 100 μm). (*Courtesy of C. Schmidt, Ph.D.*)

moderately hydrophilic surfaces are well defined, indicating active binding by integrin and outside-in signaling due to the proteins, such as fibronectin, adsorbed onto the surface (McClary et al., 2000), so the increased cell attachment on moderately hydrophilic surfaces could be due to preferential binding of cells to ECM proteins that adsorbed to the surfaces (Khang et al., 1999).

Spatial control of cells is achieved by including zones that permit cell attachment with adjoining zones that inhibit attachment. Very hydrophilic surfaces are relatively resistant to protein adsorption and can be used as an inhibitory surface to generate patterns of attached cells on a biomaterial. High-molecular-weight PEG (above 18,500 g/mol) is known to be resistant to protein adsorption and cell adhesion and can be easily modified for the covalent coupling of other molecules (Desai and Hubbell, 1991; Gombotz et al., 1991). When PEG chains were grafted onto silica films, significantly less protein adsorption was observed as compared to unmodified surfaces (Alcantar et al., 2000). PEG chains can also reduce cell adhesion. Collagen, known for its ability to promote cell attachment, can be modified into a nonpermissive substrate by attaching PEG to the collagen (PEG-collagen) (Tiller et al., 2001). PEG can confer a stealthlike property preventing cell attachment or protein absorption, making it useful for drug delivery when applied to polyelectrolyte microcapsules (Wattendorf et al., 2008) or liposomes (Pohlen et al., 2004). These and other methods can be used to create regions of differing hydrophilicity to control cell micropatterns on surfaces.

Charge. In addition to preferring moderately hydrophilic surfaces, cell attachment is improved on positively charged surfaces. Polymers that carry a positive charge at physiological pH, approximately 7.4, augment cell attachment and growth in the presence of proteins (McKeehan and Ham, 1976). In the absence of proteins, cells still prefer positively charged hydrophilic surfaces to those with a neutral or negative charge (Webb et al., 1998). When polylysine (a positively charged protein) was coated onto PLLA and PGLA nonwoven structures, chondrocyte attachment increased (Sittinger et al., 1996). When fluorinated ethylene propylene films were surface-modified with patterns of amine groups, preadsorption with albumin resulted in neuroblastoma cell attachment along the amine patterns (Ranieri et al., 1993). Human umbilical vein endothelial cells showed greater cell spreading on the positively charged poly(L-lysine)-terminated film than on the negatively charged dextran sulfate-terminated film (Wittmer et al., 2007). Also, neurite extension, an important element of nerve tissue regeneration, has been shown to depend on the polarity of the substrate in which the cells are cultured. When embryonic chick DRGs were cultured in 3D agarose hydrogels, negatively charged dermatan sulfate coupled to the hydrogel-inhibited neurite extension, whereas positively charged chitosan coupled to the hydrogel-enhanced neurite extension (Dillon et al., 2000). To determine the effect of charge on the ability of collagen to support cells, collagen was modified to have either a net positive or negative charge. However, the charge difference had minimal effect, with 90 percent of mouse fibroblasts and endothelial cells attaching after 60 minutes, regardless of the substrate's net charge. When PEG collagen, which did not support cell attachment, was given a net positive charge through amination, fibroblast and endothelial cell attachment returned to the levels of attachment on unmodified collagen (Tiller et al., 2001). To enhance adhesion of smooth muscle cells onto the arterial bypass graft, fibronectinlike engineered polymer protein was coated on the surface of poly(carbonate-urea)urethane and the retention of smooth muscle cells was increased because of its repeating sequences of RGD and its positive charge (Rashid et al., 2004). As demonstrated by these studies, positive charges added to biomaterial scaffolds can induce tissue growth.

Biodegradation. Biomaterials for some applications like total-hip replacements and synthetic vascular grafts are designed to be long-lived and even permanent, if possible. However, many tissue regeneration implants are best-designed using materials that can completely degrade in vivo to be replaced with autologous tissue. The lack of a synthetic remnant is advantageous, because it reduces the likelihood of infection and chronic inflammation that are often seen with permanent implants. Biodegradable materials are also ideal for tissues that are still growing and developing, such as bones and heart valves in pediatric patients.

The chemistry of certain materials allows them to degrade in vivo, typically due to cleavable bonds. The most commonly used degradable polyester polymers include PLLA, PDLLA, PGA, and PLGA. These polymers undergo bulk degradation into lactic and glycolic acid by hydrolysis of the ester bonds. The degradation by-products are nontoxic and easily metabolized, and the rate of degradation of PLGA can be controlled by the ratio of PLLA to PGA—the high-molecular-weight PLLA degrades slowly so PLGA having a higher ratio of PLLA than PGA degrades more slowly. Polyanhydrides are another type of biodegradable polymer used for drug delivery and tissue engineering. Due to the hydrophobicity of the polymer chains, they degrade by predictable surface erosion rather than bulk degradation as observed with the polyesters. Polyorthoester is a hydrophobic biodegradable material that degrades by surface erosion through hydrolysis, and the degradation rate can be controlled. A widely used biodegradable material is polycaprolactone. A variety of other synthetic and natural polymers are also biodegradable.

The time course of degradation should be planned and controlled. A degradable scaffold must support cell growth and provide the appropriate mechanical properties until the tissue is capable of fulfilling these functions. In the vasculature, a human artery typically experiences an average pressure of at least 100 mmHg (Guyton and Hall, 1996a). A material implanted to promote vessel regeneration must therefore supply the necessary strength and compliance until the native smooth muscle cells and fibroblasts are able to support the load. After the tissue is self-sufficient, it is optimal for the implanted material to completely degrade. The degradation timing can be controlled by adjusting polymer properties, such as the type, ratio between monomeric units, pH, and location of the degradable bonds. New methods of modifying polyanhydride networks have allowed for controlled variation of porosity, rate of degradation, and interactions with cells (Burkoth et al., 2000). Electron-beam radiation can also be used to modify the degradation of biodegradable polymers. PLA and PLGA were irradiated with electron-beam radiation and lost mass earlier than samples that were not irradiated (Leonard et al., 2009).

One must also consider the fact that the rate of tissue regeneration and polymer degradation will vary among individuals. The environment will affect the degradation rate as well. It has been shown that events such as fluid flow around a degradable PLGA scaffold will decrease the degradation rate (Agrawal et al., 2000). A novel approach to bioresorbable scaffolds involves enzyme-dependent degradation, currently under development by Hubbell and coworkers (Kraehenbuehl et al., 2008; Schense et al., 2000; Ye et al., 2000). Rather than relying on the chemistry of the environment to degrade the material, this approach depends on the cells to control degradation. Until the cells enzymatically trigger degradation, the scaffold retains its mechanical and structural properties. They developed a synthetic 3D matrix metalloproteinase (MMP) sensitive PEG-based hydrogel. To direct differentiation of P19 embryonal carcinoma cells by mimicking embryonic cardiac tissue, matrix elasticity, MMP sensitivity, and the concentration of matrix-bound RGDSP peptide were modulated. This promising method has the potential to allow for individualized degradation that is completely dependent on the tissue regeneration process for therapeutic application.

Polymer degradation usually produces small degradation products, as some materials may degrade into small, toxic by-products, even though the original material as a whole is nontoxic. When PLGA degrades into lactic acid and glycolic acid, the local pH may drop if the area is not well perfused (Wake et al., 1998). Also, if the by-products are immunogenic, the immune system may attack the area of desired tissue regeneration, and successful regeneration will not occur. To ensure biocompatibility, the toxicity of the degradation products ought to be evaluated.

21.3 BIOCHEMICAL COMPONENT

Once a material has been optimized based on its structural properties, bioactive agents can be incorporated to mimic normal regenerative environments found in vivo and further enhance tissue regeneration. These bioactive agents could consist of peptides, proteins, chemicals, oligonucleotides, genes, or living cells and can be included by two methods: (1) immobilization to the material and (2) release as diffusible agents. A combination of these two approaches could result in a diffusible signal that is chemoattractive and an immobilized signal that encourages cell attachment and proliferation. Table 21.4 provides a sampling of biochemical components incorporated into materials to enhance tissue growth.

21.3.1 Presentation of Immobilized Signals on the Scaffold

A scaffold material can provide cues that will direct and control the cell-matrix interactions to promote and regulate tissue regeneration. Biochemical signals such as ECM proteins, adhesive peptides, and growth factors can be incorporated into a material by nonspecific adsorption or through covalent immobilization. Since many mammalian cells require adhesion for cell viability, these molecules can provide the essential cues for cell attachment.

ECM Proteins for Cell Adhesion. Cell adhesion in a receptor-mediated fashion is key for cellular processes such as intracellular signaling, synthesis of ECM proteins, and mitosis and these could result in cell viability, spreading, proliferation, migration, differentiation, and ECM secretion. Specific cell adhesion to scaffolds often occurs via ECM molecules that are presented on the scaffold surface. One adhesion study confirmed that smooth muscle cells adhere via integrins to extracellular matrix proteins such as collagen, fibronectin, and vitronectin (Nikolovski and Mooney, 2000). By immobilizing matrix proteins to the material, cell adhesion can be facilitated.

TABLE 21.4 Examples of Biochemical Components Incorporated into Biomaterials for Tissue Regeneration

Design parameter	Biomaterial	Biochemical agent	Application	References
Presentation of immobilized signals				
ECM proteins	Polypropylene mesh	Collagen-GAG	Hernia repair	Butler et al., 2001
Adhesive peptides	Glass	RGD peptide	Pulmonary artery endothelial cells	Kouvroukoglou et al., 2000
Growth factors	Polystyrene	Gradient of EGF	Epidermal keratinocytes	Stefonek and Masters 2007
Presentation of chemoattractive, diffusible signals				
One-component system	3D PLGA scaffold	IGF-I and TGF-β 1	Cartilage tissue engineering	Jaklenec et al., 2008
	PLLA/PGA	Tetracycline	Bone regeneration	Park et al., 2000
Two-component system	Gelatin and collagen	bFGF	Angiogenesis	Kawai et al., 2000
	Laminin-gradianted agarose and lipid microtubule	NGF	Nerve regeneration	Dodla et al., 2008
Gene delivery	*PLGA matrices*	*PDGF-B plasmids*	Wound healing	Shea et al., 1999
	Collagen carrier	BMP-7 adenovirus	Bone regeneration	Franceschi et al., 2000
Presentation of a living component				
Cell seeding	PLGA foams	Stromal osteoblasts	Osteogenic activity	Ishaug et al., 1997
	PGA fiber matrix	Smooth muscle cells	Cell density	Kim et al., 1998
Differentiated cell-scaffold systems	Collagen-coated dextran microcarriers	Keratinocytes	Epithelium reconstitution	Voigt et al., 1999
	Collagen sponge	Fibroblasts	Skin regeneration	Kuroyanagi et al., 2001
Cell-scaffolds for neuroregeneration	Glass beads	Adrenal chromaffin cells	Neuroregeneration	Cherksey et al., 1996
	Alginate-PLL-alginate capsule	Bovine chromaffin cells	Neuroregeneration	Xue et al., 2001
Combination therapy	Matrigel 3D scaffolds	Myoblasts and bFGF	Myogenesis and angiogenesis	Barbero et al., 2001
	PLGA-HA scaffold	Stromal cells with BMP-2 genes	Bone regeneration	Laurencin et al., 2001
Stem cell-scaffold systems	Hyaluronan-based 3D scaffolds	Mesenchymal stem cells	Osteochondral repair	Radice et al., 2000
	3D collagen sponge/ PGA fibers	Mesenchymal stem cells with BMP-2 genes	BMP-2 expression	Hosseinkhani et al., 2006
Cell-based products	Collagen	Fibroblasts and keratinocytes	Venous ulcer treatment	Eaglstein et al., 1999

These adhesive ECM proteins such as collagen include the Arg-Gly-Asp (RGD) amino acid sequence that has been considered as a binding domain to the cells via ligand-integrin receptors interactions (Culp et al., 1997). Collagen has been covalently immobilized on PLGA surfaces to increase cell attachment (Zheng et al., 1998) and on polycarbonate and polyester membranes to enhance corneal epithelial tissue migration (Steele et al., 2000). A porous collagen membrane placed around a titanium implant resulted in increased bone repair in a model of alveolar ridge deficiency as compared to uncoated titanium implants (Zhang et al., 1999b), and collagen/hydroxyapatite nanocomposite thin films on titanium substrates accelerated the rate of cell proliferation and osteogenic potentials (Teng et al., 2008). Collagen has also been used in combination with other ECM components to improve a polypropylene mesh for hernia repair. A collagen-glycosaminoglycan (GAG) matrix was placed around the mesh and shown to facilitate tissue growth and vascularization (Butler et al., 2001). Also collagen has been applied with other growth factors. Collagen and basic fibroblast growth factor (bFGF) were immobilized on a 3D porous PLLA scaffold. When cultured on the modified scaffold, chondrocytes showed significantly improved cell spreading and growth (Ma et al., 2005). The numerous applications for abundant ECM proteins like collagen illustrate the usefulness of matrix proteins in tissue regeneration.

Laminin, another ECM protein, has also been used to modify materials, particularly for neural applications. When laminin was covalently immobilized on 3D agarose hydrogels, neurite extension from embryonic chick DRGs was stimulated. Further, immobilization was necessary, since laminin simply mixed into the agarose gel was unable to stimulate neurite extension (Yu et al., 1999). Uniform laminin substrates have also been used for the attachment of Schwann cells, but no preferential cell orientation was shown. When micropatterns of laminin and albumin were fabricated on glass coverslips, Schwann cells attached only on the laminin surfaces and were oriented with the laminin patterns (Thompson and Buettner, 2001). A gradient of laminin has enhanced neurite extension. Gradients of laminin were photoimmobilized into the 3D agarose gel scaffold, and neurite extension rate of dorsal root ganglia from chicken embryos was significantly higher in gradient scaffold than in the scaffold with uniform laminin concentration (Dodla and Bellamkonda 2006). These studies demonstrate how a more specialized protein like laminin can also be used to enhance and direct tissue outgrowth.

To improve biocompatibility and optimize the function of applied proteins, there are other parameters to address, including density of surface functional groups, thickness of functional layers, density of protein surfaces, and bioactivity of proteins after immobilization processes. Protein adsorption studies have demonstrated the importance of surface protein conformation. For effective interactions between cells and ECM proteins, the active domains of the proteins should be available for cell recognition. However, when a protein is adsorbed onto a surface to promote cell adhesion, the adhesion sequences will not necessarily be available. Changes in fibronectin conformation due to adsorption to glass and silane surfaces decreased endothelial cell adhesion strength and spreading (Iuliano et al., 1993). On the contrary, adsorption of vitronectin onto nanophase alumina resulted in a conformational change of the protein that increased the adhesion of rat osteoblasts, perhaps due to an increased exposure of the adhesive epitopes (Webster et al., 2001). Nanosized particles are used widely as drug-delivery carriers and with implants, therefore the biological activity of immobilized proteins on nanosized surfaces is important. The immobilized lipase on the multiwalled carbon nanotubes showed significantly increased biocatalyst compared to the lyophilized powdered enzyme (Shah et al., 2007). The interaction between lipase and hydrophobic surface resulted in a conformational change of the enzyme. Thus, conformational changes should be considered when designing immobilization strategies.

Cellular attachment and proliferation are not the only parameters of regeneration to evaluate when optimizing tissue regeneration. It has been shown that increased cell adhesion due to adhesion-promoting surface modifications can result in a decrease of ECM production (Mann et al., 1999). When a biodegradable biomaterial is used, the cells must be self-sufficient when the material is gone, and this includes making their own ECM. A biomaterial with strong adhesive properties may be detrimental to overall tissue function. This example illustrates the importance of balancing cellular activities, such as cell adhesion and matrix production.

Adhesive Peptides. Immobilizing adhesion peptides to the material can also encourage cell attachment to biomaterials. Protein adsorption can result in a loss of quaternary and tertiary structure, but peptides should not denature or change conformation when immobilized to a surface. The most commonly used amino acid sequence for cell adhesion is the RGD sequence found in a variety of ECM proteins, including collagen, fibronectin, and vitronectin. Other peptide sequences used include Tyr-Ile-Gly-Ser-Arg (YIGSR) and Ile-Lys-Val-Ala-Val (IKVAV) from laminin, as well as Arg-Glu-Asp-Val (REDV) and Leu-Asp-Val-Pro-Ser (LDVPS) from fibronectin. All of these sequences are short, so they are often contained within a slightly larger peptide to facilitate immobilization on scaffolds as well as interactions with cells using a spacer arm.

RGD peptides work via interactions with cell surface integrin receptors, as shown by the receptor-mediated attachment of human umbilical vein endothelial cells (HUVECs) to silica substrates modified with RGD peptides (Porte-Durrieu et al., 1999). When immobilized on a surface, the RGD peptides typically localized in clusters, rather than distributing uniformly (Kouvroukoglou et al., 2000). Clustering is advantageous since it has been shown to decrease the average peptide density required to support migration (Maheshwari et al., 2000). Moreover, the peptide surface density should be at or below the saturation level of the cellular receptors, because peptide densities beyond that level have shown no further increase in cell attachment, spreading, or matrix production (Rezania and Healy, 2000). Consequently, there is an optimum surface density for RGD peptides that depends on the application.

Peptides are often used to enhance specific cellular activity with the materials. RGD peptides were covalently linked to quartz surfaces to examine their effect on rat calvaria osteoblast-like cell (RCO) adhesion. Although RCOs adhered and spread on both modified and unmodified quartz in the presence of serum proteins, the RGD-modified surfaces stimulated an increase in mineralization from the RCOs (Rezania and Healy, 1999). The RGD peptide has also been coupled to alginate hydrogels. Since these hydrogels are highly hydrophilic, they have minimal interaction with cells. C2C12 mouse skeletal myoblasts were cultured on 2D membranes of alginate with and without RGD-containing peptides. Only with the RGD peptides present did the myoblasts attach and spread (Rowley et al., 1999). Other studies have immobilized RGD peptides to a hyaluronic matrix to accelerate wound healing and regeneration on mice (Cooper et al., 1996) and skin healing and regeneration for pediatric burn patients (Hansbrough et al., 1995). Immobilizing RGD to polystyrene via Pluronic F108 allowed for increased fibroblast adhesion and spreading (Neff et al., 1998). In addition, bovine pulmonary artery endothelial cells were shown to have an increased migration on glass surfaces modified with either RGD- or YIGSR-containing peptides (Kouvroukoglou et al., 2000). The versatility of RGD peptides demonstrated by these studies suggests that RGD peptides can play an influential role in enhancing tissue regeneration.

Neurite extension can be controlled using immobilized peptides. RGD peptides linked to PLLA-PEG-biotin surfaces via a streptavidin linker were shown to spatially control the adhesion and the direction of neurite extension from PC12 cells (Patel et al., 1998). Neurite extension was also spatially controlled using laminin-derived peptides YIGSR and IKVAV bound to substrates. Growth cones of chick embryo DRGs turned until they were oriented in the up-gradient direction of IKVAV-containing peptide (Adams et al., 2005). Hyaluronic acid hydrogels with IKVAV peptide were implanted in the lesion site of rat cerebrum (Wei et al., 2007). Six weeks after implantation, axons, glial cells, and blood vessels grew into the implant. These studies demonstrate the potential impact of peptides on the regeneration of nerve tissues.

Another method of immobilizing peptides to a surface is to use self-assembled monolayers (SAMs) to modify a surface. Using the microcontact printing technique to create SAMs that both promoted (via RGD peptide) and inhibited (via PEG) cell adhesion, patterns of cell adhesion were established (Zhang et al., 1999a). A different self-assembly method used a molecule with a hydrophobic tail and a peptide head group that contains a collagenlike structural motif. These peptide amphiphiles were able to promote the adhesion and spreading of human melanoma cells on tissue culture plates (Fields et al., 1998). Attachment and growth of cortical neurons also improved by deposition of amino-terminated akanethiol SAMs on a gold substrate without adhesion protein application (Palyvoda et al., 2008). Whether the immobilization technique involves SAMs or covalent chemistry, adhesive peptides are useful for modifying biomaterials to induce cell adhesion.

Growth Factor Presentation. In addition to ECM-related molecules, growth factors have been coupled to materials to provide a biochemical stimulus for proliferation and differentiation. Vascular endothelial growth factor (VEGF) immobilized to fibrin matrices had a greater mitogenic effect on human endothelial cells in vitro than soluble VEGF (Zisch et al., 2001). Also, basic fibroblast growth factor (bFGF) immobilized onto gas-plasma-modified polystyrene accelerated the formation of a confluent HUVEC layer in vitro, whereas soluble bFGF in culture medium was ineffective (Bos et al., 1999).

To stimulate osteoblastic activity of mouse pluripotent fibroblastic C3H cells for differentiation, bone morphogenetic protein-4 (BMP-4) was immobilized on a titanium alloy (Ti-6Al-4V) surface animated by plasma surface modification (Puleo et al., 2002). Studies such as these indicate that immobilized growth factors can sometimes provide a more potent stimulation than soluble growth factors. In another study, TGF-β1 was covalently immobilized to PEG hydrogels and found to increase the matrix production of vascular smooth muscle cells (Mann et al., 2001). Peptides based on the active domains of growth factors have also been utilized as biochemical cues. Alginate hydrogels have been covalently modified with a 20 amino acid sequence derived from bone morphogenic protein-2 (BMP-2) to induce bone formation in vivo. After 8 weeks, the gel was vascularized, and osteoblasts had formed new trabecular bone within the alginate pores (Suzuki et al., 2000). Gradient of growth factor on the surface has also been applied to promote cell migration, which could be a critical issue for wound healing. Epidermal growth factor (EGF) was covalently immobilized with gradient patterns and human epidermal keratinocytes migrated to the direction of higher EGF concentration under serum-free conditions (Stefonek and Masters 2007). Therefore, by immobilizing growth factors to biomaterials, a range of cell responses can be achieved.

21.3.2 Presentation of Chemoattractive, Diffusible Signals on the Scaffold

In addition to immobilized signals, the body also creates chemoattractive gradients using diffusible factors to guide cell migration. To imitate this approach, a bioactive agent can be incorporated into the biomaterial to diffuse away and provide a biochemical cue. For agent release, the biomaterial could consist of one component that fulfills both the role of the scaffold to support the cells and the role of the delivery system to release the biochemicals. Alternatively, a two-component system using one material for the scaffold and a different material for the delivery system could be employed.

Scaffold-Drug Delivery: One-Component System. Using the biomaterial scaffold as a drug-delivery device is a simple means of incorporating a diffusible agent into the material. A bioactive agent incorporated into the biomaterial will slowly diffuse away after implantation to create a concentration gradient. Diffusible agents have been included in matrices by adding them either during or after the fabrication process.

Biodegradable polyesters are among the materials usually loaded by adding the biochemicals during fabrication, and the bioactive agents are then released during degradation of the scaffold. Acidic fibroblast growth factor (aFGF) was incorporated into PDLLA-PELA copolymers for nerve regeneration (Maquet et al., 2001), and Tetracycline was added to a PLLA film/PGA mesh to stimulate bone regeneration and marrow formation in a rat craniotomy defect (Park et al., 2000). PLLA and PLLA-TCP membranes designed to release platelet-derived growth factor-BB (PDGF-BB) enhanced bone formation and allowed for complete bony reunion in a critical size defect in rats (Lee et al., 2001; Park et al., 1998). PLGA microspheres encapsulating insulinlike growth factor-I (IGF-I) and transforming growth factor-β1 (TGF-β1) were fused into a 3D PLGA scaffold for cartilage tissue engineering (Jaklenec et al., 2008). IGF-I and TGF-β1 were sequentially released from the PLGA microsphere-based scaffolds by a combination of burst release and delayed release. Fabricating scaffolds in the presence of bioactive agents is an effective method to include diffusible factors in biomaterials.

Another method for loading a biomaterial is to add the bioactive agent after the matrix has already been formed, such as by soaking a matrix in the agent solution. This method is frequently utilized for loading collagen scaffolds. An absorbable, macroporous collagen sponge soaked in a recombinant human bone morphogenic protein (BMP) solution increased the osteoinductive activity of the material (Uludag et al., 1999). To promote cartilage formation, collagen sponges were soaked in bFGF. They induced tissue regeneration at 1 week and mature chondrocytes at 4 weeks postimplantation, whereas sponges without bFGF did not show significant cartilage regeneration (Fujisato et al., 1996). These studies suggest that growth factor release can be a potent stimulator of tissue regeneration.

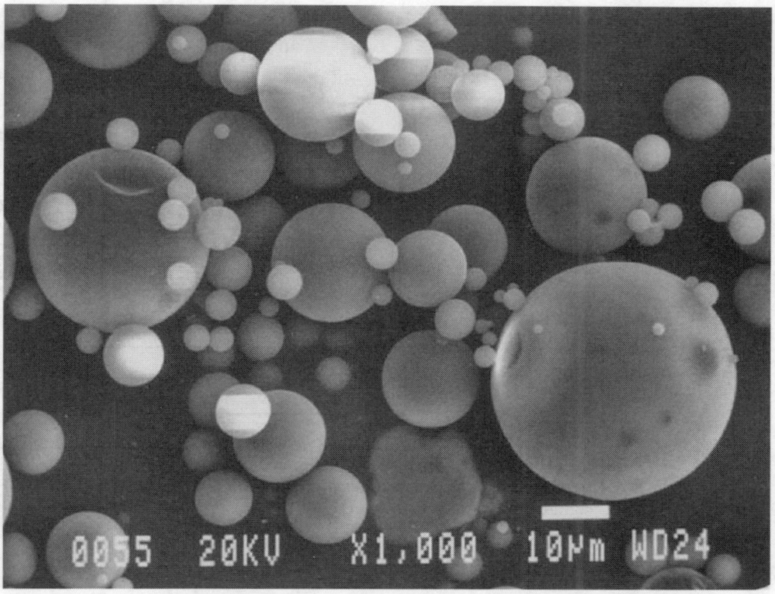

FIGURE 21.4 Scanning electron microscope image of PLGA microspheres of various sizes. After microsphere fabrication, sieves can be used to select a specific size range (bar = 10 μm). (*Courtesy of J. Gao, Ph.D.*)

The release of angiogenic factors to encourage neovascularization allows for increased tissue survival. Methods to support this facet of tissue regeneration have included the slow release of angiogenic factors such as VEGF (Eiselt et al., 1998). PLGA foam scaffolds fabricated to release VEGF have been shown to increase the proliferation of human dermal microvascular endothelial cells as compared to scaffolds without VEGF (Murphy et al., 2000). Thus, various aspects of regeneration can be enhanced by appropriately selecting the material and the bioactive agent to be released.

Scaffold-Drug Delivery: Two-Component System. An assortment of drug-delivery systems is available and can be incorporated into a scaffold for tissue regeneration. The two-component method of delivering agents is particularly useful for biomaterials that cannot be loaded with agents by the previously described methods or are not capable of providing adequate slow release. One designated delivery system is the PLGA microsphere system (Fig. 21.4). As loaded microspheres degrade, they release the particles trapped within and provide the diffusible agent. PLGA microspheres loaded with heparin, known for its antiproliferative and anticoagulate activity, were embedded in alginate films. These films were then wrapped around vein grafts and denuded carotid arteries in rats and shown to reduce intimal hyperplasia as compared to control films without heparin (Edelman et al., 2000). PLGA microspheres have also been loaded with VEGF for human dermal microvascular endothelial cells (Eiselt et al., 1998). BSA-encapsulated PLGA microspheres were incorporated in nerve guidance channels (NGCs), and BSA was released from microsphere-loaded NGCs for 84 days and EGF was released for 56 days (Goraltchouk et al., 2006). To promote angiogenesis, gelatin microspheres were loaded with bFGF and incorporated into an artificial dermis consisting of an outer silicone layer and an inner collagen sponge layer. Implants with the bFGF-loaded microspheres were shown to accelerate fibroblast proliferation and capillary formation in vivo (Kawai et al., 2000).

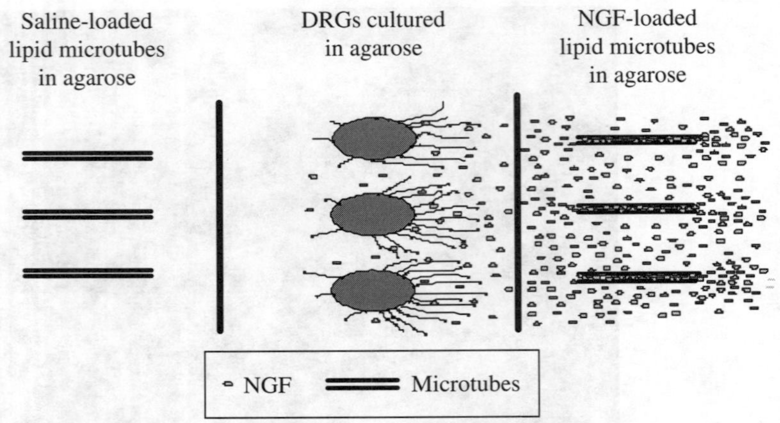

FIGURE 21.5 Schematic of directional neurite extension from chick DRGs in a 3D agarose hydrogel culture. NGF concentration gradients were established by the lipid microtube delivery system, and neurite extension was directed preferentially toward the NGF-loaded microtubes (diagram not to scale).

Another delivery system used to provide chemical gradients is the lipid microtube delivery system (Meilander et al., 2001). Lipid microtubes are hollow tubes that can be loaded with a bioactive agent and embedded into the biomaterial. Due to the concentration gradient between the tubes and the external environment, the agent is released. Lipid microtubes loaded with nerve growth factor (NGF) and incorporated into agarose hydrogels have been shown to directionally stimulate neurite extension from 3D cultures of chick embryonic DRGs (Yu et al., 1999), as depicted in Fig. 21.5. There are also examples of combination of immobilized and diffusible signals. For sciatic nerve regeneration across a challenging 20 mm gap, nerve-growth-factor-loaded lipid microtubes were mixed into agarose-hydrogel-scaffold-containing gradients of photoimmobilized laminin (Dodla et al., 2008). Animals treated with scaffolds-containing gradients of both NGF and laminin showed higher density of axons and better functional recovery. These studies demonstrate that a specialized delivery system is an effective means to provide a diffusible biochemical signal within a scaffold.

Gene-Delivery Scaffolds. Gene therapy can also provide a biochemical component to promote tissue regeneration. Instead of releasing a protein, the gene for that protein can be released to transduce cells for local protein synthesis. This is especially useful for sensitive proteins with short in vivo half-lives. One application that has benefited from gene delivery is wound healing. Gas-foamed PLGA matrices loaded with plasmid DNA encoding PDGF-B increased the formation of granulation tissue and vascularization following subcutaneous implantation in rodents (Shea et al., 1999). Likewise, collagen matrices containing adenoviral or plasmid DNA for PDGF-A or PDGF-B increased granulation tissue, reepithelialization, and neovascularization, resulting in accelerated wound healing (Chandler et al., 2000).

Gene delivery has also been used to enhance bone regeneration in vivo. An adenovirus encoding bone morphogenic protein-7 (BMP-7) was mixed with a collagen carrier and implanted in mice to produce ectopic formation of cortical and trabecular bone with a marrow cavity after 4 weeks (Franceschi et al., 2000). Similarly, plasmid DNA encoding a fragment of parathyroid hormone (PTH) was incorporated in a collagen gel to reproducibly promote bone regeneration in a canine model of bone injury. Since the DNA was shown to be incapable of diffusing out of the initial form of the gel, the DNA remained localized at the injury site until cells arrived and degraded the collagen matrix (Bonadio et al., 1999).

To test the effects of using two plasmids simultaneously, collagen sponges were soaked in a solution of plasmid DNA encoding either the osteoinductive bone morphogenic protein-4 (BMP-4), a fragment of PTH, or both BMP-4 and the PTH fragment. The loaded sponges were implanted in critical defects in the femoral diaphysis of adult rats. Defects with either the BMP-4 or PTH fragment plasmid healed completely and demonstrated the same mechanical strength as the unoperated femur. Moreover, combination gene therapy, with a collagen sponge containing plasmid DNA encoding both BMP-4 and the PTH fragment, was found to further enhance bone regeneration (Fang et al., 1996).

As these examples illustrate, gene therapy is a useful method to stimulate tissue regeneration, especially with the use of multiple genes. Advances in the field of gene therapy will extend the use of this promising technique to a variety of tissue-regeneration applications.

21.3.3 Presentation of a Living Component

A more recent approach to enhance the regenerative effort incorporates cells into tissue-engineered biomaterials. Rather than relying entirely on the migration of host cells into the implant, cells can be seeded in the biomaterial. Differentiated cells, as well as stem cells, are being used for regenerative therapies. In addition, cells can be used in combination with other biochemical therapies to further enhance regeneration.

Cell Seeding. The seeding density of cells on the implanted material can be adjusted for each application. It was shown that the final cell concentration of smooth muscle cells on PGA fiber matrices was proportional to the seeding density (Kim et al., 1998). Likewise, the osteogenic activity of stromal osteoblasts cultured on 3D PLGA foams was found to be dependent on the seeding density of the cells (Ishaug et al., 1997). An appropriate seeding density can be chosen based on the rate of implanted cell proliferation and host tissue proliferation. An implant with a low density of cells allows for the proliferation and migration of both implanted and host cells. If the cellular density on the implant is similar to that of the tissue in vivo, minimal proliferation of the host tissue is necessary. This could be useful in tissues, such as central nervous system tissue, that only have minimal regenerative capacity. In addition, the seeding method affects the cell distribution. Dynamic seeding methods result in a larger number of adherent cells as well as a more uniform distribution of the cells (Kim et al., 1998). Accordingly, the effective use of cells to stimulate tissue regeneration will involve choosing an appropriate cell seeding density and method.

Differentiated Cell-Scaffold Systems. A number of differentiated cell types have been used to aid in the regeneration of tissue in vivo. Endothelial cells are often included for vascular tissue regeneration or for neovascularization of scaffolds. Endothelial cells were perivascularly transplanted in Gelfoam matrices around balloon-denuded rat carotid arteries to control the tissue healing response and reduce intimal hyperplasia (Nathan et al., 1995). Endothelial cells have also been used in the sodding of expanded polytetrafluoroethylene (ePTFE) vascular grafts to enhance the regeneration of an endothelial cell lining in a rat aortic graft model (Ahlswede and Williams, 1994). Endothelial cells and vascular myofibroblasts were seeded onto polyglycolic-acid/poly-4-hydroxybutyrate copolymers to create small diameter vascular grafts (Hoerstrup et al., 2001). To improve scaffold vascularization, endothelial cells and dermal fibroblasts were added to a skin equivalent consisting of a chitosan-linked collagen-GAG sponge with keratinocytes. The endothelial cells and fibroblasts promoted the formation of a network of capillarylike structures in vitro and may serve as a framework to facilitate vascularization upon implantation (Black et al., 1998). Other studies have incorporated fibroblasts on spongy collagen to aid in the healing of skin defects (Kuroyanagi et al., 2001), chondrocytes in fibrin glues to result in actively proliferating and ECM-producing cells (Sims et al., 1998), keratinocytes on collagen-coated dextran microcarriers to reconstitute epithelium (Voigt et al., 1999), and hepatocytes on polyanhydrides, polyorthoesters, or PLGA fibers for possible liver regeneration (Vacanti et al., 1988). These studies suggest that numerous cell types have the potential to provide a living component in biomaterials.

Scaffold Prevascularization. Vascularization is important in implants seeded with cells because these cells will immediately require a source of nourishment, most likely via the bloodstream. Also, regenerated tissue into the implant needs to maintain initial volume. One of the approaches to improve vascularization of implant is prevascularization of scaffolds before cell seeding. One approach to ensure an adequate vascular supply when cells are implanted is to implant a cell-free scaffold to allow for fibrovascular tissue ingrowth prior to seeding the cells. Using a PVA foam, the timing of in vivo fibrovascular tissue formation was determined. It was concluded that cells should be seeded into the material as soon as the fibrovascular tissue has reached all the way to the center of the implant (Wake et al., 1995). A similar method implanted an encapsulation chamber prior to adding the cells with the intent of increasing vasculature around the chamber, since normal wound healing results in vessel regression during the second week. Cellulose membranes with 8-μm pores were able to increase the vascularization of the fibrous capsule that surrounded the membrane beyond 2 weeks, allowing for a sustained vascular supply (Padera and Colton, 1996). Such methods may provide improved local vascularization and mass transport at the time of cell implantation. However, these strategies may have limited application since they require two implantation procedures, one for the scaffold and one for the cells. Therefore, recently other approaches were used more widely. Several angiogenic growth factors such as VEGF, bFGF, and hepatocyte growth factor (HGF) can be used or endothelial cells can be incorporated with other cells to bioengineer the implant.

Cell-Scaffold Constructs for Neuroregeneration. Neurodegenerative diseases are prime candidates for cell therapy approaches to tissue regeneration. One disease that has received considerable attention for cell therapy approaches is Parkinson's disease (PD). In one study, rat adrenal chromaffin cells (ACC) were seeded on collagen-coated dextran or glass beads and injected into the brains of hemiparkinsonian rats. These animals showed significant behavioral recovery over the 12-month study. Animals receiving only the ACC without the microcarriers showed improvement at 1 month but reverted to the original diseased state by 2 months, demonstrating that the scaffold was necessary for prolonged treatment and recovery (Borlongan et al., 1998; Cherksey et al., 1996). Bovine chromaffin cells have also been used to treat hemiparkinsonian rats. Using alginate-polylysine-alginate as a microencapsulator, the cells were implanted in hemiparkinsonian rats and shown to decrease apomorphine-induced rotation (Xue et al., 2001). Likewise, human and rat fetal ventral mesencephalon cells have also been seeded onto collagen-coated dextran microcarriers as a possible treatment for Parkinson's disease. The cells had an increased survival when attached to the microcarriers versus cell suspensions (Saporta et al., 1997). To supply dopamine, PC12 cells capable of secreting dopamine were encapsulated in agarose/poly(styrene sulfonic acid) and grafted into the corpus striatum of guinea pigs. The cells were stained with a tyrosine hydroxylase antibody, suggesting that they continued to secrete dopamine in the brain. In addition, there was no immunological rejection or tumor formation when the biomaterial was used (Date et al., 1996).

Cell therapy also has potential to treat Alzheimer's disease. In one such effort, baby hamster kidney cells were genetically engineered to overexpress NGF. They were then mixed with vitrogen and infused into poly(acrylonitrile-co-vinyl chloride) copolymers (PAN/PVC) to reduce the degeneration of basal forebrain cholinergic neurons (Emerich et al., 1994). These findings regarding Parkinson's disease and Alzheimer's disease suggest that biomaterials, either as a scaffold or as a means of encapsulation, play an important role when using cells as a treatment for neurodegenerative diseases.

Combination Therapy. In vivo, cells interpret and react to numerous signals simultaneously. Taking advantage of this ability, multiple biochemical cues, such as a combination of cell therapy and growth factor delivery, can be provided for tissue regeneration. Combination strategies can be applied for cultured skin substitutes. Fibroblasts and keratinocytes were grafted on to full-thickness wounds to provide epidermal and dermal components. By adding bFGF-encapsulated gelatin microspheres, neovascularization was significantly accelerated, and epidermal thickness, dermal thickness, and cellular components were increased (Tsuji-Saso et al., 2007). Growth factors that encourage neovascularization can also be included with the cells. In one such approach, murine myoblasts were cultured in 3D scaffolds of Matrigel containing either bFGF or hepatocyte growth factor to promote angiogenesis. When the scaffolds were implanted in a model of ectopic muscle regeneration, the presence of the growth factors increased angiogenesis, resulting in improved cell viability and enhanced myogenesis (Barbero et al., 2001).

Gene therapy and cell therapy have been combined to result in murine stromal cells transduced to produce BMP-2. The cells were seeded on a PLGA-HA matrix and found to induce heterotopic bone regeneration (Laurencin et al., 2001). In another study, fibroblasts engineered to express neurotrophic factors were seeded onto poly *N*-(2-hydroxypropyl)-methacrylamide hydrogels with RGD-containing peptides. This therapy, incorporating cells, DNA, and adhesive peptides into one material, was shown to enhance optic nerve regeneration. In addition, when the cells produced two neurotrophic factors, axonal growth into the hydrogels was greater than with either growth factor alone (Loh et al., 2001). One study showed gene delivery incorporated into nanofibrous scaffolds (Liang et al., 2005). Plasmid DNA encoding β-galactosidase was condensed into globules and encapsulated by triblock copolymer, PLA-PEG-PLA. The solution mixture of DNA encapsulated nanoparticles and PLGA was formed into a nanofibrous scaffold by electrospinning, and the bioactive plasmid DNA was released from the scaffold in a controlled manner by degradation of the PLGA scaffold. Cells were transfected in vitro, and the PLGA nanofibrous scaffold supported cell adhesion. Recently, many studies have developed treatments combining more than two factors. These examples illustrate the positive regenerative effects when a biomaterial is designed to utilize several parameters in concert.

Stem Cell–Scaffold Systems. Stem cells, also known as progenitor cells, are pluripotent cells with the ability to differentiate into a variety of cell types. The most widely studied stem cell is the mesenchymal stem cell (MSC) derived from bone marrow. In the embryo, these cells give rise to skeletal tissues, including bone, cartilage, tendon, ligament, marrow stroma, adipocytes, dermis, muscle, and connective tissue (Caplan, 1991).

Mesenchymal stem cells are relevant for tissue regeneration because of their ability to differentiate, a trait they share with many cells that facilitate tissue repair in vivo. Harnessing this capability by combining MSCs, biomaterials, and the appropriate cues for differentiation should allow for the regeneration of the skeletal tissues mentioned above. A composite matrix of gelatin and esterified hyaluronic acid matrix seeded with MSCs enabled osteochondrogenic cell differentiation when implanted subcutaneously in mice (Angele et al., 1999). Similarly, MSCs were harvested from rabbit bone marrow and seeded on a hyaluronan-based 3D scaffold to fill an osteochondral defect in rabbits. While the plain scaffold was able to enhance osteochondral repair, the morphology of the repair improved when progenitor cells were included (Radice et al., 2000). For cartilage regeneration, MSCs were seeded onto collagen sponges and shown to augment meniscus cartilage regeneration in rabbits (Walsh et al., 1999). Another study demonstrated the effectiveness of MSCs for bone regeneration. MSCs were seeded onto coral scaffolds and implanted in a bone defect in sheep. The MSC scaffolds were more likely to develop into new cortical bone with a medullary canal for clinical union than the coral scaffold alone (Petite et al., 2000). MSCs have also been suspended in collagen gels and implanted into tendon defects to improve tendon regeneration and biomechanical properties (Awad et al., 1999; Young et al., 1998). These studies with MSCs are just beginning to realize the potential of stem cells as tools for tissue regeneration.

As a combination therapy, stem cells were used in conjunction with gene therapy to further enhance regeneration. Human bone marrow–derived mesenchymal stem cells were infected with an adenovirus containing the BMP-2 gene, cultured on a collagen matrix, and transplanted in murine radial defects. Unlike the sham-infected MSCs, BMP-2–infected MSCs were able to differentiate into chondrocytes in vivo, regenerate bone, and bridge the radial gap (Turgeman et al., 2001). Genetically engineered pluripotent mesenchymal cells expressing BMP-2 were compared to a nonprogenitor cell line also genetically engineering to express BMP-2. The cells were seeded onto collagen sponges and transplanted into a bone defect in mice. Even though the nonprogenitor cells had a much higher BMP-2 expression in vitro, they showed no organized bone formation in vivo (Gazit et al., 1999). In a similar model, dextran-spermine cationic polysaccharide was used as a nonviral gene carrier of plasmid DNA of BMP-2 for MSC. MSCs were seeded into 3D collagen sponges reinforced by PGA fibers and 2D culture system and cationized dextran-plasmid DNA was added to the scaffold (Hosseinkhani et al., 2006). The BMP-2 expression level was significantly higher in 3D collagen-PGA scaffold than in

2D culture. Again, materials designed with more than one factor to enhance regeneration proved superior to single-factor designs.

Commercial Cell-Based Tissue Engineered Products. Tissue-engineering products containing cells are beginning to appear on the commercial market. Apligraf, a bilayered product developed and manufactured by Organogenesis (Canton, MA) and marketed by Novartis Pharmaceuticals Corporation (East Hanover, NJ), is composed of neonatal-derived dermal fibroblasts, keratinocytes, and bovine collagen. It has been approved for the treatment of venous ulcers in the United States (Eaglstein et al., 1999). Carticel from Genzyme (Cambridge, MA) consists of healthy autologous chondrocytes that are harvested, proliferated in vitro, and implanted into sites of injured cartilage to improve the tissue. Dermagraft (Dermagraft), a human fibroblast–derived dermal substitute on a resorbable substrate, received FDA approval, and Epicel (Genzyme Biosurgery, Cambridge, MA) which is a sheet of autologous keratinocytes to replace the epidermal is used in Europe and was also approved by the FDA in October, 2007. There are more commercially available treatments such as Transcyte (temporary skin substitute; Smith & Nephew), Integra (dermal regeneration template; Intergra), and Alloderm (acellular dermal matrix; Lifecell), and many other tissue regeneration products are currently used in clinical trials.

21.4 CONCLUSIONS

Tissue regeneration allows for the development of self-renewing, responsive tissue that can remodel itself and its matrix. A number of methods to encourage tissue regeneration are currently available, most of which place the host tissue in the primary role and the biomaterial in a supportive role, mimicking permissive in vivo environments. Since a barrage of structural and biochemical cues orchestrate tissue regeneration in vivo, the design of biomaterials for tissue regeneration must progress to include a combination of design parameters described previously. As the knowledge of cell and molecular biology, materials, and bioactive agents continue to advance, more parameter combinations and new therapeutic approaches will be discovered, and the effectiveness of biomaterials designed for tissue regeneration will undoubtedly improve and extend to a variety of organs.

ACKNOWLEDGMENTS

The authors wish to thank Prof. Jinming Gao (Case Western Reserve University, Cleveland OH), Prof. Christine Schmidt (University of Texas at Austin, Austin TX) for their generous contributions to the figures in the chapter, Michael Tanenbaum for his editorial assistance, and funding from NIH R01 NS44409, NSF CBET0651716, NSF EEC9731643, the Georgia Cancer Coalition, and the Nora L. Redman Fund.

REFERENCES

Adams DN, Kao EY, Hypolite CL, Distefano MD, Hu WS, Letourneau PC. Growth cones turn and migrate up an immobilized gradient of the laminin IKVAV peptide. *J Neurobiol* 2005;**62**(1):134–147.

Aebischer P, Guénard V, Valentini RF. The morphology of regenerating peripheral nerves is modulated by the surface microgeometry of polymeric guidance channels. *Brain Res* 1990;**531**(1–2):211–218.

Agrawal CM, McKinney JS, Lanctot D, Athanasiou KA. Effects of fluid flow on the in vitro degradation kinetics of biodegradable scaffolds for tissue engineering. *Biomaterials* 2000;**21**(23):2443–2452.

Ahlswede KM, Williams SK. Microvascular endothelial cell sodding of 1-mm expanded polytetrafluoroethylene vascular grafts. *Arterioscler Thromb Vasc Biol* 1994;**14**(1):25–31.

Alcantar NA, Aydil ES, Israelachvili JN. Polyethylene glycol-coated biocompatible surfaces. *J Biomed Mater Res* 2000;**51**(3):343–351.

Angele P, Kujat R, Nerlich M, Yoo J, Goldberg V, Johnstone B. Engineering of osteochondral tissue with bone marrow mesenchymal progenitor cells in a derivatized hyaluronan-gelatin composite sponge. *Tissue Eng* 1999;**5**(6):545–554.

Attawia MA, Herbert KM, Laurencin CT. Osteoblast-like cell adherance and migration through 3-dimensional porous polymer matrices. *Biochem Biophys Res Commun* 1995;**213**(2):639–644.

Awad HA, Butler DL, Boivin GP, Smith FN, Malaviya P, Huibregtse B, Caplan AI. Autologous mesenchymal stem cell-mediated repair of tendon. *Tissue Eng* 1999;**5**(3):267–277.

Balgude AP, Yu X, Szymanski A, Bellamkonda RV. Agarose gel stiffness determines rate of DRG neurite extension in 3D cultures. *Biomaterials* 2001 May;**22**(10):1077–1084

Barber FA, Elrod BF, McGuire DA, Paulos LE. Bioscrew fixation of patellar tendon autografts. *Biomaterials* 2000;**21**(24):2623–2629.

Barbero A, Benelli R, Minghelli S, Tosetti F, Dorcaratto A, Ponzetto C, Wernig A, Cullen MJ, Albini A, Noonan DM. Growth factor supplemented matrigel improves ectopic skeletal muscle formation—a cell therapy approach. *J Cell Physiol* 2001;**186**(2):183–192.

Bellamkonda R, Ranieri JP, Bouche N, Aebischer P. Hydrogel-based three-dimensional matrix for neural cells. *J Biomed Mater Res* 1995;**29**(5):663–671.

Black AF, Berthod F, L'Heureux N, Germain L, Auger FA. In vitro reconstruction of a human capillary-like network in a tissue-engineered skin equivalent. *Faseb J* 1998;**12**(13):1331–1340.

Bonadio J, Smiley E, Patil P, Goldstein S. Localized, direct plasmid gene delivery in vivo: prolonged therapy results in reproducible tissue regeneration. *Nat Med* 1999;**5**(7):753–759.

Borlongan CV, Saporta S, Sanberg PR. Intrastriatal transplantation of rat adrenal chromaffin cells seeded on microcarrier beads promote long-term functional recovery in hemiparkinsonian rats. *Exp Neurol* 1998;**151**(2):203–214.

Bos GW, Scharenborg NM, Poot AA, Engbers GH, Beugeling T, van Aken WG, Feijen J. Proliferation of endothelial cells on surface-immobilized albumin-heparin conjugate loaded with basic fibroblast growth factor. *J Biomed Mater Res* 1999;**44**(3):330–340.

Burkoth AK, Burdick J, Anseth KS. Surface and bulk modifications to photocrosslinked polyanhydrides to control degradation behavior. *J Biomed Mater Res* 2000;**51**(3):352–359.

Buschmann MD, Gluzband YA, Grodzinsky AJ, Hunziker EB. Mechanical compression modulates matrix biosynthesis in chondrocyte/agarose culture. *J Cell Sci* 1995;**108**(Pt 4):1497–1508.

Butler CE, Navarro FA, Orgill DP. Reduction of abdominal adhesions using composite collagen-GAG implants for ventral hernia repair. *J Biomed Mater Res* 2001;**58**(1):75–80.

Caplan AI. Mesenchymal stem cells. *J Orthop Res* 1991;**9**(5):641–650.

Chandler LA, Gu DL, Ma C, Gonzalez AM, Doukas J, Nguyen T, Pierce GF, Phillips ML. Matrix-enabled gene transfer for cutaneous wound repair. *Wound Repair Regen* 2000;**8**(6):473–479.

Chang SJ, Kuo SM, Lan JW, Wang YJ. Amination of polycarbonate surface and its application for cell attachment. *Artif Cells Blood Substit Immobil Biotechnol* 1999;**27**(3):229–244.

Chen Y, T Mak A, Wang M, Li J. Biomimetic coating of apatite/collagen composite on poly L-lactic acid facilitates cell seeding. *Conf Proc IEEE Eng Med Biol Soc* 2005;**4**:4087–4090.

Cheng H, Huang YC, Chang PT, Huang YY. Laminin-incorporated nerve conduits made by plasma treatment for repairing spinal cord injury. *Biochem Biophys Res Commun* 2007;**357**(4):938–944.

Cherksey BD, Sapirstein VS, Geraci AL. Adrenal chromaffin cells on microcarriers exhibit enhanced long-term functional effects when implanted into the mammalian brain. *Neuroscience* 1996;**75**(2):657–664.

Chu CR, Monosov AZ, Amiel D. In situ assessment of cell viability within biodegradable polylactic acid polymer matrices. *Biomaterials* 1995;**16**(18):1381–1384.

Chvatal SA, Kim YT, Bratt-Leal AM, Lee H, Bellamkonda RV. Spatial distribution and acute anti-inflammatory effects of methylprednisolone after sustained local delivery to the contused spinal cord. *Biomaterials* 2008;**29**(12):1967–1975.

Clark P, Connolly P, Curtis AS, Dow JA, Wilkinson CD. Cell guidance by ultrafine topography in vitro. *J Cell Sci* 1991;**99**(Pt 1):73–77.

Clark P, Connolly P, Curtis AS, Dow JA, Wilkinson CD. Topographical control of cell behaviour: II. Multiple grooved substrata. *Development* 1990;**108**(4):635–644.

Collier JH, Camp JP, Hudson TW, Schmidt CE. Synthesis and characterization of polypyrrole-hyaluronic acid composite biomaterials for tissue engineering applications. *J Biomed Mater Res* 2000;**50**(4):574–584.

Cooper ML, Hansbrough JF, Polarek JW. The effect of an arginine-glycine-aspartic acid peptide and hyaluronate synthetic matrix on epithelialization of meshed skin graft interstices. *J Burn Care Rehabil* 1996;**17**(2):108–116.

Corey JM, Lin DY, Mycek KB, Chen Q, Samuel S, Feldman EL, Martin DC. Aligned electrospun nanofibers specify the direction of dorsal root ganglia neurite growth. *J Biomed Mater Res A* 2007;**83**(3):636–645

Culp LA, O'Conner KL, Lechner R. Extracellular matrix adhesion: biological, molecular, and pathogenic mechanisms. In: Bittar EE, Bittar N, eds. Principles of Medical Biology: JAI Press, Inc., 1997:573–607.

Date I, Miyoshi Y, Ono T, Imaoka T, Furuta T, Asari S, Ohmoto T, Iwata H. Preliminary report of polymer-encapsulated dopamine-secreting cell grafting into the brain. *Cell Transplant* 1996;**5**(5 Suppl 1):S17–S19.

Desai NP, Hubbell JA. Biological responses to polyethylene oxide modified polyethylene terephthalate surfaces. *J Biomed Mater Res* 1991;**25**(7):829–843.

Devin JE, Attawia MA, Laurencin CT. Three-dimensional degradable porous polymer-ceramic matrices for use in bone repair. *J Biomater Sci Polym Ed* 1996;**7**(8):661–669.

Dillon GP, Yu X, Bellamkonda RV. The polarity and magnitude of ambient charge influences three-dimensional neurite extension from DRGs. *J Biomed Mater Res* 2000;**51**(3):510–519.

Dillon GP, Yu X, Sridharan A, Ranieri JP, Bellamkonda RV. The influence of physical structure and charge on neurite extension in a 3D hydrogel scaffold. *J Biomater Sci Polym Ed* 1998;**9**(10):1049–1069.

Dodla MC, Bellamkonda RV. Anisotropic scaffolds facilitate enhanced neurite extension in vitro. *J Biomed Mater Res A* 2006;**78**(2):213–221.

Dodla MC, Bellamkonda RV. Differences between the effect of anisotropic and isotropic laminin and nerve growth factor presenting scaffolds on nerve regeneration across long peripheral nerve gaps. *Biomaterials* 2008;**29**(1):33–46.

Eaglstein WH, Alvarez OM, Auletta M, Leffel D, Rogers GS, Zitelli JA, Norris JE, Thomas I, Irondo M, Fewkes J, Hardin-Young J, Duff RG, Sabolinski ML. Acute excisional wounds treated with a tissue-engineered skin (Apligraf). *Dermatol Surg* 1999;**25**(3):195–201.

Edelman ER, Nathan A, Katada M, Gates J, Karnovsky MJ. Perivascular graft heparin delivery using biodegradable polymer wraps. *Biomaterials* 2000;**21**(22):2279–2286.

Eiselt P, Kim BS, Chacko B, Isenberg B, Peters MC, Greene KG, Roland WD, Loebsack AB, Burg KJ, Culberson C, Halberstadt CR, Holder WD, Mooney DJ. Development of technologies aiding large-tissue engineering. *Biotechnol Prog* 1998;**14**(1):134–140.

Elder SH, Goldstein SA, Kimura JH, Soslowsky LJ, Spengler DM. Chondrocyte differentiation is modulated by frequency and duration of cyclic compressive loading. *Ann Biomed Eng* 2001;**29**(6):476–482.

Elder SH, Kimura JH, Soslowsky LJ, Lavagnino M, Goldstein SA. Effect of compressive loading on chondrocyte differentiation in agarose cultures of chick limb-bud cells. *J Orthop Res* 2000;**18**(1):78–86.

El-Ghannam AR, Ducheyne P, Risbud M, Adams CS, Shapiro IM, Castner D, Golledge S, Composto RJ. Model surfaces engineered with nanoscale roughness and RGD tripeptides promote osteoblast activity. *J Biomed Mater Res A* 2004;**68**(4):615–627.

Emerich DF, Winn SR, Harper J, Hammang JP, Baetge EE, Kordower JH. Implants of polymer-encapsulated human NGF-secreting cells in the nonhuman primate: rescue and sprouting of degenerating cholinergic basal forebrain neurons. *J Comp Neurol* 1994;**349**(1):148–164.

Evans GR, Brandt K, Widmer MS, Lu L, Meszlenyi RK, Gupta PK, Mikos AG, Hodges J, Williams J, Gurlek A, Nabawi A, Lohman R, Patrick CW, Jr. In vivo evaluation of poly(L-actic acid) porous conduits for peripheral nerve regeneration. *Biomaterials* 1999a;**20**(12):1109–1115.

Evans MD, Dalton BA, Steele JG. Persistent adhesion of epithelial tissue is sensitive to polymer topography. *J Biomed Mater Res* 1999b;**46**(4):485–493.

Fang J, Zhu YY, Smiley E, Bonadio J, Rouleau JP, Goldstein SA, McCauley LK, Davidson BL, Roessler BJ. Stimulation of new bone formation by direct transfer of osteogenic plasmid genes. *Proc Natl Acad Sci U S A* 1996;**93**(12):5753–5758.

Fassett J, Tobolt D, Hansen LK. Type I collagen structure regulates cell morphology and EGF signaling in primary rat hepatocytes through cAMP-dependent protein kinase A. *Curr Top Dev Biol* 2006;**72**:205–236.

Feinberg AW, Feigel A, Shevkoplyas SS, Sheehy S, Whitesides GM, Parker KK. Muscular thin films for building actuators and powering devices. *Science* 2007;**317**(5843):1366–1370.

Fields GB, Lauer JL, Dori Y, Forns P, Yu YC, Tirrell M. Protein-like molecular architecture: biomaterial applications for inducing cellular receptor binding and signal transduction. *Biopolymers* 1998;**47**(2): 143-151.

Fine EG, Valentini RF, Bellamkonda R, Aebischer P. Improved nerve regeneration through piezoelectric vinylidenefluoride-trifluoroethylene copolymer guidance channels. *Biomaterials* 1991;**12**(8):775–780.

Folkman J, Hochberg M. Self-regulation of growth in three dimensions. *J Exp Med* 1973;**138**(4):745–753.

Franceschi RT, Wang D, Krebsbach PH, Rutherford RB. Gene therapy for bone formation: in vitro and in vivo osteogenic activity of an adenovirus expressing BMP7. *J Cell Biochem* 2000;**78**(3):476–486.

Frayssinet P, Mathon D, Lerch A, Autefage A, Collard P, Rouquet N. Osseointegration of composite calcium phosphate bioceramics. *J Biomed Mater Res* 2000;**50**(2):125–130.

Frondoza C, Sohrabi A, Hungerford D. Human chondrocytes proliferate and produce matrix components in microcarrier suspension culture. *Biomaterials* 1996;**17**(9):879–888.

Fujisato T, Sajiki T, Liu Q, Ikada Y. Effect of basic fibroblast growth factor on cartilage regeneration in chondrocyte-seeded collagen sponge scaffold. *Biomaterials* 1996;**17**(2):155–162.

Furukawa T, Matsusue Y, Yasunaga T, Nakagawa Y, Okada Y, Shikinami Y, Okuno M, Nakamura T. Histomorphometric study on high-strength hydroxyapatite/poly(L-lactide) composite rods for internal fixation of bone fractures. *J Biomed Mater Res* 2000;**50**(3):410–419.

Gazit D, Turgeman G, Kelley P, Wang E, Jalenak M, Zilberman Y, Moutsatsos I. Engineered pluripotent mesenchymal cells integrate and differentiate in regenerating bone: a novel cell-mediated gene therapy. *J Gene Med* 1999;**1**(2):121–133.

Giardino R, Fini M, Nicoli Aldini N, Giavaresi G, Rocca M. Polylactide bioabsorbable polymers for guided tissue regeneration. *J Trauma* 1999;**47**(2):303–308.

Giordano GG, Thomson RC, Ishaug SL, Mikos AG, Cumber S, Garcia CA, Lahiri-Munir D. Retinal pigment epithelium cells cultured on synthetic biodegradable polymers. *J Biomed Mater Res* 1997;**34**(1):87–93.

Gombotz WR, Wang GH, Horbett TA, Hoffman AS. Protein adsorption to poly(ethylene oxide) surfaces. *J Biomed Mater Res* 1991;**25**(12):1547–1562.

Goodman SL, Sims PA, Albrecht RM. Three-dimensional extracellular matrix textured biomaterials. *Biomaterials* 1996;**17**(21):2087–2095.

Goraltchouk A, Scanga V, Morshead CM, Shoichet MS. Incorporation of protein-eluting microspheres into biodegradable nerve guidance channels for controlled release. *J Control Release* 2006;**110**(2):400–407.

Gorodetsky R, Clark RA, An J, Gailit J, Levdansky L, Vexler A, Berman E, Marx G. Fibrin microbeads (FMB) as biodegradable carriers for culturing cells and for accelerating wound heating. *J Invest Dermatol* 1999;**112**(6):866–872.

Gosiewska A, Rezania A, Dhanaraj S, Vyakarnam M, Zhou J, Burtis D, Brown L, Kong W, Zimmerman M, Geesin JC. Development of a three-dimensional transmigration assay for testing cell-polymer interactions for tissue engineering applications. *Tissue Eng* 2001;**7**(3):267–277.

Guénard V, Valentini RF, Aebischer P. Influence of surface texture of polymeric sheets on peripheral nerve regeneration in a two-compartment guidance system. *Biomaterials* 1991;**12**(2):259–263.

Guyton AC, Hall JE. *Textbook of Medical Physiology*. 9th ed. Philadelphia: W.B. Saunders Company, 1996a, 175–176.

Guyton AC, Hall JE. *Textbook of Medical Physiology*. 9th ed. Philadelphia: W.B. Saunders Company, 1996b, 513–523.

Halka AT, Turner NJ, Carter A, Ghosh J, Murphy MO, Kirton JP, Kielty CM, Walker MG. The effects of stretch on vascular smooth muscle cell phenotype in vitro. *Cardiovasc Pathol* 2008;**17**(2):98–102

Hansbrough JF, Herndon DN, Heimbach DM, Solem LD, Gamelli RL, Tompkins RG. Accelerated healing and reduced need for grafting in pediatric patients with burns treated with arginine-glycine-aspartic acid peptide matrix. RGD Study Group. *J Burn Care Rehabil* 1995;**16**(4):377–387.

Hasirci V, Litman AE, Trantolo DJ, Gresser JD, Wise DL, Margolis HC. PLGA bone plates reinforced with crosslinked PPF, *J Mater Sci Mater Med* 2002;**13**(2):159–167.

Hausner T, Schmidhammer R, Zandieh S, Hopf R, Schultz A, Gogolewski S, Hertz H, Redl H. Nerve regeneration using tubular scaffolds from biodegradable polyurethane. *Acta Neurochir Suppl.* 2007;**100**:69–72.

Heijkants RG, van Calck RV, van Tienen TG, de Groot JH, Pennings AJ, Buma P, Veth RP, Schouten AJ. Polyurethane scaffold formation via a combination of salt leaching and thermally induced phase separation. *J Biomed Mater Res A* 2008;**87**(4):921–32.

Hoerstrup SP, Zund G, Sodian R, Schnell AM, Grunenfelder J, Turina MI. Tissue engineering of small caliber vascular grafts. *Eur J Cardiothorac Surg* 2001;**20**(1):164–169.

Holy CE, Shoichet MS, Davies JE. Engineering three-dimensional bone tissue in vitro using biodegradable scaffolds: investigating initial cell-seeding density and culture period. *J Biomed Mater Res* 2000;**51**(3): 376–382.

Holy CE, Yakubovich R. Processing cell-seeded polyester scaffolds for histology. *J Biomed Mater Res* 2000;**50**(2):276–279.

Hosseinkhani H, Azzam T, Kobayashi H, Hiraoka Y, Shimokawa H, Domb AJ, Tabata Y. Combination of 3D tissue engineered scaffold and non-viral gene carrier enhance in vitro DNA expression of mesenchymal stem cells. *Biomaterials* 2006;**27**(23):4269–4278.

Huhtala A, Pohjonen T, Salminen L, Salminen A, Kaarniranta K, Uusitalo H. In vitro biocompatibility of degradable biopolymers in cell line cultures from various ocular tissues: direct contact studies. *J Biomed Mater Res A* 2007;**83**(2):407–413.

Hunter SK, Kao JM, Wang Y, Benda JA, Rodgers VG. Promotion of neovascularization around hollow fiber bioartificial organs using biologically active substances. *Asaio J* 1999;**45**(1):37–40.

Ishaug SL, Crane GM, Miller MJ, Yasko AW, Yaszemski MJ, Mikos AG. Bone formation by three-dimensional stromal osteoblast culture in biodegradable polymer scaffolds. *J Biomed Mater Res* 1997;**36**(1):17–28.

Iuliano DJ, Saavedra SS, Truskey GA. Effect of the conformation and orientation of adsorbed fibronectin on endothelial cell spreading and the strength of adhesion. *J Biomed Mater Res* 1993;**27**(8):1103–1113.

Jaklenec A, Hinckfuss A, Bilgen B, Ciombor DM, Aaron R, Mathiowitz E. Sequential release of bioactive IGF-I and TGF-beta 1 from PLGA microsphere-based scaffolds. *Biomaterials* 2008;**29**(10):1518–1525.

Johansson F, Carlberg P, Danielsen N, Montelius L, Kanje M. Axonal outgrowth on nano-imprinted patterns. *Biomaterials* 2006;**27**(8):1251–1258

Jun IK, Koh YH, Lee SH, Kim HE. Novel hydroxyapatite (HA) dual-scaffold with ultra-high porosity, high surface area, and compressive strength. *J Mater Sci Mater Med* 2007 Jun;**18**(6):1071–1077.

Kawai K, Suzuki S, Tabata Y, Ikada Y, Nishimura Y. Accelerated tissue regeneration through incorporation of basic fibroblast growth factor-impregnated gelatin microspheres into artificial dermis. *Biomaterials* 2000;**21**(5):489–499.

Keely PJ, Conklin MW, Gehler S, Ponik SM, Provenzano PP. Investigating integrin regulation and signaling events in three-dimensional systems. *Methods Enzymol* 2007;**426**:27–45

Khang G, Lee SJ, Lee JH, Kim YS, Lee HB. Interaction of fibroblast cells on poly(lactide-co-glycolide) surface with wettability chemogradient. *Biomed Mater Eng* 1999;**9**(3):179–187.

Kim BS, Putnam AJ, Kulik TJ, Mooney DJ. Optimizing seeding and culture methods to engineer smooth muscle tissue on biodegradable polymer matrices. *Biotechnol Bioeng* 1998;**57**(1):46–54.

Kim YT, Haftel VK, Kumar S, Bellamkonda RV. The role of aligned polymer fiber-based constructs in the bridging of long peripheral nerve gaps. *Biomaterials* 2008;**29**(21):3117–3127

Kouvroukoglou S, Dee KC, Bizios R, McIntire LV, Zygourakis K. Endothelial cell migration on surfaces modified with immobilized adhesive peptides. *Biomaterials* 2000;**21**(17):1725–1733.

Kraehenbuehl TP, Zammaretti P, Van der Vlies AJ, Schoenmakers RG, Lutolf MP, Jaconi ME, Hubbell JA. Three-dimensional extracellular matrix-directed cardioprogenitor differentiation: systematic modulation of a synthetic cell-responsive PEG-hydrogel. *Biomaterials* 2008;**29**(18):2757–2766.

Kuroyanagi Y, Yamada N, Yamashita R, Uchinuma E. Tissue-engineered product: allogeneic cultured dermal substitute composed of spongy collagen with fibroblasts. *Artif Organs* 2001;**25**(3):180–186.

LaFrance ML, Armstrong DW. Novel living skin replacement biotherapy approach for wounded skin tissues. *Tissue Eng* 1999;**5**(2):153–170

Laurencin CT, Attawia MA, Lu LQ, Borden MD, Lu HH, Gorum WJ, Lieberman JR. Poly(lactide-co-glycolide)/hydroxyapatite delivery of BMP-2-producing cells: a regional gene therapy approach to bone regeneration. *Biomaterials* 2001;**22**(11):1271–1277.

Lee DA, Bader DL. Compressive strains at physiological frequencies influence the metabolism of chondrocytes seeded in agarose. *J Orthop Res* 1997;**15**(2):181–188.

Lee H, Bellamkonda RV, Sun W, Levenston ME. Biomechanical analysis of silicon microelectrode-induced strain in the brain. *J Neural Eng* 2005;**2**(4):81–89

Lee M, Wu BM, Dunn JC. Effect of scaffold architecture and pore size on smooth muscle cell growth. *J Biomed Mater Res A* 2008;**87**(4):1010–1016.

Lee SJ, Park YJ, Park SN, Lee YM, Seol YJ, Ku Y, Chung CP. Molded porous poly(L-lactide) membranes for guided bone regeneration with enhanced effects by controlled growth factor release. *J Biomed Mater Res* 2001;**55**(3):295–303.

Leonard DJ, Pick LT, Farrar DF, Dickson GR, Orr JF, Buchanan FJ. The modification of PLA and PLGA using electron-beam radiation. *J Biomed Mater Res A* 2009;**89**(3):567–574.

Liang D, Luu YK, Kim K, Hsiao BS, Hadjiargyrou M, Chu B. In vitro non-viral gene delivery with nanofibrous scaffolds. *Nucleic Acids Res* 2005;**33**(19):e170

Loh NK, Woerly S, Bunt SM, Wilton SD, Harvey AR. The regrowth of axons within tissue defects in the CNS is promoted by implanted hydrogel matrices that contain BDNF and CNTF producing fibroblasts. *Exp Neurol* 2001;**170**(1):72–84.

Lu L, Garcia CA, Mikos AG. Retinal pigment epithelium cell culture on thin biodegradable poly(DL-lactic-co-glycolic acid) films. *J Biomater Sci Polym Ed* 1998;**9**(11):1187–205.

Lundgren AK, Lundgren D, Wennerberg A, Hammerle CH, Nyman S. Influence of surface roughness of barrier walls on guided bone augmentation: experimental study in rabbits. *Clin Implant Dent Relat Res* 1999;**1**(1):41–48.

Lysaght MJ, Nguy NA, Sullivan K. An economic survey of the emerging tissue engineering industry. *Tissue Eng* 1998;**4**(3):231–238.

Lysaght MJ, Reyes J. The growth of tissue engineering. *Tissue Eng* 2001;**7**(5):485–493.

Ma PX, Choi JW. Biodegradable polymer scaffolds with well-defined interconnected spherical pore network. *Tissue Eng* 2001;**7**(1):23–33.

Ma Z, Gao C, Gong Y, Shen J. Cartilage tissue engineering PLLA scaffold with surface immobilized collagen and basic fibroblast growth factor. *Biomaterials* 2005;**26**(11):1253–1259.

Madsen S-K, Mooney DJ. Delivering DNA with polymer matrices: applications in tissue engineering and gene therapy. *Pharmaceut Sci Technol Today* 2000;**3**(11):381–384.

Maheshwari G, Brown G, Lauffenburger DA, Wells A, Griffith LG. Cell adhesion and motility depend on nanoscale RGD clustering. *J Cell Sci* 2000;**113**(Pt 10):1677–1686.

Mann BK, Schmedlen RH, West JL. Tethered-TGF-beta increases extracellular matrix production of vascular smooth muscle cells. *Biomaterials* 2001;**22**(5):439–444.

Mann BK, Tsai AT, Scott-Burden T, West JL. Modification of surfaces with cell adhesion peptides alters extracellular matrix deposition. *Biomaterials* 1999;**20**(23–24):2281–2286.

Maquet V, Martin D, Scholtes F, Franzen R, Schoenen J, Moonen G, Jer me R. Poly(D, L-lactide) foams modified by poly(ethylene oxide)-block-poly(D, L-lactide) copolymers and a-FGF: in vitro and in vivo evaluation for spinal cord regeneration. *Biomaterials* 2001;**22**(10):1137–1146.

Maynard EM, Fernandez E, Normann RA. A technique to prevent dural adhesions to chronically implanted microelectrode arrays. *J Neurosci Methods* 2000;**97**(2):93–101.

McClary KB, Ugarova T, Grainger DW. Modulating fibroblast adhesion, spreading, and proliferation using self-assembled monolayer films of alkylthiolates on gold. *J Biomed Mater Res* 2000;**50**(3):428–439.

McKeehan WL, Ham RG. Stimulation of clonal growth of normal fibroblasts with substrata coated with basic polymers. *J Cell Biol* 1976;**71**(3):727–734.

Meffert RM. Ceramic-coated implant systems. *Adv Dent Res* 1999;**13**:170–172.

Meilander NJ, Pasumarthy MK, Kowalczyk TH, Cooper MJ, Bellamkonda RV. Sustained release of plasmid DNA using lipid microtubules and agarose hydrogel. *J Control Release* 2003;**88**(2):321–331.

Meilander NJ, Yu X, Ziats NP, Bellamkonda RV. Lipid-based microtubular drug delivery vehicles. *J Control Release* 2001;**71**(1):141–152.

Mikos AG, Sarakinos G, Leite SM, Vacanti JP, Langer R. Laminated three-dimensional biodegradable foams for use in tissue engineering. *Biomaterials* 1993;**14**(5):323–330.

Mooney DJ, Organ G, Vacanti JP, Langer R. Design and fabrication of biodegradable polymer devices to engineer tubular tissues. *Cell Transplant* 1994;**3**(2):203–210.

Mooney DJ, Park S, Kaufmann PM, Sano K, McNamara K, Vacanti JP, Langer R. Biodegradable sponges for hepatocyte transplantation. *J Biomed Mater Res* 1995;29(8):959–965.

Murphy WL, Mooney DJ. Controlled delivery of inductive proteins, plasmid DNA and cells from tissue engineering matrices. *J Periodontal Res* 1999;**34**(7):413–419.

Murphy WL, Peters MC, Kohn DH, Mooney DJ. Sustained release of vascular endothelial growth factor from mineralized poly(lactide-co-glycolide) scaffolds for tissue engineering. *Biomaterials* 2000;**21**(24):2521–2527.

Nakayama Y, Ishibashi-Ueda H, Takamizawa K. In vivo tissue-engineered small-caliber arterial graft prosthesis consisting of autologous tissue (biotube). *Cell Transplant* 2004;**13**(4):439–449.

Narayan D, Venkatraman SS. Effect of pore size and interpore distance on endothelial cell growth on polymers. *J Biomed Mater Res A* 2008;**87**(3):710–718.

Nathan A, Nugent MA, Edelman ER. Tissue engineered perivascular endothelial cell implants regulate vascular injury. *Proc Natl Acad Sci U S A* 1995;**92**(18):8130–8134.

Neff JA, Caldwell KD, Tresco PA. A novel method for surface modification to promote cell attachment to hydrophobic substrates. *J Biomed Mater Res* 1998;**40**(4):511–519.

Niklason LE, Gao J, Abbott WM, Hirschi KK, Houser S, Marini R, Langer R. Functional arteries grown in vitro. *Science* 1999;**284**(5413):489–493.

Nikolovski J, Mooney DJ. Smooth muscle cell adhesion to tissue engineering scaffolds. *Biomaterials* 2000;**21**(20):2025–2032.

Padera RF, Colton CK. Time course of membrane microarchitecture-driven neovascularization. *Biomaterials* 1996;**17**(3):277–284.

Palyvoda O, Bordenyuk AN, Yatawara AK, McCullen E, Chen CC, Benderskii AV, Auner GW. Molecular organization in SAMs used for neuronal cell growth. *Langmuir* 2008;**24**(8):4097–4106.

Pankajakshan D, Krishnan VK, Krishnan LK. Vascular tissue generation in response to signaling molecules integrated with a novel poly(epsilon-caprolactone)-fibrin hybrid scaffold. *J Tissue Eng Regen Med* 2007;**1**(5):389–397.

Park YJ, Ku Y, Chung CP, Lee SJ. Controlled release of platelet-derived growth factor from porous poly(L-lactide) membranes for guided tissue regeneration. *J Control Release* 1998;**51**(2–3):201–211.

Park YJ, Lee YM, Park SN, Lee JY, Ku Y, Chung CP, Lee SJ. Enhanced guided bone regeneration by controlled tetracycline release from poly(L-lactide) barrier membranes. *J Biomed Mater Res* 2000;**51**(3):391–397.

Paszek MJ, Zahir N, Johnson KR, Lakins JN, Rozenberg GI, Gefen A, Reinhart-King CA, Margulies SS, Dembo M, Boettiger D, Hammer DA, Weaver VM. Tensional homeostasis and the malignant phenotype. *Cancer Cell* 2005;**8**(3):241–254.

Patel N, Padera R, Sanders GH, Cannizzaro SM, Davies MC, Langer R, Roberts CJ, Tendler SJ, Williams PM, Shakesheff KM. Spatially controlled cell engineering on biodegradable polymer surfaces. *Faseb J* 1998;**12**(14):1447–1454.

Peltola SM, Melchels FP, Grijpma DW, Kellomäki M. A review of rapid prototyping techniques for tissue engineering purposes. *Ann Med* 2008;**40**(4):268–280

Peter SJ, Lu L, Kim DJ, Stamatas GN, Miller MJ, Yaszemski MJ, Mikos AG. Effects of transforming growth factor beta1 released from biodegradable polymer microparticles on marrow stromal osteoblasts cultured on poly(propylene fumarate) substrates. *J Biomed Mater Res* 2000;**50**(3):452–462.

Peter SJ, Miller MJ, Yasko AW, Yaszemski MJ, Mikos AG. Polymer concepts in tissue engineering. *J Biomed Mater Res* 1998a;**43**(4):422–427.

Peter SJ, Miller ST, Zhu G, Yasko AW, Mikos AG. In vivo degradation of a poly(propylene fumarate)/beta-tricalcium phosphate injectable composite scaffold. *J Biomed Mater Res* 1998b;**41**(1):1–7.

Petite H, Viateau V, Bensaid W, Meunier A, de Pollak C, Bourguignon M, Oudina K, Sedel L, Guillemin G. Tissue-engineered bone regeneration. *Nat Biotechnol* 2000;**18**(9):959–963.

Pohlen U, Binnenhei M, Reszka R, Buhr HJ, Berger G. Intra-aortal therapy with 5-fluorouracil- polyethylene glycol stealth liposomes: does the metabolism of 5-fluorouracil into 5-fluoro-2'-deoxyuridine depend on pH value? An animal study in VX-2 liver tumor-bearing rabbits. *Chemotherapy* 2004 Jun;**50**(2):67–75.

Porte-Durrieu MC, Labrugere C, Villars F, Lefebvre F, Dutoya S, Guette A, Bordenave L, Baquey C. Development of RGD peptides grafted onto silica surfaces: XPS characterization and human endothelial cell interactions. *J Biomed Mater Res* 1999;**46**(3):368–375.

Provenzano PP, Eliceiri KW, Campbell JM, Inman DR, White JG, Keely PJ. Collagen reorganization at the tumor-stromal interface facilitates local invasion. *BMC Med* 2006;**4**(1):38

Puleo DA, Kissling RA, Sheu MS. A technique to immobilize bioactive proteins, including bone morphogenetic protein-4 (BMP-4), on titanium alloy. *Biomaterials* 2002;**23**(9):2079–2087.

Radice M, Brun P, Cortivo R, Scapinelli R, Battaliard C, Abatangelo G. Hyaluronan-based biopolymers as delivery vehicles for bone-marrow-derived mesenchymal progenitors. *J Biomed Mater Res* 2000;**50**(2):101–109.

Rajnicek A, Britland S, McCaig C. Contact guidance of CNS neurites on grooved quartz: influence of groove dimensions, neuronal age and cell type. *J Cell Sci* 1997;**110**(Pt 23):2905–2913.

Ranieri JP, Bellamkonda R, Jacob J, Vargo TG, Gardella JA, Aebischer P. Selective neuronal cell attachment to a covalently patterned monoamine on fluorinated ethylene propylene films. *J Biomed Mater Res* 1993;**27**(7):917–925.

Ranucci CS, Moghe PV. Polymer substrate topography actively regulates the multicellular organization and liver-specific functions of cultured hepatocytes. *Tissue Eng* 1999;**5**(5):407–420.

Rashid ST, Salacinski HJ, Button MJ, Fuller B, Hamilton G, Seifalian AM. Cellular engineering of conduits for coronary and lower limb bypass surgery: role of cell attachment peptides and pre-conditioning in optimizing smooth muscle cells (SMC) adherence to compliant poly(carbonate-urea)urethane (MyoLink) scaffolds. *Eur J Vasc Endovasc Surg* 2004;**27**(6):608–616.

Rezania A, Healy KE. Biomimetic peptide surfaces that regulate adhesion, spreading, cytoskeletal organization, and mineralization of the matrix deposited by osteoblast-like cells. *Biotechnol Prog* 1999;**15**(1):19–32.

Rezania A, Healy KE. The effect of peptide surface density on mineralization of a matrix deposited by osteogenic cells. *J Biomed Mater Res* 2000;**52**(4):595–600.

Rowley JA, Madlambayan G, Mooney DJ. Alginate hydrogels as synthetic extracellular matrix materials. *Biomaterials* 1999;**20**(1):45–53.

Rubin AL, Drake MP, Davison PF, Pfahl D, Speakman PT, Schmitt FO. Effects of pepsin treatment on the interaction properties of tropocollagen macromolecules. *Biochemistry* 1965;**4**(2):181–190.

Sah RL, Kim YJ, Doong JY, Grodzinsky AJ, Plaas AH, Sandy JD. Biosynthetic response of cartilage explants to dynamic compression. *J Orthop Res* 1989;**7**(5):619–636.

Saporta S, Borlongan C, Moore J, Mejia-Millan E, Jones SL, Bonness P, Randall TS, Allen RC, Freeman TB, Sanberg PR. Microcarrier enhanced survival of human and rat fetal ventral mesencephalon cells implanted in the rat striatum. *Cell Transplant* 1997;**6**(6):579–584.

Schense JC, Bloch J, Aebischer P, Hubbell JA. Enzymatic incorporation of bioactive peptides into fibrin matrices enhances neurite extension. *Nat Biotechnol* 2000;**18**(4):415–419.

Schmidt CE, Shastri VR, Vacanti JP, Langer R. Stimulation of neurite outgrowth using an electrically conducting polymer. *Proc Natl Acad Sci U S A* 1997;**94**(17):8948–8953.

Schreiber RE, Dunkelman NS, Naughton G, Ratcliffe A. A method for tissue engineering of cartilage by cell seeding on bioresorbable scaffolds. *Ann N Y Acad Sci* 1999;**875**:398–404.

Selden C, Shariat A, McCloskey P, Ryder T, Roberts E, Hodgson H. Three-dimensional in vitro cell culture leads to a marked upregulation of cell function in human hepatocyte cell lines—an important tool for the development of a bioartificial liver machine. *Ann N Y Acad Sci* 1999;**875**:353–363.

Shah S, Solanki K, Gupta MN. Enhancement of lipase activity in non-aqueous media upon immobilization on multi-walled carbon nanotubes. *Chem Cent J* 2007;**1**:30.

Shea LD, Smiley E, Bonadio J, Mooney DJ. DNA delivery from polymer matrices for tissue engineering. *Nat Biotechnol* 1999;**17**(6):551–554.

Shved IuA, Kukhareva LV, Zorin IM, Blinova MI, Bilibin AIu, Pinaev GP. Cultured skin cells interaction with polylactide surface coated by different collagen structures *Tsitologiia* 2007;**49**(1):32–39.

Sims CD, Butler PE, Cao YL, Casanova R, Randolph MA, Black A, Vacanti CA, Yaremchuk MJ. Tissue engineered neocartilage using plasma derived polymer substrates and chondrocytes. *Plast Reconstr Surg* 1998;**101**(6):1580–1585.

Sittinger M, Reitzel D, Dauner M, Hierlemann H, Hammer C, Kastenbauer E, Planck H, Burmester GR, Bujia J. Resorbable polyesters in cartilage engineering: affinity and biocompatibility of polymer fiber structures to chondrocytes. *J Biomed Mater Res* 1996;**33**(2):57–63.

Smith DH, Wolf JA, Meaney DF. A new strategy to produce sustained growth of central nervous system axons: continuous mechanical tension. *Tissue Eng* 2001;**7**(2):131–139.

Steele JG, Johnson G, McLean KM, Beumer GJ, Griesser HJ. Effect of porosity and surface hydrophilicity on migration of epithelial tissue over synthetic polymer. *J Biomed Mater Res* 2000;**50**(4):475–482.

Stefonek TJ, Masters KS. Immobilized gradients of epidermal growth factor promote accelerated and directed keratinocyte migration. *Wound Repair Regen* 2007;**15**(6):847–855.

Steinmeyer J, Knue S. The proteoglycan metabolism of mature bovine articular cartilage explants superimposed to continuously applied cyclic mechanical loading. *Biochem Biophys Res Commun* 1997;**240**(1):216–221.

Stover NP, Bakay RA, Subramanian T, Raiser CD, Cornfeldt ML, Schweikert AW, Allen RC, Watts RL. Intrastriatal implantation of human retinal pigment epithelial cells attached to microcarriers in advanced Parkinson disease. *Arch Neurol* 2005;**62**(12):1833–1837

Suzuki Y, Tanihara M, Suzuki K, Saitou A, Sufan W, Nishimura Y. Alginate hydrogel linked with synthetic oligopeptide derived from BMP-2 allows ectopic osteoinduction in vivo. *J Biomed Mater Res* 2000;**50**(3):405–409.

Tan W, Krishnaraj R, Desai TA. Evaluation of nanostructured composite collagen-chitosan matrices for tissue engineering. *Tissue Eng* 2001;**7**(2):203–210.

Teng SH, Lee EJ, Park CS, Choi WY, Shin DS, Kim HE. Bioactive nanocomposite coatings of collagen/hydroxyapatite on titanium substrates. *J Mater Sci Mater Med* 2008;**19**(6):2453–2461.

Thakker MM, Fay AM, Pieroth L, Rubin PA. Fibrovascular ingrowth into hydroxyapatite and porous polyethylene orbital implants wrapped with acellular dermis. *Ophthal Plast Reconstr Surg* 2004;**20**(5):368–373.

Thompson DM, Buettner HM. Schwann cell response to micropatterned laminin surfaces. *Tissue Eng* 2001; **7**(3):247–265.

Thomson RC, Giordano GG, Collier JH, Ishaug SL, Mikos AG, Lahiri-Munir D, Garcia CA. Manufacture and characterization of poly(alpha-hydroxy ester) thin films as temporary substrates for retinal pigment epithelium cells. *Biomaterials* 1996;**17**(3):321–327.

Thomson RC, Yaszemski MJ, Powers JM, Mikos AG. Hydroxyapatite fiber reinforced poly(alpha-hydroxy ester) foams for bone regeneration. *Biomaterials* 1998;**19**(21):1935–1943.

Tiller JC, Bonner G, Pan LC, Klibanov AM. Improving biomaterial properties of collagen films by chemical modification. *Biotechnol Bioeng* 2001;**73**(3):246–252.

Tsuji-Saso Y, Kawazoe T, Morimoto N, Tabata Y, Taira T, Tomihata K, Utani A, Suzuki S. Incorporation of basic fibroblast growth factor into preconfluent cultured skin substitute to accelerate neovascularization and skin reconstruction after transplantation. *Scand J Plast Reconstr Surg Hand Surg* 2007;**41**(5):228–235.

Turgeman G, Pittman DD, Muller R, Kurkalli BG, Zhou S, Pelled G, Peyser A, Zilberman Y, Moutsatsos IK, Gazit D. Engineered human mesenchymal stem cells: a novel platform for skeletal cell mediated gene therapy. *J Gene Med* 2001;**3**(3):240–251.

Uludag H, Friess W, Williams D, Porter T, Timony G, D'Augusta D, Blake C, Palmer R, Biron B, Wozney J. rhBMP-collagen sponges as osteoinductive devices: effects of in vitro sponge characteristics and protein pI on in vivo rhBMP pharmacokinetics. *Ann N Y Acad Sci* 1999;**875**:369–378.

Vacanti JP, Morse MA, Saltzman WM, Domb AJ, Perez-Atayde A, Langer R. Selective cell transplantation using bioabsorbable artificial polymers as matrices. *J Pediatr Surg* 1988;**23**(1 Pt 2):3–9.

Vallbacka JJ, Nobrega JN, Sefton MV. Tissue engineering as a platform for controlled release of therapeutic agents: implantation of microencapsulated dopamine producing cells in the brains of rats. *J Control Release* 2001;**72**(1–3):93–100.

Van Wachem PB, Beugeling T, Feijen J, Bantjes A, Detmers JP, van Aken WG. Interaction of cultured human endothelial cells with polymeric surfaces of different wettabilities. *Biomaterials* 1985;**6**(6):403–408.

Voigt M, Schauer M, Schaefer DJ, Andree C, Horch R, Stark GB. Cultured epidermal keratinocytes on a microspherical transport system are feasible to reconstitute the epidermis in full-thickness wounds. *Tissue Eng* 1999;**5**(6):563–572.

Wake MC, Gerecht PD, Lu L, Mikos AG. Effects of biodegradable polymer particles on rat marrow-derived stromal osteoblasts in vitro. *Biomaterials* 1998;**19**(14):1255–1268.

Wake MC, Gupta PK, Mikos AG. Fabrication of pliable biodegradable polymer foams to engineer soft tissues. *Cell Transplant* 1996;**5**(4):465–473.

Wake MC, Mikos AG, Sarakinos G, Vacanti JP, Langer R. Dynamics of fibrovascular tissue ingrowth in hydrogel foams. *Cell Transplant* 1995;**4**(3):275–279.

Walboomers XF, Ginsel LA, Jansen JA. Early spreading events of fibroblasts on microgrooved substrates. *J Biomed Mater Res* 2000;**51**(3):529–534.

Waldman SD, Couto DC, Grynpas MD, Pilliar RM, Kandel RA. Multi-axial mechanical stimulation of tissue engineered cartilage: review. *Eur Cell Mater* 2007;**13**:66–73; discussion 73–74.

Walsh CJ, Goodman D, Caplan AI, Goldberg VM. Meniscus regeneration in a rabbit partial meniscectomy model. *Tissue Eng* 1999;**5**(4):327–337.

Wattendorf U, Kreft O, Textor M, Sukhorukov GB, Merkle HP. Stable stealth function for hollow polyelectrolyte microcapsules through a poly(ethylene glycol) grafted polyelectrolyte adlayer. *Biomacromolecules* 2008 Jan;**9**(1):100–108.

Webb K, Hlady V, Tresco PA. Relative importance of surface wettability and charged functional groups on NIH 3T3 fibroblast attachment, spreading, and cytoskeletal organization. *J Biomed Mater Res* 1998;**41**(3):422–430.

Webster TJ, Schadler LS, Siegel RW, Bizios R. Mechanisms of enhanced osteoblast adhesion on nanophase alumina involve vitronectin. *Tissue Eng* 2001;**7**(3):291–301.

Wei YT, Tian WM, Yu X, Cui FZ, Hou SP, Xu QY, Lee IS. Hyaluronic acid hydrogels with IKVAV peptides for tissue repair and axonal regeneration in an injured rat brain. *Biomed Mater* 2007;**2**(3):S142–S146.

Widmer MS, Gupta PK, Lu L, Meszlenyi RK, Evans GR, Brandt K, Savel T, Gurlek A, Patrick CW, Jr., Mikos AG. Manufacture of porous biodegradable polymer conduits by an extrusion process for guided tissue regeneration. *Biomaterials* 1998;**19**(21):1945–1955.

Williams JC, Rennaker RL, Kipke DR. Long-term neural recording characteristics of wire microelectrode arrays implanted in cerebral cortex. *Brain Res Brain Res Protoc* 1999;**4**(3):303–313.

Wittmer CR, Phelps JA, Saltzman WM, Van Tassel PR. Fibronectin terminated multilayer films: protein adsorption and cell attachment studies. *Biomaterials* 2007;**28**(5):851–860.

Wozniak MA, Desai R, Solski PA, Der CJ, Keely PJ. ROCK-generated contractility regulates breast epithelial cell differentiation in response to the physical properties of a three-dimensional collagen matrix. *J Cell Biol* 2003;**163**(3):583–595.

Xu HH, Simon CG Jr. Self-hardening calcium phosphate cement-mesh composite: reinforcement, macropores, and cell response. *J Biomed Mater Res A* 2004;**69**(2):267–278.

Xue Y, Gao J, Xi Z, Wang Z, Li X, Cui X, Luo Y, Li C, Wang L, Zhou D, Sun R, Sun AM. Microencapsulated bovine chromaffin cell xenografts into hemiparkinsonian rats: a drug-induced rotational behavior and histological changes analysis. *Artif Organs* 2001;**25**(2):131–135.

Yaszemski MJ, Payne RG, Hayes WC, Langer R, Mikos AG. In vitro degradation of a poly(propylene fumarate)-based composite material. *Biomaterials* 1996;**17**(22):2127–2130.

Ye Q, Zund G, Benedikt P, Jockenhoevel S, Hoerstrup SP, Sakyama S, Hubbell JA, Turina M. Fibrin gel as a three dimensional matrix in cardiovascular tissue engineering. *Eur J Cardiothorac Surg* 2000;**17**(5):587–591.

Young RG, Butler DL, Weber W, Caplan AI, Gordon SL, Fink DJ. Use of mesenchymal stem cells in a collagen matrix for Achilles tendon repair. *J Orthop Res* 1998;**16**(4):406–413.

Yu X, Dillon GP, Bellamkonda RB. A laminin and nerve growth factor-laden three-dimensional scaffold for enhanced neurite extension. *Tissue Eng* 1999;**5**(4):291–304.

Zhang Q, Yao K, Liu L, Sun Y, Xu L, Shen X, Lai Q. Evaluation of porous collagen membrane in guided tissue regeneration. *Artif Cells Blood Substit Immobil Biotechnol* 1999b;**27**(3):245–253.

Zhang R, Ma PX. Synthetic nano-fibrillar extracellular matrices with predesigned macroporous architectures. *J Biomed Mater Res* 2000;**52**(2):430–438.

Zhang S, Yan L, Altman M, Lassle M, Nugent H, Frankel F, Lauffenburger DA, Whitesides GM, Rich A. Biological surface engineering: a simple system for cell pattern formation. *Biomaterials* 1999a;**20**(13):1213–1220.

Zheng J, Northrup SR, Hornsby PJ. Modification of materials formed from poly(L-lactic acid) to enable covalent binding of biopolymers: application to high-density three-dimensional cell culture in foams with attached collagen. *In Vitro Cell Dev Biol Anim* 1998;**34**(9):679–684.

Zipfel WR, Williams RM, Christie R, Nikitin AY, Hyman BT, Webb WW. Live tissue intrinsic emission microscopy using multiphoton-excited native fluorescence and second harmonic generation. *Proc Natl Acad Sci U S A* 2003;**100**(12):7075–7080.

Zisch AH, Schenk U, Schense JC, Sakiyama-Elbert SE, Hubbell JA. Covalently conjugated VEGF-fibrin matrices for endothelialization. *J Control Release* 2001;**72**(1–3):101–113.

P · A · R · T · 4

BIOELECTRONICS

CHAPTER 22

BIOELECTRICITY AND ITS MEASUREMENT

Bruce C. Towe
Arizona State University, Tempe, Arizona

22.1 INTRODUCTION

Bioelectricity is fundamental to all of life's processes. Indeed, placing electrodes on the human body, or on any living thing, and connecting them to a sensitive voltmeter will show an assortment of both steady and time-varying electric potentials depending on where the electrodes are placed. These biopotentials result from complex biochemical processes, and their study is known as *electrophysiology*. We can derive much information about the function, health, and well-being of living things by the study of these potentials. To do this effectively, we need to understand how bioelectricity is generated, propagated, and optimally measured.

22.2 THE NATURE OF BIOELECTRICITY

In an electrical sense, living things can be modeled as a bag of water having various dissolved salts. These salts ionize in solution and create an electrolyte where the positive and negative ionic charges are available to carry electricity. Positive electric charge is carried primarily by sodium and potassium ions, and negative charges often are carried by chloride and hydroxyl. On a larger scale, the total numbers of positive and negative charges in biological fluids are equal, as illustrated in Fig. 22.1. This, in turn, maintains net electroneutrality of living things with respect to their environment.

Biochemical processes at the cell molecular level are intimately associated with the transfer of electric charge. From the standpoint of bioelectricity, living things are analogous to an electrolyte container filled with millions of small chemical batteries. Most of these batteries are located at cell membranes and help define things such as cell osmotic pressure and selectivity to substances that

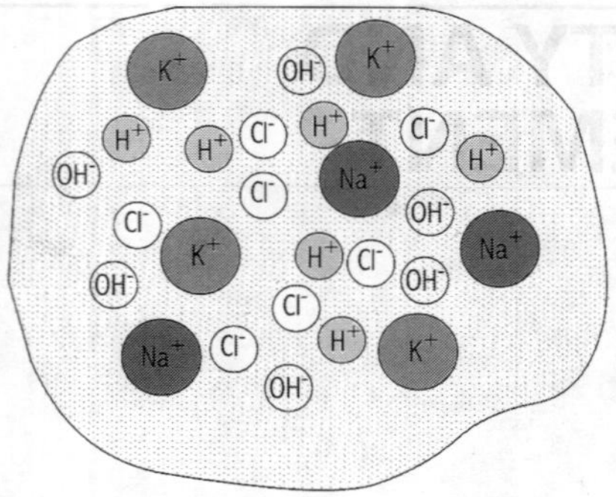

FIGURE 22.1 All living things have a net electroneutrality, meaning that they contain equal numbers of positive and negatively charged ions within their biological fluids and structure.

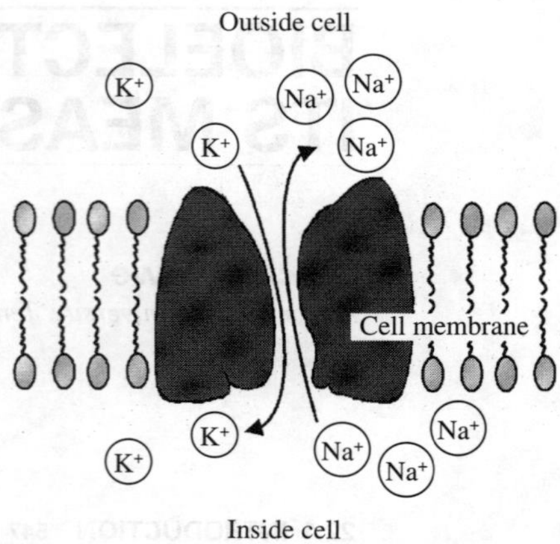

FIGURE 22.2 Concept of a sodium-potassium ionic pump within the phospholipid structure of the cell membrane. The molecular pump structures are not exactly known.

cross the membrane. These fields can vary transiently in time and thus carry information and so underlie the function of the brain and nervous system.

The most fundamental bioelectric processes of life occur at the level of membranes. In living things, there are many processes that create segregation of charge and so produce electric fields within cells and tissues. Bioelectric events start when cells expend metabolic energy to actively transport sodium outside the cell and potassium inside the cell. The movement of sodium, potassium, chloride, and, to a lesser extent, calcium and magnesium ions occurs through the functionality of molecular pumps and selective channels within the cell membrane.

Membrane ion pumps consist of assemblies of large macromolecules that span the thickness of the phospholipid cell membrane, as illustrated in Fig. 22.2. The pumps for sodium and potassium ions are coupled and appear to be a single structure that acts somewhat like a turnstile. Their physical construction transports sodium and potassium in opposite directions in a 3:2 atomic ratio, respectively.

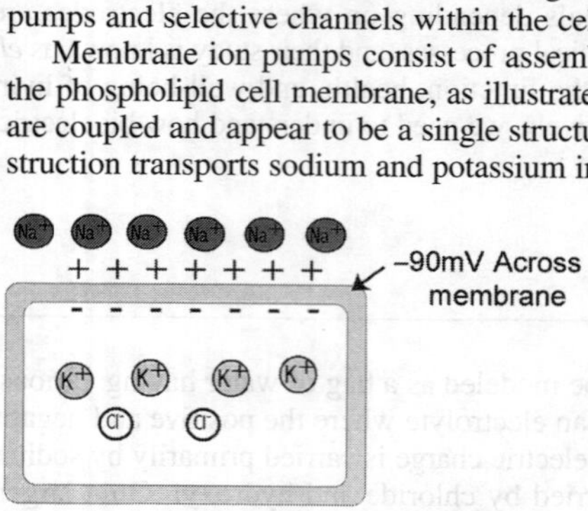

FIGURE 22.3 Electric field across the membrane due to action of the sodium-potassium pump.

As shown in Fig. 22.3, the unbalance of actively transported charge causes a low intracellular sodium ion concentration and relatively higher potassium concentration than the extracellular environment. Chloride is not actively transported. The unbalance in ionic charge creates a negative potential in the cell interior relative to the exterior and gives rise to the resting transmembrane potential (TMP).

This electric field, appearing across an approximately 70-Å-thick cell membrane, is very large by standards of the macro physical world. For example, a cellular TMP of −70 mV creates an electric field of 10^7 V/m across the membrane. In air, electric breakdown would occur and would produce lightning-bolt-sized discharges over meter-order distances. Electric breakdown is resisted in the microcellular environment by the high dielectric qualities of the cell membrane. Even so, the intensity of these fields produces large forces on ions and other charged molecules and is a major factor in ionic transfer across the cell membrane. When a cell is weakened or dies by lack of oxygen, its transmembrane field also declines or vanishes. It both regulates and results from the life and function of the cell.

In addition to ion pumps, the membrane has ion channels. These are partially constructed of helical-shaped proteins that longitudinally align to form tubes that cross the cell membrane. These proteins are oriented such that parts of their charged structure are aligned along the inside of the channels. Due to this alignment and the specific diameter of the formed channel lumen, there results selectivity for specific ionic species. For example, negatively charged protein carboxylic acid groups lining the channel wall will admit positively charged ions of a certain radius, such as sodium, and exclude negatively charged ions, such as chloride.

Some membrane ionic channels respond to changes in the surrounding membrane electric field by modulating their ionic selectivity and conductance. These are known as *voltage-gated ion channels*. Their behavior is important in excitable cells, such as nerve and muscle, where the membrane permeability and its electric potential transiently change in response to a stimulus. This change accompanies physiological events such as the contraction of muscle cells and the transmission of information along nerve cells.

22.2.1 Bioelectric Currents

Electric fields can arise from a static distribution of charge, whereas electric currents are charges in motion. Since current flow in a volume of fluid is not confined to a linear path as in a wire, currents can flow in many directions. When describing bioelectric currents, we often use a derivation of Ohm's law:

$$J = \sigma E$$

where J = current density, A/m^2
σ = medium conductivity, S/m
E = electric field, V/m

Thus, within the conductivity of living tissue, electric current flows are driven by electric field differences.

Electric currents in a wire always move from a source to a sink. Ionic currents in an electrolyte flow in a similar way. Charged ions, such as sodium, move from some origin to a destination, thereby producing an electric current flow. The magnitude of these currents is directly proportional to the number of ions flowing. This idea is shown in Fig. 22.4.

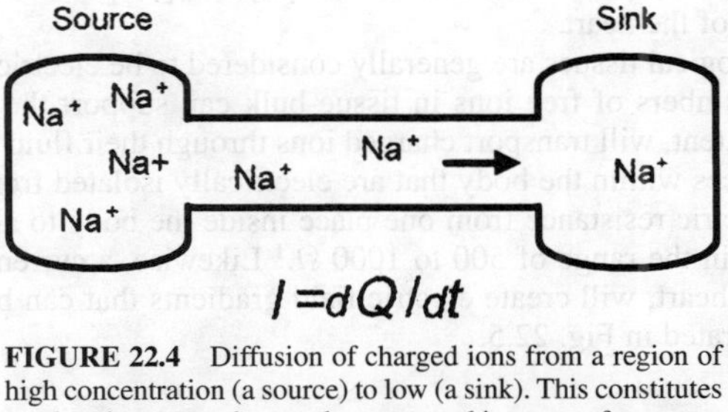

FIGURE 22.4 Diffusion of charged ions from a region of high concentration (a source) to low (a sink). This constitutes an electric current that can be expressed in terms of amperes.

Current flow I in amperes is defined as the time rate of charge Q movement:

$$I = dQ/dt$$

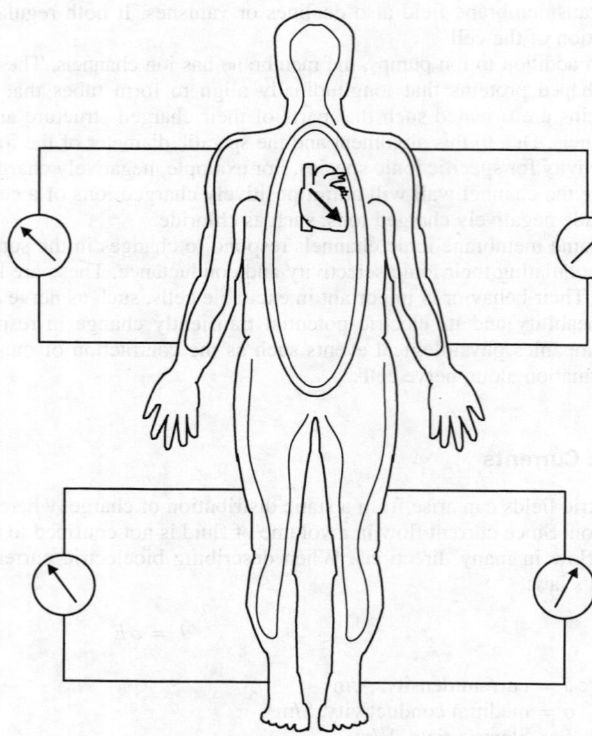

FIGURE 22.5 The volume conductivity of the body means that bioelectric current generators such as the heart produce electric fields detectable elsewhere on the body.

Thus, given the charge of 1.6×10^{-23} C, approximately 10^{23} sodium ions, for example, moving in one direction each second will produce an electric current of 1 A. Such large numbers of ions do not ordinarily flow in one direction over a second in biologic organisms. Currents in the milliampere region, however, are associated with physiologic processes such as muscular contraction and the beating of the heart.

Biological tissues are generally considered to be electric volume conductors. This means that the large numbers of free ions in tissue bulk can support the conduction of currents. Even bones, to some extent, will transport charged ions through their fluid phase. On a macroscopic scale, there are few places within the body that are electrically isolated from the whole. This is reflected in the fact that electric resistance from one place inside the body to almost any other will show a finite value, usually in the range of 500 to 1000 Ω.[1] Likewise, a current generator within the body, such as the beating heart, will create electric field gradients that can be detected from most parts of the body, as illustrated in Fig. 22.5.

22.2.2 Nernst Potentials

The origin and equilibrium of electric fields at the cellular level can be understood in terms of Nernst potentials. These potentials arise where any kind of membrane, not just living ones, selectively passes certain ions and blocks others.

If, for example, a membrane selective for potassium separates a compartment of high-concentration potassium chloride solution from another of lower concentration, there is a diffusion-driven current J_{diff} across the membrane. The value of this is given by a version of Fick's law:

$$J_{diff} = -\frac{RT}{f}\left[\frac{dC}{dx}\right]$$

where dC/dx = ion concentration gradient
R = universal gas constant
T = absolute temperature, K
f = frictional constant related to the membrane permeability

In this situation, it might be expected that potassium ions would continue to diffuse until their concentration is the same on both sides of the membrane. However, since potassium is charged and the membrane prevents charged counter-ions such as chloride from also moving across, there arises an electric field across the membrane. This electric field creates forces that tend to inhibit further potassium diffusion. The electric field tends to cause a flux of potassium J_{elect} back across the membrane. It can be shown that the flux due to this electric field dV/dx is given by

$$J_{elect} = -\left[\frac{dV}{dx}\right]nCF\frac{1}{f}$$

where n = charge on each ion
C = concentration of ions
F = Faraday's constant

At some point of equilibrium, the forward flux of ions moving under forces of diffusion equals the reverse flux of ions driven by the electric field. The *Nernst potential* of a membrane is thus defined as the electric field where the diffusive flux of ions exactly counterbalances the electric field flux such that

$$J_{diff} = -J_{elect}$$

The negative sign on the electric field term is needed for balance, since the positive direction of ionic diffusion is from a high to a low concentration. Thus an equilibrium condition is established where the forces of diffusion are exactly balanced by the forces of the electric field. This situation is illustrated in Fig. 22.6.

Substituting and solving the equation by integration for the potential difference $V_{in} - V_{out}$ across a membrane gives

$$V_{in} - V_{out} = \frac{RT}{nF}\ln\left[\frac{C_{in}}{C_{out}}\right]$$

where C_{in} and C_{out} are the respective ionic concentrations inside and outside the cell membrane. At a body temperature of 37°C and for univalent ions, the value of $RT/nF \times 2.303$ (to convert the natural log to log base 10) gives a result of 61 mV per decade of concentration ratio.

This Nernst relationship can be applied to living cell membranes. Cells are most permeable to potassium, and if we substitute known concentration values of potassium inside and outside the cell, we find that the cell TMP is near this value, but not exactly.

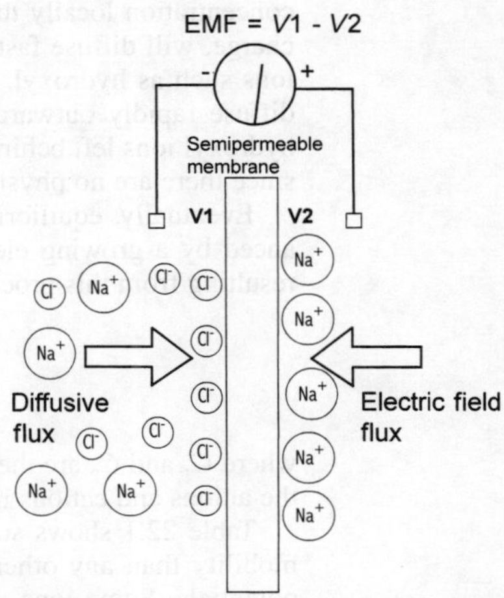

FIGURE 22.6 Nernst potentials arise across semipermeable membranes due to opposing forces of electric field and diffusion.

22.2.3 The Goldman Equation

Actually, in living cells there are many ionic species, with the important ones being potassium, sodium, and chloride. All these individually have their own Nernst potential that contributes to the total membrane potential. The fraction to which each adds to the total TMP depends on the membrane's permeability for the specific ion. Each ionic potential might be imagined as a battery in series with a specific electric conductance (related to the membrane's ionic permeability) and all connected across the membrane. Each ion species contributes according to the membrane's intrinsic permeability for that ion like batteries in parallel.

The Goldman equation accounts for multiple ionic contributors to the cell membrane potential. It assumes that the membrane permeability P is equivalent to the internal resistance of an ionic battery. Thus, with multiple ionic species that all contribute, the cell TMP is given by

$$\mathrm{TMP} = V_{\mathrm{in}} - V_{\mathrm{out}} = (-RT/F)\ln\frac{\left\{P_{\mathrm{Na}^+}\left[\mathrm{Na}^+\right]_{\mathrm{in}} + P_{\mathrm{K}^+}\left[\mathrm{K}^+\right]_{\mathrm{in}} + P_{\mathrm{Cl}^-}\left[\mathrm{Cl}^-\right]_{\mathrm{out}}\right\}}{\left[P_{\mathrm{Na}^+}\left[\mathrm{Na}^+\right]_{\mathrm{out}} + P_{\mathrm{K}^+}\left[\mathrm{K}^+\right]_{\mathrm{out}} + P_{\mathrm{Cl}^-}\left[\mathrm{Cl}^-\right]_{\mathrm{in}}\right]}$$

where the quantities in brackets are the concentrations of the ionic species. Chloride ion is negatively charged, and hence its concentration ratio in the equation is inverted compared with those of sodium and potassium.

This equation produces a result that is very close to the measured cell TMP. The activity of membrane pumps is also known to contribute a few millivolts. Together, all these sources can account for the cell TMP.

22.2.4 Diffusion Potentials

Tissue sometimes is found to be electrically polarized even where there is no membrane that would give rise to Nernst or Goldman potentials. The origin of this polarization can often be attributed to what are called *diffusion potentials*. These arise from differences in ionic mobilities in the tissue volume conductivity and because metabolic processes produce a range of different kinds of free ions.

Living processes of metabolism and biochemistry constantly liberate ions that are higher in concentration locally than at more distant locations. Small ions, e.g., hydrogen carrying a positive charge, will diffuse faster away from a site of their production than will larger, negatively charged ions such as hydroxyl. This ionic separation process, however, is self-limiting. As hydrogen ions diffuse rapidly outward, this creates an electric field in tissue relative to the negatively charged hydroxyl ions left behind. The increasing electric field slows the outward diffusion of hydrogen, but since there are no physical barriers, both ions continue to move.

Eventually, equilibrium occurs, where the rapid outward diffusion of charged fast ions is balanced by a growing electric field from slower, oppositely charged ions. The potential magnitude resulting from this process that exists across some region of tissue is given by

$$V = RT/nF\left(\frac{\mu_a - \mu_c}{\mu_i - \mu_c}\right)\ln\left(\frac{C_1}{C_2}\right)$$

where C_1 and C_2 are the differential concentrations, respectively, and μ_a and μ_c are the mobilities of the anions and cations involved.

Table 22.1 shows some representative values of ionic mobilities. Hydrogen has a much larger mobility than any other ion. Therefore, local tissue pH changes are a prime source of diffusion potentials. Some ions such as sodium tend to collect water molecules around them, resulting in a larger hydrated radius, and even though they are small, they diffuse more slowly than might be expected from their size.

TABLE 22.1 Mobilities of Various Ions[2]

Ion	Mobility of ions at infinite dilution in water, (cm/s)/(V/cm)
Hydrogen	$\mu_c = 36 \times 10^{-4}$
Hydroxyl	$\mu_a = 20.5 \times 10^{-4}$
Sodium	$\mu_c = 5.2 \times 10^{-4}$
Potassium	$\mu_c = 7.6 \times 10^{-4}$
Chloride	$\mu_a = 7.9 \times 10^{-4}$

Unlike Nernst potentials, where ions are in equilibrium and create a static electric field, diffusion potentials result from ions in motion, making them electric currents in tissue. If diffusion is isotropic, there would be an outward-directed electric field and current flow from their source. This situation is shown in Fig. 22.7.

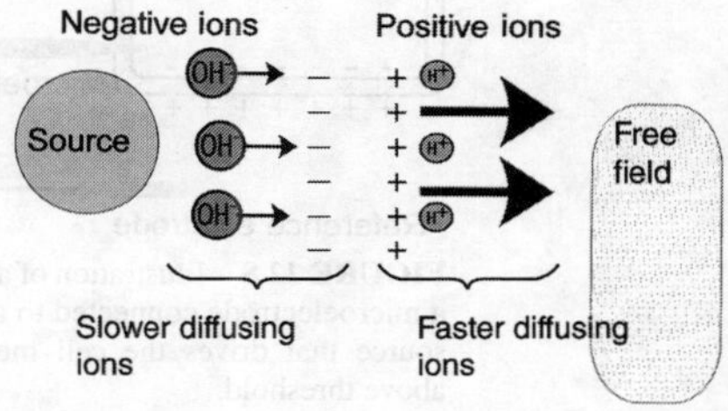

FIGURE 22.7 Fast-diffusing positively charged hydrogen ions move away from slower negatively charged hydroxyl ions, creating an electric field known as the *diffusion potential.*

Sustained diffusion currents depend on the active generation of free ions. Otherwise, the currents will decay as ionic concentration gradients move toward equilibrium. In biological organisms, diffusion currents often flow over time scales that are minutes, hours, or continuous if the source of production of the ions is continuous. Diffusion currents, in principle, can be differentiated from steady electric fields in tissue since currents can be detected using biomagnetometers that respond to ionic flow rather than to an electric field.

Diffusion currents are often associated with biological processes such as growth, development, wound healing, and tissue injury of almost any sort. For example, depriving heart tissue of oxygen, which occurs during a heart attack, produces an immediate diffusion current, known as a *current of injury*. This current is believed to result mostly from potassium ions released from inside the heart cells. Without aerobic metabolism, cells can no longer support the membrane pumps that maintain the cellular TMP. Potassium ions then flow out of the cells and diffuse outward from the injured tissues. Electrodes used to map bioelectricity during coronary vessel blockage will show a steady current flowing radially outward from the affected site. Likewise, it is known that skin wounds, bruises, other tissue traumas, and even cancer[3] can produce injury currents.

Nernst potentials, Goldman potentials, membrane ion pumps, and diffusion potentials are thus primary drivers for bioelectric currents that flow in organisms. Since natural bioelectric generators have a maximum of about −100 mV at the cellular level, most bioelectric events measured by electrodes do not exceed this millivoltage. There are a few exceptions. Certain species of electric fish, such as the electric eel, have tissues that effectively place the TMP of cells in electric series. Some remarkably high bioelectric voltages can be achieved by this arrangement, in the range of hundreds of volts. On synchronized cellular depolarization, large eels are known to discharge currents in the ampere range into seawater.

22.3 ACTION EVENTS OF NERVE

Excitable cells are those that can respond to variously electric, chemical, optical, and mechanical stimuli by sudden changes in their cell TMP. Ordinarily, a loss of a cell's membrane potential is lethal. However, fast transient changes in cell TMP, called *action events*, are part of the natural function of excitable cells.

Action events involve a multiphase biochemical-bioelectric process. A localized stimulus to an excitable cell can launch a series of cascading molecular events affecting the membrane's ionic permeability. The accompanying changes in TMP feed back on the membrane by way of voltage-gated channels and magnify the effect of the stimulus. If the stimulus amplitude reaches a threshold value, this causes further and more dramatic changes in the membrane's ionic permeability.

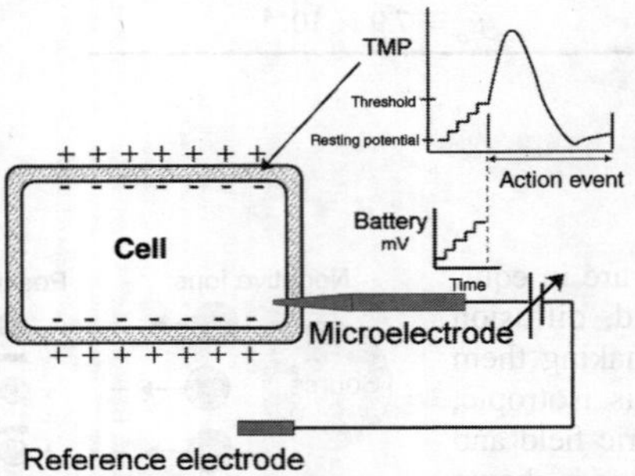

FIGURE 22.8 Illustration of a cell punctured by a microelectrode connected to a stepwise current source that drives the cell membrane potential above threshold.

The threshold behavior of excitable cells can be observable by placing a tiny (usually a 1-μm tip diameter) microelectrode inside a cell. Sufficient charge injection from an external voltage source can drive the TMP toward zero. Now if the TMP is moved stepwise more positive, an action event will occur above some threshold. At this point, the membrane potential will suddenly jump of its own accord from a negative TMP to a positive value. Figure 22.8 shows a setup where a battery is used to stepwise drive the cell TMP more positive.

During an action event, membrane sodium conductance abruptly increases, allowing the higher concentration of sodium in the extracellular medium to rush into the cell. The net negative electric field inside the cell is thereby reduced toward zero through the positive charge on sodium. This is known as *depolarization*. Shortly after the sodium inrush, there is an increase in membrane potassium conductance. This allows the higher concentration of potassium ions inside the cell to move outward. Because of a flow of positive charge to the outside of the cell, the net negative charge inside the cell is restored. This is known as *repolarization*. These changes in sodium and potassium membrane conductance are illustrated in Fig. 22.9.

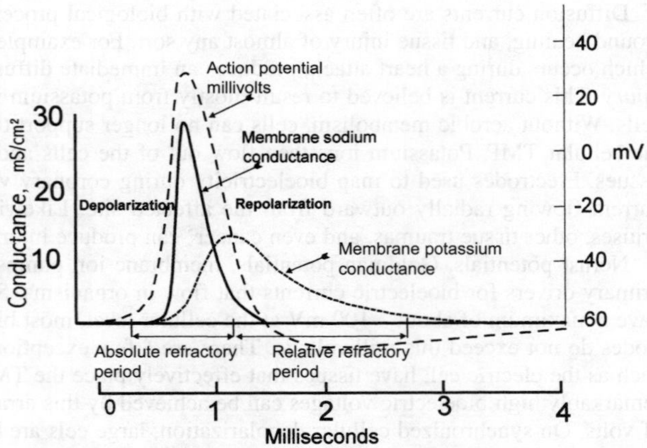

FIGURE 22.9 Illustration of the cycle of ionic conductances associated with action events.

The depolarization and repolarization phases of action events can occur quickly over intervals of tens of microseconds, although the actual durations depend very much on the cell type. During the time when the cell is depolarized, it cannot be restimulated to another action event. This interval is known as the cell's *absolute refractory period*. The cell's *relative refractory period* is the interval from partial to complete repolarization. During this time, the cell can be restimulated, but a higher stimulus is required to produce an action potential event, and it is lower in magnitude.

22.3.1 Membrane Bioelectrical Models

Cell membranes separate charges, and this causes a potential across their thickness. This aspect of the membrane can be modeled as a charged capacitor that follows the relationship

$$V = Q/C$$

where V = potential
Q = charge separation
C = capacitance

In an action potential event, the total amount of charge Q transferred across the membrane by movements of sodium and potassium is relatively little, just sufficient to charge the membrane capacitance C_m. The amplitude of potential change and time course of an action event depend on the type of excitable cell being studied.

Membranes also have a finite and distributed electric resistance both across their thickness and along their length. These resistances tend to short circuit the membrane capacitor and cause its stored charge to decay to zero if the membrane ion pumps cease. There are several different models of the cell membrane that describe its static and transient bioelectric behavior. Models of the cell membrane are useful because they help explain the propagation of action events, such as that along a nerve.

The electric nature of the membrane is usually modeled as distributed capacitors and resistors, as shown in Fig. 22.10. The value of R_m is the membrane equivalent electric resistance. R_e and R_i are the resistances of the external and internal membrane environments. The stored charge across the membrane is electrically represented by a capacitance C_m, and the action of the ionic pumps is represented by E_m.

With local membrane depolarization caused by some stimulus, the longitudinal membrane conduction causes the local rise in TMP to spread along the adjacent regions of the membrane. Adjacent voltage-gated membrane channels are driven above threshold, propagating the depolarization event. This effect on adjacent membrane is illustrated in Fig. 22.11 for a nerve axon. By this mechanism, bioelectric action events spread outward from the point of stimulus, move along the cell membrane, and cease when the entire membrane is depolarized.

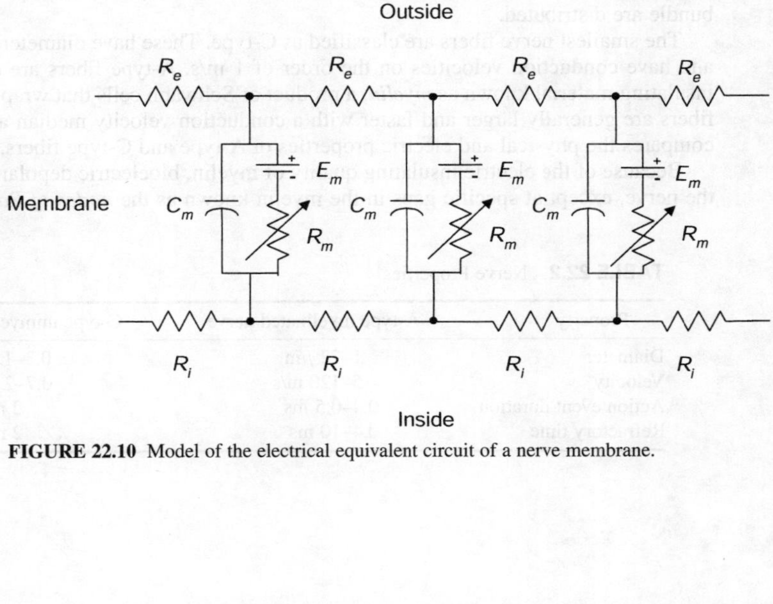

FIGURE 22.10 Model of the electrical equivalent circuit of a nerve membrane.

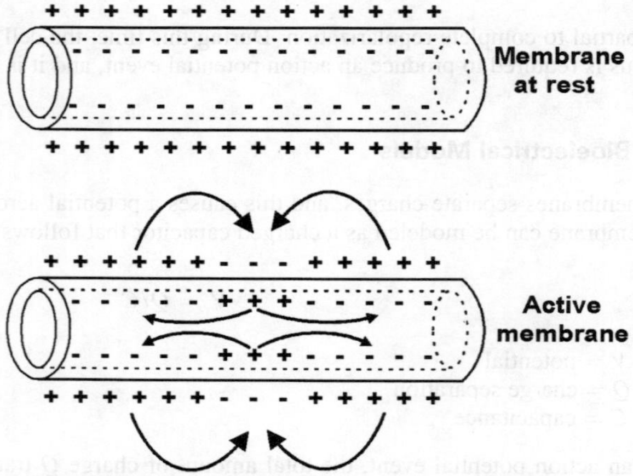

FIGURE 22.11 Depolarization of a nerve cell membrane creating a circulating flow of ionic currents.

22.3.2 Propagation of Action Events

Nerves in higher biological organisms are bundles of long, excitable cells that can extend to meter-order lengths. A sufficient stimulus to a point on a nerve cell membrane will rapidly conduct along its length. Bioelectric action currents generated in a single nerve fiber by the depolarization wavefront are relatively small, in the tens of nanoampere region. They can range into the microampere region, though, with synchronous depolarizations of many fibers within large nerve bundles. As these currents travel along the nerve length, they can produce detectable electric fields at nearby recording electrodes. The time course of these recorded biopotentials depends largely on the velocity of the action current wave as it passes by the point of measurement.

The velocity of action event propagation depends on the nerve diameter d as well as on passive electric properties of the membrane. Assuming that these electric properties are constant along the membrane, it can be shown that the depolarization wave velocity of a nerve is proportional to

$$\text{Action potential velocity (m/s)} \quad \sqrt{d}$$

Thus larger-diameter nerves propagate the depolarization wave faster. In a given bundle of individual nerve fibers, there are clusters of different fiber diameters, and hence propagation speeds within a bundle are distributed.

The smallest nerve fibers are classified as C-type. These have diameters on the order of a micron and have conduction velocities on the order of 1 m/s. A-type fibers are coated with a layer of an insulating material known as *myelin*, a product of Schwann cells that wrap around them. Myelinated fibers are generally larger and faster with a conduction velocity median around 50 m/s. Table 22.2 compares the physical and electric properties of A-type and C-type fibers.

Because of the electric insulating quality of myelin, bioelectric depolarization is prevented along the nerve, except at specific gaps in the myelin known as the *nodes of Ranvier*. At these points the

TABLE 22.2 Nerve Properties[4]

Property	A-type myelinated nerve	C-type unmyelinated nerve
Diameter	1–22 μm	0.3–1.3 μm
Velocity	5–120 m/s	0.7–2.3 m/s
Action event duration	0.4–0.5 ms	2 ms
Refractory time	0.4–10 ms	2 ms

extracellular sodium and potassium ionic currents flow during action events. The nodes confine the bioelectric current sources to relatively small areas on the nerve membrane, and the current flows appear to hop from node to node down the length of the fiber. An example of current flow in a myelinated fiber is shown in Fig. 22.12.

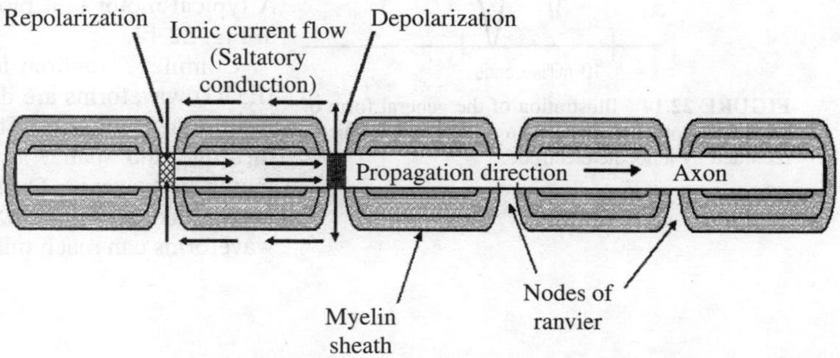

FIGURE 22.12 Myelin sheath around a nerve that limits action currents to the nodes of Ranvier.

However, there are still electrode-detectable bioelectric fields from myelinated nerves during action events, since volume currents flow, as shown in Fig. 22.13. These bioelectric currents are dipolar in nature, meaning that ionic currents flow spatially from the source at the leading edge of depolarization to a sink at the repolarization edge. Separation distances between these nodes in mammals are on the order of a millimeter.

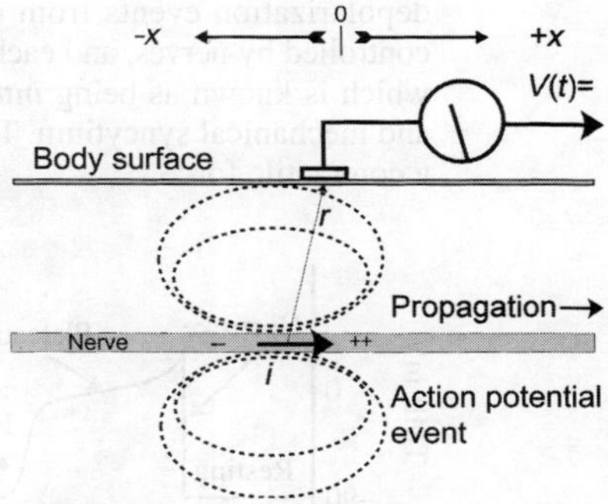

FIGURE 22.13 Electric dipole equivalent of a traveling depolarization event in nerve.

22.3.3 Action Events of Muscle

Skeletal muscles produce some of the larger bioelectric signals within the body. Muscle is composed of many small and elongated myofibers of about 50 μm in diameter. Myofibers are made of myofibril cells, which contain filaments of contractile proteins—actin and myosin. Actin and myosin are oriented longitudinal to the direction of their contraction. These proteins are believed to engage in a walk-along movement by a sliding filament process that coincides with internal fluxes of calcium ions triggered by an action event. Myofibers are in turn organized into innervated functional groups known as *motor units*. Motor units are bundled together and interwoven with others and are then called *fascicles*, ultimately forming the whole muscle.

Single motor units are actuated by a nerve fiber that terminates at the synaptic cleft of the myoneural junction. The neurotransmitter acetylcholine opens up membrane ion channels, allowing the influx of sodium and causing an action event followed by a short, twitchlike mechanical contraction.

Both an increase in recruitment of individual motor units and an increase in their firing rates control muscle force. Single-motor-unit action events produce bioelectric currents of 3 to 15 ms in duration. Under sustained nervous stimulation, these can occur with repetition rates of 5 to 30 per second. Even though the myofibril bioelectric events are pulsatile, muscle contraction can be smooth because at high firing frequencies there is a blending of the forces together. Increases in skeletal muscle contractile force are accompanied by an increase in the recruitment of myofibrils.

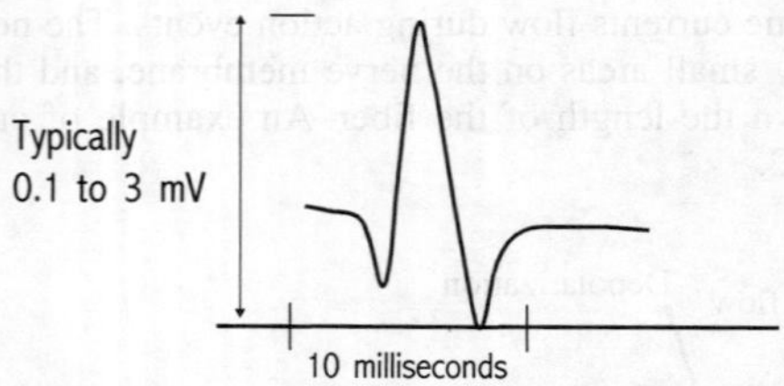

FIGURE 22.14 Illustration of the general form of an action potential event of a single motor unit as recorded by a needle electrode.

The forces of the individual motor units sum together, producing a relatively larger force. When monitored by a local invasive needle electrode, motor unit action events produce a triphasic extracellular waveform in the range of a few tens of microvolts to 1 mV. A typical motor unit bioelectric waveform is shown in Fig. 22.14.

Complex, random-looking electromyographic (EMG) waveforms are detected by electrodes placed near skeletal muscle. These waveforms result from the time and spatial superposition of thousands of motor unit events. During a strong contraction of a large skeletal muscle, monitored skin bioelectric waveforms can reach millivolt amplitudes.

22.3.4 Action Events of the Heart

Heart cells are unique compared with skeletal muscle cells because they are in electric contact with each other through electric tight junctions between cell membranes and so propagate bioelectric depolarization events from one cell to the next. By contrast, motor units of skeletal muscle are controlled by nerves, and each unit has a separate junction. Heart cells are also physically intertwined, which is known as being *intercalated*. The overall result is that the heart acts as both an electrical and mechanical syncytium. That is, the heart cells act together to conduct bioelectricity and produce a contractile force.

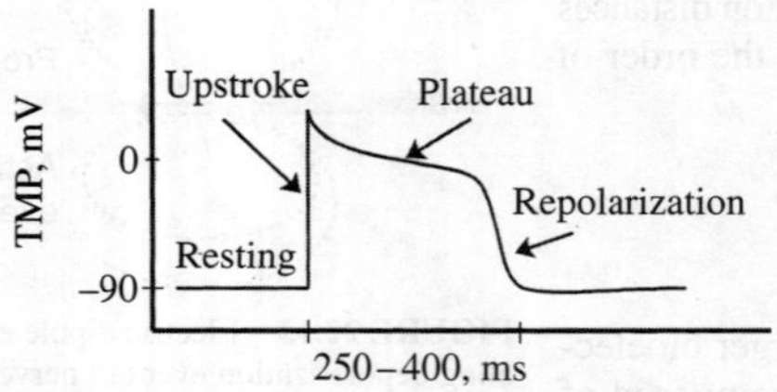

FIGURE 22.15 Illustration of a cardiac cell action potential event.

The action potential event of the heart is different from that of skeletal muscle. It has a prolonged depolarization phase that varies from tens of milliseconds for cells of the atria to about 250 to 400 ms for cells of the ventricle. The general waveform shape for an action event of the ventricle is shown in Fig. 22.15.

The prolongation of the heart action event results from the activity of slow calcium channels in the cell membranes. These act in concert with the fast sodium channels to maintain a longer depolarization phase of the heart. This prolongation is important in the physiological function of the heart since it defines the timing and duration of the mechanical events required for a contraction.

The mechanical contraction of the heart follows the time course of its longer bioelectric current flows. Bioelectric currents initiate and define the motor activity of the heart cells. If the heart cells simply twitched during an action event rather than producing a sustained force over a longer duration, there would not be time for the myocardium to move against the inertia of blood in the ventricles.

The bioelectric depolarization that leads to contraction starts in the pacemaker cells in the sinoatrial node. There it passes as a narrow band of depolarization from the atria toward the ventricles. Although the process of depolarization is complex and not spatially uniform, it can be thought of as a moving band of current flow from top to bottom of the heart. For example, assuming a depolarization velocity of 25 m/s and a sodium channel-opening rise time of 30 μs, a traveling band of current approximately 0.75 mm wide would move through the heart during the contraction phase (systole). This simplified notion is illustrated in Fig. 22.16. In actuality, specialized nodal tracts of the atria, the bundle of His, and the Purkinje fibers in the ventricles direct the propagation wave and affect its dipolar length.

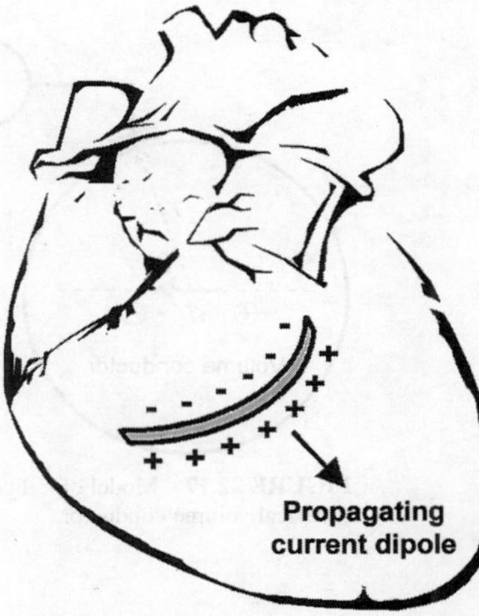

FIGURE 22.16 Illustration showing the simplified concept of a traveling band of depolarization creating a net current dipole in the heart.

Subsequently, heart cells repolarize during the resting (diastole) phase of the heart cycle. The repolarization wave event is again a cellular current flow creating a bioelectric potential. In humans, many millions of cells participate in this depolarization. Each cell is a tiny bioelectric current generator. The sum of the generators produces biopotentials on the order of 1 to 3 mV on the chest wall surface. A recording of these cardiac potentials is known as an *electrocardiogram* (ECG, or sometimes EKG, from the German, *electrokardiogram*).

22.4 VOLUME CONDUCTOR PROPAGATION

Living things create and conduct current within their tissues and so produce remotely detectable electric fields. Excitable tissue function is both initiated and followed by bioelectric events. Thus there exists the possibility of monitoring physiological function through the use of remote and noninvasive potential-sensing electrodes. Measurement of the bioelectric magnitude and time course may allow us to gain an understanding of biological function and performance. Indeed, changes in monitored biocurrent flows have been found to be useful indicators of disease. Unfortunately, it is not straightforward to use noninvasive surface electrodes to infer the location and time courses of biocurrent flows inside tissue.

22.4.1 Dipolar Current Sources in Volume Conductors

When discussing bioelectric currents, electrophysiologists usually use the term *dipole moment p*. This is defined as

$$p = id$$

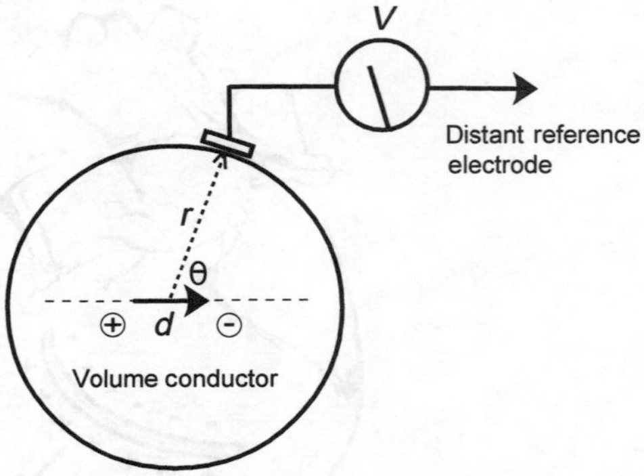

FIGURE 22.17 Model of a dipolar current within a large spherical volume conductor.

where i is the ionic current in milliamperes and d is the separation distance between the current's source and sink. The reason for this usage is that the magnitude of potential remotely detected from an ionic current flow depends not only on the current amplitude but also on its source-sink separation.

A model situation often used is a dipolar current source immersed in a large spherical volume conductor. The surface potential is monitored with respect to a distant electrode, as seen in Fig. 22.17. Due to spherical symmetry, the potential V at a point on the sphere surface is given by a fairly simple volume-conductor relationship:

$$V = \frac{id\cos\theta}{4\pi\sigma r^2}$$

where θ is the angle formed by the current vector to the remote monitoring point. This equation defines the fraction of the electric potential seen by remote monitoring electrodes. Biological tissues have widely varying conductivities σ at low biopotential frequencies (10 Hz) ranging from 0.6 S/m for blood,[5] which is a relatively good conductor, to 0.04 S/m for fat, which is a relatively poor one.

Bioelectric dipole moments range from milliampere-millimeter currents associated with the heart and skeletal muscle to nanoampere-millimeter for nerve currents. The volume-conductor relation shows that the detection of these current moments depends on a number of variables besides their strength. For example, surface potentials depend both on the dipole distance and on the orientation of the dipole moment with respect to the electrode.

22.4.2 The Problem of Biocurrent Localization

The task of the electrophysiologist or the physician is often to interpret recorded bioelectric waveform shapes in terms of physiological events. Bioelectric field propagation in biological objects, however, is complex partly because of nonuniformities in tissue conductivity. Therefore, skin surface potentials often do not directly follow the pattern distribution of the internal currents that produce them.

If we know the distribution of biocurrents in tissue and know or can estimate tissue conductivities, it is possible to calculate the biopotential distribution on the body surface. In electrophysiology, this is known as the *forward problem*. Conversely, inferring the magnitude and distribution of biocurrent generators from surface biopotentials is called the *inverse problem*. Indeed, solving this problem would be very useful for medical diagnostics and to allow us to gain a greater understanding of physiology. Unfortunately, the inverse problem is known to be mathematically ill-posed, bearing no direct solution. This derives from the fact that there are too many variables and too few measurements possible to define a three-dimensional current from potentials on a two-dimensional surface.

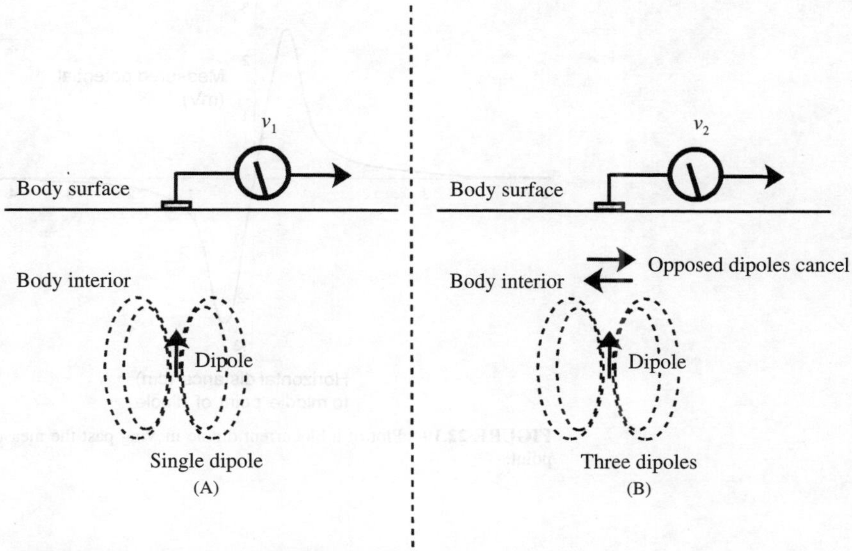

FIGURE 22.18 Illustration of the bioelectrical inverse problem.

For example, multiple biocurrent vector directions and variable dipole distances can create a situation where, if they are close together and have opposite vector directions, they can cancel, rendering no trace of their existence. Figure 22.18 illustrates the problem of vector cancellation. When far enough away from the skin, one current source in (A) creates the same surface potential as the three sources seen in (B). This is just one of many different geometric possibilities of dipole orientation and body surface distance that create identical surface potentials.

There are, however, constraints that can be put on the inverse problem to make it somewhat more tractable. Estimates of tissue conductivity, knowledge of how currents flow in biological tissues, and knowledge of the normal biocurrent time course can simplify the problem. Complex computer models have been developed to derive medical diagnostic and other electrophysiological data from maps of surface potentials. These are still the subject of research.

Another example of ambiguity in what a waveform shows is that the biocurrent dipole amplitude may appear to be changing when really it is moving. A model situation is where a biopotential electrode is placed on the surface of a volume conductor and a dipole moment p moves past it. The distance from the center of the dipole to the electrode is r, and θ is the angle that the dipole makes with respect to the vertical. Plotting the potential V at the electrode measurement point as the current dipole moves past, assuming that the dipole is relatively far away from the measuring point compared with its length, we see that motion of the dipole produces a complex biopotential, as plotted in Fig. 22.19. It has a biphasic component where, in fact, there is no change in amplitude or reversal of the biocurrent source.

Another factor that makes it difficult to use skin biopotential amplitudes as quantitative indicators of physiologic events is that there are significant variations between people relative to body fat, muscle distribution, and size and position of tissue biocurrent sources.

In practice, simple observation of the biopotential waveform is often very useful. For example, a common biopotential recording is the fetal ECG. Electrodes are placed on the mother's abdomen to bring the bioelectric monitoring point close to the source; however, the fetal current generators are still relatively weak. Furthermore, the mother's ECG is also captured in the recording. Nonetheless, the two waveforms are easily discriminated by a trained eye. The fetal ECG is typically faster,

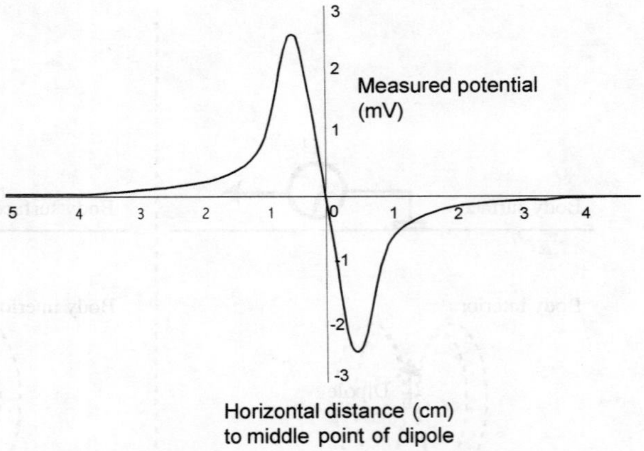

FIGURE 22.19 Plot of a biocurrent dipole moving past the measuring point.

smaller in amplitude, and may exhibit a simpler waveform than the maternal ECG, making the detected waveform rather obvious to the physician.

22.5 DETECTION OF BIOELECTRIC EVENTS

22.5.1 Bioelectrodes and the Electrode-Skin Interface

Biopotentials from the human body are generally low-level signals, maximally in the millivolt range; however, in many cases, microvolt-level signals are of significant interest. Although these potentials are not difficult to amplify, the detection and measurement of bioelectric potentials from tissue or skin are not straightforward processes. Many people have found through hard experience that the placement of electrodes on the skin often creates an assortment of biopotential measurement problems. These include baseline drifts, motion artifacts, and interference originating from power wiring and radiofrequency sources. Some of these problems originate from a lack of understanding of electrode characteristics. Careful electrode selection and placement, with a solid understanding of electrode use, are important in achieving good-quality biopotential recordings.

Electrode metals used to monitor low-level biopotentials perform the function of transducing ionic electrochemical reactions into a current carried by electrons in wires. Electrochemical reactions must occur at the interface of the electrode surface. Otherwise, no charge transfer will occur to the electrode wire, and a recording apparatus would not measure a biopotential.

22.5.2 Electrode-Electrolyte Interface

When metals are placed in electrolytes, such as in the saline environment of tissue or skin, atoms of the metal slightly dissolve into solution. This slight dissolution of metal is accompanied by a loss of electrons to the atoms that remain with the parent metal. It leaves the parent metal with a net negative charge and the dissolved metal ions with a positive charge. The created electric field tends to draw the ions back to the vicinity of the metal surface; however, energy is required for their recombination, so the ions are just held close to the metal surface. An interfacial double layer of charged ions is formed, as seen in the model in Fig. 22.20.

This model is attributable to the great nineteenth-century scientist Herman von Helmholtz, although there are several other models. The dissolved metal ions line up in a double layer of atomically thin sheets immediately next to the parent metal. This layer has electric qualities of a battery, a capacitor, and an electric resistor. These qualities profoundly affect bioelectrode performance and its ability to accurately report biopotentials.

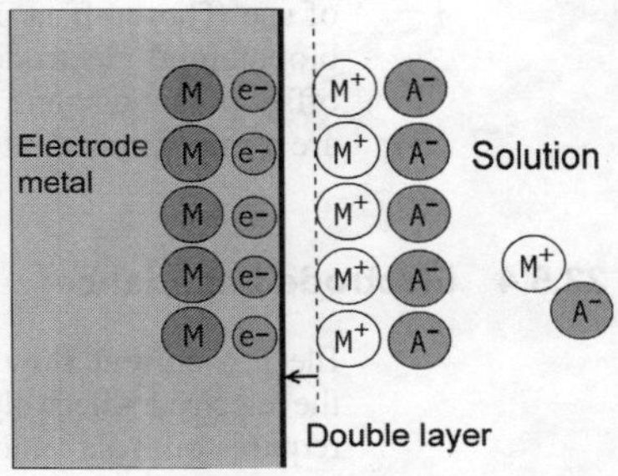

FIGURE 22.20 The Helmholtz layer is an electric double layer of charged metal ions (M^+) and anions (A^-) facing each other at the electrode-electrolyte interface.

22.5.3 Electrode Half-Cell Potential

Two metal electrodes placed into an electrolytic solution constitute what is called an *electrochemical cell*. A potential arises at the solution interface of each electrode due to the separation of charged ions across its double layer. This potential is known as the *electrode half-cell potential*. It cannot be measured directly since it requires some reference potential for comparison.

Two dissimilar metal electrodes placed in an electrolyte will show a potential difference that is a function of the metals used, the electrolyte composition, and the temperature. Half-cell potential differences can be up to several volts and are the basis of the electric batteries used to power appliances. Theoretically, the cell potential difference between two electrodes E_{cell} can be determined by knowing the half-cell potential of each electrode E_{hc1} and E_{hc2} with respect to some common reference electrode. Thus the cell potential difference is given by

$$E_{cell} = E_{hc1} - E_{hc2}$$

The value of this electric field depends on the electrochemical potentials of the electrode metals and is related to their position in the electrochemical series. Table 22.3 shows some values for some common electrode metals at room temperature. Electrochemists have by convention adopted the hydrogen electrode as a standard of reference potential and assigned it a value of 0 V. All other metals have a nonzero potential with respect to it. Metal half-cell potentials depend on their electrochemical oxidation state, and they are usually arranged in a table showing their activity relative to others, such as seen in Table 22.3.

In theory, if two electrodes are of the same metal, their individual half-cell potentials are the same, and so the cell potential difference should equal zero. This is desirable for biopotential monitoring. Otherwise, the electrode pair would add an offset potential to the biopotential being monitored.

Unfortunately, unbalanced half-cell potentials are often the case with biopotential electrodes. Primarily, this is due to different electrode metal surface states that occur through oxidation occurring with air exposure, tarnishing, metallurgical preparation, previous electrolyte exposure, or past history

TABLE 22.3 Half-Cell Potentials of Some Common Metals at 25°C[6]

Metal and reaction	Electrode potential E_{hc}
$Al \rightarrow Al^{3+} + 3e^-$	−1.67
$Fe \rightarrow Fe^{2+} + 2e^-$	−0.441
$H_2 \rightarrow 2H^+ + 2e^-$	0 by definition
$Cu \rightarrow Cu^{2+} + 2e^-$	+0.340
$Ag^+ + Cl^- \rightarrow AgCl$	+0.223
$Ag \rightarrow Ag^+ + e^-$	+0.799

of use. These offset potentials typically range from several tens of millivolts with commercial silver biopotential electrodes to hundreds of millivolts with electrodes such as stainless steel. Electrode offset potentials tend to be unstable and drift in amplitude with time and accumulated use. Electrodes are a major contributor to slow baseline drifts in biopotential measurements.

22.5.4 Electrode Impedance

Electric current flow though electrodes occurs through the agency of electrochemical reactions at the electrode-electrolyte interface layer. These reactions do not always occur readily and usually require some activation energy, and so the electrode interface can be a source of electrical resistance. Depending on the electrode composition and its area, electrode-electrolyte resistance is on the order of a few hundred ohms with typical ECG skin electrodes and thousands to millions of ohms with small wire electrodes and microelectrodes. Electrode interface resistance is usually not large compared with other resistance in the electrode-biological circuit.

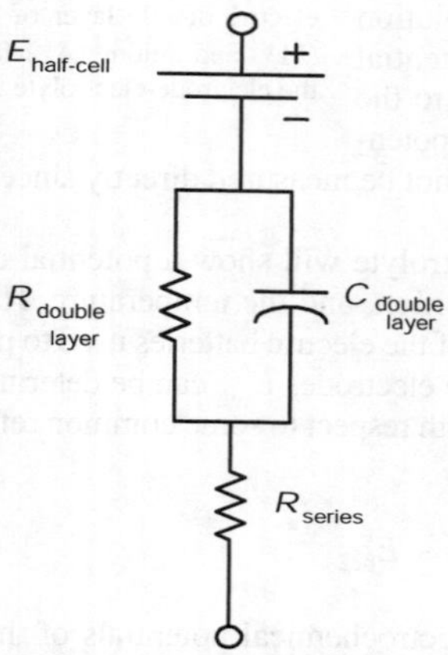

FIGURE 22.21 Electric equivalent circuit of a biopotential electrode.

The separation and storage of charge across the electrode double layer are equivalent to an electric capacitance. This capacitance is relatively high per unit area, on the order of 10 to 100 μF/cm^2 with many metals in physiologic electrolytes. Together the electrode resistance and capacitance form a complex impedance to electric current flows. A simple diagram of an equivalent electric circuit is given in Fig. 22.21. The electrode-electrolyte interface is somewhat more complicated than linear models can easily show. For example, the equivalent capacitance and resistance of an electrode R_e and C_e are not fixed but fall in value roughly as a square-root function of frequency.

The result is that bioelectrodes more easily pass alternating or time-varying currents at frequencies above a few hundred hertz than they do with steady currents or low frequencies. Fortunately, this has little impact on most bioelectric recording applications, such as ECG or electroencephalography (EEG). Even higher-frequency EMG recordings are only nominally impacted. This is so because high-input-impedance bioelectric amplifiers are relatively insensitive to moderate changes in electrode impedance that occur as a function of frequency.

The frequency-dependent behavior of electrode impedance is of more concern in intracellular microelectrode recording applications, where electrode resistances are very high. In conjunction with the electrode capacitance and that of the recording circuit, a low-pass filter is formed at the microelectrode interface that tends to distort high-frequency portions of action events.

Frequency-dependent electrode impedance is also important in bioelectric stimulation applications, where relatively larger currents and complex waveforms are often used to stimulate excitable tissues.

22.5.5 Electrode Electrochemistry

In most metal electrodes, a process of chemical oxidation and reduction transfers current. At the anode, oxidation occurs, and electrons are given up to the parent metal. Reduction occurs at the cathode, where metal ions in solution accept electrons from the metal.

Actually, this is a process of mass transfer since, with oxidation, metal ions leave the electrode and move into solution and, with reduction, metal ions form a metal precipitate on the electrode. Ordinarily, current flow in biopotential recording electrodes is very small. Therefore, only minuscule quantities of the electrode metal are transferred to or from electrode surfaces. Biocurrent flows are also generally oscillating, so the transference of ions is cyclic between the electrodes with no net mass transfer. This process of electrode mass transfer through dissolution and precipitation of metal ions is depicted in Fig. 22.22.

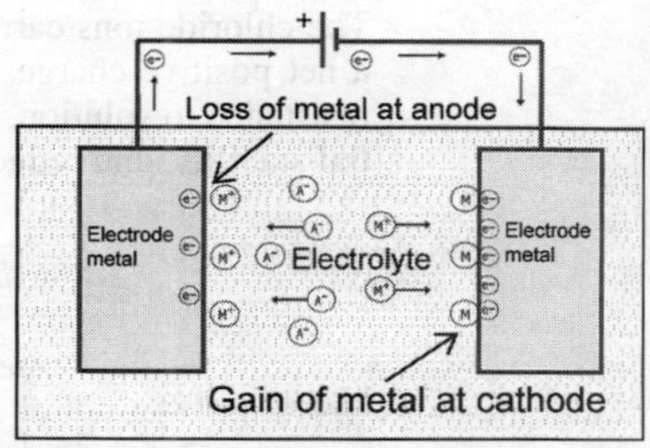

FIGURE 22.22 Transfer of charge due to transfer of ionized atoms of the electrode mass.

There are exceptions to electric conduction by electrode mass transfer. Noble metals such as platinum, iridium, and gold are electrochemically inert. When placed into solution, they usually do not significantly lose their substance to ionization. They are still useful as bioelectrodes, however, because they catalyze electrochemical reactions in solution by donating or accepting electrons without actually contributing their mass to the electrochemical process. They participate by catalyzing reactions at their surface but are not consumed. They are often electrically modeled as capacitors, but this is not a perfect model since they will pass steady currents. Although unconsumed, noble metal electrodes are generally not as electrically stable as other kinds of electrodes used in monitoring applications.

22.5.6 Electrode Polarization

Metal electrodes present a complex electrochemical interface to solution that often does not allow electric charge to traverse with equal ease in both current directions. For example, in some metal-electrolyte systems, such as iron-saline solutions, there is a greater tendency for iron to oxidize than to reduce.

Common experience reveals that iron easily oxidizes (rusts) but resists reversal back to the iron base metal. In electrochemistry, this process is known as *electrode polarization*. A result of polarization is higher electrode resistance to current flow in one direction versus the other. With polarization, the electrode half-cell potential value also tends to vary from table values and depends on the direction and magnitude of electrode current flow. It is desirable for electrodes to be electrochemically reversible since this prevents the process of polarization. Electrode polarization is a problem in biopotential measurements because it is associated with electric instability. It gives rise to offset potentials between electrodes, electrode noise, and high resistance.

Electrodes made from electrically conductive metals such as pure silver, copper, tin, or aluminum are not electrochemically reversible and so do not provide the best or lowest-resistance pathway to electrolytic solutions or to tissue. These metals are electrochemically reactive (corrode) in (physiologic) electrolytes, even with no current flow.

The best bioelectric interfaces are combinations of metals and their metallic salts, usually chlorides. The metal salt is used as a coating on the base metal and acts as an intermediary in the electrode-electrolyte processes. Silver, in combination with a chloride coating, is the most widely used biopotential recording electrode. Silver chemically reacts in chloride-bearing fluids such as saline, skin sweat, and body fluids containing potassium and sodium chloride. After a few hours of immersion, a silver electrode will become coated with a thin layer of silver chlorides. This occurs by the spontaneous reaction:

$$\mathrm{Ag + NaCl \rightarrow AgCl + Na^+}$$

The outer layer of silver chloride is highly reversible with chloride ions in physiologic electrolytes, and the silver is highly reversible with its salts. Thus current can reversibly flow across the electrode by a two-stage chemical reaction:

$$\mathrm{Ag \leftrightarrow Ag^+} + e^-$$
$$\mathrm{Ag^+ + Cl^- \leftrightarrow AgCl}$$

The chloride ions carry net negative charges in chloride-bearing electrolytes, and silver ions carry a net positive charge. This two-stage process of electric charge transfer greatly lowers electrode resistance to solution, reduces electrode polarization to near zero, improves electrode offset potential stability, and reduces electrochemical noise.

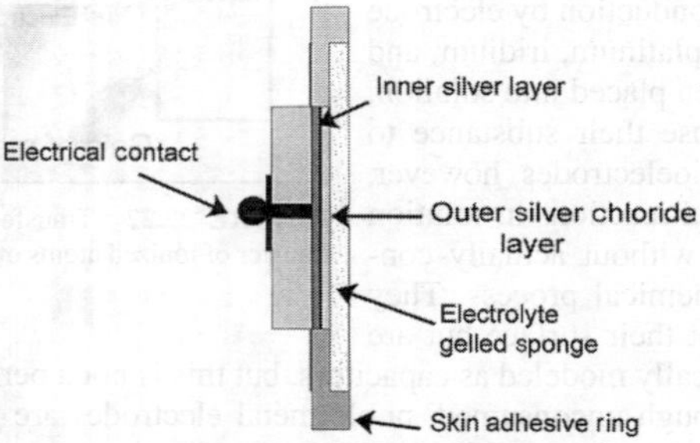

FIGURE 22.23 Silver–silver chloride electrode construction.

To conserve silver metal, commercial silver–silver chloride electrodes, sold for clinical and other high-volume biopotential monitoring, consist of thin layers of silver deposited over an underlying steel electrode. A thin layer of silver chloride is then formed electrochemically on the silver surface by the manufacturer. It may also be formed during recording by a chemical reaction with an applied gel containing high concentrations of potassium chloride. Usually, a thin sponge pad holds a gel electrolyte in contact with the silver, as shown in Fig. 22.23. It provides a suitable wick or electrolyte contact with the skin. Thus coupling of the silver chloride with the skin occurs through the electrolyte gel rather than by direct contact.

Thin-layer silver electrodes are usually designed for single-use application, not chronic or continuous monitoring applications, since the silver surface and chloride layer are easily scratched. When the underlying silver base metal is exposed, the silver electrode becomes polarizable, degrading its performance. An example of a single-use silver–silver chloride electrode can be seen in Fig. 22.24A. The pure-silver electrodes seen in Fig. 22.24B are sometimes used in EEG recording. These electrodes develop a chloride layer with the application of a salty gel during their use and can be cleaned afterwards for reuse.

The most rugged and reusable electrodes are made of a matrix of fused silver and silver chloride powders. These composite electrodes form a hard and durable pellet. They are relatively expensive but offer superior performance. A photograph of this type is shown in Fig. 22.24C. If the surface of this composite electrode is scratched or damaged, it can be resurfaced with abrasion to provide a renewed composition of silver–silver chloride. Furthermore, these reusable electrodes exhibit low polarization, low electrical noise, and low electrical impedance.

22.5.7 Stimulating Bioelectrodes

Stimulating electrodes pass significant currents to biological fluids for evoking action potential events and for other purposes. They must satisfy a different set of performance requirements than those for biopotential monitoring. For stimulation, silver–silver chloride electrodes are not usually the best choice, particularly when stimulating current pulses are not symmetrical in polarity through the electrode. High-current monophasic pulses, for example, can cause significant amounts of silver to be lost from the anode, and silver or other metal ions in solution will precipitate on the cathode. This leads to an asymmetry in chemical composition of the electrodes, differential impedance, and the usually undesirable introduction of silver metal into biological media, which may have toxic consequences.

To avoid injection of metal ions into biological tissues, electrodes using the noble metals are the best choice. Although they are expensive, their resistance to corrosion and good biocompatibility often outweigh the expense. Like all metal-electrolyte systems, their electric impedance and ability to transfer charge to solution depends on the current frequency. At higher frequencies, the high capacitive nature of noble electrodes in solution permits good charge transfer.

Stainless steel and certain other noncorrodable alloys are often used for cost reasons when the electrode surface area is relatively large. Also, graphite powder dispersed in a polymer binder has been used as a low-cost, large-area electrode for such applications as skeletal muscle stimulation.

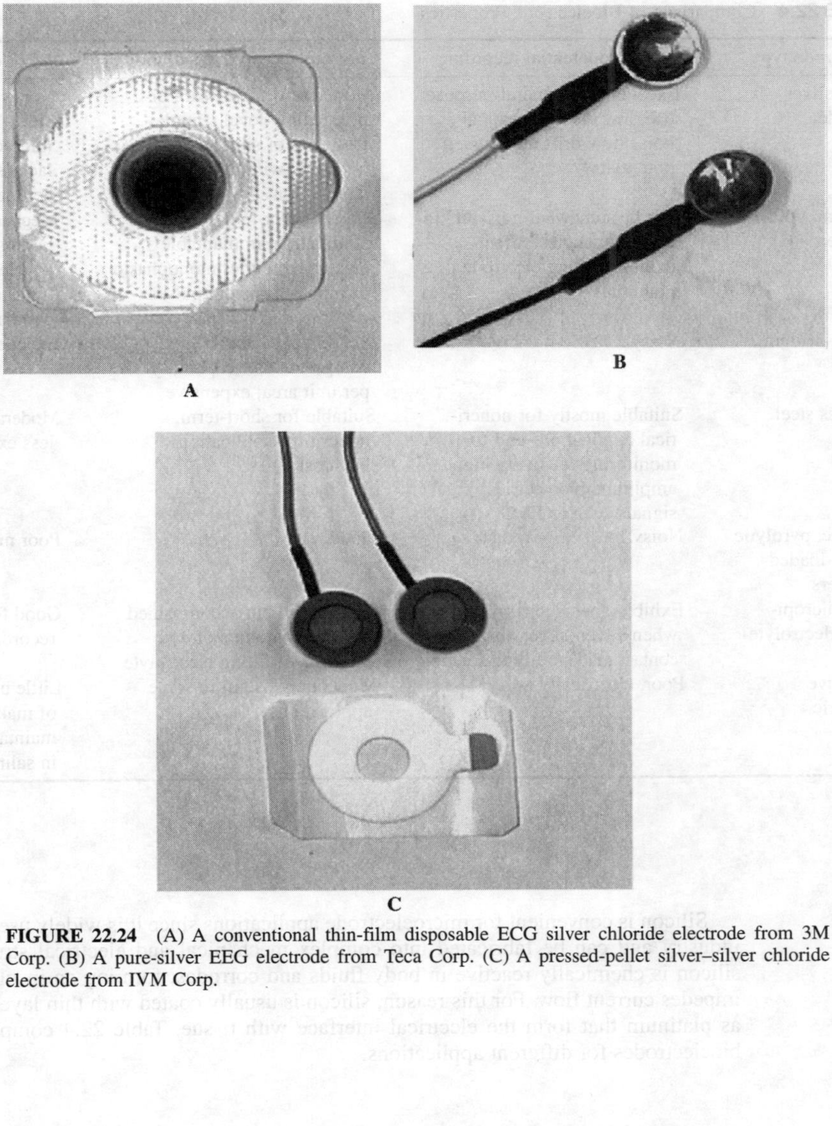

FIGURE 22.24 (A) A conventional thin-film disposable ECG silver chloride electrode from 3M Corp. (B) A pure-silver EEG electrode from Teca Corp. (C) A pressed-pellet silver–silver chloride electrode from IVM Corp.

Although stainless steel and graphite electrodes generally have high impedance per unit area, this becomes less of a concern when electrodes have large (several square centimeter) surface areas because the overall impedance is low. Tungsten is not a noble metal, but it is minimally reactive in physiologic fluids when current densities are low and the stimulating current is biphasic. Tungsten is often used for penetrating microelectrodes since it has a high stiffness and good mechanical qualities.

The reversible electrode tin–tin chloride is available commercially at about half the cost of silver-based electrodes. Tin electrodes are approved in the United States for EEG monitoring applications; however, they seem not as durable as silver electrodes and are not as widely used.

TABLE 22.4 Comparison of Bioelectrode Properties

Electrode type	For biopotential recording	For bioelectrical stimulation	For cellular microelectrodes
Silver–silver chloride	Excellent for general-purpose use; low electrochemical noise, low drift, low offset potentials	Moderately useful with biphasic, low-level stimulation; loss of silver chloride on anode with monophasic stimulation	Works well for placement inside glass barrel liquid-coupled microelectrodes; silver itself lacks sufficient stiffness for cell penetration
Platinum, gold, tungsten	Can be somewhat noisy at low frequencies; often exhibit drifting electrode potentials	Excellent for long-term stimulation, implantable electrodes, either monophasic or biphasic current pulses	Mechanical and physical qualities are useful and often outweigh problems of higher noise; tungsten has high stiffness for cellular penetration
Iridium–iridium oxide	Noisy	Good; a particularly high charge-transfer capability per unit area; expensive	Excellent for microstimulation
Stainless steel	Suitable mostly for noncritical applications and for monitoring relatively high amplitude bioelectric signals such as ECG	Suitable for short-term, noncritical applications; low cost	Moderately useful for stimulation; less expensive
Graphite, pyrolytic carbon-loaded polymers	Noisy	Good	Poor mechanical qualities
Glass micropipette, electrolyte-filled	Exhibits low electrical noise when silver–silver chloride contact made to filling solution	Often used, but accompanied by small amounts of iono-phoresis of filling electrolyte	Good for low-noise intracellular recordings
Capacitive dielectric	Poor, electrically noisy	Moderately useful in some applications	Little used due to the difficulty of making thin dielectrics that maintain a high resistivity in saline

Silicon is convenient for microelectrode applications since it is widely used in the semiconductor industry and can be fabricated into complex mechanical and electrical structures. Unfortunately, silicon is chemically reactive in body fluids and corrodes, forming an insulating glass (SiO_2) that impedes current flow. For this reason, silicon is usually coated with thin layers of other metals such as platinum that form the electrical interface with tissue. Table 22.4 compares different types of bioelectrodes for different applications.

22.5.8 Electrode-Skin Interface

Perhaps the greatest problems encountered in biopotential recording are noise, motion artifacts, and a general instability of the biopotential monitored signal. These problems are most severe when electrodes are placed on dry skin. They are less of an issue with invasive, implanted, or intracellular electrodes.

Placement of electrodes directly on the skin will show a large electrical resistance, often in the megohm (10^6) region. This is due mostly to the surface layer of dead and dehydrated skin cells on the epidermis, known as the *corneum*. Below the epidermis, the next sublayer is the living part of the skin, known as the *dermis*. It exhibits a complex electrical behavior having a resistance, capacitance, and potential generators similar in some respects to that of electrodes.

More stable bioelectric recordings from the skin are achieved with application of a liquid or gel electrolyte between the skin and electrode, as shown in Fig. 22.25. This bridges the electrode surface to the skin. The gel is an aqueous chloride-bearing solution that will hydrate the skin, reduce the impedance of the corneum, and produce a more uniform medium for charge transfer. Skin-electrode impedance can drop below 5 kΩ across the hydrated skin and abraded corneum. High impedances in the range of 20 to 100 kΩ are not uncommon if the skin is not adequately prepared, i.e., abraded and clean.

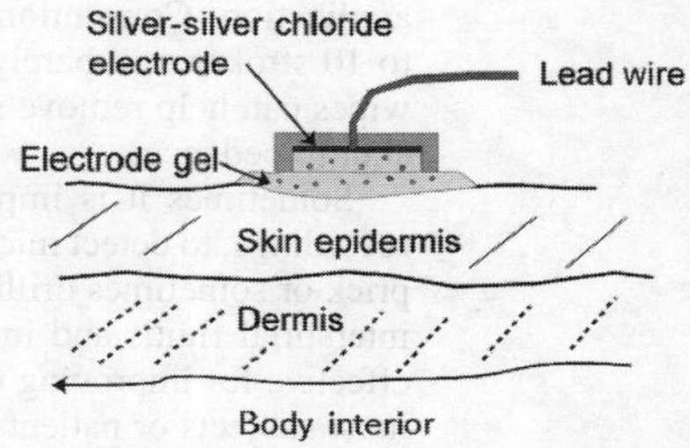

FIGURE 22.25 Electrode-skin coupling using a gel electrolyte.

Gel electrolytes provide a convenient method of coupling between the silver–silver chloride electrodes to the skin surface. The gel also helps protect the thin silver chloride layer on the electrode from abrasion with the skin surface as well as to hydrate the skin. After several minutes, gel electrolytes saturate the outer resistive layers of dead skin and form a low-impedance pathway to the body interior.

Commercial electrode gels usually use relatively high concentrations of potassium or sodium chlorides at a neutral pH. Since these concentration levels can irritate the skin, there are different types of gels on the market offering trade-offs of low resistance versus gentleness to the skin.

The living nature of the dermis also creates an electrochemical potential called a *skin battery*.[7] This battery is associated with the function of the sweat glands. It is very pressure-sensitive. Small movements or forces on the electrodes cause transient millivolt-order changes in the skin-battery magnitude.[8] These changes appear as motion artifacts and wandering baselines on biopotential traces.

The skin potential due to electrolytes placed on the skin E_{skin} and the intrinsic battery potential generated by the sweat glands E_{sweat} are usually modeled as two batteries in parallel with internal resistances, as shown in Fig. 22.26.

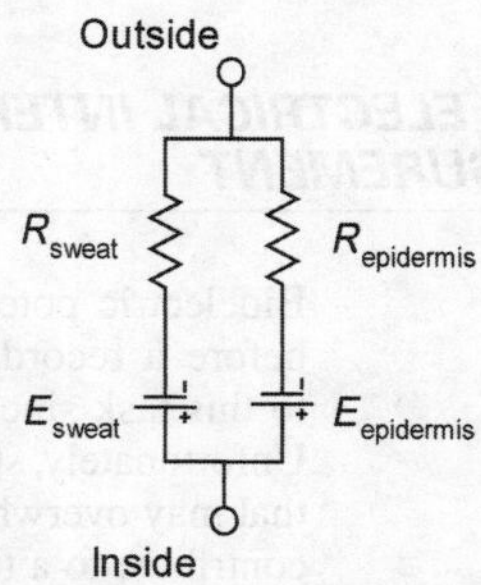

FIGURE 22.26 Illustration of the electric nature of the skin.

The electric sources in the skin vary with time, temperature, hydration, and pressure. For example, a buildup of sweat under the electrodes will cause slow changes in the monitored dc potential. Pressure on the electrodes causes deformation of the skin and consequent resistance change that shunts the skin battery and changes its magnitude. These effects are particularly frustrating to the recording of low-frequency biopotentials since they produce a wandering baseline.

The skin battery is partially modulated by sympathetic nervous system activity. This interesting effect is known as the *skin potential response* (SPR). It arises due to a varying electric shunt resistance across the skin that occurs with both capillary vasodilatation and changes in sweat duct activity that are under autonomic nervous control.[9,10] Fast-changing emotional states such as excitement or alarm can produce millivolt-order changes in the skin potential that are then superimposed on the monitored biopotential. This effect is similar to the better-known *galvanic skin response* (GSR), which directly measures the changes in skin resistance as a function of emotional stress. GSR recording is sometimes used in forensic applications, such as lie detectors.

22.5.9 Skin Preparation

The key to fast electrode equilibration with the skin is removing or abrogating the skin corneum. This is usually performed by skin abrasion. Fine-grit abrasive materials are sometimes incorporated into commercial electric coupling creams so that outer layers of dead skin will be removed on application. Conventional 320- to 400-grit sandpaper applied with light pressure using about 6 to 10 strokes will barely redden the skin but dramatically reduce the skin resistance.[11–13] Alcohol wipes can help remove skin oils in preparation for gel application but are not used alone to reduce skin impedance.

Sometimes it is important to reduce skin resistance to the lowest possible value, as in EEG recordings, to detect microvolt-level signals. In this case, the skin barrier is punctured by using a pinprick or sometimes drilling with small abrasive tools.[14] The abraded region or puncture fills up with interstitial fluids and immediately forms a low-resistance pathway to the body interior. Although effective for improving bioelectrode performance, it is often not popular (for obvious reasons) with most subjects or patients.

Commercial skin electrodes are usually packaged in metal foil wrappers that are impervious to moisture. These wrappers help prevent evaporation of the gel and should not be removed until the electrodes are to be used. The electrodes should always be examined for adequate gel prior to application.

Although electrode gels are needed for good skin contact, hydrating electrolytes produce another source of electric potential, known as a *skin diffusion potential*, in addition to the skin battery. This diffusion potential arises because skin membranes are semipermeable to ions. The magnitude of this skin potential varies as a function of the salt composition in the electrolyte.

Thus there are multiple electric potentials in addition to the biopotential detected by skin electrodes. These electrode and skin potentials drift with skin temperature, pressure, equilibration time, and emotional excitement. Whether these potentials are significant in recording depends on the frequency of the biopotential signal. The diagnostic ECG, for example, requires the recording of relatively low-frequency (0.05 Hz) signals and is vulnerable to these effects. The higher-frequency EMG recordings can largely filter these out.

22.6 ELECTRICAL INTERFERENCE PROBLEMS IN BIOPOTENTIAL MEASUREMENT

Bioelectric potentials are relatively low-level electric signals and must be substantially amplified before a recording can be easily displayed. Modern integrated-circuit amplifiers are well suited to this task since they have high gains and contribute little noise to the biopotential measurement. Unfortunately, skin-monitored biopotentials typically show a complexity of interfering electric signals that may overwhelm the desired signals. This is so because the size and bulk of animals and humans contribute to a type of antenna effect for environmental electric fields.

22.6.1 Power-Line Interference

In modern society we are immersed in a complex electromagnetic environment originating from power wiring in buildings, radio transmitters of various sorts, radiofrequency-emitting appliances such as computers, and natural sources such as atmospheric electricity. Within the home, environmental electric fields will typically induce in the human body a few tens of millivolts with respect to a ground reference. These fields can be much larger, as high as a few volts, if someone is using a cell phone or is located within a foot of power-line wiring or near a radio station. These induced voltages are thousands of times larger than the bioelectric signals from the heart as recorded on the chest surface.

Electric coupling of the body to environmental sources is usually due to proximity capacitance and, to a lesser extent, inductive (magnetic) fields. Capacitive coupling between two objects results from the electric field between them. The space or air gap separating the objects acts as a dielectric. The coupling can be simply modeled as a parallel-plate capacitor, which can be determined by

$$C = \frac{\epsilon A}{d}$$

where $\epsilon = \epsilon_0 \epsilon_r$, where the individual ϵ dielectric constants are for free space and air, respectively
A = area of mutual conductor plate interception
d = separation distance

For example, let A be equal to the surface area of the human body intercepted by a power line and d be a distance less than 1 m from it. In this situation, only fractions of a picofarad (10^{-12} F) coupling results. However, due to the closer proximity to the floor, a person usually will have greater coupling to ground than to the power line, perhaps by a factor of 100 or more. As a result, a voltage divider is created, and the body acquires a potential, known as a *floating potential* V_{float}. Its magnitude, as measured by a voltmeter with a ground reference, is determined by the ratio of impedances of the body to the power line Z_{line}, where $Z_{line} = 2\pi f C_{line}$, and ground Z_{ground}, where $Z_{ground} = 2\pi f C_{ground}$. This arrangement is shown in Fig. 22.27 and ignores any ground resistance since it is usually negligible. The body itself is a volume conductor with such a low relative resistance that it is not significant to this analysis.

In this case, a subject's floating potential is given by the impedance divider relationship:

$$V_{float} = V_{line} \frac{Z_{ground}}{Z_{line} + Z_{ground}}$$

The floating potential can be a relatively large induced potential. Take, for example, a person sitting in a metal chair. If the person's proximity capacitance to the power line is assumed to be 1 pF, the ground impedance Z_{ground} is $10^7\ \Omega$, and the line voltage is 120 V_{rms} (338 $V_{pk\text{-}pk}$) at 60 Hz (in the USA), then the calculated floating potential is

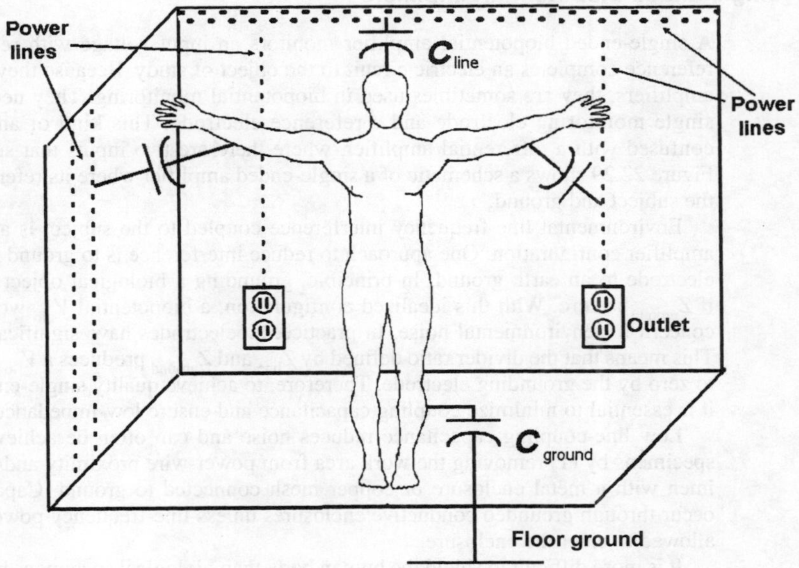

FIGURE 22.27 Illustration of body capacitive line coupling.

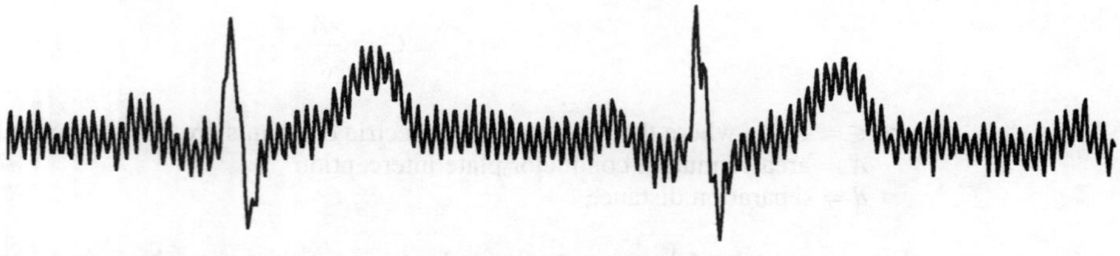

FIGURE 22.28 Power-line coupling interference in an ECG waveform.

$$Z_{\text{line}} = \frac{1}{2\pi fC} = \frac{1}{2\pi(60)(10^{-12})} = 2.65 \times 10^{0}\,\Omega$$
$$V_{\text{float}} = 338(10^{7} / 2.65 \times 10^{9} + 10^{7}) = 1.27\ V_{\text{pk-pk}}$$

This V_{float} is present uniformly over the body and will sum with a skin biopotential V_{bio}. The output of the amplifier V_{out} is the sum of all potentials at its input. Thus the floating potential is summed with the biopotential:

$$V_{\text{out}} = V_{\text{float}} + V_{\text{bio}}$$

In the preceding example, the line-induced interference is more than 10,000 times greater than could be tolerated in a recording. It is an artifact with a sinusoidal waveform characteristic. Figure 22.28 provides an example of this type of power-line interference in an ECG recording.

22.6.2 Single-Ended Biopotential Amplifiers

A single-ended biopotential amplifier monitors an input voltage with respect to its reference. Its reference completes an electric circuit to the object of study. Because they are simple, single-ended amplifiers, they are sometimes used in biopotential monitoring. They need only two electrodes, a single monitoring electrode and a reference electrode. This kind of amplifier should not to be confused with a differential amplifier, where there are two inputs that subtract from one another. Figure 22.29 shows a schematic of a single-ended amplifier where its reference is connected to both the subject and ground.

Environmental line-frequency interference coupled to the subject is a major challenge for this amplifier configuration. One approach to reduce interference is to ground the body with a reference electrode to an earth ground. In principle, grounding a biological object will reduce V_{float} to zero if Z_{ground} is zero. With this idealized configuration, a biopotential V_{bio} would be amplified without concern for environmental noise. In practice, bioelectrodes have significant electrical impedances. This means that the divider ratio defined by Z_{line} and Z_{ground} produces a V_{float} value that is not reduced to zero by the grounding electrode. Therefore, to achieve quality single-ended amplifier recordings, it is essential to minimize coupling capacitance and ensure low-impedance reference electrodes.

Low line-coupling capacitance reduces noise and can often be achieved with small biological specimens by (1) removing the work area from power-wire proximity and/or (2) shielding the specimen with a metal enclosure or copper mesh connected to ground. Capacitive coupling does not occur through grounded conductive enclosures unless line-frequency power wires to equipment are allowed to enter the enclosure.

It is more difficult to shield the human body than biological specimens because of the body's bulk and greater surface area. Skin-electrode resistance is also greater than that of invasive electrodes used in biological specimens, and this causes higher floating potentials on the human body. Except under

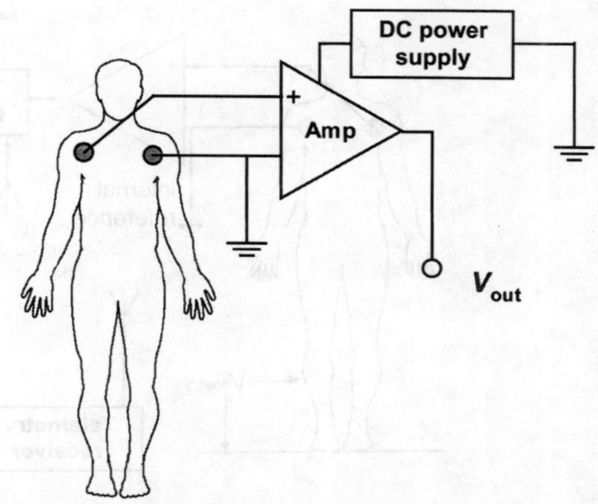

FIGURE 22.29 Recording of a biopotential using a single-ended amplifier.

certain conditions discussed later, these circumstances can create frustration in using single-ended amplifiers for human recording.

For example, if a subject's electrode-skin impedance $Z_{electrode}$ is 20 kΩ, this value is low enough that it dominates over his or her ground capacitance such that essentially $Z_{ground} = Z_{electrode}$. Assuming the same line-coupling capacitance as before (1 pF) and using the voltage-divider relation given earlier, the calculated floating potential V_{float} is now much lower:

$$V_{float} = 338 \frac{20\,\text{k}\Omega}{20\,\text{k}\Omega + 2.65 \times 10^9\,\Omega}$$
$$= 2.5\,\text{mV at 60 Hz}$$

Under these electric capacitive coupling circumstances (which are rather severe), this example shows that a single-ended amplifier referenced to a grounded body experiences power-main interference 250 percent larger than a 1-mV ECG. The ECG will appear to be undesirably riding on a large oscillatory artifact.

22.6.3 Biotelemetry

Isolating the amplifier and recording system from earth ground can significantly reduce problems with line-noise interference. Remember, a subject's floating potential appears with respect to an earth-ground reference since it originates from capacitive coupling to power lines. Power lines from the electric service are referenced to earth ground in the electric distribution system. Thus, isolating the biopotential amplifier and its reference from earth ground would eliminate the appearance of floating potentials across the amplifier inputs. An isolated system, however, still must have an amplifier reference on the subject's body in order to complete the electric circuit.

Biotelemetry is one way to provide this kind of isolation. In conjunction with battery-powered amplifiers, biotelemetry can be a very effective way to reduce electromagnetic interference in biopotential recordings since it can be isolated from ground reference. This is depicted in Fig. 22.30. Here, the isolated system reference is shown by the triangle symbol rather than the segmented lines of earth ground.

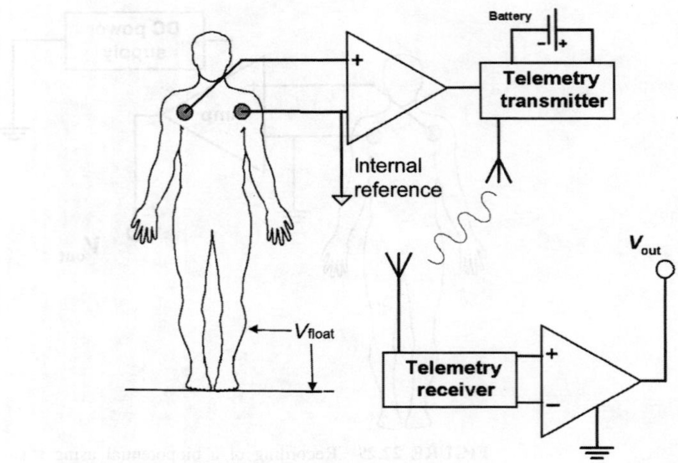

FIGURE 22.30 Biotelemetry recording system.

An isolated amplifier is referenced only to the body under measurement and so in principle does not detect any of the V_{float}. It is not that V_{float} is zero; it is just that it does not appear at the amplifier input and so is not in the equations. Thus, for an amplifier gain of $A = 1$,

$$V_{out} = V_{bio}$$

Biotelemetry also has the significant advantage of allowing the use of single-ended amplifiers that only require two electrodes for measurement. Three electrodes are required by differential amplifier recording techniques. Fewer electrodes simplify measurement and require less labor in electrode application and maintenance.

In practice, biopotential recording by battery-powered biotelemetry works quite well in interference rejection. The remaining sources of signal interference have to do with magnetically coupled potentials induced into the lead wires, and these problems are specific to certain environments, such as those in close proximity to high-current-carrying wires or high-power appliances.

Miniature telemetry systems are becoming more widely used for biopotential recording applications. However, the added cost and complexity are often a disadvantage. Their greatest utility has so far been in patient ambulatory applications in the clinic, such as ECG monitoring. However, small wireless systems for multichannel monitoring the EMG in biomechanics applications are often useful, as are microsized systems for neural recordings in brain research on animals. In this latter case, the wireless nature of the link can essentially eliminate power-line interferences that are a problem in recording the microvolt-level signals from EEG.

Battery-powered amplifiers are isolated and convenient for portable applications but are not the same as biotelemetry. Unfortunately, connection of a battery-powered amplifier to a recording system without any other isolation in the connecting cables unavoidably interconnects the amplifier reference to the recording instrument reference, the latter of which itself is usually connected to a power-line ground. This abrogates the advantage of battery isolation on the power supply. Solutions can consist of using optical isolators on the signal output leads or using commercial isolation amplifiers.

22.6.4 Differential Biopotential Amplifiers

The use of differential amplifiers is common in biopotential measurements because of a greater ability to reject environmental interference compared with ground-referenced single-ended amplifiers. Differential amplifiers subtract the electric potential present at one place on the body from that of another. Both potentials are measured with respect to a third body location that serves as a common point of reference.

Differential amplifiers are useful because biopotentials generated within the body vary over the body surface, but line-coupled noise does not. For example, subtraction of the heart electric potential at two points on the chest surface will produce a resulting potential since the local biopotential amplitudes and wave shapes at each electrode are different. Environmental electric fields from the power line are more remote and couple such that they are present uniformly over the body. This is partly due to the distributed nature of capacitive coupling. It is also because the low 50- to 60-Hz line frequencies have electric field wavelengths so long (hundreds of meters) that a person's body can be considered to be, in some sense, an antenna in the uniform near field of an electric field source.

The induced body potential V_{float} is present at both inputs of a difference amplifier, and as used here, it is also known as the common-mode potential V_{cm}. This is so because it is common (equal) in amplitude and phase at each of the two amplifier inputs. Thus, for our differential amplifier,

$$V_{\text{cm}} = V_{\text{float}}$$

The connection of a differential amplifier always requires three electrodes since a common reference point for the amplifier is needed. This point can be anywhere on the body, but by convention in ECG measurements, for example, the right leg is used as this reference. Figure 22.31 illustrates this situation.

Differential amplifiers of gain A perform the following operation:

$$V_{\text{out}} = A(V_1 - V_2)$$

where V_1 and V_2 are the signal levels on each of the noninverting and inverting inputs of the amplifier, respectively, with respect to a reference. In practice, differential amplifiers very closely approach this ideal. Modern differential amplifiers can have common-mode rejection ratios of 120 dB or better, meaning that they perform the subtraction to better than one part per million.

The grounding electrode, as in the preceding single-ended case, also reduces the common-mode potential on the body surface. Even if the ground were not effective due to a large electrode resistance,

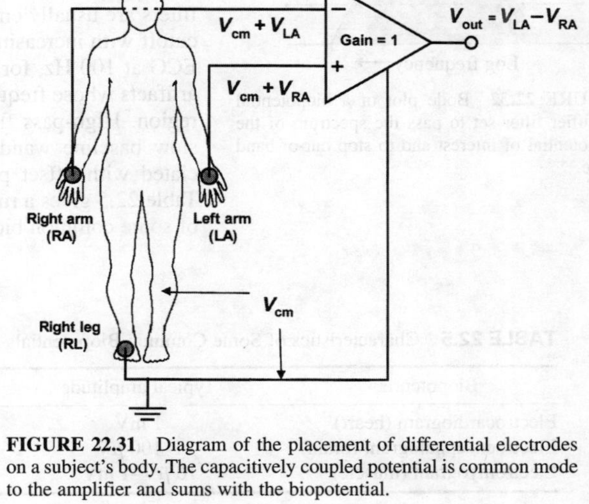

FIGURE 22.31 Diagram of the placement of differential electrodes on a subject's body. The capacitively coupled potential is common mode to the amplifier and sums with the biopotential.

within a fairly large range of common-mode levels, the differential amplifier would be capable of near-perfect cancellation of the common-mode signal.

In ECG monitoring, for example, the common-mode interference on the body sums with the arm-lead potentials V_{RA} and V_{LA}. If we calculate V_{out} under these circumstances, we get

$$V_{out} = A[(V_{cm} + V_{LA}) - (V_{cm} + V_{RA})] = A(V_{LA} - V_{RA})$$
$$= AV_{ECG}$$

The quantity $V_{LA} - V_{RA}$ is the definition of ECG lead I.

In practice, this interference cancellation process works fairly well; however, the assumption that the power-line-induced signal is common mode (uniform) over the body does not hold perfectly in all situations. Slight differences in its phase or amplitude over the subject's body when in close proximity to some electric field source or unbalanced electrode impedances can cause this cancellation process to be less than perfect. Some line noise may still pass through into the recording. Usually, improvements in skin electrode preparation can remedy this problem.

22.6.5 Bandpass Filtering

An understanding of the frequency content of bioelectric signals can be helpful in maximizing the biopotential recording quality. Cell membrane sodium channel activation is probably the fastest of bioelectric events in living things. In heart cells, for example, these occur over time scales on the order of 30 μs. In practice, most bioelectric recordings of fast body surface potentials such as the EMG and cell neural spikes show no significant difference in wave shape with amplifier bandwidths at about 5 kHz. Wider bandwidths than this tend to admit disproportionately more noise than signal.

Both high-pass and low-pass filters are generally needed in biopotential recordings. Setting the filter cutoffs implies knowledge of the biopotential frequency spectrum of interest. In general, it is desirable to narrow amplifier bandwidths as much as possible to reduce power-line noise, radio-station interference, digital computer noise, and electric fields in the tens of kilohertz range such as those associated with the cathode-ray-tube monitors.

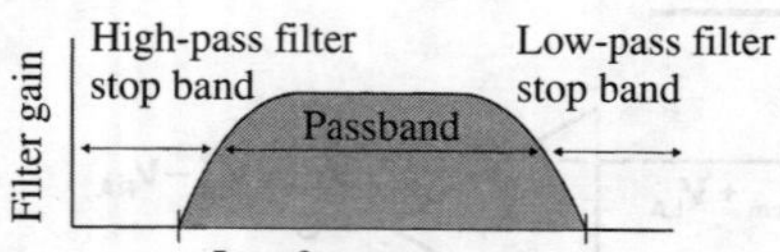

FIGURE 22.32 Bode plot of a biopotential amplifier filter set to pass the spectrum of the biopotential of interest and to stop out-of-band noise.

Figure 22.32 shows a Bode plot of the desirable situation. The roll-off of the filters brackets the frequency spectrum of interest in the biopotential. This produces the greatest rejection of out-of-band noise. Simple single-pole filters are usually employed that give a relatively gentle cutoff with increasing frequency. Low-pass filtering the ECG at 100 Hz, for example, can greatly reduce EMG artifacts whose frequencies extend up into the kilo hertz region. High-pass filtering at 0.5 or 1 Hz helps reject slow baseline wander from electrode potentials associated with offset potential and skin hydration drifts. Table 22.5 gives a rule of thumb for the spectral content of some common biopotentials.

TABLE 22.5 Characteristics of Some Common Biopotentials

Biopotential	Typical amplitude	Frequency spectrum
Electrocardiogram (heart)	1 mV	0.05–100 Hz (diagnostic)
Electroencephalogram (brain)	1–100 μV	0.1–50 Hz
Electromyogram (muscle)	10 μV–1 mV	10 Hz–5 kHz

It is also tempting to use low-pass filters set at 30 Hz and below to reduce the level of 50- or 60-Hz line-frequency interference, but the monitored biopotential waveform shape may change. The ECG is probably the best example where waveform shape is fundamental to its utility as a medical diagnostic. Subtle changes in the shape of the QRS or ST segment, for example, can be indicative of myocardial pathology or infarction. Any waveform filtering or processing operation that affects the waveform shape can be misleading to a physician trained to interpret subtle ECG waveform changes as clues to pathology.

Because the bioelectric wave shape is so important in diagnosis, ECG machines are required in the United States to have filtering of 0.05 Hz high pass and 100 Hz low pass at the −3-dB breakpoints. Some commercial machines have 150-Hz bandpass capability.

If exact waveform fidelity does not need to be maintained, as is often the case in the EMG and even occasionally in the EEG, bandwidths can be narrowed with concomitant improvements in recording noise rejection. Even with the ECG, not all monitoring circumstances require high-fidelity waveform reproduction. In some clinical ECG machines, a front-panel switch can change the waveform filtering to a nondiagnostic monitor mode where the bandpass is 1 to 30 Hz. These filter breakpoints substantially reduce problems with electrode motion artifact at the low-frequency end and reduce EMG skeletal muscle signals from the electrodes at the high-frequency end. The result is more ECG waveform distortion but with the advantage of less false heart-rate and loss-of-signal alarms for clinical staff and a more stable and easier-to-read waveform display. The effect of 3-Hz highpass filtering on ECG baseline wander can be seen in Fig. 22.33. It effectively eliminates the large drifts of the waveform trace.

Sharp cutoff filters should be avoided in biopotential measurements where the bioelectric waveform shape is of interest. Filtering can greatly distort waveforms where waveform frequencies are near the filter breakpoints. Phase and amplitude distortions are more severe with higher-order sharp-cutoff filters. Filters such as the Elliptic and the Tchebyscheff exhibit drastic phase distortion that can seriously distort bioelectric waveforms. Worse still for biopotential measurements, these filters have a tendency to "ring" or overshoot in an oscillatory way with transient events. The result can be addition of features in the bioelectric waveform that are not really present in the raw signal, time delays of parts of the waveforms, and inversion of phase of the waveform peaks. Figure 22.34 shows that the sharp cutoff of a fifth-order elliptical filter applied to an ECG waveform produces a dramatically distorted waveform shape.

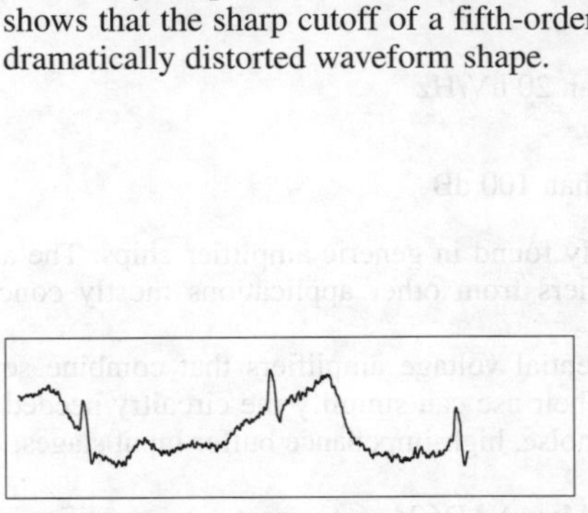

FIGURE 22.33 (A) Electrocardiogram showing muscle noise and baseline wander. (B) The effect of introducing an analog 3-Hz (−3-dB) high-pass filter into the signal path. There is a marked reduction in baseline wander.

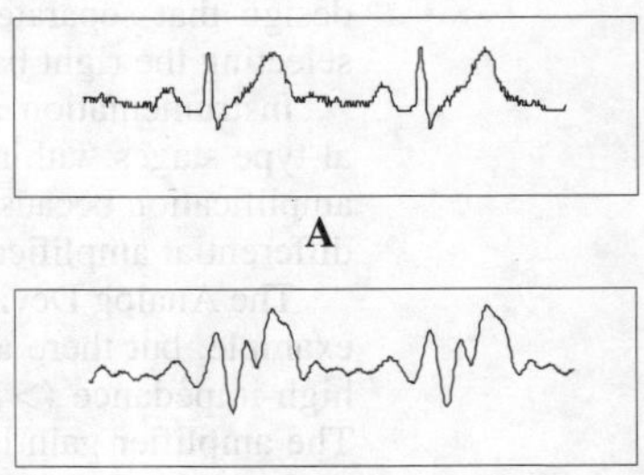

FIGURE 22.34 (A) Electrocardiogram with slight muscle tremor. (B) Electrocardiogram with a strong fifth-order analog Elliptic filter introduced into the signal path. Considerable amplitude and phase distortion of the waveform in (B) is evident, obscuring most of the ECG features and introducing spurious waveform artifacts.

22.6.6 Electrode Lead Wires

Some care must be taken with lead wires to biopotential recording electrodes. Commercial bioelectrodes are often sold with 100-cm lengths of an insulated but unshielded signal-carrying wire. Unshielded wires increase capacitive coupling, in proportion to their length, to environmental sources of electrical interference. In electrically quiet environments or with low electrode impedances to the skin, these may work satisfactorily without coupling excessive noise. Keeping the electrode wires close to grounded objects or near the body can be helpful in reducing line-frequency noise pickup.

In more demanding applications, the electrode lead wires should be shielded, preferably by purchasing the type that has a fine coaxial braided copper wire around the central signal-carrying lead. The shield should be connected to the amplifier reference but not connected to the electrode signal wire itself since this would abrogate its shielding effect.

Interference by ac magnetic induction into the electrode lead wires is a possible but often not a serious problem in most recording environments. The exceptions are where nearby machinery draws large current (many amperes) or where electrode lead wires pass close to current-carrying wiring. In these situations, the amplitude of the induced electric field is defined by Ampere's law and is roughly proportional to the open area defined by the perimeter of the loop formed by two electrode wires. Twisting the electrode lead wires together can reduce this area to near zero, and this approach can be an effective method of reducing this source of electromagnetic noise.

22.6.7 Biopotential Amplifier Characteristics

Modern integrated-circuit amplifiers, and even most inexpensive op-amps, are capable of giving good-quality recordings of millivolt-level biopotentials such as from the heart and muscles. Higher-quality integrated-circuit instrumentation amplifier chips are more suited to measuring microvolt-level signals such as associated with the electroneurography (ENG), EEG, and intracortical events.

Some of the desirable characteristics of bioelectric amplifiers are

- Gains of 10^3 to 10^4
- Amplifier broad-spectrum noise less than 20 nV/Hz
- Input impedance greater than $10^8\ \Omega$
- Common-mode rejection ratio greater than 100 dB

Most of these characteristics are easily found in generic amplifier chips. The aspects of circuit design that separate biopotential amplifiers from other applications mostly concern the ease of selecting the right bandpass filtering.

Instrumentation amplifiers are differential voltage amplifiers that combine several operational-type stages within a single package. Their use can simplify the circuitry needed for biopotential amplification because they combine low-noise, high-impedance buffer input stages, and high-quality differential amplification stages.

The Analog Devices, Inc. (Norwood, Mass.) AD624 instrumentation amplifier is used here as an example, but there are other chips by other manufacturers that would serve as well. This chip has high-impedance ($>10^9\ \Omega$) input buffers that work well with even high-impedance bioelectrodes. The amplifier gain is easily selected from several standard gains by interconnection of pins on the package or, alternatively, by adjusting the value of a single external resistor.

Figure 22.35 shows its configuration, and it can be used to monitor many different biopotentials. Its gain is conveniently determined by adjusting R_G to select an amplifier gain A according to the relation $A = (40k/R_G) + 1$. Gains of 1 to 1000 can be easily selected; however, it is desirable to keep the gain of this part of the circuit less than about 50 since higher gains will tend to saturate the amplifier if electrode dc offset potentials become large.

The instrumentation amplifier is connected to a bandpass filter consisting of simple single-pole high-pass and low-pass filter. The component values on the filter stage are variable and selected

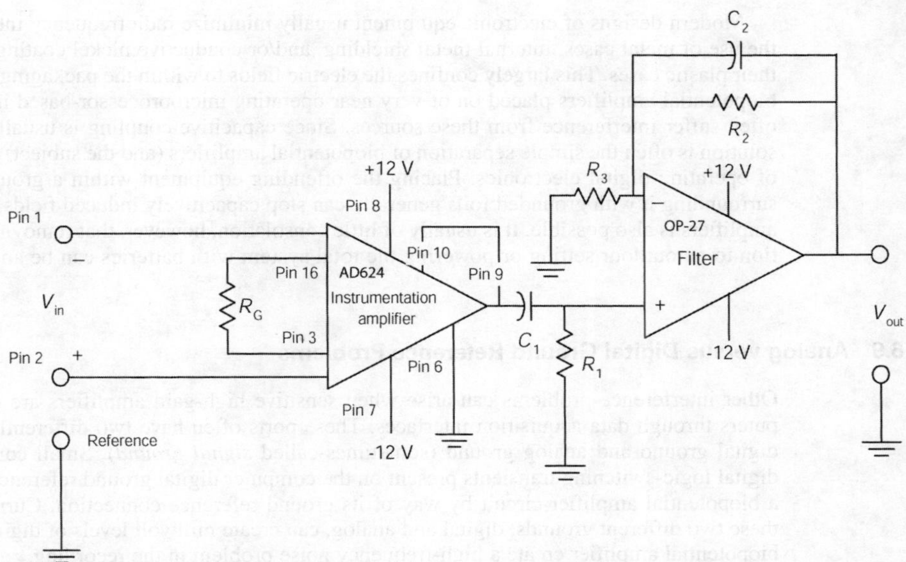

FIGURE 22.35 A simple biopotential amplifier design based on an integrated-circuit instrumentation amplifier.

for frequency cutoffs suitable for a specific biopotential monitoring application. Generic but good-quality operational amplifiers such as the industry-standard OP-27 are used in the filter stage.

The −3-dB low-pass and high-pass cutoff frequencies of the filter, formed by R_2 and C_2 and R_1 and C_1, respectively, are given by $f_c = 1/(2\pi RC)$. Typical values for EMG recording, for example, using cutoffs approximately at 10 Hz high pass and 3 kHz low pass would be $R_1 = 10\ \text{k}\Omega$, $C_1 = 1.6\ \mu\text{F}$, $R_2 = 50\ \text{k}\Omega$, and $C_2 = 1$ nF. $R_3 = 10\ \text{k}\Omega$ for an in-band gain of 5. Overall, this circuit with an R_G of 800 Ω provides an in-band gain of 250, meaning that a 1-mV EMG signal will give a 0.25-V output. Good-quality electrodes are required for optimal performance.

Improvements in this simple design might include protection on the amplifier inputs by using series input lead resistors of 50 kΩ or more and capacitive input couplings. Zener diodes across the input leads offer further protection from defibrillator and static electricity by shorting transients to ground. Selectable gains and added filtering options would give the amplifier more flexibility in application.

22.6.8 Other Sources of Measurement Noise

In addition to power-line coupled noise, computers and cathode-ray-tube monitors can be a troublesome source of interference in many clinical and laboratory situations. Digital logic electronics often involve fast switching of large currents, particularly in the use of switching-type solid-state power supplies. These produce and can radiate harmonics that spread over a wide frequency spectrum. Proximity of the amplifier or the monitored subject to these devices can sometimes result in pulselike biopotential interference.

Cathode-ray-tube monitors internally generate large electric fields (tens of thousands of volts) at frequencies of 15.75 to 70 kHz needed to drive the horizontal beam deflection on the cathode-ray tube. These fields are strong and have a high frequency, so they would have the possibility of being a major problem in biopotential recording. However, since the 1970s, the radiated electric field emissions from these devices have been regulated by government agencies in most countries, and this considerably reduces the likelihood of their interference.

Modern designs of electronic equipment usually minimize radiofrequency interference (RFI) by the use of metal cases, internal metal shielding, and/or conductive nickel coatings on the insides of their plastic cases. This largely confines the electric fields to within the packaging. Even so, sensitive biopotential amplifiers placed on or very near operating microprocessor-based instrumentation can often suffer interference from these sources. Since capacitive coupling is usually the problem, the solution is often the simple separation of biopotential amplifiers (and the subject) from the proximity of operating digital electronics. Placing the offending equipment within a grounded metal box or surrounding it with grounded foils generally can stop capacitively induced fields. Shielding the bioamplifiers is also possible. It is usually of little consolation, however, that removing the instrumentation to an outdoor setting or powering the total system with batteries can be an effective solution.

22.6.9 Analog versus Digital Ground Reference Problems

Other interference problems can arise when sensitive high-gain amplifiers are connected to computers through data-acquisition interfaces. These ports often have two differently labeled grounds, digital ground and analog ground (sometimes-called *signal ground*). Small currents arising from digital logic-switching transients present on the computer digital ground reference can pass through a biopotential amplifier circuit by way of its ground reference connection. Current flows between these two different grounds, digital and analog, can create millivolt levels of digital noise that in the biopotential amplifier create a high-frequency noise problem in the recording.

This problem is particularly severe with high-gain bioamplifiers, such as those used for microvolt-level EEG measurements. This problem is alleviated in most commercial instrumentation designs by internally isolating the analog signal ground from digital ground.

22.6.10 Ground Loops

Ground loops can create seemingly intractable problems with line-frequency (50 or 60 Hz) interference in low-level biopotential recordings. They often occur when biopotential amplifiers are connected to signal processing or recording systems such as filters, oscilloscopes, or computer-based data-acquisition systems. The root cause is often that the reference wire of signal cables interconnect the ground references of all the instruments. However, each instrument is also referenced to a power-line ground through its third-wire grounding pin on the power-line plug, as required by electrical safety codes.

Interference arises from the fact that all power grounds and signal-ground references are not equal. Line-powered instruments and appliances are only supposed to draw current through the hot and neutral wires of the line. However, the third-pin instrument power ground conducts small capacitive and resistive leakage currents from its power supply to wall-outlet ground. These ground leakage currents originate mostly in the instrument power-line transformer winding capacitance to ground and in resistive leakage from less than perfect wire insulation. Appliances having heavy motors, such as refrigerators, air conditioners, etc., that draw high currents tend to have greater leakage currents.

Currents flowing in the power-line ground cause voltage drops in the resistance of the building wiring ground. As a result, a voltmeter will often show several tens of millivolts between one power-outlet ground and another even in the same room. Since recording amplifier grounds are usually referenced to the instrument power-line ground, millivolt-level potential differences can create circulating currents between power-ground and instrument-ground references. By the same process, there can also arise current flows between various instruments through their individual ground references.

The result is that small line-frequency currents flow in loops between different instruments interconnected by multiple signal and ground references. Line-frequency voltage drops in the interconnecting reference path wiring can appear as a signal across the amplifier inputs.

The solutions are often varied and cut and dry for each application. Some typical solutions include

- Plugging all instruments into the same power bus feeding off a single power socket
- Using battery-powered equipment where possible or feasible
- Earth grounding the amplifier input stages
- Independent ground wires from the subject to the bioamplifier
- Identifying and replacing certain offending instruments that contribute disproportionately to induced noise
- Use of isolation modules on the amplifier
- Grounding the work tables, patient beds, or surrounding area

Within modern work environments, it is not infrequent for interference in biopotential recordings to appear from the following sources when they are near (perhaps a meter) the recording site:

- Computers, digital electronics, digital oscilloscopes
- Cathode-ray-tube displays
- Brush-type electric motors
- Fluorescent light fixtures
- Operating televisions, VCRs

Less frequent but also possible sources include

- Local radio stations, cell phone repeaters, amateur radio transmitters, military radars
- Arc welding equipment, medical diathermy, and HVAC systems
- Digital cell phones
- Institutional carrier-current control signals sent through power wiring to synchronize clocks and remotely control machinery

Not usually a problem are portable radios, CD players, stereos, and regular telephones.

22.6.11 Electrical Safety

Whenever a person is connected to an electrical device by a grounded conductive pathway that is low resistance, such as through biopotential electrodes, there is a concern about electrical safety. Electric voltages that ordinarily would be harmless to casual skin contact can become dangerous or even lethal if someone happens to be well grounded. Wetted skin can provide low resistance, and from this stems the old adage about the inadvisability of standing in pools of water when around electric appliances.

Electric shock hazard is particularly a concern in clinical biopotential monitoring where the patient may be in a vulnerable state of health. Bioelectrodes are desirably low-resistance connections to the body for amplifier performance reasons. As discussed earlier, they similarly can offer a low-resistance pathway to ground for electric fault currents.

These fault currents could arise from many sources, including within the amplifier itself through some internal failure of its insulation or from a patient coming into contact with defective electric devices in the immediate environment. These might include such things as a table lamp, a reclining bed controller, electric hand appliances (e.g., hair dryers), and computers, radios, television sets, etc. All have potential failure modes that can place the hot lead of the power main to the frame or case of the device. Current flows of about 6 mA or greater at line frequencies cause muscle paralysis, and the person may be in serious straits indeed and unable to let go. In some failure modes, the device can still appear to function quite normally.

Ground-Fault Circuit Interrupters. Commercial ground-fault circuit interrupters (GFCIs) detect unbalanced current flows between the hot and neutral sides of a power line. Small fault current flows through a person's body to ground will trip a GFCI circuit breaker, but large currents through a normally functioning appliance will not. Building codes for power outlets near water in many countries now requires these devices. GFCI devices can significantly increase safety when used with bioinstrumentation. These devices are often incorporated into the wall socket itself and can be identified since they usually show a red test-reset button near the electrical socket.

A GFCI can shut off the power supply to a device or bioinstrumentation amplifier within 15 to 100 ms of the start of a fault current to ground. This interruption process is so fast that a person may not experience the sensation of a fault shock and even may then wonder why the instrument is not working.

It should be noted that GFCI devices are not foolproof, nor are they absolute protection against electric shock from an instrument. They only are effective with fault currents that follow a path to ground. It is still possible to receive a shock from an appliance fault where a person's body is across the hot-to-neutral circuit, requiring a simultaneous contact with two conductors. This is a more unusual situation and implies exposed wiring from the appliance.

Isolation Amplifiers. Isolation amplifiers increase safety by preventing fault currents from flowing through the body by way of a ground-referenced biopotential electrode. Isolation amplifiers effectively create an electric system similar to biotelemetry. They eliminate any significant resistive coupling between the isolated front-end stages of the amplifier and the output stages to the recorder. They also reduce the amplifier capacitive proximity coupling to ground to a few dozen picofarads or less, depending on manufacture. This provides very high isolation impedance at the power frequency. In principle, isolation amplifiers give many of the advantages of biotelemetry in terms of safety.

Isolated amplifiers are universally used in commercial biopotential monitoring instruments and are mandated in many countries by government regulatory agencies for ECG machines. There are a number of commercial prepackaged modules that conveniently perform this function, so the researcher or design engineer can concentrate on other areas of system design. Isolation amplifiers can be small, compact modules of dimensions 2 by 7.5 cm, as seen in Fig. 22.36.

From an electronic design standpoint, isolation requires considerable sophistication in the bioamplifier. Isolation amplifiers use special internal transformers that have a low interwinding capacitance. They employ a carrier-frequency modulation system for signal coupling between isolated stages and use a high-frequency power-induction system that is nearly equivalent to battery power in isolation. The isolation module effectively creates its own internal reference known as a *guard* (triangle symbol in Fig. 22.37) that connects to the biopotential reference electrode on the subject. The functional components in an isolated amplifier are seen in Fig. 22.37.

In addition to an improvement in electrical safety, isolated amplifiers in principle should eliminate line-frequency noise in biopotential recordings in the same way as does biotelemetry. The biopotential amplifier reference electrode provides the needed current return path, but because it is isolated,

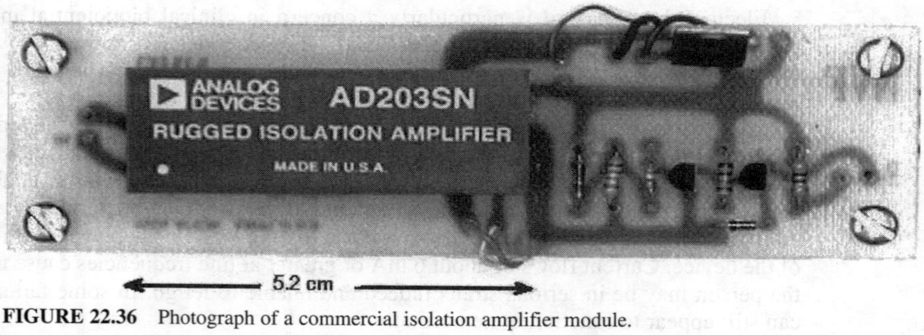

FIGURE 22.36 Photograph of a commercial isolation amplifier module.

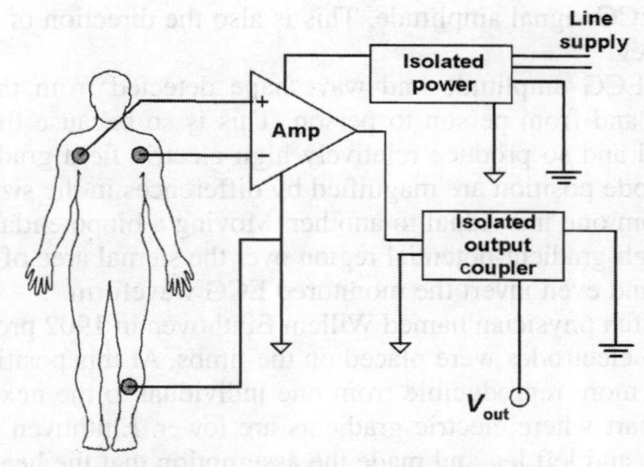

FIGURE 22.37 An isolation amplifier configuration.

however, it does not reduce the patient's floating potential with respect to ground. This means that V_{float} does not appear between the amplifier input and guard but only with respect to ground, and the bioamplifier has no connection to ground. V_{float} then does not appear in any current nodal analysis, and the isolated bioamplifier effectively ignores this potential.

In practice, the performance advantages are not quite as great as what might be expected. The few picofarads of capacitive coupling that remain to ground as a result of imperfect isolation still can allow the amplifier to be ground referenced to a slight degree. For this reason, isolated bioamplifiers are not totally immune to capacitively coupled power-line interference. There is often a small floating potential present at the amplifier input; however, its amplitude is greatly reduced over the nonisolated case.

22.7 BIOPOTENTIAL INTERPRETATION

22.7.1 Electrocardiography

A recording of the heart's bioelectrical activity is called an ECG. It is one of the most frequently measured biopotentials. The study of the heart's bioelectricity is a way of understanding its physiological performance and function. Dysfunction of the heart as a pump often shows up as a characteristic signature in the ECG because its mechanical events are preceded and initiated by electrical events.

Measurement of the ECG is performed using a differential amplifier. Two limb electrodes at a time are selected for the input to the differential amplifier stage. ECG amplifiers typically have gains of about 1000 and so increase the nominally 1-mV biopotential to about 1 V for driving a strip-chart recorder, cathode-ray-tube display, or computer data-acquisition card. Chart speeds in ECG recording have been standardized at 25 and 50 mm/s.

The heart's depolarization is an electric vector called the *cardiac equivalent vector*. The placement of two electrodes creates a direction between them called the *electrode lead*. The electrode-detected bioelectric signal V results from a dot-product relationship of the cardiac equivalent vector **m** with the electrode lead **a** such that

$$V = \mathbf{m} \bullet \mathbf{a} = \mathrm{ma}\cos\theta$$

One of the contributors to the ECG waveform morphology is the changing direction of the cardiac depolarization front. Placing electrodes on the chest such that they are in line with the general direction of the cardiac biocurrent flow, from the sinoatrial node to the heart apex, provides the largest ECG signal amplitude. This is also the direction of a line connecting the right shoulder and the left leg.

The ECG amplitude and waveshape detected from the chest surface change with electrode position and from person to person. This is so because the biocurrents in the heart are relatively localized and so produce relatively high electric field gradients on the chest surface. Small errors in electrode position are magnified by differences in the size, shape, and position of the heart in the chest from one individual to another. Moving a biopotential electrode as little as a centimeter or so in the high-gradient-potential region over the sternal area of the chest, for example, can substantially change and even invert the monitored ECG waveform.

A Dutch physician named Willem Einthoven in 1902 proposed a measurement convention where the ECG electrodes were placed on the limbs. At this position, the monitored electric activity wave shape is more reproducible from one individual to the next because they are in a relative far field to the heart where electric gradients are lower. Einthoven used electrodes placed on the right and left arms and left leg and made the assumption that the heart was at the electric center of a triangle defined by the electrodes.

Einthoven's electrode placement has been adopted and standardized into the ECG lead system known as the *Einthoven triangle* and is shown in Fig. 22.38. Electric potential differences are measured between the three limb electrodes along the line between the electrode placements, and their potentials are called lead I, II, and III such that

$$\text{Lead I} = V_{\text{LA}} - V_{\text{RA}}$$
$$\text{Lead II} = V_{\text{LL}} - V_{\text{RA}}$$
$$\text{Lead III} = V_{\text{LL}} - V_{\text{LA}}$$

These three leads create an electrical perspective of the heart from three different vectorial directions.

The letter designations of the major features of the ECG wave are derived from the Dutch. The first wave (the preliminary) resulting from atrial contraction was designated as P and is followed in sequence by the triphasic ventricular depolarization called the QRS, and the electric repolarization wave follows as the T wave. Lead II is often used in monitoring heart rhythm because it gives the largest biopotential during ventricular contraction. The normal ECG is seen in Fig. 22.39.

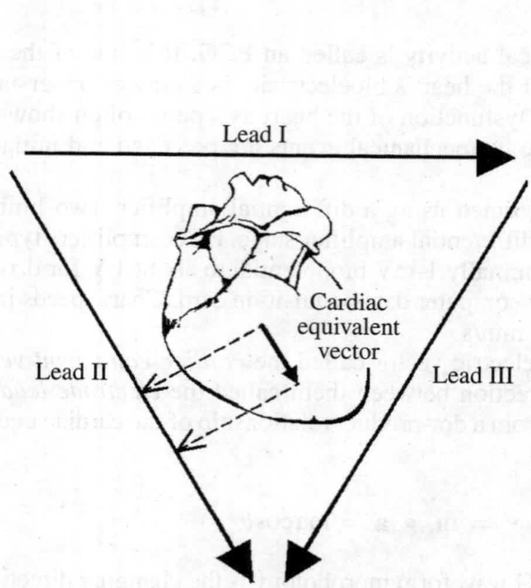

FIGURE 22.38 The ECG lead vectors are based on the Einthoven triangle placement of electrodes.

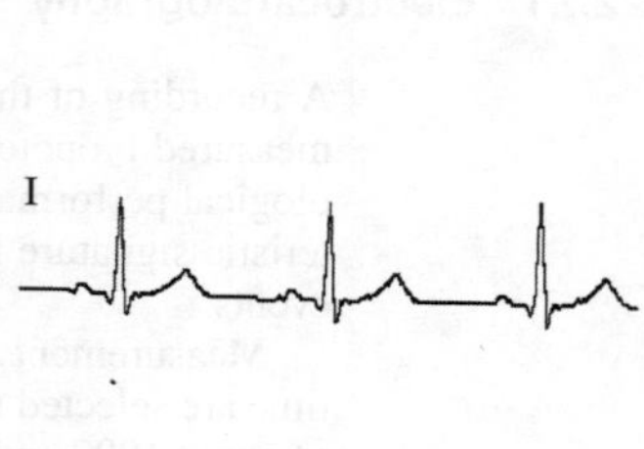

FIGURE 22.39 The normal ECG for leads I, II, and III.

The right-leg electrode is an important electrode even though it does not explicitly appear in the ECG Lead system. It provides the common reference point for the differential amplifier, and in older ECG machines, it is a grounding point for the body to reduce electric noise.

Other Lead systems are also possible and have been standardized into what is known as the *12-lead system* that constitutes the clinical ECG. In addition to leads I, II, and III, there are three others known as the augmented leads aVR, aVL, and aVF. These leads use an electric addition process of the limb-electrode signals to create a virtual signal reference point in the center of the chest known as the *Wilson central terminal* (WCT). From the WCT reference point, the augmented lead vectors point to the right arm, left arm, and left leg, respectively.

There are also six precordial leads, V_1 to V_6, that track along the rib cage over the lower heart region that are used to give more localized ECG spatial information. This total of 12 leads are used clinically to allow the cardiologist to view the electric activity of the heart from a variety of electrical perspectives and to enable a diagnosis based on a more comprehensive data set.

In the plane of the surface electrodes, the signals from the various electrode leads provide sufficient information to define the time-varying biocurrent amplitude and direction in the heart. When this is done, the recording is called a *vectorcardiogram*.

ECG Waveforms in Pathology. ECG waveform interpretation has over the years evolved into a powerful tool for assessing pathologies of the heart. Although its diagnostic interpretation requires considerable training, gross waveform changes that occur in common pathologies can be easily seen even by the inexperienced. Myocardial infarction (heart attack), for example, often is accompanied by an ST-segment elevation. The usually isoelectric (flat) part of the ECG between the S wave and the onset of the T wave is elevated from zero, as can be seen in the sequential waveform comparison in Fig. 22.40.

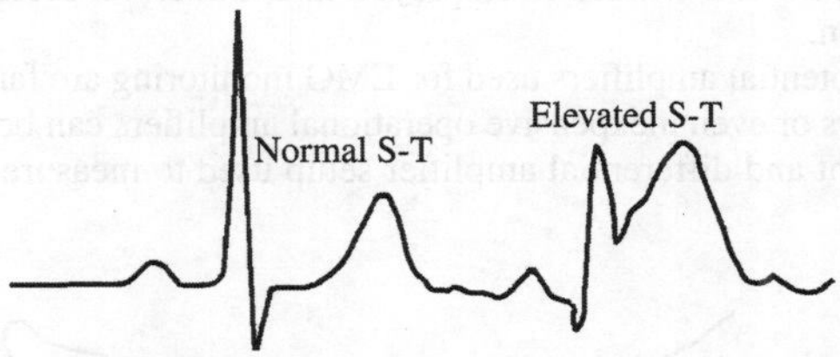

FIGURE 22.40 A dramatic ST-segment elevation subsequent to a myocardial infarction.

This ST-segment displacement is known to be a result of a bioelectric injury current flowing in the heart. This injury current arises from oxygen deprivation of the heart muscle and is usually due to blockage of one or more of the coronary vessels. The elevated ST segment can be 20 percent or more of the ECG amplitude and is sometimes taken as an indicator, along with other factors, of the relative degree of cardiac injury.

After infarction, this injury current slowly subsides over a period of hours or days as the affected cells either live or die. Some cells near the border of the affected region continue to survive but are on the threshold of ischemia (poor blood flow resulting in oxygen deprivation). When stressed, these cells are particularly vulnerable to increased demands placed on the heart, and they are sources of injury currents during exercise. Treadmill exercise, for example, will often stress these cells, and the presence or absence of ST-segment elevation can give insight into amount of ischemic tissue and so indicate the degree of healing in the patient's recovery from infarction. ST-segment monitoring can also be useful for gaining insight into a progressive coronary vessel blockage that creates the pain in the chest known as *angina*.

22.7.2 Electromyography

Skin-surface electrodes placed over contracting skeletal muscles will record a complex time-varying biopotential waveform known as an *electromyogram* (EMG). This electric signal arises from the summed action potential events of individual muscle motor units. Because a large number of cells are undergoing action events during muscle contraction, bioelectric current flows are relatively large and can produce skin potentials as high as 10 mV, although more usually it is in the range of a few millivolts.

The amplitude of the EMG as measured on the skin surface is related, although not linearly, to muscle contraction force. In general, an increasing frequency and complexity of the myogram biopotential follows increasing muscular contraction. This results from both the increased motor unit firing rate and the increased recruitment of muscle fibrils.

The EMG waveform looks random and is fairly well represented by random noise having a Gaussian distribution function. The peak energy is roughly in the 30- to 150-Hz range with some low-energy components as high as 500 Hz. As the muscle fatigues, the EMG frequency spectrum shifts toward the lower frequencies, and the bioelectric amplitude decreases.

Many attempts have been made to use the skin-surface-detected EMG as an indicator of the strength of voluntary muscle force generation, but with often less than hoped-for success. The biopotential frequency and amplitude tend to change little over a range of low contractile force, rise quickly with small changes in moderate force, and vary relatively little with progressively larger forces. In applications where the EMG is used for control of prosthetics, there have been problems due to a relatively little range of proportional control.

Even so, the EMG is widely monitored and used for many applications in research and medicine partly because it is so accessible and easily recorded. For example, the EMG is often used in biomechanics research where it is desired to monitor which muscle groups are active and/or their timing and sequence of contraction. Frequency-spectrum analysis of the EMG can be used to detect the degree of muscle fatigue and to gain insight into muscle performance. EMG monitoring of jaw and neck muscle tension is employed in commercial biofeedback monitors designed to encourage relaxation.

Biopotential amplifiers used for EMG monitoring are fairly simple since standard instrumentation amplifiers or even inexpensive operational amplifiers can be used in a differential mode. An electrode placement and differential amplifier setup used to measure the EMG is shown in Fig. 22.41.

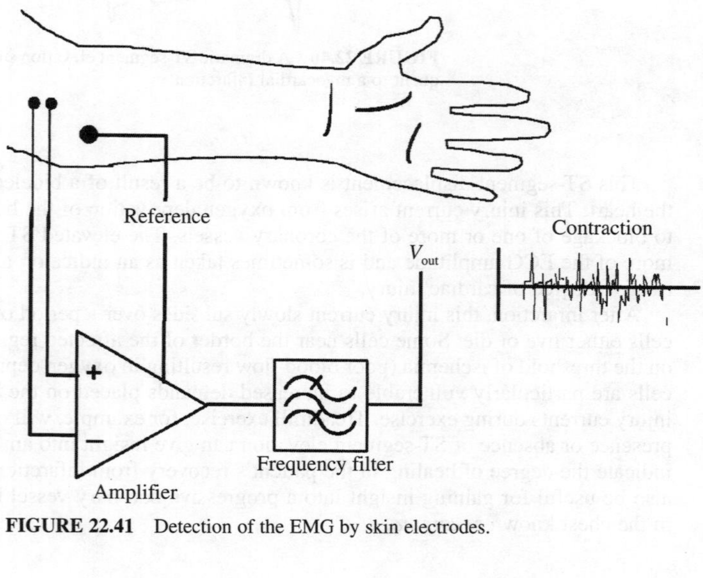

FIGURE 22.41 Detection of the EMG by skin electrodes.

Frequency filtering can be an important aspect of EMG biopotential measurement. For example, electrode movement artifacts can appear with strong muscle contractions, and these add to the EMG waveform, giving the illusion of a larger signal than is really present. With some relatively poor electrode placements and skin preparations, electrode motion artifacts can be the largest signal measured. High-pass filtering helps reject electrode motion artifacts that can accompany forceful skeletal muscle contraction. Analog filters set for 20 to 500 Hz can often be adequate, but some special research applications set the filter as low as 1 to 2 Hz to monitor low-frequency muscle tremors in some cases associated with disease states.

The raw EMG waveform is usually not directly utilized in applications but rather is first subjected to signal processing. One method consists of EMG signal full wave rectification and then low-pass filtering to give the envelope of the muscle-effort waveform. Threshold detectors, slope proportional controllers, and integral control can be implemented using the resulting envelope waveform. Multiple channels derived from different voluntary muscle groups can be used for more complex applications.

For example, Fig. 22.42 shows the results of an experiment using the bicep muscle EMG as a control signal. Two gelled silver–silver chloride electrodes were applied to the upper arm of a volunteer near the bicep about 2 cm apart, and a third reference electrode was placed near the wrist. The EMG biopotentials resulting from two strong voluntary contractions of the bicep were amplified with a gain about 500 in a bandpass of 10 Hz to 1 kHz. The amplified signal was then applied to the data-acquisition interface of a computer. The analog EMG signal was sampled at 10 kHz to avoid aliasing and to capture a high-fidelity EMG waveform. Figure 22.42A shows this raw digitized EMG signal. It has a complex waveform, whereas the average amplitude of its envelope rises and falls twice as a result of two discrete muscle efforts over a period of 5 seconds.

To use this signal as a control, we need to integrate the EMG signal over time since its frequency components are far too high. First, it is necessary to take the absolute value of the waveform to provide full wave rectification; otherwise, the alternating waveform integrates to zero. This operation is conveniently done in the digital domain, as shown in Fig. 22.42B. Rectification can also be accomplished by using an analog electronic system before the waveform is digitally sampled. Next, calculating a running average of the amplitudes digitally smoothes the rectified waveform. This result is shown in Fig. 22.42C. The degree of smoothing determines the response time of the system, as well as its sensitivity to false triggering. The user can display the smoothed EMG waveform to set a threshold. When the computer detects a threshold crossing, it then performs subsequent control steps according to a program.

Low-pass filtering can also be performed prior to computer sampling by conventional analog filtering. This allows a designer to be less concerned about the speed of computer processing needed for real-time signals.

EMG Waveforms in Pathology. Various forms of needle electrodes introduced into the muscle are used clinically to detect biopotentials from the firing of single motor units. Although invasive, the biopotentials monitored from needle electrodes contain medically diagnostic information in a waveshape that is otherwise obscured by the placement of electrodes on the surface of the skin. Needle EMG is used to help detect loss of neurons innervating a muscle, which may be seen in cases of nerve root compression, disk herniation, and peripheral nerve injury, all leading to axonal degeneration.

In muscular disease, needle EMG waveforms vary in strength, waveshape, and frequency content. For example, in muscular dystrophy, the EMG action events are low in amplitude, short in duration (1 to 2 ms), and high in frequency (up to 40 per second). When the bioelectric signals are introduced into a loudspeaker so that they can be heard, there is a high-pitched characteristic sound. These diseased muscles fatigue easily, and this is reflected in their action events that are greatly reduced with sustained contraction.

When the innervation of muscles is severed by accident or disease, spontaneous action events known as *fibrillation waves* appear several weeks after the trauma. These waves result from weak random contraction and relaxation of individual motor units and produce no muscle tension. Fibrillation potentials persist as long as denervation persists and as long as the muscles are present.

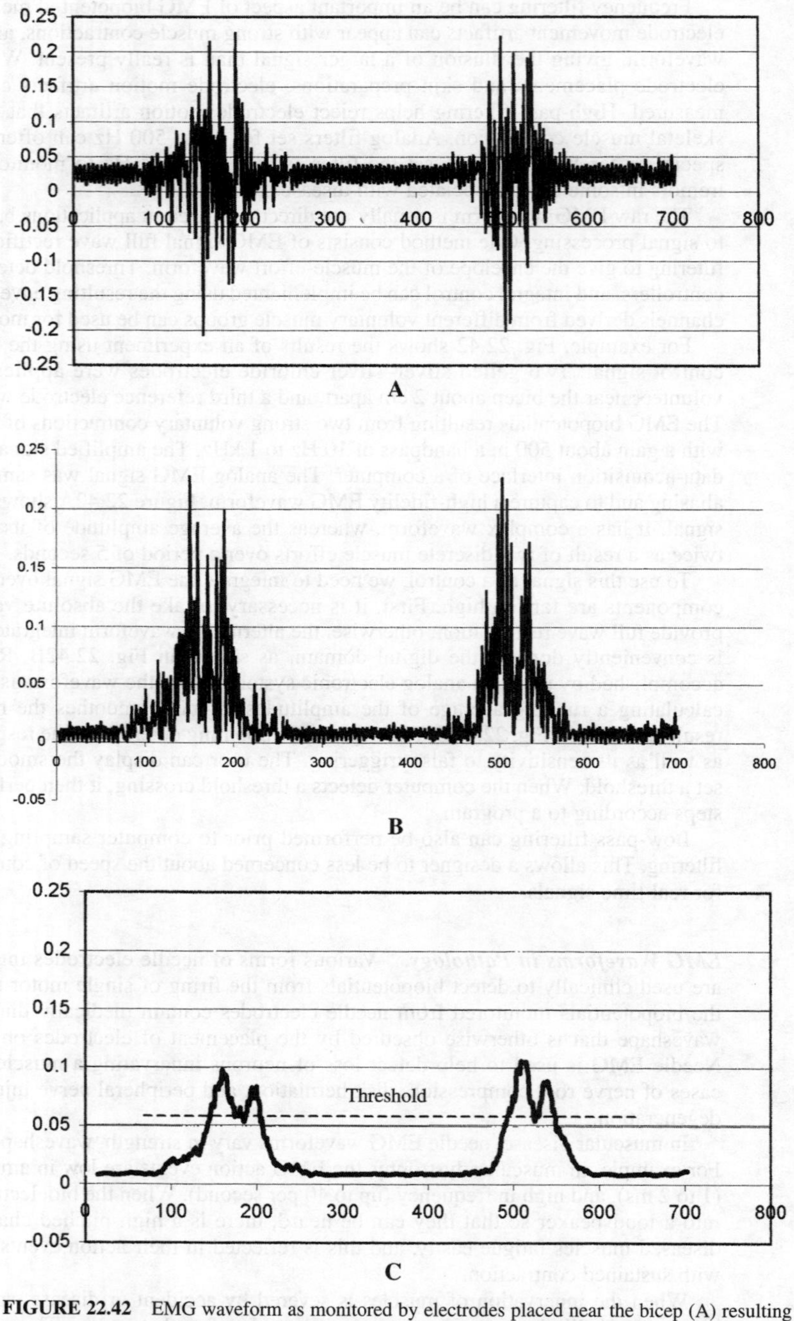

FIGURE 22.42 EMG waveform as monitored by electrodes placed near the bicep (A) resulting from two strong contractions of this muscle, (B) the absolute value of the EMG waveform, and (C) a smoothed moving average that could be used to trigger a threshold circuit to actuate an EMG-controlled prosthetic device.

The waves slowly fade away, as the muscle atrophies. If reinnervation occurs as the injury heals, low-amplitude EMG events can be seen long before the muscle produces signs of visible contraction.

22.7.3 Electroencephalography

Biopotential recordings from the head reflect the bioelectric function of the brain. This recording is known as an *electroencephalogram* (EEG). The first systematic recording of the human EEG is attributed to the Austrian psychiatrist Dr. Hans Berger, who published his results in 1929. By using a primitive galvanometer and surface electrodes placed on his son's scalp, he showed the EEG as a rhythmic pattern of electrical oscillation.

The EEG is produced by electrical dipoles in the outer brain cortex. The waveform is too low in frequency to be the summed result of fast action potential events. Instead, the electric signal is believed to be attributable to the aggregate of excitatory and inhibitory postsynaptic potentials (EPSPs/IPSPs).

The EEG monitored on the top of the head originates primarily from the pyramidal cell layer of the neocortex. These cells have a dipolar nature and are organized with their dendrites in vertical columns. This sets up what is called a *dendrosomatic dipole*, which oscillates in amplitude with the arrival of excitatory or inhibitory postsynaptic potentials. Changes in membrane polarization, as well as EPSPs/IPSPs, impress voltages that are conducted throughout the surrounding medium. A highly conductive layer of cerebrospinal fluid (CSF) between the dura and the skull tends to spatially diffuse biopotentials from the brain cortex. Furthermore, the skull bone is a relatively poor electric conductor. The properties of both the CSF and the skull together reduce millivolt-level bioelectric events in the brain to only microvolts of biopotential on the brain surface.

EEG waveforms are typically 1 to 50 μV in amplitude with frequencies of 2 to 50 Hz. During brain disease states, such as in epileptic seizures, the EEG amplitudes can be much greater, nearing 1000 μV. In some research applications, their frequency spectrum of interest can extend above 100 Hz. Alternatively, invasive electrodes can be placed directly on or in the brain. This electric measurement is known as an *electrocortiogram*, and it has frequency components that extend into the kilohertz range.

The EEG is known to be a composite of many different bioelectric generators within the brain. However, it has not proved to be a powerful technique in studying brain function. The brain is a complex organ that has enormous numbers of bioelectrically active neurons and glial cells. Millions of these cells fire at any given time, and their potentials do not organize well or sum in ways that are characteristic of an activity of a specific part of the brain. Even so, spectral analysis of the EEG shows certain peaks, and study of the EEG suggests that characteristics of the waveforms can be associated with certain mental states. Table 22.6 shows the major brain rhythms categorized according to their major frequency component.

From wakefulness to deep sleep, there is a progression of EEG activity, slowing from beta wave activity (about 18 Hz) to theta-delta wave activity (3.5 to 8 Hz). Figure 22.43 shows the appearances of the major brain wave frequencies. The delta waves occur in deep sleep or coma. Theta waves are

TABLE 22.6 The Major Brain Wave Frequencies

Brain rhythm	Frequency range, Hz
Alpha	8–13
Beta	14–30
Theta	4–7
Delta	<3.5

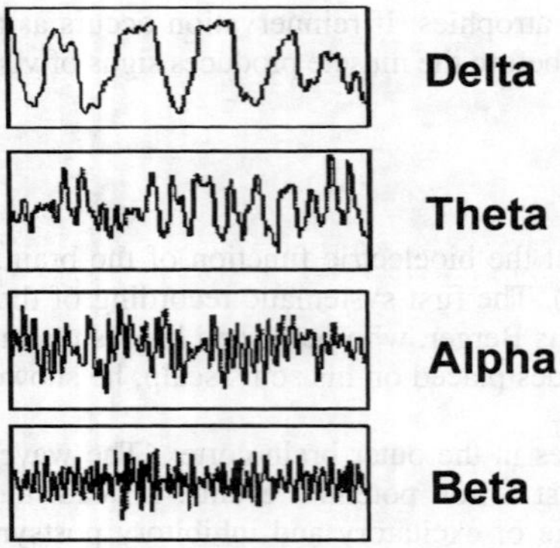

FIGURE 22.43 Waveform appearances of four brain rhythms in order of increasing frequency.

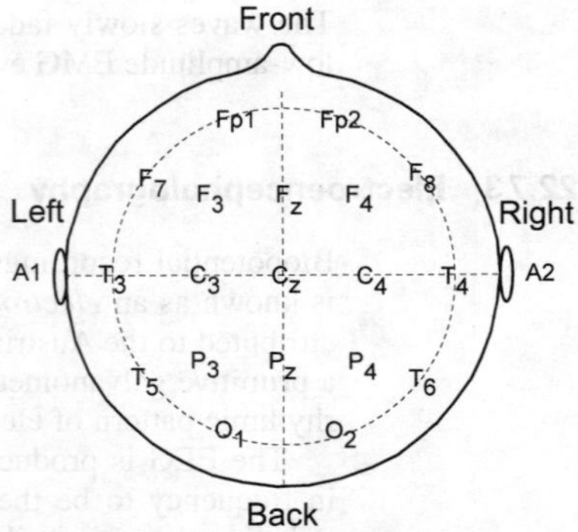

FIGURE 22.44 The 10-20 lead system is the standard for placement of EEG electrodes.

around 7 Hz and are believed to reflect activity in the hippocampus and limbic system. They appear to mediate and/or motivate adaptive, complex behaviors, such as learning and memory.

Alpha waves are around 10 Hz and strongest over the occipital and frontal lobes of the brain. They occur whenever a person is alert and not actively processing information. Alpha waves have been linked to extraversion and creativity, since subjects manifest alpha waves when coming to a solution for creative problems. During most of waking consciousness, the active brain produces beta waves at around 12 to 18 Hz. There also is a high-frequency EEG wave band known as gamma that is above 35 Hz. These waves are relatively small in amplitude and carry little power. The origin of these waves is unclear, and they are not listed in many reference books.

The EEG is widely used in the study of sleep patterns, the various stages of sleep, and the effects of various pharmaceuticals on sleep. The EEG is also used in the study of epilepsy, both in its diagnosis and in research applications that seek to predict epileptic seizure onset.

The clinical EEG is generally monitored using high-quality silver–silver chloride electrodes attached to the scalp in a specific arrangement. This arrangement is known as the *10-20 lead system* and is shown in Fig. 22.44. This lead system gains its name from the fact that electrodes are spaced apart by either 10 or 20 percent of the total distances from landmarks on the skull. Along a line front to back, this is between the bridge of the nose, the nasion, and the bump at the rear base of the skull, the inion. Side to side, the ears form the landmarks.

The electrodes are labeled by letters according to their positions on the scalp, such as frontal, parietal, temporal, or occipital regions. Intermediate positions are labeled by two letters, such as Fp1, meaning the first of a frontal-parietal electrode placement. EEG electrodes are often, but not exclusively, used in differential pairs. This allows a greater sensitivity to biopotentials located between a specific pair of electrodes in an attempt to gain a greater spatial specificity to the generators within the brain. The various electrode placements also allow a greater sensitivity to specific rhythm generators. The alpha rhythm, for example, is known to be the strongest in the occipital electrodes, whereas the beta activity is typically greatest in the frontal electrodes.

Mapping of the brain electric activity using more densely spaced sets of electrodes has been accomplished in combination with computer data-acquisition systems. Maps of the instantaneous distribution of bioelectricity over the head are a research tool used to help study the functionality of the brain.

Evoked EEG Potentials. When a stimulus is applied to the brain through the sensory system, such as a tone burst in the ear, a flash of light to the eye, or a mechanical or electric stimulus to the skin or nerve, there is a subtle response in the EEG. This is known as an *evoked response*, and it reflects the detection and processing of these bioelectric sensory events within the brain. The amplitude of evoked potentials is quite variable but is typically in the range of 3 to 20 μV.

Ordinarily, the brain response to these stimuli is so subtle that they are undetectable in the noise of other brain electric activity. However, if the stimuli is repetitive, then a powerful computer-based technique known as *signal averaging* can be used to extract the corresponding bioelectric events from the rest of the larger but uncorrelated EEG brain activity.

The most well known of these evoked potentials are the auditory evoked response (AER), the visual evoked response (VER), and the somatosensory evoked response (SSER). The somatosensory system evoked signal can result from multiple types of stimuli to the body—light touch, pain, pressure, temperature, and proprioception (also called joint and muscle position sense).

The procedures for evoked waveform monitoring and signal extraction are all basically the same. In each case, electrodes are placed over or near the brain structures most involved in processing the sensory signal. The pulsed stimulus is applied at rates that do not produce fatigue or accommodation of the brain or nervous system. Computer data acquisition and processing create an averaged waveform that has noise suppressed and provides a display of the evoked potential waveform. A physician then evaluates the recording. Experience has shown that certain waveform shapes are associated with normal function, and so deviations, such as different propagation delays or amplitudes, may indicate pathology and be of clinical interest.

Evoked EEG Waveforms in Pathology. The VER is used clinically as a test for optic neuritis or other demyelinating events along the optic nerve or further back along the optic pathways. The test involves stimulating the visual pathways by having a patient watch a black and white checkered pattern on a TV screen in a darkened room. The black and white squares alternate on a regular cycle that generates electrical potentials along the optic nerve and the brain. Electrodes are placed over the visual centers on the occipital scalp. The pattern reversal stimulates action events along the optic nerve, the optic chiasm, and the optic tract through complex processing pathways that ultimately feed to the occipital cortex.

The whole trip of the bioelectric wave propagation (the latency) normally takes about 100 ms. The VER averaged waveforms take on morphology having characteristic peaks such as the P100. This waveform is given this designation because it is a positive-polarity electric event that is delayed by 100 ms after the visual stimulus. White-matter brain lesions anywhere along this pathway will slow or even stop the signal.

Figure 22.45 shows two overlying VER waveforms. Each waveform is the average of 128 individual EEG responses from a visual stimulus. The slight variation of the two waveforms gives an indication of the noise in the measurement that is not fully averaged out, as well as the physiologic variability from trial to trial.

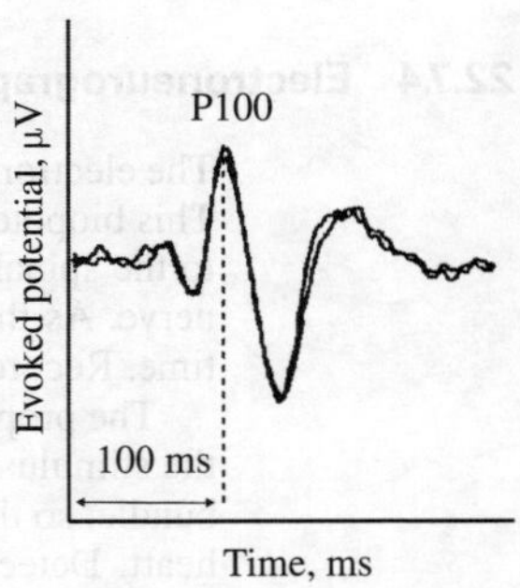

FIGURE 22.45 A visual evoked response waveform showing the P100 peak. It is delayed 100 ms from the onset of a visual flash stimulus in healthy people.

Signal Processing of Evoked Biopotential Waveforms. Due to the relatively low amplitude of evoked waveforms, bandpass filtering is not sufficient to show their responses against the background noise. Noise originates from uncorrelated EEG activity, low-level EMG activity of the head and neck, and sometimes even cardiac bioelectricity.

The signal-to-noise ratio (SNR) is an indicator of the quality of the biopotential recording in terms of being able to identify the biopotential of interest apart from the noise:

$$\text{SNR} = \frac{\text{signal power}}{\text{noise power}}$$

An SNR of 1 means that the signal and noise are of equal power, and hence the signal waveform is indistinguishable from the noise. SNRs of at least 3 to 5 are needed to reliably see the presence of biopotential waveforms, and much higher SNRs, perhaps 10 to 20, are needed for diagnosis.

Signal averaging is a very powerful method of improving the SNR and extracting low-level repetitive signals from uncorrelated noise. It can be employed as long as one can repetitively evoke the biopotential. Signal theory provides that when the interfering noise is random and thus uniformly distributed in the frequency spectrum, signal averaging increases the ratio of the signal amplitude to noise amplitude by

$$\text{SNR ratio improvement} \propto \sqrt{n}$$

where n is the number of waveforms averaged.

EMG noise in evoked bioelectric recordings often does not strictly meet the criteria of randomness and flat frequency spectrum since it is somewhat peaked at certain frequencies. Line-frequency interference has a single, large-frequency peak but is otherwise uncorrelated with the evoked waveform. Despite these variations from the optimum, signal averaging can still be quite useful in improving the SNR when bioelectric responses can be repetitively evoked.

A computer-based data-acquisition system has an analog-to-digital converter that is triggered to sample the bioelectric waveform in synchrony with, and just following, the sensory stimulus. The evoked biopotential along with the noise is digitally sampled and stored in memory as a sequence of numbers representing the signal's instantaneous amplitude over time. Successively sampled waveforms are then numerically added in a pointwise fashion with the previous corresponding time intervals for each past event. The resulting ensemble of added waveforms are then digitally scaled in amplitude by the number of events, and the averaged waveform is displayed. Many commercial signal-processing software packages can perform this function.

The improvement in the ability to see the evoked waveform is limited only by the degree to which the noise deviates from the ideal, the practical limitations on the time one can wait to accumulate evoked events, and physiological variability. Generally, averaging as few as 64 to perhaps greater than 1024 evoked events can provide the needed waveform fidelity.

22.7.4 Electroneurography

The electroneurogram (ENG) is a bioelectric recording of a propagating nerve action potential event. This biopotential is usually evoked by an electric stimulus applied to a portion of the nerve proximal to the spinal cord. The ENG is of interest in assessing nerve function, particularly after injury to a nerve. As the nerve heals and regrows, the ENG amplitude becomes detectable and increases over time. Recording this waveform can give insight into the progress of nerve healing.

The propagated bioelectric response is detected with skin bioelectrodes some distance away from the stimulus. Nerve action events are transient and not synchronous with other fibers within a nerve bundle, so these action currents do not sum together in the same way as they do, for example, in the heart. Detection of the skin surface potential created by an action event from a single nerve fibril within a larger bundle is very difficult, perhaps impossible.

The exception is when a large external electric stimulus is applied to the nerve bundle causing a synchronous depolarization of many fibers. This causes a relatively larger action potential that is more detectable; however, the skin potential signals are still only in the range of 10 to 30 μV. Even with total suppression of line-frequency noise, this signal can be easily obscured by small EMG activity from unrelaxed local muscles. The solution is to evoke the ENG by repetitive stimulation of the nerve. This allows computer-based signal averaging, which increases the ENG signal-to-noise ratio.

An example method of recording the ENG involves stimulation of the ulnar nerve on the upper forearm under the bicep. This stimulation produces a twitching of the muscles in the fingers. The ENG is detected as the efferent action potential passes two biopotential electrodes straddling the nerve at the wrist. Figure 22.46 shows the placement of electrodes and an illustration of the propagation delay in the ENG waveform.

The ENG in this case arises from the depolarization of many myelinated nerve fibrils within the bundle. ENG amplitude is usually on the order of a few tens of microvolts and creates a transient, sinusoidal-looking waveform as it passes the electrodes. The finite propagation velocity causes

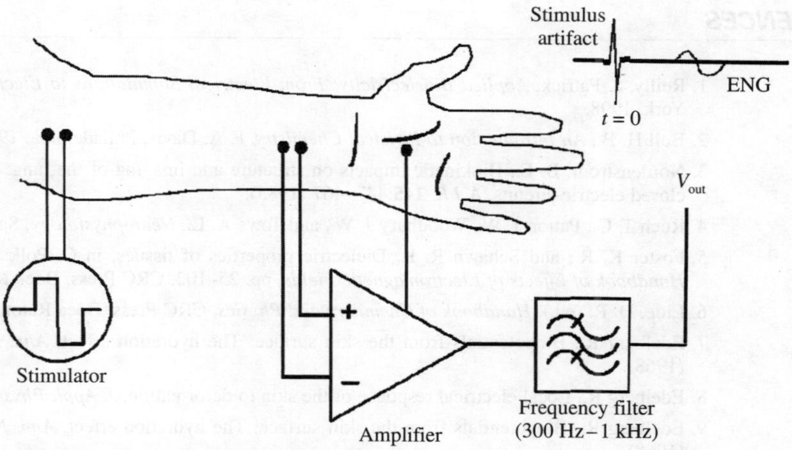

FIGURE 22.46 Illustration of the instrumentation setup for monitoring the ENG.

a several-millisecond delay between the stimulus and the electrode recording. The nerve action potential conduction velocity V can be determined from

$$\text{Nerve conduction velocity } V = \frac{d}{t}$$

where d is the separation distance of the electrodes and t is the propagation delay time. The propagation velocity is slowed in nerve trauma and stretch injuries. Monitoring nerve conduction through the affected region of the nerve can help a physician assess the progress of nerve repair.

22.7.5 Other Biopotentials

Bioelectrodes placed on or near many major organs having bioelectrically active tissue will often register a bioelectric potential associated with their function. For example, electrodes placed over the stomach will register a slowly varying biopotential associated with digestion. This recording is known as an *electrogastrogram* (EGG).

Electrodes placed on the skin around the eye will detect a biopotential due to a dipolar current flow from the cornea to the retina. The dot product of this biocurrent dipole with an electrode pair will change in amplitude according to the gaze angle. This is known as an *electroocculogram* (EOG), and it can be used to determine the eye's angular displacement.

Finally, there are also bioelectric currents flowing in the retina. They are detectable using corneal electrodes, and the monitored biopotential is known as an *electroretinogram* (ERG). It changes in amplitude and waveshape with pulsed illumination. A strobe light, for example, will produce a transient ERG biopotential of nearly 1 mV.

ACKNOWLEDGMENT

I would like to acknowledge the help and contributions of Mr. William Phillips in the creation of the illustrations and in manuscript editing.

REFERENCES

1. Reilly, J. Patrick, *Applied Bioelectricity: From Electrical Stimulations to Electropathology,* Springer, New York, 1998.
2. Bull H. B., *An Introduction to Physical Chemistry,* F. A. Davis, Philadelphia, 1971.
3. Nordenstrom, B. E., Biokinetic impacts on structure and imaging of the lung: The concept of biologically closed electric circuits, *A.J.R.* **145**:447–467 (1985).
4. Ruch T. C., Patton J. W., Woodbury J. W., and Towe A. L., *Neurophysiology*, Saunders, Philadelphia, 1968.
5. Foster K. R., and Schawn R. P., Dielectric properties of tissues, in C. Polk and E. Postow (eds.), CRC *Handbook of Effects of Electromagnetic Fields*, pp. 25–102, CRC Press, Boca Raton, Fla., 1986.
6. Lide, D. R. (ed.), *Handbook of Chemistry and Physics*, CRC Press, Boca Raton, Fla., 1972.
7. Edelberg R., Biopotentials from the skin surface: The hydration effect, *Ann. N.Y. Acad Sci* **148**:252–262 (1968).
8. Edelberg R., Local electrical response of the skin to deformation, *J. Appl. Physiol.* **34**(3):334–340 (1973).
9. Edelberg R., Biopotentials from the skin surface: The hydration effect, *Ann. N.Y. Acad. Sci.* **148**:252–262 (1968).
10. Wilcott R. C., Arousal sweating and electrodermal phenomena, *Psychol. Bull.* **67**(1):58–72 (1967).
11. Tam H. W., and Webster J. G., Minimizing electrode motion artifact by skin abrasion. *IEEE Trans. Biomed. Eng*. **24**(2):134–139 (1977).
12. Burbank D. P., and Webster J. G., Reducing skin potential motion artifact by skin abrasion, *Med. Biol. Eng. Comput.* **16**:31–38 (1978).
13. Thakor N. V., and Webster J. G., The origin of skin potential and its variations, presented at the 31st Annual Conference on Engineering in Medicine and Biology (ACEMB), Georgia, Alliance for Engineering and Biology, Bethesda, 1978.
14. Shackel B., Skin drilling: A method of diminishing galvanic skin potentials, *Am. Jo. Physiol*. 72:114–121 (1959).

CHAPTER 23
BIOMEDICAL SIGNAL ANALYSIS

Jit Muthuswamy
Arizona State University, Tempe, Arizona

23.1 INTRODUCTION

Any signal transduced from a biological or medical source could be called a *biosignal*. The signal source could be at the molecular level, cell level, or a systemic or organ level. A wide variety of such signals are commonly encountered in the clinic, research laboratory, and sometimes even at home. Examples include the electrocardiogram (ECG), or electrical activity from the heart; speech signals; the electroencephalogram (EEG), or electrical activity from the brain; evoked potentials (EPs, i.e., auditory, visual, somatosensory, etc.), or electrical responses of the brain to specific peripheral stimulation; the electroneurogram, or field potentials from local regions in the brain; action potential signals from individual neurons or heart cells; the electromyogram (EMG), or electrical activity from the muscle; the electroretinogram from the eye; and so on.

Clinically, biomedical signals are primarily acquired for monitoring (detecting or estimating) specific pathological/physiological states for purposes of diagnosis and evaluating therapy. In some cases of basic research, they are also used for decoding and eventual modeling of specific biological systems. Furthermore, current technology allows the acquisition of multiple channels of these signals. This brings up additional signal-processing challenges to quantify physiologically meaningful interactions among these channels.

Goals of signal processing in all these cases usually are noise removal, accurate quantification of signal model and its components through analysis (system identification for modeling and control purposes), feature extraction for deciding function or dysfunction, and prediction of future pathological or functional events as in prosthetic devices for heart and brain. Typical biological applications may involve the use of signal-processing algorithms for more than one of these reasons. The monitored biological signal in most cases is considered an additive combination of signal and noise. Noise can be from instrumentation (sensors, amplifiers, filters, etc.), from electromagnetic interference (EMI), or in general, any signal that is asynchronous and uncorrelated with the underlying physiology of interest. Therefore different situations warrant different assumptions for noise characteristics, which will eventually lead to an appropriate choice of signal-processing method.

The focus of this chapter is to help the biomedical engineer or the researcher choose the appropriate representation or analysis of the signal from the available models and then guide the engineer toward an optimal strategy for quantification. This chapter is not meant to be an exhaustive review of biosignals and techniques for analyzing. Only some of the fundamental signal-processing techniques that find wide application with biosignals are discussed in this chapter. It is not structured to suit the reader who has a scholarly interest in biomedical signal-processing techniques. For a more detailed overview of biomedical signal-processing techniques, the reader is referred to Refs. 1 and 2. This chapter will not deal with measurement issues of the signal. The reader is assumed to have acquired the signal reliably and is poised to make decisions based on the signals. This chapter will help the reader navigate his or her way from the point of signal acquisition to the point where it is useful for decision making.

A general classification of biomedical signals is attempted in Sec. 23.2. This will enable the reader (user) to place his or her signal of interest in the appropriate class. Subsequently, the sections are outlined according to different techniques for signal analysis. As far as possible, the first paragraph of each section generally outlines the class(es) of signals for which the corresponding technique is best suited. Toward the end of each section, appropriate MATLAB functions useful for analysis are indicated. Each section is then illustrated by an application.

23.2 CLASSIFICATIONS OF SIGNALS AND NOISE

The biomedical signal sources can be broadly classified into *continuous processes* and *discrete-time* or *point processes*. Each of these types of signals could be deterministic (or predictable), stochastic (or random), fractal, or chaotic. The continuous processes are typically encountered in one of the following situations.

23.2.1 Deterministic Signals in Noise

Examples of this type are ECG or single-fiber EMG signals in noise. The measured signal $x(t)$ can be represented as follows:

$$x(t) = s(t) + n(t)$$

where $s(t)$ is the actual deterministic signal and $n(t)$ is the additive noise. A segment of blood pressure shown in Fig. 23.1*A* is an example of a deterministic periodic signal. A Gaussian white noise assumption is valid in many biological cases. The goal in many situations is feature extraction under noisy (could be EMI, ambient, or instrumentation noise) conditions and subsequently correlating with the underlying physiological or pathological state.

23.2.2 Deterministic Signals (Synchronized to Another Stimulus Signal or Perturbation) in Noise

Examples of this type include all the different evoked responses (auditory, somatosensory, visual, etc.) and event-related potentials recorded in response to controlled stimuli administered to the body (or any biological system in general). These signals usually reveal functional characteristics of specific pathways in the body. For instance, evoked responses to peripheral somatosensory stimulation reveal the performance of the somatosensory pathway leading to the sensory cortex. A segment of cortical somatosensory evoked potential is shown in Fig. 23.1*B* that was obtained after averaging 100 stimulus-response pairs. Evoked responses or event-related potentials are usually superimposed over

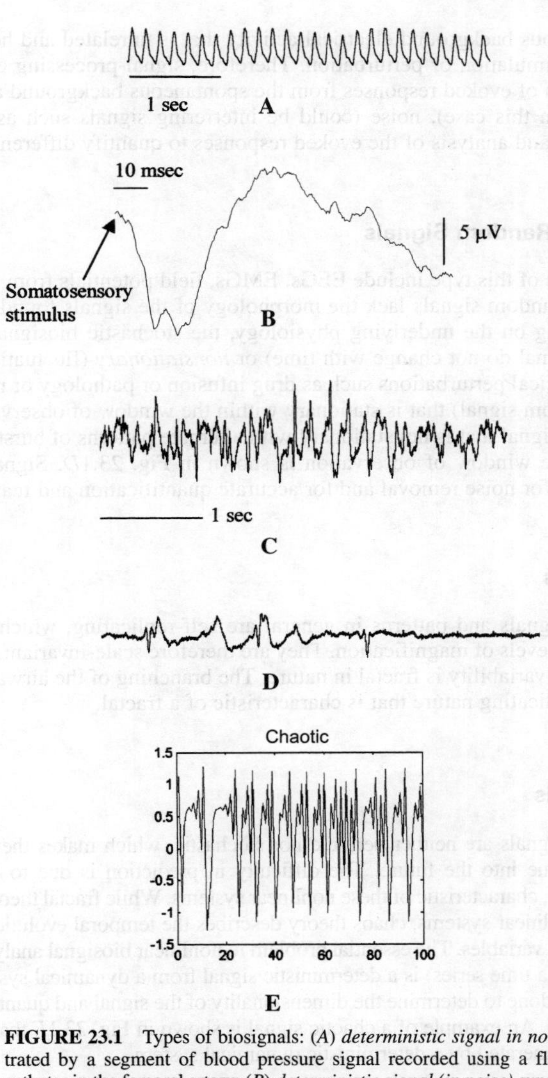

FIGURE 23.1 Types of biosignals: (*A*) *deterministic signal in noise*, illustrated by a segment of blood pressure signal recorded using a fluid-filled catheter in the femoral artery; (*B*) *deterministic signal (in noise) synchronized to an external cue or perturbation*, illustrated by an epoch of somatosensory evoked potential recorded from the somatosensory cortex in response to an electrical stimulus to the forelimb; (*C*) *stationary stochastic signal*, illustrated by a segment of EEG from the cortex that shows no specific morphology or shape, but the statistics of the signals are more or less stable or stationary in the absence of any physiological perturbations; (*D*) *nonstationary stochastic signal*, illustrated by a segment of EEG recorded from an adult rat recovering from a brain injury showing bursts of activity, but the statistics of this signal change with time; (*E*) *a chaotic signal* that was artificially generated resembles a stochastic signal but is actually generated by a deterministic dynamical system.

spontaneous background electrical activity that is unrelated and hence asynchronous to the administered stimulation or perturbation. Therefore, signal-processing efforts have been directed toward extraction of evoked responses from the spontaneous background activity (could also be considered "noise" in this case), noise (could be interfering signals such as ECG, EMG, or ambient noise) removal, and analysis of the evoked responses to quantify different components.

23.2.3 Stochastic or Random Signals

Examples of this type include EEGs, EMGs, field potentials from the brain, and R-R intervals from ECGs. Random signals lack the morphology of the signals found in the preceding two categories. Depending on the underlying physiology, the stochastic biosignals could be *stationary* (statistics of the signal do not change with time) or *nonstationary* (fluctuations in the signal statistics due to physiological perturbations such as drug infusion or pathology or recovery). A segment of EEG signal (random signal) that is stationary within the window of observation is shown in Fig. 23.1*C*, and an EEG signal that is nonstationary with alternate patterns of bursts and suppressions in amplitudes within the window of observation is shown in Fig. 23.1*D*. Signal-analysis techniques have been typically for noise removal and for accurate quantification and feature extraction.

23.2.4 Fractal Signals

Fractal signals and patterns in general are self-replicating, which means that they look similar at different levels of magnification. They are therefore scale-invariant. There is evidence to suggest that heart rate variability is fractal in nature. The branching of the airway into bronchioles seems to have a self-replicating nature that is characteristic of a fractal.

23.2.5 Chaotic Signals

Chaotic signals are neither periodic nor stochastic, which makes them very difficult to predict beyond a short time into the future. The difficulty in prediction is due to their extreme sensitivity to initial conditions, characteristic of these nonlinear systems. While fractal theory details the spatial characteristics of the nonlinear systems, chaos theory describes the temporal evolution of the system parameters or the dynamical variables. The essential problem in nonlinear biosignal analysis is to determine whether a given biosignal (a time series) is a deterministic signal from a dynamical system. Subsequently, signal analysis is usually done to determine the dimensionality of the signal and quantification of the dynamical states of the system. An example of a chaotic signal is shown in Fig. 23.1*E* that resembles a random signal but is actually generated by a deterministic dynamical system.

23.2.6 Multichannel Signals

Multichannel signals could include signals of any of the preceding five types but acquired using multichannel recording technology. Analysis and interpretation usually involve a matrix formulation of the single-channel analysis technique. A segment of four-channel multiunit activity (extracellular action potential signals) from thalamic and cortical structures is shown in Fig. 23.2. The goals of signal analysis are usually to identify correlation and hence synchrony among different channels, to achieve feature extraction under noisy conditions, and to identify underlying physiology.

The same six broad types of signals are found among point processes as well. The most common example of a point process is the action potential traces (recorded from either the extracellular or the intracellular space). Derived measures such as the neuronal firing rate histograms or cross-correllograms that are continuous in time are often used for analysis of these point processes.

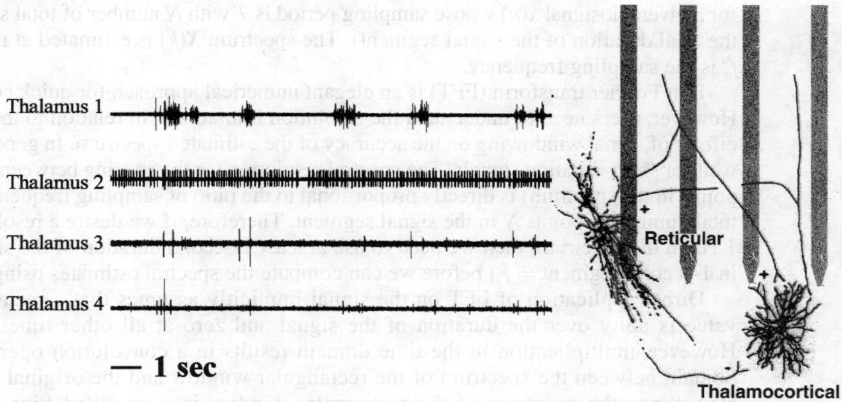

FIGURE 23.2 An example of a *multichannel biosignal* acquired using a multichannel microelectrode implanted in the thalamus and cortex of an adult rat. Each channel is a trace of multiunit activity (action potentials from a few neurons in the vicinity of each microelectrode as illustrated in the adjacent cartoon).

The following sections are organized as follows. Section 23.3 deals with analysis of deterministic and stationary stochastic signals. Analysis of nonstationary signals is discussed in Sec. 23.4. Subsequently, Sec. 23.5 deals with alternative orthogonal basis of representing biosignals that are optimal in certain physiological situations. Techniques for dealing with pairs of signals (both stochastic or a combination of stochastic and deterministic) are discussed in Sec. 23.6. Finally, Sec. 23.7 deals with analysis of fractal and chaotic signals. The statistics of the estimates are discussed wherever appropriate. By discussing these techniques separately, I am not suggesting that each of these techniques should be used in isolation. My hope is that the reader will get a deeper appreciation for each technique and will be driven toward creative solutions based on the data that could very well include a combination of several techniques.

23.3 SPECTRAL ANALYSIS OF DETERMINISTIC AND STATIONARY RANDOM SIGNALS

One of the most common analysis techniques that is used for biological signals is aimed at breaking down the signal into its different spectral (or frequency) components.

23.3.1 Fast Fourier Transforms

Signal Types—Deterministic Biosignals (with or without Noise). Fast Fourier transform (FFT) is commonly used in analyzing the spectral content of any deterministic biosignal (with or without noise). I will discuss the issue of estimating the spectrum of the signal under noisy conditions in the following subsections. Discrete Fourier transform (DFT) allows the decomposition of discrete time signals into sinusoidal components whose frequencies are multiples of a fundamental frequency. The amplitudes and phases of the sinusoidal components can be estimated using the DFT and is represented mathematically as

$$X(k) = \frac{1}{N}\sum_{n=0}^{N-1} x(n)e^{-j(2\pi kn/NT)} \tag{23.1}$$

for a given biosignal $x(n)$ whose sampling period is T with N number of total samples (NT is therefore the total duration of the signal segment). The spectrum $X(k)$ is estimated at multiples of f_s/N, where f_s is the sampling frequency.

Fast Fourier transform (FFT) is an elegant numerical approach for quick computation of the DFT. However, users need to understand the resolution limitations (in relation to the signal length) and the effects of signal windowing on the accuracy of the estimated spectrum. In general, FFT does not work well for short-duration signals. The spectral resolution (or the spacing between ordinates of successive points in the spectrum) is directly proportional to the ratio of sampling frequency f_s of the signal to the total number of points N in the signal segment. Therefore, if we desire a resolution of approximately 1 Hz in the spectrum, then we need to use at least 1-second duration of the signal (number of points in 1-second segment $= f_s$) before we can compute the spectral estimates using FFT.

Direct application of FFT on the signal implicitly assumes that a rectangular window whose value is unity over the duration of the signal and zero at all other times multiplies the signal. However, multiplication in the time domain results in a convolution operation in the frequency domain between the spectrum of the rectangular window and the original spectrum of the signal $x(n)$. Since the spectrum of the rectangular window is a so-called Sinc function consisting of decaying sinusoidal ripples, the convolved spectrum $X(f)$ can be a distorted version of the original spectrum of $x(n)$. Specifically, spectral contents from one frequency component (usually the dominating spectral peak) tend to leak into neighboring frequency components due to the convolution operation. Therefore, it is often advisable to window the signals (particularly when one expects a dominating spectral peak adjacent to one with lower amplitude in the signal spectrum). Several standard windows, such as Hamming, Hanning, Kaiser, Blackman-Tukey, etc., are available in any modern signal-processing toolbox, each with its own advantages and disadvantages. For a thorough review on different windows and their effect on the estimation of spectral contents, the reader is referred to Refs. 3 and 4.

23.3.2 Periodogram Approach

Signal Types—Deterministic Signals in Noise or Pure Stationary Random Signals. For deterministic signals in noise or pure random signals, Welch's periodogram approach can be used for estimating the power spectrum of the signal. The given length of the signal N is segmented into several (K) overlapping or nonoverlapping epochs each of length M. The power spectrum of each epoch is evaluated using FFT and averaged over K epochs to obtain the averaged periodogram. An implicit assumption in this method is that the statistical properties of the noise or the signal do not change over the length of the given sequence of data (assumption of *stationarity*). Periodogram leads to statistically unbiased estimates (the mean value of the *estimate* of the power spectrum equals the true value of the power spectrum). Further, the variance (or uncertainty) in the individual estimates is inversely proportional to K. Therefore, it is desirable to increase the number of segments K in order to decrease the uncertainty in the estimates. However, increasing K will also decrease the resolution in the power spectra for reasons discussed in the preceding subsection. The power spectra using Welch's periodogram approach can be estimated using *spectrum.welch* function in MATLAB. Since the power spectral values are estimates, one has to specify the confidence in these estimates for a complete description. When the epochs are nonoverlapping, the ratio of the power spectral estimate at each frequency to its actual value can be approximated to be a χ^2_{2K} random variable with $2K$ degrees of freedom.[5] Therefore, the interval within which the actual value is likely to lie can be estimated easily, given the desired level of confidence. Other functions in MATLAB that may be worth considering are *spectrum.burg, spectrum.periodogram, spectrum.mtm,* etc.

23.3.3 Parametric Methods

Signal Types—Short-Duration Signals and Stationary Random Signals in Noise. When a high-resolution spectrum is desired and only a short-duration signal is available, parametric approaches outlined in this subsection provide a better alternative (as long as the parametric model is accurate) to FFT-based approaches for power spectral estimation in the case of *random or stochastic signals in noise*. For deterministic or periodic signals (with or without noise), Fourier transform–based approaches will still be preferable.[6] Examples of parametric modeling include the autoregressive (AR) model, the autoregressive moving-average (ARMA) model, and the moving-average (MA) model. So far there is no automatic method to choose from AR, ARMA, or MA. The given signal is treated as the output of a linear time-invariant system (more advanced adaptive methods can be used to track time-varying model parameters) driven by a white Gaussian noise. The AR model can also be treated as an attempt to predict the current signal sample based on p past values of the signal weighted by constant coefficients. We estimate the best model by trying to minimize the mean squared error between the signal sample predicted by the model and the actual measured signal sample.

In an AR model, the signal $x(n)$ is represented in terms of its prior samples as follows:

$$x(n) = e(n) - a_1 x(n-1) - a_2 x(n-2) - \cdots - a_p x(n-p) \tag{23.2}$$

where $e(n)$ = assumed to be zero mean white Gaussian noise with a variance of σ^2
p = order of the AR model
$x(n-i)$ = signal sample i time periods prior to the current sample at n
a_i = coefficients or parameters of the AR model

This representation can also be seen as a system model in which the given biosignal is assumed to be the output of a linear time-invariant system that is driven by a white noise input $e(n)$. The coefficients or parameters of the AR model a_i become the coefficients of the denominator polynomial in the transfer function of the system and therefore determine the locations of the poles of the system model. As long as the biosignal is stationary, the estimated model coefficients can be used to reconstruct any length of the signal sequence. Theoretically, therefore, power spectral estimates of any desired resolution can be obtained. The three main steps in this method are

1. Estimation of approximate model order (p)
2. Estimation of model coefficients (a_i)
3. Estimation of the power spectrum using the model coefficients or parameters

It is critical to estimate the right model order because this determines the number of poles in the model transfer function (between the white noise input and the signal output). If the model order is too small, then the power spectral estimate tends to be biased more toward the dominant peaks in the power spectrum. If the model order is larger than required, it often gives rise to spurious peaks in the power spectral estimate of the signal.

Several asymptotic model order selection methods use a form of generalized information criteria (GIC) that could be represented as GIC(α, p) = $N \ln(\rho_p) - \alpha p$, where p is the model order, α is a constant, N is the number of data points, and ρ_p is the variance in the residual or error for model p.[7] The error or residual variance ρ_p can be determined using a (forward) prediction error $e_p(n)$ defined as

$$e_p(n) = \sum_{k=0}^{p} a_p(k)x(n-k)$$

where $a_p(k)$ is a parameter in the AR model of order p. The error variance is then simply a summation of squared forward prediction errors given by

$$\rho_p = \sum_{n=0}^{N-1} |e_p(n)|^2$$

When the value of α is 2 in the expression for GIC, it takes the form of the Akaike information criterion (AIC).[8,9] The optimum model order p is one that minimizes the generalized or Akaike information criterion.[9] More recent methods to estimate model order for signal sequences with a finite number of sample points include predictive least squares (PLS) and finite sample information criteria (FSIC).[7]

Having determined the optimal model order for the given segment of signal, the model can be estimated using one of the following MATLAB functions: *arburg, arcov* (uses a covariance approach), *armcov* (uses a modified covariance approach), or *aryule* (uses the Yule-Walker equations for estimation). The *arburg* function uses Burg's method[10] that minimizes both forward and backward prediction errors to arrive at the estimates of the AR model (similar to the modified covariance approach in *armcov*). The AIC model order estimation works well in combination with the Burg's method. Each of these functions uses different numerical procedures to arrive at the minimum mean square estimate of the AR model. The *aryule* function uses the autocorrelation estimates of the signal to determine the AR coefficients, which could potentially degrade the resolution of the spectrum. A brief discussion of the different AR parameter estimators and their application in ultrasonic tissue characterization is found in Ref. 11. Once the AR model has been estimated, the power spectra can be estimated by using the following expression:

$$P(f) = \frac{\sigma_p^2 T}{\left|1 + \sum_{k=0}^{p} a_p(k)\exp(-j2\pi fkT)\right|^2} \tag{23.3}$$

where $P(f)$ = power spectral estimate at the frequency f
σ^2_p = variance of the white noise input to the model
T = sampling period of the signal

The power spectrum of the signal can be estimated using the *pburg, pcov, pmcov*, or *pyulear* functions in MATLAB.

Statistics of the Spectral Estimates. The exact results for the statistics of the AR spectral estimator are not known. For large samples of stationary processes, the spectral estimates have approximately a Gaussian probability density function and are asymptotically unbiased and consistent estimates of the power spectral density. The variance of the estimate is given by

$$\mathrm{Var}[P(f)] = \begin{cases} \dfrac{4p}{N}P^2(f) & f = 0 \text{ and } \dfrac{f_s}{2} \\ \dfrac{2p}{N}P^2(f) & \text{otherwise} \end{cases} \tag{23.4}$$

where f_s = sampling frequency of the signal
N = number of samples
p = model order[4]

In general, parametric methods are preferred for stochastic signals, provided the estimations of model order and the model parameters are done carefully.

APPLICATION *An 8000-point EEG signal segment sampled at 278 Hz is shown in Fig. 23.3A. The power spectrum of the signal as evaluated using Welch's periodogram method is shown in Fig. 23.3B. The MATLAB function spectrum was used with a Hanning window of length 512, allowing*

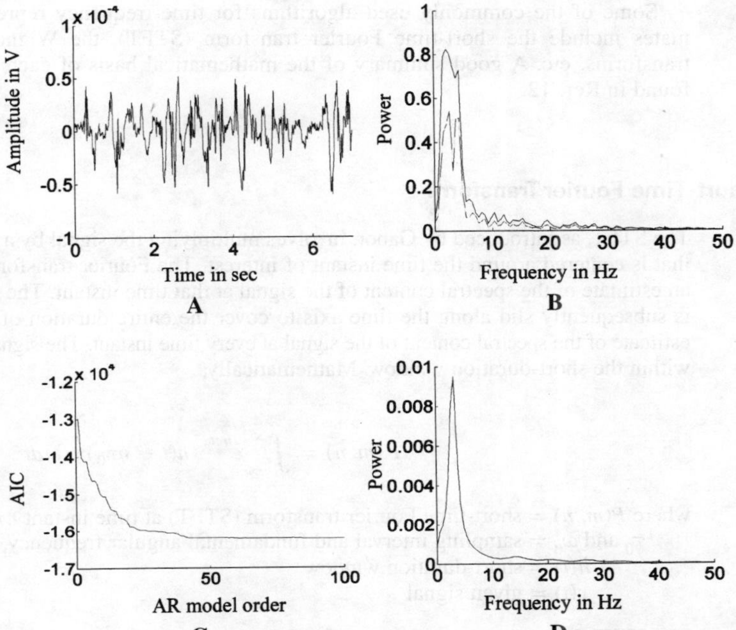

FIGURE 23.3 Comparison of a periodogram-based approach and a parametric approach to spectral analysis of stochastic signals. (*a*) A typical segment of EEG. (*b*) The power spectrum estimated using the periodogram approach (lower curve) along with the 95 percent confidence interval (upper curve). There is a higher uncertainty in the estimates in the low-frequency regime. (*c*) The autoregressive (AR) model order is estimated using an AIC criteria. The value of AIC seems to reach a minimum at approximately a model order of 50. (*d*) The power spectrum of the EEG signal estimated using an AR model of order 50. The power spectrum from the AR model has a higher resolution than (*b*).

for 256-point overlap between successive segments. The resolution of the spectrum is the ratio of the sampling frequency to the number of points, which turns out to be 0.54 Hz. The corresponding 95 percent confidence interval shown (upper curve) along with the power spectral estimate (lower curve) indicates the slightly higher uncertainty in the estimates around 5 Hz. An AR model order of 40 was chosen using the AIC shown in Fig. 23.3C. The power spectral estimate from the AR model using Burg's method in Fig. 23.3D shows a much higher resolution.

23.4 SPECTRAL ANALYSIS OF NONSTATIONARY SIGNALS

A signal is nonstationary when the statistics of the signal (mean, variance, and higher-order statistics) change with time. The traditional spectral estimation methods just outlined will only give an averaged estimate in these cases and will fail to capture the dynamics of the underlying generators. Alternative analysis techniques that determine time-localized spectral estimates can be used when the user suspects that the signal sequence under consideration is not under steady-state physiological conditions. These methods work well with both deterministic and random signals in noise.

Some of the commonly used algorithms for time-frequency representations of spectral estimates include the short-time Fourier transform (STFT), the Wigner-Ville transform, wavelet transforms, etc. A good summary of the mathematical basis of each of these techniques can be found in Ref. 12.

23.4.1 Short-Time Fourier Transform

The STFT, as introduced by Gabor, involves multiplying the signal by a short-duration time window that is centered around the time instant of interest. The Fourier transform of the product then gives an estimate of the spectral content of the signal at that time instant. The short-time-duration window is subsequently slid along the time axis to cover the entire duration of the signal and to obtain an estimate of the spectral content of the signal at every time instant. The signal is assumed to be stationary within the short-duration window. Mathematically,

$$P(m, n) = \int_{-\infty}^{\infty} e^{imt\omega_0} h(t - n\tau_0) x(t)\, dt \tag{23.5}$$

where $P(m, n)$ = short-time Fourier transform (STFT) at time instant $n\tau_0$ and frequency $m\omega_0$
τ_0 and ω_0 = sampling interval and fundamental angular frequency, respectively
$h(t)$ = short-duration window
$x(t)$ = given signal

The STFT thus results in a spectrum that depends on the time instant to which the window is shifted. The choice of Gaussian functions for the short-duration window gives excellent localization properties despite the fact that the functions are not limited in time. Alternatively, STFT can also be viewed as filtering the signal "at all times" using a bandpass filter centered around a given frequency *f* whose impulse response is the Fourier transform of the short-duration window modulated to that frequency. However, the duration and bandwidth of the window remain the same for all frequencies.

23.4.2 Wavelet Transforms

The wavelet transform, in contrast, is a signal-decomposition (or analysis) method on a set of orthogonal basis functions obtained by dilations, contractions, and shifts of a prototype wavelet. Wavelets have been used extensively for processing biomedical images[13–16] and for processing almost every kind of biosignal with nonstationarities.[17–26] The main distinction between Fourier transform–based methods such as the STFT and wavelet transforms is that the former use windows of constant width, whereas the latter use windows that are frequency-dependent.[8,27] Wavelet transforms enable arbitrarily good time resolution for high-frequency components and arbitrarily good frequency resolution for low-frequency components by using windows that are narrow for high-frequency components and broad for low-frequency components. In general, the continuous wavelet transform can be represented mathematically as

$$S(a, b) = \int x(t)\psi^*_{a,b}(t)\, dt \tag{23.6}$$

where $x(t)$ = given signal
a = scale factor
b = time
$*$ = complex conjugate

The orthogonal basis functions denoted by $\psi_{a,b}(t)$ are obtained by scaling and shifting a prototype wavelet function $\psi(t)$ (also sometimes called a *mother wavelet*) by scale a and time b, respectively, as shown below:

$$\psi_{a,b}(t) = \frac{1}{\sqrt{|a|}}\psi\left(\frac{t-b}{a}\right) \tag{23.7}$$

By adjusting the scale factor, the window duration can be arbitrarily changed for different frequencies. By choosing a and b appropriately, a discrete time version of the orthogonal basis functions can be represented as follows:

$$\psi(m, n) = a_0^{-m/2}\psi(a_0^{-m}t - nb_0) \tag{23.8}$$

where a_0 and b_0 are fundamental scale factor and time shift, respectively (m and n represent multiples of scale factor and the time shift).

Wavelet analysis works especially well with signals that have short durations of high-frequency components and long durations of low-frequency components, for example, EEG signals or signals or variations in interbeat (R-R) intervals, etc. I describe in this subsection a simple procedure for obtaining time-frequency representation of signals using wavelet transforms, as outlined in Refs. 8, 28, and 29.

1. Using FFT, find the Fourier transform $X(\omega)$ of the discrete time signal N-point signal $x(n)$.
2. For every equally spaced discrete frequency of interest f_i (>0), ($f_{min} < f_i < f_{max}$),
   a. Determine the scale factor $a_i = 1/f_i$.
   b. Denoting the analyzing wavelet by $\psi(n)$ (being implicitly dependent on the scale factor a) and its DFT by $\psi(\omega)$, which is centered around ω_0, evaluate the product vector $Z(\omega) = \psi(a\omega)X(\omega)$ for $\omega = -N/2$ to $N/2 - 1$.
   c. Determine the inverse Fourier transform of $Z(\omega)$ and scale the resulting time series by $\sqrt{a}$.

$$P(m, n) = \int_{-\infty}^{\infty} e^{imt\omega_0} h(t - n\tau_0)x(t)\,dt \tag{23.9}$$

   d. Repeat steps a to c for every discrete frequency within the range f_{min} and f_{max}.
   e. The resulting output $S(n, \omega)$ is the time-frequency representation of the signal $x(n)$.

The Fourier transform of one of the prototype wavelets (called a *Morlet wavelet*) is given by

$$\psi(\omega) = \exp[-(\omega - \omega_0)^2/2] + \text{small correction terms}$$

The correction terms are theoretically necessary to make the negative-frequency components of the term $\exp[-(\omega - \omega_0)^2/2]$ zero (an additional constraint imposed by Kronland-Martinet et al.[28]). In order to make the correction terms negligible, the center frequency ω_0 is chosen to be anywhere between 5.0 and 6.0. The corresponding time-domain form of the analyzing wavelet is a modulated Gaussian of the form (up to a constant normalization factor)

$$\psi(n) = e^{i\omega_0 n}\exp(-n^2/2)$$

The square of $S(n, \omega)$ is often referred to as a *scalogram*, and it gives an estimate of the time-localized power spectrum. An exhaustive tutorial on wavelet transforms and the appropriate MATLAB functions to be used can be found in Ref. 30.

APPLICATION *I have used wavelet transforms to track the changes in the spectral components of the somatosensory evoked potentials with an ischemic injury (induced by asphyxia) to the brain in a rodent model, as illustrated in Fig. 23.4. The high-frequency components disappear first at the*

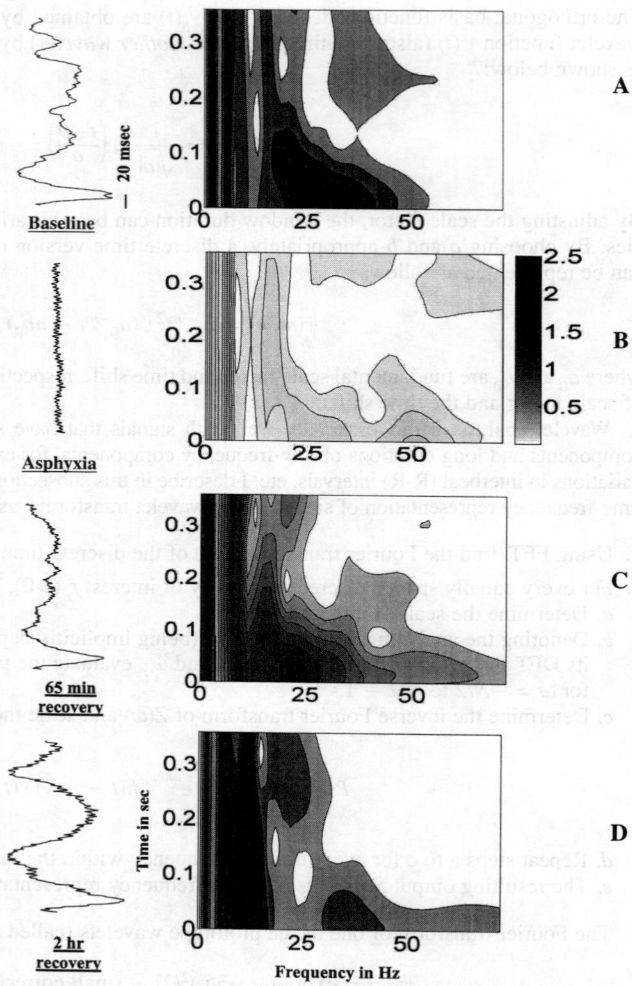

FIGURE 23.4 Analysis of a *nonstationary stochastic biosignal* using a wavelet-based approach for time-frequency localization of signal power. Somatosensory evoked potentials in response to an electrical stimulation to the contralateral forelimb recorded at different stages of brain injury are shown to the left of the vertical axis of the colored contour plots. The signals are recorded (*A*) at baseline—before the rat was subject to a controlled duration of asphyxia or oxygen deprivation; (*B*) during asphyxia—showing electrical silence or isoelectric behavior; (*C*) after approximately 65 minutes into recovery from the injury—showing partial recovery of low-frequency amplitudes; (*D*) after approximately 2 hours into recovery—showing greater recovery of the low-frequency and high-frequency generators in the evoked potentials. The time-frequency distribution of evoked potentials seems to indicate a greater vulnerability of the high-frequency generators in the brain to oxygen deprivation.

induction of injury and recover long after recovery of the low-frequency components after resuscitation of the animal. The results seem to suggest differential vulnerabilities in the generators of brain potentials. The somatosensory responses were obtained by averaging 100 stimulus-response pairs.

23.5 PRINCIPAL COMPONENTS ANALYSIS

Signal Types—Deterministic or Stochastic Signals in Colored Noise. So far we have represented (by projection) biosignals in terms of Fourier basis functions, autoregressive parameters, or wavelet-basis functions, depending on application. In general, the signal can be represented in terms of any convenient set of orthogonal basis functions. One such orthogonal basis, called the *principal components* of the given signal, has been widely used for analysis of biosignals. It is also called *Karhoenen-Loeve analysis* for signals with zero mean.

Broadly speaking, principal component analysis (PCA) has been used for at least two different applications where signal representation using other basis functions does not provide the optimal solution. First, when the presence of a known signal waveform (hence deterministic) has to be detected in colored (implying correlation among noise terms) Gaussian noise, projecting the noisy signal along its principal components allows for optimal detection of signal. When the noise is white (independent, identically distributed) Gaussian, a matched filter (or a correlator, to be discussed in a subsequent subsection on cross-correlation) provides the most optimal detection. The second broad application of principal components analysis has been in pattern classification, where it has been used for identifying the feature vectors that are most discriminating. Selecting the most discriminating features leads to a reduction in the dimensionality of input feature vectors. Indeed, one could reasonably argue that the first application is a special case of the second. Nevertheless, I will treat them distinctly in this section and outline methods for both applications.

23.5.1 Detecting Deterministic or Known Signals in Colored Gaussian Noise

The observation vectors (successive time samples could also be used to construct the observation vector) are the sum of a known signal and noise terms that are correlated. The key idea in this application is to emphasize the projection of the signal along directions where the noise energy is minimal. The assumption is that we know the covariance matrix of the noise a priori. Even if it is not known, it can be easily estimated from the covariance of a *training set* (trial observations) of observation vectors. The element K_{ij} of the covariance matrix K is the estimated covariance between ith and jth components of the observation vector. Having estimated K, we find the eigenvalues and the corresponding eigenvectors of the matrix. If the matrix is positive definite, all the eigenvalues will be distinct, and the corresponding eigenvectors will be orthogonal. By suitably scaling the eigenvectors, we obtain a set of orthonormal basis functions ϕ_i, $i = 1, 2, \ldots, N$, where N is the dimensionality of the observation vector. The known signal vector $\mathbf{S}$ and the observation vector $\mathbf{X}$ are projected onto the set of orthonormal eigenvectors. Mathematically, the $(N \times N)$ matrix

$$\Phi = \begin{bmatrix} \phi_1^T \\ \phi_2^T \\ \vdots \\ \phi_N^T \end{bmatrix}$$

represents the set of N orthonormal eigenvectors (each of dimension $N \times 1$). $\mathbf{S}' = \mathbf{\Phi S}$ represents the projection of the known signal vector along each eigenvector. Similarly $\mathbf{X}'$ represents the projection of the received observation vectors (known signal plus colored noise) along the orthonormal eigenvectors. The optimal detector is designed by evaluating

$$\sum_{i=1}^{N} \frac{S_i'}{\lambda_i} X_i'$$

for every observation vector, where λ_i are the corresponding eigenvalues. This ratio (also called the *likelihood ratio* after normalization by the norm of $\mathbf{S}'$; it is really a cross-correlation of lag zero between projections of the known signal and projections of the observation vector) is compared against a threshold that is calculated from a priori known probabilities to detect the presence of the known signal. As the ratio indicates, the signal projection is emphasized (amplified) in directions where the eigenvalues are small, implying smaller noise energy in that direction. The threshold Λ_0 for an optimal Bayes detector is given by Ref. 31,

$$\Lambda_0 = \frac{p_0(C_{10} - C_{00})}{p_1(C_{01} - C_{11})} \tag{23.10}$$

where p_1 = a known priori probability of the presence of the known signal (the frequency of occurrence of the known signal can be estimated by prior observation or knowledge of the generating process)

$p_0 = (1 - p_1)$

$C_{ij} (0 \le C_{ij} \le 1)$ = cost of deciding i when j actually occurred (where 0 indicates absence and 1 indicates presence of known signal in the noise)

Typically, C_{00} and C_{11} can be assumed to be zero, whereas C_{01} and C_{10} can each be assumed to be unity. However, sometimes the cost of false-positive C_{10} (detecting a signal when there is none) may be different from the cost of false-negative C_{01} (missing the known signal when it was actually present), depending on the application. Therefore, when the likelihood ratio exceeds the Bayes threshold, the detector indicates the presence of the known signal, and vice versa.

In the statistical analysis toolbox of MATLAB, functions *princomp* and *pcacov* enable the computation of principal components. The same method can be extended to detecting a finite number M of known signals. For further information on M-ary detection, the reader is referred to Ref. 31.

23.5.2 Principal Components Analysis for General Pattern Classification

Biosignals are often examined for recognizable patterns that indicate change in pathology or underlying physiology and hence aid diagnosis. In the absence of any signal analysis, the sample points in the measured biosignals have to be directly used to discriminate changes in underlying physiology. Analysis of the signal along spectral or wavelet components may not be the most discriminating since the components are not optimized for *discrimination* but are optimized for *spectral decomposition* and localization of energy. However, principal components analysis offers an elegant way to choose a set of orthonormal basis functions that are optimized specifically for maximum discrimination between two or more known classes of biosignals. In most cases, this method results in a drastic reduction in the number of signal components that one has to work with and also improves the classification or diagnosis as well.

Given a set of observation vectors (containing samples of the biosignals) from two different physiological or pathological states, we form a scatter matrix, which is really a scaled version of the sample covariance matrix. The scatter matrix $\mathbf{K}$ is defined as[32]

$$\mathbf{K} = \sum_{k=1}^{L} (\mathbf{X}_k - \mathbf{M})(\mathbf{X}_k - \mathbf{M})^t \tag{23.11}$$

where L = number of N-dimensional observation vectors $\mathbf{X}_i$
$\mathbf{M}$ = sample mean of the observation vectors
t = transpose operator

All the observations from different physiological states are pooled together to form the scatter matrix. Since the scatter matrix is real and positive, all the eigenvectors of **K** are orthogonal. The eigenvectors are then normalized as in the preceding application to yield an orthonormal set of basis vectors. The magnitude of the corresponding eigenvalues indicates the degree of scatter along those eigenvectors. We then choose the eigenvectors corresponding to the largest eigenvalues as the preferred directions of projections and determine the projections of the subsequent observations along those directions.

APPLICATION *PCA is commonly used for sorting neuronal spikes (action potentials). Extracellular data collected using microelectrodes implanted in the brain typically record action potentials or spikes from more than one neuron. Different neurons typically register action potentials of different shapes and sizes at the microelectrode. A trace of multineuronal action potential data (or multiunit data) is shown in Fig. 23.5B. The three different action potentials found in the trace are shown separately in an enlarged fashion in Fig. 23.5A. The result of principal components analysis of the three action potential waveforms is shown in Fig. 23.5C. When plotted in the space spanned by the two most dominant principal components, the corresponding projections of the three different action potentials show three distinct clusters that are easily separable. Instead of using all the time samples that constitute the waveform of the action potentials, principal components analysis identifies just two features (projections along two dominant principal components or eigenvectors) that are sufficient for discrimination.*

23.5.3 Independent Components Analysis

Signal Types—Stochastic Signals in Noise and Mixtures of Several Stochastic Signals. An extension of principal components analysis called *independent components analysis* (ICA) was originally used for *blind-source separation.*[33] In other words, when the measured signal vector (the number of channels of measured signal is given by the dimension of the vector) is an unknown linear mixture or combination of an equal number of independent, non-Gaussian sources, then this technique is useful in arriving at an estimate of the unknown original sources of the signal. For instance, when multiple channels of EEG are collected from several locations on the scalp, the potentials are presumably generated by mixing some underlying components of brain activity. While principal components analysis is useful in identifying the orthogonal directions (eigenvectors) that contain significant signal energy, independent components analysis is useful in identifying the independent, non-Gaussian components of the signal. This technique will not work if there is a strong indication that the original independent sources are Gaussian (if just one of the independent components is Gaussian, the ICA model may still be estimated[33]).

If the independent signal sources are represented by $\mathbf{s} = \{s_1, s_2, \ldots, s_N\}$ (could be N different kinds of sources) and an unknown *mixing* matrix **A** (inherent to the generating source or the medium between the source and the measurement point) generates the measured or received signals $\mathbf{r} = \{r_1, r_2, \ldots, r_n\}$, then the ICA signal model can be represented as $\mathbf{r} = \mathbf{As}$. This technique has been used successfully on EEG signals,[34,35] to decompose evoked potentials,[36] and to remove artifacts in magnetoencephalography (MEG).[37]

The goal of ICA is to design a matrix **F** specifying linear spatial filters that inverts the mixing process due to the **A** matrix. The matrix **F** is therefore often referred to as the *separation matrix* that helps to generate a scaled and permuted version $\mathbf{y} = \{y_1, y_2, \ldots, y_N\} = \mathbf{Fr}$ of the original sources **s**. The basic principle of ICA is centered on the central limit theorem in statistics, which states that the distribution of a sum of independent random variables tends toward a Gaussian distribution under certain conditions. Therefore, the signal **r** (mixture of several independent non-Gaussian sources) will be more Gaussian. The idea then is to formulate a measure of non-Gaussianity and then project

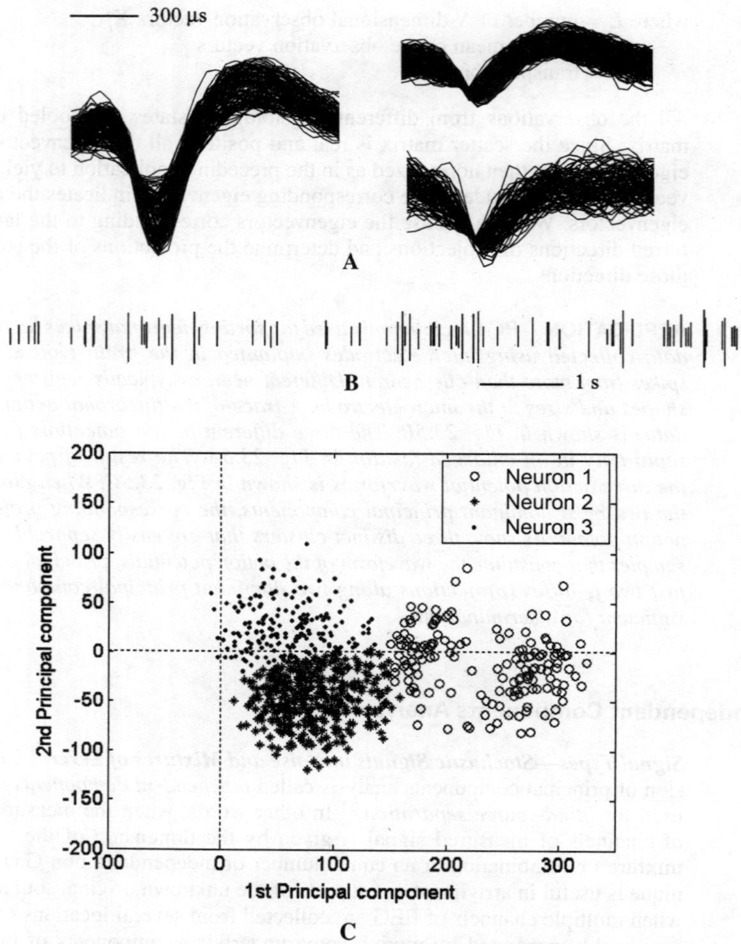

FIGURE 23.5 The measured biosignal (multiunit activity from a single microelectrode) is projected along an alternate (as opposed to Fourier basis functions shown earlier) set of orthogonal basis vectors (eigenvectors or principal components) for the purpose of *sorting* action potentials belonging to different neurons. The three different action potentials recorded by the microelectrode are shown in (*A*). Multiple traces within each action potential indicate multiple occurrences of similar action potentials superimposed to demonstrate variability. The three action potentials differ from each other in duration and peak amplitudes. On a more compressed scale in (*B*) the three action potentials appear as spikes of different heights. Plotting the action potential waveforms along two of their principal components in (*C*) gives a clear separation between the three different action potentials. Thus, instead of using all the points of the action potential waveform for sorting or classification, the use of projections along the principal components reduces the number of features required for sorting to just two.

the measured or received signal along specific directions in an iterative manner (as specified by the **F** matrix), which will maximize the measure of non-Gaussianity. Different measures of non-Gaussianity have been used to determine the optimal matrix **F**, such as the information-maximization approach[38] or methods based on cumulants[39] and negentropy.[40]

Using kurtosis (or the fourth-order cumulant) of a signal as a measure of its non-Gaussianity, an implementation of ICA originally derived by Hyvarinen and Oja[41] is discussed here. For the kth source signal s_k, the kurtosis is defined as

$$\text{Kurt}(s_k) = E\{s_k^4\} - 3[E\{s_k^2\}]^2 \tag{23.12}$$

where $E\{\cdot\}$ denotes the mathematical expectation. The kurtosis is negative for source signals whose amplitude has sub-Gaussian probability densities (probability distributions flatter than Gaussian), positive for super-Gaussian (probability distributions sharper than Gaussian), and zero for Gaussian densities. Maximizing the norm of the kurtosis leads to identification of the independent sources. This method was used in Ref. 35 to eliminate ECG interference in EEG signals.

A brief outline is presented here. For a more detailed presentation, the reader is referred to an excellent review.[33] The first step in ICA processing is to center **r** by subtracting its mean vector **m** so as to make **r** a zero-mean variable. After estimating the mixing matrix with centered data, the procedure is completed by adding the mean vector **m** of **r** back to the centered estimate that was subtracted in the first step. Subsequent to centering, the measured vector is sometimes whitened as part of preprocessing the signal before applying the ICA algorithm. Whitening the observed vector **r** (resulting in a flat power spectrum) removes the second-order relationships and produces a new vector $\mathbf{u} = \{u_1, u_2, \ldots, u_n\}$ whose components are uncorrelated. The variance of the individual components of **u** is unity. In matrix notation, this is

$$\mathbf{u} = \mathbf{U}\mathbf{r} \tag{23.13}$$

where **U** is the whitening matrix. Expressing **r** in terms of **s** and **A**, the model **u** becomes

$$\mathbf{u} = \mathbf{U}\mathbf{A}\mathbf{s} \tag{23.14}$$

The solution is

$$\mathbf{y} = \mathbf{W}\mathbf{u} \tag{23.15}$$

where **W** is the separating matrix for the measured signals after whitening (Fig. 23.6).

Maximizing the absolute value of the kurtosis of the components of **y** [Eq. (23.12)], one of the columns of the separating matrix **W** is found, and so one independent component at a time is identified. The other columns are estimated subsequently. The algorithm has a cubic convergence and typically convergence by 20 iterations.[35] From Eqs. (23.13), (23.14), and (23.15), the output matrix of independent components **y** can be written as

$$\mathbf{y} = \mathbf{W}\mathbf{u} = \mathbf{W}\mathbf{U}\mathbf{r} = \mathbf{F}\mathbf{r} \tag{23.16}$$

The rows of this matrix are the time course of activation of the individual ICA components. A MATLAB implementation of the algorithm (FastICA) is available at http://www.cis.hut.fi/projects/ica/fastica/.[33]

APPLICATION *ICA has been used to separate ECG interference in EEG signals recorded from adult rats undergoing controlled ischemic brain injury and subsequent recovery.*[35] *The measured signal vector* **r** *consisted of two EEG signals recorded from right and left parietal cortex areas and one channel of ECG, as illustrated in Fig. 23.7. The signals shown at the top in Fig. 23.7 were recorded right after an asphyxic injury to the brain during which the EEGs became isoelectric. The early recovery from such injury is characterized by low-amplitude waveforms in the EEG that carry information about the early recovery mechanisms in the cortex. However, they are prone to corruption from the larger-amplitude ECG signals. The reconstructed EEG is free from any interference*

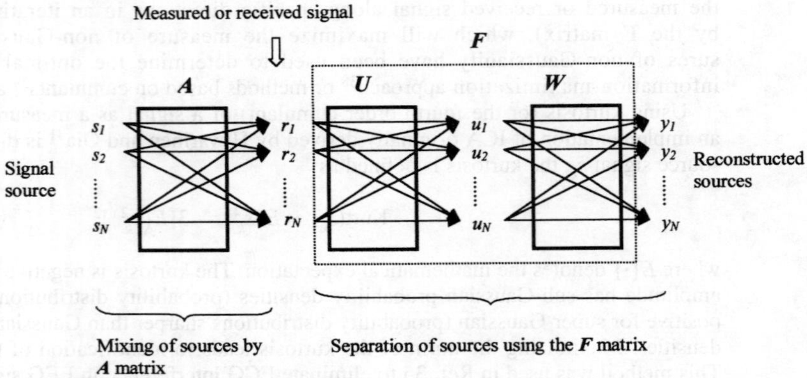

FIGURE 23.6 Schematic of independent components analysis technique for a blind source separation application. The signal from the sources gets mixed by an unknown mixing matrix **A** before being measured. The goal of ICA is to design a separating matrix **F** of linear spatial filters that will invert the measured signal vector **r** back into the independent components represented by the vector **y**. The components of **y** should be approximations of the source vector **s**, although they (the reconstructed sources) do not have to match the order in which they appear in **s**.

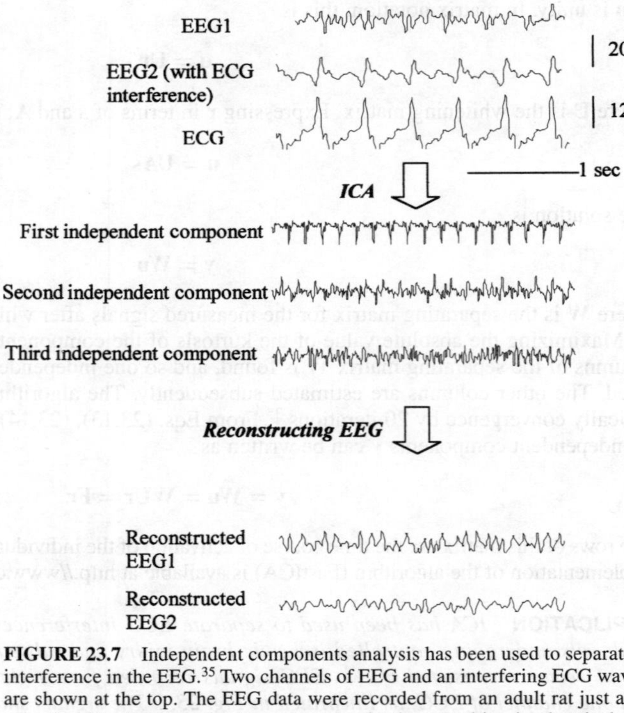

FIGURE 23.7 Independent components analysis has been used to separate ECG interference in the EEG.[35] Two channels of EEG and an interfering ECG waveform are shown at the top. The EEG data were recorded from an adult rat just after an episode of brain injury due to oxygen deprivation, resulting in electrical silence in the brain. EEG during the early recovery stages shows very low-amplitude activity, resulting in pronounced interference from the ECG waveforms. The independent components are used for reconstructing the two EEG waveforms shown at the bottom.

from ECG. The EEG was reconstructed from the independent components by setting the independent component in $\mathbf{y}$ *that corresponds to ECG to zero and evaluating* $\mathbf{r} = \mathbf{F}^{-1}\mathbf{y}$ *[from Eq. (23.16)].*

23.6 CROSS-CORRELATION AND COHERENCE ANALYSIS

Signal Types—Pairs of Stochastic Signals, Pairs of Stochastic and a Deterministic Signal, and Multichannel Signal Analysis. The signal-analysis methods discussed so far represented the measured signals along a set of orthogonal basis functions (Fourier, wavelet, or principal components) for noise removal (thus enhancing the signal-to-noise ratio), feature extraction, signal-source separation, etc. A bioengineer will also find situations where he or she has to deal with pairs of signals. Cross-correlation and coherence analysis are often simple tools that are extremely effective in quantifying relationships among pairs of biosignals.[42–48] Some of the typical application situations are as follows:

1. Detecting a known (deterministic) signal in a noisy environment
2. Estimating time delay or propagation delay between two biosignals (deterministic or stochastic signals in noise)
3. Estimating the transfer function of the signal-generating system (deconvolution, estimating the degree of linearity, etc.)

The cross-correlation between two measured biosignals $x(n)$ and $y(n)$ is defined statistically as $R_{yx}(k) = E[y(n)x(n+k)]$, where the operator E represents the statistical expectation or mean and k is the amount of time signal $x(n)$ delayed with respect to $y(n)$. Given two time sequences of $x(n)$ and $y(n)$ each of N points, the commonly used estimate of cross-covariance $c_{yx}(k)$ is as follows[5]:

$$c_{yx}(k) = \begin{cases} \dfrac{1}{N}\displaystyle\sum_{n=0}^{N-k-1}[y(n)-\hat{m}_y][x(n+k)-\hat{m}_x] & k \ge 0 \\ \dfrac{1}{N}\displaystyle\sum_{n=0}^{N-k-1}[y(n+k)-\hat{m}_y][x(n)-\hat{m}_x] & k \le 0 \end{cases} \tag{23.17}$$

where $\hat{m}_y$ and $\hat{m}_y$ are the sample means of the signal sequences $y(n)$ and $x(n)$, respectively. The sample means can be omitted in this expression if the signals have been detrended using a MATLAB function such as *detrend*.

Statistics of the Estimate. The cross-correlation estimator is however biased[5] because

$$E[c_{yx}(k)] = \left(1 - \frac{|k|}{N}\right)C_{yx}(k) \tag{23.18}$$

where $C_{yx}(k)$ is the true value of the cross-covariance or cross-correlation at a lag of k. The bias reduces for increasing length N of the signal sequence. However, the variance of this estimate is complicated. If the two sequences are Gaussian and completely uncorrelated, then the variance in the estimate of the cross-correlation is $\sigma_x^2\sigma_y^2/N$, where σ_x^2 and σ_y^2 are variances of $x(n)$ and $y(n)$ (the white noise sequences), respectively. In general, estimation of correlation between two sequences has to be done cautiously, as outlined in Ref. 5. Each individual signal sequence is modeled using a parametric model outlined in Sec. 23.3.3. The cross-correlation between the two error sequences (should be white Gaussian noise if the model is accurate) that were generated by modeling each signal must be estimated. The 95-percent confidence limits on the cross-correlation between the error sequences must be computed using the variance expression given earlier. Finally, the cross-correlation between the two signal sequences $x(n)$ and $y(n)$ can be estimated. Values that exceed the 95-percent confidence limits of the cross-correlation between the two error sequences indicate statistically significant correlation.

23.6.1 Detection of Known Signals (Deterministic) in White Gaussian Noise

The simple cross-correlation estimator is used extensively in the form of a matched filter implementation to detect a finite number of known signals (in other words, simultaneous acquisition of multiple channels of known signals). When these deterministic signals are embedded in white Gaussian noise, the matched filter (obtained from cross-correlation estimate at zero lag, $k = 0$, between the known signal sequence and the observed noisy signal sequence) gives the optimum detection performance (in the Bayes' sense[31]).

If the known N-dimensional signal vector is $\mathbf{S}$ (could be any signal of fixed morphology, such as the ECG, evoked potential, action potentials, etc.) and the measured N-dimensional observation vector with white Gaussian noise is $\mathbf{X}$, then we evaluate a likelihood ratio that is defined as

$$\sum_{i=1}^{N} \frac{S_i X_i}{\|S\|^2}$$

and compare it against a Bayes threshold Λ_0 identical to the one described in the section on PCA. When the likelihood ratio exceeds the threshold, the detector flags the presence of the known signal in the measurement.

APPLICATION *Matched filters can be used to detect and sort action potentials in noise. The multiunit data in Fig. 23.8B were collected from the ventral posteriolateral thalamic nuclei using a microelectrode. The segment shows two different types of action potentials (corresponding to two*

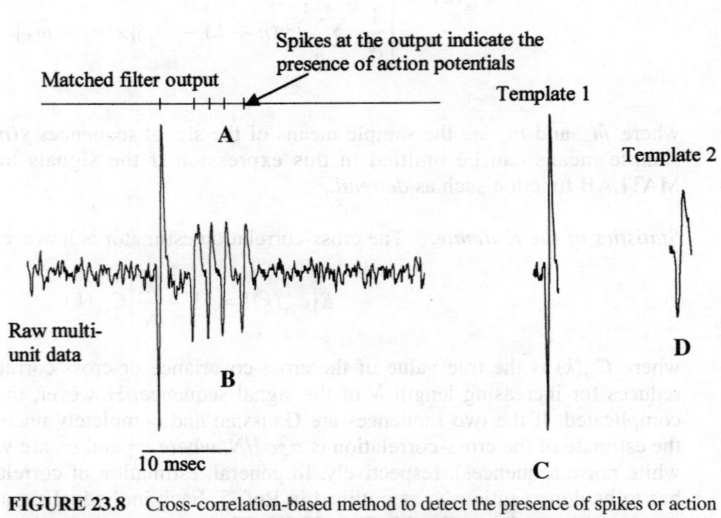

FIGURE 23.8 Cross-correlation-based method to detect the presence of spikes or action potentials in multiunit activity. The continuous waveform with the action potentials is shown in (*B*). The shapes of the action potentials to be detected are known a priori (deterministic signal). Using a cross-correlation of the known signal [templates (*C*) and (*D*)] with the measured signal, the presence of action potentials is indicated by a vertical line in (*A*). This approach is optimal in the presence of white Gaussian noise.

different neurons at different locations relative to the microelectrode). Action potential shapes from trial data were recognized and stored as templates. Two of the templates presumably corresponding to two different neurons are shown in Fig. 23.8C and D. Action potentials (or spikes) in the subsequent data set are detected (indicated by vertical lines in the detector output in Fig. 23.8A) and sorted based on these templates (detecting a known signal in noise). The noise is assumed to be white Gaussian, and the matched filter works reasonably well in detecting these spikes. However, the detector often fails when two action potentials overlap.

In contrast to the PCA–based approach for detection and discrimination, the cross-correlation or matched-filter approach is based on a priori knowledge of the shape of the deterministic signal to be detected. However, the PCA-based method also requires some initial data (although the data could be noisy, and the detector does not need to know a priori the label or the class of the different signals) to evaluate the sample covariance matrix **K** and its eigenvectors. In this sense, the PCA-based detector operates in an unsupervised mode. Further, the matched-filter approach is optimal only when the interfering noise is white Gaussian. When the noise is colored, the PCA-based approach will be preferred.

23.6.2 Coherence Estimation

The estimation of coherence is useful to determine if *spectral* components between two signal sequences are significantly correlated. It is also useful in determining the linearity of biological systems. Although most biological systems can be expected to be nonlinear, changes in the degree of nonlinearity often are correlated with changes in underlying physiology or pathology. For instance, Kong et al.[49] used coherence to monitor changes in blood oxygenation level in the brain by calculating the linearity of the somatosensory evoked responses. Assuming that $x(n)$ and $y(n)$ are the input and output of a linear system, the cross-spectral density $S_{yx}(f)$ is given by $S_{yx}(f) = S_x(f)H(f)$, where $S_x(f)$ is the amplitude spectral density of the input signal at f and $H(f)$ is the transfer function of the linear system. A coherence function defined as

$$C\hat{o}h_{xy}(f) = \frac{|S_{yx}(f)|^2}{S_y(f)S_x(f)} \qquad (23.19)$$

is therefore unity (maximum value) for linear systems. Consequently, any deviation from unity can be used as an indicator of the presence of nonlinearity in the system. The coherence function is estimated using the values of $S_x(f)$, $S_y(f)$, and $S_{yx}(f)$ obtained through FFTs. In MATLAB, the *spectrum* and *cohere* functions can be used to evaluate the cross-spectral density and the coherence.

Statistics of the Estimates. The mean and the variance of the sample estimates of the coherence function are derived in Ref. 5, and I only reproduce the final results here. In general, the cross-spectral density is evaluated by doing the Fourier transform of a windowed (using a lag window) sequence of cross-correlation estimates. The choice of the smoothing window therefore determines the variance in the estimates of cross-spectral density (numerator in the expression of coherence). The variance of the smoothed coherence estimator is given by[5]

$$\frac{1}{2V}[1 - C\hat{o}h_{xy}(f)]^2 \qquad (23.20)$$

where V is a variance reduction factor that depends on the smoothing window used. The different types of windows and their respective variance reduction factors can be found in Ref. 5. In general, the user has to be careful in choosing a large enough lag window that it includes all the largest cross-correlation estimates. An insufficient length in the lag window can give unreasonably large bias in the estimate of cross-spectral density. The coherence estimate is also biased because

$$E[C\hat{o}h_{xy}(f)] \approx \left(1 - \frac{\tau}{NT}\right) Coh_{xy}(f) \tag{23.21}$$

where τ is the time shift between the two sequences[5,50] that can be found by locating the lag corresponding to the peak estimate of cross-correlation. The source of bias can then be minimized by aligning the signals so that τ becomes negligibly small before estimating the cross-spectral density.

APPLICATION *An adaptive implementation of coherence estimation has been used in Ref. 49 to track hypoxic injury-related changes in somatosensory-evoked potential signals, as shown in Fig. 23.9. Figure 23.9A shows the change in amplitude of one of the peaks in the somatosensory evoked response (SEP amplitude) from a cat at different levels of oxygen concentration in the inhaled air. After the administration of 9 percent oxygen, the SEP amplitude shows a gradual decrease until the oxygen is restored to 100 percent. A linearity index derived using the coherence measure gives a more sensitive indication of injury, as shown in Fig. 23.9B.*

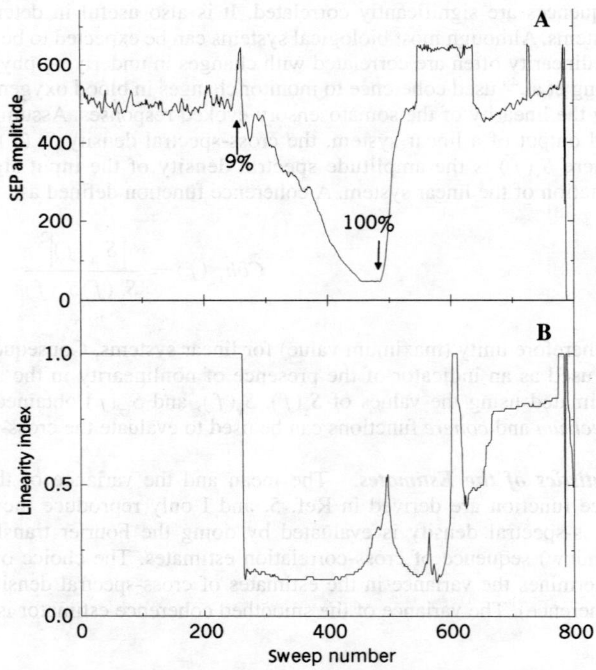

FIGURE 23.9 Adaptive coherence method to track changes in the somatosensory evoked potentials (SEPs).[49] A linearity index [shown in (*B*)] derived from the coherence of SEPs from the brain under low oxygen conditions with the SEPs derived during normal oxygen conditions was shown to be a very sensitive indicator of changes in brain oxygen content. The conventional amplitude of the SEP [shown in (*A*)] was not found to be that sensitive.

23.7 CHAOTIC SIGNALS AND FRACTAL PROCESSES

Signal Types—Random Signals That Are Not Stochastic But Are Generated by a Nonlinear Dynamic System. Fractal signals are scale-invariant, meaning that they look very similar at all levels of magnification. There is very good evidence to indicate that the beat-to-beat interval in heart rate is a fractal. Chaotic signals, on the other hand, are deterministic signals that cannot be predicted beyond a short time in the future.[2] They are extremely sensitive to initial conditions. Further, their behavior does not depend on any random inputs. The nonlinear time-series analysis techniques discussed briefly here have been used to analyze heart rate,[51–53] nerve activity,[54] renal flow,[55] arterial pressure, EEG,[56,57] and respiratory waveforms.[58]

The randomness of a chaotic time series is not due to noise but rather due to deterministic dynamics of a small number of dynamical variables in the nonlinear generating system. Therefore, they need to be distinguished from stochastic processes discussed earlier and analyzed appropriately. The randomness in a chaotic signal is therefore not revealed by statistical analysis but by dynamical analysis based on phase-space reconstruction. The phase space of a dynamical system (both nonlinear and linear) is the space spanned by its dynamical variables, and the phase plot is the plot of the time variation in the dynamical variables within the phase space. The phase plot of a dynamical system generating a chaotic time series is a strange attractor whose dimensionality (dimension of the set of points comprising the phase plot) is not an integer but a fraction. Hence they are said to have a *fractal* dimension. Standard objects in Euclidean geometry have integer dimensions. For instance, the dimension of a point in space is zero, that of a line is one, and that of an area is two. The fractal dimension D of a strange attractor (name of the phase plot of a nonlinear system generating a chaotic signal) is related to the minimum number of dynamical variables needed to model the dynamics of the strange attractor. Analysis of chaotic signals typically is geared toward (1) understanding how complex the nonlinear system is, (2) determining if it is chaotic or not, (3) determining the number of dynamic variables that dominate the system, and (4) assessing the changes in dynamic behavior of a system with different rhythms.

The following subsection details some methods to find out if a given random time series from a biological source is chaotic. Further, methods to determine the dimensionality and draw the phase plot or portrait of the chaotic signal are outlined briefly.

23.7.1 Analysis of Chaotic Signals

Frequency Analysis. The statistical analysis of chaotic signals includes spectral analysis to confirm the absence of any spectral lines, since chaotic signals do not have any periodic deterministic component. Absence of spectral lines would indicate that the signal is either chaotic or stochastic. However, chaos is a complicated nonperiodic motion distinct from stochastic processes in that the amplitude of the high-frequency spectrum shows an exponential decline. The frequency spectrum can be evaluated using FFT-based methods outlined in the earlier sections.

Estimating Correlation Dimension of a Chaotic Signal. One of the ways to measure the dimensionality of the phase portrait of a chaotic signal is through what is known as the *correlation dimension* D_2. It is defined as

$$D_2 = \frac{\log C(r)}{\log r}$$

as $r \to 0$, where r is the length of the side of the hypercubes that are needed to cover the phase plot and $C(r)$ is correlation sum. The correlation sum is defined as $C(r) = \Sigma_{i=1}^{M(r)} p_i^2$, where p_i is the probability of finding a single point belonging to the phase plot within the hypercube. $M(r)$ is the number of m-dimensional cells or hypercubes of side r needed to cover the entire phase plot.

One of the key steps in the analysis is therefore to reconstruct the phase plot or phase space of the dynamical system. The embedding theorems of Takens[59] and Sauer et al.[60,61] help us in reconstructing the phase space using a time series from the dynamical system rather than using the dynamical variables of the system. Given a discrete time series $x(n)$ from a biological source, we construct a k-dimensional point in the phase space using $k - 1$ time-delayed samples of the same series as represented by

$$\mathbf{x}(n) = \{x(n), x(n+\tau), x(n+2\tau), \ldots, x[n+(k-1)\tau]\}$$

The selection of the time delay τ is done in such a way that it makes every component of phase space uncorrelated. Therefore, τ is determined from estimate of the autocorrelation function of the time series. The time lag that corresponds to the first zero in the autocorrelation is often chosen as a good approximation for τ.[62,63] The determination of D_2 in practice can be done using the Grassberger-Procaccia algorithm[64] outlined below. Consider a pair of points in space with m dimensions ($m < k$) at time instants i and j:

$$\mathbf{x}_m(i): \{x(i), x(i+\tau), x(i+2\tau), \ldots, x[i+(m-1)\tau]\}$$

$$\mathbf{x}_m(j): \{x(j), x(j+\tau), x(j+2\tau), \ldots, x[j+(m-1)\tau]\}$$

where m is called the *embedding dimension* of the phase plot. However, m is not known a priori. Therefore, we determine the correlation dimension D_2 for different embedding dimensions of the attractor in the phase space. The minimum embedding dimension is then given by $m + 1$, where m is the embedding dimension above which the measured value of the correlation dimension D_2 for the corresponding phase plot remains constant. The Euclidean distance between the two points is given by $r_{ij}(m) = \|\mathbf{x}_m(i) - \mathbf{x}_m(j)\|$. For a critical distance r, a correlation integral (an approximation of the correlation sum defined earlier) is evaluated that gives the probability of the distance between the two given points being less than r:

$$C_2(r, m) = \frac{1}{N^2} \sum_{\substack{i,j=1 \\ i \neq j}}^{N} \theta[r - \|x_m(i) - x_m(j)\|]$$

where $N = k - (m-1)\tau$
$\theta =$ Heaviside function
$C_2(r, m) =$ correlation integral

An estimate of the correlation dimension D_2 is given by

$$D_2(m) = \frac{\log[C_2(r, m)]}{\log(r)}$$

The log-log plot of $C_2(r, m)$ versus r corresponding to the given m has a linear region called the *scaling region*, the slope of which gives an estimate of the correlation dimension. The reliability of the estimated slope in the linear scaling region can be a major source of error in the Grassberger-Procaccia algorithm. If N_c point pairs $\{\log[C_2(r_i, m)], \log(r_i) | i = 1, 2, \ldots, N_c\}$ exist in the scaling region, then $D_2(m)$ is given by[65]

$$D_2(m) = \frac{N_c \sum_{i=1}^{N_c} \log(r_i) \log[C_2(r_i, m)] - \sum_{i=1}^{N_c} \log(r_i) \sum_{i=1}^{N_c} \log[C_2(r_i, m)]}{N_c \sum_{i=1}^{N_c} [\log(r_i)]^2 - \left[\sum_{i=1}^{N_c} \log(r_i)\right]^2}$$

The value of m beyond which $D_2(m)$ gradually saturates determines the embedding dimension m_c. That is, $D_2(m_c) = D_2(m_c + 1) = D_2(m_c + 2) = \cdots = D_2(m_c)$ gives an estimate of the correlation dimension.

Phase-Space Analysis. Having determined the time lag τ for decorrelating the components of the phase space and the embedding dimension, a line joining the m_c dimensional points given by

$$\mathbf{x}_{mc}(j):\{x(j), x(j+\tau), x(j+2\tau), \ldots, x[j+(m_c-1)\tau]\}$$

(where $j = 1, 2, \ldots, n$) gives a portrait of the evolution of dynamical variables of the system. According to the Takens theorem, for an attractor having an integer-dimension manifold, the phase plot obtained from the time series preserves the topological properties (such as dimension) of the attractor. Phase-plane analysis of chaotic processes enables quantitative description subsequently through calculation of Lyapunov exponents, Poincare mapping, etc. The goal of this characterization is to obtain a portrait of evolution of the state variables of the system. Additional parameters such as the Lyapunov exponents and complexity measures can be determined as well once the biological process begins to exhibit chaotic behavior. The user is referred to Refs. 66 to 68 for further information.

There are several issues that a user has to be aware of while doing a nonlinear time-series analysis. If the biosignal in question is indeed generated by a deterministic dynamical system, then the sampling frequency of the time series should be sufficiently large to capture the deterministic rule governing the evolution of the series. The length of the sequence should also be sufficiently large. Fortunately, there is a rule of thumb given by Ruelle[69] for the minimum length of time series that is quite helpful. It states that estimates of the dimension of the phase plot $D \geq 2 \log_{10} N$ should be regarded as unreliable, where N is the length of the time series. Finally, noise contamination during measurement could obscure detection of deterministic dynamics and hence degrade forecasting of biologically significant events. The user is referred to Ref. 68 for MATLAB codes for the Grassberger-Procaccia algorithm, phase-space reconstruction, and forecasting.

Surrogate Data to Compare Chaotic and Stochastic Processes. Surrogate data are used in nonlinear time-series analysis to make useful comparisons between the given biosignal, which could be chaotic, and a set of artificially generated stochastic signals that share the same essential statistical properties (mean, variance, and the power spectrum) with the biosignal.[68,70] If the measured topological properties of the biosignal lie within the standard deviation of the topological properties measured from the artificially generated surrogate data, then the null hypothesis that the biosignal is just random noise cannot be ruled out. A systematic method for generating surrogate data with the same mean, variance, and power spectrum as a given biosignal is detailed in Ref. 70, and a MATLAB code is available in Ref. 68. The main steps in the procedure are outlined below.

The DFT $X(k)$ of the observed signal sequence $x(n)$ is evaluated using Eq. (23.1). Keeping the magnitudes of the Fourier coefficients intact, the phases of the Fourier coefficients are randomized (maintaining symmetry about the midpoint so that we still get a real time series after inverse Fourier transform). The Fourier sequence is now inverted to produce a real time series that is a surrogate of the original data. With different random assignments for the phase values of Fourier coefficients, a different time series can be generated every iteration. All the different time series generated using this procedure would be part of the surrogate data to the biosignal. The random phase assignments are done as follows: If the length of the measured sequence is N (assumed to be even), a set of random phase values $\phi_m \in [0, \pi]$, for $m = 2, 3, \ldots, N/2$, is generated using a function such as *rand* in MATLAB. The phase of the Fourier coefficients are randomized to generate a new sequence of Fourier coefficients $X_s(k)$ as shown below:

$$X_s(k) = \begin{cases} X(k) & \text{for } k = 1 \text{ and } \dfrac{N}{2}+1 \\ |X(k)|e^{j\phi_m} & \text{for } k = 2,3\ldots,\dfrac{N}{2} \\ |X(N-k+2)|e^{j\phi_{N-k+2}} & \text{for } k = \dfrac{N}{2}+2, \dfrac{N}{2}+3, \ldots, N \end{cases}$$

For every new set of $\phi_m \in [0, \pi]$, we can generate a new surrogate time series $x_s(n)$ by performing the inverse Fourier transform of $X_s(k)$.

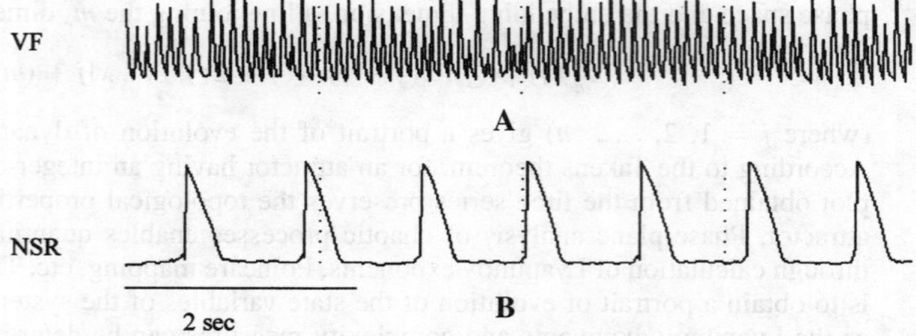

FIGURE 23.10 Action potential waveforms from an isolated heart (Langendorff preparation) are shown[65] (*A*) during ventricular fibrillation (VF) and (*B*) during normal sinus rhythm (NSR).

APPLICATION *Myocardial cell action potentials collected from a Langendorff setup of an isolated rabbit heart experiment have been found to exhibit chaotic behavior.[65] Two different cardiac cell action potential waveforms are illustrated in Fig. 23.10 corresponding to ventricular fibrillation (VF) in (A) and normal sinus rhythm (NSR) in (B). The corresponding frequency spectrum is shown in Fig. 23.11. VF certainly shows chaotic characteristics in Fig. 23.11A, whereas NSR shows distinct spectral lines in Fig. 23.11B, indicating the presence of deterministic components. Using the calculated correlation dimensions for the two different action potentials (VF = 5.629, NSR = 2.704),*

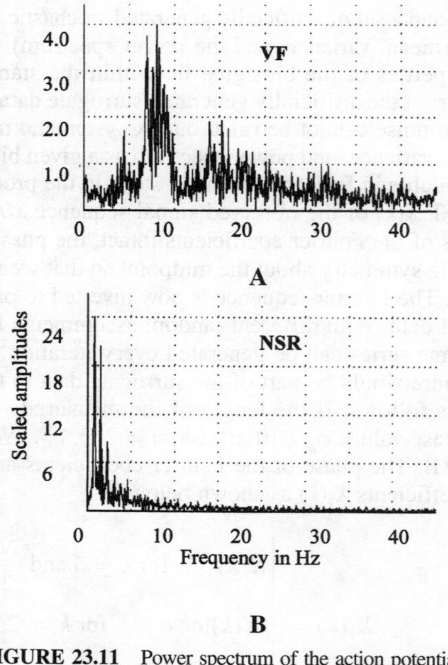

FIGURE 23.11 Power spectrum of the action potential waveform during[65] (*A*) VF and (*B*) NSR. The power spectrum of VF has no spectral components or peaks in contrast with the power spectrum of NSR, which has distinct spectral lines indicating that it is a periodic and not a stochastic or chaotic waveform.

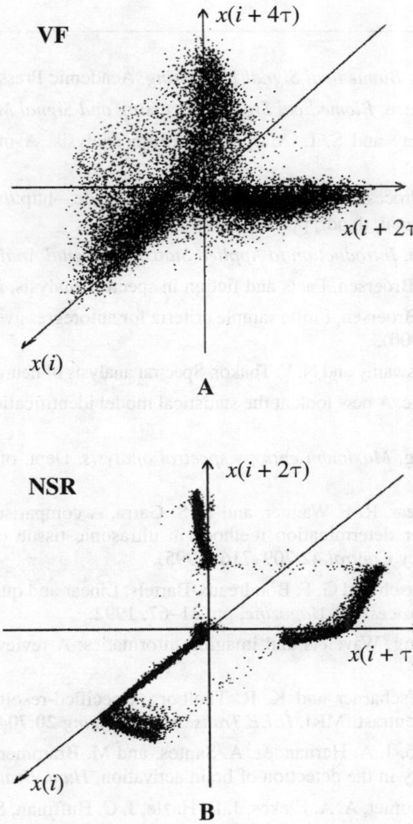

FIGURE 23.12 Phase plots of the action potential waveform during[65] (*A*) VF and (*B*) NSR. The time delay required to make the individual components of the phase plot uncorrelated was determined to be $6\delta t$, and $41\delta t$, respectively, where $\delta t = 5$ msec is the sampling interval. The embedding dimension of the VF waveform was determined to be 6, and that of the NSR waveform was 3. The phase plot of the VF waveform is shown in (*A*) spanned by $\{x(i), x(i + 2\tau), x(i + 4\tau)\}$, demonstrating a strange attractor, whereas the phase plot of the NSR waveform is shown in (*B*) spanned by $\{x(i), x(i + \tau), x(i + 2\tau)\}$.

the embedding dimension is $m = 6$ for VF. The projections of the trajectories for VF in a three-dimensional phase space spanned by $\{x(i), x(i + 2\tau), x(i + 4\tau)\}$ is shown in Fig. 23.12A, whereas for NSR the embedding dimension $m = 3$. The corresponding three-dimensional phase portrait spanned by $\{x(i), x(i + \tau), x(i + 2\tau)\}$ is shown in Fig. 23.12B. For VF and NSR, the decorrelating time τ was determined to be $6\delta\tau$ and $41\delta\tau$, respectively, where $\delta\tau = 5$ msec is the sampling interval. Obviously, VF demonstrates chaotic character, whereas NSR demonstrates a periodic or quasiperiodic nature.

REFERENCES

1. M. Akay, *Biomedical Signal Processing*, Academic Press, San Diego, 1994.
2. E. N. Bruce, *Biomedical Signal Processing and Signal Modeling*, Wiley, New York, 2001.
3. S. M. Kay and S. L. Marple, Spectrum analysis: A modern perspective, *Proc. IEEE* **69**(11):1380–1419 (1981).
4. Signal Processing ToolboxTM 6, user's guide—http://www.mathworks.com/access/helpdesk/help/pdf_doc/signal/signal_tb.pdf, pp. 3.2–3.14.
5. R. Shiavi, *Introduction to Applied Statistical Signal Analysis*, 2d ed. Academic Press, San Diego, 1999.
6. P. M. T. Broersen, Facts and fiction in spectral analysis, *IEEE Trans. Instum. Measur.* **49**:766–772 (2000).
7. P. M. T. Broersen, Finite sample criteria for autoregressive order selection, *IEEE Trans Signal Proc.* **48**:3550–3558 (2000).
8. J. Muthuswamy and N. V. Thakor, Spectral analysis of neurological signals, *J. Neurosci. Methods* **83**:1–14 (1998).
9. H. Akaike, A new look at the statistical model identification, *IEEE Trans. Automatic Control* **AC-19**:716–723 (1974).
10. J. P. Burg, *Maximum entropy spectral analysis*, Dept. of Geophysics, Stanford University, Stanford, Calif., 1975.
11. K. A. Wear, R. F. Wagner, and B. S. Garra, A comparison of autoregressive spectral estimation algorithms and order determination methods in ultrasonic tissue characterization, *IEEE Trans Ultrason. Ferroelect. Frequency Control* **42**:709–716 (1995).
12. F. Hlawatsch and G. F. Boudreaux-Bartels, Linear and quadratic time-frequency signal representations, *IEEE Signal Processing Magazine*, pp. 21–67, 1992.
13. J. Z. Wang, Wavelets and imaging informatics: A review of the literature, *J. Biomed. Inform.* **34**:129–141 (2001).
14. V. von Tscharner and K. R. Thulborn, Specified-resolution wavelet analysis of activation patterns from BOLD contrast fMRI, *IEEE Trans. Med. Imaging* **20**:704–714 (2001).
15. M. Desco, J. A. Hernandez, A. Santos, and M. Brammer, Multiresolution analysis in fMRI: Sensitivity and specificity in the detection of brain activation, *Hum. Brain Mapp.* **14**:16–27 (2001).
16. D. F. Schomer, A. A. Elekes, J. D. Hazle, J. C. Huffman, S. K. Thompson, C. K. Chui, and W. A. Murphy, Jr., Introduction to wavelet-based compression of medical images, *Radiographics* **18**:469–481 (1998).
17. K. Wang, H. Begleiter, and B. Porjesz, Spatial enhancement of event-related potentials using multiresolution analysis, *Brain Topogr.* **10**:191–200 (1998).
18. R. Q. Quiraga, Z. Nadasdy, and Y. Ben-Shawl, Unsupervised spike detection and sorting with wavelets and superparamagnetic clustering, *Neural Comput.* **16**:1661–1687 (2004).
19. K. L. Park, K. J. Lee, and H. R. Yoon, Application of a wavelet adaptive filter to minimise distortion of the ST-segment, *Med. Biol. Eng. Comput.* **36**:581–586 (1998).
20. N. D. Panagiotacopulos, J. S. Lee, M. H. Pope, and K. Friesen, Evaluation of EMG signals from rehabilitated patients with lower back pain using wavelets, *J. Electromyogr. Kinesiol.* **8**:269–278 (1998).
21. J. Jalife, O. Berenfeld, A. Skanes, and R. Mandapati, Mechanisms of atrial fibrillation: Mother rotors or multiple daughter wavelets, or both? *J. Cardiovasc. Electrophysiol.* **9**:S2–12 (1998).
22. R. Gobbele, H. Buchner, and G. Curio, High-frequency (600 Hz) SEP activities originating in the subcortical and cortical human somatosensory system, *Electroencephalogr. Clin. Neurophysiol.* **108**:182–189 (1998).
23. Q. Fang and I. Cosic, Protein structure analysis using the resonant recognition model and wavelet transforms, *Australas. Phys. Eng. Sci. Med.* **21**:179–185 (1998).
24. P. Carre, H. Leman, C. Fernandez, and C. Marque, Denoising of the uterine EHG by an undecimated wavelet transform, *IEEE Trans. Biomed. Eng.* **45**:1104–1113 (1998).
25. N. Aydin, S. Padayachee, and H. S. Markus, The use of the wavelet transform to describe embolic signals, *Ultrasound Med. Biol.* **25**:953–958 (1999).
26. V. J. Samar, A. Bopardikar, R. Rao, and K. Swartz, Wavelet analysis of neuroelectric waveforms: A conceptual tutorial, *Brain Lang.* **66**:7–60 (1999).
27. M. Akay and C. Mello, Wavelets for biomedical signal processing, presented at 19th International Conference of IEEE/EMBS, Chicago, 1997.

28. R. Kronland-Martinet, J. Morlet, and A. Grossmann, Analysis of sound patterns through wavelet transforms, *Int. J. Pattern Recog. Artif. Intell.* **1**:273–301 (1987).

29. B. Gramatikov, S. Yi-chun, P. Caminal, H. Rix, and N. V. Thakor, Multiresolution wavelet analysis of the body surface ECG before and after angioplasty, *Ann. Biomed. Eng.* **23**:553–561 (1995).

30. M. Misiti, Y. Misiti, G. Oppenheim, and J-M Poggi, Wavelet Toolbox^{TM} 4, user's guide—www.mathworks.com/ access/helpdesk/help/pdf_doc/wavelet/wavelet_ug.pdf.

31. H. L. van Trees, *Detection, Estimation and Modulation Theory*, Vol. I, Wiley, New York, 1969.

32. R. O. Duda, P. E. Hart, and D. G. Stork, *Pattern Classification*, Wiley, New York, 2001.

33. A. Hyvarinen and E. Oja, Independent component analysis: Algorithms and applications, *Neural Networks* **13**:411–430 (2000).

34. S. Makeig, A. Bell, T. P. Jung, and T. J. Sejnowski, Independent component analysis of electroencephalographic data, in *Advances in Neural Information Processing Systems*, Vol. **8**, pp. 145–151, MIT Press, Cambridge, Mass., 1996.

35. S. Tong, A. Bezerianos, J. Paul, Y. Zhu, and N. Thakor, Removal of ECG interference from the EEG recordings in animals using independent component analysis, *J. Neurosci. Methods* **108**:11–17 (2001).

36. R. Vigario, J. Sarela, and E. Oja, Independent component analysis in wave decomposition of auditory evoked fields, presented at International Conference on Artificial Neural Networks (ICANN '98), Skovde, Sweden, 1998.

37. R. Vigario, V. Jousmaki, M. Hamalainen, R. Hari, and E. Oja, Independent component analysis for identification of artifacts in magnetoencephalographic recordings, in *Advances in Neural Information Processing Systems*, pp. 229–235, MIT Press, Cambridge, Mass., 1998.

38. J. P. Nadal and N. Parga, Nonlinear neurons in the low noise limit: A factorial code maximized information transfer, *Network* **5**:565–581 (1994).

39. P. Comon, Independent component analysis: A new concept? *Signal Processing* **36**:287–314 (1994).

40. M. Girolami and C. Fyfe, Extraction of independent signal sources using a deflationary exploratory projection pursuit network with lateral inhibition, *IEEE Proc. Vision Image Signal Proc.* **14**:299–306 (1997).

41. A. Hyvarinen and E. Oja, A fast fixed-point algorithm for independent component analysis, *Neural Comput.* **9**:1483–1492 (1997).

42. P. H. Boeijinga and F. H. Lopes da Silva, A new method to estimate time delays between EEG signals applied to beta activity of the olfactory cortical areas, *Electroencephalogr. Clin. Neurophysiol.* **73**:198–205 (1989).

43. Z. Bohdanecky, P. Lansky, and T. Radil, An integral measure of the coherence function between pairs of EEG recordings, *Electroencephalogr. Clin. Neurophysiol.* **54**:587–590 (1982).

44. P. Brown, A. Oliviero, P. Mazzone, A. Insola, P. Tonali, and V. Di Lazzaro, Dopamine dependency of oscillations between subthalamic nucleus and pallidum in Parkinson's disease, *J. Neurosci.* **21**:1033–1038 (2001).

45. S. Cerutti, M. Alberti, G. Baselli, O. Rimoldi, A. Malliani, M. Merri, and M. Pagani, Automatic assessment of the interaction between respiration and heart rate variability signal, *Med. Prog. Technol.* **14**:7–19 (1988).

46. M. P. Davey, J. D. Victor, and N. D. Schiff, Power spectra and coherence in the EEG of a vegetative patient with severe asymmetric brain damage, *Clin. Neurophysiol.* **111**:1949–1954 (2000).

47. L. Fendelander, P. W. Hsia, and R. J. Damiano, Jr., Spatial coherence: A new method of quantifying myocardial electrical organization using multichannel epicardial electrograms, *J. Electrocardiol.* **30**:9–19 (1997).

48. T. B. Kuo, C. C. Yang, and S. H. Chan, Transfer function analysis of ventilatory influence on systemic arterial pressure in the rat, *Am. J. Physiol.* **271**:H2108–2115 (1996).

49. X. Kong and N. Thakor, Adaptive coherence estimation reveals nonlinear processes in injured brain, in *IEEE Proc. Intl. Conf. Acoustics, Speech, and Signal Processing, ICASSP-93*, **1**:89–90 (1993).

50. G. Carter, Coherence and time-delay estimation, in C. Chen (ed.), *Signal Processing Handbook*, Dekker, New York, 1988.

51. M. R. Guevara, L. Glass, and A. Shrier, Phase locking, period doubling bifurcations, and irregular dynamics in periodically stimulated cardiac cells, *Science* **214**:1350–1352 (1981).

52. D. R. Chialvo, D. C. Michaels, and J. Jalife, Supernormal excitability as a mechanism of chaotic dynamics of activation in cardiac purkinje fibers, *Circ. Res.* **66**:525–545 (1990).

53. K. M. Stein, N. Lippman, and P. Kligfield, Fractal rhythms of the heart, *J. Electrocardiol.* **24**(suppl.):72–76 (1992).

54. Z. S. Huang, G. L. Gebber, S. Zhong, and S. Barman, Forced oscillations in sympathetic nerve discharge, *Am. J. Physiol*. **263**:R564–R571 (1992).

55. K. P. Yip, N. H. Holstein-Rathlou, and D. J. Marsh, Chaos in blood flow control in genetic and renovascular hypertensive rats, *Am. J. Physiol*. **261**:F400–F408 (1991).

56. L. D. Iasemidis, L. D. Olson, R. S. Savit, and J. C. Sackellares, Time dependencies in the occurrences of epileptic seizures, *Epilepsy Res*. **17**:81–94 (1994).

57. C. A. Skarda and W. J. Freeman, How brains make chaos in order to make sense of the world, *Behav. Brain Sci*. **10**:161–195 (1987).

58. D. Hoyer, K. Schmidt, R. Bauer, U. Zwiener, M. Kohler, B. Luthke, and M. Eiselt, Nonlinear analysis of heart rate and respiratory dynamics, *IEEE Eng. Med. Biol. Mag*. **16**:31–39 (1997).

59. F. Takens, Detecting strange attractors in turbulence, D. A. Rand and L. S. Young (eds.), in *Dynamical Systems and Turbulence*, Springer, Berlin, 1981.

60. T. Sauer and J. A. Yorke, Rigorous verification of trajectories for computer simulation of dynamical systems, *Nonlinearity* **4**:961–979 (1991).

61. T. Sauer, J. Yorke, and M. Casdagli, Embedology, *J. Stat. Phys*. **65**:579–616 (1994).

62. D. Holton and R. M. May, Distinguishing chaos from noise, in *The Nature of Chaos*, Chap. 7, Oxford University Press, Oxford, England, 1993.

63. A. M. Fraser and H. L. Swinney, Using mutual information to find independent coordinates of strange attractors, *Phys. Rev. [A]* **33**:1134–1139 (1986).

64. P. Grassberger and I. Procaccia, Characterization of strange attractors, *Phys. Rev. Lett*. **50**:346–349 (1983).

65. X. S. Zhang and Y. S. Zhu, The extraction of dynamical information of myocardial cell electrophysiology by fractal and chaotic analysis methods, *Automedica* **18**:9–26 (1999).

66. F. Kasper and H. G. Schuster, Easily calculable measure for the complexity of spatiotemporal patterns, *Phys. Rev. [A]* **36**:842–848 (1987).

67. A. Lempel and J. Ziv, On the complexity of finite sequences, *IEEE Trans. Inform. Technol*. **22**:75–81 (1976).

68. B. Henry, N. Lovell, and F. Camacho, Nonlinear dynamics time series analysis, M. Akay (ed.), in *Nonlinear Biomedical Signal Processing*, Vol. II, pp. 1–39, IEEE Press, New York, 2000.

69. D. Ruelle, Deterministic chaos: The science and the fiction, *Proc. R. Soc. Lond. [A]* **427**:241–248 (1990).

70. J. Theiler, B. Galdrikian, A. Longtin, S. Eubank, and J. D. Farmer, Using surrogate data to detect nonlinearity in time series, M. Casdagli and S. Eubank (eds.), in *Nonlinear Modeling and Forecasting*, Addison-Wesley, Reading, Mass., 1992.

CHAPTER 24
BIOSENSORS

Prem C. Pandey
Banaras Hindu University, Varanasi, India

Govind Pandey
King George Medical University, Lucknow, India

Bonnie Pierson
University of North Carolina and North Carolina State University, Raleigh, North Carolina

Roger J. Narayan
University of North Carolina and North Carolina State University, Raleigh, North Carolina

24.1 INTRODUCTION

With the trend toward miniaturization of medical devices, biosensors have recently emerged as economical devices of small size for performing tasks, which previously required larger amounts of materials and larger device geometries. This chapter is intended to provide a brief overview on the subject of biosensors and provide an overview of recent developments in this discipline.

No single definition for the term "biosensor" has been universally agreed upon. Biosensors integrate several core disciplines into a highly flexible field. While this interdisciplinary approach makes the subject ripe for innovation, it also makes it difficult for researchers from several different backgrounds to communicate well with one another or even agree upon an area of focus of the field. Biosensors commonly utilize a biological element as a sensor and transducing element in order to translate the response of a biological element into a measurable signal. The biological elements can be any number of things, including proteins, nucleic acids, enzymes, or whole cells. These components are selected for their highly specialized interactions with biological species, which correspond with the sensing mechanism of the biosensor. For example, antibodies have extremely specific binding sites, as shown in Fig. 24.1, which will selectively bind with a particular antigen. Biosensors exploit the specialized nature of these biological elements to produce analytical systems that can measure one or more explicitly identified target substances or analytes (Vikesland and Rule,

FIGURE 24.1 Illustration of the specificity of the antigen-antibody binding site

2008). The transducing element is then used to measure the number and/or type of reactions that involve the biological element. These transducers can measure biological interactions directly (e.g., the optical detection of fluorescently tagged antibodies) or indirectly (e.g., the monitoring of reaction by-products like carbon dioxide).

There are a large variety of biosensors that are currently being studied, which contain any number of combinations of biosensors and transducers. With this wide assortment and ample room for deviation, there are devices which push the bounds of the definition of biosensors. One prime example is the case of excitable cells. It has been suggested that an excitable cell, such as an intact neuron, should be considered a complete biosensor, as it can both sense a specific analyte (e.g., a neurotransmitter) and transduce the biological response into an electrical signal (e.g., an action potential). While this does not strictly suit the traditionally accepted notion of a biosensor, it does appear to meet the basic criteria of possessing both a biological sensor and a transducing element. Similarly, genetically engineered proteins that are fluorescent but experience a change in luminescence when they interact with a specific analyte could be considered biosensors as they both detect the target molecule and transduce the reaction into a visible spectra signal (Doi and Yanagawa, 1999). Nevertheless, the integration of the sensing element with the transducing element determines the success of a commercial biosensor. In this chapter, we will examine common biological sensing mechanisms, traducing elements, and manufacturing methods for fabrication of biosensors.

24.2 BIOLOGICAL SENSING MECHANISMS

The fundamental genius of many advanced biosensors is that they can investigate specific substances or reactions under realistic biological conditions by taking advantage of the known behavior of other biological substances. Countless types of biological elements have been considered for use as biomolecular recognition tools in biosensors and detection assays (Setti et al., 2004). In particular, three broad categories of biological components have emerged as the basis for both research and commercial biosensors: antibodies, enzymes, and whole cells. These biological components can be used in a large assortment of biomolecular mechanisms, including electrical potentials, fluorescent molecular tags, conformational changes, and reaction by-products. And each of these mechanisms, in turn, can be used with a variety of transducing or detecting methods, further increasing the unique attributes of each biosensor. This multitude of options and possibilities makes the selection of every component and mechanism an important step in the development and optimization of a biosensor for a particular application.

24.2.1 Commonly Used Biological Materials

The biological sensing component of biosensors is an integral part to the function of the overall biosensor. The most frequently employed biological materials in this field are proteins and whole cells. Proteins, or long chains of amino acids, are nearly innumerable in variation when encountered in a living organism and can serve diverse functions in the biological environment. The proteins of most use in biosensors are enzymes. These proteins possess specific binding attributes that make them very well suited for use in biosensors, where specificity is critical to ensure accurate detection and data.

Enzymes are traditionally discussed in terms of their ability to accelerate or inhibit biochemical reactions; it is for precisely this reason that they are frequently used in biosensors and other medical devices. Enzymes catalyze reactions by very specifically binding with a particular analyte (i.e., activating molecule), and transforming it into a different biomolecular product (or products). In some cases, the activating analyte can even cause a change in the enzyme, which induces a conformational change in the enzyme structure. The first generation of biosensors relied on enzymes to initiate readings in electrodes through the release of ions or oxidation-reduction reactions. Though in recent years, technology has expanded to monitor other aspects of the enzymatic behavior, such as nonionic molecular by-products and conformational changes. Enzymes can also be engineered to have specific traits or characteristics, which can allow one to further exploit the site-specific binding that makes this type of protein ideal for biosensor applications.

Antibodies are another type of material with a highly specialized and explicit binding site that exhibit highly specific binding with other molecules. Developed by organisms in response to an immune challenge, antibodies react to specific molecules that are considered "foreign," which are termed antigens. Since there are a large number of potentially harmful substances that an organism may come in contact with, there is a correspondingly large number of antibodies that can be generated. Antibodies may also be engineered or fluorescently tagged to enable monitoring of antibody-antigen interactions. One advantage associated with using antibodies is that the antibody structure is well understood, which allows for greater control of immobilization and orientation of these materials on the surface of a biosensor.

Cells may also be used as sensing mechanisms, and their incorporation into sensors is well-established, with numerous studies demonstrating the practicality of their use. Specialized cells are more frequently employed, such as sensory cells that contain specific chemoreceptors or neurons that detect specific neurotransmitter molecules. An electrical charge or action potential is generated by the cell-molecule interaction; this electrical charge or action potential can be monitored to assess the target molecule concentration. For instance, cells with sensitivity to changes in glucose and glibenclamide were used detect insulin secretion of other cells; a series of current spikes was detected via the patch clamp approach (Hazama et al., 1998). Intact cells that are not as specialized have also been used in biosensors, mainly to investigate and take advantage of the properties of the organelles, cellular proteins, and membrane receptors that cells possess. These biosensors often monitor metabolic variations or changes in transmembrane potential that reflect the activity of cellular components.

In one study, cells were used to evaluate complex mixtures after sorting by electrophoresis through a microcolumn. In the first experiment, binding at specific cell receptor sites was scrutinized using optical transduction of fluorescence from intracellular calcium levels. In another experiment, a specific receptor site was engineered into a cell using RNA transcription; interaction with the analyte was measured by the electrical current changes across the cell membrane (Shear et al., 1995). These investigations further demonstrate the ability of cells to function as accurate detectors of single specific substances. The most important potential application of cell-based biosensing involves the monitoring of many types of analytes using whole cells. While the transduction of such a multi-analyte cell detection process poses a formidable challenge, appropriately selected or engineered cells are useful for this application since they contain many different types of proteins with precise binding sites. In contrast to extracellular proteins, proteins contained within cells do not exhibit steric hindrance or denaturation; these changes are associated with direct immobilization of a protein on the sensor surface. Furthermore, unlike antibodies or enzymes that must be carefully harvested and separated for use in biosensors, a cellular biosensor would be self-replicating, allowing for a reduction in manufacturing cost and a potentially reusable product.

24.2.2 Direct Binding

The most straightforward way in which an unmodified protein can interact with an unmodified analyte is through direct binding using specific binding sites. This fundamental mechanism can have an array of characteristics that can, in turn, be used to monitor and record information about the protein-analyte interaction. One such characteristic that can be measured is the discharge of ions that accompanies some biomolecular interactions. Such discharges and changes in the balance of ions on the cellular level can result in the development of recordable membrane potentials and even the generation of action potentials. Several of the protein-analyte contacts produce recordable electrical signals either through a change in ion concentration, as in transmembrane potentials and action potentials created by cells, or through oxidation and reduction reactions that occur with the by-products of biomolecular protein interactions at the membrane surface.

Mechanisms that monitor protein-analyte binding directly are particularly useful for researchers who are interested in gaining detailed information about these interactions; these techniques do not alter the participating molecules as many other sensing mechanisms do. However, use of indirect mechanisms on a large scale, such as mechanisms that gauge cell behavior in order to extrapolate information about protein binding, can be too broad to provide information on the specifics of the protein-analyte binding mechanism. However, use of indirect mechanisms on a large scale may still give useful information for screening applications such as pharmaceutical development.

Transmembrane Potential. The actions of proteins within cells can, in most instances, generate a change in potential as a result of the production or movement of ions associated with normal biochemical reactions. The potential gradients, known as transmembrane potentials, can be monitored through the use of a patch-clamp or a similar recording device, which isolates a single membrane receptor and records changes in the membrane potential. However, this method is invasive and will eventually result in the death of the cell being investigated. As a result, this method is not widely used in commercial biosensor applications as it requires considerable resources and effort to obtain information from the cell. Furthermore, the information that may be ascertained may not be as specific or as helpful as the information that may be collected using sensors that detect singular biochemical interactions outside of the complex environment of the cell. It should be noted, however, that this method is of use for some specific applications that require feedback from generalized biological receptors. While biosensors traditionally focus on specific binding, the generalized behavior of a cell in response to a particular molecule can be extremely useful in screening for toxic compounds and in the development of pharmaceutical products. The transmembrane potential can also be used to monitor the function of organelles and other subcellular processes. For example, researchers have used the change in transmembrane potential of mitochondria to indicate toxicity (da Silvaa et al., 1998). Given the importance of mitochondria to the generation of ATP as well as the general importance of smaller cellular functions to overall biological health, these studies remain a viable and important area of investigation.

Action Potentials. In response to a particular stimulus or analyte, certain specialized and excitable cells can generate a charge gradient that moves along the membrane of the cell, which is known as an action potential. Neurons, cardiac muscle cells, and sensory cells are widely used for their capacity to create distinct electrical outputs in response to biochemical interactions. The cells that operate through an action potential mechanism are ideal for biosensor applications because they demonstrate the very same specificity that is present in protein detectors. For example, neurons contain neuroreceptors that respond to a corresponding neurotransmitter. Depending upon the family of neuron, it can contain many different types of neuroreceptors or a limited range of neuroreceptors; many types of cells could provide useful information in appropriate applications. The presence of a neurotransmitter or a conformationally similar biological molecule in sufficient quantities will activate an action potential response.

The type of action potential generated in this process can provide supplementary information about the properties of the triggering molecule. Through rate coding and amplitude changes, the concentration of the analyte can be determined. With extensive activation over time, cells can adapt to the repeated or continuous presence of the stimulus. As a result, cell responsiveness and the number of action potentials may be decreased. This homeostatic mechanism limits the lifetime and reusability of the action potential biosensor process. Similarly, cardiac muscle cells can change their pacing and electrical potential discharge in response to the concentration of surrounding ions. Sensory cells, such as chemoreceptors, may recognize specific molecules or changes in the concentration of specific molecules (e.g., carbon dioxide, oxygen, or odor molecules).

As discussed previously, the direct transduction of a biochemical stimulus into a recordable electrical signal might qualify these cells as biosensors in their own right; however, further transduction technology must be used to record and analyze these electrical signals. Most frequently, the action potentials generated by cells are recorded by an external-monitoring method, such as an electrode array.

Oxidation and Reduction Reactions. Some reactions result in the release or absorption of free ions through oxidation and reduction reactions, which occur during biochemical interaction between multiple molecules. For example, certain enzymes will produce by-products (e.g., hydrogen peroxide) during interaction with a specific molecule. This by-product can, in turn, oxidize other susceptible materials. When the enzyme is attached to the surface of a biosensor or a transducing substrate, these reactions can be further encouraged and extrapolated by the biosensor material. This process allows for the transfer of electrons and ions, which can then be directly measured using transduction technology. This process gives an indication of the analyte concentration that is being detected on the surface of the biosensor.

Biomolecular sensing components that are not capable of producing oxidation-reduction reactions can be modified by attaching enzymes that are capable of these reactions in order to allow for electrical transduction. For example, one highly cited experiment compared the performance of a monolayer composed of ferrocene (an electron mediator) and an antibody on the surface of an electrode to an electrode covered in a redox-modified glucose oxidase and found that both methods produced better data than traditional, unmediated antigen-antibody interactions due to the amplification of the signal provided by oxidation-reduction reactions (Blonder et al., 1996).

Oxidation-reduction reactions caused by enzyme by-products are perhaps the earliest and one of the most widely used mechanisms utilized in biosensors. The direct transfer of the electrons between biological molecules and the biosensor surface allows this technology to be miniaturized, allowing for the development of rapid and portable sensors. However, oxidation and reduction reactions permanently alter and degrade the biosensor surface over time, causing devices based on this mechanism to have limited lifetimes. The materials that serve as electron donors or acceptors of these devices are inexpensive; as a result, disposable products that rely on oxidation-reduction reactions have been rapidly manufactured and widely distributed. A typical example of the oxidation-reduction reaction at a commercial scale is the blood glucose sensor. During blood glucose sensing, the displayed signal is the function of mostly glucose oxidase–catalyzed reaction. First-generation glucose biosensors based on electrochemical mode of signal transduction rely on the natural enzymatic reaction and glucose oxidase–catalyzed reaction; oxygen acts as an electron donor to regenerate the reduced glucose oxidase. This blood glucose sensing technology involves either the consumption of oxygen or formation of hydrogen peroxide as a function of glucose oxidase–catalyzed transformation of blood glucose. Oxygen consumption is detected with the oxygen electrode, and the scheme of first commercial design of glucose sensor based on such reaction was launched by Yellow Spring. Hydrogen peroxide undergoes both reduction and oxidation on the surface of the electrode and may also be explored for glucose biosensing. The limitations associated with electroanalysis of hydrogen peroxide include poor sensitivity of the sensor response based on the reduction of hydrogen peroxide which takes place at relatively low potential, and high overvoltage associated with oxidation of hydrogen peroxide. These problems directed the introduction of another reaction scheme that allows the regeneration of reduced enzyme in absence of oxygen as reported by Cass et al. (1984). The second-generation enzyme electrode was introduced, involving the participation of the oxidized form of the redox mediator at the site of enzymatic reaction, which reacts with reduced glucose oxidase, converts to the native form of enzyme, and in turn becomes reduced. The reduced form of the redox mediator is regenerated electrochemically. During this process the second-order rate constant for the

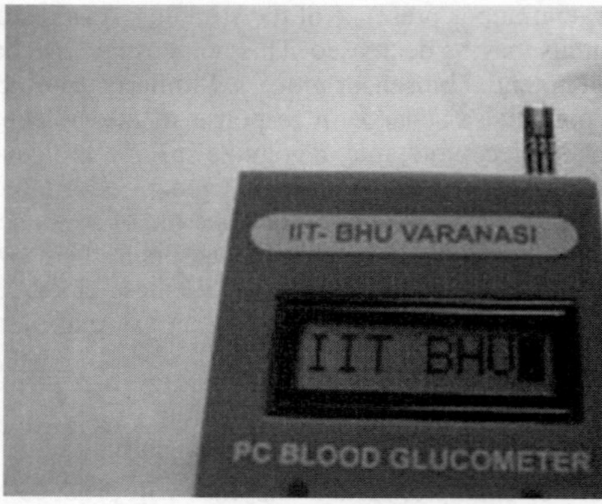

FIGURE 24.2 Commercial blood glucometer.

reaction between reduced glucose oxidase and oxidized form of redox mediator governs the signal amplification and overall response of the sensor. Many commercial blood glucose sensors (Fig. 24.2) function on this concept involving an electronic component and disposable enzyme, printed test strip for blood glucose sensing.

The use of redox mediator has been more reliable for single application as in the case of commercially available blood glucometer; however, during subsequent measurements these mediators are leached out from the surface and many a time causes rate-determining step thus affecting the rate of enzyme-catalyzed reaction. Such limitations directed us to use the components of organic metals such as tetracyanoquinodimethane (TCNQ) and tetrathiafulvalene (TTF) and served as efficient mediator in probing glucose oxidase–catalyzed reaction within graphite paste (Pandey et al. 1991). Some of the limitations as discussed herein directed us to explore another artificial system for effective regeneration of redox enzyme during enzymatic reaction, and another concept of third-generation enzyme electrode was introduced. The third-generation TCNQ and TTF enzyme electrodes show good redox activity and serve as efficient mediator for regeneration of reduced enzyme or cofactor. However, TCNQ is anionic in nature, whereas TTF is cationic and allows charges transfer complexation when mixed together forming organic metal; this material acts as an efficient electrocatalyst and enables the regeneration of glucose oxidase.

24.2.3 Optical Tagging

The ability to closely monitor molecular interactions has also been extrapolated to instances in which fluorescent or other tags are attached to either the sensing material or analyte involved in the sensor to indicate movement and/or chemical reaction. In such a way, the sensing material used in the biosensor can be fundamentally altered in order to provide a quantitative indicator of the desired interaction or property.

Molecular tags frequently involve modifying the sensing material with the addition of a short molecular chain. This tag can then be visualized either directly or through the addition of a reagent, which interacts with the tag to form a visible precipitate or other recordable change. Initially, tags used radioactive labels to monitor the presence and movement of an analyte. However, the inherent difficulties involved with preparation, storage, and use of radioactive labels has diminished the popularity of radioactive methods. Other molecules are commonly used in research and commercial applications; for example, fluorescent molecules and other molecules can be monitored for decay characteristics and can be used safely in clinical settings. Depending on the type of molecule used to tag the sensing material, this method can be cost efficient and can involve minimal processing by the end user.

Fluorophores, molecular components that exhibit fluorescent qualities, are one notable family of molecular tags. A fluorophore can be attached to a sensing material through biomolecular engineering methods. With specific selection, they can be attached in such a way as to illuminate continuously or in response to conformational changes in the larger structure of the enzyme or antibody. Thus, fluorophore tags can be used to directly monitor the movement and the concentration of particular analyte. In addition, these molecules can provide details about analyte-fluorophore interaction. In addition, they can be used to indirectly detect the replacement of an analyte by a competing substance, when it is not possible to tag the actual desired analyte of interest.

One of the biggest challenges with the use of fluorescent tags is the limited number of fluorescent molecules that have adequate properties to warrant inclusion in biosensors (Hellinga and Marvin, 1998). This restriction can be especially troublesome for researchers as it places constraints on the quantity and contrast properties of available tagging agents. The limited options regarding selection of wavelength reduce the number of specific interactions that can be investigated at one time and diminish the potential for fluorescent mechanisms to be used in large, multianalyte biosensors. It is worth noting, however, that researchers are investigating the creation of new or altered fluorophores that have more desirable properties and distinctive characteristics, which can distinguish them from currently used tags (Rizzo et al., 2004). To date, the development of novel tags has not significantly impacted the number and type of tags that are utilized in research or commercial biosensors. Yet, for biosensors designed to monitor a conservative number of sensing material-analyte interactions, the fluorescent tag mechanism works exceedingly well. It is a moderately economical method for observing interactions between biological molecules that do not produce noticeable molecular by-products and cannot be investigated using other methods.

Direct Monitoring. In order to quantify the specific interaction between a sensing material and its corresponding analyte, fluorophore molecular tags can be attached to the analyte and used to "wash" the biosensor, which allows for maximum binding. By exposing the sensor interface to a biologically neutral solution, excess analyte can be removed from the sensor. The resulting fluorescence indicates interaction between the sensor and analyte.

This simplified method can prove useful in quantifying the concentration of analyte present in a given sample solution; indeed, it is most frequently used for this purpose. Detection of toxins and nonpathogenic bacteria has been demonstrated using this technique (Rowe-Taitt et al., 2000). This method has also been shown to be useful for determining if a specific antibody or other analyte has been adsorbed onto a sensor substrate. Similarly, this basic mechanism may be valuable in evaluating the functionality of a biosensor, particularly in the distribution and immobilization of detection proteins.

Competitive Binding. In some instances, one may not want to modify the sensor or the analyte through the addition of molecular tags. This situation is especially true in applications in which it is important to record information about the interaction between two unmodified biological molecules. In these occasions, it is useful to employ a competitive binding method. In the competitive binding mechanism, a fluorescently tagged molecule with a low binding affinity for the enzyme or antibody is exposed to the sensing component of the biosensor. The analyte interacts with the sensor; as a result, the location and number of binding sites can be ascertained from fluorescence analysis. The analyte of interest, which possesses a higher binding affinity, is exposed to the biosensor and actively displaces the fluorescently tagged molecules. By comparing the fluorescence produced by the sensor before and after the addition of the second sample, investigators can determine if the analyte of interest was present in the second sample. In addition, the number of binding sites that interact with this sample can be resolved. As a variation, two molecules tagged with fluorophores that exhibit different spectra can be used, which provides more accurate information on the affinity of the second molecular sample.

This mechanism has been utilized for the detection of toxins and drugs; it can also be utilized for environmental monitoring, clinical screening, or hazard detection. For example, a competitive binding sensor has recently been designed to detect cocaine, which contained an antibody attached to nanobeads. This device used a major metabolite of cocaine as an analog and a first binding substance with weaker affinity. The detecting beads were placed in a container. A flow tube provided input of a fluid sample containing cocaine as well as output of a fluid containing displaced fluorescently tagged metabolites to a fluorescence detector (Ligler et al., 1992). Since the binding affinity between the antibody and cocaine is much higher than the binding affinity between the antibody and the metabolite, it is not an easily reversible reaction. As such, the device can only be used effectively once. The lack of reusability makes it difficult to establish normal calibration curves and increases the expense of the device. Results from this biosensor suggest that competitive binding works well in microfluidic sensors and chips, since a sample can be used to "wash" a prepared sensor and displacement of the initial analyte exhibiting lower affinity can be immediately monitored. With the reduction in biosensor size, a correspondingly smaller sample size is needed. This is an evident advantage in clinical settings over current screening devices, which may require large sample quantities. In research applications, the reduction of sample size may also enable a decrease in cost.

Conformation-Initiated. Some engineered proteins undergo conformational changes upon binding or absorption that prevent or initiate fluorescence, which allow for direct monitoring of a specific binding action. This process is termed an allosteric mechanism as it relates to the change in shape that occurs at the interface of two chemically interacting molecules. For example, researchers have covalently attached fluorophores to glucose binding sites on *Escherichia coli* bacteria and have demonstrated that the degree to which glucose molecule(s) occupy the binding site is directly related to the degree of fluorescence that is observed (Marvin and Hellinga, 1998). Fluorescent tags cannot only indicate the presence of a specific interaction, but can provide information about the degree of interaction.

Other research efforts involve designing fluorescent proteins to have appropriate binding properties or activation site(s) for use in a biosensor. In one well-cited instance, a green fluorescent protein with appropriate optical characteristics for monitoring was progressively mutated to contain the active binding site of the EM1 β-lactamase enzyme, which is responsive to the β-lactamase-inhibitory protein. After what the investigators termed "directed evolution," the engineered green fluorescent protein demonstrated a change in fluorescent intensity in proportion to the amount of inhibitory protein that was present. In addition, the protein maintained a constant fluorescent intensity in the presence of another nonactivating protein (Doi and Yanagawa, 1999). The placement of receptor site and fluorophore must be carefully considered in order to obtain the desired change in fluorescence without interfering with the function of either the fluorophore or the binding site in the absence of a suitable analyte.

While fluorescent indicators provide a significant opportunity to monitor the protein behavior, this method does not necessarily work well with every type of protein that can potentially be used in a biosensor. This statement is particularly true for direct transduction based on change in conformation and subsequent fluorescence, since a large number of proteins do not undergo significant conformational change upon binding of a specific receptor site (Doi and Yanagawa, 1999). Still, this method is very popular in both research and commercial setting as the technique works very well with those proteins that exhibit a favorable conformational change.

24.2.4 Immobilization Issues

While the biological detection mechanisms used by biosensors are exceedingly useful, they do suffer from significant limitations. In particular, the need to immobilize the detecting protein or other biological material on the surface of the biosensor can result in conformational and functional interference. Protein orientation and conformation is an important concern. When immobilized on the surface of a biosensor and not free moving, proteins are susceptible to issues such as steric hindrance and adsorption.

The manner in which proteins are adsorbed onto a surface can affect their ability to function completely and appropriately. Access to the protein active site can be effectively blocked at certain orientations. Furthermore, protein conformation may be altered when the protein is in contact with a surface, potentially resulting in the degradation of the active site. Binding sites can also be blocked by steric hindrance, obstruction caused by accumulation of material in one region. This stresses the importance of achieving a surface with evenly distributed and correctly oriented proteins. Researchers are addressing this issue through attempts to modify the surface or sensor-biological material interface in order to promote monodispersed layers and appropriate protein orientation. Although a conclusive method is unlikely to emerge in the near future, it is apparent that protein immobilization is an important factor in the function and degree of biosensor sensitivity.

24.2.5 Multianalyte

An interesting avenue of emerging research is the engineering of proteins to detect multiple types of analytes or a family of analytes. This move toward generalization of binding sites, in stark contrast to the specificity that traditionally characterizes biosensors, reflects the need to create more cost-effective sensors. For instance, an antibody that will react to an entire family or evolving strain of antigens will be more useful in clinical settings for initial diagnosis than an extremely specific antibody which can only react to one strain or one specific type of antigen. This approach is already being performed to an extent; as discussed in the subsection "Competitive Binding," under Sec. 24.2.3, biosensors are often sensitive to molecules that are similar in structure to the optimal analyte. However, while many drugs and toxins act through related mechanisms, they are rarely analogous in molecular composition to the extent that a single-sensing mechanism will detect multiple analytes.

By engineering either a protein with a generalized binding site or a series of very similar proteins that specifically bind to a number of analytes, a type of "effective-mass" fluorescent biosensor may be developed. Research by De Lorimier and others has examined the use of bacterial periplasmic binding proteins labeled with fluorophores to detect conformational changes and to function as a generalized multianalyte detection system. The proteins they selected are sensitive to a wide variety of molecular analytes, including amino acids, sugars, and other materials. All of the proteins engineered in the study were also capable of using the same fluorescent detection system, making them ideal for placement on a single substrate as a multianalyte biosensor (De Lorimier et al., 2002). However, even in this single study of 11 proteins, the researchers were only able to use eight types of fluorophores. Their results demonstrate the limitations of the fluorescent tagging process in fabricating multiple detection biosensors using engineered proteins.

An alternate mechanism for expanding the flexibility of biosensor technology involves the incorporation of multiple, specific sensing proteins into one biosensor. This can create a sensor that provides information about the presence of multiple molecules through testing of only one sample. This type of sensor can serve as a lab-on-a-chip and can allow multiple screening tests to be done concurrently, which saves both time and expense of multiple samples and reagents.

The development of multianalyte biosensors focuses a great deal on features that will impact commercialization, such as rapidity of results and minimization of required materials. A prime example is an array biosensor that was recently developed by Golden, in which attention changed to refining the design by miniaturizing components and establishing autonomous operation after sensitivity to several analytes was verified (Golden et al., 2005). Rowe noted an emphasis on the simultaneous detection of multiple factors; for example, detection by a biosensor of both (1) multiple analytes in columns divided by detecting protein and (2) multiple analytes in combination columns. This process effectively demonstrated the presence of various mixtures of analytes (Rowe et al., 1999). Furthermore, this particular biosensor recognized three distinct types of biological analytes: viral, bacterial, and amino acid. This result was particularly ambitious since most sensors, even multianalyte sensors, tend to focus on a single type or family of analyte. Their results demonstrate the potential to fabricate truly extensive sensors.

24.3 TRANSDUCTION METHODS

While the biological sensor component allows one to monitor biological molecules through a variety of mechanisms, corresponding transduction processes must be incorporated in order to collect data and precisely monitor analyte-sensor interactions. Methods of detection frequently used in biosensors include (1) indirect monitoring of the reaction through detection of reaction by-products or other chemical changes or (2) direct monitoring through creation of a detectable signal from the biological sensing component itself. Distinguishable and quantitative reaction feedbacks can take the form of changes in electrical potential, changes in emission of energy or light, and changes in the physical state of interacting biological materials.

24.3.1 Optical

This transduction method was greatly popularized by the increased availability of tagged or modified fluorescent biomolecular detectors. Optical transduction methods have experienced a surge in use with the development of increasingly sensitive equipment. Some of the more common optical transduction methods are described below.

Fluorescence Spectroscopy. Described by some researchers as "the most flexible 'transduction' technique," fluorescence spectroscopy is an analytical method that records the emission spectrum of a sample (e.g., biosensor surface) after applying an excitation stimulus (e.g., a laser or an ultraviolet light source) (Lakey and Ragget, 1998). The recorded spectra can then be used to extrapolate information about the number and location of fluorescently tagged molecules present on the sample. Furthermore, it can monitor conformational changes that result from both binding and biological molecule interaction, thus making it useful for examining the behavior of a sample over time. Spectroscopic detection of fluorescence has been extended to the molecular level, which provides an extensive spectrum of detection levels from which to choose (Fernandes, 1998). The ability to function optimally in the presence of small sample sizes, with minimum amounts of fluorescent molecules, makes this process well suited for biosensor applications in which miniaturization and small-scale components are required.

While this procedure is well established, there is some interest in making improvements and alterations. Gas-monitoring systems have been developed in which an enzymatic reaction can lead to generation of a particular gas (e.g., oxygen or carbon dioxide), which in turn can be physically examined through optical fluorescent or pH detection (Leiner, 1991). Fluorescence spectroscopy equipment is widely used and sufficient for current biosensors. One of the distinct advantages of using this transduction technology is that it can be utilized for the analysis of many biological sensing components over the device lifetime and it can be readily adapted to new developments in detection tools; however, spectroscopic approaches do not lend themselves to use in mobile, disposable, or multianalyte biosensors.

Fiber Optic. Fluorescence can be optically recorded by detecting the light that is generated by fluorescent molecules through one or more fiber optic tubes. The refractory path of light in the fiber optic strands can be taken into account in the quantification of fluorescence, which provides information as to the concentration and location of tagged molecules. Given the minimal amount of sensing material and sample size traditionally used in biosensors, researchers have attached the sensing biological elements directly to the end of one or more fiber optic tubes in order to get more continuous monitoring throughout the biochemical interaction between the sensing material and the analyte. The detection of periplasmic binding proteins commonly observed in bacteria such as *E. coli* and *Salmonella* has been achieved using fiber optic transducers. The sensing proteins were placed against the optical fibers; this construct was placed behind a dialysis membrane, which allowed access to the sample (Salins et al., 2004).

Fiber optic detectors can also transduce fluorescence data, much like fluorescence spectroscopy. One example used a laser reflecting off of the solid-phase component of the sensor, which contained fluorescently tagged proteins, in order to enhance the emission of the fluorophores. The output was then conveyed through the fiber optic system to a photomultiplier tube (Schult et al., 1999). In another instance, the detection of *Yersinia pestis* was accomplished using a laser to generate evanescent waves, which were then reflected into fiber optic detectors (Wei et al., 2007). The use of fiber optic materials can provide extremely accurate results with relatively portable equipment. Use of a fluorescence spectrometer allows for evaluation of many fluorescent biosensors. Fiber optic transducers are relatively inexpensive compared to other equipment and provide similar accuracy.

Surface Plasmon Resonance. One technique for examining interactions on the surfaces of metal involves assessing the resonance of surface plasmons. Surface plasmons refer to electromagnetic waves that tend to move parallel to a metal. This process effectively forms an interface between the metal and the surrounding environment. These waves can be monitored and can vary based on alterations to the metal surface, such as changes in adsorbed proteins and other biological molecules. This process is of particular interest to researchers because it permits extremely detailed examination of the interactions that take place on the biosensor surface. Complex factors such as the mechanism of molecular assembly and biochemical rate limitations can be examined using the surface plasmon resonance technique. It is important to note that artifacts may be present in data obtained using this technique due to steric hindrance in the immobilization of biological molecules on the surface or adsorption of the analyte on the immobilization substrate (Schuck, 1997). Comparison of surface plasmon resonance methods to direct assay methods show that surface plasmon resonance methods enjoy a much lower threshold of detection for many proteins, such as fibronectin and human factor B (Sun et al., 2007). This technique can accelerate the development of effective sensors with improved accuracy and precision.

Fret and Quantum Dots. The resonant energy present in fluorescently tagged molecules can also be used to monitor biochemical reactions at specific binding sites. Fluorescent indicators can be excited and amplified with specific wavelengths. Under similar environments, one protein labeled with a given fluorophore may emit light brightly while another fluorophore may remain unaffected. Due to the resonant energy phenomenon, when two materials come in close contact during a reaction on the biosensor surface and the energy is redistributed, which enables the initially unaffected fluorophore to emit light. Forster resonant energy transfer (FRET) utilizes this valuable property to examine transferable resonant energy before and during biochemical reactions between various biological materials. The interesting properties of quantum dots (e.g., emission of light at a specific wavelength) have allowed these materials to play a growing role in FRET analysis. The accuracy of FRET analysis is related to the overlap of the spectra of the materials (Clapp et al., 2004).

The creation of a multianalyte variation based on FRET technology could prove extremely useful. This technique is limited by the limited current selection of fluorescent tags. Efforts are underway to develop improved fluorescent tags with specific features and characteristics for FRET detection. In one instance, a cyan fluorophore was mutagenetically altered to improve the quantum yield and the extinction coefficient; as a result, these modified materials may provide more accurate data with less noise (Rizzo et al., 2004). Quantum dots provide better emission and a wider range of distinct emission wavelengths than other fluorophore tags. Optical methods hold great potential for detection of multiple substances. As such, optical tags are a viable option for use in next-generation biosensors.

24.3.2 Electrical

As noted in the discussion of biological sensing mechanisms, many interactions between biological materials produce a change in potential or voltage. Potentiometric detectors can record changes in voltage. Alternatively, a potential may be applied to a biological material; if a reaction occurs, the corresponding current change can be detected (amperometric detection). This section describes electrical transduction techniques that have been developed.

Field Effect Transistors. A popular device that is widely used in commercial biosensors is the field-effect transistor (FET), which uses an input junction with a high impedance to conduct current flow with the application of electrons present in a voltage gradient. There are a large number of variations concerning the materials and gating structures used in the construction of solid-state field-effect transistors, but they function in the same fundamental manner. Recent efforts have involved manufacturing field-effect transistors from organic materials and processing field-effect transistor thin films. These adaptions hold the potential for developing in vivo, highly portable, or flexible sensors. Field-effect transistors are particularly sensitive to changes in pH; as a result, they can indirectly monitor reactions through the oxidation of products of chemical reactions (Sevilla et al., 1994). Ion-sensitive systems have been developed; however, these systems have limited applications because they cannot distinguish between ion types and cannot be readily used in multianalyte applications.

Microbeads and Nanoparticles. Recent research efforts have involved development of multianalyte lab-on-a-chip biosensors based on microbeads and nanoparticles; these materials offer a novel medium on which to immobilize biological sensing agents. The small, spherical dimensions of these materials allow for maximization of surface area and minimization of space, which can assist in the miniaturization of biosensors. The shape is also useful for microfluidic applications, both (1) permitting the free movement of the spheres through the fluid containing the analyte and (2) increasing exposure of the analyte to the sensing material. The material from which the sphere is created can affect sensor performance in several ways. The material may be chosen for protein immobilization properties. For other applications, a material may be chosen with magnetic properties, which may offer control over sphere movement and transduction.

Microspheres are often preferred over nanoparticles for use in biosensors and other medical devices because they are larger in size and can be more easily detected. Microspheres are also capable of being optically tagged with fluorescent materials (Han, 2001). Due to their small size, nanoparticles also exhibit several desirable characteristics for use in biosensors; for example, nanoparticles exhibit minimal size and high mobility, which minimizes the possibility of nanoparticle interference with small-scale interactions between biological molecules. In addition, a higher number of nanoparticles can be placed in a given location, which may improve the sensitivity of the biosensor (Graham et al., 2004).

Microbeads and nanoparticles with magnetic properties are commonly used in biosensors. Magnetic nanoparticles are generally made from inherently magnetic metals, such as iron. On the other hand, microbeads or spheres are often made out of polymeric materials, in which nanometer-sized particles of metal are scattered throughout the polymeric matrix (Baselt et al., 1998). The metal particles only exhibit magnetic behavior in the presence of a magnetic field, which limits concerns regarding aggregation of material. Nanoparticles, given their significantly smaller size, are less likely than microspheres to exhibit agglomeration at the same concentration (Graham et al., 2004). Sensing materials or analytes can then be attached to the sphere surface. In most sensing mechanism, the spheres are exposed to the corresponding material, which is sometimes immobilized on the sensor (Fig. 24.3). The change in resistance of the sensor can be measured directly. A magnetic field can be applied in order to determine the force of the chemical bonds between the sensing material and analyte. Nonmagnetic microspheres can also be used for optical detection; these materials often consist of polymer spheres that are coated or embedded with quantum dots (Han, 2001). Using these materials, one can combine the optical qualities of quantum dots with the analyte immobilization properties of certain polymers.

One of the first uses of magnetic microspheres was as a measurement method in microscopy. By applying an increasing magnetic force to an analyte that was bound to a superparamagnetic bead, the amount of force required to disrupt the bond could be determined. From this information, information about the energetics of the interaction could be inferred. It is believed that magnetic force microscopy, through the attachment of the microsphere to the recording magnetic cantilever after bond cleavage, can circumvent some artifacts in atomic force microscopy data caused by the recording cantilever (Baselt et al., 1998).

Both magnetic microbeads and nanoparticles are currently used in biosensors; these materials have been shown to be effective transducers of biomolecular interactions. One first mechanism, giant magnetoresistance (GMR), makes use of the random scattering of spin orientations in a material composed of alternating magnetic and nonmagnetic sheets or thin films (Graham et al., 2004). Application of a magnetic field aligns the magnetism of the films. As a result, a greater number of electron spins are oriented in the same direction, which causes a drop in resistance in the plane of the films (Megens and Prinns, 2005). Magnetoresistive plates can attract microbeads and nanoparticles

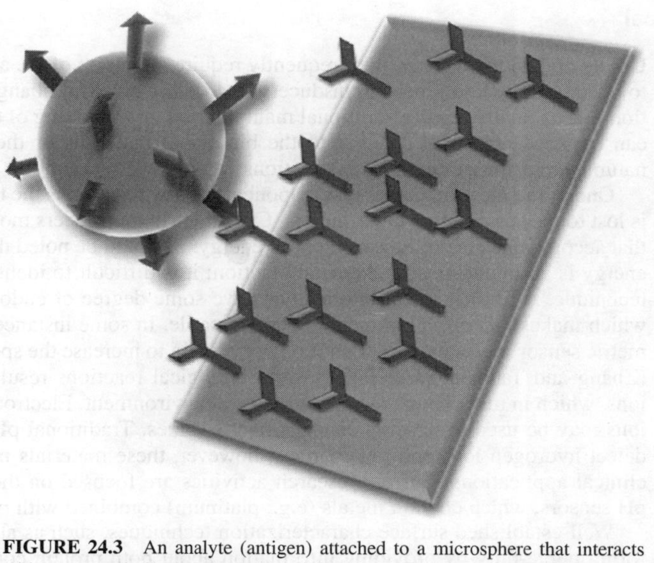

FIGURE 24.3 An analyte (antigen) attached to a microsphere that interacts with a corresponding antibody immobilized on a sensor surface, which can be monitored for changes in electrical resistance.

upon application of a magnetic field. As an example, researchers have attached an analyte to magnetic microbeads and immobilized a corresponding sensing material to the surface of magnetoresistive plates. They allowed the materials to interact and removed excess microbeads with a small magnetic field. The number of microbeads attached to the surface of the sensor could be determined by the change in resistance (Rife et al., 2003).

Another transduction mechanism that is frequently employed also involves the use of magneto-resistive plates. In this case, the application of multiple magnetic fields is used to change the orientation of each magnetic layer individually. These transducers known as spin valves allow one to directly control the resistance of the plates (Megens and Prinns, 2005). In the presence of only one magnetic field, the electrons in all of the magnetic layers will align according to the magnetic gradient. The application of two or more magnetic fields perpendicularly to the plates (to prevent in-plane interference) results in changes in resistance, which can directly be related to the movement and arrangement of electrons in the plates. This transduction technique can be applied to similar situations as the GMR technique; however, it does provide greater control over the orientation and recorded resistance. For measurement of individual particles, or small magnetic fields, "Hall-effect" sensors, which have a linear response, can be used. These sensors exhibit a cross shape, which better lends itself to detection of individual molecules or microbeads (Ejsing et al., 2005). Magnetic tags have substantial advantages over optical tagging methods in that they can provide direct transduction of the biological interactions; quantifiable and easily recordable data can be obtained. On the other hand, fluorescent tags require more complex transduction and transformation processes to convert recorded images into useful statistical data. Unlike some fluorescent and molecular tags, microspheres and nanoparticles are robust for general use; no changes in shape, size, or properties of these materials have been noted after 19 months exposure to air (Gee et al., 2003). The inert chemical stability of these materials, coupled with a lack of interference in biological interactions, makes this method of transduction very useful. Magnetic microbeads are also being investigated as a new method for data storage, including use as random access memory (Megens and Prinns, 2005).

24.3.3 Physical

Unlike optical methods, which frequently require alteration of the analyte in order to make it visible to spectroscopy equipment, transducers that detect physical changes caused by biochemical reactions occasionally require additional manipulation or processing of the materials. These mechanisms can transduce physical changes to the biological materials or their surroundings that occur as a natural extension of chemical interactions.

One of the most fundamental components of any reaction is the transfer of energy, some of which is lost to the surrounding environment. Calorimetric transducers monitor for a change in temperature that accompanies the release of thermal energy. It should be noted that generation or consumption of energy is an indicator of a chemical reaction; it is difficult to identify a specific reaction using this technique. All biochemical interactions have some degree of endothermal or exothermal behavior, which makes this detection method very versatile. In some instances, researchers will coat a calorimetric sensor with a particular antibody or protein to increase the specificity of the detected reactions (Zhang and Tadigadapa, 2004). Several biological reactions result in the production of hydrogen ions, which in turn change the pH of the local environment. Electrodes that are sensitive to hydrogen ions may be used to observe changes in pH values. Traditional pH electrodes use metal oxides to detect hydrogen ions and pH changes; however, these materials may not be appropriate for some clinical applications. Current research activities are focused on the development of biocompatible pH sensors, which contain metals (e.g., platinum) combined with polymers (Lakard et al., 2004).

Well-established surface characterization techniques, such as atomic force microscopy, can perform double-duty by providing information about both protein conformation on the surface of the sensor and information on the location of bonds between the sensing material and analyte. These methods can employ a myriad of devices but involve detection of a physical change that occurs at the sensor surface. Though surface characterization techniques cannot be easily translated into widely manufactured biosensors, physical methods remain useful tools for sensing biological materials.

24.3.4 Piezoelectric

The piezoelectric properties of certain crystals allow an electrical field to be transduced into a mechanical vibrational movement. This property can be exploited for use in biosensors by directly attaching sensing materials to the surface of a piezoelectric crystal. When the biological sensing mechanism interacts with the analyte, the added molecular weight changes the frequency at which the crystal will vibrate. This mechanism allows investigators to quantify the amount of sensing material that attached to the piezoelectric crystal and the amount of analyte that was bound by the sensing material (Fig. 24.4). The method in which the sensing material is immobilized on the crystal is particularly important to prevent nonspecific binding and achieve an accurate resonant frequency; however, it is often difficult to achieve a high-quality monolayer of biological sensing agent. This technology offers significant advantages to researchers involved in isolating particular genes. In addition, piezoelectric materials may be used to detect reversible reactions, thereby creating reusable sensors. In a more recent study, researchers created a specific biosensor for hepatitis B and compared two methods of immobilization, reporting better results for protein probes attached through polyethyleneimine adhesion and through glutaraldehyde cross-linking than through unaided physical adsorption. This biosensor was able to reproduce similar results for five uses, indicating a high degree of reusability (Zhou et al., 2002). Piezoelectric crystals hold enormous potential for many biological applications.

24.4 MANUFACTURE OF BIOSENSORS

It is important to consider the approaches used for manufacturing of biosensors. The cost for biosensor manufacturing as well as the manufacturing errors must be minimized. One hurdle associated with biosensor commercialization is the absence of established and validated biosensor

FIGURE 24.4 Accumulation of biological materials changes the resonant frequency of a piezoelectric crystal.

manufacturing procedures (Gonzalez-Martinez et al., 2007). There is a wide variety of potential biological sensing mechanisms, methods of transduction, methods of detection, and manufacturing methods. While this wide variety allows for significant innovation of new fabrication techniques, it is difficult to standardize a given protocol across producers. Many successful biosensors have been successfully developed; however, the transition from basic research to product development to the approval and marketing of a biosensor may be simplified by evaluating various manufacturing processes. These studies would have the added benefit of providing an expectation of performance from each method and could assist in the development of quality control measures for mass-produced biosensors. The quality of commercially marketed biosensors is extremely important, not only to the manufacturer, but to the end user, for whom the results may have considerable implications. Therefore, the manufacturing process should be considered a crucial and guiding factor in the development of biosensors.

24.4.1 Lithography

Lithography involves processing of biosensor components by depositing and etching thin layers of material. Chemical treatments are applied to select areas of the layered substrate to enable each deposition or etching step. There are limitations in terms of types of materials and geometries that can be processed using lithographic methods.

Mechanics. Photolithography, stereolithography, and electron beam lithography are the primary mechanisms used in for lithographic processing of biosensors. Photolithography utilizes the exposure of material to ultraviolet light for depositing or removing a layer of material. Stereolithography uses a laser or a lamp to selectively solidify layers of a photosensitive liquid; the material is processed in a layer-by-layer manner to create three-dimensional structure. The electron beam lithography methods utilizes an electron beam to selectively etch surface features. Electrochemical methods for lithographic processing are also available (Lai et al., 2006). All of the lithographic methods involve the addition or removal of layers of material using templates or patterns.

All of the lithographic methods are used to prepare materials with small-scale features for biosensor applications. Stereolithography can be used for manufacturing of three-dimensional biosensor components. If the geometry of the biosensor component made by stereolithography contains overhangs, support structures must be manufactured alongside the component. In some cases, these support structures may need to be removed before the biosensor can be used, which adds to the cost of manufacturing.

Mass Manufacturing. Given the variety and versatility of the lithographic procedures available to manufacturers, the inclusion of lithographic techniques in biosensor manufacturing processes seems straightforward. Methods that are less expensive and less labor intensive (e.g., lithographic processes) find greater use in large-scale biosensor fabrication. More expensive methods, such as electron beam lithography, may provide superior quality in small dimensions; however, they are not feasible to manufacturers outside of a university or research and development setting.

FIGURE 24.5 Screen printing conductive circuitry onto a transducing electrode.

24.4.2 Screen Printing

One popular method for processing biosensor components is screen printing; this method is used to deposit patterns containing sensing materials or circuitry onto the surface of a biosensor component. This method is inexpensive and enables the production of patterns containing small-scale features. It is currently used for the manufacture of electrodes and disposable transducers. This mechanism has also been used for the immobilization of sensing materials on the transducer surface of a biosensor.

Mechanics. Screen printing uses one or more templates to create high resolution printing of inks on a substrate. This mechanism can be used in the creation of the circuitry. Electrically conductive or insulating inks are deposited on the surface; the inks then dry and/or cool to form a continuously connected pattern that serves as an electronic component (Fig. 24.5). The immobilization of biological materials on the surface of a transducer can be accomplished by applying a solution containing the material of interest through the screen pattern onto the desired areas of the electrode or transducer. For example, screen printing of ink containing either glucose oxidase or horseradish peroxidase in a sol-gel has been demonstrated, which is then cured after printing to form a disposable electrode (Wang et al., 1996).

Further steps are often taken to protect the integrity of the patterned material in order to maintain the performance and accuracy of the biosensor. For example, the biological agent may be embedded in a polymer matrix for protection. Environmental factors play a major role in the success and durability of screen-printed biological materials.

Viability of Printed Biological Materials. One notable advantage of screen printing is that it does not require high temperatures or stresses in order to prepare the biological material in a precise pattern. This is particularly useful given the sensitivity of many biological materials to slight changes in environmental conditions. There is significant concern about evaporation of solutions containing biological materials; these processes may reduce the efficiency of reactions during use of the biosensor. A possible solution involves incorporation of a layer that requires drying or hardening as part of the finishing process; however, use of the protective layer is not particularly useful in most applications in which the biological sensing element must be readily available for contact with biological materials. The environmental conditions during sensor production, storage, and use can influence the performance of the biological component of a biosensor. For example, Patel et al. (2001) demonstrated that enzymatic screen-printed biosensors experience increased degradation at moderate-elevated temperatures. These processes accelerate the enzymatic reactions (Patel et al., 2001).

This manufacturing process may be augmented by the use of biocomposite inks, which reduces the number of steps required to place multiple layers of biological materials on the substrate. Many biological materials require separate handling and placement steps in order to function correctly; this factor limits the use of composite inks to those that have been verified as effective. Screen printing alone cannot be used to complete the processing of many sensor materials. In a review of screen printing mechanisms for enzymes, Albareda-Sirvent notes that most processes currently in use also require intermediary steps that are done either by hand or electrochemically, which reduces the efficiency of this process.

Requirement of Sample Volume during Biosensing. The operation of commercially electrochemical biosensors requires the interaction of a finite amount of the blood sample with the sensing components to yield a quantitative signal as a function of the analyte concentration present in the blood sample. Such requirements suggest the use of an invasive technology to perform blood sampling for clinical diagnostic applications. One of the parameters associated with self-monitoring of blood glucose is that the sample volume is dependent on the reaction area of the sensor. The higher the volume of blood sample, the less user-friendly the biosensor design. Accordingly, technology has been innovated that gradually required a lower volume of blood sample. In many blood glucose sensors, a fingerprick is used to obtain a small quantity of blood sample, which is directly applied to the reaction area. Through the use of capillary action during the application of blood on the sensing area of enzyme electrode, a sample volume of $< 2\ \mu L$ blood is required; this approach facilitates the use of minimally invasive technology for blood glucose sensing. Another approach that involves minimally invasive technology for blood glucose monitoring is wearable sensors. Wearable sensors are point of care devices, which allow for minimally invasive monitoring of physiological functions and eliminate fluid transfer between the subject and the device; these devices are capable of providing real-time analysis (Windmiller and Wang, 2013). Novel epidermal electronic devices containing printed flexible circuits that can be stretched and bent to mimic skin elasticity can perform electrophysiological measurements (e.g., measure temperature and hydration) and detect electrical changes associated with brain and muscle activity (Kim et al., 2011). Temporary tattoos integrated with screen-printed electrodes for use on the skin were recently described for sensing lactate in sweat. The goal of future efforts in point of care diagnostics is a minimally invasive biosensor that can provide real-time data with high sensitivity.

Microneedle-Based Glucose Monitoring. There have been recent efforts to develop a microneedle-enabled analytical system that is capable of minimally invasive interrogation due to its ability to puncture the stratum corneum layer of the skin and access interstitial fluid while not interacting with deeper layers of the skin, which contain tissues that are associated with pain and blood flow (Miller et al., 2016). For example, Zimmermann et al. demonstrated passive diffusion of interstitial fluid from a human finger with hollow microneedle devices; they detected glucose levels using enzymatic electrochemical electrodes located beneath the microneedle array (Zimmermann et al., 2003). Interstitial fluid was wicked through eight 200-mm tall microneedles and combined with a buffer solution. The biosensor showed a readily discernible signal at the outset of testing; however, the responsiveness of the sensor was not sustained during the study. The limitations of the device were related to the fact that the functionality of the device relied on the transfer of a small volume of interstitial fluid through channels in the device. Recently, we demonstrated the fabrication of a screen-printed electrode (SPE) and a microneedle-assembled electrochemical sensor for transdermal biosensing (Pandey et al., 2018). In this work, gold nanoparticles were mixed with Prussian blue nanoparticles; the homogeneous suspension was layered over freshly made SPE, followed by curing of the structure. The modified SPE was used to fix the microneedle assembly as shown in Fig. 24.6. Figure 24.6*A* contains the electrochemical detector connected to the microneedle-fixed assembly on the SPE, which shows the novel design of the microneedle-based transdermal biosensor containing the polyethylenimine-modified Prussian blue-gold nanohybrid-enzyme ink for on-chip electrochemical biosensing; the microneedle interface of this device may be fixed on the skin with a simple adhesive bandage (Fig. 24.6*B*). The microneedle-based sensor assembly is shown in Fig. 24.6*C*. The PBNP-modified SPE shows excellent electrochemical behavior.

Mass Manufacturing. Screen printing is currently a widely used fabrication method for disposable electrodes and other biosensor components (Ricci, 2003). For example, this method is used for the production of carbon electrodes that are utilized in glucose sensors (Dequaire and Heller, 2002).

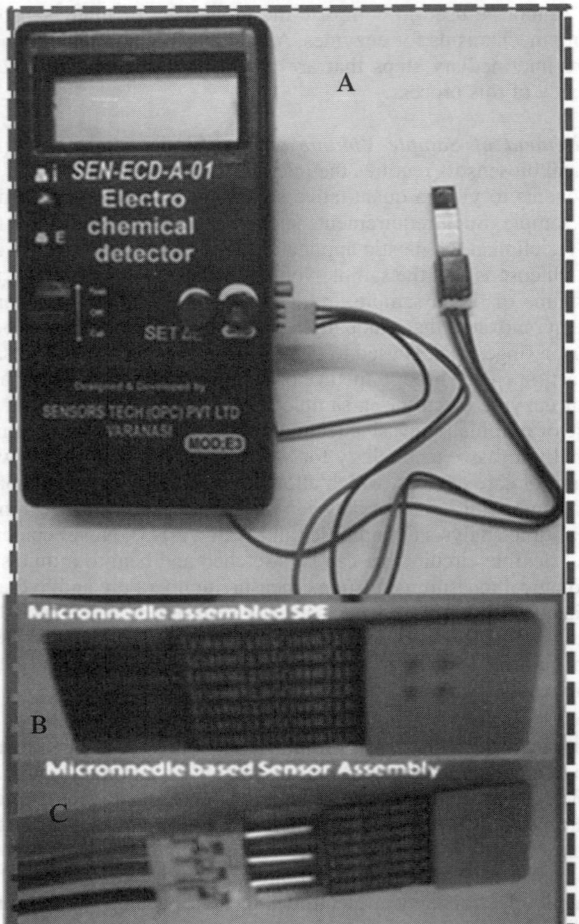

FIGURE 24.6 (*A*) Electrochemical detector connected to a microneedle-assembled screen-printed electrode in a microneedle-based H_2O_2 sensor. (*B*) Microneedle-assembled screen-printed electrode. (*C*) Microneedle-based sensor assembly.

While the simplicity of the concepts behind screen printing is apparent, it is far from a flawless manufacturing technique. It is hindered by the cumbersome and time-consuming nature of placing and removing screens. This method is excellent for large-scale enterprises, but it is not adaptable and cannot be easily used by researchers and other small groups. A distinct advantage of the screen printing process is that the same procedure can be used to produce both transduction and sensing components. Separate screens may be needed for each step, raising start-up costs. In addition, intermediary treatments may be needed.

Furthermore, the creation of a biosensor fabricated by screen printing requires both highly precise geometries and ink placement. In multistep processes, the placement of layers must be accurate with respect to one another. This high level of precision may be difficult to maintain outside of small screen printing operations and may require extensive quality control. Albareda-Sirvent states that screen printing is exceptionally useful in both speed and simplicity but requires significant and complicated optimization processes to make a successful device that functions as intended (Albareda-Sirvent et al., 2000).

Comparative studies have been done between manufacturing processes, which assess the overall suitability of several processes for a specific application. In one such study, however, it is noted that both screen printing and inkjet printing are useful and feasible machine manufacturing techniques for the production of lactate sensors (Hart et al., 1996). Nonetheless, additional comparisons will be required to develop a comprehensive understanding of the advantages and disadvantages of various manufacturing methods for fabrication of biosensors.

24.4.3 Inkjet Printing

Inkjet printing is a versatile technology that has been utilized for many biosensor manufacturing steps, including fabrication of the transducer as well as deposition of biological materials for the sensor. Inkjet printers are able to process many components of the biosensor, including the circuit, electrode, and transducer. In addition, inkjet printing provides the ability to precisely place materials in patterns with small feature sizes. In addition, the process allows for the fabrication of three-dimensional structures (e.g., transduction units) through layering of materials. Inkjet printers have demonstrated the ability to print nucleic acids, proteins, and other biological materials in accurate patterns (feature sizes of 20 mm and above). This capability has enabled the use of inkjet printing in biosensor and immunoassay manufacturing.

Mechanics. Inkjet printing is a commonly used approach for the specific placement and patterning of any substance that can homogeneously be dispersed in solution in the form of an "ink." The accuracy of drop placement in inkjet printing is dependent on the ink attributes such as the viscosity and the degree of heterogeneity. Inkjet printers have been used to process patterns containing polymers, metals, and nanoparticles. More recent inkjet printing research has involved patterning of proteins and other types of biological materials. A cartridge holds the desired solution and disperses it in a controlled manner onto the surface in the form of droplets through a piezoelectric or thermal mechanism. This method does not involve contact between the printer nozzle and the substrate, which limits contamination or other undesirable processes.

There are two primary types of inkjet printing mechanisms that have been utilized for the production of biosensors, piezoelectric, and thermal printers (Fig. 24.7). In piezoelectric inkjet printing, an actuator containing a piezoelectric material (e.g., lead zirconate titanate) vibrates when a voltage is applied. The mechanical movement of the piezoelectric material creates pressure gradients, which lead to the movement of fluid from the cartridge to the surface. This process does not involve heating of the ink. In thermal printing mechanism, a voltage waveform is used to actuate a heat source, which vaporizes the ink and forms a bubble. A pressure gradient forms when the bubble is discharged at the nozzle tip, which pulls ink through the nozzle (Sen and Darabi, 2007). The application of high temperatures as well as high pressures in this technique is a cause for concern when patterning sensitive biological materials. It is known that inks containing inorganic molecules may be altered (e.g., changes in viscosity or premature curing) at high temperatures. Other researchers maintain that the heating process has minimal effects due to stabilizing materials (e.g., glycerol) in the ink that prevent excess injury to the biological materials during the printing process (Setti et al., 2004). Both mechanisms of printing provide very accurate, reproducible patterning of biological materials. Carter et al. (2006) suggest that use of inkjet printing to process multianalyte arrays may minimize issues of cross sensitivity or incompatibility, which would make inkjet printing an appropriate biosensor manufacturing process. Processing details are important parameters for evaluating a product created using inkjet technologies. As with inkjet printers used in graphic arts and publishing, inkjet printers used in biosensor manufacturing frequently have multiple nozzles attached to a single cartridge. As a result, these inkjet printers often have the option of selecting the number of jets in the multiple-nozzle array that will be used for patterning of a biological material. For example, it has been observed that two active nozzles that are spaced a certain distance apart can achieve high-quality printing performance by depositing material in dense patterns, which form a three-dimensional pattern when layered

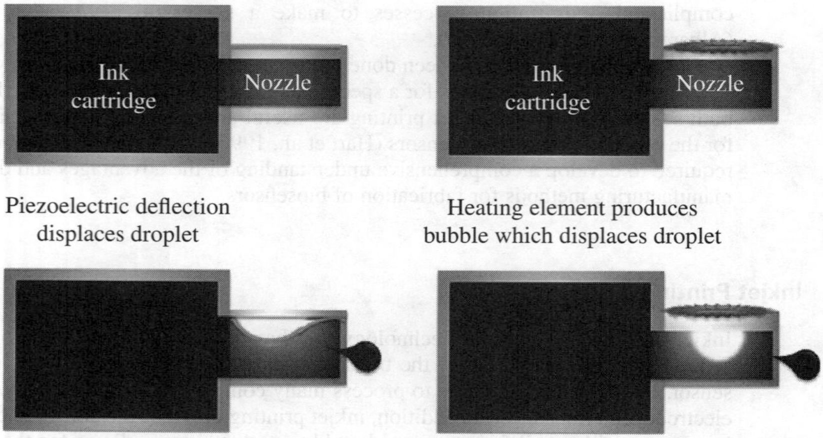

FIGURE 24.7 A cross-sectional illustration of thermal and piezoelectric inkjet nozzles.

(Ibrahim et al., 2006). The ability to select certain nozzles from the printhead and to monitor the droplets being formed at the nozzle provides a high degree of control over the precision of an inkjet printed pattern. Many commercially produced inkjet printers are altered for use in biosensor fabrication. For example, research labs adjust the inkjet printing mechanism in order to better fit a project or object of investigation. Researchers have published information regarding the use of conventional desktop inkjet printers for patterning conductive polymers (Yoshioka and Jabbour, 2006). Another group has produced conducting lines of silver colloids using a commercially marketed inkjet printer (Lee et al., 2005). These results demonstrate that inkjet technologies are flexible and can be readily implemented in a large-scale manufacturing process.

Capability of Printed Transducers. Inkjet printing is a useful method for producing electrodes and other transducers. Inkjet printing is able to deposit multiple layers, is able to process a large variety of materials, and is capable of precise patterning of biological materials on a small scale (>20 mm). Polymers and nanoparticles may be processed using this technique to create biosensor circuitry.

Polymers are useful for inkjet fabrication of biosensor transducers and other components because the materials can be inkjet printed and then cured (or processed in other ways) to obtain appropriate properties for use in a biosensor. Polymers can be inkjet printed for use in signal transducers and other electronic components. These structures often exhibit better surface contact properties and conduction properties; in addition, they may be used in flexible devices. The properties of the polymer (e.g., viscosity) must be matched with the inkjet nozzle settings. The properties of the ink have a significant impact on droplet size and drop position accuracy; for example, ringlike droplets have sometimes been observed (de Gans et al., 2004). In addition, the ink undergoes high pressures and stretching during droplet ejection from the nozzle, which can cause cross-linking and other changes in material properties (Xu et al., 2007). Careful consideration of the inkjet material and the solvent can minimize unwanted changes to the inkjet material or the inkjet pattern.

Inkjet printing is also of particular interest to researchers working with nanoparticles, since the size of the inkjet nozzle enables printing of nanoparticle patterns with no nozzle blockage by nanoparticle aggregates. Recently, electrodes have been fabricated by inkjet printing of polyaniline nanoparticles; polyaniline is particularly troublesome polymer to process using conventional manufacturing methods. These polyaniline structures may be used to prepare a successful ammonia sensor at low cost (Crowley et al., 2008). Metal nanoparticles that are inkjet printed for circuitry applications must be heat treated to metallize the patterns and ensure pattern continuity (Lee et al., 2006). The addition of heat is commonly provided using a laser, since a laser can precisely interact with a region of the device without damaging other parts of the device. Inkjet printing of nanoparticles suffers from the complications that are observed in inkjet printing of other materials, including the effect of solvent selection on droplet size and droplet shape. To improve the accuracy of inkjet printing, hydrophobic interactions and other forces may be used to enable more precise patterning. This surface energy patterning process has been used with excellent results. The properties of the ink also contribute to the feature size of inkjet-printed patterns (Wang et al., 2004). Sirringhaus et al. (2000) have noted that inkjet printing must be capable of producing an entire circuit with few steps and few interactions with the equipment operator in order to be an effective biosensor fabrication technique.

Viability of Inkjet-Printed Biological Materials. Inkjet printers may also be used to produce the biological sensing component of a biosensor; for example, inkjet printing may be used to fabricate monitoring sensors for environmental pollutants (e.g., organic chlorinated compounds). Inkjetting may also be used to fabricate microarrays for pharmacologic agents and biological molecules; these devices have several potential applications, including use in pharmaceutical development. These devices may also be used to identify genetic markers and biochemical interactions (Lemmo et al., 1998). For example, inkjet printing was used to place a DNA multiarray on a membrane, which was later hybridized by cDNA in genetic analysis probe (Goldmann and Gonzalez, 2000). This type of diagnostic device can advance other fields of research by providing prompt information on a large quantity of samples.

There are concerns that the inkjet-printing process may damage the functionality of proteins and other biological materials. Many studies have examined this issue, and have provided encouraging results. Nishioka et al. (2004) evaluated damage to the protein peroxidase that was processed using a piezoelectric inkjet printer; this material is a commonly used enzyme indicator. They determined that protein processed using higher compression rates exhibited greater damage. However, the addition of surfactants and sugars to the ink may stabilize the protein and reduce protein damage (Nishoika et al., 2004). In addition, surfactant- and sugar-modified inks may prevent blockage of the inkjet nozzles (Setti et al., 2004). Most inkjet solutions containing biological materials include surfactants.

Several authors have raised concerns about ink storage, specifically the potential for accumulation of biological material in the ink. Inhomogeneous inks may cause nozzle blockages and may interfere with printing accuracy. Ink aggregation varies based on the type of material being printed; one researcher noticed aggregation of cells in an ink after only 20 minutes (Saunders et al., 2008). This problem may limit large-scale manufacture of biosensors, since many manufacturing processes minimize costs through bulk storage of materials. This limitation requires frequent changing of cartridges to prevent agglomeration of biological materials, or a mechanism to occasionally disperse the biological ink in the cartridge without damaging the biological materials. Extensive biosensor production using inkjet printers may require the development of monitoring procedures or instruments that maintain uniform ink properties.

The functionality of biological materials deposited by means of inkjet printing is generally accepted as sufficient for many applications; the inkjet-printing method has been incorporated into many device fabrication processes. For example, inkjet printing has been used extensively in the production of protein microarrays for use in diagnostics and screening (Heller, 2002).

Surface Modification Potential. In previous section, the successful use of inkjet printers for depositing both organic and inorganic materials for biosensor applications was discussed; additional modifications to the transducer or biological component can also be achieved using inkjet printing. For example, inkjet technology may be used to modify the surface of the transducer in order to improve protein orientation and performance of the biosensor. One researcher found that inkjet printing of thiols followed by inkjet printing of a superimposed layer of proteins reduced the nonspecific protein adsorption and promoted appropriate protein conformation (Hasenbank et al., 2008). Other surface treatments that may be provided using inkjet printing include chemical functionalization, oxidation, and protein coating (Henares et al., 2008; Miettinen, 2008). Also, inkjet printing may be used to modify the surface of the transducing element. In one recent example, an inkjet-printed polymer film was used for the detection of organic vapors (Mabrook et al., 2006).

Mass Manufacturing. With the ability to form a transduction element, perform surface modification, and deposit biological materials, inkjet printing is uniquely poised to produce biosensors with fewer processing steps than other conventional biosensor fabrication processes. As such, use of inkjet printers may serve to greatly reduce the overall cost of biosensor production. In addition, inkjet printing is able to incorporate increasing degrees of automation while enabling a reduction of costs.

Inkjet printing is certainly a feasible mechanism for mass manufacturing. For example, Fisher and Zhang (2007) have produced an automated inkjet system, which can fabricate protein microarrays by means of visual monitoring, precision machining motions, automated handling of intermediate components, and automated handling of completed assays. Their study demonstrates the practical use of inkjet-printing technology for mass production.

In addition, inkjet printing is capable of more precise placement of material than many other conventional manufacturing methods. Inkjet printing is also able to repeat the accurate placement of material in order to perform bottom-to-top fabrication of biosensors and create other three-dimensional devices. Hasenbank et al. (2008) evaluated the patterning capabilities and flexibility of piezoelectric inkjet printers by direct and sequential deposition of proteins onto a substrate. Specifically, multiprotein patterning was achieved using multiple biological inks, each containing a different protein complex. Both good protein adhesion to the substrate and minimal cross-reactivity were noted (Hasenbank et al., 2008). These studies confirm the accuracy of inkjet-printing method and will help to establish this method as a significant biosensor manufacturing process.

Inkjet printing represents a significant development in biosensor manufacturing as it allows for straightforward and inexpensive printing of biological materials and other sensor components on a given substrate. It is capable of processing many, if not all, of the materials commonly used in biosensor fabrication. Due to this unique capability, an inkjet printer may be used alone to develop a fully functional biosensor. The incorporation of transduction tools, such as spectroscopy tools to detect fluorescence or dye-labeled biological reactants, could provide greater functionality to these sensors.

24.5 APPLICATIONS

Due to their flexible capabilities, biosensors have found numerous uses in a wide variety of fields. Research, clinical, and commercial applications of biosensors are discussed below; it should be noted that these categories frequently overlap.

24.5.1 Research

In addition to the research that is underway to develop biosensors, biosensors themselves can be used as investigative tools to facilitate the exploration of other topics. These devices have been used to better understand molecular interactions in order to identify toxins and potential biochemical warfare tools (Shah and Wilkins, 2003); create lab-on-a-chip devices (Weigl et al., 2003); and develop drugs (Giuliano and Taylor, 1998).

One of the key challenges for pharmaceutical companies is the large number of potential pharmacologic agents that must be screened in order to determine the useful properties of these materials. As such, the low cost and high sensitivity of biosensors make them ideal for selecting and comparing pharmacologic agents. One case in point was the evaluation of association and dissociation behavior of several HIV-1 protease inhibitor drugs using the surface plasmon resonance process (Markgren et al., 2000).

Biosensors may also be used to examine the effects of toxins and investigate the mechanism of action for a biological agent. These activities may assist in work to inactivate or counter biological agents. One notable model is the BARC biosensor that has been developed by Edelstein et al. (2000), which uses a combination of hybridized DNA protein fragments and selectively magnetic microbeads in order to measure the presence of a number of potential biological warfare agents with extremely high sensitivity. These examples demonstrate the growing use of biosensors in public health, defense, and environmental protection.

24.5.2 Clinical

Biosensors have demonstrated tremendous suitability for use in the clinical health care setting. Rapid, inexpensive, and sensitive biosensors serve as diagnostic tools and monitoring devices for health care professionals. Diagnostic equipment has been developed for any number of clinical applications, including indication of dental disease by quantities of salivary peroxidase (Ivnitski et al., 2003). Drug screening is another instance in which biosensors can be used to provide rapid results that can improve patient treatment (Moeller, 2008). Biosensors have been developed that can provide genetic information on the chemical interaction between sequences of DNA (Wang, 2002). This technology opens the possibility for developing multianalyte or multiarray sensors that screen for many genetic diseases simultaneously.

In vivo monitoring of patients for electrolytes balance can be performed using biosensors. One recent paper by Jiang and Gud (2004) examined sensing of zinc in vivo using biosensors, noting the changes in fluorescent detection methods over the years. More commonly, biosensors are used in general clinical practice to monitor the ratio of gases in the blood. These sensors utilize optical detection or fluorescent sensor methods (Leiner, 1991). A large number of other biosensors are actively utilized in clinical practice.

24.5.3 Commercial

Biosensors have become widely available in a wide variety of fields, including food manufacturing and environmental monitoring. For example, biosensors have been used for assessing the presence of *Salmonella* in food (Fu et al., 2008) and for determining the moisture and oil content in commercially produced batches of cookies (Ozanich et al., 1992). Optical immunosensors have been used for the detection of pesticides, including triazine compounds (Bier et al., 1992). Additionally, biosensors that were initially developed for clinical purposes are now being utilized for home health care and monitoring. For example, glucose sensors are commonly used by individuals with diabetes to monitor their blood glucose level.

24.6 CONCLUDING REMARKS

The process of creating a biosensor can encompass many disciplines and processes. This review discusses several parameters relevant to biosensor detection processes, biosensor transduction processes, and biosensor manufacturing processes; however, there is a continuous development of new procedures and refinement of current processes. In particular, development of cost-effective and reproducible manufacturing processes is a critical step in the commercialization of biosensors including microneedle-based biosensing. Additional studies are needed to compare various biosensor fabrication processes, biosensor materials, and biosensor manufacturing protocols. This lack of comparative information may hinder commercialization and development of novel biosensors (Gonzalez-Martinez et al., 2007). Future advances in biosensor development will be made by integrating novel materials and fabrication processes.

REFERENCES

Albareda-Sirvent, M., Merkoçi, A., and Alegret, A. (2000). Configurations used in the design of screen-printed biosensors. *Sensors and Actuators B: Chemical*, **69**(1–2), 153–163.

Baselt, D. R., Lee, G. U., Natesan, M., Metzger, S. W., Sheehan, P. E., Colton, R. J. (1998). A biosensor based on magnetoresistance technology. *Biosensors and Bioelectronics*, **13**(7–8), 731–739.

Bier, F. F., Stocklein, W., Bocher, M., Bilitewski, U., and Schmid, R. D. (1992). Use of a fiber optic immunosensor for the detection of pesticides. *Sensors and Actuators B: Chemical*, **7**(1–3), 509–512.

Blonder, R., Katz, E., Cohen, Y. Itzhak, N., et al. (1996). Application of redox enzymes for probing the antigen- antibody association at monolayer interfaces: development of amperometric immunosensor electrodes. *Analytical Chemistry*, **68**, 3151–3157.

Carter, J. C., Alvis, R. M., Brown, S. B., Langry, K. C., Wilson, T. S., McBride, M. T., et al. (2006). Fabricating optical fiber imaging sensors using inkjet printing technology: a pH sensor proof-of-concept. *Biosensors and Bioelectronics*, **21**(7), 1359–1364.

Cass, A. E. G., Davis, G., Francis, G. D., Hill, H. A. O., Aston, W. J., Higgins, I. J., Plotkin, E. V., Scott, L. D. L., Turner, A. P. F. (1984). Ferrocene-mediated enzyme electrode for amperometric determination of glucose. *Analytical Chemistry*, **56**(4), 44667–44671.

Clapp, A. R., Medintz, I. L., Mauro, J. M., Fisher, B. R., Bawendi, M. G., and Mattoussi, H. (2004). Fluorescence resonance energy transfer between quantum dot donors and dye-labeled protein acceptors. *Journal of American Chemical Society*, **126**(1), 301–310.

Crowley, K., O'Malley, E., Morrin, A., Smyth, M., and Killard, A. (2008). An aqueous ammonia sensor based on an inkjet-printed polyaniline nanoparticles-modified electrode. *Analyst*, **133**, 391–399.

da Silvaa, E. M., Soares, A., and Moreno, A. (1998). The use of the mitochondrial transmembrane electric potential as an effective biosensor in ecotoxicological research. *Chemosphere*, **36**(10), 2375–2390.

de Gans, B., Duinveld, P., and Schubert, U. (2004). Inkjet printing of polymers: state of the art and future developments. *Advanced Materials*, **16**(3), 203–213.

de Lorimier, R. M., Smith, J. J., Dwyer, M. A., Looger, L. L., Sali, K. M., Paavola, C. D., et al. (2002). Construction of a fluorescent biosensor family. *Protein Science*, **11**(11), 2655–2675.

Dequaire, M., and Heller, A. (2002). Screen printing of nucleic acid detecting carbon electrodes. *Analytical Chemistry*, **74**, 4370–4377.

Doi, N., and Yanagawa, H. (1999). Design of generic biosensors based on green fluorescent proteins with allosteric sites by directed evolution. *FEBS Letters*, **453**(3), 305–307.

Edelstein, R., Tamanaha, C., Sheehan, P., Miller, M., et al. (2000) The BARC biosensor applied to the detection of biological warfare agents. *Biosensors and Bioelectronics*, **14**(10–11), 805–813.

Ejsing, L., Hansen, M., Menon, A., Ferreira, H., et al. (2005). Magnetic microbead detection using the planar Hall effect. *Journal of Magnetism and Magnetic Material*, **293**(1), 677–684.

Fernandes, P. B. (1998). Technological advances in high-throughput screening. *Current Opinion in Chemical Biology*, **2**(5), 597–603.

Fisher, W., and Zhang, M. J. (2007). A biochip microarray fabrication system using inkjet technology. *IEEE Transactions on Automation Science and Engineering*, **4**(4), 488–500.

Fu, J., Park, B. Siragusa, G., Jones, L., et al. (2008). An Au/SI hetero-nanorod-based biosensor for *Salmonella* detection. *Nanotechnology*, **19**(15), 155502.

Gee, S., Hong, Y., Erickson, D., Sur, J., and Park, M.(2003). Synthesis and aging effect of spherical magnetite (FeO) nanoparticles for biosensor applications. *Journal of Applied Physics*, **93**(10), 7560–7563.

Giuliano, K., and Taylor, D. (1998). Fluorescent-protein biosensors: new tools for drug discovery. *Trends in Biotechnology*, **16**(3), 135–140.

Golden, J., Taitt, C., Shriver-Lake, L., Shubin, Y., and Ligler, F. (2005). A portable automated multianalyte biosensor. *Talanta*, **65**(5), 1078–1085.

Goldmann, T., and Gonzalez, J. (2000). DNA-printing: utilization of a standard inkjet printer for the transfer of nucleic acids to solid supports. *Journal of Biochemical and Biophysical Methods*, **42**(3), 105–110.

González-Martínez, M. A., Puchades, R., and Maquieira, A. (2007). Optical immunosensors for environmental monitoring: how far have we come? *Analytical and Bioanalytical Chemistry*, **387**(1), 205–218.

Graham, D., Ferreira, H., and Freitas, P. (2004). Magnetoresistive-based biosensors and biochips. *Trends in Biotechnology*, **22**(9), 455–462.

Han, M., Gao, X., Su, J. Z., and Nie, S. (2001). Quantum-dot-tagged microbeads for multiplexed optical coding of biomolecules. *Nature Biotechnology,* **19**, 631–635.

Hart, A. L., Turner, A. P. F., and Hopcroft, D. (1996). On the use of screen- and ink-jet printing to produce amperometric enzyme electrodes for lactate. *Biosensors and Bioelectronics*, **11**(3), 263–270.

Hasenbank, M. S., Edwards, T., Fu, E., Garzon, R., Kosar, T. F., Look, M., et al. (2008). Demonstration of multianalyte patterning using piezoelectric inkjet printing of multiple layers. *Analytica Chimica Acta*, **611**(1), 80–88.

Heller, M. (2002). DNA microarray technology: devices, systems, and applications. *Annual Review of Biomedical Engineering*, **4**, 129–153.

Hellinga, H. W., and Marvin, J. S. (1998). Protein engineering and the development of generic biosensors. *Trends in Biotechnology*, **16**(4), 183–189.

Hazama, A., Hayashi, S., and Okada, Y. (1998). Cell surface measurements of ATP release from single pancreatic β cells using a novel biosensor technique. *Pflügers Archiv European Journal of Physiology*, **437** (1), 31–35.

Henares, T. G., Mizutani, F., and Hisamoto, H. (2008). Current development in microfluidic immunosensing chip. *Analytica Chimica Acta*, **611**(1), 17–30.

Ibrahim, M., Otsubo, T., Narahara, H., Koresawa, H., and Suzuki, H. (2006). Inkjet printing resolution study for multi-material rapid prototyping. *JSME International Journal Series C-Mechanical Systems Machine Elements and Manufacturing*, **49**(2), 353–360.

Ivnitski, D., Sitdikov, R., and Ivnitski, N. (2003). Non-invasive electrochemical hand-held biosensor as diagnostic indicator of dental diseases. *Electrochemistry Communication*, **5**(3), 225–229.

Jiang, P. J., and Guo, Z. J. (2004). Fluorescent detection of zinc in biological systems: recent development on the design of chemosensors and biosensors. *Coordination Chemistry Reviews*, **248**(1–2), 205–229.

Kim , D., N. Lu , R. Ma , Y. Kim , R. Kim , S. Wang , J. Wu , S. M. Won, H. Tao, and A. Islam. (2011). Epidermal Electronics, *Science,* **33**, 838.

Lai, R., Lee, S., Soh, H., Plaxco, K., and Heeger, A. (2006). Differential labeling of closely spaced biosensor electrodes via electrochemical lithography. *Langmuir*, **22**, 1932–1936.

Lakard, B., Herlem, G., Labachelerie, M., Daniau, W., Martin, G., et al. (2004). Miniaturized pH biosensors based on electrochemically modified electrodes with biocompatible polymers. *Biosensors and Bioelectronics*, **19**(6), 595–606.

Lakey, J. H., and Raggett, E. M. (1998). Measuring protein-protein interactions. *Current Opinion Structural Biology*, **8**(1), 119–123.

Lee, H. H., Chou, K. S., and Huang, K. C. (2005). Inkjet printing of nanosized silver colloids. *Nanotechnology*, **16**(10), 2436–2441.

Lee, K. J., Jun, B. H., Kim, T. H., and Joung, J. (2006). Direct synthesis and inkjetting of silver nanocrystals toward printed electronics. *Nanotechnology*, **17**(9), 2424–2428.

Leiner, M. J. P. (1991). Luminescence chemical sensors for biomedical applications-scope and limitations. *Analytica Chimica Acta*, **255**(2), 209–222.

Lemmo, A., Rose, D., and Tisone, T. (1998). Inkjet dispensing technology: applications in drug discovery. *Current Opinion in Biotechnology*, **9**(6), 615–617.

Ligler, F., Kusterbeck, A., Ogert, K., and Wemhoff, G. (1992). Drug detection using the flow immunosensor. *Biosensor Design and Application*, 511, 73–80.

Mabrook, M. F., Pearson, C., and Petty, M. C. (2006). Inkjet-printed polymer films for the detection of organic vapors. *IEEE Sensors Journal*, **6**(6), 1435–1444.

Markgren, P., Hämäläinen, M., and Danielson, U. (2000). Kinetic analysis of the interaction between HIV-1 protease and inhibitors using optical biosensor technology. *Analytical Biochemistry*, **279**(1), 71–78.

Marvin, J. S., and Hellinga, H. W. (1998). Engineering biosensors by introducing fluorescent allosteric signal transducers: construction of a novel glucose sensor. *Journal of American Chemical Society*, **120**(1), 7–11.

Megens, M., and Prinns, M. (2005). Magnetic biochips: a new option for sensitive diagnostics. *Journal of Magnetism and Magnetic Material*, **293**, 702–708.

Miettinen, J., Pekkanen, V., Kaija, K., Mansikkamäki, P., et al. (2008). Inkjet printed system-in-package design and manufacturing. *Microelectronics J,* **39**(12), 1740–1750.

Miller P. R., Narayan, R. J., and Polsky, R. (2016). Microneedle-based sensors for medical diagnosis. *Journal of Materials Chemistry B*, **4**, 1379–1383.

Miller, P. R., Xiao, X., Brener, I., Burckel, D. B., Narayan, R., and Ronen Polsky, R. (2014). Microneedle-based transdermal sensor for on-chip potentiometric determination of K^+. *Advanced Healthcare Materials*, **3**(6), 876–881.

Moeller, K. E., Lee, K. and Kissack, J. C. (2008). Urine drug screening: practical guide for clinicians. *Mayo Clinic Proceedings,* **83**(1), 66–76.

Nishioka, G., Markey, A., and Holloway, C. (2004). Protein damage in drop-on-demand printers. *Journal of American Chemical Society*, **126**(50), 16320–16321.

Ozanich, R., Schrattenholzer, M., and Callis, J. (1992). Noninvasive determination of moisture and oil content of wheat-flour cookies: near-infrared spectroscopy in the wavelength range 700–1100 nm. *Biosensors Design and Application*, 511, 137–164.

Pandey, P. C., Pandey, G., and Narayan, R. J. (2018). A process for making microneedle-based transdermal biosensor involving polyethylenimine-modified Prussian blue gold nanohybrids-enzyme ink for on-chip electrochemical biosensing in body fluid. Indian Patent, 201811044930, November 2018.

Pandey, P. C., Tran-Minh, C., and Lantreibecq, F. (1991). Electrochemical studies on tetrathiafulvalene-tetracyanoquinodimethane modified acetylcholine/choline sensor. *Applied Biochemistry and Biotechnology*, **31**(2), 145–158.

Patel, N., Meier, S., Cammann, K., and Chemnitius, G. (2001). Screen-printed biosensors using different alcohol oxidases. *Sensors and Actuators B*, **75**, 101–110.

Ricci, F., Amine, A., Palleschi, G., and Moscone, D. (2003). Prussian blue based screen printed biosensors with improved characteristics of long-term lifetime and pH stability. *Biosensors and Bioelectronics,* **18**, 165.

Rife, J., Miller, M., Sheehan, P., Tamanaha, C., Tondra, M., and Whitman, L. (2003). Design and performance of GMR sensors for the detection of magnetic microbeads in biosensors. *Sensors and Actuators A*, **107**, 209–218.

Rizzo, M. A., Springer, G. H., Granada, B., and Piston, D. W. (2004). An improved cyan fluorescent protein variant useful for FRET. *Nature Biotechnology*, **22**(4), 445–449.

Rowe, C., Tender, L., Feldstein, M., Golden, J., et al. (1999). Array biosensor for simultaneous identification of bacterial, viral, and protein analytes. *Analytical Chemistry*, **71**(17), 3846–3852.

Rowe-Taitt, C., Golden, J., Feldstein, M., Cras, J., Hoffman, K., and Ligler, F. (2000). Array biosensor for detection of biohazards. *Biosensors and Bioelectronics*, **14**(10–11), 785–794.

Salins, L., Deo, S., and Daunert, S. (2004). Phosphate binding protein as the biorecognition element in a biosensor for phosphate. *Sensors and Actuators B: Chemical*, **97**(1), 81–89.

Saunders, R. E., Gough, J. E., and Derby, B. (2008). Delivery of human fibroblast cells by piezoelectric drop-on-demand inkjet printing. *Biomaterials*, **29**(2), 193–203.

Schuck, P. (1997). Use of surface plasmon resonance to probe the equilibrium and dynamic aspects of interactions between biological macromolecules. *Annual Review of Biophysics and Biomolecular Structure*, **26**, 541–566.

Schult, K., Katerkamp, A., Trau, D., Grawe, F., Cammann, K., and Meusel, M. (1999). Disposable optical sensor chip for medical diagnostics: new ways in bioanalysis. *Analytical Chemistry*, **71**(23), 5430–5435.

Sen, A. K., and Darabi, J. (2007). Droplet ejection performance of a monolithic thermal inkjet print head. *Journal of Micromechanics and Microengineering*, **17**(8), 1420–1427.

Setti, L., Piana, C., Bonazzi, S., Ballarin, B., Frascaro, D., Fraleoni-Morgera, A., et al. (2004). Thermal inkjet technology for the microdeposition of biological molecules as a viable route for the realization of biosensors. *Analytical Letters*, **37**(8), 1559–1570.

Sevilla, F., Kullick, T., and Scheper, T. (1994). FET sensor for lactose based on co-immobilized β-galactosidase/glucose dehydrogenase. *Biosensors and Bioelectronics*, **9**, 275–281.

Shah, J., and Wilkins, E. (2003). Electrochemical biosensors for detection of biological warfare agents. *Electroanalysis*, **15**(3), 157–167.

Shear, J. B., Fishman, H. A., Allbritton, N. L., Garigan, D., Zare, R. N., and Scheller, R. H. (1995). Single cells as biosensors for chemical separations. *Science*, **267**(5194), 74–77.

Sirringhaus, H., Kawase, T., Friend, R., Shimoda, T., et al. (2000). High-resolution inkjet printing of all-polymer transistor circuits. *Science*, **290**(5499), 2123–2126.

Sun, Y., Liu, X., Song, D., Tian, Y., Bi, S., and Zhang, H. (2007). Sensitivity enhancement of surface plasmon resonance immunosensing by antibody–antigen coupling. *Sensors and Actuators B: Chemical*, **122**(2), 469–474.

Vikesland, P. J., and Rule, K. (2008). Nanotechnology-enabled immunoassays for drinking water protection. (cover story). *Innovation*, **8**(1), 25–26.

Wang, J. (2002). Electrochemical nucleic acid biosensors. *Analytica Chimica Acta.*, **469**(1), 63–71.

Wang, J., Pamidi, P. V. A., and Park, D. S. (1996). Screen-printable sol-gel enzyme-containing carbon inks. *Analytical Chemistry*, **68**(15), 2705–2708.

Wang, J., Zheng, Z., Huck, W., and Sirringshaus, H. (2004). Polymer field effect transistors fabricated by dewetting. *Synthetic Materials*, **146**(3), 287.

Wei, H., Zhao, Y., Bi, Y., Guo, Z., et al. (2007). Direct detection of *Yersinia pestis* from the infected animal specimens by a fiber optic biosensor. *Sensors and Actuators B: Chemical*, **123**(1), 204–210.

Weigl, B., Bardell, R., and Cabrera, C. (2003). Lab-on-a-chip for drug development. *Advanced Drug Delivery Reviews*, **55**(3), 349–377.

Windmiller, R., and Wang, J. (2013). Wearable electrochemical sensors and biosensors: a review. *Electroanalysis*, **25**, 29–46.

Xu, D., Sanchez-Romaguera, V., Barbosa, S., Travis, W., de Wit, J., Swan, P., et al. (2007). Inkjet printing of polymer solutions and the role of chain entanglement. *Journals of Materials Chemistry*, **17**(46), 4902–4907.

Yoshioka, Y., and Jabbour, G. E. (2006). Desktop inkjet printer as a tool to print conducting polymers. *Synthetics Metals*, **156**(11–13), 779–783.

Zhang, Y., and Tadigadapa, S. (2004). Calorimetric biosensors with integrated microfluidics channels. *Biosensors and Bioelectronics*, **19**(12), 1733–1743.

Zhou, X., Liu, L., Hu, M., Wang, L., and Hu, J. (2002). Detection of hepatitis B virus by piezoelectric biosensor. *Journal of Pharmaceutical and Biomedical Analysis*, **27**(1–2), 341–345.

Zimmermann, S., Fienbork, D., Stoeber, B., Flounders, A.W., and Liepmann, D. (2003). A microneedle-based glucose monitor: fabricated on a wafer-level using in-device enzyme immobilization, in 12th International Conference on TRANSDUCERS, Solid-State Sensors, Actuators and Microsystems, **1**, 99–102.

CHAPTER 25
BIOMICROELECTROMECHANICAL SYSTEMS—BioMEMS TECHNOLOGIES

Teena James
Department of Biomedical Engineering and Microelectronics Research Center, New Jersey Institute of Technology, Newark, New Jersey

Manu Sebastian Mannoor
Department of Biomedical Engineering and Microelectronics Research Center, New Jersey Institute of Technology, Newark, New Jersey

Dentcho Ivanov
Microelectronics Fabrication Center, New Jersey Institute of Technology, Newark, New Jersey

25.1 INTRODUCTION

Microelectromechanical systems (MEMSs) was introduced in the late 1980s as an extension of the traditional semiconductor very-large-scale-integration (VLSI) technologies for the fabrication of integrated devices with numerous applications in communication systems, navigation systems, integrated sensors, actuators, hybrid integrated circuits (IC), and optoelectronics devices. One of the first MEMS devices with specific biomedical application has been MEMS microphones used to help people with impaired hearing. Currently, various mechanical, optical, thermal, electrochemical, and acoustoelectronics devices have been developed using MEMS technologies with applications in microsurgery, prosthesis, therapeutics, and diagnostics. The introduction of the science of miniaturization has enabled the development of devices which are commensurable with cellular and subcellular components (Fig. 25.1).

The most attractive element in MEMS technologies has always been the possibility to use the same design and microfabrication tools used in the industrial manufacturing of silicon-based integrated circuits silicon semiconductor technologies were developed during the second half of the twentieth century after the discovery of the transistor and the replacement of vacuum tubes in the consumer electronics by integrated systems. Silicon technologies have been highly optimized both financially and technically, which has made the expansion into the MEMS field fast and easy. Still using the same microfabrication techniques and cleanroom equipment as IC manufacturing industry,

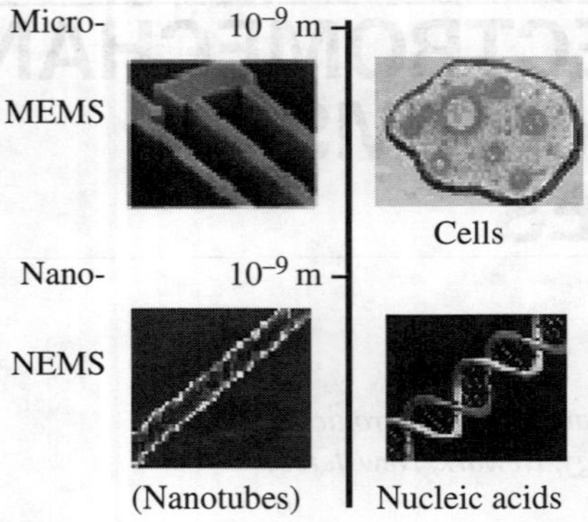

FIGURE 25.1 MEMSs are commensurable with living cells.

MEMS technologies have started developing on their own by introducing many new elements that have not been used prior by the semiconductor industry such as bulk micromachining techniques, microfluidic devices, and various substrates other than silicon such as glass, ceramics, and polymers.

In principle, silicon is not a harmful material to the human body; however, other materials that have already established a good reputation in the biomedical world as friendly to the living cells have quickly attracted the attention of the MEMS designers. The development of new MEMS techniques capable of performing bulk and surface micromachining on such materials used as basic device substrates has given a powerful push in the direction of developing a new MEMS technology with various biomedical applications—BioMEMS. BioMEMS design and microfabrication is an interdisciplinary world that changes every day by adding new techniques, design methods, and applications. The first MEMS device to be used for medical applications was the silicon micromachined disposable blood pressure sensors in the early 1970s.[1] Currently there are numerous MEMS devices such as DNA chips,[2] pumps,[3] blood glucose detectors,[4] cochlear implants,[5] blood analyzers,[6] and catheters[7–8] which have found tremendous applications in various fields of biology and medicine.

25.2 DESIGN OF BIOMEMS DEVICES

The design of integrated BioMEMS systems and arrays uses a set of computer-aided design (CAD) and simulation tools that enables using advanced models for evaluating specification, materials characteristics, biocompatibility, figures of merits through developing photolithography mask layouts, and detailed travelers for the microfabrication process (Fig. 25.2).

Because of the complexity of the devices various design phases are interconnected and cannot be processed separately. The final goal is to get a set of photolithography masks, microfabrication travelers (set of microfabrication recipes), and device substrates (wafers). This can be done only after performing all simulations, evaluations of figures of merit, choice of substrate material, and all dielectric and metal

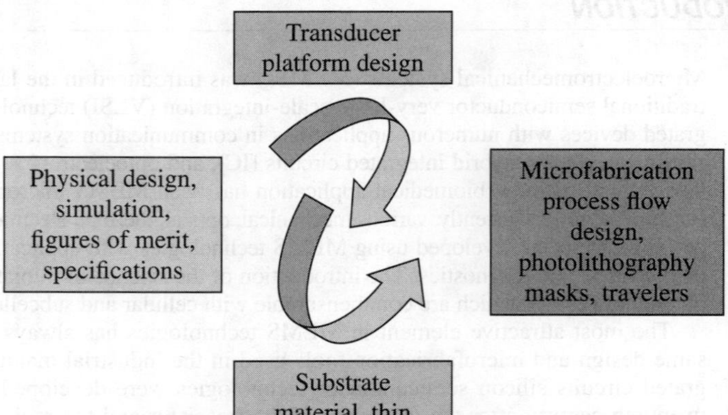

FIGURE 25.2 BioMEMS design process showing the various interconnected steps.

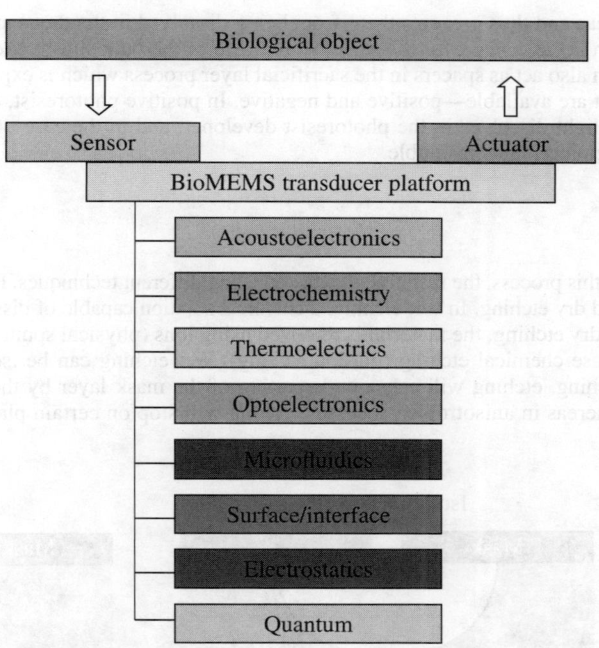

FIGURE 25.3 Transducer platforms for BioMEMS devices.

thin films involved in the fabrication process. If the BioMEMS device is a sensor or an actuator, the transducer platform that will be used is an important step of the design (Fig. 25.3).

The general design idea in many BioMEMS systems is an integrated biochip that can be fabricated using micro- or nanofabrication technologies.

25.3 MEMS PROCESS STEPS

The substrate for most of the MEMS devices is silicon. Single crystal silicon wafers are obtained from silicon boule, which is grown by techniques such as Czochralski process, float-zone process, etc. These silicon wafers undergo different processes such as photolithography, thin film deposition, oxidation, wet and dry chemical etching, diffusion, ion implantation, wafer bonding, and metallization during the development of MEMS devices.

The process steps involved in MEMS fabrication can generally be categorized as bulk and surface micromachining. Bulk micromachining consists of developing microstructures by the direct etching of bulk substrates such as single crystal silicon. These process steps enable the use of active devices and integrated circuit technology. Many complex 3D structures such as V-grooves, channels, pyramidal pits, and membranes can be formed using these techniques by utilizing the predictable anisotropic characteristics of silicon.[9] Surface micromachining involves fabrication of MEMS structures by the patterning and etching of deposited thin films on the bulk substrates.

25.3.1 Photolithography

The wafer is first coated with photoresist and then exposed to ultraviolet light through a patterned lithographic mask made of either quartz or glass. The light polymerizes the photoresist in the exposed areas and thus prevents them from being dissolved in the developer. The patterned photoresist layer can act as a mask for the selective removal of the bulk substrate or deposited thin films. Photoresist can also act as spacers in the sacrificial layer process which is explained below. Two type of photoresist are available—positive and negative. In positive photoresist, the area of the photoresist exposed to light dissolves in the photoresist developer, and in the case of negative photoresist, the exposed region remains insoluble.

25.3.2 Etching

In this process, the material is removed using different techniques. Etching is classified into wet etching and dry etching. In wet etching, a chemical solution capable of dissolving the material is used whereas in dry etching, the material is removed using ions (physical sputtering, reactive ion etching) or vapor phase chemical etching (plasma etching). Wet etching can be isotropic or anisotropic. In isotropic etching, etching will cause undercutting of the mask layer by the same distance as the etch depth, whereas in anisotropic processes etching will stop on certain planes in the substrate (Fig. 25.4).

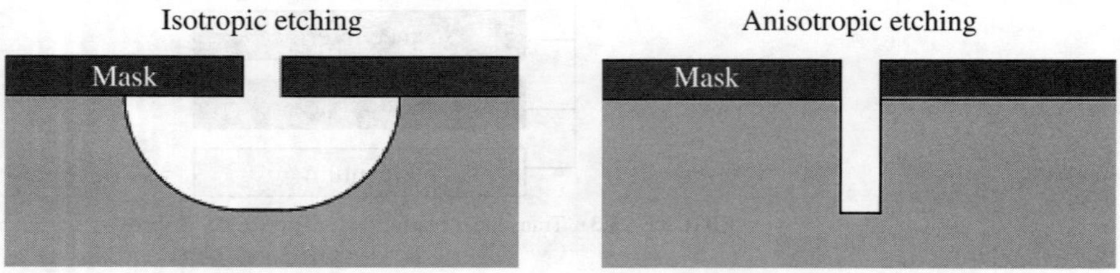

FIGURE 25.4 Isotropic and anisotropic etching.

25.3.3 Thin Film Deposition

In this process, material is added onto the substrate. Thin films such as silicon dioxide, polysilicon, silicon nitride, metals, etc. are deposited using this process. This process is categorized into chemical and physical deposition. Chemical deposition occurs as a result of a chemical reaction happening in the vapor phase leading to deposition of a solid layer of material on the substrate surface (CVD, PECVD). In physical deposition, thin films are produced by mechanical and thermal processes. The material is melted by electron beam and deposited in e-beam evaporation. In the case of sputtering, energetic ions strike the surface of the target, causing atoms to be ejected and it condenses on the substrate.

25.3.4 Structures with Sacrificial Layer

Sacrifical layer technique was developed to create partially or totally movable structures. This is done by the selective removal of underlying thin film referred as sacrificial layer and keeping the overlaying structural layer intact. Thin films of photoresist, silicon dioxide, and metals such as copper are usually used as sacrificial layers (Fig. 25.5).

For in-depth coverage of micromachining technologies, the reader is referred to *Micromachined Transducers Sourcebook* by Kovacs[10] or *Fundamentals of Microfabrication: The Science of Miniaturization* by Marc Madou.[11] The incorporation of new materials and new processes into the traditional IC fabrication techniques has allowed MEMS techniques to tremendously influence the biological and medical field. BioMEMS, in particular microfluidic devices, have made use of

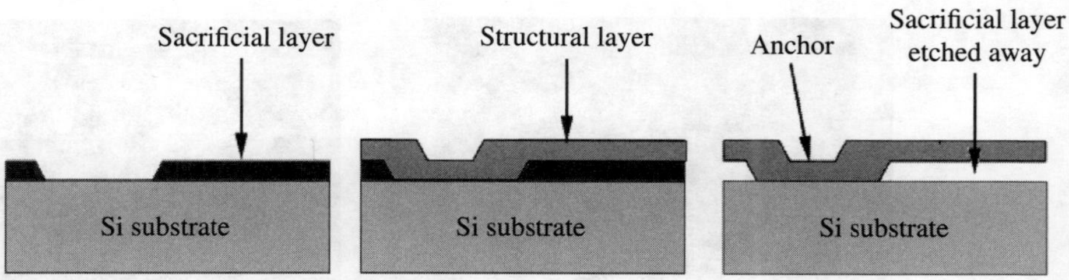

FIGURE 25.5 Patterning using sacrificial layer.

polymers and plastics as their structural and substrate layers. Typical fabrication techniques for these materials include micromolding, injection molding, and hot embossing.

Miniaturization of devices holds great promises for applications such as minimally invasive surgery with micrometer control, point-of-care diagnostics, high throughput analysis of genetic information, and autonomous therapeutic delivery. The successful development of such devices has huge impact on the health care improvement, including shortening of postsurgical recovery time, early identification of diseases, and more accessible health care delivery. The application of MEMS devices in the broad field of biomedical instrumentation is innumerable. Major applications of MEMS in the biomedical field for the purpose of this chapter has been broadly classified as

- MEMS for surgical application
- MEMS in drug delivery devices
- MEMS in bioelectric interfaces
- MEMS-based diagnostics

25.4 SURGICAL APPLICATIONS OF MEMS

This is one of the fastest growing areas as MEMS technology has the potential to improve surgical outcomes, lower risks, and help reduce cost due to miniaturization. The advent of MEMS in the surgical field has greatly modified the traditional concept of cutting and sewing of tissue. Open surgery, wherein large incisions are made in a patient's body for allowing the surgeon full access to the surgical area, is being replaced by minimally invasive procedure. Minimally invasive surgery (MIS) offers quick recovery, reduced operative pain, short hospital stays, and ultimately lower cost to the patient. In MIS procedure, the limitations are that the surgeon does not have full access to the surgical area, and therefore his view is restricted. The advances in the MEMS technology offer tools that give the surgeon more control during these procedures. MEMS devices with their small size, improved performance, and ability to interface with the existing computer systems has tremendously improved the precision and accuracy in the surgical procedures[12] (Fig. 25.6).

25.4.1 Micromachined Cutting Tools

The art of miniaturization also has other advantages such as developing miniature knives which makes smaller incision and thus causes lesser bleeding (Fig. 25.7). Silicon scalpels are more advantageous than the diamond and stainless steel blades since they can be batch fabricated and made sharper to atomic level along their crystal planes. The possibility to integrate measurement electrodes

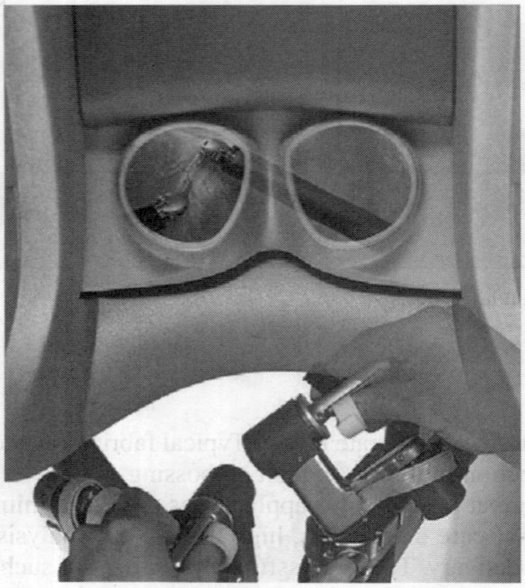

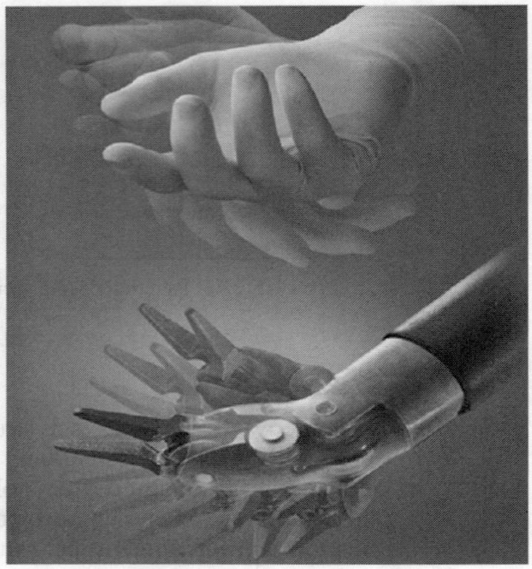

FIGURE 25.6 MEMS in surgery.[12]

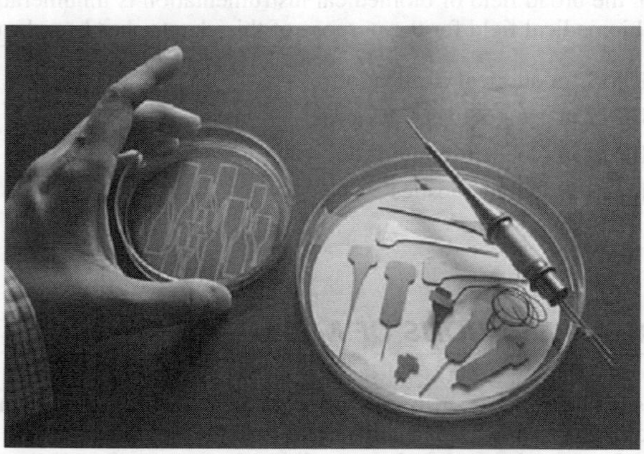

FIGURE 25.7 Micromachined cutting tools.[14]

and the related circuitry onto the same structure makes these tools more attractive. In the work done by Ruzzu et al., a MEMS rotary cutter is presented which is designed for removing sclerotic plaque inside partially occluded vessels.[13]

A surgical device called data knife was developed by Verimetra, Inc., Pittsburg, PA (Fig. 25.8). It consists of a scalpel outfitted with different strain sensors along the edges of the blade to sense the amount of force being applied. The pressure of the surrounding fluid is measured to identify the location of the tissue.

25.4.2 Eye Surgery

A good example of using MEMS technology in eye surgical devices is the ultrasonic cutting tool which is used for the removal of cataract. The tip of the cutter is resonated at ultrasonic frequencies using an attached piezoelectric material. The device can easily cut through even tough tissues like

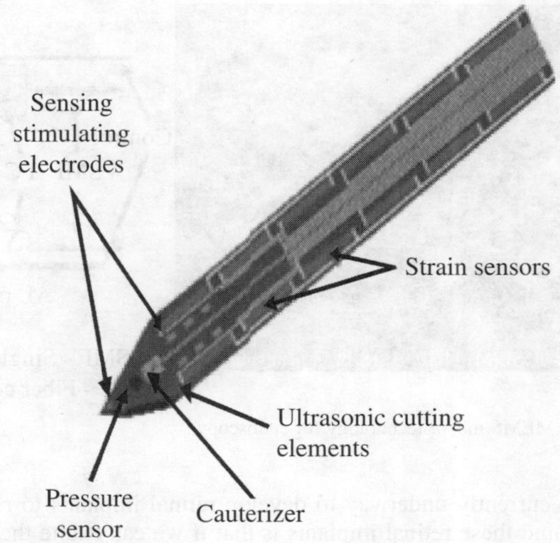

FIGURE 25.8 Data knife[42] Verimetra, Inc.

hardened lens of a cataract patient when activated.[42] The posterior capsule tissue underneath the lens is extremely delicate when compared to the crystalline lens. Therefore, a piezoelectric sensor integrated onto the phacoemulsification (cataract removal) hand piece has been developed and has undergone clinical trials.[15] This gives the surgeon a feedback on the type of tissue he is cutting and lets him differentiate between the hard and soft tissue during surgery. Precision piezoelectric micromotors for intraocular delivery of replacement lenses after cataract removal is an interesting example for a MEMS actuator as a surgical tool.[16]

Retinal Implant. Retina is the inner layer of eye which receives images formed by the lens and transmits them to the brain through the optic nerve (Fig. 25.9). It has photoreceptive cells, capable of phototransduction. In diseases such as retinitis pigmentosa and age-related macular degeneration, these retinal cells die off but the nerve cells leading the signal to the brain remains intact. Researches

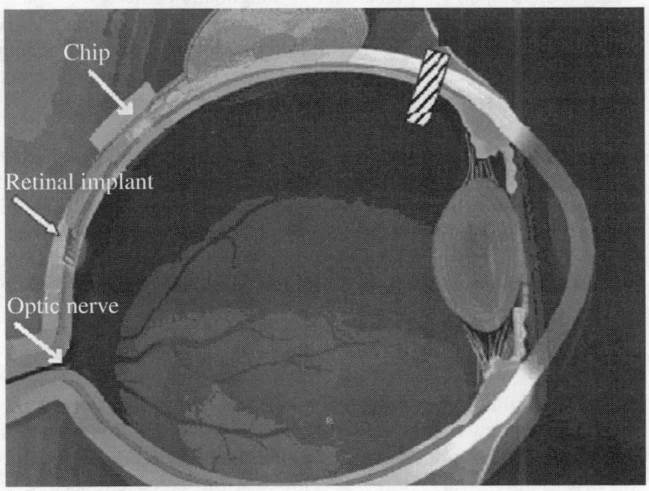

FIGURE 25.9 Retinal implant.[17]

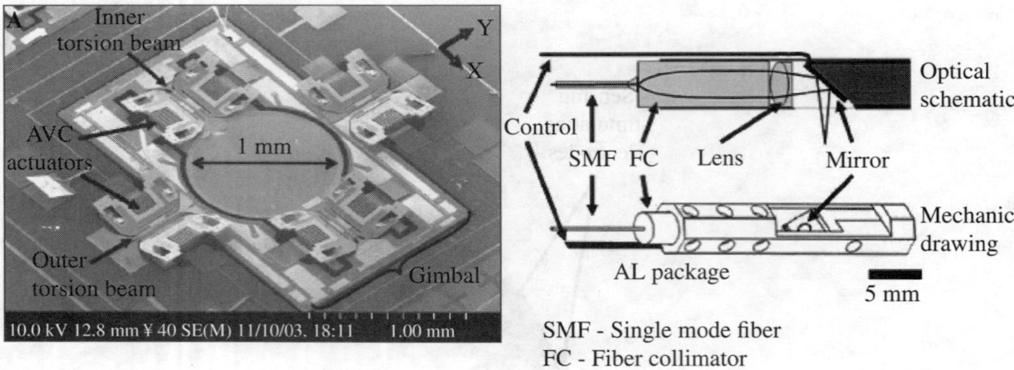

FIGURE 25.10 MEMS mirror technology for endoscopy.[24]

are currently underway to develop retinal implants to restore visions in such cases. The approach behind these retinal implants is that if we can excite the retinal nerve cells mimicking the photoreceptors, the brain will be able to process the information coming through the optic nerve as vision.

Researchers at MIT have developed such an implant which consists of a few electrodes that's implanted in the eye. The processor in the video camera attached to the patients glasses translates visual information into radio signals that are sent to a chip attached to the white of the eye. This chip in turn excites the implanted retinal electrodes wirelessly making them to stimulate appropriate ganglion cells by current pulses.[17]

25.4.3 Catheters/Stents

Medical tools for use in the human body, such as catheters and endoscopic tools, need to be small, thin, multifunctional, and of high performance. These, therefore, represent other major applications of miniaturization in surgery.[18–20] MEMS-based pressure sensors are now used on catheter devices and MEMS transducers in intravascular ultrasound imaging. Many other types of MEMS sensors to measure blood flows, pressures, temperatures, oxygen content, and chemical concentrations are also being looked upon for placement on diagnostic catheters.[21–23]

Aguirre et al.[24] describes a two-axis scanning MEMS catheter based on MEMS mirror technology for endoscopic OCT imaging (high-resolution in situ cross-sectional imaging of biological tissues). The scanner has a larger 1-mm-diameter mirror and uses angled vertical comb (AVC) actuators to produce large angle scan for high-resolution imaging (Fig. 25.10).

Active Catheter. A major limitation of the conventional catheters is that they cannot move actively and thus can only offer limited directional movements causing pain and damage for the patients. Recently, studies have been reported on the development of MEMS-based active catheters incorporated with actuating elements such as shape memory alloy or polyelectrolyte gel actuators.[25–26] Haga et al.[27] describe the development of an active bending electric endoscope using SMA microcoil actuators for intestinal use and also for inspection within the abdominal cavity.

25.4.4 Endoscopy

This is a minimally invasive procedure wherein a fiber optic tube is passed through the gastrointestinal tract to view the inside and perform procedures such as biopsies. The end of the endoscope has an objective lens and a camera and on the other end is a light delivery system.

Eric Seibel et al.[28] have developed a pill-sized endoscope called tethered capsule endoscope (Fig. 25.11A). This device consists of a single optical fiber for illumination and six fibers for collecting

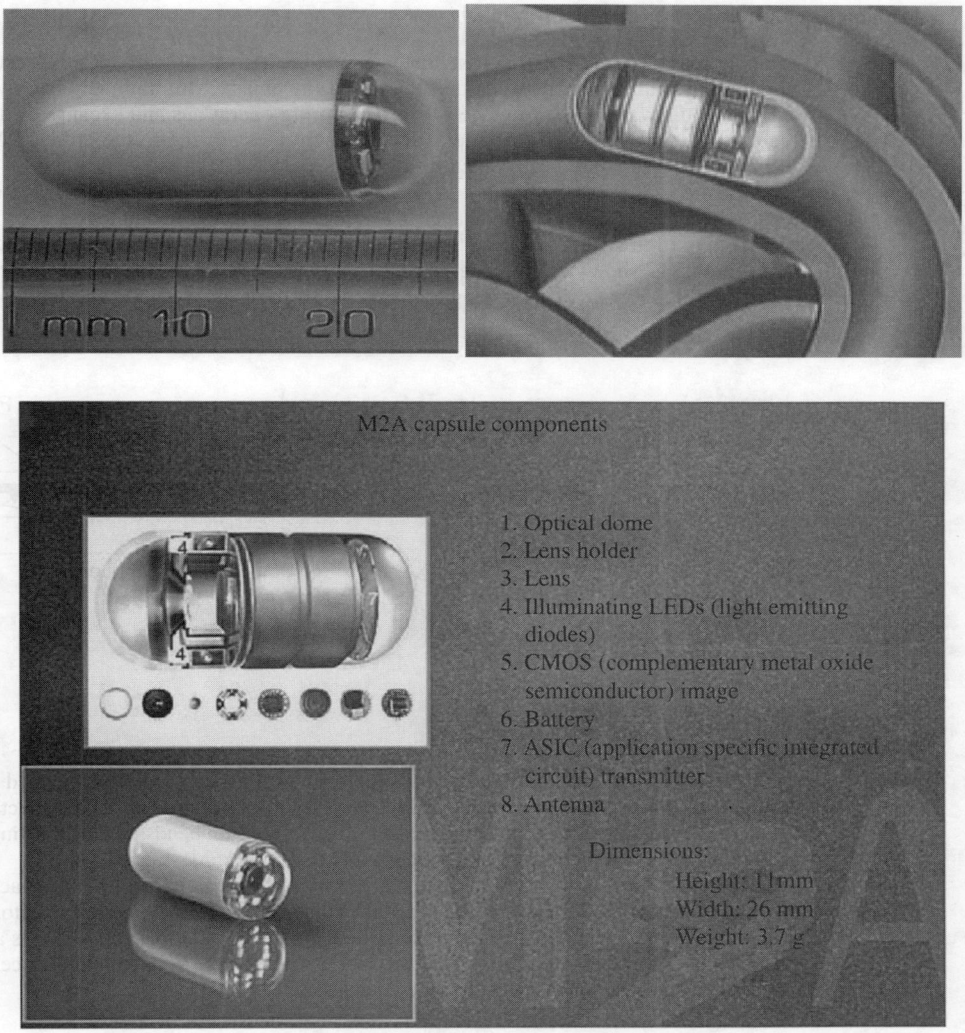

FIGURE 25.11 (A) Pill-sized endoscope,[29] (B) M2A capsule components.

light, all encased in a pill. When inside the body, an electric current flowing through the endoscope causes the fiber to bounce back and forth so that it sees the surrounding one pixel at a time. The fiber also spins and its tip projects red, green, and blue laser light. The image processing combines all this to create a 2D picture.

Given Imaging Ltd. has developed an imaging pill (M2A capsule) that moves through the gastrointestinal tract to image and diagnose conditions associated with the GI tract. It is about 26 mm long, 11 mm wide, and weighs under 4 g and contains a color video camera with a viewing angle of 140°, a wireless radiofrequency transmitter, four LED lights, and battery (Fig. 25.11B). The capsule is made of a specially sealed biocompatible material that is resistant to stomach acid and powerful digestive enzymes.[30]

25.4.5 Tactile Sensing

A tactile sensor is a device or system that can measure a given property of an object or contact event through physical contact between the sensor and the object.[31] In minimally invasive procedure, the surgeon is unaware of the force he is exerting during operations and because of the lack of tactile feedback, he is not aware of the elasticity and firmness of the tissue either.[32] MEMS offer the techniques to overcome this problem using force feedback devices.

A tactile sensor can be thought to be made of four layers: a sensing layer, an electronics layer, a protective layer, and a support layer.[33] The main transducer technologies used in these sensing elements used are piezoelectric,[34] piezoresistive,[35,36] capacitive,[37] optical,[38] and mechanical.[39]

Figure 25.12 shows a millimeter-sized sensor that can sense the magnitude and the position of an applied force, slippage of a grasping tool, and the softness of an object. The sensor is designed to be compatible with the grasper of many MIS tools, as well as to be easily fabricated by MEMS techniques. Piezoelectric poly vinylidene fluoride (PVDF) film is chosen as the transduction in the sensor. When the sensor comes in contact with a soft object, the beam bends inward, causing the PVDF film to develop an output electric charge proportional to the bending stress.[40]

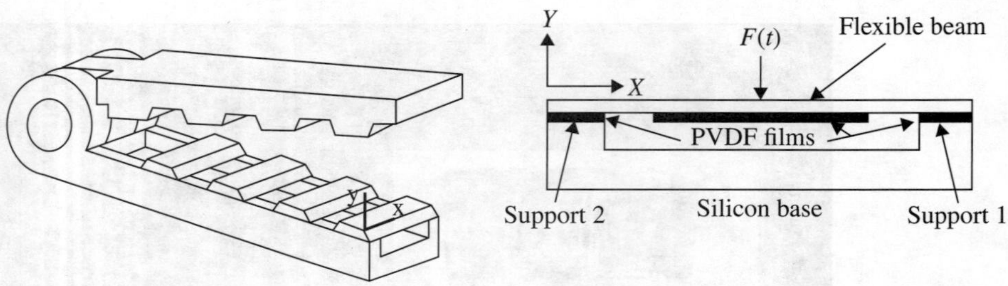

FIGURE 25.12 MEMS grasping device.[40]

Another example of this type of device is given by Chu et al. in his three-axis tactile sensor based on a differential capacitive principle.[41] In this device each tactile uses one capacitor array with four identical quadratic capacitors. Once forced, the membrane (the top electrode) tilts and deflects, and consequently, every capacitance in the array varies in response to the applied force. Thus, the force can be decoupled from these capacitance changes.

25.5 MEMS IN DRUG-DELIVERY SYSTEMS

It is well known in the fields of medicine that the therapeutic efficacy of a drug can be greatly impacted by the method by which it is delivered.[43] BioMEMS devices offer many advantages to drug-delivery systems, by providing controlled, targeted, and precise delivery of therapeutic agents along with automated or semiautomated feedback control. MEMS-based systems is, therefore, a powerful platform for delivering potent therapeutic agents and other substances, and it is a new area of study that is only beginning to be explored. The target of MEMS-based drug-delivery systems is to deliver precise quantities of drugs at the right time as close as possible to the treatment spot. There are various ways to provide a timed delivery of drugs which includes microencapsulation, transdermal patches, and implants. In the case of therapeutic applications wherein a timed delivery of drug is required, implantable devices are chosen. A microscale drug-delivery system consists of micropumps, microsensors, microfluid channels, and necessary circuitry. It is, therefore, important to discuss the approaches that are being done to develop MEMS components such as microreservoirs, micropumps, valves, and microneedles.

25.5.1 Microreservoirs

A drug depot or supply is required in order to develop drug-delivery system. For oral drug-delivery systems, Desai and team have tested reservoir-containing silicon microparticles.[44] The surfaces of these devices were functionalized with avidin linked to biotinylated lectins, and thus were designed to adhere onto specific cells in the digestive tract to deliver drugs. In the case of injectable devices, a slow dissolving cap over each reservoir fabricated from gelatin or starch, for example, could deliver therapeutic agents to cancer cells.[45]

Santini et al. developed a silicon-based MEMS device consisting of an array of microreservoirs covered with a gold membrane, each of which contained a dosage of drug that could be released separately.[46] Application of an anodic voltage to the required membrane causes electrochemical dissolution of the membrane in the presence of chloride ions. This causes the membrane to weaken and rupture, allowing the drug within the reservoir to dissolve and diffuse into the surrounding tissue. The device allows the release of potent substances in a digitized manner, such that small pulses of drug can be combined to produce a complex release profile or one with tight dosage control.[47] One major challenge in the design of the devices was that it was not possible to seal the electronics, reservoirs, etc. by conventional welding techniques as it damaged the biological compounds contained within the well. This problem has now been solved by Santini et al. by using cold-compression technique that forms an unbreakable bond to seal all the components. The microchip developed by Santini et al.[48] measured $15 \times 15 \times 1$ mm^3, and contained 100 individually addressable, 300-nL reservoirs which could be individually addressed and opened remotely (Fig. 25.13).

Nontraditional MEMS fabrication techniques and materials are also being explored to form microwell- or microreservoir-based drug-delivery devices to achieve greater biocompatibility. For

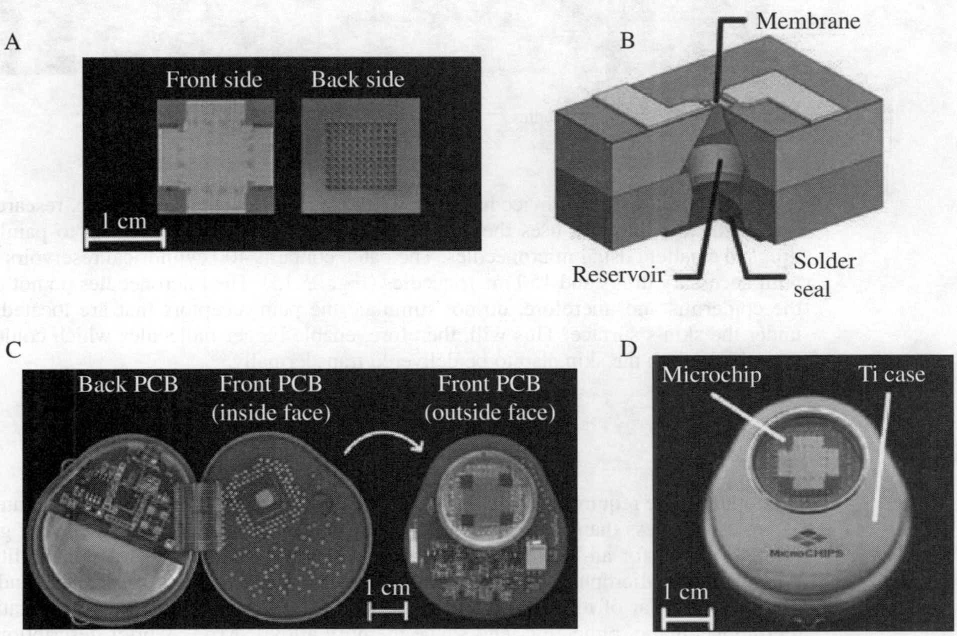

FIGURE 25.13 Microchips.[48]

example, microwells of varying sizes have been fabricated by micromolding of poly(dimethylsiloxane) (PDMS) on a photoresist-coated silicon wafer that is photolithographically patterned.[49]

25.5.2 Microneedles

Microneedles were first developed as a method for transdermal drug delivery (Fig. 25.14).[50,51] Various schemes have been proposed in this field, including microhypodermic needles, disposable arrays of microneedles for use with syringe, and solid needles to increase skin permeability for use with a transdermal patch.[52–54] The delivery of macromolecules such as oligodeoxynucleotides and ovalbumin has been demonstrated using stainless steel microprojection arrays (Macroflux, manufactured by Alza).[55,56]

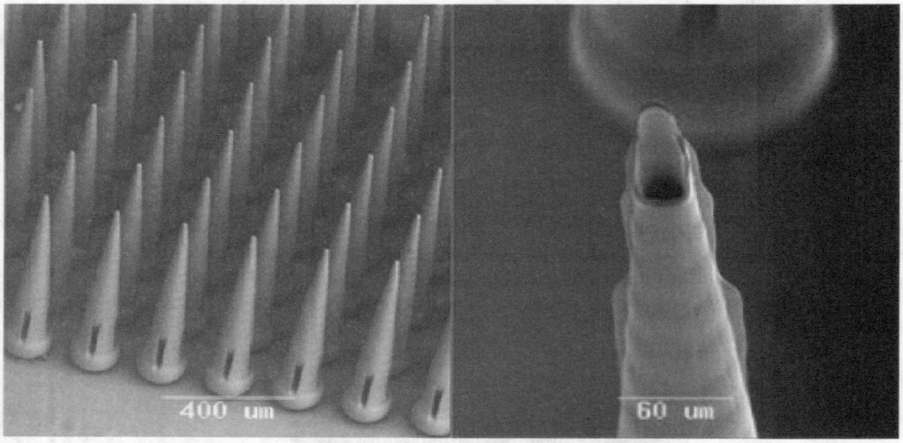

FIGURE 25.14 Microneedles.[57]

A new drug-delivery device has been developed by Hewlett-Packard Co. researchers in the form of a medical patch that uses thermal inkjet technology found in printers to painlessly administer drugs to a patient using microneedles. The patch contains 400 cylindrical reservoirs that can be filled with necessary drugs and 150 microneedles (Fig. 25.15). The microneedles do not penetrate beyond the epidermis and, therefore, do not stimulate the pain receptors that are located about 0.75 mm under the skin's surface. This will, therefore, enable bigger molecules which couldn't be absorbed directly through the skin also to be delivered transdermally.[58]

25.5.3 Micropumps

Micropumps are required in drug delivery for the fine control of fluids. The flow rates in these devices are usually less than 10 μL/min and precise metering of the therapeutics is of great importance. Design criteria for an implantable micropump include small size, biocompatibility, and sufficient pressure head. Micropumps are basically categorized into two types: mechanical and nonmechanical. The most popular of mechanical pumps applied in MEMS are, namely, electrostatic, piezoelectric, thermopneumatic, bimetallic, and shape memory alloy (SMA). A brief description of some of the actuating mechanisms used in micropumps are given below (Fig. 25.16).[60]

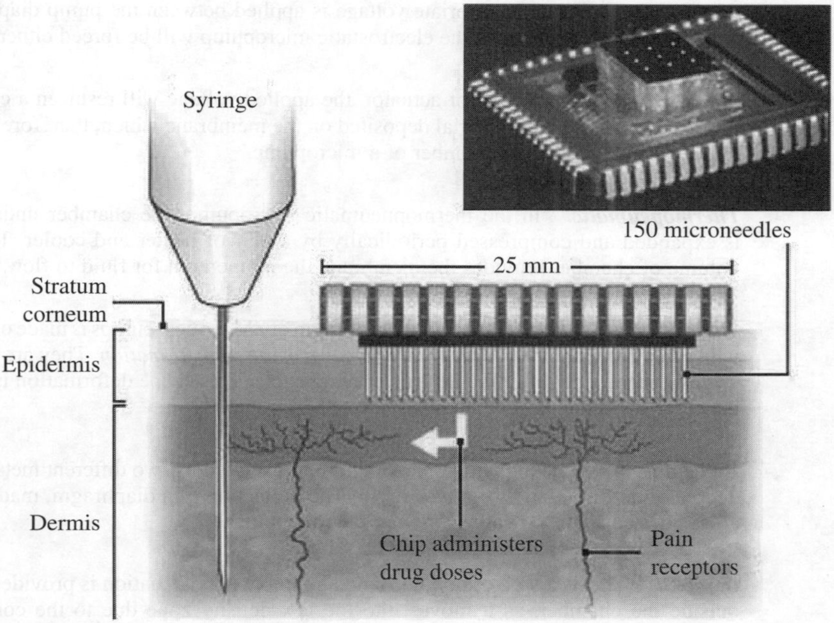

FIGURE 25.15 Microneedles from HP.[59]

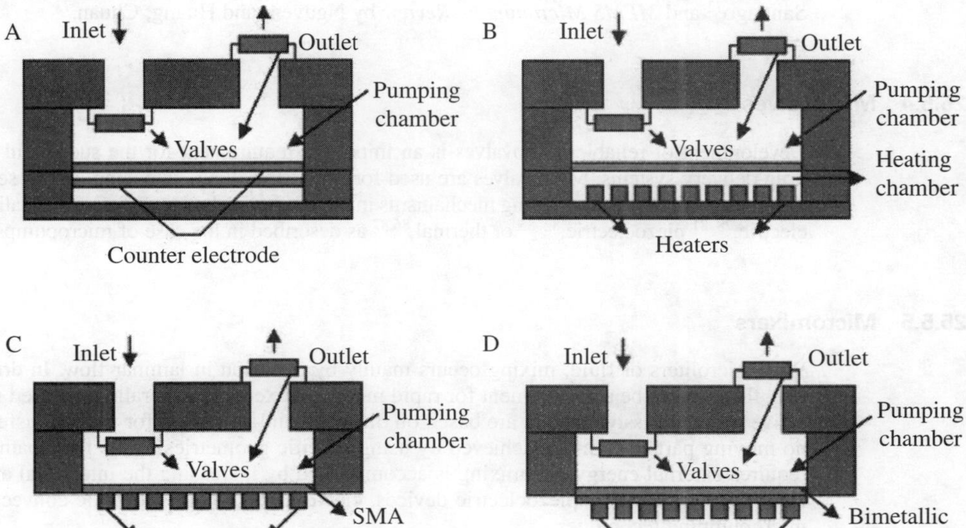

FIGURE 25.16 Different actuating mechanisms.[60]

Electrostatic. When appropriate voltage is applied between the pump diaphragm and the bottom electrode, the diaphragm of the electrostatic micropump will be forced either up or down.[61]

Piezoelectric. In this type of actuator, the applied voltage will result in a certain degree of deformation of piezoelectric material deposited on the membrane which, therefore, acts as a push plate to expel the fluid out of the chamber of a micropump.[62]

Thermopeumatic. In the thermopneumatic micropump, the chamber underneath the diaphragm is expanded and compressed periodically by a pair of heater and cooler. The periodic change in volume of chamber provides the membrane the momentum for fluid to flow.[63]

Shape Memory Alloy (SMA). The diaphragm of SMA micropumps is made of shape-memory-alloys which has the property of *thermoelastic martensitic transformation.* They are capable of restoring its original shape right after the heating/cooling cycle. This shape deformation is utilized as the actuating force upon the diaphragm of a micro-SMA pump.[64,65]

Bimetallic. A bimetallic microdiaphragm is constituted by two different metals that exhibit different degree of deformation when heated.[66,67] The deflection of a diaphragm, made of bimetallic materials is utilized as the actuating force in the micropump.

Osmotic. This is a type of nonmechanical pump where actuation is provided by the working fluid, outside the chamber, as it moves into the low-density zone due to the concentration difference. The inertia force of the moving flow directly transfers a kinetic momentum upon the actuation diaphragm.

Other micropumps have also been proposed which uses nonmechanical technique such as Lorenz force[68] electrohydrodynamic ion-drag micropump,[69] electrosmotic,[70] electrowetting,[71] etc. For further information on micropumps, the reader is referred to *A Review of Micropumps* by Laser and Santiago[72] and *MEMS Micropumps: Review* by Nguyen, and Huang, Chuan.[73]

25.5.4 Microvalves

Development of reliable microvalves is an important requirement for the successful development of drug-delivery systems. Microvalves are used for flow controlling, switching on/off, sealing of liquids, gases, or vacuums. The actuating mechanisms in the mechanical microvalves are usually magnetic,[74–77] electric,[78–81] piezoelectric,[82–85] or thermal,[86,87] as described in the case of micropumps.

25.5.5 Micromixers

With microliters of fluid, mixing occurs mainly by diffusion in laminar flow. In drug-delivery system, there might be a requirement for rapid mixing. Mixers are generally classified into passive and active mixers. Passive mixers are based on diffusion and advection for mass transfer and they have no moving parts. Mixing is achieved by using specific geometries of the fluid path. Active mixing requires external energy and mixing is accomplished by increasing the interfacial area between the fluids. This is done by piezoelectric devices, electrokinetic mixers, chaotic convections, and other micropumping techniques.

Biocompatibility of MEMS Materials. A key issue to be seriously taken into account for implantable MEMS drug-delivery devices is biocompatibility as immune system may identify them as foreign object and thus attack and destroy them. For this reason, and also due to the mechanical stress applied on tissues due to dynamics of devices such as micropumps, low-stiffness polymer MEMS has become more and more popular for these applications. Polymers such as poly(methyl methacrylate) (PMMA), poly(dimethylsiloxane) (PDMS), SU-8 photoresist, or Parylene C, has been proven to have better biocompatibility and, therefore, has the potential to be used in BioMEMS devices.[60]

25.6 BIOELECTRIC INTERFACE DEVICES

Modern patient care involves detailed measurement of bioelectric signals like electrocardiogram (ECG), electroencephalogram (EEG), and evoked potentials (EP). Efforts have been directed at miniaturizing the electrodes used to reduce the potential damage it causes to the tissues. Microelectrodes, fabricated by the micromachining technology has been shown successful in measuring impedance of nearby tissue, stimulating cells, and even for monitoring release of neurotransmitters. The microelectrode tips are usually between one-half and 5 μm in diameter, that when inserted close enough to a cell such as neuron, it can detect its individual electrical signals (Fig. 25.17).

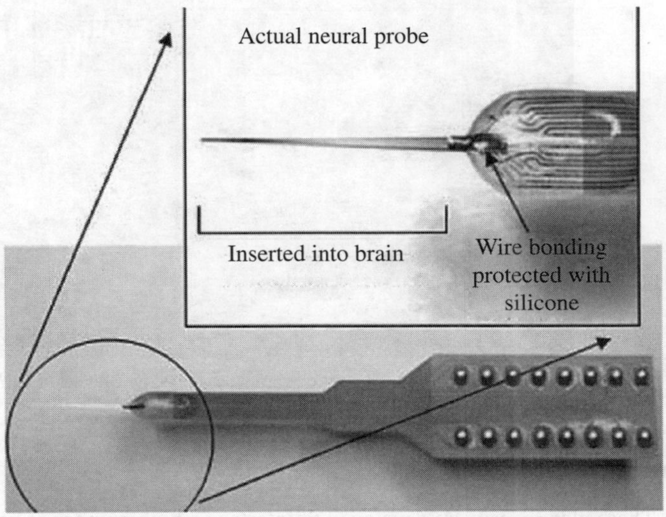

FIGURE 25.17 Penetrating electrodes developed at University of Michigan.[88] *(From Neuronexus, Inc.)*

25.6.1 Design Considerations

A neural probe, from an engineering point, is a bidirectional transducer that establishes a neurotechnical contact between a technical device and a neural structure within the body. The objective of this transducer is to record bioelectrical signals from natural sensors of the body.[88] From a biological point of view, such an interface is a foreign body. Both views have to be brought together to consider the requirements and complex aspects of biocompatibility.[89,90] Suitable devices to be used in this regard have to be biocompatible both in its structural as well as material properties.

The design has to ensure temporally stable transducer properties of the electrode–electrolyte interface throughout the lifetime of the implant. Due to the good ohmic electrode–tissue contacts, metals such as gold, platinum (Pt), platinum-iridium, tungsten, and tantalum are the best choices as materials for these devices.[91,92] Minimal energy consumption during stimulation, stable electrochemical characteristics, and stability against artifacts and noises are other factors to be considered in the choice of electrode materials.[93]

25.6.2 Microelectrode Arrays

Arrays of electrodes using silicon-glass technology have been produced with varying height from 250 to 600 μm.[94,95] A slanted array with electrodes of varying length, ranging from 0.5 to 1.5 mm with 0.1 mm difference in length between rows of neighboring electrodes (Fig. 25.18), was developed by Branner et al. to provide access to nerve fascicles.[97] Electrodes of this array were capable of selectively recording single-unit responses from mechanoreceptors. Various other design approaches have also been demonstrated for the fabrication of these microelectrode arrays.[98–103]

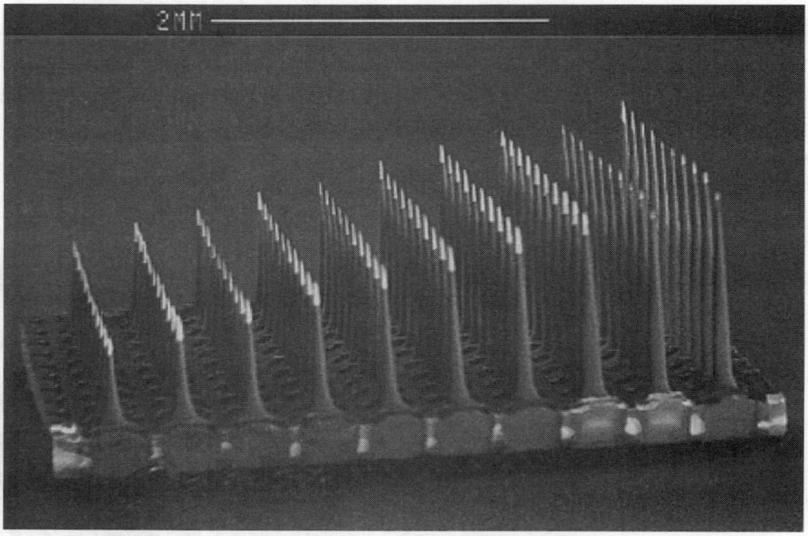

FIGURE 25.18 Slanted electrode array developed by Branner et al.[104]

25.6.3 Regenerative Electrodes

These electrodes were developed to interface a high number of nerve fibers by using an array of holes (Fig. 25.19), with electrodes built around them, implanted between the severed stumps of a peripheral nerve.[105–108]

Researches have shown that neural activity recording is possible using these multiple hole silicon arrays.[110–114] The limitation of these structures is that the size of the holes in the silicon limits the elongation of regenerating axons.[115–117] Although an ideal design-one hole for one regenerated axon is preferred (~2 μm), the failure of nerve regeneration in these small holes has led to a more optimized design wherein the diameter of holes is in the range of 40 to 65 μm (Fig. 25.20).

25.6.4 Biohybrid Sensors

In these sensors, an attempt to combine both cell culturing and technical device is made. This is done by culturing cells on the surface of microelectrode arrays, so that their physiological state can be monitored by technical recording instrument.[118] Metallic electrodes are mostly used for these sensors. Both simulation and recording of signals is possible using these sensors. These sensors can be used to monitor the reaction of cells for drug testing.

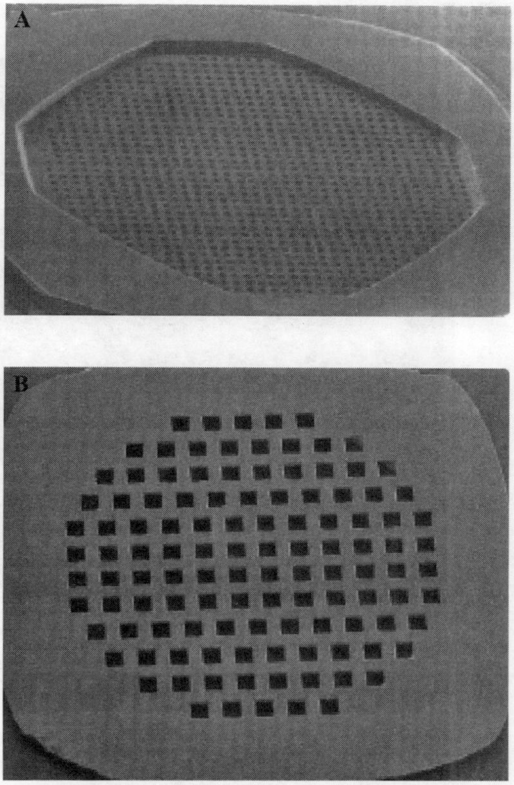

FIGURE 25.19 Multiple holes with electrode built around them for recording activity of each regenerating nerve fiber.[109]

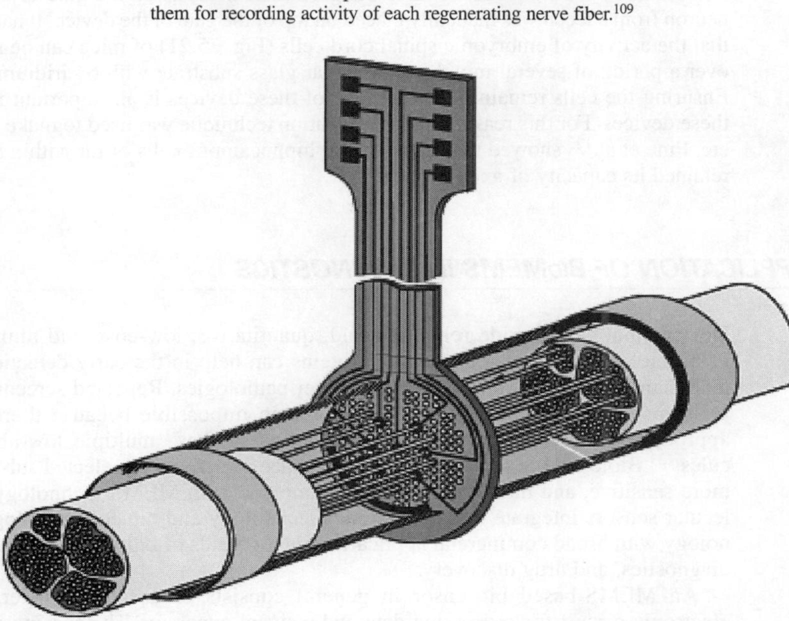

FIGURE 25.20 Concept of regenerative electrode—the nerve fibers of a sectioned nerve grow through the holes of the electrode.[88]

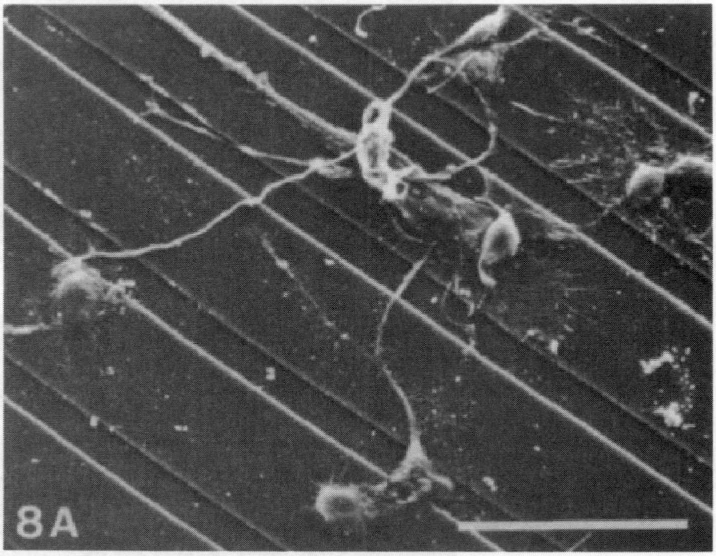

Chick embryo hemisphere neurons on poly-L-lysine-coated 8 μm grooves, separated by 20 μm ridges

FIGURE 25.21 Chick embryo on polylysine.[119]

Fromherz et al.[120] demonstrated the growth of neurons on the gate of a field-effect transistor. A neuron from a leech was manually placed on top of the gate of the device. It has also been demonstrated that the activity of embryonic spinal cord cells (Fig. 25.21) of mice can be recorded simultaneously over a period of several months on a planar glass substrate with 64 iridium tin oxide electrodes.[121] Ensuring the cells remain on the surface of these devices is an important factor for the success of these devices. For this reason, microfabrication technique was used to make 3D structures like wells, etc. Pine et al.[122] showed that transplanted hippocampus cells of rat within a 3D microcompartment retained its capacity of axon growth.

25.7 APPLICATION OF BIOMEMS IN DIAGNOSTICS

Devices that can provide reliable, rapid, quantitative, low-cost, and multichannel identification of biomolecules such as genes and proteins can help in the early detection and the treatment of malignant diseases such as cancer and other pathologies. Repeated screening of large populations for signs of such malignant diseases has been impossible because there are no contemporary approaches for reliable, quantitative detection of these multiple low-abundance protein molecules.[123] Biological tests measuring the presence or activity of selected substances become quicker, more sensitive, and more flexible when combined with MEMS technology. MEMS-based biomolecular sensors integrate microelectronics technology and molecular biology into a platform technology with broad commercial applications in the fields of biomedical research, genomics, medical diagnostics, and drug discovery.

An MEMS-based biosensor in general consists of a sensing layer, a transducer, and an electronic circuit for processing data and a signal generator. The sensing layer is a layer that will produce a signal in relation to the concentration of the specific chemical or biological agent that

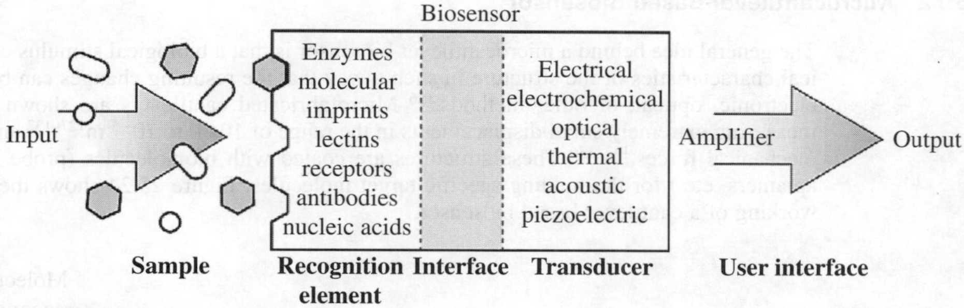

FIGURE 25.22 Schematic of a biosensor.[124]

is present in its vicinity which has to be detected. This layer can either contain bioreceptors (proteins, DNA, etc.) or be made of bioreceptors covalently attached to the transducer. The key factor that has to be considered when designing such sensing layer is that the biomolecules should be very specific to their target molecules. The presence of target molecules in the sample is converted to a measurable electronic output as it binds on to the respective probe molecules forming a probe-target complex, this signal being directly proportional to the concentration of target in the analyte. Different signal transduction mechanisms have been tested for this purpose, including optical, mechanical, electrochemical, piezoelectric, etc. A general configuration of a biosensor is shown in Fig. 25.22.

25.7.1 Optical Sensing

In these BioMEMS sensors, the output transduced signal is light. These sensors can be based on various phenomenon like optical diffraction, electrochemiluminescence, absorbance, or fluorescence of an appropriate indicator compound or resonance. In optical diffraction-based devices, a silicon wafer is coated with a protein via covalent bonds. The wafer is exposed to UV light through a photo mask, and the antibodies become inactive in the exposed regions. When the diced wafer chips are incubated in an analyte, antigen-antibody bindings are formed in the active regions, thus creating a diffraction grating. This grating produces a diffraction signal when illuminated with a light source such as a laser.[125] Surface plasmon resonance devices detect target analytes by measuring the refractive index changes that occur when a target binds to the surface of a metal-coated (generally gold) surface. Gene chip microarrays produced by Affymetrix is another example of MEMS technology used for biosensing (Fig. 25.23). A unique photolithographic manufacturing process produces these arrays with millions of DNA probes on a small glass chip.

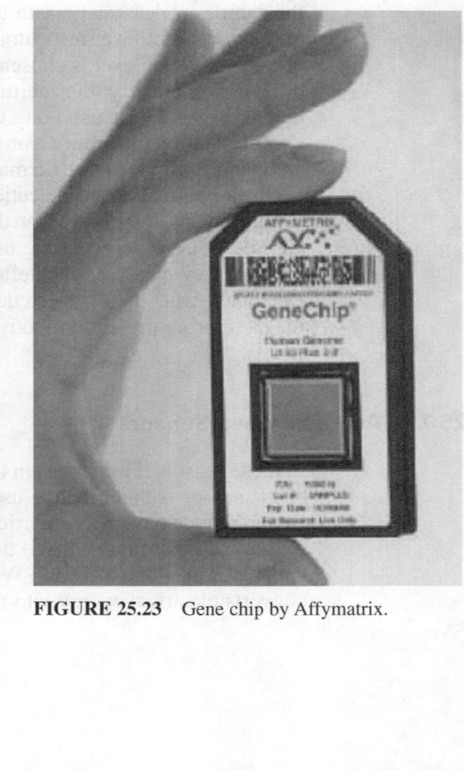

FIGURE 25.23 Gene chip by Affymatrix.

25.7.2 Microcantilever-Based Biosensor

The general idea behind a microcantilever biosensor is that a biological stimulus can affect mechanical characteristics of the structure in such a way that the resulting changes can be measured using electronic, optical, or other methods.[126] Microfabricated cantilevers are shown to be capable of measuring extremely small displacements in the range of 10^{-12} to 10^{-6} m[127–132] and extremely small mechanical forces.[133–136] These structures are coated with biomolecules (probe DNA, antibodies, aptamers, etc.) for the binding specific target molecules. Figure 25.24 shows the schematic of the working of a cantilever-based biosensor.

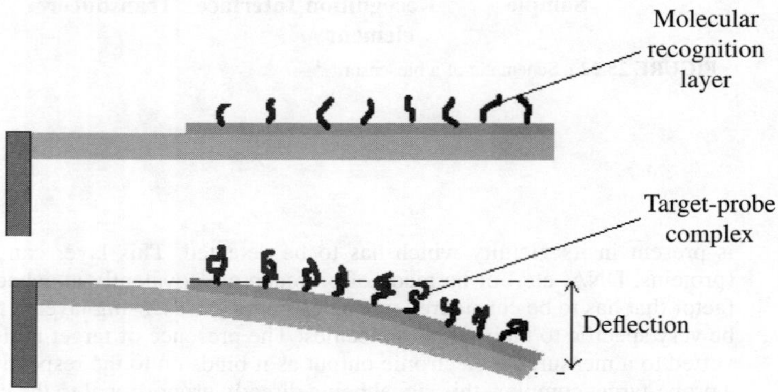

FIGURE 25.24 Schematic of the working of a cantilever-based biosensor.

Cantilever-based biosensors can operate in two modes: static and dynamic. In static mode of operation, the deflection of the cantilever structure from the original state resulting from the mass loading is used to detect the presence of analyte molecules. Several signal transduction mechanisms such as optical, peizoresistive, and capacitive methods are used to produce a measurable signal from the cantilever deformation. In the dynamic mode of operation, the changes in resonance frequency of the microcantilever resonator structures are used for the analyte detection. The structural material used for the cantilever is chosen in accordance with the type of biomolecule immobilized, the immobilization chemistry, the inertness to the environment, the mode of sensor operation, etc. Mostly metals like gold are used due to their inertness to the external environment and due to the simple immobilization procedure using the thiol chemistry.[137,138] The microcantilever resonator structures are made from piezoelectric materials.

In the optical-based detection method, a laser beam is usually focused on the free end of the cantilever and the position of the reflected beam is identified using a position-sensitive photodetector. Yoo et al.[139] reported the use of microcantilever-based biosensing for protein detection. In this method, they measured the deflection of the microcantilever using two readout methods: optical and electrical. Arntz et al.[140] also demonstrated the application of optical-readout-based microcantilever for monitoring protein-antibody recognition.

25.7.3 Acoustic Wave Sensors

In these sensors the changes in the wave properties caused by biomolecule interactions at the surface of the sensor is the principle used for transduction in these sensors. Various surface acoustic waves can propagate on a piezoelectric substrate.[141] These sensors are configured in different ways such as transverse shear mode (TSM) devices (QCM-based devices), surface acoustic wave (SAW) devices, and flexural plate wave (FPW) devices. These devices consist of a piezoelectric substrate and converts electrical energy into mechanical energy in the form of acoustic waves.

In quartz crystal microbalance, the resonant frequency f of an AT-cut quartz crystal is directly proportional to the mass loading on its surface. When the target-probe complex formation occurs on surface due to the molecular recognition layer, a mass change occurs. This is shown as a change in its resonant frequency. For a typical TSM device fabricated on quartz crystal (AT-cut) operating at 10 MHz, a mass change of 1 ng produces a frequency change of 1 Hz.

Figure 25.25 shows the configuration of a SAW device. An anisotropically etched silicon substrate holding a gold membrane coated with a ZnO piezoelectric film.[142] The SAW is stimulated by applying an AC voltage to the fingers of the interdigitated electrode on the piezoelectric crystal surface.

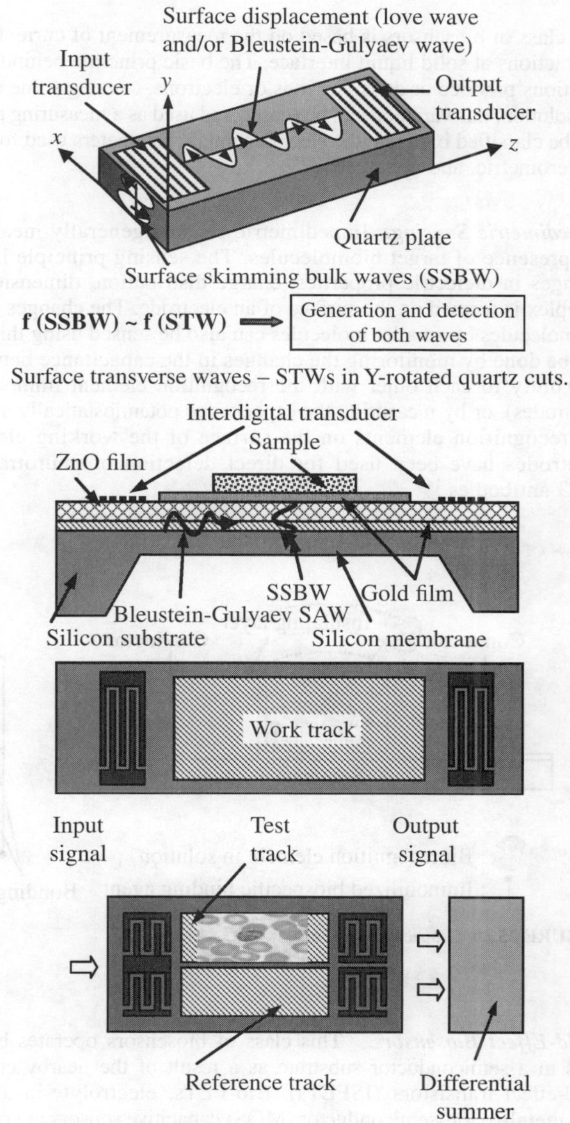

FIGURE 25.25 Setup of a differential detector using both BG and skimming waves.

Changes in the properties of the piezoelectric crystal surface due to biomolecular interaction affect the propagation of these surface acoustic waves. Bacteria colonies growing on the resonator surface can be monitored using a differential device composed by two tracks: one working and one reference track. The output signals of both tracks go to a differential summer. The reference track is covered and isolated from the surrounding so that bacteria cannot penetrate into this track, while the work track is exposed to bacteria.

25.7.4 Electrochemical Sensing

The class of biosensors is based on the measurement of current and or voltages to detect molecular interactions at solid liquid interface. The basic principle behind these sensors is that many chemical reactions produce or consume ions or electrons, causing some change in the electrical properties of the solution, this variation can be sensed and used as a measuring parameter. Electrochemical biosensors can be classified based on the electrochemical parameters used for detection purposes as impedimetric, amperometric, and voltametric.[125]

Impedimetric Sensing. Impedimetric sensors generally measure capacitance changes to detect the presence of target biomolecules. The sensing principle in capacitive sensors is based on the changes in dielectric properties, charge distribution, dimension, and shape, when a probe-target complex is formed on the surface of an electrode. The changes caused by the displacement of larger biomolecules by smaller molecules can also be sensed using this type of mechanisms.[143] Biosensing can be done by monitoring the changes in the capacitance between two metal conductors in close proximity to each other with the recognition element immobilized between them (interdigitated electrodes), or by measuring the capacitance potentiostatically at an electrode-solution interface with the recognition elements on the surface of the working electrode (Fig. 25.26). Interdigitated electrodes have been used for direct detection of neurotransmitters,[144] acetylcholine,[145] and hIgG antibodies.[146]

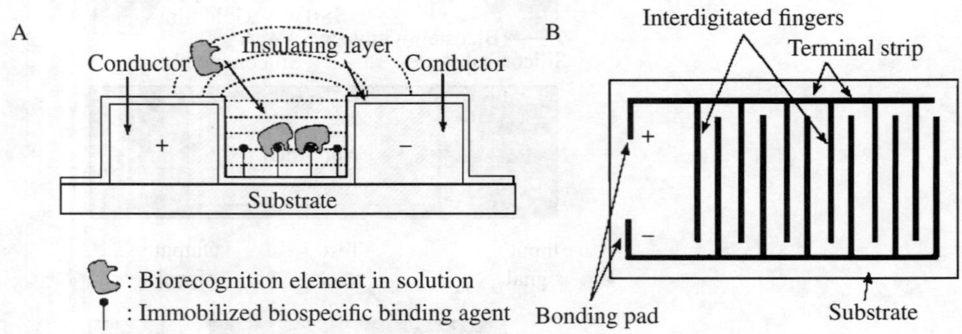

FIGURE 25.26 Capacitive biosensor.

Field-Effect Biosensors. This class of biosensors operates by the field-effect modulation of carriers in a semiconductor substrate as a result of the nearby charged biomolecules.[147] Ion-sensitive field-effect transistors (ISFETs), Bio-FETs, electrolyte-insulator-semiconductor (EIS) sensors, and metal-oxide-semiconductor (MOS) capacitive sensors are canonical examples.[148–151] Most of the experiments for detecting charged macromolecules reported in the literature with field-effect principle have used a transistor structure.[152–160]

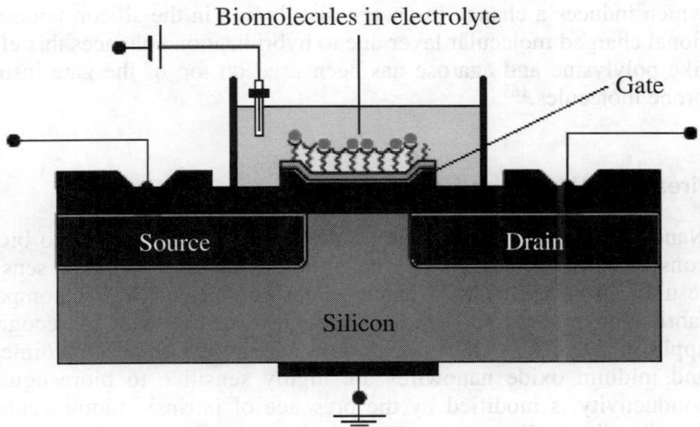

FIGURE 25.27 A field-effect-transistor-based DNA hybridization sensor.

The physical structure of a FET-type biosensor for detecting DNA and protein molecules is very similar to the MOSFET structure, and hence the operating principle can be explained based on the MOSFET operation theory (Fig. 25.27). Probe molecules are immobilized on the gate material utilizing the appropriate linking chemistries. The presence of charged macromolecules as a result of immobilization will modify the distribution of charge carriers in the channel region of the semiconductor and these changes will be visible in the I-V characteristics of the device. The addition of charged macromolecules as a result of hybridization or other biomolecular interaction will enhance this change.

Another major field-effect configuration used for biomolecular detection includes the capacitive electrolyte-insulator-semiconductor (EIS) structures (Fig. 25.28) and the metal-oxide-semiconductive (MOS) structures.[161–167] During the immobilization of DNA molecules, the intrinsic negative charge due to the phosphate backbone will effectively alter the surface potential at the gate metal (Au)

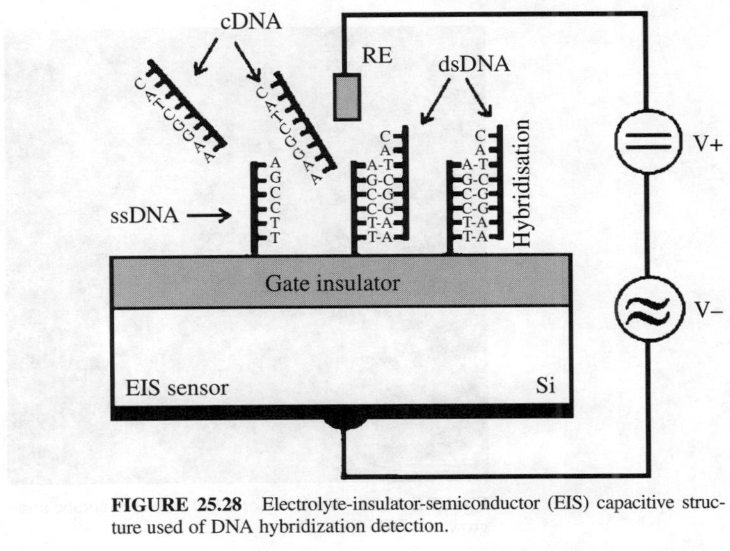

FIGURE 25.28 Electrolyte-insulator-semiconductor (EIS) capacitive structure used of DNA hybridization detection.

which induces a change in charge distribution in the silicon underneath. The presence of an additional charged molecular layer due to hybridization enhances this effect. Different biomimetic layer like polylysine and agarose has been used on top of the gate insulator for the immobilization of probe molecules.[168]

25.7.5 Nanowires and Nanotube-Based Sensors

Nanomaterials possess unique properties that are amenable to biosensing applications. They are considered to be one-dimensional structure and are extremely sensitive to electronic perturbations resulting from the charged biomolecular interactions.[169] The compatibility with the semiconductor fabrication process and readiness to functionalize with biorecognition layers are promising for applications such as DNA microarrays and protein chips. One-dimensional silicon nanowires[170–172] and inidium oxide nanowires are highly sensitive to biorecognition events as their electronic conductivity is modified by the presence of intrinsic biomolecular charges. Field sensors using functionalized silicon nanowires have been demonstrated sensitive to detect protein cancer markers with femtomolar sensitivity. Single-walled carbon nanotube (SWNT)-based field-effect transistors have proven promising for detection of biomolecules such as DNA and antibodies (Figs. 25.29 and 25.30).

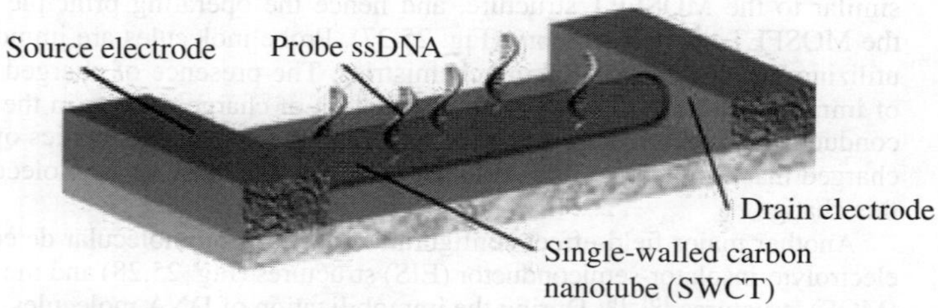

FIGURE 25.29 Carbon-nanotube-transistor-based DNA sensor.

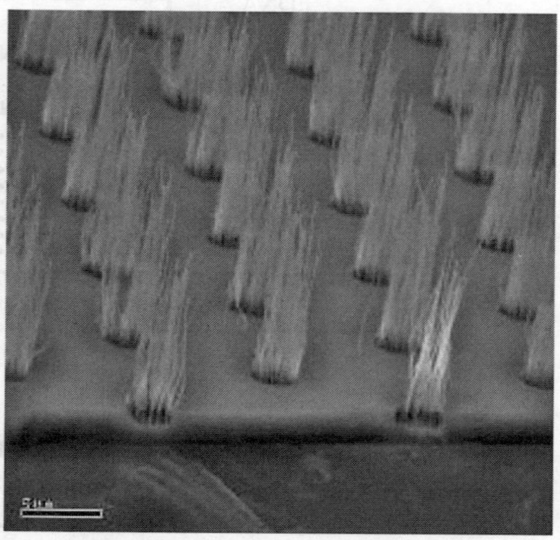

FIGURE 25.30 Vertically oriented carbon nanotube array grown by DC PECVD.

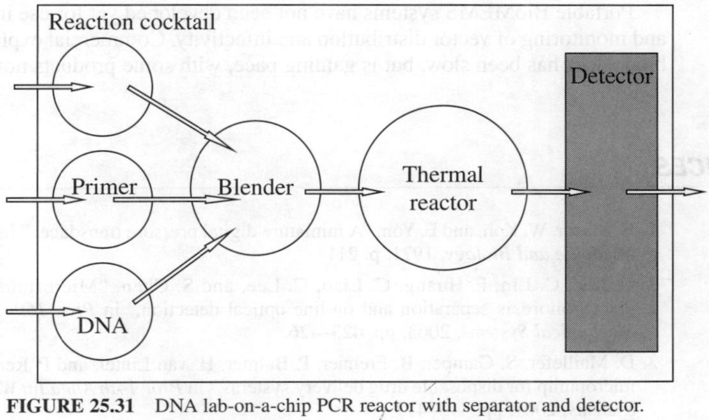

FIGURE 25.31 DNA lab-on-a-chip PCR reactor with separator and detector.

25.7.6 Lab-on-a-Chip Device

Miniaturized devices that have the ability to perform laboratory operations on small scales are known as lab-on-a-chip (LOC) devices. These devices can offer point-of-care diagnostic abilities that could revolutionize medicine. Figure 25.31 shows a schematic of such a lab-on-a-chip device for DNA analysis. These devices consist of thermal polymerase-chain-reaction (PCR) modules and numerous microfluidic channels for mixing and reproducing DNA samples for the analysis. Some MEMS manufacturers have already commercialized the whole PCR feature except the detection module, which is still at research stage. The detection module is the heart of the DNA lab-on-a-chip analyzer. Developing and integrating efficient detection modules into the PCR microfluidic system represents a challenging task.

Figure 25.32 shows protein lab chips developed by Agilent Technologies to analyze protein, DNA, and RNA in fluid samples. The analysis of the sample takes place as fluids are moving through the chip in a process called electrophoresis. The chip consists of a network of tiny channels manufactured in glass that serve as pathways for the movement of fluid samples. Fluids move as voltage gradients are created across the fluid, simulating the action of much larger valves and pumps.

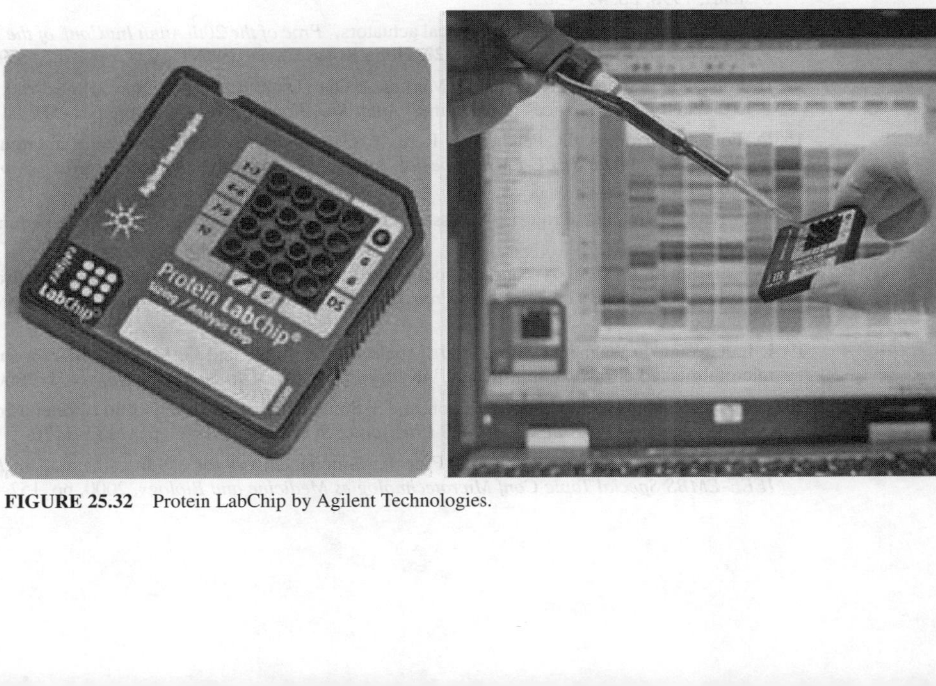

FIGURE 25.32 Protein LabChip by Agilent Technologies.

Portable BioMEMS systems have not been developed yet for use in bacterial infection diagnostics and monitoring of vector distribution and infectivity. Commercial exploitation for these MEMS-based biodevices has been slow, but is gaining pace, with some products now on the market.

REFERENCES

1. E. Blazer, W. Koh, and E. Yon, "A miniature digital pressure transducer," in *Proc 24th Annu Conf Engineering Medicine and Biology*, 1971, p. 211.
2. G. Lee, C. Lin, F. Huang, C. Liao, C. Lee, and S. Chen, "Microfluidic chips for DNA amplification, electrophoresis separation and on-line optical detection," in *Proc 16th Annu Int Workshop Micro Electro Mechanical Systems*, 2003, pp. 423–426.
3. D. Maillefer, S. Gamper, B. Frehner, P. Balmer, H. van Lintel, and P. Renaud, "A high-performance silicon micropump for disposable drug delivery systems," in *Proc 14th Annu Int Workshop Micro Electro Mechanical Systems*, 2001, pp. 413–417.
4. J. Kim, B. Kim, E. Yoon, and C. Han, "A new monolithic microbiosensor for blood analysis," in *Proc 14th Annu Int Workshop Micro Electro Mechanical Systems*, 2001, pp. 443–446.
5. K. Wise and K. Najafi, "Fully-implantable auditory prostheses: restoring hearing to the profoundly deaf," in *Int Electron Devices Meeting Dig* (IDEM'02), pp. 499–502.
6. I. Lauks, "Microfabricated biosensors and microanalytical systems for blood analysis," *Acc Chem Res*, vol. **31**, no. 5, pp. 317–324, 1998.
7. K. T. Park and M. Esashi, "An active catheter with integrated circuit for communication and control," in *Proc 12th Annu Int Workshop Micro Electro Mechanical Systems*, 1999, pp. 400–405.
8. H. Takizawa, H. Tosaka, R. Ohta, S. Kaneko, and Y. Ueda, "Development of a microfine active bending catheter equipped with MIF tactile sensors," in *Proc 12th Annu Int Workshop Micro Electro Mechanical Systems*, 1999, pp. 412–417.
9. K. E. Peterson, "Silicon as a mechanical material," *Proc of the IEEE*, vol. **70**, no. 5, 1982, pp. 420–457.
10. G. T. A. Kovacs, *Micromachined Transducers Sourcebook*, Boston, MA: McGraw-Hill, 2002.
11. Marc J. Madou, *Fundamentals of Microfabrication, the Science of Miniaturization*, CRC Press, 2002.
12. K. J. Rebello, "Applications of MEMS in surgery," *Proc IEEE*, vol. **92**, no. 1, Jan 2004.
13. A. Ruzzu, J. Fahrenberg, M. Muller, C. Rembe, and U. Wallrabe, "A cutter with rotational-speed dependent diameter for interventional catheter systems," in *Proc 11th Annu Int Workshop on Micro Electro Mechanical Systems*, 1998, pp. 499–503.
14. A. Lal, "Silicon-based ultrasonic surgical actuators," *Proc of the 20th Annu Int Conf. of the IEEE Engineering in Medicine and Biology Society*, vol. **20**, Hong Kong, China, 29 Oct. 1998, pp. 2785–2790.
15. D. Polla, A. Erdman, W. Robbins, D. Markus, J. Diaz-Diaz, R. Rizq, Y. Nam, H. T. Brickner, A. Wang, and P. Krulevitch, "Microdevices in medicine," *Annu Rev Biomed Eng*, vol. **2**, pp. 551–576, 2002.
16. D. Polla, A. Erdman, D. Peichel, R. Rizq, Y. Gao, and D. Markus "Precision micromotor for surgery," in *Proc 1st Annu Int IEEE-EMBS Special Topics Conf. Microtechnologies Medicine and Biology*, 2000, pp. 180–183.
17. The Retinal Implant Project, Accessed on April 20, 2008, http://www.rle.mit.edu/rleonline/Progress Reports/1999 16.pdf
18. A. Fleischman, R. Modi, A. Nair, G. Lockwood, and S. Roy, "Focused high frequency ultrasonic transducers for minimally invasive imaging," in *Proc 15th Annu Int Workshop on Micro Electro Mechanical Systems*, 2002, pp. 300–303.
19. I. Ladabaum, P. Wagner, C. Zanelli, J. Mould, P. Reynolds, and G. Wojcik, "Silicon substrate ringing in microfabricated ultrasonic transducers," in *Proc 2000 IEEE Ultrasonics Symp*, vol. **1**, 2000, pp. 943–946.
20. J. Zara, S. Bobbio, S. Goodwin-Johansson, and S. Smith, "Intracardiac ultrasound catheter using a micromachine (MEMS) actuator," in *Proc 1999 IEEE Ultrasonics Symp*, vol. **2**, 1999, pp. 1173–1176.
21. J. F. L. Goosen, D. Tanase, and P. J. French, "Silicon sensors for use in catheters," in *Proc 1st Annu Int IEEE-EMBS Special Topic Conf Microtechnologies Medicine and Biology*, 2000, pp. 152–155.

22. J. F. L. Goosen, P. J. French, and P. M. Sarro, "Pressure, flow, and oxygen saturation sensors on one chip for use in catheters," in *Proc 13th Annu Int Workshop on Micro Electro Mechanical Systems*, 2000, pp. 537–540.
23. Y. Haga, T. Mineta, and M. Esashi, "Active catheter, active guidewire and related sensor systems," in *Proc 5th Biannu World Automation Congress*, vol. **14**, 2002, pp. 291–296.
24. A. D. Aguirre, P. R. Hertz, Y. Chen, J. G. Fujimoto, W. Piyawattanametha, L. Fan, and M. C. Wu, "Two-axis MEMS scanning catheter for ultrahigh resolution three-dimensional and en face imaging," *Opt Express*, vol. **15**, pp. 2445–2453, 2007.
25. G. Lim, K. Minami, and M. Esashi, "Active catheter which have SMA actuator and bias spring," *Tech Digest of the 14th Sensor Symp*, Kawasaki, Japan, June 4–5, 1996, pp. 263–266.
26. Y. Haga, K. Park, and M. Esashi, "Active catheter using polymer links," *Tech Digest of the 15th Sensor Symp*, Kawasaki, Japan, June 3–4, 1997, pp. 177–180.
27. Y. Haga, T. Matsunaga, W. Makishi, K. Totsu, T. Mineta, and M. Esashi, "Minimally invasive diagnostics and treatment using micro/nano machining," *Minim Invasive Ther Allied Technol*, vol. **15**, no. 4, pp. 218–225, 2006.
28. Seibel, Eric, et al., "Tethered capsule endoscopy, a low-cost high-performance alternative technology for the screening of esophageal cancer and Barrett's esophagus," *IEEE Trans Biomed Eng*, vol. **55**, no. 3, March 2008, prepublication issue.
29. D. Panescu, "Emerging technologies. An imaging pill for gastrointestinal endoscopy," *IEEE Eng Med Biol Mag*, vol. **24**, no. 4, July–Aug, 2005.
30. D. Panescu, "An imaging pill for gastrointestinal endoscopy," *IEEE Eng Med Biol Mag,* vol. **24**, no. 4, pp. 12–14, 2005.
31. M. H. Lee and H. R. Nicholls, "Tactile sensing for mechatronics—a state-of-the-art survey," *Mechatronics*, vol. **9**, no. 1, pp. 1–31, 1999.
32. G. F. Buess, M. O. Schurr, and S. C. Fischer, "Robotics and allied technologies in endoscopic surgery," *Arch Surg*, vol. **135**, pp. 229–235, 2000.
33. M. E. H. Eltaib and J. R. Hewit, "Tactile sensing technology for minimal access surgery—a review," *Mechatronics*, vol. **13**, no. 109, pp. 1163–1177, 2003.
34. J. Darghi, "A piezoelectric tactile sensor with three sensing elements for robotic, endoscopic and prothetic applications," *Sens Actuat*, vol. **80**, no. 1, pp. 23–30, 2000.
35. V. Hatzivasiliou and S. G. Tzafestas, "Analysis and design of a new piezoresistive tactile sensor system for robotic applications," *J Intell Robot Syst*, vol. **10**, pp. 243–256, 1994.
36. W. D. Hillis, "A high-resolution imaging touch sensor," *Int J Robot Res*, vol. **1**, no. 2, pp. 33–44, 1982.
37. J. L. Novak, "Initial design and analysis of a capacitive sensor for shear and normal force measurement," in *Proc of 1989 IEEE Int Conf Robotics and Automation*, Scottsdale, Arizona, 1989, pp. 137–145.
38. A. Pugh, (ed.), *Robot sensors,* vol. **2**: *Tactile and Non-Vision*, Springer-Verlag, UK/Berlin: IFS Publications, 1986.
39. H. R. Nicholls and M. H. Lee, "A survey of robot tactile sensing technology," *Int J Robot Res*, vol. **8**, no. 3, 1989, pp. 3–30.
40. S. Sokhanvar1, M. Packirisamy, and J. Dargahi, "A multifunctional PVDF-based tactile sensor for minimally invasive surgery," *Smart Mater Struct*, vol. **16**, pp. 989–998, 2007.
41. Z. Chu, P. M. Sarro, and S. Middelhoek, "Silicon three-axial tactile sensor," *Sens Actuat*, vol. **54**, pp. 505–510, 1996.
42. K. Rebello, K. Lebouitz, and M. Migliuolo, "MEMS tactile sensors for surgical instruments," presented at the *2003 MRS Symp*, San Francisco, CA.
43. E. E. Bakken and K. Heruth, "Temporal control of drugs: an engineering perspective," *Ann NY Acad Sci*, vol. **618**, pp. 422–427, 1991.
44. A. Ahmed, C. Bonner, and T. A. Desai, "Bioadhesive microdevices for drug delivery: a feasibility study," *Biomed Microdevices*, vol. **3**, pp. 89–95, 2001.
45. F. J. Martin and C. Grove, "Microfabricated drug delivery systems: concepts to improve clinical benefit," *Biomed Microdevices*, vol. **3**, pp. 97–108, 2001.
46. J. T. Santini, M. J. Cima, and R. Langer, "A controlled-release microchip," *Nature*, vol. **397**, pp. 335–338, 1999.

47. J. T. Santini Jr., A. C. Richards, R. A. Scheidt, M. J. Cima, and R. Langer, "Microchips as controlled drug delivery devices," *Angew Chem Int Ed*, vol. **39**, pp. 2396–2407, 2000.

48. J. H. Prescott, S. Lipka, S. Baldwin, N. F. Sheppard Jr., J. M. Maloney, J. Coppeta, B. Yomtov, M. A. Staples, and J. T. Santini Jr. "Chronic, programmed polypeptide delivery from an implanted, multireservoir microchip device," *Nat Biotechnol*, vol. **24**, pp. 437–438, 2006.

49. R. J. Jackman, D. C. Duffy, E. Ostuni, N. D. Willmore, and G. M. Whitesides, "Fabricating large arrays of microwells with arbitrary dimensions and filling them using discontinuous dewetting," *Anal Chem*, vol. **70**, pp. 2280–2287, 1998.

50. S. Henry, D. V. McAllister, M. G. Allen, and M. R. Prausnitz, "Microfabricated microneedles: a novel approach to transdermal drug delivery," *J Pharm Sci*, vol. **87**, pp. 922–925, 1998.

51. S. Kaushik, A. H. Hord, D. D. Denson, D. V. McAllister, S. Smitra, M. G. Allen, and M. R. Prausnitz, "Lack of pain associated with microfabricated microneedles," *Anesth Analg*, pp. 502D–504D, 2001.

52. V. McAllister, M. G. Allen, and M. R. Prausnitz, "Microfabricated microneedles for gene and drug delivery," *Annu Rev Biomed Eng*, vol. **2**, pp. 289–313, 2000.

53. M. R. Prausnitz, "Overcoming skin's barrier: the search for effective and user-friendly drug delivery," *Diab Technol Ther*, vol. **3**, pp. 233–236, 2001.

54. S. Henry, D. V. McAllister, M. G. Allen, and M. R. Prausnitz, "Microfabricated microneedles: a novel approach to transdermal drug delivery," *J Pharm Sci*, vol. **87**, pp. 922–925, 1998.

55. W. Q. Lin, M. Cormier, A. Samiee, A. Griffin, B. Johnson, C. -L. Teng, G. E. Hardee, and P. E. Daddona, "Transdermal delivery of antisense oligonucleotides with microprojection patch (Macroflux) technology," *Pharm Res*, vol. **18**, pp. 1789–1793, 2001.

56. J. A. Matriano, M. Cormier, J. Johnson, W. A. Young, M. Buttery, K. Nyam, and P. E. Daddona, "Macroflux microprojection array patch technology: a new and efficient approach for intracutaneous immunization," *Pharm Res*, vol. **19**, pp. 63–70, 2002.

57. A. Doraiswamy, C. Jin, R. J. Narayan, P. Mageswaran, P. Mente, R. Modi, R. Auyeung, D. B. Chrisey, A. Ovsianikov, and B. Chichkov, "Two photon induced polymerization of organic-inorganic hybrid biomaterials for microstructured medical devices," *Acta Biomaterialia*, vol. **2**, no. 3, pp. 267–275, 2006.

58. Painless Drug Injections, Accessed on April 12, 2008, http://www.technologyreview.com/Biotech/19365/?a=f

59. Hewlett Packard, http://newsimg.bbc.co.uk/media/images/44125000/gif/_44125474_drug_microchip_hp_ 416.gif

60. N. C. Tsai and C. Y. Sue, "Review of MEMS-based drug delivery and dosing systems," *Sens Actuators B Phys*, vol. **134**, no. 2, pp. 555–564, 15 March 2007.

61. R. Zengerle, J. Ulrich, S. Kluge, M. Richter, and A. Richter, "A bidirectional silicon micropump," Sens *Actuators A Phys*, vol. **50**, pp. 81–86, 1995.

62. M. Koch, N. Harris, A. G. R. Evans, N. M. White, and A. Brunnschweiler, "A novel micromachined pump based on thick-film piezoelectric actuation," *Sens Actuators A Phys*, vol. **70**, pp. 98–103, 1998.

63. O. C. Jeong and S. S. Yang, "Fabrication and test of a thermopneumatic micropump with a corrugated p+ diaphragm," *Sens Actuators A Phys*, vol. **83**, pp. 249–255, 2000.

64. D. Xu, L. Wang, G. Ding, Y. Zhou, A. Yu, and B. Cai, "Characteristics and fabrication of NiTi/Si diaphragm micropump," *Sens Actuators A Phys*, vol. **93**, pp. 87–92, 2001.

65. W. L. Benard, H. Kahn, A. H. Heuer, and M. A. Huff, "A titanium–nickel shape-memory alloy actuated micropump," *International Conference on Solid-State Sensors and Actuators, Proc*, vol. **1**, pp. 361–364, 1997.

66. C. Zhan, T. Lo, L. Liu, and P. Tsien, "A silicon membrane micropump with integrated bimetallic actuator," *Chin J Electron*, vol. **5**, pp. 29–35, 1996.

67. Y. Yang, Z. Zhou, X. Ye, and X. Jiang, "Bimetallic thermally actuated micropump," *American Society of Mechanical Engineers, Dynamic Systems and Control Division*, (Publication) DSC, vol. **59**, pp. 351–354, 1996.

68. J. Jang and S. S. Lee, "Theoretical and experimental study of MHD (magnetohydrodynamic) micropump," *Sens Actuators A Phys*, vol. **80**, pp. 84–89, 2000.

69. J. Darabi, M. Rada, M. Ohadi, and J. Lawler, "Design, fabrication, and testing of an electrohydrodynamic ion-drag micropump," *J Microelectromech Syst*, vol. **11**, pp. 684–690, 2002.

70. C. H. Chen and J. G. Santiago, "A planar electroosmotic micropump," *J MEMS*, vol. **11**, pp. 672–683, 2002.

71. K. S. Yun, I. J. Cho, J. U. Bu, C. J. Kim, and E. Yoon, "A surface-tension driven micropump for low-voltage and low-power operations," *J MEMS*, vol. **11**, pp. 454–461, 2002.

72. D. J. Laser and J. G. Santiago, "A review of micropumps," *J Micromech Microeng*, vol. **14**, R35–R64, 2004.

73. N. -T. Nguyen, X. Chuan, and T. K. Huang, "MEMS-micropumps: a review," *J Fluids Eng (Transactions of the ASME)*, vol. **124**, no. 2, pp. 384–392, June 2002.

74. K. Yanagisawa, H. Kuwano, and A. Tapo, "An electromagnetically driven microvalve," *Proc Transducers '93*, pp. 102–105, 1993.

75. A. Meckes, J. Behrens, O. Kayser, W. Benecke, T. Becker, and G. Muller, "Microfluidic system for the integration and cyclic operation of gas sensors," *Sens Actuators A*, vol. **76**, pp. 478–483, 1999.

76. B. Bae, H. Kee, S. Kim, Y. Lee, T. Sim, Y. Kim, and K. Park, "In vitro experiment of the pressure regulating valve for a glaucoma implant," *J Micromech Microeng*, vol. **13**, pp. 613–619, 2003.

77. B. Bae, N. Kim, H. Kee, S. -H. Kim, Y. Lee, S. Lee, and K. Park, "Feasibility test of an electromagnetically driven valve actuator for glaucoma treatment," *J Microelectromech Syst*, vol. **11**, pp. 344–354, 2002.

78. K. Sato and M. Shikida, "An electrostatically actuated gas valve with an S-shaped film element," *J Micromech Microeng*, vol. **4**, pp. 205–209, 1994.

79. M. Shikida, K. Sato, S. Tanaka, Y. Kawamura, and Y. Fujisaki, "Electrostatically driven gas valve with high conductance," *J Microelectromech Syst*, vol. **3**, pp. 76–80, 1994.

80. C. Goll, W. Bacher, B. Bustgens, D. Maas, R. Ruprecht, and W. K. Schomburg, "An electrostatically actuated polymer microvalve equipped with a movable membrane electrode," *J Micromech Microeng*, vol. **7**, pp. 224–226, 1997.

81. J. K. Robertson and K. D. Wise, "A low pressure micromachined flow modulator," *Sens Actuators A*, vol. **71**, pp. 98–106, 1998.

82. H. Q. Li, D. C. Roberts, J. L. Steyn, K. T. Turner, O. Yaglioglu, N. W. Hagood, S. M. Spearing, and M. A. Schmidt, "Fabrication of a high frequency piezoelectric microvalve," *Sens Actuators A*, vol. **111**, pp. 51–56, 2004.

83. D. C. Roberts, H. Li, J. L. Steyn, O. Yaglioglu, and S. M. Spearing, "A piezoelectric microvalve for compact high-frequency, high-differential pressure hydraulic micropumping systems," *J Microelectromech Syst*, vol. **12**, pp. 81–92, 2003.

84. T. Rogge, Z. Rummler, and W. K. Schomburg, "Polymer micro valve with a hydraulic piezo-drive fabricated by the AMANDA process," *Sens Actuators A*, vol. **110**, 206–212, 2004.

85. P. Shao, Z. Rummler, and W. K. Schomburg, "Polymer micro piezo valve with a small dead volume," *J Micromech Microeng*, vol. **14**, pp. 305–309, 2004.

86. C. A. Rich and K. D. Wise, "A high-flow thermopneumatic microvalve with improved efficiency and integrated state sensing," *J Microelectromech Syst*, vol. **12**, pp. 201–208, 2003.

87. H. Takao, K. Miyamura, H. Ebi, M. Ashiki, K. Sawada, and K. Ishida, "A MEMS microvalve with PDMS diaphragm and two-chamber configuration of thermo-pneumatic actuator for integrated blood test system on silicon," *Sens Actuators A*, vol. **119**, pp. 468–475, 2005.

88. X. Navarro, T. B. Krueger, N. Lago, S. Micera, T. Stieglitz, and P. Dario, "A critical review of interfaces with the peripheral nervous system for the control of neuroprostheses and hybrid bionic systems," *J Peripher Nerv Syst*, vol. **10**, no. 3, pp. 229–258, 2005.

89. P. Heiduschka and S. Thanos, "Implantable bioelectronic interfaces for lost nerve functions," *Prog Neurobiol*, vol. **55**, pp. 433–461, 1998.

90. T. Stieglitz, "Considerations on surface and structural biocompatibility as prerequisite for long-term stability of neural prostheses," *J Nanosci Nanotechnol*, vol. **4**, pp. 496–503, 2004.

91. L. A. Geddes and R. Roeder, "Measurement of the direct-current (faradic) resistance of the electrode-electrolyte interface for commonly used electrode materials," *Ann Biomed Eng*, vol. **29**, pp. 181–186, 2001.

92. L. A. Geddes and R. Roeder, "Criteria for the selection of materials for implanted electrodes," *Ann Biomed Eng*, vol. **31**, pp. 879–890, 2003.

93. T. Stieglitz and J. U. Meyer, "Microtechnical interfaces to neurons," *Microsyst Technol Chem Life Sci*, pp. 131–162, 1997.

94. W. L. C. Rutten, J. P. A. Smit, T. H. Rozijn, and J. H. Meier, "3D neuro-electronic interface devices for neuromuscular control: design studies and realization steps," *Biosens Bioelectron*, vol. **10**, pp. 141–153, 1995.

95. W. L. C. Rutten, J. P. A. Smit, T. A. Frieswijk, J. A. Bielen, A. L. H. Brouwer, J. R. Buitenweg, and C. Heida, "Neuro-electronic interfacing with multielectrode arrays," *IEEE Eng Med Biol Mag*, vol. **18**, pp. 47–55, 1999.

96. W. L. C. Rutten, "Selective electrical interfaces with the nervous system," *Ann Rev Biomed Eng*, vol. **4**, pp. 407–452, 2002.

97. A. Branner, R. B. Stein, and R. A. Normann, "Selective stimulation of cat sciatic nerve using an array of varying-length microelectrodes," *J Neurophysiol*, vol. **85**, pp. 1585–1594, 2001.

98. K. L. Drake, K. D. Wise, J. Farraye, D. J. Anderson, and S. L. BeMent, "Performance of planar multisite microprobes in recording extracellular single-unit intracortical activity," *IEEE Trans Biomed Eng*, vol. **35**, pp. 719–732, 1988.

99. W. Ehrfeld and D. Munchmeyer, "LIGA method, three dimensional microfabrication using synchrotron radiation," *Nucl Instrum Methods Phys Res A*, vol. **303**, pp. 523–531, 1991.

100. R. A. Normann, E. M. Maynard, P. J. Rousche, and D. J. Warren, "A neural interface for a cortical vision prosthesis," *Vision Res*, vol. **12**, pp. 2577–2587, 1998.

101. T. H. Yoon, E. J. Hwang, D. Y. Shin, S. I. Park, S. J. Oh, S. C. Jung, H. C. Shin, et al., "A micromachined silicon depth probe for multichannel neural recording," *IEEE Trans Biomed Eng*, vol. **47**, pp. 1082–1087, 2000.

102. T. Stieglitz and M. Gross, "Flexible BIOMEMS with electrode arrangements on front and back side as key component in neural prostheses and biohybrid systems," *Sens Actuators B*, vol. **12**, pp. 1–7, 2002.

103. S. Takeuchi, T. Suzuki, K. Mabuchi, and H. Fujita, "3D flexible multichannel neural probe array," *J Micromech Microeng*, vol. **14**, pp. 104–107, 2004.

104. A. Branner, R. B. Stein, and R. A. Normann, "Selective stimulation of cat sciatic nerve using an array of varying-length microelectrodes," *J Neurophysiol*, vol. **85**, pp. 1585–1594, 2001.

105. R. Llinás, C. Nicholson, and K. Johnson, "Implantable monolithic wafer recording electrodes for neurophysiology," In: *Brain Unit Activity During Behaviour*. Phillips M. I. (ed.), Springfield, IL: Charles C. Thomas., pp. 105–110, 1973.

106. D. J. Edell, "A peripheral nerve information transducer for amputees: long-term multichannel recordings from rabbit peripheral nerves," *IEEE Trans Biomed Eng*, vol. **33**, pp. 203–214, 1986.

107. G. T. A. Kovacs, C. W. Storment, and J. M. Rosen, "Regeneration microelectrode array for peripheral nerve recording and stimulation," *IEEE Trans Biomed Eng*, vol. **39**, pp. 893–902, 1992.

108. P. Dario, P. Garzella, M. Toro, S. Micera, M. Alavi, U. Meyer, E. Valderrama, et al., "Neural interfaces for regenerated nerve stimulation and recording," *IEEE Trans Rehabil Eng*, vol. **6**, pp. 353–363, 1998.

109. L. Wallman, Y. Zhang, T. Laurell, and N. Danielsen, "The geometric design of micromachined silicon sieve electrodes influences functional nerve regeneration," *Biomaterials*, vol. **22**, pp. 1187–1193, 2001.

110. G. T. A. Kovacs, C. W. Storment, M. Halks-Miller, C. R. Belczynski, C. C. Della Santina, E. R. Lewis, and N. I. Maluf, "Silicon-substrate microelectrode array for parallel recording of neural activity in peripheral and cranial nerves," *IEEE Trans Biomed Eng*, vol. **41**, pp. 567–577, 1994.

111. X. Navarro, S. Calvet, M. Butí, N. Gómez, E. Cabruja, P. Garrido, R. Villa, and E. Valderrama, "Peripheral nerve regeneration through microelectrode arrays based on silicon technology," *Restor Neurol Neurosci*, vol. **9**, pp. 151–160, 1996.

112. R. M. Bradley, X. Cao, T. Akin, and K. Najafi, "Long term chronic recordings from peripheral sensory fibers using a sieve electrode array," *J Neurosci Methods*, vol. **73**, pp. 177–186, 1997.

113. C. C. Della Santina, G. T. A. Kovacs, and E. R. Lewis, "Multi-unit recording from regenerated bullfrog eighth nerve using implantable silicon-substrate microelectrodes," *J Neurosci Methods*, vol. **72**, pp. 71–86, 1997.

114. A. F. Mensinger, D. J. Anderson, C. J. Buchko, M. A. Johnson, D. C. Martin, P. A. Tresco, R. B. Silver, and S. M. Highstein, "Chronic recording of regenerating VIIIth nerve axons with a sieve electrode," *J Neurophysiol*, vol. **83**, pp. 611–615, 2000.

115. D. J. Edell, "A peripheral nerve information transducer for amputees: long-term multichannel recordings from rabbit peripheral nerves," *IEEE Trans Biomed Eng*, vol. **33**, pp. 203–214, 1986.

116. J. M. Rosen, M. Grosser, and V. R. Hentz, "Preliminary experiments in nerve regeneration through laser-drilled holes in silicon chips," *Restor Neurol Neurosci*, vol. **2**, pp. 89–102, 1990.

117. Q. Zhao, J. Drott, T. Laurell, L. Wallman, K. Lindström, L. M. Bjursten, G. Lundborg, L. Montelius, and N. Danielsen, "Rat sciatic nerve regeneration through a micromachined silicon chip," *Biomaterials*, vol. **18**, pp. 75–80, 1997.

118. C. A. Thomas Jr., P. A. Springer, G. E. Loeb, Y. Berwald-Netter, and L. M. Okun, "A miniature microelectrode array to monitor the bioelectric activity of cultured cells," *Exp Cell Res*, vol. **74**, pp. 61–66, 1972.

119. P. Clark, P. Connolly, A. S. G. Curtis, J. A. T. Dow, and C. D. W Wilkinson, "Topographical control of cell behaviour: II. Multiple grooved substrata," *Development*, vol. **108**, pp. 635–644, 1990.

120. P. Fromherz, H. Schaden, and T. Vetter, "Guided outgrowth of leech neurons in culture," *Neurosci Lett*, vol. **129**, pp. 77–80, 1991b.

121. M. H. Droge, G. W. Gross, M. H. Hightower, and L. E. Czisny, "Multielectrode analysis of coordinated, multisite, rhythmic bursting in cultured CNS monolayer networks," *J Neurosci*, vol. **6**, pp. 1583–1592, 1986.

122. J. Pine, Y.-C. Tai, G. Buzsaki, A. Bragin, and D. Carpi, The cultured neuron probe. Quarterly Progress Report, NIH-NINDS, Neural Prosthesis Program No. 4, NO1-NS-3-2393.

123. M. M. Cheng, G. Cuda, Y. L. Bunimovich, M. Gaspari, J. R. Heath, H. D. Hill, et al., "Nanotechnologies for biomolecular detection and medical diagnostics," *Curr Opin Chem Biol*, vol. **10**, pp. 11–19, 2006.

124. J. P. Chambers, B. P. Arulanandam, L. L. Matta, A. Weis, and J. J. Valdes, "Biosensor Recognition Elements," *Curr Issues Mol Biol*, vol. **10**, pp. 1–12.

125. S. P. Mohanty and E. Kougianos, "Biosensors: a tutorial review," *IEEE, Potentials* vol. **25**, no. 2, pp. 35–40, March–April 2006.

126. N. V. Lavrik, M. J. Sepaniak, and P. G. Datskos, "Cantilever transducers as a platform for chemical and biological sensors," *Rev Sci Instrum*, vol. **75**, no. 7, July 2004.

127. H. J. Butt, R. Berger, E. Bonaccurso, Y. Chen, and J. Wang, "Impact of atomic force microscopy on interface and colloid science," *J Colloid Interface Sci*, vol. **133**, pp. 91–104, 2007.

128. J. Samuel, C. J. Brinker, L. J. D. Frink, and F. van Swol, *Langmuir*, vol. **14**, p. 2602, 1998.

129. L. J. D. Frink and F. van Swol, *Colloids Surf*, ser. A, vol. **162**, p. 25, 2000.

130. J. E. Sader, *J Appl Phys*, vol. **91**, p. 9354, 2002.

131. J. E. Sader, *J Appl Phys*, vol. **89**, p. 2911, 2001.

132. M. Godin, V. Tabard-Cossa, P. Grutter, and P. Williams, *Appl Phys Lett*, vol. **79**, p. 551, 2001.

133. K. J. Bruland, J. L. Garbini, W. M. Dougherty, and J. A. Sidles, *J Appl Phys*, vol. **83**, p. 3972, 1998.

134. D. Rugar, C. S. Yannoni, and J. A. Sidles, *Nature*, London, vol. **360**, p. 563, 1992.

135. H. J. Mamin and D. Rugar, *Appl Phys Lett*, vol. **79**, p. 3358, 2001.

136. P. Streckeisen, S. Rast, C. Wattinger, E. Meyer, P. Vettiger, C. Gerber, and H. J. Guntherodt, *Appl Phys A Mater Sci Process*, vol. **66**, S341, 1998.

137. J. Fritz, M. K. Baller, H. P. Lang, T. Strunz, E. Meyer, H. J. Guntherodt, E. Delamarche, C. Gerber, and J. K. Gimzewski, *Langmuir*, vol. **16**, p. 9694, 2001.

138. J. Fritz, M. K. Baller, H. P. Lang, H. Rothuizen, P. Vettiger, E. Meyer, H. J. Guntherodt, C. Gerber, and J. K. Gimzewski, *Science*, vol. **288**, p. 316, 2000.

139. K. A. Yoo, J. H. Kim, B. H. Nahm, C. J. Kang, and Y. S. Kim, *Journal of Physics: Conference*, Ser 61, pp. 1308–1311, 2007.

140. Y. Arntz, J. D. Seelig, H. P. Lang, J. Zhang, P. Hunziker, J. P. Ramseyer, E. Meyer, M. Hegner, and C. Gerber, *Nanotechnol*, vol. **14**, no. 1, pp. 86–90, 2003.

141. Y. V. Gulyaev, *IEEE Trans On Ultrasonics, Ferroelectrics, and Frequency Control*, vol. **45**, pp. 935–942, 1998.

142. D. Ivanov, "BioMEMS sensor system for bacterial infection detection," *BioDrug*, vol. **20**, no. 6, pp. 351–356, 2006.

143. E. Souteyrand, J. P. Cloarec, J. R. Martin, C. Wilson, I. Lawrence, S. Mikkelson, and M. F. Lawrence, "Direct detection of the hybridization of synthetic homo-oligomer DNA sequences by field effect," *J Phys Chem B*, vol. **101**, pp. 2980–2985, 1997.

144. Y. Han, A. Offenhäusser, and S. Ingebrandt, "Detection of DNA hybridization by a field-effect transistor with covalently attached catcher molecules," *Surf Interf Anal*, vol. **38**, pp. 176–181, 2006.

145. F. Pouthas, C. Gentil, D. Cote, and U. Bockelmann, "DNA detection on transistor arrays following mutation-specific enzymatic amplification," *Appl Phys Lett*, vol. **84**, pp. 1594–1596, 2004.

146. M. W. Dashiell, A. T. Kalambur, R. Leeson, K. J. Roe, J. F. Rabolt, and J. Kolodzey, in: *Proc. IEEE Lester Eastman Conference*, pp. 259–264, Delaware, 2002.

147. M. J. Schoning, A. Pogossian. "Bio FEDs (field-effect devices): state-of-the-art and new directions," *Electroanalysis*, vol. **18**, pp. 1983, 2006.

148. P. Estrela, A. G. Stewart, F. Yan, and P. Migliorato, "Field effect detection of biomolecular interactions," *Electrochemica Acta*, vol. **50**, pp. 4995–5000, 2005.

149. G. Xuan, J. Kolodzey, V. Kapoor, and G. Gonye, *Appl. Phys. Lett.*, vol. **87**, p. 103903, 2005.

150. A. Poghossian, A. Cherstvy, S. Ingebrandt, A. Offenhausser, and M. J. Schoning, *Sens Actuators B Chem*, vol. **11**, pp. 470–480, 2005.

151. A. Poghossian, S. Ingebrandt, M. H. Abouzar, and M. J. Schoning, "Label-free detection of charged macromolecules by using a field-effect-based sensor platform: experiments and possible mechanisms of signal generation," *Appl Phys A*, vol. **87**, pp. 517–524, 2007.

152. E. Souteyrand, J. P. Cloarec, J. R. Martin, C. Wilson, I. Lawrence, S. Mikkelson, and M. F. Lawrence, "Direct detection of the hybridization of synthetic homo-oligomer DNA sequences by field effect," *J Phys Chem B*, vol. **101**, pp. 2980–2985, 1997.

153. F. Uslu, S. Ingebrandt, D. Mayer, S. Böcker-Meffert, M. Odenthal, and A. Offenhäusser, "Labelfree fully electronic nucleic acid detection system based on a field-effect transistor device," *Biosens Bioelectron*, vol. **19**, pp. 1723–1731, 2004.

154. Y. Han, A. Offenhäusser, and S. Ingebrandt, "Detection of DNA hybridization by a field-effect transistor with covalently attached catcher molecules," *Surf Interf Anal*, vol. **38**, pp. 176–181, 2006.

155. F. Pouthas, C. Gentil, D. Cote, and U. Bockelmann, "DNA detection on transistor arrays following mutation-specific enzymatic amplification," *Appl Phys Lett*, vol. **84**, pp. 1594–1596, 2004.

156. M. W. Dashiell, A. T. Kalambur, R. Leeson, K. J. Roe, J. F. Rabolt, and J. Kolodzey, in: *Proc IEEE Lester Eastman Conference*, pp. 259–264, Delaware, 2002.

157. D. -S. Kim, Y. -T. Jeong, H. -K. Lyu, H. -J. Park, H. S. Kim, J. -K. Shin, P. Choi, J. -H. Lee, G. Lim, and M. Ishida, "Field effect transistor-based bimolecular sensor employing a Pt reference electrode for the detection of deoxyribonucleic acid sequence," *Jpn J Appl Phys*, vol. **43**, pp. 3855–3859, 2004.

158. J. -K. Shin, D. -S. Kim, H. -J. Park, and G. Lim, , "Detection of DNA and protein molecules using an FET-type biosensor with gold as a gate metal," *Electroanalysis*, vol. **16**, pp. 1912–1918, 2004.

159. D. -S. Kim, Y. -T. Jeong, H. -K. Lyu, H. -J. Park, J. -K. Shin, P. Choi, J. -H. Lee, and G. Lim, "An FET-type charge sensor for highly sensitive detection of DNA sequence," *Biosens Bioelectron*, vol. **20**, pp. 69–74, 2004.

160. D. -S. Kim, H. -J. Park, H. -M. Jung, J. -K. Shin, Y. -T. Jeong, P. Choi, J. -H. Lee, and G. Lim, "Field effect transistor-based bimolecular sensor employing a Pt reference electrode for the detection of deoxyribonucleic acid sequence," *Jpn J Appl Phys*, vol. **43**, pp. 3855–3859, 2004.

161. J. Fritz, E. B. Cooper, S. Gaudet, P. K. Sorger, and S. R. Manalis, "Electronic detection of DNA by its intrinsic molecular charge," *Proc Nat Acad Sci*, vol. **99**, pp. 14142–14146, 2002.

162. T. Sakata and Y. Miyahara, "Potential behavior of biochemically modified gold electrode for extended-gate field-effect transistor," *Jpn J Appl Phys*, vol. **44**, pp. 2860–2863, 2005.

163. J. Fritz, E. B. Cooper, S. Gaudet, P. K. Sorger, and S. Manalis, "Electronic detection of DNA by its intrinsic molecular charge," *Proc Natl Acad Sci*, vol. **99**, pp. 14142–14146, 2002.

164. A. Star, E. Tu, J. Niemann, Jean-Christophe P. Gabriel, C. Steve Jolner, and C. Valcke, "Label-free detection of DNA hybridization using carbon nanotube network field-effect transistors," *Proc Natl Acad Sc USA*, 2005.

165. J. Hahm and C. M. Lieber, "Direct ultrasensitive electrical detection of DNA and DNA sequence variations using nanowire nanosensors," *Nano Lett*, vol. **4**, pp. 51–54, 2004.

166. F. Patolsky, G. F. Zheng, O. Hayden, M. Lakadamyali, X. W. Zhuang, and C. M. Lieber, "Electrical detection of single viruses," *Proc Natl Acad Sci USA*, vol. **101**, pp. 14017–14022, 2004.

167. J. Li, H. T. Ng, A. Cassell, W. Fan, H. Chen, Q. Ye, J. Koehne, J. Han, and M. Meyyappan, "Carbon nanotube nanoelectrode array for ultrasensitive DNA detection," *Nano Lett*, vol. **3**, pp. 597–602, 2003.

168. M. Curreli, C. Li, Y. Sun, B. Lei, M. A. Gundersen, M. E. Thompson, and C. Zhou, "Selective functionalization of In2O3 nanowire mat devices for biosensing applications," *J Am Chem Soc*, vol. **127**, pp. 6922–6923, 2005.

169. R. J. Chen, S. Bangsaruntip, K. A. Drouvalakis, N. Wong Shi Kam, M. Shim, Y. Li, W. Kim, P. J. Utz, and H. Dai, "Noncovalent functionalization of carbon nanotubes for highly specific electronic biosensor," *Proc Natl Acad Sci USA*, vol. **100**, pp. 4984–4989, 2003.

170. A. Star, J. -C. P. Gabriel, K. Bradley, and G. Grüner, "Electronic detection of specific protein binding using nanotube FET devices," *Nano Lett*, vol. **3**, pp. 459–463, 2003.

171. C. Berggren, B. Bjarnason, and G. Johansson, "Capacitive biosensors," *Electroanalysis*, vol. **13**, pp. 173–180, 2001.

172. Agilent Technologies, http://www.chem.agilent.com/cag/feature/10-00/feature.html

CHAPTER 26

NEURAL INTERFACES

Jit Muthuswamy
Arizona State University, Tempe, Arizona

26.1 INTRODUCTION

This chapter focuses primarily on implantable neural interfaces and the key design requirements in developing interfaces for recording electrical activity from single neurons in the brain and peripheral nervous system (PNS). Larger-scale interfaces for recording electroencephalogram (EEG), electrocorticogram (ECoG), or evoked responses that are mounted on the scalp or the surface of the brain and not implanted in the brain tissue face significantly less challenges in terms of reliability. The chapter outlines some key mechanical and electrical design requirements that a neural engineer needs to consider in the development of an implantable chronic neural interface. Subsequent design considerations regarding materials and related fabrication processes are not within the scope of this chapter. Please refer to a book chapter on MEMS neural interfaces for more detail [1]. Similarly, packaging and interconnect issues that are critical to the overall design and development of chronic neural interfaces are also out of scope of this chapter. Typically, packaging and interconnects are an after-thought in the design and development process and these issues have the potential to stymie the entire development exercise if it is not seriously considered very early in the design and development cycle. In addition, safety and efficacy issues related to neural stimulation are out of scope of this chapter. We refer the reader to other good resources on design considerations for neuronal stimulation [2, 3].

26.2 NEURAL INTERFACES

Neural interfaces are optimally engineered systems with specifically designed functional features to communicate with neural tissue in the central system and/or the PNS. They are typically used to read/monitor or write/modulate the function of the neural tissue in the vicinity of the interface with a variety of different applications. For instance, macroscale interfaces such as superficial scalp electrodes (in either wet or dry configuration) for measuring EEG have been used in clinical sleep studies and for monitoring epileptic seizures for several decades now. These macroscale neural interfaces for EEG permit monitoring of the function of several thousand cells in specific regions of the brain. Similar interfaces placed on the brain by surgically opening the skull (craniotomy) permit the monitoring of ECoG signals. These signals are also volume-conducted electrical signals that reflect the spatiotemporal summation of the electrical activity of several thousands of cells in the vicinity of the interface. Implantable neural interfaces, on the other hand, are typically used to monitor or modulate the function (electrical activity or neurochemical activity) of a targeted group of cells in the brain. These interfaces are generally smaller (microscale or in rare cases even nanoscale) in order to interface with targeted cell(s) and simultaneously reduce tissue damage resulting from implantation. The function of these implants varies widely according to application. For instance, if one is interested in building a neuroprosthetic system for upper or lower limb amputees, implantable neural interfaces will enable both sensing motor activity in specific neural fibers (that might drive actuators in external robotic limbs) and also stimulating sensory neural fibers to communicate afferent sensations (such as touch, heat, and proprioception) to the brain. Such implants will typically have to last the lifetime of the patient.

Implants in the brain to monitor function of specific neurons reveal how the behavior of organisms is encoded in neuronal circuits. These studies use brain monitoring technologies in an attempt to decode brain function. Since it is often difficult to ascertain which neuronal circuits are involved in accomplishing a given brain function leading to a behavior, it is desirable to monitor a large ensemble of neurons using several thousands of interfaces/implants, each monitoring the function of one or a few neurons. The other two nonobvious but highly desirable needs in these decoding studies are that (a) we monitor neuronal function unhindered in awake, behaving subjects to overcome the confounding effects of anesthesia or sedatives and (b) this monitoring lasts for long periods of time so we can understand long-term physiological changes such as learning and memory. All of these needs may never be met using conventional implantable neural interfaces, but nonetheless they have motivated much of the neural interface development over the past several decades. They are also central to the current, massive technology development effort as part of the BRAIN (Brain Research through Advancing Innovative Neurotechnologies) initiative of the federal government in the United States and similar initiatives in the European Union. One of the key strengths of implantable neural interfaces is that they are capable of monitoring single neurons real-time in both superficial and deep brain structures in behaving animals.

The limitations of the implantable microelectrode technology are quite well known now. In general, microelectrodes are biased toward the sample of neurons that are active or have higher firing rates during the time of implantation or recording. When using multiple neural interfaces in a bundle or multichannel microelectrodes, the yield (in terms of number of microelectrodes that actually capture neuronal activity) is not consistent across experiments and depends on the level of anesthesia, location of the microelectrodes, user skills, experimental protocol used, and the type of microelectrode used. Meeting the above-mentioned needs of a neural interface, therefore, raises several huge engineering challenges in batch-fabricating large numbers of reliable neural interfaces and associated interconnects to communicate the neuronal data to the outside world. Significant additional challenges are also involved in packaging the implantable devices to last through chronic experimentation. Reliability of neural interfaces under chronic implantation conditions remains a serious challenge due to numerous biological failure modes (such as surgical injury and foreign body response) and material failure modes at the interface that are yet to be fully understood [4–8]. Signal-to-noise ratios (SNR) of implantable neural interfaces used for monitoring neuronal function remain highly variable, and interfaces can often become nonfunctional after a period of implantation.

26.3 SIGNALS FROM THE BRAIN

Extracellular signals from single neurons can range from tens to hundreds of microvolts buried in typically 10 to 20 μV of background noise signals, as shown in Fig. 26.1. On occasion, extracellular action potential signals can be a few millivolts, and these have been usually associated with microelectrodes with very sharp tips. Local field potential signals and EEG signals can range from a few hundreds of microvolts to few millivolts. Intracellular electrical signals recorded using penetrating microelectrodes can range several tens of millivolts capturing both subthreshold and action potential membrane potential fluctuations with the highest spatial resolution of all approaches.

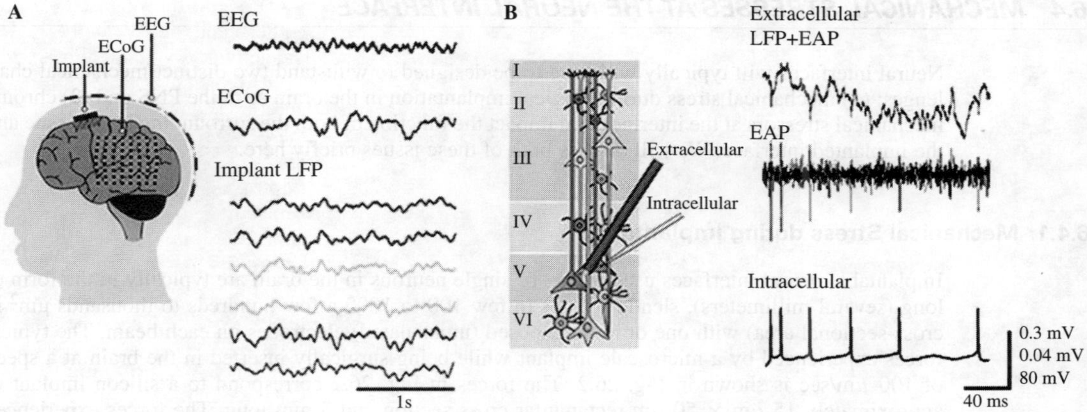

FIGURE 26.1 Illustration of different types of electrical signals obtained using conventional brain monitoring approaches. Macroscale electrodes placed on the scalp measure EEG and grid electrodes on the brain surface measure ECoG signals, while implantable microscale electrodes can be used to monitor electrical activity from single cells extracellularly or in rare occasions intracellularly. The typical morphology and scales of these different electrical signals are also indicated. (*Copyright © 2015 Obien, Deligkaris, Bullmann, Bakkum and Frey, from MEJ Obien, K Deligkaris, T Bullman, DJ Bakkum, and U Frey, "Revealing neuronal function through microelectrode array recordings," Front. Neurosci. 06 January 2015, https://doi.org/10.3389/fnins.2014.00423.*)

Neural interfaces/implants to stimulate and modulate function of specific neuronal circuits in the brain or in the PNS face additional needs and design challenges. They are generally used to deliver current or voltage pulses, so efficacy and safety are two primary needs. Efficacy is generally determined by the ability of the neural interface in combination with the current or voltage pulse to achieve the desired behavioral/functional change in an end organ such as reduction in tremor (in response to deep brain stimulation of subthalamic nuclei), reduction in the occurrence of seizures (in response to vagal nerve stimulation), etc. Safety is determined primarily by any undesirable tissue dysfunction or damage. A related safety issue is determined by the degree of any off-target stimulation leading to undesirable side-effects such as cognitive or mood changes. While some degree of off-target stimulation is generally expected, the goal is to minimize the ratio of off-target effects to target effects of neural stimulation. There are a variety of good software available such as SimNIBS (software for simulating noninvasive brain stimulation, simNIBS.org), BrainStimulator (http://www.sci.utah.edu/cibc-software/scirun/brainstimulator.html), and others funded by the NIH BRAIN initiative that allow one to estimate the regions of the brain that get stimulated using electrodes placed on the scalp.

As mentioned earlier, the most significant challenge in developing implantable neural interfaces is their reliability in chronic conditions. Several strategies have been attempted with varying degrees of success. They include (a) bioactive coatings on the surface of implants to mitigate injury and inflammatory response, (b) soft neural interfaces to reduce the mismatch in mechanical stiffness between the brain tissue and the material implant, (c) thin and flexible neural interfaces that float with the brain tissue, and finally (d) neural interfaces that autonomously move in the brain tissue in response to failure [9–11]. As a result, neural engineers will need to adapt one of the above strategies if they require the neural interfaces to function reliably over a period of several months or years. Each of the above design strategies is accompanied by its own material and fabrication challenges. In principle, any conductor or a doped semiconductor that is insulated everywhere except over an area that is typically a few tens of microns in diameter (if the exposed area is a circle) or a few tens of microns in dimension over each side of a rectangle should be capable of interfacing with neurons in the brain or the PNS and record their electrical activity. However, the following design requirements to minimize acute and chronic mechanical stresses will need to be met in order to have a successful *chronic* neural interface.

26.4 MECHANICAL STRESSES AT THE NEURAL INTERFACE

Neural interfaces will typically will have to be designed to withstand two distinct mechanical challenges: (1) mechanical stress during surgical implantation in the brain or in the PNS and (2) chronic mechanical stressors at the interface that impact the function of both the surrounding brain tissue and the implanted interface. We will discuss both of these issues briefly here.

26.4.1 Mechanical Stress during Implantation

Implantable neural interfaces used to record single neurons in the brain are typically in the form of long (several millimeters), slender beams (a few 100 to 1000 a few hundreds to thousands μm^2 in cross-sectional area) with one or more exposed (uninsulated) electrodes on each beam. The typical forces experienced by a microscale implant while being surgically inserted in the brain at a speed of 100 μm/sec is shown in Fig. 26.2. The forces in Fig. 26.2 correspond to a silicon implant of approximately 15 μm $\times$ 50 μm rectangular cross section and 5 mm long. The forces experienced by the implant are a function of the dimensions of the implant, shape of the implant tip that makes the first contact with the brain, whether it is a single neural implant or an array of neural implants, the speed with which the implant is driven through the brain to its target location, the nature of the implant motion (whether bidirectional or unidirectional) while being implanted, the use of mechanical positioning systems for implantation versus implantation by hand, etc. We will initially discuss the design of a single shank neural implant and examine the mechanical design issues involved. The requirement is that the implant penetrates the brain without significant buckling and bending and reaches the target brain location. Typically, the surgery involves incision and retraction of the scalp, a craniotomy to open up an area of the skull for implantation, and incising or removing the dura mater on the brain, as shown in Fig. 26.2.

The first design requirement is that these rather long, slender beams be able to penetrate the brain without causing significant damage to the implant or the brain tissue. It is always possible to make an implant sufficiently "stiff" (by increasing the elastic modulus of the implant material or the cross-sectional dimensions relative to the length), but as we will discuss later, both of the above strategies will lead directly to an increase in damage to the surrounding tissue. Therefore, the focus is really on how to design closer to the lower bounds of elastic modulus and cross-sectional dimensions and still penetrate the brain surface and cause minimal damage to the surrounding tissue. The key design equation to guide in this initial design is the one for Euler's critical load for buckling in beams that are fixed on both ends. The critical load P_{cr} (in Newtons, N) beyond which a slender

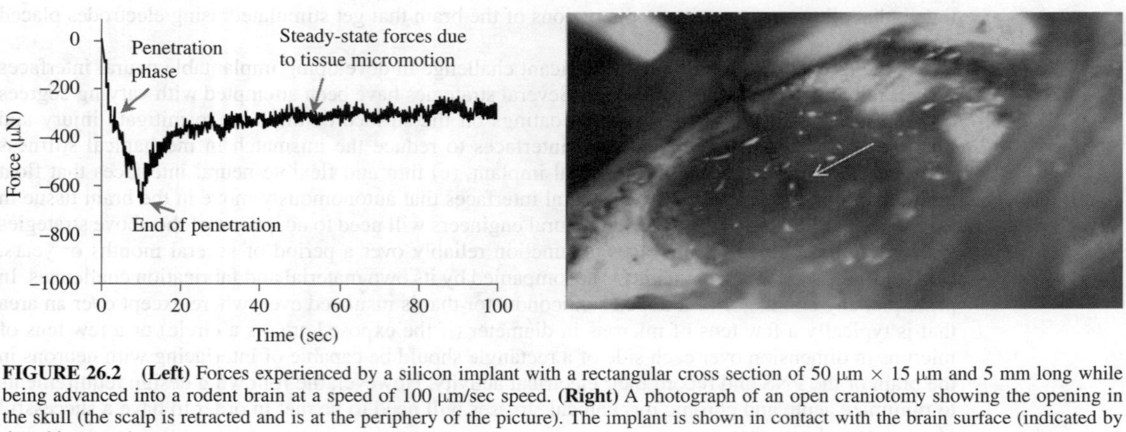

FIGURE 26.2 **(Left)** Forces experienced by a silicon implant with a rectangular cross section of 50 μm × 15 μm and 5 mm long while being advanced into a rodent brain at a speed of 100 μm/sec speed. **(Right)** A photograph of an open craniotomy showing the opening in the skull (the scalp is retracted and is at the periphery of the picture). The implant is shown in contact with the brain surface (indicated by the white arrow).

implant will buckle in its first mode (where the ends of the implant are fixed with zero bending and the bending increases to a maximum value at the middle of the free-section of the implant before decreasing back to zero at the other end) while penetrating the brain tissue is given by the following Euler's relationship:

$$P_{\text{cr}} = \frac{\pi^2 EI}{l^2} \tag{26.1}$$

where E is the elastic moduli of the material, I is the area moment of Inertia, and l in the denominator is the length of the implant. For implants with a solid, circular cross section (long cylindrical implants) and a diameter of d, the well-known relationship for moment of inertia is given by

$$I = \frac{\pi d^4}{32} \tag{26.2}$$

For an implant with solid, rectangular cross section, the moment of inertia is given by

$$I = \frac{bh^3}{12} \tag{26.3}$$

where b is the width of the implant and h is the thickness of the implant (in the direction of bending). As indicated by Eq. (26.3), the thickness (or diameter) has a dominant effect in the ability of the implant to penetrate the brain. For instance, for interfaces ~5 mm long made of materials such as insulated metals (tungsten, platinum-iridium, stainless steel, etc.) or semiconductor materials whose elastic modulus is typically in several hundred GPa, implants with very thin cross-sectional profiles (as low as a few tens of square micrometers in cross-sectional area) can successfully penetrate the brain at appropriate penetration speeds. However, if one uses softer polymers such as polyimide or parylene-C, whose elastic modulus is typically a few hundred MPa, one will need to increase the cross-sectional area to minimally several hundreds or thousands of square micrometers to enable successful penetration of the brain surface at typical implantation speeds.

Acute Mechanical Stress during Implantation Can be Minimized using Bidirectional Movement Strategy Mechanical stress build-up of the kind illustrated in Fig. 26.2 during implantation of neural interfaces can lead to tissue fracture and damage of vasculature and cells in the brain tissue. More importantly, it can lead to inaccuracies in the positioning of neural implants used to monitor or stimulate targeted regions of the brain. The build-up of stress is due to the viscoelastic nature of brain tissue. One of the ways to minimize build-up of mechanical stress at the interface during implantation is to advance the implant by pushing it in the brain tissue a few tens of micrometers and retracting it by a smaller distance so as to achieve a net movement into the brain by a few tens of micrometers. A successful demonstration of this strategy is shown in Fig. 26.3 [12], where a bidirectional movement of the neural implant resulted in net zero stress build-up (black traces) in the tissue as it is advanced into the brain tissue. The above approach also works for multichannel neural implants that involve multiple shanks penetrating the brain tissue.

Acute Mechanical Stress due to Tissue Micromotion Can be Minimized using Soft Interfaces In addition to build-up of mechanical stress during implantation, there is also a steady-state pulsatile mechanical stress in the neural interface due to tissue micromotion induced by breathing and vascular pulsations in the vicinity. Soft interfaces such as polymers, hydrogels, and siloxanes can significantly reduce the steady-state mechanical stresses due to tissue micromotion. Table 26.1 summarizes the micromotion-induced mechanical stresses at steady state under acute conditions for implants with different elastic moduli.

However, a good design for penetration may not always be a good design postimplantation, when the brain tissue surrounding the implant moves several tens to hundreds of micrometers (depending on the species these numbers increase with brain size) relative to the implant creating chronic, repetitive mechanical stresses (ranging from hundreds to thousands of Pascals) which can potentially

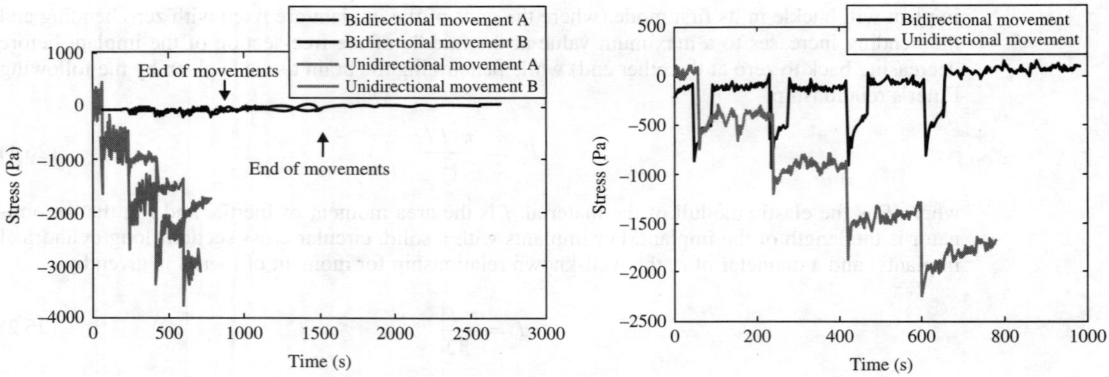

FIGURE 26.3 Stress build-up as a neural implant is advanced at a speed of 100 μm/sec into the brain tissue unidirectionally (red/gray trace) and bidirectionally (black trace).

TABLE 26.1 Average Steady-State Mechanical Stress due to Tissue Micromotion Immediately after Implantation

Elastic modulus of implant material	Average steady-state mechanical stress due to tissue micromotion (Pa)
~200 GPa (silicon)	221
~200 GPa (stainless steel)	136
~80 GPa (silicon coated with soft polyvinyl alcohol)	82.2
~5.2 GPa (nanocomposite before softening)	99.1
~12 MPa (nanocomposite after softening)	49.8

exacerbate tissue damage [13, 14]. Indeed, the design requirement for successful penetration of the brain surface or the tough epineurium around a peripheral nerve may be often at odds with the design requirements for chronic implantation, as we will discuss next. This has led to several clever design strategies for neural interfaces that will allow successful penetration and post implantation mechanical compatibility. We will discuss in more detail four of the most successful strategies (outlined earlier at the end of Sec. 26.1) after a brief discussion on the chronic mechanical stressors postimplantation at the neural interface.

26.4.2 Chronic Mechanical Stressors at the Neural Interface

Under chronic conditions, there are several sources of mechanical stressors at the implant–tissue interface. Tissue micromotion (due to pressure waves caused by periodic breathing and vascular pulsations or episodic behavioral factors) against a rigid and often stationary implant can lead to significant repetitive mechanical stressors that change with time of implantation. The functional impact of such mechanical stressors on neurons and glia at the interface is not yet clear. In addition, there can be significant mechanical stressors due to episodic behavior that induces mechanical stresses at the interface of brain tissue and a fixed implant. Interconnects (if they are not zero-insertion-force or ZIF connectors) to connect with the external recording or stimulation systems can also introduce significant mechanical stresses on the implants and the underlying brain tissue even when the implants are anchored firmly to the skull. Any permanent displacement of the neurons in the brain tissue relative to the implant due to any of the above mechanical factors can result in the catastrophic loss of electrical interface with the targeted set of neurons or neuronal circuits. Unlike mechanical stressors in acute implantation conditions, the chronic mechanical stressors are less known and the engineer is often forced to design using empirical principles to minimize chronic mechanical stressors at the neural interface. Dynamic remodeling of brain tissue (including microvasculature, neurons, glia, and microglia) around neural implants over a period lasting 4 to 8 weeks postimplant makes estimating and designing for mechanical stresses at the interface under chronic conditions more challenging. For instance, the elastic modulus of brain tissue at the interface (within a distance of 150 μm from the surface of the implant) of a 100-μm-diameter stainless steel implant can change approximately tenfold from a few kPa (on the day of implantation) to approx. 30 kPa over a duration of 4 weeks of implantation [14]. Subsequently, from week 4 to week 8 of implantation, the elastic moduli of the brain tissue at the interface appears to return back to baseline values of <10 kPa probably due to healing and compacting of scar tissue around the neural implant. Such dynamic changes make the design effort to minimize chronic stressors more challenging.

Nevertheless, over the past 15 years, several key design principles leading to significantly lower foreign body response and improved functional reliability of the interface have emerged empirically from multiple studies.

1. Nevertheless, over the past 15 years, several key design principles have emerged from multiple empirical lines of evidence demonstrating significantly lower foreign body response and improved functional reliability of the interface. A variety of different materials such as hydrogels and polymers have been used in the design of neural interfaces either as a coating over an underlying rigid metal implant, or as the substrate material of the implant itself. The materials have consistently demonstrated lower reactive astrocytes and higher neuronal densities around these implants under chronic conditions [15–19]. The experimental data reported in Sec. 26.4.1 [20] and modeling studies [21] predict significantly lower mechanical stresses with softer interfaces that are expected to be sustained under chronic conditions. The key challenge using this approach is no longer in identifying a biocompatible soft material but in designing an appropriate scalable fabrication method that will allow the handling and micromachining of soft materials and integration with associated interconnect technology. This challenge is yet to be adequately addressed.
2. Implants that were slender with cross-sectional diameters or dimensions smaller than 12 μm [22, 23] have been demonstrated to significantly mitigate reactive astrocytes and activated microglia at the interface under chronic conditions. These prior studies have led to the design and development of several successful carbon microelectrode arrays (with diameters of individual fibers in the range of 5 to 8.4 μm) and injectable mesh electrode technologies (with electrodes having similar dimensions as neuronal cell bodies) that have shown great success in mitigating tissue reaction and enhancing reliability under chronic conditions [24–30]. The key challenge using this approach is finding strategies to penetrate the brain tissue with these ultrathin microelectrodes. Several clever approaches have been used to overcome the above challenge. For instance, Chestek et al. have used a biodegradable polyethylene glycol (PEG) to hold an array of carbon microelectrodes (~8.4 μm diameter each) together as they are inserted into the brain tissue [26]. The array is inserted slowly as the PEG matrix holding the array dissolves in contact just above the brain tissue. The Lieber research group at Harvard University has used an injection strategy where the array of microelectrodes and interconnects are squeezed into a needle and injected into the brain tissue (while simultaneously retracting the needle). Once inside, the mesh unfurls inside the brain tissue creating interfaces with neurons in the brain.
3. A very useful meta-analysis of nine prior studies (2005 to 2016) reported a high correlation between the inflammatory response in the first 50 μm of brain tissue around the implant and the implant bending stiffness as opposed to either the elastic modulus or the cross-sectional dimensions of the implant independently [31]. The implant bending stiffness S (units of N/m) in the above meta-analysis was defined as follows:

$$S = \frac{3EI}{l^3} \tag{26.4}$$

where E is the elastic modulus of the implant material, I is the second area moment of the implant, and l in the denominator is the length of the implant. Equations (26.1) and (26.4), therefore, give critical design guidance that will enable neural implants to meet both the force requirements for penetration and the chronic design requirement of minimizing inflammatory response in the brain tissue around the implant.

Finite element analysis of mechanical stresses at a typical rigid silicon neural interface is shown in Fig. 26.4. Maximum Tresca stresses are observed at the sharp tip and at the surface along the length of the implant. Shear (Tresca) stress gradients (with respect to time) are calculated from the stress profiles along a line extending away from the tip of the tapered silicon implant (point of highest stresses) and going into the brain. The rectangular cross-sectional dimensions of the implant are 50 μm × 5 μm and the brain tissue displacement rate is 20 μm over a period of 2 seconds simulating breathing-induced micromotion in rodent brain tissue. The brain tissue was modeled as a hyperelastic, viscoelastic material in the above simulation. The first boundary condition imposed on the model was a "tie" condition between the implant and the brain at the contact surfaces to achieve

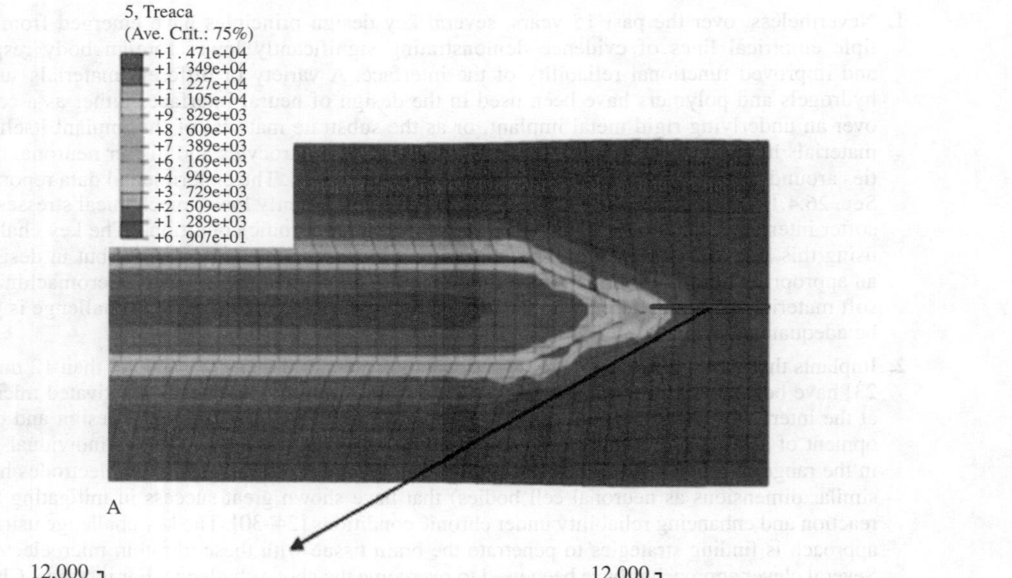

FIGURE 26.4 (*a*) Shear (Tresca) stress gradients (with respect to time) calculated from the stress profiles along a line (shown in red) starting from one corner of the tip of the tapered silicon implant (highest stresses) and going into the brain. The gradients were calculated by differentiating the stress profiles in time (*b*, *c*).

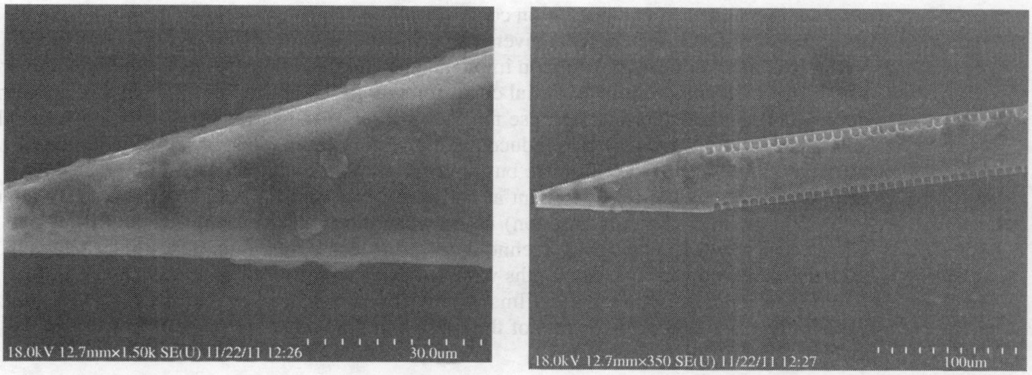

FIGURE 26.5 Scanning electron micrographs (SEMs) of polysilicon implants after 8 months of implantation in rodent somatosensory cortex show no signs of corrosion.

a no-slip condition between the contact surfaces of the brain tissue and the implant. The above "tie" condition to achieve a "no-slip" condition between the contact surfaces of the brain tissue and the implant surface models the chronic condition when the implant is surrounded by a glial sheath with adherent cells on the implant surface.

Neuronal viability has been shown to express a shear rate dependency [32]. At a shear stress rate of 5600 Pa/sec (and resting stress of 2 Pa), it has been shown that 24 hours after insult, cell viability decreased to 30 to 40 percent for neurons while remaining at 100 percent for astrocytes [32]. Apart from direct injury, rapid stretching of neurons (at substantially lower stress) has been shown to trigger a cascade of cellular events that leads to an increase in intracellular free-calcium concentration [33, 34] and subsequently excitotoxicity and cell-death in in vitro systems. The increased membrane permeability following a traumatic insult can lead to the leakage of cytosolic components [35]. Neurons show significant intracellular (Ca^{2+}) response at fluid shear stress impulse loading of 85 Pa/sec for a 25 msec linear increase [35]. It has been shown previously that the neuronal injury was load-dependent [33]. Consequently, when the mechanical stimulus was delivered slowly, there was no response. Based on the above data from prior studies, it appears regions within 20 μm (approx. 2 neuronal cell body diameters juxtaposed) from the tip of the tapered silicon implant are vulnerable to necrosis at least for some time during brain tissue micromotion due to respiration. For brain tissue micromotion due to vascular pulsatility, the stress rates within brain tissue stay much lower than 5600 Pa/sec in most cases (except for the tip of the silicon implants) and hence we do not expect any cellular necrosis due to chronic vascular pulsations. We also observed that in each of our modeling conditions, the stress rates exceeded 85 Pa/sec (that is likely sufficient to cause an increase in intracellular Ca^{2+}) at the tip of the implants. In most cases, this stress rate is reached by all the elements within our modeled brain tissue of thickness 100 μm. Hence, it is likely that there is some rise in intracellular Ca^{2+} concentrations leading to impaired cell function within neurons in the immediate vicinity of all the implants.

26.4.3 Other Design Considerations

Other abiotic factors that could lead to potential failure of the interface include cracking or corrosion of insulation, conductive leads and/or the substrate of the implant under exposure to cerebrospinal fluid, and blood and ions in the brain and PNS. The choice of materials, fabrication process used, and electrical stimulation parameters (if the neural interface is used for stimulation) play a critical role in the corrosion rate and resultant structural failure of the neural implant. Design engineers should pay close attention to all three of the above factors in the development and use of neural interfaces. Commonly used neural interface materials such as platinum/iridium, silicon, carbon, and stainless-steel that are insulated with Teflon, parylene-C, silicon nitride/oxide, etc. generally perform very well under chronic implantation conditions. The design considerations involved in the design of safe stimulation parameters for a given implanted electrode is discussed at length in Refs. 2 and 3. In the case of silicon and polysilicon implants, the choice of dopants and the fabrication process can often play a defining role in material corrosion rate in the brain. For instance, boron or phosphorus doping and galvanic biasing (to raise the Fermi level of the surrounding solution above that of the silicon substrate) were shown to reduce the dissolution (corrosion) of polysilicon from 1 μm/day to 90 Å/day at 93°C [36] in phosphate buffered saline. The study concluded that dissolution of silicon or polysilicon may not be significant at body temperature. Similarly, in our own lab, the thin films (with 50 μm $\times$ 5 μm cross section) of polysilicon fabricated using the SUMMiTV^{TM} (Sandia's Ultraplanar Multi-level MEMS Technology V) process of the Sandia National labs and insulated with epoxy lasted well over 8 months with no visible signs of corrosion as shown in Fig. 26.5. The minimal residual stress in the thin films of polysilicon produced by the SUMMiTV^{TM} process might explain the minimal corrosion rate of these films in the body.

REFERENCES

1. J. Muthuswamy, A. Sridharan, and M. Okandan, "MEMS neural probes," in *Encyclopedia of Nanotechnology*, 2nd ed., B. Bhushan (ed.), Springer, Dordrecht, Netherlands, 2016.
2. S. F. Cogan, S. Hara, and K. A. Ludwig, "The Safe delivery of electrical currents and neuromodulation," in *Neuromodulation*, Elliot S. Krames, P. Hunter Peckham, Ali R. Rezai (eds.), Academic Press, Cambridge, MA, 2018.
3. S. F. Cogan, K. A. Ludwig, C. G. Welle, and P. Takmakov, "Tissue damage thresholds during therapeutic electrical stimulation," vol. 13, no. 2, *Journal of Neural Engineering*, 2016, doi:10.1088/1741-2560/13/2/021001.
4. W. M. Grill, S. E. Norman, and R. V. Bellamkonda, "Implanted neural interfaces: Biochallenges and engineered solutions," vol. 11, pp. 1–24, *Annual Review of Biomedical Engineering*, 2009.
5. V. S. Polikov, P. A. Tresco, and W. M. Reichert, "Response of brain tissue to chronically implanted neural electrodes," vol. 148, no. 1, pp. 1–18, *Journal of Neuroscience Methods*, 2005.
6. A. K. Engel, C. K. E. Moll, I. Fried, and G. A. Ojemann, "Invasive recordings from the human brain: Clinical insights and beyond," vol. 6, no. 1, pp. 35–47, *Nature Reviews Neuroscience*, 2005.
7. R. J. Vetter, J. C. Williams, J. F. Hetke, E. A. Nunamaker, and D. R. Kipke, "Chronic neural recording using silicon-substrate microelectrode arrays implanted in cerebral cortex," vol. 51, no. 6, pp. 896–904, *IEEE Transactions on Biomedical Engineering*, 2004.
8. D. McCreery, S. Cogan, S. Kane, and V. Pikov, "Correlations between histology and neuronal activity recorded by microelectrodes implanted chronically in the cerebral cortex," vol. 13, no. 3, *Journal of Neural Engineering*, 2016, doi: 10.1088/1741-2560/13/3/036012.
9. N. Jackson, A. Sridharan, S. Anand, M. Baker, M. Okandan, and J. Muthuswamy, "Long-term neural recordings using MEMS based movable microelectrodes in the brain," vol. 3, *Frontiers in Neuroengineering*, 2010, doi: 10.3389/fneng.2010.00010.
10. J. Muthuswamy, S. Anand, and A. Sridharan, "Adaptive movable neural interfaces for monitoring single neurons in the brain," *Frontiers in Neuroscience*, 2011, https://doi.org/10.3389/fnins.2011.00094.
11. S. Anand, J. Sutanto, M. S. Baker, M. Okandan, and J. Muthuswamy, "Electrothermal microactuators with peg drive improve performance for brain implant applications," vol. 21, no. 5, pp. 1172–1186, *Journal of Microelectromechanical Systems*, 2012.
12. S. Anand, S. S. Kumar, and J. Muthuswamy, "Autonomous control for mechanically stable navigation of microscale implants in brain tissue to record neural activity," vol. 18, no. 4, p. 72, *Biomedical Microdevices*, 2016.
13. A. Gilletti and J. Muthuswamy, "Brain micromotion around implants in the rodent somatosensory cortex," vol. 3, no. 3, pp. 189–195, *Journal of Neural Engineering*, 2006.
14. A. Sridharan, S. D. Rajan, and J. Muthuswamy, "Long-term changes in the material properties of brain tissue at the implant-tissue interface," vol. 10, no. 6, *Journal of Neural Engineering*, 2013, doi: 10.1088/1741-2560/10/6/066001.

15. A. Sridharan and J. Muthuswamy, "Performance of soft, brain-like neural implants in rodents in chronic experiments," in *Front. Bioeng. Biotechnol. Conference Abstract: 10th World Biomaterials Congress*, 2016, doi: 10.3389/conf.FBIOE.2016.01.00550.

16. J. R. Capadona, K. Shanmuganathan, D. J. Tyler, S. J. Rowan, and C. Weder, "Stimuli-responsive polymer nanocomposites inspired by the sea cucumber dermis," vol. **319**, pp. 1370–1374, *Science*, 2008

17. K. C. Spencer, J. C. Sy, K. B. Ramadi, A. M. Graybiel, R. Langer, and M. J. Cima, "Characterization of mechanically matched hydrogel coatings to improve the biocompatibility of neural implants," vol. 7, no. 1, *Scientific Reports*, 2017, doi: 10.1038/s41598-017-02107-2.

18. Z. J. Du, et al., "Ultrasoft microwire neural electrodes improve chronic tissue integration," vol. 53, pp. 46–58, *Acta Biomaterialia*, 2017.

19. J. P. Harris, et al., "Mechanically adaptive intracortical implants improve the proximity of neuronal cell bodies," vol. 8, no. 6, *Journal of Neural Engineering*, 2011, doi: 10.1088/1741-2560/8/6/066011.

20. A. Sridharan, J. K. Nguyen, J. R. Capadona, and J. Muthuswamy, "Compliant intracortical implants reduce strains and strain rates in brain tissue in vivo," vol. 12, no. 3, *Journal of Neural Engineering*, 2015, doi: 10.1088/1741-2560/12/3/036002.

21. H. Lee, R. V. Bellamkonda, W. Sun, and M. E. Levenston, "Biomechanical analysis of silicon microelectrode-induced strain in the brain," vol. 2, no. 4, pp. 81–89, *Journal of Neural Engineering*, 2005.

22. P. Stice, A. Gilletti, A. Panitch, and J. Muthuswamy, "Thin microelectrodes reduce GFAP expression in the implant site in rodent somatosensory cortex," vol. 4, no. 2, pp. 42–53, *Journal of Neural Engineering*, 2007.

23. J. P. Seymour and D. R. Kipke, "Neural probe design for reduced tissue encapsulation in CNS," vol. 28, no. 25, pp. 3594–3607, *Biomaterials*, 2007.

24. P. R. Patel, et al., "Insertion of linear 8.4 μm diameter 16 channel carbon fiber electrode arrays for single unit recordings," vol. 12, no. 4, *Journal of Neural Engineering*, 2015, doi: 10.1088/1741-2560/12/4/046009.

25. T. G. Schuhmann, J. Yao, G. Hong, T. M. Fu, and C. M. Lieber, "Syringe-injectable electronics with a plug-and-play input/output interface," vol. 17, no. 9, pp. 5836–5842, *Nano Letters*, 2017.

26. P. R. Patel, et al., "Chronic in vivo stability assessment of carbon fiber microelectrode arrays," vol. 13, no. 6, *Journal of Neural Engineering*, 2016, doi: 10.1088/1741-2560/13/6/066002.

27. T. Zhou, et al., "Syringe-injectable mesh electronics integrate seamlessly with minimal chronic immune response in the brain," vol. 114, no. 23, pp. 5894–5899, *Proceedings of the National Academy of Sciences of the United States of America*, 2017.

28. T. G. Schuhmann, et al., "Syringe-injectable mesh electronics for stable chronic rodent electrophysiology," vol. 2018, no. 137, *Journal of Visualized Experiments*, 2018. doi: 10.3791/58003

29. T. D. Yoshida Kozai, et al., "Ultrasmall implantable composite microelectrodes with bioactive surfaces for chronic neural interfaces," vol. 11, no. 12, pp. 1065–1073, *Nature Materials*, 2012.

30. G. Guitchounts, J. E. Markowitz, W. A. Liberti, and T. J. Gardner, "A carbon-fiber electrode array for long-term neural recording," vol. 10, no. 4, *Journal of Neural Engineering*, 2013, doi: 10.1088/1741-2560/10/4/046016.

31. A. M. Stiller, et al., "A meta-analysis of intracortical device stiffness and its correlation with histological outcomes," vol. 9, no. 9, *Micromachines*, 2018, doi: 10.3390/mi9090443.

32. G. R. Prado and M. C. LaPlaca, "Differential response of primary neurons and astrocytes to a controlled hydrodynamic insult in cultured neural cells," vol. 50, pp. 627-628, *American Society of Mechanical Engineers, Bioengineering Division (Publication) Bed* 2001.

33. M. C. Laplaca, V. M. Y. Lee, and L. E. Thibault, "An in vitro model of traumatic neuronal injury: Loading rate-dependent changes in acute cytosolic calcium and lactate dehydrogenase release," vol. 14, no. 6, pp. 355–368, *Journal of Neurotrauma*, 1997.

34. R. S. Cargill and L. E. Thibault, "Acute alterations in [Ca^{2+}](i) in NG108-15 cells subjected to high strain rate deformation and chemical hypoxia: An in vitro model for neural trauma," vol. 13, no. 7, pp. 395–407, *Journal of Neurotrauma*, 1996.

35. M. C. LaPlaca and L. E. Thibault, "Dynamic mechanical deformation of neurons triggers an acute calcium response and cell injury involving the *N*-methyl-D-Aspartate glutamate receptor," vol. 52, no. 2, pp. 220–229, *Journal of Neuroscience Research*, 1998.

36. B. H. Stark, M. R. Dokmeci, and K. Najafi, "Improving corrosion-resistance of polysilicon using boron doping and self-induced galvanic bias," vol. 26, no. 3, pp. 295–301, *IEEE Transactions on Advanced Packaging*, 2003.

INDEX

Note: Page numbers followed by *f* refer to figures; page numbers followed by *t* refer to tables.